SECOND CANADIAN EDITION

CORPORATE
FINANCE

JONATHAN BERK
STANFORD UNIVERSITY

PETER DEMARZO
STANFORD UNIVERSITY

DAVID STANGELAND
UNIVERSITY OF MANITOBA

CONTRIBUTOR
JERROD FALK
UNIVERSITY OF MANITOBA

Pearson Canada
Toronto

To Rebecca, Natasha, and Hannah for the love and for being there. —J. B.
To Kaui, Pono, Koa, and Kai for all the love and laughter. —P. D.
To my family and friends for all the love, support, encouragement, and motivation. —D. S.

Library and Archives Canada Cataloguing in Publication

Berk, Jonathan B., 1962–
Corporate finance / Jonathan Berk, Peter DeMarzo, David Stangeland.—2nd Canadian ed.

Includes index.
ISBN 978-0-321-70872-4

1. Corporations—Finance—Textbooks.   I. DeMarzo, Peter M.   II. Stangeland,
David, 1964–   III. Title.

HG4026.B48 2011   658.15   C2010-906851-3

ISBN 978-0-321-70872-4

Vice-President, Editorial Director:
   Gary Bennett
Editor-in-Chief: Nicole Lukach
Acquisitions Editor: Claudine O'Donnell
Marketing Manager: Leigh-Anne Graham
Senior Developmental Editor: Paul Donnelly
Project Manager: Imee Salumbides
Production Editors: Heather Sangster
   (Strong Finish), Laura Neves
Copy Editor: Andrea Nemeth (Strong Finish)

Proofreaders: Suzanne Needs (Strong Finish),
   Camille Isaacs, Kelli Howey
Compositor: MPS Limited, a Macmillan
   Company
Art Director: Julia Hall
Cover and Interior Designer:
   Jennifer Stimson Design
Cover Image: Getty Images/Piecework
   Productions

1 2 3 4 5   15 14 13 12 11

Printed and bound in the United States of America.

Brief Contents

Contents

About the Authors

Peter DeMarzo and Jonathan Berk

JONATHAN BERK is the A.P. Giannini Professor of Finance at the Graduate School of Business, Stanford University and is a Research Associate at the National Bureau of Economic Research. Before coming to Stanford, he was the Sylvan Coleman Professor of Finance at Haas School of Business at the University of California, Berkeley. Prior to earning his Ph.D., he worked as an Associate at Goldman Sachs (where his education in finance really began).

Professor Berk's research interests in finance include corporate valuation, capital structure, mutual funds, asset pricing, experimental economics, and labor economics. His work has won a number of research awards including the TIAA-CREF Paul A. Samuelson Award, the Smith Breeden Prize, Best Paper of the Year in *The Review of Financial Studies*, and the FAME Research Prize. His paper, "A Critique of Size-Related Anomalies," was selected as one of the two best papers ever published in *The Review of Financial Studies*. In recognition of his influence on the practice of finance he has received the Bernstein-Fabozzi/Jacobs Levy Award, the Graham and Dodd Award of Excellence, and the Roger F. Murray Prize. He served as an Associate Editor of the *Journal of Finance* for eight years and is currently an Advisory Editor of the journal.

Born in Johannesburg, South Africa, Professor Berk is married, with two daughters, and is an avid skier and biker.

PETER DEMARZO is the Mizuho Financial Group Professor of Finance and Senior Associate Dean for Academic Affairs at the Stanford Graduate School of Business. He is also a Research Associate at the National Bureau of Economic Research. He currently teaches MBA and Ph.D. courses in Corporate Finance and Financial Modeling. In addition to his experience at the Stanford Graduate School of Business, Professor DeMarzo has taught at the Haas School of Business and the Kellogg Graduate School of Management, and he was a National Fellow at the Hoover Institution.

Professor DeMarzo received the Sloan Teaching Excellence Award at Stanford in 2004 and 2006, and the Earl F. Cheit Outstanding Teaching Award at U.C. Berkeley in 1998. Professor DeMarzo has served as an Associate Editor for *The Review of Financial Studies, Financial Management*, and the *B.E. Journals in Economic Analysis and Policy*, as well as a Director of the American Finance Association. He has served as Vice President and is currently President-elect of the Western Finance Association. Professor DeMarzo's research is in the area of corporate finance, asset securitization, and contracting, as well as market structure and regulation. His recent work has examined issues of the optimal design of contracts and securities, the regulation of insider trading and broker-dealers, and the influence of information asymmetries on corporate investment. He has received numerous awards including the Western Finance Association Corporate Finance Award and the Barclays Global Investors/Michael Brennan best-paper award from *The Review of Financial Studies*.

Professor DeMarzo was born in Whitestone, New York, and is married with three boys. He and his family enjoy hiking, biking, and skiing.

David Stangeland

DAVID STANGELAND, PhD, BComm (Distinction), CMA, did his undergraduate and graduate university education at the University of Alberta in Edmonton. In 1991, he moved to Winnipeg where he joined the Accounting & Finance Department in the I. H. Asper School of Business at the University of Manitoba. Dr. Stangeland is a Professor of Finance, was Head of the Department of Accounting & Finance Department for two terms, and is now the Associate Dean of the I. H. Asper School responsible for programs and administration.

Professor Stangeland teaches finance courses at the University of Manitoba and in the Canadian Executive MBA program at the Warsaw School of Economics in Poland. His teaching spans undergraduate, MBA, and PhD courses in corporate finance, investment banking, and international finance.

Professor Stangeland's research interests are in the areas of corporate governance, corporate control, and corporate finance. His work is well cited and has been published in several journals including the *Journal of Financial and Quantitative Analysis*, the *Journal of Banking & Finance*, the *Journal of Corporate Finance*, *Financial Management*, the *Stanford Journal of Law, Business, & Finance*, and numerous others.

Dr. Stangeland served on the Board of Directors of CMA Canada and he chaired CMA Canada's Pension Committee. He is a member of the Board of Trustees for the University of Manitoba Pension Plans, a member of the Investment Committee for the Teachers Retirement Allowance Fund, and serves on the Independent Review Committee for a mutual fund company. Professor Stangeland is a two-time recipient of the CMA Canada Academic Merit Award for Teaching and Research, a four-time winner of the University of Manitoba Teaching Services Award, and a recipient of the Associates Award for Research.

Professor Stangeland was born and raised in Edmonton, Alberta, where he learned to appreciate the outdoors including running, cycling, hiking, and skiing and, in the winter, travelling to warmer climates.

Preface

The first Canadian edition was written just as the financial crisis of 2008–2009 was unfolding. One thing that was reinforced by the financial crisis is the need to understand finance so that correct decision making is done. As we said in the first edition, understanding finance is important and is the purpose of this book:

In our over 50 years of combined teaching experience, we have found that leaving out core material deemed "too hard" actually makes the subject matter less accessible. The core concepts in finance are simple and intuitive. What makes the subject challenging is that it is often difficult for a novice to distinguish between these core ideas and other intuitively appealing approaches that, if used in financial decision making, will lead to incorrect decisions. De-emphasizing the core concepts that underlie finance strips students of the essential intellectual tools they need to differentiate between good and bad decision making. Therefore, our primary motivation for writing this book was to equip students with a solid grounding in the core financial concepts and tools needed to make good decisions.

There is little doubt that one of the most important contributing factors to the financial crisis was that many practitioners who should have known better did not understand, or chose to ignore, the core concepts that underlie finance in general, and the pedagogy in this book in particular, leading them to make many very bad decisions.

We present corporate finance as an application of a set of simple, powerful ideas. At the heart is the principal of the absence of arbitrage opportunities, or Law of One Price: In life, you don't get something for nothing. This simple concept is a powerful and important tool in financial decision making. By relying on it, and the other core principles in this book, financial decision makers can avoid the bad decisions brought to light by the financial crisis. We use the Law of One Price as a compass; it keeps financial decision makers on the right track and is the backbone of the entire book.

NEW TO THIS EDITION

We have updated all text discussions and figures, tables and facts to accurately reflect developments in the field in the last two years. Given the success of the first edition, we focused substantive changes on areas where there was clear evidence that such change would be beneficial. Specific highlights include the following:

- As painful as the financial crisis was, there is a silver lining: it provides a valuable pedagogical illustration of what can go wrong when practitioners ignore the core concepts that underlie financial decision making. We integrate this important lesson into the book in a series of contextual boxes we call Financial Crisis boxes. These boxes bring the relevance of the crisis home to students by illustrating and analyzing key details about the financial crisis, ranging from Madoff's fraud to Lehman Brothers' bankruptcy and beyond.

- We reorganized the flow of topics in Part 4, Risk and Return to better meet course needs. Instead of spreading the theoretical derivation of the CAPM over two chapters, we have combined this material into one chapter—Chapter 11, Optimal Portfolio Choice and the Capital Asset Pricing Model. We stuck to the original concept from the first edition that allows instructors the option to cover this material without necessarily getting into the details of the CAPM. Instructors can skip Chapter 11 and move directly from Chapter 10 to Chapter 12, without losing continuity.

- Chapter 12, Estimating the Cost of Capital, is a new chapter written in response to the many adopters who wanted a single place in the book that explained how to calculate the cost of capital. The chapter is a practical guide on how to implement the risk–return model.

- We made extensive revisions to Chapter 13, Investor Behaviour and Capital Market Efficiency, and renamed the chapter to reflect its new content. In this chapter we review the evidence on investor behaviour and explain how this behaviour might impact the efficiency of the market portfolio.

- We have updated many of our practitioner interviews to incorporate an "inside" perspective on the financial crisis. We have also added a number of new interviews with, for example, Frederic S. Mishkin, former Federal Reserve Board governor and David Holland, Senior Vice President and Treasurer of Cisco.

- Another area that we have made significant additions and improvements to are the problems found at the end of each chapter and on MyFinanceLab. We added 200 new problems to the Second Canadian Edition. As in the first edition, we personally wrote and solved every problem. In addition, every single problem is available on MyFinanceLab, the groundbreaking homework and tutorial system that accompanies the book. MyFinanceLab upgrades include context-dependent hints based on prior user data. The system recognizes typical mistakes and provides immediate feedback, allowing the student to learn instantaneously from the mistake.

THE LAW OF ONE PRICE AS THE UNIFYING PRINCIPLE OF VALUATION

This book presents corporate finance as an application of a small set of simple core ideas. Modern finance theory and practice is grounded in the idea of the absence of arbitrage (or the Law of One Price) as the unifying concept in valuation. We introduce the Law of One Price concept as the basis for net present value and the time value of money in Chapter 3, *Arbitrage and Financial Decision Making*. In the opening of each part, and as pertinent throughout the remaining chapters, we relate major concepts to the Law of One Price, creating a framework to ground the student and connect theory to practice.

PART-BY-PART OVERVIEW

Parts 1 and 2 lay the foundation for our study of corporate finance. Chapter 1 introduces the corporation and other business forms. We examine the roles of the financial manager and financial markets, as well as conflicts surrounding ownership and control of corporations. Chapter 2 reviews basic corporate accounting principles and financial statements. It now includes a number of additional ratios and the DuPont identity.

Part 2 presents the basic tools that are the cornerstones of corporate finance. As we have already pointed out, Chapter 3 introduces the Law of One Price and net present value as the basis of the unifying framework that will guide the student through the course. An optional appendix provides a brief introduction to risk for those who want to include an emphasis on risk in the early introduction to capital budgeting. It can be covered with Chapter 3 or at a later point, if desired. Chapter 4 introduces the time value of money and describes methods for estimating the timing of cash flows and computing the net present value of various types of cash flow patterns. Chapter 5, *Interest Rates*, provides an extensive overview of issues that arise in estimating the appropriate discount rate.

Part 3 opens with Chapter 6, in which we present and critique alternatives to net present value for evaluating projects. We restructured the IRR coverage for the Second Canadian Edition. We then turn to applying valuation principles from Part 2 for discounting cash flows to both real and financial assets. We explain the basics of valuation for capital projects (Chapter 7), bonds (Chapter 8), and stocks (Chapter 9). Chapter 7 provides a clear and systematic presentation of the difference between earnings and free cash flow and gives a solid understanding of Canadian tax effects from capital cost allowance (CCA). We apply these concepts to stocks in Chapter 9, providing a unifying treatment of projects within the firm and the valuation of the firm as a whole. In addition, Chapter 9 also discusses the issue of market efficiency and implications for financial managers.

The flexible structure of Part 4 allows professors to tailor coverage of risk and return to their needs—be it for a theory- or practice-heavy emphasis. Chapter 10, *Capital Markets and the Pricing of Risk*, provides the keys to understanding risk and return. The chapter also explains the distinction between diversifiable and systematic risk. After this comprehensive yet succinct treatment, professors can choose to continue on to the theory, now centralized in Chapter 11, *Optimal Portfolio Choice and the Capital Asset Pricing Model*, which presents the CAPM and develops the details of mean-variance portfolio optimization. Alternatively, professors can proceed directly to Chapter 12, *Estimating the Cost of Capital Pricing Model*, which is a new practically-focused chapter on the cost of capital. Chapter 13 examines the role of behavioural finance and ties investor behaviour to the topic of market efficiency and alternative models of risk and return.

Part 5 addresses how a firm should raise the funds it needs to undertake its investments and the firm's resulting capital structure. We focus on examining how the choice of capital structure affects the value of the firm in the perfect world in Chapter 14, and with frictions such as taxes and agency issues in Chapters 15 and 16. Chapter 16 features new coverage of the asset substitution problem and debt overhang. We focus on payout policy in Chapter 17.

In Part 6, we return to the capital budgeting decision with the complexities of the real world. Chapter 18 introduces the three main methods for capital budgeting with leverage and market imperfections: the weighted average cost of capital (WACC) method, the adjusted present value (APV) method, and the flow-to-equity (FTE) method. We present these traditionally difficult but important ideas by emphasizing the underlying assumptions and core principles behind them, moving through progressively more complex ideas. This organization allows professors to delve as deeply into these techniques as is appropriate for their needs. Chapter 19 presents a capstone case for the first six parts of the book that applies the techniques developed up to this point to build a valuation model for a firm, Ideko Corp., using Excel.

Part 7 focuses on the role of options in investing and financing decisions. Chapter 20 introduces financial options and Chapter 21 presents commonly used techniques for pricing options. Chapter 22 highlights the role of real options in capital budgeting and features a new section on ordering multi-stage investments.

In Part 8, we explain the institutional details associated with alternative long-term financing sources. Chapter 23 describes the process a company goes through when it raises equity capital. In Chapter 24, we review how firms can use the debt markets to raise capital and the role of asset-backed securities, collateralized debt obligations, and mortgage-backed securities in the financial crisis. Chapter 25 introduces leasing as an alternative and in the lease analysis treats the CCA tax shields in a manner consistent with the presentation in Chapter 7.

In Part 9, we turn to the details of running the financial side of a corporation on a day-to-day basis. In Chapter 26, we discuss how firms manage their working capital. In Chapter 27, we explain how firms manage their short-term cash needs.

Part 10 addresses special topics. Chapter 28 discusses mergers and acquisitions, and Chapter 29 provides an overview of corporate governance. In Chapter 30, we consider corporations' use of insurance and financial derivatives to manage risk. Chapter 31 introduces the issues a firm faces when making a foreign investment and addresses the valuation of foreign projects.

CUSTOMIZE YOUR APPROACH

Corporate Finance offers coverage of the major topical areas for introductory-level MBA students, as well as the depth required in a reference textbook for upper-division courses. Most professors customize their classes by selecting a subset of chapters reflecting the subject matter they consider most important. We designed this book from the outset with this need for flexibility in mind. Parts 2 through 6 are the core chapters in the book. We envision that most MBA programs will cover this material—yet even within these core chapters instructors can pick and choose.

Single quarter course: Cover Chapters 3–15; if time allows, or students are previously familiar with the time value of money, add on Chapters 16–19.

Semester-long course: Incorporate chapters from Part 7, *Options*, and Part 10, *Special Topics*, as desired.

Single mini-semester: Assign Chapters 3–10, 14, and 15 if time allows.

CANADIAN CONTENT AND CONTEXT

A Canadian text should reflect Canadian realities, and show how they fit into the bigger picture. The Canadian tax system, for example, differs significantly from that of the United States in regards to dividends, capital gains, capital cost allowance, and leasing. We use the relevant Canadian tax code to make the examples more realistic to students and to give them exposure to how Canadian taxation works. There are many institutional and market differences between Canada and the United States. We have incorporated information on both countries' institutions and markets and often include comparisons with other countries. We feel it is important that students understand Canada's relative positioning on a number of issues related to markets, the financial crisis, corporate governance, and corporate finance. To this end, we have selected Canadian examples, when appropriate, for use in the text. Many of the companies we use as examples are ones known by Canadian students, companies that have had interesting successes or failures. We feel that, in addition to learning corporate finance, students should have familiarity with Canadian business and its rich history.

STUDENT SUPPORT

MYFINANCELAB

MyFinanceLab is a critical component of the text. This resource will give all students the practice and tutorial help they need to succeed. For more details, see the full description at the beginning of the book.

COURSESMART

CourseSmart goes beyond traditional expectations–providing instant, online access to the textbooks and course materials you need at an average savings of 60%. With instant access from any computer and the ability to search your text, you'll find the content you need quickly, no matter where you are. And with online tools like highlighting and note-taking, you can save time and study efficiently. See all the benefits at www.coursesmart.com/students.

INSTRUCTOR SUPPORT

SOLUTIONS MANUAL

This essential companion to the text provides detailed, accuracy-verified solutions to every chapter problem. Spreadsheet solutions to selected chapter problems and Data Cases are available on the Instructor's Resource CD-ROM.

INSTRUCTOR'S MANUAL

Corresponding to each chapter, the Instructor's Manual provides a chapter overview and outline correlated to the PowerPoint Lecture Notes, learning objectives, a guide to worked examples in the PowerPoint Lecture Notes, and a listing of chapter problems with Excel Spreadsheets (available on the Instructor's Resource CD-ROM).

TEST BANK

The Test Bank provides a wealth of accuracy-verified testing material. It is made available in Word format (Test Item File) and in electronic format (TestGen). The wide selection of multiple-choice, short answer, and essay questions—with over 500 new questions for the Second Canadian Edition—are qualified by difficulty level and skill type and correlated to chapter topics. Numerical-based problems include step-by-step solutions.

POWERPOINT LECTURE PRESENTATION

The PowerPoint Lecture Presentation offers outlines of each chapter with graphs, tables, and key terms and concepts. Fresh worked examples—50 of them new for the Second Canadian Edition—provide detailed, step-by-step solutions in the same format as the boxes from the text and correlated to parallel specific textbook examples. The PowerPoints are included on the Instructor's Resource CD-ROM and are also available for download from Pearson's online catalogue (vig.pearsoned.ca).

INSTRUCTOR'S RESOURCE CD-ROM

Compatible with PC and Macintosh computers, this CD-ROM offers the complete set of instructor supplements, including Microsoft Word and Adobe PDF files of the Instructor's Manual, Solutions Manual, and Test Bank; complete PowerPoint Lecture Presentations; Excel Spreadsheet Solutions to selected chapter problems and Data Cases; and the Computerized Test Bank in TestGen.

COURSESMART FOR INSTRUCTORS

CourseSmart goes beyond traditional expectations–providing instant, online access to the textbooks and course materials you need at a lower cost for students. And even as students save money, you can save time and hassle with a digital eTextbook that allows you to search for the most relevant content at the very moment you need it. Whether it's evaluating textbooks or creating lecture notes to help students with difficult concepts, CourseSmart can make life a little easier. See how when you visit www.coursesmart.com/instructors.

TECHNOLOGY SPECIALISTS. Pearson's Technology Specialists work with faculty and campus course designers to ensure that Pearson technology products, assessment tools, and online course materials are tailored to meet your specific needs. This highly qualified team is dedicated to helping schools take full advantage of a wide range of educational resources, by assisting in the integration of a variety of instructional materials and media formats. Your local Pearson Education sales representative can provide you with more details on this service program.

ACKNOWLEDGMENTS

Now that we have explained what is in this book, we can turn to thanking the people that made it happen. As any textbook writer will tell you, you cannot write a textbook of this scope without a substantial amount of help. First and foremost, we thank Gary Bennett, VP and editorial director of Higher Education at Pearson Canada, whose vision of a high-quality corporate finance text for the Canadian market continues to inspire our writing. Claudine O'Donnell's knowledge, experience, leadership, and patience kept the various aspects of the project moving along smoothly. Paul Donnelly needs special thanks for his hard work and perseverance in his role as senior developmental editor. His focus on getting the chapters written and moved through the developmental process was amazing. No less amazing was his patience and tactful encouragement to meet the many deadlines along the way. We also thank Imee Salumbides, as project manager, who managed the stages of the book with skill. Andrea Nemeth provided excellent copy editing, and we thank her for making the chapters more readable and grammatical. Bruce Price, the technical checker, also gets our thanks for his keen eye to detail and the ability to catch and correct any error before the final printing. We are also thankful to Jennifer Parks for her skilful oversight of the MyFinanceLab project—a formidable undertaking in its own right. Of course, we also thank Leigh-Anne Graham for leading the successful marketing of the text in the Canadian market.

A corporate finance textbook is the product of the talents and hard work of many talented colleagues. We're appreciative of the work of Marlene Bellamy and Conor Vibert in conducting the interviews that provide a critically important perspective, and to the interviewees who graciously provided their time and insights.

Mark Rubinstein inspired us with his passion to get the history of finance right by correctly attributing the important ideas to the people who first enunciated them. Inspiration is one thing; actually undertaking the task is another. His book, *A History of the Theory of Investments: My Annotated Bibliography*, was indispensable—it provided the only available reference of the history of finance. As will be obvious to any reader, we have used it extensively in this text and we, as well as the profession as a whole, owe him a debt of gratitude for taking the time to write it all down.

We could not have written this text if we were not once ourselves students of finance. As any student knows, the key to success is having a great teacher. In our case we are lucky to have been taught and advised by the people who helped create modern finance: Ken Arrow, Darrell Duffie, Mordecai Kurz, Randall Morck, Stephen Ross, Richard Roll, and Gordon Sick. It was from them that we learned the importance of the core principles of finance, including the Law of One Price, on which this book is based. The learning process does not end at graduation and, like most people, we have had especially influential colleagues and mentors from which we learned a great deal during our careers and we would like to recognize them explicitly here: Mike Fishman, Richard Green, David Manry, Charles Mossman, Vasant Naik, Art Raviv, Mark Rubinstein, Harry Turtle, Joe Williams, and Jeff Zwiebel. We continue to learn from our colleagues and we are grateful to all of them. Finally, we would like to thank those with whom we have taught finance classes over the years: Anat Admati, Paul Brockman, Tim Burt, Jerrod Falk, Ming Huang, Gady Jacoby, Robert Korajczyk, Cyril Oickle, Paul Pfleiderer, Hugh Pratt, Sergio Rebelo, Richard Stanton, Raman Uppal, and Steven Zheng. Their ideas and teaching strategies have, without a doubt, influenced our own sense of pedagogy and found their way into this text.

Jonathan Berk
Peter DeMarzo
David Stangeland

MAJOR CONTRIBUTOR

Jerrod Falk deserves special thanks as a major contributor to the Second Canadian Edition. Jerrod graduated with his Bachelor of Commerce (Honours) at the University of Manitoba in 1992 and went on to complete his Certified Management Accountant designation (and was the Gold Medal winner) in 1997. His career in corporate finance has spanned both business and government organizations in various roles including corporate controller. Since 2000, Jerrod has been an instructor at the University of Manitoba and is a recipient of multiple teaching awards. His work on the chapter revisions was invaluable and we are honoured to have him as part of the team in the production of the Second Canadian Edition.

CONTRIBUTORS

The original US editions of this text involved the contributions of over 200 manuscript reviewers, class testers, and focus group participants. We strived to incorporate every contributor's input and are truly grateful for the time each individual took to provide comments and suggestions. Their work helped to prepare the strong foundation on which the Canadian editions are built. We also owe a great debt of thanks to the discerning and conscientious reviewers of the Second Canadian Edition manuscript, whose names are listed below.

Sandra Betton, *Concordia University*
Esther Eiling, *University of Toronto, Scarborough*
Dave Kennedy, *Lethbridge College*
Andrey Pavlov, *Simon Fraser University*
Wei Wang, *Queen's University*

Teaching Students to Think Finance

With a consistency in presentation and an innovative set of learning aids, *Corporate Finance, Second Canadian Edition,* simultaneously meets the needs of both future financial managers and non-financial managers. This textbook truly shows every student how to "think finance."

SIMPLIFIED PRESENTATION OF MATHEMATICS

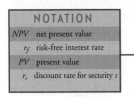

NOTATION	
NPV	net present value
r_f	risk-free interest rate
PV	present value
r_s	discount rate for security s

One of the hardest parts of learning finance is mastering the jargon, math, and non-standardized notation. *Corporate Finance,* Second Canadian Edition, systematically uses:

- **Notation Boxes:** Each chapter begins with a Notation box that defines the variables and the acronyms used in the chapter and serves as 'legend' for students' reference.

Future Value of an Annuity

$$FV(\text{annuity}) = PV \times (1 + r)^N$$
$$= \frac{C}{r}\left(1 - \frac{1}{(1 + r)^N}\right) \times (1 + r)^N$$
$$= C \times \frac{1}{r}\left((1 + r)^N - 1\right) \qquad (4.8)$$

- **Numbered and Labeled Equations:** The first time a full equation is given in notation form it is numbered. Key equations are titled and revisited in the summary and in end papers.

- **Spreadsheet Tables:** Select tables are available on MyFinanceLab as Excel files, enabling students to change inputs and manipulate the underlying calculations.

PRACTICE FINANCE TO LEARN FINANCE

Working problems is the proven way to cement and demonstrate an understanding of finance.

- **Concept Check questions** at the end of each section enable students to test their understanding and target areas in which they need further review.

- **End-of-chapter problems written personally by Jonathan Berk, Peter DeMarzo and David Stangeland** offer instructors the opportunity to assign first-rate materials to students for homework and practice with the confidence that the problems are consistent with the chapter content. Both the problems and solutions, which were also written by the authors, have been class-tested and accuracy checked to ensure quality.

END-OF-CHAPTER MATERIALS REINFORCE LEARNING

Testing understanding of central concepts is crucial to learning finance.

DATA CASE

Assume today is July 31, 2009. Natasha Kingery is 30 years old and has a Bachelor of Science degree in computer science. She is currently employed at Open Text Corporation in Ottawa and earns $38,000 a year, which she anticipates will grow at 3% per year. Natasha hopes to retire at age 65 and has just begun to think about the future.

Natasha has $75,000 that she recently inherited from her aunt. She invested this money in 10-year Government of Canada bonds. She is considering whether she should further her education and would use her inheritance to pay for it.

She has investigated a couple of programs and is asking for your help as a financial planning intern to determine the financial consequences associated with each option. Natasha has already been accepted to both of these programs, and could start either one soon.

One alternative that Natasha is considering is attaining a certification in network design. This certification would automatically promote her to a new position and give her a raise of $10,000. This salary differential will grow at a rate of 3% a year as long as she keeps working. The certification program requires the completion of 20 Web-based courses and a score of 80% or better on an exam at the end of the course work. She has learned that the average amount of time necessary to finish the program is one year. The total cost of the program is

- **Chapter Summaries and Key Terms lists** are vital aids for studying and review.

- **Data Cases** present in-depth scenarios in a business setting with questions designed to guide students' analysis. Many questions involve the use of Internet resources.

- **Further Readings** direct the student reader to seminal studies and late-breaking research to encourage independent study.

Bridging Theory and Practice

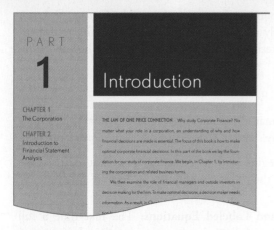

THE LAW OF ONE PRICE AS THE UNIFYING VALUATION FRAMEWORK

The Law of One Price framework reflects the modern idea that the absence of arbitrage is the unifying concept of valuation. This critical insight is introduced in Chapter 3, revisited in each Part Opener, and integrated throughout the text—motivating all major concepts and connecting theory to practice.

STUDY AIDS WITH A PRACTICAL FOCUS

To be successful, students need to master the core concepts and learn to identify and solve problems that today's practitioners face.

- **Common Mistakes** boxes alert students to frequently made mistakes stemming from misunderstanding core concepts and calculations, as well as mistakes made in practice.

- **Worked Examples** accompany every important concept using a step-by-step procedure that illustrates both Problem and Solution. Clear labels make them easy to find for help with homework or studying. Many include an Excel spreadsheet calculator.

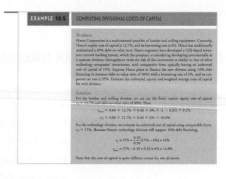

APPLICATIONS THAT REFLECT REAL PRACTICE

Corporate Finance, Second Canadian Edition, features actual companies and leaders in the field.

- Real-company examples open each chapter
- Interviews with notable practitioners are featured in many chapters
- General Interest boxes highlight timely material from financial publications that shed light on business problems and real-company practices

PART

1

Introduction

CHAPTER 1

The Corporation

CHAPTER 2

Introduction to
Financial Statement
Analysis

THE LAW OF ONE PRICE CONNECTION. Why study Corporate Finance? No matter what your role in a corporation, an understanding of why and how financial decisions are made is essential. The focus of this book is how to make optimal corporate financial decisions. In this part of the book we lay the foundation for our study of corporate finance. We begin, in Chapter 1, by introducing the corporation and related business forms.

We then examine the role of financial managers and outside investors in decision making for the firm. To make optimal decisions, a decision maker needs information. As a result, in Chapter 2 we review an important source of information for corporate decision making—the firm's accounting statements.

The Corporation

Corporations have existed in Canada since before Canada was a nation. One of the oldest and most recognized corporations in Canada is the Hudson's Bay Company (HBC). HBC was given its charter in 1670 and still continues in operation today. In 1970, the head office of HBC moved from London, England, to Winnipeg; it now resides in Toronto. Ownership and control of the HBC has changed over the years too: originally domiciled in England, then in Canada, and currently in the United States.

Corporations are arguably the most important business organizations in Canada and around the world because of their dominance in terms of products produced, revenues and profits generated, and people employed. The corporate form is not static, though; it evolves through time. The financial and broader economic crisis that began in 2007 has transformed the financial landscape, bringing down multinationals such as AIG and multiple banks around the world. As governments seek to prevent a similar crisis in the future, new regulations will shape corporations and the environment in which they operate. There has never been a more exciting time to study corporate finance.

This book is about how corporations make financial decisions. Canadian corporate law has evolved from British Common Law and brought in aspects of U.S. corporate law. The purpose of this chapter is to introduce the corporation, as well as explain alternative business organizational forms common in Canada. A key factor in the success of corporations is the ability to easily trade ownership shares, and so we will also explain the role of stock markets in facilitating trading among investors in a corporation and the implications that has for the ownership and control of corporations.

1.1 THE THREE TYPES OF FIRMS

We begin our study of corporate finance by introducing the three major types of firms: sole proprietorships, partnerships, and corporations. We explain each organizational form in turn, but our primary focus is on the most important form—the corporation. In addition to describing what a corporation is, we also provide an overview of why corporations are so successful.

SOLE PROPRIETORSHIPS

A **sole proprietorship** is a business owned and run by one person. Sole proprietorships are usually very small with few, if any, employees. Although they are the most common type of business unit in the economy, sole proprietorships are relatively small in terms of revenues and profits produced and people employed. Sole proprietorships share the following key characteristics:

1. Sole proprietorships are straightforward to set up. Because of this advantage, many new businesses use this organizational form.

2. The principal limitation of a sole proprietorship is that there is no separation between the firm and the owner; the firm can have only one owner and business income is taxed at the personal level. If there are other investors, they cannot hold an ownership stake in the firm; this limits the ability of the owner to raise money for the business.

3. The owner of a sole proprietorship has unlimited personal liability for any of the firm's debts. That is, if the firm defaults on any debt payment, the lender can (and will) require the owner to repay the loan from personal assets. An owner who cannot afford to repay the loan must declare personal bankruptcy.

4. The life of a sole proprietorship is limited to the life of the owner. It is also difficult to transfer ownership of a sole proprietorship.

For most businesses, the disadvantages of a sole proprietorship outweigh the advantages. As soon as the firm reaches the point at which it can borrow without the owner agreeing to be personally liable, the owner typically converts the business into a form that limits the owner's liability.

PARTNERSHIPS

A **partnership** is similar to a sole proprietorship but it has more than one owner. Key features of a partnership are as follows:

1. Income is taxed at the personal level. The income is split among partners according to their ownership in the partnership.

2. *All* partners have unlimited personal liability. This applies to the firm's debt. That is, a lender can require *any* partner to repay *all* the firm's outstanding debts. Similarly, the unlimited liability applies in a legal judgment against the partnership; each partner is fully liable. Thus, partners must be chosen carefully, as any single partner's actions can affect the exposure of all the partners.

3. The partnership ends on the death or withdrawal of any single partner. However, partners can avoid liquidation if the partnership agreement provides for alternatives such as a buyout of a deceased or withdrawn partner.

Some old and established businesses remain partnerships or sole proprietorships. Often these firms are the types of businesses in which the owners' personal reputations are the basis for the businesses. For example, law firms and accounting firms are often organized as partnerships. For such enterprises, the partners' personal liability increases the confidence of the firm's clients that the partners will strive to maintain their reputation.

A **limited partnership** is a partnership with two kinds of owners, general partners and limited partners. There must be at least one general partner. General partners have the same rights and privileges as partners in a (general) partnership—they are personally liable for the firm's debt obligations. Limited partners, however, have **limited liability**—that is, their liability is limited to their investment. Their private property cannot be seized to pay off the firm's outstanding debts. Furthermore, the death or withdrawal of a limited partner does not dissolve the partnership, and a limited partner's interest is transferable. However, a limited partner has no management authority and cannot legally be involved in the managerial decision making for the business.

Private equity funds and venture capital funds are two examples of industries dominated by limited partnerships. In these firms, a few general partners contribute some of their own capital and raise additional capital from outside investors who are limited partners. The general partners control how all the capital is invested. Most often they will actively participate in running the businesses in which they choose to invest. The outside investors play no active role in running the partnership; their concern is with how their investments are performing.

In Canada a special type of partnership called a **limited liability partnership (LLP)** can be used in the legal and accounting professions. The LLP is similar to a general partnership in that the partners can be active in the management of the firm and they do have a degree of unlimited liability. The limitation on a partner's liability takes effect only in cases related to actions of negligence of other partners or those supervised by other partners. In all other respects, including a particular partner's own negligence or the negligence of those supervised by the particular partner, that partner has unlimited personal liability. In addition, the assets of the business are potentially at risk of seizure due to the actions of anyone within the partnership. Thus, while a partner's personal assets are protected from the negligent actions of other partners, the investment into the overall partnership may be lost.

CORPORATIONS

The distinguishing feature of a **corporation** is that it is a legally defined, artificial being (a judicial person or legal entity), separate from its owners. As such, it has many of the legal powers that people have. It can enter into contracts, acquire assets, incur obligations, and it receives similar protection against the seizure of its property as received by an individual. Because a corporation is a legal entity separate and distinct from its owners, it is solely responsible for its own obligations. Consequently, the owners of a corporation (its **shareholders**) have limited liability; they are not liable for any obligations the corporation enters into. Similarly, the corporation is not liable for any personal obligations of its owners.

FORMATION OF A CORPORATION.   In most provinces corporations are defined under the provincial Business Corporations Act or the Canada Business Corporations Act. Corporations must be legally formed, which means that the **articles of incorporation** must be filed with the relevant registrar of corporations. The articles of incorporation, sometimes referred to as the corporate charter, are like a corporate constitution that sets out the terms of the corporation's ownership and existence. Setting up a corporation is therefore considerably more costly than setting up a sole proprietorship. Most firms hire lawyers to create the formal articles of incorporation and a set of bylaws.

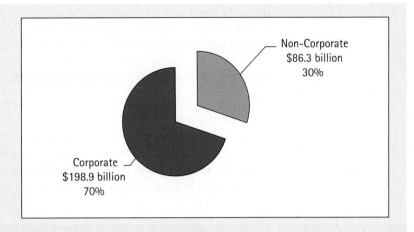

FIGURE 1.1

2006 Canadian Business Net Income Before Tax: Corporate Versus Non-Corporate

Comparing incorporated firms to unincorporated firms, even though there are more unincorporated businesses, 70% of business income is generated by corporations.

Source: Statistics Canada, Table 380-0016

OWNERSHIP OF A CORPORATION. There is no limit on the number of owners a corporation can have. Because most corporations have many owners, each owner owns only a fraction of the corporation. The entire ownership stake of a corporation is divided into shares known as **stock**. The collection of all the outstanding shares of a corporation is known as the **equity** of the corporation. An owner of a share of stock in the corporation is known as a shareholder, **stockholder**, or **equity holder** and is entitled to **dividend payments**, that is, payments made at the discretion of the corporation's Board of Directors to the equity holders. Shareholders usually receive voting rights and dividend rights that are proportional to the amount of stock they own. For example, a shareholder who owns 30% of the firm's shares will be entitled to 30% of the votes at an annual meeting and 30% of the total dividend payment. In Canada, many corporations have a dominant shareholder (controlling in excess of 25% of the equity); in the United States, more corporations are considered widely held (with the largest shareholder holding less than 5% of the equity). About 19% of Canadian corporations listed on the Toronto Stock Exchange (TSX) have multiple classes of stock such that some classes may have more voting rights than others, even though they have the same rights to dividends.

A unique feature of a corporation is that there is no limitation on who can own its stock. That is, an owner of a corporation need not have any special expertise or qualification. This feature allows free trade in the shares of the corporation and provides one of the most important advantages of organizing a firm as a corporation rather than as sole proprietorship or partnership. Corporations can raise substantial amounts of capital because they can sell ownership shares to anonymous outside investors.

The availability of outside funding has enabled corporations to dominate the economy compared to unincorporated businesses (see Figure 1.1). Let's take the world's largest corporation ranked by sales in the Fortune Global 500 survey, Wal-Mart Stores Inc., headquartered in Bentonville, Arkansas. For the fiscal year ended January 31, 2007, Wal-Mart's annual report indicated revenue was about $345 billion and the total value of the company (the wealth in the company the owners collectively owned) was over $200 billion. It employed 1.9 million people. Let's put these numbers into perspective. A country with $345 billion gross domestic product (GDP) in 2006 would rank just ahead of Poland as the 22nd richest *country* (out of more than 200).[1] Poland has more than 38 million people,

---

1. To see the World Bank Quick Reference Tables on GDP and Population, go to http://go.worldbank.org/B5PYF93QF0.

about 20 times as many people as employees at Wal-Mart. Indeed, if the number of employees were used as the "population" of Wal-Mart, it would rank as the 142nd largest country, just behind Slovenia.

TAX IMPLICATIONS FOR CORPORATE ENTITIES

An important difference between the types of organizational forms is the way they are taxed. Because a corporation is a separate legal entity, a corporation's profits are subject to taxation separate from its owners' tax obligations. In effect, shareholders of a corporation pay taxes twice. First, the corporation pays tax on its profits, and then when the remaining profits are distributed to the shareholders, the shareholders pay their own personal income tax on this income. This system is sometimes referred to as *double taxation*.

EXAMPLE 1.1

TAXATION OF CORPORATE EARNINGS

Problem

You are a shareholder in a corporation. Some of your shares are held inside your registered retirement savings plan (RRSP) so any earnings there are not taxed as long as the money is kept in the RRSP; any income from shares held outside your RRSP is taxable. The corporation earns $5 per share before taxes. After it has paid taxes, it will distribute the rest of its earnings to you as a dividend. The corporate tax rate is 35% and your tax rate on dividend income outside your RRSP is 24%.[2] How much of the earnings remains after all taxes are paid (calculate this twice—for the shares in the RRSP and for the shares outside of the RRSP)?

Solution

First, the corporation pays taxes. It earned $5 per share, but must pay $0.35 \times \$5 = \$1.75$ to the government in corporate taxes. That leaves $3.25 to distribute. However, for the shares outside your RRSP you must pay $0.24 \times \$3.25 = 78$ cents in income taxes, leaving $\$3.25 - \$0.78 = \$2.47$ per share after all taxes are paid. As a shareholder owning shares outside your RRSP you end up with only $2.47 of the original $5 in earnings; the remaining $\$1.75 + \$0.78 = \$2.53$ is paid as taxes. Thus, your total effective tax rate on the corporation's earnings is $2.53/5 = 50.6\%$ if your shares are held outside your RRSP. The shares you hold within your RRSP are not subject to taxes on the dividends paid; thus, there is only the corporate tax of 35% and your RRSP keeps the full $3.25 dividend. Note, eventually when you withdraw money from your RRSP, the *full* amount withdrawn will be taxed at your regular income tax rate. Hopefully, though, when you are retired and withdraw the money, you will have a lower tax rate.

In most countries, there is some relief from double taxation. Thirty countries make up the Organization for Economic Co-operation and Development (OECD), and of these countries, only Ireland offers no relief from double taxation. In Canada, the dividend tax

---

2. Your tax on dividend income from a Canadian corporation is determined by Canada Revenue Agency's requirement to gross up the dividend amount by 45%, apply your tax rate to the grossed up amount, and then receive a dividend tax credit of 27.5% of the actual dividend. In the 2007 tax year, this resulted in combined federal and provincial tax rates on dividends that ranged from 17.45% in Alberta to 30.63% in Newfoundland and was around 24% in many of the other provinces.

credit gives some relief by effectively giving a lower tax rate on dividend income than on other sources of income. In the 2007 tax year, for most provinces, dividend income was taxed at a rate about 20% less than ordinary income; for example, in Ontario the effective personal tax rates (combined provincial and federal) were 24.64% for dividends and 46.41% for regular income for individuals in the top tax bracket. A few countries, including Australia, Finland, Mexico, New Zealand, and Norway, offer complete relief by effectively not taxing dividend income.

The corporate organizational structure is the only organizational structure subject to double taxation. However, Canada Revenue Agency allows an exemption from double taxation for certain **flow through entities** where all income produced by the business flows to the investors and virtually no earnings are retained within the business. These entities are called **income trusts** and come in three forms. A **business income trust** holds all the debt and equity securities of a corporation (the underlying business) in trust for the trust's owners, called the **unit holders**. An **energy trust** either holds resource properties directly or holds all the debt and equity securities of a resource corporation within the trust. A **real estate investment trust (REIT)** either holds real estate properties directly or holds all the debt and equity securities of a corporation that owns real estate properties. For income trusts formed before November 2006, there is no tax at the business level until 2011. REITs will continue to have no tax at the business level beyond 2011 but the other forms of income trusts will be taxed.

EXAMPLE 1.2   TAXATION OF INCOME TRUSTS

Problem

Rework Example 1.1 assuming the corporation in that example had all its debt and equity held in an income trust and flowed through all earnings to trust unit owners. We will assume you hold some of the trust units within your RRSP, so they are not subject to personal taxes. For the trust units held outside your RRSP, suppose you pay tax at a rate of 46%.

Solution

In this case, there is no corporate tax. If the business earned $5 per unit, then the $5 is paid out to the trust unit holders. For your units held within your RRSP, there is no personal tax. Thus there is no tax whatsoever in the year the business income is generated—giving the government 0% of the business earnings. Eventually, when you withdraw money from your RRSP for retirement, some tax will be paid, but that may not be for 30 years, and the tax rate may be for a low tax bracket, as you may have lower earnings during retirement. For your units held outside your RRSP, there will be personal tax of $0.46 \times \$5 = \$2.30$. The net tax collected by the government is the 46% collected from you.

On October 31, 2006, the government changed the taxation of business and energy trusts so they would be taxable at the business level (beginning in 2011). Its concern was that many of these trust units were held within non-taxable RRSPs or pension funds or by foreign investors, and thus much of the tax that would normally be collected from corporate earnings was being lost by the government. Since that time, many of these income trusts have been converting back to the standard corporate form because of the loss of their special non-taxable status.

CONCEPT CHECK 1. What are the advantages and disadvantages of organizing a business as a corporation?

2. What is a limited liability partnership (LLP)? How does it differ from a limited partnership?

3. What is an income trust? Which type of trust will still get preferential tax treatment after 2011?

1.2 OWNERSHIP VERSUS CONTROL OF CORPORATIONS

Unlike the owner of a sole proprietorship, which has direct control of the firm, it is often not feasible for the owners of a corporation to have direct control of the firm because there are many owners of a corporation, each of whom can freely trade their stock. That is, in a corporation, direct control and ownership are often separate. Rather than the owners, the *board of directors* and *chief executive officer* possess direct control of the corporation. In this section, we explain how the responsibilities for the corporation are divided between these two entities and how together they shape and execute the goals of the firm.

THE CORPORATE MANAGEMENT TEAM

The shareholders of a corporation exercise their control by electing a **board of directors**, a group of people that has the ultimate decision-making authority in the corporation. In most corporations, each share of stock gives a shareholder one vote in the election of each position on the board of directors, so investors with more shares have more influence. When one or two shareholders own a very large proportion of the outstanding stock, these shareholders might either be on the board of directors themselves or they may have the right to appoint a number of directors.

The board of directors makes rules on how the corporation should be run (including how the top managers in the corporation are compensated), sets policy, and monitors the performance of the company. The board of directors delegates most decisions that involve day-to-day running of the corporation to its management—headed by the **chief executive officer** (or **CEO**). The CEO is charged with running the corporation by instituting the rules and policies set by the board of directors. The size of the rest of the management team varies from corporation to corporation. The separation of powers within corporations between the board of directors and CEO is not always distinct. In fact, it is not uncommon for the CEO also to be the chairman of the board of directors. The most senior financial manager is the **chief financial officer (CFO)**, who usually reports directly to the CEO. Figure 1.2 presents part of a typical organizational chart for a corporation, highlighting the key positions a financial manager may take.

THE FINANCIAL MANAGER

Within the corporation, financial managers are responsible for three main tasks: making investment decisions, making financing decisions, and managing the firm's cash flows.

INVESTMENT DECISIONS. The financial manager's most important job is to make the firm's investment decisions. The financial manager must weigh the costs and benefits of each investment or project and decide which of them qualify as good uses of the money shareholders have invested in the firm. These investment decisions fundamentally shape what the firm does and whether it will add value for its owners. In this book, we will develop all the tools necessary to make these investment decisions.

FIGURE 1.2

Organizational Chart of a Typical Corporation
The board of directors, representing the shareholders, controls the corporation and hires the Chief Executive Officer, who is then responsible for running the corporation. The Chief Financial Officer overseas the financial operations of the firm, with the Controller managing both tax and accounting functions, and the Treasurer responsible for capital budgeting, risk management, and credit management activities.

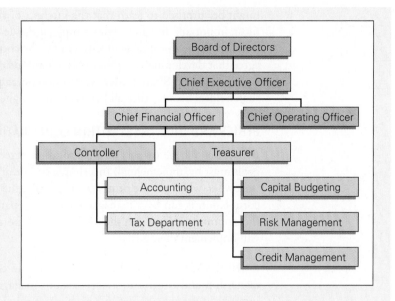

FINANCING DECISIONS.   Once the financial manager has decided which investments to make, he or she also decides how to pay for them. Large investments may require the corporation to raise additional money. The financial manager must decide whether to raise more money from new and existing owners by selling more shares of stock (equity) or to borrow the money instead (debt). In this book, we will discuss the characteristics of each source of money and how to decide which one to use in the context of the corporation's overall mix of debt and equity.

CASH MANAGEMENT.   The financial manager must ensure that the firm has enough cash on hand to meet its obligations from day to day. This job, also commonly known as managing working capital, may seem straightforward, but in a young or growing company, it can mean the difference between success and failure. Even companies with great products require significant amounts of money to develop and bring those products to market. Consider the costs to Apple of launching the iPhone, which included developing the technology and creating a massive marketing campaign, or the costs to Boeing of producing the 787—the firm spent billions of dollars before the first 787 left the ground. A company typically burns through a significant amount of cash before the sales of the product generate income. The financial manager's job is to make sure that access to cash does not hinder the firm's success.

OWNERSHIP AND CONTROL OF CORPORATIONS

In theory, the goal of a firm should be determined by the firm's owners. A sole proprietorship has a single owner who runs the firm, so the goals of a sole proprietorship are the same as the owner's goals. But in organizational forms with multiple owners, the appropriate goal of the firm—and thus its managers—is not as clear.

Many corporations have thousands of owners (shareholders). Each owner is likely to have different interests and priorities. Whose interests and priorities determine the goals of the firm? Later in the book, we examine this question in more detail. However, you might be surprised to learn that the interests of shareholders are aligned for many, if not most, important decisions. For example, if the decision is whether to develop a new product that will be a profitable investment for the corporation, all shareholders will very likely agree that developing this product is a good idea because it will increase the value of the shares they own. **Shareholder wealth maximization** is the one goal that generally unites shareholders because they all benefit from a higher stock price.

ETHICS AND INCENTIVES WITHIN CORPORATIONS

Even when all the owners of a corporation agree on the goals of the corporation, these goals must be implemented. In a simple organizational form such as a sole proprietorship, the owner, who runs the firm, can ensure that the firm's goals match his or her own. But a corporation is run by a management team, separate from its owners, giving rise to conflicts of interest. How can the owners of a corporation ensure that the management team will implement their goals?

PRINCIPAL-AGENT PROBLEM.   Many people claim that because of the separation of ownership and control in a corporation, managers have little incentive to work in the interests of the shareholders when this means working against their own self-interests. As a manager, wouldn't it be more fun to relax all day and freely eat in the company's gourmet dining room? Unfortunately for shareholders, **shirking** or consuming **perquisites** do little to benefit them even though the manager can benefit a lot. Economists call this a **principal-agent problem** (or just an **agency problem**) when managers, despite being hired as the agents of shareholders, put their own self-interest ahead of the interests of shareholders. Managers face the ethical dilemma of whether to adhere to their responsibility to put the interests of shareholders first, or to do what is in their own personal best interest.

The most common way the principal-agent problem is addressed in practice is by minimizing the number of decisions managers must make for which their own self-interest substantially differs from the interests of the shareholders. For example, managers' compensation contracts are designed to ensure that most decisions in the shareholders' interest are also in the managers' interests; shareholders often tie the compensation of top managers to the corporation's profits or perhaps to its stock price. Thus, if managers shirk or consume too many perquisites, the corporation's profit and stock price will drop and managers' compensation will decline. This encourages managers not to shirk or consume too many perquisites. There is, however, a limitation to this strategy. By tying compensation too closely to performance, the shareholders might be asking managers to take on more risk than they are comfortable taking. As a result, managers may not make decisions that the shareholders want them to, or it might be hard to find talented managers willing to accept the job.

THE CEO'S PERFORMANCE.   Another way shareholders can encourage managers to work in the interests of shareholders is to discipline them if they don't. If shareholders are unhappy with a CEO's performance, they could, in principle, pressure the board to oust the CEO. However, directors and top executives are very rarely replaced through a grassroots shareholder uprising. Instead, dissatisfied investors often choose to sell their shares. Of course, somebody must be willing to buy the shares from the dissatisfied shareholders. If enough shareholders are dissatisfied, the only way to entice investors to buy the shares is to have a low price. Similarly, investors who see a well-managed corporation will want to purchase shares; this drives up the stock price. Thus, the stock price of the corporation is a barometer for corporate leaders that continuously gives them feedback on their shareholders' opinion of their performance.

When the stock performs poorly, the board of directors might react by replacing the CEO. In some corporations, however, the senior executives are entrenched because boards of directors do not have the will to replace them. Often the reluctance to fire results because the board consists of people who are close friends of the CEO and lack objectivity. In corporations in which the CEO is entrenched and doing a poor job, the expectation of continued poor performance will cause the stock price to be low. Low stock prices create a profit opportunity. In a **hostile takeover**, an individual or organization—sometimes known as a corporate raider—can purchase a large fraction of the stock and in doing so get enough votes to replace the board of directors and the CEO. With a new superior management team, the stock is a much more attractive investment, which would likely result in a price rise and a profit for the corporate raider and the other shareholders. Although the words "hostile" and "raider" have negative connotations, corporate raiders themselves provide an important service to shareholders. The mere threat of being removed as a result of a hostile takeover is often enough to discipline bad managers and motivate boards of directors to make difficult decisions. Consequently, when a corporation's shares are publicly traded, a "market for corporate control" is created that encourages managers and boards of directors to act in the interests of their shareholders.

If there is a dominant shareholder, or a shareholder that owns a class of shares with multiple votes, it may be impossible for the market for corporate control to work as desired because not enough shares can be purchased on the market to accumulate enough votes to change control. Shareholder rights activists point out this problem for many Canadian firms that have multiple voting classes or a dominant shareholder; thus, as investors we might want to reconsider investing in such firms. In response to the concern about multiple voting stocks, in 2004 the TSX added extensions to stocks' ticker symbols to indicate whether a share had lesser or greater voting power than other shares from the same corporation. However, due to intense lobbying pressure, these symbol extensions were removed by the end of June 2006.

SHAREHOLDERS VERSUS STAKEHOLDERS.   Shareholders are not the only ones interested in what a corporation does. Employees are interested in their jobs with the corporation. Customers are interested in the quality of the corporation's products. Suppliers are interested in being paid for their supplies and making a profit on what they sell to corporations. The community is interested in the environmental impact of the corporation and the government is interested in the tax dollars it collects. These groups and others (including shareholders and debt holders) can be considered **stakeholders** of the corporation, as they each have an interest (or stake) in how the corporation operates. In Canada, the United States, and the United Kingdom, the prevailing view in terms of the corporate goal is shareholder wealth maximization. In Japan and some European countries, a sometimes more popular view is that of **stakeholder satisfaction**. Stakeholder satisfaction as the desired corporate objective is a view also held by many critics of corporations and free enterprise economies.

How big, though, is the difference between caring for stakeholders versus shareholder wealth maximization? Consider a corporation that harasses employees, sacrifices quality, delays paying suppliers, breaks environmental protection laws, and sets up schemes to avoid taxes. These actions are obviously detrimental to many of the corporation's stakeholders, but do they accomplish shareholder wealth maximization? Some would argue that they do because they may allow the corporation to report a higher profit in the current year. This, however, is short-sighted, as it ignores the problems caused by these actions in future periods. When employees feel harassed, they may quit or consider becoming unionized. When customers experience defective products, they will stop buying from the corporation. When suppliers realize they are not going to be paid on time, they will either stop selling to the corporation, or they will adjust their prices higher to recoup the lost money due to delayed collections. When it is discovered that environmental laws are broken, the corporation will be fined and forced to clean up its operations. Tax avoidance by the corporation may also result in penalties or the government changing the tax laws. In all these cases, there will be long-term damage to the corporation's reputation and profits. Since shareholders own stock that is a claim to the company's current *and future* earnings, these actions will actually be harmful to the current value of the company's stock. In the vast majority of cases, corporations that take care of their stakeholders also add value for their stockholders, so there is a convergence between shareholder wealth maximization and stakeholder satisfaction. Management that is being criticized for acting against stakeholders can usually be equally criticized for not acting for shareholder wealth maximization. Of course there are limits in both directions. If managers are excessively generous to some stakeholders, it may border on corporate welfare at the expense of shareholder wealth maximization.

CORPORATE BANKRUPTCY. Ordinarily, a corporation is run on behalf of its shareholders. But when a corporation borrows money, the holders of the firm's debt also become investors in the corporation. While the debt holders do not normally exercise control over the firm, if the corporation fails to repay its debts the debt holders are entitled to seize the assets of the corporation in compensation for the default. To prevent such a seizure, the firm may attempt to renegotiate with the debt holders, or file for bankruptcy protection. (We describe the details of the bankruptcy process and its implications for corporate decisions in much more detail in Part 5 of the text.)

In bankruptcy, management is given the opportunity to reorganize the firm and renegotiate with debt holders. If this process fails, control of the corporation generally passes to the debt holders. In most cases, the original equity holders are left with little or no stake in the firm. Thus, when a firm fails to repay its debts, the end result is often a change in ownership of the firm, with control passing from equity holders to debt holders. Importantly, bankruptcy need not result in a **liquidation** of the firm, which involves shutting down the business and selling off its assets. Even if control of the firm passes to the debt holders, it is in the debt holders' interest to run the firm in the most profitable way possible. Doing so often means keeping the business operating. For example, in April 2003, Air Canada declared bankruptcy. After 18 months working on restructuring, the airline emerged from bankruptcy as ACE Aviation. Old shareholders of Air Canada were left with virtually nothing—owning only 0.01% of the shares of ACE Aviation. Affected creditors were given about 46% of the shares in ACE and rights to purchase additional shares. If they did not exercise their rights to purchase additional shares, Deutsche Bank stood by to buy up to 42% of ACE Aviation's shares. Other investors injected $250 million by buying preferred shares in ACE Aviation. In order to make ACE Aviation a viable company and to get the required financing, employees had to accept concessions on their union contracts, aircraft leases had to be renegotiated, and the operating units of Air Canada were reconfigured so they could compete for third-party business. These changes, while difficult, were better than what would have resulted if Air Canada had been shut

INTERVIEW WITH MICHAEL SCOTT

Michael Scott is chairman and CEO of Precision BioLogic Incorporated, which develops, manufactures, and markets very specialized products that are used in the diagnosis of blood coagulation disorders.

QUESTION: **Business schools teach the concept of shareholder wealth maximization as the overriding corporate goal. Do you agree?**

ANSWER: That is an important goal. As a company, we are an engine for value creation. That value has three prongs: creating value for customers, for employees, and for shareholders. Shareholder value creation comes from the first two. If you have engaged employees looking for ways to create value for customers, you will have a successful business and create value for shareholders.

We provide good jobs, with a good work-life balance, that people are happy to be doing. Our company is participatory and consensus-based. We ensure that people across the company participate in the processes we go through with customers as we listen for product ideas, as we develop ideas, and as we work together. We want engaged people who are committed to their work, rather than compliant with a regime.

The medical products industry is all about trust. We are known for service and have built strong relationships over the years with the largest players in the industry. That pays off for us in collaborations, in development, and in ongoing sustainable profitable business. The collaborative way in which we develop products is incredibly important. Our job is to produce fairly priced, high-quality products so our customers can make a positive buying decision.

So we have strong relationships with our customers and are responsive to their needs. That, combined with dedicated, committed, engaged employees, makes us successful. Obviously, that all results in value being created for our shareholders.

QUESTION: **Is maximizing profit or quarterly income the same as shareholder wealth maximization?**

ANSWER: No, and I think that is where many people go wrong. You have to look at profitability over time and how it affects value. One reason we remain a private company is to avoid the game of trying to match the quarter-by-quarter demands of analysts who track publicly traded companies. We may make a business decision to invest in expensive new marketing or development efforts. That may negatively affect our profitability in the short run. Value recognizes the whole future stream of profits our company will produce. We have, year by year, been increasingly profitable as a matter of developing the business.

QUESTION: **Some argue that other stakeholders (e.g., employees, suppliers, customers, government, community) need to be looked after and that this conflicts with shareholder wealth maximization. Can you comment on that?**

ANSWER: I don't think that shareholder wealth maximization is compromised by paying attention to other stakeholders. In the short run you might squeeze out more profits by pressing harder on suppliers or employees. But for the long run, and for a sustainable entity, you need an ecosystem of players who are all benefiting from the activities of the company. That includes customers, suppliers, and particularly employees. If you have a healthy organization, with employees who are happy and engaged in what they are doing, that will help to ensure the long-run success of the company, which then reflects on shareholder value.

QUESTION: **Can you comment on plans for the future ownership of your company?**

ANSWER: We could take the company public, we could keep it private, or we could sell it. We do not think going public is the right thing for us now, because we are not big consumers of external capital. We are profitable and growing quite strongly and steadily at about 15 to 20% per year. Also, we like the flexibility of being a private company. We like what we have built, we like the culture, and we are creating and extracting value for shareholders while recognizing those things. At this time we don't want to sell the company. So we are coming up with a slow transition of ownership that involves key employees coming in through an earn-in over time and the exiting over time of a number of existing shareholders—potentially eventually even myself. There is no particular hurry to that. We want to make sure the transition is solid and will work for everybody.

FINANCIAL **CRISIS**
LEHMAN BROTHERS BANKRUPTCY

On September 15, 2008, Lehman Brothers investment bank announced it was filing for bankruptcy protection. With liabilities exceeding $700 billion, Lehman's bankruptcy was by far the largest bankruptcy in history, and it helped to trigger a worldwide financial crisis. In reporting the bankruptcy of this 158-year-old investment bank, the *International Herald Tribune* claimed, "It certainly is over for Lehman's 25,000 employees, who have lost a large portion of their fortunes as the firm's stock has fallen and who are now frantically searching for work."[1] But was it really "over"?

Despite the bankruptcy filing, Lehman continued to operate. Within a week of the filing, Barclays PLC had purchased Lehman's North American investment-banking and trading units as going concerns and so all the employees of these units became employees of Barclays. Within a month Nomura Holdings had purchased Lehman's non-U.S. subsidiaries as going concerns, and so Lehman's foreign employees became employees of Nomura. Finally, by the end of the year Lehman Brothers' Investment Management business was bought by its senior managers.

As catastrophic as this bankruptcy was to the economy, it did not result in the cessation of Lehman Brothers' underlying business activities. Instead, it precipitated a change in who owned and controlled the firm.

1. Landon Thomas, *International Herald Tribune*, September 15, 2008.

down completely—leaving the company's creditors with less, displacing all the employees, and terminating the leases from the aircraft suppliers. Air Canada regained its status in the Canadian aviation industry with ACE Aviation's income jumping from $261 million in 2005 to $1.4 billion in 2007. How Air Canada and other airlines will fare in the future is always a good question. Airlines are quite cyclical in their profitability and by the end of 2008, in the midst of the economic crisis, Ace Aviation's annual net income had slipped to a $120 million loss. Not until the second quarter of 2009 did ACE Aviation return to positive net income.

Thus, a useful way to understand corporations is to think of there being two sets of investors with claims to its cash flows: debt holders and equity holders. As long as the corporation can satisfy the claims of the debt holders, ownership remains in the hands of the equity holders. If the corporation fails to satisfy debt holders' claims, debt holders may take control of the firm. Thus a corporate bankruptcy is best thought of as a *change in ownership* of the corporation, and not necessarily as a failure of the underlying business.

CONCEPT CHECK

1. What is a principal-agent problem that may exist in a corporation?

2. How does the board of directors control a corporation?

3. How does shareholder wealth maximization converge with stakeholder satisfaction?

4. How may a corporate bankruptcy filing affect the ownership of a corporation?

1.3 THE STOCK MARKET

As we have discussed, shareholders would like the firm's managers to maximize the value of their investment in the firm. The value of their investment is determined by the price of a share of the corporation's stock. Because **private companies** have a limited set of shareholders and their shares are not regularly traded, the value of their shares can be difficult to determine. But many corporations are **public companies**, whose shares trade on organized markets called a **stock market** (or **stock exchange**). These markets provide *liquidity* and determine a market price for the company's shares. An investment is said to be **liquid** if it is possible to sell it quickly and easily for a price very close to the price at which you could contemporaneously buy it. This liquidity is attractive to outside investors, as it provides flexibility regarding the timing and duration of their investment in the firm. In this section we provide an overview of the world's major stock markets. The research and trading of participants in these markets give rise to share prices that provide constant feedback to managers regarding investors' views of their decisions.

PRIMARY AND SECONDARY STOCK MARKETS

When a corporation itself issues new shares of stock and sells them to investors they do so on the **primary market.** After this initial transaction between the corporation and investors, the shares continue to trade in a **secondary market** between investors without the involvement of the corporation. For example, if you wish to buy 100 shares of Tim Hortons, you would place an order on a stock exchange, where Tim Hortons trades under the ticker symbol THI. You would buy your shares from someone who already held shares of Tim Hortons, not from Tim Hortons itself.

THE LARGEST STOCK MARKETS

The best-known stock market and the largest stock market in the world is the New York Stock Exchange (NYSE). The largest stock exchange in Canada is the Toronto Stock Exchange (TSX), which is part of the TMX Group (formed by the merger of the TSX and the Montreal Exchange—a market for derivatives trading that will be discussed later in the book). The TSX is the ninth largest exchange in the world as measured by total market capitalization in 2008. Most countries have at least one stock market. Other than the NYSE and NASDAQ (which stands for National Association of Securities Dealers Automated Quotations) in the United States, the biggest stock markets are the London Stock Exchange, NYSE Euronext, and the Tokyo Stock Exchange.

Figure 1.3 ranks the world's 20 largest stock markets by two of the most common measures: the total value of all domestic corporations listed on the exchange and the total annual volume of shares traded on the exchange. Table 1.1 shows the actual data for the world's 50 largest stock markets for the same measures.

TSX

The TSX is an electronic exchange. Investors (individuals and institutions) can post orders onto the TSX trading system from anywhere. The highest price being quoted to buy a stock is called the **bid price**. The lowest price being quoted to sell a stock is called the **ask** (or **offer**) **price**. When the bid and ask prices are at the same price, the trade is completed; then the next highest bid and next lowest ask become the quoted bid and ask prices respectively.

Ask prices exceed bid prices. This difference between the posted ask price and bid price is called the **bid-ask spread**. If you enter the market wanting to buy a stock, you can post your order, but until your order matches the ask price (the amount for which someone will sell the stock to you), no trade will take place. Because customers end up always buying at the ask (the higher price) and selling at the bid (the lower price), the

FIGURE 1.3

Worldwide Stock Markets Ranked by Two Common Measures

The 20 biggest stock markets in the world ranked (a) by total value of all domestic corporations listed on the exchange at year-end 2008 and (b) by total value of the volume of shares traded on the exchange in 2008.

Source: www.world-exchanges.org.

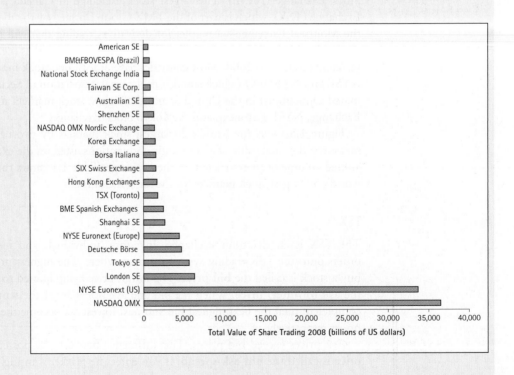

WORLDWIDE STOCK MARKETS RANKED BY TWO COMMON MEASURES

TABLE 1.1

The 50 biggest stock markets in the world ranked (a) by total value of all domestic corporations listed on the exchange at year-end 2008 and (b) by total value of the volume of shares traded on the exchange in 2008.

Top 50 Stock Markets by Domestic Capitalization			Top 50 Stock Markets by Value of Shares Traded		
Rank	Exchange	USD billions 2008	Rank	Exchange	USD billions 2008
1	NYSE Euronext (US)	9,208.9	1	NASDAQ OMX	36,446.5
2	Tokyo SE Group	3,115.8	2	NYSE Euonext (US)	33,638.9
3	NASDAQ OMX	2,396.3	3	London SE	6,271.5
4	NYSE Euronext (Europe)	2,101.7	4	Tokyo SE	5,607.3
5	London SE	1,868.2	5	Deutsche Börse	4,678.8
6	Shanghai SE	1,425.4	6	NYSE Euronext (Europe)	4,411.2
7	Hong Kong Exchanges	1,328.8	7	Shanghai SE	2,600.2
8	Deutsche Börse	1,110.6	8	BME Spanish Exchanges	2,410.7
9	TSX (Toronto)	1,033.4	9	TSX (Toronto)	1,716.2
10	BME Spanish Exchanges	948.4	10	Hong Kong Exchanges	1,629.8
11	SIX Swiss Exchange	857.3	11	SIX Swiss Exchange	1,500.4
12	Australian SE	683.9	12	Borsa Italiana	1,499.5
13	Bombay SE	647.2	13	Korea Exchange	1,432.5
14	National Stock Exchange India	600.3	14	NASDAQ OMX Nordic Exchange	1,338.2
15	BM&FBOVESPA (Brazil)	592.0	15	Shenzhen SE	1,248.7
16	NASDAQ OMX Nordic Exchange	563.1	16	Australian SE	1,213.2
17	Borsa Italiana	522.1	17	Taiwan SE Corp.	829.6
18	Johannesburg SE	482.7	18	National Stock Exchange India	725.4
19	Korea Exchange	470.8	19	BM&FBOVESPA (Brazil)	724.2
20	Taiwan SE Corp.	356.7	20	American SE	561.6
21	Shenzhen SE	353.4	21	Oslo Børs	442.6
22	Singapore Exchange	265.0	22	Johannesburg SE	395.2
23	Mexican Exchange	234.1	23	Bombay SE	301.6
24	Bursa Malaysia	189.1	24	Singapore Exchange	259.9
25	Osaka SE	147.4	25	Istanbul SE	247.9
26	Oslo Børs	145.9	26	Osaka SE	235.6
27	Tel Aviv SE	134.8	27	Thailand SE	116.0
28	American SE	132.4	28	Athens Exchange	113.7
29	Santiago SE	131.8	29	Mexican Exchange	110.5
30	Istanbul SE	118.3	30	Tel Aviv SE	110.1
31	Thailand SE	103.1	31	Indonesia SE	109.4
32	Indonesia SE	98.8	32	Wiener Börse	104.7
33	Jasdaq (Japan)	93.2	33	Bursa Malaysia	93.8
34	Athens Exchange	90.9	34	Egyptian Exchange	93.5
35	Warsaw SE	90.8	35	Irish SE	81.9
36	Colombia SE	87.7	36	Warsaw SE	69.5
37	Egyptian Exchange	85.2	37	Jasdaq (Japan)	45.0
38	Wiener Börse (Vienna)	76.3	38	Santiago SE	36.2
39	Luxembourg SE	66.6	39	Budapest SE	30.7
40	Philippine SE	52.0	40	Amman SE	28.7
41	Irish SE	49.5	41	Colombia SE	20.3
42	Tehran SE	48.7	42	New Zealand Exchange	18.1
43	Buenos Aires SE	39.9	43	Philippine SE	17.1
44	Lima SE	37.9	44	Tehran SE	15.2
45	Amman SE	35.9	45	Buenos Aires SE	6.6
46	New Zealand Exchange	24.2	46	Lima SE	6.3
47	Budapest SE	18.5	47	Ljubljana SE	2.3
48	Ljubljana SE	11.8	48	Cyprus SE	2.1
49	Cyprus SE	8.0	49	Luxembourg SE	1.9
50	Mauritius SE	4.7	50	Colombo SE	1.0

Source: www.world-exchanges.org.

bid-ask spread is an implicit **transaction cost** investors have to pay in order to trade. Companies that are more interesting to investors are frequently traded and many investors put in orders to buy and sell the stock. In these cases, the bid-ask spread is generally quite small. Other companies that attract less investor interest are said to be **thinly traded**. Because not many investors want to trade these stocks, the bid-ask spreads tend to be much larger. Stocks that trade on the TSX tend to have lower bid-ask spreads than those that trade on the TSX Venture Exchange (an exchange for relatively small company stocks).

NYSE

The NYSE is one of the last major stock exchanges to have an active trading floor to which orders are routed for the trading of shares of stock. The NYSE also has **specialists** (or **market makers**) who are given preferential access to orders but must also stand ready to buy or sell shares at their posted bid and ask prices. Recently, the NYSE has combined electronic trading with the trading on the floor. It is likely that the role of floor trading and the importance of the specialist will decline as the need for a specialist to make a market in a company's stock is replaced by the ability of investors to access an electronic exchange and post their own bid and ask prices directly.

CONCEPT CHECK

1. What is the TSX?
2. What advantage does a stock market provide to corporate investors?

In this chapter, we provided an overview of corporate finance, described the financial manager's role, and stressed the importance of stock markets. In the coming chapters, we will develop the tools of financial analysis together with a clear understanding of when to apply them and why they work. These tools will provide the foundation that will allow you to use the financial market information provided by stock markets and other sources to make the best possible financial management decisions.

SUMMARY

1. There are three types of firms in Canada: sole proprietorships, partnerships, and corporations. In addition, there are income trusts that may hold all of a company's securities so that the company's income can flow through to investors with no tax at the business level.

2. Firms with unlimited personal liability include sole proprietorships and partnerships.

3. Firms with limited liability include limited partnerships; limited liability partnerships (to some extent, although there is also unlimited liability to some extent); and corporations.

4. A corporation is a legally defined artificial being (a judicial person or legal entity) that has many of the legal powers people have. It can enter into contracts, acquire assets, and incur obligations.

5. The shareholders in a corporation effectively must pay tax twice. The corporation pays tax once and then investors must pay personal tax on any funds that are distributed as dividends.

6. Income trusts are structured to be exempt from tax at the business level. Business trusts and energy trusts will lose this exemption in 2011; real estate investment trusts will retain this exemption.

7. The ownership of a corporation is divided into shares of stock collectively known as equity. Investors in these shares are called shareholders, stockholders, or equity holders.

8. The ownership and control of a corporation are separated. Shareholders exercise their control indirectly through the board of directors.

9. Financial managers within the firm are responsible for three main tasks: making investment decisions, making financing decisions, and managing the firm's cash flows.

10. Shareholder wealth maximization as the corporate goal is the predominant view in Canada, the U.S., and the U.K. A contrasting view emphasizes stakeholder satisfaction, but shareholder wealth maximization, for the most part, also requires corporations to take care of their stakeholders.

11. Corporate bankruptcy can be thought of as a change in ownership and control of the corporation. The equity holders give up their ownership and control to the debt holders.

12. The shares of public corporations are traded on stock markets. The shares of private corporations do not trade on a stock market.

KEY TERMS

agency problem *p. 10*
articles of incorporation *p. 4*
ask (offer) price *p. 15*
bid price *p. 15*
bid-ask spread *p. 15*
board of directors *p. 8*
business income trust *p. 7*
chief executive officer (CEO) *p. 8*
chief financial officer (CFO) *p. 8*
corporation *p. 4*
dividend payments *p. 5*
energy trust *p. 7*
equity *p. 5*
equity holder *p. 5*
flow through entities *p. 7*
hostile takeover *p. 11*
income trust *p. 7*
limited liability *p. 4*
limited liability partnership (LLP) *p. 4*
limited partnership *p. 4*
liquid *p. 15*
liquidation *p. 12*

market makers *p. 18*
partnership *p. 3*
perquisites *p. 10*
principal-agent problem *p. 10*
primary market *p. 15*
private companies *p. 14*
public companies *p. 15*
real estate investment trust (REIT) *p. 7*
secondary market *p. 15*
shareholder *p. 4*
shareholder wealth maximization *p. 10*
shirking *p. 10*
sole proprietorship *p. 3*
specialists *p. 18*
stakeholder *p. 11*
stakeholder satisfaction *p. 11*
stock *p. 5*
stockholder *p. 5*
stock markets (stock exchanges) *p. 15*
thinly traded *p. 18*
transaction cost *p. 18*
unit holder *p. 7*

PROBLEMS

The Three Types of Firms

1. What is the most important difference between a corporation and *all* other organizational forms?

2. What does the phrase *limited liability* mean in a corporate context?

3. Which organizational forms give their owners complete limited liability?

4. What are the main advantages and disadvantages of organizing a firm as a corporation?

5. Explain the difference between a corporation and a corporation held by an income trust.

6. You are a shareholder in a corporation. The corporation earns $2 per share before taxes. Once it has paid taxes it will distribute the rest of its earnings to you as a dividend. The corporate tax rate is 34%, the personal tax rate on dividend income is 18%, and the personal tax rate on other income is 40%. How much is left for you after all taxes are paid?

7. Repeat Problem 6 assuming the corporation is within an income trust and you own units in the trust during 2010.

Ownership Versus Control of Corporations

8. You have decided to form a new start-up company developing applications for the iPhone. Give examples of the three distinct types of financial decisions you will need to make.

9. Corporate managers work for the owners of the corporation. Consequently, they should make decisions that are in the interests of the owners, rather than their own. What strategies are available to shareholders to help ensure that managers are motivated to act this way?

10. Suppose your local supermarket manager decides that to increase profit, the store will no longer refrigerate milk held in the storage room. Milk on the shelf will still be refrigerated. What stakeholders might this impact? Will the impact of this decision be positive or negative for the stakeholders? Will it be positive or negative for the shareholders? Explain.

11. Suppose you are considering renting an apartment. You, the renter, can be viewed as an agent while the company that owns the apartment can be viewed as the principal. What principal-agent conflicts do you anticipate? Suppose, instead, that you work for the apartment company. What features would you put into the lease agreement that would give the renter incentives to take good care of the apartment?

12. You are the CEO of a company and you are considering entering into an agreement to have your company buy another company. You think the price might be too high, but you will be the CEO of the combined, much larger company. You know that when the company gets bigger, your pay and prestige will increase. What is the nature of the agency conflict here and how is it related to ethical considerations?

13. Are hostile takeovers necessarily bad for firms or their investors? Explain.

The Stock Market

14. What is the difference between a public and private corporation?

15. Explain why the bid-ask spread is a transaction cost.

16. The following quote on Yahoo! stock appeared on February 11, 2009, on Yahoo! Finance:

Yahoo! Inc. (NasdaqGS: YHOO)
Real-Time: 12:57 ↓0.18 (1.41%) 12:34PM ET

Last Trade:	**12.53**	Day's Range:	12.42 − 12.91
Trade Time:	12:19PM ET	52wk Range:	8.94 − 30.25
Change:	↓0.22 (1.71%)	Volume:	5,996,715
Prev Close:	12.75	Avg Vol (3m):	21,536,800
Open:	12.86	Market Cap:	17.39B
Bid:	12.53 × 100	P/E (ttm):	41.35 ×
Ask:	12.54 × 13500	EPS (ttm):	0.30
1y Target Est:	15.00	Div & Yield:	N/A (N/A)

If you wanted to buy Yahoo!, what price would you pay? How much would you receive if you wanted to sell Yahoo!?

Introduction to Financial Statement Analysis

As we discussed in Chapter 1, one of the great advantages of the corporate organizational form is that it places no restriction on who can own shares in the corporation. Anyone with money to invest is a potential investor. As a result, corporations are often widely held, with investors ranging from individuals who hold 100 shares to mutual funds and institutional investors who own millions of shares. For example, in 2008, International Business Machines Corporation (IBM) had almost 1.4 billion shares outstanding held by over 583,000 shareholders. Although the corporate organizational structure greatly facilitates the firm's access to investment capital, it also means that stock ownership is most investors' sole tie to the company. How, then, do investors learn enough about a company to know whether or not they should invest in it? How can financial managers assess the success of their own firm and compare it to competitors? One way firms evaluate their performance and communicate this information to investors is through their *financial statements*.

Firms issue financial statements regularly to communicate financial information to the investment community. A detailed description of the preparation and analysis of these statements is sufficiently complicated that to do it justice would require an entire book. Here we briefly review the subject, emphasizing only the material that investors and corporate financial managers need in order to make the corporate-finance decisions we discuss in the text.

We review four main types of financial statements, present examples of these statements for a firm, and discuss where an investor or manager might find various types of information about the company. We also discuss some of the financial ratios that investors and analysts use to assess a firm's performance and value. We close the chapter with a look at highly publicized financial reporting abuses at Enron and WorldCom.

2.1 THE DISCLOSURE OF FINANCIAL INFORMATION

Financial statements are firm-issued accounting reports with past performance information that a firm issues periodically (usually quarterly and annually). Canadian public companies are required to file these reports (called **interim financial statements** and **annual reports**) with their provincial securities commissions. This process is centralized nationally through the System for Electronic Document Analysis and Retrieval (**SEDAR**). At www.sedar.com, Canadian company filings can be easily accessed. U.S. public companies are required to file their financial statements with the U.S. Securities and Exchange Commission (SEC) on a quarterly basis on form **10-Q** and annually on form **10-K**. Companies in Canada and the United States must also send an annual report with their financial statements to their shareholders each year. Private companies often also prepare financial statements, but they usually do not have to disclose these reports to the public. Financial statements are important tools through which investors, financial analysts, and other interested outside parties (such as creditors) obtain information about a corporation. They are also useful for managers within the firm as a source of information for corporate financial decisions. In this section, we examine the guidelines for preparing financial statements and the types of financial statements.

PREPARATION OF FINANCIAL STATEMENTS

Reports about a company's performance must be understandable and accurate. **Generally Accepted Accounting Principles (GAAP)** (and the incoming International Financial Reporting Standards [IFRS]) provide a framework including a common set of rules and a standard format for public companies to use when they prepare their reports. This standardization also makes it easier to compare the financial results of different firms.

Investors also need some assurance that the financial statements are prepared accurately. Corporations are required to hire a neutral third party, known as an **auditor**, to check the annual financial statements, ensure they are prepared according to GAAP, and verify that the information is reliable.

TYPES OF FINANCIAL STATEMENTS

Under IFRS, every public company is required to produce a *balance sheet, statement of comprehensive income* (which includes the *income statement*), *statement of cash flows, statement of changes in equity,* and *notes including accounting policies.* These financial statements provide investors and creditors with an overview of the firm's financial performance. In the sections that follow, we take a close look at the content of these financial statements.

CONCEPT CHECK   1. What are the financial statements that all public companies must produce?

2. What is the role of an auditor?

INTERNATIONAL FINANCIAL REPORTING STANDARDS

Because Generally Accepted Accounting Principles (GAAP) differ among countries, companies face tremendous accounting complexities when they operate internationally. Investors also face difficulty interpreting financial statements of foreign companies, which is often considered a major barrier to international capital mobility. As companies and capital markets become more global, however, interest in harmonization of accounting standards across countries has increased.

The most important harmonization project began in 1973 when representatives of 10 countries (including Canada) established the International Accounting Standards Committee. This effort led to the creation of the International Accounting Standards Board (IASB) in 2001, with headquarters in London. Now the IASB has issued a set of International Financial Reporting Standards (IFRS).

The IFRS are taking root throughout the world. The European Union (EU) approved an accounting regulation in 2002 requiring all publicly traded EU companies to follow IFRS in their consolidated financial statements starting in 2005. Canadian publicly accountable companies (we will simply refer to them as public companies from this point on) must follow IFRS in their financial statements for fiscal years beginning January 1, 2011, or later. Many other countries have adopted IFRS for all listed companies, including Australia and several countries in Latin America and Africa. Indeed all major stock exchanges around the world accept IFRS except the United States and Japan, which maintain their local GAAP. In November 2007, the United States' SEC allowed foreign companies listed on U.S. exchanges to use IFRS rather than U.S. GAAP. This will be important for Canadian companies, as they will no longer have to reconcile their statements with U.S. GAAP if their filings correspond to IFRS.

The main conceptual difference between U.S. GAAP and IFRS is that U.S. GAAP are based primarily on accounting rules with specific guidance in applying them, whereas IFRS are based more on principles requiring professional judgment by accountants, and specific guidance in application is limited. In implementation, the main difference is how assets and liabilities are valued. Whereas U.S. GAAP are based primarily on historical cost accounting, IFRS places more emphasis on "fair value" of assets and liabilities, or estimates of market values. In the past, Canadian GAAP were being harmonized with U.S. GAAP. This harmonization has stopped as Canadian GAAP moves to IFRS. As the outgoing Canadian GAAP are more principle-based, they fall between U.S. GAAP and IFRS and the change to IFRS will not be as large as the eventual change between U.S. GAAP and IFRS. Effort to achieve convergence between U.S. GAAP and IFRS was spurred by the Sarbanes-Oxley Act (SOX) of 2002 in the United States. It included a provision that U.S. accounting standards move toward international convergence on high-quality accounting standards.

2.2 THE BALANCE SHEET

The **balance sheet**, or **statement of financial position**,[1] lists the firm's *assets* and *liabilities*, providing a snapshot of the firm's financial position at a given point in time. Table 2.1 shows the balance sheet for a fictitious company, Global Conglomerate Corporation. Notice that the balance sheet is divided into two parts ("sides"): the assets on the left side and the liabilities on the right. The **assets** list the cash, inventory, property, plant, and equipment, and other investments the company has made; the **liabilities** show the firm's obligations to creditors. Also shown with liabilities on the right side of the balance sheet is the *shareholders' equity*. **Shareholders' equity**, the difference between the firm's assets and liabilities, is an accounting measure of the firm's net worth.

The assets on the left side show how the firm uses its capital (its investments), and the right side summarizes the sources of capital, or how a firm raises the money it needs.

---

1. In IFRS and recent U.S. GAAP pronouncements, the balance sheet is referred to as the *statement of financial position*.

TABLE 2.1 GLOBAL CONGLOMERATE CORPORATION BALANCE SHEET FOR 2011 AND 2010

GLOBAL CONGLOMERATE CORPORATION
Consolidated Balance Sheet
As at December 31 (in $ millions)

Assets	2011	2010	Liabilities and Shareholders' Equity	2011	2010
Current Assets			**Current Liabilities**		
Cash	21.2	19.5	Accounts payable	29.2	24.5
Accounts receivable	18.5	13.2	Notes payable/short-term debt	3.5	3.2
Inventories	15.3	14.3	Current maturities of long-term debt	13.3	12.3
Other current assets	2.0	1.0	Other current liabilities	2.0	4.0
Total current assets	57.0	48.0	Total current liabilities	48.0	44.0
Long-Term Assets			**Long-Term Liabilities**		
Land	22.2	20.7	Long-term debt	99.9	76.3
Buildings	36.5	30.5	Capital lease obligations	—	—
Equipment	39.7	33.2	Total debt	99.9	76.3
Less accumulated depreciation	(18.7)	(17.5)	Future income tax	7.6	7.4
Net property, plant, and equipment	79.7	66.9	Other long-term liabilities	—	—
Goodwill	20.0	20.0	Total long-term liabilities	107.5	83.7
Other long-term assets	21.0	14.0	**Total Liabilities**	**155.5**	**127.7**
Total long-term assets	120.7	100.9	**Shareholders' Equity**	**22.2**	**21.2**
Total Assets	**177.7**	**148.9**	**Total Liabilities and Shareholders' Equity**	**177.7**	**148.9**

Because of the way shareholders' equity is calculated, the left and right sides must balance:

The Balance Sheet Identity

$$\text{Assets} = \text{Liabilities} + \text{Shareholders' Equity} \tag{2.1}$$

In Table 2.1, total assets for 2011 ($177.7 million) are equal to total liabilities ($155.5 million) plus shareholders' equity ($22.2 million).

We now examine the assets, liabilities, and shareholders' equity in more detail. Finally, we evaluate the firm's financial standing by analyzing the information contained in the balance sheet.

ASSETS

In Table 2.1, Global's assets are divided into current and long-term assets. We discuss each in turn.

CURRENT ASSETS.   **Current assets** are either cash or assets that could be converted into cash within one year. This category includes:

1. Cash and other **marketable securities**, which are short-term, low-risk investments that can be easily sold and converted to cash (for example, money market investments such as government debt that matures within a year);

2. **Accounts receivable**, which are amounts owed to the firm by customers who have purchased goods or services on credit;

3. **Inventories**, which are composed of raw materials as well as work-in-progress and finished goods;

4. Other current assets, which is a catch-all category that includes items such as prepaid expenses (expenses, such as rent or insurance, that have been paid in advance).

LONG-TERM ASSETS.   The first category of long-term assets is net property, plant, and equipment. These include assets such as real estate or machinery that produce tangible benefits for more than one year. If Global spends $2 million on new equipment, this $2 million will be included with property, plant, and equipment on the balance sheet. Because equipment tends to wear out or become obsolete over time, Global will reduce the value recorded for this equipment each year by deducting an amount called **depreciation**. The firm reduces the value of fixed assets (other than land) over time according to a depreciation schedule that depends on the asset's life span. Depreciation is not an actual cash expense that the firm pays; it is a way of recognizing that buildings and equipment wear out and thus become less valuable the older they get. The **book value** of an asset is equal to its acquisition cost less accumulated depreciation. Net property, plant, and equipment shows the total book value of these assets.

When a firm acquires another company, it will acquire a set of assets that will then be listed on its balance sheet. In many cases, however, the firm may pay more for the company than the total fair market value of the assets it acquires. In this case, the difference between the price paid for the company and the fair value assigned to its assets is recorded as **goodwill**. For example, Global paid $25 million in 2009 for a firm whose assets had a fair value of $5 million. Thus, $20 million is recorded as goodwill in Table 2.1. Goodwill captures the value of other "intangibles" that the firm acquired through the acquisition (e.g., brand names and trademarks, patents, customer relationships, and employees). If the value of these intangible assets declines over time, the amount of goodwill listed on the balance sheet will be reduced by a write-down that captures the change in value of the acquired assets. Like depreciation, the write-down is not an actual cash expense.

Other long-term assets can include such items as property not used in business operations, start-up costs in connection with a new business, trademarks and patents, and property held for sale. The sum of all the firm's assets is the total assets at the bottom of the left side of the balance sheet in Table 2.1.

LIABILITIES

We now examine the liabilities shown on the right side of the balance sheet, which are divided into *current* and *long-term liabilities.*

CURRENT LIABILITIES.   Liabilities that will be satisfied within one year are known as **current liabilities**. They include:

1. **Accounts payable**, the amounts owed to suppliers for products or services purchased with credit;

2. Notes payable, short-term debt, and current maturities of long-term debt, which are all repayments of debt that will occur within the next year;

3. Items such as salary or taxes that are owed but have not yet been paid, and deferred or unearned revenue, which is revenue that has been received for products that have not yet been delivered.

The difference between current assets and current liabilities is the firm's **net working capital**, the capital available in the short term to run the business. For example, in 2011, Global's net working capital totalled $9.0 million ($57.0 million in current assets − $48.0 million in current liabilities). Firms with low (or negative) net working capital may face a shortage of funds.

LONG-TERM LIABILITIES.   Long-term liabilities are liabilities that extend beyond one year. We describe the main types below.

1. **Long-term debt** is any loan or debt obligation with a maturity of more than a year. When a firm needs to raise funds to purchase an asset or make an investment, it may borrow those funds through a long-term loan.

2. **Capital leases** are long-term lease contracts that obligate the firm to make regular lease payments in exchange for use of an asset.[2] They allow a firm to gain use of an asset by leasing it from the asset's owner. For example, a firm may lease a building to serve as its corporate headquarters.

3. **Future income tax** is an account that shows taxes that have been recognized on the firm's financial statements but are not yet charged according to tax law. Firms generally keep two sets of financial statements: one for financial reporting and one for tax purposes. Occasionally, the rules for the two types of statements differ. A future income tax liability generally arises when the firm's financial income exceeds its income for tax purposes. Because future tax liabilities will eventually be paid, they appear as a liability on the balance sheet.[3]

SHAREHOLDERS' EQUITY

The sum of the current liabilities and long-term liabilities is total liabilities. The difference between the firm's assets and liabilities is the shareholders' equity; it is also called the **book value of equity**. As we stated earlier, it represents the net worth of the firm from an accounting perspective.

Ideally, the balance sheet would provide us with an accurate assessment of the true value of the firm's equity. Unfortunately, this is unlikely to be the case. First, many of the assets listed on the balance sheet are valued based on their historical cost rather than their true value today. For example, an office building is listed on the balance sheet according to its historical cost net of depreciation. But the actual value of the office building today may be very different from this amount, and it may be much *more* than the amount the firm paid for it years ago. The same is true for other property, plant, and equipment, as

---

2. See Chapter 25 for a precise definition of a capital lease.

3. A common cause of a future tax liability is when a firm's depreciation deduction for financial reporting purposes is less than capital cost allowance, CCA, that can be deducted for tax purposes. A firm may also have a future tax asset related to tax that has already been paid to the Canada Revenue Agency but not yet reported on the financial statements.

well as goodwill: the true value today of an asset may be very different from, and even exceed, its book value. A second, and probably more important, problem is that *many of the firm's valuable assets are not captured on the balance sheet.* For example, the expertise of the firm's employees, the firm's reputation in the marketplace, the relationships with customers and suppliers, and the quality of the management team are all assets that add to the value of the firm that do not appear on the balance sheet.

For these reasons, the book value of equity is an inaccurate assessment of the actual value of the firm's equity. Thus, it is not surprising that it will often differ substantially from the amount investors are willing to pay for the equity. The total market value of a firm's equity equals the market price per share times the number of shares, referred to as the company's **market capitalization**. The market value of a stock does not depend on the historical cost of the firm's assets; instead, it depends on what investors expect those assets to produce in the future.

EXAMPLE **2.1**	MARKET VERSUS BOOK VALUE

Problem

If Global has 3.6 million shares outstanding, and these shares are trading for a price of $14 per share, what is Global's market capitalization? How does the market capitalization compare to Global's book value of equity?

Solution

Global's market capitalization is (3.6 million shares) $\times$ ($14/share) = $50.4 million. This market capitalization is significantly higher than Global's book value of equity of $22.2 million. In fact, the ratio of its market value to its book value is 50.4/22.2 = 2.27, meaning that investors are willing to pay more than twice the amount Global's shares are "worth" according to their book value.

Finally, we note that the book value of equity can be negative (liabilities exceed assets), and that a negative book value of equity is not necessarily an indication of poor performance. Successful firms are often able to borrow in excess of the book value of their assets because creditors recognize that the market value of the assets is far higher. For example, in June 2005, Amazon.com had total liabilities of $2.6 billion and a book value of equity of −$64 million. At the same time, the market value of its equity was over $15 billion. Clearly, investors recognized that Amazon's assets were worth far more than their book value.

CONCEPT CHECK

1. What is the balance sheet identity?

2. The book value of a company's assets usually does not equal the market value of those assets. What are some reasons for this difference?

2.3   BALANCE SHEET ANALYSIS

What can we learn from analyzing a firm's balance sheet? Although the book value of a firm's equity is not a good estimate of its true value as an ongoing firm, it is sometimes used as an estimate of the **liquidation value** of the firm, the value that would be left if its assets were sold and liabilities paid. Unfortunately, it is unlikely that book value of equity is any more accurate an estimate of liquidation value than market value. We can also learn a great deal of useful information from a firm's balance sheet that goes beyond the book value of the firm's equity. We now discuss analyzing the balance sheet to assess the firm's value, its leverage, and its short-term cash needs.

MARKET-TO-BOOK RATIO.   In Example 2.1, we computed the **market-to-book ratio** (also called the **price-to-book [P/B] ratio**) for Global, which is the ratio of its market capitalization to the book value of shareholders' equity.

$$\text{Market-to-Book Ratio} = \frac{\text{Market Value of Equity}}{\text{Book Value of Equity}} \qquad (2.2)$$

It is one of many financial ratios used by analysts to evaluate a firm. The market-to-book ratio for most successful firms substantially exceeds 1, indicating that the value of the firm's assets when put to use exceeds their historical cost (or liquidation value). Variations in this ratio reflect differences in fundamental firm characteristics as well as the value added by management.

In mid-2006, Ford Motor Company (F) had a market-to-book ratio of 0.89, a reflection of investors' assessment that many of Ford's plants and other assets were unlikely to be profitable and were worth less than their book value. In the two following years Ford had such large losses that its book value of equity fell below zero and the market-to-book ratio fell to −5.08 by the end of December 2009. In 2006, the average market-to-book ratio for the auto industry was about 1.5, and for large U.S. firms it was close to 4.0. In contrast, consider that Google (GOOG) had a market-to-book ratio of over 15, and the average for technology firms was about 6.0. Analysts often classify firms with low market-to-book ratios as **value stocks**, and those with high market-to-book ratios as **growth stocks.** Negative market-to-book ratios (like Ford's for 2008) are not considered meaningful because we normally associate a higher ratio with a better assessment of a firm's future performance. With a negative market-to-book ratio, a higher ratio (closer to zero) can occur when the market value of the firm is close to zero or when the book value of equity is far below zero. A near-zero market value is consistent with expectations that the firm will likely not survive. In contrast, a firm with a book value of equity far below zero may be a turnaround prospect and its future may be quite bright. It simply is not clear what a negative market-to-book-value ratio implies.

DEBT-EQUITY RATIO.   Another important piece of information that we can learn from a firm's balance sheet is the firm's **leverage**, or the extent to which it relies on debt as a source of financing. The **debt-equity ratio** is a common ratio used to assess a firm's leverage. We calculate this ratio by dividing the total amount of short- and long-term debt (including current maturities) by the total shareholders' equity:

$$\text{Debt-Equity Ratio} = \frac{\text{Total Debt}}{\text{Total Equity}} \qquad (2.3)$$

We can calculate this ratio using either book or market values for equity and debt. From Table 2.1, note Global's debt in 2011 includes notes payable ($3.5 million), current maturities of long-term debt ($13.3 million), and long-term debt ($99.9 million), for a total of $116.7 million. Therefore, its *book* debt-equity ratio is 116.7/22.2 = 5.3, using the book value of equity. Note the large increase from 2010, when the book debt-equity ratio was only (3.2 + 12.3 + 76.3)/21.2 = 4.3.

Because of the difficulty interpreting the book value of equity, the book debt-equity ratio is not especially useful. It is more informative to compare the firm's debt to the market value of its equity. Global's debt-equity ratio in 2011 using the market value of equity (from Example 2.1) is 116.7/50.4 = 2.3, which means Global's debt is a bit more than double the market value of its equity.[4] As we see later in the text, a firm's *market* debt-equity ratio has important consequences for the risk and return of its stock.

ENTERPRISE VALUE.   A firm's market capitalization measures the market value of the firm's equity, or the value that remains after the firm has paid its debts. But what is the value of the business itself? The **enterprise value** of a firm assesses the value of the underlying business assets, unencumbered by debt and separate from any cash and marketable securities. We compute it as follows:

$$\text{Enterprise Value} = \text{Market Value of Equity} + \text{Debt} - \text{Cash} \qquad (2.4)$$

For example, given its market capitalization from Example 2.1, Global's enterprise value in 2011 is 50.4 + 116.7 − 21.2 = $145.9 million. The enterprise value can be interpreted as the cost to take over the business. That is, it would cost 50.4 + 116.7 = $167.1 million to buy all of Global's equity and pay off its debts, but because we would acquire Global's $21.2 million in cash, the net cost is only 167.1 − 21.2 = $145.9 million.

EXAMPLE 2.2	COMPUTING ENTERPRISE VALUE

Problem

On December 31, 2009, Maple Leaf Foods Inc. (MFI) had a share price of $11.67, 136.8 million shares outstanding, a market-to-book ratio of 1.34, a book debt-equity ratio of 0.88, and cash of $29 million. What was Maple Leaf's market capitalization? What was its enterprise value?

Solution

Maple Leaf Foods had a market capitalization of $11.67/share × 136.8 million shares = $1.60 billion. We divide the market value of equity by Maple Leaf's market-to-book ratio to calculate Maple Leaf's book value of equity as 1.60/1.34 = $1.19 billion. Given a book debt-equity ratio of 0.88, Maple Leaf Foods had total debt of 0.88 × 1.19 = $1.05 billion. Thus, Maple Leaf's enterprise value was 1.60 + 1.05 − 0.028 = $2.62 billion.

OTHER BALANCE SHEET INFORMATION.   Creditors often compare a firm's current assets and current liabilities to assess whether the firm has sufficient working capital to meet its short-term needs. This comparison is sometimes summarized in the firm's **current ratio**, the ratio of current assets to current liabilities, or its **quick ratio**, the ratio of current assets other than inventory to current liabilities. A higher current or quick ratio implies less risk of the firm experiencing a cash shortfall in the near future.

---

4. In this calculation, we have compared the market value of equity to the book value of debt. Strictly speaking, it would be best to use the market value of debt. But because the market value of debt is generally not very different from its book value, this distinction is often ignored in practice.

Analysts also use the information on the balance sheet to watch for trends that could provide information regarding the firm's future performance. For example, an unusual increase in inventory could be an indicator that the firm is having difficulty selling its products.

CONCEPT CHECK   1. What is the difference between a firm's book debt-equity ratio and its market debt-equity ratio?

2. What is a firm's enterprise value?

2.4 THE INCOME STATEMENT

When you want somebody to get to the point, you might ask them for the "bottom line." This expression comes from the *income statement*. The **income statement** or **statement of financial performance**[5] lists the firm's revenues and expenses over a period of time. The last or "bottom" line of the income statement shows the firm's **net income**, which is a measure of its profitability during the period. The income statement is sometimes called a statement of earnings, a statement of operations, or a profit and loss (P&L) statement. The net income is also referred to as the firm's **earnings**. In this section, we examine the components of the income statement in detail and introduce ratios we can use to analyze this data.

EARNINGS CALCULATIONS

Whereas the balance sheet shows the firm's assets and liabilities at a given point in time, the income statement shows the flow of revenues and expenses generated by those assets and liabilities between two dates. Table 2.2 shows Global's income statement for 2011. We examine each category on the statement.

GROSS PROFIT.   The first two lines of the income statement list the revenues from sales of products and the costs incurred to make and sell the products. The cost of sales are costs directly related to producing the goods or services being sold, such as manufacturing costs. Other costs such as administrative expenses, research and development and interest expenses are not included in the cost of sales. The third line is **gross profit**, the difference between sales revenues and the costs.

OPERATING EXPENSES.   The next group of items is operating expenses. These are expenses from the ordinary course of running the business that are not directly related to producing the goods or services being sold. They include administrative expenses and overhead, salaries, marketing costs, and research and development expenses. The third type of operating expense, depreciation and **amortization**, is not an actual cash expense but represents an estimate of the costs that arise from wear and tear or obsolescence of the firm's assets.[6] The firm's gross profit net of operating expenses is called **operating income**.

---

5. In IFRS and recent U.S. GAAP pronouncements, the income statement is referred to as the *statement of financial performance*.

6. Depreciation and amortization are not deductible for tax purposes. Instead, capital cost allowance (CCA) is used by the Canada Revenue Agency (CRA) for tax purposes. CCA rates vary depending on the asset type (or class) and cover tangible and intangible assets (e.g., patents).

GLOBAL CONGLOMERATE CORPORATION INCOME STATEMENT FOR 2011 AND 2010

TABLE 2.2

GLOBAL CONGLOMERATE CORPORATION
Income Statement
Year ended December 31 (in $ millions, except per share amounts)

	2011	2010
Total sales	186.7	176.1
Cost of sales	(153.4)	(147.3)
Gross Profit	33.3	28.8
Selling, general, and administrative expenses	(13.5)	(13.0)
Research and development	(8.2)	(7.6)
Depreciation and amortization	(1.2)	(1.1)
Operating Income	10.4	7.1
Other income	—	—
Earnings Before Interest and Taxes (EBIT)	10.4	7.1
Interest expense	(7.7)	(4.6)
Earnings Before Taxes (EBT)	2.7	2.5
Taxes	(0.7)	(0.6)
Net Income	2.0	1.9
Earnings per share:	$0.556	$0.528
Diluted earnings per share:	$0.526	$0.500

EARNINGS BEFORE INTEREST AND TAXES. We next include other sources of income or expenses that arise from activities that are not the central part of a company's business. Cash flows from the firm's financial investments are one example of other income that would be listed here. After we have adjusted for other sources of income or expenses, we have the firm's earnings before interest and taxes, or **EBIT**.

EARNINGS BEFORE TAXES AND NET INCOME. From EBIT, we deduct the interest paid on outstanding debt to compute Global's earnings before taxes, and then we deduct corporate taxes to determine the firm's net income.

Net income represents the total earnings of the firm's equity holders. It is often reported on a per-share basis as the firm's **earnings per share (EPS)**. We compute EPS by dividing net income by the total number of shares outstanding:

$$\text{EPS} = \frac{\text{Net Income}}{\text{Shares Outstanding}} = \frac{\$2.0 \text{ Million}}{3.6 \text{ Million Shares}} = \$0.556 \text{ per Share} \qquad (2.5)$$

Although Global has only 3.6 million shares outstanding as of the end of 2011, the number of shares outstanding may grow if Global compensates its employees or executives with **stock options** that give the holder the right to buy a certain number of shares by a specific date at a specific price. If the options are "exercised," the company issues new shares and the number of shares outstanding will grow. The number of shares may also grow if the firm issues **convertible bonds**, a form of debt that can be converted to shares. Because there will be more total shares to divide the same earnings, this growth in the number of shares is referred to as **dilution**. Firms disclose the potential for dilution from options they have awarded by reporting **diluted EPS**, which shows the earnings per share the company would have if dilutive convertible bonds were converted or stock options were exercised. For example, if Global has awarded 200,000 stock options to its key executives, its diluted EPS is $2.0 million/3.8 million shares = $0.526.

CONCEPT CHECK

1. What it is the difference between a firm's gross profit and its net income?

2. What is the diluted earnings per share?

2.5 INCOME STATEMENT ANALYSIS

The income statement provides very useful information regarding the profitability of a firm's business and how it relates to the value of the firm's shares. We now discuss several ratios that are often used to evaluate a firm's performance and value.

PROFITABILITY RATIOS

We introduce three ratios that assess a firm's profitability.

GROSS MARGIN. The **gross margin** of a firm is the ratio of gross profit to revenues (sales):

$$\text{Gross Margin} = \frac{\text{Gross Profit}}{\text{Sales}} \qquad (2.6)$$

A firm's gross margin reflects its ability to sell a product for more than the cost of producing it. For example, in 2011 Global had gross margin of 33.3/186.7 = 17.8%.

OPERATING MARGIN. Because there are additional expenses of operating a business beyond the direct costs of goods sold, another important profitability ratio is the **operating margin**, the ratio of operating income to revenues:

$$\text{Operating Margin} = \frac{\text{Operating Income}}{\text{Sales}} \qquad (2.7)$$

The operating margin reveals how much a company earns before interest and taxes from each dollar of sales. Global's operating margin in 2011 was 10.4/186.7 = 5.57%, an increase from its 2010 operating margin of 7.1/176.1 = 4.03%. By comparing operating margins across firms within an industry, we can assess the relative efficiency of firms' operations. For example, in 2008, Air Canada (AC.B) had an operating margin of −1.5%. However, competitor WestJet Airlines (WJA) had an operating margin of 11.48%.

Differences in operating margins can also result from differences in strategy. For example, in November 2008, high-end U.S. retailer Nordstrom (JWN) had an operating margin of 11.9%; Wal-Mart Stores (WMT) had an operating margin of only 5.8%. In this case, Wal-Mart's lower operating margin is not a result of its inefficiency but is part of its strategy of offering lower prices to sell common products in high volume. Indeed, Wal-Mart's sales were more than 50 times higher than those of Nordstrom.

NET PROFIT MARGIN.   A firm's **net profit margin** is the ratio of net income to revenues:

$$\text{Net Profit Margin} = \frac{\text{Net Income}}{\text{Total Sales}} \tag{2.8}$$

The net profit margin shows the fraction of each dollar in revenues that is available to equity holders after the firm pays interest and taxes. Global's net profit margin in 2011 was $2.0/186.7 = 1.07\%$. Differences in net profit margins can be due to differences in efficiency, but they can also result from differences in leverage, which determines the amount of interest payments.

WORKING CAPITAL DAYS.   We can use the combined information in the firm's income statement and balance sheet to gauge how efficiently the firm is utilizing its net working capital. For example, we can express the firm's accounts receivable in terms of the number of days' worth of sales that it represents, called the **accounts receivable days**:[7]

$$\text{Accounts Receivable Days} = \frac{\text{Accounts Receivable}}{\text{Average Daily Sales}} \tag{2.9}$$

Given average daily sales of $\$186.7$ million$/365 = \$0.51$ million in 2011, Global's receivables of $\$18.5$ million represent $18.5/0.51 = 36$ days' worth of sales. In other words, Global takes a little over one month to collect payment from its customers, on average. In 2010, Global's accounts receivable represented only 27 days' worth of sales. Although the number of receivable days can fluctuate seasonally, a significant unexplained increase could be a cause for concern (perhaps indicating the firm is doing a poor job collecting from its customers or is trying to boost sales by offering generous credit terms). Accounts payable can also be expressed in terms of the number of days' worth of cost of goods sold, as can inventory.

EBITDA.   Financial analysts often compute a firm's earnings before interest, taxes, depreciation, and amortization, or **EBITDA**. Because depreciation and amortization are not cash expenses for the firm, EBITDA reflects the cash a firm has earned from its operations. Global's EBITDA in 2011 was $10.4 + 1.2 = \$11.6$ million.

LEVERAGE RATIOS.   Lenders often assess a firm's leverage by computing an **interest coverage ratio**. Common ratios consider operating income, EBIT, or EBITDA as a multiple of the firm's interest expenses. When this ratio is high, it indicates that the firm is earning much more than is necessary to meet its required interest payments.

INVESTMENT RETURNS.   Analysts often evaluate the firm's return on investment by comparing its income to its investment using ratios such as the firm's **return on equity (ROE)**:[8]

$$\text{Return on Equity} = \frac{\text{Net Income}}{\text{Book Value of Equity}} \tag{2.10}$$

---

7. Accounts Receivable Days can also be calculated based on the average accounts receivable at the end of the current and prior years.

8. Because net income is measured over the year, the ROE can also be calculated based on the average book value of equity at the end of the current and prior years.

Global's ROE in 2011 was 2.0/22.2 = 9.0%. The ROE provides a measure of the return the firm has earned on its past investments. A high ROE may indicate the firm is able to find investment opportunities that are very profitable. Of course, one weakness of this measure is the difficulty in interpreting the book value of equity. Another common measure is the **return on assets (ROA)**, which is net income divided by the total assets.

THE DUPONT IDENTITY

We can analyze the determinants of a firm's ROE using a tool called the **DuPont Identity**, named for the company that popularized its use, which expresses the ROE in terms of the firm's profitability, asset efficiency, and leverage:

$$\text{ROE} = \underbrace{\left(\frac{\text{Net Income}}{\text{Sales}}\right)}_{\text{Net Profit Margin}} \times \underbrace{\left(\frac{\text{Sales}}{\text{Total Assets}}\right)}_{\text{Asset Turnover}} \times \underbrace{\left(\frac{\text{Total Assets}}{\text{Book Value of Equity}}\right)}_{\text{Equity Multiplier}} \quad (2.11)$$

$$\underbrace{}_{\text{Return on Assets}}$$

The first term in the DuPont Identity is the firm's net profit margin, which measures its overall profitability. The second term is the firm's **asset turnover**, which measures how efficiently the firm is utilizing its assets to generate sales. The final term is a measure of leverage called the **equity multiplier**, which indicates the value of assets held per dollar of shareholder equity. The equity multiplier will be higher the greater the firm's reliance on debt financing. Applying this identity to Global, we see that in 2011 its asset turnover is 186.7/170.1 = 1.1, with an equity multiplier of 170.1/22.2 = 7.66. Given its net profit margin of 1.07%, we can compute its ROE as

$$\text{ROE} = 9.0\% = 1.07\% \times 1.1 \times 7.66$$

EXAMPLE 2.3

DETERMINANTS OF ROE

Problem

For the year ended November 2008, Wal-Mart Stores had sales of $403.9 billion, net income of $13.7 billion, assets of $167.8 billion, and a book value of equity of $65.5 billion. For the same period, Target (TGT) had sales of $65.3 billion, net income of $2.6 billion, total assets of $47.0 billion, and a book value of equity of $13.6 billion. Compare these firms' profitability, asset turnover, equity multipliers, and return on equity during this period. If Target had been able to match Wal-Mart's asset turnover in 2008, what would its ROE have been?

Solution

Wal-Mart's net profit margin was 13.7/403.9 = 3.39%, which was below Target's net profit margin of 2.6/65.3 = 3.98%. On the other hand, Wal-Mart used its assets more efficiently, with an asset turnover of 403.9/167.8 = 2.41, compared to only 65.3/47.0 = 1.39 for Target. Finally, Target had greater leverage (in terms of book value), with an equity multiplier of 47.0/13.6 = 3.46, relative to Wal-Mart's equity multiplier of 167.8/65.5 = 2.56. Next, let's compute the ROE of each firm directly using the DuPont Identity:

$$\text{Wal-Mart ROE} = \frac{13.7}{65.5} = 20.91\% = 3.39\% \times 2.41 \times 2.56$$

$$\text{Target ROE} = \frac{2.6}{13.6} = 19.1\% = 3.98\% \times 1.39 \times 3.46$$

Note that due to its lower asset turnover, Target had a lower ROE than Wal-Mart despite its higher net profit margin and leverage. If Target had been able to match Wal-Mart's asset turnover, its ROE would have been 3.98% × 2.41 × 3.46 = 33.2%.

VALUATION RATIOS.   Analysts use a number of ratios to gauge the market value of the firm. The most important is the firm's **price-earnings (P/E) ratio**:

$$\text{P/E Ratio} = \frac{\text{Market Capitalization}}{\text{Net Income}} = \frac{\text{Share Price}}{\text{Earnings per Share}} \tag{2.12}$$

That is, the P/E ratio is the ratio of the value of equity to the firm's earnings, either on a total basis or on a per-share basis. For example, Global's P/E ratio in 2011 was 50.4/2.0 = 14/0.556 = 25.2. The P/E ratio is a simple measure that is used to assess whether a stock is over- or undervalued based on the idea that the value of a stock should be proportional to the level of earnings it can generate for its shareholders. P/E ratios can vary widely across industries and tend to be higher for industries with high growth rates. P/E ratios also vary widely across time and tend to be low when the economy is headed for a downturn but high when an economy starts rebounding.

The P/E ratio considers the value of the firm's equity and so depends on its leverage. To assess the market value of the underlying business, it is common to consider valuation ratios based on the firm's enterprise value. Common ratios include the ratio of enterprise value to revenue, or enterprise value to operating income or EBITDA. These ratios compare the value of the business to its sales, operating profits, or cash flow. Like the P/E ratio, these ratios are used to make intra-industry comparisons of how firms are priced in the market.

The P/E ratio is not useful when the firm's earnings are negative. In this case, it is common to look at the firm's enterprise value relative to sales. The risk in doing so, however, is that earnings might be negative because the firm's underlying business model is fundamentally flawed, as was the case for many Internet firms in the late 1990s.

COMMON MISTAKE MISMATCHED RATIOS

When considering valuation (and other) ratios, be sure that the items you are comparing both represent amounts related to the entire firm or both represent amounts related solely to equity holders. For example, a firm's share price and market capitalization are values associated with the firm's equity. Thus, it makes sense to compare them to the firm's earnings per share or net income, which are amounts accruing to equity holders after interest has been paid to debt holders. We must be careful, however, if we compare a firm's market capitalization to its revenues, operating income, or EBITDA because these amounts are related to the whole firm, and both debt and equity holders have a claim to them. Thus, it is better to compare revenues, operating income, or EBITDA to the enterprise value of the firm, which includes both debt and equity.

| EXAMPLE 2.4 | COMPUTING PROFITABILITY AND VALUATION RATIOS |

Problem

Consider the following data from December 31, 2008, for CP and CN Rail ($ millions):

	Canadian Pacific Railway Limited (CP)	Canadian National Railway Company (CNR)
Revenues	4,815	8,482
Operating Income	1,057	2,894
Net Income	619	1,895
Market Capitalization	6,299	20,990
Cash	118	413
Debt	4,880	7,911

Compare CP's and CN's operating margin, net profit margin, P/E ratio, and the ratio of enterprise value to operating income and sales.

Solution

CP had an operating margin of 1057/4815 = 22.0%, a net profit margin of 619/4815 = 12.9%, and a P/E ratio of 6299/619 = 10.2. Its enterprise value was 6299 + 4880 − 118 = $11,061 million, which has a ratio of 11,061/1057 = 10.5 to operating income and 11,061/4815 = 2.30 to revenues.

CN had an operating margin of 2894/8482 = 34.1%, a net profit margin of 1895/8482 = 22.3%, and a P/E ratio of 20,990/1895 = 15.0. Its enterprise value was 20,990 + 7911 − 413 = $28,488 million, which has a ratio of 28,488/2894 = 9.8 to operating income and 28,488/8482 = 3.36 to sales.

Note that despite their large difference in size, CP's and CN's P/E ratios were very similar. CP's net profit margin was somewhat lower than CN's, however, explaining the difference in the ratio of enterprise value to sales.

CONCEPT CHECK

1. What is the DuPont Identity?

2. How do you use the price-earnings (P/E) ratio to gauge the market value of a firm?

2.6 THE STATEMENT OF CASH FLOWS

The income statement provides a measure of the firm's profit over a given time period. However, it does not indicate the amount of *cash* the firm has earned. There are two reasons that net income does not correspond to cash earned. First, there are non-cash entries on the income statement, such as depreciation and amortization. Second, certain uses of cash, such as the purchase of a building or expenditures on inventory, are not reported on the income statement. The firm's **statement of cash flows** utilizes the information from the income statement and balance sheet to determine how much cash the firm has generated, and how that cash has been allocated, during a set period. As we will see, from the perspective of an investor attempting to value the firm, the statement of cash flows provides what may be the most important information of the five financial statements.

The statement of cash flows is divided into three sections: operating activity, investment activity, and financing activity. The first section, operating activity, starts with net income from the income statement. It then adjusts this number by adding back all non-cash entries related to the firm's operating activities. The next section, investment activity, lists the cash used for investment. The third section, financing activity, shows the flow of cash between the firm and its investors. Global Conglomerate's statement of cash flows is shown in Table 2.3. In this section, we take a close look at each component of the statement of cash flows.

OPERATING ACTIVITY

The first section of Global's statement of cash flows adjusts net income by all non-cash items related to operating activity. For instance, depreciation is deducted when computing net income, but it is not an actual cash expense. Thus, we add it back to net income when determining the amount of cash the firm has generated. Similarly, we add back any other non-cash expenses (for example, future income taxes).

GLOBAL CONGLOMERATE CORPORATION STATEMENT OF CASH FLOWS FOR 2011 AND 2010

TABLE 2.3	**GLOBAL CONGLOMERATE CORPORATION** Statement of Cash Flows Year ended December 31 (in $ millions)		
		2011	**2010**
Operating activity			
Net income		2.0	1.9
Depreciation and amortization		1.2	1.1
Other non-cash items		(2.8)	(1.0)
Cash effect of changes in			
Accounts receivable		(5.3)	(0.3)
Accounts payable		4.7	(0.5)
Inventory		(1.0)	(1.0)
Cash from Operating Activities		**(1.2)**	**0.2**
Investment activity			
Capital expenditures		(14.0)	(4.0)
Acquisitions and other investing activity		(7.0)	(2.0)
Cash from Investing Activities		**(21.0)**	**(6.0)**
Financing activity			
Dividends paid		(1.0)	(1.0)
Sale or purchase of stock		—	—
Increase in short-term borrowing		1.3	3.0
Increase in long-term borrowing		23.6	2.5
Cash from Financing Activities		**23.9**	**4.5**
Change in Cash		**1.7**	**(1.3)**

Next, we adjust for changes to net working capital that arise from changes to accounts receivable, accounts payable, or inventory. When a firm sells a product, it records the revenue as income even though it may not receive the cash from that sale immediately. Instead, it may grant the customer credit and let the customer pay in the future. The customer's obligation adds to the firm's accounts receivable. We use the following guidelines to adjust for changes in working capital:

1. Accounts Receivable: When a sales is recorded as part of net income, but the cash has not yet been received from the customer, we must adjust the cash flows by *deducting* the increases in accounts receivable. This increase represents additional lending by the firm to its customers, and it reduces the cash available to the firm.

2. Accounts Payable: Similarly, we *add* increases in accounts payable. Accounts payable represents borrowing by the firm from its suppliers. This borrowing increases the cash available to the firm.

3. Inventory: Finally, we *deduct* increases to inventory. Increases to inventory are not recorded as an expense and do not contribute to net income (the cost of the goods are only included in net income when the goods are actually sold). However, the cost of increasing inventory is a cash expense for the firm and must be deducted.

The changes in these working capital items can be found from the balance sheet. For example, from Table 2.1, Global's accounts receivable increased from $13.2 million in 2010 to $18.5 million in 2011. We deduct the increase of $18.5 - 13.2 = \$5.3$ million on the statement of cash flows. Note that although Global showed positive net income on the income statement, it actually had a negative $1.2 million cash flow from operating activity, in large part because of the increase in accounts receivable.

INVESTMENT ACTIVITY

The next section of the statement of cash flows shows the cash required for investment activities. Purchases of new property, plant, and equipment are referred to as **capital expenditures**. Recall that capital expenditures do not appear immediately as expenses on the income statement. Instead, the firm depreciates these assets and deducts depreciation expenses over time. To determine the firm's cash flow, we already added back depreciation because it is not an actual cash expense. Now, we subtract the actual capital expenditure that the firm made. Similarly, we also deduct other assets purchased or investments made by the firm, such as acquisitions. In Table 2.3, we see that in 2011, Global spent $21 million in cash on investing activities.

FINANCING ACTIVITY

The last section of the statement of cash flows shows the cash flows from financing activities. Dividends paid to shareholders are a cash outflow. Global paid $1 million to its shareholders as dividends in 2011. The difference between a firm's net income and the amount it spends on dividends is referred to as the firm's **retained earnings** for that year:

$$\text{Retained Earnings} = \text{Net Income} - \text{Dividends} \qquad (2.13)$$

Global retained $2 million - $1 million = $1 million, or 50% of its earnings in 2011.

Also listed under financing activity is any cash the company received from the sale of its own stock, or cash spent buying (repurchasing) its own stock. Global did not issue or repurchase stock during this period. The last items to include in this section result from changes to Global's short-term and long-term borrowing. Global raised money by issuing debt, so the increases in short-term and long-term borrowing represent cash inflows.

The final line of the statement of cash flows combines the cash flows from these three activities to calculate the overall change in the firm's cash balance over the period of the statement. In this case, Global had cash inflows of $1.7 million. By looking at the statement in Table 2.3 as a whole, we can determine that Global chose to borrow (mainly in the form of long-term debt) to cover the cost of its investment and operating activities. Although the firm's cash balance has increased, Global's negative operating cash flows and relatively high expenditures on investment activities might give investors some reasons for concern. If that pattern continues, Global will need to continue to borrow to remain in business.

EXAMPLE 2.5	THE IMPACT OF DEPRECIATION ON CASH FLOW

Problem

Suppose Global had an additional $1 million depreciation expense in 2011. If Global's tax rate on pre-tax income is 26%, what would be the impact of this expense on Global's earnings? How would it impact Global's cash at the end of the year?

Solution

Depreciation is an operating expense, so Global's operating income, EBIT, and pre-tax income would fall by $1 million. This decrease in pre-tax income would reduce Global's tax bill by 26% × $1 million = $0.26 million.[9] Therefore, net income would fall by 1 − 0.26 = $0.74 million.

On the statement of cash flows, net income would fall by $0.74 million, but we would add back the additional depreciation of $1 million because it is not a cash expense. Thus, cash from operating activities would rise by −0.74 + 1 = $0.26 million. Thus, Global's cash balance at the end of the year would increase by $0.26 million, the amount of the tax savings that resulted from the additional depreciation deduction.

CONCEPT CHECK	1. Why does a firm's net income not correspond to cash generated?
	2. What are the components of the statement of cash flows?

2.7 OTHER FINANCIAL STATEMENT INFORMATION

The most important elements of a firm's financial statements are the balance sheet, income statement, and the statement of cash flows, which we have already discussed. Several other pieces of information contained in the financial statements warrant brief mention: the management discussion and analysis, the statement of shareholders' equity, the statement of comprehensive income, and notes to the financial statements.

MANAGEMENT DISCUSSION AND ANALYSIS

The **management discussion and analysis (MD&A)** is a preface to the financial statements in which the company's management discusses the recent year (or quarter),

---

9. We will assume that both depreciation for financial reporting and capital cost allowance (CCA) for tax purposes increase by the same amount. This will give us the tax reduction and there will be no change to the future income tax liability on the balance sheet.

INTERVIEW WITH SUE FRIEDEN

Sue Frieden is Ernst & Young's Global Managing Partner, Quality & Risk Management. A member of the Global Executive board, she is responsible for every aspect of quality and risk management: employees, services, procedures, and clients.

QUESTION: Do today's financial statements give the investing public what they need?

ANSWER: Globally, we are seeing an effort to provide more forward-looking information to investors. But fundamental questions remain, such as how fully do investors understand financial statements and how fully do they read them? Research shows that most individual investors don't rely on financial statements much at all. We need to determine how the financial statement and related reporting models can be improved. To do that we will need a dialogue involving investors, regulators, analysts, auditors, stock exchanges, academics, and others to ensure that financial statements and other reporting models are as relevant as they can be.

QUESTION: Ernst & Young is a global organization. How do accounting standards in the U.S. compare to those elsewhere?

ANSWER: In January of 2005, 100 countries outside the U.S. began the process of adopting new accounting standards (International Financial Reporting Standards) that would in large measure be based on principles rather than rules. As global markets become more complex, it is clear that we all need to be playing by the same set of rules, but as a first step we need to have consistency from country to country. There are definite challenges to overcome in reconciling principle-based and rules-based systems, but we are optimistic that these challenges will inevitably get resolved. At the same time, there are efforts underway to ensure that auditing standards are globally consistent. Ultimately, financial statements prepared under global standards and audited under consistent global auditing standards will better serve investors.

QUESTION: What role does the audit firm play in our financial markets, and how has that changed since the collapse of Arthur Andersen?

ANSWER: All of us—the entire business community—have gone through a pivotal, historic moment. And certainly the accounting profession has seen unprecedented change in the past few years as well. The passage of Sarbanes-Oxley and other changes are helping to restore public trust. Things are certainly very different from what we've known before. We're now engaging on a regular basis with a wider range of stakeholders: companies, boards, policy-makers, opinion leaders, investors, and academia. And we've had the chance to step back and ask ourselves why we do what we do as accounting professionals, and why it matters. In terms of the services we offer, much of what we do helps companies comply with regulations, guard against undue risks, and implement sound transactions. And part of the value in what we do is providing the basis to all stakeholders to understand whether companies are playing by the rules—whether it is accounting rules, financial reporting rules, or tax rules. We help create confidence in financial data. The public may not fully understand precisely what auditors do or how we do it, but they care that we exist because it provides them the confidence they so badly need and want.

QUESTION: How does a global accounting firm such as Ernst & Young ensure that each of its partners adheres to the appropriate standards?

ANSWER: People often tell me, as the global leader for quality and risk management, how hard my job is and how much is on my shoulders. The truth is, doing the right thing—adhering and often exceeding the standards expected of us as independent public auditors—rests on the shoulders of everyone in the organization. All of our more than 107,000 people around the world know it is their responsibility to make this happen. What's more, they know it is their responsibility to raise questions when they have concerns. Perhaps most importantly, all of our people know that no client is too big to walk away from if we sense the company's management is not committed to doing the right thing.

providing a background on the company and any significant events that may have occurred. Management may also discuss the coming year, and outline goals and new projects.

Management should also discuss any important risks that the firm faces or issues that may affect the firm's liquidity or resources. Management is also required to disclose any **off-balance sheet transactions**, which are transactions or arrangements that can have a material impact on the firm's future performance yet do not appear on the balance sheet. For example, if a firm has made guarantees that it will compensate a buyer for losses related to an asset purchased from the firm, these guarantees represent a potential future liability for the firm that must be disclosed as part of the MD&A.

STATEMENT OF SHAREHOLDERS' EQUITY

The **statement of shareholders' equity** breaks down the shareholders' equity computed on the balance sheet into the amount that came from issuing new shares versus retained earnings. Because the book value of shareholders' equity is not a useful assessment of value for financial purposes, the information contained in the statement of shareholders' equity is also not particularly insightful.

STATEMENT OF COMPREHENSIVE INCOME

The **statement of comprehensive income** shows the total income and expenses for a period by combining net income (or profit) from the income statement with information not reported on the income statement such as gains and losses that affect equity through reserve or other accounts.

NOTES TO THE FINANCIAL STATEMENTS

In addition to the financial statements, companies provide extensive notes with further details on the information provided in the statements. For example, the notes document important accounting assumptions that were used in preparing the statements. They often provide information specific to a firm's subsidiaries or its separate product lines. They show the details of the firm's stock-based compensation plans for employees and the different types of debt the firm has outstanding. Details of acquisitions, spin-offs, leases, taxes, and risk management activities are also given. The information provided in the notes is often very important to interpret fully the firm's financial statements.

| EXAMPLE **2.6** | SALES BY BUSINESS SEGMENT |

Problem

In the notes to its financial statements, Maple Leaf Foods Inc. (MFI) reported the following sales revenues by business segment ($ thousands):

	2009	**2008**
Meat Products Group	$3,310,393	$3,303,694
Agribusiness Group	206,064	232,999
Bakery Products Group	1,705,145	1,705,909
Total	$5,221,602	$5,242,602

Which segment showed the highest percentage growth? If Maple Leaf has the same percentage growth by category from 2008 to 2009, what will its total revenues be in 2010?

Solution

The percentage growth in sales in the Meat Products Group, was (3,310,393 − 3,303,694)/3,310,393 = 0.2%. Growth in sales in the Agribusiness Group was −11.6% and in the Bakery Products Group was −0.04%. The Meat Products Group showed is the only group in which sales did not decline.

If these growth rates continue for another year, sales in the Meat Products Group will be 3,310,393 × (1 + 0.002) = $3.32 billion, and the other categories will be $0.18 billion, and $1.70 billion, respectively, for total revenues of $5.20 billion.

CONCEPT CHECK

1. Where do off-balance sheet transactions appear in a firm's financial statements?
2. What information do the notes to financial statements provide?

2.8 ACCOUNTING MANIPULATION

The various financial statements we have examined are of critical importance to investors and financial managers alike. Even with safeguards such as GAAP and auditors, though, financial reporting abuses unfortunately do take place. We now review two of the most infamous recent examples.

ENRON

Enron was the most well known of the accounting scandals of the early 2000s. Enron started as an operator of natural-gas pipelines but evolved into a global trader dealing in a range of products including gas, oil, electricity, and even broadband Internet capacity. A series of events unfolded that led Enron to file the largest bankruptcy filing in U.S. history in December 2001. By the end of 2001, the market value of Enron's shares had fallen by over $60 billion.

Interestingly, throughout the 1990s and up to late 2001, Enron was touted as one of the most successful and profitable companies in the United States. *Fortune* rated Enron "The Most Innovative Company in America" for six straight years, from 1995 to 2000. But while many aspects of Enron's business were successful, subsequent investigations suggest that Enron executives had been manipulating Enron's financial statements to mislead investors and artificially inflate the price of Enron's stock and maintain its credit rating. In 2000, for example, 96% of Enron's reported earnings were the result of accounting manipulation.[10]

Although the accounting manipulations that Enron used were quite sophisticated, the essence of most of the deceptive transactions was surprisingly simple. Enron sold assets at inflated prices to other firms (or, in many cases, business entities that Enron's CFO Andrew Fastow had created), together with a promise to buy back those assets at an even

---

10. John R. Kroger, "Enron, Fraud and Securities Reform: An Enron Prosecutor's Perspective," *University of Colorado Law Review* (December 2005): 57–138.

FINANCIAL **CRISIS**
BERNARD MADOFF'S PONZI SCHEME

It's only when the tide goes out that you learn who's been swimming naked. — *Warren Buffett*

On December 11, 2008, federal agents arrested Bernie Madoff, one of the world's most successful hedge fund managers. It turned out that the $50 billion[11] fund he ran was in fact a fraud. His spectacular performance of the last 17 years, generating consistent annual returns between 10% and 15%, was actually a complete fabrication. Madoff had been running the world's largest Ponzi scheme: that is, he used the capital contributed by new investors to pay off old investors. His strategy was so successful that for more than a decade investors ranging from Steven Spielberg to New York University, as well as a number of large banks and investment advisors, lined up to invest with him. Indeed, Madoff quite likely would have been able to hide the fraud until his deathbed had not the global financial crisis spurred many investors to seek to withdraw funds from their Madoff accounts in order to raise cash and cover losses elsewhere in their portfolios. In addition, the financial crisis meant there were few new investors with both the cash and the willingness to invest. As a result, Madoff did not have enough new capital to pay off the investors who wanted to withdraw their capital, and the scheme finally collapsed.

How was Madoff able to hide perhaps the largest fraud of all time for so long? Rather than simply manipulate his accounting statements, Madoff *made them up* with the assistance of a virtually unknown accounting firm with only one active accountant. Although many investors may have questioned why such a large fund, with $50 billion in assets, would choose an unknown and tiny audit firm, not enough of them recognized this choice as a potential red flag. In addition, because Madoff's firm was private, it was not subject to the strict regulatory requirements for public companies (such as the Sarbanes-Oxley Act) and so had weak reporting requirements. As this case makes clear, when making an investment decision, it is important not only to review the firm's financial statements, but also to consider the reliability and reputation of the auditors who prepared the statements in the first place.

higher future price. Thus, Enron was effectively borrowing money, receiving cash today in exchange for a promise to pay more cash in the future. But Enron recorded the incoming cash as revenue and then hid the promises to buy them back in a variety of ways.[12] In the end, much of its revenue growth and profits in the late 1990s were the result of this type of manipulation.

WORLDCOM

On July 21, 2002, WorldCom entered the largest bankruptcy of all time. At its peak, WorldCom had a market capitalization of $120 billion. Again, a series of accounting manipulations beginning in 1998 hid the firm's financial problems from investors.

In WorldCom's case, the fraud was to reclassify $3.85 billion in operating expenses as long-term investment. The immediate impact of this change was to boost WorldCom's reported earnings; operating expenses are deducted from earnings immediately, whereas long-term investments are depreciated slowly over time. Of course, this manipulation would not boost WorldCom's cash flows, because long-term investments must be deducted on the cash flow statement at the time they are made.

---

11. $50 billion is the total amount Madoff states that he reported to his investors, including (fictitious) returns; investigators are still trying to determine the exact amount that investors had actually contributed to the fund.

12. In some cases, these promises were called "price risk management liabilities" and hidden with other trading activities; in other cases they were off-balance sheet transactions that were not fully disclosed.

Some investors were concerned by WorldCom's excessive investment compared to the rest of the industry. As one investment advisor commented, "Red flags [were] things like big deviations between reported earnings and excess cash flow . . . [and] excessive capital expenditures for a long period of time. That was what got us out of WorldCom in 1999."[13]

SARBANES-OXLEY ACT

Enron and WorldCom highlight the importance to investors of accurate and up-to-date financial statements for firms they choose to invest in. The problems at Enron, World-Com, and elsewhere were kept hidden from boards and shareholders until it was too late. In the wake of these scandals, many people felt that the accounting statements of these companies did not present an accurate picture of the financial health of the company. In 2002, the United States Congress passed the **Sarbanes-Oxley Act** that requires, among other things, that CEOs and CFOs certify the accuracy and appropriateness of their firm's financial statements and increases the penalties against them if the financial statements later prove to be fraudulent.[14] Following the Sarbanes-Oxley Act in United States, Canadian regulators adopted similar measures that came into effect in 2005.

CONCEPT CHECK

1. Describe the transactions Enron used to increase its reported earnings.

2. What is the Sarbanes-Oxley Act?

SUMMARY

1. Financial statements are accounting reports that a firm issues periodically to describe its past performance.

2. Investors, financial analysts, managers, and other interested parties such as creditors rely on financial statements to obtain reliable information about a corporation.

3. The main types of financial statements are the balance sheet, the income statement, and the statement of cash flows.

4. The balance sheet shows the current financial position (assets, liabilities, and shareholders' equity) of the firm at a single point in time.

5. The two sides of the balance sheet must balance:

$$\text{Assets} = \text{Liabilities} + \text{Shareholders' Equity} \qquad (2.1)$$

6. Shareholders' equity is the book value of the firm's equity. It differs from market value of the firm's equity, its market capitalization, because of the way assets and liabilities are recorded for accounting purposes. A successful firm's market-to-book ratio typically exceeds 1.

7. A common ratio used to assess a firm's leverage is

$$\text{Debt-Equity Ratio} = \frac{\text{Total Debt}}{\text{Total Equity}} \qquad (2.3)$$

This ratio is most informative when computed using the market value of equity. It indicates the degree of leverage of the firm.

---

13. Robert Olstein, as reported in *The Wall Street Journal*, August 23, 2002.

14. We discuss these and other related corporate governance issues further in Chapter 29.

8. The enterprise value of a firm is the total value of its underlying business operations:

$$\text{Enterprise Value} = \text{Market Capitalization} + \text{Debt} - \text{Cash} \qquad (2.4)$$

9. The income statement reports the firm's revenues and expenses, and it computes the firm's bottom line of net income, or earnings.

10. Net income is often reported on a per-share basis as the firm's earnings per share:

$$\text{Earnings per Share (EPS)} = \text{Net Income/Shares Outstanding} \qquad (2.5)$$

We compute diluted EPS by adding to the number of shares outstanding the possible increase in the number of shares from the exercise of stock options the firm has awarded.

11. Profitability ratios show the firm's operating or net income as a fraction of sales, and they are an indication of a firm's efficiency and its pricing strategy.

12. Working capital ratios express the firm's working capital as a number of days of sales (for receivables) or cost of sales (for inventory or payables).

13. Interest coverage ratios indicate the ratio of the firm's income or cash flows to its interest expenses, and they are a measure of financial strength.

14. Return on investment ratios such as ROE or ROA express the firm's net income as a return on the book value of its equity or total assets.

15. The DuPont Identity expresses a firm's ROE in terms of its profitability, asset efficiency, and leverage:

$$\text{ROE} = \underbrace{\underbrace{\left(\frac{\text{Net Income}}{\text{Sales}}\right)}_{\text{Net Profit Margin}} \times \underbrace{\left(\frac{\text{Sales}}{\text{Total Assets}}\right)}_{\text{Asset Turnover}}}_{\text{Return on Assets}} \times \underbrace{\left(\frac{\text{Total Assets}}{\text{Book Value of Equity}}\right)}_{\text{Equity Multiplier}} \qquad (2.11)$$

16. Valuation ratios compute market capitalization or enterprise value of the firm relative to its earnings or operating income.

17. The P/E ratio computes the value of a share of stock relative to the firm's EPS. P/E ratios tend to be high for fast-growing firms.

18. When comparing valuation ratios, it is important to be sure both numerator and denominator match in terms of whether they include debt.

19. The statement of cash flows reports the sources and uses of the firm's cash. It shows the adjustments to net income for non-cash expenses and changes to net working capital, as well as the cash used (or provided) from investing and financing activities.

20. The management discussion and analysis section of the financial statements contains management's overview of the firm's performance, as well as disclosure of risks the firm faces, including those from off-balance sheet transactions.

21. The statement of shareholders' equity breaks down the shareholders' equity computed on the balance sheet into the amount that came from issuing new shares versus retained earnings. It is not particularly useful for financial valuation purposes.

22. The notes to a firm's financial statements generally contain important details regarding the numbers used in the main statements.

23. Recent accounting scandals have drawn attention to the importance of financial statements. New legislation has increased the penalties for fraud, and tightened the procedures firms must use to assure that statements are accurate.

KEY TERMS

accounts payable *p. 26*
accounts receivable *p. 26*
accounts receivable days *p. 34*
amortization *p. 31*
annual report *p. 23*
assets *p. 24*
asset turnover *p. 35*
auditor *p. 23*
balance sheet *p. 24*
book value *p. 26*
book value of equity *p. 27*
capital expenditures *p. 39*
capital leases *p. 27*
convertible bonds *p. 33*
current assets *p. 26*
current liabilities *p. 26*
current ratio *p. 30*
debt-equity ratio *p. 29*
depreciation *p. 26*
diluted EPS *p. 33*
dilution *p. 33*
DuPont Identity *p. 35*
earnings per share (EPS) *p. 32*
EBIT *p. 32*
EBITDA *p. 34*
enterprise value *p. 30*
equity multiplier *p. 35*
financial statements *p. 23*
future income tax *p. 27*
Generally Accepted Accounting Principles (GAAP) *p. 23*
goodwill *p. 26*
gross margin *p. 33*
gross profit *p. 31*
growth stocks *p. 29*
income statement *p. 31*
interest coverage ratio *p. 34*

interim financial statement *p. 23*
inventories *p. 26*
leverage *p. 29*
liabilities *p. 24*
liquidation value *p. 28*
long-term debt *p. 27*
management discussion and analysis (MD&A) *p. 40*
market capitalization *p. 28*
marketable securities *p. 26*
market-to-book ratio (price-to-book [P/B] ratio) *p. 29*
net income or earnings *p. 31*
net profit margin *p. 34*
net working capital *p. 27*
off-balance sheet transactions *p. 42*
operating income *p. 31*
operating margin *p. 33*
price-earnings (P/E) ratio *p. 36*
quick ratio *p. 30*
retained earnings *p. 39*
return on assets (ROA) *p. 35*
return on equity (ROE) *p. 34*
Sarbanes-Oxley Act (SOX) *p. 45*
SEDAR *p. 23*
shareholders' equity *p. 24*
statement of cash flows *p. 37*
statement of comprehensive income *p. 42*
statement of financial performance *p. 31*
statement of financial position *p. 24*
statement of shareholders' equity *p. 42*
stock options *p. 32*
10-K *p. 23*
10-Q *p. 23*
value stocks *p. 29*

PROBLEMS

The Disclosure of Financial Information

1. What financial statements can be found in a firm's annual report? What checks are there on the accuracy of these statements?

2. Who reads financial statements? List at least three categories of people. For each category, provide an example of the type of information they might be interested in and discuss why.

3. Find the most recent financial statements for Starbucks Corporation (SBUX) using the following sources:

   a. From the company's Web page http://www.starbucks.com. (*Hint:* Search for "investor relations.")

   b. From the SEC Web site www.sec.gov. (*Hint:* Search for company filings in the EDGAR database.)

   c. From the Yahoo finance Web site http://finance.yahoo.com.

   d. From at least one other source. (*Hint:* Enter "SBUX 10K" at www.google.com.)

   e. Repeat the analysis for Tim Hortons www.timhortons.com. In addition to the EDGAR site, check www.sedar.com for the Canadian filings.

The Balance Sheet

4. Consider the following potential events that might have occurred to Global Conglomerate on December 30, 2011. For each one, indicate which line items in Global's balance sheet would be affected and by how much. Also indicate the change to Global's book value of equity.

   a. Global used $20 million of its available cash to repay $20 million of its long-term debt.

   b. A warehouse fire destroyed $5 million worth of uninsured inventory.

   c. Global used $5 million in cash and $5 million in new long-term debt to purchase a $10 million building.

   d. A large customer owing $3 million for products it already received declared bankruptcy, leaving no possibility that Global would ever receive payment.

   e. Global's engineers discover a new manufacturing process that will cut the cost of its flagship product by over 50%.

   f. A key competitor announces a radical new pricing policy that will drastically undercut Global's prices.

5. What was the change in Global Conglomerate's book value of equity from 2010 to 2011 according to Table 2.1? Does this imply that the market price of Global's shares increased in 2011? Explain.

6. Use Google Finance to find the balance sheet date for Qualcomm as of September 27, 2009.

   a. How much did Qualcomm have in cash and short-term investments?

   b. What were Qualcomm's total accounts receivable?

   c. What were Qualcomm's total assets?

   d. What were Qualcomm's total liabilities? How much of this was long-term debt?

   e. What was the book value of Qualcomm's equity?

7. Find online the annual 10-K report for Peet's Coffee & Tea, Inc. (PEET) for 2008. Answer the following questions from its balance sheet:

   a. How much cash did Peet's have at the end of 2008?

   b. What was Peet's total assets?

   c. What was Peet's total liabilities? How much debt did Peet's have?

   d. What was the book value of Peet's equity?

Balance Sheet Analysis

8. In March 2005, General Electric (GE) had a book value of equity of $113 billion, 10.6 billion shares outstanding, and a market price of $36 per share. GE also had cash of $13 billion, and total debt of $370 billion. Four years later, in early 2009, GE had a book value of equity of $105 billion, 10.5 billion shares outstanding with a market price of $10.80 per share, cash of $48 billion, and total debt of $524 billion. Over this period, what was the change in GE's

   a. market capitalization?

   b. market-to-book ratio?

   c. book debt-equity ratio? market debt-equity ratio?

   d. enterprise value?

9. In July 2007, Apple (AAPL) had cash of $7.12 billion, current assets of $18.75 billion, current liabilities of $6.99 billion, and inventories of $0.25 billion.

   a. What was Apple's current ratio?

   b. What was Apple's quick ratio?

   c. In July 2007, Dell (DELL) had a quick ratio of 1.25 and a current ratio of 1.30. What can you say about the asset liquidity of Apple relative to Dell?

10. In November 2007, Abercrombie and Fitch (ANF) had a book equity of $1,458 million, a price per share of $75.01, and 86.67 million shares outstanding. At the same time, Gap Inc. (GPS) had a book equity of $5,194 million, a share price of $20.09, and 798.22 million shares outstanding.

   a. What is the market-to-book ratio of each of these clothing retailers?

   b. What conclusions can you draw comparing the two ratios?

The Income Statement and Income Statement Analysis

11. Find online the annual 10-K report for Peet's Coffee & Tea, Inc. (PEET) for 2008. Answer the following questions from the income statement:

   a. What were Peet's revenues for 2008? By what percentage did revenues grow from 2007?

   b. What was Peet's operating and net profit margin in 2008? How do they compare with its margins in 2007?

   c. What was Peet's diluted earnings per share in 2008? What number of shares is this EPS based on?

12. Suppose that in 2012, Global launched an aggressive marketing campaign that boosts sales by 15%. However, its operating margin fell from 5.57% to 4.50%. Suppose that it has no other income, interest expenses are unchanged, and taxes are the same percentage of pre-tax income as in 2011.

   a. What is Global's EBIT in 2012?

   b. What is Global's income in 2012?

   c. If Global's P/E ratio and number of shares outstanding remains unchanged, what is Global's share price in 2012?

13. Suppose a firm's tax rate is 35%.

    a. What effect would a $10 million operating expense have on this year's earnings? What effect would it have on next year's earnings?

    b. What effect would a $10 million capital expense have on this year's earnings, if the capital is depreciated at a rate of $2 million per year for five years? What effect would it have on next year's earnings?

14. You are analyzing the leverage of two firms and you note the following (all values in millions of dollars):

	Debt	Book Equity	Market Equity	Operating Income	Interest Expense
Firm A	500	300	400	100	50
Firm B	80	35	40	8	7

    a. What is the market debt-to-equity ratio of each firm?

    b. What is the book debt-to-equity ratio of each firm?

    c. What is the interest coverage ratio of each firm?

    d. Which firm may have more difficulty meeting its debt obligations? Explain.

*15. Quisco Systems has 6.5 billion shares outstanding and a share price of $18. Quisco is considering developing a new networking product in-house at a cost of $500 million. Alternatively, Quisco can acquire a firm that already has the technology for $900 million worth (at the current price) of Quisco stock. Suppose that absent the expense of the new technology, Quisco will have EPS of $0.80.

    a. Suppose Quisco develops the product in-house. What impact would the development cost have on Quisco's EPS? Assume all costs are incurred this year and are treated as an R&D expense, Quisco's tax rate is 35%, and the number of shares outstanding is unchanged.

    b. Suppose Quisco does not develop the product in-house but instead acquires the technology. What effect would the acquisition have on Quisco's EPS this year? (Note that acquisition expenses do not appear directly on the income statement. Assume the acquired firm has no revenues or expenses of its own, so that the only effect on EPS is due to the change in the number of shares outstanding.)

    c. Which method of acquiring the technology has a smaller impact on earnings? Is this method cheaper? Explain.

16. In January 2009, American Airlines (AMR) had a market capitalization of $1.7 billion, debt of $11.1 billion, and cash of $4.6 billion. American Airlines had revenues of $23.8 billion. British Airways (BAB) had a market capitalization of $2.2 billion, debt of $4.7 billion, cash of $2.6 billion, and revenues of $13.1 billion.

    a. Compare the market capitalization-to-revenue ratio (also called the price-to-sales ratio) for American Airlines and British Airways.

    b. Compare the enterprise value-to-revenue ratio for American Airlines and British Airways.

    c. Which of these comparisons is more meaningful? Explain.

*17. Find online the annual 10-K for Peet's Coffee and Tea (PEET) for 2008.

    a. Compute Peet's net profit margin, total asset turnover, and equity multiplier.

    b. Use this data to compute Peet's ROE using the DuPont Identity.

    c. If Peet's managers wanted to increase its ROE by 1 percentage point, how much higher would their asset turnover need to be?

d. If Peet's net profit margin fell by 1 percentage point, by how much would their asset turnover need to increase to maintain their ROE?

18. Repeat the analysis of parts (a) and (b) in the previous problem for Starbucks Coffee (SBUX). Use the DuPont Identity to understand the difference between the two firms' ROEs.

19. Consider a retailing firm with a net profit margin of 3.5%, a total asset turnover of 1.8, total assets of $44 million, and a book value of equity of $18 million.

   a. What is the firm's current ROE?

   b. If the firm increased its net profit margin to 4%, what would its ROE be?

   c. If, in addition, the firm increased its revenues by 20% (while maintaining this higher profit margin and without changing its assets or liabilities), what would be its ROE?

The Statement of Cash Flows

20. Find online the annual 10-K report for Peet's Coffee & Tea, Inc. (PEET) for 2008. Answer the following questions from its cash flow statement:

   a. How much cash did Peet's generate from operating activities in 2008?

   b. What was Peet's depreciation expense in 2008?

   c. How much cash was invested in new property and equipment (net of any sales) in 2008?

   d. How much did Peet's raise from the sale of shares of its stock (net of any purchases) in 2008?

21. Can a firm with positive net income run out of cash? Explain.

22. See the cash flow statement here for H.J. Heinz (HNZ) (in $ thousands):

   a. What was Heinz's cumulative earnings over these four quarters? What was its cumulative cash flows from operating activities?

   b. What fraction of the cash from operating activities was used for investment over the four quarters?

   c. What fraction of the cash from operating activities was used for financing activities over the four quarters?

PERIOD ENDING	29-Oct-08	30-Jul-08	30-Apr-08	30-Jan-08
Net Income	**276,710**	**228,964**	**194,062**	**218,532**
Operating Activities, Cash Flows Provided By or Used In				
Depreciation	69,997	75,733	74,570	73,173
Adjustments to net income	14,359	(13,142)	48,826	(47,993)
Changes in accounts receivables	(38,869)	(53,218)	100,732	(84,711)
Changes in liabilities	82,816	(111,577)	201,725	39,949
Changes in inventories	(195,186)	(114,121)	85,028	57,681
Changes in other operating activities	17,675	(26,574)	12,692	(2,097)
Total Cash Flow from Operating Activities	**227,502**	**(13,935)**	**717,635**	**254,534**
Investing Activities, Cash Flows Provided By or Used In				
Capital expenditures	(82,584)	(41,634)	(100,109)	(69,170)
Investments	(5,465)	5,465	(93,153)	(48,330)
Other cash flows from investing activities	(108,903)	732	(58,069)	20,652
Total Cash Flows from Investing Activities	**(196,952)**	**(35,437)**	**(251,331)**	**(96,848)**

Financing Activities, Cash Flows Provided By or Used In				
Dividends paid	(131,483)	(131,333)	(119,452)	(121,404)
Sale purchase of stock	78,774	1,210	(76,807)	(79,288)
Net borrowings	515,709	114,766	(283,696)	64,885
Other cash flows from financing activities	(282)	2,000	(46,234)	39,763
Activities	**462,718**	**(13,357)**	**(526,189)**	**(96,044)**
Effect of exchange rate changes	(119,960)	(610)	32,807	6,890
Change in Cash and Cash Equivalents	**$373,308**	**(63,339)**	**(27,078)**	**$68,532**

23. Suppose your firm receives a $5 million order on the last day of the year. You fill the order with $2 million worth of inventory. The customer picks up the entire order the same day and pays $1 million upfront in cash; you also issue a bill for the customer to pay the remaining balance of $4 million within 30 days. Suppose your firm's tax rate is 0% (i.e., ignore taxes). Determine the consequences of this transaction for each of the following:

    a. Revenues   d. Inventory

    b. Earnings   e. Cash

    c. Receivables

24. Nokela Industries purchases a $40 million cyclo-converter. The cyclo-converter will be depreciated by $10 million per year over four years, starting this year. Suppose Nokela's tax rate is 40%.

    a. What impact will the cost of the purchase have on earnings for each of the next four years?

    b. What impact will the cost of the purchase have on the firm's cash flow for the next four years?

Other Financial Statement Information

25. The balance sheet information for Clorox Co. (CLX) in 2004–2005 is shown here, with data in $ thousands:

    a. What change in the book value of Clorox's equity took place at the end of 2004?

    b. Is Clorox's market-to-book ratio meaningful? Is its book debt-equity ratio meaningful? Explain.

Balance Sheet:	31-Mar-05	31-Dec-04	30-Sep-04	30-Jun-04
Assets				
Current Assets				
Cash and cash equivalents	293,000	300,000	255,000	232,000
Net receivables	401,000	362,000	385,000	460,000
Inventory	374,000	342,000	437,000	306,000
Other current assets	60,000	43,000	53,000	45,000
Total Current Assets	**1,128,000**	**1,047,000**	**1,130,000**	**1,043,000**
Long-term investments	128,000	97,000	—	200,000
Property, plant, and equipment	979,000	991,000	995,000	1,052,000
Goodwill	744,000	748,000	736,000	742,000
Other assets	777,000	827,000	911,000	797,000
Total Assets	**3,756,000**	**3,710,000**	**3,772,000**	**3,834,000**

Liabilities				
Current Liabilities				
Accounts payable	876,000	1,467,000	922,000	980,000
Short/current long-term debt	410,000	2,000	173,000	288,000
Total Current Liabilities	**1,286,000**	**1,469,000**	**1,095,000**	**1,268,000**
Long-term debt	2,381,000	2,124,000	474,000	475,000
Other liabilities	435,000	574,000	559,000	551,000
Total Liabilities	**4,102,000**	**4,167,000**	**2,128,000**	**2,294,000**
Total Shareholder Equity	**−346,000**	**−457,000**	**1,644,000**	**1,540,000**
Total Liabilities & Shareholder Equity	**$3,756,000**	**$3,710,000**	**$3,772,000**	**$3,834,000**

    c. Find online Clorox's other financial statements from that time. What was the cause of the change to Clorox's book value of equity at the end of 2004?

    d. Does Clorox's book value of equity in 2005 imply that the firm is unprofitable? Explain.

26. Find online the annual 10-K report for Peet's Coffee & Tea, Inc. (PEET) for 2008. Answer the following questions from the notes to its financial statements:

    a. Under stock-based compensation, what was Peet's net income in 2008 after deducting the fair value of options granted to employees?

    b. What was Peet's inventory (including green coffee and other inventories) at the end of 2008?

    c. What was the fair value of Peet's holdings of marketable government securities at the end of 2008?

    d. What property does Peet's lease? What are the minimum lease payments due in 2009?

    e. How many stock options did Peet's grant in 2008?

    f. What fraction of Peet's 2008 sales came from coffee beans and tea products? What fraction came from beverages and pastries?

Accounting Manipulation

27. Find online the annual 10-K report for Peet's Coffee & Tea Inc. (PEET) for 2008.

    a. Which auditing firm certified these financial statements?

    b. Which officers of Peet's certified the financial statements?

28. WorldCom reclassified $3.85 billion of operating expenses as capital expenditures. Explain the effect this reclassification would have on WorldCom's cash flows. (*Hint:* Consider taxes.) WorldCom's actions were illegal and clearly designed to deceive investors. But if a firm could legitimately choose how to classify an expense for tax purposes, which choice is truly better for the firm's investors?

DATA CASE

This is your second interview with a prestigious brokerage firm for a job as an equity analyst. You survived the morning interviews with the department manager and the vice-president of equity. Everything has gone so well that they want to test your ability as an analyst. You are seated in a room with a computer and a list with the names of two companies: Ford (F) and Microsoft (MSFT). You have 90 minutes to complete the following tasks:

    1. Download the annual income statements, balance sheets, and cash flow statements for the last four fiscal years from MarketWatch (www.marketwatch.com). Enter each company's

stock symbol and then go to "financials." Export the statements to Excel by right-clicking while the cursor is inside each statement.

2. Find historical stock prices for each firm from Yahoo! Finance (http://finance.yahoo.com). Enter your stock symbol, click on "Historical Prices" in the left column, and enter the proper date range to cover the last day of the month corresponding to the date of each financial statement. Use the closing stock prices (not the adjusted close). To calculate the firm's market capitalization at each date, we multiply the number of shares outstanding (see "Basic Weighted Shares Outstanding" on the income statement) by the firm's historic stock price.

3. For each of the four years of statements, compute the following ratios for each firm:

   Valuation Ratios
   Price-Earnings Ratio (for EPS use Diluted EPS Total)
   Market-to-Book Ratio
   Enterprise Value-to-EBITDA
   (For debt, include long-term and short-term debt; for cash, include marketable securities.)

   Profitability Ratios
   Operating Margin (Use Operating Income After Depreciation)
   Net Profit Margin
   Return on Equity

   Financial Strength Ratios
   Current Ratio
   Book Debt–Equity Ratio
   Market Debt–Equity Ratio
   Interest Coverage Ratio (EBIT ÷ Interest Expense)

4. Obtain industry averages for each firm from Reuters.com (www.reuters.com/finance/stocks). Click on "Stocks," enter the symbol, then click on "Ratios."

   a. Compare each firm's ratios to the available industry ratios for the most recent year. (Ignore the "Company" column, as your calculations will be different.)

   b. Analyze the performance of each firm versus the industry and comment on any trends in each individual firm's performance. Identify any strengths or weaknesses you find in each firm.

5. Examine the market-to-book ratios you calculated for each firm. Which, if any, of the two firms can be considered "growth firms" and which, if any, can be considered "value firms"?

6. Compare the valuation ratios across the two firms. How do you interpret the difference between them?

7. Consider the enterprise value of each firm for each of the four years. How have the values of each firm changed over the time period?

Tools

THE LAW OF ONE PRICE CONNECTION. In this part of the text, we introduce the basic tools for making financial decisions. We begin by introducing the most important idea in this book, the concept of *the absence of arbitrage*, or the **Law of One Price**. The Law of One Price states that we can use market prices to determine the value of an investment opportunity to the firm. We will demonstrate that the Law of One Price is the one unifying principle that underlies all of financial economics and links all of the ideas throughout this book. We will return to this theme throughout our study of Corporate Finance.

For a financial manager, evaluating financial decisions involves computing the net present value of a project's future cash flows. In Chapter 3 we explain how to compute the net present value of an investment opportunity. In Chapter 4 we use the Law of One Price to derive a central concept in financial economics—the time value of money. We explain how to value a stream of future cash flows and derive a few useful shortcuts for computing the net present value of various types of cash flow patterns. Chapter 5 considers how to use market interest rates to determine the appropriate discount rate for a set of cash flows. We apply the Law of One Price to demonstrate that the discount rate will depend on the rate of return of investments with maturity and risk similar to the cash flows being valued. This observation leads to the important concept of the *cost of capital* of an investment decision.

Arbitrage and Financial Decision Making

On July 24, 2007, Tom Albanese, CEO of the Anglo-Australian mining company Rio Tinto, offered to buy Montreal-headquartered Alcan for U.S. $101 per share, or about U.S.$38.1 billion in cash. The same month, Robert Meers, CEO of Vancouver-based Lululemon, raised U.S.$327.6 million in the initial public offering of Lululemon's stock. Lululemon's stock price rose 55.6% on the first day of trading, rising from U.S.$18 per share to U.S.$28. Most of the proceeds from the stock issue went to previous shareholders who were selling their shares, but about $38 million of new money was injected into Lululemon and was targeted to fund new store openings and provide working capital. Also in September 2010, Mike Lazaridis, president and co-CEO of Waterloo-based Research In Motion (RIM), announced the introduction of the BlackBerry PlayBook that would compete with the just-released Apple iPad. How did these CEOs decide that these decisions were good for their firms?

Every decision has future consequences, and these consequences can be either beneficial or costly. For example, after extending the deadline for its offer, Rio Tinto ultimately succeeded in its attempt to acquire Alcan. The acquisition made Rio Tinto the world's largest producer of aluminum. The benefits of the acquisition include the future revenues from Alcan's resource properties and greater control and influence over the markets for aluminum. Purchasing Alcan was a good decision if the future benefits justify the upfront and future costs. If the benefits exceed the costs, the decision will increase the value of the firm and therefore the wealth of its investors.

Comparing costs and benefits is complicated because they often occur at different points in time, may be in different currencies, or may have different risks associated with them. To make a valid comparison, we must use the tools of finance to express all costs and benefits in common terms. In this chapter, we introduce a central principle of finance, which we name the *Valuation Principle*, which states that we can use current market prices to determine the value today of the costs and benefits associated with a decision. This principle allows us to apply the concept of *net present value* (NPV) as a way to compare the costs and benefits of a project in terms of a common unit—namely, dollars today. We will then be able to evaluate a decision by answering this question: *Does the cash value today of its benefits exceed the cash value today of its costs?* In addition, we will see that the NPV indicates the net amount by which the decision will increase wealth.

We then turn to financial markets, and apply these same tools to determine the prices of securities that trade in the market. We discuss strategies called *arbitrage* that allow us to exploit situations in which the prices of publicly available investment opportunities do not conform to these values. Because investors trade rapidly to take advantage of arbitrage opportunities, we argue that equivalent investment opportunities trading simultaneously in competitive markets must have the same price. This *Law of One Price* is the unifying theme of valuation that we use throughout this text.

3.1 VALUING DECISIONS

A financial manager's job is to make decisions on behalf of the firm's investors. For example, when faced with an increase in demand for the firm's products, a manager may need to decide whether to raise prices or increase production. If the decision is to increase production and a new facility is required, is it better to rent or purchase the facility? If the facility will be purchased, should the firm pay cash or borrow the funds needed to pay for it?

Our objective in this book is to explain how to make decisions that increase the value of the firm to its investors. In principle, the idea is simple and intuitive: For good decisions, the benefits exceed the costs. Of course, real-world opportunities are usually complex and so the costs and benefits are often difficult to quantify. The analysis will often involve skills from other management disciplines, as in these examples:

Marketing: to determine the increase in revenues resulting from an advertising campaign

Economics: to determine the increase in demand from lowering the price of a product

Organizational Behaviour: to determine the productivity impact of a change in management structure

Strategy: to determine a competitor's response to a price increase

Operations: to determine production costs after the modernization of a manufacturing plant

For the remainder of this text, we assume that the analyses of these other disciplines have been completed to quantify the costs and benefits associated with a decision. With those tasks done, the financial manager must compare the costs and benefits and determine the best decision to make so as to maximize the value of the firm.

ANALYZING COSTS AND BENEFITS

The first step in decision making is to identify the costs and benefits of a decision. The next step is to quantify these costs and benefits. In order to compare the costs and benefits, we need to evaluate them in the same terms—cash today. Let's make this concrete with a simple example.

Suppose a jewellery manufacturer has the opportunity to trade 400 ounces of silver for 10 ounces of gold today. Because an ounce of gold differs in value from an ounce of silver, it is incorrect to compare 400 ounces to 10 ounces and conclude that the larger quantity is better. Instead, to compare the costs and benefits, we first need to quantify their values in equivalent terms.

Consider the silver. What is its cash value today? Suppose silver can be bought and sold for a current market price of $15 per ounce. Then the 400 ounces of silver we give up has a cash value of[1]

$$(400 \text{ ounces of silver today}) \times (\$15/\text{ounce of silver today}) = \$6000 \text{ today}$$

If the current market price for gold is $900 per ounce, then the 10 ounces of gold we receive has a cash value of

$$(10 \text{ ounces of gold today}) \times (\$900/\text{ounce of gold today}) = \$9000 \text{ today}$$

Now that we have quantified the costs and benefits in terms of a common measure of value, cash today, we can compare them. The jeweller's opportunity has a benefit of $9000 today and a cost of $6000 today, so the net value of the decision is $9000 − $6000 = $3000 today. By accepting the trade, the jewellery firm will be richer by $3000.

USING MARKET PRICES TO DETERMINE CASH VALUES

In evaluating the jeweller's decision, we used the current market price to convert from ounces of silver or gold to dollars. We did not concern ourselves with whether the jeweller thought that the price was fair or whether the jeweller would use the silver or gold. Do such considerations matter? Suppose, for example, that the jeweller does not need the gold, or thinks the current price of gold is too high. Would he value the gold at less than $9000? The answer is no—he can always sell the gold at the current market price and receive $9000 right now. Similarly, he would not value the gold at more than $9000, because even if he really needs the gold or thinks the current price of gold is too low, he can always buy 10 ounces of gold for $9000. Thus, independent of his own views or preferences, the value of the gold to the jeweller is $9000.

This example illustrates an important general principle: whenever a good trades in a **competitive market**—by which we mean a market in which it can be bought *and* sold at the same price—that price determines the cash value of the good. As long as a competitive market exists, the value of the good will not depend on the views or preferences of the decision maker.

---

1. You might worry about commissions or other transactions costs that are incurred when buying or selling gold, in addition to the market price. For now, we will ignore transactions costs; we will discuss their effect in Section 3.7.

| EXAMPLE **3.1** | **COMPETITIVE MARKET PRICES DETERMINE VALUE** |

Problem

You have just won a radio contest and are disappointed to find out that the prize is four tickets to the Def Leppard reunion tour (face value $40 each). Not being a fan of 1980s power rock, you have no intention of going to the show. However, there is a second choice: two tickets to your favourite band's sold-out show (face value $45 each). You notice that on eBay, tickets to the Def Leppard show are being bought and sold for $30 apiece and tickets to your favourite band's show are being bought and sold at $50 each. Which prize should you choose?

Solution

Competitive market prices, not your personal preferences (nor the face value of the tickets), are relevant here:

> four Def Leppard tickets at $30 apiece = $120 market value
> two of your favourite band's tickets at $50 apiece = $100 market value

Instead of taking the tickets to your favourite band, you should accept the Def Leppard tickets, sell them on eBay, and use the proceeds to buy two tickets to your favourite band's show. You'll even have $20 left over to buy a T-shirt.

Thus, by evaluating cost and benefits using competitive market prices, we can determine whether a decision will make the firm and its investors wealthier. This point is one of the central and most powerful ideas in finance, which we call the **Valuation Principle**:

> *The value of an asset to the firm or its investors is determined by its competitive market price. The benefits and costs of a decision should be evaluated using these market prices, and when the value of the benefits exceeds the value of the costs, the decision will increase the market value of the firm.*

The Valuation Principle provides the basis for decision making throughout this text. In the remainder of this chapter, we first apply it to decisions whose costs and benefits occur at different points in time and develop the main tool of project evaluation, the *Net Present Value Rule*. We then consider its consequences for the prices of assets in the market and develop the concept of the *Law of One Price*.

| EXAMPLE **3.2** | **APPLYING THE VALUATION PRINCIPLE** |

Problem

You are the operations manager at your firm. Due to a pre-existing contract, you have the opportunity to acquire 200 barrels of oil and 3000 kilograms of copper for a total of $12,000. The current competitive market price of oil is $50 per barrel and of copper is $2 per kilogram. You are not sure you need all of the oil and copper, and are concerned that the value of both commodities may fall in the future. Should you take this opportunity?

Solution

To answer this question, you need to convert the costs and benefits to their cash values using market prices:

$$(200 \text{ barrels of oil}) \times (\$50/\text{barrel of oil today}) = \$10,000 \text{ today}$$

$$(3000 \text{ kilograms of copper}) \times (\$2/\text{kilogram of copper today}) = \$6000 \text{ today}$$

The net value of the opportunity is $10,000 + $6000 − $12,000 = $4000 today. Because the net value is positive, you should take it. This value depends only on the *current* market prices for oil and copper. Even if you do not need all the oil or copper, or expect their values to fall, you can sell them at current market prices and obtain their value of $16,000. Thus, the opportunity is a good one for the firm, and will increase its value by $4000.

WHEN COMPETITIVE MARKET PRICES ARE NOT AVAILABLE

Competitive market prices allow us to calculate the value of a decision without worrying about the tastes or opinions of the decision maker. When competitive prices are not available, we can no longer do this. Prices at retail stores, for example, are one sided: you can buy at the posted price, but you cannot sell the good to the store at that same price. We cannot use these one-sided prices to determine an exact cash value. They determine the maximum value of the good (since it can always be purchased at that price), but an individual may value it for much less depending on his or her preferences for the good.

EXAMPLE 3.3	WHEN VALUE DEPENDS ON PREFERENCES

Problem

The local Lexus dealer hires you as an extra in a commercial. As part of your compensation, the dealer offers to sell you today a new Lexus for $53,000. The best available retail price for the Lexus is $60,000, and the price you could sell it for in the used car market is $55,000. How would you value this compensation?

Solution

If you plan to buy a Lexus anyway, then the value to you of the Lexus is $60,000, the price you would otherwise pay for it. In this case, the value of the dealer's offer is $60,000 − $53,000 = $7000. But suppose you do not want or need a Lexus. If you were to buy it from the dealer and then sell it, the value of taking the deal would be $55,000 − $53,000 = $2000. Thus, depending on your desire to own a new Lexus, the dealer's offer is worth somewhere between $2000 (you don't want a Lexus) and $7000 (you definitely want one). Because the price of the Lexus is not competitive (you cannot buy and sell at the same price), the value of the offer is ambiguous and depends on your preferences.

CONCEPT CHECK

1. In order to compare the costs and benefits of a decision, what must we determine?

2. If crude oil trades in a competitive market, would an oil refiner that has a use for the oil value it differently from another investor?

3.2 INTEREST RATES AND THE TIME VALUE OF MONEY

For most financial decisions, unlike in the examples presented so far, costs and benefits occur at different points in time. For example, typical investment projects incur costs upfront and provide benefits in the future. In this section, we show how to account for this time difference when evaluating a project.

THE TIME VALUE OF MONEY

Consider an investment opportunity with the following certain cash flows:

Cost: $100,000 today
Benefit: $105,000 in one year

Because both are expressed in dollar terms, it might appear that the cost and benefit are directly comparable so that the project's net value is $105,000 − $100,000 = $5000. But this calculation ignores the timing of the costs and benefits, and it treats money today as equivalent to money in one year.

In general, a dollar today is worth more than a dollar in one year. If you have $1 today, you can invest it. For example, if you deposit it in a bank account paying 7% interest, you will have $1.07 at the end of one year. We call the difference in value between money today and money in the future the **time value of money**.

THE INTEREST RATE: AN EXCHANGE RATE ACROSS TIME

By depositing money into a savings account, we can convert money today into money in the future with no risk. Similarly, by borrowing money from the bank, we can exchange money in the future for money today. The rate at which we can exchange money today for money in the future is determined by the current interest rate. In the same way that an exchange rate allows us to convert money from one currency to another, the interest rate allows us to convert a currency in one point of time to the same currency in another point in time. In essence, an interest rate is like an exchange rate across time. It tells us the market price today of money in the future.

Suppose the current annual interest rate is 7%. By investing or borrowing at this rate, we can exchange $1.07 in one year for each $1 today. More generally, we define the **risk-free interest rate**, r_f for a given period as the interest rate at which money can be borrowed or lent without risk over that period. We can exchange $(1 + r_f)$ dollars in the future per dollar today, and vice versa, without risk. We refer to $(1 + r_f)$ as the **interest rate factor** for risk-free cash flows; it defines the exchange rate across time, and has units of "$ in one year/$ today."

As with other market prices, the risk-free interest rate depends on supply and demand. In particular, at the risk-free interest rate the supply of savings equals the demand for borrowing. After we know the risk-free interest rate, we can use it to evaluate other decisions in which costs and benefits are separated in time without knowing the investor's preferences.

VALUE OF INVESTMENT IN ONE YEAR. Let's reevaluate the investment we considered earlier, this time taking into account the time value of money. If the interest rate is 7%, then we can express our costs as

$$\text{Cost} = (\$100,000 \text{ today}) \times (1.07 \text{ \$ in one year/\$ today})$$
$$= \$107,000 \text{ in one year}$$

Think of this amount as the opportunity cost of spending $100,000 today: we give up the $107,000 we would have had in one year if we had left the money in the bank. Alternatively, if we were to borrow the $100,000, we would owe $107,000 in one year.

Both costs and benefits are now in terms of "dollars in one year," so we can compare them and compute the investment's net value:

$$\$105{,}000 - \$107{,}000 = -\$2000 \text{ in one year}$$

In other words, we could earn $2000 more in one year by putting our $100,000 in the bank rather than making this investment. We should reject the investment: if we took it, we would be $2000 poorer in one year than if we didn't.

VALUE OF INVESTMENT TODAY.   The previous calculation expressed the value of the costs and benefits in terms of dollars in one year. Alternatively, we can use the interest rate factor to convert to dollars today. Consider the benefit of $105,000 in one year. What is the equivalent amount in terms of dollars today? That is, how much would we need to have in the bank today so that we would end up with $105,000 in the bank in one year? We find this amount by dividing by the interest rate factor:

$$\text{Benefit} = (\$105{,}000 \text{ in one year}) \div (1.07 \text{ \$ in one year/\$ today})$$

$$= \$105{,}000 \times \frac{1}{1.07} \text{ today}$$

$$= \$98{,}130.84 \text{ today}$$

This is also the amount the bank would lend to us today if we promised to repay $105,000 in one year.[2] Thus, it is the competitive market price at which we can "buy" or "sell" *today* an amount of $105,000 in one year.

Now we are ready to compute the net value of the investment:

$$\$98{,}130.84 - \$100{,}000 = -\$1869.16 \text{ today}$$

Once again, the negative result indicates that we should reject the investment. Taking the investment would make us $1869.16 poorer today because we have given up $100,000 for something worth only $98,130.84.

PRESENT VERSUS FUTURE VALUE.   This calculation demonstrates that our decision is the same whether we express the value of the investment in terms of dollars in one year or dollars today: we should reject the investment. Indeed, if we convert from dollars today to dollars in one year,

$$(-\$1869.16 \text{ today}) \times (1.07 \text{ \$ in one year/\$ today}) = -\$2000 \text{ in one year}$$

we see that the two results are equivalent, but expressed as values at different points in time. When we express the value in terms of dollars today, we call it the **present value** (**PV**) of

---

2. We are assuming the bank will both borrow and lend at the risk-free interest rate. We discuss the case when these rates differ in Section 3.7.

the investment. If we express it in terms of dollars in the future, we call it the **future value** of the investment.

DISCOUNT FACTORS AND RATES. In the preceding calculation, we can interpret

$$\frac{1}{1+r} = \frac{1}{1.07} = 0.93458$$

as the *price* today of $1 in one year. Note that the value is less than $1—money in the future is worth less today, and so its price reflects a discount. Because it provides the discount at which we can purchase money in the future, the amount $\frac{1}{1+r}$ is called the one-year **discount factor**. The risk-free interest rate is also referred to as the **discount rate** for a risk-free investment.

EXAMPLE 3.4

COMPARING COSTS AT DIFFERENT POINTS IN TIME

Problem
The cost of building the Canada Line that extends Vancouver's rapid transit from downtown to Richmond and the airport was projected to be about $2.05 billion in 2005. The Canada Line opened in 2009 in advance of the 2010 Vancouver Winter Olympics. In 2005, projections for Vancouver-area construction costs indicated that costs were rising by about 10% per year. If the interest rate was 3.25%, what would be the cost of a one-year delay in terms of dollars in 2005?

Solution
If the project were delayed, it would cost $2.05 billion $\times$ (1.10) = $2.255 billion in 2006. To compare this amount to the cost of $2.05 billion in 2005, we must convert it using the interest rate of 3.25%:

$2.255 billion in 2006 ÷ ($1.0325 in 2006/$ in 2005) = $2.184 billion in 2005

Therefore, the cost of a delay of one year was

$2.184 billion − $2.05 billion = $134 million in 2005

That is, delaying the project for one year was equivalent to giving up $134 million in cash.

We can use the risk-free interest rate to determine values in the same way we used competitive market prices. Figure 3.1 illustrates how we use competitive market prices, exchange rates, and interest rates to convert between dollars today and other goods, currencies, or dollars in the future.

CONCEPT CHECK
1. How do you compare costs at different points in time?
2. If interest rates rise, what happens to the value *today* of a promise of money in one year?

FIGURE 3.1

Converting Between Dollars Today and Gold, Euros, or Dollars in the Future

We can convert dollars today to different goods, currencies, or points in time by using the competitive market price, exchange rate, or interest rate.

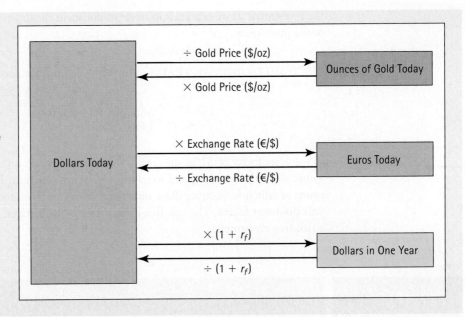

3.3 PRESENT VALUE AND THE NPV DECISION RULE

In Section 3.2, we converted between cash today and cash in the future using the risk-free interest rate. As long as we convert costs and benefits to the same point in time, we can compare them to make a decision. In practice, however, most corporations prefer to measure values in terms of their present value—that is, in terms of cash today. In this section we apply the Valuation Principle to derive the concept of the *net present value*, or *NPV*, and define the "golden rule" of financial decision making, the *NPV Decision Rule*.

NET PRESENT VALUE

When the value of a cost or benefit is computed in terms of cash today, we refer to it as the present value (PV). Similarly, we define the **net present value (NPV)** of a project or investment as the difference between the present value of its benefits and the present value of its costs:

Net Present Value
$$NPV = PV(\text{Benefits}) - PV(\text{Costs}) \qquad (3.1)$$

If we use positive cash flows to represent benefits and negative cash flows to represent costs, and calculate the present value of multiple cash flows as the sum of present values for individual cash flows, we can write this definition as

$$NPV = PV(\text{All project cash flows}) \qquad (3.2)$$

That is, the NPV is the total of the present values of all project cash flows.

Let's consider a simple example. Suppose you are offered the following investment opportunity: in exchange for $500 today, you will receive $550 in one year with certainty. If the risk-free interest rate is 8% per year then

$$PV(\text{Benefit}) = (\$550 \text{ in one year}) \div (1.08 \text{ \$ in one year/\$ today})$$

$$= \$509.26 \text{ today}$$

This PV is the amount we would need to put in the bank today to generate $550 in one year ($509.26 × 1.08 = $550). In other words, *the present value is the cash cost today of "doing it yourself"—it is the amount you need to invest at the current interest rate to recreate the cash flow.*

Once the costs and benefits are in present value terms, we can compute the investment's NPV:

$$NPV = \$509.26 - \$500 = \$9.26 \text{ today}$$

But what if you don't have the $500 needed to cover the initial cost of the project? Does the project still have the same value? Because we computed the value using competitive market prices, it should not depend on your tastes or the amount of cash you have in the bank. If you don't have the $500, suppose you borrow $509.26 from the bank at the 8% interest rate and then take the project. What are your cash flows in this case?

Today: $509.26 (loan) − $500 (invested in the project) = $9.26

In one year: $550 (from project) − $509.26 × 1.08 (loan balance) = $0

This transaction leaves you with exactly $9.26 extra cash in your pocket today and no future net obligations. So taking the project is like having an extra $9.26 in cash up front. Thus, the NPV expresses the value of an investment decision as an amount of cash received today. *As long as the NPV is positive, the decision increases the value of the firm and is a good decision regardless of your current cash needs or preferences regarding when to spend the money.*

THE NPV DECISION RULE

The NPV represents the value of the project in terms of cash today. Therefore, good projects are those with a positive NPV—they make the investor wealthier. Projects with negative NPVs have costs that exceed their benefits, and accepting them is equivalent to losing money today.

Because NPV is expressed in terms of cash today, it simplifies decision making. As long as we have correctly captured all of the costs and benefits of the project, decisions with positive NPV will increase the wealth of the firm and its investors. We capture this logic in the **NPV decision rule**:

> *When making an investment decision, take the alternative with the highest NPV. Choosing this alternative is equivalent to receiving its NPV in cash today.*

ACCEPTING OR REJECTING A PROJECT. A common financial decision is whether to accept or reject a project. Because rejecting the project generally has *NPV* = 0 (there are no new costs or benefits from not doing the project), the NPV decision rule implies that we should

- Accept those projects with positive NPV because accepting them is equivalent to receiving their NPV in cash today, and

- Reject those projects with negative NPV; accepting them would reduce the wealth of investors, whereas not doing them has no cost (NPV = 0).

If the NPV is exactly zero, you will neither gain nor lose by accepting the project rather than rejecting it. It is not a bad project because it does not reduce firm value, but it does not add value either.

| EXAMPLE **3.5** | THE NPV IS EQUIVALENT TO CASH TODAY |

Problem

Your firm needs to buy a new $9500 copier. As part of a promotion, the manufacturer has offered to let you pay $10,000 in one year, rather than pay cash today. Suppose the risk-free interest rate is 7% per year. Is this offer a good deal? Show that its NPV represents cash in your pocket.

Solution

If you take the offer, the benefit is that you won't have to pay $9500 today, which is already in PV terms. The cost, however, is $10,000 in one year. We therefore convert the cost to a present value at the risk-free interest rate:

$$PV(\text{Cost}) = (\$10,000 \text{ in one year}) \div (1.07 \text{ \$ in one year/\$ today}) = \$9345.79 \text{ today}$$

The NPV of the promotional offer is the difference between the benefits and the costs:

$$NPV = \$9500 - \$9345.79 = \$154.21 \text{ today}$$

The NPV is positive, so the investment is a good deal. It is equivalent to getting a cash discount today of $154.21, and only paying $9345.79 today for the copier. To confirm our calculation, suppose you take the offer and invest $9345.79 in a bank paying 7% interest. With interest, this amount will grow to $9345.79 × 1.07 = $10,000 in one year, which you can use to pay for the copier.

CHOOSING AMONG PROJECTS.   We can also use the NPV decision rule to choose among projects. To do so, we must compute the NPV of each alternative, and then select the one with the highest NPV. This alternative is the one which will lead to the largest increase in the value of the firm.

| EXAMPLE **3.6** | CHOOSING AMONG ALTERNATIVE PLANS |

Problem

Suppose you started a Web site hosting business and then decided to return to school. Now that you are back in school, you are considering selling the business within the next year. An investor has offered to buy the business for $200,000 whenever you are ready. If the interest rate is 10%, which of the following three alternatives is the best choice?

1. Sell the business now.
2. Scale back the business and continue running it while you are in school for one more year, and then sell the business (requiring you to spend $30,000 on expenses now, but generating $60,000 in profit at the end of the year).
3. Hire someone to manage the business while you are in school for one more year, and then sell the business (requiring you to spend $50,000 on expenses now, but generating $100,000 in profit at the end of the year).

CASH FLOWS AND NPVS FOR WEB SITE BUSINESS ALTERNATIVES

TABLE 3.1

	Today	In One Year	NPV
Sell Now	$200,000	0	$200,000
Scale Back Operations	−$30,000	$50,000 $200,000	$-30,000 + \dfrac{\$250,000}{1.10} = \$197,273$
Hire a Manager	−$50,000	$100,000 $200,000	$-50,000 + \dfrac{\$300,000}{1.10} = \$222,727$

Solution

The cash flows and NPVs are given in Table 3.1.

Faced with these three alternatives, the best choice is the one with highest NPV: Hire a manager and sell in one year. Choosing this alternative is equivalent to receiving $222,727 today.

NPV AND INDIVIDUAL'S CONSUMPTION PREFERENCES

When we compare projects with different patterns of present and future cash flows, we may have preferences regarding when we want to consume and thus when we want to receive the cash. Some may prefer consuming now and need cash today; others may prefer to defer consumption so they can save for the future. In the Web site hosting business example, hiring a manager and selling in one year has the highest NPV. However, this option requires an initial outlay of $50,000, as opposed to selling the business and receiving $200,000 immediately. Suppose you need $60,000 in cash now for consumption today (e.g., to pay for school and other expenses). Would selling the business be a better choice in that case?

As was true for the jeweller considering trading silver for gold in Section 3.1, the answer is again no. As long as you can borrow and lend at the 10% interest rate, hiring a manager is the best choice whatever your preferences regarding the timing of the cash flows. To see why, suppose you borrow $110,000 at the rate of 10% and hire the manager. Then you will owe $110,000 × 1.10 = $121,000 in one year, for total cash flows shown in Table 3.2. Compare these cash flows with those from selling now, and investing the excess $140,000 (which, at the rate of 10%, will grow to $140,000 × 1.10 = $154,000 in one year). Both strategies provide $60,000 in cash today, but the combination of hiring a manager and borrowing generates an additional $179,000 − $154,000 = $25,000 in one year.[3] Thus, even if you need $60,000 now, hiring the manager and selling in one year is still the best option.

This example illustrates our first separation principle, namely the **Separation of Individual's Consumption Preferences from the Optimal Investment Decision**:

Regardless of our consumption preferences that dictate whether we prefer cash today versus cash in the future, we should always maximize NPV first. We can then borrow or lend to shift cash flows through time so as to match our most preferred consumption spending pattern through time. In effect our preferences regarding consumption spending through time are separate from our optimal investment decision.

---

3. Note also that the present value of this additional cash flow, $25,000 × 1.10 = $22,727, is exactly the difference in NPVs between the two alternatives.

CASH FLOWS OF HIRING AND BORROWING VERSUS SELLING AND INVESTING

TABLE 3.2

	Today	In One Year
Hire a Manager	−$50,000	$300,000
Borrow	$110,000	−$121,000
Total Cash Flow	$60,000	$179,000
Versus		
Sell Now	$200,000	$0
Invest	−$140,000	$154,000
Total Cash Flow	$60,000	$154,000

CONCEPT CHECK

1. What is the NPV decision rule?

2. Why doesn't the NPV decision rule depend on the investor's preferences?

3.4   ARBITRAGE AND THE LAW OF ONE PRICE

So far, we have emphasized the importance of using competitive market prices to compute the NPV. But is there always only one such price? What if the same good trades for different prices in different markets? Consider gold. Gold trades in many different markets, with the largest markets in New York and London. To value an ounce of gold we could look up the competitive price in either of these markets. But suppose gold is trading for $850 per ounce in New York and $900 per ounce in London. Which price should we use?

Fortunately, such situations do not arise, and it is easy to see why. Recall that these are competitive market prices, at which you can both buy *and* sell. Thus, you can make money in this situation simply by buying gold for $850 per ounce in New York and then immediately selling it for $900 per ounce in London.[4] You will make $900 − $850 = $50 per ounce for each ounce you buy and sell. Trading 1 million ounces at these prices, you would make $50 million with no risk or investment! This is a case where that old adage, "Buy low, sell high," can be followed perfectly.

Of course, you will not be the only one making these trades. Everyone who sees these prices will want to trade as many ounces as possible. Within seconds, the market in New York would be flooded with buy orders, and the market in London would be flooded with sell orders. Although a few ounces (traded by the lucky individuals who spotted this opportunity first) might be exchanged at these prices, the price of gold in New York would quickly rise in response to all the orders, and the price in London would rapidly fall.[5] Prices would continue to change until they were equalized somewhere in the middle, such as $875 per ounce.

---

4. There is no need to transport the gold from New York to London because investors in these markets trade ownership rights to gold that is stored securely elsewhere.

5. As economists would say, supply would not equal demand in these markets. In New York, demand would be infinite because everyone would want to buy. For equilibrium to be restored so that supply equals demand, the price in New York would have to rise. Similarly, in London there would be infinite supply until the price there fell.

AN OLD JOKE

There is an old joke that many finance professors enjoy telling their students. It goes like this:

A finance professor and a student are walking down a street. The student notices a $100 bill lying on the pavement and leans down to pick it up. The finance professor immediately intervenes and says, "Don't bother; there is no free lunch. If that were a real $100 bill lying there, somebody would already have picked it up!"

This joke invariably generates much laughter because it makes fun of the principle of no arbitrage in competitive markets. But once the laughter dies down, the professor then asks whether anyone has ever *actually* found a real $100 bill lying on the pavement. The ensuing silence is the real lesson behind the joke.

This joke sums up the point of focusing on markets in which no arbitrage opportunities exist. Free $100 bills lying on the pavement, like arbitrage opportunities, are extremely rare for two reasons: (1) Because $100 is a large amount of money, people are especially careful not to lose it, and (2) in the rare event when someone does inadvertently drop $100, the likelihood of you finding it before someone else does is extremely small.

ARBITRAGE

The practice of buying and selling equivalent goods in different markets to take advantage of a price difference is known as **arbitrage**. More generally, we refer to any situation in which it is possible to make a profit without taking any risk or making any investment as an **arbitrage opportunity**. Because an arbitrage opportunity has positive NPV, whenever an arbitrage opportunity appears in financial markets, investors will race to take advantage of it. Those investors who spot the opportunity first and who can trade quickly will have the ability to exploit it. Once they place their trades, prices will respond, causing the arbitrage opportunity to evaporate.

Arbitrage opportunities are like money lying in the street; once spotted, they will quickly disappear. Thus the normal state of affairs in markets should be that no arbitrage opportunities exist. We call a competitive market in which there are no arbitrage opportunities a **normal market**.[6]

LAW OF ONE PRICE

In a normal market, the price of gold at any point in time will be the same in London and New York. The same logic applies more generally whenever equivalent investment opportunities trade in two different competitive markets. If the prices in the two markets differ, investors will profit immediately by buying in the market where it is cheap and selling in the market where it is expensive. In doing so, they will equalize the prices. As a result, prices will not differ (at least not for long). This important property is the Law of One Price:

If equivalent investment opportunities trade simultaneously in different competitive markets, then they must trade for the same price in both markets.

One useful consequence of the Law of One Price is that when evaluating costs and benefits to compute a net present value, we can use any competitive price to determine a cash value, without checking the price in all possible markets.

---

6. The term *efficient market* is also sometimes used to describe a market that, along with other properties, is without arbitrage opportunities. We avoid the term because it is often vaguely (and inconsistently) defined.

1. If the Law of One Price were violated, how could investors profit?

2. When investors exploit an arbitrage opportunity, how do their actions affect prices?

3.5 NO-ARBITRAGE AND SECURITY PRICES

An investment opportunity that trades in a financial market is known as a **financial security** (or, more simply, a **security**). The notions of arbitrage and the Law of One Price have important implications for security prices. We begin exploring its implications for the prices of individual securities as well as market interest rates. We then broaden our perspective to value a package of securities. Along the way, we will develop some important insights about firm decision making and firm value that will underpin our study throughout this textbook.

VALUING A SECURITY WITH THE LAW OF ONE PRICE

The Law of One Price tells us that the prices of equivalent investment opportunities should be the same. We can use this idea to value a security if we can find another equivalent investment whose price is already known. Consider a simple security that promises a one-time payment to its owner of $1000 in one year's time. Suppose there is no risk that the payment will not be made. One example of this type of security is a **bond**, a security sold by governments and corporations to raise money from investors today in exchange for the promised future payment. If the risk-free interest rate is 5%, what can we conclude about the price of this bond in a normal market?

To answer this question, consider an alternative investment that would generate the same cash flow as this bond. Suppose we invest money at the bank at the risk-free interest rate. How much do we need to invest today to receive $1000 in one year? As we saw in Section 3.3, the cost today of recreating a future cash flow on our own is its present value:

$$PV(\$1000 \text{ in one year}) = (\$1000 \text{ in one year}) \div (1.05 \text{ \$ in one year/\$ today})$$

$$= \$952.38 \text{ today}$$

If we invest $952.38 today at the 5% risk-free interest rate, we will have $1000 in one year's time with no risk.

We now have two ways to receive the same cash flow: (1) buy the bond or (2) invest $952.38 at the 5% risk-free interest rate. Because these transactions produce equivalent cash flows, the Law of One Price implies that in a normal market, they must have the same price (or cost). Therefore,

$$Price(Bond) = \$952.38$$

IDENTIFYING ARBITRAGE OPPORTUNITIES WITH SECURITIES.   Recall that the Law of One Price is based on the possibility of arbitrage: If the bond had a different price, there would be an arbitrage opportunity. For example, suppose the bond traded for a price of $940. How could we profit in this situation?

In this case, we can buy the bond for $940 and at the same time borrow $952.38 from the bank. Given the 5% interest rate, we will owe the bank $952.38 × 1.05 = $1000 in one year. Our overall cash flows from this pair of transactions are as shown in Table 3.3. Using this strategy we can earn $12.38 in cash today for each bond that we buy, without taking any risk or paying any of our own money in the future. Of course, as we—and others

NET CASH FLOWS FROM BUYING THE BOND AND BORROWING

TABLE 3.3

	Today ($)	In One Year ($)
Buy the bond	−940.00	+1000.00
Borrow from the bank	+952.38	−1000.00
Net cash flow	+12.38	0.00

NET CASH FLOWS FROM SELLING THE BOND AND INVESTING

TABLE 3.4

	Today ($)	In One Year ($)
Sell the bond	+960.00	−1000.00
Invest at the bank	−952.38	+1000.00
Net cash flow	+7.62	0.00

who see the opportunity—start buying the bond, its price will quickly rise until it reaches $952.38 and the arbitrage opportunity disappears.

A similar arbitrage opportunity arises if the bond price is higher than $952.38. For example, suppose the bond is trading for $960. In that case, we should sell the bond and invest $952.38 at the bank. As shown in Table 3.4, we then earn $7.62 in cash today, yet keep our future cash flows unchanged by replacing the $1000 we would have received from the bond with the $1000 we will receive from the bank. Once again, as people begin selling the bond to exploit this opportunity, the price will fall until it reaches $952.38 and the arbitrage opportunity disappears.

When the bond is overpriced, the arbitrage strategy involves selling the bond and investing some of the proceeds. But if the strategy involves selling the bond, does this mean that only the current owners of the bond can exploit it? The answer is no; in financial markets it is possible to sell a security you do not own by doing a *short sale*. In a **short sale**, the person who intends to sell the security first borrows it from someone who already owns it. Later, that person must either return the security by buying it back or pay the owner the cash flows he or she would have received. For example, we could short sell the bond in the example by promising to repay the current owner $1000 in one year. By executing a short sale, it is possible to exploit the arbitrage opportunity when the bond is overpriced even if you do not own it.

DETERMINING THE NO-ARBITRAGE PRICE

We have shown that at any price other than $952.38, an arbitrage opportunity exists for our bond. Thus, in a normal market, the price of this bond must be $952.38. We call this price the **no-arbitrage price** for the bond.

By applying the reasoning for pricing the simple bond, we can outline a general process for pricing other securities:

1. Identify the cash flows that will be paid by the security.

2. Determine the "do-it-yourself" cost of replicating those cash flows on our own; that is, the present value of the security's cash flows.

NASDAQ SOES BANDITS

Many Canadian companies have their shares listed on NASDAQ in the United States in addition to being listed on the TSX in Canada. The NASDAQ stock market differs from other markets in that it includes multiple dealers who all trade the same stock. For example, on a given day, as many as 10 or more dealers may post prices at which they are willing to trade Apple Computer stock (AAPL). The NASDAQ also has a Small Order Execution System (SOES) that allows individual investors to execute trades of up to 1000 shares instantly through an electronic system.

A type of trader sometimes referred to as a "SOES bandit" exploits the ability to execute trades instantly.

These traders watch the quotes of different dealers, waiting for arbitrage opportunities to arise. If one dealer is offering to sell AAPL at $20.25 and another is willing to buy at $20.30, the SOES bandit can profit by instantly buying 1000 shares at $20.25 from the first dealer and selling 1000 shares at $20.30 to the second dealer. Such a trade yields an arbitrage profit of $1000 \times \$0.05 = \$50$.

In the past, by making trades like this one many times per day, these traders could make a reasonable amount of money. Before long, the activity of these traders forced dealers to monitor their own quotes much more actively so as to avoid being "picked off" by these bandits. Today, this sort of arbitrage opportunity rarely appears.*

*SOES bandits can still profit by trading on information before dealers have updated their quotes. See J. Harris and P. Schultz, "The Trading Profits of SOES Bandits," *Journal of Financial Economics* 50 (2) (October 1998): 39–62.

Unless the price of the security equals this present value, an arbitrage opportunity will appear. Thus, the general formula is

No-Arbitrage Price of a Security

$$\text{Price(Security)} = PV(\text{All cash flows paid by the security}) \tag{3.3}$$

DETERMINING THE INTEREST RATE FROM BOND PRICES

Given the risk-free interest rate, the no-arbitrage price of a risk-free bond is determined by Eq. 3.3. The reverse is also true: If we know the price of a risk-free bond, we can use Eq. 3.3 to determine what the risk-free interest rate must be if there are no arbitrage opportunities.

For example, suppose a risk-free bond that pays $1000 in one year is trading with a competitive market price of $929.80 today. From Eq. 3.3, we know that the bond's price equals the present value of the $1000 cash flow it will pay:

$$\$929.80 \text{ today} = (\$1000 \text{ in one year}) \div (1 + r_f \ \$ \text{ in one year}/\$ \text{ today})$$

EXAMPLE 3.7	COMPUTING THE NO-ARBITRAGE PRICE

Problem

Consider a security that pays its owner $100 today and $100 in one year, without any risk. Suppose the risk-free interest rate is 10%. What is the no-arbitrage price of the security today (before the first $100 is paid)? If the security is trading for $195, what arbitrage opportunity is available?

> **Solution**
>
> We need to compute the present value of the security's cash flows. In this case there are two cash flows: $100 today, which is already in present value terms, and $100 in one year. The present value of the second cash flow is
>
> $$\$100 \text{ in one year} \div (1.10 \ \$ \text{ in one year}/\$ \text{ today}) = \$90.91 \text{ today}$$
>
> Therefore, the total present value of the cash flows is $100 + $90.91 = $190.91 today, which is the no-arbitrage price of the security.
>
> If the security is trading for $195, we can exploit its overpricing by selling it for $195. We can then use $100 of the sale proceeds to replace the $100 we would have received from the security today and invest $90.91 of the sale proceeds at 10% to replace the $100 we would have received in one year. The remaining $195 − $100 − $90.91 = $4.09 is an arbitrage profit.

We can rearrange this equation to determine the risk-free interest rate:

$$1 + r_f = \frac{\$1000 \text{ in one year}}{\$929.80 \text{ today}} = 1.0755 \ \$ \text{ in one year}/\$ \text{ today}$$

That is, if there are no arbitrage opportunities, the risk-free interest rate must be 7.55%.

In practice, this method is the way interest rates are actually calculated. When financial news services report current interest rates, they have derived these rates based on the current prices of risk-free government bonds trading in the market.

Note that the risk-free interest rate equals the percentage gain that you earn from investing in the bond, which is called the bond's **return**:

$$\text{Return} = \frac{\text{Gain at end of year}}{\text{Initial cost}}$$

$$= \frac{1000 - 929.80}{929.80} = \frac{1000}{929.80} - 1 = 7.55\% \tag{3.4}$$

Thus, if there is no arbitrage, the risk-free interest rate is equal to the return from investing in a risk-free bond. If the bond offered a higher return, then investors would earn a profit by borrowing at the risk-free interest rate and investing in the bond. If the bond had a lower return, investors would sell the bond and invest the proceeds at the risk-free interest rate. No arbitrage is therefore equivalent to the idea that *all risk-free investments should offer investors the same return.*

THE NPV OF TRADING SECURITIES AND THE OPTIMAL INVESTMENT DECISION

We have established that positive-NPV decisions increase the wealth of the firm and its investors. Think of buying a security as an investment decision. The cost of the decision is the price we pay for the security, and the benefit is the cash flows that we will receive from owning the security. When securities trade at no-arbitrage prices, what can we conclude about the value of trading them? From Eq. 3.3 the cost and benefit are equal in a normal market and so the NPV of buying a security is zero:

$$NPV(\text{Buy security}) = PV(\text{All cash flows paid by the security}) - \text{Price}(\text{Security})$$
$$= 0$$

Similarly, if we sell a security, the price we receive is the benefit and the cost is the cash flows we give up. Again the NPV is zero:

$$NPV(\text{Sell security}) = \text{Price(Security)} - PV(\text{All cash flows paid by the security})$$
$$= 0$$

Thus, the NPV of trading a security in a normal market is zero. This result is not surprising. If the NPV of buying a security were positive, then buying the security would be equivalent to receiving cash today—that is, it would present an arbitrage opportunity. Because arbitrage opportunities do not exist in normal markets, the NPV of all security trades must be zero.

Another way to understand this result is to remember that every trade has both a buyer and a seller. If the trade offered a positive NPV to one, it must give a negative NPV to the other. But then one of the two parties would not agree to the trade. Because all trades are voluntary, they must occur at prices at which neither party is losing value, and therefore for which the trade is zero NPV.

The insight that security trading in a normal market is a zero-NPV transaction is a critical building block in our study of corporate finance. Trading securities in a normal market neither creates nor destroys value. Instead, value is created by the real investment projects in which the firm engages, such as developing new products, opening new stores, or creating more efficient production methods. Financial transactions are not sources of value but merely serve to adjust the timing and risk of the cash flows to best suit the needs of the firm or its investors.

An important consequence of this result is the idea that we can evaluate a decision by focusing on its real components, rather than its financial ones. That is, we can separate the firm's investment decision from its financing choice. This is the second separation principle we have discovered, namely, the **Separation of the Investment and Financing Decisions**:

> *Security transactions in a normal market neither create nor destroy value on their own. Therefore, we can evaluate the NPV of an investment decision separately from the decision the firm makes regarding how to finance the investment or any other security transactions the firm is considering.*

EXAMPLE 3.8

SEPARATING INVESTMENT AND FINANCING

Problem

Your firm is considering a project that will require an upfront investment of $10 million today and will produce $12 million in cash flow for the firm in one year without risk. Rather than pay for the $10 million investment entirely using its own cash, the firm is considering raising additional funds by issuing a security that will pay investors $5.5 million in one year. Suppose the risk-free interest rate is 10%. Is pursuing this project a good decision without issuing the new security? Is it a good decision with the new security?

Solution

Without the new security, the cost of the project is $10 million today and the benefit is $12 million in one year. Converting the benefit to a present value

$$\$12 \text{ million in one year} \div (1.10 \ \$ \text{ in one year}/\$ \text{ today}) = \$10.91 \text{ million today}$$

we see that the project has $NPV = \$10.91 \text{ million} - \$10 \text{ million} = \$0.91 \text{ million today.}$

Now suppose the firm issues the new security. In a normal market, the price of this security will be the present value of its future cash flow:

$$\text{Price(Security)} = \$5.5 \text{ million} \div 1.10 = \$5 \text{ million today}$$

Thus, after it raises \$5 million by issuing the new security, the firm will only need to invest an additional \$5 million to take the project.

To compute the project's NPV in this case, note that in one year the firm will receive the \$12 million payout of the project, but owe \$5.5 million to the investors in the new security, leaving \$6.5 million for the firm. This amount has a present value of

$$\$6.5 \text{ million in one year} \div (1.10 \text{ \$ in one year} / \text{\$ today}) = \$5.91 \text{ million today}$$

Thus, the project has $NPV = \$5.91 \text{ million} - \$5 \text{ million} = \$0.91 \text{ million}$ today, as before.

In either case, we get the same result for the NPV. The separation principle indicates that we will get the same result for any choice of financing for the firm that occurs in a normal market. We can therefore evaluate the project without explicitly considering the different financing possibilities the firm might choose.

VALUING A PORTFOLIO

So far, we have discussed the no-arbitrage price for individual securities. The Law of One Price also has implications for packages of securities. Consider two securities, A and B. Suppose a third security, C, has the same cash flows as A and B combined. In this case, security C is equivalent to a combination of securities A and B. We use the term **portfolio** to describe a collection of securities. What can we conclude about the price of security C as compared to the prices of A and B?

VALUE ADDITIVITY. Because security C is equivalent to the portfolio of A and B, by the Law of One Price, they must have the same price. This idea leads to the relationship known as **value additivity**; that is, the price of C must equal the price of the portfolio, which is the combined price of A and B:

Value Additivity

$$\text{Price(C)} = \text{Price(A + B)} = \text{Price(A)} + \text{Price(B)} \tag{3.5}$$

Because security C has cash flows equal to the sum of A and B, its value or price must be the sum of the values of A and B. Otherwise, an obvious arbitrage opportunity would exist. For example, if the total price of A and B were lower than the price of C, then we could make a profit buying A and B and selling C. This arbitrage activity would quickly push prices until the price of security C equals the total price of A and B.

More generally, value additivity implies that the value of a portfolio is equal to the sum of the values of its parts. That is, the "à la carte" price and the package price must coincide.[7]

---

7. This feature of financial markets does not hold in many other, noncompetitive markets. For example, a round-trip airline ticket often costs much less than two separate one-way tickets. Of course, airline tickets are not sold in a competitive market; you cannot buy *and* sell the tickets at the listed prices. Only airlines can sell tickets, and they have strict rules against reselling tickets. Otherwise, you could make money buying round-trip tickets and selling them to people who need one-way tickets.

NO-ARBITRAGE PRICES OF EXCHANGE-TRADED FUNDS

Value additivity is the principle behind a type of trading activity known as ETF arbitrage. Common stock indices (such as the S&P/TSX 60) represent portfolios of individual stocks. It is possible to trade the individual stocks in an index on the TSX. It is also possible to trade the entire index (as a single security) using an exchange-traded fund (ETF) that is traded on the TSX. When the price of the ETF is below the total price of the individual stocks, traders buy the index and sell the stocks to capture the price difference. This can be done because most ETFs allow designated institutional traders to exchange a prescribed number of units of the ETF for the stocks that make up the ETF. Similarly, when the price of the ETF is above the total price of the individual stocks, traders sell the ETF and buy the individual stocks. The designated traders that engage in ETF arbitrage can automate the process by tracking the prices and submitting the orders via computer; as a result, this activity is also referred to as "program trading." The actions of these arbitrageurs ensure that the ETF prices and the individual stock prices track each other very closely.

VALUE ADDITIVITY AND FIRM VALUE.   Value additivity has an important consequence for the value of an entire firm. The cash flows of the firm are equal to the total cash flows of all projects and investments within the firm. Therefore, by value additivity, the price or value of the entire firm is equal to the sum of the values of all projects and investments within it. In other words, our NPV decision rule coincides with maximizing the value of the entire firm:

> *To maximize the value of the entire firm, managers should make decisions that maximize NPV. The NPV of the decision represents its contribution to the overall value of the firm.*

EXAMPLE 3.9   VALUING AN ASSET IN A PORTFOLIO

Problem
Horton Holdings is a publicly traded company with only two assets: It owns 60% of Tim's Donuts chain and 100% of the Caribou hockey team. Suppose the market value of Horton Holdings is $160 million, and the market value of the entire Tim's Donuts chain (which is also publicly traded) is $120 million. What is the market value of the Caribou hockey team?

Solution
We can think of Horton as a portfolio consisting of a 60% stake in Tim's Donuts and 100% of the Caribou hockey team. By value additivity, the sum of the value of the stake in Tim's Donuts and the Caribou hockey team must equal the $160 million market value of Horton. Because the 60% stake in Tim's Donuts is worth 60% × $120 million = $72 million, the Caribou hockey team has a value of $160 million − $72 million = $88 million.

WHERE DO WE GO FROM HERE?

The key concepts we have developed in this chapter—the Valuation Principle, Net Present Value, and the Law of One Price—provided the foundation for financial decision making. The Law of One Price allows us to determine the value of stocks, bonds, and other securities, based on their cash flows, and validates the optimality of the NPV decision rule in

FINANCIAL **CRISIS**
LIQUIDITY AND THE INFORMATIONAL ROLE OF PRICES

In the first half of 2008, as the extent and severity of the decline in the U.S. housing market became apparent, investors became increasingly worried about the value of securities that were backed by residential home mortgages. As a result, the volume of trade in the multi-trillion dollar market for mortgage-backed securities plummeted over 80% by August 2008. Over the next two months, trading in many of these securities ceased altogether, making the markets for these securities increasingly illiquid.

Competitive markets depend upon liquidity; there must be sufficient buyers and sellers of a security so that it is possible to trade at any time at the current market price. When markets become illiquid it may not be possible to trade at the posted price. As a consequence, we can no longer rely on market prices as a measure of value.

The collapse of the mortgage-backed securities market created two problems. First was the loss of trading opportunities, making it difficult for holders of these securities to sell them. But a potentially more significant problem was the loss of *information*. Without a liquid, competitive market for these securities, it became impossible to reliably value these securities. In addition, given that the value of the banks holding these securities was based on the sum of all projects and investments within them, investors could not value the banks either. Investors reacted to this uncertainty by selling both the mortgage-backed securities and securities of banks—worldwide—that held mortgage-backed securities. These actions further compounded the problem by driving down prices to seemingly unrealistically low levels and thereby threatening the solvency of the entire world financial system.

The loss of information precipitated by the loss of liquidity played a key role in the breakdown of credit markets. As both investors and government regulators found it increasingly difficult to assess the solvency of the banks, banks found it difficult to raise new funds on their own and also shied away from lending to other banks because of their concerns about the financial viability of their competitors. The result was a breakdown in lending. Ultimately, governments were forced to step in and spend hundreds of billions of dollars in order to (1) provide new capital to support banks and (2) provide liquidity by ensuring a market for "toxic" asset-backed securities.

identifying projects and investments that create value. In the remainder of the text, we will build on this foundation and explore the details of applying these principles in practice.

For simplicity, we have focused in this chapter on projects that were not risky, and thus had known costs and benefits. The same fundamental tools of the Valuation Principle and the Law of One Price can be applied to analyze risky investments as well, and we will look in detail at methods to assess and value risk in Part 4 of the text. Those seeking some early insights into this topic, however, are encouraged to read the appendix to this chapter. There we use the principle of no arbitrage developed in this chapter to demonstrate two fundamental insights regarding the impact of risk on valuation:

1. When cash flows are risky, we must discount them at a rate equal to the risk-free interest rate plus an appropriate risk premium; and,

2. The appropriate risk premium will be higher the more the project's returns tend to vary with the overall risk in the economy.

Finally, the chapter appendix also addresses the important practical issue of transactions costs. There we show that when purchase and sale prices, or borrowing and lending rates, differ, the Law of One Price will continue to hold, but only up to the level of transactions costs.

CONCEPT CHECK
1. If a firm makes an investment that has a positive NPV, how does the value of the firm change?
2. Explain the two separation principles.
3. In addition to trading opportunities, what else do liquid markets provide?

SUMMARY

1. To evaluate a decision, we must value the incremental costs and benefits associated with that decision. A good decision is one for which the value of the benefits exceeds the value of the costs.

2. To compare costs and benefits that occur at different points in time, in different currencies, or with different risks, we must put all costs and benefits in common terms. Typically, we convert costs and benefits into cash today.

3. A competitive market is one in which a good can be bought and sold at the same price. We use prices from competitive markets to determine the cash value of a good.

4. The time value of money is the difference in value between money today and money in the future. The rate at which we can exchange money today for money in the future by borrowing or investing is the current market interest rate. The risk-free interest rate, r_f, is the rate at which money can be borrowed or lent without risk.

5. The present value (PV) of a cash flow is its value in terms of cash today.

6. The net present value (NPV) of a project is

$$PV(\text{Benefits}) - PV(\text{Costs}) \qquad (3.1)$$

7. A good project is one with a positive net present value. The NPV decision rule states that when choosing from among a set of alternatives, choose the one with the highest NPV. The NPV of a project is equivalent to the cash value today of the project.

8. Regardless of our preferences for consumption today versus in the future (and thus our preferred pattern of cash flows through time), we should always first maximize NPV. We can then borrow or lend to shift cash flows through time and attain a pattern of cash flows that matches our consumption preferences through time. This is the separation of Consumption Preferences from the Optimal Investment Decision—our preferences regarding consumption through time (and thus cash-flow patterns) are separate from our optimal investment decision.

9. Arbitrage is the process of trading to take advantage of equivalent goods that have different prices in different competitive markets.

10. A normal market is a competitive market with no arbitrage opportunities.

11. The Law of One Price states that if equivalent goods or securities trade simultaneously in different competitive markets, they will trade for the same price in each market. This law is equivalent to saying that no arbitrage opportunities should exist.

12. The no-arbitrage price of a security is

$$PV(\text{All cash flows paid by security}) \qquad (3.3)$$

13. Value additivity implies that the value of a portfolio is equal to the sum of the values of its parts.

14. To maximize the value of the entire firm, managers should make decisions that maximize the NPV. The NPV of the decision represents its contribution to the overall value of the firm.

15. The second separation principle, the Separation of Investment and Financing Decisions, states that security transactions in a normal market neither create nor destroy value on their own. As a consequence, we can evaluate the NPV of an investment decision separately from the financing of the investment (the security transactions the firm is considering).

KEY TERMS

arbitrage *p. 69*
arbitrage opportunity *p. 69*
bond *p. 70*
competitive market *p. 58*
discount factor *p. 63*
discount rate *p. 63*
financial security *p. 70*
future value *p. 63*
interest rate factor *p. 61*
Law of One Price *p. 55*
net present value (NPV) *p. 64*
no-arbitrage price *p. 71*
normal market *p. 69*
NPV decision rule *p. 65*

portfolio *p. 75*
present value (PV) *p. 62*
return *p. 73*
risk-free interest rate *p. 61*
security *p. 70*
Separation of Individual's
    Consumption Preferences from the
    Optimal Investment Decision *p. 67*
Separation of the Investment and
    Financing Decisions *p. 74*
short sale *p. 71*
time value of money *p. 61*
valuation principle *p. 59*
value additivity *p. 75*

PROBLEMS

The problems marked in green can be found on MyFinanceLab at www.myfinancelab.com. Visit your MyFinanceLab for additional practice. An asterisk (*) indicates problems with a higher level of difficulty. Additional readings for this chapter may be found in the Textbook Resources section on MyFinanceLab.

Valuing Decisions

1. Honda Motor Company is considering offering a $2000 rebate on its minivan, lowering the vehicle's price from $30,000 to $28,000. The marketing group estimates that this rebate will increase sales over the next year from 40,000 to 55,000 vehicles. Suppose Honda's profit margin with the rebate is $6000 per vehicle. If the change in sales is the only consequence of this decision, what are its costs and benefits? Is it a good idea?

2. You are an international shrimp trader. A food producer in the Czech Republic offers to pay you 2 million Czech koruna today in exchange for a year's supply of frozen shrimp. Your Thai supplier will provide you with the same supply for 3 million Thai baht today. If the current competitive market exchange rates are 25.50 koruna per dollar and 41.25 baht per dollar, what is the value of this deal?

3. Suppose the current market price of corn is $3.75 per bushel. Your firm has a technology that can convert 1 bushel of corn to 3 gallons of ethanol. If the cost of conversion is $1.60 per bushel, at what market price of ethanol does conversion become attractive?

4. Suppose your employer offers you a choice between a $5000 bonus and 100 shares of the company stock. Whichever one you choose will be awarded today. The stock is currently trading for $63 per share.

   a. Suppose that if you receive the stock bonus, you are free to trade it. Which form of the bonus should you choose? What is its value?

   b. Suppose that if you receive the stock bonus, you are required to hold it for at least one year. What can you say about the value of the stock bonus now? What will your decision depend on?

5. You have decided to take your daughter skiing in Whistler. The best price you have been able to find for a round-trip air ticket is $359. You notice that you have 20,000 frequent flyer miles that are about to expire, but you need 25,000 miles to get her a free ticket. The airline offers to sell you 5000 additional miles for 3¢ per mile.

    a. Assuming that if you don't use the miles for your daughter's ticket they will become worthless, what should you do?

    b. What additional information would your decision depend on if the miles were not expiring? Why?

**Interest Rates and the
Time Value of Money**

6. Suppose the risk-free interest rate is 4%.

    a. Having $200 today is equivalent to having what amount in one year?

    b. Having $200 in one year is equivalent to having what amount today?

    c. Which would you prefer, $200 today or $200 in one year? Does your answer depend on when you need the money? Why or why not?

7. You have an investment opportunity in Japan. It requires an investment of $1 million today and will produce a cash flow of ¥114 million in one year with no risk. Suppose the risk-free interest rate in Canada is 4%, the risk-free interest rate in Japan is 2%, and the current competitive exchange rate is ¥110 per $1. What is the NPV of this investment? Is it a good opportunity?

8. Your firm has a risk-free investment opportunity where it can invest $160,000 today and receive $170,000 in one year. For what level of interest rates is this project attractive?

**Present Value and the
NPV Decision Rule**

9. You run a construction firm. You have just won a contract to build a government office building. Building it will require an investment of $10 million today and $5 million in one year. The government will pay you $20 million in one year upon the building's completion. Suppose the cash flows and their times of payment are certain, and the risk-free interest rate is 10%.

    a. What is the NPV of this opportunity?

    b. How can your firm turn this NPV into cash today?

10. Your firm has identified three potential investment projects. The projects and their cash flows are shown here:

Project	Cash Flow Today ($)	Cash Flow in One Year ($)
A	−10	20
B	5	5
C	20	−10

Suppose all cash flows are certain and the risk-free interest rate is 10%.

    a. What is the NPV of each project?

    b. If the firm can choose only one of these projects, which should it choose?

    c. If the firm can choose any two of these projects, which should it choose?

11. Your computer manufacturing firm must purchase 10,000 keyboards from a supplier. One supplier demands a payment of $100,000 today plus $10 per keyboard payable in one year. Another supplier will charge $21 per keyboard, also payable in one year. The risk-free interest rate is 6%.

    a. What is the difference in their offers in terms of dollars today? Which offer should your firm take?

b. Suppose your firm does not want to spend cash today. How can it take the first offer and not spend $100,000 of its own cash today?

Arbitrage and the Law of One Price

12. Suppose the Royal Bank offers a risk-free interest rate of 5.5% on both savings and loans, and Scotiabank offers a risk-free interest rate of 6% on both savings and loans.

    a. What arbitrage opportunity is available?

    b. Which bank would experience a surge in the demand for loans? Which bank would receive a surge in deposits?

    c. What would you expect to happen to the interest rates the two banks are offering?

13. Throughout the 1990s, interest rates in Japan were lower than interest rates in Canada. As a result, many Japanese investors were tempted to borrow in Japan and invest the proceeds in Canada. Explain why this strategy does not represent an arbitrage opportunity.

14. Many Canadian stocks are interlisted on both the TSX and an American exchange such as the NYSE or NASDAQ. For example, CN Rail trades with symbol CNR on the TSX and with symbol CNI on the NYSE. Suppose the NYSE price of CN is U.S.$49.85 and the TSX price of CN is $50.40 (in Canadian funds). Use the Law of One Price to determine the current CAD/USD exchange rate (where CAD stands for Canadian dollars and USD stands for U.S. dollars).

No-Arbitrage and Security Prices

15. The promised cash flows of three securities are listed here. If the cash flows are risk-free, and the risk-free interest rate is 5%, determine the no-arbitrage price of each security before the first cash flow is paid.

Security	Cash Flow Today ($)	Cash Flow in One Year ($)
A	500	500
B	0	1000
C	1000	0

16. An exchange-traded fund (ETF) is a security that represents a portfolio of individual stocks. Consider an ETF for which each share represents a portfolio of two shares of CN Rail (CNR), one share of Canadian Pacific (CP), and three shares of WestJet (WJA). Suppose the current stock prices of each individual stock are as shown here:

Stock	Current Market Price
CNR	$50
CP	$69
WJA	$17

    a. What is the price per share of the ETF in a normal market?

    b. If the ETF currently trades for $200, what arbitrage opportunity is available? What trades would you make?

    c. If the ETF currently trades for $250, what arbitrage opportunity is available? What trades would you make?

EXCEL   17. Consider two securities that pay risk-free cash flows over the next two years and that have the current market prices shown here:

Security	Price Today ($)	Cash Flow in One Year ($)	Cash Flow in Two Years ($)
B1	94	100	0
B2	85	0	100

a. What is the no-arbitrage price of a security that pays cash flows of $100 in one year and $100 in two years?

b. What is the no-arbitrage price of a security that pays cash flows of $100 in one year and $500 in two years?

c. Suppose a security with cash flows of $50 in one year and $100 in two years is trading for a price of $130. What arbitrage opportunity is available?

18. Suppose a security with a risk-free cash flow of $150 in one year trades for $140 today. If there are no arbitrage opportunities, what is the current risk-free interest rate?

EXCEL   19. Xia Corporation is a company whose sole assets are $100,000 in cash and three projects that it will undertake. The projects are risk-free and have the following cash flows:

Project	Cash Flow Today ($)	Cash Flow in One Year ($)
A	−20,000	30,000
B	−10,000	25,000
C	−60,000	80,000

Xia plans to invest any unused cash today at the risk-free interest rate of 10%. In one year, all cash will be paid to investors and the company will be shut down.

a. What is the NPV of each project? Which projects should Xia undertake and how much cash should it retain?

b. What is the total value of Xia's assets (projects and cash) today?

c. What cash flows will the investors in Xia receive? Based on these cash flows, what is the value of Xia today?

d. Suppose Xia pays any unused cash to investors today, rather than investing it. What are the cash flows to the investors in this case? What is the value of Xia now?

e. Explain the relationship in your answers to parts (b), (c), and (d).

<table>
<tr><td>

CHAPTER 3 APPENDIX

notation

r_s discount rate for security s

</td></tr>
</table>

THE PRICE OF RISK

Thus far we have considered only cash flows that have no risk. But in many settings, cash flows are risky. If something is risky, then its actual outcome may be different from its expected outcome. So a risky cash flow may turn out to be better or worse, in reality, than what was originally expected. In this section, we examine how to determine the present value of a risky cash flow.

RISKY VERSUS RISK-FREE CASH FLOWS

Suppose the risk-free interest rate is 4% and that over the next year the economy is equally likely to strengthen or weaken. Consider an investment in a risk-free bond, and one in the stock market index (a portfolio of all stocks in the market). The risk-free bond has no risk and will pay $1100 whatever the state of the economy. The cash flow from an investment in the market index, however, depends on the strength of the economy. Let's assume that the market index will be worth $1400 if the economy is strong but only $800 if the economy is weak. Table 3A.1 summarizes these payoffs.

In Section 3.5 we saw that the no-arbitrage price of a security is equal to the present value of its cash flows. For example, the price of the risk-free bond corresponds to the 4% risk-free interest rate:

$$\text{Price (Risk-Free Bond)} = \text{PV (Cash Flows)}$$
$$= (\$1100 \text{ in one year}) \div (1.04 \ \$ \text{ in one year/\$ today})$$
$$= \$1058 \text{ today}$$

Now consider the market index. An investor who buys it today can sell it in one year for a cash flow of either $800 or $1400, with an expected payoff of $\frac{1}{2}(\$800) + \frac{1}{2}(\$1400) =$ $1100. Although this expected payoff is the same as the risk-free bond, the market index has a lower price today. It pays $1100 *on average*, but its actual cash flow is risky, so investors are only willing to pay $1000 for it today rather than $1057.69. What accounts for this lower price?

RISK AVERSION AND THE RISK PREMIUM

Intuitively, investors pay less to receive $1100 on average than to receive $1100 with certainty because they don't like risk. In particular, it seems likely that for most individuals, *the personal cost of losing a dollar in bad times is greater than the benefit of an extra dollar in good times.* Thus, the benefit from receiving an extra $300 ($1400 versus $1100) when the

CASH FLOWS AND MARKET PRICES (IN $) OF A RISK-FREE BOND AND AN INVESTMENT IN THE MARKET PORTFOLIO

TABLE 3A.1			

| Security | Market Price Today | Cash Flow in One Year | |
		Weak Economy	**Strong Economy**
Risk-free bond	1057.69	1100	1100
Market index	1000	800	1400

economy is strong is less important than the loss of $300 ($800 versus $1100) when the economy is weak. As a result, investors prefer to receive $1100 with certainty.

The notion that investors prefer to have a safe income rather than a risky one of the same expected amount is called **risk aversion**. It is an aspect of an investor's preferences, and different investors may have different degrees of risk aversion. The more risk averse investors are, the lower the current price of the market index will be compared to a risk-free bond with the same expected payoff.

Because investors care about risk, we cannot use the risk-free interest rate to compute the present value of a risky future cash flow. When investing in a risky project, investors will expect a return that appropriately compensates them for the risk. For example, investors who buy the market index for its current price of $1000 receive $1100 on average at the end of the year, which is an average gain of $100, or a 10% return on their initial investment. When we compute the return of a security based on the payoff we expect to receive on average, we call it the **expected return**:

$$\text{Expected return of a risky investment} = \frac{\text{Expected gain at end of year}}{\text{Initial cost}} \quad (3A.1)$$

Of course, although the expected return of the market index is 10%, its *actual* return will be higher or lower. If the economy is strong, the market index will rise to 1400, which represents a return of

$$\text{Market return if economy is strong} = (1400 - 1000)/1000 = 40\%$$

If the economy is weak, the index will drop to 800, for a return of

$$\text{Market return if economy is weak} = (800 - 1000)/1000 = -20\%$$

We can also calculate the 10% expected return by computing the expectation of these actual returns:

$$\tfrac{1}{2}(40\%) + \tfrac{1}{2}(-20\%) = 10\%$$

Thus, investors in the market index earn an expected return of 10% rather than the risk-free interest rate of 4% on their investment. The difference of 6% between these returns is called the market index's **risk premium**. The risk premium of a security represents the additional return that investors expect to earn to compensate them for the security's risk. Because investors are risk averse, the price of a risky security cannot be calculated by simply discounting its expected cash flow at the risk-free interest rate. Rather,

When a cash flow is risky, to compute its present value we must discount the cash flow we expect on average at a rate that equals the risk-free interest rate plus an appropriate risk premium.

THE NO-ARBITRAGE PRICE OF A RISKY SECURITY

The risk premium of the market index is determined by investors' preferences toward risk. And in the same way we used the risk-free interest rate to determine the no-arbitrage price of other risk-free securities, we can use the risk premium of the market index to value other risky securities. For example, suppose some security A will pay investors $600 if the economy is strong and nothing if it is weak. Let's see how we can determine the market price of security A using the Law of One Price.

As shown in Table 3A.2, if we combine security A with a risk-free bond that pays $800 in one year, the cash flows of the portfolio in one year are identical to the cash flows of the market index. By the Law of One Price, the total market value of the bond and security A

DETERMINING THE MARKET PRICE OF SECURITY A (CASH FLOWS IN $)

TABLE 3A.2

Security	Market Price Today	Cash Flow in One Year	
		Weak Economy	Strong Economy
Risk-free bond	769.23	800	800
Security A	?	0	600
Market index	1000	800	1400

must equal $1000, the value of the market index. Given a risk-free interest rate of 4%, the market price of the bond is

$$(\$800 \text{ in one year}) \times (1.04 \text{ \$ in one year/\$ today}) = \$769.23 \text{ today}$$

Therefore, the initial market price of security A is $1000 − 769.23 = $230.77. If the price of security A were higher or lower than $230.77, then the value of the portfolio of the bond and security A would differ from the value of the market index, violating the Law of One Price and creating an arbitrage opportunity.

RISK PREMIUMS DEPEND ON RISK

Given an initial price of $230.77 and an expected payoff of $\frac{1}{2}(0) + \frac{1}{2}(600) = 300$, security A has an expected return of

$$\text{Expected return of security A} = \frac{300 - 230.77}{230.77} = 30\%$$

Note that this expected return exceeds the 10% expected return of the market portfolio. Investors in security A earn a risk premium of 30% − 4% = 26% over the risk-free interest rate, compared to a 6% risk premium for the market portfolio. Why are the risk premiums so different?

The reason for the difference becomes clear if we compare the actual returns for the two securities. When the economy is weak, investors in security A lose everything, for a return of −100%, and when the economy is strong, they earn a return of (600 − 230.77)/230.77 = 160%. In contrast, the market index loses 20% in a weak economy and gains 40% in a strong economy. Given its much more variable returns, it is not surprising that security A must pay investors a higher risk premium.

RISK IS RELATIVE TO THE OVERALL MARKET

The example of security A suggests that the risk premium of a security will depend on how variable its returns are. But before drawing any conclusions, it is worth considering one further example.

EXAMPLE 3A.1   A NEGATIVE RISK PREMIUM

Problem

Suppose security B pays $600 if the economy is weak and $0 if the economy is strong. What are its no-arbitrage price, expected return, and risk premium?

Solution

If we combine the market index and security B together in a portfolio, we earn the same payoff as a risk-free bond that pays $1400, as shown here (cash flows in $):

Security	Market Price Today	Cash Flow in One Year	
		Weak Economy	**Strong Economy**
Market index	1000	800	1400
Security B	?	600	0
Risk-free bond	1346.15	1400	1400

Because the market price of the risk-free bond is $1400 × 1.04 = $1346.15 today, we can conclude from the Law of One Price that security B must have a market price of $1346.15 − 1000 = $346.15 today.

   If the economy is weak, security B pays a return of (600 − 346.15)/346.15 = 73.3%. If the economy is strong, security B pays nothing, for a return of −100%. The expected return of security B is therefore $\frac{1}{2}(73.3\%) + \frac{1}{2}(-100\%) = -13.3\%$. Its risk premium is −13.3% − 4% = −17.3%; that is, security B pays investors 17.3% less on average than the risk-free interest rate.

The results for security B are quite striking. Looking at securities A and B in isolation, they seem very similar—both are equally likely to pay $600 or $0. Yet security A has a much lower market price than security B ($230.77 vs. $346.15). In terms of returns, security A pays investors an expected return of 30%; security B pays −13.3%. Why are their prices and expected returns so different? And why would risk-averse investors be willing to buy a risky security with an expected return below the risk-free interest rate?

To understand this result, note that security A pays $600 when the economy is strong, and B pays $600 when the economy is weak. Recall that our definition of risk aversion is that investors value an extra dollar of income more in bad times than in good times. Thus, because security B pays $600 when the economy is weak and the market index performs poorly, it pays off when investors' wealth is low and they value money the most. In fact, security B is not really "risky" from an investor's point of view; rather, security B is an insurance policy against an economic decline. By holding security B together with the market index, we can eliminate our risk from market fluctuations. Risk-averse investors are willing to pay for this insurance by accepting a return below the risk-free interest rate.

This result illustrates an extremely important principle. The risk of a security cannot be evaluated in isolation. Even when a security's returns are quite variable, if the returns vary in a way that offsets other risks investors are holding, the security will reduce rather than increase investors' risk. As a result, risk can only be assessed relative to the other risks that investors face; that is,

The risk of a security must be evaluated in relation to the fluctuations of other investments in the economy. A security's risk premium will be higher the more its returns tend to vary with the overall economy and the market index. If the security's returns vary in the opposite direction of the market index, it offers insurance and will have a negative risk premium.

Table 3A.3 compares the risk and risk premiums for the different securities we have considered thus far. For each security we compute the difference in its return when the economy is strong versus weak. Note that the risk premium for each security is proportional to this difference, and the risk premium is negative when the returns vary in the opposite direction of the market.

RISK AND RISK PREMIUMS FOR DIFFERENT SECURITIES

TABLE 3A.3

Security	Returns		Difference in Returns	Risk Premium
	Weak Economy	Strong Economy		
Risk-free bond	4%	4%	0%	0%
Market index	−20%	40%	60%	6%
Security A	−100%	160%	260%	26%
Security B	73.3%	−100%	−173.3%	−17.3%

RISK, RETURN, AND MARKET PRICES

We have shown that when cash flows are risky, we can use the Law of One Price to compute present values by constructing a portfolio that produces cash flows with identical risk. As shown in Figure 3A.1, computing prices in this way is equivalent to converting between cash flows today and the *expected* cash flows received in the future using a discount rate, r_s, that includes a risk premium appropriate for the investment's risk:

$$r_s = r_f + (\text{risk premium for investment } s) \tag{3A.2}$$

For the simple setting considered here with only a single source of risk (the strength of the economy), we have seen that the risk premium of an investment depends on how its returns vary with the overall economy. In Part 4 of the text we show that this result holds for more general settings with many sources of risk and more than two possible states of the economy.

EXAMPLE 3A.2

USING THE RISK PREMIUM TO COMPUTE A PRICE

Problem

Consider a risky bond with a cash flow of $1100 when the economy is strong and $1000 when the economy is weak. Suppose a 1% risk premium is appropriate for this bond. If the risk-free interest rate is 4%, what is the price of the bond today?

Solution

From Eq. 3A.2, the appropriate discount rate for the bond is

$$r_b = r_f + (\text{Risk premium for the bond}) = 4\% + 1\% = 5\%$$

The expected cash flow of the bond is $\frac{1}{2}(\$1100) + \frac{1}{2}(\$1000) = \$1050$ in one year. Thus, the price of the bond today is

$$\text{Bond Price} = (\text{Average cash flow in one year}) \div (1 + r_b \ \$ \text{ in one year/\$ today})$$

$$= (\$1050 \text{ in one year}) \div (1.05 \ \$ \text{ in one year/\$ today})$$

$$= \$1000 \text{ today}$$

FIGURE 3A.1

Converting Between Dollars Today and Dollars in One Year with Risk
When cash flows are risky, Eq. 3A.2 determines the expected return, r_s, that we can use to convert between prices or present values today and the expected cash flow in the future.

Given this price, the bond's return is 10% when the economy is strong, and 0% when the economy is weak. (Note that the difference in the returns is 10%, which is $\frac{1}{6}$ as variable as the market index; see Table 3A.3. Correspondingly, the risk premium of the bond is $\frac{1}{6}$ that of the market index as well.)

CONCEPT CHECK

1. Why does the expected return of a risky security generally differ from the risk-free interest rate? What determines the size of its risk premium?

2. Explain why the risk of a security should not be evaluated in isolation.

ARBITRAGE WITH TRANSACTIONS COSTS

In our examples up to this point, we have ignored the costs of buying and selling goods or securities. In most markets, you must pay **transactions costs** to trade securities. As discussed in Chapter 1, when you trade securities in markets such as the TSX, you must pay two types of transactions costs. First, you must pay your broker a commission on the trade. Second, because you will generally pay a slightly higher price when you buy a security (the ask price) than you receive when you sell (the bid price), you will also pay the bid-ask spread. For example, a share of Lululemon stock (ticker symbol LLL) might be quoted as follows:

Bid: $34.30
Ask: $34.70

We can interpret these quotes as if the competitive price for Lululemon is 34.50, but there is a transaction cost of $0.20 per share when buying or selling.[8]

What consequences do these transactions costs have for no-arbitrage prices and the Law of One Price? Earlier we stated that the price of gold in New York and London must be identical in competitive markets. Suppose, however, that total transactions costs of $5 per ounce are associated with buying gold in one market and selling it in the other. Then

---

8. Any price in between the bid price and the ask price could be the competitive price, with differing transactions costs for buying and selling.

if the price of gold is $850 per ounce in New York and $852 per ounce in London, the "Buy low, sell high" strategy no longer works:

Cost: $850 per ounce (buy gold in New York) + $5 (transactions costs)

Benefit: $852 per ounce (sell gold in London)

NPV: $852 − $850 − $5 = −$3 per ounce

Indeed, there is no arbitrage opportunity in this case until the prices diverge by more than $5, the amount of the transactions costs.

In general, we need to modify our previous conclusions about no-arbitrage prices by appending the phrase "up to transactions costs." In this example, there is only one competitive price for gold—up to a discrepancy of the $5 transactions cost. The other conclusions of this chapter have the same qualifier. The package price should equal the à la carte price, up to the transactions costs associated with packaging and unpackaging. The price of a security should equal the present value of its cash flows, up to the transactions costs of trading the security and the cash flows.

Fortunately, for most financial markets, these costs are small. For example, in February 2008, typical bid-ask spreads for large, actively traded TSX stocks were between 1 and 5 cents per share, although they can be much greater for more thinly traded stocks. As a first approximation we can ignore these spreads in our analysis. Only in situations in which the NPV is small (relative to the transactions costs) will any discrepancy matter. In that case, we will need to carefully account for all transactions costs to decide whether the NPV is positive or negative.

EXAMPLE 3A.3 — THE NO-ARBITRAGE PRICE RANGE

Problem

Consider a bond that pays $1000 at the end of the year. Suppose the market interest rate for deposits is 6%, but the market interest rate for borrowing is 6.5%. What is the no-arbitrage price *range* for the bond? That is, what is the highest and lowest price the bond could trade for without creating an arbitrage opportunity?

Solution

The no-arbitrage price for the bond equals the present value of the cash flows. In this case, we can use either of two interest rates to compute the present value, depending on whether we are borrowing or lending. For example, the amount we would need to put in the bank today to receive $1000 in one year is

($1000 in one year) ÷ (1.06 $ in one year/$ today) = $943.40 today

where we have used the 6% interest rate that we will earn on our deposit. The amount that we can borrow today if we plan to repay $1000 in one year is

($1000 in one year) ÷ (1.065 $ in one year/$ today) = $938.97 today

where we have used the higher 6.5% rate that we will have to pay if we borrow.

Suppose the bond price P exceeded $943.40. Then you could profit by selling the bond at its current price and investing $943.40 of the proceeds at the 6% interest rate. You would still receive $1000 at the end of the year, but you would get to keep the difference $(P − 943.40) today. This arbitrage opportunity will keep the price of the bond from going higher than $943.40.

> Alternatively, suppose the bond price P were less than $938.97. Then you could borrow $938.97 at 6.5% and use P of it to buy the bond. This would leave you with $($938.97 $- P)$ today, and no obligation in the future because you can use the $1000 bond payoff to repay the loan. This arbitrage opportunity will keep the price of the bond from falling below $938.97.
>
> If the bond price P is between $938.97 and $943.40, then both of the preceding strategies will lose money, and there is no arbitrage opportunity. Thus no arbitrage implies a narrow range of possible prices for the bond ($938.97 to $943.40), rather than an exact price.

To summarize, when there are transactions costs, arbitrage keeps prices of equivalent goods and securities close to each other. Prices can deviate, but not by more than the transactions costs of the arbitrage.

CONCEPT CHECK

1. In the presence of transactions costs, why might different investors disagree about the value of an investment opportunity?

2. By how much could this value differ?

SUMMARY

A.1. When cash flows are risky, we cannot use the risk-free interest rate to compute present values. Instead, we can determine the present value by constructing a portfolio that produces cash flows with identical risk, and then applying the Law of One Price.

A.2. The risk of a security must be evaluated in relation to the fluctuations of other investments in the economy. A security's risk premium will be higher the more its returns tend to vary with the overall economy and the market index. If the security's returns vary in the opposite direction of the market index, it offers insurance and will have a negative risk premium.

A.3. When there are transactions costs, the prices of equivalent securities can deviate from each other, but not by more than the transactions costs of the arbitrage.

KEY TERMS

expected return *p. 84*   risk premium *p. 84*
risk aversion *p. 84*   transactions costs *p. 88*

PROBLEMS

The Price of Risk

A.1. The table here shows the no-arbitrage prices of securities A and B that we calculated.

Security	Market Price Today	Cash Flow in One Year	
		Weak Economy	**Strong Economy**
Security A	231	0	600
Security B	346	600	0

a. What are the payoffs of a portfolio of one share of security A and one share of security B?

b. What is the market price of this portfolio? What expected return will you earn from holding this portfolio?

A.2. Suppose security C has a payoff of $600 when the economy is weak and $1800 when the economy is strong. The risk-free interest rate is 4%.

a. Security C has the same payoffs as what portfolio of the securities A and B in problem A.1?

b. What is the no-arbitrage price of security C?

c. What is the expected return of security C if both states are equally likely? What is its risk premium?

d. What is the difference between the return of security C when the economy is strong and when it is weak?

e. If security C had a risk premium of 10%, what arbitrage opportunity would be available?

*A.3. You work for Innovation Partners and are considering creating a new security. This security would pay out $1000 in one year if the last digit in the closing value of the Dow Jones Industrial index in one year is an even number and zero if it is odd. The one-year risk-free interest rate is 5%. Assume that all investors are averse to risk.

a. What can you say about the price of this security if it were traded today?

b. Say the security paid out $1000 if the last digit of the Dow is odd and zero otherwise. Would your answer to part (a) change?

c. Assume both securities (the one that paid out on even digits and the one that paid out on odd digits) trade in the market today. Would that affect your answers?

*A.4. Suppose a risky security pays an expected cash flow of $80 in one year. The risk-free rate is 4%, and the expected return on the market index is 10%.

a. If the returns of this security are high when the economy is strong and low when the economy is weak, but the returns vary by only half as much as the market index, what risk premium is appropriate for this security?

b. What is the security's market price?

Arbitrage with Transactions Costs

*A.5. Suppose Hewlett-Packard (HPQ) stock is currently trading on the NYSE with a bid price of $28 and an ask price of $28.10. At the same time, a NASDAQ dealer posts a bid price for HPQ of $27.85 and an ask price of $27.95.

a. Is there an arbitrage opportunity in this case? If so, how would you exploit it?

b. Suppose the NASDAQ dealer revises his or her quotes to a bid price of $27.95 and an ask price of $28.05. Is there an arbitrage opportunity now? If so, how would you exploit it?

c. What must be true of the highest bid price and the lowest ask price for no arbitrage opportunity to exist?

*A.6. Consider a portfolio of two securities: one share of Johnson and Johnson (JNJ) stock and a bond that pays $100 in one year. Suppose this portfolio is currently trading with a bid price of $141.65 and an ask price of $142.25, and the bond is trading with a bid price of $91.75 and an ask price of $91.95. In this case, what is the no-arbitrage price range for JNJ stock?

CHAPTER

4

NOTATION

r	interest rate
C	cash flow
FV_n	future value on date n
PV	present value; annuity spreadsheet notation for the initial amount
C_n	cash flow at date n
N	date of the last cash flow in a stream of cash flows
NPV	net present value
P	initial principal or deposit, or equivalent present value
FV	future value; annuity spreadsheet notation for the extra final payment
g	growth rate
$NPER$	annuity spreadsheet notation for the number of periods or dates of the last cash flow
$RATE$	annuity spreadsheet notation for interest rate
PMT	annuity spreadsheet notation for cash flow
IRR	internal rate of return
PV_n	present value on date n

The Time Value of Money

As discussed in Chapter 3, to evaluate a project a financial manager must compare its costs and benefits. In most cases, the cash flows in financial investments involve more than one future period. For example, early in 2003, the Boeing Company announced that it was developing the 7E7, now known as the 787 Dreamliner, a highly efficient, long-range airplane able to seat 200 to 250 passengers. Boeing's project involves revenues and expenses that will occur many years or even decades into the future. Components of the 787 Dreamliner planes will be produced in Boeing plants in the United States and around the world (including Boeing Winnipeg in Canada). How can financial managers evaluate a project such as the 787 Dreamliner airplane?

As we learned in Chapter 3, Boeing should make the investment in the 787 Dreamliner if the NPV is positive. Calculating the NPV requires tools to evaluate cash flows lasting several periods. We develop these tools in this chapter. The first tool is a visual method for representing a stream of cash flows: the *timeline*. After constructing a timeline, we establish three important rules for moving cash flows to different points in time. Using these rules, we show how to compute the present and future values of the costs and benefits of a general stream of cash flows, and how to compute the NPV. Although these techniques can be used to value any type of asset, certain types of assets have cash flows that follow a regular pattern. We develop shortcuts for *annuities*, *perpetuities*, and other special cases of assets with cash flows that follow regular patterns.

4.1 THE TIMELINE

We begin our look at valuing cash flows lasting several periods with some basic vocabulary and tools. We refer to a series of cash flows lasting several periods as a **stream of cash flows**. We can represent a stream of cash flows on a **timeline**, a linear representation of the timing of the expected cash flows. Timelines are an important first step in organizing and then solving a financial problem. We use them throughout this text.

To illustrate how to construct a timeline, assume that a friend owes you money. He has agreed to repay the loan by making two payments of $10,000 at the end of each of the next two years. We represent this information on a timeline as follows:

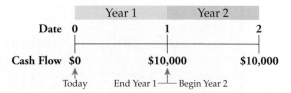

Date 0 represents the present. Date 1 is one year later and represents the end of the first year. The $10,000 cash flow below date 1 is the payment you will receive at the end of the first year. Date 2 is two years from now; it represents the end of the second year. The $10,000 cash flow below date 2 is the payment you will receive at the end of the second year.

You will find the timeline most useful in tracking cash flows if you interpret each point on the timeline as a specific date. The space between date 0 and date 1 then represents the time period between these dates, in this case, the first year of the loan. Date 0 is the beginning of the first year, and date 1 is the end of the first year. Similarly, date 1 is the beginning of the second year, and date 2 is the end of the second year. By denoting time in this way, date 1 signifies *both* the end of year 1 and the beginning of year 2, which makes sense since those dates are effectively the same point in time.[1]

In this example, both cash flows are inflows. In many cases, however, a financial decision will involve both inflows and outflows. To differentiate between the two types of cash flows, we assign a different sign to each: Inflows are positive cash flows, whereas outflows are negative cash flows.

To illustrate, suppose you're still feeling generous and have agreed to lend your brother $10,000 today. Your brother has agreed to repay this loan in two instalments of $6000 at the end of each of the next two years. The timeline is:

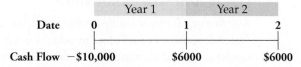

Notice that the first cash flow at date 0 (today) is represented as −$10,000 because it is an outflow. The subsequent cash flows of $6000 are positive because they are inflows.

So far, we have used timelines to show the cash flows that occur at the end of each year. Actually, timelines can represent cash flows that take place at the end of any time period. For example, if you pay rent each month, you could use a timeline like the one in our first example to represent two rental payments, but you would replace the "year" label with "month."

---

1. That is, there is no real time difference between a cash flow paid at 11:59 P.M. on December 31 and one paid at 12:01 A.M. on January 1, although there may be some other differences such as taxation that we overlook for now.

Many of the timelines included in this chapter are very simple. Consequently, you may feel that it is not worth the time or trouble to construct them. As you progress to more difficult problems, however, you will find that timelines identify events in a transaction or investment that are easy to overlook. If you fail to recognize these cash flows, you will make flawed financial decisions. Therefore, we recommend that you approach *every* problem by drawing the timeline as we do in this chapter.

EXAMPLE **4.1**	CONSTRUCTING A TIMELINE

Problem
Suppose you must pay tuition and residence fees of $10,000 per year for the next two years. Assume your tuition and residence fees must be paid in equal instalments at the start of each semester. What is the timeline of your tuition and residence fee payments?

Solution
Assuming today is the start of the first semester, your first payment occurs at date 0 (today). The remaining payments occur at semester intervals. Using one semester as the period length, we can construct a timeline as follows:

Date (Semesters)	0	1	2	3	4
Cash Flow	−$5000	−$5000	−$5000	−$5000	$0

CONCEPT CHECK	1. What are the key elements of a timeline?
	2. How can you distinguish cash inflows from cash outflows on a timeline?

4.2 THE THREE RULES OF TIME TRAVEL

Financial decisions often require comparing or combining cash flows that occur at different points in time. In this section, we introduce three important rules central to financial decision making that allow us to compare or combine values.

RULE 1: ONLY CASH FLOW VALUES AT THE SAME POINT IN TIME CAN BE COMPARED OR COMBINED

Our first rule is that it is only possible to compare or combine values at the same point in time. This rule restates a conclusion introduced in Chapter 3: Only cash flows in the same units can be compared or combined. *A dollar today* and *a dollar in one year* are not equivalent. Having money now is more valuable than having money in the future; if you have the money today you can earn interest on it.

To compare or combine cash flows that occur at different points in time, you first need to convert the cash flows into the same units or *move* them to the same point in time. The next two rules show how to move the cash flows on the timeline.

RULE 2: TO MOVE A CASH FLOW FORWARD IN TIME, YOU MUST COMPOUND IT

Suppose we have $1000 today, and we wish to determine the equivalent amount in one year's time. If the current market interest rate is 10%, we can use that rate as an exchange rate to move the cash flow forward in time. That is,

$$(\$1000 \text{ today}) \times (1.10 \ \$ \text{ in one year}/\$ \text{ today}) = \$1100 \text{ in one year}$$

In general, if the market interest rate for the year is r, then we multiply by the interest rate factor, $(1 + r)$, to move the cash flow from the beginning to the end of the year. This process of moving a value or cash flow forward in time is known as **compounding**. *Our second rule stipulates that to move a cash flow forward in time, you must compound it.*

We can apply this rule repeatedly. Suppose we want to know how much the $1000 is worth in two years' time. If the interest rate for year 2 is also 10%, then we convert as we just did:

($1100 in one year) $\times$ (1.10 $ in two years/$ in one year) = $1210 in two years

Let's represent this calculation on a timeline:

Given a 10% interest rate, all of the cash flows—$1000 at date 0, $1100 at date 1, and $1210 at date 2—are equivalent. They have the same value but are expressed in different units (different points in time). An arrow that points to the right indicates that the value is being moved forward in time, that is, compounded.

The value of a cash flow that is moved forward in time is known as its **future value**. In the preceding example, $1210 is the future value of $1000 two years from today. Note that the value grows as we move the cash flow further in the future. The equivalent value of two cash flows at two different points in time is sometimes referred to as the **time value of money**. By having money sooner, you can invest it and end up with more money later. Note also that the equivalent value grows by $100 the first year, but by $110 the second year. In the second year we earn interest on our original $1000 principal, plus we earn interest on the $100 accrued interest from the first year. If an investment only earns interest on principal and no interest on accrued interest, it is said to earn **simple interest**. Most investments earn interest on the original principal amount invested and earn interest on the accrued interest; the combined effect is known as **compound interest**.

How does the future value change if we move the cash flow three years? Continuing to use the same approach, we compound the cash flow a third time. Assuming the competitive market interest rate is fixed at 10%, we get

$$\$1000 \times (1.10) \times (1.10) \times (1.10) = \$1000 \times (1.10)^3 = \$1331$$

In general, to take a cash flow C forward n periods into the future, we must compound it by the n intervening interest rate factors. If the interest rate r is constant, this calculation yields

Future Value of a Cash Flow

$$FV_n = C \times \underbrace{(1 + r) \times (1 + r) \times \cdots \times (1 + r)}_{n \text{ times}} = C \times (1 + r)^n \tag{4.1}$$

Figure 4.1 shows the importance of earning "interest on interest" in the growth of the account balance over time. The type of growth that results from compounding is called geometric or exponential growth. As Example 4.2 shows, over a long horizon, the effect of compounding can be quite dramatic.

FIGURE 4.1   The Composition of Interest over Time

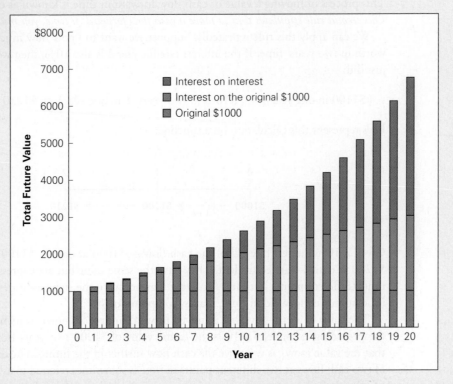

This bar graph shows how the account balance and the composition of the interest changes over time when an investor starts with an original deposit of $1000, represented by the red area, in an account earning 10% interest over a 20-year period. Note that the turquoise area representing interest on interest grows, and by year 15 has become larger than the interest on the original deposit, shown in green. Over the 20 years of the investment, the interest on interest the investor earned is $3727.50, while the interest earned on the original $1000 principal is $2000. The total compound interest over the 20 years is $5727.50 (the sum of the interest on interest and the interest on principal). Combining the original principal of $1000 with the total compound interest gives the future value after 20 years of $6727.50.

EXAMPLE 4.2   **THE POWER OF COMPOUNDING**

Problem

Suppose you invest $1000 in an account paying 10% interest per year. How much will you have in the account in 7 years? in 20 years? in 75 years?

Solution

We can apply Eq. 4.1 to calculate the future value in each case:

7 years:	$1000 \times (1.10)^7 = \$1948.72$
20 years:	$1000 \times (1.10)^{20} = \$6727.50$
75 years:	$1000 \times (1.10)^{75} = \$1,271,895.37$

Note that at 10% interest, our money will nearly double in 7 years. After 20 years, it will increase almost 7-fold. And if we invest for 75 years, we will be millionaires!

Solution

The timeline of the cash flows you want to provide is

This is a standard perpetuity of $30,000 per year. The funding you would need to give the university in perpetuity is the present value of this cash flow stream. From the formula,

$$PV = C/r = \$30{,}000/0.08 = \$375{,}000 \text{ today}$$

if you donate $375,000 today, and if the university invests it at 8% per year forever, then the graduates will have $30,000 every year for their party. Hopefully, they will invite you back to attend!

COMMON MISTAKE DISCOUNTING ONE TOO MANY TIMES

The perpetuity formula assumes that the first payment occurs at the end of the first period (at date 1). Sometimes perpetuities have cash flows that start later in the future. In this case, we can adapt the perpetuity formula to compute the present value, but we need to do so carefully to avoid a common mistake.

To illustrate, consider the graduation party described in Example 4.6. Rather than starting immediately, suppose that the first party will be held two years from today. How would this delay change the amount of the donation required?

Now the timeline looks like this:

We need to determine the present value of these cash flows, as it tells us the amount of money in the bank needed today to finance the future parties. We cannot apply the perpetuity formula directly, however, because these cash flows are not *exactly* a perpetuity as we defined it. Specifically, the cash flow in the first period is "missing." But consider the situation on date 1—at that point, the first party is one period away and then the cash flows are periodic. From the perspective of date 1, this *is* a perpetuity, and we can apply the formula. From the preceding calculation, we know we need $375,000 on date 1 to have

enough to start the parties on date 2. We rewrite the timeline as follows:

Our goal can now be restated more simply: How much do we need to invest today to have $375,000 in one year? This is a simple present value calculation:

$$PV = \$375{,}000/1.08 = \$347{,}222 \text{ today}$$

A common mistake is to discount the $375,000 twice because the first party is in two periods. *Remember—the present value formula for the perpetuity already discounts the cash flows to one period prior to the first cash flow.* Note that the length of the period is determined by the time period between cash flows. In the above example, the present value for the perpetuity brings the cash flows back one year before the first cash flow because the cash flows and interest rate are yearly. If a perpetuity had monthly cash flows (and we used the appropriate monthly discount rate), then the present value formula for the perpetuity would bring the cash flows back one month before the first cash flow. Keep in mind that this applies to perpetuities, annuities, and all of the other special cases discussed in this section. All of these formulas discount the cash flows to one period prior to the first cash flow.

ANNUITIES

An **annuity** is a stream of N equal cash flows paid at regular intervals. The difference between an annuity and a perpetuity is that an annuity ends after some fixed number of payments. Most car loans, mortgages, and some bonds are annuities. We represent the cash flows of an annuity on a timeline as follows.

Note that just as with the perpetuity, we adopt the convention that the first payment takes place at date 1, one period from today. The present value of an N-period annuity with payment C and interest rate r is

$$PV = \frac{C}{(1 + r)} + \frac{C}{(1 + r)^2} + \frac{C}{(1 + r)^3} + \cdots + \frac{C}{(1 + r)^N} = \sum_{n=1}^{N} \frac{C}{(1 + r)^n}$$

To find a simpler formula, we use the same approach we followed with the perpetuity: Find a way to create an annuity. To illustrate, suppose you invest $100 in a bank account paying 5% interest. At the end of one year, you will have $105 in the bank—your original $100 plus $5 in interest. Using the same strategy as for a perpetuity, suppose you withdraw the $5 interest and reinvest the $100 for a second year. Once again you will have $105 after one year, and you can repeat the process, withdrawing $5 and reinvesting $100, every year. For a perpetuity, you left the principal in forever. Alternatively, you might decide after 20 years to close the account and withdraw the principal. In that case, your cash flows will look like this:

With your initial $100 investment, you have created a 20-year annuity of $5 per year, plus you will receive an extra $100 at the end of 20 years. By the Law of One Price, because it took an initial investment of $100 to create the cash flows on the timeline, the present value of these cash flows is $100, or

$$\$100 = PV(\text{20-year annuity of \$5 per year}) + PV(\$100 \text{ in 20 years})$$

Rearranging terms gives

$$PV(\text{20-year annuity of \$5 per year}) = \$100 - PV(\$100 \text{ in 20 years})$$

$$= 100 - \frac{100}{(1.05)^{20}} = \$62.31$$

So the present value of $5 for 20 years is $62.31. Intuitively, the value of the annuity is the initial investment in the bank account minus the present value of the principal that will be left in the account after 20 years.

We can use the same idea to derive the general formula. First, we invest P in the bank, and withdraw only the interest $C = r \times P$ each period. After N periods, we close the account. Thus, for an initial investment of P, we will receive an N-period annuity of C per period, *plus* we will get back our original P at the end. P is the total present value of the two sets of cash flows,[4] or

$$P = PV(\text{annuity of } C \text{ for } N \text{ periods}) + PV(P \text{ in period } N)$$

By rearranging terms, we compute the present value of the annuity:

$$PV(\text{annuity of } C \text{ for } N \text{ periods}) = P - PV(P \text{ in period } N)$$

$$= P - \frac{P}{(1 + r)^N} = P\left(1 - \frac{1}{(1 + r)^N}\right) \quad (4.6)$$

Recall that the periodic payment C is the interest earned every period; that is, $C = r \times P$ or, equivalently, solving for P provides the upfront cost in terms of C,

$$P = C/r$$

Making this substitution for P, in Eq. 4.6, provides the formula for the present value of an annuity of C for N periods.

Present Value of an Annuity[5]

$$PV(\text{annuity of } C \text{ for } N \text{ periods with interest rate } r) = C \times \frac{1}{r}\left(1 - \frac{1}{(1 + r)^N}\right) \quad (4.7)$$

EXAMPLE 4.8

PRESENT VALUE OF A LOTTERY PRIZE ANNUITY

Problem

On a recent trip to the U.S., you purchased a ticket in a state lottery. Now you discover that you are the lucky winner of the $30 million prize. You can take your prize money as either (a) 30 payments of $1 million per year (starting today), or (b) $15 million paid today. If the interest rate is 8%, which option should you take?

Solution

Option (a) provides $30 million in prize money but paid over time. To evaluate it correctly, we must convert it to a present value. Here is the timeline:

Because the first payment starts today, the last payment will occur in 29 years (for a total of 30 payments).[6] The $1 million at date 0 is already stated in present value terms, but we need

---

4. Here we are using value additivity (see Chapter 3) to separate the present value of the cash flows into separate pieces.

5. An early derivation of this formula is attributed to the astronomer Edmond Halley ("Of Compound Interest," published after Halley's death by Henry Sherwin, *Sherwin's Mathematical Tables*, London: W. and J. Mount, T. Page and Son, 1761).

6. An annuity in which the first payment occurs immediately is sometimes called an *annuity due*. Throughout this text, we always use the term "annuity" to mean one that is paid in arrears.

to compute the present value of the remaining payments. Fortunately, this case looks like a 29-year annuity of $1 million per year, so we can use the annuity formula:

$$PV(\text{29-year annuity of \$1 million}) = \$1 \text{ million} \times \frac{1}{0.08}\left(1 - \frac{1}{1.08^{29}}\right)$$

$$= \$1 \text{ million} \times 11.16$$

$$= \$11.16 \text{ million today}$$

Thus, the total present value of the cash flows is $1 million + $11.16 million = $12.16 million. In timeline form:

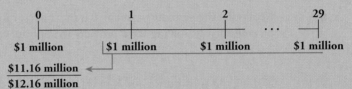

Option (b), $15 million upfront, is more valuable—even though the total amount of money paid is half that of option (a). The reason for the difference is the time value of money. If you have the $15 million today, you can use $1 million immediately and invest the remaining $14 million at an 8% interest rate. This strategy will give you $14 million × 8% = $1.12 million per year in perpetuity! Alternatively, you can spend $15 million − $11.16 million = $3.84 million today, and invest the remaining $11.16 million, which will still allow you to withdraw $1 million each year for the next 29 years before your account is depleted.

Now that we have derived a simple formula for the present value of an annuity, it is easy to find a simple formula for the future value. If we want to know the value N years in the future, we move the present value N periods forward on the timeline; that is, we compound the present value for N periods at interest rate r:

Future Value of an Annuity

$$FV(\text{annuity}) = PV \times (1 + r)^N$$

$$= \frac{C}{r}\left(1 - \frac{1}{(1 + r)^N}\right) \times (1 + r)^N$$

$$= C \times \frac{1}{r}\left((1 + r)^N - 1\right) \tag{4.8}$$

This formula is useful if we want to know how a savings account will grow over time.

EXAMPLE 4.9

REGISTERED RETIREMENT SAVINGS PLAN (RRSP) ANNUITY

Problem

Ellen just turned 35 years old, and she has decided it is time to plan seriously for her retirement. On each birthday, beginning in one year and ending when she turns 65, she will save $10,000 in an RRSP account. If the account earns 10% per year, how much will Ellen have saved at age 65?

Solution

As always, we begin with a timeline. In this case, it is helpful to keep track of both the dates and Ellen's age:

Ellen's RRSP looks like an annuity of $10,000 per year for 30 years. (*Hint:* It is easy to become confused when you just look at age, rather than at both dates and age. A common error is to think there are only $65 - 36 = 29$ payments. Writing down both dates and age avoids this problem.)

To determine the amount Ellen will have in the RRSP at age 65, we compute the future value of this annuity:

$$FV = \$10,000 \times \frac{1}{0.10} \left(1.10^{30} - 1 \right)$$

$$= \$10,000 \times 164.49$$

$$= \$1.645 \text{ million at age 65}$$

GROWING CASH FLOWS

So far, we have considered only cash flow streams that have the same cash flow every period. If instead the cash flows are expected to grow at a constant rate in each period, we can also derive a simple formula for the present value of the future stream.

GROWING PERPETUITY.   A **growing perpetuity** is a stream of cash flows that occur at regular intervals and grow at a constant rate forever. For example, a growing perpetuity with a first payment of $100 that grows at a rate of 3% has the following timeline:

In general, a growing perpetuity with a first payment C_1 and a growth rate g will have the following series of cash flows:

As with perpetuities with equal cash flows, we adopt the convention that the first payment occurs at date 1. Since the first payment, C_1, occurs at date 1 and the nth payment, C_n, occurs at date n, there are only $n - 1$ periods of growth between these payments. Substituting the cash flows from the preceding timeline into the general formula for the present value of a cash flow stream gives

$$PV = \frac{C_1}{(1 + r)} + \frac{C_1(1 + g)}{(1 + r)^2} + \frac{C_1(1 + g)^2}{(1 + r)^3} + \cdots = \sum_{n=1}^{\infty} \frac{C_1(1 + g)^{n-1}}{(1 + r)^n}$$

Suppose $g > r$. Then the cash flows grow even faster than they are discounted; each term in the sum gets larger, rather than smaller. In this case, the sum is infinite! What does an infinite present value mean? Remember that the present value is the "do-it-yourself" cost of creating the cash flows. An infinite present value means that no matter how much money you start with, it is *impossible* to reproduce those cash flows on your own. Growing perpetuities of this sort cannot exist in practice because no one would be willing to offer one at any finite price. A promise to pay an amount that forever grew faster than the interest rate is also unlikely to be kept (or believed by any savvy buyer).

The only viable growing perpetuities are those where the growth rate is less than the interest rate, so that each successive term in the sum is less than the previous term and the overall sum is finite. Consequently, we assume that $g < r$ for a growing perpetuity.

To derive the formula for the present value of a growing perpetuity, we follow the same logic used for a regular perpetuity: Compute the amount you would need to deposit today to create the perpetuity yourself. In the case of a regular perpetuity, we created a constant payment forever by withdrawing the interest earned each year and reinvesting the principal. To increase the amount we can withdraw each year, the principal that we reinvest each year must grow. We can accomplish this by withdrawing less than the full amount of interest earned each period, using the remaining interest to increase our principal.

Let's consider a specific case. Suppose you want to create a perpetuity growing at 2%, so you invest $100 in a bank account that pays 5% interest. At the end of one year, you will have $105 in the bank—your original $100 plus $5 in interest. If you withdraw only $3, you will have $102 to reinvest—2% more than the amount you had initially.

This amount will then grow to $102 \times 1.05 = \$107.10$ in the following year, and you can withdraw $\$3 \times 1.02 = \$3.06$, which will leave you with principal of $\$107.10 - \$3.06 = \$104.04$. Note that $\$102 \times 1.02 = \$104.04$. That is, both the amount you withdraw and the principal you reinvest grow by 2% each year. On a timeline, these cash flows look like this:

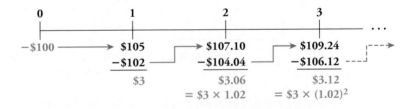

By following this strategy, you have created a growing perpetuity that starts at $3 and grows 2% per year. This growing perpetuity must have a present value equal to the cost of $100.

We can generalize this argument. In the case of an equal-payment perpetuity, we deposited an amount P in the bank and withdrew the interest each year. Because we always left the principal P in the bank, we could maintain this pattern forever. If we want to increase the amount we withdraw from the bank each year by g, then the principal in the bank will have to grow by the same factor g. That is, instead of reinvesting P in the second year, we should reinvest $P(1 + g) = P + gP$. In order to increase our principal by gP, we can only withdraw $C_1 = rP - gP = P(r - g)$.

From the timeline, we see that after one period we can withdraw $C_1 = P(r - g)$ and keep our account balance and cash flow growing at a rate of g forever. Solving this equation for P gives

$$P = \frac{C_1}{r - g}$$

The present value of the growing perpetuity with initial cash flow C_1 is P, the initial amount deposited in the bank account:

Present Value of a Growing Perpetuity

$$PV(\text{growing perpetuity}) = \frac{C_1}{r - g} \tag{4.9}$$

To understand the formula for a growing perpetuity intuitively, start with the formula for a perpetuity. In the earlier case, you had to put enough money in the bank to ensure that the interest earned matched the cash flows of the regular perpetuity. In the case of a growing perpetuity, you need to put more than that amount in the bank because you have to finance the growth in the cash flows. How much more? If the bank pays interest at a rate of 10%, then all that is left to take out if you want to make sure the principal grows 3% per year is the difference: 10% − 3% = 7%. So instead of the present value of the perpetuity being the first cash flow divided by the interest rate, it is now the first cash flow divided by the *difference* between the interest rate and the growth rate.

EXAMPLE 4.10

ENDOWING A GROWING PERPETUITY

Problem

In Example 4.7, you planned to donate money to your university to fund an annual $30,000 graduation party. Given an interest rate of 8% per year, the required donation was the present value of

$$PV = \$30,000/0.08 = \$375,000 \text{ today}$$

Before accepting the money, however, the president of the student association has asked that you increase the donation to account for the effect of inflation on the cost of the party in future years. Although $30,000 is adequate for next year's party, the president estimates that the party's cost will rise by 4% per year thereafter. To satisfy the president's request, how much do you need to donate now?

Solution

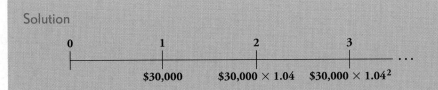

The cost of the party next year is $30,000, and the cost then increases 4% per year forever. From the timeline, we recognize the form of a growing perpetuity. To finance the growing cost, you need to provide the present value today of

$$PV = \$30{,}000/(0.08 - 0.04) = \$750{,}000 \text{ today}$$

You need to double the size of your gift. Now you can be sure they will invite you to the future parties!

GROWING ANNUITY. A **growing annuity** is a stream of N growing cash flows, paid at regular intervals. It is a growing perpetuity that eventually comes to an end. The following timeline shows a growing annuity with initial cash flow C_1, growing at rate g every period until period N:

As with growing perpetuities discussed earlier, we adopt the convention that the first payment occurs at date 1. Since the first payment, C_1, occurs at date 1 and the Nth payment, C_N, occurs at date N, there are only $N - 1$ periods of growth between these payments.

The present value of an N-period growing annuity with initial cash flow C_1, growth rate g, and interest rate r is given by

Present Value of a Growing Annuity

$$PV = C_1 \times \frac{1}{r - g}\left(1 - \left(\frac{1 + g}{1 + r}\right)^N\right) \qquad (4.10)$$

Because the annuity has only a finite number of terms, Eq. 4.10 also works when $g > r$.[7] The process of deriving this simple expression for the present value of a growing annuity is the same as for a regular annuity. Interested readers may consult the online appendix for details.

EXAMPLE 4.11   RETIREMENT SAVINGS WITH A GROWING ANNUITY

Problem

In Example 4.9, Ellen considered saving $10,000 per year for her retirement. Although $10,000 is the most she can save in the first year, she expects her salary to increase each year so that she will be able to increase her savings by 5% per year. With this plan, if she earns

---

7. Eq. 4.10 does not work for $g = r$. But in that case, growth and discounting cancel out, and the present value, equivalent to receiving all the cash flows, is $PV = N \times C_1/(1 + r)$.

10% per year in her RRSP, what is the present value of her planned savings and how much will Ellen have saved at age 65?

Solution

Her new savings plan is represented by the following timeline:

This example involves a 30-year growing annuity, with a growth rate of 5%, and an initial cash flow of $10,000. The present value of this growing annuity is given by

$$PV = \$10,000 \times \frac{1}{0.10 - 0.05}\left(1 - \left(\frac{1.05}{1.10}\right)^{30}\right)$$

$$= \$10,000 \times 15.0463$$

$$= \$150,463 \text{ today}$$

Ellen's proposed savings plan is equivalent to having $150,463 in the bank *today*. To determine the amount she will have at age 65, we need to move this amount forward 30 years:

$$FV = \$150,463 \times 1.10^{30}$$

$$= \$2.625 \text{ million in 30 years}$$

Ellen will have saved $2.625 million at age 65 using the new savings plan. This sum is almost $1 million more than she would have had in her RRSP without the additional annual increases in savings.

Similar to what we did with regular annuities, it is easy to find a simple formula for the future value of a growing annuity. If we want to know the value N years in the future, we move the present value N periods forward on the timeline; that is, we compound the present value for N periods at interest rate r:

Future Value of a Growing Annuity

$$PV = C \times \frac{1}{r - g}\left(1 - \left(\frac{1 + g}{1 + r}\right)^{N}\right)$$

$$FV = PV \times (1 + r)^{N} = C \times \frac{1}{r - g}\left(1 - \left(\frac{1 + g}{1 + r}\right)^{N}\right) \times (1 + r)^{N}$$

$$FV = C \times \frac{1}{r - g}\left((1 + r)^{N} - (1 + g)^{N}\right) \qquad (4.11)$$

Try using this formula in Example 4.11 to get the future value of Ellen's savings when she is 65.

The formula for the growing annuity is a general solution. In fact, we can deduce all of the other formulas in this section from the expression for a growing annuity. To see how to derive the other formulas from this one, first consider a growing perpetuity. It is a growing annuity with $N = \infty$. If $g < r$, then

$$\frac{1 + g}{1 + r} < 1$$

and so

$$\left(\frac{1+g}{1+r}\right)^n \to 0 \text{ as } N \to \infty$$

The formula for a growing annuity when $N = \infty$ therefore becomes

$$PV = \frac{C_1}{r-g}\left(1 - \left(\frac{1+g}{1+r}\right)^N\right) = \frac{C_1}{r-g}(1-0) = \frac{C_1}{r-g}$$

which is the formula for a growing perpetuity. The formulas for a regular annuity and perpetuity also follow from the formula if we let the growth rate $g = 0$.

CONCEPT CHECK

1. How do you calculate the present value of a
   a. Perpetuity?
   b. Annuity?
   c. Growing perpetuity?
   d. Growing annuity?

2. How are the formulas for the present value of a perpetuity, annuity, growing perpetuity, and growing annuity related?

3. How do you calculate the future value of a
   a. Annuity?
   b. Growing annuity?

4.6 SOLVING PROBLEMS WITH A SPREADSHEET PROGRAM

In the previous section, we derived formulas that were shortcuts for computing the present values of cash flows that have special patterns. Two other kinds of shortcuts simplify the calculation of present values—the use of spreadsheets and financial calculators. In this section we focus on spreadsheets.

Spreadsheet programs such as Excel have a set of functions that perform the calculations that finance professionals do most often. In Excel, the functions are called NPER, RATE, PV, PMT, and FV. The functions are all based on the timeline of an annuity:

together with an interest rate, denoted by *RATE*. Thus, there are a total of five variables: *NPER, RATE, PV, PMT,* and *FV.* Each function takes four of these variables as inputs and returns the value of the fifth one that ensures that the NPV of the cash flows is zero. That is, the functions all solve the problem

$$NPV = PV + PMT \times \frac{1}{RATE}\left(1 - \frac{1}{(1+RATE)^{NPER}}\right) + \frac{FV}{(1+RATE)^{NPER}} = 0 \quad (4.12)$$

In words, the present value of the annuity payments *PMT*, plus the present value of the final payment *FV*, plus the initial amount *PV*, has a net present value of zero. Let's tackle a few examples.

EXAMPLE 4.12	COMPUTING THE FUTURE VALUE IN EXCEL

Problem

Suppose you plan to invest $20,000 in an account paying 8% interest. How much will you have in the account in 15 years?

Solution

We represent this problem with the following timeline:

$$
\begin{array}{ccccc}
0 & 1 & 2 & & NPER = 15 \\
\hline
PV = -\$20{,}000 & PMT = \$0 & \$0 & \cdots & FV = ? \\
\end{array}
$$

To compute the solution, we enter the four variables we know ($NPER = 15$, $RATE = 8\%$, $PV = -20{,}000$, $PMT = 0$) and solve for the one we want to determine (FV) using the Excel function FV (RATE, NPER, PMT, PV). The spreadsheet here calculates a future value of $63,443.

	NPER	RATE	PV	PMT	FV	Excel Formula
Given	15	8.00%	−20,000	0		
Solve for FV					63,443	=FV(0.08,15,0,−20000)

Note that we entered *PV* as a negative number (the amount we are putting *into* the bank), and *FV* is shown as a positive number (the amount we can take *out* of the bank). It is important to use signs correctly to indicate the direction in which the money is flowing when using the spreadsheet functions.

To check the result, we can solve this problem directly:

$$FV = \$20{,}000 \times 1.08^{15} = \$63{,}443$$

This Excel spreadsheet in Example 4.12 is available at the text Web site and is set up to allow you to compute any one of the five variables. We refer to this spreadsheet as the **annuity spreadsheet**. You simply enter the four input variables on the top line and leave the variable you want to compute blank. The spreadsheet computes the fifth variable and displays the answer on the bottom line. The spreadsheet also displays the Excel function that is used to get the answers. Let's work through a more complicated example that illustrates the convenience of the annuity spreadsheet.

EXAMPLE 4.13

USING THE ANNUITY SPREADSHEET

Problem

Suppose that you invest $20,000 in an account paying 8% interest. You plan to withdraw $2000 at the end of each year for 15 years. How much money will be left in the account after 15 years?

Solution

Again, we start with the timeline:

$$PV = -\$20,000 \qquad PMT = \$2000 \qquad \$2000 \qquad \$2000 + FV = ?$$

The timeline indicates that the withdrawals are an annuity payment that we receive from the bank account. Note that PV is negative (money *into* the bank), while PMT is positive (money *out* of the bank). We solve for the final balance in the account, FV, using the annuity spreadsheet:

	NPER	RATE	PV	PMT	FV	Excel Formula
Given	15	8.00%	−20,000	2000		
Solve for FV					9139	=FV(0.08,15,2000,−20000)

We will have $9139 left in the bank after 15 years.

   We can also compute this solution directly. One approach is to think of the deposit and the withdrawals as being separate accounts. In the account with the $20,000 deposit, our savings will grow to $63,443 in 15 years, as we computed in Example 4.11. Using the formula for the future value of an annuity, if we borrow $2000 per year for 15 years at 8%, at the end our debt will have grown to

$$\$2000 \times \frac{1}{0.08} \left(1.08^{15} - 1\right) = \$54,304$$

After paying off our debt, we will have $63,443 − $54,304 = $9139 remaining after 15 years.

You can also use a handheld financial calculator to do the same calculations. The calculators work in much the same way as the annuity spreadsheet. You enter any four of the five variables, and the calculator calculates the fifth variable.

CONCEPT CHECK

1. What tools can you use to simplify the calculation of present values?

2. What is the process for using the annuity spreadsheet?

3. Why do you enter some cash flows as negative and some as positive when using the spreadsheet's or financial calculator's functions?

4.7 SOLVING FOR VARIABLES OTHER THAN PRESENT VALUE OR FUTURE VALUE

So far, we have calculated the present value or future value of a stream of cash flows. Sometimes, however, we know the present value or future value but do not know one of the variables we have previously been given as an input. For example, when you take out a loan, you may know the amount you would like to borrow, but may not know the loan payments that will be required to repay it. Or, if you make a deposit into a bank account, you may want to calculate how long it will take before your balance reaches a certain level. In such situations, we use the present and/or future values as inputs, and solve for the variable we are interested in. We examine several special cases in this section.

SOLVING FOR THE CASH FLOWS

Let's consider an example where we know the present value of an investment but do not know the cash flows. The best example is a loan—you know how much you want to borrow (the present value) and you know the interest rate, but you do not know how much you need to repay each year. Suppose you are opening a business that requires an initial investment of $100,000. Your bank manager has agreed to lend you this money. The terms of the loan state that you will make equal annual payments for the next 10 years and will pay an interest rate of 8% with the first payment due one year from today. What is your annual payment?

From the bank's perspective, the timeline looks like this:

The bank will give you $100,000 today in exchange for 10 equal payments over the next decade. You need to determine the size of the payment C that the bank will require. For the bank to be willing to lend you $100,000, the loan cash flows must have a present value of $100,000 when evaluated at the bank's interest rate of 8%. That is,

$$100,000 = PV(\text{10-year annuity of } C \text{ per year, evaluated at the loan rate})$$

Using the formula for the present value of an annuity,

$$100,000 = C \times \frac{1}{0.08}\left(1 - \frac{1}{1.08^{10}}\right) = C \times 6.71008$$

solving this equation for C gives

$$C = \frac{100,000}{6.71008} = \$14,902.95$$

You will be required to make 10 annual payments of $14,902.95 in exchange for $100,000 today.

We can also solve this problem with the annuity spreadsheet:

	NPER	RATE	PV	PMT	FV	Excel Formula
Given	10	8.00%	100,000		0	
Solve for PMT				−14,903		=PMT(0.08,10,100000,0)

In general, when solving for a loan payment, think of the amount borrowed (the loan principal) as the present value of the payments. If the payments of the loan are an annuity, we can solve for the payment of the loan by inverting the annuity formula. Writing this procedure formally, we begin with the timeline (from the bank's perspective) for a loan with principal P, requiring N periodic payments of C and interest rate r:

Setting the present value of the payments equal to the principal,

$$P = PV(\text{annuity of } C \text{ for } N \text{ periods}) = C \times \frac{1}{r}\left(1 - \frac{1}{(1 + r)^N}\right)$$

Solving this equation for C gives the general formula for the loan payment in terms of the outstanding principal (amount borrowed), P; interest rate, r; and number of payments, N:

Loan Payment

$$C = \frac{P}{\dfrac{1}{r}\left(1 - \dfrac{1}{(1 + r)^N}\right)} \tag{4.13}$$

EXAMPLE 4.14 — COMPUTING A LOAN PAYMENT

Problem

Your firm plans to buy a warehouse for $100,000. The bank offers you a 30-year loan with equal annual payments and an interest rate of 8% per year. The bank requires that your firm pay 20% of the purchase price as a down payment, so you can borrow only $80,000. What is the annual loan payment?

Solution

We start with the timeline (from the bank's perspective):

Using Eq. 4.12, we can solve for the loan payment, C, as follows:

$$C = \frac{P}{\dfrac{1}{r}\left(1 - \dfrac{1}{(1 + r)^N}\right)} = \frac{80,000}{\dfrac{1}{0.08}\left(1 - \dfrac{1}{(1.08)^{30}}\right)}$$

$$= \$7106.19$$

Using the annuity spreadsheet:

	NPER	RATE	PV	PMT	FV	Excel Formula
Given	30	8.00%	−80,000		0	
Solve for PMT				7106		=PMT(0.08,30,−80000,0)

Your firm will need to pay $7106.19 each year to repay the loan.

We can use this same idea to solve for the cash flows when we know the future value rather than the present value. As an example, suppose you have just had a child. You decide to be prudent and start saving this year for her university education. You would like to have $60,000 saved by the time your daughter is 18 years old. If you can earn 7% per year on your savings, how much do you need to save each year to meet your goal?

The timeline for this example is

That is, you plan to save some amount C per year, and then withdraw $60,000 from the bank in 18 years. Therefore, we need to find the annuity payment that has a future value of $60,000 in 18 years. Using the formula for the future value of an annuity from Eq. 4.8,

$$60{,}000 = FV\,(\text{annuity}) = C \times \frac{1}{0.07}\left(1.07^{18} - 1\right) = C \times 34$$

Therefore, $C = \frac{60{,}000}{34} = \$1764.76$. So you need to save $1764.76 per year. If you do, then at a 7% interest rate your savings will grow to $60,000 by the time your child is 18 years old.

Now let's solve this problem with the annuity spreadsheet:

	NPER	RATE	PV	PMT	FV	Excel Formula
Given	18	7.00%	0		60,000	
Solve for PMT				−1765		=PMT(0.07,18,0,60000)

Once again, we find that we need to save $1764.76 for 18 years to accumulate $60,000.

INTERNAL RATE OF RETURN

In some situations, you know the present value and cash flows of an investment opportunity but you do not know the interest rate that equates them. This interest rate is called the **internal rate of return** (IRR), defined as the interest rate that sets the net present value of the cash flows equal to zero.

For example, suppose that you have an investment opportunity that requires a $1000 investment today and will have a $2000 payoff in six years. On a timeline,

One way to analyze this investment is to ask the question: What interest rate, r, would you need so that the NPV of this investment is zero?

$$NPV = -1000 + \frac{2000}{(1 + r)^6} = 0$$

Rearranging gives

$$1000 \times (1 + r)^6 = 2000$$

That is, r is the interest rate you would need to earn on your $1000 to have a future value of $2000 in six years. We can solve for r as follows:

$$1 + r = \left(\frac{2000}{1000}\right)^{1/6} = 1.122462$$

or $r = 12.2462\%$. This rate is the IRR of this investment opportunity. Making this investment is equivalent to earning 12.2462% per year on your money for six years.

When there are just two cash flows, as in the preceding example, it is easy to compute the IRR. Consider the general case in which you invest an amount P today, and receive FV in N years. Then

$$P \times (1 + \text{IRR})^N = FV$$
$$1 + \text{IRR} = (FV/P)^{1/N}$$

That is, we take the total return of the investment over N years, FV/P, and convert it to an equivalent one-year rate by raising it to the power $1/N$.

Now let's consider a more sophisticated example. Suppose your firm needs to purchase a new forklift. The dealer gives you two options: (1) a price for the forklift if you pay cash and (2) annual payments if you take out a loan from the dealer. To evaluate the loan that the dealer is offering you, you will want to compare the rate on the loan with the rate that your bank is willing to offer you. Given the loan payment that the dealer quotes, how do you compute the interest rate charged by the dealer?

In this case, we need to compute the IRR of the dealer's loan. Suppose the cash price of the forklift is $40,000, and the dealer offers financing with no down payment and four annual payments of $15,000. This loan has the following timeline:

From the timeline it is clear that the loan is a four-year annuity with a payment of $15,000 per year and a present value of $40,000. Setting the NPV of the cash flows equal to zero requires that the present value of the payments equals the purchase price:

$$40{,}000 = 15{,}000 \times \frac{1}{r}\left(1 - \frac{1}{(1+r)^4}\right)$$

The value of r that solves this equation, the IRR, is the interest rate charged on the loan. Unfortunately, in this case there is no simple way to solve for the interest rate r.[8] The only way to solve this equation is to guess values of r until you find the right one.

Start by guessing $r = 10\%$. In this case, the value of the annuity is

$$15{,}000 \times \frac{1}{0.10}\left(1 - \frac{1}{(1.10)^4}\right) = 47{,}548$$

The present value of the payments is too large. To lower it, we need to use a higher interest rate. We guess 20% this time:

$$15{,}000 \times \frac{1}{0.20}\left(1 - \frac{1}{(1.20)^4}\right) = 38{,}831$$

Now the present value of the payments is too low, so we must pick a rate between 10% and 20%. We continue to guess until we find the right rate. Let us try 18.45%:

$$15{,}000 \times \frac{1}{0.1845}\left(1 - \frac{1}{(1.1845)^4}\right) = 40{,}000$$

The interest rate charged by the dealer is 18.45%.

An easier solution than guessing the IRR and manually calculating values is to use a spreadsheet or calculator to automate the guessing process. When the cash flows are an annuity, as in this example, we can use the annuity spreadsheet in Excel to compute the IRR. Recall that the annuity spreadsheet solves Eq. 4.12. It ensures that the NPV of investing in the annuity is zero. When the unknown variable is the interest rate, it will solve for the interest rate that sets the NPV equal to zero—that is, the IRR. For this case,

	NPER	RATE	PV	PMT	FV	Excel Formula
Given	4		40,000	−15,000	0	
Solve for Rate		18.45%				=RATE(4,−15000,40000,0)

The annuity spreadsheet correctly computes an IRR of 18.45%.

EXAMPLE 4.15

COMPUTING THE INTERNAL RATE OF RETURN WITH THE ANNUITY SPREADSHEET IN EXCEL

Problem

Jessica has just graduated with her MBA. Rather than take the investment banking job she was offered at CIBC World Markets, she has decided to go into business for herself. However, CIBC World Markets was so impressed with Jessica that it has decided to fund her business. In return for an initial investment of $1 million, Jessica has agreed to pay the

---

8. With five or more periods and general cash flows, there is *no* general formula to solve for r; trial and error and interpolation (by hand, computer, or financial calculator) is the *only* way to compute the IRR.

bank $125,000 at the end of each year for the next 30 years. What is the internal rate of return on CIBC World Markets' investment in Jessica's company, assuming she fulfills her commitment?

Solution

Here is the timeline (from CIBC World Markets' perspective):

The timeline shows that the future cash flows are a 30-year annuity. Setting the NPV equal to zero requires

$$1,000,000 = 125,000 \times \frac{1}{r}\left(1 - \frac{1}{(1 + r)^{30}}\right)$$

Using the annuity spreadsheet to solve for r,

	NPER	RATE	PV	PMT	FV	Excel Formula
Given	30		−1,000,000	125,000	0	
Solve for Rate		12.09%				=RATE(30,125000,−1000000,0)

the IRR on this investment is 12.09%.

In a few cases, it is possible to solve for the IRR directly. The next example demonstrates one such case.

EXAMPLE 4.16   **COMPUTING THE INTERNAL RATE OF RETURN DIRECTLY**

Problem

CIBC World Markets offers Jessica a second option for repayment of the loan. She can pay $100,000 the first year, increase the amount by 4% each year, and continue to make these payments forever, rather than for 30 years. What is the IRR in this case?

Solution

The timeline is

The timeline shows that the future cash flows are a growing perpetuity with a growth rate of 4%. Setting the NPV equal to zero requires

$$1,000,000 = \frac{100,000}{r - 0.04}$$

We can solve this equation for r

$$r = 0.04 + \frac{100,000}{1,000,000} = 0.14$$

The IRR on this investment is 14%.

SOLVING FOR THE NUMBER OF PERIODS

In addition to solving for cash flows or the interest rate, we can solve for the amount of time it will take a sum of money to grow to a known value. In this case, the interest rate, present value, and future value are all known. We need to compute how long it will take for the present value to grow to the future value.

Suppose we invest $10,000 in an account paying 10% interest, and we want to know how long it will take for the amount to grow to $20,000.

COMMON MISTAKE EXCEL'S NPV AND IRR FUNCTIONS

Although spreadsheets and financial calculators can simplify the process of solving problems, their designers have adopted specific conventions that you will need to be aware of to avoid making mistakes. In particular, before using any built-in financial function, always read the documentation for that function carefully to be aware of the correct format and any assumptions that are made by the software. Here we describe two functions in Excel, NPV and IRR, and some pitfalls to watch out for.

NPV
Excel's NPV function has the format, NPV(rate, value1, value2, . . .) where "rate" is the interest rate per period used to discount the cash flows, and "value1," "value2," etc., are the cash flows (or ranges of cash flows). The NPV function computes the present value of the cash flows *assuming the first cash flow occurs at date 1*. Therefore, if a project's first cash flow occurs at date 0, we cannot use the NPV function by itself to compute the NPV. We can use the NPV function to compute the present value of the cash flows from date 1 onward, and then must add the date 0 cash flow to that result to calculate the NPV.

Another pitfall with the NPV function is that cash flows that are left blank are treated differently from cash flows that are equal to zero. If the cash flow is left blank, *both the cash flow and the period are ignored*. For example,

the NPV function is used to evaluate the two equivalent cash flow streams shown below. In the second case, the NPV function ignores the blank cell at date 2 and assumes the cash flow is 10 at date 1 and 110 at date 2, which is clearly not what is intended and is incorrect.

NPV @ 10%	Date 1	Date 2	Date 3
$91.74	10	0	110
$100.00	10		110

Because of these idiosyncrasies, we avoid using Excel's NPV function, and find it to be more reliable to compute the present value of each cash flow separately in Excel, and then sum them to determine the NPV.

IRR
Excel's IRR function has the format, IRR(values, guess), where "values" is the range containing the cash flows, and "guess" is an optional starting guess where Excel begins its search for an IRR. There are two things to note about the IRR function. First, the values given to the IRR function should include all of the cash flows of the project, including the one at date 0. In this sense, the IRR and NPV functions in Excel are inconsistent. Second, like the NPV function, the IRR ignores the period associated with any blank cells.

We want to determine N.

In terms of our formulas, we need to find N so that the future value of our investment equals $20,000:

$$FV = \$10,000 \times 1.10^N = \$20,000 \qquad (4.14)$$

One approach is to use trial and error to find N, as with the IRR. For example, with $N = 7$ years, $FV = \$19,487$, so it will take longer than 7 years. With $N = 8$ years, $FV = \$21,436$, so it will take between 7 and 8 years. Alternatively, this problem can be solved on the annuity spreadsheet. In this case, we solve for N:

	NPER	RATE	PV	PMT	FV	Excel Formula
Given		10.00%	−10,000	0	20,000	
Solve for NPER	7.27					=NPER(0.10,0,−10000,20000)

It will take about 7.3 years for our savings to grow to $20,000.

Finally, this problem can be solved mathematically. Dividing both sides of Eq. 4.14 by $10,000, we have

$$1.10^N = 20{,}000/10{,}000 = 2$$

To solve for an exponent, we take the logarithm of both sides, and use the fact that $\ln(x^y) = y\ln(x)$:

$$N\ln(1.10) = \ln(2)$$

$$N = \ln(2)/\ln(1.10) = 0.6931/0.0953 \approx 7.3 \text{ years}$$

EXAMPLE 4.17

SOLVING FOR THE NUMBER OF PERIODS IN A SAVINGS PLAN

Problem
You are saving to make a down payment on a house. You have $10,050 saved already, and you can afford to save an additional $5000 per year at the end of each year. If you earn 7.25% per year on your savings, how long will it take you to save $60,000?

Solution
The timeline for this problem is

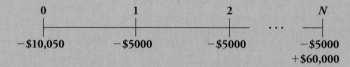

We need to find N so that the future value of our current savings plus the future value of our planned additional savings (which is an annuity) equals our desired amount:

$$10{,}050 \times 1.0725^N + 5000 \times \frac{1}{0.0725}(1.0725^N - 1) = 60{,}000$$

To solve mathematically, rearrange the equation to

$$1.0725^N = \frac{60{,}000 \times 0.0725 + 5000}{10{,}050 \times 0.0725 + 5000} = 1.632$$

We can then solve for N:

$$N = \frac{\ln(1.632)}{\ln(1.0725)} = 7 \text{ years}$$

It will take seven years to save the down payment. We can also solve this problem using the annuity spreadsheet:

	NPER	RATE	PV	PMT	FV	Excel Formula
Given		7.25%	−10,050	−5000	60,000	
Solve for N	7.00					=NPER(0.0725,−5000,−10050,60000)

RULE OF 72

Another way to think about the effect of compounding and discounting is to consider how long it will take your money to double given different interest rates. Suppose we want to know how many years it will take for $1 to grow to a future value of $2. We want the number of years, N, to solve

$$FV = \$1 \times (1 + r)^N = \$2$$

If you solve this formula for different interest rates, you will find the following approximation:

Years to double ≈ 72 ÷ (interest rate in percent)

This simple "Rule of 72" is fairly accurate (i.e., within one year of the exact doubling time) for interest rates higher than 2%. For example, if the interest rate is 9%, the doubling time should be about 72 ÷ 9 = 8 years. Indeed, $1.09^8 = 1.99$! So, given a 9% interest rate, your money will approximately double every 8 years.

In this chapter we developed the tools a financial manager needs to apply the NPV rule when cash flows occur at different points in time. As we have seen, the interest rate we use to discount or compound the cash flows is a critical input to any of our present or future value calculations. Throughout the chapter, we have taken the interest rate as given.

What determines the interest rate that we should use when discounting cash flows? The Law of One Price implies that we must rely on market information to assess the value of cash flows across time. In the next chapter, we learn the drivers of market interest rates as well as how they are quoted. Understanding interest rate quoting conventions will also allow us to extend the tools we developed in this chapter to situations where the cash flows are paid, and interest is compounded, more or less than once per year.

CONCEPT CHECK

1. How do you solve for the cash flow of an annuity?

2. What is the internal rate of return, and how do you calculate it?

3. How do you solve for the number of periods to pay off an annuity?

SUMMARY

1. Timelines are a critical first step in organizing the cash flows in a financial problem.

2. There are three rules of time travel:
   a. Only cash flow values that occur at the same point in time can be compared or combined.

b. To move a cash flow forward in time, you must compound it.

c. To move a cash flow backward in time, you must discount it.

3. The future value in n years of a cash flow C today is

$$C \times (1 + r)^n \qquad (4.1)$$

4. The present value today of a cash flow C received in n years is

$$\frac{C}{(1 + r)^n} \qquad (4.2)$$

5. The present value of a cash flow stream is

$$PV = \sum_{n=0}^{N} \frac{C_n}{(1 + r)^n} \qquad (4.3)$$

6. The future value on date n of a cash flow stream with a present value of PV is

$$FV_n = PV \times (1 + r)^n \qquad (4.4)$$

7. The NPV of an investment opportunity is PV(benefits − costs).

8. A perpetuity is a constant cash flow C paid every period, forever. The present value of a perpetuity is

$$\frac{c}{r} \qquad (4.5)$$

9. An annuity is a constant cash flow C paid every period for N periods. The present value of an annuity is

$$C \times \frac{1}{r}\left(1 - \frac{1}{(1 + r)^N}\right) \qquad (4.7)$$

The future value of an annuity at the end of the annuity is

$$C \times \frac{1}{r}\left((1 + r)^N - 1\right) \qquad (4.8)$$

10. In a growing perpetuity or annuity, the cash flows grow at a constant rate g each period. The present value of a growing perpetuity is

$$\frac{C_1}{r - g} \qquad (4.9)$$

The present value of a growing annuity is

$$C_1 \times \frac{1}{r - g}\left(1 - \left(\frac{1 + g}{1 + r}\right)^N\right) \qquad (4.10)$$

The future value of a growing annuity at the end of the growing annuity is

$$FV = C \times \frac{1}{r - g}\left((1 + r)^N - (1 + g)^N\right) \qquad (4.11)$$

11. The annuity and perpetuity formulas can be used to solve for the annuity payments when either the present value or the future value is known. The periodic payment on an N-period loan with principal P and interest rate r is

$$C = \frac{P}{\frac{1}{r}\left(1 - \frac{1}{(1+r)^N}\right)} \qquad (4.13)$$

12. The internal rate of return (IRR) of an investment opportunity is the interest rate that sets the NPV of the investment opportunity equal to zero.

13. The annuity formulas can be used to solve for the number of periods it takes to save a fixed amount of money.

KEY TERMS

annuity *p. 108*
annuity spreadsheet *p. 117*
compound interest *p. 95*
compounding *p. 95*
consol *p. 104*
discounting *p. 97*
future value *p. 95*
growing annuity *p. 114*

growing perpetuity *p. 111*
internal rate of return (IRR) *p. 121*
perpetuity *p. 104*
simple interest *p. 95*
stream of cash flows *p. 93*
timeline *p. 93*
time value of money *p. 95*

PROBLEMS

The problems marked in green can be found in MyFinanceLab at www.myfinancelab.com. Visit your MyFinanceLab for additional practice. An asterisk (*) indicates problems with a higher level of difficulty. Additional readings for this chapter may be found in the Textbook Resources section on MyFinanceLab.

The Timeline

1. You have just taken out a five-year loan from a bank to buy an engagement ring. The ring costs $5000. You plan to put down $1000 and borrow $4000. You will need to make annual payments of $1000 at the end of each year. Show the timeline of the loan from your perspective. How would the timeline differ if you created it from the bank's perspective?

2. You currently have a four-year-old mortgage outstanding on your house. You make monthly payments of $1500. You have just made a payment. The mortgage has 26 years to go (i.e., it had an original term of 30 years). Show the timeline from your perspective. How would the timeline differ if you created it from the bank's perspective?

The Three Rules of Time Travel

3. Calculate the future value of $2000 in
   a. 5 years at an interest rate of 5% per year.
   b. 10 years at an interest rate of 5% per year.

    c. 5 years at an interest rate of 10% per year.

    d. Why is the amount of interest earned in part a less than half the amount of interest earned in part b?

4. What is the present value of $10,000 received

    a. 12 years from today when the interest rate is 4% per year?

    b. 20 years from today when the interest rate is 8% per year?

    c. 6 years from today when the interest rate is 2% per year?

5. Your brother has offered to give you either $5000 today or $10,000 in 10 years. If the interest rate is 7% per year, which option is preferable?

6. Consider the following alternatives:

    i. $100 received in 1 year

    ii. $200 received in 5 years

    iii. $300 received in 10 years

    a. Rank the alternatives from most valuable to least valuable if the interest rate is 10% per year.

    b. What is your ranking if the interest rate is only 5% per year?

    c. What is your ranking if the interest rate is 20% per year?

7. Suppose you invest $1000 in an account paying 8% interest per year.

    a. What is the balance in the account after 3 years? How much of this balance corresponds to "interest on interest"?

    b. What is the balance in the account after 25 years? How much of this balance corresponds to interest on interest?

8. Your daughter is currently 8 years old. You anticipate that she will be going to university in 10 years. You would like to have $100,000 in a registered education savings plan (RESP) to fund her education at that time. If the account promises to pay a fixed interest rate of 3% per year, how much money do you need to put into the account today (ignoring government grants) to ensure that you will have $100,000 in 10 years?

9. You are thinking of retiring. Your retirement plan will pay you either $250,000 immediately on retirement or $350,000 five years after the date of your retirement. Which alternative should you choose if the interest rate is

    a. 0% per year?

    b. 8% per year?

    c. 20% per year?

10. Your grandfather put some money in an account for you on the day you were born. You are now 18 years old and are allowed to withdraw the money for the first time. The account currently has $3996 in it and pays an 8% interest rate.

    a. How much money would be in the account if you left the money there until your 25th birthday?

    b. What if you left the money until your 65th birthday?

    c. How much money did your grandfather originally put in the account?

Valuing a Stream of Cash Flows

11. Suppose you receive $100 at the end of each year for the next 3 years.

    a. If the interest rate is 8%, what is the present value of these cash flows?

    b. What is the future value in 3 years of the present value you computed in (a)?

c. Suppose you deposit the cash flows in a bank account that pays 8% interest per year. What is the balance in the account at the end of each of the next 3 years (after your deposit is made)? How does the final bank balance compare with your answer in (b)?

EXCEL 12. You have just received a windfall from an investment you made in a friend's business. He will be paying you $10,000 at the end of this year, $20,000 at the end of the following year, and $30,000 at the end of the year after that (three years from today). The interest rate is 3.5% per year.

a. What is the present value of your windfall?

b. What is the future value of your windfall in three years (on the date of the last payment)?

EXCEL 13. You have a loan outstanding. It requires making three annual payments at the end of the next three years of $1000 each. Your bank has offered to allow you to skip making the next two payments in lieu of making one large payment at the end of the loan's term in three years. If the interest rate on the loan is 5%, what final payment will the bank require you to make so that it is indifferent between the two forms of payment?

Calculating the Net Present Value

EXCEL 14. You have been offered a unique investment opportunity. If you invest $10,000 today, you will receive $500 one year from now, $1500 two years from now, and $10,000 ten years from now.

a. What is the NPV of the opportunity if the interest rate is 6% per year? Should you take the opportunity?

b. What is the NPV of the opportunity if the interest rate is 2% per year? Should you take it now?

EXCEL 15. Marian Nowak owns her own business and is considering an investment. If she undertakes the investment, it will pay $4000 at the end of each of the next three years. The opportunity requires an initial investment of $1000 plus an additional investment at the end of the second year of $5000. What is the NPV of this opportunity if the interest rate is 2% per year? Should Marian take it?

Perpetuities, Annuities, and Other Special Cases

16. Your buddy in mechanical engineering has invented a money machine. The main drawback of the machine is that it is slow. It takes one year to manufacture $100. However, once built, the machine will last forever and will require no maintenance. The machine can be built immediately, but it will cost $1000 to build. Your buddy wants to know if he should invest the money to construct it. If the interest rate is 9.5% per year, what should your buddy do?

17. How would your answer to Problem 16 change if the machine takes one year to build?

18. The British government has a consol bond outstanding paying £100 per year forever. Assume the current interest rate is 4% per year.

a. What is the value of the bond immediately after a payment is made?

b. What is the value of the bond immediately before a payment is made?

19. What is the present value of $1000 paid at the end of each of the next 100 years if the interest rate is 7% per year?

*20. You are head of the Schwartz Family Endowment for the Arts. You have decided to fund an arts school in Toronto in perpetuity. Every five years, you will give the school $1 million. The first payment will occur five years from today. If the interest rate is 8% per year, what is the present value of your gift?

*21.   When you purchased your house, you took out a 30-year annual-payment mortgage with an interest rate of 6% per year. The annual payment on the mortgage is $1200. You have just made a payment and have now decided to pay the mortgage off by repaying the outstanding balance. What is the payoff amount if

    a. You have lived in the house for 12 years (so there are 18 years left on the mortgage)?

    b. You have lived in the house for 20 years (so there are 10 years left on the mortgage)?

    c. You have lived in the house for 12 years (so there are 18 years left on the mortgage) and you decide to pay off the mortgage immediately *before* the twelfth payment is due?

22.   You are 25 years old and decide to start saving for your retirement. You plan to save $5000 at the end of each year (so the first deposit will be one year from now), and will make the last deposit when you retire at age 65. Suppose you earn 8% per year on your retirement savings.

    a. How much will you have saved for retirement?

    b. How much will you have saved if you wait until age 35 to start saving (again, with your first deposit at the end of the year)?

`EXCEL`   23.   Your grandmother has been putting $1000 into a savings account on every birthday since your first (that is, when you turned one). The account pays an interest rate of 3%. How much money will be in the account on your 18th birthday immediately after your grandmother makes the deposit on that birthday?

`EXCEL`   24.   A rich relative has bequeathed you a growing perpetuity. The first payment will occur in a year and will be $1000. Each year after that, you will receive a payment on the anniversary of the last payment that is 8% larger than the last payment. This pattern of payments will go on forever. If the interest rate is 12% per year,

    a. What is today's value of the bequest?

    b. What is the value of the bequest immediately after the first payment is made?

*25.   You are thinking of building a new machine that will save you $1000 in the first year. The machine will then begin to wear out so that the savings *decline* at a rate of 2% per year forever. What is the present value of the savings if the interest rate is 5% per year?

26.   You work for a pharmaceutical company that has developed a new drug. The patent on the drug will last 17 years. You expect that the drug's profits will be $2 million in its first year and that this amount will grow at a rate of 5% per year for the next 17 years. Once the patent expires, other pharmaceutical companies will be able to produce the same drug and competition will likely drive profits to zero. What is the present value of the new drug if the interest rate is 10% per year?

`EXCEL`   27.   Your oldest daughter is about to start kindergarten at a private school. Tuition is $10,000 per year, payable at the *beginning* of the school year. You expect to keep your daughter in private school through high school. You expect tuition to increase at a rate of 5% per year over the 13 years of her schooling. What is the present value of the tuition payments if the interest rate is 5% per year?

`EXCEL`   28.   A rich aunt has promised you $5000 one year from today. In addition, each year after that, she has promised you a payment (on the anniversary of the last payment) that is 5% larger than the last payment. She will continue to show this generosity for 20 years, giving a total of 20 payments. If the interest rate is 5%, what is her promise worth today?

`EXCEL`   *29.   You are running a hot Internet pharmacy company. Analysts predict that its earnings will grow at 30% per year for the next five years. After that, as competition increases, earnings growth is expected to slow to 2% per year and continue at that level forever. Your company has just announced earnings of $1,000,000. What is the present value of all future earnings if the interest rate is 8%? (Assume all cash flows occur at the end of the year.)

Solving Problems with a
Spreadsheet Program

    *30. Your brother has offered to give you $100, starting next year, and after that growing at 3% for the next 20 years. You would like to calculate the value of this offer by calculating how much money you would need to deposit in the local bank so that the account will generate the same cash flows as he is offering you. Your local bank will guarantee a 6% annual interest rate so long as you have money in the account.

a. How much money will you need to deposit into the account today?

b. Using an Excel spreadsheet, show explicitly that you can deposit this amount of money into the account, and every year withdraw what your brother has promised, leaving the account with nothing after the last withdrawal.

Solving for Variables
Other Than Present Value
or Future Value

31. You have decided to buy a perpetuity. The bond makes one payment at the end of every year forever and has an interest rate of 5%. If you initially put $1000 into the bond, what is the payment every year?

    32. You are thinking of purchasing a house. The house costs $350,000. You have $50,000 in cash that you can use as a down payment on the house, but you need to borrow the rest of the purchase price. The bank is offering a 30-year mortgage that requires annual payments and has an interest rate of 7% per year. What will your annual payment be if you sign up for this mortgage?

*33. You are thinking about buying a piece of art that costs $50,000. The art dealer is proposing the following deal: He will lend you the money, and you will repay the loan by making the same payment every two years for the next 20 years (i.e., a total of 10 payments). If the interest rate is 4%, how much will you have to pay every two years?

EXCEL   *34. You would like to buy the house and take the mortgage described in Problem 32. You can afford to pay only $23,500 per year. The bank agrees to allow you to pay this amount each year, yet still borrow $300,000. At the end of the mortgage (in 30 years), you must make a *balloon* payment; that is, you must repay the remaining balance on the mortgage. How much will this balloon payment be?

EXCEL   35. You are saving for retirement. To live comfortably, you decide you will need to save $2 million in your RRSP by the time you are 65. Today is your 30th birthday, and you decide that, starting today and continuing on every birthday up to and including your 65th birthday, you will put the same amount into a savings account. If the interest rate is 5%, how much must you set aside each year to make sure that you will have $2 million in the RRSP on your 65th birthday?

EXCEL   *36. You realize that the plan in Problem 35 has a flaw. Because your income will increase over your lifetime, it would be more realistic to save less now and more later. Instead of putting the same amount aside each year, you decide to let the amount that you set aside grow by 7% per year. Under this plan, how much will you put into the account today? (Recall that you are planning to make the first contribution to the RRSP account today.)

*37. You are 35 years old, and decide to save $5000 each year (with the first deposit one year from now), in an account paying 8% interest per year. You will make your last deposit 30 years from now when you retire at age 65. During retirement, you plan to withdraw funds from the account at the end of each year (so your first withdrawal is at age 66). What constant amount will you be able to withdraw each year if you want the funds to last until you are 90?

38.   You have an investment opportunity that requires an initial investment of $5000 today and will pay $6000 in one year. What is the IRR of this opportunity?

39.   Suppose you invest $2000 today and receive $10,000 in five years.
   a. What is the IRR of this opportunity?
   b. Suppose another investment opportunity also requires $2000 upfront, but pays an equal amount at the end of each year for the next five years. If this investment has the same IRR as the first one, what is the amount you will receive each year?

40.   You are shopping for a car and read the following advertisement in the newspaper: "Own a new Spitfire! No money down. Four annual payments of just $10,000." You have shopped around and know that you can buy a Spitfire for cash for $32,500. What is the interest rate the dealer is advertising (what is the IRR of the loan in the advertisement)? Assume that you must make the annual payments at the end of each year.

41.   A local bank is running the following advertisement in the newspaper: "For just $1000 we will pay you $100 forever!" The fine print in the ad says that for a $1000 deposit, the bank will pay $100 every year in perpetuity, starting one year after the deposit is made. What interest rate is the bank advertising (what is the IRR of this investment)?

*42.   The Laiterie de Coaticook in the Eastern Townships of Quebec produces several types of cheddar cheese. It sells the cheese in four varieties: aged 2 months, 9 months, 15 months, and 2 years. At the producer's store, it sells 2 pounds of each variety for the following prices: $7.95, $9.49, $10.95, and $11.95, respectively. Consider the cheese maker's decision whether to continue to age a particular 2-pound block of cheese. At 2 months, he can either sell the cheese immediately or let it age further. If he sells it now, he will receive $7.95 immediately. If he ages the cheese, he must give up the $7.95 today to receive a higher amount in the future. What is the IRR (expressed in percent per month) of the investment of giving up $79.50 today by choosing to store 20 pounds of cheese that is currently 2 months old and instead selling 10 pounds of this cheese when it has aged 9 months, 6 pounds when it has aged 15 months, and the remaining 4 pounds when it has aged 2 years?

*43.   Your grandmother bought an annuity from Manulife Financial for $200,000 when she retired. In exchange for the $200,000, Manulife will pay her $25,000 per year until she dies. The interest rate is 5%. How long must she live after the day she retired to come out ahead (that is, to get more in *value* than what she paid in)?

EXCEL   *44.   You are thinking of making an investment in a new plant. The plant will generate revenues of $1 million per year for as long as you maintain it. You expect that the maintenance cost will start at $50,000 per year and will increase 5% per year thereafter. Assume that all revenue and maintenance costs occur at the end of the year. You intend to run the plant as long as it continues to make a positive cash flow (as long as the cash generated by the plant exceeds the maintenance costs). The plant can be built and become operational immediately. If the plant costs $10 million to build, and the interest rate is 6% per year, should you invest in the plant?

EXCEL   *45.   You have just turned 30 years old, have just received your MBA, and have accepted your first job. Now you must decide how much money to put into your RRSP. Your RRSP works as follows: Every dollar in the plan earns 7% per year. You cannot make withdrawals until your 65th birthday. After that point, you can make withdrawals as you see fit. You decide that you will plan to live to 100 and work until you turn 65. You estimate that to live comfortably in retirement, you will need $100,000 per year starting at the end of the first year of retirement (i.e., when you turn 66) and ending on your 100th birthday. You will contribute the same amount to the plan at the end of every year that you work. How much do you need to contribute each year to fund your retirement?

EXCEL   *46.   Problem 45 is not very realistic because most people do not contribute a fixed amount to their RRSP each year. Instead, you would prefer to contribute a fixed percentage of your salary each year. Assume that your starting salary is $75,000 per year and it will grow 2% per year until you retire. Assuming everything else stays the same as in Problem 45, what percentage of your income do you need to contribute to the plan every year to fund the same retirement income?

DATA CASE

Assume today is July 31, 2009. Natasha Kingery is 30 years old and has a Bachelor of Science degree in computer science. She is currently employed at Open Text Corporation in Ottawa and earns $38,000 a year, which she anticipates will grow at 3% per year. Natasha hopes to retire at age 65 and has just begun to think about the future.

Natasha has $75,000 that she recently inherited from her aunt. She invested this money in 10-year Government of Canada bonds. She is considering whether she should further her education and would use her inheritance to pay for it.[9]

She has investigated a couple of programs and is asking for your help as a financial planning intern to determine the financial consequences associated with each option. Natasha has already been accepted to both of these programs, and could start either one soon.

One alternative that Natasha is considering is attaining a certification in network design. This certification would automatically promote her to a new position and give her a raise of $10,000. This salary differential will grow at a rate of 3% a year as long as she keeps working. The certification program requires the completion of 20 Web-based courses and a score of 80% or better on an exam at the end of the course work. She has learned that the average amount of time necessary to finish the program is one year. The total cost of the program is $5,000, due when she enrols in the program. Because she will do all the work for the certification on her own time, Natasha does not expect to lose any income during the certification.

Another option is going back to school for an MBA degree. With an MBA degree, Natasha expects to be promoted to a managerial position at Open Text. The managerial position pays $20,000 a year more than her current position. She expects that this salary differential will also grow at a rate of 3% per year for as long as she keeps working. The evening program, which will take three years to complete, costs $25,000 per year, due at the beginning of each of her three years in school. Because she will attend classes in the evening, Natasha doesn't expect to lose any income while she is earning her MBA if she chooses to undertake the MBA.

1. Determine the interest rate she is currently earning on her inheritance by going to the Bank of Canada Web site (www.bankofcanada.ca) and clicking on Interest Rates under the Rates and Statistics tab. Then click on "Canadian Bonds." Once there, click on "10-year lookup." Enter the appropriate date you want, July 31, 2009, and check off the desired bond, "10 year" (daily prices) to obtain the average yield or interest rate that she is earning. Use this interest rate as the average discount rate for the remainder of this problem.

2. Create a timeline in Excel for her current situation, as well as the certification program and MBA degree options, using the following assumptions:

    ■ Salaries for the year are paid only once, at the end of the year.

    ■ The salary increase becomes effective immediately upon graduating from the MBA program or being certified. That is, because the increases become effective immediately

---

9. If Natasha lacked the cash to pay for her tuition up front, she could borrow the money. More intriguingly, she could sell a fraction of her future earnings, an idea that has received attention from researchers and entrepreneurs; see Miguel Palacios, *Investing in Human Capital: A Capital Markets Approach to Student Funding,* Cambridge University Press, 2004.

but salaries are paid at the end of the year, the first salary increase will be paid exactly one year after graduation or certification.

3. Calculate the present value of the salary differential for completing the certification program. Subtract the cost of the program to get the NPV of undertaking the certification program.

4. Calculate the present value of the salary differential for completing the MBA degree. Calculate the present value of the cost of the MBA program. Based on your calculations, determine the NPV of undertaking the MBA.

5. Based on your answers to Questions 3 and 4, what advice would you give to Natasha? What if the two programs are mutually exclusive? That is, if Natasha undertakes one of the programs there is no further benefit to undertaking the other program. Would your advice change?

Interest Rates

NOTATION

EAR   effective annual rate

   r   interest rate or discount rate

PV   present value

FV   future value

  C   cash flow

APR   annual percentage rate

  k   number of compounding periods per year

  r_r real interest rate

  i   rate of inflation

NPV   net present value

  C_n cash flow that arrives in period *n*

  n   number of periods

  r_n interest rate or discount rate for an *n*-year term

  τ tax rate

In Chapter 4, we explored the mechanics of computing present values and future values given a market interest rate. But how do we determine that interest rate? In practice, interest is paid and interest rates are quoted in different ways. For example, in March 2010, ING Direct offered a 5-year guaranteed investment certificate (GIC) with an interest rate of 3% per year with annual compounding, while President's Choice Financial offered an interest rate of 3% per year, but with the interest compounded on a monthly basis. Interest rates can also change through time and differ depending on the investment horizon. On January 31, 1990, investors earned about 11% on one-year risk-free (Government of Canada) investments, but only earned about 9.3% on twenty-year risk-free investments. This is in sharp contrast to February 16, 2010, when investors only earned 0.63% on one-year risk-free investments, but earned 4.06% on twenty-year risk-free investments. Interest rates can also vary due to risk or tax consequences. For example, the Canadian government is able to borrow at a much lower interest rate than Molson Coors Brewing Company.

In this chapter, we consider the factors that affect interest rates and discuss how to determine the appropriate discount rate for a set of cash flows. We begin by looking at the way interest is paid and interest rates are quoted, and we show how to calculate the effective interest paid in one year given different quoting conventions. We then consider some of the main determinants of interest rates—namely, inflation and government policy. Because interest rates tend to change over time, investors will demand different interest rates for different investment horizons based on their expectations. Finally, we examine the role of risk in determining interest rates and show how to adjust interest rates to determine the effective amount received (or paid) after accounting for taxes.

5.1   INTEREST RATE QUOTES AND ADJUSTMENTS

To determine the appropriate discount rate from an interest rate, we need to understand the ways that interest rates are quoted. Also, because interest rates may be quoted for different time intervals, such as monthly, semiannual, or annual, it is often necessary to adjust the interest rate to a time period that matches that of our cash flows. We explore these mechanics of interest rates in this section.

THE EFFECTIVE ANNUAL RATE

Interest rates are often stated as an **effective annual rate (EAR)**, which indicates the total amount of interest that will be earned at the end of one year.[1] This method of quoting the interest rate is the one we have used thus far in this textbook, and in Chapter 4 we used the EAR as the discount rate r in our time value of money calculations. For example, with an EAR of 5%, a $100,000 investment grows to

$$\$100,000 \times (1 + r) = \$100,000 \times (1.05) = \$105,000$$

in one year. After two years it will grow to

$$\$100,000 \times (1 + r)^2 = \$100,000 \times (1.05)^2 = \$110,250$$

ADJUSTING THE EFFECTIVE ANNUAL RATE TO AN EFFECTIVE RATE OVER DIFFERENT TIME PERIODS

The preceding example shows that earning an effective annual rate of 5% for two years is equivalent to earning 10.25% in total interest over the entire period:

$$\$100,000 \times (1.05)^2 = \$100,000 \times 1.1025 = \$110,250$$

In general, by raising the interest rate factor $(1 + r)$ to the appropriate power, we can compute an equivalent effective interest rate for a longer time period.

We can use the same method to find the equivalent effective interest rate for periods shorter than one year. In this case, we raise the interest rate factor $(1 + r)$ to the appropriate fractional power. For example, earning 5% interest in one year is equivalent to receiving

$$(1 + r)^{0.5} = (1.05)^{0.5} = \$1.0247$$

for each $1 invested every six months. That is, a 5% effective annual rate is equivalent to an interest rate of approximately 2.47% earned every six months; this would be an effective six-month rate. We can verify this result by computing the interest we would earn in one year by investing for two six-month periods at this rate:

$$(1 + r)^2 = (1.0247)^2 = \$1.05$$

In general, we can convert an effective rate of r for one period to an equivalent effective rate for n periods using the following formula:

$$\text{Equivalent } n\text{-Period Effective Rate} = (1 + r)^n - 1 \qquad (5.1)$$

In this formula, n can be larger than 1 (to compute an effective rate over more than one period) or smaller than 1 (to compute an effective rate over a fraction of a period). When

---

1. The effective annual rate is often referred to as the *effective annual yield* (EAY) or the *annual percentage yield* (APY).

computing present or future values, it is convenient to adjust the discount rate to match the time period of the cash flows. This adjustment is *necessary* to apply the perpetuity or annuity formulas, as in the following example.

EXAMPLE 5.1

VALUING MONTHLY CASH FLOWS

Problem
Suppose your bank account pays interest monthly with an effective annual rate of 6%. What amount of interest will you earn each month? If you have no money in the bank today, how much will you need to save at the end of each month to accumulate $100,000 in 10 years?

Solution
From Eq. 5.1, a 6% EAR is equivalent to earning $(1.06)^{1/12} - 1 = 0.4868\%$ per month. To determine the amount to save each month to reach the goal of $100,000 in 10 years, we must determine the amount C of the monthly payment that will have a future value of $100,000 in 10 years, given an interest rate of 0.4868% per month. We can use the annuity formula from Chapter 4 to solve this problem if we write the timeline for our savings plan using *monthly* periods:

Month:	0	1	2	120
Cash flow:		C	C	C

That is, we can view the savings plan as a monthly annuity with $10 \times 12 = 120$ monthly payments. From the future value of an annuity formula, Eq. 4.8:

$$FV(\text{annuity}) = C \times \frac{1}{r}\left[(1 + r)^n - 1\right]$$

we can solve for the payment C using the equivalent monthly interest rate $r = 0.4868\%$, and $n = 120$ months:

$$C = \frac{FV(\text{annuity})}{\frac{1}{r}\left[(1 + r)^n - 1\right]} = \frac{\$100,000}{\frac{1}{0.004868}\left[(1.004868)^{120} - 1\right]} = \$615.47 \text{ per month}$$

we can also compute this result using the annuity spreadsheet:

	NPER	RATE	PV	PMT	FV	Excel Formula
Given	120	0.4868%	0		100,000	
Solve for PMT				−615.47		=PMT(0.004868,120,0,100000)

Thus, if we save $615.47 per month and we earn interest monthly at an effective annual rate of 6%, we will have $100,000 in 10 years.

ANNUAL PERCENTAGE RATES

Banks quote interest rates in terms of an **annual percentage rate (APR)**, which indicates the amount of **simple interest** earned in one year, that is, the amount of interest earned *without* the effect of compounding even though compounding may occur. Because it does not include the effect of compounding, the APR quote is typically less than the actual amount of interest that you will earn. To compute the actual amount that you will earn in one year, the APR must first be converted to an effective annual rate.

For example, suppose Scotiabank advertises savings accounts with an interest rate of "6% per year with monthly compounding." By convention, this rate quote implies you will earn an effective monthly rate of 6%/12 = 0.5% every month. So an APR with monthly compounding is actually a way of indirectly quoting an *effective monthly* interest rate, rather than an effective annual interest rate. Because the interest compounds each month, you will earn

$$\$1 \times (1.005)^{12} = \$1.061678$$

at the end of one year, for an effective annual rate of 6.1678%. The 6.1678% that you earn on your deposit is higher than the quoted 6% APR due to compounding: In later months, you earn interest on the interest paid in earlier months.

It is important to remember that because the APR does not reflect the true amount you will earn over one year, *the APR itself cannot be used as a discount rate and it is not an effective annual rate.* Instead, the APR with k compounding periods is a way of indirectly quoting the actual interest earned each compounding period.

$$\text{Implied Effective Interest Rate per Compounding Period} = \frac{\text{APR}}{k \text{ periods/year}} \qquad (5.2)$$

We call this rate an *implied effective* rate because it shows the actual interest earned over the period and, by convention, it is what is implied from an APR quote. In our example, this will be an effective rate per month. Once we have computed the implied effective rate per compounding period from Eq. 5.2, we can compute the equivalent effective rate

---

EXAMPLE 5.2

FUTURE VALUES OF SAVINGS ANNUITIES WITH DIFFERENT PAYMENT FREQUENCIES

Problem

You want to save for a special vacation that you will take in six years. Given a rate of 6% per year with monthly compounding for your savings account at Scotiabank, you wish to know what will be the future value of an annuity of deposits you will make to your account. This information will help you decide the best way to save. You are considering the following annuities over a six-year time frame:

1. Equal monthly deposits of $100 each.
2. Equal semiannual deposits of $600 each.
3. Equal annual deposits of $1200 each.
4. Equal biannual deposits (every two years) of $2400 each.

Solution

The four different annuities are represented on the following timelines:

Year:	0	1	2		6
3. Annual cash flows:		$1,200	$1,200	...	$1,200

Two-year period:	0	1	2		3
4. Biannual cash flows:		$2,400	$2,400	...	$2,400

For each of the annuities, you can calculate the future value using Eq. 4.8,

$$FV(\text{annuity}) = C \times \frac{1}{r}\left((1 + r)^N - 1\right)$$

It is necessary to ensure that the rate, r, in the equation is an effective rate per period where the period of the rate matches the period of time between the individual cash flows of the annuity. Using Eq. 5.2, you know the implied effective rate per month is $\frac{6\%}{12} = 0.5\%$. This can be used in the first case (as it has monthly cash flows). For the other cases, the effective rate per month of 0.5% needs to be converted into equivalent effective rates for periods corresponding to the cash flows of the respective annuities. Use Eq. 5.1 to do these conversions.

When using the annuity formula, Eq. 4.8, you also need to ensure that the number of cash flows is correctly specified based on the number of years and the cash flows per year. Over six years, there are $6 \times 12 = 72$ monthly cash flows, $6 \times 2 = 12$ semiannual cash flows, $6 \times 1 = 6$ annual cash flows, or $6 \times \frac{1}{2} = 3$ biannual cash flows. It is important to use both the correct interest rates and the correct number of cash flows, both of which depend on the period of time that elapses between cash flows.

Annuity	Effective rate needed for the FV(annuity) calculation	FV(annuity) =
1: $100 per month	Effective rate per month = 0.5%	$\$100 \times \dfrac{1}{0.005}\left(1.005^{72} - 1\right)$ $= \$8640.89$
2: $600 per semiannual period	Effective rate per semiannual period $= (1 + 0.005)^6 - 1$ $= 3.0378\%$	$\$600 \times \dfrac{1}{0.030378}\left(1.030378^{12} - 1\right)$ $= \$8533.53$
3: $1200 per year	Effective rate per year (EAR) $= (1 + 0.005)^{12} - 1$ $= 6.1678\%$	$\$1200 \times \dfrac{1}{0.061678}\left(1.061678^6 - 1\right)$ $= \$8405.83$
4: $2400 per two-year period	Effective rate per two-year period $= (1 + 0.005)^{24} - 1$ $= 12.7160\%$	$\$2400 \times \dfrac{1}{0.12716}\left(1.12716^3 - 1\right)$ $= \$8154.36$

So, what is your conclusion? If you have the money available each month, the first annuity is best. It gives the highest future value because the earlier each dollar is deposited, the more time it has to earn interest. You will have almost $500 more to spend on your vacation if you do monthly savings instead of biannual savings.

EFFECTIVE ANNUAL RATES FOR A 6 % APR WITH DIFFERENT COMPOUNDING PERIODS

TABLE 5.1

Compounding Interval	Effective Annual Rate
Annual	$(1 + 0.06/1)^1 - 1 = 6\%$
Semiannual	$(1 + 0.06/2)^2 - 1 = 6.09\%$
Monthly	$(1 + 0.06/12)^{12} - 1 = 6.1678\%$
Daily	$(1 + 0.06/365)^{365} - 1 = 6.1831\%$

for any other time interval using Eq. 5.1. The effective annual rate corresponding to an APR with k compounding periods per year is given by the following conversion formula:

Converting an APR to an EAR

$$1 + EAR = \left(1 + \frac{APR}{k}\right)^k \tag{5.3}$$

Table 5.1 shows the effective annual rates that correspond to an APR of 6% with different compounding intervals. The EAR increases with the frequency of compounding because of the ability to earn interest on interest sooner. Investments can compound even more frequently than daily. In principle, the compounding interval could be hourly or every second. In the limit we approach the idea of **continuous compounding**, in which we compound the interest every instant.[2] As a practical matter, compounding more frequently than daily has a negligible impact on the effective annual rate and is rarely observed.

Converting APRs to EARs is useful if you need to compare APRs that are quoted with different compounding periods. EARs are also useful to know as they tell you how much an investment held for one year will grow over the year.

When working with APRs, we must first convert the APR to an implied effective discount rate per compounding interval using Eq. 5.2. We can then use Eq. 5.1 to convert the effective rate per compounding period to an equivalent effective rate per *different* compounding period. If we need to convert our APR to an effective rate per year, i.e., an EAR, we can use Eq. 5.3 (which is a special case of applying both equations 5.2 and 5.1 simultaneously).

CONCEPT CHECK

1. What is the difference between an EAR and an APR quote?

2. Why can't the APR itself be used as a discount rate?

5.2 APPLICATION: DISCOUNT RATES AND LOANS

Now that we have explained how to compute the discount rate from an interest rate quote, let's apply the concept to solve two common financial problems: calculating a loan payment and calculating the remaining balance on a loan.

---

2. A 6% APR with continuous compounding results in an EAR of approximately 6.1837%, which is almost the same as daily compounding. See the appendix to Chapter 5 for further discussion of continuous compounding.

COMPUTING LOAN PAYMENTS. To calculate a loan payment, we first compute the discount rate from the quoted interest rate of the loan, and then equate the outstanding loan balance with the present value of the loan payments and solve for the loan payment.

Many loans, such as consumer loans and car loans, have monthly payments and are quoted in terms of an APR with monthly compounding. These types of loans are **amortizing loans**, which means that each month you pay interest on the loan plus some part of the loan balance. Each monthly payment is the same, and the loan is fully repaid with the final payment. Typical terms for a new car loan might be "6.75% APR for 60 months." Most provinces in Canada have harmonized their cost of credit disclosure requirements so that when the compounding interval for the APR is not stated explicitly, it is equal to the interval between the payments, or one month in this case.[3] Thus this quote means that the loan will be repaid with 60 equal monthly payments, computed using a 6.75% APR with monthly compounding. Consider the timeline for a $30,000 car loan with these terms:

The payment, C, is set so that the present value of the cash flows, evaluated using the loan interest rate, equals the original principal amount of $30,000. In this case, the 6.75% APR with monthly compounding corresponds to a one-month discount rate of 6.75%/12 = 0.5625%. Because the loan payments are an annuity, we can use Eq. 4.12 to find C:

$$C = \frac{P}{\frac{1}{r}\left(1 - \frac{1}{(1+r)^N}\right)} = \frac{30,000}{\frac{1}{0.005625}\left(1 - \frac{1}{(1+0.005625)^{60}}\right)} = \$590.50$$

Alternatively, we can solve for the payment C using the annuity spreadsheet:

	NPER	RATE	PV	PMT	FV	Excel Formula
Given	60	0.5625%	30,000		0	
Solve for PMT				−590.50		=PMT(0.005625,60,30000,0)

COMPUTING CANADIAN MORTGAGE PAYMENTS. When you buy a home, you usually need to borrow money. This is done using a **mortgage**, which is a loan where the borrower offers property as security for the lender. Canadian banks quote mortgage rates as APRs with semiannual compounding. The most common payment schedule calls for monthly payments; thus, before using the quoted APR, you must convert the quoted APR into an equivalent effective rate per month.

EXAMPLE 5.3

CONVERTING A CANADIAN MORTGAGE APR TO A DISCOUNT RATE

Suppose you need to borrow $400,000 and the Bank of Montreal offers you a five-year term at a mortgage with a rate of 7.252% to be amortized over 25 years of monthly payments. To

3. An important exception is Canadian mortgages. These are quoted with APRs using semiannual compounding even though payments are usually monthly.

determine your monthly payments, you need to convert the 7.252% APR with semiannual compounding into an equivalent effective rate per month. This requires two steps. First, you can use Eq. 5.2 to get the implied effective interest rate per semiannual period:

$$\frac{7.252\%}{2} = 3.626\% \text{ per semiannual period}$$

Then you can use Eq. 5.1 to convert the effective semiannual rate to the equivalent effective monthly rate:

$$(1.03656)^{1/6} - 1 = 0.005954 \text{ or } 0.5954\% \text{ per month}$$

You can calculate the monthly payments using the same method as shown above for loan payments. However, you might get confused by the terms of the mortgage. It is a five-year mortgage but amortized over 25 years of monthly payments. What does this mean? The five-year term of the mortgage means that the quoted rate is fixed for the five years. At the end of the five years, you must renegotiate the mortgage at prevailing rates or pay off the outstanding balance. The amortization over 25 years means that your payments are calculated as though the interest rate will stay at the quoted APR for the full 25 years and the same 300 monthly payments will be made over this entire time. So using Eq. 4.12, we can solve for the monthly mortgage payments, C:

$$C = \frac{P}{\frac{1}{r}\left(1 - \frac{1}{(1 + r)^N}\right)} = \frac{400{,}000}{\frac{1}{0.005954}\left(1 - \frac{1}{(1 + 0.005954)^{300}}\right)} = \$2864.17$$

Although the payments are calculated as though 300 monthly payments will be made, they are only paid over the term of the mortgage (5 years or 60 months). When the term of the mortgage is over, you can either repay the outstanding balance in full or you can refinance it (usually by renewing your mortgage).

COMPUTING THE OUTSTANDING LOAN BALANCE.   The outstanding balance on a loan, also called the outstanding principal, is equal to the present value of the remaining future loan payments, again evaluated using the loan interest rate. We calculate the outstanding loan balance by determining the present value of the remaining loan payments using the loan rate as the discount rate.

EXAMPLE 5.4   COMPUTING THE OUTSTANDING LOAN BALANCE

Problem
Returning to our hypothetical mortgage at the Bank of Montreal from Example 5.3, we are interested in what your outstanding balance will be at the end of the mortgage's initial term.

Solution
Since the mortgage was amortized over 25 years and the term is 5 years, you will have paid 60 monthly payments and have 240 payments remaining on the amortization at the end of the mortgage's term. The present value (a moment after the 60th payment) of the remaining

240 payments, evaluated using the mortgage rate as the discount rate, gives us the outstanding balance.

$$\text{Balance after 5 years} = \$2864.17 \times \frac{1}{0.005954}\left(1 - \frac{1}{1.005954^{240}}\right) = \$365{,}321.11$$

You might also be interested in knowing how much of your payments went to paying principal and how much went to paying interest. Since your initial principal was $400,000 and your outstanding balance at the end of the mortgage's term is $365,321.11, you paid a total of $34,678.89 toward principal. Since you paid 60 payments of $2864.17 summing to $171,850.20, the amount of your payments that went to interest charges is $171,850.20 − $34,678.89 = $137,171.31.

CONCEPT CHECK

1. How can you compute the outstanding balance on a loan?

2. What is an amortizing loan?

3. What is special about APR quotes for Canadian mortgages?

5.3 THE DETERMINANTS OF INTEREST RATES

How are interest rates determined? Fundamentally, interest rates are determined in the market based on individuals' willingness to borrow and lend. In this section, we look at some of the factors that may influence interest rates, such as inflation, government policy, and expectations of future growth.

INFLATION AND REAL VERSUS NOMINAL RATES

The interest rates that are quoted by banks and other financial institutions, and that we have used for discounting cash flows, are **nominal interest rates**, which indicate the rate at which your money will grow if invested for a certain period. Of course, if prices in the economy are also growing due to inflation, the nominal interest rate does not represent the increase in purchasing power that will result from investing. The rate of growth of your purchasing power, after adjusting for inflation, is determined by the **real interest rate,** which we denote by r_r. If r is the nominal interest rate and i is the rate of inflation, we can calculate the rate of growth of purchasing power as follows:

$$\text{Growth in Purchasing Power} = 1 + r_r = \frac{1 + r}{1 + i} = \frac{\text{Growth of Money}}{\text{Growth of Prices}} \quad (5.4)$$

We can rearrange Eq. 5.4 to find the following formula for the real interest rate, together with a convenient approximation for the real interest rate when inflation rates are low:

The Real Interest Rate

$$r_r = \frac{r - i}{1 + i} \approx r - i \quad (5.5)$$

That is, the real interest rate is approximately equal to the nominal interest rate less the rate of inflation.[4]

---

4. The real interest rate should not be used as a discount rate for future cash flows. It can be used as a discount rate only if the cash flows are not the expected cash flows that will be paid, but are the equivalent cash flows before adjusting them for growth due to inflation (in that case, we say the cash flows are in *real terms*). This approach is error prone, however, so throughout this book we will always forecast cash flows including any growth due to inflation, and discount using nominal interest rates.

| EXAMPLE **5.5** | CALCULATING THE REAL INTEREST RATE |

Problem

In the year 2000, short-term Canadian government bond rates were about 5.8% and the rate of inflation was about 3%. In 2003, interest rates were about 2.7% and inflation was about 3.1%. What was the real interest rate in 2000 and 2003?

Solution

Using Eq. 5.5, the real interest rate in 2000 was (0.058% − 0.03%)/(1.03) = 0.0272 or 2.72% (which is approximately equal to the difference between the nominal rate and inflation: 5.8% − 3% = 2.8%). In 2003, the real interest rate was (0.027% − 0.031%)/ (1.031) = −0.0039 or −0.39%. Note that the real interest rate was negative in 2003, indicating that interest rates were insufficient to keep up with inflation: Investors in Canadian government bonds were able to buy less at the end of the year than they could have purchased at the start of the year.

Figure 5.1 shows the history of nominal interest rates and inflation rates in Canada since 1962. Note that the nominal interest rate tends to move with inflation. Intuitively, individuals' willingness to save will depend on the growth in purchasing power they can expect (given by the real interest rate). Thus, when the inflation rate is high, a higher nominal interest rate is needed to induce individuals to save.

INVESTMENT AND INTEREST RATE POLICY

Interest rates affect not only individuals' propensity to save, but also firms' incentive to raise capital and invest. Consider a risk-free investment opportunity that requires an upfront investment of $10 million and generates a cash flow of $3 million per year for

| FIGURE 5.1 |

Canadian Interest Rates and Inflation Rates, 1962–2009

Interest rates are average three-month Treasury Bill rates and inflation rates are based on year-to-year changes in the Consumer Price Index (CPI) compiled by Statistics Canada.
Source: Statistics Canada.

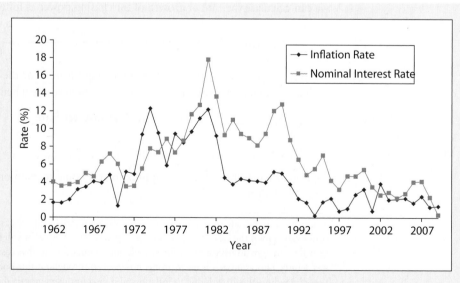

four years. If the risk-free interest rate is 5%, this investment has an NPV of

$$NPV = -10 + \frac{3}{1.05} + \frac{3}{1.05^2} + \frac{3}{1.05^3} + \frac{3}{1.05^4} = \$0.638 \text{ million}$$

If the interest rate is 9%, the NPV falls to

$$NPV = -10 + \frac{3}{1.09} + \frac{3}{1.09^2} + \frac{3}{1.09^3} + \frac{3}{1.09^4} = -\$0.281 \text{ million}$$

and the investment is no longer profitable. The reason, of course, is that we are discounting the positive cash flows at a higher rate, which reduces their present value. The cost of $10 million occurs today, however, so its present value is independent of the discount rate.

More generally, when the costs of an investment precede the benefits, an increase in the interest rate will decrease the investment's NPV. All else being equal, higher interest rates will therefore tend to shrink the set of positive-NPV investments available to firms. The Bank of Canada and central banks in other countries use this relationship between interest rates and investment incentives when trying to guide the economy. They can lower interest rates to stimulate investment if the economy is slowing (such as in 2008 and 2009), and they can raise interest rates to reduce investment if the economy is "overheating" and inflation is on the rise.

THE YIELD CURVE AND DISCOUNT RATES

You may have noticed that the interest rates that banks offer on investments or charge on loans depend on the horizon, or *term*, of the investment or loan. The relationship between the investment term and the interest rate is called the **term structure** of interest rates. We can plot this relationship on a graph called the **yield curve**. Figure 5.2 shows the term structure and corresponding yield curve of risk-free Canadian interest rates that were available to investors in January of 2004, 2005, 2008, and 2009. In each case, note that the interest rate depends on the horizon, and that the difference between short-term and long-term interest rates was especially pronounced in 2004 and 2009.

We can use the term structure to compute the present and future values of a risk-free cash flow over different investment horizons. For example, $100 invested for one year at the one-year interest rate in January 2004 would grow to a future value of

$$\$100 \times 1.025875 = \$102.59$$

at the end of one year, and $100 invested for ten years at the ten-year interest rate in January 2004 would grow to[5]

$$\$100 \times (1.048969)^{10} = \$161.30$$

The same logic can be applied when computing the present value of cash flows with different maturities. A risk-free cash flow received in two years should be discounted at the two-year interest rate, and a cash flow received in ten years should be discounted at the ten-year interest rate. In general, a risk-free cash flow of C_n received in n years has present value

$$PV = \frac{C_n}{(1 + r_n)^n} \tag{5.6}$$

---

5. We could also invest for ten years by investing at the one-year interest rate for ten years in a row. However, because we do not know what future interest rates will be, our ultimate payoff would not be risk free.

INTERVIEW WITH FREDERIC S. MISHKIN

Frederic Mishkin, Alfred Lerner Professor of Banking and Financial Institutions at Columbia University Graduate School of Business, served as a governor of the Federal Reserve Board from 2006 to 2008.

QUESTION: **What are the main policy instruments used by central banks to control the economy?**

ANSWER: Short-term interest rates are one of the main policy instruments used by central banks to control the economy. Specifically, central banks like the U.S. Federal Reserve [the Fed] will act to lower short-term interest rates in order to stimulate investment if the economy is in a recession. For example, while the economy was slowing down in 2007 and 2008, the Fed cut its short-term interest rate target aggressively, from 5.25% down to 0% by year's end.

The Fed can affect interest rates by changing the amount of liquidity in the financial system. By purchasing U.S. Treasury and federal agency securities or making loans to the financial system, the Fed increases banks' available reserves. This expansion of banks' liquidity increases the availability of credit, thereby lowering interest rates. Similarly, if the Fed sells securities to financial firms, the cash they use to purchase the securities is no longer available to be lent, and this shortage of liquidity raises interest rates.

QUESTION: **We often hear that central banks are concerned about inflation—why? How does the Fed act to fight inflation?**

ANSWER: A primary objective of a central bank is price stability, maintaining a low and stable inflation rate. Getting to the "right" number—an inflation rate that is neither too high nor too low—is one of the key challenges of monetary policy today. High inflation is almost always accompanied by high variability of inflation, making it difficult for consumers, businesses, and government to plan for the future and thus reducing economic efficiency.

The Federal Reserve tries to curb inflation by raising interest rates. Higher interest rates constrain demand in the economy, bringing it into balance with supply and preventing inflation from heating up. Consumers reduce spending when faced with higher interest rates on mortgages, credit cards, and car loans. Likewise, firms cut back on projects when the cost to finance them goes up.

QUESTION: **During the 2007–2009 financial crisis, the Fed and other central banks around the world became concerned about the risk of deflation. Why is deflation a concern?**

ANSWER: The dangers of *deflation*—or a negative inflation rate—are every bit as serious as the dangers of inflation. Deflation also creates uncertainty about future price levels and makes debt more expensive to repay in terms of goods and services. When borrowers struggle to repay debt or default on their debt obligations, the economy suffers.

Deflation also limits the effectiveness of monetary policy. The Federal Reserve can only control nominal interest rates. But investors' decisions to save or invest are determined by real interest rates, which determine the amount they will actually earn after accounting for inflation. If the inflation rate falls significantly below the nominal interest, then the real interest rate can remain high and offset the Fed's attempt to stimulate the economy.

QUESTION: **Recently, the Fed has been buying long-term Treasury Bonds. Why would the Fed do this?**

ANSWER: When traditional monetary policy tools fall short, the Federal Reserve pursues other options. So in 2008–2009, the Fed provided liquidity directly to certain credit markets, lowering interest rates on loans and on securities that have credit risk.

The Fed's purchase on long-term Treasury Bonds is another example. In 2009, when short-term rates were close to 0 percent, the Fed bought long-term Treasury Bonds. Because of the inverse relationship between bond prices and interest rates, this action lowered long-term interest rates relative to short-term rates.

FIGURE 5.2   Term Structure of Risk-Free Canadian Interest Rates, January 2004, 2005, 2008, and 2009

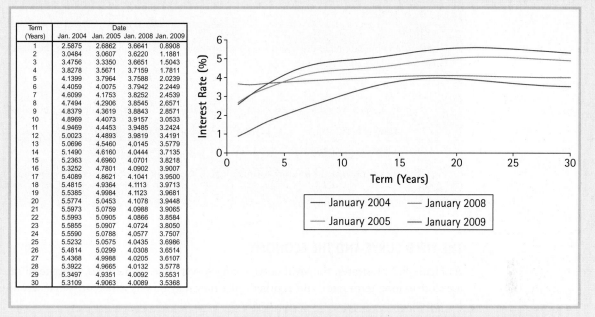

Term (Years)	Jan. 2004	Jan. 2005	Jan. 2008	Jan. 2009
1	2.5875	2.6862	3.6641	0.8908
2	3.0484	3.0607	3.6220	1.1881
3	3.4756	3.3350	3.6651	1.5043
4	3.8278	3.5671	3.7159	1.7811
5	4.1399	3.7964	3.7588	2.0239
6	4.4059	4.0075	3.7942	2.2449
7	4.6099	4.1753	3.8252	2.4539
8	4.7494	4.2906	3.8545	2.6571
9	4.8379	4.3619	3.8843	2.8571
10	4.8969	4.4073	3.9157	3.0533
11	4.9469	4.4453	3.9485	3.2424
12	5.0023	4.4893	3.9819	3.4191
13	5.0696	4.5460	4.0145	3.5779
14	5.1490	4.6160	4.0444	3.7135
15	5.2363	4.6960	4.0701	3.8218
16	5.3252	4.7801	4.0902	3.9007
17	5.4089	4.8621	4.1041	3.9500
18	5.4815	4.9364	4.1113	3.9713
19	5.5385	4.9984	4.1123	3.9681
20	5.5774	5.0453	4.1078	3.9448
21	5.5973	5.0759	4.0988	3.9065
22	5.5993	5.0905	4.0866	3.8584
23	5.5855	5.0907	4.0724	3.8050
24	5.5590	5.0788	4.0577	3.7507
25	5.5232	5.0575	4.0435	3.6986
26	5.4814	5.0299	4.0308	3.6514
27	5.4368	4.9988	4.0205	3.6107
28	5.3922	4.9665	4.0132	3.5778
29	5.3497	4.9351	4.0092	3.5531
30	5.3109	4.9063	4.0089	3.5368

Each curve in the figure shows the interest rates available (at a point in time) from investing in risk-free Government of Canada securities with different terms to maturity. In each case, the interest rates differ depending on the investment horizon.

Source: Bank of Canada zero-coupon yield curve data.

where r_n is the risk-free interest rate for an n-year term. In other words, when computing a present value we must match the term of the cash flow and term of the discount rate.

Combining Eq. 5.6 for cash flows in different years leads to the general formula for the present value of a cash flow stream:

Present Value of a Cash Flow Stream Using a Term Structure of Discount Rates

$$PV = \frac{C_1}{1 + r_1} + \frac{C_2}{(1 + r_2)^2} + \cdots + \frac{C_N}{(1 + r_N)^N} = \sum_{n=1}^{N} \frac{C_n}{(1 + r_n)^n} \qquad (5.7)$$

Note the difference between Eq. 5.7 and Eq. 4.3. Here, we use a different discount rate for each cash flow, based on the rate from the yield curve with the same term. When the yield curve is relatively flat, as it was in January 2008, this distinction is relatively minor and is often ignored by discounting using a single "average" interest rate r. But when short-term and long-term interest rates vary widely, as they did in January 2004 and January 2009, Eq. 5.7 should be used.

Warning: All of our shortcuts for computing present values (annuity and perpetuity formulas, the annuity spreadsheet) are based on discounting all of the cash flows *at the same rate*. They *cannot* be used in situations in which cash flows need to be discounted at different rates.

| EXAMPLE **5.6** | USING THE TERM STRUCTURE TO COMPUTE PRESENT VALUES |

Problem

Compute the present value of a risk-free five-year annuity of $1000 per year, given the yield curve for January 2005 in Figure 5.2.

Solution

To compute the present value, we discount each cash flow by the corresponding interest rate:

$$PV = \frac{1000}{1.026862} + \frac{1000}{1.030607^2} + \frac{1000}{1.033350^3} + \frac{1000}{1.035671^4} + \frac{1000}{1.037964^5} = \$4520.80$$

Note that we cannot use the annuity formula here because the discount rates differ for each cash flow.

THE YIELD CURVE AND THE ECONOMY

As Figure 5.2 illustrates, the yield curve changes over time. Sometimes, short-term rates are close to long-term rates, and at other times they may be very different. What accounts for the changing shape of the yield curve?

The Bank of Canada determines very short-term interest rates through its influence on the **overnight rate**, which is the rate at which banks can borrow cash reserves on an overnight basis. All other interest rates on the yield curve are set in the market and are adjusted until the supply of lending matches the demand for borrowing at each loan term. As we shall see in a moment, expectations of future interest rate changes have a major effect on investors' willingness to lend or borrow for longer terms and, therefore, on the shape of the yield curve.

Suppose short-term interest rates are equal to long-term interest rates. If interest rates are expected to rise in the future, investors would not want to make long-term investments.

COMMON MISTAKE   USING THE ANNUITY FORMULA WHEN DISCOUNT RATES VARY

When computing the present value of an annuity, a common mistake is to use the annuity formula with a single interest rate even though interest rates vary with the investment horizon. For example, we *cannot* compute the present value of the five-year annuity in Example 5.6 using the five-year interest rate from January 2005:

$$PV \neq \$1000 \times \frac{1}{0.037964}\left(1 - \frac{1}{1.037964^5}\right)$$

$$= \$4477.40$$

If we want to find the single interest rate that we could use to value the annuity, we must first compute the present value of the annuity using Eq. 5.7 and then solve for its IRR. For the annuity in Example 5.6, we use the annuity spreadsheet below to find its IRR of 3.4551%. The IRR of the annuity is always between the highest and lowest discount rates used to calculate its present value, as is the case in this example.

	NPER	RATE	PV	PMT	FV	Excel Formula
Given	5		−4,520.8	1,000	0	
Solve for Rate		3.4551%				=RATE(5,1000,−4520.80,0)

Instead, they could do better by investing on a short-term basis and then reinvesting after interest rates rose. Thus, if interest rates are expected to rise, long-term interest rates will tend to be higher than short-term rates to attract investors.

Similarly, if interest rates are expected to fall in the future, then borrowers would not wish to borrow at long-term rates that are equal to short-term rates. They would do better by borrowing on a short-term basis, and then taking out a new loan after rates fall. So, if interest rates are expected to fall, long-term rates will tend to be lower than short-term rates to attract borrowers.

These arguments imply that the shape of the yield curve will be strongly influenced by interest rate expectations. A sharply increasing (*steep*) yield curve, with long-term rates much higher than short-term rates, generally indicates that interest rates are expected to rise in the future. A decreasing (*inverted*) yield curve, with long-term rates lower than short-term rates, generally signals an expected decline in future interest rates. Because interest rates tend to drop in response to a slowdown in the economy, an inverted yield curve is often interpreted as a negative forecast for economic growth. Conversely, the yield curve tends to be steep as the economy comes out of a recession and interest rates are expected to rise.[6]

Clearly, the yield curve provides extremely important information for a business manager. In addition to specifying the discount rates for risk-free cash flows that occur at different horizons, it is also a potential leading indicator of future economic growth.

EXAMPLE 5.7

COMPARING SHORT- AND LONG-TERM INTEREST RATES

Problem

Suppose the current one-year interest rate is 1%. If it is known with certainty that the one-year interest rate will be 2% next year and 4% the following year, what will the interest rates r_1, r_2, and r_3 of the yield curve be today? Is the yield curve flat, increasing, or inverted?

Solution

We are told already that the one-year rate $r_1 = 1\%$. To find the two-year rate, note that if we invest \$1 for one year at the current one-year rate and then reinvest next year at the new one-year rate, after two years we will earn

$$\$1 \times (1.01) \times (1.02) = \$1.0302$$

We should earn the same payoff if we invest for two years at the current two-year rate r_2:

$$\$1 \times (1 + r_2)^2 = \$1.0302$$

Otherwise, there would be an arbitrage opportunity: If investing at the two-year rate led to a higher payoff, investors could invest for two years and borrow at the one-year rate. If investing at the two-year rate led to a lower payoff, investors could invest at the one-year rate and borrow at the two-year rate.

Solving for r_2, we find that

$$r_2 = (1.0302)^{1/2} - 1 = 1.499\%$$

---

6. Other factors besides interest rate expectations—most notably risk—can have an impact on the shape of the yield curve. See Chapter 8 for further discussion.

Similarly, investing for three years at the one-year rates should have the same payoff as investing at the current three-year rate:

$$(1.01) \times (1.02) \times (1.04) = 1.0714 = (1 + r_3)^3$$

We can solve for $r_3 = (1.0714)^{1/3} - 1 = 2.326\%$. Therefore, the current yield curve has $r_1 = 1\%$, $r_2 = 1.499\%$, and $r_3 = 2.326\%$. The yield curve is increasing as a result of the anticipated higher interest rates in the future.

CONCEPT CHECK

1. What is the difference between a nominal and real interest rate?

2. How are interest rates and the level of investment made by businesses related?

5.4   RISK AND TAXES

In this section, we discuss two other factors that are important when evaluating interest rates: risk and taxes.

RISK AND INTEREST RATES

We have already seen that interest rates vary with the investment horizon. Interest rates also vary based on the identity of the borrower. For example, Table 5.2 lists the interest rates paid by a number of different borrowers in August 2007 for a four-year loan.

Why do these interest rates vary so widely? The lowest interest rate is the rate paid on Government of Canada bonds. These bonds are widely regarded to be risk free because there is virtually no chance the government will fail to pay the interest and default on these bonds. Thus, when we refer to the "risk-free interest rate," we mean the rate on Government of Canada bonds (for shorter terms, we also look at Government of Canada treasury bills).

All other borrowers have some risk of default. For these loans, the stated interest rate is the *maximum* amount that investors will receive. Investors may receive less if the company has financial difficulties and is unable to fully repay the loan. To compensate for the risk that they will receive less if the firm defaults, investors demand a higher interest rate than the rate on Government of Canada bonds. The difference between the interest rate of the

INTEREST RATES ON FOUR-YEAR LOANS FOR VARIOUS BORROWERS, AUGUST 2007

TABLE 5.2

Borrower	Interest Rate
Government of Canada	4.33%
Hydro Québec	4.58%
Hydro One	4.84%
TD Canada Trust	4.99%
CIBC	5.05%
Royal Bank of Canada	5.18%
Domtar	6.98%

loan and the Government of Canada bond rate will depend on investors' assessment of the likelihood that the firm will default.

Later in the textbook we will develop tools to evaluate the risk of different investments and determine the interest rate or discount rate that appropriately compensates investors for the level of risk they are taking. For now, we should remember that when discounting future cash flows, it is important to use a discount rate that matches both the horizon and the risk of the cash flows. Specifically, *the right discount rate for a cash flow is the rate of return available in the market on other investments of comparable risk and term.*

EXAMPLE 5.8	DISCOUNTING RISKY CASH FLOWS

Problem

Suppose the Canadian government owes your firm $1000, to be paid in four years. Based on the interest rates in Table 5.2, what is the present value of this cash flow? Suppose instead Domtar owes your firm $1000. Estimate the present value in this case.

Solution

Assuming we can regard the government's obligation as risk free (there is no chance you won't be paid), then we discount the cash flow using the risk-free interest rate of 4.33%:

$$PV = \$1000 \div (1.0433)^4 = \$844.04$$

The obligation from Domtar is not risk free. There is no guarantee that Domtar will not have financial difficulties and fail to pay the $1000. Because the risk of this obligation is likely to be comparable to the four-year loan quoted in Table 5.2, the 6.98% interest rate of the loan is a more appropriate discount rate to use to compute the present value in this case:

$$PV = \$1000 \div (1.0698)^4 = \$763.47$$

Note the substantially lower present value in this case, due to the risk of default.

AFTER-TAX INTEREST RATES

If the cash flows from an investment are taxed, the actual cash flow that the investor will get to keep will be reduced by the amount of the tax payments. We will discuss the taxation of corporate investments in detail in later chapters. Here, we consider the effect of taxes on the interest earned on savings (or paid on borrowing). Taxes reduce the amount of interest the investor can keep, and we refer to this reduced amount as the **after-tax interest rate**.

Consider an investment that pays 8% interest (EAR) for one year. If you invest $100 at the start of the year, you will earn 8% $\times$ $100 = $8 in interest at year-end. This interest may be taxable as income.[7] If you are in a 40% tax bracket, you will owe

$$(40\% \text{ income tax rate}) \times (\$8 \text{ interest}) = \$3.20 \text{ tax liability}$$

Thus you will receive only $8 − $3.20 = $4.80 after paying taxes. This amount is equivalent to earning 4.80% interest and not paying any taxes, so the after-tax interest rate is 4.80%.

---

7. In Canada, interest income for individuals is taxable unless it is earned by investments held inside a retirement account such as an RRSP or RRIF, in a registered education savings plan (RESP), or in a tax-free savings account (TFSA).

In general, if the interest rate is r and the tax rate is τ, then for each \$1 invested you will earn interest equal to r and owe tax of $\tau \times r$ on the interest. The equivalent after-tax interest rate is therefore

After-Tax Interest Rate

$$r - (\tau \times r) = r(1 - \tau) \tag{5.8}$$

Applying this formula to our previous example of an 8% interest rate and a 40% tax rate, we find the interest rate is $8\% \times (1 - 0.40) = 4.80\%$ after taxes.

The same calculation can be applied to loans. In some cases, the interest on loans is tax-deductible.[8] In that case, the cost of paying interest on the loan is offset by the benefit of the tax deduction. The net effect is that when interest on a loan is tax-deductible, the effective after-tax interest rate is $r(1 - \tau)$. In other words, the ability to deduct the interest expense lowers the effective after-tax interest rate paid on the loan.

EXAMPLE 5.9

COMPARING AFTER-TAX INTEREST RATES

Problem

Suppose you have a credit card with a 19.9% APR with daily compounding, a bank savings account paying 5% EAR, and a car loan with a 4.8% APR with monthly compounding. Your income tax rate is 40%. The interest on the savings account is taxable, and the interest on the car loan is not tax-deductible. What is the effective after-tax interest rate of each instrument, expressed as an EAR? What should your priorities be in terms of your financial situation?

Solution

At first glance it looks like you should pay down your credit card because it carries a high interest rate, and then you should save because your savings account earns more than the interest charged on your car loan. However, tax effects are important and may change your priorities.

Because taxes are typically paid annually, we must first convert each interest rate to an EAR to determine the actual amount of interest earned or paid during the year. The savings account has a 5% EAR. Using Eq. 5.3, the EAR of the credit card is $(1 + 0.199/365)^{365} - 1 = 22.01\%$ and the EAR of the car loan is $(1 + 0.048/12)^{12} - 1 = 4.91\%$.

Next, we compute the after-tax interest rate for each. Because the credit card interest is not tax-deductible, its after-tax interest rate is the same as its pre-tax interest rate, 22.01%. The same holds for the car loan: its after-tax interest rate is the same as its pre-tax interest rate, 4.91%. The savings account's interest is taxed, though, so the after-tax interest rate that we will earn on the savings account is $5\% \times (1 - 0.40) = 3\%$.

What should your financial priorities be? Certainly you should pay off the credit card, as its after-tax interest cost (over 22%) is higher than the after-tax interest you can earn in your savings account (only 3%). In addition, even though your savings appear to have a higher rate of interest than the car loan, the after-tax return on your savings, 3%, is less than the after-tax cost of the car loan, 4.91%. Thus, you should use your savings to pay down the car loan, too. So your priorities are first to pay off the credit card (in full) and, second, pay down the car loan. If you have money left over, you can put it in your savings account.

---

8. In Canada, interest is tax-deductible for individuals only for loans used for the purchase of income-generating assets (e.g., stocks, bonds, or rental property).

1. Why do corporations pay higher interest rates on their loans than the Government of Canada?

2. How do taxes affect the interest earned on an investment? What about the interest paid on a loan?

5.5 THE OPPORTUNITY COST OF CAPITAL

As we have seen in this chapter, the interest rates we observe in the market will vary based on quoting conventions, the term of the investment, and risk. The actual return kept by an investor will also depend on how the interest is taxed. In this chapter, we have developed the tools to account for these differences and gained some insights into how interest rates are determined.

In Chapter 3, we argued that the "market interest rate" provides the exchange rate that we need to compute present values and evaluate an investment opportunity. But with so many interest rates to choose from, the term "market interest rate" is inherently ambiguous. Therefore, going forward in the textbook, we will base the discount rate that we use to evaluate cash flows on the investor's **opportunity cost of capital** (or more simply, the **cost of capital**), which is *the best available expected return offered in the market on an investment of comparable risk and term to the cash flow being discounted.*

The opportunity cost of capital is the return the investor forgoes when the investor takes on a new investment. Consider a firm that is evaluating an investment project. For the firm, if investing in the new project requires the firm to raise new financing from outside security holders, then the cost of capital is the marginal cost of new funds to be raised. In order to attract funds, the firm must offer an expected return comparable to what the firm's security holders could earn elsewhere with the same risk and horizon. The same logic applies when a firm considers a project it can fund internally. Because any funds invested in a new project could be returned to the firm's security holders to invest elsewhere, the new project should be taken only if it offers a better return than security holders' other opportunities.

Thus, the opportunity cost of capital provides the benchmark against which the cash flows of the new investment should be evaluated. For a risk-free project, it will typically correspond to the interest rate on Government of Canada securities with a similar term. The cost of capital for risky projects will often exceed this amount, depending on the nature and magnitude of the risk. We will develop tools for estimating the cost of capital for risky projects in Part 4 of the text.

1. What is the opportunity cost of capital?

2. Why do different interest rates exist, even in a competitive market?

SUMMARY

1. The effective annual rate (EAR) indicates the actual amount of interest earned in one year. The EAR can be used as a discount rate for annual cash flows.

2. Given an EAR r, the equivalent discount rate for an n-year time interval, where n may be a fraction, is

$$(1 + r)^n - 1 \tag{5.1}$$

3. An annual percentage rate (APR) indicates the total amount of interest earned in one year without considering the effect of compounding. APRs cannot be used as discount rates.

4. An APR can be converted to an equivalent implied effective rate per its compounding period by dividing by the number of compounding periods, k, that occur per year:

$$\text{Implied Effective Interest Rate per Compounding Period} = \frac{APR}{k \text{ periods/year}} \quad (5.2)$$

5. We can combine equations 5.1 and 5.2 to convert an APR to an EAR:

$$1 + EAR = \left(1 + \frac{APR}{k}\right)^k \quad (5.3)$$

6. Loan rates are typically stated as APRs. The outstanding balance of a loan is equal to the present value of the loan cash flows, when evaluated using the equivalent effective interest rate per payment interval based on the loan rate.

7. Quoted interest rates are nominal interest rates, which indicate the rate of growth of the money invested. The real interest rate indicates the rate of growth of one's purchasing power after adjusting for inflation.

8. Given a nominal interest rate r and an inflation rate i, the real interest rate is

$$r_r = \frac{r - i}{1 + i} \approx r - i \quad (5.5)$$

9. Nominal interest rates tend to be high when inflation is high and low when inflation is low.

10. Higher interest rates tend to reduce the NPV of typical investment projects. The Bank of Canada raises interest rates to moderate investment and combat inflation, and lowers interest rates to stimulate investment and economic growth.

11. Interest rates differ with the investment horizon according to the term structure of interest rates. The graph plotting interest rates as a function of the horizon is called the yield curve.

12. Cash flows should be discounted using the discount rate that is appropriate for their horizon. Thus the PV of a cash flow stream is

$$PV = \frac{C_1}{1 + r_1} + \frac{C_2}{(1 + r_2)^2} + \cdots + \frac{C_N}{(1 + r_N)^N} = \sum_{n=1}^{N} \frac{C_n}{(1 + r_n)^n} \quad (5.7)$$

13. Annuity and perpetuity formulas cannot be applied when discount rates vary with the horizon.

14. The shape of the yield curve tends to vary with investors' expectations of future economic growth and interest rates. It tends to be inverted prior to recessions and to be steep coming out of a recession.

15. Canadian government treasury-bill and bond rates are regarded as risk-free interest rates. Other borrowers will pay higher interest rates on their loans because of the possibility that they may default.

16. The correct discount rate for a cash flow is the expected return available in the market on other investments of comparable risk and term.

17. If the interest on an investment is taxed at rate τ, or if the interest on a loan is tax-deductible, then the effective after-tax interest rate is

$$r(1 - \tau) \quad (5.8)$$

KEY TERMS

after-tax interest rate *p. 153*
amortizing loan *p. 143*
annual percentage rate (APR) *p. 139*
continuous compounding *p. 142*
(opportunity) cost of capital *p. 155*
effective annual rate (EAR) *p. 138*
mortgage *p. 143*
nominal interest rate *p. 145*

overnight rate *p. 150*
real interest rate *p. 145*
simple interest *p. 139*
term structure *p. 147*
yield curve *p. 147*

PROBLEMS

The problems marked in green can be found on MyFinanceLab at www.myfinancelab.com. Visit your MyFinanceLab for additional practice. An asterisk (*) indicates problems with a higher level of difficulty. Additional readings for this chapter may be found in the Textbook Resources section on MyFinanceLab.

Interest Rate Quotes and Adjustments

1. Your bank is offering you an account that will pay 20% interest in total for a two-year deposit. Determine the equivalent discount rate for a period length of
   a. Six months.
   b. One year.
   c. One month.

EXCEL

2. Which do you prefer: a bank account that pays 5% per year (EAR) for three years or
   a. An account that pays 2½% every six months for three years?
   b. An account that pays 7½% every 18 months for three years?
   c. An account that pays ½% per month for three years?

EXCEL

3. Many academic institutions offer a sabbatical policy. Every seven years a professor is given a year free of teaching and other administrative responsibilities at full pay. For a professor earning $70,000 per year who works for a total of 42 years, what is the present value of the amount she will earn while on sabbatical if the interest rate is 6% (EAR)?

4. You have found three investment choices for a one-year deposit: 10% APR compounded monthly, 10% APR compounded annually, and 9% APR compounded daily. Compute the EAR for each investment choice. (Assume that there are 365 days in the year.)

5. You are considering moving your money to a new bank offering a one-year GIC that pays an 8% APR with monthly compounding. Your current bank's manager offers to match the rate you have been offered. The account at your current bank would pay interest every 6 months. How much interest will you need to earn every 6 months to match the GIC?

6. Your bank account pays interest with an EAR of 5%. What is the APR quote for this account based on semiannual compounding? What is the APR with monthly compounding?

7. Suppose the interest rate is 8% APR with monthly compounding. What is the present value of an annuity that pays $100 every six months for five years?

8. You can earn $50 in interest on a $1000 deposit for 8 months. If the EAR is the same regardless of the length of the investment, how much interest will your earn on a $1000 deposit for
   a. 6 month?
   b. 1 year?
   c. 1½ years?

9. Suppose you invest $100 in a bank account, and 5 years later it has grown to $134.39.
   a. What APR did you receive, if the interest was compounded semi-annually?
   b. What APR did you receive, if the interest was compounded monthly?

EXCEL
10. Your son has been accepted into university. This university guarantees that your son's tuition will not increase for the four years that he attends. The first $10,000 tuition payment is due in six months. After that, the same payment is due every six months until you have made a total of eight payments. The university offers a bank account that allows you to withdraw money every six months and has a fixed APR of 4% (with semiannual compounding) guaranteed to remain the same over the next four years. How much money must you deposit today if you intend to make no further deposits and would like to make all the tuition payments from this account, leaving the account empty when the last payment is made?

11. You make monthly payments on your mortgage. It has a quoted APR of 5% (with semiannual compounding). What percentage of the outstanding principal do you pay in interest each month?

Application: Discount Rates and Loans

12. Capital One is advertising a 60-month, 5.99% APR motorcycle loan. If you need to borrow $8000 to purchase your dream Harley Davidson, what will your monthly payment be?

13. The Bank of Montreal is offering a mortgage with an EAR of 5⅜%. If you plan to borrow $150,000, what will your monthly payment be assuming a 30-year amortization?

14. You have decided to refinance your mortgage. You plan to borrow whatever is outstanding on your current mortgage. The current monthly payment is $2356 and you have made every payment on time. The original term of the mortgage was 30 years, and the mortgage is exactly four years and eight months old. You have just made your monthly payment. The mortgage interest rate is 6.2% (APR with semiannual compounding). How much do you owe on the mortgage today?

15. You have just sold your house for $1,000,000 in cash. Your mortgage was originally a 30-year mortgage with monthly payments and an initial balance of $800,000. The mortgage is currently exactly 18½ years old, and you have just made a payment. If the interest rate on the mortgage is 7.75% (APR with semiannual compounding), how much cash will you have from the sale once you pay off the mortgage?

16. You have just purchased a home and taken out a $500,000 mortgage. The mortgage has a 30-year term with monthly payments and an APR (with semiannual compounding) of 6.5%.
   a. How much will you pay in interest, and how much will you pay in principal, during the first year?
   b. How much will you pay in interest, and how much will you pay in principal, during the twentieth year (i.e., between 19 and 20 years from now)?

17. Your mortgage has 25 years left, and has an APR of 8% (with semiannual compounding) and monthly payments of $1500.

    a. What is the outstanding balance?

    b. Suppose you cannot make the mortgage payment and you are in danger of losing your house to foreclosure. The bank has offered to renegotiate your loan. The bank expects to get $150,000 for the house if it forecloses. They will lower your payment as long as they will receive at least this amount (in present value terms). If current 25-year mortgage interest rates have dropped to 5% (APR with semiannual compounding), what is the lowest monthly payment you could make for the remaining life of your loan that would be attractive to the bank?

EXCEL   ***18.** You have an outstanding student loan with required payments of $500 per month for the next four years. The interest rate on the loan is 9% APR (monthly). You are considering making an extra payment of $100 today (that is, you will pay an extra $100 that you are not required to pay). If you are required to continue to make payments of $500 per month until the loan is paid off, what is the amount of your final payment? What effective rate of return (expressed as an APR with monthly compounding) have you earned on the $100?

EXCEL   ***19.** Consider again the setting of Problem 18. Now that you realize your best investment is to prepay your student loan, you decide to prepay as much as you can each month. Looking at your budget, you can afford to pay an extra $250 per month in addition to your required monthly payments of $500, or $750 in total each month. How long will it take you to pay off the loan?

    *20. If you decide to take the mortgage in Problem 13, the Bank of Montreal will offer you the following deal: Instead of making the monthly payment you computed in that problem every month, you can make half the payment every two weeks (so that you will make 52/2 = 26 payments per year). How long will it take to pay off the mortgage if the EAR remains the same at 5⅜%?

EXCEL   ***21.** Your friend tells you he has a very simple trick for taking one-third off the time it takes to repay your mortgage: Use your Christmas bonus to make an extra payment on January 1 of each year (that is, pay your monthly payment due on that day twice). If you take out your mortgage on July 1, so your first monthly payment is due August 1, and you make an extra payment every January 1, how long will it take to pay off the mortgage? Assume that the mortgage has an original term of 30 years and an APR (with semiannual compounding) of 12%.

EXCEL   **22.** You need a new car and the dealer has offered you a price of $20,000, with the following payment options: (a) pay cash and receive a $2000 rebate, or (b) pay a $5000 down payment and finance the rest with a 0% APR loan over 30 months. But having just quit your job and started an MBA program, you are in debt and you expect to be in debt for at least the next 2½ years. You plan to use credit cards to pay your expenses; luckily you have one with a low (fixed) rate of 15% APR (with monthly compounding). Which payment option is best for you?

    23. The mortgage on your house in Winnipeg is 5 years old. It required monthly payments of $1402, had an original term of 30 years, and had an interest rate of 9% (APR with semiannual compounding). In the intervening 5 years, interest rates have fallen, housing prices in the U.S. have fallen, and you have decided to retire to Florida. You have decided to sell your house in Winnipeg and use your equity for the down payment on a condo in Florida. You will roll over the outstanding balance on your old mortgage into a new mortgage in Florida. The new mortgage has a 30-year term, requires monthly payments, and has an interest rate of 6⅝% (APR with *monthly* compounding, which is typical for U.S. mortgages).

    a. What monthly repayments will be required with the new loan?

    b. If you still want to pay off the mortgage in 25 years, what monthly payment should you make on your new mortgage?

    c. Suppose you are willing to continue making monthly payments of $1402. How long will it take you to pay off the new mortgage?

    d. Suppose you are willing to continue making monthly payments of $1402, and you want to pay off the mortgage in 25 years. How much additional cash can you borrow today as part of the new financing?

24. You have credit card debt of $25,000 that has an APR (with monthly compounding) of 15%. Each month you only pay the minimum monthly payment. You are required to pay only the outstanding interest. You have received an offer in the mail for an otherwise identical credit card with an APR of 12%. After considering all your alternatives, you decide to switch cards, roll over the outstanding balance on the old card into the new card, and borrow additional money as well. How much can you borrow today on the new card without changing the minimum monthly payment you will be required to pay?

The Determinants of Interest Rates

25. In 1974, interest rates were 7.782% and the rate of inflation was 12.299% in Canada. What was the real interest rate in 1974? How would the purchasing power of your savings have changed over the year?

26. If the rate of inflation is 5%, what nominal interest rate is necessary for you to earn a 3% real interest rate on your investment?

27. Can the nominal interest rate available to an investor be negative? (*Hint:* Consider the interest rate earned from saving cash "under the mattress.") Can the real interest rate be negative? Explain.

28. Consider a project that requires an initial investment of $100,000 and will produce a single cash flow of $150,000 in five years.

    a. What is the NPV of this project if the five-year interest rate is 5% (EAR)?

    b. What is the NPV of this project if the five-year interest rate is 10% (EAR)?

    c. What is the highest five-year interest rate such that this project is still profitable?

EXCEL   29. Suppose the term structure of risk-free interest rates is as shown below:

Term	1 year	2 years	3 years	5 years	7 years	10 years	20 years
Rate (EAR, %)	1.99	2.41	2.74	3.32	3.76	4.13	4.93

    a. Calculate the present value of an investment that pays $1000 in two years and $2000 in five years for certain.

    b. Calculate the present value of receiving $500 per year, with certainty, at the end of the next five years. To find the rates for the missing years in the table, linearly interpolate between the years for which you do know the rates. (For example, the rate in year 4 would be the average of the rate in year 3 and year 5.)

    *c. Calculate the present value of receiving $2300 per year, with certainty, for the next 20 years. Infer rates for the missing years using linear interpolation. (*Hint:* Use a spreadsheet.)

EXCEL 30. Using the term structure in Problem 29, what is the present value of an investment that pays $100 at the end of each of years 1, 2, and 3? If you wanted to value this investment correctly using the annuity formula, which discount rate should you use?

EXCEL 31. What is the shape of the yield curve given the term structure in Problem 29? What expectations are investors likely to have about future interest rates?

EXCEL 32. Suppose the current one-year interest rate is 6%. One year from now, you believe the economy will start to slow and the one-year interest rate will fall to 5%. In two years, you expect the economy to be in the midst of a recession, causing the Bank of Canada to cut interest rates drastically and the one-year interest rate to fall to 2%. The one-year interest rate will then rise to 3% the following year, and continue to rise by 1% per year until it returns to 6%, where it will remain from then on.

    a. If you were certain regarding these future interest rate changes, what two-year interest rate would be consistent with these expectations?

    b. What current term structure of interest rates, for terms of 1 to 10 years, would be consistent with these expectations?

    c. Plot the yield curve in this case. How does the one-year interest rate compare to the ten-year interest rate?

Risk and Taxes

33. Based on the data in Table 5.2, which would you prefer: $500 from Domtar paid today or a promise that the firm will pay you $700 in six years? Which would you choose if the Government of Canada offered you the same alternatives?

34. Your best taxable investment opportunity has an EAR of 4%. Your best tax-free investment opportunity has an EAR of 3%. If your tax rate is 30%, which opportunity provides the higher after-tax interest rate?

35. Your best friend consults you for investment advice. You learn that his tax rate is 35%, and he has the following current investments and debts:

- A car loan with an outstanding balance of $5000 and a 4.8% APR (monthly compounding)
- Credit cards with an outstanding balance of $10,000 and a 14.9% APR (monthly compounding)
- A regular savings account with a $30,000 balance, paying a 5.50% EAR
- A money market savings account with a $100,000 balance, paying a 5.25% APR (daily compounding)

    a. Which savings account pays a higher after-tax interest rate?

    b. Should your friend use his savings to pay off any of his outstanding debts? Explain.

36. Suppose you have outstanding debt with an 8% interest rate that can be repaid anytime, and the interest rate on Government of Canada treasury bills is only 5%. You plan to repay your debt using cash that you don't invest elsewhere. Until your debt is repaid, what cost of capital should you use when evaluating a new risk-free investment opportunity? Why?

The Opportunity Cost of Capital

37. In the summer of 2008 in Heathrow airport in London, BB (bestofthebest), a private company, offered a lottery to win a Ferrari or 90,000 British pounds, equivalent at the time to about $180,000. Both the Ferrari and the money, in 100-pound notes, were on display. If the U.K. interest rate was 5% per year (EAR), how much did it cost the company in pounds each

month to keep the cash on display? That is, what was the opportunity cost of keeping it on display rather than in a bank account? (Ignore taxes.)

38. Your firm is considering the purchase of a new office phone system. You can either pay $32,000 now, or $1000 per month for 36 months.

   a. Suppose your firm currently borrows at a rate of 6% per year (APR with monthly compounding). Which payment plan is more attractive?

   b. Suppose your firm currently borrows at a rate of 18% per year (APR with monthly compounding). Which payment plan would be more attractive in this case?

CHAPTER 5 APPENDIX

Notation

e	2.71828 ...
ln	natural logarithm
r_{cc}	continuously compounded discount rate
g_{cc}	continuously compounded growth rate
$\overline{C}_1$	total cash flows received in first year

CONTINUOUS RATES AND CASH FLOWS

In this appendix we consider how to discount cash flows when interest is paid, or cash flows are received, on a continuous basis.

DISCOUNT RATES FOR A CONTINUOUSLY COMPOUNDED APR

Some investments compound more frequently than daily. As we move from daily to hourly ($k = 24 \times 365$) to compounding every second ($k = 60 \times 60 \times 24 \times 365$), we approach the limit of continuous compounding, in which we compound every instant ($k = \infty$). Equation 5.3 cannot be used to compute the discount rate from an APR quote based on continuous compounding. In this case, the discount rate for a period length of one year—that is, the EAR—is given by Eq. 5A.1:

The EAR for a Continuously Compounded APR

$$(1 + EAR) = e^{APR} \tag{5A.1}$$

where the mathematical constant[9] $e = 2.71828. . . .$ Once you know the EAR, you can compute the discount rate for any compounding period length using Eq. 5.2.

Alternatively, if we know the EAR and want to find the corresponding continuously compounded APR, we can invert Eq. 5A.1 by taking the natural logarithm (ln) of both sides:[10]

The Continuously Compounded APR for an EAR

$$APR = \ln(1 + EAR) \tag{5A.2}$$

Continuously compounded rates are not often used in practice. Sometimes, banks offer them as a marketing gimmick, but there is little actual difference between daily and continuous compounding. For example, with a 6% APR, daily compounding provides an EAR of $(1 + 0.06/365)^{365} - 1 = 6.18313\%$, whereas with continuous compounding the EAR is $e^{0.06} - 1 = 6.18365\%$.

CONTINUOUSLY ARRIVING CASH FLOWS

How can we compute the present value of an investment whose cash flows arrive continuously? For example, consider the cash flows of an online book retailer. Suppose the firm forecasts cash flows of $10 million per year. The $10 million will be received throughout each year, not at year-end, that is, the $10 million is paid *continuously* throughout the year.

We can compute the present value of cash flows that arrive continuously using a version of the growing perpetuity formula. If cash flows arrive, starting immediately, at an initial rate of $$C$ per year, and if the cash flows grow at rate g per year, then given a discount rate (expressed as an EAR) of r per year, the present value of the cash flows is

Present Value of a Continuously Growing Perpetuity[11]

$$PV = \frac{C}{r_{cc} - g_{cc}} \tag{5A.3}$$

---

9. The constant e raised to a power is also written as the function *exp*. That is, $e^{APR} = exp(APR)$. This function is built into most spreadsheets and calculators.

10. Recall that $\ln(e^x) = x$.

11. Given the perpetuity formula, we can value an annuity as the difference between two perpetuities.

where $r_{cc} = \ln(1 + r)$ and $g_{cc} = \ln(1 + g)$ are the discount and growth rates expressed as continuously compounded APRs, respectively.

There is another, approximate method for dealing with continuously arriving cash flows. Let $\overline{C}_1$ be the total cash flows that arrive during the first year. Because the cash flows arrive throughout the year, we can think of them arriving "on average" in the middle of the year. In that case, we should discount the cash flows by ½ year less:

$$\frac{C}{r_{cc} - g_{cc}} \approx \frac{\overline{C}_1}{r - g} \times (1 + r)^{1/2} \tag{5A.4}$$

In practice, the approximation in Eq. 5A.4 works quite well. More generally, it implies that when cash flows arrive continuously, we can compute present values reasonably accurately by pretending that all of the cash flows for the year arrive in the middle of the year.

EXAMPLE 5A.1   VALUING PROJECTS WITH CONTINUOUS CASH FLOWS

Problem

Your firm is considering buying an oil rig. The rig will initially produce oil at a rate of 30 million barrels per year. You have a long-term contract that allows you to sell the oil at a profit of $1.25 per barrel. If the rate of oil production from the rig declines by 3% over the year and the discount rate is 10% per year (EAR), how much would you be willing to pay for the rig?

Solution

According to the estimates, the rig will generate profits at an initial rate of (30 million barrels per year) × ($1.25/barrel) = $37.5 million per year. The 10% discount rate is equivalent to a continuously compounded APR of $r_{cc} = \ln(1 + 0.10) = 9.531\%$; similarly, the growth rate has an APR of $g_{cc} = \ln(1 - 0.03) = -3.046\%$. From Eq. 5A.3, the present value of the profits from the rig is

$$PV(\text{profits}) = 37.5/(r_{cc} - g_{cc}) = 37.5/(0.09531 + 0.03046) = \$298.16 \text{ million}$$

Alternatively, we can closely approximate the present value as follows. The initial profit rate of the rig is $37.5 million per year. By the end of the year, the profit rate will have declined by 3% to 37.5 × (1 − 0.03) = $36.375 million per year. Therefore, the average profit rate during the year is approximately (37.5 + 36.375)/2 = $36.938 million. Valuing the cash flows as though they occur at the middle of each year, we have

$$PV(\text{profits}) = [36.938/(r - g)] \times (1 + r)^{1/2}$$
$$= [36.938/(0.10 + 0.03)] \times (1.10)^{1/2} = \$298.01 \text{ million}$$

Note that both methods produce very similar results.

Basic Valuation

THE LAW OF ONE PRICE CONNECTION. Now that the basic tools for financial decision making are in place, we can begin to apply them. One of the most important decisions facing a financial manager is the choice of which investments the corporation should make. In Chapter 6, we compare the net present value rule to other investment rules firms sometimes use and explain why the net present value rule is superior. The process of allocating the firm's capital for investment is known as capital budgeting, and in Chapter 7 we outline the discounted cash flow method for making such decisions. Both chapters provide a practical demonstration of the power of the tools that were introduced in Part 2.

Firms raise the capital they need to make investments by issuing securities such as bonds and stocks. In the following two chapters, we use the tools to explain how to value these securities. In Chapter 8, Valuing Bonds, the Law of One Price allows us to link bond prices and their yields to the term structure of market interest rates. Similarly, in Chapter 9, Valuing Stocks, we show how the Law of One Price leads to several alternative methods for valuing a firm's equity by considering its future dividends, free cash flows, or how its value compares to that of similar, publicly traded companies.

CHAPTER

6

Investment Decision Rules

When Onex Corporation was deciding whether to acquire Cineplex Entertainment in 1998, it needed to consider both the costs and the benefits of the proposed acquisition. The costs included the initial purchase price and the ongoing costs of operating the business. Benefits would be the future revenues from Cineplex Entertainment. The right way to evaluate such a decision is to compare the cash value today of the costs to the cash value today of the benefits by computing the NPV of the acquisition; Onex should have undertaken the Cineplex Entertainment acquisition only if it had a positive NPV.

Although the NPV investment rule maximizes the value of the firm, some firms nevertheless use other techniques to evaluate investments and decide which projects to pursue. In this chapter, we explain several commonly used techniques—namely, the *payback rule* and the *internal rate of return rule*. In each case, we define the decision rule and compare decisions based on this rule to decisions based on the NPV rule. We also illustrate the circumstances in which some of the alternative rules are likely to lead to bad investment decisions. After establishing these rules in the context of a single, stand-alone project, we broaden our perspective to include deciding among mutually exclusive investment opportunities. We conclude with a look at project selection when the firm faces resource constraints.

6.1 NPV AND STAND-ALONE PROJECTS

We begin our discussion of investment decision rules by considering a take-it-or-leave-it decision involving a single, stand-alone project. By undertaking this project, the firm does not constrain its ability to take other projects. We initiate our analysis with the familiar NPV rule from Chapter 3: *When making an investment decision, take the alternative with the highest NPV. Choosing this alternative is equivalent to receiving its NPV in cash today.* In the case of a stand-alone project, we must choose between accepting and rejecting the project. The NPV rule then says we should compare the project's NPV to zero (the NPV of doing nothing) and accept the project if its NPV is positive.

APPLYING THE NPV RULE

Researchers at Saskatchewan Fertilizer Corporation (SFC) have made a breakthrough. They believe that they can produce a new, environmentally friendly fertilizer at a substantial cost saving over the company's existing line of fertilizer. The fertilizer will require a new plant that can be built immediately at a cost of $250 million. Financial managers estimate that the benefits of the new fertilizer will be $35 million per year, starting at the end of the first year and lasting forever, as shown by the following timeline:

As we explained in Chapter 4, the NPV of this cash flow stream, given a discount rate r, is

$$\text{NPV} = -250 + \frac{35}{r}$$

Figure 6.1 plots the NPV as a function of the discount rate, r. Notice that the NPV is positive only for discount rates that are less than 14%, the internal rate of return (IRR). To decide whether to invest (using the NPV rule), we need to know the cost of capital. The financial managers responsible for this project estimate a cost of capital of 10% per year. Referring to Figure 6.1, we see that when the discount rate is 10%, the NPV is $100 million, which is positive. The NPV investment rule indicates that by making the investment, SFC will increase the value of the firm by $100 million, so SFC should undertake this project.

MEASURING SENSITIVITY WITH IRR

If you are unsure of your cost of capital estimate, it is important to determine how sensitive your analysis is to errors in this estimate. The IRR can provide this information. For SFC, if the cost of capital estimate is more than the 14% IRR, the NPV will be negative (see Figure 6.1). In general, *the difference between the cost of capital and the IRR is the maximum amount of estimation error in the cost of capital estimate that can exist without altering the original decision.*

ALTERNATIVE RULES VERSUS THE NPV RULE

The NPV rule indicates that SFC should undertake the investment in fertilizer technology. As we evaluate alternative rules for project selection, keep in mind that sometimes other investment rules may give the same answer as the NPV rule, but at other times they may disagree. When the rules conflict, following the alternative rule means we are not

FIGURE 6.1

NPV of SFC's New Project
The graph shows the NPV as a function of the discount rate. The NPV is positive only for discount rates that are less than 14%, the internal rate of return (IRR). Given the cost of capital of 10%, the project has a positive NPV of $100 million.

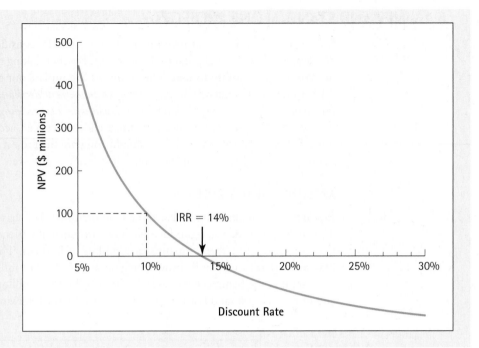

taking a positive NPV project and thus we are not maximizing wealth. In these cases, the alternative rules lead to bad decisions.

In a 2001 study, John Graham and Campbell Harvey[1] found that 74.9% of the firms they surveyed used the NPV rule for making investment decisions. In a 1995 study, Vijay Jog and Ashwani Srivastava[2] found that less than 50% of Canadian firms used NPV, but about 75% used some form of discounted cash flow analysis. These results are substantially different from that found in an earlier study in 1977 by L. J. Gitman and J. R. Forrester,[3] who found that only 9.8% of firms used the NPV rule. MBA students in recent years have been listening to their finance professors! Even so, the two more recent studies indicate that over one-fourth of corporations do not use the NPV rule. Exactly why other capital budgeting techniques are used in practice is not always clear. However, because you may encounter these techniques in the business world, you should know what they are, how they are used, and how they compare to NPV. In this section, we examine alternative decision rules for single, stand-alone projects within the firm. The focus here is on the *payback rule, IRR rule,* and *Economic Value Added.*

CONCEPT CHECK

1. Explain the NPV rule for stand-alone projects.

2. How can you interpret the difference between the cost of capital and the IRR?

1. John Graham and Campbell Harvey, "The Theory and Practice of Corporate Finance: Evidence from the Field," *Journal of Financial Economics* 60 (2001): 187–243.

2. Vijay Jog and Ashwani Srivastava, "Capital Budgeting Practices in Corporate Canada," *Financial Practice and Education* 50 (1995): 37–43.

3. L. J. Gitman and J. R. Forrester, Jr., "A Survey of Capital Budgeting Techniques Used by Major U.S. Firms," *Financial Management* 6 (1977): 66–71.

INTERVIEW WITH DICK GRANNIS

Dick Grannis is senior vice-president and treasurer of QUALCOMM Incorporated, a world leader in digital wireless communications technology and semiconductors, headquartered in San Diego. He joined the company in 1991 and oversees the company's $10 billion cash investment portfolio. He works primarily on investment banking, capital structure, and international finance.

QUESTION: **QUALCOMM has a wide variety of products in different business lines. How does your capital budgeting process for new products work?**

ANSWER: QUALCOMM evaluates new projects (such as new products, equipment, technologies, research and development, acquisitions, and strategic investments) by using traditional financial measurements including discounted cash flow/NPV models, IRR levels, peak funding requirements, the time needed to reach cumulative positive cash flows, and the short-term impact of the investment on our reported net earnings. For strategic investments, we consider the possible value of financial, competitive, technology and/or market value enhancements to our core businesses—even if those benefits cannot be quantified. Overall, we make capital budgeting decisions based on a combination of objective analyses and our own business judgment.

We do not engage in capital budgeting and analysis if the project represents an immediate and necessary requirement for our business operations. One example is new software or production equipment to start a project that has already received approval.

We are also mindful of the opportunity costs of allocating our internal engineering resources on one project vs. another project. We view this as a constantly challenging but worthwhile exercise, because we have many attractive opportunities but limited resources to pursue them.

QUESTION: **How often does QUALCOMM evaluate its hurdle rates and what factors does it consider in setting them? How do you allocate capital across areas and regions and assess the risk of non-U.S. investments?**

ANSWER: QUALCOMM encourages its financial planners to utilize hurdle (or discount) rates that vary according to the risk of the particular project. We expect a rate of return commensurate with the project's risk. Our finance staff considers a wide range of discount rates and chooses one that fits the project's expected risk profile and time horizon. The range can be from 6.00% to 8.00% for relatively safe investments in the domestic market to 50% or more for equity investments in foreign markets that may be illiquid and difficult to predict. We re-evaluate our hurdle rates at least every year.

We analyze key factors including: (i) market adoption risk (whether or not customers will buy the new product or service at the price and volume we expect), (ii) technology development risk (whether or not we can develop and patent the new product or service as expected), (iii) execution risk (whether we can launch the new product or service cost effectively and on time), and (iv) dedicated asset risk (the amount of resources that must be consumed to complete the work).

QUESTION: **How are projects categorized and how are the hurdle rates for new projects determined? What would happen if QUALCOMM simply evaluated all new projects against the same hurdle rate?**

ANSWER: We primarily categorize projects by risk level, but we also categorize projects by the expected time horizon. We consider short-term and long-term projects to balance our needs and achieve our objectives. For example, immediate projects and opportunities may demand a great amount of attention, but we also stay focused on long-term projects because they often create greater long-term value for stockholders.

If we were to evaluate all new projects against the same hurdle rate, then our business planners would, by default, consistently choose to invest in the highest risk projects because those projects would appear to have the greatest expected returns in DCF models or IRR analyses. That approach would probably not work well for very long.

6.2 THE INTERNAL RATE OF RETURN RULE

One interpretation of the internal rate of return is that it is the average return for taking on the investment opportunity. The **internal rate of return (IRR) investment rule** is based on this idea: If the average return on the investment opportunity (i.e., the IRR) is greater than the return on other alternatives in the market with equivalent risk and maturity (i.e., the project's cost of capital), then you should undertake the investment opportunity. We state the rule formally as follows:

IRR Investment Rule: Take any investment opportunity where the IRR exceeds the opportunity cost of capital. Turn down any opportunity whose IRR is less than the opportunity cost of capital.

IRR RULE EXAMPLE

Like the NPV rule, the internal rate of return investment rule is applied to single, stand-alone projects within the firm. The IRR investment rule will give the correct answer (that is, the same answer as the NPV rule) in many—but not all—situations. For instance, it gives the correct answer for SFC's fertilizer opportunity. From Figure 6.1, whenever the cost of capital is below the IRR (14%), the project has a positive NPV and you should undertake the investment. In general, *the IRR rule works for a stand-alone project if all of the project's negative cash flows precede its positive cash flows.* But in other cases, the IRR rule may disagree with the NPV rule and thus be incorrect. Let's examine several situations in which the IRR fails.

UNCONVENTIONAL CASH FLOWS

John Star, the founder of SuperTech, the most successful company in the last 20 years, has just retired as CEO. A major publisher has offered him a $1 million "how I did it" book deal. That is, the publisher will pay him $1 million upfront if Star agrees to write a book about his experiences. He estimates that it will take him three years to write the book. The time that he spends writing will cause him to forgo alternative sources of income amounting to $500,000 per year. Considering the risk of his alternative income sources and available investment opportunities, Star estimates his opportunity cost of capital to be 10%. The timeline of Star's investment opportunity is:

0	1	2	3
$1,000,000	−$500,000	−$500,000	−$500,000

The NPV of Star's investment opportunity is

$$NPV = 1,000,000 - \frac{500,000}{1 + r} - \frac{500,000}{(1 + r)^2} - \frac{500,000}{(1 + r)^3}$$

By setting the NPV equal to zero and solving for r, we find the IRR. Using the annuity spreadsheet:

	NPER	RATE	PV	PMT	FV	Excel Formula
Given	3		1,000,000	−500,000	0	
Solve for I		23.38%				RATE(3, 500000, 1000000, 0)

The 23.38% IRR is larger than the 10% opportunity cost of capital. According to the IRR rule, Star should sign the deal. But what does the NPV rule say?

$$NPV = 1,000,000 - \frac{500,000}{1.1} - \frac{500,000}{1.1^2} - \frac{500,000}{1.1^3} = -\$243,426$$

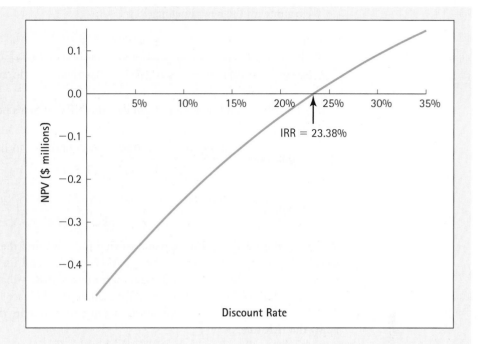

FIGURE 6.2

NPV of Star's $1 Million Book Deal

When the benefits of an investment occur before the costs, the NPV is an *increasing* function of the discount rate.

At a 10% discount rate, the NPV is negative, so signing the deal would reduce Star's wealth. He should not sign the book deal.

Figure 6.2 plots the NPV of the investment opportunity. It shows that, no matter what the cost of capital is, the IRR rule and the NPV rule will give exactly opposite recommendations. That is, the NPV is positive only when the opportunity cost of capital is *above* 23.38% (the IRR). In fact, Star should accept the investment only when the opportunity cost of capital is greater than the IRR, the opposite of what the IRR rule recommends.

Figure 6.2 illustrates the problem with using the IRR rule in this case. For most conventional investment opportunities, expenses occur initially and cash is received later. In this case, Star gets cash *upfront* and incurs the costs of producing the book *later*. It is as if Star borrowed money, and when you borrow money you prefer as *low* a rate as possible. Star's optimal rule is to borrow money so long as the rate at which he borrows is *less* than the cost of capital. Thus the normal IRR rule must be reversed for projects with **unconventional cash flows** (or borrowing-style cash flows): that is, with unconventional cash flows, projects should be accepted if their IRR is less than the cost of capital.

Even though the normal IRR rule fails to give the correct answer in this case, the IRR itself still provides useful information *in conjunction* with the NPV rule. As mentioned earlier, the IRR provides information on how sensitive the investment decision is to uncertainty in the cost of capital estimate. In this case. The difference between the cost of capital and the IRR is large—13.38%. Star would have to have underestimated the cost of capital by 13.38% to make the NPV positive.

MULTIPLE IRRS

Star has informed the publisher that it needs to sweeten the deal before he will accept it. In response, the publisher has agreed to make royalty payments. Star expects these payments to amount to $20,000 per year forever, starting once the book is published in three years. Should he accept or reject the new offer?

We begin with the new timeline:

Using the annuity and perpetuity formulas, the NPV of Star's new investment opportunity is

$$NPV = 1,000,000 - \frac{500,000}{1+r} - \frac{500,000}{(1+r)^2} - \frac{500,000}{(1+r)^3} + \frac{20,000}{(1+r)^4} + \frac{20,000}{(1+r)^5} + \cdots$$

$$= 1,000,000 - \frac{500,000}{r}\left(1 - \frac{1}{(1+r)^3}\right) + \frac{1}{(1+r)^3}\left(\frac{20,000}{r}\right)$$

By setting the NPV equal to zero and solving for r, we find the IRR. (Note, this is not solvable algebraically; we set up the equation in Excel and used the Solver Add-In to determine the results for r.) In this case, there are *two* IRRs—that is, there are two values of r that set the NPV equal to zero. You can verify this fact by substituting IRRs of 4.723% and 19.619% into the equation. Because there is more than one IRR, we cannot apply the IRR rule.

For guidance, let's turn to the NPV rule. Figure 6.3 plots the NPV of the opportunity. If the cost of capital is *either* below 4.723% or above 19.619%, Star should undertake the opportunity. Otherwise, he should turn it down. Notice that even though the IRR rule fails in this case, the two IRRs are still useful as bounds on the cost of capital. If the cost of capital estimate is wrong, and it is actually smaller than 4.723% or larger than 19.619%, the decision not to pursue the project will change. Because these bounds are far from the actual cost of capital of 10%, Star can have a high degree of confidence in his decision to reject the deal.

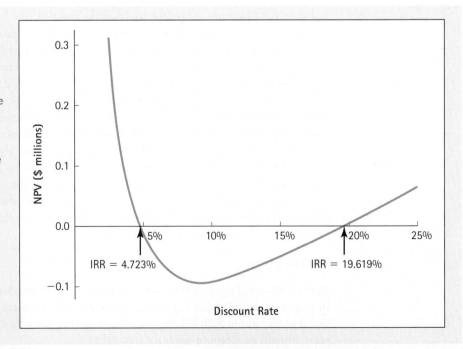

FIGURE 6.3

NPV of Star's Book Deal with Royalties

In this case, there is more than one IRR, invalidating the IRR rule. If the opportunity cost of capital is *either* below 4.723% or above 19.619%, Star should make the investment.

There is no easy fix for the IRR rule when there are multiple IRRs. Although the NPV is negative between the IRRs in this example, the reverse is also possible (see Problem 9). In this case, the project would have a positive NPV for discount rates between the IRRs rather than for discount rates lower or higher than the IRRs. Furthermore, there are situations in which more than two IRRs exist.[4] In such situations, our only choice is to rely on the NPV rule.

NONEXISTENT IRR

Luckily for John Star, he has other opportunities available to him. An agent has approached him and guaranteed $1 million in each of the next three years if he will agree to give four lectures per month over that period. Star estimates that preparing and delivering the lectures would take the same amount of time as writing the book—that is, the cost would be $500,000 per year. Therefore, his net cash flow will be $500,000 per year. What is the IRR of this opportunity? Here is the new timeline:

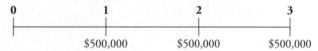

The NPV of Star's new investment opportunity is

$$NPV = \frac{500{,}000}{1 + r} + \frac{500{,}000}{(1 + r)^2} + \frac{500{,}000}{(1 + r)^3}$$

By setting the NPV equal to zero and solving for r, we find the IRR. In this case, however, there is *no* discount rate that will set the NPV equal to zero. As shown in Figure 6.4, the NPV of this opportunity is always positive, no matter what the cost of capital is. But do

FIGURE 6.4

NPV of Lecture Contract
No IRR exists because the NPV is positive for all values of the discount rate. Thus the IRR rule cannot be used.

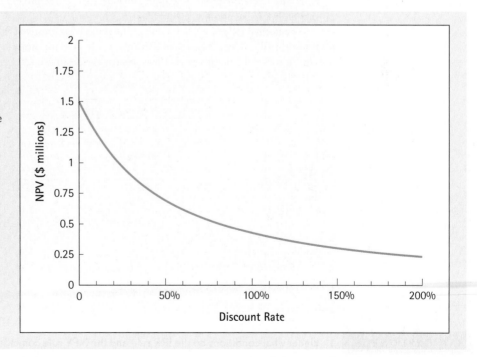

---

4. In general, there can be as many IRRs as the number of times the project's cash flows change sign over time.

not be fooled into thinking that whenever the IRR does not exist the NPV will always be positive. It is quite possible for no IRR to exist when the NPV is always negative (see Problem 11).

In such situations, we cannot use the IRR rule because it provides no recommendation at all. Thus, our only choice is to rely on the NPV rule.

EXAMPLE 6.1 PROBLEMS WITH THE IRR RULE

Problem
Consider projects with the following cash flows:

Project	0	1	2
A	−375	−300	900
B	−22,222	50,000	−28,000
C	400	400	−1,056
D	−4,300	10,000	−6,000

Which of these projects have an IRR close to 20%? For which of these projects is the IRR rule valid?

Solution
Let's plot the NPV profile for each project. From the NPV profiles, we can see that projects A, B, and C each have an IRR approximately 20%, while project D has no IRR. Note also that project C has another IRR of 5%.

The normal IRR rule is valid only if the project has positive NPV for every discount rate below the IRR. Thus, the normal IRR rule is only valid for project A. This project is the only one for which the negative cash flows precede the positive ones.

CONCEPT CHECK

1. Under what conditions do the IRR rule and the NPV rule coincide for a stand-alone project?

2. If the IRR rule and the NPV rule lead to different decisions for a stand-alone project, which should you follow? Why?

THE IRR VERSUS THE IRR RULE

The examples in this section illustrate the potential shortcomings of the IRR rule when choosing to accept or reject a stand-alone project. As we said at the outset, we can only avoid these problems if all of the negative cash flows of the project precede the positive cash flows. Otherwise, we cannot rely on the IRR rule. However, the IRR itself remains a very useful tool. The IRR measures the average return over the life of an investment and indicates the sensitivity of the NPV to estimation error in the cost of capital. Thus, knowing the IRR can be very useful, but relying on it to make investment decisions can be hazardous.

An erroneous reason for using the IRR rule is that you do not need to know the opportunity cost of capital to calculate the IRR. On a superficial level, this is true: The IRR does not depend on the cost of capital. However, you may not need to know the cost of capital to calculate the IRR, but you certainly need to know the cost of capital when you apply the IRR *rule*. Consequently, the opportunity cost is as important to the IRR rule as it is to the NPV rule. In our opinion, some firms use the IRR rule exclusively because the IRR sums up the attractiveness of investment opportunity in a single number without requiring the person running the numbers to make an assumption about the cost of capital. However, if a CFO wants a brief summary of an investment opportunity but does not want her employee to make a cost of capital assumption, she can also request a plot of the NPV as a function of the discount rate. Neither this request nor a request for the IRR requires knowing the cost of capital, but the NPV graph has the distinct advantage of being much more informative and reliable.

If you are employed by a firm that uses the IRR rule exclusively, our advice is to always calculate the NPV. If the two rules agree, you can feel comfortable reporting the IRR rule recommendation. If they do not agree, you should investigate why the IRR rule failed by using the concepts in this section. Once you have identified the problem, you can alert your superiors to it and perhaps persuade them to adopt the NPV rule.

6.3 THE PAYBACK RULE

The simplest investment rule is the **payback investment rule**, which is based on the notion that an opportunity that pays back its initial investment quickly is a good idea. To apply the payback rule, you first calculate the amount of time it takes to pay back the initial investment, called the **payback period**. If the payback period is less than a prespecified length of time—called the **cut-off period**—which is usually a few years, then you accept the project. Otherwise, you turn it down. For example, a firm might adopt any project with a payback period of less than two years.

APPLYING THE PAYBACK RULE

To illustrate the payback rule, we return to the Saskatchewan Fertilizer Corporation (SFC) example.

EXAMPLE 6.2   USING THE PAYBACK RULE

Problem

Assume SFC requires all projects to have a payback period of five years or less. Would the firm undertake the fertilizer project under this rule?

Solution

The sum of the cash flows from year 1 to year 5 is $35 \times 5 = \$175$ million, which will not cover the initial investment of $250 million. In fact, it will not be until year 8 that the initial investment will be paid back ($35 × 8 = $280 million). Because the payback period for this project is 8 years and exceeds the 5-year cut-off period, SFC will reject the project. (Note, if you assume the yearly cash flows are actually distributed evenly over the course of each year, then the payback period for the project will be $\frac{\$250 \text{ million}}{\$35 \text{ million}}$ = 7.1428 years. This assumption, though, would be inconsistent with how we were calculating the NPV (which assumed all cash flows were at the end of each year.)

As a result of the payback rule analysis in Example 6.2, SFC rejected the project. However, as we saw earlier, with a cost of capital of 10%, the NPV is $100 million. Following the payback rule would be a mistake because SFC would pass up a project worth $100 million.

PAYBACK RULE PITFALLS IN PRACTICE

The payback rule is not as reliable as the NPV rule because it (i) ignores the project's cost of capital and the time value of money, (ii) ignores cash flows after the payback period, and (iii) relies on an ad hoc decision criterion (what is the right number of years to require for the payback period?).[5] Despite this failing, both the Graham and Harvey study and the Jog and Srivastava study found that about 50% of the firms they surveyed reported using the payback rule for making decisions.

Why do some companies consider the payback rule? The answer probably relates to its simplicity. This rule is typically used for small investment decisions, for example, whether to purchase a new copy machine or to service the old one. In such cases, the cost of making an incorrect decision might not be large enough to justify the time required to calculate the NPV. The payback rule also provides budgeting information regarding the length of time capital will be committed to a project. Some firms are unwilling to commit capital to long-term investments without greater scrutiny. Also, if the required payback period is short (one or two years), then most projects that satisfy the payback rule will have a positive NPV. So firms might save effort by first applying the payback rule, and only if it fails take the time to compute NPV.

CONCEPT CHECK

1. Can the payback rule reject projects that have positive NPV? Can it accept projects that have negative NPV?

2. If the payback rule does not give the same answer as the NPV rule, which rule should you follow? Why?

6.4   CHOOSING BETWEEN PROJECTS

Thus far, we have considered only decisions where the choice is either to accept or to reject a single, stand-alone project. Sometimes, however, a firm must choose just one project from among several possible projects, that is, they are **mutually exclusive projects**. For example, a manager may be evaluating alternative package designs for a new product. When choosing any one project excludes us from taking the others, we are facing mutually exclusive projects.

---

5. Some companies address the first failing by computing the payback period using discounted cash flows (called discounted payback). Unfortunately, with discounted payback, the main benefit of payback—its simplicity—is lost.

NPV RULE AND MUTUALLY EXCLUSIVE PROJECTS

When projects are mutually exclusive, we need to determine which projects have positive NPV and then rank the projects to identify the best one. In this situation, the NPV rule provides a straightforward answer: *Pick the project with the highest NPV.* Because the NPV expresses the value of the project in terms of cash today, picking the project with the highest NPV leads to the greatest increase in wealth.

| EXAMPLE 6.3 | NPV AND MUTUALLY EXCLUSIVE PROJECTS |

Problem

A small commercial property is for sale near your university. Given its location, you believe a student-oriented business would be very successful there. You have researched several possibilities and come up with the following cash flow estimates (including the cost of purchasing the property). Which investment should you choose?

Project	Initial Investment	First Year Cash Flow	Growth Rate	Cost of Capital
Bookstore	$300,000	$63,000	3.0%	8%
Coffee Shop	$400,000	$80,000	3.0%	8%
Music Store	$400,000	$104,000	0.0%	8%
Electronics Store	$400,000	$100,000	3.0%	11%

Solution

Assuming each business lasts indefinitely, we can compute the present value of the cash flows from each as a constant growth perpetuity. The NPV of each project is

$$NPV \text{ (Bookstore)} = -300,000 + \frac{63,000}{8\% - 3\%} = \$960,000$$

$$NPV \text{ (Coffee Shop)} = -400,000 + \frac{80,000}{8\% - 3\%} = \$1,200,000$$

$$NPV \text{ (Music Store)} = -400,000 + \frac{104,000}{8\%} = \$900,000$$

$$NPV \text{ (Electronics Store)} = -400,000 + \frac{100,000}{11\% - 3\%} = \$850,000$$

Thus, all of the alternatives have positive NPV. But because we can only choose one, the coffee shop is the best alternative.

IRR RULE AND MUTUALLY EXCLUSIVE PROJECTS

Because the IRR is a measure of the expected return of investing in the project, you might be tempted to extend the IRR investment rule to the case of mutually exclusive projects by picking the project with the highest IRR. Unfortunately, picking one project over another simply because it has a larger IRR can lead to mistakes. In particular, *when projects differ in their scale of investment, the timing of their cash flows, or their riskiness, then their IRRs cannot be meaningfully compared.*

DIFFERENCES IN SCALE

Would you prefer a 500% return on $1, or a 20% return on $1 million? While a 500% return certainly sounds impressive, at the end of the day you will only make $5. The latter return sounds much more mundane, but you will make $200,000. This comparison illustrates an important shortcoming of IRR: Because it is a return, you cannot tell how much value will actually be created without knowing the scale of the investment.

If a project has a positive NPV, and if we can double its size, its NPV will double: By the Law of One Price, doubling the cash flows of an investment opportunity must make it worth twice as much. However, the IRR rule does not have this property—it is unaffected by the scale of the investment opportunity because the IRR measures the average return of the investment. Hence the IRR rule cannot be used to compare projects of different scales.

As an illustration of this situation, consider the investment in the bookstore versus the coffee shop in Example 6.3. We can compute the IRR of each as follows:

$$\text{Bookstore:} \quad -300{,}000 + \frac{63{,}000}{IRR - 3\%} = 0 \implies IRR = 24\%$$

$$\text{Coffee Shop:} \quad -400{,}000 + \frac{80{,}000}{IRR - 3\%} = 0 \implies IRR = 23\%$$

Both projects have IRRs that exceed their cost of capital of 8%. But although the coffee shop has a lower IRR, because it is on a larger scale of investment ($400,000 versus $300,000), it generates a higher NPV ($1.2 million versus $960,000) and thus is more valuable.

DIFFERENCES IN TIMING

Even when projects have the same scale, the IRR may lead you to rank them incorrectly due to difference in the timing of the cash flows: The IRR is expressed as a return, but the dollar value of earning a given return—and therefore its NPV—depends on how long the return is earned. Earning a very high annual return is much more valuable if you earn it for several years than if you earn it for only a few days.

As an example, consider the following short-term and long-term projects:

Both projects have an IRR of 50%, but one lasts for one year, while the other has a five-year horizon. If the cost of capital for both projects is 10%, the short-term project has an

NPV of $-100 + 150/1.10 = \$36.36$, whereas the long-term project has an NPV of $-100 + 759.375/1.10^5 = \$371.51$. Notice that despite having the same IRR, the long-term project is more than 10 times as valuable as the short-term project.

Even when projects have the same horizon, the pattern of cash flows over time will often differ. Consider again the coffee shop and music store investment alternatives in Example 6.3. Both of these investments have the same initial scale, and the same horizon (infinite). The IRR of the music store investment is

$$\text{Music Store:} \quad -400,000 + \frac{104,000}{IRR} = 0 \implies IRR = 26\%$$

But although the music store has a higher IRR than the coffee shop (26% versus 23%), it has a lower NPV ($900,000 versus $1.2 million). The reason the coffee shop has a higher NPV despite having a lower IRR is its higher growth rate. The coffee shop has lower initial cash flows but higher long-run cash flows than the music store. The fact that its cash flows are relatively delayed makes the coffee shop effectively a longer-term investment.

DIFFERENCES IN RISK

To know whether the IRR of a project is attractive, we must compare it to the project's cost of capital, which is determined by the project's risk. Thus, an IRR that is attractive for a safe project need not be attractive for a much riskier project. As a simple example, while you might be quite pleased to earn a 10% return on a risk-free investment opportunity, you might be much less satisfied to earn a 10% return on an investment in a risky start-up company.

Looking again at Example 6.3, consider the investment in the electronics store. The IRR of the electronics store is

$$\text{Electronics Store:} \quad -400,000 + \frac{100,000}{IRR - 3\%} = 0 \implies IRR = 28\%$$

This IRR is higher than those of all the other investment opportunities. Yet the electronics store has the lowest NPV. In this case, the investment in the electronics store is riskier, and its higher cost of capital means that despite having a higher IRR, its expected future cash flows are not sufficiently high to make the investment as attractive as the safer alternatives.

THE INCREMENTAL IRR RULE

When considering a pair of mutually exclusive projects, we can avoid comparing the IRRs directly by computing the **incremental IRR**, which is the IRR of the difference between the cash flows of the two alternatives (the *increment* to the cash flows of one investment over the other). The incremental IRR tells us the IRR associated with switching from one project to another. Then, instead of comparing the projects, we can evaluate the decision to switch as a stand-alone decision, and apply the IRR rule using the incremental IRR.

| EXAMPLE **6.4** | USING THE INCREMENTAL IRR TO COMPARE ALTERNATIVES |

Problem

Your firm is considering overhauling its production plant. The engineering team has come up with two proposals, one for a minor overhaul and one for a major overhaul. The two options have the following cash flows (in millions of dollars):

Proposal	0	1	2	3
Minor Overhaul	−10	6	6	6
Major Overhaul	−50	25	25	25

What is the IRR of each proposal? What is the incremental IRR? If the cost of capital for both of these projects is 12%, what should your firm do?

Solution

We can compute the IRR of the each proposal using the annuity calculator. For the minor overhaul, the IRR is 36.3%:

	NPER	RATE	PV	PMT	FV	Excel Formula
Given	3		−10	6	0	
Solve for Rate		36.3%				=RATE(3,6,−10,0)

For the major overhaul, the IRR is 23.4%:

	NPER	RATE	PV	PMT	FV	Excel Formula
Given	3		−50	25	0	
Solve for Rate		23.4%				=RATE(3,25,−50,0)

The IRR of both projects exceeds the cost of capital of 12%. Because the negative cash flows of each project precede the positive ones, we can apply the IRR rule to conclude that each project has positive NPV. But which project is best? Because the projects have different scales, we cannot compare their IRRs directly. To compute the incremental IRR of switching from the minor overhaul to the major overhaul, we first compute the incremental cash flows:

Proposal	0	1	2	3
Major Overhaul	−50	25	25	25
Less: Minor Overhaul	−10	6	6	6
Incremental Cash Flow	−40	19	19	19

These cash flows have an IRR of 20.0%:

	NPER	RATE	PV	PMT	FV	Excel Formula
Given	3		−40	19	0	
Solve for Rate		20.0%				=RATE(3,19,−40,0)

Because the incremental IRR exceeds the 12% cost of capital, switching to the major overhaul looks attractive (i.e., its larger scale is sufficient to make up for its lower IRR). We can check this result using Figure 6.5, which shows the NPV profiles for each project. At the 12% cost of capital, the NPV of the major overhaul does indeed exceed that of the minor overhaul, despite its lower IRR. Note also that the incremental IRR determines the crossover point of the NPV profiles, the discount rate for which the best project choice switches from the major overhaul to the minor one.

FIGURE 6.5

Comparison of Minor and Major Overhaul

Comparing the NPV profiles of the minor and major overhauls in Example 6.4, we can see that despite its lower IRR, the major overhaul has a higher NPV at the cost of capital of 12%. Note also that the incremental IRR of 20% determines the crossover point or discount rate at which the optimal decision changes.

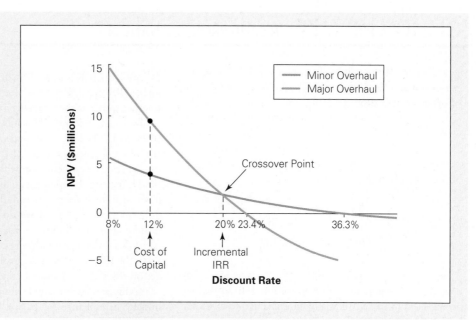

SHORTCOMINGS OF THE INCREMENTAL IRR RULE. Although the incremental IRR rule resolves some problems with mutually exclusive investments, it still uses the IRR rule on the incremental cash flows. As a result, it shares several problems with the regular IRR rule:

- You must keep track of which project is the incremental project and ensure that the incremental cash flows are initially negative and then become positive. Otherwise, the incremental IRR rule will have the unconventional cash flow problem and will give the wrong answer.

- The incremental IRR need not exist.

- Many incremental IRRs could exist. In fact, the likelihood of multiple IRRs is greater with the incremental IRR rule than with the regular IRR rule.

In addition to the regular problems possible with the IRR rule, two additional problems arise:

- When the incremental IRR rule indicates that one of the two projects is better, it does not imply that the better project should be accepted. It is possible that a bad project will look good when compared to a project that is even worse. The incremental IRR rule can show which is better, but, in fact, you would do best by avoiding both projects. This problem does not occur if you compare the NPVs of the two projects; if they are both negative, then reject both projects.

- The incremental IRR rule assumes that the riskiness of the two projects is the same. When the risks are different, the cost of capital of the incremental cash flows is not obvious, making it difficult to know whether the incremental IRR exceeds the cost of capital. In this case only the NPV rule, which allows each project to be discounted at its own cost of capital, will give a reliable answer.

In summary, although the incremental IRR rule can provide a reliable method for choosing among projects, it can be difficult to apply correctly. It is much simpler to use the NPV rule.

COMMON MISTAKE   IRR AND PROJECT FINANCING

Because the IRR is not itself a measure of value, it is easy to manipulate by restructuring the project's cash flows. In particular, it is easy to increase the IRR of a project by financing a portion of the initial investment. A common mistake in practice is to regard this higher IRR as an indication that the financing is attractive. For example, consider an investment in new equipment that will have the following cash flows:

This investment has an IRR of 30%. Now suppose that seller of the equipment offers to lend us $80, so that we only need to pay $20 initially. In exchange we must pay $100 in one year. By financing the project in this way, the cash flows become:

The project's IRR is now $(30/20) - 1 = 50\%$. Does this higher IRR mean that the project is now more attractive? In other words, is the financing a good deal?

The answer is no. Remember, we cannot compare IRRs, so a 50% IRR is not necessarily better than a 30% IRR. In this case, the project with financing is a much smaller scale investment than without financing. In addition, it may not be appropriate to mix the financing cash flows with the investment's cash flows as they are likely of different risks. Finally, if we do consider the leveraged cash flows, they will likely be riskier and need to be compared to a different opportunity cost of capital in order to apply the IRR rule. (We'll see explicitly the effect of leverage on risk in Parts 4 and 5 of the text.)

In this particular example, note that we borrowed $80 initially in exchange for paying $100 in one year. The IRR of this loan is $(100/80) - 1 = 25\%$ (this is also the incremental IRR of rejecting the financing). This rate is probably much higher than our firm's borrowing cost if it borrowed through other means. If so, including this financing with the project would be a mistake, despite the higher IRR.

WHEN CAN RETURNS BE COMPARED?

In this chapter we have highlighted the many pitfalls that arise when attempting to compare the IRRs of different projects. But there are many situations in which it is quite reasonable to compare returns. For example, if we were thinking of saving money in a savings account for the next year, we would likely compare the effective annual rates associated with different accounts and choose the highest option.

When is it reasonable to compare returns in this way? Remember, *we can only compare returns if the investments (i) have the same scale, (ii) have the same timing, and*

(iii) have the same risk. While one or more of these conditions are typically violated when we compare two investment projects, they are much more likely to be met when one of the investments is an investment in publicly traded securities or with a bank. When we invest with a bank or in traded securities, we can usually choose the scale of our investment, as well as our investment horizon, so that the opportunities match. In this case, as long as we are comparing opportunities with the same risk, comparing returns is meaningful. (Indeed, this condition was the basis for our definition of the cost of capital in Chapter 5.)

CONCEPT CHECK   1.   What is the incremental IRR rule and what are its shortcomings as a decision rule?

2.   For mutually exclusive projects, explain why picking one project over another because it has a larger IRR can lead to mistakes.

6.5   PROJECT SELECTION WITH RESOURCE CONSTRAINTS

In some situations, different investment opportunities demand different amounts of a particular resource. If there is a fixed supply of the resource so that you cannot undertake all possible opportunities, simply picking the highest NPV opportunity might not lead to the best decision.

EVALUATION OF PROJECTS WITH DIFFERENT RESOURCE REQUIREMENTS

Assume you are considering the three projects in Table 6.1, all of which require warehouse space. Table 6.1 shows the NPV of each project and the amount of available warehouse space that each project requires. Project A has the highest NPV but it uses up the entire resource (the warehouse); thus it would be a mistake to take this opportunity. Projects B and C can *both* be undertaken (together they use all the available space), and their combined NPV exceeds the NPV of project A; thus you should initiate them both. Together their NPV is $150 million, compared to just $100 million for project A alone.

PROFITABILITY INDEX

In this simple example, identifying the optimal combination of projects to undertake is straightforward. In actual situations replete with projects and resources, finding the optimal combination can be difficult. Practitioners often use the **profitability index** to identify the optimal combination of projects to undertake in such situations:

Profitability Index[6]

$$\text{Profitability Index (PI)} = \frac{\text{Value Created}}{\text{Resource Consumed}} = \frac{\text{NPV}}{\text{Resource Consumed}} \quad (6.1)$$

The profitability index measures the "bang for your buck," that is, the value created in terms of NPV per unit of resource consumed. After computing the profitability index, we can rank projects based on it. Starting with the project with the highest index, we move down the ranking, taking all projects until the resource is consumed. In Table 6.1, we

POSSIBLE PROJECTS REQUIRING WAREHOUSE SPACE

TABLE 6.1

Project	NPV ($ millions)	Fraction of Warehouse Required (%)	Profitability Index
A	100	100	1
B	75	60	1.25
C	75	40	1.875

---

6. Some people use alternative versions of the profitability index (e.g., PI = $PV_{\text{cash inflows}} \div PV_{\text{cash outflows}}$). This is useful if the constrained resource is the cash with which to invest. Our version of the profitability index is more general so it can be applied to any problem with a constrained resource.

have calculated the profitability index for each of the three projects. Note how the profitability index rule would select projects B and C.

EXAMPLE 6.5   PROFITABILITY INDEX WITH A HUMAN RESOURCE CONSTRAINT

Problem

Your division at Northern Networks, a large networking company, has put together a project proposal to develop a new home networking router. The expected NPV of the project is $17.7 million, and the project will require 50 software engineers. Northern Networks has a total of 190 engineers available, and the router project must compete with the following other projects for these engineers:

Project	NPV ($ millions)	Engineering Headcount
Router	17.7	50
Project A	22.7	47
Project B	8.1	44

Project	NPV ($ millions)	Engineering Headcount
Project C	14.0	40
Project D	11.5	61
Project E	20.6	58
Project F	12.9	32
Total	**107.5**	**332**

How should Northern Networks prioritize these projects?

Solution

The goal is to maximize the total NPV we can create with 190 employees (at most). We compute the profitability index for each project, using Engineering Headcount in the denominator, and then sort projects based on the index:

Project	NPV ($ millions)	Engineering Headcount (EHC)	Profitability Index (NPV per EHC)	Total EHC Required
Project A	22.7	47	0.483	47
Project F	12.9	32	0.403	79
Project E	20.6	58	0.355	137
Router	17.7	50	0.354	187
Project C	14.0	40	0.350	
Project D	11.5	61	0.189	
Project B	8.1	44	0.184	

We now assign the resource to the projects in descending order according to the profitability index. The final column shows the cumulative use of the resource as each project is taken on until the resource is used up. To maximize NPV within the constraint of 190 employees, Northern Networks should choose the first four projects on the list. The resource constraint forces Northern Networks to forgo three otherwise valuable projects.

POSSIBLE PROJECTS FOR $100 MILLION BUDGET

TABLE 6.2

Project	NPV ($ millions)	Initial Investment ($ millions)	Profitability Index NPV/Investment
I	110	100	1.1
II	70	50	1.4
III	60	50	1.2

CAPITAL RATIONING CONSTRAINTS

In some circumstances a firm may not be able to raise additional funds for investment or a manager may only be allocated a limited budget for making investments. When funds are limited, there is said to be a **capital rationing** constraint. Without the capital rationing, you would accept all positive NPV projects. When there is capital rationing, though, ranking projects by their profitability index is useful. Suppose you are considering the three projects shown in Table 6.2 but you have a budget of at most $100 million to invest. While Project I has the highest NPV, it uses up the entire budget. Projects II and III can both be undertaken (together they also take up the entire budget), and their combined NPV exceeds the NPV of Project I. Thus, with a budget of $100 million, the best choice is to take Projects II and III (the projects with the highest profitability indices) for a combined NPV of $130 million, compared to just $110 million for Project I alone.

SHORTCOMINGS OF THE PROFITABILITY INDEX

Although the profitability index is simple to compute and use, in some situations it does not give an accurate answer. For example, suppose in Example 6.5 that Northern Networks has an additional small project with an NPV of only $100,000 that requires 3 engineers. The profitability index in this case is $0.1/3 = 0.03$, so this project would appear at the bottom of the ranking. However, notice that 3 of the 190 employees are not being used after the first four projects are selected. As a result, it would make sense to take on this project even though it would be ranked last.

A more serious problem occurs when multiple resource constraints apply. In this case, the profitability index can break down completely. The only surefire way to find the best combination of projects is to search through all of them. Although this process may sound exceedingly time-consuming, linear and integer programming techniques have been developed specifically to tackle this kind of problem. By using these techniques on a computer, the solution can usually be obtained almost instantaneously (for references, see additional readings for this chapter in the Textbook Resources section on MyFinanceLab).

CONCEPT CHECK

1. Explain why picking the project with the highest NPV might not be optimal when you evaluate mutually exclusive projects with different resource requirements.

2. How can the profitability index be used to identify attractive projects when there are resource constraints?

SUMMARY

1. If your objective is to maximize wealth, the NPV rule always gives the correct answer.

2. The difference between the cost of capital and the IRR is the maximum amount of estimation error that can exist in the cost of capital estimate without altering the original decision.

3. IRR investment rule: Take any investment opportunity whose IRR exceeds the opportunity cost of capital. Turn down any opportunity whose IRR is less than the opportunity cost of capital.

4. The IRR rule may give the wrong answer if the project has unconventional cash flows (an upfront cash inflow followed by outflows—similar to a borrowing arrangement). When there are multiple IRRs or the IRR does not exist, the IRR rule cannot be used.

5. When choosing among mutually exclusive investment opportunities, pick the opportunity with the highest NPV. Do not compare individual projects' IRRs to choose among mutually exclusive investment opportunities.

6. Incremental IRR rule: Assume you are comparing two mutually exclusive opportunities, A and B, and the IRRs of both opportunities exceed the cost of capital. If you subtract the cash flows of opportunity B from the cash flows of opportunity A (and the result is a conventional set of cash flows: outflows followed by inflows), then you should take opportunity A if the incremental IRR exceeds the cost of capital. Otherwise, take opportunity B. The incremental IRR indicates the discount rate at which the optimal project choice changes.

7. We cannot use the IRR to compare investment opportunities unless the investments have the same scale, timing, and risk.

8. Payback investment rule: Calculate the amount of time it takes to pay back the initial investment (the payback period). If the payback period is less than a prespecified length of time (the cut-off period), then accept the project. Otherwise, turn it down.

9. The payback rule is simple, and favours short-term investments. But it is often incorrect.

10. When choosing among projects competing for the same resource, ranking the projects by their profitability indices and picking the set of projects with the highest profitability indices that can still be undertaken given the limited resource often produces the best result.

$$\text{Profitability Index (PI)} = \frac{\text{Value Created}}{\text{Resource Consumed}} = \frac{\text{NPV}}{\text{Resource Consumed}} \qquad (6.1)$$

11. The profitability index is only completely reliable if the set of projects taken following the profitability index ranking completely exhausts the available resource and there is only a single relevant resource constraint.

KEY TERMS

PROBLEMS

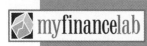

NPV and Stand-Alone Projects

1. Your brother wants to borrow $10,000 from you. He has offered to pay you back $12,000 in a year. If the cost of capital of this investment opportunity is 10%, what is its NPV? Should you undertake the investment opportunity? Calculate the IRR and use it to determine the maximum deviation allowable in the cost of capital estimate to leave the decision unchanged.

2. You are considering investing in a start-up company. The founder asked you for $200,000 today and you expect to get $1,000,000 in 9 years. Given the riskiness of the investment opportunity, your cost of capital is 20%. What is the NPV of the investment opportunity? Should you undertake the investment opportunity? Calculate the IRR and use it to determine the maximum deviation allowable in the cost of capital estimate to leave the decision unchanged.

3. You are considering opening a new plant. The plant will cost $100 million upfront and will take one year to build. After that, it is expected to produce profits of $30 million at the end of every year of production. The cash flows are expected to last forever. Calculate the NPV of this investment opportunity if your cost of capital is 8%. Should you make the investment? Calculate the IRR and use it to determine the maximum deviation allowable in the cost of capital estimate to leave the decision unchanged.

EXCEL
4. Your firm is considering the launch of a new product, the XJ5. The upfront development cost is $10 million, and you expect to earn a cash flow of $3 million per year for the next 5 years. Plot the NPV profile for this project for discount rates ranging from 0% to 30%. For what range of discount rates is the project attractive?

EXCEL
5. Bill Clinton reportedly was paid $10 million to write his book *My Life*. The book took three years to write. In the time he spent writing, Clinton could have been paid to make speeches. Given his popularity, assume that he could earn $8 million per year (paid at the end of the year) speaking instead of writing. Assume his cost of capital is 10% per year.

   a. What is the NPV of agreeing to write the book (ignoring any royalty payments)?

   b. Assume that, once the book is finished, it is expected to generate royalties of $5 million in the first year (paid at the end of the year) and these royalties are expected to decrease at a rate of 30% per year in perpetuity. What is the NPV of the book with the royalty payments?

EXCEL
*6. FastTrack Bikes Inc. is thinking of developing a new composite road bike. Development will take six years and the cost is $200,000 per year. Once in production, the bike is expected to make $300,000 per year for 10 years. Assume the cost of capital is 10%.

   a. Calculate the NPV of this investment opportunity. Should the company make the investment?

   b. Calculate the IRR and use it to determine the maximum deviation allowable in the cost of capital estimate to leave the decision unchanged.

   c. Calculate the NPV of this investment opportunity assuming the cost of capital is 14%. Should the company make the investment given this new assumption?

7. OpenSeas Inc. is evaluating the purchase of a new cruise ship. The ship would cost $500 million, and would operate for 20 years. OpenSeas expects annual cash flows from operating the ship to be $70 million (at the end of each year) and its cost of capital is 12%.

    a. Prepare an NPV profile of the purchase.

    b. Use Excel and Solver to determine the IRR.

    c. Is the purchase attractive based on these estimates?

    d. How far off could OpenSeas' cost of capital be before your purchase decision would change?

The Internal Rate of Return Rule

(*Note:* In most cases you will find it helpful to use Excel to compute the IRR.)

8. You are considering an investment in a clothes distributor. The company needs $100,000 today and expects to repay you $120,000 in a year from now. What is the IRR of this investment opportunity? Given the riskiness of the investment opportunity, your cost of capital is 20%. What does the IRR rule say about whether you should invest?

9. You have been offered a very long-term investment opportunity to increase your money 100-fold. You can invest $1000 today and expect to receive $100,000 in 40 years. Your cost of capital for this (very risky) opportunity is 25%. What does the IRR rule say about whether the investment should be undertaken? What about the NPV rule? Do they agree?

10. Does the IRR rule agree with the NPV rule in Problem 3? Explain.

EXCEL 11. How many IRRs are there in part a of Problem 5? Does the IRR rule give the right answer in this case? How many IRRs are there in part b of Problem 5? Does the IRR rule work in this case?

12. Professor Wendy Smith has been offered the following deal: A law firm would like to retain her for an upfront payment of $50,000. In return, for the next year the firm would have access to 8 hours of her time every month. Smith's rate is $550 per hour and her opportunity cost of capital is 15% (EAR). What does the IRR rule advise regarding this opportunity? What about the NPV rule?

13. Innovation Company is thinking about marketing a new software product. Upfront costs to market and develop the product are $5 million. The product is expected to generate profits of $1 million per year for 10 years; following that, the company will have to provide product support expected to cost $100,000 per year in perpetuity. Assume all profits and expenses occur at the end of the year.

    a. What is the NPV of this investment if the cost of capital is 6%? Should the firm undertake the project? Repeat the analysis for discount rates of 2% and 15%.

    b. How many IRRs does this investment opportunity have?

    EXCEL
    c. What does the IRR rule indicate about this investment? Explain.

EXCEL *14. You own a coal mining company and are considering opening a new mine. The mine itself will cost $120 million to open. If this money is spent immediately, the mine will generate $20 million for each of the next 10 years. After that, the coal will run out and the site must be cleaned and maintained at environmental standards. The cleaning and maintenance are expected to cost $2 million per year in perpetuity. What does the IRR rule say about whether you should accept this opportunity? If the cost of capital is 8%, what does the NPV rule say?

15. Your firm spends $500,000 per year in regular maintenance of its equipment. Due to the economic downturn, the firm considers forgoing these maintenance expenses for the next 3 years. If it does so, it expects it will need to spend $2 million in year 4 replacing failed equipment.

    a. What is the IRR of the decision to forgo maintenance of the equipment?

    b. Does the IRR rule work for this decision?

    c. For what costs of capital is forgoing maintenance a good decision?

EXCEL *16. You are considering investing in a new gold mine in South Africa. Gold in South Africa is buried very deep, so the mine will require an initial investment of $250 million. Once this investment is made, the mine is expected to produce revenues of $30 million per year for the next 20 years. It will cost $10 million per year to operate the mine. After 20 years, the gold will be depleted. The mine must then be stabilized on an ongoing basis, which will cost $5 million per year in perpetuity. Calculate the IRR of this investment. (*Hint:* Plot the NPV as a function of the discount rate to estimate the IRR or use Excel and Solver to get a precise IRR number.)

EXCEL *17. You are considering constructing a new plant to manufacture a new product. You anticipate that the plant will take a year to build and cost $100 million upfront. Once built, it will generate cash flows of $15 million at the end of every year over the life of the plant. The plant will wear out 20 years after its completion. At that point you expect to get $10 million in salvage value for the plant. Using a cost of capital of 12%, calculate the NPV. What is the IRR? Do the NPV and IRR rules agree in this case? Explain.

18. You work for a company that uses IRR exclusively. The reason is that the CEO does not like to read long memos. He is fond of saying, "I don't like two-handed economists!"[7] He likes to distil all decisions down to a single number like the IRR. Your boss has asked you to calculate the IRR of a project. He refuses to give you the cost of capital for the project, but you know that once you compute the IRR he will compare it to the cost of capital and use that information to make the investment decision. What should you do?

19. Your firm has been hired to develop new software for the university's class registration system. Under the contract, you will receive $500,000 as an upfront payment. You expect the development costs to be $450,000 per year for the next 3 years. Once the new system is in place, you will receive a final payment of $900,000 from the university 4 years from now.

   a. What are the IRRs of this opportunity?

   b. If your cost of capital is 10%, is the opportunity attractive?

   Suppose you are able to renegotiate the terms of the contract so that your final payment in year 4 will be $1 million.

   c. What is the IRR of the opportunity now?

   d. Is it attractive at these terms?

EXCEL 20. You are considering constructing a new plant in a remote wilderness area to process the ore from a planned mining operation. You anticipate that the plant will take a year to build and cost $100 million upfront. Once built, it will generate cash flows of $15 million at the end of every year over the life of the plant. The plant will be useless 20 years after its completion once the mine runs out of ore. At that point you expect to pay $200 million to shut the plant down and restore the area to its pristine state. Using a cost of capital of 12%,

   a. What is the NPV of the project?

   b. Is using the IRR rule reliable for this project? Explain.

   c. What are the IRR's of this project?

The Payback Rule

21. You are a real estate agent thinking of placing a sign advertising your services at a local bus stop. The sign will cost $5000 and will be posted for one year. You expect that it will generate additional revenue of $500 per month. What is the payback period?

---

7. Former U.S. President Harry Truman is purported to have complained that the problem with all economists is that they always have two hands. When asked to give advice, they always said, "On the one hand . . . but on the other hand . . ."

22. You are considering making a movie. The movie is expected to cost $10 million upfront and take a year to make. After that, it is expected to make $5 million in the year it is released and $2 million for the following four years. What is the payback period of this investment? If you require a payback cut-off period of two years, will you make the movie? Does the movie have positive NPV if the cost of capital is 10%?

Choosing Between Projects

23. You are deciding between two mutually exclusive investment opportunities. Both require the same initial investment of $10 million. Investment A will generate $2 million per year (starting at the end of the first year) in perpetuity. Investment B will generate $1.5 million at the end of the first year and its revenues will grow at 2% per year for every year after that.

    a. Which investment has the higher IRR?

    b. Which investment has the higher NPV when the cost of capital is 7%?

    c. In this case, when does picking the higher IRR give the correct answer as to which investment is the best opportunity?

 24. You have just started your summer internship, and your boss asks you to review a recent analysis that was done to compare three alternative proposals to enhance the firm's manufacturing facility. You find that the prior analysis ranked the proposals according to their IRR, and recommended the highest IRR option, Proposal A. You are concerned and decide to redo the analysis using NPV to determine whether this recommendation was appropriate. But while you are confident the IRRs were computed correctly, it seems that some of the underlying data regarding the cash flows that were estimated for each proposal was not included in the report. For Proposal B, you cannot find information regarding the total initial investment that was required in year 0. And for Proposal C, you cannot find the data regarding additional salvage value that will be recovered in year 3. Here is the information you have:

Proposal	IRR	Year 0	Year 1	Year 2	Year 3
A	60.0%	−100	30	153	88
B	55.0%	?	0	206	95
C	50.0%	−100	37	0	204 + ?

    a. Determine the two missing data amounts.

    b. Suppose the appropriate cost of capital for each alternative is 10%. Using this information, determine the NPV of each project. Which project should the firm choose?

    c. Why is ranking the projects by their IRR not valid in this situation?

25. Use the incremental IRR rule to correctly choose between the investments in Problem 23 when the cost of capital is 7%.

26. You work for an outdoor play structure manufacturing company and are trying to decide between two projects:

	Year-End Cash Flows ($ thousands)			
Project	0	1	2	IRR
Playhouse	−30	15	20	10.4%
Fort	−80	39	52	8.6%

You can undertake only one project. If your cost of capital is 8%, use the incremental IRR rule to make the correct decision.

 *27. Use the incremental IRR to determine the range of discount rates for which each project is optimal in Problem 24.

28. Consider two investment projects, which both require an upfront investment of $10 million, and which both pay a constant amount each year for the next 10 years. Under what conditions can you rank these projects by comparing their IRRs?

29. You are considering a safe investment opportunity that requires a $1000 investment today, and will pay $500 two years from now and another $750 five years from now.

    a. What is the IRR of this investment?

    b. If you are choosing between this investment and putting your money in a safe bank account that pays an EAR of 5% per year for the next 5 years, can you make the decision by simply comparing this EAR with the IRR of the investment? Explain.

30. AOL is considering two proposals to overhaul its network infrastructure. They have received two bids. The first bid, from Huawei, will require a $20 million upfront investment and will generate $20 million in savings for AOL each year for the next 3 years. The second bid, from Cisco, requires a $100 million upfront investment and will generate $60 million in savings each year for the next 3 years.

    a. What is the IRR for AOL associated with each bid?

    b. If the cost of capital for this investment is 12%, what is the NPV for AOL of each bid?

    Suppose Cisco modifies its bid by offering a lease contract instead. Under the terms of the lease, AOL will pay $20 million upfront, and $35 million per year for the next 3 years. AOL's savings will be the same as with Cisco's original bid.

    c. Including its savings, what are AOL's net cash flows under the lease contract? What is the IRR of the Cisco bid now?

    d. Is this new bid a better deal for AOL than Cisco's original bid? Explain.

Project Selection with Resource Constraints

31. Natasha's Flowers, a local florist, purchases fresh flowers each day at the local flower market. The buyer has a budget of $1000 per day to spend. Different flowers have different profit margins, and also a maximum amount the shop can sell. Based on past experience the shop has estimated the following NPV of purchasing each type:

	NPV per Bunch	Cost per Bunch	Max. Bunches
Roses	$3	$20	25
Lilies	$8	$30	10
Pansies	$4	$30	10
Orchids	$20	$80	5

What combination of flowers should the shop purchase each day?

32. You own a car dealership and are trying to decide how to configure the showroom floor. The floor has 2000 square feet of usable space. You have hired an analyst and asked her to estimate the NPV of putting a particular model on the floor and how much space each model requires:

Model	NPV	Space Requirement (sq. ft.)
MB345	$3,000	200
MC237	$5,000	250
MY456	$4,000	240
MG231	$1,000	150
MT347	$6,000	450
MF302	$4,000	200
MG201	$1,500	150

In addition, the showroom also requires office space. The analyst has estimated that office space generates an NPV of $14 per square foot. What models should be displayed on the floor and how many square feet should be devoted to office space?

33. Kaimalino Properties (KP) is evaluating six real estate investments. Management plans to buy the properties today and sell them five years from today. The following table summarizes the initial cost and the expected sale price for each property, as well as the appropriate discount rate based on the risk of each venture.

Project	Cost Today	Discount Rate	Expected Sale Price in Year 5
Mountain Ridge	$ 3,000,000	15%	$18,000,000
Ocean Park Estates	15,000,000	15%	75,500,000
Lakeview	9,000,000	15%	50,000,000
Seabreeze	6,000,000	8%	35,500,000
Green Hills	3,000,000	8%	10,000,000
West Ranch	9,000,000	8%	46,500,000

KP has a total capital budget of $18,000,000 to invest in properties.

a. What is the IRR of each investment?

b. What is the NPV of each investment?

c. Given its budget of $18,000,000, which properties should KP choose?

d. Explain why the profitably index method could not be used if KP's budget were $12,000,000 instead. Which properties should KP choose in this case?

*34. Orchid Biotech Company is evaluating several development projects for experimental drugs. Although the cash flows are difficult to forecast, the company has come up with the following estimates of the initial capital requirements and NPVs for the projects. Given a wide variety of staffing needs, the company has also estimated the number of research scientists required for each development project (all cost values are given in millions of dollars).

Project Number	Initial Capital	Number of Research Scientists	NPV
I	$10	2	$10.1
II	15	3	19.0
III	15	4	22.0
IV	20	5	25.0
V	30	10	60.2

a. Suppose that Orchid has a total capital budget of $60 million. How should it prioritize these projects?

b. Ignore the constraint in part a. Suppose that Orchid currently has 12 research scientists and does not anticipate being able to hire any more in the near future. How should Orchid prioritize these projects?

c. If instead Orchid had 15 research scientists available, explain why the profitability index ranking cannot be used to prioritize projects. Which projects should it choose now?

equipment and the relevant **CCA rate**, denoted as *d*, for the asset class. Assume this computer equipment falls under asset class 45 and has a CCA rate of $d = 45\%$. Canada Revenue Agency has a "**half-year rule**" that is meant to compensate for the fact that sometimes assets are bought at the beginning of the year and other times they are bought at the end of the year. CRA assumes assets qualify for half a year's worth of CCA in the first tax year. (The full cost is denoted as **CapEx**.) Thus, when an asset is purchased, one-half of its cost is added to the **undepreciated capital cost (UCC)** for the **asset pool** (the collection of assets) in the same class. We denote this addition to the UCC as UCC_1. Thus $UCC_1 = 0.5 \times CapEx$. For a particular asset, the incremental CCA deduction that can be claimed at the end of the tax year is equal to the incremental undepreciated capital cost associated with that asset multiplied by the CCA rate, *d*,

$$CCA_t = UCC_t \times d \tag{7.1}$$

where CCA_t is the incremental CCA deduction for an asset taken in tax year *t*; UCC_t is the incremental undepreciated capital cost for an asset in tax year *t* prior to the asset's CCA deduction in year *t*; *d* is the CCA rate that determines the proportion of UCC that can be claimed as a CCA deduction.

After a CCA deduction is claimed, the UCC is reduced for the next year. However, for the second tax year we must also remember to add in the other half of CapEx into the incremental UCC. In general, we can determine the incremental UCC for an asset as follows.

Year *t*	Incremental UCC Used for Calculating the CCA for Tax Year
$t = 1$	$UCC_1 = 0.5 \times CapEx$
$t \geq 2$	$UCC_t = CapEx \times \left(1 - \dfrac{d}{2}\right) \times (1 - d)^{t-2} \qquad (7.2)$

We assume the asset is purchased sometime during the first tax year so the first CCA deduction affects the end-of-year calculation of taxable income. The UCC calculation above is the undepreciated capital cost remaining in year *t* just before the CCA deduction of year *t*.

RIM's calculation of the CCA amounts for the first five years of the BlackBerry Presenter project are shown in the spreadsheet below. There will still be a positive UCC balance after the CCA deduction in year 5. This means that RIM can claim CCA deductions in future years too. In fact, because the CCA calculation always deducts a proportion of the UCC, UCC will never fall to zero (as long as the asset is not sold), so *CCA deductions can continue forever*. For now we will ignore the CCA deductions beyond year 5. In Section 7.2, we will address how to properly deal with all the CCA effects.

Deducting CCA amounts in the spreadsheet in Table 7.2 completes the forecast for the BlackBerry Presenter's earnings before interest and taxes (EBIT) shown in line 7 of the spreadsheet in Table 7.1. Since the capital expenditures do not show up as a cash outflow in the earnings calculation and the non-cash CCA deduction does, we can see why earnings are not an accurate representation of cash flows.

INTEREST EXPENSES. In Chapter 2, we saw that to compute a firm's net income, we must first deduct interest expenses from EBIT. When evaluating a capital budgeting decision like the BlackBerry Presenter project, however, we generally *do not include interest expenses*. Any incremental interest expenses will be related to the firm's decision regarding

TABLE 7.2	THE BLACKBERRY PRESENTER'S SCHEDULE OF CCA AND UCC FOR THE FIRST FIVE YEARS

Year	0	1	2	3	4	5
Capital Expenditure, CCA and UCC Forecasts ($000s)						
1 CapEx (half added into UCC$_1$, half added into UCC$_2$)	7,500	—	—	—	—	—
2 UCC$_t$	—	3,750	5,813	3,197	1,758	967
3 CCA$_t$ = UCC$_t$ × d	—	1,688	2,616	1,439	791	435
4 CCA rate, d	45%					

Notes: UCC$_1$ = 0.5 × CapEx

Ucc$_2$ = UCC$_1$ − CCA$_1$ + (0.5 × CapEx)

For the yellow cells, UCC$_t$ = UCC$_{t-1}$ − CCA$_{t-1}$.

Since CCA$_5$ < UCC$_5$, there will be a positive balance remaining for UCC$_6$.

how to finance the project. Here we wish to evaluate the project on its own, separate from the financing decision.[2] Thus we evaluate the BlackBerry Presenter project *as if* RIM will not use any debt to finance it (whether or not that is actually the case), and we postpone the consideration of alternative financing choices until Part 5 of this book. For this reason, we refer to the net income we compute in Table 7.1 as the **unlevered net income** of the project, to indicate that it does not include any interest expenses associated with leverage.

TAXES. The final expense we must account for is corporate taxes. The correct tax rate to use is the firm's **marginal corporate tax rate**, which is the tax rate it will pay on an *incremental* dollar of pre-tax income. In Table 7.1, we assume the marginal corporate tax rate for the BlackBerry Presenter project to be 40% each year. The incremental income tax expense is calculated in line 8 as

$$\text{Income Tax} = \text{EBIT} \times \tau_c \tag{7.3}$$

where τ_c is the firm's marginal corporate tax rate.

In year 1, the BlackBerry Presenter will contribute an additional $10.513 million to RIM EBIT, which will result in an additional $10.513 million × 40% = $4.205 million in corporate tax that RIM will owe. We deduct this amount to determine the BlackBerry Presenter's after-tax contribution to net income.

In year 0, however, the BlackBerry Presenter's EBIT is negative. Are taxes relevant in this case? Yes. The BlackBerry Presenter will reduce RIM's taxable income in year 0 by $15 million. As long as RIM earns taxable income elsewhere in year 0 against which it can offset the BlackBerry Presenter's losses, RIM will owe $15 million × 40% = $6 million *less* in taxes in year 0. The firm should credit this tax savings to the BlackBerry Presenter project. Similar credits apply in year 6 (and beyond), when the firm claims CCA deductions for the lab equipment.

---

2. This approach is motivated by the Separation Principle from Chapter 3: When securities are fairly priced, the net present value of a fixed set of cash flows is independent of how those cash flows are financed. Later in the text we will consider cases in which financing may influence the project's value, and we will extend our capital budgeting techniques accordingly in Chapter 18.

| EXAMPLE 7.1 | TAXING LOSSES FOR PROJECTS IN PROFITABLE COMPANIES |

Problem

Kellogg Company plans to launch a new line of high-fibre, zero-trans-fat breakfast pastries. The heavy advertising expenses associated with the new product launch will generate operating losses of $15 million next year for the product. Kellogg expects to earn pre-tax income of $460 million from operations other than the new pastries next year. If Kellogg pays a 40% tax rate on its pre-tax income, what will it owe in taxes next year without the new pastry product? What will it owe with the new pastries?

Solution

Without the new pastries, Kellogg will owe $460 million × 40% = $184 million in corporate taxes next year. With the new pastries, Kellogg's pre-tax income next year will be only $460 million − $15 million = $445 million, and it will owe $445 million × 40% = $178 million in tax. Thus, launching the new product reduces Kellogg's taxes next year by $184 million − $178 million = $6 million.

UNLEVERED NET INCOME CALCULATION. We can express the calculation in the spreadsheet of Table 7.1 as the following shorthand formula for unlevered net income:

$$\text{Unlevered Net Income} = \text{EBIT} \times (1 - \tau_c)$$

$$= (\text{Revenues} - \text{Costs} - \text{CCA}) \times (1 - \tau_c) \qquad (7.4)$$

That is, a project's unlevered net income is equal to its incremental revenues less costs and CCA, evaluated on an after-tax basis. *Note:* The EBIT calculated in Table 7.1 used CCA instead of accounting depreciation. When you see EBIT numbers in financial reports, they are normally based on accounting depreciation. If this is the case, then the EBIT in Eq. 7.4 must be replaced with (EBIT + Depreciation − CCA).

INDIRECT EFFECTS ON INCREMENTAL EARNINGS

When computing the incremental earnings of an investment decision, we should include *all* changes between the firm's earnings with the project versus without the project. Thus far, we have analyzed only the direct effects of the BlackBerry Presenter project. But the BlackBerry Presenter may have indirect consequences for other operations within RIM. Because these indirect effects will also affect RIM's earnings, we must include them in our analysis.

OPPORTUNITY COSTS. Many projects use a resource that the company already owns. Because the firm does not need to pay cash to acquire this resource for a new project, it is tempting to assume that the resource is available for free. However, in many cases the resource could provide value for the firm in another opportunity or project. The **opportunity cost** of using a resource is the value it could have provided in its best alternative use.[3] Because this value is lost when the resource is used by another project, we

---

3. In Chapter 5, we defined the opportunity cost of capital as the rate you could earn on an alternative investment with equivalent risk. We similarly define the opportunity cost of using an existing asset in a project as the cash flow generated by the next-best alternative use for the asset.

should include the opportunity cost as an incremental cost of the project. In the case of the BlackBerry Presenter project, space will be required for the new lab. Even though the lab will be housed in an existing facility, we must include the opportunity cost of not using the space in an alternative way.

| EXAMPLE 7.2 | THE OPPORTUNITY COST OF THE BLACKBERRY PRESENTER'S LAB SPACE |

Problem
Suppose the BlackBerry Presenter's lab will be housed in warehouse space that the company would have otherwise rented out for $200,000 per year during years 1–4. How does this opportunity cost affect the BlackBerry Presenter's incremental earnings?

Solution
In this case, the opportunity cost of the warehouse space is the forgone rent. This cost would reduce the BlackBerry Presenter's incremental earnings during years 1–4 by $200,000 × (1 − 40%) = $120,000.

PROJECT EXTERNALITIES. **Project externalities** are indirect effects of the project that may increase or decrease the profits of other business activities of the firm. For instance, in the Kellogg example in the chapter introduction, some purchasers of Kellogg's new Low-Sugar Frosted Flakes would otherwise have bought Kellogg's regular Frosted Flakes. When sales of a new product displace sales of an existing product, the situation is often referred to as **cannibalization**. Suppose that approximately 25% of the BlackBerry Presenter's sales come from customers who would have purchased an existing BlackBerry if the BlackBerry Presenter were not available. Because this reduction in sales of the existing BlackBerrys is a consequence of the decision to develop the BlackBerry Presenter, we must include it when calculating the BlackBerry Presenter incremental earnings.

The spreadsheet in Table 7.3 recalculates the BlackBerry Presenter's incremental earnings forecast including the opportunity cost of the lab space and the expected cannibalization of

THE BLACKBERRY PRESENTER'S INCREMENTAL EARNINGS FORECAST INCLUDING CANNIBALIZATION AND LOST RENT

TABLE 7.3

Year	0	1	2	3	4	5
Incremental Earnings Forecast ($000s)						
1 Sales	—	23,500	23,500	23,500	23,500	—
2 Cost of Goods Sold	—	(9,500)	(9,500)	(9,500)	(9,500)	—
3 **Gross Profit**	—	14,000	14,000	14,000	14,000	—
4 Selling, General, and Administrative	—	(3,000)	(3,000)	(3,000)	(3,000)	—
5 Research and Development	(15,000)	—	—	—	—	—
6 Capital Cost Allowance (CCA)	—	(1,688)	(2,616)	(1,439)	(791)	(435)
7 **EBIT**	(15,000)	9,313	8,384	9,561	10,209	(435)
8 Income Tax at 40%	6,000	(3,725)	(3,354)	(3,825)	(4,084)	174
9 **Unlevered Net Income**	(9,000)	5,588	5,031	5,737	6,125	(261)

the existing product. The opportunity cost of the lab space in Example 7.2 increases selling, general, and administrative expenses from $2.8 million to $3.0 million. For the cannibalization, suppose that the existing BlackBerry wholesales for $100 so the expected loss in sales is

$$25\% \times 100{,}000 \text{ units} \times \$100/\text{unit} = \$2.5 \text{ million}$$

Compared to Table 7.1, the sales forecast falls from $26 million to $23.5 million. In addition, suppose the cost of the existing BlackBerry is $60 per unit. Then the cost of goods sold is reduced by

$$25\% \times 100{,}000 \text{ units} \times (\$60 \text{ cost per unit}) = \$1.5 \text{ million}$$

Thus, because RIM will no longer need to produce as many of its existing BlackBerrys, the incremental cost of goods sold of the BlackBerry Presenter project drops from $11 million to $9.5 million. The BlackBerry Presenter's incremental gross profit therefore declines by $2.5 million − $1.5 million = $1 million once we account for this externality.

Thus, comparing the spreadsheets in Tables 7.1 and 7.3, our forecast for the BlackBerry Presenter's unlevered net income in years 1–4 declines due to the lost rent of the lab space and the lost sales of the existing BlackBerry. For example, year 1 unlevered net income has declined from $6.308 million to $5.588 million.

COMMON MISTAKE THE OPPORTUNITY COST OF AN IDLE ASSET

A common mistake is to conclude that if an asset is currently idle, its opportunity cost is zero. For example, the firm might have a warehouse that is currently empty or a machine that is not being used. Often, the asset may have been idled in anticipation of taking on the new project, and would have otherwise been put to use by the firm.

Even if the firm has no alternative use for the asset, the firm could choose to sell or rent the asset. The value obtained from the asset's alternative use, sale, or rental represents an opportunity cost that must be included as part of the incremental cash flows.

SUNK COSTS AND INCREMENTAL EARNINGS

A **sunk cost** is any unrecoverable cost for which the firm is already liable. Sunk costs have been or will be paid regardless of the decision whether or not to proceed with the project. Therefore, they are not incremental with respect to the current decision and should not be included in its analysis. For this reason, we did not include in our analysis the $300,000 already expended on the marketing and feasibility studies for the BlackBerry Presenter. Because this $300,000 has already been spent, it is a sunk cost. A good rule to remember is that *if our decision does not affect a cash flow, then the cash flow should not affect our decision.* Following are some common examples of sunk costs you may encounter.

FIXED OVERHEAD EXPENSES. **Overhead expenses** are associated with activities that are not directly attributable to a single business activity but instead affect many different areas of the corporation. These expenses are often allocated to the different business activities for accounting purposes. To the extent that these overhead costs are fixed and will be incurred in any case, they are not incremental to the project and should not be included. Only include as incremental expenses the *additional* overhead expenses that arise because of the decision to take on the project.

PAST RESEARCH AND DEVELOPMENT EXPENDITURES. When a firm has already devoted significant resources to develop a new product, there may be a tendency to continue investing in the product even if market conditions have changed and the product is unlikely to be viable. The rationale that is sometimes given is that if the product is abandoned, the money that has already been invested will be "wasted." In other cases, a decision is made to abandon a project because it cannot possibly be successful enough to recoup the investment that has already been made. In fact, neither argument is correct: Any money that has already been spent is a sunk cost and therefore irrelevant. The decision to continue or abandon should be based only on the incremental costs and benefits of the product going forward.

REAL-WORLD COMPLEXITIES

We have simplified the BlackBerry Presenter example in an effort to focus on the types of effects that financial managers consider when estimating a project's incremental earnings. For a real project, however, the estimates of these revenues and costs are likely to be much more complicated. For instance, our assumption that the same number of the BlackBerry Presenter units will be sold each year is probably unrealistic. A new product typically has lower sales initially, as customers gradually become aware of the product. Sales will then accelerate, plateau, and ultimately decline as the product nears obsolescence or faces increased competition.

Similarly, the average selling price of a product and its cost of production will generally change over time. Prices and costs tend to rise with the general level of inflation in the economy. The prices of technology products, however, often fall over time as newer, superior technologies emerge and production costs decline. For most industries, competition tends to reduce profit margins over time. These factors should be considered when estimating a project's revenues and costs.

THE SUNK COST FALLACY

Sunk cost fallacy is a term used to describe the tendency of people to be influenced by sunk costs and to "throw good money after bad." That is, people sometimes continue to invest in a project that has a negative NPV because they have already invested a large amount in the project and feel that by not continuing it, the prior investment will be wasted. The sunk cost fallacy is also sometimes called the "Concorde effect," a term that refers to the British and French governments' decision to continue funding the joint development of the Concorde aircraft even after it was clear that sales of the plane would fall far short of what was necessary to justify its continued development. Although the project was viewed by the British government as a commercial and financial disaster, the political implications of halting the project—and thereby publicly admitting that all past expenses on the project would result in nothing—ultimately prevented either government from abandoning the project.

| EXAMPLE 7.3 | PRODUCT ADOPTION AND PRICE CHANGES |

Problem

Suppose sales of the BlackBerry Presenter were expected to be 100,000 units in year 1, 125,000 units in years 2 and 3, and 50,000 units in year 4. Suppose also that the BlackBerry Presenter's sale price and manufacturing cost are expected to decline by 10% per year, as with other wireless products. By contrast, selling, general, and administrative expenses are expected to rise with inflation by 4% per year. Update the incremental earnings forecast in the spreadsheet in Table 7.3 to account for these effects.

Solution

The BlackBerry Presenter's incremental earnings with these new assumptions are shown in the spreadsheet below:

Year	0	1	2	3	4	5
Incremental Earnings Forecast ($000s)						
1 Sales	—	23,500	26,438	23,794	8,566	—
2 Cost of Goods Sold	—	(9,500)	(10,688)	(9,619)	(3,463)	—
3 Gross Profit	—	14,000	15,750	14,175	5,103	—
4 Selling, General, and Administrative	—	(3,000)	(3,120)	(3,245)	(3,375)	—
5 Research and Development	(15,000)	—	—	—	—	—
6 Capital Cost Allowance (CCA)	—	(1,688)	(2,616)	(1,439)	(791)	(435)
7 EBIT	(15,000)	9,313	10,014	9,492	937	(435)
8 Income Tax at 40%	6,000	(3,725)	(4,006)	(3,797)	(375)	174
9 Unlevered Net Income	(9,000)	5,588	6,009	5,695	562	(261)

For example, sale prices in year — will be $260 × 0.90 = $234 per unit for the BlackBerry Presenter, and $100 × 0.90 = $90 per unit for the cannibalized product. Thus incremental sales in year — are equal to 125,000 units × ($234 per unit) − 31,250 cannibalized units × ($90 per unit) = $26.438 million.

| CONCEPT CHECK | 1. Should we include sunk costs in the cash flows of a project? Why or why not? |

2. Explain why you must include the opportunity cost of using a resource as an incremental cost of a project.

3. How do we forecast unlevered net income?

7.2 DETERMINING FREE CASH FLOW AND NPV

As discussed in Chapter 2, earnings are an accounting measure of the firm's performance. They do not represent real profits: The firm cannot use its earnings to buy goods, pay employees, fund new investments, or pay dividends to shareholders. To do those things, a firm needs cash. Thus, to evaluate a capital budgeting decision, we must determine its consequences for the firm's available cash. The incremental effect of a project on the firm's available cash is the project's **free cash flow**.

In this section, we forecast the free cash flow of the BlackBerry Presenter project using the earnings forecasts we developed in Section 7.1. We then use this forecast to calculate the NPV of the project.

CALCULATING THE FREE CASH FLOW FROM EARNINGS

As discussed in Chapter 2, there are important differences between earnings and cash flow. Earnings include non-cash charges, such as CCA (or depreciation for financial reporting purposes), but do not include the cost of capital investment (the capital expenditures). To determine the BlackBerry Presenter's free cash flow from its incremental earnings, we must adjust for these differences.

CAPITAL EXPENDITURES AND CAPITAL COST ALLOWANCE. Capital cost allowance, CCA, is not a cash expense that is paid by the firm. Rather, it is a method used for tax purposes to allocate the original purchase cost of the asset. Capital expenditures should include both the cost of the asset plus any other costs needed to get the asset up and running. Expenses such as transportation, installation, and set-up charges all form part of this cost. Under the CCA method, this capital expenditure cost is only depreciable once the asset has been put into use by the business. Because CCA is not a cash flow, we do not include it in the cash flow forecast. Instead, we include the actual cash cost of the asset when it is purchased.

To compute the BlackBerry Presenter's free cash flow, we must add back to earnings the CCA deduction for the lab equipment (a non-cash charge) and subtract the actual capital expenditure of $7.5 million that will be paid for the equipment in year 0. We show these adjustments in lines 10 and 11 of the spreadsheet in Table 7.4 (which is based on the incremental earnings forecast of Table 7.3).

NET WORKING CAPITAL (NWC). We defined net working capital in Chapter 2 as the difference between current assets and current liabilities. The main components of net working capital are cash, inventory, receivables, and payables:

$$\text{Net Working Capital} = \text{Current Assets} - \text{Current Liabilities}$$

$$= \text{Cash} + \text{Inventory} + \text{Receivables} - \text{Payables} \quad (7.5)$$

CALCULATION OF THE BLACKBERRY PRESENTER'S FREE CASH FLOW (INCLUDING CANNIBALIZATION AND LOST RENT)

TABLE 7.4

	Year	0	1	2	3	4	5
Incremental Earnings Forecast ($000s)							
1	Sales	–	23,500	23,500	23,500	23,500	–
2	Cost of Goods Sold	–	(9,500)	(9,500)	(9,500)	(9,500)	–
3	**Gross Profit**	–	14,000	14,000	14,000	14,000	–
4	Selling, General, and Administrative	–	(3,000)	(3,000)	(3,000)	(3,000)	–
5	Research and Development	(15,000)	–	–	–	–	–
6	Capital Cost Allowance (CCA)	–	(1,688)	(2,616)	(1,439)	(791)	(435)
7	**EBIT**	(15,000)	9,313	8,384	9,561	10,209	(435)
8	Income Tax at 40%	6,000	(3,725)	(3,354)	(3,825)	(4,084)	174
9	**Unlevered Net Income**	(9,000)	5,588	5,031	5,737	6,125	(261)
Free Cash Flow ($000s)							
10	Plus: CCA	–	1,688	2,616	1,439	791	435
11	Less: Capital Expenditures	(7,500)					
12	Less: Increases in NWC	–	(2,100)	–	–	–	2,100
13	**Free Cash Flow**	(16,500)	5,175	7,646	7,175	6,916	2,274

THE BLACKBERRY PRESENTER'S NET WORKING CAPITAL REQUIREMENTS

TABLE 7.5

Year	0	1	2	3	4	5
Net Working Capital Forecast ($000s)						
1 Cash Requirements	—	—	—	—	—	—
2 Inventory	—	—	—	—	—	—
3 Receivables (15% of Sales)	—	3,525	3,525	3,525	3,525	—
4 Payables (15% of COGS)	—	(1,425)	(1,425)	(1,425)	(1,425)	—
5 Net Working Capital	—	2,100	2,100	2,100	2,100	—

Most projects will require the firm to invest in net working capital. Firms may need to maintain a minimum cash balance[4] to meet unexpected expenditures, and inventories of raw materials and finished product to accommodate production uncertainties and demand fluctuations. Also, customers may not pay for the goods they purchase immediately. While sales are immediately counted as part of earnings, the firm does not receive any cash until the customers actually pay. In the interim, the firm includes the amount that customers owe in its receivables. Thus the firm's receivables measure the total credit that the firm has extended to its customers. In the same way, payables measure the credit the firm has received from its suppliers. The difference between receivables and payables is the net amount of the firm's capital that is consumed as a result of these credit transactions, known as **trade credit**.

Suppose that the BlackBerry Presenter will have no incremental cash or inventory requirements (products will be shipped directly from the contract manufacturer to customers). However, receivables related to the BlackBerry Presenter are expected to account for 15% of annual sales, and payables are expected to be 15% of the annual cost of goods sold (COGS).[5] The BlackBerry Presenter's net working capital requirements are shown in Table 7.5.

Table 7.5 shows that the BlackBerry Presenter project will require no net working capital in year 0, $2.1 million in net working capital in years 1–4, and no net working capital in year 5. How does this requirement affect the project's free cash flow? Any increases in net working capital represent an investment that reduces the cash available to the firm and so reduces free cash flow. We define the increase in net working capital in year t as

$$\Delta NWC_t = NWC_t - NWC_{t-1} \qquad (7.6)$$

We can use our forecast of the BlackBerry Presenter's net working capital requirements to complete our estimate of the BlackBerry Presenter's free cash flow in Table 7.4. In year 1, net working capital increases by $2.1 million. This increase represents a cost to the firm as shown in line 12 of the spreadsheet in Table 7.4. This reduction of free cash flow corresponds to the fact that $3.525 million of the firm's sales in year 1, and $1.425 million of its costs, have not yet been paid.

In years 2–4, net working capital does not change, so no further contributions are needed. In year 5, when the project is shut down, net working capital falls by $2.1 million as the

4. The cash included in net working capital is cash that is *not* invested to earn a market rate of return. It includes non-invested cash such as that held in the firm's chequing account, in a company safe or cash box, in cash registers (for retail stores), and other sites. This is cash that is required to be kept on hand in order to run the business.

5. If customers take N days to pay on average, then accounts receivable will consist of those sales that occurred in the last N days. If sales are evenly distributed throughout the year, receivables will equal $(N/365)$ times annual sales. Thus, receivables equal to 15% of sales corresponds to an average payment period of $N = 15\% \times 365 = 55$ days. The same is true for payables. (See also Eq. 2.9 in Chapter 2.)

payments of the last customers are received and the final bills are paid. We add this $2.1 million to free cash flow in year 5, as shown in line 12 of the spreadsheet in Table 7.4.

Now that we have adjusted the BlackBerry Presenter's unlevered net income for CCA, capital expenditures, and increases to net working capital, we compute the BlackBerry Presenter's free cash flow as shown in line 13 of the spreadsheet in Table 7.4. Note that in years 0 and 1, free cash flow is lower than unlevered net income, reflecting the upfront investment in equipment and net working capital required by the project. In later years, free cash flow exceeds unlevered net income because CCA is not a cash expense. In the last year, the firm ultimately recovers the investment in net working capital, further boosting the free cash flow.

EXAMPLE 7.4	NET WORKING CAPITAL WITH CHANGING SALES

Problem

Forecast the required investment in net working capital for the BlackBerry Presenter under the scenario in Example 7.3.

Solution

Required investments in net working capital are shown below:

	Year	0	1	2	3	4	5
Net Working Capital Forecast ($000s)							
1 Receivables (15% of Sales)		—	3,525	3,966	3,569	1,285	—
2 Payables (15% of COGS)		—	(1,425)	(1,603)	(1,443)	(519)	—
3 **Net Working Capital**		—	2,100	2,363	2,126	766	—
4 Increases in NWC		—	2,100	263	(237)	(1,360)	(766)

In this case, working capital changes each year. A large initial investment in working capital is required in year 1, followed by a small investment in year 2 as sales continue to grow. Working capital is recovered in years 3–5 as sales decline.

CALCULATING FREE CASH FLOW DIRECTLY

As we noted at the outset of this chapter, because practitioners usually begin the capital budgeting process by first forecasting earnings, we have chosen to do the same. However, we could have calculated the BlackBerry Presenter's free cash flow directly by using the following shorthand formula:

Free Cash Flow

$$\text{Free Cash Flow} = \overbrace{(\text{Revenues} - \text{Costs} - \text{CCA}) \times (1 - \tau_c)}^{\text{Unlevered Net Income}}$$
$$+ \text{CCA} - \text{CapEx} - \Delta NWC \tag{7.7}$$

Note that we first deduct CCA when computing the project's incremental earnings, and then add it back (because it is a non-cash expense) when computing free cash flow. Thus the only effect of CCA is to reduce the firm's taxable income. Indeed, we can rewrite Eq. 7.7 as

$$\text{Free Cash Flow} = (\text{Revenues} - \text{Costs}) \times (1 - \tau_c) - \text{CapEx} - \Delta NWC$$
$$+ \tau_c \times \text{CCA} \tag{7.8}$$

The last term in Eq. 7.8, $\tau_c \times$ CCA is called the **CCA tax shield**. It is the tax savings that results from the ability to deduct CCA from taxable income. As a consequence, CCA deductions have a *positive* impact on free cash flow. As stated earlier, firms often report a different depreciation deduction for accounting purposes and use CCA for tax purposes. Because only the tax consequences of CCA are relevant for free cash flow, we should use the CCA deduction that the firm will use for tax purposes in our forecast.

CALCULATING THE NPV

To compute the BlackBerry Presenter's NPV, we must discount its free cash flow at the appropriate cost of capital.[6] As discussed in Chapter 5, the cost of capital for a project is the expected return that investors could earn on their best alternative investment with similar risk and maturity. We will develop the techniques needed to estimate the cost of capital in Part 5 of the text, when we discuss capital structure. For now, we assume that RIM's managers believe that the BlackBerry Presenter project will have similar risk to other projects within RIM, and that the appropriate cost of capital for these projects is 12%.

Given this cost of capital, we compute the present value of each of the expected free cash flows. As explained in Chapter 4, if the cost of capital $r = 12\%$, the present value of the free cash flow in year t (or FCF_t) is

$$PV(FCF_t) = \frac{FCF_t}{(1 + r)^t} = FCF_t \times \underbrace{\frac{1}{(1 + r)^t}}_{t\text{–year discount factor}} \tag{7.9}$$

We compute the NPV of the BlackBerry Presenter project in Table 7.6. Line 3 calculates the discount factor, and line 4 multiplies the free cash flow by the discount factor to get the present value. The NPV of the project is the sum of the present values of each free cash flow, reported on line 5:

$$NPV = -16{,}500 + 4621 + 6096 + 5107 + 4396 + 1290$$
$$= 5009$$

We can also compute the NPV using the Excel NPV function to calculate the present value of the cash flows in year 1 through 5, and then add the cash flow in year 0 (i.e., "$=NPV(r, FCF_1:FCF_5) + FCF_0$").

Based on our estimates, the BlackBerry Presenter's NPV is $5.009 million. While the BlackBerry Presenter's upfront cost is $16.5 million, the present value of the additional free cash flow that RIM will receive from the project is $21.509 million. Thus, taking the BlackBerry Presenter project is equivalent to RIM having an extra $5.009 million in the bank today.

COMPUTING THE BLACKBERRY PRESENTER'S NPV

TABLE 7.6

Year		0	1	2	3	4	5
Net Present Value ($000s)							
1 Free Cash Flow		(16,500)	5,175	7,646	7,175	6,916	2,274
2 Project Cost of Capital	12%						
3 Discount Factor		1.0000	0.8929	0.7972	0.7118	0.6355	0.5674
4 PV of Free Cash Flow		(16,500)	4,621	6,096	5,107	4,396	1,290
5 NPV		5,009					

---

6. Rather than draw a separate timeline for these cash flows, we can interpret the final line of the spreadsheet in Table 7.4 as the timeline.

1. What adjustments must you make to a project's unlevered net income to determine its free cash flows?

2. What is the CCA tax shield?

7.3 CHOOSING AMONG ALTERNATIVES

Thus far, we have considered the capital budgeting decision to launch the BlackBerry Presenter product line. To analyze the decision, we computed the project's free cash flow and calculated the NPV. Because *not* launching the BlackBerry Presenter produces an additional NPV of zero for the firm, launching the BlackBerry Presenter is the best decision for the firm if its NPV is positive. In many situations, however, we must compare mutually exclusive alternatives, each of which has consequences for the firm's cash flows. As we explained in Chapter 6, in such cases we can make the best decision by first computing the free cash flow associated with each alternative and then choosing the alternative with the highest NPV.

EVALUATING MANUFACTURING ALTERNATIVES. Suppose RIM is considering an alternative manufacturing plan for the BlackBerry Presenter product. The current plan is to fully outsource production at a cost of $110 per unit. Alternatively, RIM could assemble the product in-house at a cost of $95 per unit. However, the latter option will require $5 million in upfront operating expenses to reorganize the assembly facility, and RIM will need to maintain inventory equal to one month's production.

To choose between these two alternatives, we compute the free cash flow associated with each choice and compare their NPVs to see which is most advantageous for the firm. When comparing alternatives, we need to compare only those cash flows that differ between them. We can ignore any cash flows that are the same under either scenario (e.g., the BlackBerry Presenter's revenues).

Table 7.7 compares the two assembly options, computing the NPV of the cash costs for each. The difference in EBIT results from the upfront cost of setting up the in-house

NPV COST OF OUTSOURCED VERSUS IN-HOUSE ASSEMBLY OF THE BLACKBERRY PRESENTER

TABLE 7.7

Year	0	1	2	3	4	5
Outsourced Assembly ($000s)						
1 EBIT	—	(11,000)	(11,000)	(11,000)	(11,000)	—
2 Income Tax at 40%	—	4,400	4,400	4,400	4,400	—
3 Unlevered Net Income	—	(6,600)	(6,600)	(6,600)	(6,600)	—
4 Less: Increases in NWC	—	1,650	—	—	—	(1,650)
5 Free Cash Flow	—	(4,950)	(6,600)	(6,600)	(6,600)	(1,650)
6 NPV at 12%	(19,510)					

Year	0	1	2	3	4	5
In-House Assembly ($000s)						
7 EBIT	(5,000)	(9,500)	(9,500)	(9,500)	(9,500)	—
8 Income Tax at 40%	2,000	3,800	3,800	3,800	3,800	—
9 Unlevered Net Income	(3,000)	(5,700)	(5,700)	(5,700)	(5,700)	—
10 Less: Increases in NWC	—	633	—	—	—	(633)
11 Free Cash Flow	(3,000)	(5,067)	(5,700)	(5,700)	(5,700)	(633)
12 NPV at 12%	(20,107)					

facility in year 0, and the differing assembly costs: $110/unit $\times$ 100,000 units/yr = $11 million/yr outsourced, versus $95/unit $\times$ 100,000 units/yr = $9.5 million/yr in-house. Adjusting for taxes, we see the consequences for unlevered net income on lines 3 and 9.

Because the options do not differ in terms of capital expenditures (there is none associated with assembly), to compare the free cash flow for each, we only need to adjust for their different net working capital requirements. If assembly is outsourced, payables account for 15% of the cost of goods, or 15% $\times$ $11 million = $1.65 million. This amount is the credit RIM will receive from its supplier in year 1 and will maintain until year 5. Because RIM will borrow this amount from its supplier, net working capital *falls* by $1.65 million in year 1, adding to RIM's free cash flow. In year 5, RIM's net working capital will increase as RIM pays its suppliers, and free cash flow will fall by an equal amount.

If assembly is done in-house, payables are 15% $\times$ $9.5 million = $1.425 million. However, RIM will need to maintain inventory equal to one month's production, which has a cost of $9.5 million $\div$ 12 = $0.792 million. Thus RIM's net working capital will decrease by $1.425 million − $0.792 million = $0.633 million in year 1 and will increase by the same amount in year 5.

COMPARING FREE CASH FLOWS FOR RIM'S ALTERNATIVES. Adjusting for increases to net working capital, we compare the free cash flow of each alternative on lines 5 and 11 and compute their NPVs using the project's 12% cost of capital.[7] In each case, the NPV is negative, as we are evaluating only the costs of production. Outsourcing, however, is somewhat cheaper, with a present value cost of −$19.5 million versus −$20.1 million if the units are produced in-house.[8]

CONCEPT CHECK   1. How do you choose between mutually exclusive capital budgeting projects?

2. When choosing between alternatives, what cash flows can be ignored?

7.4 FURTHER ADJUSTMENTS TO FREE CASH FLOW

In this section, we consider a number of complications that can arise when estimating a project's free cash flow, such as non-cash items, timing of cash flows, alternative assumptions about CCA deductions and tax shields, liquidation and salvage values, and tax loss carryforwards.

OTHER NON-CASH ITEMS. In general, other non-cash items that appear as part of incremental earnings should not be included in the project's free cash flow. The firm should

---

7. The risks of these options could potentially differ from the risk of the project overall and from the risks of each other, requiring a different cost of capital for each case. We ignore any such differences here.

8. It is also possible to compare these two cases in a single spreadsheet where we compute the difference in the free cash flows directly, rather than compute the free cash flows separately for each option. We prefer to do them separately, as it is clearer and generalizes to the case when there are more than two options.

include only actual cash revenues or expenses. For example, the firm adds back any amortization of intangible assets (such as patents) to unlevered net income when calculating free cash flow.

TIMING OF CASH FLOWS. For simplicity, we have treated the cash flows for the Black-Berry Presenter as if they occur at annual intervals. In reality, cash flows will be spread throughout the year. We can forecast free cash flow on a quarterly, monthly, or even continuous basis when greater accuracy is required.

PERPETUAL CCA TAX SHIELDS. The free cash flows we estimated over the five years of the project will miss the value of CCA tax shields that occur after the project has ended. If an asset is not sold, it will generate CCA deductions and the resulting tax shields every year into perpetuity. Since the CCA deducted each year is a proportion of the UCC, UCC never falls to zero. In Table 7.2 we have the CCA deductions for the first five years. You may not see an obvious pattern in the CCA deductions, but there is one and it relates to the way the Canada Revenue Agency requires CCA to be calculated. Recall that one-half of CapEx is added into the UCC initially and the second half of CapEx is added into the UCC in the second year. In effect, one-half of the CapEx starts having CCA applied initially and the other half of the CapEx starts having CCA applied in the second year. Table 7.8 shows the CCA calculation using the formula $CCA_t = UCC_t \times d$ where the CapEx amount is split across two years.

Line 7 of the spreadsheet in Table 7.8 shows the sum of the CCAs calculated from line 3 and line 6. If you compare the CCAs in line 7 to those shown in Table 7.2 you will see that they are the same. Why is this useful? Because it will help us calculate the present value of the CCA tax shields including those that continue on perpetually.

Recall that each year we can determine the CCA tax shield as $\tau_c \times CCA$. The CCA tax shields in Table 7.9 are calculated from the two streams of CCA amounts shown in Table 7.8. The two streams of CCA amounts are calculated using the formula $CCA_t = UCC_t \times d$ where the CapEx amount is split across two years (i.e., half of CapEx is added to UCC_1 and half is added to UCC_2).

BREAKING DOWN THE CCA INTO TWO PERPETUITIES

TABLE 7.8 .

	Year	0	1	2	3	4	5
	Capital Expenditure, CCA and UCC Forecasts ($000s)						
1	CapEx added to UCC_1	3,750					
2	UCC_t	–	3,750	2,063	1,134	624	343
3	$CCA_t = UCC_t \times d$	–	1,688	928	510	281	154
4	CapEx added to UCC_2	3,750					
5	UCC_t		–	3,750	2,063	1,134	624
6	$CCA_t = UCC_t \times d$		–	1,688	928	510	281
7	CCA (line 3) + CCA (line 6)		1,688	2,616	1,439	791	435
8	CCA rate, d	45%					

Notes: For the yellow cells, $UCC_t = UCC_{t-1} - CCA_{t-1}$

Since $CCA_5 < UCC_5$, there will be a positive balance remaining for UCC_6.

TABLE 7.9	BREAKING DOWN THE CCA TAX SHIELDS INTO TWO PERPETUITIES

Year	0	1	2	3	4	5	6	...
Capital Expenditure, CCA and UCC Forecasts ($000s)								
1 CapEx added to UCC_1	3,750							
2 UCC_t		3,750	2,063	1,134	624	343	189	...
3 $CCA_t = UCC_t \times d$		1,688	928	510	281	154	85	...
4 CCA tax shield $= \tau_c \times$ CCA		675	371	204	112	62	34	...
5 CapEx added to UCC_2	3,750							
6 UCC_t			3,750	2,063	1,134	624	343	...
7 $CCA_t = UCC_t \times d$			1,688	928	510	281	154	...
8 CCA tax shield $= \tau_c \times$ CCA			675	371	204	112	62	...
9 Total CCA = CCA (line 3) + CCA (line 7)		1,688	2,616	1,439	791	435	239	...
10 Total CCA tax shield $= \tau_c \times$ Total CCA		675	1,046	575	316	174	96	...
11 CCA rate, d	45%							
12 Tax rate, τ_c	40%							

The CCA tax shields in line 4 of the spreadsheet in Table 7.9 are nothing more than a growing perpetuity with growth rate equal to –45% (thus growth $= -d$). The first cash flow of this perpetuity occurs in one year and the cash flow amount is

$$0.5 \times \text{CapEx} \times d \times \tau_c$$

The CCA tax shields in line 8 of the spreadsheet in Table 7.9 are identical, except that they are delayed one additional year. To determine the present value of the total CCA tax shields, we can use the Law of One Price and add the present value of the perpetuity in line 4 to the present value of the perpetuity in line 8. We use the formula for the present value of a growing perpetuity and insert $-d$ for the growth rate.

PV of CCA tax shields from line 4: $PV = \dfrac{0.5 \times \text{CapEx} \times d \times \tau_c}{r + d}$

PV of CCA tax shields from line 8: $PV = \dfrac{0.5 \times \text{CapEx} \times d \times \tau_c}{r + d} \times \dfrac{1}{(1 + r)}$

Summing these two amounts together and simplifying, we get the following:

$$PV = \frac{0.5 \times \text{CapEx} \times d \times \tau_c}{r + d} \times \frac{(1 + r)}{(1 + r)} + \frac{0.5 \times \text{CapEx} \times d \times \tau_c}{r + d} \times \frac{1}{(1 + r)}$$

$$= \frac{0.5 \times \text{CapEx} \times d \times \tau_c}{r + d} \times \frac{(2 + r)}{(1 + r)}$$

This results in our formula for the present value of the CCA tax shield perpetuity:

$$PV_{\text{CCA tax shields}} = \frac{\text{CapEx} \times d \times \tau_c}{r + d} \times \frac{\left(1 + \dfrac{r}{2}\right)}{(1 + r)} \quad (7.10)$$

If the asset is not sold, then Eq. 7.10 gives the present value of all the CCA tax shields, including those that continue beyond the end of the project.

If we use Eq. 7.10 to get the present value of all the CCA tax shields, then we must adjust our calculation of free cash flows so that we do not double count any CCA tax shields. The free cash flows we estimated for the BlackBerry Presenter in Table 7.4 include the CCA tax shields for the first five years. To remove the CCA tax shields we can adjust Eqs. 7.7 or 7.8 by removing all references to CCA. Eq. 7.11, below, shows the calculation of free cash flows excluding CCA tax shields.

$$FCF_{\text{excluding CCA tax shield}} = (\text{Revenues} - \text{Costs}) \times (1 - \tau_c) - \text{CapEx} - \Delta NWC \quad (7.11)$$

Eq. 7.11 can be used only when we account for the value of CCA tax shields separately (as done with Eq. 7.10 above, Eq. 7.15 below or, in the Appendix, Eqs. 7A.2 or 7A.4). Table 7.10 shows the free cash flows and NPV recalculated when we separate the CCA tax shields in the analysis.

The PV of CCA tax shields shown in line 17 is calculated as follows:

$$PV_{\text{CCA tax shields}} = \frac{7500 \times .45 \times .40}{.12 + .45} \times \frac{\left(1 + \dfrac{.12}{2}\right)}{(1 + .12)} = 2242$$

TABLE 7.10   **THE BLACKBERRY PRESENTER'S FCF AND NPV WITH CCA TAX SHIELDS TREATED SEPARATELY**

	Year	0	1	2	3	4	5
Incremental Earnings Forecast ($000s)							
1 Sales		–	23,500	23,500	23,500	23,500	–
2 Cost of Goods Sold		–	(9,500)	(9,500)	(9,500)	(9,500)	–
3 Gross Profit		–	14,000	14,000	14,000	14,000	–
4 Selling, General, and Administrative		–	(3,000)	(3,000)	(3,000)	(3,000)	–
5 Research and Development		(15,000)	–	–	–	–	–
6 Capital Cost Allowance (CCA)		not included, as analyzed separately					
7 EBIT		(15,000)	11,000	11,000	11,000	11,000	–
8 Income Tax at 40%		6,000	(4,400)	(4,400)	(4,400)	(4,400)	–
9 Unlevered Net Income		(9,000)	6,600	6,600	6,600	6,600	–
Free Cash Flow ($000s)							
10 Plus: CCA		not included, as analyzed separately					
11 Less: Net Capital Expenditures		(7,500)					
12 Less: Increases in NWC		–	(2,100)	–	–	–	2,100
13 Free Cash Flow_excluding CCA tax shields		(16,500)	4,500	6,600	6,600	6,600	2,100
14 Project Cost of Capital	12%						
15 Discount Factor		1.0000	0.8929	0.7972	0.7118	0.6355	0.5674
16 PV of Free Cash Flow_excluding CCA tax shields		(16,500)	4,018	5,261	4,698	4,194	1,192
17 PV of CCA Tax Shields (Eq. 7.10)		2,242					
18 NPV		5,105					

The NPV shown in line 18 of the spreadsheet in Table 7.10 is the sum of the present values of the free cash flows (excluding CCA tax shields) shown in line 16 and the PV of the CCA tax shield perpetuity shown in line 17:

$$\text{NPV} = -16,500 + 4,018 + 5,261 + 4,698 + 4,194 + 1,192 + 2,242 = 5,105$$

As you can see, the NPV rises from $5.009 million to $5.105 million when we include all the CCA tax shield effects. If we were to forget to include the CCA tax shields after year five, then we would underestimate the NPV by about $96,000.

LIQUIDATION OR SALVAGE VALUE. Assets that are no longer needed often have a resale value, or some salvage value if the parts are sold for scrap. Some assets may have a negative liquidation value. For example, it may cost money to remove and dispose of the used equipment.

In the calculation of expected free cash flow for date t, we include the expected liquidation value of any assets that are expected to be sold during year t. In addition, we need to include the expected tax effects from selling the asset. There are two main tax effects. First, there will be a **capital gains tax** if the asset is sold for an amount greater than its original purchase price, denoted by CapEx. Canada Revenue Agency taxes half of the gain at the corporate tax rate.

$$\text{Capital Gains Tax} = \frac{1}{2} \times \left(\text{Sale Price} - \text{CapEx}\right) \times \tau_c \qquad (7.12)$$

The capital gains tax will be paid in the tax year the asset is sold and will be included in the free cash flow for that year as a negative effect. When we discussed purchasing an asset at date 0, we assumed the tax effect (the CCA tax shield) would occur at date 1 because the asset was purchased just after the year 0 end-of-year for tax purposes. To be consistent, we will assume that an asset sale at date t is actually at the beginning of the tax year $t + 1$. Thus, given an asset sale at date t, the capital gains tax should be deducted from the free cash flow for date $t + 1$.[9]

The second tax effect from selling an asset is that the subsequent CCA deductions and tax shields will change. The UCC for the asset will be reduced by the asset sale in the tax year of the asset sale. The minimum of the sale price and the original purchase price, CapEx, is subtracted from the UCC to get the post-sale UCC. If the asset is sold at date t, we will continue our assumption that the sale is at the beginning of tax year $t + 1$.

$$\text{Post-Sale UCC}_{t+1} = \text{UCC}_{t+1} - \text{minimum of (Sale Price}_t, \text{CapEx)} \qquad (7.13)$$

Post-sale UCC_{t+1} will be used as the basis to determine CCA_{t+1} and subsequent CCA deductions.

The way post-sale CCA deductions are calculated depends on whether post-sale UCC_{t+1} for the asset pool is positive or negative, whether or not the firm still owns any

---

9. Other assumptions can be made about the timing of the asset sale. If the asset sale occurs within tax year t rather than at the beginning of tax year $t + 1$, then the capital gains tax would reduce the free cash flow for date t.

assets in that asset pool, and whether or not the firm will be buying additional assets in that pool with value greater than the asset's expected sale price. For now, we will assume that other assets remain in the asset pool and post-sale UCC_{t+1} for the asset pool remains positive. With this assumption we have what is called a **continuing pool**. We will also assume that in the tax year of the asset sale, future purchases of assets (for other projects) will be less than the asset's expected sale price; this is referred to as **negative net additions**. Other cases are discussed in the appendix.

CONTINUING POOL, NEGATIVE NET ADDITIONS.   With a continuing pool and negative net additions, adjustments must be made to the post-sale CCA amounts and resulting tax shields. The effect of the asset sale is fully recognized in the tax year of the sale and the UCC is reduced accordingly. Utilizing what we know from deriving Eq. 7.10, the present value of the reduction in CCA tax shields can be calculated as follows.

$$PV_{\text{lost CCA tax shields}} = \frac{\min(\text{Sale Price}_t, \text{CapEx}) \times d \times \tau_c}{r + d} \times \frac{1}{(1 + r)^t} \quad (7.14)$$

In Eq. 7.14, the first reduction in CCA tax shields is in year $t + 1$. The growing perpetuity formula discounts the lost CCA tax shields back to date t, the last term in Eq. 7.14 discounts from date t to date 0.

We can combine Eqs. 7.10 and 7.14 to get the overall present value of expected CCA tax shields under the condition of an expected continuing pool of assets and negative net additions when the asset is sold.

$$PV_{\text{CCA tax shields}} = \frac{\text{CapEx} \times d \times \tau_c}{r + d} \times \frac{\left(1 + \dfrac{r}{2}\right)}{(1 + r)}$$

$$- \frac{\min(\text{Sale Price}_t, \text{CapEx}) \times d \times \tau_c}{r + d} \times \frac{1}{(1 + r)^t} \quad (7.15)^{[10]}$$

Remember to consider all the effects of the asset sale. Given our assumptions about the timing of the asset purchase and sale with respect to the relevant tax years, we consider the sale price, CCA tax shield effects, and capital gains tax as follows. We add the sale price to the free cash flow for year t. We use Eq. 7.15 instead of Eq. 7.10 in order to calculate the present value of all the expected CCA tax shields. If there is a **capital gain**, we subtract the capital gains tax (Eq. 7.12) from the free cash flow for year $t + 1$.

---

10. Alternative assumptions about the timing of the asset purchase or sale can be easily accommodated. For instance, if the asset is purchased at the end of tax year 0 rather than the beginning of tax year 1, the first term of Eq. 7.15 would have to be multiplied by $(1 + r)$. If the asset is expected to be sold at the end of tax year t rather than the beginning of tax year $t + 1$, then the last term of Eq. 7.15 would be multiplied by $(1 + r)$. Often business reasons drive the timing of the asset sale (rather than just the tax implications), so it is important to understand how to adjust these formulas.

EXAMPLE 7.5	ADDING SALVAGE VALUE AND CCA EFFECTS TO THE ANALYSIS

Problem

RIM is expected to sell the specialized computer equipment at date 4 (or the beginning of tax year 5) as the lab will be shut down at that point. The expected *Sale Price*$_4$ is high, $8 million, because of the expected appreciation of precious minerals used within the computer equipment. It is expected that RIM will still own other computer equipment at that time but will not be making such purchases in excess of $8 million in tax year 5.

Solution

Add in the $8 million to the free cash flow for year 4 and replace Eq. 7.10 with Eq. 7.15 to take into account how CCA tax shields will be changed by the asset sale. Since there is a capital gain, calculate the capital gains tax and deduct it from the free cash flow for year 5. The results are shown in the spreadsheet below.

	Year	0	1	2	3	4	5
Incremental Earnings Forecast ($000s)							
1 Sales		–	23,500	23,500	23,500	23,500	–
2 Cost of Goods Sold		–	(9,500)	(9,500)	(9,500)	(9,500)	–
3 Gross Profit		–	14,000	14,000	14,000	14,000	–
4 Selling, General, and Administrative		–	(3,000)	(3,000)	(3,000)	(3,000)	–
5 Research and Development		(15,000)	–	–	–	–	–
6 Capital Cost Allowance (CCA)		not included, as analyzed separately					
7 EBIT		(15,000)	11,000	11,000	11,000	11,000	–
8 Income Tax at 40%		6,000	(4,400)	(4,400)	(4,400)	(4,400)	–
9 Unlevered Net Income		(9,000)	6,600	6,600	6,600	6,600	–
Free Cash Flow ($000s)							
10 Plus: CCA		not included, as analyzed separately					
11 Less: Net Capital Expenditures		(7,500)	–	–	–	8,000	–
12 Less: Increases in NWC		–	(2,100)	–	–	–	2,100
13 Less: Capital Gains Tax		–	–	–	–	–	(100)
14 Free Cash Flow$_{excluding\ CCA\ tax\ shields}$		(16,500)	4,500	6,600	6,600	14,600	2,000
15 Project Cost of Capital	12%						
16 Discount Factor		1.0000	0.8929	0.7972	0.7118	0.6355	0.5674
17 PV of Free Cash Flow$_{excluding\ CCA\ tax\ shields}$		(16,500)	4,018	5,261	4,698	9,279	1,135
18 PV of CCA Tax Shields (Eq. 7.15)		736					
19 NPV		8,627					

Note that the $8 million from the asset sale is the same as a negative capital expenditure. It is reflected on line 11 of the spreadsheet and is added into the free cash flow for year 4. The capital gains tax shown on line 13 is calculated using Eq. 7.12 as follows:

$$\text{Capital Gains Tax} = \frac{1}{2} \times (8000 - 7500) \times 0.40 = 100$$

Since the asset is sold at the beginning of tax year 5, the capital gains tax reduces free cash flow for year 5. The present value of CCA tax shields using Eq. 7.15 on line 18 is calculated as follows:

$$PV_{\text{CCA tax shields}} = \frac{7500 \times .45 \times .40}{.12 + .45} \times \frac{\left(1 + \frac{.12}{2}\right)}{(1 + .12)} - \frac{7500 \times .45 \times .40}{.12 + .45} \times \frac{1}{(1 + .12)^4}$$

The NPV (line 19) is the sum of the present values of the free cash flows (excluding CCA tax shields) plus the PV of CCA tax shields calculated with Eq. 7.15.

$$NPV = -16{,}500 + 4{,}018 + 5{,}261 + 4{,}698 + 9{,}279 + 1{,}135 + 736 = 8{,}627$$

You should notice that the NPV is much higher than what was calculated in Table 7.10. The reason it is higher is because of the large asset sale price. Also note that the PV of CCA tax shields is lower and there is a capital gain; these are the other effects of the asset sale.

TERMINAL OR CONTINUATION VALUE.   Sometimes the firm explicitly forecasts free cash flow over a shorter horizon than the full horizon of the project or investment. This is necessarily true for investments with an indefinite life, such as an expansion of the firm. In this case, we estimate the value of the remaining free cash flow beyond the forecast horizon by including an additional, one-time cash flow at the end of the forecast horizon called the **terminal** or **continuation value** of the project. This amount represents the market value (as of the last forecast period) of the free cash flow from the project at all future dates.

Depending on the setting, we use different methods for estimating the continuation value of an investment. For example, when analyzing investments with long lives, it is common to explicitly calculate free cash flow over a short horizon, and then assume that cash flows grow at some constant rate beyond the forecast horizon.

EXAMPLE 7.6   **CONTINUATION VALUE WITH PERPETUAL GROWTH**

Problem
Home Again Hardware is considering opening a set of new retail stores. The free cash flow projections for the new stores are shown below (in millions of dollars):

After year 4, Home Again Hardware expects free cash flow from the stores to increase at a rate of 5% per year. If the appropriate cost of capital for this investment is 10%, what continuation value in year 3 captures the value of future free cash flows in year 4 and beyond? What is the NPV of the new stores?

Solution
The expected free cash flow from the store in year 4 is $1.30 million, with future free cash flow beyond year 4 expected to grow at 5% per year. The continuation value in year 3 of

the free cash flow in year 4 and beyond can therefore be calculated as a constant growth perpetuity:

Continuation Value in Year 3 = PV(FCF in year 4 and beyond)

$$= \frac{FCF_4}{r - g} = \frac{\$1.30 \text{ million}}{0.10 - 0.05} = \$26 \text{ million}$$

We can restate the free cash flows of the investment as follows (in thousands of dollars):

Year	0	1	2	3
Free Cash Flow (Years 0–3)	(10,500)	(5,500)	800	1,200
Continuation Value				26,000
Free Cash Flow	(10,500)	(5,500)	800	27,200

The NPV of the investment in the new stores is

$$NPV = -10{,}500 - \frac{5500}{1.10} + \frac{800}{1.10^2} + \frac{27{,}200}{1.10^3} = \$5597$$

or $5.597 million.

TAX LOSS CARRYFORWARDS. A firm generally identifies its marginal tax rate by determining the tax bracket that it falls into based on its overall level of pre-tax income. Two additional features of tax law, called **tax loss carryforwards and carry-backs**, allow corporations to take losses during a current year and offset them against gains in nearby years. In Canada, companies can "carry back" losses for three years, and for tax years after 2005, companies can "carry forward" losses for 20 years. This tax rule means that the firm can offset losses during one year against income for the previous three years, or save the losses to be offset against income during the next 20 years. When a firm can carry back losses, it receives a refund for back taxes in the current year. Otherwise, the firm must carry forward the loss and use it to offset future taxable income. When a firm has tax loss carryforwards well in excess of its current pre-tax income, then the additional income it earns today will not increase the taxes it owes until after it exhausts its carryforwards. This delay reduces the present value of the tax liability.

EXAMPLE 7.7   **TAX LOSS CARRYFORWARDS**

Problem

Engem Exploration has outstanding tax loss carryforwards of $100 million from losses over the past six years. If Engem Exploration earns $30 million per year in pre-tax income from now on, when will it first pay taxes? If Engem Exploration earns an extra $5 million this coming year, in which year will its taxes increase?

Solution

With pre-tax income of $30 million per year, Engem Exploration will be able to use its tax loss carryforwards to avoid paying taxes until year 4 (in millions of dollars):

Year	1	2	3	4	5
Pre-tax Income	30	30	30	30	30
Tax Loss Carryforward Used	−30	−30	−30	−10	
Taxable Income	0	0	0	20	30

If Engem Exploration earns an additional $5 million the first year, it will owe taxes on an extra $5 million in year 4:

Year	1	2	3	4	5
Pre-tax Income	35	30	30	30	30
Tax Loss Carryforward Used	−35	−30	−30	−5	
Taxable Income	0	0	0	25	30

Thus, when a firm has tax loss carryforwards, the tax impact of current earnings will be delayed until the carryforwards are exhausted. This delay reduces the present value of the tax impact, and firms sometimes approximate the effect of tax loss carryforwards by using a lower marginal tax rate.

CONCEPT CHECK

1. What is the continuation or terminal value of a project?

2. What is a tax loss carryforward and how does it affect the amount of tax paid on newly generated income of a project?

7.5 ANALYZING THE PROJECT

When evaluating a capital budgeting project, financial managers should make the decision that maximizes NPV. As we have discussed, to compute the NPV for a project, you need to estimate the incremental cash flows and choose a discount rate. Given these inputs, the NPV calculation is relatively straightforward. The most difficult part of capital budgeting is deciding how to estimate the cash flows and cost of capital. These estimates are often subject to significant uncertainty. In this section, we look at methods that assess the importance of this uncertainty and identify the drivers of value in the project.

BREAK-EVEN ANALYSIS

When we are uncertain regarding the input to a capital budgeting decision, it is often useful to determine the **break-even** level of that input, which is the level for which the investment has an NPV of zero. One example that we have already considered is the calculation of the internal rate of return (IRR). Recall from Chapter 6 that the difference between the IRR of a project and the cost of capital tells you how much error in the cost of capital it would take to change the investment decision. Assume the data used to generate Table 7.6

THE BLACKBERRY PRESENTER'S IRR CALCULATION

TABLE 7.11

	Year	0	1	2	3	4	5
Net Present Value ($000s) and IRR							
1 Free Cash Flow		(16,500)	5,175	7,646	7,175	6,916	2,274
2 NPV @ 12%	5,009						
3 IRR	24.3%						

BREAK-EVEN LEVELS FOR THE BLACKBERRY PRESENTER

TABLE 7.12

Parameter	Break-Even Level
Units sold	81,326 units per year
Wholesale price	$231.99 per unit
Cost of goods	$138.01 per unit
Cost of capital	24.5%

represent all of the information about the BlackBerry Presenter project. Using Excel's IRR function, the spreadsheet in Table 7.11 uses the free cash flows from Table 7.6 and calculates an IRR of 24.3% for the project.[11] Hence, the true cost of capital can be as high as 24.3% and the project will still have positive NPV.

Recall that the free cash flows in Tables 7.6 and 7.11 omitted the CCA tax shields after year 5. Since the missing tax shields add to the NPV, the IRR of the BlackBerry Presenter project is actually greater than the 24.3% estimated. We can use the spreadsheet in Table 7.10 and Excel's Solver tool to determine the IRR for the BlackBerry Presenter project without omitting the CCA tax shields after year 5. The resulting IRR is 24.5%, slightly higher than the earlier estimate of 24.3% with the missing CCA tax shields.[12]

There is no reason to limit our attention to the uncertainty in the cost of capital estimate. In a **break-even analysis**, for each parameter, we calculate the value at which the NPV of the project is zero. Table 7.12 shows the break-even level for several key parameters calculated by changing the inputs for Table 7.10 (the analysis that includes all CCA tax shield effects). For example, based on the initial assumptions, the BlackBerry Presenter project will break even with a sales level of just under 81,326 units per year. Alternatively, at a sales level of 100,000 units per year, the project will break even with a sales price of $231.99 per unit.

---

11. Use the IRR function over the range of cells for the free cash flows, = IRR(FCF0:FCF5).

12. To use Solver to determine the IRR, we want the target cell (the cell containing the final NPV) to be set to zero by having Solver change the cell that contains the project cost of capital. The cost of capital that makes NPV zero is the project's IRR.

We have examined the break-even levels in terms of the project's NPV, which is the most useful perspective for decision making. Other accounting notions of break-even are sometimes considered, however. For example, we could compute the **EBIT break-even** for sales, which is the level of sales for which the project's EBIT is zero. Because the CCA deduction is different each year, the EBIT break-even level of sales will be different each year. Because break-even analysis based on EBIT or other accounting results ignores the time value of money, such break-even values lead to negative NPV results; thus they really are not that useful for decision-making purposes.

SENSITIVITY ANALYSIS

Another important capital budgeting tool is sensitivity analysis. **Sensitivity analysis** breaks the NPV calculation into its component assumptions and shows how the NPV varies as the underlying assumptions change. In this way, sensitivity analysis allows us to explore the effects of errors in our NPV estimates for the project. By conducting a sensitivity analysis, we learn which assumptions are the most important; we can then invest further resources and effort to refine these assumptions. Such an analysis also reveals which aspects of the project are most critical when we are actually managing the project.

To determine the importance of this uncertainty, we recalculate the NPV of the BlackBerry Presenter project under the best- and worst-case assumptions for each parameter. For example, if the number of units sold is only 70,000 per year, the NPV of the project falls to –$3.1 million. We repeat this calculation for each parameter. The result is shown in Figure 7.1, which reveals that the most important parameter assumptions are the number of units sold and the sale price per unit. These assumptions deserve the greatest scrutiny during the estimation process. In addition, as the

---

FIGURE 7.1

The BlackBerry Presenter's NPV Under Best- and Worst-Case Parameter Assumptions

Green bars show the change in NPV under the best-case assumption for each parameter; red bars show the change under the worst-case assumption. Also shown are the break-even levels for each parameter. Under the initial assumptions, the BlackBerry Presenter's NPV is $5.105 million (the centre of the horizontal axis).

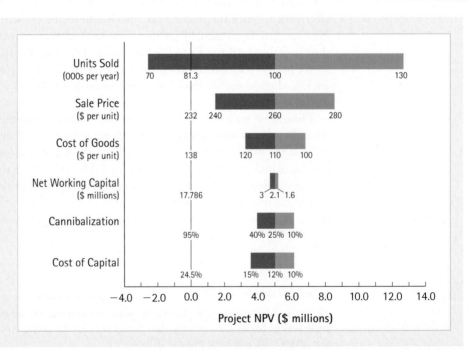

TABLE 7.13

BEST- AND WORST-CASE PARAMETER ASSUMPTIONS FOR THE BLACKBERRY PRESENTER

Parameter	Initial Assumption	Worst Case	Best Case
Units sold (thousands)	100	70	130
Sale price ($/unit)	260	240	280
Cost of goods ($/unit)	110	120	100
NWC ($ thousands)	2100	3000	1600
Cannibalization	25%	40%	10%
Cost of capital	12%	15%	10%

most important drivers of the project's value, these factors deserve close attention when managing the project.

To illustrate, consider the assumptions underlying the calculations (shown in Table 7.10) of the BlackBerry Presenter's NPV. There is likely to be significant uncertainty surrounding each revenue and cost assumption. Table 7.13 shows the base-case assumptions, together with the best and worst cases, for several key aspects of the project.

EXAMPLE 7.8

SENSITIVITY TO MARKETING AND SUPPORT COSTS

Problem

The current forecast for the BlackBerry Presenter's marketing and support costs is $3 million per year during years 1–4. Suppose the marketing and support costs may be as high as $4 million per year. What is the BlackBerry Presenter's NPV in this case?

Solution

We can answer this question by changing the selling, general, and administrative expense to $4 million in the spreadsheet and computing the NPV of the project. We can also calculate the impact of this change as follows: A $1 million increase in marketing and support costs will reduce EBIT by $1 million and will, therefore, decrease BlackBerry Presenter's free cash flow by an after-tax amount of $1 million $\times$ (1 $-$ 40%) = $0.6 million per year. The present value of this decrease is

$$PV = \frac{-0.6}{1.12} + \frac{-0.6}{1.12^2} + \frac{-0.6}{1.12^3} + \frac{-0.6}{1.12^4} = -\$1.822 \text{ million}$$

The BlackBerry Presenter's NPV would fall to $5.105 million $-$ $1.822 million = $3.283 million.

SCENARIO ANALYSIS OF ALTERNATIVE PRICING STRATEGIES

TABLE 7.14

Strategy	Sale Price ($/unit)	Expected Units Sold (thousands)	NPV ($ thousands)
Current strategy	260	100	5105
Price reduction	245	110	4831
Price increase	275	90	4831

FIGURE 7.2

Price and Volume Combinations for the BlackBerry Presenter with Equivalent NPV

The graph shows alternative price per unit and annual volume combinations that lead to an NPV of $5.105 million. Pricing strategies with combinations above this line will lead to a higher NPV and are superior.

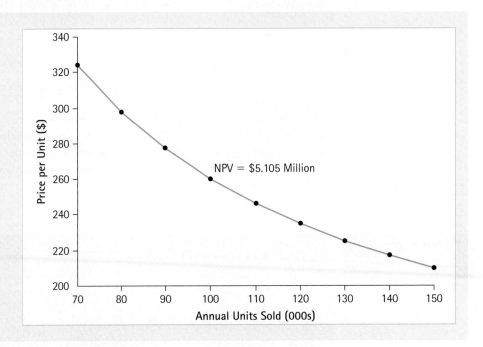

SCENARIO ANALYSIS

In the analysis thus far, we have considered the consequences of varying only one parameter at a time. In reality, certain factors may affect more than one parameter. **Scenario analysis** considers the effect on NPV of changing multiple project parameters. For example, lowering the BlackBerry Presenter's price may increase the number of units sold. We can use scenario analysis to evaluate alternative pricing strategies for the BlackBerry Presenter product in Table 7.14. In this case, the current strategy is optimal. Figure 7.2 shows the combinations of price and volume that lead to the same NPV of $5.105 million for the BlackBerry Presenter as the current strategy. Only strategies with price and volume combinations above the line will lead to a higher NPV.

CONCEPT CHECK

1. What is sensitivity analysis?

2. How does scenario analysis differ from sensitivity analysis?

INTERVIEW WITH DAVID HOLLAND

Dav id Holland is senior vice-president and treasurer of Cisco, responsible for managing all funding, risk, and capital market activities related to the firm's $50 billion balance sheet.

QUESTION: What is the importance of considering free cash flow, as opposed to just the earnings implications of a financial decision?

ANSWER: There is an adage saying, "Cash flow is a fact and earnings are an opinion." Earnings use an accounting framework and are governed by many rules, making it hard to know what earnings tell the investor. The economics of cash flow are clear: We can't dispute whether cash has come in or gone out. Cisco's investment decisions are based primarily on cash flow models because they take project risk into account and show the impact on value creation for owners of the business.

QUESTION: What key financial metrics does Cisco use to make investment decisions?

ANSWER: Cisco focuses primarily on net present value (NPV) for investment decisions. Robust NPV analysis goes beyond simply accepting projects with positive NPVs and rejecting those with negative NPVs. It identifies the key drivers that affect project success and demonstrates the interplay between factors that affect cash flow. For example, running a model using a lower margin approach shows us the impact on revenue growth and on operating cost structures. We can compare that to a higher margin (premium pricing) approach. The business unit manager learns how to control aspects of the business model to alleviate risk or accelerate the upside potential.

We prefer NPV to internal rate of return (IRR), which may return multiple answers or give false signals as to an investment's profitability, depending on the organization of cash flows. An attraction of IRR analysis is the ease of comparing percentage returns. However, this method hides the scope of a project. A project with a 25 percent return may generate $1 million in shareholder value, while another with a 13 percent IRR might produce $1 billion. NPV captures the size of the return in dollar terms and shows a project's impact on share price. NPV also creates an ownership framework for employees whose compensation package includes some form of stock ownership, directly tying the decision-making criteria to stock price.

QUESTION: When developing a model to analyze a new investment, how do you deal with the uncertainty surrounding estimates, especially for new technologies?

ANSWER: Cisco relies on strong financial modelling for the thousands of investment decisions we make every year. Our 2500 finance people worldwide work with the internal client—the business lead—to understand the assumptions in the model and to check the model's result against alternative assumptions. Evaluating the cash flows for technology projects, especially new technology, is difficult. When you buy an oil refinery, you can see the throughput and the cash flows. Identifying the relevant savings from a component technology for a larger router or switch product or a strategic move into a new area is more complex and intangible. Scenario and sensitivity analyses and game theory help us control risk by adjusting our strategy. We also look at the qualitative aspects, such as how the strategy fits into the customer sector and the directions customers are moving with their tech platforms.

QUESTION: How does Cisco adjust for risk?

ANSWER: To stay competitive in the technology space, we must be prepared to take some level of risk, even in down markets. We apply the same discount rate to all projects in a category, based on their market risk (i.e., sensitivity to market conditions). We do not adjust the discount rate to account for project-specific risks, because our required return has not changed and that would distort the true value of the company. To assess a project's unique risks, we model the upside or downside of cash flows with scenario and sensitivity analysis. We might analyze the sensitivity of a project's NPV to a 1 percent change in both revenue growth and operating costs. Then we run the model with other assumptions, developing base, optimistic, and bearish cases. We discuss these models with the business lead and rerun the models based on their input. This process improves our potential outcome and project profitability.

SUMMARY

1. Capital budgeting is the process of analyzing investment opportunities and deciding which ones to accept. A capital budget is a list of all projects that a company plans to undertake during the next period.

2. We use the NPV rule to evaluate capital budgeting decisions, making decisions that maximize NPV. When deciding to accept or reject a project, we accept projects with a positive NPV.

3. The incremental earnings of a project comprise the amount by which the project is expected to change the firm's earnings.

4. Incremental earnings should include all incremental revenues and costs associated with the project, including project externalities and opportunity costs, but excluding sunk costs and interest expenses.

   a. Project externalities are cash flows that occur when a project affects other areas of the company's business.

   b. An opportunity cost is the cost of using an existing asset.

   c. A sunk cost is an unrecoverable cost that has already been incurred.

   d. Interest and other financing-related expenses are excluded to determine the project's unlevered net income.

5. We estimate taxes using the marginal tax rate, based on the net income generated by the rest of the firm's operations, as well as any tax loss carrybacks or carryforwards.

6. When evaluating a capital budgeting decision, we first consider the project on its own, separate from the decision regarding how to finance the project. Thus, we ignore interest expenses.

7. We compute free cash flow from incremental earnings by eliminating all non-cash deductions and including all capital investment.

   a. Capital Cost Allowance (CCA) is a non-cash deduction so it is added back.

   b. Actual capital expenditures are deducted.

   c. Increases in net working capital are deducted. Net working capital is defined as

$$\text{Cash} + \text{Inventory} + \text{Receivables} - \text{Payables} \qquad (7.5)$$

8. The basic calculation for free cash flow is

$$\text{Free Cash Flow} = \overbrace{(\text{Revenues} - \text{Costs} - \text{CCA}) \times (1 - \tau_c)}^{\text{Unlevered Net Income}}$$
$$+ \text{CCA} - \text{CapEx} - \Delta NWC \qquad (7.7)$$

Free cash flow should also include the (after-tax) liquidation or salvage value of any assets that are disposed of and the resulting tax effects. It may also include a terminal (continuation) value if the project continues beyond the forecast horizon.

9. CCA deductions affect free cash flow only through the CCA tax shield.

10. The discount rate for a project is its cost of capital, that is, the expected return of securities with comparable risk and horizon.

11. When choosing between alternatives, we only need to include those components of free cash flow that differ among the alternatives.

12. Break-even analysis computes the level of a parameter that makes the project's NPV equal zero.

13. Sensitivity analysis breaks the NPV calculation down into its component assumptions, showing how the NPV varies as the values of the underlying assumptions change.

14. Scenario analysis considers the effect of changing multiple parameters simultaneously.

KEY TERMS

asset class *p. 196*
asset pool *p. 197*
break-even *p. 218*
break-even analysis *p. 219*
cannibalization *p. 200*
CapEx *p. 197*
capital budget *p. 195*
capital budgeting *p. 195*
capital cost allowance (CCA) *p. 196*
capital gain *p. 214*
capital gains tax *p. 213*
CCA rate *p. 197*
CCA tax shield *p. 207*
continuing pool *p. 214*
EBIT break-even *p. 220*
free cash flow *p. 203*
half-year rule *p. 197*
incremental earnings *p. 195*

marginal corporate tax rate *p. 198*
negative net additions *p. 214*
opportunity cost *p. 199*
overhead expenses *p. 201*
positive net additions *p. 233*
project externalities *p. 200*
scenario analysis *p. 222*
sensitivity analysis *p. 220*
sunk cost *p. 201*
tax loss carryforwards and
    carrybacks *p. 217*
tax year *p. 196*
terminal (continuation) value *p. 216*
terminating pool *p. 233*
trade credit *p. 205*
undepreciated capital cost (UCC) *p. 197*
unlevered net income *p. 198*

PROBLEMS

The problems marked in green can be found on MyFinanceLab at www.myfinancelab.com. Visit your MyFinanceLab for additional practice. An asterisk (*) indicates problems with a higher level of difficulty. Additional readings for this chapter may be found in the Textbook Resources section on MyFinanceLab.

Forecasting Earnings

1. Pisa Pizza, a seller of frozen pizza, is considering introducing a healthier version of its pizza that will be low in cholesterol and contain no trans fats. The firm expects that sales of the new pizza will be $20 million per year. While many of these sales will be to new customers, Pisa Pizza estimates that 40% will come from customers who switch to the new, healthier pizza instead of buying the original version.

   a. Assume customers will spend the same amount on either version. What level of incremental sales is associated with introducing the new pizza?

   b. Suppose that 50% of the customers who will switch from Pisa Pizza's original pizza to its healthier pizza will switch to another brand if Pisa Pizza does not introduce a healthier pizza. What level of incremental sales is associated with introducing the new pizza in this case?

2. Kokomochi is considering the launch of an advertising campaign for its latest dessert product, the Mini Mochi Munch. Kokomochi plans to spend $5 million on TV, radio, and print advertising this year for the campaign. The ads are expected to boost sales of the Mini Mochi Munch by $9 million this year and by $7 million next year. In addition, the company expects that new consumers who try the Mini Mochi Munch will be more likely to try Kokomochi's other products. As a result, sales of other products are expected to rise by $2 million each year.

   Kokomochi's gross profit margin for the Mini Mochi Munch is 35%, and its gross profit margin averages 25% for all other products. The company's marginal corporate tax rate is 35% both this year and next year. What are the incremental earnings associated with the advertising campaign?

3. Home Builder Supply, a retailer in the home improvement industry, currently operates seven retail outlets in the Maritimes. Management is contemplating building an eighth retail store in Dartmouth, Nova Scotia. Its most successful retail outlet is in Halifax. The company already owns the land for the Dartmouth store, which currently has an abandoned warehouse located on it. Last month, the marketing department spent $10,000 on market research to determine the extent of customer demand for the new store. Now Home Builder Supply must decide whether to build and open the new store.

   Which of the following should be included as part of the incremental earnings for the proposed new retail store?

   a. The cost of the land where the store will be located.

   b. The cost of demolishing the abandoned warehouse and clearing the lot.

   c. The loss of sales in the existing retail outlet, if customers who previously drove from Dartmouth to Halifax to shop at the existing outlet become customers of the new store instead.

   d. The $10,000 in market research spent to evaluate customer demand.

   e. Construction costs for the new store.

   f. The value of the land if sold.

   g. Interest expense on the debt borrowed to pay the construction costs.

4. Hyperion Inc. currently sells its latest high-speed colour printer, the Hyper 500, for $350. It plans to lower the price to $300 next year. Its cost of goods sold for the Hyper 500 is $200 per unit, and this year's sales are expected to be 20,000 units.

   a. Suppose that if Hyperion drops the price to $300 immediately, it can increase this year's sales by 25% to 25,000 units. What would be the incremental impact on this year's EBIT of such a price drop?

   b. Suppose that for each printer sold, Hyperion expects additional sales of $75 per year on ink cartridges for the next three years, and Hyperion has a gross profit margin of 70% on ink cartridges. What is the incremental impact on EBIT for the next three years of a price drop this year?

EXCEL

5. Royal Mount Games would like to invest in a division to develop software for video games. To evaluate this decision, the firm first attempts to project the working capital needs for this operation. Its chief financial officer has developed the following estimates (in millions of dollars):

	Year 1	Year 2	Year 3	Year 4	Year 5
Cash	6	12	15	15	15
Accounts receivable	21	22	24	24	24
Inventory	5	7	10	12	13
Accounts payable	18	22	24	25	30

Assuming that Royal Mount currently does not have any working capital invested in this division, calculate the cash flows associated with changes in working capital for the first five years of this investment.

Determining Free Cash Flow and NPV

6. Etobicoke Enterprises is deciding whether to expand its production facilities. Although long-term cash flows are difficult to estimate, management has projected the following cash flows for the first two years (in millions of dollars):

	Year 1	Year 2
Revenues	125	160
Cost of goods sold and operating expenses other than depreciation	40	60
Capital Cost Allowance	25	36
Increase in working capital	5	8
Capital expenditures	30	40
Marginal corporate tax rate	35%	35%

a. What are the incremental earnings for this project for years 1 and 2?

b. What are the free cash flows for this project for the first two years?

EXCEL

7. You are a manager at Northern Fibre, which is considering expanding its operations in synthetic fibre manufacturing. Your boss comes into your office, drops a consultant's report on your desk, and complains, "We owe these consultants $1 million for this report, and I am not sure their analysis makes sense. Before we spend the $25 million on new equipment needed for this project, look it over and give me your opinion." You open the report and find the following estimates (in thousands of dollars):

	Project Year				
	1	2	. . .	9	10
Sales revenue	30,000	30,000		30,000	30,000
− Cost of goods sold	18,000	18,000		18,000	18,000
= Gross profit	12,000	12,000		12,000	12,000
− General, sales, and administrative expenses	2,000	2,000		2,000	2,000
− Depreciation	2,500	2,500		2,500	2,500
= Net operating income	7,500	7,500		7,500	7,500
− Income tax	2,625	2,625		2,625	2,625
= Net income	4,875	4,875		4,875	4,875

All of the estimates in the report seem correct. You note that the consultants used straight-line depreciation for the new equipment that will be purchased today (year 0), which is what the accounting department recommended for financial reporting purposes. Canada Revenue Agency allows a CCA rate of 30% on the equipment for tax purposes. The report concludes that because the project will increase earnings by $4.875 million per year for 10 years, the project is worth $48.75 million. You think back to your halcyon days in finance class and realize there is more work to be done!

First, you note that the consultants have not factored in the fact that the project will require $10 million in working capital upfront (year 0), which will be fully recovered in year 10. Next, you see they have attributed $2 million of selling, general, and administrative expenses to the project, but you know that $1 million of this amount is overhead that will be incurred even if the project is not accepted. Finally, you know that accounting earnings are not the right thing to focus on!

  a. Given the available information, what are the free cash flows in years 0 through 10 that should be used to evaluate the proposed project?

  b. If the cost of capital for this project is 14%, what is your estimate of the value of the new project?

8. Atlantic Telecom reported a net income of $250 million for the most recent fiscal year. The firm had CCA deductions of $100 million (assume reported depreciation was equal to this CCA), capital expenditures of $200 million, and no interest expenses. Working capital increased by $10 million. Calculate the free cash flow for Atlantic Telecom for the most recent fiscal year.

Further Adjustments to Free Cash Flow

9. Spherical Manufacturing recently spent $15 million to purchase some equipment used in the manufacture of disk brakes. This equipment has a CCA rate of 25% and Spherical's marginal corporate tax rate is 35%.

  a. What are the annual CCA deductions associated with this equipment for the first five years?

  b. What are the annual CCA tax shields for the first five years?

  c. What is the present value of the first five CCA tax shields if the appropriate discount rate is 10% per year?

  d. What is the present value of all the CCA tax shields assuming the equipment is never sold if the appropriate discount rate is 10% per year?

  e. How might your answer to part d change if Spherical anticipates that its marginal corporate tax rate will increase substantially over the next five years?

10. Hudson Bay Properties is considering starting a commercial real estate division. It has prepared the following four-year forecast of free cash flows for this division:

	Year 1	Year 2	Year 3	Year 4
Free cash flow	−$185,000	−$12,000	$99,000	$240,000

Assume cash flows after year 4 will grow at 3% per year, forever. If the cost of capital for this division is 14%, what is the continuation value in year 4 for cash flows after year 4? What is the value today of this division?

11. Your firm would like to evaluate a proposed new operating division. You have forecasted cash flows for this division for the next five years, and have estimated that the cost of capital is 12%.

You would like to estimate a continuation value. You have made the following forecasts for the last year of your five-year forecasting horizon (in millions of dollars):

	Year 5
Revenues	1,200
Operating income	100
Net income	50
Free cash flows	110
Book value of equity	400

a. You forecast that future free cash flows after year 5 will grow at 2% per year, forever. Estimate the continuation value in year 5, using the growing perpetuity formula.

b. You have identified several firms in the same industry as your operating division. The average P/E ratio for these firms is 30. Estimate the continuation value assuming the P/E ratio for your division in year 5 will be the same as the average P/E ratio for the comparable firms today.

c. The average market/book ratio for the comparable firms is 4.0. Estimate the continuation value using the market/book ratio.

 12. One year ago, your company purchased a machine used in manufacturing for $110,000. You have learned that a new machine is now available that offers many advantages; you can purchase it for $150,000 today. The CCA rate applicable to both machines is 40%; neither machine will have any long-term salvage value. You expect that the new machine will produce EBITDA (earnings before interest, taxes, depreciation, and amortization) of $40,000 per year for the next 10 years. The current machine is expected to produce EBITDA of $20,000 per year. All other expenses of the two machines are identical. The market value today of the current machine is $50,000. Your company's tax rate is 45%, and the opportunity cost of capital for this type of equipment is 10%. Should your company replace its year-old machine?

Choosing Among Alternatives

13. Big Rock Brewery currently rents a bottling machine for $50,000 per year, including all maintenance expenses. It is considering purchasing a machine instead, and is comparing two options:

a. Purchase the machine it is currently renting for $150,000. This machine will require $20,000 per year in ongoing maintenance expenses.

b. Purchase a new, more advanced machine for $250,000. This machine will require $15,000 per year in ongoing maintenance expenses and will lower bottling costs by $10,000 per year. Also, $35,000 will be spent upfront in training the new operators of the machine.

Suppose the appropriate discount rate is 8% per year and the machine is purchased today. Maintenance and bottling costs are paid at the end of each year, as is the rental of the machine. Assume also that the machines are subject to a CCA rate of 25% and there will be a negligible salvage value. The marginal corporate tax rate is 35%. Should Big Rock continue to rent, purchase its current machine, or purchase the advanced machine?

Analyzing the Project

14. Buhler Industries is a farm implement manufacturer. Management is currently evaluating a proposal to build a plant that will manufacture lightweight tractors. Buhler plans to use a cost of capital of 12% to evaluate this project. Based on extensive research, it has prepared the following incomplete incremental free cash flow projections (in millions of dollars):

	Year 0	Years 1–9	Year 10
Revenues		100.0	100.0
− Manufacturing expenses (other than depreciation)		−35.0	−35.0
− Marketing expenses		−10.0	−10.0
− CCA		?	?
= EBIT		?	?
− Taxes (35%)		?	?
= Unlevered net income		?	?
+ CCA		?	?
− Increases in net working capital		−5.0	−5.0
− Capital expenditures	−150.0		
+ Continuation value			+12.0
= Free cash flow	−150.0	?	?

The relevant CCA rate for capital expenditures is 10%. Assume assets are never sold.

a. For this base-case scenario, what is the NPV of the plant to manufacture lightweight tractors?

b. Based on input from the marketing department, Buhler is uncertain about its revenue forecast. In particular, management would like to examine the sensitivity of the NPV to the revenue assumptions. What is the NPV of this project if revenues are 10% higher than forecast? What is the NPV if revenues are 10% lower than forecast?

c. Rather than assuming that cash flows for this project are constant, management would like to explore the sensitivity of its analysis to possible growth in revenues and operating expenses. Specifically, management would like to assume that revenues, manufacturing expenses, and marketing expenses are as given in the table for year 1 and grow by 2% per year every year starting in year 2. Management also plans to assume that the initial capital expenditures (and therefore CCA), additions to working capital, and continuation value remain as initially specified in the table. What is the NPV of this project under these alternative assumptions? How does the NPV change if the revenues and operating expenses grow by 5% per year rather than by 2%?

d. To examine the sensitivity of this project to the discount rate, management would like to compute the NPV for different discount rates. Create a graph, with the discount rate on the *x*-axis and the NPV on the *y*-axis, for discount rates ranging from 5% to 30%. For what ranges of discount rates does the project have a positive NPV?

*15. Buckingham Packaging is considering expanding its production capacity by purchasing a new machine, the XC-750. The cost of the XC-750 is $2.75 million. Unfortunately, installing this machine will take several months and will partially disrupt production. The firm has just completed a $50,000 feasibility study to analyze the decision to buy the XC-750, resulting in the following estimates:

■ *Marketing:* Once the XC-750 is operating next year, the extra capacity is expected to generate $10 million per year in additional sales, which will continue for the 10-year life of the machine.

■ *Operations:* The disruption caused by the installation will decrease sales by $5 million this year. Once the machine is operating next year, the cost of goods for the products produced by the XC-750 is expected to be 70% of their sale price. The increased production will require additional inventory on hand of $1 million, to be added in year 0 and depleted in year 10.

■ *Human Resources:* The expansion will require additional sales and administrative personnel at a cost of $2 million per year.

■ *Accounting:* The XC-750 has a CCA rate of 30%, and no salvage is expected. The firm expects receivables from the new sales to be 15% of revenues and payables to be 10% of the cost of goods sold. Buckingham's marginal corporate tax rate is 35%.

   a. Determine the incremental earnings (using CCA) from the purchase of the XC-750.

   b. Determine the free cash flow from the purchase of the XC-750 for the first 10 years.

   c. If the appropriate cost of capital for the expansion is 10%, compute the NPV of the purchase (including all CCA tax shield effects).

   d. While the expected new sales will be $10 million per year from the expansion, estimates range from $8 million to $12 million. What is the NPV in the worst case? In the best case?

   e. What is the NPV break-even level of new sales from the expansion? What is the NPV break-even level for the cost of goods sold?

   f. Buckingham could instead purchase the XC-900, which offers even greater capacity. The cost of the XC-900 is $4 million. The extra capacity would not be useful in the first two years of operation, but would allow for additional sales in years 3–10. What level of additional sales (above the $10 million expected for the XC-750) per year in those years would justify purchasing the larger machine?

DATA CASE

EXCEL

You have just been hired by Dell Computers in their capital budgeting division. Your first assignment is to determine the net cash flows and NPV of a proposed new type of portable computer system similar in size to a BlackBerry, which has the operating power of a high-end desktop system.

Development of the new system will require an initial investment equal to 10% of net Property, Plant, and Equipment (PPE) for the fiscal year ended Feb. 3, 2010. The project will then require an additional investment equal to 10% of initial investment after the first year of the project, a 5% increase after the second year, and a 1% increase after the third, fourth, and fifth years. The product is expected to have a life of five years. First-year revenues for the new product are expected to be 3% of total revenue for Dell's fiscal year ended Feb. 3, 2010. The new product's revenues are expected to grow at 15% for the second year, then 10% for the third, and 5% annually for the final two years of the expected life of the project. Your job is to determine the rest of the cash flows associated with this project. Your boss has indicated that the operating costs and net working capital requirements are similar to the rest of the company and that depreciation is straight-line for capital budgeting purposes (so CCA is not applicable here). Welcome to the "real world." Since your boss hasn't been much help, here are some tips to guide your analysis:

   1. Obtain Dell's financial statements. (If you "really" worked for Dell you would already have this data, but at least you won't get fired if your analysis is off target.) Download the annual income statements, balance sheets, and cash flow statements for the last four fiscal

years from MarketWatch (www.marketwatch.com). Enter Dell's ticker symbol and then go to "financials." Export the statements to Excel by right-clicking while the cursor is inside each statement.

2. You are now ready to determine the Free Cash Flow. Compute the Free Cash Flow for each year using Eq. 7.7 from this chapter (replacing CCA with Depreciation for the U.S. company):

$$\overbrace{\text{Free Cash Flow} = (\text{Revenues} - \text{Costs} - \text{Depreciation}) \times (1 - \tau_c)}^{\text{Unlevered net income}}$$
$$+ \text{ Depreciation} - \text{CapEx} - \Delta NWC$$

Set up the timeline and computation of free cash flow in separate, contiguous columns for each year of the project life. Be sure to make outflows negative and inflows positive.

   a. Assume that the project's profitability will be similar to Dell's existing projects in 2009 and estimate (revenues − costs) each year by using the 2009 EBITDA/Sales profit margin.

   b. Determine the annual depreciation by assuming Dell depreciates these assets by the straight-line method over a 10-year life.

   c. Determine Dell's tax rate by using the income tax rate in 2009.

   d. Calculate the net working capital required each year by assuming that the level of NWC will be a constant percentage of the project's sales. Use Dell's 2009 NWC/Sales to estimate the required percentage. (Use only accounts receivable, accounts payable, and inventory to measure working capital. Other components of current assets and liabilities are harder to interpret and not necessarily reflective of the project's required NWC, e.g., Dell's cash holdings.)

   e. To determine the free cash flow, calculate the *additional* capital investment and the *change* in net working capital each year.

3. Determine the IRR of the project and the NPV of the project at a cost of capital of 12% using the Excel functions. For the calculation of NPV, include cash flows 1 through 5 in the NPV function and then subtract the initial cost (i.e., $=NPV(\text{rate}, CF_1:CF_5) + CF_0$). For IRR, include cash flows zero through five in the cash flow range.

<table>
<tr><td></td></tr>
</table>

THE EFFECTS OF ASSET SALES ON CCA CALCULATIONS

If an asset is sold at date t (the beginning of tax year $t + 1$), then the way post-sale CCA deductions are calculated depends on whether post-sale UCC_{t+1} for the asset pool is positive or negative, whether or not the firm still owns any assets in that asset pool, and whether or not the firm will be buying additional assets in that pool with value greater than the asset's expected sale price. If the asset sold was the last asset in its asset class, or if post-sale UCC_{t+1} *for the pool of all assets in the same class* drops below zero, then we have what is called a **terminating pool** (the asset pool is said to terminate). If other assets remain in the class and post-sale UCC_{t+1} for the asset pool remains positive, then the asset pool is said to continue. The tax effects differ depending on whether there is a terminating pool or continuing pool of assets. For a continuing asset pool, there are different effects depending on whether we assume the firm will be purchasing new assets (for other projects) in the same asset pool with prices greater than the current project's asset sale price (this is called a continuing pool with **positive net additions**). In the main chapter we showed how to do the analysis for the case of a continuing pool of assets where future purchases will be less than the expected sale price of our asset (negative net additions). The other cases are discussed below.

CONTINUING POOL, POSITIVE NET ADDITIONS

Following the sale of the asset at date t (the beginning of tax year $t + 1$), there is a reduction to UCC_{t+1} that is used to determine CCA_{t+1} and, by extension, future CCA deductions. At the expected time of the asset's sale, if the firm is expected to be making additional purchases in the same asset class and these purchases will exceed the sale amount, the pool is said to continue with positive net additions. With positive net additions, the reduction of the UCC is spread over two years (much like the half-year rule spreads an asset's purchase effect over two years). We can use Eq. 7.10 to determine the present value of the lost CCA tax shields by replacing the CapEx amount with the adjustment for the asset sale (the minimum of the sale price or CapEx).

$$PV_{\text{lost CCA tax shields}} = \frac{\min(\text{Sale Price}_t, \text{CapEx}) \times d \times \tau_c}{r + d} \times \frac{\left(1 + \frac{r}{2}\right)}{(1 + r)} \times \frac{1}{(1 + r)^t}$$

Note that Eq. 7.10 discounts the CCA tax shields (the first of which is received at time 1) to time 0. In the above equation, the first CCA tax shield reduction is in time $t + 1$, so Eq. 7.10 would discount the CCA tax shield reductions back to date t; therefore, we have to discount the entire amount back another t periods to get the present value at date 0. The above equation can be simplified as follows for a continuing pool with positive net additions.

$$PV_{\text{lost CCA tax shields}} = \frac{\min(\text{Sale Price}_t, \text{CapEx}) \times d \times \tau_c}{r + d} \times \frac{\left(1 + \frac{r}{2}\right)}{(1 + r)^{t+1}} \quad (7\text{A}.1)$$

We can combine Eqs. 7.10 and 7A.1 to get the overall present value of expected CCA tax shields under the condition of an expected continuing pool of assets and positive net additions when the asset is sold.

$$PV_{\text{CCA tax shields}} = \frac{\text{CapEx} \times d \times \tau_c}{r + d} \times \frac{\left(1 + \dfrac{r}{2}\right)}{(1 + r)}$$

$$- \frac{\min(\text{Sale Price}_t, \text{CapEx}) \times d \times \tau_c}{r + d} \times \frac{\left(1 + \dfrac{r}{2}\right)}{(1 + r)^{t+1}} \qquad (7A.2)$$

Remember to consider all the effects of the asset sale. Given the asset is sold at date t (the beginning of tax year $t + 1$) the following must be done. First, we add the asset's sale price$_t$ to the free cash flow for date t. Then we replace Eq. 7.10 with Eq. 7A.2 in order to calculate the present value of all the expected CCA tax shields. Finally, if there is a capital gain, we must subtract the capital gains tax (Eq. 7.12) from the free cash flow for year $t + 1$.

| EXAMPLE 7A.1 | PRESENT VALUE OF CCA TAX SHIELDS FOR A CONTINUING POOL WITH POSITIVE NET ADDITIONS |

Problem

NorthVan Processing Ltd. is considering acquiring some processing equipment for a proposed project. The cost of the equipment is $2 million. The equipment will be used for the next five years and then sold for an amount expected to be $200,000. Such equipment falls under asset class 43 for the purpose of calculating CCA deductions and the relevant CCA rate is 30%. Management at NorthVan has asked for your help in determining the year-by-year CCA deductions, the relevant tax shields, and their present value. They want this information so they can use it in an NPV analysis for the project. NorthVan's marginal tax rate is 40% and the relevant cost of capital is 9%. NorthVan's management indicated that they own several other assets in the same class and expect to be making purchases in excess of $200,000 most years.

Solution

To determine the year-by-year CCA deductions, you can use Eqs. 7.1 and 7.2 to make the following spreadsheet. Note, with a continuing pool and positive net additions, the effect of the asset sale at date = (the beginning of tax year 6) is that half of the sale price is an incremental reduction to UCC$_6$ and half of the sale price is an incremental reduction to UCC$_7$.

UCC, CCA, and Tax Shield Calculations Given a Continuing Pool with Positive Net Additions

Year, t	0	1	2	3	4	5	6	7	8	9	...
Capital Expenditure, CCA and UCC Forecasts ($000s)											
1 CapEx	2,000					(200)					
2 UCC$_t$		1,000	1,700	1,190	833	583	308	116	81	57	...
3 CCA$_t$ = UCC$_t \times d$		300	510	357	250	175	92	35	24	17	...
4 CCA tax shield = $\tau_C \times$ CCA		120	204	143	100	70	37	14	10	7	...
5 Present value of CCA tax shield = $(\tau_C \times$ CCA$_t)/(1 + r)^t$		110	172	110	71	45	22	8	5	3	...
6 CCA rate, d	30%										
7 Tax rate, τ_C	40%			Note the asset sale causes a reduction to the UCC for years 6 and 7.							
8 Project cost of capital, r	9%			Under positive net additions, half of the sale reduces UCC$_6$, the other half reduces UCC$_7$.							
9 Sum of PV$_{\text{CCA tax shields}}$ from $t = 1$ to 25	551.62955			The sum shown on line 9 includes the individual PV of CCA tax shields calculated out to year 25.							
10 PV$_{\text{CCA tax shields}}$ (equation 7A.2)	551.63425			Line 9 and line 10 differ because line 9 omits CCA tax shields after year 25.							

The calculation of the present value of CCA tax shields in line 10 of the spreadsheet uses Eq. 7A.2 as follows.

$$PV_{\text{CCA tax shields}} = \frac{2,000 \times .3 \times .4}{.09 + .3} \times \frac{\left(1 + \dfrac{.09}{2}\right)}{(1 + .09)}$$

$$- \frac{200 \times .3 \times .4}{.09 + .3} \times \frac{\left(1 + \dfrac{.09}{2}\right)}{(1 + .09)^{5+1}} = 551.63$$

This is roughly equal to the sum of the present values of the individual CCA tax shields with the result shown in line 9 of the spreadsheet. So the present value of the CCA tax shields, $551,634.25, would be added into the NPV calculation for the evaluation of the project under consideration at NorthVan Processing. In addition, you would advise management not to forget to deduct the cost of the equipment and add the present value of the Sale Price when calculating the NPV.

TERMINATING POOL

If an asset is sold at date t (the beginning of tax year $t + 1$) and the asset pool terminates, then no CCA deductions will occur in tax year $t + 1$ or following years. If post-sale UCC_{t+1} will be negative, it is as though the firm will have claimed too much CCA over the time it owned the asset. The absolute value of post-sale UCC_{t+1} will then be added into taxable income for year $t + 1$ as recaptured CCA. The effect of this is that more tax will have to be paid in year $t + 1$. If post-sale UCC_{t+1} will be positive, it is as though the firm will not have claimed enough CCA over the time it owned the asset. In effect, the firm will have sold the asset for less than its undepreciated capital cost. The positive post-sale UCC_{t+1} is called a terminal loss and it will be a deduction from taxable income for year $t + 1$. A terminal loss in year $t + 1$ means less taxable income for year $t + 1$ and thus less tax paid in year $t + 1$.

$$\text{Terminal Loss (Recaptured CCA) Cash Flow}_{t+1} = \text{Post-Sale } UCC_{t+1} \times \tau_c \qquad \text{(7A.3)}$$

If the amount calculated in Eq. 7A.3 is positive (due to a terminal loss), then taxes are reduced and this saving is added into the firm's free cash flow for year $t + 1$. If it is negative (due to recaptured CCA), then taxes are increased, resulting in a lower free cash flow for year $t + 1$.

With a terminating asset pool, no further CCA deductions are allowed after the asset is sold. This means that there would be no CCA deductions in tax year $t + 1$ or in following years. If we wanted to use Eq. 7.10 to determine the present value of CCA tax shields, we would need to adjust it to eliminate the CCA tax shields from tax year $t + 1$ onward. This is equivalent to subtracting a perpetuity of CCA tax shields generated from UCC_{t+1} (the UCC that remained after the CCA deduction claimed in year t). The adjustment to

Eq. 7.10 for a terminating asset pool due to a sale at date t (the beginning of tax year $t + 1$) is as follows.

$$PV_{\text{CCA tax shields}} = \frac{\text{CapEx} \times d \times \tau_c}{r + d} \times \frac{\left(1 + \frac{r}{2}\right)}{(1 + r)}$$
$$- \frac{\text{UCC}_{t+1} \times d \times \tau_c}{r + d} \times \frac{1}{(1 + r)^t} \qquad (7A.4)^{[13]}$$

where UCC_{t+1} is calculated using Eq. 7.2.

It is important to remember all the effects of a terminating pool caused by the sale of an asset at date t (the beginning of tax year $t + 1$). We just saw that Eq. 7A.4 must be used in place of Eq. 7.10. As in other cases, the Sale Price$_t$ received at date t is added to the free cash flow for date t. The tax effect of the terminal loss (or recaptured CCA) shown in Eq. 7A.3 is added to the free cash flow for date $t + 1$. Finally, if there is a capital gain, then the capital gains tax (Eq. 7.12) is subtracted from the free cash flow for year $t + 1$.

EXAMPLE 7A.2	PRESENT VALUE OF CCA TAX SHIELDS FOR A TERMINATING POOL

Problem

Surrey Seeds is considering a project that will require them to build a greenhouse on land that it can lease for four years. Surrey Seeds does not own any other buildings or greenhouses as their other operations are in premises for which they have short-term leases. The cost of the greenhouse is $1 million. After the end of the land's lease, Surrey Seeds will sell the greenhouse to the landowner for $250,000. Greenhouses fall under asset class 8 for the purpose of calculating CCA deductions and the relevant CCA rate is 20%. Management at Surrey Seeds has asked for your help in determining the year-by-year CCA deductions, all relevant tax effects related to the greenhouse, and their present value. They want this information so they can use it in an NPV analysis for the project. Surrey Seeds' marginal tax rate is 40% and the relevant cost of capital is 11%.

Solution

To determine the year-by-year CCA deductions, you can use Eqs. 7.1 and 7.2 to make the following spreadsheet. Note, given the situation described, this will be the case of a terminating pool. You can use Eq. 7A.4 to determine the present value of CCA tax shields. You will need Eq. 7.2 to calculate UCC_5 for Eq. 7A.4. You will also need to determine the post-sale UCC_5 to know if there is a tax effect due to a terminal loss or recaptured CCA.

---

13. If the asset sale was timed to be at the end of tax year t rather than at the beginning of tax year $t + 1$, then in Eq. 7A.4 we would use UCC_t instead of UCC_{t+1} and the exponent on the last term of the equation would be $t - 1$ instead of t.

UCC, CCA, and Tax Shield Calculations Given a Terminating Pool

	Year, t	0	1	2	3	4	5
Capital Expenditure, CCA and UCC Forecasts ($000s)							
1	CapEx	1,000				(250)	
2	UCC_t		500	900	720	576	461
3	$CCA_t = UCC_t \times d$		100	180	144	115	
4	CCA tax shield $= \tau_c \times CCA$		40	72	58	46	
5	Present value of CCA tax shield $= (\tau_c \times CCA_t)/(1+r)^t$		36	58	42	30	
6	CCA rate, d	20%					
7	Tax rate, τ_c	40%	Note that there are no CCA deductions following				
8	Project cost of capital, r	11%	the termination of the pool.				
9	Sum of $PV_{CCA\ tax\ shields}$ from $t = 1$ to 4	166.94380					
10	$PV_{CCA\ tax\ shields}$ (equation 7A.4)	166.94380					
11	Post-sale $UCC_5 = UCC_5 -$ sale price$_4$	211					
12	Terminal loss (recapture) tax effect$_5$	84					
13	PV terminal loss (recapture) tax effect	50.03982					
14	Sum of PV of tax effects	216.98361					

The calculation of the present value of CCA tax shields in line 10 of the spreadsheet uses Eq. 7A.4 as follows.

$$PV_{CCA\ tax\ shields} = \frac{1{,}000 \times .2 \times .4}{.11 \times .2} \times \frac{\left(1 + \dfrac{.11}{2}\right)}{(1 + .11)}$$
$$- \frac{461 \times .2 \times .4}{.11 + .2} \times \frac{1}{(1 + .11)^4} = 166.94$$

This is exactly equal to the sum of the present values of the individual CCA tax shields with the result shown in line 9 of the spreadsheet. The reason for the two amounts being exactly the same is that in neither case are there any CCA deductions for date 5 or onward.

The Post-Sale $UCC_5 = UCC_5 -$ Sale Price$_4 = 461 - 250 = 211$. Since this is positive, Surrey Seeds will have a terminal loss. The terminal loss reduces taxes and thus generates a positive tax shield in the amount of $211 \times 40\% = 84$. The present value of the terminal loss tax shield is approximately 50.

Putting it all together (and remembering all the above values were in thousands of dollars), you add the present value of the CCA tax shields to the present value of the terminal loss tax shield to get the present value of the tax effects of $216,983.61. This would be added into the NPV calculation for the evaluation of the project under consideration at Surrey Seeds. Of course, you would advise management to deduct the initial cost of the greenhouse and add the present value of the sale price into the NPV calculation too.

CHAPTER

8

Valuing Bonds

NOTATION

CPN	coupon payment on a bond
n	number of periods
y,YTM	yield to maturity
P	initial price of a bond
FV	face value of a bond
YTM_n	yield to maturity on a zero-coupon bond with *n* periods to maturity
r_n	interest rate or discount rate for a cash flow that arrives in period *n*
PV	present value
NPER	annuity spreadsheet notation for the number of periods or dates of the last cash flow
RATE	annuity spreadsheet notation for interest rate
PMT	annuity spreadsheet notation for cash flow
APR	annual percentage rate

The Government of Canada had a budget deficit in 1996/97, prior to which it only had two surpluses in the previous 36 years. To finance budget deficits, governments must borrow money. The accumulated debt of the Government of Canada (face value of bonds and Treasury Bills outstanding) peaked at over $468 billion in 1997. Since that time, until 2009, the Canadian government has consistently run budget surpluses. This means more money was collected (through taxes) than was spent on programs. The surplus funds could be used to pay down the Government of Canada debt. In May 2007, the debt of the Government of Canada dropped below $397 billion, of which Treasury Bills accounted for $113.5 billion and Canadian dollar denominated Government of Canada bonds accounted for $274.6 billion. Provincial governments had another $286.6 billion of Canadian dollar denominated bonds outstanding, while municipalities had $34.5 billion and corporations had $267.2 billion outstanding. All together, in 2007, there were over $1.1 trillion of Canadian dollar denominated debt outstanding and over $1.5 trillion of debt (of all currencies) issued by Canadian institutions.[1]

In this chapter we look at the basic types of bonds and consider their valuation. Understanding bonds and their pricing is useful for several reasons. First, the prices of risk-free government bonds can be used to determine the risk-free interest rates that produce the yield curve discussed in Chapter 5. As we saw there, the yield curve provides important information for valuing risk-free cash flows and assessing expectations of inflation and economic growth. Second, firms often issue bonds to fund their own investments, and the returns investors receive on those bonds is one factor that determines a firm's cost of capital. Finally, bonds provide

---

1. CANSIM, database Table 176-0071 and 0022.

an opportunity to begin our study of how securities are priced in a competitive market. The ideas we develop in this chapter will be helpful when we turn to the topic of valuing stocks in Chapter 9.

As we explained in Chapter 3, the Law of One Price implies that the price of a security in a competitive market should be the present value of the cash flows an investor will receive from owning it. Thus we begin the chapter by evaluating the promised cash flows for different types of bonds. If a bond is risk-free, so that the promised cash flows will be paid with certainty, we can use the Law of One Price to directly relate the return of a bond and its price. We also describe how bond prices change dynamically over time and examine the relationship between the prices and returns of different bonds. Finally, we consider bonds for which there is a risk of default, so that their cash flows are not known with certainty.

8.1   BOND CASH FLOWS, PRICES, AND YIELDS

In this section we look at how bonds are defined and then study the basic relationship between bond prices and their yield to maturity.

BOND TERMINOLOGY

Recall from Chapter 3 that a bond is a security sold by governments and corporations to raise money from investors today in exchange for the promised future payment. The terms of the bond are described as part of the **bond indenture**, which indicates the amounts and dates of all payments to be made. These payments are made until a final repayment date, called the **maturity date** of the bond. The time remaining until the repayment date is known as the **term** of the bond.

Bonds typically make two types of payments to their holders. The promised interest payments of a bond are called **coupons**. The bond indenture typically specifies that the coupons will be paid periodically (for example, semiannually) until the maturity date of the bond. The principal or **face value** of a bond is the notional amount we use to compute the interest payments. Usually, the face value is repaid at maturity. It is generally denominated in standard increments such as $1000. A bond with a $1000 face value, for example, is often referred to as a "$1000 bond."

The amount of each coupon payment is determined by the **coupon rate** of the bond. This coupon rate is set by the issuer and stated on the bond indenture. The coupon rate indicates the percentage of face value paid out as coupons each year, so the amount of each coupon payment, CPN, is

Coupon Payment

$$CPN = \frac{\text{Coupon Rate} \times \text{Face Value}}{\text{Number of Coupon Payments per Year}} \tag{8.1}$$

For example, a "$1000 bond with a 10% coupon rate and semiannual payments" will pay coupon payments of $1000 × 10%/2 = $50 every six months.

ZERO-COUPON BONDS

The simplest type of bond is a **zero-coupon bond**, a bond that does not make coupon payments. The only cash payment the investor receives is the face value of the bond on the maturity date. **Treasury Bills**, which are **Government of Canada bonds** with a maturity of up to one year, are zero-coupon bonds. Recall from Chapter 3 that the present value of a future cash flow is less than the cash flow itself. As a result, prior to its maturity date, the price of a zero-coupon bond is always less than its face value. That is, zero-coupon bonds always trade at a **discount** (a price lower than the face value), so they are also called **pure discount bonds**.

Suppose that a one-year, risk-free, zero-coupon bond with a $100,000 face value has an initial price of $96,618.36. If you purchased this bond and held it to maturity, you would have the following cash flows:

Although the bond pays no "interest" directly, as an investor you are compensated for the time value of your money by purchasing the bond at a discount to its face value.

YIELD TO MATURITY.   Recall that the IRR of an investment opportunity is the discount rate at which the NPV of the investment opportunity is equal to zero. The IRR of an investment in a zero-coupon bond is the rate of return that investors will earn on their money if they buy the bond at its current price and hold it to maturity. The IRR of an investment in a bond is given a special name, the **yield to maturity (YTM)** or just the *yield*:

> *The yield to maturity of a bond is the discount rate that sets the present value of the promised bond payments equal to the current market price of the bond.*

Intuitively, the yield to maturity for a zero-coupon bond is the return you will earn as an investor from holding the bond to maturity and receiving the promised face value payment.

Let's determine the yield to maturity of the one-year zero-coupon bond discussed earlier. According to the definition, the yield to maturity of the one-year bond solves the following equation:

$$96,618.36 = \frac{100,000}{1 + YTM_1} \tag{8.2}$$

In this case,

$$1 + YTM_1 = \frac{100,000}{96,618.36} = 1.035$$

That is, the yield to maturity for this bond is 3.5%. Because the bond is risk free, investing in this bond and holding it to maturity is like earning 3.5% interest on your initial investment. Thus, by the Law of One Price, the competitive market risk-free interest rate is 3.5%, meaning all one-year risk-free investments must earn 3.5%.

Similarly, the yield to maturity for a zero-coupon bond with n periods to maturity, current price P, and face value FV is[2]

$$P = \frac{FV}{(1 + YTM_n)^n} \tag{8.2}$$

Rearranging this expression, we get

Yield to Maturity of an n-Year Zero-Coupon Bond

$$YTM_n = \left(\frac{FV}{P}\right)^{1/n} - 1 \tag{8.3}$$

The yield to maturity (YTM_n) in Eq. 8.3 is the effective rate of return per period for holding the bond from today until maturity on date n.

EXAMPLE 8.1	YIELDS FOR DIFFERENT MATURITIES

Problem

Suppose the following zero-coupon bonds are trading at the prices shown below per $100 face value. Determine the corresponding yield to maturity for each bond.

Maturity	1 Year	2 Years	3 Years	4 Years
Price	$96.62	$92.45	$87.63	$83.06

Solution

Using Eq. 8.3, we have

$$YTM_1 = (100/96.62) - 1 \quad = 3.50\%$$
$$YTM_2 = (100/92.45)^{1/2} - 1 = 4.00\%$$
$$YTM_3 = (100/87.63)^{1/3} - 1 = 4.50\%$$
$$YTM_4 = (100/83.06)^{1/4} - 1 = 4.75\%$$

RISK-FREE INTEREST RATES. In earlier chapters, we discussed the competitive market interest rate r_n available from today until date n for risk-free cash flows; we used this interest rate as the cost of capital for a risk-free cash flow that occurs on date n. Because a default-free zero-coupon bond that matures on date n provides a risk-free return over the same period, the Law of One Price guarantees that the risk-free interest rate equals the yield to maturity on such a bond.

Risk-Free Interest Rate with Maturity n

$$r_n = YTM_n \tag{8.4}$$

Consequently, we will often refer to the yield to maturity of the appropriate maturity, zero-coupon risk-free bond as *the* risk-free interest rate. Some financial professionals also use the term **spot interest rates** to refer to these default-free, zero-coupon yields.

---

2. In Chapter 4, we used the notation FV_n for the future value on date n of a cash flow. Conveniently, for a zero-coupon bond, the future value is also its face value, so the abbreviation FV is easy to remember.

FINANCIAL **CRISIS**
PURE DISCOUNT BONDS TRADING AT A PREMIUM

On December 9, 2008, in the midst of one of the worst financial crises in history, the unthinkable happened—for the first time since the Great Depression, U.S. Treasury Bills traded at a negative yield. That is, these risk-free pure discount bonds traded at premium. As Bloomberg.com reported: "If you invested $1 million in three-month bills at today's negative discount rate of 0.01 percent, for a price of 100.002556, at maturity you would receive the par value for a loss of $25.56."

A negative yield on a Treasury Bill implies that investors have an arbitrage opportunity: By *selling* the bill, and holding the proceeds in cash, they would have a risk-free *profit* of $25.56. Why did investors not rush to take advantage of the arbitrage opportunity and thereby eliminate it?

Well, first, the negative yields did not last very long, suggesting that in, fact, investors did rush to take advantage of this

opportunity. But second, after closer consideration, the opportunity might not have been a sure risk-free arbitrage. When selling a Treasury security, the investor must choose where to invest, or at least hold, the proceeds. In normal times investors would be happy to deposit the proceeds with a bank, and consider this deposit to be risk free. But these were not normal times—many investors had great concerns about the financial stability of banks and other financial intermediaries. Perhaps investors shied away from this "arbitrage" opportunity because they were worried that the cash they would receive could not be held safely anywhere (even putting it "under the mattress" has a risk of theft!). Thus, we can view the $25.56 as the price investors were willing to pay to have the U.S. Treasury hold their money safely for them at a time when no other investments seemed truly safe.

In Chapter 5, we introduced the yield curve, which plots the risk-free interest rate for different maturities. These risk-free interest rates correspond to the yields of risk-free zero-coupon bonds. Thus the yield curve we introduced in Chapter 5 is also referred to as the **zero-coupon yield curve**.

COUPON BONDS

Like zero-coupon bonds, **coupon bonds** pay investors their face value at maturity. In addition, these bonds make regular coupon interest payments. When the Government of Canada sells bonds, they are normally issued with maturities of 2, 5, 10, or 30 years.

EXAMPLE 8.2

THE CASH FLOWS OF A COUPON BOND

Problem
The Government of Canada has just issued a five-year, $1000 bond with a 5% coupon rate and semiannual coupons. What cash flows will you receive if you hold this bond until maturity?

Solution
The face value of this bond is $1000. Because this bond pays coupons semiannually, from Eq. 8.1 you will receive a coupon payment every six months of CPN = $1000 × 5%/2 = $25. Here is the timeline, based on a six-month period:

Note that the last payment occurs five years (10 six-month periods) from now and is composed of both a coupon payment of $25 and the face value payment of $1000.

We can also compute the yield to maturity of a coupon bond. Recall that the yield to maturity for a bond is the IRR of investing in the bond and holding it to maturity; it is the *single* discount rate that equates the present value of the bond's remaining cash flows to its current price, shown in the following timeline:

Because the coupon payments represent an annuity, the yield to maturity is the interest rate y that solves the following equation:[3]

Yield to Maturity of a Coupon Bond

$$P = CPN \times \frac{1}{y}\left(1 - \frac{1}{(1 + y)^N}\right) + \frac{FV}{(1 + y)^N} \qquad (8.5)$$

Unfortunately, unlike in the case of zero-coupon bonds, there is no simple formula to solve for the yield to maturity directly. Instead, we need to use a financial calculator, trial-and-error, or the annuity spreadsheet we introduced in Chapter 4 (or Excel's IRR function).

When we calculate a bond's yield to maturity by solving Eq. 8.5, the yield we compute will be an effective rate *per coupon interval*. This yield is typically stated as an annual rate by multiplying it by the number of coupons per year, thereby converting it to an APR with the same compounding interval as the coupon rate.

EXAMPLE 8.3	COMPUTING THE YIELD TO MATURITY OF A COUPON BOND

Problem

Consider the five-year, $1000 bond with a 5% coupon rate and semiannual coupons described in Example 8.2. If this bond is currently trading for a price of $957.35, what is the bond's yield to maturity?

Solution

Because the bond has ten remaining coupon payments, we compute its yield y by solving:

$$957.35 = 25 \times \frac{1}{y}\left(1 - \frac{1}{(1 + y)^{10}}\right) + \frac{1000}{(1 + y)^{10}}$$

We can solve it by trial-and-error, or we can easily solve it by using a financial calculator or the annuity spreadsheet.

	NPER	RATE	PV	PMT	FV	Excel Formula
Given	10		−957.35	25	1,000	
Solve for Rate		3.00%				=Rate(10,25,−957.35,1000)

---

3. In Eq. 8.5, we have assumed that the first cash coupon will be paid one period from now. If the first coupon is less than one period away, the cash price of the bond can be found by adjusting the price in Eq. 8.5 by multiplying by $(1 + y)^f$, where f is the fraction of the coupon interval that has already elapsed. (Also, bond prices are often quoted in terms of the *clean price*, which is calculated by deducting from the cash price P an amount, called *accrued interest*, equal to $f \times CPN$. See the box on page 248.)

Therefore, $y = 3\%$. Because the bond pays coupons semiannually, this yield is an effective rate per six-month period. We convert it to an APR by multiplying by the number of coupon payments per year. Thus the bond has a quoted yield to maturity equal to a 6% APR with semiannual compounding; this is the standard way coupon-paying bonds' yields are quoted.

We can also use Eq. 8.5 to compute a bond's price based on its yield to maturity. We simply discount the cash flows using the yield, as in Example 8.4.

EXAMPLE 8.4

COMPUTING A BOND PRICE FROM ITS YIELD TO MATURITY

Problem

Consider again the five-year, $1000 bond with a 5% coupon rate and semiannual coupons in Example 8.3. Suppose you are told that its yield to maturity has increased to 6.30% (expressed as an APR with semiannual compounding). What price is the bond trading for now?

Solution

Given the yield, we can compute the price using Eq. 8.5. First, note that a 6.30% APR is equivalent to an effective semiannual rate of 3.15%; this is needed to discount the semiannual annuity of the coupons. Therefore, the bond price is

$$P = 25 \times \frac{1}{0.0315}\left(1 - \frac{1}{1.0315^{10}}\right) + \frac{1000}{1.0315^{10}} = \$944.98$$

We can also use the annuity spreadsheet:

	NPER	RATE	PV	PMT	FV	Excel Formula
Given	10	3.15%		25	1,000	
Solve for PV			−944.98			=PV(0.0315,10,25,1000)

Because we can convert any price into a yield, and vice versa, prices and yields are often used interchangeably. For example, the bond in Example 8.4 could be quoted as having a yield of 6.30% or a price of $944.98 per $1000 face value. Indeed, bond traders generally quote bond yields rather than bond prices. One advantage of quoting the yield to maturity rather than the price is that the yield is independent of the face value of the bond. When prices are quoted in the bond market, they are conventionally quoted as a percentage of their face value. Thus the bond in Example 8.4 would be quoted as having a price of 94.498, which would imply an actual price of $944.98 given the $1000 face value of the bond.

CONCEPT CHECK

1. What is the relationship between a bond's price and its yield to maturity?

2. The risk-free interest rate for a maturity of *n* years can be determined from the yield of what type of bond?

8.2   DYNAMIC BEHAVIOUR OF BOND PRICES

As we mentioned earlier, zero-coupon bonds always trade at a discount, that is, prior to maturity, their price is less than their face value. Coupon bonds may trade at a discount, at a **premium** (a price greater than their face value), or at **par** (a price equal to their face value). In this section, we identify when a bond will trade at a discount or premium as well as how the bond's price will change due to the passage of time and fluctuations in interest rates.

DISCOUNTS AND PREMIUMS

If the bond trades at a discount, an investor who buys the bond will earn a return both from receiving the coupons *and* from receiving a face value that exceeds the price paid for the bond. As a result, if a bond trades at a discount, its yield to maturity will exceed its coupon rate. Given the relationship between bond prices and yields, the reverse is clearly also true: If a coupon bond's yield to maturity exceeds its coupon rate, the present value of its cash flows at the yield to maturity will be less than its face value, and the bond will trade at a discount.

A bond that pays a coupon can also trade at a premium to its face value. In this case, an investor's return from the coupons is diminished by receiving a face value less than the price paid for the bond. Thus, a bond trades at a premium whenever its yield to maturity is less than its coupon rate.

When a bond trades at a price equal to its face value, it is said to trade at par. A bond trades at par when its coupon rate is equal to its yield to maturity. A bond that trades at a discount is also said to trade below par, and a bond that trades at a premium is said to trade above par.

Table 8.1 summarizes the properties of coupon bond prices.

TABLE 8.1	BOND PRICES IMMEDIATELY AFTER A COUPON PAYMENT		
When the bond price is . . .	greater than the face value	equal to the face value	less than the face value
We say the bond trades . . .	"above par" or "at a premium"	"at par"	"below par" or "at a discount"
This occurs when the . . .	Coupon Rate > Yield to Maturity	Coupon Rate = Yield to Maturity	Coupon Rate < Yield to Maturity

EXAMPLE 8.5	DETERMINING THE DISCOUNT OR PREMIUM OF A COUPON BOND

Problem

Consider three 30-year Government of Canada bonds with annual coupon payments. One bond has a 10% coupon rate, one has a 5% coupon rate, and one has a 3% coupon rate. If the yield to maturity of each bond is 5%, what is the price of each bond per $100 face value? Which bond trades at a premium, which trades at a discount, and which trades at par?

Solution

We can compute the price of each bond using Eq. 8.5. Therefore, the bond prices are

$$P(10\% \text{ coupon}) = 10 \times \frac{1}{0.05}\left(1 - \frac{1}{1.05^{30}}\right) + \frac{100}{1.05^{30}} = \$176.86 \quad \text{(trades at a premium)}$$

$$P(5\% \text{ coupon}) = 5 \times \frac{1}{0.05}\left(1 - \frac{1}{1.05^{30}}\right) + \frac{100}{1.05^{30}} = \$100.00 \quad \text{(trades at par)}$$

$$P(3\% \text{ coupon}) = 3 \times \frac{1}{0.05}\left(1 - \frac{1}{1.05^{30}}\right) + \frac{100}{1.05^{30}} = \$69.26 \quad \text{(trades at a discount)}$$

Most issuers of coupon bonds choose a coupon rate so that the bonds will *initially* trade at, or very close to, par (i.e., at face value). For example, the Government of Canada sets the coupon rates on its bonds in this way. After the issue date, the market price of a bond generally changes over time for two reasons. First, as time passes, the bond gets closer to its maturity date. Holding fixed the bond's yield to maturity, the present value of the bond's remaining cash flows changes as the time to maturity decreases. Second, at any point in time, changes in market interest rates affect the bond's yield to maturity and its price (the present value of the remaining cash flows). We explore these two effects in the remainder of this section.

TIME AND BOND PRICES

Let's consider the effect of time on the price of a bond. Suppose you purchase a 30-year, zero-coupon bond with a yield to maturity of 5%. For a face value of $100, the bond will initially trade for

$$P(30 \text{ years to maturity}) = \frac{100}{1.05^{30}} = \$23.14$$

Now let's consider the price of this bond five years later, when it has 25 years remaining until maturity. If the bond's yield to maturity remains at 5%, the bond price in five years will be

$$P(25 \text{ years to maturity}) = \frac{100}{1.05^{25}} = \$29.53$$

Note that the bond price is higher, and hence the discount from its face value is smaller, when there is less time to maturity. The discount shrinks because the yield has not changed, but there is less time until the face value will be received. If you purchased the bond for $23.14 and then sold it after five years for $29.53, the IRR of your investment would be

$$\left(\frac{29.53}{23.14}\right)^{1/5} - 1 = 5.0\%$$

That is, your return is the same as the yield to maturity of the bond. This example illustrates a more general property for bonds. If a bond's yield to maturity does not change, then the IRR of an investment in the bond equals its yield to maturity even if you sell the bond early.

These results also hold for coupon bonds. The pattern of price changes over time is a bit more complicated for coupon bonds, however, because as time passes most of the cash flows get closer but some of the cash flows disappear as the coupons get paid. Example 8.6 illustrates these effects.

EXAMPLE 8.6

THE EFFECT OF TIME ON THE PRICE OF A COUPON BOND

Problem

Consider a 30-year Government of Canada bond with a 10% coupon rate (annual payments) and a $100 face value. What is the initial price of this bond if it has a 5% yield to maturity? If the yield to maturity is unchanged, what will the price be immediately before and after the first coupon is paid?

Solution

We computed the price of this bond with 30 years to maturity in Example 8.5:

$$P = 10 \times \frac{1}{0.05}\left(1 - \frac{1}{1.05^{30}}\right) + \frac{100}{1.05^{30}} = \$176.86$$

Now consider the cash flows of this bond in one year, immediately before the first coupon is paid. The bond now has 29 years until it matures, and the timeline is as follows:

Again, we compute the price by discounting the cash flows by the yield to maturity. Note that there is a cash flow of $10 at date zero, the coupon that is about to be paid. In this case, it is easiest to treat the first coupon separately and value the remaining cash flows as in Eq. 8.5:

$$P(\text{just before first coupon}) = 10 + 10 \times \frac{1}{0.05}\left(1 - \frac{1}{1.05^{29}}\right) + \frac{100}{1.05^{29}} = \$185.71$$

Note that the bond price is higher than it was initially. It will make the same total number of coupon payments, but an investor does not need to wait as long to receive the first one. We could also compute the price by noting that because the yield to maturity remains at 5% for the bond, investors in the bond should earn a return of 5% over the year: $176.86 \times 1.05 = \$185.71$.

What happens to the price of the bond just after the first coupon is paid? The timeline is the same as that given earlier, except the new owner of the bond will not receive the coupon at date zero. Thus, just after the coupon is paid, the price of the bond (given the same yield to maturity) will be

$$P(\text{just after first coupon}) = 10 \times \frac{1}{0.05}\left(1 - \frac{1}{1.05^{29}}\right) + \frac{100}{1.05^{29}} = \$175.71$$

The price of the bond will drop by the amount of the coupon ($10) immediately after the coupon is paid, reflecting the fact that the owner will no longer receive the coupon. In this case, the price is lower than the initial price of the bond. Because there are fewer coupon payments remaining, the premium investors will pay for the bond declines. Still, an investor who buys the bond initially, receives the first coupon, and then sells it, earns a 5% return if the bond's yield does not change: $(10 \times 175.71)/176.86 = 1.05$.

The Effect of Time on Bond Prices
The graph illustrates the effects of the passage of time on bond prices when the yield remains constant. The price of a zero-coupon bond rises smoothly. The price of a coupon bond also rises between coupon payments, but tumbles on the coupon date, reflecting the amount of the coupon payment. For each coupon bond, the grey line shows the trend of the bond price just after each coupon is paid.

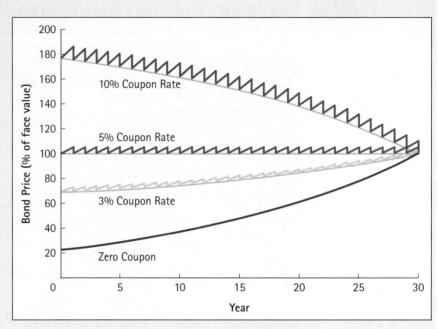

CLEAN AND DIRTY PRICES FOR COUPON BONDS

As Figure 8.1 illustrates, coupon bond prices fluctuate around the time of each coupon payment in a saw tooth pattern: The value of the coupon bond rises as the next coupon payment gets closer and then drops after it has been paid. This fluctuation occurs even if there is no change in the bond's yield to maturity.

Because bond traders are more concerned about changes in the bond's price that arise due to changes in the bond's yield, rather than these predictable patterns around coupon payments, they often do not quote the price of a bond in terms of its actual cash price, which is also called the **dirty price** or **invoice price** of the bond. Instead, bonds are often quoted in terms of a **clean price**, which is the bond's cash price less an adjustment for accrued interest, the amount of the next coupon payment that has already accrued:

Clean price = Cash (dirty) price − Accrued interest

Accrued interest = Coupon Amount ×

$$\left(\frac{\text{Days since last coupon payment}}{\text{Days in current coupon period}}\right)$$

Note that immediately before a coupon payment is made, the accrued interest will equal the full amount of the coupon, whereas immediately after the coupon payment is made, the accrued interest will be zero. Thus, accrued interest will rise and fall in a saw tooth pattern as each coupon payment passes:

If we subtract accrued interest from the bond's cash price and compute the clean price, the saw-tooth pattern is eliminated. Thus, absent changes in the bond's yield to maturity, its clean price converges smoothly over time to the bond's face value, as shown in the grey lines in Figure 8.1.

Figure 8.1 illustrates the effect of time on bond prices, assuming the yield to maturity remains constant. Between coupon payments, the prices of all bonds rise at a rate equal to the yield to maturity as the remaining cash flows of the bond become closer. But as each coupon is paid, the price of a bond drops by the amount of the coupon. When the bond is trading at a premium, the price drop when a coupon is paid will be larger than the price increase between coupons, so the bond's premium will tend to decline as time passes. If the bond is trading at a discount, the price increase between coupons will exceed the drop when a coupon is paid, so the bond's price will rise and its discount will decline as time passes. Ultimately, the prices of all bonds approach the bonds' face value when the bonds mature and their last coupon is paid.

For each of the bonds illustrated in Figure 8.1, if the yield to maturity remains at 5%, investors will earn a 5% return on their investment. For the zero-coupon bond, this return is earned solely due to the price appreciation of the bond. For the 10% coupon bond, this return comes from the combination of coupon payments and price depreciation over time.

INTEREST RATE CHANGES AND BOND PRICES

As interest rates in the economy fluctuate, the yields that investors demand to invest in bonds will also change. Let's evaluate the effect of fluctuations in a bond's yield to maturity on its price.

Consider again a 30-year, zero-coupon bond with a yield to maturity of 5%. For a face value of $100, the bond will initially trade for

$$P(5\% \text{ yield to maturity}) = \frac{100}{1.05^{30}} = \$23.14$$

But suppose interest rates suddenly rise so that investors now demand a 6% yield to maturity before they will invest in this bond. This change in yield implies that the bond price will fall to

$$P(6\% \text{ yield to maturity}) = \frac{100}{1.06^{30}} = \$17.41$$

Relative to the initial price, the bond price changes by $(17.41 - 23.14)/23.14 = -24.8\%$, a substantial price drop.

This example illustrates a general phenomenon. A higher yield to maturity implies a higher discount rate for a bond's remaining cash flows, reducing their present value and hence the bond's price. Therefore, *as interest rates and bond yields rise, bond prices will fall, and vice versa*.

The sensitivity of a bond's price to changes in interest rates depends on the timing of its cash flows. Because it is discounted over a shorter period, the present value of a cash flow that will be received in the near future is less dramatically affected by interest rates than a cash flow in the distant future. Thus shorter-maturity zero-coupon bonds are less sensitive to changes in interest rates than are longer-term zero-coupon bonds. Similarly, bonds with higher coupon rates—because they pay higher cash flows upfront—are less sensitive to interest rate changes than otherwise identical bonds with lower coupon rates. The sensitivity of a bond's price to changes in interest rates is measured by the bond's **duration**.[4] Bonds with high durations are highly sensitive to interest rate changes.

---

4. We define duration formally and discuss this concept more thoroughly in Chapter 30.

| EXAMPLE 8.7 | THE INTEREST RATE SENSITIVITY OF BONDS |

Problem

Consider a 15-year zero-coupon bond and a 30-year coupon bond with 10% annual coupons. Both bonds have a $100 face value. By what percentage will the price of each bond change if its yield to maturity increases from 5% to 6%?

Solution

First we compute the price of each bond for each yield to maturity:

Yield to Maturity	15-Year, Zero-Coupon Bond	30-Year, 10% Annual Coupon Bond
5%	$\dfrac{100}{1.05^{15}} = \$48.10$	$10 \times \dfrac{1}{0.05}\left(1 - \dfrac{1}{1.05^{30}}\right) + \dfrac{100}{1.05^{30}} = \$176.86$
6%	$\dfrac{100}{1.06^{15}} = \$41.73$	$10 \times \dfrac{1}{0.06}\left(1 - \dfrac{1}{1.06^{30}}\right) + \dfrac{100}{1.06^{30}} = \$155.06$

The price of the 15-year zero-coupon bond changes by $(41.73 - 48.10)/48.10 = -13.2\%$ if its yield to maturity increases from 5% to 6%. For the 30-year bond with 10% annual coupons, the price change is $(155.06 - 176.86)/176.86 = -12.3\%$. Even though the 30-year bond has a longer maturity, because of its high coupon rate its sensitivity to a change in yield is actually less than that of the 15-year zero coupon bond.

In actuality, bond prices are subject to the effects of both the passage of time and changes in interest rates. Bond prices converge to the bond's face value due to the time effect, but simultaneously move up and down due to unpredictable changes in bond yields. Figure 8.2 illustrates this behaviour by demonstrating how the price of the 30-year, zero-coupon bond might change over its life. Note that the bond price tends to converge to the face value as the bond approaches the maturity date, but also moves higher when its yield falls and lower when its yield rises.

As Figure 8.2 demonstrates, prior to maturity the bond is exposed to interest rate risk. If an investor chooses to sell and the bond's yield to maturity has decreased, then the investor will receive a high price and earn a high return. If the yield to maturity has increased, the bond price is low at the time of sale and the investor will earn a low return. In the appendix to this chapter, we discuss one way corporations manage this type of risk.

CONCEPT CHECK

1. If a bond's yield to maturity does not change, how does its cash price change between coupon payments?

2. What risk does an investor in a default-free bond face if she plans to sell the bond prior to maturity?

3. How does a bond's coupon rate affect its duration—the bond price's sensitivity to interest rate changes?

Yield to Maturity and Bond Price Fluctuations over Time

The graphs illustrate changes in price and yield for a 30-year zero-coupon bond over its life. The top graph illustrates the changes in the bond's yield to maturity over its life.

In the bottom graph, the actual bond price is shown in blue. Because the yield to maturity does not remain constant over the bond's life, the bond's price fluctuates as it converges to the face value over time. Also shown is the price if the yield to maturity remained fixed at 4%, 5%, or 6%.

8.3 THE YIELD CURVE AND BOND ARBITRAGE

Thus far, we have focused on the relationship between the price of an individual bond and its yield to maturity. In this section, we explore the relationship between the prices and yields of different bonds. Using the Law of One Price, we show that given the spot interest rates, which are the yields of default-free zero-coupon bonds, we can determine the price and yield of any other default-free bond. As a result, the yield curve provides sufficient information to evaluate all such bonds.

REPLICATING A COUPON BOND

Because it is possible to replicate the cash flows of a coupon bond using zero-coupon bonds, we can use the Law of One Price to compute the price of a coupon bond from the prices of zero-coupon bonds. For example, we can replicate a three-year, $1000 bond that pays 10% annual coupons using three zero-coupon bonds as follows:

We match each coupon payment to a zero-coupon bond with a face value equal to the coupon payment and a term equal to the time remaining to the coupon date. Similarly, we match the final bond payment (final coupon plus return of face value) in three years to a three-year, zero-coupon bond with a corresponding face value of $1100. Because the coupon bond cash flows are identical to the cash flows of the portfolio of zero-coupon bonds, the Law of One Price states that the price of the portfolio of zero-coupon bonds must be the same as the price of the coupon bond.

To illustrate, assume that current zero-coupon bond yields and prices are as shown in Table 8.2 (they are the same as in Example 8.1). We can calculate the cost of the zero-coupon bond portfolio that replicates the three-year coupon bond as follows:

Zero-Coupon Bond	Face Value Required	Cost
1 year	100	96.62
2 years	100	92.45
3 years	1100	$11 \times 87.63 = 963.93$
	Total Cost:	$1153.00

By the Law of One Price, the three-year coupon bond must trade for a price of $1153. If the price of the coupon bond were higher, you could earn an arbitrage profit by selling the coupon bond and buying the zero-coupon bond portfolio. If the price of the coupon bond were lower, you could earn an arbitrage profit by buying the coupon bond and short selling the zero-coupon bonds.

VALUING A COUPON BOND USING ZERO-COUPON YIELDS

To this point, we have used the zero-coupon bond *prices* to derive the price of the coupon bond. Alternatively, we can use the zero-coupon bond *yields*. Recall that the yield to maturity of a zero-coupon bond is the competitive market interest rate for a risk-free investment

YIELDS AND PRICES (PER $100 FACE VALUE) FOR ZERO-COUPON BONDS

TABLE 8.2

Maturity	1 Year	2 Years	3 Years	4 Years
YTM_n	3.50%	4.00%	4.50%	4.75%
Price	$96.62	$92.45	$87.63	$83.06

with a term equal to the term of the zero-coupon bond. Therefore, the price of a coupon bond must equal the present value of its coupon payments and face value discounted at the competitive market interest rates (see Eq. 5.7 in Chapter 5):

Price of a Coupon Bond

$$P = PV(\text{Bond Cash Flows})$$

$$= \frac{CPN}{1 + YTM_1} + \frac{CPN}{(1 + YTM_2)^2} + \cdots + \frac{CPN + FV}{(1 + YTM_n)^n} \quad (8.6)$$

where CPN is the bond coupon payment, YTM_n is the yield to maturity of a *zero-coupon* bond that matures at the same time as the nth coupon payment, and FV is the face value of the bond. For the three-year, $1000 bond with 10% annual coupons considered earlier, we can use Eq. 8.6 to calculate its price using the zero-coupon yields in Table 8.2:

$$P = \frac{100}{1.035} + \frac{100}{1.04^2} + \frac{100 + 1000}{1.045^3} = \$1153$$

This price is identical to the price we computed earlier by replicating the bond. Thus we can determine the no-arbitrage price of a coupon bond by discounting its cash flows using the zero-coupon yields. In other words, the information in the zero-coupon yield curve is sufficient to price all other risk-free bonds.

COUPON BOND YIELDS

Given the yields for zero-coupon bonds, we can use Eq. 8.6 to price a coupon bond. In Section 8.1, we saw how to compute the yield to maturity of a coupon bond from its price. Combining these results, we can determine the relationship between the yields of zero-coupon bonds and coupon-paying bonds.

Consider again the three-year, $1000 bond with 10% annual coupons. Given the zero-coupon yields in Table 8.2, we calculate a price for this bond of $1153. From Eq. 8.5, the yield to maturity of this bond is the rate y that satisfies

$$P = 1153 = \frac{100}{(1 + y)} + \frac{100}{(1 + y)^2} + \frac{100 + 1000}{(1 + y)^3}$$

We can solve for the yield by using the annuity spreadsheet:

	NPER	RATE	PV	PMT	FV	Excel Formula
Given	3		−1,153	100	1,000	
Solve for Rate		4.44%				=RATE(3,100,−1153,1000)

Therefore, the yield to maturity of the bond is 4.44%. We can check this result directly as follows:

$$P = \frac{100}{1.0444} + \frac{100}{1.0444^2} + \frac{100 + 1000}{1.0444^3} = \$1153$$

Because the coupon bond provides cash flows at different points in time, the yield to maturity of a coupon bond is a weighted average of the yields of the zero-coupon bonds of equal and shorter maturities. The weights depend (in a complex way) on the magnitude of the cash flows each period. In this example, the zero-coupon bond yields were 3.5%, 4.0%, and 4.5%. For this coupon bond, most of the value in the present value calculation comes from the present value of the third cash flow because it includes the principal, so the yield is closest to the three-year, zero-coupon yield of 4.5%.

EXAMPLE 8.8	YIELDS ON BONDS WITH THE SAME MATURITY

Problem

Given the following zero-coupon yields, compare the yield to maturity for a three-year, zero-coupon bond; a three-year coupon bond with 4% annual coupons; and a three-year coupon bond with 10% annual coupons. All of these bonds are default free.

Maturity	1 year	2 years	3 years	4 years
Zero-coupon YTM$_n$	3.50%	4.00%	4.50%	4.75%

Solution

From the information provided, the yield to maturity of the three-year, zero-coupon bond is 4.50%. Also, because the yields match those in Table 8.2, we already calculated the yield to maturity for the 10% coupon bond as 4.44%. To compute the yield for the 4% coupon bond, we first need to calculate its price. Using Eq. 8.6, we have

$$P = \frac{40}{1.035} + \frac{40}{1.04^2} + \frac{40 + 1000}{1.045^3} = \$986.98$$

The price of the bond with a 4% coupon is $986.98. From Eq. 8.5, its yield to maturity solves the following equation:

$$\$986.98 = \frac{40}{(1 + y)} + \frac{40}{(1 + y)^2} + \frac{40 + 1000}{(1 + y)^3}$$

We can calculate the yield to maturity using the annuity spreadsheet:

	NPER	RATE	PV	PMT	FV	Excel Formula
Given	3		−986.98	40	1,000	
Solve for Rate		4.47%				=RATE(3,40,−986.98,1000)

To summarize, for the three-year bonds considered,

Coupon rate	0%	4%	10%
YTM	4.50%	4.47%	4.44%

Example 8.8 shows that coupon bonds with the same maturity can have different yields depending on their coupon rates. The yield to maturity of a coupon bond is a weighted average of the yields on the zero-coupon bonds. As the coupon increases, earlier cash flows become relatively more important than later cash flows in the calculation of the present value. If the yield curve is upward sloping (as it is for the yields in Example 8.8), the resulting yield to maturity decreases with the coupon rate of the bond. Alternatively, when the zero-coupon yield curve is downward sloping, the yield to maturity will increase with the coupon rate. When the yield curve is flat, all zero-coupon and coupon-paying bonds will have the same yield, independent of their maturities and coupon rates.

COUPON-PAYING YIELD CURVE

As we have shown in this section, we can use the zero-coupon yield curve to determine the price and yield to maturity of other risk-free bonds. The plot of the yields of coupon bonds of different maturities is called the **coupon-paying yield curve**. The Bank of Canada reports the yields on 2-, 3-, 5-, 7-, 10-, and 30-year bonds. If we plotted these yields, we would have a coupon-paying yield curve. As we showed in Example 8.8, two coupon-paying bonds with the same maturity may have different yields; therefore, it is important to know the specific bond issues that are used by the Bank of Canada and practitioners—these are called the benchmark bonds. Fortunately, the Bank of Canada gives the precise maturity dates and coupon rates of the **benchmark bonds**. Using similar methods to those employed in this section, we can apply the Law of One Price to determine the zero-coupon bond yields using the coupon-paying yield curve (see Problem 22). Thus either type of yield curve provides enough information to value all other risk-free bonds.

CONCEPT CHECK

1. How do you calculate the price of a coupon bond from the prices of zero-coupon bonds?
2. How do you calculate the price of a coupon-paying bond from the yields of zero-coupon bonds?
3. Explain why two coupon bonds with the same maturity may each have a different yield to maturity.

8.4   CORPORATE BONDS

So far in this chapter, we have focused on default-free bonds such as Government of Canada securities, for which the cash flows are known with certainty. For other bonds such as **corporate bonds** (bonds issued by corporations), the issuer may default—that is, it might not pay back the full amount promised in the bond indenture. This risk of default, which is known as the **credit risk** of the bond, means that the bond's cash flows are not known with certainty.

CORPORATE BOND YIELDS

How does the credit risk of default affect bond prices and yields? Because the cash flows promised by the bond are the most that bondholders can hope to receive, the cash flows that a purchaser of a bond with credit risk *expects* to receive may be less than that amount. As a result, investors pay less for bonds with credit risk than they would for an otherwise identical default-free bond. Because the yield to maturity for a bond is calculated using the *promised* cash flows, the yield of bonds with credit risk will be higher than that of otherwise identical default-free bonds. Let's illustrate the effect of credit risk on bond yields and investor returns by comparing different cases.

NO DEFAULT.   Suppose that the one-year, zero-coupon Treasury Bill has a yield to maturity of 4%. What are the price and yield of a one-year, $1000, zero-coupon bond issued by Loblaw Companies Limited? First, suppose that all investors agree that there is *no* possibility that Loblaw's bond will default within the next year. In that case, investors will receive $1000 in one year for certain, as promised by the bond. Because this bond is risk free, the Law of One Price guarantees that it must have the same yield as the one-year, zero-coupon Treasury Bill. The price of the bond will therefore be

$$P = \frac{1000}{1 + YTM_1} = \frac{1000}{1.04} = \$961.54$$

CERTAIN DEFAULT. Now suppose that investors believe that Loblaw will default with certainty at the end of one year and will be able to pay only 90% of its outstanding obligations. Then, even though the bond promises $1000 at year-end, bondholders know they will receive only $900. Investors can predict this shortfall perfectly, so the $900 payment is risk free, and the bond is still a one-year risk-free investment. We therefore compute the price of the bond by discounting this cash flow using the risk-free interest rate as the cost of capital:

$$P = \frac{900}{1 + YTM_1} = \frac{900}{1.04} = \$865.38$$

The prospect of default lowers the cash flow investors expect to receive and hence the price they are willing to pay.

Given the bond's price, we can compute the bond's yield to maturity. When computing this yield, we use the *promised* rather than the *actual* cash flows. Thus

$$YTM = \frac{FV}{P} - 1 = \frac{1000}{865.38} - 1 = 15.56\%$$

The 15.56% yield to maturity of Loblaw's bond is much higher than the yield to maturity of the default-free Treasury Bill. But this result does not mean that investors who buy the bond will earn a 15.56% return. Because Loblaw will default, the expected return of the bond equals its 4% cost of capital:

$$\frac{900}{865.38} = 1.04$$

Note that *the yield to maturity of a defaultable bond is not equal to the expected return of investing in the bond.* Because we calculate the yield to maturity using the promised cash flows rather than the expected cash flows, the yield will always be higher than the expected return of investing in the bond.

RISK OF DEFAULT. The two Loblaw examples were extreme cases, of course. In the first case, we assumed the probability of default was zero; in the second case, we assumed Loblaw would definitely default. In reality, the chance that Loblaw will default lies somewhere in between these two extremes (and for most firms, is probably much closer to zero).

To illustrate, again consider the one-year, $1000, zero-coupon bond issued by Loblaw. This time, assume that the bond payoffs are uncertain. In particular, there is a 50% chance that the bond will repay its face value in full and a 50% chance that the bond will default and you will receive $900. Thus, on average, you will receive $950.

To determine the price of this bond, we must discount this expected cash flow using a cost of capital equal to the expected return of other securities with equivalent risk. If

INTERVIEW WITH LISA BLACK

*L*isa Black is managing director at Teachers Insurance and Annuity Association, a major financial services company. A chartered financial analyst, she oversees a variety of fixed income funds, including money market, intermediate bond, high-yield, emerging market debt, and inflation-linked bond funds.

QUESTION: When many people think about the financial markets, they picture the equity markets. How big and how active are the bond markets compared to the equity markets?

ANSWER: The dollar volume of bonds traded daily is about ten times that of equity markets. For example, a single $15 billion issue of 10 year Treasury bonds will sell in one day. The Lehman Brothers U.S. Universal Index of dollar-denominated debt outstanding totals almost $10 trillion, and its biggest component is the $8.3 trillion U.S. aggregate index, a broad index of investment grade debt. It includes treasuries, agencies, corporate bonds, and mortgage-backed securities. Other major sectors include corporate high yield bonds, Eurodollar bonds, emerging markets, and private placements.

QUESTION: How do the bond markets operate?

ANSWER: Firms and governments turn to bond markets when they need to borrow money to fund new construction projects, cover budget deficits, and similar reasons. On the other side, you have institutions like TIAA-CREF, endowments, and foundations with funds to invest.

Wall Street investment bankers serve as intermediaries between capital raisers and investors, matching up borrowers with creditors in terms of maturity needs and risk appetite. Because we provide annuities for college professors, for example, we invest money for longer periods of time than an insurance company that needs funds to pay claims. In the institutional world, such as the bond funds we manage, we typically trade in blocks of bonds ranging from $5 million to $50 million at a time.

QUESTION: What drives changes in the values of Treasury bonds?

ANSWER: The simple answer is that when interest rates rise, bond prices fall. The key is to dig below that reality to see *why* interest rates rise and fall. A major factor is investors' expectations for inflation and economic growth.

Interest rates generally rise when the expectation is that growth will accelerate, because inflation won't be far behind. During the 2008–2009 recession, interest rates dropped as the Federal Reserve injected liquidity into the system. There was also a flight to quality after the bankruptcy of Lehman Brothers. The value of the Reserve Fund fell drastically as its holdings of about $785 million of Lehman's short-term debt securities became all but worthless. Worried retail and institutional investors sold their money market funds and purchased U.S. Treasury Bills and notes to protect their principal. With increased demand, interest rates on risk-free Treasury securities fell sharply. At one point T-bills even had a negative yield.

QUESTION: What impact did the 2008–2009 financial crisis have on the bond market? What changes do you anticipate going forward as a result?

ANSWER: While the effects of the crisis on equity markets have been widely discussed, the effects on the bond market have been just as profound. Particularly noteworthy is the role governments and central bankers have played—and likely will continue to play—to stabilize financial institutions deemed too big or important to fail. The Fed introduced an unprecedented number of stimulus programs to unfreeze credit markets, including programs to guarantee money funds. The challenge will be how and when the various support programs and financial infusions will end and/or be paid back. In addition, the rating agencies' role and ratings methodologies will likely be subject to greater scrutiny, both from regulators and investors.

In the corporate sector, many borrowers—the automotive industries, for example—could not raise debt financing during the crisis. Credit spreads widened dramatically as investors shunned even AAA- and AA-rated credits. Major institutional investors sat on the sidelines for several months, and the corporate bond new issue market was essentially nonexistent. Not until the federal government announced programs to increase liquidity did institutional investors reenter the market, first buying only the highest credit quality instruments, such as first mortgage bonds issued by utilities and government-guaranteed mortgage-backed securities. Investors then began to move down the credit quality chain, selectively focusing on issuers that could weather an economic downtown.

Loblaw is more likely to default if the economy is weak than if the economy is strong, the results of Chapter 3 suggest that investors will demand a risk premium to invest in this bond. Thus Loblaw's debt cost of capital, which is the expected return Loblaw's debt holders will require to compensate them for the risk of the bond's cash flows, will be higher than the 4% risk-free interest rate.

Let's suppose investors demand a risk premium of 1.1% for this bond, so that the appropriate cost of capital is 5.1%. Then the present value of the bond's cash flow is:

$$P = \frac{950}{1.051} = \$903.90$$

Consequently, in this case the bond's yield to maturity is 10.63%:

$$YTM = \frac{FV}{P} - 1 = \frac{1000}{903.90} - 1 = 0.1063$$

Of course, the 10.63% promised yield is the most investors will receive. If Loblaw defaults, they will receive only $900, for a return of $900/903.90 - 1 = -0.43\%$. The average return is $0.50(10.63\%) + 0.50(-0.43\%) = 5.1\%$, the bond's cost of capital.

Table 8.3 summarizes the prices, expected return, and yield to maturity of the Loblaw bond under the various default assumptions. Note that the bond's price decreases, and its yield to maturity increases, with a greater likelihood of default. Conversely, *the bond's expected return, which is equal to the firm's debt cost of capital, is less than the yield to maturity if there is a risk of default. Moreover, a higher yield to maturity does not necessarily imply that a bond's expected return is higher.*

BOND RATINGS

It would be both difficult and inefficient for every investor to privately investigate the default risk of every bond. Consequently, several companies rate the creditworthiness of bonds and make this information available to investors. By consulting these ratings, investors can assess the creditworthiness of a particular bond issue. The ratings therefore encourage widespread investor participation and relatively liquid markets. The three best-known bond-rating companies in Canada are the Dominion Bond Rating Service (DBRS), a privately held Canadian firm; Standard & Poor's (which acquired the Canadian Bond Rating Service); and Moody's Investors Service. Table 8.4 summarizes the rating classes each company uses. Bonds with the highest rating are judged to be least likely to default.

PRICE, EXPECTED RETURN, AND YIELD TO MATURITY OF A ONE-YEAR, ZERO-COUPON LOBLAW BOND WITH DIFFERENT LIKELIHOODS OF DEFAULT

TABLE **8.3**	Loblaw Bond (1-year, zero-coupon)	Bond Price	Yield to Maturity	Expected Return
	Default Free	$961.54	4.00%	4%
	50% Chance of Default	$903.90	10.63%	5.1%
	Certain Default	$865.38	15.56%	4%

Bonds in the top four categories are often referred to as **investment-grade bonds** because of their low default risk. Bonds in the bottom five categories are often called **speculative bonds**, **junk bonds**, or **high-yield bonds** because their likelihood of default is high. The rating depends on the risk of bankruptcy as well as the bondholders' ability to lay claim to the firm's assets in the event of such a bankruptcy. Thus debt issues with a low-priority claim in bankruptcy will have a lower rating than issues from the same company that have a high priority in bankruptcy or that are backed by a specific asset such as a building or a plant.

CORPORATE YIELD CURVES

Just as we can construct a yield curve from risk-free Government of Canada securities, we can plot a similar yield curve for corporate bonds. Figure 8.3 shows the average yields of Canadian banks, which are representative of a low-AA DBRS credit rating for

TABLE 8.4 BOND RATINGS

Dominion Bond Rating Service (DBRS)	Moody's	Standard & Poor's	Description (Moody's)
Investment Grade Debt			
AAA	Aaa	AAA	Judged to be of the best quality. They carry the smallest degree of investment risk and are generally referred to as "gilt edged." Interest payments are protected by a large or an exceptionally stable margin and principal is secure. While the various protective elements are likely to change, such changes as can be visualized are most unlikely to impair the fundamentally strong position of such issues.
AA	Aa	AA	Judged to be of high quality by all standards. Together with the Aaa group, they constitute what are generally known as high-grade bonds. They are rated lower than the best bonds because margins of protection may not be as large as in Aaa securities or fluctuation of protective elements may be of greater amplitude or there may be other elements present that make the long-term risk appear somewhat larger than the Aaa securities.
A	A	A	Possess many favourable investment attributes and are considered as upper-medium-grade obligations. Factors giving security to principal and interest are considered adequate, but elements may be present that suggest a susceptibility to impairment some time in the future.

(Continued)

| TABLE 8.4 | | | *(CONTINUED)* |

Dominion Bond Rating Service (DBRS)	Moody's	Standard & Poor's	Description (Moody's)
Investment Grade Debt			
BBB	Baa	BBB	Are considered as medium-grade obligations (i.e., they are neither highly protected nor poorly secured). Interest payments and principal security appear adequate for the present but certain protective elements may be lacking or may be characteristically unreliable over any great length of time. Such bonds lack outstanding investment characteristics and, in fact, have speculative characteristics as well.
Speculative Bonds			
BB	Ba	BB	Judged to have speculative elements; their future cannot be considered as well assured. Often the protection of interest and principal payments may be very moderate, and thereby not well safeguarded during both good and bad times over the future. Uncertainty of position characterizes bonds in this class.
B	B	B	Generally lack characteristics of a desirable investment. Assurance of interest and principal payments of maintenance of other terms of the contract over any long period of time may be small.
CCC	Caa	CCC	Are of poor standing. Such issues may be in default or there may be present elements of danger with respect to principal or interest.
CC	Ca	CC	Are speculative to a high degree. Such issues are often in default or have other marked shortcomings.
C, D	C	C, D	Lowest-rated class of bonds, and issues so rated can be regarded as having extremely poor prospects of ever attaining any real investment standing

Source: www.moodys.com, www.dbrs.com, TD Waterhouse Canada Inc.

corporate bonds. Figure 8.3 also includes yields for Province of Ontario bonds and Government of Canada bonds. We refer to the difference between the yields of the various bonds and the Government of Canada yields as the **default spread** or **credit spread**. Credit spreads fluctuate as perceptions regarding the probability of default change. Note that the credit spread is higher for bonds with lower ratings and therefore a greater likelihood of default.

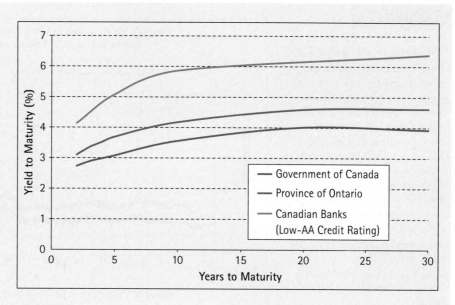

FIGURE 8.3

Corporate and Provincial Yield Curves for March 25, 2007
This figure shows the yield curve for Government of Canada securities, Province of Ontario bonds, and yield curves for banks rated as Low-AA. Note how the yield to maturity is higher for lower-rated bonds, which have a higher probability of default.

Source: Special thanks to Scotia Capital Inc. for this customized data.

The Ontario bonds have a positive credit spread between 0.37% and 0.69% (as of March 25, 2008), but the banks have a larger credit spread ranging from 1.4% to 2.45%. You might wonder why there would be any credit spread for Ontario, as it seems unimaginable that a province would default on its debt. In fact, the province with the lowest current credit spread, Alberta, is also the only province to have defaulted on its debt; this occurred in 1936.

CONCEPT CHECK

1. There are two reasons the yield of a defaultable bond exceeds the yield of an otherwise identical default-free bond. What are they?

2. What is a bond rating?

FINANCIAL **CRISIS**
THE CREDIT CRISIS AND BOND YIELDS

The financial crisis that engulfed the world's economies in 2008 originated as a credit crisis that first emerged in August 2007. At that time, problems in the mortgage market had led to the bankruptcy of several large mortgage lenders. The default of these firms, and the downgrading of many of the bonds backed by mortgages these firms had made, caused many investors to reassess the risk of other bonds in their portfolios. As perceptions of risk increased, and investors attempted to move into safer U.S. Treasury securities, the prices of corporate bonds fell and their spreads rose relative to Treasuries, as shown in Figure 8.4. Panel A of the figure shows

the yield spreads for long-term corporate bonds, where we can see that spreads of even the highest-rated Aaa bonds increased dramatically, from a typical level of 0.5% to over 2% by the fall of 2008. Panel B shows a similar pattern for the rate banks had to pay on short-term loans compared to the yields of short-term Treasury Bills. This increase in borrowing costs made it more costly for firms to raise the capital needed for new investment, slowing economic growth. The decline in these spreads in early 2009 was viewed by many as an important first step in mitigating the ongoing impact of the financial crisis on the rest of the economy

FIGURE 8.4

Yield Spreads and the Financial Crisis
Panel A shows the yield spread
between long-term (30 year) U.S.
corporate and Treasury bonds.
Panel B shows the yield spread
of short-term loans to major
international banks (LIBOR) and
U.S. Treasury Bills (also referred to
as the Treasury-Eurodollar or
"TED" spread).
Note the dramatic increase in these
spreads beginning in August 2007
and again in September 2008,
before beginning to decline in late
2008/early 2009.
Source: Bloomberg.com (www.bloomberg.
com/apps/cbuilder?ticker1=.TEDSP%
3AIND).

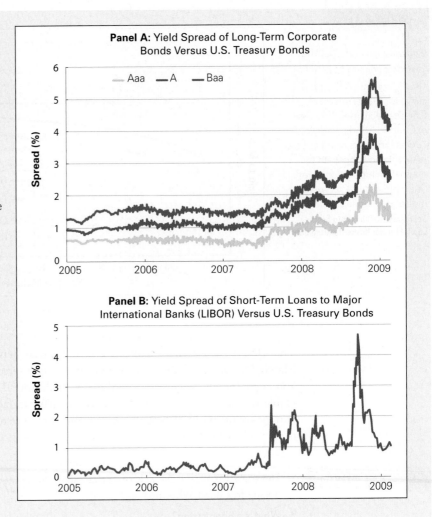

Panel A: Yield Spread of Long-Term Corporate Bonds Versus U.S. Treasury Bonds

Panel B: Yield Spread of Short-Term Loans to Major International Banks (LIBOR) Versus U.S. Treasury Bonds

SUMMARY

1. Bonds pay both coupon and principal or face value payments to investors. By convention, the coupon rate of a bond indicates the percent of face value paid out as coupons each year, so the amount of each coupon payment, *CPN*, is

$$CPN = \frac{\text{Coupon Rate} \times \text{Face Value}}{\text{Number of Coupon Payments per Year}} \tag{8.1}$$

2. Zero-coupon bonds make no coupon payments, so investors receive only the bond's face value.

3. The internal rate of return of a bond is called its yield to maturity (or yield). The yield to maturity of a bond is the discount rate that sets the present value of the promised bond payments equal to the current market price of the bond.

4. The yield to maturity for a zero-coupon bond is given by

$$YTM_n = \left(\frac{FV}{P}\right)^{1/n} - 1 \tag{8.3}$$

5. The risk-free interest rate for an investment until date n equals the yield to maturity of a risk-free zero-coupon bond that matures on date n. A plot of these rates against maturity is called the zero-coupon yield curve.

6. The yield to maturity for a coupon bond is the discount rate, y, that equates the present value of the bond's future cash flows with its price:

$$P = CPN \times \frac{1}{y}\left(1 - \frac{1}{(1+y)^N}\right) + \frac{FV}{(1+y)^N} \tag{8.5}$$

7. A bond will trade at a premium if its coupon rate exceeds its yield to maturity. It will trade at a discount if its coupon rate is less than its yield to maturity. If a bond's coupon rate equals its yield to maturity, it trades at par.

8. As a bond approaches maturity, the price of the bond approaches its face value.

9. If a bond's yield to maturity does not change, then the IRR of an investment in the bond equals its yield to maturity even if you sell the bond early.

10. Bond prices change as interest rates change. When interest rates rise, bond prices fall, and vice versa.

    a. Long-term zero-coupon bonds are more sensitive to changes in interest rates than are short-term zero-coupon bonds.

    b. Bonds with low coupon rates are more sensitive to changes in interest rates than similar maturity bonds with high coupon rates.

    c. The duration of a bond measures the sensitivity of its price to changes in interest rates.

11. Because we can replicate a coupon-paying bond using a portfolio of zero-coupon bonds, the price of a coupon-paying bond can be determined based on the zero-coupon yield curve using the Law of One Price:

$$P = PV(\text{Bond Cash Flows})$$
$$= \frac{CPN}{1 + YTM_1} + \frac{CPN}{(1 + YTM_2)^2} + \cdots + \frac{CPN + FV}{(1 + YTM_n)^n} \tag{8.6}$$

12. When the yield curve is not flat, bonds with the same maturity but different coupon rates will have different yields to maturity.

13. When a bond issuer does not make a bond payment in full, the issuer has defaulted.

    a. The risk that default can occur is called default or credit risk.

    b. Government of Canada debt securities are free of default risk.

14. The expected return of a corporate bond, which is the firm's debt cost of capital, equals the risk-free rate of interest plus a risk premium. The expected return is less than the bond's yield to maturity because the yield to maturity of a bond is calculated using the promised cash flows, not the expected cash flows.

15. Bond ratings summarize the creditworthiness of bonds for investors.

16. The difference between yields on Government of Canada bonds and yields on corporate bonds is called the credit spread or default spread. The credit spread compensates investors for the difference between promised and expected cash flows and for the risk of default.

KEY TERMS

benchmark bonds *p. 255*
bond indenture *p. 239*
clean price *p. 248*
corporate bonds *p. 255*
coupon bonds *p. 242*
coupon rate *p. 239*
coupon-paying yield curve *p. 255*
coupons *p. 239*
credit risk *p. 255*
default spread (credit spread) *p. 260*
dirty price *p. 248*
discount *p. 240*
duration *p. 249*
face value *p. 239*
Government of Canada bonds *p. 240*

high-yield bonds *p. 259*
investment-grade bonds *p. 259*
invoice price *p. 248*
junk bonds *p. 259*
maturity date *p. 239*
par *p. 245*
premium *p. 245*
pure discount bonds *p. 240*
speculative bonds *p. 259*
spot interest rates *p. 241*
term *p. 239*
Treasury Bills *p. 240*
yield to maturity (YTM) *p. 240*
zero-coupon bond *p. 240*
zero-coupon yield curve *p. 242*

PROBLEMS

The problems marked in green can be found on MyFinanceLab at www.myfinancelab.com. Visit your MyFinanceLab for additional practice. An asterisk (*) indicates problems with a higher level of difficulty. Additional readings for this chapter may be found in the Textbook Resources section on MyFinanceLab.

Bond Cash Flows, Prices, and Yields

1. A 30-year bond with a face value of $1000 has a coupon rate of 5.5%, with semiannual payments.
    a. What is the coupon payment for this bond?
    b. Draw the cash flows for the bond on a timeline.

2. Assume that a bond will make payments every six months as shown on the following timeline (using six-month periods):

    a. What is the maturity of the bond (in years)?
    b. What is the coupon rate (in percent)?
    c. What is the face value?

EXCEL

3. The following table summarizes prices of various default-free zero-coupon bonds (expressed as a percentage of face value):

Maturity (years)	1	2	3	4	5
Price (per $100 face value)	$95.51	$91.05	$86.38	$81.65	$76.51

    a. Compute the yield to maturity for each bond.
    b. Plot the zero-coupon yield curve (for the first five years).
    c. Is the yield curve upward sloping, downward sloping, or flat?

EXCEL

4. Suppose the current zero-coupon yield curve for risk-free bonds is as follows:

Maturity (years)	1	2	3	4	5
YTM_n	5.00%	5.50%	5.75%	5.95%	6.05%

   a. What is the price per $100 face value of a two-year, zero-coupon, risk-free bond?

   b. What is the price per $100 face value of a four-year, zero-coupon, risk-free bond?

   c. What is the risk-free interest rate for a five-year maturity?

5. A three-month Treasury Bill sold for a price of $100.002556 per $100 face value. What is the yield to maturity of this bond, expressed as an EAR?

6. Suppose a ten-year, $1000 bond with an 8% coupon rate and semiannual coupons is trading for a price of $1034.74.

   a. What is the bond's yield to maturity (expressed as an APR with semiannual compounding)?

   b. If the bond's yield to maturity changes to 9% APR, what will the bond's price be?

7. Suppose a five-year, $1000 bond with annual coupons has a price of $900 and a yield to maturity of 6%. What is the bond's coupon rate?

Dynamic Behaviour of Bond Prices

8. The prices of several bonds with face values of $1000 are summarized in the following table:

Bond	A	B	C	D
Price	$972.50	$1040.75	$1150.00	$1000.00

   For each bond, state whether it trades at a discount, at par, or at a premium.

9. Explain why the yield of a bond that trades at a discount exceeds the bond's coupon rate.

10. Suppose a seven-year, $1000 bond with an 8% coupon rate and semiannual coupons is trading with a yield to maturity of 6.75%.

   a. Is this bond currently trading at a discount, at par, or at a premium? Explain.

   b. If the yield to maturity of the bond rises to 7.00% (APR with semiannual compounding), what price will the bond trade for?

11. Suppose that General Motors Acceptance Corporation issued a bond with ten years until maturity, a face value of $1000, and a coupon rate of 7% (annual payments). The yield to maturity on this bond when it was issued was 6%.

   a. What was the price of this bond when it was issued?

   b. Assuming the yield to maturity remains constant, what is the price of the bond immediately before it makes its first coupon payment?

   c. Assuming the yield to maturity remains constant, what is the price of the bond immediately after it makes its first coupon payment?

12. Suppose you purchase a ten-year bond with 6% annual coupons. You hold the bond for four years, and sell it immediately after receiving the fourth coupon. If the bond's yield to maturity was 5% when you purchased and sold the bond,

   a. What cash flows will you pay and receive from your investment in the bond per $100 face value?

   b. What is the internal rate of return of your investment?

EXCEL

13. Consider the following bonds:

Bond	Coupon Rate (annual payments)	Maturity (years)
A	0%	15
B	0%	10
C	4%	15
D	8%	10

a. What is the percentage change in the price of each bond if its yield to maturity falls from 6% to 5%?

b. Which of the bonds A–D is most sensitive to a 1% drop in interest rates from 6% to 5% and why? Which bond is least sensitive? Provide an intuitive explanation for your answer.

EXCEL

14. Suppose you purchase a 30-year, zero-coupon bond with a yield to maturity of 6%. You hold the bond for five years before selling it.

a. If the bond's yield to maturity is 6% when you sell it, what is the internal rate of return of your investment?

b. If the bond's yield to maturity is 7% when you sell it, what is the internal rate of return of your investment?

c. If the bond's yield to maturity is 5% when you sell it, what is the internal rate of return of your investment?

d. Even if a bond has no chance of default, is your investment risk free if you plan to sell it before it matures? Explain.

15. Suppose you purchase a 30-year Government of Canada bond with a 5% annual coupon, initially trading at par. In 10 years' time, the bond's yield to maturity has risen to 7% (EAR).

a. If you sell the bond now, what internal rate of return will you have earned on your investment in the bond?

b. If instead you hold the bond to maturity, what internal rate of return will you earn on your investment in the bond?

c. Is comparing the IRRs in (a) versus (b) a useful way to evaluate the decision to sell the bond? Explain.

16. Suppose the current yield on a one-year zero coupon bond is 3%, while the yield on a five-year zero coupon bond is 5%. Neither bond has any risk of default. Suppose you plan to invest for one year. You will earn more over the year by investing in the five-year bonds as long as their yield does not rise above what level?

The Yield Curve and Bond Arbitrage

For Problems 17–22, assume zero-coupon yields on default-free securities are as summarized in the following table:

Maturity (years)	1	2	3	4	5
Zero-coupon YTM_n	4.00%	4.30%	4.50%	4.70%	4.80%

17. What is the price today of a two-year, default-free security with a face value of $1000 and an annual coupon rate of 6%? Does this bond trade at a discount, at par, or at a premium?

18. What is the price of a five-year, zero-coupon, default-free security with a face value of $1000?

19. What is the price of a three-year, default-free security with a face value of $1000 and an annual coupon rate of 4%? What is the yield to maturity for this bond?

20. What is the maturity of a default-free security with annual coupon payments and a yield to maturity of 4.0%? Why?

*21. Consider a four-year, default-free security with annual coupon payments and a face value of $1000 that is issued at par. What is the coupon rate of this bond?

22. Consider a five-year, default-free bond with annual coupons of 5% and a face value of $1000.

   a. Without doing any calculations, determine whether this bond is trading at a premium or at a discount. Explain.

   b. What is the yield to maturity on this bond?

   c. If the yield to maturity on this bond increased to 5.2%, what would the new price be?

*23. Prices of zero-coupon, default-free securities with face values of $1000 are summarized in the following table.

Maturity (years)	1	2	3
Price (per $1000 face value)	$970.87	$938.95	$904.56

Suppose you observe that a three-year, default-free security with an annual coupon rate of 10% and a face value of $1000 has a price today of $1183.50. Is there an arbitrage opportunity? If so, show specifically how you would take advantage of this opportunity. If not, why not?

*24. Assume there are four default-free bonds with the following prices and future cash flows:

Bond	Price Today	Cash Flows		
		Year 1	Year 2	Year 3
A	$ 934.58	1,000	0	0
B	881.66	0	1,000	0
C	1,118.21	100	100	1,100
D	839.62	0	0	1,000

Do these bonds present an arbitrage opportunity? If so, how would you take advantage of this opportunity? If not, why not?

EXCEL *25. Suppose you are given the following information about the default-free, coupon-paying yield curve:

Maturity (years)	1	2	3	4
Coupon rate (annual payments)	0.00%	10.00%	6.00%	12.00%
YTM	2.000%	3.908%	5.840%	5.783%

   a. Use arbitrage to determine the yield to maturity of a two-year, zero-coupon bond.

   b. What is the zero-coupon yield curve for years 1 through 4?

Corporate Bonds

26. Explain why the expected return of a corporate bond does not equal its yield to maturity.

27. Grummon Corp. has issued zero-coupon corporate bonds with a five-year maturity. Investors believe there is a 20% chance that Grummon will default on these bonds. If Grummon does default, investors expect to receive only 50 cents per dollar they are owed. If investors require

a 6% expected return on their investment in these bonds, what will be the price and yield to maturity on these bonds?

28. The following table summarizes the yields to maturity on several one-year, zero-coupon securities:

Security	Yield (%)
Treasury Bill	3.1
AAA corporate	3.2
BBB corporate	4.2
B corporate	4.9

    a. What is the price (expressed as a percentage of the face value) of a one-year, zero-coupon corporate bond with an AAA rating?

    b. What is the credit spread on AAA-rated corporate bonds?

    c. What is the credit spread on B-rated corporate bonds?

    d. How does the credit spread change with the bond rating? Why?

29. Andrew Industries is contemplating issuing a 30-year bond with a coupon rate of 7% (annual coupon payments) and a face value of $1000. Andrew believes it can get a rating of A from DBRS. However, due to recent financial difficulties at the company, DBRS is warning that it may downgrade Andrew Industries' bonds to BBB. Yields on A-rated, long-term bonds are currently 6.5%, and yields on BBB-rated bonds are 6.9%.

    a. What is the price of the bond if Andrew maintains the A rating for the bond issue?

    b. What will the price of the bond be if it is downgraded?

EXCEL 30. HMK Enterprises would like to raise $10 million to invest in capital expenditures. The company plans to issue five-year bonds with a face value of $1000 and a coupon rate of 6.5% (annual payments). The following table summarizes the yield to maturity for five-year (annual-pay) coupon corporate bonds of various ratings:

Rating	AAA	AA	A	BBB	BB
YTM	6.20%	6.30%	6.50%	6.90%	7.50%

    a. Assuming the bonds will be rated AA, what will the price of the bonds be?

    b. How much total principal amount of these bonds must HMK issue to raise $10 million today, assuming the bonds are AA rated? (Because HMK cannot issue a fraction of a bond, assume that all fractions are rounded to the nearest whole number.)

    c. What must the rating of the bonds be for them to sell at par?

    d. Suppose that when the bonds are issued, the price of each bond is $959.54. What is the likely rating of the bonds? Are they junk bonds?

31. A BBB-rated corporate bond has a yield to maturity of 8.2%. A Government of Canada bond has a yield to maturity of 6.5%. These yields are quoted as APRs with semiannual compounding. Both bonds pay semiannual coupons at a rate of 7% and have five years to maturity.

    a. What is the price (expressed as a percentage of the face value) of the Government of Canada bond?

    b. What is the price (expressed as a percentage of the face value) of the BBB-rated corporate bond?

    c. What is the credit spread on the BBB bonds?

32. The Isabelle Corporation rents prom dresses in its stores across eastern Canada. It has just issued a five-year zero-coupon corporate bond at a price of $74. You have purchased this bond and intend to hold it until maturity.

a. What is the yield to maturity of the bond?

b. What is the expected return on your investment (expressed as an EAR) if there is no chance of default?

c. What is the expected return (expressed as an EAR) if there is a 100% probability of default and you will recover 90% of the face value?

d. What is the expected return (expressed as an EAR) if the probability of default is 50%, the likelihood of default is higher in bad times than good times, and, in the case of default, you will recover 90% of the face value?

e. For parts b to d, what can you say about the five-year risk-free interest rate in each case?

DATA CASE

EXCEL

You are an intern with Sirius Satellite Radio in their corporate finance division. The firm is planning to issue $50 million of 12% annual coupon bonds with a 10-year maturity. The firm anticipates an increase in its bond rating. Your boss wants you to determine the gain in the proceeds of the new issue if the issue is rated above the firm's current bond rating. To prepare this information, you will have to determine Sirius' current debt rating and the yield curve for their particular rating. Strangely, no one at Sirius seems to have this information; apparently they are still busy trying to figure out who decided it was a good idea to hire Howard Stern. *Note:* Because Sirius is a U.S. company, you will need U.S. data.

1. Begin by finding the current U.S. Treasury yield curve. At the Treasury Web site (www.treas.gov), search using the term "yield curve" and select "US Treasury—Daily Treasury Yield Curve." *Beware:* There will likely be two links with the same title. Look at the description below the link and select the one that does *not* say "Real Yield . . ." You want the nominal rates. The correct link is likely to be the first link on the page. Download that table into Excel by right clicking with the cursor in the table and selecting "Export to Microsoft Excel."

2. Find the current yield spreads for the various bond ratings. Unfortunately, the current spreads are available only for a fee, so you will use old ones. Go to BondsOnline (www.bondsonline.com) and click on "Today's Market." Next click on "Corporate Bond Spreads." Download this table to Excel and copy and paste it to the same file as the Treasury yields.

3. Find the current bond rating for Sirius. Go to Standard & Poor's Web site (www.standardandpoors.com). Select "Find a Rating" from the list at the left of the page, then select "Credit Ratings Search." At this point you will have to register (it's free) or enter the username and password provided by your instructor. Next you will be able to search by Organization Name: enter Sirius and select Sirius Satellite Radio. Use the credit rating for the organization, not the specific issue ratings.

4. Return to Excel and create a timeline with the cash flows and discount rates you will need to value the new bond issue.

   a. To create the required spot rates for Sirius' issue add the appropriate spread to the Treasury yield of the same maturity.

   b. The yield curve and spread rates you have found do not cover every year that you will need for the new bonds. Specifically, you do not have yields or spreads for four-, six-, eight-, and nine-year maturities. Fill these in by linearly interpolating the given yields and spreads. For example, the four-year spot rate and spread will be the average of the three- and five-year rates. The six-year rate and spread will be the average of the five- and seven-year rates. For years eight and nine you will have to spread the difference between years seven and ten across the two years.

    c. To compute the spot rates for Sirius' current debt rating, add the yield spread to the Treasury rate for each maturity. However, note that the spread is in basis points, which are 1/100th of a percentage point.

    d. Compute the cash flows that would be paid to bondholders each year and add them to the timeline.

5. Use the spot rates to calculate the present value of each cash flow paid to the bondholders.

6. Compute the issue price of the bond and its initial yield to maturity.

7. Repeat steps 4–6 based on the assumption that Sirius is able to raise its bond rating by one level. Compute the new yield based on the higher rating and the new bond price that would result.

8. Compute the additional cash proceeds that could be raised from the issue if the rating were improved.

<table>
<tr><td>

CHAPTER 8 APPENDIX

notation

f_n one-year forward rate for year n

</td></tr>
</table>

FORWARD INTEREST RATES

Given the risk associated with interest rate changes, corporate managers require tools to help manage this risk. One of the most important is the interest rate forward contract. An **interest rate forward contract** (also called a **forward rate agreement**) is a contract today that fixes the interest rate for a loan or investment in the future. In this appendix, we explain how to derive forward interest rates from zero-coupon yields.

COMPUTING FORWARD RATES

A **forward interest rate** (or **forward rate**) is an interest rate that we can guarantee today for a loan or investment that will occur in the future. Throughout this section, we will consider only interest rate forward contracts for one-year investments; thus when we refer to the forward rate for year 5, we mean the rate available *today* on a one-year investment that begins four years from today and is repaid five years from today.

We can use the Law of One Price to calculate the forward rate from the zero-coupon yield curve. The forward rate for year 1 is the rate on an investment that starts today and is repaid in one year; it is equivalent to an investment in a one-year, zero-coupon bond. Therefore, by the Law of One Price, these rates must coincide:

$$f_1 = YTM_1 \tag{8A.1}$$

Now consider the two-year forward rate. Suppose the one-year, zero-coupon yield is 5.5% and the two-year, zero-coupon yield is 7.0%. There are two ways to invest money risk free for two years. First, we can invest in the two-year, zero-coupon bond at rate of 7.0% and earn $\$(1.07)^2$ after two years per dollar invested. Second, we can invest in the one-year bond at a rate of 5.5%, which will pay \$1.055 at the end of one year, and simultaneously guarantee the interest rate we will earn by reinvesting the \$1.055 for the second year by entering into an interest rate forward contract for year 2 at rate f_2. In that case, we will earn $\$(1.055)(1 + f_2)$ at the end of two years.

Because both strategies are risk free, by the Law of One Price, they must have the same return:

$$(1.07)^2 = (1.055)(1 + f_2)$$

Rearranging, we have

$$(1 + f_2) = \frac{1.07^2}{1.055} = 1.0852$$

Therefore, in this case the forward rate for year 2 is $f_2 = 8.52\%$.

In general, we can compute the forward rate for year n by comparing an investment in an n-year, zero-coupon bond to an investment in an $(n - 1)$ year, zero-coupon bond, with the interest rate earned in the nth year being guaranteed through an interest rate forward contract. Because both strategies are risk free, they must have the same payoff or else an arbitrage opportunity would be available. Comparing the payoffs of these strategies, we have

$$(1 + YTM_n)^n = (1 + YTM_{n-1})^{n-1}(1 + f_n)$$

We can rearrange this equation to find the general formula for the forward interest rate:

$$f_n = \frac{(1 + YTM_n)^n}{(1 + YTM_{n-1})^{n-1}} - 1 \tag{8A.2}$$

EXAMPLE 8A.1	**COMPUTING FORWARD RATES**

Problem

Calculate the forward rates for years 1 through 5 from the following zero-coupon yields:

Maturity	1	2	3	4
YTM_n	5.00%	6.00%	6.00%	5.75%

Solution

Using Eqs. 8A.1 and 8A.2:

$$f_1 = YTM_1 = 5.00\%$$

$$f_2 = \frac{(1 + YTM_2)^2}{(1 + YTM_1)} - 1 = \frac{1.06^2}{1.05} - 1 = 7.01\%$$

$$f_3 = \frac{(1 + YTM_3)^3}{(1 + YTM_2)^2} - 1 = \frac{1.06^3}{1.06^2} - 1 = 6.00\%$$

$$f_4 = \frac{(1 + YTM_4)^4}{(1 + YTM_3)^3} - 1 = \frac{1.0575^4}{1.06^3} - 1 = 5.00\%$$

Note that when the yield curve is increasing in year n (that is, when $YTM_n > YTM_{n-1}$), the forward rate is higher than the zero-coupon yield, $f_n > YTM_n$. Similarly, when the yield curve is decreasing, the forward rate is less than the zero-coupon yield. When the yield curve is flat, the forward rate equals the zero-coupon yield.

COMPUTING BOND YIELDS FROM FORWARD RATES

Equation 8A.2 computes the forward interest rate using the zero-coupon yields. It is also possible to compute the zero-coupon yields from the forward interest rates. To see this, note that if we use interest rate forward contracts to lock in an interest rate for an investment in year 1, year 2, and so on through year n, we can create an n-year, risk-free investment. The return from this strategy must match the return from an n-year, zero-coupon bond. Therefore:

$$(1 + f_1) \times (1 + f_2) \times \cdots \times (1 + f_n) = (1 + YTM_n)^n \qquad (8A.3)$$

For example, using the forward rates from Example 8A.1, we can compute the four-year zero-coupon yield:

$$\begin{aligned} 1 + YTM_4 &= [(1 + f_1)(1 + f_2)(1 + f_3)(1 + f_4)]^{1/4} \\ &= [(1.05)(1.0701)(1.06)(1.05)]^{1/4} \\ &= 1.0575 \end{aligned}$$

FORWARD RATES AND FUTURE INTEREST RATES

A forward rate is the rate that you contract for today for an investment in the future. How does this rate compare to the interest rate that will actually prevail in the future? It is tempting to believe that the forward interest rate should be a good predictor of future interest rates. In reality, this will generally not be the case. Instead, it is a good predictor only when investors do not care about risk.

EXAMPLE 8A.2	FORWARD RATES AND FUTURE SPOT RATES

Problem

JoAnne Wilford is corporate treasurer for Wafer Thin Semiconductor. She must invest some of the cash on hand for two years in risk-free bonds. The current one-year, zero-coupon yield is 5%. The one-year forward rate is 6%. She is trying to decide between three possible strategies: (i) buy a two-year bond, (ii) buy a one-year bond and enter into an interest rate forward contract to guarantee the rate in the second year, or (iii) buy a one-year bond and forgo the forward contract, reinvesting at whatever rate prevails next year. Under what scenarios would she be better off following the risky strategy?

Solution

From Eq. 8A.3, both strategies (i) and (ii) lead to the same risk-free return of $(1 + YTM_2)^2 = (1 + YTM_1)(1 + f_2) = (1.05)(1.06)$. The third strategy returns $(1.05)(1 + r)$, where r is the one-year interest rate next year. If the future interest rate turns out to be 6%, then the two strategies will offer the same return. Otherwise Wafer Thin Semiconductor is better off with strategy (iii) if the interest rate next year is greater than the forward rate—6%—and worse off if the interest rate is lower than 6%.

As Example 8A.2 makes clear, we can think of the forward rate as a break-even rate. If this rate actually prevails in the future, investors will be indifferent between investing in a two-year bond and investing in a one-year bond and rolling over the money in one year. If investors did not care about risk, then they would be indifferent between the two strategies whenever the expected one-year spot rate equals the current forward rate. However, investors *do* generally care about risk. If the expected returns of both strategies were the same, investors would prefer one strategy or the other depending on whether they want to be exposed to future interest rate risk fluctuations. In general, the expected future spot interest rate will reflect investors' preferences toward the risk of future interest rate fluctuations. Thus

$$\text{Expected Future Spot Interest Rate}$$
$$= \text{Forward Interest Rate} + \text{Risk Premium} \tag{8A.4}$$

This risk premium can be either positive or negative depending on investors' preferences. If investors prefer long-term investments instead of short-term investments, the risk premium will be positive. If investors have a liquidity preference and prefer short-term investments instead of longer-term investments, the risk premium will be negative.[5] As a result, forward rates by themselves tend not to be ideal predictors of future spot rates, but with more information about the yield curve, they can provide some information about future spot rates.

---

5. Empirical research suggests that the risk premium tends to be negative when the yield curve is upward sloping (the more typical case) and positive when it is downward sloping. See Eugene F. Fama and Robert R. Bliss, "The Information in Long-Maturity Forward Rates," *American Economic Review* 77(4) (1987): 680–692; and John Y. Campbell and Robert J. Shiller, "Yield Spreads and Interest Rate Movements: A Bird's Eye View," *Review of Economic Studies* 58(3) (1991): 495–514.

forward interest rate (forward rate) *p. 271*   interest rate forward contract *p. 271*
forward rate agreement *p. 271*

PROBLEMS

The problems marked in green can be found on MyFinanceLab at www.myfinancelab.com. **Visit your MyFinanceLab for additional practice. An asterisk (*) indicates problems with a higher level of difficulty.**

Problems A.1–A.4 refer to the following table:

Maturity (years)	1	2	3	4	5
Zero-coupon YTM$_n$	4.0%	5.5%	5.5%	5.0%	4.5%

A.1.   What is the forward rate for year 2 (the forward rate quoted today for an investment that begins in one year and matures in two years)?

A.2.   What is the forward rate for year 3 (the forward rate quoted today for an investment that begins in two years and matures in three years)? What can you conclude about forward rates when the yield curve is flat?

A.3.   What is the forward rate for year 5 (the forward rate quoted today for an investment that begins in four years and matures in five years)?

*A.4.   Suppose you wanted to lock in an interest rate for an investment that begins in one year and matures in five years. What rate would you obtain if there are no arbitrage opportunities?

*A.5.   Suppose the yield on a one-year, zero-coupon bond is 5%. The forward rate for year 2 is 4%, and the forward rate for year 3 is 3%. What is the yield to maturity of a zero-coupon bond that matures in three years?

Valuing Stocks

On January 16, 2006, footwear and apparel maker Kenneth Cole Productions Inc. announced that its president, Paul Blum, had resigned to pursue "other opportunities." The price of the company's stock had already dropped more than 16% over the prior two years, and the firm was in the midst of a major undertaking to restructure its brand. News that its president, who had been with the company for more than 15 years, was now resigning was taken as a bad sign by many investors. The next day, Kenneth Cole's stock price dropped by more than 6% on the New York Stock Exchange to $26.75, with over 300,000 shares traded, more than twice its average daily volume. How might an investor decide whether to buy or sell a stock such as Kenneth Cole at this price? Why would the stock suddenly be worth 6% less on the announcement of this news? What actions can Kenneth Cole's managers take to increase the stock price?

To answer these questions, we turn to the Law of One Price. As we demonstrated in Chapter 3, the Law of One Price implies that the price of a security should equal the present value of the expected cash flows an investor will receive from owning it. In this chapter, we apply this idea to stocks. Thus, to value a stock, we need to know the expected cash flows an investor will receive and the appropriate cost of capital with which to discount those cash flows. Both of these quantities can be challenging to estimate, and many of the details needed to do so will be developed throughout the remainder of the text. In this chapter, we will begin our study of stock valuation by identifying the relevant cash flows and developing the main tools that practitioners use to evaluate them.

Our analysis begins with a consideration of the dividends and capital gains received by investors who hold the stock for different periods, from which we develop the *dividend-discount model* of stock valuation. Next, we apply Chapter 7's tools to value stocks based on the free cash flows generated by the firm. Having developed these stock valuation methods based on discounted cash flows, we then relate them to the practice of using valuation multiples based on comparable firms. We conclude the chapter by discussing the role of competition in the information contained in stock prices and its implications for investors and corporate managers.

9.1   THE DIVIDEND-DISCOUNT MODEL

The Law of One Price implies that to value any security, we must determine the expected cash flows an investor will receive from owning it. Thus, we begin our analysis of stock valuation by considering the cash flows for an investor with a one-year investment horizon. We then consider the perspective of investors with long investment horizons. We show that, if investors have the same beliefs, their valuation of the stock will not depend on their investment horizon. Using this result, we then derive the first method to value a stock: the *dividend-discount model.*

A ONE-YEAR INVESTOR

There are two potential sources of cash flows from owning a stock. First, the firm might pay out cash to its shareholders in the form of a dividend. Second, the investor might generate cash by choosing to sell the shares at some future date. The total amount received in dividends and from selling the stock will depend on the investor's investment horizon. Let's begin by considering the perspective of a one-year investor.

When an investor buys a stock, she will pay the current market price for a share, P_0. While she continues to hold the stock, she will be entitled to any dividends the stock pays. Let Div_1 be the total dividends paid per share of the stock during the year. At the end of the year, the investor will sell her share at the new market price, P_1. Assuming for simplicity that all dividends are paid at the end of the year, we have the following timeline for this investment:

Of course, the future dividend payment and stock price in the timeline above are not known with certainty; rather, these values are based on the investor's expectations at the time the stock is purchased. Given these expectations, the investor will be willing to pay a price today up to the point that this transaction has a zero NPV, that is, up to the point at which the current price equals the present value of the expected future dividend and sale price. Because these cash flows are risky, we cannot discount them using the risk-free interest rate. Instead, we must discount them based on the **equity cost of capital**, r_E, for the stock, which is the expected return of other investments available in the market with equivalent risk to the firm's shares. Doing so leads to the following equation for the stock price:

$$P_0 = \frac{Div_1 + P_1}{1 + r_E} \tag{9.1}$$

If the current stock price were less than this amount, it would be a positive-NPV investment opportunity. We would therefore expect investors to rush in and buy it, driving up the stock's price. If the stock price exceeded this amount, selling it would have a positive NPV and the stock price would quickly fall. As we discovered in Chapter 3, in a competitive market, buying or selling a share of stock must be a zero-NPV investment opportunity.

DIVIDEND YIELDS, CAPITAL GAINS, AND TOTAL RETURNS

We can reinterpret Eq. 9.1 if we multiply by $(1 + r_E)$, divide by P_0, and subtract 1 from both sides:

Total Return

$$r_E = \frac{Div_1 + P_1}{P_0} - 1 = \underbrace{\frac{Div_1}{P_0}}_{\text{Dividend Yield}} + \underbrace{\frac{P_1 - P_0}{P_0}}_{\text{Capital Gain Rate}} \tag{9.2}$$

The first term on the right side of Eq. 9.2 is the stock's **dividend yield**, which is the expected annual dividend of the stock divided by its current price. The dividend yield is the percentage return the investor expects to earn from the dividend paid by the stock. The second term on the right side of Eq. 9.2 reflects the **capital gain** the investor will earn on the stock, which is the difference between the expected sale price and purchase price for the stock, $P_1 - P_0$. We divide the capital gain by the current stock price to express the capital gain as a percentage return, called the **capital gain rate**.

The sum of the dividend yield and the capital gain rate is called the **total return** of the stock. The total return is the expected return that the investor will earn for a one-year investment in the stock. Thus Eq. 9.2 states that the stock's total return should equal the equity cost of capital. In other words, *the expected total return of the stock should equal the expected return of other investments available in the market with equivalent risk.*

This result is what we should expect: The firm must pay its shareholders a return commensurate with the return they can earn elsewhere while taking the same risk. If the stock offered a higher return than other securities with the same risk, investors would sell those other investments and buy the stock instead. This activity would drive up the stock's current price, lowering its dividend yield and capital gain rate until Eq. 9.2 holds true. If the stock offered a lower expected return, investors would sell the stock and drive down its price until Eq. 9.2 was again satisfied.

EXAMPLE 9.1

STOCK PRICES AND RETURNS

Problem

Suppose you expect Shoppers Drug Mart's stock to pay dividends of $0.56 per share in the coming year and trade for $45.50 per share at the end of the year. If investments with equivalent risk to Shoppers Drug Mart's stock have an expected return of 6.80%, what is the most you would pay today for Shoppers Drug Mart's stock? What dividend yield and capital gain rate would you expect at this price?

Solution

Using Eq. 9.1, we have

$$P_0 = \frac{Div_1 + P_1}{1 + r_E} = \frac{0.56 + 45.50}{1.0680} = \$43.13$$

At this price, Shoppers Drug Mart's dividend yield is $Div_1/P_0 = 0.56/43.13 = 1.30\%$. The expected capital gain is $45.50 - $43.13 = $2.37 per share, for a capital gain rate of $2.37/43.13 = 5.50\%$. Therefore, at this price Shoppers Drug Mart's expected total return is $1.30\% + 5.50\% = 6.80\%$, which is equal to its equity cost of capital.

A MULTIYEAR INVESTOR

Equation 9.1 depends upon the expected stock price in one year, P_1. But suppose we planned to hold the stock for two years. Then we would receive dividends in both year 1 and year 2 before selling the stock, as shown in the following timeline:

Setting the stock price equal to the present value of the future cash flows in this case implies[1]

$$P_0 = \frac{Div_1}{1 + r_E} + \frac{Div_2 + P_2}{(1 + r_E)^2} \tag{9.3}$$

Equations 9.1 and 9.3 are different: As a two-year investor we care about the dividend and stock price in year 2, but these terms do not appear in Eq. 9.1. Does this difference imply that a two-year investor will value the stock differently than a one-year investor?

The answer to this question is no. While a one-year investor does not care about the dividend and stock price in year 2 directly, she will care about them indirectly because they will affect the price for which she can sell the stock at the end of year 1. For example, suppose the investor sells the stock to another one-year investor with the same beliefs. The new investor will expect to receive the dividend and stock price at the end of year 2, so he will be willing to pay

$$P_1 = \frac{Div_2 + P_2}{1 + r_E}$$

for the stock. Substituting this expression for P_1 into Eq. 9.1, we get the same result as in Eq. 9.3:

$$P_0 = \frac{Div_1 + P_1}{1 + r_E} = \frac{Div_1}{1 + r_E} + \frac{1}{1 + r_E}\overbrace{\left(\frac{Div_2 + P_2}{1 + r_E}\right)}^{P_1}$$

$$= \frac{Div_1}{1 + r_E} + \frac{Div_2 + P_2}{(1 + r_E)^2}$$

Thus the formula for the stock price for a two-year investor is the same as the one for a sequence of two one-year investors.

THE DIVIDEND-DISCOUNT MODEL EQUATION

We can continue this process for any number of years by replacing the final stock price with the value that the next holder of the stock would be willing to pay. Doing so leads to the general **dividend-discount model** for the stock price, where the

---

1. By using the same equity cost of capital for both periods, we are assuming that the equity cost of capital does not depend on the term of the cash flows. Otherwise, we would need to adjust for the term structure of the equity cost of capital (as we did with the yield curve for risk-free cash flows in Chapter 5). This step would complicate the analysis but would not change the results.

horizon N is arbitrary:

Dividend-Discount Model

$$P_0 = \frac{Div_1}{1 + r_E} + \frac{Div_2}{(1 + r_E)^2} + \cdots + \frac{Div_N}{(1 + r_E)^N} + \frac{P_N}{(1 + r_E)^N} \qquad (9.4)$$

Equation 9.4 applies to a single N-year investor, who will collect dividends for N years and then sell the stock, or to a series of investors who hold the stock for shorter periods and then resell it. Note that Eq. 9.4 holds for *any* horizon N. Thus all investors (with the same beliefs) will attach the same value to the stock, independent of their investment horizons. How long they intend to hold the stock and whether they collect their return in the form of dividends or capital gains is irrelevant. For the special case in which the firm eventually pays dividends and is never acquired, it is possible to hold the shares forever. Consequently, we can let N go to infinity in Eq. 9.4 and write it as follows:

$$P_0 = \frac{Div_1}{1 + r_E} + \frac{Div_2}{(1 + r_E)^2} + \frac{Div_3}{(1 + r_E)^3} + \cdots = \sum_{n=1}^{\infty} \frac{Div_n}{(1 + r_E)^n} \qquad (9.5)$$

That is, *the price of the stock is equal to the present value of the expected future dividends it will pay.*

1. How do you calculate the total return of a stock?
2. What discount rate do you use to discount the future cash flows of a stock?
3. Why will a short-term and long-term investor with the same beliefs be willing to pay the same price for a stock?

9.2 APPLYING THE DIVIDEND-DISCOUNT MODEL

Equation 9.5 expresses the value of the stock in terms of the expected future dividends the firm will pay. Of course, estimating these dividends—especially for the distant future—is difficult. A common approximation is to assume that in the long run, dividends will grow at a constant rate. In this section, we will consider the implications of this assumption for stock prices and explore the tradeoff between dividends and growth.

CONSTANT DIVIDEND GROWTH

The simplest forecast for the firm's future dividends states that they will grow at a constant rate, g, forever. That case yields the following timeline for the cash flows for an investor who buys the stock today and holds it:

Because the expected dividends are a constant growth perpetuity, we can use Eq. 4.9 to calculate their present value. We then obtain the following simple formula for the stock price:[2]

Constant Dividend Growth Model

$$P_0 = \frac{Div_1}{r_E - g} \qquad (9.6)$$

---

2. As we discussed in Chapter 4, this formula requires that $g < r_E$. Otherwise, the present value of the growing perpetuity is infinite. The implication here is that it is impossible for a stock's dividends to grow at a rate $g > r_E$ *forever*. If the growth rate does exceed r_E, it must be temporary, and the constant growth model cannot be applied in such a case.

According to the **constant dividend growth model**, the value of the firm depends on the current dividend level, divided by the equity cost of capital adjusted by the growth rate.

EXAMPLE 9.2

VALUING A FIRM WITH CONSTANT DIVIDEND GROWTH

Problem

Hydro One is a regulated utility company that provides transmission and distribution of electricity in Ontario. Suppose Hydro One plans to pay $2.30 per share in dividends in the coming year. If its equity cost of capital is 7% and dividends are expected to grow by 2% per year in the future, estimate the value of Hydro One's stock.

Solution

If dividends are expected to grow perpetually at a rate of 2% per year, we can use Eq. 9.6 to calculate the price of a share of Hydro One stock:

$$P_0 = \frac{Div}{r_E - g} = \frac{\$2.30}{0.07 - 0.02} = \$46.00$$

For another interpretation of Eq. 9.6, note that we can rearrange it as follows:

$$r_E = \frac{Div_1}{P_0} + g \tag{9.7}$$

Comparing Eq. 9.7 with Eq. 9.2, we see that g equals the expected capital gain rate. In other words, with constant expected dividend growth, the expected growth rate of the share price matches the growth rate of dividends.

DIVIDENDS VERSUS INVESTMENT AND GROWTH

In Eq. 9.6, the firm's share price increases with the current dividend level, Div_1, and the expected growth rate, g. To maximize its share price, a firm would like to increase both these quantities. Often, however, the firm faces a tradeoff: Increasing growth may require investment, but money spent on investment cannot be used to pay dividends. We can use the constant dividend growth model to gain insight into this tradeoff.

A SIMPLE MODEL OF GROWTH.   What determines the rate of growth of a firm's dividends? If we define a firm's **dividend payout rate** as the fraction of its earnings that the firm pays as dividends each year, we can write the firm's dividend per share at date t as follows:

$$Div_t = \underbrace{\frac{Earnings_t}{Shares\ Outstanding_t}}_{EPS_t} \times Dividend\ Payout\ Rate_t \tag{9.8}$$

That is, the dividend each year is the firm's earnings per share (EPS) multiplied by its dividend payout rate. Thus the firm can increase its dividend in three ways:

1. It can increase its earnings (net income).

2. It can increase its dividend payout rate.

3. It can decrease its shares outstanding.

Let's suppose for now that the firm does not issue new shares (or buy back its existing shares), so that the number of shares outstanding is fixed, and explore the tradeoff between options 1 and 2.

A firm can do one of two things with its earnings: It can pay them out to investors, or it can retain and reinvest them. By investing cash today, a firm can increase its future dividends. For simplicity, let's assume that if no investment is made, the firm does not grow, so the current level of earnings generated by the firm remains constant. If all increases in future earnings result exclusively from new investment made with retained earnings, then

$$\text{Change in Earnings} = \text{New Investment} \times \text{Return on New Investment} \quad (9.9)$$

New investment equals earnings multiplied by the firm's **retention rate**, the fraction of current earnings that the firm retains:

$$\text{New Investment} = \text{Earnings} \times \text{Retention Rate} \quad (9.10)$$

Substituting Eq. 9.10 into Eq. 9.9 and dividing by earnings gives an expression for the growth rate of earnings:

$$\text{Earnings Growth Rate} = \frac{\text{Change in Earnings}}{\text{Earnings}}$$
$$= \text{Retention Rate} \times \text{Return on New Investment} \quad (9.11)$$

If the firm chooses to keep its dividend payout rate constant, then the growth in dividends will equal growth of earnings:

$$g = \text{Retention Rate} \times \text{Return on New Investment} \quad (9.12)$$

PROFITABLE GROWTH.   Equation 9.12 shows that a firm can increase its growth rate by retaining more of its earnings. However, if the firm retains more earnings, it will be able to pay out less of those earnings, which from Eq. 9.8 means that the firm will have to reduce its dividend. If a firm wants to increase its share price, should it cut its dividend and invest more, or should it cut investment and increase its dividend? Not surprisingly, the answer will depend on the profitability of the firm's investments. Let's consider an example.

EXAMPLE 9.3	CUTTING DIVIDENDS FOR PROFITABLE GROWTH

Problem

The Forzani Group Ltd. expects to have earnings per share of $6 in the coming year. Rather than reinvest these earnings and grow, the firm plans to pay out all of its earnings as a dividend. With the expectation of no growth, The Forzani Group's current share price is $60.

Suppose The Forzani Group could cut its dividend payout rate to 75% for the foreseeable future and use the retained earnings to open new stores. The return on its investment in these stores is expected to be 12%. Assuming its equity cost of capital is unchanged, what effect would this new policy have on The Forzani Group's stock price?

Solution

First, let's estimate The Forzani Group's equity cost of capital. Currently, The Forzani Group plans to pay a dividend equal to its earnings of $6 per share. Given a share price of $60, The Forzani Group's dividend yield is $6/$60 = 10%. With no expected growth ($g = 0$), we can use Eq. 9.7 to estimate r_E:

$$r_E = \frac{Div_1}{P_0} + g = 10\% + 0\% = 10\%$$

In other words, to justify The Forzani Group's stock price under its current policy, the expected return of other stocks in the market with equivalent risk must be 10%.

Next, we consider the consequences of the new policy. If The Forzani Group reduces its dividend payout rate to 75%, then from Eq. 9.8 its dividend this coming year will fall to $Div_1 = EPS_1 \times 75\% = \$6 \times 75\% = \$4.50$. At the same time, because the firm will now retain 25% of its earnings to invest in new stores, from Eq. 9.12 its growth rate will increase to

$$g = \text{Retention Rate} \times \text{Return on New Investment} = 25\% \times 12\% = 3\%$$

Assuming The Forzani Group can continue to grow at this rate, we can compute its share price under the new policy using the constant dividend growth model of Eq. 9.6:

$$P_0 = \frac{Div_1}{r_E - g} = \frac{\$4.50}{0.10 - 0.03} = \$64.29$$

Thus, The Forzani Group's share price should rise from $60 to $64.29 if it cuts its dividend to increase investment and growth, implying the investment has positive NPV. By using its earnings to invest in projects that offer a rate of return (12%) greater than its equity cost of capital (10%), Forzani has created value for its shareholders.

In Example 9.3, cutting the firm's dividend in favour of growth raised the firm's stock price. But this is not always the case, as the next example demonstrates.

EXAMPLE 9.4

UNPROFITABLE GROWTH

Problem

Suppose The Forzani Group decides to cut its dividend payout rate to 75% to invest in new stores, as in Example 9.3. But now suppose that the return on these new investments is 8%, rather than 12%. Given its expected earnings per share this year of $6 and its equity cost of capital of 10%, what will happen to The Forzani Group's current share price in this case?

Solution

Just as in Example 9.3, The Forzani Group's dividend will fall to $6 \times 75\% = \$4.50$. Its growth rate under the new policy, given the lower return on new investment, will now be $g = 25\% \times 8\% = 2\%$. The new share price is therefore

$$P_0 = \frac{Div_1}{r_E - g} = \frac{\$4.50}{0.10 - 0.02} = \$56.25$$

Thus, even though The Forzani Group will grow under the new policy, the new investments have negative NPV. Forzani's share price will fall if it cuts its dividend to make new investments with a return of only 8% when its investors can earn 10% on other investments with comparable risk.

INTERVIEW WITH MARILYN FEDAK

Marilyn G. Fedak is the vice-chair, Investment Services, and was formerly head of Global Value Equities at AllianceBernstein, a publicly traded global asset management firm with approximately $450 billion in assets.

QUESTION: **What valuation methods do you use to identify buying opportunities?**

ANSWER: We use both a dividend-discount model (DDM) and a proprietary quantitative return model called the Global Edge Model (GEM). For our non-U.S. portfolios, we use the GEM model; in the U.S., we use a combination of GEM and the DDM. At its most basic level, the DDM provides a way to evaluate how much we need to pay today for a company's future earnings. All things being equal, we are looking to buy as much earnings power as cheaply as we can.

It is a very reliable methodology, *if* you have the right forecasts for companies' future earnings. Our GEM model encompasses a variety of valuation measures, such as P/E and price-to-book ratios and selected success factors—for example, ROE and price momentum.

In both the U.S. and non-U.S. portfolios, we use these valuation tools to rank companies from the most undervalued to the most expensive. We focus on the stocks that rank the highest. Our decision making bodies, the investment policy groups, meet with analysts to quality control the forecasts for the highest ranked group of stocks. Once the forecasts are approved, we add risk tools to construct optimal portfolios.

QUESTION: **Are there drawbacks to these models?**

ANSWER: Both models have advantages and drawbacks. The DDM is a very reliable valuation methodology. However, its focus on forecasts of cash flow or earnings over some future period requires a large, highly skilled body of research analysts. And, it is oriented to the long term so the timing of purchases and sales can be too early.

The Global Edge Model is very useful to efficiently evaluate investments within large universes. However, it is very oriented to current profitability and valuation metrics—not the future. As such, judgment has to be applied to determine if a company is likely to sustain similar characteristics going forward.

QUESTION: **Has the precipitous decline in stock prices in late 2008 and early 2009 caused you to retool your valuation methodology?**

ANSWER: In 2006, we began studying the interaction of the DDM and GEM models and determined that combining the two models gives us superior results to a single methodology when evaluating U.S. securities. The DDM focuses on forecasts of a company's future, whereas the quantitative return model captures a company's history and current status. This new methodology was very helpful to us in 2008, when the GEM model signalled caution for certain sectors that looked inexpensive based on the DDM.

We have also broadened our research to incorporate more external inputs and have assigned a higher probability to unlikely events such as the recent government intervention in the financial and auto industries. On the risk side, we have added a refinancing risk tool and are tracking short interest in various equities.

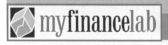 Visit MyFinanceLab at www.myfinancelab.com to see the accompanying video for this interview.

Comparing Example 9.3 with Example 9.4, we see that the effect of cutting the firm's dividend to grow crucially depends on the return on new investment. In Example 9.3, the return on new investment of 12% exceeds the firm's equity cost of capital of 10%, so the investment has positive NPV. In Example 9.4, the return on new investment is only 8%, so the new investment has negative NPV (even though it will lead to earnings growth). Thus *cutting the firm's dividend to increase investment will raise the stock price if, and only if, the new investments have a positive NPV.*

CHANGING GROWTH RATES

Successful young firms often have very high initial earnings growth rates. During this period of high growth, it is not unusual for these firms to retain 100% of their earnings to exploit profitable investment opportunities. As they mature, their growth slows to rates more typical of established companies. At that point, their earnings exceed their investment needs and they begin to pay dividends.

We cannot use the constant dividend growth model to value the stock of such a firm, for several reasons. First, these firms often pay *no* dividends when they are young. Second, their growth rate continues to change over time until they mature. However, we can use the general form of the dividend-discount model to value such a firm by applying the constant growth model to calculate the future share price of the stock P_N once the firm matures and its expected growth rate stabilizes:

0	1	2		N	$N+1$	$N+2$	$N+3$	
	Div_1	Div_2	...	Div_N $+ P_N$	Div_{N+1}	Div_{N+1} $\times(1+g)$	Div_{N+1} $\times(1+g)^2$	...

Specifically, if the firm is expected to grow at a long-term rate g after year $N+1$, then from the constant dividend growth model:

$$P_N = \frac{Div_{N+1}}{r_E - g} \qquad (9.13)$$

We can then use this estimate of P_N as a terminal (continuation) value in the dividend-discount model. Combining Eq. 9.4 with Eq. 9.13, we have

Dividend-Discount Model with Constant Long-Term Growth

$$P_0 = \frac{Div_1}{1 + r_E} + \frac{Div_2}{(1 + r_E)^2} + \cdots + \frac{Div_N}{(1 + r_E)^N} + \frac{1}{(1 + r_E)^N}\left(\frac{Div_{N+1}}{r_E - g}\right) \qquad (9.14)$$

EXAMPLE 9.5

VALUING A FIRM WITH TWO DIFFERENT GROWTH RATES

Problem

Small Fry Inc. has just invented a potato chip that looks and tastes like a French fry. Given the phenomenal market response to this product, Small Fry is reinvesting all of its earnings to expand its operations. Earnings were $2 per share this past year and are expected to grow at a rate of 20% per year until the end of year 4. At that point, other companies are likely to bring out competing products. Analysts project that at the end of year 4, Small Fry will cut investment and begin paying 60% of its earnings as dividends and its growth will slow to a long-run rate of 4%. If Small Fry's equity cost of capital is 8%, what is the value of a share today?

Solution

We can use Small Fry's projected earnings growth rate and payout rate to forecast its future earnings and dividends as shown in the following spreadsheet:

Year	0	1	2	3	4	5	6
Earnings							
1 EPS Growth Rate (versus prior year)		20%	20%	20%	20%	4%	4%
2 EPS	$2.00	$2.40	$2.88	$3.46	$4.15	$4.31	$4.49
Dividends							
3 Dividend Payout Rate		0%	0%	0%	60%	60%	60%
4 Div		$ —	$ —	$ —	$2.49	$2.59	$2.69

Starting from $2.00 in year 0, EPS grows by 20% per year until year 4, after which growth slows to 4%. Small Fry's dividend payout rate is zero until year 4, when competition reduces its investment opportunities and its payout rate rises to 60%. Multiplying EPS by the dividend payout ratio, we project Small Fry's future dividends in line 4.

From year 4 onward, Small Fry's dividends will grow at the expected long-run rate of 4% per year. Thus we can use the constant dividend growth model to project Small Fry's share price at the end of year 3. Given its equity cost of capital of 8%,

$$P_3 = \frac{Div_4}{r_E - g} = \frac{\$2.49}{0.08 - 0.04} = \$62.25$$

We then apply the dividend-discount model (Eq. 9.4) with this terminal value:

$$P_0 = \frac{Div_1}{1 + r_E} + \frac{Div_2}{(1 + r_E)^2} + \frac{Div_3}{(1 + r_E)^3} + \frac{P_3}{(1 + r_E)^3} = \frac{\$62.25}{(1.08)^3} = \$49.42$$

LIMITATIONS OF THE DIVIDEND-DISCOUNT MODEL

The dividend-discount model values the stock based on a forecast of the future dividends paid to shareholders. But unlike a Government of Canada bond, whose cash flows are known with virtual certainty, a tremendous amount of uncertainty is associated with any forecast of a firm's future dividends.

Let's consider the example of Kenneth Cole Productions (KCP), mentioned in the introduction to this chapter. In early 2006, KCP paid annual dividends of $0.72. With an equity cost of capital of 11% and expected dividend growth of 8%, the constant dividend growth model implies a share price for KCP of

$$P_0 = \frac{Div_1}{r_E - g} = \frac{\$0.72}{0.11 - 0.08} = \$24$$

which is reasonably close to the $26.75 share price the stock had at the time. With a 10% dividend growth rate, however, this estimate would rise to $72 per share; with a 5% dividend growth rate, the estimate falls to $12 per share. As we see, even small changes in the assumed dividend growth rate can lead to large changes in the estimated stock price.

Furthermore, it is difficult to know which estimate of the dividend growth rate is more reasonable. KCP more than doubled its dividend between 2003 and 2005, but earnings remained relatively flat during that time. Consequently, this rapid rate of dividend growth was not likely to be sustained. Forecasting dividends requires forecasting the firm's earnings, dividend payout rate, and future share count. But future earnings will depend on interest expenses (which in turn depend on how much the firm borrows), and its share

JOHN BURR WILLIAMS' *THEORY OF INVESTMENT VALUE*

The first formal derivation of the dividend-discount model appeared in the *Theory of Investment Value*, written by John Burr Williams in 1938. The book was an important landmark in the history of corporate finance, because Williams demonstrated for the first time that corporate finance relied on certain principles that could be derived using formal analytical methods. As Williams wrote in the preface:

The truth is that the mathematical method is a new tool of great power whose use promises to lead to notable advances in Investment Analysis. Always it has been the rule in the history of science that the invention of new tools is the key to new discoveries, and we may expect the same rule to hold true in this branch of Economics as well.

While his book was not widely appreciated in its day (indeed, legend has it there was a lively debate at Harvard whether it was acceptable as his Ph.D. dissertation), by the time Williams died in 1989, the importance of the mathematical method in corporate finance was indisputable and the discoveries that resulted from this "new" tool had fundamentally changed its practice. He is today regarded as the founder of fundamental analysis, and his book also pioneered the pro forma modelling of financial statements and firm cash flows, as well as many other ideas now central to modern finance (see Chapter 14 for further reference).

count and dividend payout rate will depend on whether the firm uses a portion of its earnings to repurchase shares. Because borrowing and repurchase decisions are at management's discretion, they can be more difficult to forecast reliably than other, more fundamental aspects of the firm's cash flows.[3] We look at two alternative methods that avoid some of these difficulties in the next section.

CONCEPT CHECK

1. In what three ways can a firm increase its future dividend per share?

2. Under what circumstances can a firm increase its share price by cutting its dividend and investing more?

9.3   TOTAL PAYOUT AND FREE CASH FLOW VALUATION MODELS

In this section, we outline two alternative approaches to valuing the firm's shares that avoid some of the difficulties of the dividend-discount model. First, we consider the *total payout model*, which allows us to ignore the firm's choice between dividends and share repurchases. Then we consider the *discounted free cash flow model*, which focuses on the cash flows to all of the firm's investors, both debt and equity holders, and allows us to avoid estimating the impact of the firm's borrowing decisions on earnings.

SHARE REPURCHASES AND THE TOTAL PAYOUT MODEL

In our discussion of the dividend-discount model, we implicitly assumed that any cash paid out by the firm to shareholders takes the form of a dividend. However, in recent years, an increasing number of firms have replaced dividend payouts with share repurchases. In a **share repurchase**, the firm uses excess cash to buy back its own stock. Share repurchases have two consequences for the dividend-discount model. First, the more cash the firm uses to repurchase shares, the less it has available to pay dividends. Second, by

---

3. We discuss management's decision to borrow funds or repurchase shares in Part 5 of the text.

repurchasing shares, the firm decreases its share count, which increases its earning and dividends on a per-share basis.

In the dividend-discount model, we valued a share from the perspective of a single shareholder, discounting the dividends the shareholder will receive:

$$P_0 = PV(\text{Future Dividends per Share}) \tag{9.15}$$

An alternative method that may be more reliable when a firm repurchases shares is the **total payout model**, which values *all* of the firm's equity, rather than a single share. To do so, we discount the total payouts that the firm makes to shareholders, which is the total payouts that the firm makes to shareholders, which is the total amount spent on both dividends *and* share repurchases.[4] Then we divide by the current number of shares outstanding to determine the share price.

Total Payout Model

$$P_0 = \frac{PV(\text{Future Total Dividends and Repurchases})}{\text{Shares Outstanding}_0} \tag{9.16}$$

We can apply the same simplifications that we obtained by assuming constant growth in Section 9.2 to the total payout method. The only change is that *we discount total dividends and share repurchases and use the growth rate of earnings (rather than earnings per share) when forecasting the growth of the firm's total payouts.* This method can be more reliable and easier to apply when the firm uses share repurchases.

EXAMPLE 9.6	VALUATION WITH SHARE REPURCHASES

Problem

Suppose Buhler Industries has 217 million shares outstanding and expects earnings at the end of this year of $860 million. Buhler plans to pay out 50% of its earnings in total, paying 30% as a dividend and using 20% to repurchase shares. If Buhler's earnings are expected to grow by 7.5% per year and these payout rates remain constant, determine Buhler's share price assuming an equity cost of capital of 10%.

Solution

Buhler will have total payouts this year of 50% × $860 million = $430 million. Based on the equity cost of capital of 10% and an expected earnings growth rate of 7.5%, the present value of Buhler's future payouts can be computed as a constant growth perpetuity:

$$PV(\text{Future Total Dividends and Repurchases}) = \frac{\$430 \text{ million}}{0.10 - 0.075} = \$17.2 \text{ billion}$$

This present value represents the total value of Buhler's equity (i.e., its market capitalization). To compute the share price, we divide by the current number of shares outstanding:

$$P_0 = \frac{\$17.2 \text{ billion}}{217 \text{ million shares}} = \$79.26 \text{ per share}$$

---

4. You can think of the total payouts as the amount you would receive if you owned 100% of the firm's shares: You would receive all of the dividends, plus the proceeds from selling shares back to the firm in the share repurchase.

Using the total payout method, we did not need to know the firm's split between dividends and share repurchases. To compare this method with the dividend-discount model, note that Buhler will pay a dividend of 30% × $860 million/(217 million shares) = $1.19 per share, for a dividend yield of 1.19/79.26 = 1.50%. From Eq. 9.7, Buhler's expected EPS, dividend, and share price growth rate is $g = r_E - Div_1/P_0 = 8.50\%$. This growth rate exceeds the 7.50% growth rate of earnings because Buhler's share count will decline over time due to share repurchases.[5]

THE DISCOUNTED FREE CASH FLOW MODEL

In the total payout model, we first value the firm's equity, rather than just a single share. The **discounted free cash flow model** goes one step further and begins by determining the total value of the firm to all investors—both equity *and* debt holders. That is, we begin by estimating the firm's enterprise value, which we defined in Chapter 2 as[6]

$$\text{Enterprise Value} = \text{Market Value of Equity} + \text{Debt} - \text{Cash} \qquad (9.17)$$

The enterprise value is the value of the firm's underlying business, unencumbered by debt and separate from any cash or marketable securities. We can interpret the enterprise value as the net cost of acquiring the firm's equity, taking its cash, paying off all debt, and thus owning the unlevered business. The advantage of the discounted free cash flow model is that it allows us to value a firm without explicitly forecasting its dividends, share repurchases, or its use of debt.

VALUING THE ENTERPRISE.   How can we estimate a firm's enterprise value? To estimate the value of the firm's equity, we computed the present value of the firm's total payouts to equity holders. Likewise, to estimate a firm's enterprise value, we compute the present value of the *free cash flow* (FCF) that the firm has available to pay all investors, both debt and equity holders. We saw how to compute the free cash flow for a project in Chapter 7; we now perform the same calculation for the entire firm:

$$\text{Free Cash Flow} = \overbrace{EBIT \times (1 - \tau_c)}^{\text{Unlevered Net Income}} + \text{Depreciation}$$
$$- \text{Capital Expenditures} - \text{Increases in Net Working Capital} \qquad (9.18)$$

Note: As in Chapter 7, if capital cost allowance (CCA) replaces depreciation for tax purposes, then CCA would be used in the calculation of EBIT and would replace depreciation in Eq. 9.18.

---

5. We can check that an 8.5% EPS growth rate is consistent with 7.5% earnings growth and Buhler's repurchase plans as follows. Given an expected share price of $79.26 × 1.085 = $86.00 next year, Buhler will repurchase 20% × $860 million ÷ ($86.00 per share) = 2 million shares next year. With the decline in the number of shares from 217 million to 215 million, EPS grows by a factor of 1.075 × (217/215) = 1.085 or 8.5%.

6. To be precise, by cash we are referring to the firm's cash in excess of its working capital needs, which is the amount of cash it has invested at a competitive market interest rate. Note, for free cash flow we are using free cash flow to the firm. In Chapter 18 we discuss free cash flow to equity and discuss how it can be used for valuation purposes.

When we are looking at the entire firm, it is natural to define the firm's **net investment** as its capital expenditures in excess of depreciation:

$$\text{Net Investment} = \text{Capital Expenditures} - \text{Depreciation} \qquad (9.19)$$

With that definition, we can also write the free cash flow formula as

$$\begin{aligned} \text{Free Cash Flow} = {} & EBIT \times (1 - \tau_c) - \text{Net Investment} \\ & - \text{Increases in Net Working Capital} \end{aligned} \qquad (9.20)$$

Free cash flow measures the cash generated by the firm before any payments to debt or equity holders are considered. Thus, just as we determine the value of a project by calculating the NPV of the project's free cash flow, we estimate a firm's current enterprise value V_0 by computing the present value of the firm's free cash flow:

Discounted Free Cash Flow Model

$$V_0 = PV(\text{Future Free Cash Flow of Firm}) \qquad (9.21)$$

Given the enterprise value, we can estimate the share price by using Eq. 9.17 to solve for the value of equity and then divide by the total number of shares outstanding:

$$P_0 = \frac{V_0 + \text{Cash}_0 - \text{Debt}_0}{\text{Shares Outstanding}_0} \qquad (9.22)$$

Intuitively, the difference between the discounted free cash flow model and the dividend-discount model is that in the dividend-discount model, the firm's cash and debt are included indirectly through the effect of interest income and expenses on earnings. In the discounted free cash flow model, we ignore interest income and expenses because free cash flow is based on EBIT, but then adjust for cash and debt directly in Eq. 9.22.

IMPLEMENTING THE MODEL. A key difference between the discounted free cash flow model and the earlier models we have considered is the discount rate. In previous calculations we used the firm's equity cost of capital, r_E, because we were discounting the cash flows to equity holders. Here we are discounting the free cash flow that will be paid to both debt and equity holders. Thus we should use the firm's **weighted average cost of capital (WACC)**, denoted by r_{wacc} which is the cost of capital the firm must pay to all of its investors, both debt and equity holders. If the firm has no debt, then $r_{wacc} = r_E$. But when a firm has debt, r_{wacc} is an average of the firm's debt and equity cost of capital. In that case, because debt is generally less risky than equity, r_{wacc} is generally less than r_E. We can also interpret the WACC as reflecting the average risk of all of the firm's investments. We will develop methods to calculate the WACC explicitly in Parts 4 and 5 of the text.

Given the firm's weighted average cost of capital, we implement the discounted free cash flow model in much the same way as we did the dividend-discount model. That is, we forecast the firm's free cash flow up to some horizon, together with a terminal (continuation) value of the enterprise:

$$V_0 = \frac{FCF_1}{1 + r_{wacc}} + \frac{FCF_2}{(1 + r_{wacc})^2} + \cdots + \frac{FCF_N}{(1 + r_{wacc})^N} + \frac{V_N}{(1 + r_{wacc})^N} \qquad (9.23)$$

Often, the terminal value is estimated by assuming a constant long-run growth rate g_{FCF} for free cash flows beyond year N, so that

$$V_N = \frac{FCF_{N+1}}{r_{wacc} - g_{FCF}} = \left(\frac{1 + g_{FCF}}{r_{wacc} - g_{FCF}}\right) \times FCF_N \qquad (9.24)$$

The long-run growth rate g_{FCF} is typically based on the expected long-run growth rate of the firm's revenues.

EXAMPLE 9.7	VALUING KENNETH COLE USING FREE CASH FLOW

Problem

Kenneth Cole (KCP) had sales of $518 million in 2005. Suppose you expect its sales to grow at a 9% rate in 2006, but that this growth rate will slow by 1% per year to a long-run growth rate for the apparel industry of 4% by 2011. Based on KCP's past profitability and investment needs, you expect EBIT to be 9% of sales, increases in net working capital requirements to be 10% of any increase in sales, and net investment (capital expenditures in excess of depreciation) to be 8% of any increase in sales. If KCP has $100 million in cash, $3 million in debt, 21 million shares outstanding, a tax rate of 37%, and a weighted average cost of capital of 11%, what is your estimate of the value of KCP's stock in early 2006?

Solution

Using Eq. 9.20, we can estimate KCP's future free cash flow based on the estimates above as follows:

Year	2005	2006	2007	2008	2009	2010	2011
FCF Forecast ($ million)							
1 Sales	518.0	564.6	609.8	652.5	691.6	726.2	755.3
2 *Growth versus Prior Year*		9.0%	8.0%	7.0%	6.0%	5.0%	4.0%
3 EBIT (9% of sales)		50.8	54.9	58.7	62.2	65.4	68.0
4 Less: Income Tax (37%)		(18.8)	(20.3)	(21.7)	(23.0)	(24.2)	(25.1)
5 Plus: Depreciation		–	–	–	–	–	–
6 Less: Capital Expenditures		–	–	–	–	–	–
7 Less: Inc. in NWC (10% ΔSales)		(4.7)	(4.5)	(4.3)	(3.9)	(3.5)	(2.9)
8 **Free Cash Flow**		27.4	30.1	32.7	35.3	37.7	39.9

Because we expect KCP's free cash flow to grow at a constant rate after 2011, we can use Eq. 9.24 to compute a terminal enterprise value:

$$V_{2011} = \left(\frac{1 + g_{FCF}}{r_{wacc} - g_{FCF}} \right) \times FCF_{2011} = \left(\frac{1.04}{0.11 - 0.04} \right) \times 39.9 = \$592.8 \text{ million}$$

From Eq. 9.23 KCP's current enterprise value is the present value of its free cash flows plus terminal value:

$$V_0 = \frac{27.4}{1.11} + \frac{30.1}{1.11^2} + \frac{32.7}{1.11^3} + \frac{35.3}{1.11^4} + \frac{37.7}{1.11^5} + \frac{39.9}{1.11^6} + \frac{592.8}{1.11^6} = \$456.9 \text{ million}$$

We can now estimate the value of a share of KCP's stock using Eq. 9.22:

$$P_0 = \frac{456.9 + 100 - 3}{21} = \$26.38$$

CONNECTION TO CAPITAL BUDGETING.   There is an important connection between the discounted free cash flow model and the NPV rule for capital budgeting that we developed in Chapter 7. Because the firm's free cash flow is equal to the sum of the free cash flows from the firm's current and future investments, we can interpret the firm's enterprise value as the total NPV that the firm will earn from continuing its existing projects and initiating new ones. Hence, the NPV of any individual project represents its contribution to the firm's enterprise value. To maximize the firm's share price, we should accept projects that have a positive NPV.

Recall also from Chapter 7 that many forecasts and estimates were necessary to estimate the free cash flows of a project. The same is true for the firm: We must forecast future sales, operating expenses, taxes, capital requirements, and other factors. On the one hand, estimating free cash flow in this way gives us flexibility to incorporate many specific details about the future prospects of the firm. On the other hand, some uncertainty inevitably surrounds each assumption. It is therefore important to conduct a sensitivity analysis, as we described in Chapter 7, to translate this uncertainty into a range of potential values for the stock.

EXAMPLE 9.8

SENSITIVITY ANALYSIS FOR STOCK VALUATION

Problem

In Example 9.7, KCP's EBIT was assumed to be 9% of sales in 2006, slowing to a long-term growth rate of 4%. How would your estimate of the stock's value change if you expected revenue growth of 4% from 2006 on? How would it change if in addition you expected EBIT to be 7% of sales, rather than 9%?

Solution

With 4% revenue growth and a 9% EBIT margin, KCP will have 2006 revenues of $518 \times 1.04 = \$538.7$ million, and EBIT of $9\% \times 538.7 = \$48.5$ million. Given the increase in sales of $538.7 - 518.0 = \$20.7$ million, we expect net investment of $8\% \times 20.7 = \$1.6$ million and additional net working capital of $10\% \times 20.7 = \$2.1$ million. Thus, KCP's expected FCF in 2006 is

$$FCF_{06} = 48.5\,(1 - .37) - 1.6 - 2.1 = \$26.8 \text{ million}$$

Because growth is expected to remain constant at 4%, we can estimate KCP's enterprise value as a growing perpetuity:

$$V_0 = \$26.8/(0.11 - 0.04) = \$383 \text{ million}$$

for an initial share value of $P_0 = (383 + 100 - 3)/21 = \$22.86$. Thus, comparing this result with that of Example 9.7, we see that a higher initial revenue growth of 9% versus 4% contributes about $2 to the value of KCP's stock.

If in addition we expect KCP's EBIT margin to be only 7%, our FCF estimate would decline to

$$FCF_{06} = (.07 \times 538.7)\,(1 - .37) - 1.6 - 2.1 = \$20.0 \text{ million}$$

for an enterprise value of $V_0 = \$20/(0.11 - 0.04) = \$286$ million and a share value of $P_0 = (286 + 100 - 3)/21 = \$18.24$.

Thus, we can see that maintaining an EBIT margin of 9% versus 7% contributes more than $4.50 to KCP's stock value in this scenario.

Figure 9.1 summarizes the different valuation methods we have discussed thus far. The value of the stock is determined by the present value of its future dividends. We can estimate the total market capitalization of the firm's equity from the present value of the firm's total payouts, which includes dividends and share repurchases. Finally, the present value of the firm's free cash flow, which is the cash the firm has available to make payments to equity or debt holders, determines the firm's enterprise value.

Present Value of ...	Determines the ...
Dividend Payments	Stock Price
Total Payouts (All Dividends and Repurchases)	Equity Value
Free Cash Flow (Cash available to pay all security holders)	Enterprise Value

CONCEPT CHECK

1. How does the growth rate used in the total payout model differ from the growth rate used in the dividend-discount model?

2. What is the enterprise value of the firm?

3. How can you estimate a firm's stock price based on its projected free cash flows?

9.4 VALUATION BASED ON COMPARABLE FIRMS

Thus far, we have valued a firm or its stock by considering the expected future cash flows it will provide to its owner. The Law of One Price then tells us that its value is the present value of its future cash flows, because the present value is the amount we would need to invest elsewhere in the market to replicate the cash flows with the same risk.

Another application of the Law of One Price is the method of comparables. In the **method of comparables** (or "comps"), rather than value the firm's cash flows directly, we estimate the value of the firm based on the value of other, comparable firms or investments that we expect will generate very similar cash flows in the future. For example, consider the case of a new firm that is *identical* to an existing publicly traded company. If these firms will generate identical cash flows, the Law of One Price implies that we can use the value of the existing company to determine the value of the new firm.

Of course, identical companies do not exist. Even two firms in the same industry selling the same types of products, while similar in many respects, are likely to be of a different size or scale. In this section, we consider ways to adjust for scale differences to use comparables to value firms with similar business, and then discuss the strengths and weaknesses of this approach.

VALUATION MULTIPLES

We can adjust for differences in scale between firms by expressing their value in terms of a **valuation multiple**, which is a ratio of the value to some measure of the firm's scale. As an analogy, consider valuing an office building. A natural measure to consider would be the price per square foot for other buildings recently sold in the area. Multiplying the size of the office building under consideration by the average price per square foot would typically provide a reasonable estimate of the building's value. We can apply this same idea to stocks, replacing square footage with some more appropriate measure of the firm's scale.

THE PRICE-EARNINGS RATIO. The most common valuation multiple is the price-earnings (P/E) ratio, which we introduced in Chapter 2. A firm's P/E ratio is equal to the share price divided by its earnings per share. The intuition behind its use is that when you buy a stock, you are in a sense buying the rights to the firm's future earnings. Because differences in the scale of firms' earnings are likely to persist, you should be willing to pay proportionally more for a stock with higher current earnings. Thus we can estimate the value of a firm's share by multiplying its current earnings per share by the average P/E ratio of comparable firms.

To interpret the P/E multiple, consider the stock price formula we derived in Eq. 9.6 for the case of constant dividend growth: $P_0 = Div_1/(r_E - g)$. If we divide both sides of this equation by EPS_1, we have the following formula:

$$\text{Forward P/E} = \frac{P_0}{EPS_1} = \frac{Div_1/EPS_1}{r_E - g} = \frac{\text{Dividend Payout Rate}}{r_E - g} \quad (9.25)$$

Eq. 9.25 provides a formula for the firm's **forward P/E,** which is the P/E multiple computed based on its **forward earnings** (expected earnings over the next 12 months). We can also compute the firm's **trailing P/E** (earnings over the prior 12 months).[7] For valuation purposes, the forward P/E is generally preferred, as we are most concerned with future earnings.[8]

Equation 9.25 implies that if two stocks have the same payout and EPS growth rates, as well as equivalent risk (and therefore the same equity cost of capital), then they should have the same P/E. It also shows that firms and industries with high growth rates, and which generate cash well in excess of their investment needs so that they can maintain high payout rates, should have high P/E multiples.

EXAMPLE 9.9

VALUATION USING THE PRICE-EARNINGS RATIO

Problem
Suppose furniture manufacturer Herman Miller Inc. has earnings per share of $1.38. If the average P/E of comparable furniture stocks is 21.3, estimate a value for Herman Miller using the P/E as a valuation multiple. What are the assumptions underlying this estimate?

Solution
We estimate a share price for Herman Miller by multiplying its EPS by the P/E of comparable firms. Thus $P_0 = \$1.38 \times 21.3 = \$29.39$. This estimate assumes that Herman Miller will have similar future risk, payout rates, and growth rates to comparable firms in the industry.

---

7. Assuming EPS grows at rate g_0 between date 0 and 1,

$$\text{Trailing P/E} = P_0/EPS_0 = (1 + g_0)P_0/EPS_1 = (1 + g_0)(\text{Forward P/E})$$

so trailing multiples tend to be higher for growing firms. Thus, when comparing multiples, be sure to be consistent in the use of either trailing or forward multiples across firms.

8. Because we are interested in the persistent components of the firm's earnings, it is also common practice to exclude extraordinary items that will not be repeated when calculating a P/E ratio for valuation purposes.

ENTERPRISE VALUE MULTIPLES. It is also common practice to use valuation multiples based on the firm's enterprise value. As we discussed in Section 9.3, because it represents the total value of the firm's underlying business rather than just the value of equity, using the enterprise value is advantageous if we want to compare firms with different amounts of leverage.

Because the enterprise value represents the entire value of the firm before the firm pays its debt, to form an appropriate multiple, we divide it by a measure of earnings or cash flows before interest payments are made. Common multiples to consider are enterprise value to EBIT, EBITDA (earnings before interest, taxes, depreciation, and amortization), and free cash flow. However, because capital expenditures can vary substantially from period to period (e.g., a firm may need to add capacity and build a new plant one year, but then not need to expand further for many years), most practitioners rely on enterprise value to EBITDA multiples. From Eq. 9.24, if expected free cash flow growth is constant, then

$$\frac{V_0}{EBITDA_1} = \frac{FCF_1/EBITDA_1}{r_{wacc} - g_{FCF}} \tag{9.26}$$

As with the P/E multiple, this valuation multiple is higher for firms with high growth rates and low capital requirements (so that free cash flow is high in proportion to EBITDA).

EXAMPLE 9.10

VALUATION USING AN ENTERPRISE VALUE MULTIPLE

Problem

Suppose Rocky Shoes and Boots (RCKY) has earnings per share of $2.30 and EBITDA of $30.7 million. RCKY also has 5.4 million shares outstanding and debt of $125 million (net of cash). You believe Deckers Outdoor Corporation is comparable to RCKY in terms of its underlying business, but Deckers has no debt. If Deckers has a P/E of 13.3 and an enterprise value to EBITDA multiple of 7.4, estimate the value of RCKY's shares using both multiples. Which estimate is likely to be more accurate?

Solution

Using Decker's P/E, we would estimate a share price for RCKY of $P_0 = \$2.30 \times 13.3 = \$30.59$. Using the enterprise value to EBITDA multiple, we would estimate RCKY's enterprise value to be $V_0 = \$30.7$ million $\times 7.4 = \$227.2$ million. We then subtract debt and divide by the number of shares to estimate RCKY's share price: $P_0 = (227.2 - 125)/5.4 = \$18.93$. Because of the large difference in leverage between the firms, we would expect the second estimate, which is based on enterprise value, to be more reliable.

OTHER MULTIPLES. Many other valuation multiples are possible. Looking at enterprise value as a multiple of sales can be useful if it is reasonable to assume that the firms will maintain similar margins in the future. For firms with substantial tangible assets, the ratio of price to book value of equity per share is sometimes used. Some multiples are specific to an industry. In the cable TV industry, for example, it is natural to consider enterprise value per subscriber.

LIMITATIONS OF MULTIPLES

If comparables were identical, the firms' multiples would match precisely. Of course, firms are not identical. Thus the usefulness of a valuation multiple will depend on the nature of the differences between firms and the sensitivity of the multiples to these differences.

Table 9.1 lists several valuation multiples for Kenneth Cole as well as for other firms in the footwear industry, as of January 2006. Also shown is the average for each multiple, together with the range around the average (in percentage terms). Comparing Kenneth Cole with the industry averages, KCP looks somewhat undervalued according to the other multiples shown. For all of the multiples, a significant amount of dispersion across the industry is apparent. While the enterprise value to EBITDA multiple shows the smallest variation, even with it we cannot expect to obtain a precise estimate of value.

The differences in these multiples are most likely due to differences in expected future growth rates, profitability, and risk (and therefore costs of capital), and, in the case of Puma, differences in accounting conventions between the United States and Germany. As with Puma, differences in accounting conventions are especially problematic for Canadian firms. This is due to the lack of many comparable companies (that match based on industry and size) in Canada; the comparables are often chosen from the United States where the accounting rules sometimes differ in important ways. Aside from differences in accounting conventions across countries, a firm's accounting numbers may simply be misstated. For example, Nortel Networks Corporation had to restate its financial results for several years and advises investors not to use its historical financial reports from the fiscal years 2001 to 2005 and the first three quarters of 2006. Investors in the market understand these differences, so the stocks are priced accordingly. But when valuing a firm using multiples, there is no clear guidance about how to adjust for these differences other than by narrowing the set of comparables used and being very careful in interpreting the accounting information given.

TABLE 9.1 STOCK PRICES AND MULTIPLES FOR THE FOOTWEAR INDUSTRY, JANUARY 2006

Ticker	Name	Stock Price ($)	Market Capitalization ($ million)	Enterprise Value ($ million)	P/E	Price/ Book	Enterprise Value/ Sales	Enterprise Value/ EBITDA
NKE	Nike	84.20	21,830	20,518	16.64	3.59	1.43	8.75
PMMAY	Puma AG	312.05	5,088	4,593	14.99	5.02	2.19	9.02
RBK	Reebok International	58.72	3,514	3,451	14.91	2.41	0.90	8.58
WWW	Wolverine World Wide	22.10	1,257	1,253	17.42	2.71	1.20	9.53
BWS	Brown Shoe Co.	43.36	800	1,019	22.62	1.91	0.47	9.09
SKX	Skechers U.S.A.	17.09	683	614	17.63	2.02	0.62	6.88
SRR	Stride Rite Corp.	13.70	497	524	20.72	1.87	0.89	9.28
DECK	Deckers Outdoor Corp.	30.05	373	367	13.32	2.29	1.48	7.44
WEYS	Weyco Group	19.90	230	226	11.97	1.75	1.06	6.66
RCKY	Rocky Shoes & Boots	19.96	106	232	8.66	1.12	0.92	7.55
DFZ	R.G. Barry Corp.	6.83	68	92	9.2	8.11	0.87	10.75
BOOT	LaCrosse Footwear	10.40	62	75	12.09	1.28	0.76	8.30
				Average	15.01	2.84	1.06	8.49
				Maximum	+51%	+186%	+106%	+27%
				Minimum	−42%	−61%	−56%	−22%

Thus, a key shortcoming of the comparables approach is that it does not take into account the important differences among firms. One firm might have an exceptional management team, another might have developed an efficient manufacturing process, or secured a patent on a new technology. Such differences are ignored when we apply a valuation multiple.

Another limitation of comparables is that they provide only information regarding the value of the firm *relative to* the other firms in the comparison set. Using multiples will not help us determine if an entire industry is overvalued, for example. This issue became especially important during the dot-com boom of the late 1990s. Because many of these firms did not have positive cash flows or earnings, new multiples were created to value them (e.g., price to "page views"). While these multiples could justify the value of these firms in relation to one another, it was much more difficult to justify the stock prices of many of these firms using a realistic estimate of cash flows and the discounted free cash flow approach.

COMPARISON WITH DISCOUNTED CASH FLOW METHODS

Using a valuation multiple based on comparables is best viewed as a "shortcut" to the discounted cash flow methods of valuation. Rather than separately estimate the firm's cost of capital and future earnings or free cash flows, we rely on the market's assessment of the value of other firms with similar future prospects. In addition to its simplicity, the multiples approach has the advantage of being based on actual prices of real firms, rather than what may be unrealistic forecasts of future cash flows.

Discounted cash flows methods have the advantage that they allow us to incorporate specific information about the firm's cost of capital or future growth. Thus, because the true driver of value for any firm is its ability to generate cash flows for its investors, the discounted cash flow methods have the potential to be more accurate than the use of a valuation multiple.

STOCK VALUATION TECHNIQUES: THE FINAL WORD

In the end, no single technique provides a final answer regarding a stock's true value. All approaches require assumptions or forecasts that are too uncertain to provide a definitive assessment of the firm's value. Most real-world practitioners use a combination of these approaches and gain confidence if the results are consistent across a variety of methods.

Figure 9.2 compares the ranges of values for Kenneth Cole Productions using the different valuation methods that we have discussed in this chapter.[9] Kenneth Cole's stock price of $26.75 in January 2006 is within the range estimated by all of these methods. Hence, based on this evidence alone we would not conclude that the stock is obviously under- or over-priced.

It is important to note that when we are valuing a company's stock using any of our models, the valuations are only good at the time we do them. Every new piece of information we learn can potentially change our predictions for future data (free cash flows, EBITDA, growth, cost of capital, etc.). As our predictions or expectations change, our

---

9. Charts such as this one, showing the range of values produced by each valuation method, are often referred to as a valuation "football field" by practitioners.

| FIGURE 9.2 | Range of Valuations for KCP Stock Using Alternative Valuation Methods |

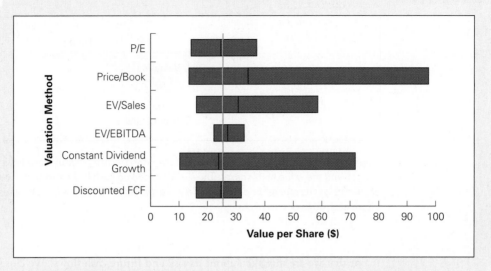

Valuations from multiples are based on the low, high, and average values of the comparable firms from Table 9.1 (see Problems 23 and 24). The constant dividend growth model is based on an 11% equity cost of capital and 5%, 8%, and 10% dividend growth rates, as discussed at the end of Section 9.2. The discounted free cash flow model is based on Example 9.7 with the range of parameters in Problem 21. (Midpoints are based on average multiples or base case assumptions. Red and blue regions show the variation between the lowest-multiple/worst-case scenario and the highest-multiple/best-case scenario. KCP's actual share price of $26.75 at the beginning of 2006 is indicated by the grey line.)

valuation models should be updated. In actuality, this is what is done in the market and this explains why stock prices constantly change. Consider the case of KCP: Its sales did not rise as we expected when we did our valuation in the beginning of 2006. By the end of 2006 sales rose to only $536.5 million (compared to our projection of $564.6 million) and by the end of 2007, sales had dropped to $510.7 million (compared to our projection of $609.8 million). So while, at the beginning of 2006, our valuations were consistent with the market price of $26.75 that existed at that time, as we learned of the new sales information, we would have revised our valuations downward. In fact, KCP's stock price dropped below $25 at the beginning of 2007, dropped to about $5 in March 2009 and was around $12 in May 2010.

CONCEPT CHECK

1. What are some common valuation multiples?

2. What implicit assumptions are made when valuing a firm using multiples based on comparable firms?

9.5 INFORMATION, COMPETITION, AND STOCK PRICES

As shown in Figure 9.3, the models described in this chapter link the firm's expected future cash flows, its cost of capital (determined by its risk), and the value of its shares. But what conclusions should we draw if the actual market price of a stock doesn't appear to be consistent with our estimate of its value? Is it more likely that the stock is mispriced

FIGURE 9.3   The Valuation Triad

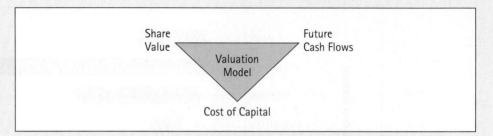

Valuation models determine the relationship among the firm's future cash flows, its cost of capital, and the value of its shares. The stock's expected cash flows and cost of capital can be used to assess its market price. Conversely, the market price can be used to assess the firm's future cash flows or cost of capital.

or that we are mistaken about its risk and future cash flows? We close this chapter with a consideration of this question and the implications for corporate managers.

INFORMATION IN STOCK PRICES

Consider the following situation. It is early 2006; you are a new junior analyst assigned to research Kenneth Cole Productions stock and assess its value. You scrutinize the company's recent financial statements, look at the trends in the industry, and forecast the firm's future earnings, dividends, and free cash flows. You carefully run the numbers and estimate the stock's value at $30 per share. On your way to present your analysis to your boss, you run into a slightly more experienced colleague in the elevator. It turns out your colleague has been researching the same stock, and has different beliefs. According to her analysis, the value of the stock is only $20 per share. What would you do?

Although you could just assume your colleague is wrong, most of us in this situation would reconsider our own analysis. The fact that someone else who has carefully studied the stock has come to a very different conclusion is powerful evidence that we might have missed something. In the face of this information from our colleague, we would probably adjust our assessment of the stock's value downward. Of course, our colleague might also revise her opinion based on our assessment. After sharing our analyses, we would likely end up with a consensus estimate somewhere between $20 and $30 per share. That is, at the end of this process our beliefs would be similar.

This type of encounter happens millions of times every day in the stock market. When a buyer seeks to buy a stock, the willingness of other parties to sell the same stock suggests that they value the stock differently, as the NPV of buying and selling the stock cannot *both* be positive. Thus, the information that others are willing to trade should lead buyers and sellers to revise their valuations. Ultimately, investors trade until they reach a consensus regarding the value of the stock. In this way, stock markets aggregate the information and views of many different investors.

Thus, if your valuation model suggests a stock is worth $30 per share when it is trading for $20 per share in the market, the discrepancy is equivalent to knowing that thousands of investors—many of them professionals who have access to the best information—disagree with your assessment. This knowledge should make you reconsider your original analysis.

INTERVIEW WITH RANDY COUSINS

Randy Cousins, CFA, is managing director at BMO Capital Markets and Equity Research Analyst within the Equity Research Department there.

QUESTION: Can you provide some background about BMO?

ANSWER: BMO is the TSX symbol for the Bank of Montreal. The Bank of Montreal is one of the original banks in Canada. Over the past 30 years, the bank purchased Nesbitt Thomson and subsequently Burns Fry to form Nesbitt Burns. BMO then reconfigured the asset pool to create BMO Capital Markets, which serves large corporations and institutional investors. The wealth management division includes Jones Heward and Nesbitt Burns. BMO owns Harris Bank, a banking operation in the United States. Then at the heart of the company is its retail banking operation with BMO Bank of Montreal branches across Canada.

QUESTION: Why are banks important?

ANSWER: A bank takes a person's savings and puts that money to work by lending the funds to other individuals or businesses. It allows for the reallocation of capital from savers to borrowers and makes money by taking a spread between its cost of funds and what it actually earns on its loans or other assets. If the bank is making smart decisions, it is allocating the capital in the most efficient manner, which in turn results in the highest growth opportunities for society.

QUESTION: How has that been working recently?

ANSWER: In banking, the costs of a bad mistake may not show up immediately, even though initially there may be positive immediate returns. The current global credit and financial crisis is an example of a financial system that made bad or possibly reckless decisions. In lending, you want to earn a rate of return but you also want to have your capital returned; it does not matter how much interest you earn on the capital if you do not get the original capital back.

QUESTION: Can you talk about your role as an equity research analyst?

ANSWER: My job is to pick stocks that outperform the market and my coverage universe. This helps capital flow to companies that can best use it. I try to identify businesses that have good growth prospects but whose current valuation may not reflect the potential of that business.

QUESTION: What are some of the valuation methods used by analysts?

ANSWER: Analysts may use a variety of valuation techniques including relative valuation, discounted cash flow analysis, or technical analysis.

There are two categories of relative valuation. The first looks at the relative value of a company with respect to other companies within the same line of business. The second approach is to look at relative value through history.

Discounted cash flow analysis looks at the present value of the cash flows the firm will produce or at a dividend-discount model. Analysts track the premium or discount to the PV and choose to buy or sell that stock based on whether it is trading at a significant premium to the PV or at a discount to the PV.

A few investors also use technical analysis. While some market players will dispute the usefulness of charts, there are other investors who use technical analysis when buying or selling stocks. To understand the operation of capital markets, it is useful to understand the many approaches used by all market participants.

As an analyst or portfolio manager, you will probably use a variety of valuation techniques. Likely you will triangulate the various valuation techniques to give you confidence that when you are buying a security for your unit holder or for your clients, you are minimizing risk and creating an opportunity for a reasonable capital gain.

QUESTION: Can you discuss value versus growth investing?

ANSWER: Value investors try to buy stocks that trade at less than the market multiple with a growth rate that is better than the market. They look for a business that is selling at a significant discount to its intrinsic value. In value investing, timing/price is usually more important. You are usually buying the stock when it is out of favour on the expectation that the market's perception of the business will improve. Growth investors focus on companies that have superior growth characteristics to the market. They try to identify a superior business; even if they do not get the timing right, the superior growth prospect carries the stock price upward.

SUMMARY

1. The Law of One Price states that the value of a stock is equal to the present value of the dividends and future sale price the investor will receive. Because these cash flows are risky, they must be discounted at the equity cost of capital, which is the expected return of other securities available in the market with equivalent risk to the firm's equity.

2. The total return of a stock is equal to the dividend yield plus the capital gain rate. The expected total return of a stock should equal its equity cost of capital:

$$r_E = \frac{Div_1 + P_1}{P_0} - 1 = \underbrace{\frac{Div_1}{P_0}}_{\text{Dividend Yield}} + \underbrace{\frac{P_1 - P_0}{P_0}}_{\text{Capital Gain Rate}} \tag{9.2}$$

3. When investors have the same beliefs, the dividend-discount model states that, for any horizon N, the stock price satisfies the following equation:

$$P_0 = \frac{Div_1}{1 + r_E} + \frac{Div_2}{(1 + r_E)^2} + \cdots + \frac{Div_N}{(1 + r_E)^N} + \frac{P_N}{(1 + r_E)^N} \tag{9.4}$$

4. If the stock eventually pays dividends and is never acquired, the dividend-discount model implies that the stock price equals the present value of all future dividends.

5. The constant dividend growth model assumes that dividends grow at a constant expected rate g. In that case, g is also the expected capital gain rate, and

$$P_0 = \frac{Div_1}{r_E - g} \tag{9.6}$$

6. Future dividends depend on earnings, shares outstanding, and the dividend payout rate:

$$Div_t = \underbrace{\frac{\text{Earnings}_t}{\text{Shares Outstanding}_t}}_{EPS_t} \times \text{Dividend Payout Rate}_t \tag{9.8}$$

7. If the dividend payout rate and the number of shares outstanding is constant, and if earnings change only as a result of new investment from retained earnings, then the growth rate of the firm's earnings, dividends, and share price is calculated as follows:

$$g = \text{Retention Rate} \times \text{Return on New Investment} \tag{9.12}$$

8. Cutting the firm's dividend to increase investment will raise the stock price if, and only if, the new investments have a positive NPV.

9. If the firm has a long-term growth rate of g after the period $N + 1$, then we can apply the dividend-discount model and use the constant dividend growth formula to estimate the terminal stock value P_N.

10. The dividend-discount model is sensitive to the dividend growth rate, which is difficult to estimate accurately.

11. If the firm undertakes share repurchases, it is more reliable to use the total payout model to value the firm. In this model, the value of equity equals the present value of future total dividends and repurchases. To determine the stock price, we divide the equity value by the initial number of shares outstanding of the firm:

$$P_0 = \frac{PV(\text{Future Total Dividends and Repurchases})}{\text{Shares Outstanding}_0} \tag{9.16}$$

12. The growth rate of the firm's total payout is governed by the growth rate of earnings, not earnings per share.

13. When a firm has leverage, it is more reliable to use the discounted free cash flow model. In this model,

   a. The enterprise value (the market value of equity plus debt, less excess cash) of the firm equals the present value of the firm's future free cash flow:

$$\text{Net Investment} = \text{Capital Expenditures} - \text{Depreciation} \qquad (9.19)$$

   b. We can estimate the firm's future free cash flow as

$$\begin{aligned} \text{Free Cash Flow} = \; & EBIT \times (1 - \tau_c) - \text{ Net Investment} \\ & - \text{Increases in Net Working Capital} \end{aligned} \qquad (9.20)$$

   c. We discount free cash flows using the weighted average cost of capital, which is the expected return the firm must pay to investors to compensate them for the risk of holding the firm's debt and equity together.

   d. We can estimate a terminal enterprise value by assuming free cash flow grows at a constant rate (typically equal to the rate of long-run revenue growth).

   e. We determine the stock price by subtracting debt and adding cash to the enterprise value, and then dividing by the initial number of shares outstanding of the firm:

$$P_0 = \frac{V_0 + \text{Cash}_0 - \text{Debt}_0}{\text{Shares Outstanding}_0} \qquad (9.22)$$

14. We can also value stocks by using valuation multiples based on comparable firms. Multiples commonly used for this purpose include the P/E ratio and the ratio of enterprise value to EBITDA. Using multiples assumes that comparable firms have the same risk, future growth, and quality of accounting data as the firm being valued.

15. No valuation model provides a definitive value for the stock. It is best to use several methods to identify a reasonable range for the value.

16. Stock prices aggregate the information of many investors. Therefore, if our valuation disagrees with the stock's market price, it is most likely an indication that our assumptions about the firm's cash flows are wrong.

17. Competition between investors tends to eliminate positive-NPV trading opportunities. Competition will be strongest when information is public and easy to interpret. Privately informed traders may be able to profit from their information, which is reflected in prices only gradually.

18. The efficient markets hypothesis states that competition eliminates all positive-NPV trades, which is equivalent to stating that securities with equivalent risk have the same expected returns.

19. In an efficient market, investors will not find positive-NPV trading opportunities without some source of competitive advantage. By contrast, the average investor will earn a fair return on his or her investment.

20. In an efficient market, to raise the stock price corporate managers should focus on maximizing the present value of the free cash flow from the firm's investments, rather than accounting consequences or financial policy. To increase investor confidence in a firm's stock, managers may consider listing the stock in a more efficient market—one that is characterized by strong competition, liquidity, and easy access to reliable information.

KEY TERMS

capital gain *p. 277*
capital gain rate *p. 277*
constant dividend growth model *p. 280*
discounted free cash flow model *p. 288*
dividend-discount model *p. 278*
dividend payout rate *p. 280*
dividend yield *p. 277*
efficient markets hypothesis *p. 290*
equity cost of capital *p. 276*
forward earnings *p. 293*
forward P/E *p. 293*

method of comparables *p. 292*
net investment *p. 289*
retention rate *p. 281*
share repurchase *p. 286*
total payout model *p. 287*
total return *p. 277*
trailing P/E *p. 293*
valuation multiple *p. 292*
weighted average cost of capital
    (WACC) *p. 289*

PROBLEMS

The problems marked in green can be found on MyFinanceLab at www.myfinancelab.com. Visit your
MyFinanceLab for additional practice. An asterisk (*) indicates problems with a higher level of difficulty.
Additional readings for this chapter may be found in the Textbook Resources section on MyFinanceLab.

The Dividend Discount Model

1. Assume Evco Inc. has a current price of $50 and will pay a $2 dividend in one year, and its equity cost of capital is 15%. What price must you expect it to sell for right after paying the dividend in one year in order to justify its current price?

2. Anle Corporation has a current price of $20, is expected to pay a dividend of $1 in one year, and its expected price right after paying that dividend is $22.
    a. What is Anle's expected dividend yield?
    b. What is Anle's expected capital gain rate?
    c. What is Anle's equity cost of capital?

3. Suppose Acap Corporation will pay a dividend of $2.80 per share at the end of this year and $3.00 per share next year. You expect Acap's stock price to be $52.00 in two years. If Acap's equity cost of capital is 10%:
    a. What price would you be willing to pay for a share of Acap stock today, if you planned to hold the stock for two years?
    b. Suppose instead you plan to hold the stock for one year. What price would you expect to be able to sell a share of Acap stock for in one year?
    c. Given your answer in part b, what price would you be willing to pay for a share of Acap stock today, if you planned to hold the stock for one year? How does this compare to your answer in part a?

4. Krell Industries has a share price of $22.00 today. If Krell is expected to pay a dividend of $0.88 this year, and its stock price is expected to grow to $23.54 at the end of the year, what is Krell's dividend yield and equity cost of capital?

Applying the Dividend-Discount Model

5. NoGrowth Corporation currently pays a dividend of $0.50 per quarter, and it will continue to pay this dividend forever. What is the price per share if its equity cost of capital is 15% per year?

6. Summit Systems will pay a dividend of $1.50 this year. If you expect Summit's dividend to grow by 6% per year, what is its price per share if its equity cost of capital is 11%?

7. Dorpac Corporation has a dividend yield of 1.5%. Dorpac's equity cost of capital is 8%, and its dividends are expected to grow at a constant rate.

   a. What is the expected growth rate of Dorpac's dividends?

   b. What is the expected growth rate of Dorpac's share price?

8. Kenneth Cole Productions (KCP), suspended its dividend at the start of 2009. Suppose you do not expect KCP to resume paying dividends until 2011. You expect KCP's dividend in 2011 to be $0.40 per year (paid at the end of the year), and you expect it to grow by 5% per year thereafter. If KCP's equity cost of capital is 11%, what is the value of a share of KCP at the start of 2009?

9. DFB Inc. expects earnings this year of $5 per share, and it plans to pay a $3 dividend to shareholders. DFB will retain $2 per share of its earnings to reinvest in new projects with an expected return of 15% per year. Suppose DFB will maintain the same dividend payout rate, retention rate, and return on new investments in the future and will not change its number of outstanding shares.

   a. What growth rate of earnings would you forecast for DFB?

   b. If DFB's equity cost of capital is 12%, what price would you estimate for DFB stock?

   c. Suppose DFB instead paid a dividend of $4 per share this year and retained only $1 per share in earnings. If DFB maintains this higher payout rate in the future, what stock price would you estimate now? Should DFB raise its dividend?

10. Cooperton Mining just announced it will cut its dividend from $4 to $2.50 per share and use the extra funds to expand. Prior to the announcement, Cooperton's dividends were expected to grow at a 3% rate, and its share price was $50. With the new expansion, Cooperton's dividends are expected to grow at a 5% rate. What share price would you expect after the announcement? (Assume Cooperton's risk is unchanged by the new expansion.) Is the expansion a positive NPV investment?

11. Gillette Corporation will pay an annual dividend of $0.65 one year from now. Analysts expect this dividend to grow at 12% per year thereafter until the fifth year. After then, growth will level off at 2% per year. According to the dividend-discount model, what is the value of a share of Gillette stock if the firm's equity cost of capital is 8%?

12. Colgate-Palmolive Company has just paid an annual dividend of $0.96. Analysts are predicting an 11% per year growth rate in earnings over the next five years. After then, Colgate's earnings are expected to grow at the current industry average of 5.2% per year. If Colgate's equity cost of capital is 8.5% per year and its dividend payout ratio remains constant, what price does the dividend-discount model predict Colgate stock should sell for?

13. What is the value of a firm with initial dividend Div, growing for n years (i.e., until year $n + 1$) at rate g_1 and after that at rate g_2 forever, when the equity cost of capital is r?

14. Halliford Corporation expects to have earnings this coming year of $3 per share. Halliford plans to retain all of its earnings for the next two years. For the subsequent two years, the firm will retain 50% of its earnings. It will then retain 20% of its earnings from that point onward. Each year, retained earnings will be invested in new projects with an expected return of 25% per year. Any earnings that are not retained will be paid out as dividends. Assume Halliford's share count remains constant and all earnings growth comes from the investment of retained earnings. If Halliford's equity cost of capital is 10%, what price would you estimate for Halliford stock?

Total Payout and Free Cash Flow Valuation Models

15. Suppose Cisco Systems pays no dividends but spent $5 billion on share repurchases last year. If Cisco's equity cost of capital is 12%, and if the amount spent on repurchases is expected to grow by 8% per year, estimate Cisco's market capitalization. If Cisco has 6 billion shares outstanding, what stock price does this correspond to?

16. Stelco Steel plans to pay a dividend of $3 this year. The company has an expected earnings growth rate of 4% per year and an equity cost of capital of 10%.

    a. Assuming Stelco's dividend payout rate and expected growth rate remains constant, and Stelco does not issue or repurchase shares, estimate Stelco's share price.

    b. Suppose Stelco decides to pay a dividend of $1 this year and use the remaining $2 per share to repurchase shares. If Stelco's total payout rate remains constant, estimate Stelco's share price.

    c. If Stelco maintains the dividend and total payout rate given in part b, at what rate are Stelco's dividends and earnings per share expected to grow?

17. Benchmark Metrics Inc. (BMI), an all-equity financed firm, just reported EPS of $5.00 per share for 2008. Despite the economic downturn, BMI is confident regarding its current investment opportunities. But due to the financial crisis, BMI does not wish to fund these investments externally. The Board has therefore decided to suspend its stock repurchase plan and cut its dividend to $1 per share (vs. almost $2.00 per share in 2007), and retain these funds instead. The firm has just paid the 2008 dividend, and BMI plans to keep its dividend at $1.00 per share in 2009 as well. In subsequent years, it expects its growth opportunities to slow, and it will still be able to fund its growth internally with a target 40 percent dividend payout ratio, and reinitiating its stock repurchase plan for a total payout rate of 60 percent. (All dividends and repurchases occur at the end of each year.)

Suppose BMI's existing operations will continue to generate the current level of earnings per share in the future. Assume further that the return on new investment is 15 percent, and that reinvestments will account for all future earnings growth (if any). Finally, assume BMI's equity cost of capital is 10%.

    a. Estimate BMI's EPS in 2009 and 2010 (before any share repurchases).

    b. What is the value of a share of BMI at the start of 2009?

EXCEL 18. Heavy Metal Corporation is expected to generate the following free cash flows over the next five years:

Year	1	2	3	4	5
FCF ($ million)	53	68	78	75	82

After then, the free cash flows are expected to grow at the industry average of 4% per year. Using the discounted free cash flow model and a weighted average cost of capital of 14%:

    a. Estimate the enterprise value of Heavy Metal.

    b. If Heavy Metal has no excess cash, debt of $300 million, and 40 million shares outstanding, estimate its share price.

19. IDX Technologies is a privately held developer of advanced security systems based in Chicago. As part of your business development strategy, in late 2008 you initiate discussions with IDX's founder about the possibility of acquiring the business at the end of 2008. Estimate the value of IDX per share using a discounted FCF approach and the following data:

    ■ Debt: $30 million

    ■ Excess cash: $110 million

    ■ Shares outstanding: 50 million

    ■ Expected FCF in 2009: $45 million

    ■ Expected FCF in 2010: $50 million

    ■ Future FCF growth rate beyond 2010

    ■ Weighted-average cost of capital: 9.4%

EXCEL   20.   Sora Industries has 60 million outstanding shares, $120 million in debt, $40 million in cash, and the following projected free cash flow for the next four years:

	Year	0	1	2	3	4
Earnings and FCF Forecast ($ million)						
1	Sales	433.0	468.0	516.0	547.0	574.3
2	*Growth versus Prior Year*		*8.1%*	*10.3%*	*6.0%*	*5.0%*
3	Cost of Goods Sold		(313.6)	(345.7)	(366.5)	(384.8)
4	**Gross Profit**		154.4	170.3	180.5	189.5
5	Selling, General, and Administrative		(93.6)	(103.2)	(109.4)	(114.9)
6	Capital Cost Allowance (CCA)		(7.0)	(7.5)	(9.0)	(9.5)
7	**EBIT**		53.8	59.6	62.1	65.2
8	Less: Income Tax at 40%		(21.5)	(23.8)	(24.8)	(26.1)
9	Plus: Capital Cost Allowance (CCA)		7.0	7.5	9.0	9.5
10	Less: Capital Expenditures		(7.7)	(10.0)	(9.9)	(10.4)
11	Less: Increase in NWC		(6.3)	(8.6)	(5.6)	(4.9)
12	**Free Cash Flow**		25.3	24.6	30.8	33.3

a. Suppose Sora's revenue and free cash flow are expected to grow at a 5% rate beyond year 4. If Sora's weighted average cost of capital is 10%, what is the value of Sora's stock based on this information?

b. Sora's cost of goods sold was assumed to be 67% of sales. If its cost of goods sold is actually 70% of sales, how would the estimate of the stock's value change?

c. Let's return to the assumptions of part a and suppose Sora can maintain its cost of goods sold at 67% of sales. However, now suppose Sora reduces its selling, general, and administrative expenses from 20% of sales to 16% of sales. What stock price would you estimate now? (Assume no other expenses, except taxes, are affected.)

*d. Sora's net working capital needs were estimated to be 18% of sales (which is their current level in year 0). If Sora can reduce this requirement to 12% of sales starting in year 1, but all other assumptions remain as in part a, what stock price do you estimate for Sora? (*Hint:* This change will have the largest impact on Sora's free cash flow in year 1.)

EXCEL   21.   Consider the valuation of Kenneth Cole Productions in Example 9.7.

a. Suppose you believe KCP's initial revenue growth rate will be between 7% and 11% (with growth slowing in equal steps to 4% by year 2011). What range of share prices for KCP is consistent with these forecasts?

b. Suppose you believe KCP's EBIT margin will be between 7% and 10% of sales. What range of share prices for KCP is consistent with these forecasts (keeping KCP's initial revenue growth at 9%)?

c. Suppose you believe KCP's weighted average cost of capital is between 10% and 12%. What range of share prices for KCP is consistent with these forecasts (keeping KCP's initial revenue growth and EBIT margin at 9%)?

d. What range of share prices is consistent if you vary the estimates as in parts (a), (b), and (c) simultaneously?

Valuation Based on Comparable Firms

22.   You notice that PepsiCo has a stock price of $52.66 and EPS of $3.20. Its competitor, the Coca-Cola Company, has EPS of $2.49. Estimate the value of a share of Coca-Cola stock using only this data.

EXCEL   23.   Suppose that in January 2006, Kenneth Cole Productions had EPS of $1.65 and a book value of equity of $12.05 per share.

a. Using the average P/E multiple in Table 9.1, estimate KCP's share price.

b. What range of share prices do you estimate based on the highest and lowest P/E multiples in Table 9.1?

c. Using the average price to book value multiple in Table 9.1, estimate KCP's share price.

d. What range of share prices do you estimate based on the highest and lowest price to book value multiples in Table 9.1?

EXCEL 24. Suppose that in January 2006, Kenneth Cole Productions had sales of $518 million, EBITDA of $55.6 million, excess cash of $100 million, $3 million of debt, and 21 million shares outstanding.

a. Using the average enterprise value to sales multiple in Table 9.1, estimate KCP's share price.

b. What range of share prices do you estimate based on the highest and lowest enterprise value to sales multiples in Table 9.1?

c. Using the average enterprise value to EBITDA multiple in Table 9.1, estimate KCP's share price.

d. What range of share prices do you estimate based on the highest and lowest enterprise value to EBITDA multiples in Table 9.1?

EXCEL 25. In addition to footwear, Kenneth Cole Productions designs and sells handbags, apparel, and other accessories. You decide, therefore, to consider comparables for KCP outside the footwear industry.

a. Suppose that Fossil Inc. has an enterprise value to EBITDA multiple of 9.73 and a P/E multiple of 18.4. What share price would you estimate for KCP using each of these multiples, based on the data for KCP in Problems 23 and 24?

b. Suppose that Tommy Hilfiger Corporation has an enterprise value to EBITDA multiple of 7.19 and a P/E multiple of 17.2. What share price would you estimate for KCP using each of these multiples, based on the data for KCP in Problems 23 and 24?

EXCEL 26. Consider the following data for the airline industry in early 2009 (EV = enterprise value, BV = book value, NM = not meaningful because divisor is negative). Discuss the usefulness of using multiples to value an airline company.

Company Name	Market Cap	EV	EV/Sales	EV/EBITDA	EV/EBIT	P/E	P/BV
Honda Motor Co. Ltd.	55,694.1	77,212.4	0.9×	8.2×	10.8×	10.9×	1.6×
DaimlerChrysler AG	47,462.2	136,069.6	0.7×	6.6×	28.7×	13.2×	1.2×
Nissan Motor Co. Ltd.	44,463.2	93,138.3	1.2×	7.3×	11.8×	NM	NM
Volkswagen AG	25,215.6	84,922.0	0.7×	5.7×	22.3×	14.5×	1.2×
General Motors Corp.	15,077.9	274,336.9	1.4×	44.3×	NM	NM	1.1×
PSA Peugeot Citroen	13,506.7	44,015.1	0.6×	7.2×	18.6×	10.6×	1.3×
Ford Motor Co.	11,931.1	145,009.1	0.8×	11.9×	NM	490.8×	2.0×
Mitsubishi Motors Corp.	7,919.4	9,633.3	0.6×	207.2×	NM	NM	3.9×
Daihatsu Motor Co. Ltd.	3,666.3	6,913.8	0.6×	7.9×	17.7×	15.9×	1.6×

Source: Capital IQ.

Information, Competition, and Stock Prices

27. You read in the paper that Summit Systems from Problem 6 has revised its growth prospects and now expects its dividends to grow at 3% per year forever.

a. What is the new value of a share of Summit Systems stock based on this information?

b. If you tried to sell your Summit Systems stock after reading this news, what price would you be likely to get and why?

28. In early 2009, Coca-Cola Company had a share price of $46. Its dividend was $1.52, and you expect Coca-Cola to raise this dividend by approximately 7% per year in perpetuity.

a. If Coca-Cola's equity cost of capital is 8%, what share price would you expect based on your estimate of the dividend growth rate?

b. Given Coca-Cola's share price, what would you conclude about your assessment of Coca-Cola's future dividend growth?

29. Roybus Inc. a manufacturer of flash memory, just reported that its main production facility in Taiwan was destroyed in a fire. While the plant was fully insured, the loss of production will decrease Roybus's free cash flow by $180 million at the end of this year and by $60 million at the end of next year.

a. If Roybus has 35 million shares outstanding and a weighted average cost of capital of 13%, what change in Roybus's stock price would you expect upon this announcement? (Assume the value of Roybus' debt is not affected by the event.)

b. Would you expect to be able to sell Roybus's stock on hearing this announcement and make a profit? Explain.

30. Apnex Inc. is a biotechnology firm that is about to announce the results of its clinical trials of a potential new cancer drug. If the trials were successful, Apnex stock will be worth $70 per share. If the trials were unsuccessful, Apnex stock will be worth $18 per share. Suppose that the morning before the announcement is scheduled, Apnex shares are trading for $55 per share.

a. Based on the current share price, what sort of expectations do investors seem to have about the success of the trials?

b. Suppose hedge fund manager Paul Kliner has hired several prominent research scientists to examine the public data on the drug and make their own assessment of the drug's promise. Would Kliner's fund be likely to profit by trading the stock in the hours prior to the announcement?

c. What would limit the fund's ability to profit on its information?

DATA CASE

As a new analyst for a large brokerage firm, you are anxious to demonstrate the skills you learned in your MBA program and prove that you are worth your attractive salary. Your first assignment is to analyze the stock of the General Electric Corporation. Your boss recommends determining prices based on both the dividend-discount model and discounted free cash flow valuation methods. GE uses a cost of equity of 10.5% and an after-tax weighted average cost of capital of 7.5%. The expected return on new investments is 12%. However, you are a little concerned because your finance professor has told you that these two methods can result in widely differing estimates when applied to real data. You are really hoping that the two methods will reach similar prices. Good luck with that!

1. Go to Yahoo! Finance (http://finance.yahoo.com) and enter the symbol for General Electric (GE). From the main page for GE gather the following information and enter it onto a spreadsheet:

a. The current stock price (last trade) at the top of the page.

b. The current dividend amount, which is in the bottom-right cell in the same box as the stock price.

2. Next click on "Key Statistics" from the left side of the page. From the Key Statistics page gather the following information and enter it on the same spreadsheet:

   a. The number of shares of stock outstanding.

   b. The Payout ratio.

3. Next click on "Analyst Estimates" from the left side of the page. From the Analyst Estimates page find the expected growth rate for the next five years and enter it onto your spreadsheet. It will be near the very bottom of the page.

4. Next click on "Income Statement" near the bottom of the menu on the left. Place the cursor in the middle of the income statements and right-click. Select "Export to Microsoft Excel." Copy and paste the entire three years of income statements into a new worksheet in your existing Excel file. Repeat this process for both the balance sheet and cash flow statement for General Electric. Keep all the different statements in the same Excel worksheet.

5. To determine the stock value based on the dividend-discount model:

   a. Create a timeline in Excel for five years.

   b. Use the dividend obtained from Yahoo! Finance as the current dividend to forecast the next five annual dividends based on the five-year growth rate.

   c. Determine the long-term growth rate based on GE's payout ratio (which is one minus the retention ratio) using Eq. 9.12.

   d. Use the long-term growth rate to determine the stock price for year five using Eq. 9.13.

   e. Determine the current stock price using Eq. 9.14.

6. To determine the stock value based on the discounted free cash flow method:

   a. Forecast the free cash flows using the historic data from the financial statements downloaded from Yahoo! to compute the three-year average of the following ratios:

      i.   EBIT/Sales

      ii. Tax Rate (Income Tax Expense/Income Before Tax)

      iii. Property Plant and Equipment/Sales

      iv. Depreciation/Property Plant and Equipment

      v.   Net Working Capital/Sales

   b. Create a timeline for the next seven years.

   c. Forecast future sales based on the most recent year's total revenue growing at the five-year growth rate from Yahoo! for the first five years and the long-term growth rate for years six and seven.

   d. Use the average ratios computed in part a to forecast EBIT, property, plant and equipment, depreciation, and net working capital for the next seven years.

   e. Forecast the free cash flow for the next seven years using Eq. 9.18.

   f. Determine the horizon enterprise value for year five using Eq. 9.24.

   g. Determine the enterprise value of the firm as the present value of the free cash flows.

   h. Determine the stock price using Eq. 9.22.

7. Compare the stock prices from the two methods to the actual stock price. What recommendations can you make as to whether clients should buy or sell General Electric's stock based on your price estimates?

8. Explain to your boss why the estimates from the two valuation methods differ. Specifically address the assumptions implicit in the models themselves as well as those you made in preparing your analysis. Why do these estimates differ from the actual stock price of GE?

PART

4

Risk and Return

THE LAW OF ONE PRICE CONNECTION.   To apply the Law of One Price correctly requires comparing investment opportunities of equivalent risk. We explain in this part of the book how to measure and compare risks across investment opportunities. Chapter 10 introduces the key insight that investors only demand a risk premium for risk they cannot remove themselves without cost by diversifying their portfolios. Hence, only non-diversifiable risk will matter when comparing investment opportunities. Intuitively, this insight suggests that an investment's risk premium will depend on its sensitivity to market risk. In Chapter 11, we quantify this idea and thereby derive investors' optimal investment portfolio choices. We then consider the implications of assuming all investors choose their portfolio of investments optimally. This assumption leads to the *Capital Asset Pricing Model* (CAPM), the central model in financial economics that quantifies what an equivalent risk is and thereby provides the relation between risk and return. In Chapter 12 we apply these ideas and consider the practicalities of estimating the cost of capital for a firm and for an individual investment project. Chapter 13 takes a closer look at the behaviour of individual as well as professional investors. Doing so reveals some strengths and weaknesses of the CAPM, as well as ways we can combine the CAPM with the principle of no arbitrage for a more model of risk and return.

NOTATION

P_R	probability of return R
$Var(R)$	variance of return R
$SD(R)$	standard deviation of return R
$E[R]$	expectation of return R
Div_t	dividend paid on date t
P_t	price on date t
R_t	realized or total return of a security from date $t-1$ to t
$\overline{R}$	average return
β_s	beta of security s
r	Cost of capital of an investment opportunity

Capital Markets and the Pricing of Risk

Between 2004 and 2007, investors in Barrick Gold Corporation earned an average return of 13.93% per year. Within this period there was some variation, with the annual return ranging from 0.03% for 2004 to 17.61% for 2007. Over the same period, investors in TransCanada Corp. earned an average return of 14.32%. These investors, however, had positive returns each year, varying between 3.47% in 2007 and 27.13% in 2005. WestJet Airlines' average return was 9.50% over the four years but the range was from a low of −36.78% in 2004 to a high of 50.77% in 2007. Finally, investors in three-month Government of Canada Treasury Bills earned an average return of 3.29% during the period, with a low return of 2.23% over 2004 and a high return of 4.28% over 2007. Clearly, these four investments offered returns that were very different in terms of their average level and their variability. What accounts for these differences?

In this chapter, we will explain why these differences exist. Our goal is to develop a theory that explains the relationship between average returns and the variability of returns and thereby derive the risk premium that investors require to hold different securities and investments. We then use this theory to explain how to determine the cost of capital for an investment opportunity.

We begin our investigation of the relationship between risk and return by examining historical data for publicly traded securities. We will see, for example, that while stocks are riskier investments than bonds, they have also earned higher average returns. We can interpret the higher average return on stocks as compensation to investors for the greater risk they are taking.

But we will also find that not all risk needs to be compensated. By holding a portfolio containing many different investments, investors can eliminate risks that are specific to individual securities. It is only those risks that cannot be eliminated by holding a large portfolio that determine the risk premium required by investors. These observations will allow us to refine our definition of what risk is, how it can be measured, and how the cost of capital is determined.

10.1   A FIRST LOOK AT RISK AND RETURN

We begin our look at risk and return by illustrating how the risk premium affects investor decisions and returns. Suppose your grandparents invested $100 on your behalf at the beginning of 1956. They instructed their broker to reinvest any dividends or interest earned in the account until the beginning of 2009. How would that $100 have grown if it were placed in one of the following investments?

1. S&P/TSX Composite Index: A portfolio, constructed by Standard & Poor's, of the largest, most liquid, stocks and income trust units traded on the Toronto Stock Exchange (TSX). As of the end of 2008, there were 250 firms in the index with market capitalizations averaging about $4.3 billion and ranging from about $60 million to over $50 billion.

2. Standard & Poor's 500 (S&P 500): A portfolio, constructed by Standard & Poor's, comprising 90 U.S. stocks up to 1957 and 500 U.S. stocks after that. The firms represented are leaders in their respective industries and are among the largest firms, in terms of market value, traded on U.S. markets. At the end of 2008, the average market capitalization of each firm was over $18 billion and ranged from about $810 million to nearly $800 billion.

3. Long-Term Government of Canada Bonds: These bonds have a maturity of approximately 30 years.

4. Government of Canada Treasury Bills: An investment in three-month Government of Canada Treasury Bills.

Figure 10.1 shows the result, through the end of 2008, of investing $100 at the beginning of 1956 in each of these four investment portfolios, ignoring transactions costs. The graph is striking: Had your grandparents invested $100 in the S&P/TSX Composite Index, the investment would be worth more than $9,300 in 2008! By contrast, if they had invested in Treasury Bills, the investment would be worth only about $2549.

For comparison, we also show how prices changed during the same period using the consumer price index (CPI). Over most of this period, smaller stocks (as represented by the S&P/TSX Composite Index) experienced the highest long-term return, followed by larger stocks (as found in the US S&P 500 Index). With the recent downturns of U.S. markets, the appreciation of the Canadian dollar through the latter part of 2009, and declining interest rates, the Government of Canada long-term bonds actually outperformed the S&P 500 over the last part of the period. Treasury Bills have the smallest fluctuations in their value, but their growth over the period was also the least. All of the investments grew faster than inflation (as measured by the CPI).

Value of $100 Invested at the Beginning of 1956 in the S&P/TSX Composite Index, the S&P 500, Long-Term Government of Canada Bonds, and Canadian Treasury Bills

These returns assume all dividends and interest are reinvested and exclude transactions costs. Also shown is the change in Canada's consumer price index (CPI).

Sources: Statistics Canada, Bank of Canada, and Chicago Center for Research in Security Prices.

A second pattern is also evident in Figure 10.1. While the S&P/TSX Composite Index performed the best in the long run, its value also experienced the largest fluctuations. For example, if your parents had invested $2,000 in the S&P/TSX Composite Index in August 1987, for your university education, it would have grown to about $7,460 by the end of 2008. In contrast, had your parents invested in long-term Government of Canada bonds, the $2,000 investment would have grown to almost $17,070 by the end of 2008 because it would have avoided the major drops caused by the market crash of October 1987, and the downturns in 1998 and 2008. Looking over the entire time frame from 1956 to 2008, there were some months when the S&P/TSX Composite Index dropped by as much as 22.5% and rose by as much as 16.5% (in one month); its average return was about 0.82% per month. Compare this to Canadian Treasury Bills that, at their worst, returned about 0% in a month but, at their best, returned about 1.9% in a month; their average return was about 0.51% per month.

In Chapter 3, we explained why investors are averse to fluctuations in the value of their investments and why riskier investments have higher expected returns. Investors do not like to be hit when they are already down; when times are bad, they do not like to have their problems further compounded by experiencing losses on their investments. In fact, even if your grandparents had actually put the $100 into the S&P/TSX Composite Index in 1956, it is unlikely you would have seen much of it in 2008. More likely, in the depths of the various recessions your grandparents would have turned to their investment to get them through the bad times. Recent recessions occurred in the early 1980s and early 1990s. At the same time, the S&P/TSX Composite Index dropped over 30% between 1980 and 1982, and dropped over 20% in the first 10 months of 1990. So, to make matters worse, at the time your grandparents would need to draw on their investments, the value of the investments had dropped significantly.

During the financial crisis of 2008 many people faced similar difficulties. The S&P/TSX dropped over 37% in the final seven months of 2008. Many investors who had all their retirement money invested in stocks saw close to half their retirement income evaporate in a matter of months. Over the previous years these individuals enjoyed large gains in their retirement portfolios. However, these high returns came at a cost—the risk of large losses in a downturn. Many investors faced a double whammy: an increased risk of being unemployed (as firms started laying off employees) precisely when the value of their savings eroded.

Although we understand the general principle explaining why investors do not like risk and demand a risk premium to bear it, our goal in this chapter is to quantify this relationship. We would like to explain *how much* investors demand (in terms of a higher expected return) to bear a given level of risk. To quantify the relationship, we must first develop tools that will allow us to measure risk and return. That is the objective of the next section.

CONCEPT CHECK

1. From 1956 to 2008, which of the following investments had the highest return: S&P/TSX Composite Index, S&P 500, Government of Canada long-term bonds, or Canadian T-Bills?

2. From 1956 to 2008, which investment grew in value in every year? Which investment had the greatest variability?

10.2 COMMON MEASURES OF RISK AND RETURN

When a manager makes an investment decision or an investor purchases a security, they have some view as to the risk involved and the likely return the investment will earn. Thus we begin our discussion by reviewing the standard ways in which risks are defined and measured.

PROBABILITY DISTRIBUTIONS

Different securities have different initial prices, pay different dividend amounts, and sell for different future amounts. To make them comparable, we express their performance in terms of their returns. The return indicates the percentage increase in the value of an investment per dollar initially invested in the security. When an investment is risky, there are different returns it may earn. Each possible return has some likelihood of occurring. We summarize this information with a **probability distribution**, which assigns a probability, P_R, that each possible return, R, will occur.

Let's consider a simple example. Suppose BFI stock currently trades for $100 per share. You believe that in one year there is a 25% chance the share price will be $140, a 50% chance it will be $110, and a 25% chance it will be $80. BFI pays no dividends, so these payoffs correspond to returns of 40%, 10%, and 220%, respectively. Table 10.1 summarizes the probability distribution for BFI's returns.

We can also represent the probability distribution with a histogram, as shown in Figure 10.2.

PROBABILITY DISTRIBUTION OF RETURNS FOR BFI

TABLE 10.1

Current Stock Price ($)	Stock Price in One Year ($)	Probability Distribution	
		Return, R	Probability, P_R
	140	0.40	25%
100	110	0.10	50%
	80	−0.20	25%

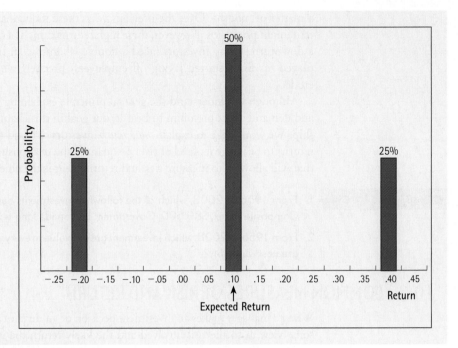

FIGURE 10.2

Probability Distribution of Returns for BFI

The height of a bar in the histogram indicates the likelihood of the associated outcome.

EXPECTED RETURN

Given the probability distribution of returns, we can compute the expected return. The **expected (or mean) return** is calculated as a weighted average of the possible returns, where the weights correspond to the probabilities.[1]

Expected (Mean) Return
$$\text{Expected Return} = E[R] = \sum_R p_R \times R \tag{10.1}$$

The expected return is the return we would earn on average if we could repeat the investment many times, with the return being drawn from the same distribution each time. In terms of the histogram, the expected return is the "balancing point" of the distribution, if we think of the probabilities as weights. The expected return for BFI is

$$E[R_{BFI}] = 25\%(-0.20) + 50\%(0.10) + 25\%(0.40) = 10\%$$

This expected return corresponds to the balancing point in Figure 10.2.

VARIANCE AND STANDARD DEVIATION

Two common measures of the risk of a probability distribution are its *variance* and *standard deviation*. The **variance** is the expected squared deviation from the mean, and the **standard deviation** is the square root of the variance.

Variance and Standard Deviation of the Return Distribution
$$Var(R) = E[(R - E[R])^2] = \sum_R p_R \times (R - E[R])^2$$
$$SD(R) = \sqrt{Var(R)} \tag{10.2}$$

---

1. The notation means that we sum the probability that each return will occur, P_R, times the return, R, for all possible returns.

If the return is riskless and never deviates from its mean, the variance is zero. Otherwise, the variance increases with the magnitude of the deviations from the mean. Therefore, the variance is a measure of how "spread out" the distribution of the return is. The variance of BFI's return is

$$Var(R_{BFI}) = 25\% \times (-0.20 - 0.10)^2 + 50\% \times (0.10 - 0.10)^2$$
$$+ 25\% \times (0.40 - 0.10)^2 = 0.045$$

The standard deviation of the return is the square root of the variance, so for BFI,

$$SD(R) = \sqrt{Var(R)} = \sqrt{0.045} = 21.2\% \qquad (10.3)$$

In finance, the standard deviation of a return is also referred to as its **volatility**. While the variance and the standard deviation both measure the variability of the returns, the standard deviation is easier to interpret because it is in the same units as the returns themselves.[2]

EXAMPLE 10.1

CALCULATING THE EXPECTED RETURN AND VOLATILITY

Problem

Suppose RIM stock is equally likely to have a 45% return or a -25% return. What are its expected return and volatility?

Solution

First we calculate the expected return by taking the probability-weighted average of the possible returns:

$$E[R] = \sum_R p_R \times R = 50\% \times 0.45 + 50\% \times (-0.25) = 10.0\%$$

To compute the volatility, we first determine the variance:

$$Var(R) = \sum_R p_R \times (R - E[R])^2 = 50\% \times (0.45 - 0.10)^2 + 50\% \times (-0.25 - 0.10)^2$$
$$= 0.1225$$

Then the volatility or standard deviation is the square root of the variance:

$$SD(R) = \sqrt{(R)} = \sqrt{0.1225} = 35\%$$

Note that both RIM and BFI have the same expected return, 10%. However, the returns for RIM are more spread out than those for BFI—the high returns are higher and the low returns are lower, as shown by the histogram in Figure 10.3. As a result, RIM has a higher variance and volatility than BFI.

---

2. While the variance and the standard deviation are the most common measures of risk, they do not differentiate between upside and downside risk. Because investors dislike only negative resolutions of uncertainty, alternative measures that focus solely on downside risk have been developed, such as the semivariance (which measures the variance of the losses only) and the expected tail loss (the expected loss in the worst $x\%$ of outcomes). These alternative measures are more complex and cumbersome to apply, and yet in many applications produce the same ranking of risk as the standard deviation (as in Example 10.1, or if returns are normally distributed). Thus they tend to be used only in special applications in which the standard deviation alone is not a sufficient characterization of risk.

FIGURE 10.3

Probability Distribution for BFI and RIM Returns
While both stocks have the same expected return, RIM's return has a higher variance and standard deviation.

If we could observe the probability distributions that investors anticipate for different securities, we could compute their expected returns and volatilities and explore the relationship between them. Of course, in most situations we do not know the explicit probability distribution, as we did for BFI. Without that information, how can we estimate and compare risk and return? A popular approach is to extrapolate from historical data, which is a sensible strategy if we are in a stable environment and believe that future returns should mirror past returns. Let's look at the historical returns of stocks and bonds, to see what they reveal about the relationship between risk and return.

CONCEPT CHECK

1. How do we calculate the expected return of a stock?

2. What are the two most common measures of risk, and how are they related to each other?

10.3   HISTORICAL RETURNS OF STOCKS AND BONDS

In this section, we explain how to compute average returns and volatilities using historical stock market data. The distribution of past returns can be helpful when we seek to estimate the distribution of returns investors may expect in the future. We begin by first explaining how to compute historical returns.

COMPUTING HISTORICAL RETURNS

Of all the possible returns, the **realized return** is the return that actually occurs over a particular time period. How do we measure the realized return for a stock? Suppose you invest in a stock on date t for price P_t. If the stock pays a dividend, Div_{t+1}, on date $t + 1$, and you sell the stock at that time for price P_{t+1}, then the realized return from your investment in the stock from t to $t + 1$ is

$$R_{t+1} = \frac{Div_{t+1} + P_{t+1}}{P_t} - 1 = \frac{Div_{t+1}}{P_t} + \frac{P_{t+1} - P_t}{P_t}$$

$$= \text{Dividend Yield} + \text{Capital Gain Rate} \tag{10.4}$$

That is, as we discussed in Chapter 9, the realized return, R_{t+1}, is the total return we earn from dividends and capital gains, expressed as a percentage of the initial stock price.[3]

CALCULATING REALIZED ANNUAL RETURNS. If you hold the stock beyond the date of the first dividend, then to compute your return you must specify how you invest any dividends you receive in the interim. To focus on the returns of a single security, let's assume that *all dividends are immediately reinvested and used to purchase additional shares of the same stock or security.* In this case, we can use Eq. 10.4 to compute the stock's return between dividend payments, and then compound the returns from each dividend interval to compute the return over a longer horizon. For example, if a stock pays dividends at the end of each quarter, with realized returns $R_{Q1}, \ldots, R_{Q4}$ each quarter, then its annual realized return, R_{annual}, is computed as

$$1 + R_{annual} = (1 + R_{Q1})(1 + R_{Q2})(1 + R_{Q3})(1 + R_{Q4}) \tag{10.5}$$

EXAMPLE 10.2

REALIZED RETURNS FOR BARRICK GOLD CORP. STOCK

Problem

What were the realized annual returns for Barrick Gold Corp. stock in 2004 and in 2008?

Solution

First we look up Barrick Gold Corp. stock price data at the start and end of the year, as well as at any dividend dates (see the book's Web site for online sources of stock price and dividend data). From these data we can construct the following table:

Barrick Gold Corp.

Date	Price ($)	Dividend ($)*	Return	Date	Price ($)	Dividend ($)*	Return
12/31/2003	29.31			12/31/2007	41.78		
6/15/2004	26.39	0.1506	−9.45%	6/16/2008	40.35	0.2042	−2.93%
12/15/2004	28.82	0.1345	9.72%	12/15/2008	40.64	0.2470	1.33%
12/31/2004	29.00		0.62%	12/31/2008	44.71		10.01%
Annual Return over 2004:			−0.03%	Annual Return over 2008:			8.21%

*Dividends were declared in USD and were converted to CAD at the exchange rate for the dates given.
Sources: Barrick Gold Corp. for Prices and Dividends, Bank of Canada for CAD/USD Exchange Rate.

We compute each period's return using Eq. 10.4. For example, the return from December 31, 2007, until June 16, 2008, is equal to

$$\frac{.2042 + 40.35}{41.78} - 1 = -2.93\%$$

Note that Barrick only paid dividends in June and December during each of these two years (most dividend-paying stocks pay quarterly dividends). Thus, we can adapt Eq. 10.5 to

---

[3]. We can compute the realized return for any security in the same way, by replacing the dividend payments with any cash flows paid by the security (for example, with a bond, coupon payments would replace dividends).

calculate the annual return. We compute the return from the start of the year to the dividend date in June, the return between the two dividend dates, and the return from the dividend date in December to the end of the year. Using a similar method to that shown in Eq. 10.5, we get the annual return compounded through these three sub-periods:

$$R_{2004} = (0.9055)(1.0972)(1.0062) - 1 = -0.03\%$$
$$R_{2008} = (.9707)(1.0133)(1.1001) - 1 = 8.21\%$$

Example 10.2 illustrates two features of the returns from holding a stock like Barrick. First, both dividends and capital gains contribute to the total realized return—ignoring either one would give a very misleading impression of Barrick's performance. Second, the returns are risky. In years like 2004 the returns are negative, meaning that shareholders lost money over the year, but in other years like 2008 they are positive, meaning Barrick's shareholders made money.

We can compute realized returns in a similar way for any investment. We can also compute the realized returns for an entire portfolio, by keeping track of the interest and dividend payments paid by the portfolio during the year, as well as the change in the market value of the portfolio. For example, the realized returns for the S&P/TSX Composite Index are shown in Table 10.2, which for comparison purposes also lists the returns for Barrick Gold Corp. and for three-month Treasury Bills.

REALIZED RETURN FOR THE S&P TSX COMPOSITE INDEX, BARRICK GOLD CORP., AND TREASURY BILLS, 1997–2008

	Year-End	S&P TSX Composite Index Return*	Barrick Gold Corp. Return*	3-Month T-Bill Return
TABLE 10.2	1998	−1.58%	12.85%	4.75%
	1999	31.59%	−12.61%	4.77%
	2000	7.51%	−3.14%	5.56%
	2001	−12.57%	4.87%	4.09%
	2002	−12.44%	−3.47%	2.53%
	2003	26.72%	22.15%	2.91%
	2004	14.48%	−0.03%	2.23%
	2005	24.13%	12.77%	2.65%
	2006	17.26%	11.15%	4.01%
	2007	9.83%	17.61%	4.28%
	2008	−33.00%	8.21%	2.65%
	Average	6.54%	6.40%	3.68%
	Variance	0.0389	0.0108	0.0001
	Standard Deviation	0.1972	0.1037	0.0112

Sources: Statistics Canada, Bank of Canada, Barrick Gold Corp.

COMPARING REALIZED ANNUAL RETURNS. Once we have calculated the realized annual returns, we can compare them to see which investments performed better in a given year. From Table 10.2, we can see that Barrick stock outperformed the S&P/TSX Composite Index in 1998, 2001, 2002, 2007, and 2008. In 2002 Treasury Bills performed better than both Barrick stock and the S&P/TSX Composite Index.

Over any particular period we observe only one draw from the probability distribution of returns. If the realized return in each period is drawn from the same probability distribution, however, we can observe multiple draws by observing the realized return over multiple periods. By counting the number of times the realized return falls within a particular range, we can estimate the underlying probability distribution. Let's illustrate this process with the data in Figure 10.1.

Figure 10.4 plots the annual returns for each investment in Figure 10.1 in a histogram. The height of each bar represents the number of months that the annual returns were in each 1% range indicated on the *x*-axis. When we plot the probability distribution in this way using historical data, we refer to it as the **empirical distribution** of the returns.

AVERAGE ANNUAL RETURNS

The **average annual return** of an investment during some historical period is simply the average of the realized returns for each year. That is, if R_t is the realized return of a security in year t, then the average annual return for years 1 through T is

Average Annual Return of a Security

$$\bar{R} = \frac{1}{T}(R_1 + R_2 + \cdots + R_T) = \frac{1}{T}\sum_{t=1}^{T} R_t \tag{10.6}$$

FIGURE 10.4

The Empirical Distribution of Monthly Returns for Canadian T-Bills, Long-Term Government of Canada Bonds, Canadian Stocks (S&P/TSX Composite), and U.S. Stocks (S&P 500) in $CAD: 1956–2008

Sources: Statistics Canada, Bank of Canada, CRSP.

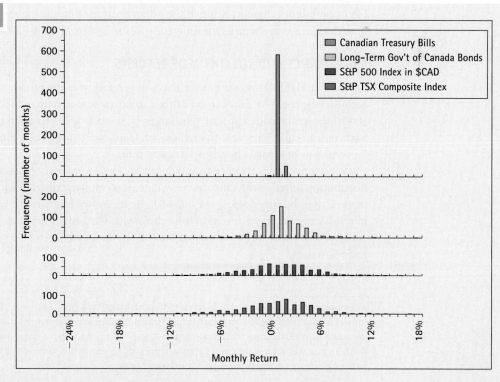

AVERAGE ANNUAL RETURNS FOR CANADIAN STOCKS (S&P/TSX COMPOSITE INDEX), LONG-TERM GOVERNMENT OF CANADA BONDS, AND CANADIAN TREASURY BILLS, 1950–2008

TABLE 10.3

Investment	Average Annual Return
Three-Month Canadian Treasury Bills	5.81%
Long-Term Government of Canada Bonds	7.54%
S&P/TSX Composite Index	11.20%

Source: Passport Financial Services Inc.

Notice that the average annual return is the balancing point of the empirical distribution—in this case, the probability of a return occurring in a particular range is measured by the number of times the realized return falls in that range. Therefore, if the probability distribution of the returns is the same over time, the average return provides an estimate of the expected return.

For example, using the data from Table 10.2, the average return for S&P/TSX Composite Index for the years 1998–2008 is

$$\overline{R} = \frac{1}{11}(-.0158 + .3159 + .0751 - .1257 - .1244$$
$$+ .2672 + .1448 + .2413 + .1726 + .0983 - .3300) = 6.54\%$$

The average Canadian Treasury Bill return from 1998–2008 was 3.68%. Therefore, investors earned 6.54% − 3.68% = 2.68% more on average holding the S&P/TSX Composite Index than investing in Canadian Treasury Bills during this period. Table 10.3 provides the average returns for different investments from 1956–2008.

THE VARIANCE AND VOLATILITY OF RETURNS

Looking at Figure 10.4, we can see that the variability of the returns is very different for each investment. The distribution of the Canadian stocks' returns (S&P/TSX Composite Index) shows the widest spread. The larger U.S. stocks that make up the S&P 500 Index have returns that vary less than those of Canadian stocks, but much more than the Government of Canada bonds or Treasury Bills.

To quantify this difference in variability, we can estimate the standard deviation of the distribution of returns. As before, we will use the empirical distribution to derive this estimate. Using the same logic as we did with the mean, we estimate the variance by computing the average squared deviation from the mean. The only complication is that we do not actually know the mean, so instead we use the best estimate of the mean—the average realized return.[4]

---

4. You may wonder why we divide by $T - 1$ rather than by T here. It is because we are not computing deviations from the true expected return; instead, we are computing deviations from the estimated average return $\overline{R}$. Because the average return is derived from the same data, we lose a degree of freedom (in essence, we use up one of the data points), so that when computing the variance we really have only $T - 1$ additional data points to base it on.

Variance Estimate Using Realized Returns

$$Var(R) = \frac{1}{T-1} \sum_{t=1}^{T} (R_t - \bar{R})^2 \qquad (10.7)$$

We estimate the standard deviation or volatility as the square root of the variance.[5]

EXAMPLE 10.3	COMPUTING A HISTORICAL VOLATILITY

Problem

Using the data from Table 10.2, what is the variance and volatility of the S&P/TSX Composite Index returns for the years 1998–2008?

Solution

Earlier we calculated the average annual return of the S&P/TSX Composite Index during this period to be 6.54%. Therefore,

$$
\begin{aligned}
Var(R) &= \frac{1}{T-1} \sum_{t=1}^{T} (R_t - \bar{R})^2 \\
&= \frac{1}{10-1}[(-0.0158 - 0.0654)^2 + (.3159 - 0.0654)^2 \\
&\quad + (0.0751 - 0.0654)^2 + \cdots + (-0.3300 - 0.0654)^2] \\
&= 0.0389
\end{aligned}
$$

The volatility or standard deviation is therefore

$$SD(R) = \sqrt{Var(R)} = \sqrt{0.0389} = 19.72\%$$

We can compute the standard deviation of the returns to quantify the differences in the variability of the distributions that we observed in Figure 10.4. These results are shown in Table 10.4.

VOLATILITY OF ANNUAL RETURNS FOR CANADIAN STOCKS (S&P/TSX COMPOSITE INDEX), LONG-TERM GOVERNMENT OF CANADA BONDS, AND CANADIAN TREASURY BILLS, 1950–2008

TABLE 10.4	

Investment	Return Volatility (standard deviation)
Three-Month Canadian Treasury Bills	3.84%
Long-Term Government of Canada Bonds	10.12%
S&P/TSX Composite Index	17.15%

Source: Passport Financial Services Inc.

---

5. If the returns used in Eq. 10.7 are not annual returns, the variance is typically converted to annual terms by multiplying by the number of periods per year. For example, when using monthly returns, we multiply the variance by 12 and, equivalently, the standard deviation by $\sqrt{12}$.

Comparing the volatilities in Table 10.4 we see that, as expected, the stocks have had the most variable historical returns. The returns of Government of Canada long-term bonds and Treasury Bills are much less variable than stocks, with Treasury Bills being the least volatile investment category.

USING PAST RETURNS TO PREDICT THE FUTURE: ESTIMATION ERROR

To estimate the cost of capital for an investment, we need to determine the expected return that investors will require to compensate them for that investment's risk. If we assume that the distribution of past returns and the distribution of future returns are the same, one approach we could take is to look at the return investors expected to earn in the past on the same or similar investments, and assume they will require the same return in the future.

Two difficulties arise with this approach.

1. *We do not know what investors expected in the past; we can only observe the actual returns that were realized.* In 2008, for example, investors lost 33% investing in the S&P/TSX Composite Index, which is surely not what they expected at the beginning of the year (or they would have invested in Treasury Bills instead!).

2. *The average return is just an estimate of the true expected return.* If we assume that investors are neither overly optimistic nor overly pessimistic on average, however, then we can use a security's historical average return to estimate its actual expected return. As with all statistics, however, an estimation error will occur. Given the volatility of stock returns, this estimation error will be large even when we have many years of data.

STANDARD ERROR.   We measure the degree of estimation error statistically through the standard error of the estimate. The **standard error** is the standard deviation of the estimated value of the mean of the actual distribution around its true value; that is, it is the standard deviation of the *average* return. The standard error provides an indication of how far the sample average might deviate from the expected return. If we assume that the distribution of a stock's return is identical each year, and that each year's return is independent of prior years' returns,[6] then the standard error of the estimate of the expected return can be found from the following formula:

Standard Error of the Estimate of the Expected Return

$$SD(\text{Average of Independent, Identical Risks}) = \frac{SD(\text{Individual Risk})}{\sqrt{\text{Number of Observations}}} \tag{10.8}$$

Because the average return will be within two standard errors of the true expected return approximately 95% of the time,[7] the standard error can be used to determine a reasonable

---

6. The assumption that the returns of a security are independent and identically distributed (IID) means that the likelihood that this year's return has a given outcome is the same as in prior years and does not depend on past returns, in the same way that the odds of a coin coming up heads do not depend on past flips. It turns out to be a reasonable first approximation for stock returns.

7. If returns are independent and from a normal distribution, then the estimated mean will be within two standard errors of the true mean 95.44% of the time. Even if returns are not normally distributed, this formula is approximately correct with a sufficient number of independent observations.

ARITHMETIC AVERAGE RETURNS VERSUS COMPOUND ANNUAL RETURNS

We compute average annual returns by calculating an *arithmetic* average. An alternative is the compound annual return (also called the compound annual growth rate, or CAGR), which is computed as the *geometric* average of the annual returns $R_1, \ldots, R_T$:

Compound Annual Return =
$$[(1 + R_1) \times (1 + R_2) \times \cdots \times (1 + R_T)]^{1/T} - 1$$

In other words, we compute the return from years 1 through T by compounding the annual returns, and then convert the result to an annual yield by taking it to the power $1/T$ and subtracting 1.

Passport Financial Services Inc. estimated the compound annual return for the S&P/TSX Composite Index from 1950 to 2008 to be 9.82%. That is, $100 invested at 9.82% for the 59 years from 1950 to 2008 would grow to

$$\$100 \times (1.0982)^{59} = \$25{,}130.72$$

This is equivalent (up to rounding error) to the growth in the S&P/TSX Composite Index during the same period. Similarly, between 1950 and 2008 the compound annual return for Long-Term Government of Canada Bonds was estimated to be 7.09%, and for Canadian Treasury Bills it was estimated to be 5.75%.

In each case, the compound annual return is below the average annual return shown in Table 10.3. This difference reflects the fact that returns are volatile. To see the effect of volatility, suppose an investment has annual returns of +20% one year and −20% the next year. The average annual return is $\frac{1}{2}(20\% - 20\%) = 0\%$. But the value of $1 invested after two years is

$$\$1 \times (1.20) \times (0.80) = \$0.96$$

That is, an investor would have lost money. Why? Because the 20% gain happens on a $1 investment, whereas the 20% loss happens on a larger investment of $1.20. In this case, the compound annual return is

$$(0.96)^{1/2} - 1 = -2.02\%$$

This logic implies that the compound annual return will always be below the average return, and the difference grows with the volatility of the annual returns. (Typically, the difference is about half of the variance of the returns.)

Which is a better description of an investment's return? The compound annual return is a better description of the long-run *historical* performance of an investment. It describes the equivalent risk-free return that would be required to duplicate the investment's performance over the same time period. The ranking of the long-run performance of different investments coincides with the ranking of their compound annual returns. Thus the compound annual return is the return that is most often used for comparison purposes. For example, mutual funds generally report their compound annual returns over the last five or ten years.

Conversely, we should use the arithmetic average return when we are trying to estimate an investment's *expected* return over a *future* horizon based on its past performance. If we view past returns as independent draws from the same distribution, then the arithmetic average return provides an unbiased estimate of the true expected return. However, for this result to hold we must compute the historical returns using the same time intervals as the expected return we are estimating (e.g., we use the average of past monthly returns to estimate the future monthly return, or the average of past annual returns to estimate the future annual return). Because of estimation error the estimate for different time intervals will generally differ from the result one would get by simply compounding the average annual return. With enough data however, the results will coincide. For example, if the investment mentioned above is equally likely to have annual returns of +20% and −20% in the future, then if we observe many 2-year periods, a $1 investment will be equally likely to grow to

$$(1.20)(1.20) = \$1.44,$$
$$(1.20)(0.80) = \$0.96,$$
$$(0.80)(1.20) = \$0.96,$$
$$\text{or } (0.80)(0.80) = \$0.64.$$

Thus, the average 2-year return will be $(1.44 + 0.96 + 0.96 + 0.64)/4 = \$1$, so that the average annual and 2-year returns will both be 0%.

range for the true expected value. The **95% confidence interval** for the expected return is defined as

$$\text{Historical Average Return} \pm (2 \times \text{Standard Error}) \qquad (10.9)$$

For example, from 1950 to 2008 the average return of the S&P/TSX Composite Index was 11.20% with a volatility of 17.15%. Assuming its returns are drawn from an independent and identical distribution (IID) each year, the 95% confidence interval for the expected return of the S&P/TSX Composite Index during this period is

$$11.2\% \pm 2\left(\frac{17.15\%}{\sqrt{59}}\right) = 11.2\% \pm 4.47\%$$

or a range from 6.73% to 15.67%. Thus, even with 59 years of data, we cannot estimate the expected return of the S&P/TSX Composite Index very accurately. If we believe the distribution may have changed over time and we can use only more recent data to estimate the expected return, then the estimate will be even less accurate.

LIMITATIONS OF EXPECTED RETURN ESTIMATES. Individual stocks tend to be even more volatile than large portfolios, and many have been in existence for only a few years, providing little data with which to estimate returns. Because of the relatively large estimation error in such cases, the average return investors earned in the past is not a reliable estimate of a security's expected return. Instead, we need to derive an alternative method to estimate the expected return—one that relies on more reliable statistical estimates. In the remainder of this chapter, the strategy we will follow is to first consider how to measure a security's risk, and then use the relationship between risk and return—which we must still determine—to estimate its expected return.

EXAMPLE 10.4   **THE ACCURACY OF EXPECTED RETURN ESTIMATES**

Problem

Using the returns for the S&P/TSX Composite Index from 1998 to 2008 only (see Table 10.2), what is the 95% confidence interval for our estimate of the S&P/TSX Composite Index's expected return?

Solution

Earlier, we calculated the average return for the S&P/TSX Composite Index during this period to be 6.54%, with a volatility of 19.72% (see Example 10.3). The standard error of our estimate of the expected return is $19.72/\sqrt{11} = 5.9\%$, and the 95% confidence interval is 6.54% $\pm$ (2 $\times$ 5.9%), or from -5.3% to 18.3%. As this example shows, with only a few years of data, we cannot reliably estimate expected returns for stocks.

CONCEPT CHECK

1. How do we estimate the average annual return of an investment?

2. Even with 59 years of data on the S&P/TSX Composite Index returns, we cannot estimate the expected return of the S&P/TSX Composite Index very accurately. Why?

10.4   THE HISTORICAL TRADEOFF BETWEEN RISK AND RETURN

In Chapter 3, we discussed the idea that investors are risk averse: The benefit they receive from an increase in income is smaller than the personal cost of an equivalent decrease in income. This idea suggests that investors would not choose to hold a portfolio that is more volatile unless they expected to earn a higher return. In this section, we quantify the historical relationship between volatility and average returns.

THE RETURNS OF LARGE PORTFOLIOS

In Tables 10.3 and 10.4, we computed the historical average returns and volatilities for several different types of investments. We combine those data in Table 10.5, which lists the volatility and excess return for each investment. The **excess return** is the difference between the average return for the investment and the average return for Treasury Bills, a risk-free investment.

In Figure 10.5, we plot the average return versus the volatility of each type of investment given in Table 10.5. We also include data for the larger U.S. stocks included in the S&P 500 Index with the returns adjusted to reflect the value of the Canadian dollar (CAD). Note the positive relationship: The investments with higher volatility have rewarded investors with higher average returns. Figure 10.5 is consistent with our view that investors are risk averse. Riskier investments must offer investors higher average returns to compensate them for the extra risk they are taking.

THE RETURNS OF INDIVIDUAL STOCKS

Figure 10.5 suggests the following simple model of the risk premium: Investments with higher volatility should have a higher risk premium and therefore higher returns. Indeed, looking at Figure 10.5 it is tempting to draw a line through the portfolios and conclude that all investments should lie on or near this line, that is, expected return should rise proportionately with volatility. This conclusion appears to be approximately

VOLATILITY VERSUS EXCESS RETURN OF CANADIAN SMALL STOCKS (S&P/TSX COMPOSITE INDEX), LONG-TERM GOVERNMENT OF CANADA BONDS, AND CANADIAN TREASURY BILLS, 1950–2008

TABLE 10.5

Investment	Return Volatility (standard deviation)	Excess Return (average return in excess of Treasury Bills)
Three-Month Canadian Treasury Bills	3.84%	0%
Long-Term Government of Canada Bonds	10.12%	1.73%
S&P/TSX Composite Index	17.15%	5.39%

Source: Passport Financial Services Inc.

FIGURE 10.5

The Historical Tradeoff Between Risk and Return in Large Portfolios, 1950–2008

Also included are Canadian Treasury Bills and Long-Term Government of Canada Bonds. Note the general increasing relationship between historical volatility and average return.

Sources: **Passport Financial Services Inc., Statistics Canada, Bank of Canada, CRSP.**

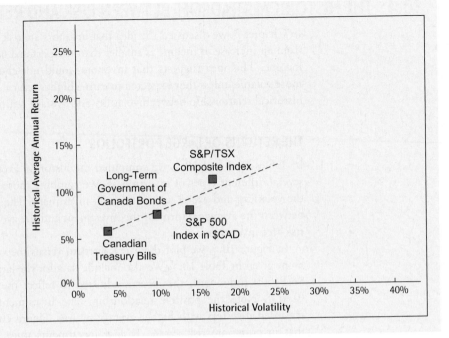

true for the large portfolios we have looked at so far. Is it correct? Does it apply to individual stocks?

Unfortunately, the answer to both questions is no. Figure 10.6 shows that, if we look at the volatility and return of individual stocks, we do not see any clear relationship between them. Each point represents the returns from 1926 to 2004 of investing in the Nth largest stock traded in the United States (updated quarterly) for $N = 1$ to 500.

FIGURE 10.6

Historical Volatility and Return for 500 Individual Stocks, by Size, Updated Quarterly, 1926–2004

Unlike the case for large portfolios, there is no precise relationship between volatility and average return for individual stocks. Individual stocks have higher volatility and lower average returns than the relationship shown for large portfolios. For comparison purposes, Figure 10.5 points are included: Canadian T-Bills, Government bonds, the S&P/TSX Composite Index, and the S&P 500 Index in CAD.

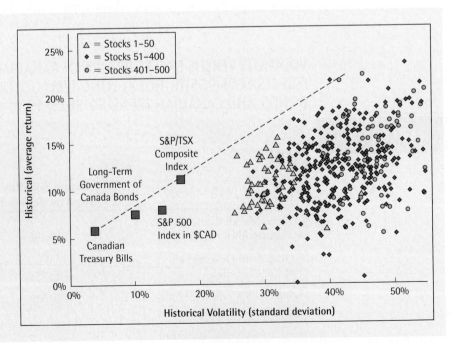

We can make several important observations from these data. First, there is a relationship between size and risk: Larger stocks have lower volatility overall. In addition, even the largest stocks are typically more volatile than a portfolio of large stocks such as the S&P 500 Index or even a portfolio of somewhat smaller stocks such as the S&P/TSX Composite Index. Finally, there is no clear relationship between volatility and return. While the smallest stocks have a slightly higher average return, many stocks have higher volatility and lower average returns than other stocks. And all stocks seem to have higher risk and lower returns than we would have predicted from a simple extrapolation of our data from large portfolios.

Thus, while volatility seems be a reasonable measure of risk when evaluating a large portfolio, it is not adequate to explain the returns of individual securities. What are we to make of this fact? Why wouldn't investors demand a higher return from stocks with a higher volatility? And how is it that portfolios such as the S&P/TSX Composite Index or the S&P 500 Index are so much less risky than all of the 500 stocks individually? To answer these questions, we need to think more carefully about how to measure risk for an investor.

CONCEPT CHECK

1. What is the excess return?

2. Is it true that expected returns for individual stocks increase proportionately with volatility?

10.5 COMMON VERSUS INDEPENDENT RISK

In this section we explain why the risk of an individual security differs from the risk of a portfolio composed of similar securities. We begin with an example from the insurance industry.

THEFT VERSUS EARTHQUAKE INSURANCE: AN EXAMPLE

Consider two types of home insurance: theft insurance and earthquake insurance. Let us assume, for the purpose of illustration, that the risk of each of these two hazards is similar for a given home in the San Francisco area. Each year there is about a 1% chance that the home will be robbed and a 1% chance that the home will be damaged by an earthquake.

In this case, the chance the insurance company will pay a claim for a single home is the same for both types of insurance policies. Suppose an insurance company writes 100,000 policies of each type for homeowners in San Francisco. We know that the risks of the individual policies are similar, but are the risks of the portfolios of policies similar?

First consider theft insurance. Because the chance of a theft for any given home is 1%, we would expect about 1% of the 100,000 homes to experience a robbery. Thus the number of theft claims will be about 1000 per year. The actual number of claims may be a bit higher or lower each year, but not by much. We can estimate the likelihood that the insurance company will receive different numbers of claims, assuming that instances of theft are independent of one another (that is, the fact that one house is robbed does not change the odds of other houses being robbed). The number of claims will almost always be between 875 and 1125 (0.875% and 1.125% of the number of policies written). In this case, if the insurance company holds reserves sufficient to cover 1200 claims, it will almost certainly have enough to meet its obligations on its theft insurance policies.

Now consider earthquake insurance. There is a 99% chance that an earthquake will not occur. All of the homes are in the same city, so if an earthquake does occur, all homes are likely to be affected and the insurance company can expect 100,000 claims. As a result, the insurance company will have to hold reserves sufficient to cover claims on all 100,000 policies it wrote to meet its obligations if an earthquake occurs.

Thus earthquake and theft insurance lead to portfolios with very different risk characteristics. For earthquake insurance, the number of claims is very risky. It will most likely be zero, but there is a 1% chance that the insurance company will have to pay claims on *all* the policies it wrote. In this case, the risk of the portfolio of insurance policies is no different from the risk of any single policy—it is still all or nothing. Conversely, for theft insurance the number of claims in a given year is quite predictable. Year in and year out, it will be very close to 1% of the total number of policies, or 1000 claims. The portfolio of theft insurance policies has almost no risk![8]

TYPES OF RISK.   Why are the portfolios of insurance policies so different when the individual policies themselves are quite similar? Intuitively, the key difference between them is that an earthquake affects all houses simultaneously, so the risk is perfectly correlated across homes. We call risk that is perfectly correlated **common risk**. In contrast, we assume that thefts in different houses are not related to each other, so the risk of theft is uncorrelated and independent across homes. We call this type of risk **independent risk**. When risks are independent, some individual homeowners are unlucky and others are lucky, but overall the number of claims is quite predictable. The averaging out of independent risks in a large portfolio is called **diversification**.[9]

THE ROLE OF DIVERSIFICATION

We can quantify this difference in terms of the standard deviation of the percentage of claims. First consider the standard deviation for an individual homeowner. At the beginning of the year, the homeowner expects a 1% chance of placing a claim for either type of insurance. But at the end of the year, the homeowner will have filed a claim (100%) or not (0%). Using Eq. 10.2 the standard deviation is

$$SD(\text{Claim}) = \sqrt{Var(\text{Claim})}$$
$$= \sqrt{0.99 \times (0 - 0.01)^2 + 0.01 \times (1 - 0.01)^2} = 9.95\%$$

For the homeowner, this standard deviation is the same for a loss from earthquake or theft.

Now consider the standard deviation of the percentage of claims for the insurance company. In the case of earthquake insurance, because the risk is common, the percentage of claims is either 100% or 0%, just as it was for the homeowner. Thus the percentage of claims received by the earthquake insurer is also 1% on average, with a 9.95% standard deviation.

While the theft insurer also receives 1% of claims on average, because the risk of theft is independent across households, the portfolio is much less risky. To quantify this difference, let's calculate the standard deviation of the average claim using Eq. 10.8. Recall that when risks are independent and identical, the standard deviation of the average is known

---

8. In the case of insurance, this difference in risk—and therefore in required reserves—can lead to a significant difference in the cost of the insurance. Indeed, earthquake insurance is generally thought to be more expensive to purchase, even though the risk to an individual household may be similar to other risks, such as theft or fire.

9. Harry Markowitz was the first to formalize the role of diversification in forming an optimal stock market portfolio. See H. M. Markowitz, "Portfolio Selection," *Journal of Finance* 7 (1952): 77–91.

as the standard error, which declines with the square root of the number of observations. Therefore,

$$SD(\text{Percentage Theft Claims}) = \frac{SD(\text{Individual Claim})}{\sqrt{\text{Number of Observations}}}$$

$$= \frac{9.95\%}{\sqrt{100,000}} = 0.03\%$$

Thus there is almost *no* risk for the theft insurer.

The principle of diversification is used routinely in the insurance industry. In addition to theft insurance, many other forms of insurance (life, health, auto) rely on the fact that the number of claims is relatively predictable in a large portfolio. Even in the case of earthquake insurance, insurers can achieve some diversification by selling policies in different geographical regions or by combining different types of policies. Diversification is used to reduce risk in many other settings. For example, many systems are designed with redundancy to decrease the risk of a disruption: Firms often add redundancy to critical parts of the manufacturing process, NASA puts more than one antenna on its space probes, automobiles contain spare tires, and so forth.

EXAMPLE 10.5   DIVERSIFICATION AND GAMBLING

Problem

Roulette wheels are typically marked with the numbers 1 through 36 plus 0 and 00. Each of these outcomes is equally likely every time the wheel is spun. If you place a bet on any one number and are correct, the payoff is 35:1; that is, if you bet $1, you will receive $36 if you win ($35 plus your original $1) and nothing if you lose. Suppose you place a $1 bet on your favourite number. What is the casino's expected profit? What is the standard deviation of this profit for a single bet? Suppose 9 million similar bets are placed throughout the casino in a typical month. What is the standard deviation of the casino's average revenues per dollar bet each month?

Solution

Because there are 38 numbers on the wheel, the odds of winning are 1/38. The casino loses $35 if you win, and makes $1 if you lose. Therefore, using Eq. 10.1, the casino's expected profit is

$$E[\text{Payoff}] = (1/38) \times (-\$35) + (37/38) \times (\$1) = \$0.0526$$

That is, for each dollar bet, the casino earns 5.26 cents on average. For a single bet, we calculate the standard deviation of this profit using Eq. 10.2 as

$$SD(\text{Payoff}) = \sqrt{(1/38) \times (-35 - 0.0526)^2 + (37/38) \times (1 - 0.0526)^2} = \$5.76$$

This standard deviation is quite large relative to the magnitude of the profits. But if many such bets are placed, the risk will be diversified. Using Eq. 10.8, the standard deviation of the casino's average revenues per dollar bet is only

$$SD(\text{Average Payoff}) = \frac{\$5.76}{\sqrt{9,000,000}} = \$0.0019$$

In other words, the 95% confidence interval for the casino's profits per dollar bet is $0.0526 ± (2 × 0.0019) = $0.0488 to $0.0564. Given $9 million in bets placed, the casino's monthly profits will almost always be between $439,200 and $507,600; thus, there is very little risk. The key assumption, of course, is that the outcome of each bet is independent of each other. If the $9 million were placed in a single bet, the casino's risk would be large—losing 35 × $9 million = $315 million if the bet wins. For this reason, casinos often impose limits on the amount of any individual bet.

CONCEPT CHECK
1. What is the difference between common risk and independent risk?

2. Under what circumstances will risk be diversified in a large portfolio of insurance contracts?

10.6 DIVERSIFICATION IN STOCK PORTFOLIOS

As the insurance example indicates, the risk of a portfolio of insurance contracts depends on whether the individual risks within it are common or independent. Independent risks are diversified in a large portfolio, whereas common risks are not. Let's consider the implication of this distinction for the risk of stock portfolios.

FIRM-SPECIFIC VERSUS SYSTEMATIC RISK

Over any given time period, the risk of holding a stock is that the dividends plus the final stock price will be higher or lower than expected, which makes the realized return risky. What causes dividends or stock prices, and therefore returns, to be higher or lower than we expect? Usually, stock prices and dividends fluctuate due to two types of news:

1. *Firm-specific news* is good or bad news about the company itself. For example, a firm might announce that it has been successful in gaining market share within its industry.

2. *Market-wide news* is news about the economy as a whole and therefore affects all stocks. For instance, the Bank of Canada might announce that it will lower interest rates to boost the economy.

Fluctuations of a stock's return that are due to firm-specific news are independent risks. Like theft across homes, these risks are unrelated across stocks. This type of risk is also referred to as **firm-specific, idiosyncratic, unsystematic, unique,** or **diversifiable risk**.

Fluctuations of a stock's return that are due to market-wide news represent common risk. As with earthquakes, all stocks are affected simultaneously by the news. This type of risk is also called **systematic, undiversifiable,** or **market risk**.

When we combine many stocks in a large portfolio, the firm-specific risks for each stock will average out and be diversified. Good news will affect some stocks, and bad news will affect others, but the amount of good or bad news overall will be relatively constant. The systematic risk, however, will affect all firms—and therefore the entire portfolio—and will not be diversified.

Let's consider an example. Suppose type S firms are affected *only* by the strength of the economy, a systematic risk which has a 50–50 chance of being either strong or weak. If the economy is strong, type S stocks will earn a return of 40%; if the economy is weak, their return will be −20%. Because these firms face systematic risk (the strength of the economy), holding a large portfolio of type S firms will not diversify the risk. When the

Volatility of Portfolios of Type S and I Stocks

Because type S firms have only systematic risk, the volatility of the portfolio does not change. Type I firms have only idiosyncratic risk, which is diversified and eliminated as the number of firms in the portfolio increases. Typical stocks carry a mix of both types of risk, so that the risk of the portfolio declines as idiosyncratic risk is diversified away, but systematic risk still remains.

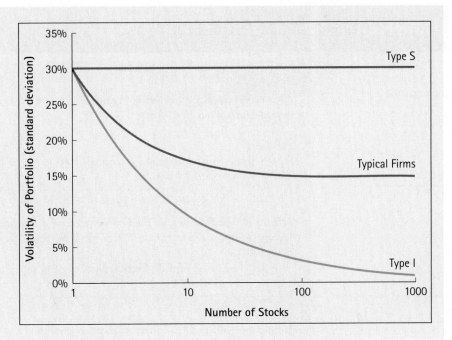

economy is strong, the portfolio will have the same return of 40% as each type S firm; when the economy is weak, the portfolio will also have a return of −20%.

Now consider type I firms, which are affected only by idiosyncratic, firm-specific risks. Their returns are equally likely to be 35% or −25%, based on factors specific to each firm's local market. Because these risks are firm specific, if we hold a portfolio of the stocks of many type I firms, the risk is diversified. About half of the firms will have returns of 35%, and half will have returns of −25%, so that the return of the portfolio will be the average return of 50% (0.35) + 50% (−0.25) = 5%.

Figure 10.7 illustrates how volatility declines with the size of the portfolio for type S and I firms. Type S firms have only systematic risk. As with earthquake insurance, the volatility of the portfolio does not change as the number of firms increases. Type I firms have only idiosyncratic risk. As with theft insurance, the risk is diversified as the number of firms increases, and volatility declines. As is evident from Figure 10.7, with a large number of firms, the risk is essentially eliminated.

Of course, actual firms are not like type S or I firms. Firms are affected by both systematic, market-wide risks and firm-specific risks. Figure 10.7 also shows how the volatility changes with the size of a portfolio containing the stocks of typical firms. When firms carry both types of risk, only the firm-specific risk will be diversified when we combine many firms' stocks into a portfolio. The volatility will therefore decline until only the systematic risk, which affects all firms, remains.

This example explains one of the puzzles in Figure 10.6. There we saw that the S&P/ TSX Composite Index and the S&P 500 Index had much lower volatility than any of the individual stocks. Now we can see why: The individual stocks each contain firm-specific risk, which is eliminated when we combine them into a large portfolio. Thus the portfolio as a whole can have lower volatility than each of the stocks within it.

| EXAMPLE 10.6 | PORTFOLIO VOLATILITY |

Problem

What is the volatility of the average return of ten type S firms? What is the volatility of the average return of ten type I firms?

Solution

Type S firms have equally likely returns of 40% or −20%. Their expected return is $\frac{1}{2}(40\%) + \frac{1}{2}(-20\%) = 10\%$, so

$$SD(R_S) = \sqrt{\tfrac{1}{2}(0.40 - 0.10)^2 + \tfrac{1}{2}(-0.20 - 0.10)^2} = 30\%$$

Because all type S firms have high or low returns at the same time, the average return of ten type S firms is also 40% or −20%. Thus it has the same volatility of 30%, as shown in Figure 10.7.

Type I firms have equally likely returns of 35% or −25%. Their expected return is $\frac{1}{2}(35\%) + \frac{1}{2}(-25\%) = 5\%$, so

$$SD(R_I) = \sqrt{\tfrac{1}{2}(0.35 - 0.05)^2 + \tfrac{1}{2}(-0.25 - 0.05)^2} = 30\%$$

Because the returns of type I firms are independent, using Eq. 10.8, the average return of ten type I firms has volatility of $30\%/\sqrt{10} = 9.5\%$, as shown in Figure 10.7.

NO ARBITRAGE AND THE RISK PREMIUM

Consider again type I firms, which are affected only by firm-specific risk. Because each individual type I firm is risky, should investors expect to earn a risk premium when investing in type I firms?

In a competitive market, the answer is no. To see why, suppose the expected return of type I firms exceeds the risk-free interest rate. Then by holding a large portfolio of many type I firms, investors could diversify the firm-specific risk of these firms and earn a return above the risk-free interest rate without taking on any significant risk.

The situation just described is very close to an arbitrage opportunity, which investors would find very attractive. They would borrow money at the risk-free interest rate and invest it in a large portfolio of type I firms, which offers a higher return with only a tiny amount of risk.[10] As more investors take advantage of this situation and purchase shares of type I firms, the current share prices for type I firms would rise, lowering their expected return (recall that the current share price P_t is the denominator when computing the stock's return as in Eq. 10.4). This trading would stop only after the return of type I firms equalled the risk-free interest rate. Competition between investors drives the return of type I firms down to the risk-free return.

The preceding argument is essentially an application of the Law of One Price: Because a large portfolio of type I firms has no risk, it must earn the risk-free interest rate. This no-arbitrage argument suggests the following more general principle:

The risk premium for diversifiable risk is zero, so investors are not compensated for holding firm-specific risk.

---

10. If investors could actually hold a large enough portfolio and completely diversify all the risk, this would be a true arbitrage opportunity.

FINANCIAL CRISIS
DIVERSIFICATION BENEFITS DURING MARKET CRASHES

The figure below illustrates the benefits of diversification over the last 40 years. The blue graph shows the historical volatility of the S&P 500 portfolio (annualized based on daily returns each quarter). The red curve is the weighted average volatility of the individual stocks in the portfolio. Thus, the red shaded area is idiosyncratic risk; risk that has been diversified away by holding the portfolio. The blue area is market risk which cannot be diversified.

Market volatility clearly varies, increasing dramatically during times of crisis. But notice also that the fraction of risk that can be diversified away also varies, and seems to decline during times of crisis. For example, since 1962, on average about 50% of the volatility of individual stocks is diversifiable

(i.e., the red area is about 50% of the total). But as the figure demonstrates, during both the 1987 crash and the 2008 financial crisis this fraction fell dramatically, so that only about 20% of the volatility of individual stocks could be diversified. The combined effect of increased volatility and reduced diversification during the 2008 financial crisis was that the risk that investors care about—market risk—increased seven-fold, from 10% to 70%, between 2006 and the last quarter of 2008.

Although you are always better off diversifying, it is important to keep in mind that the benefits of diversification depend on economic conditions. In times of extreme crisis the benefits may go down, making downturns in the market particularly painful for investors.

Source: CRSP.

This principle can be applied not just to type I firms, but to all stocks and securities. It implies that the risk premium of a stock is not affected by its diversifiable, firm-specific risk. If the diversifiable risk of stocks were compensated with an additional risk premium, then investors could buy the stocks, earn the additional premium, and simultaneously diversify and eliminate the risk. By doing so, investors could earn an additional premium without taking on additional risk. This opportunity to earn something for nothing would quickly be exploited and eliminated.[11]

Because investors can eliminate firm-specific risk "for free" by diversifying their portfolios, they will not require a reward or risk premium for holding it. However, diversification

---

11. The main thrust of this argument can be found in S. Ross, "The Arbitrage Theory of Capital Asset Pricing," *Journal of Economic Theory* 13 (December 1976): 341–360.

does not reduce systematic risk: Even holding a large portfolio, an investor will be exposed to risks that affect the entire economy and therefore affect all securities. Because investors are risk averse, they will demand a risk premium to hold systematic risk; otherwise they would be better off selling their stocks and investing in risk-free bonds. Because investors can eliminate firm-specific risk for free by diversifying, whereas systematic risk can be eliminated only by sacrificing expected returns, it is a security's systematic risk that determines the risk premium investors require to hold it. This fact leads to a second key principle:

The risk premium of a security is determined by its systematic risk and does not depend on its diversifiable risk.

This principle implies that a stock's volatility, which is a measure of total risk (that is, systematic risk plus diversifiable risk), is not especially useful in determining the risk premium that investors will earn. For example, consider again type S and I firms. As calculated in Example 10.6, the volatility of a single type S or I firm is 30%. Although both types of firms have the same volatility, type S firms have an expected return of 10% and type I firms have an expected return of 5%. The difference in expected returns derives from the difference in the kind of risk each firm bears. Type I firms have only

COMMON MISTAKE   A FALLACY OF LONG-RUN DIVERSIFICATION

We have seen that investors can greatly reduce their risk by dividing their investment dollars over many different investments, eliminating the diversifiable risk in their portfolios. It is sometimes argued that the same logic applies over time: By investing for many years, we can also diversify the risk we face during any particular year. Is this correct? In the long run, does risk still matter?

Equation 10.8 tells us that if returns each year are independent, the volatility of the average annual return declines with the number of years that we invest. Of course, as long-term investors, we don't care about the volatility of our *average* return; instead, we care about the volatility of our *cumulative* return over the period. This volatility grows with the investment horizon, as illustrated in the following example.

In 1956, the S&P/TSX Index increased in value by about 11%. In fact, if we think about the example of your grandparents investing $100 in 1956 we can see from Figure 10.1 that it would have grown to about $9300 by the start of 2009. But suppose that mining and transportation strikes had caused stocks to drop by 44.5% in 1956. Then the initial $100 invested would be worth only $100 × (1 − 44.5%) = $55.50 at the beginning of 1957. If returns from then on were unchanged, the investment would be worth about half as much at the end of 2008, or $4660.

Thus, if future returns are not affected by today's return, then an increase or a decline in the value of our portfolio today will translate into the same percentage increase or decrease in the value of our portfolio in the future, so there is no diversification over time. The only way the length of the time horizon can reduce risk is if a below-average return this year implies that returns are more likely to be above average in the future (and vice versa), a phenomenon sometimes referred to as *mean reversion*. Mean reversion implies that past low returns can be used to predict future high returns in the stock market.

For short horizons of a few years, there is no evidence of mean reversion in the stock market. For longer horizons, there is some evidence of mean reversion historically, but it is not clear how reliable this evidence is (there are not enough decades of accurate stock market data available) or whether the pattern will continue. Even if there is long-run mean reversion in stock returns, a buy-and-hold diversification strategy is still not optimal: Because mean reversion implies that past returns can be used to predict future returns, one should invest more in stocks when returns are predicted to be high, and invest less when they are predicted to be low. This strategy is very different from the diversification we achieve by holding many stocks, where we cannot predict which stocks will have good or bad firm-specific shocks.

firm-specific risk, which does not require a risk premium, so the expected return of 5% for type I firms equals the risk-free interest rate. Type S firms have only systematic risk. Because investors will require compensation for taking on this risk, the expected return of 10% for type S firms provides investors with a 5% risk premium above the risk-free interest rate.

We now have an explanation for the second puzzle of Figure 10.6. While volatility might be a reasonable measure of risk for a well-diversified portfolio, it is not an appropriate metric for an individual security. Thus, there should be no clear relationship between volatility and average returns for individual securities. Consequently, to estimate a security's expected return, we need to find a measure of a security's systematic risk.

In Chapter 3, we used a simple example to show that an investment's risk premium depends on how its returns move in relation to the overall economy. In particular, risk-averse investors will demand a premium to invest in securities that will do poorly in bad times. This idea coincides with the notion of systematic risk we have defined in this chapter. Economy-wide risk—that is, the risk of recessions and booms—is systematic risk that cannot be diversified. Therefore an asset that moves with the economy contains systematic risk and so requires a risk premium.

EXAMPLE 10.7 — DIVERSIFIABLE VERSUS SYSTEMATIC RISK

Problem
Which of the following risks of a stock are likely to be firm-specific, diversifiable risks, and which are likely to be systematic risks? Which risks will affect the risk premium that investors will demand?

a. The risk that the founder and CEO retires

b. The risk that oil prices rise, increasing production costs

c. The risk that a product design is faulty and the product must be recalled

d. The risk that the economy slows, reducing demand for the firm's products

Solution
Because oil prices and the health of the economy affect all stocks, risks (b) and (d) are systematic risks. These risks are not diversified in a large portfolio, and so will affect the risk premium that investors require to invest in a stock. Risks (a) and (c) are firm-specific risks, and so are diversifiable. While these risks should be considered when estimating a firm's future cash flows, they will not affect the risk premium that investors will require and, therefore, will not affect a firm's cost of capital.

CONCEPT CHECK

1. Explain why the risk premium of diversifiable risk is zero.

2. Why is the risk premium of a security determined only by its systematic risk?

10.7 MEASURING SYSTEMATIC RISK

As we have discussed, investors can eliminate the firm-specific risk in their investments by diversifying their portfolio. Thus, when evaluating the risk of an investment, an investor will care about its systematic risk, which cannot be eliminated through diversification. In exchange for bearing systematic risk, investors want to be compensated by earning a higher return. So, to determine the expected return investors will require to undertake an investment, we first need to measure the investment's systematic risk.

AN INVESTMENT'S SENSITIVITY TO SYSTEMATIC RISK

To determine how sensitive a stock's return is to interest rate changes, for example, we would look at how much the return tends to change on average for each 1% change in interest rates. Similarly, if we want to determine how sensitive a stock's return is to oil prices, we would examine the average change in the return for each 1% change in oil prices. In the same way, if we wanted to determine how sensitive a stock is to systematic risk, we can look at the average change in the return for each 1% change in the return of *a portfolio that fluctuates solely due to systematic risk.*

EFFICIENT PORTFOLIO.　Thus the key step to measuring systematic risk is finding a portfolio that contains *only* systematic risk. Then changes in the price of this portfolio will correspond to systematic shocks to the economy. We call such a portfolio an **efficient portfolio**. An efficient portfolio cannot be diversified further, that is, there is no way to reduce the risk of the portfolio without lowering its expected return.

MARKET PORTFOLIO.　As we will see over the next few chapters, the best way to identify an efficient portfolio is one of the key questions in modern finance. Because diversification improves with the number of stocks held in a portfolio, an efficient portfolio should be a large portfolio containing many different stocks. Thus a natural candidate for an efficient portfolio is the **market portfolio**, which is a portfolio of all stocks and securities in the market. Because it is difficult to find data for the returns of many bonds and small stocks, it is common in practice to use a large market index portfolio as an approximation for the market portfolio. In Canada, the S&P/TSX Composite Index is often used; in the U.S., the S&P 500 Index is often used. In both these cases, the assumption is that these portfolios are large enough to be essentially fully diversified.

BETA AND SYSTEMATIC RISK

If we assume that the market portfolio (or the S&P/TSX Composite Index) is efficient, then changes in the value of the market portfolio represent systematic shocks to the economy. Knowing this, we can measure the systematic risk of a security's return by its beta. The **beta (β)** of a security is the sensitivity of the security's return to the return of the overall market. More precisely,

The beta is the expected percent change in the excess return of a security for a 1% change in the excess return of the market portfolio.

EXAMPLE 10.8

ESTIMATING BETA

Problem

Suppose the market portfolio excess return tends to increase by 47% when the economy is strong and decline by 25% when the economy is weak. What is the beta of a type S firm whose excess return is 40% on average when the economy is strong and −20% when the economy is weak? What is the beta of a type I firm that bears only idiosyncratic, firm-specific risk?

Solution

The systematic risk of the strength of the economy produces a 47% − (−25%) = 72% change in the return of the market portfolio. The type S firm's return changes by 40% − (−20%) = 60% on average. Thus the firm's beta is $\beta_S = 60\%/72\% = 0.833$. That is, each 1% change in the return of the market portfolio leads to a 0.833% change in the type S firm's return on average.

The return of a type I firm that has only firm-specific risk, however, is not affected by the strength of the economy. Its return is affected only by factors that are specific to the firm. Whether the economy is strong or weak, it will have the same expected return, and thus $\beta_I = 0\%/72\% = 0$.

REAL-FIRM BETAS.   We will look at statistical techniques for estimating beta from historical data in Chapter 12. It is important to note that we can estimate beta reasonably accurately using just a few years of data (which was not the case for expected returns, as we saw in Example 10.4). Using the S&P/TSX Composite Index to represent the market's return, Table 10.6 shows the betas of several stocks, as well as the average betas for stocks within their TSX industry sectors, during 2004–2008. As shown in the table, each 1% change in the excess return of the market during this period led, on average, to a 1.714% change in the excess return for RIM, but only a 0.511% change in the excess return for Shoppers Drug Mart.

INTERPRETING BETAS.   Beta measures the sensitivity of a security to market-wide risk factors. For a stock, this value is related to how sensitive its underlying revenues and cash flows are to general economic conditions. The average beta of a stock in the market is about 1.0; that is, the average stock price tends to move about 1% for each 1% move in the overall market. Stocks in cyclical industries, in which revenues tend to vary greatly over the business cycle, are likely to be more sensitive to systematic risk and have higher betas than stocks in less sensitive industries.

For example, notice the relatively low betas of Fortis Inc. (a utility company), Maple Leaf Foods Inc. (a meat-processing company), and Loblaw Companies Limited (a food retailer). Utilities tend to be stable and highly regulated, and thus are insensitive to fluctuations in the overall market. Food production and food retailing companies are also very insensitive: the demand for their products appears to be unrelated to the booms and busts of the economy as a whole.

At the other extreme, information technology stocks tend to have the highest betas. Shocks in the economy have an amplified impact on these stocks: When the market as a whole is up, RIM tends to rise more than 1.7 times as much; but when the market stumbles, RIM tends to fall almost 1.7 times as far.

| TABLE 10.6 | BETAS WITH RESPECT TO THE S&P/TSX COMPOSITE INDEX FOR INDIVIDUAL STOCKS AND AVERAGE BETAS FOR STOCKS IN THEIR TSX INDUSTRY SECTORS (BASED ON FIVE YEARS OF MONTHLY DATA FOR 2004–2008) | | | |

Industry	Industry Beta	Company Ticker	Company Name	Company Beta
Energy	1.416	IMO	Imperial Oil Limited	1.165
		PCA	Suncor Energy Inc.	1.390
Materials	1.320	AEM	Agnico-Eagle Mines Ltd.	1.522
		ABX	Barrick Gold Corporation	0.551
		HBM	HudBay Minerals Inc.	2.666
Industrials	0.801	BBD.B	Bombardier Inc.	1.496
		CP	Canadian Pacific Railway	0.665
		SNC	SNC-Lavalin Group Inc.	0.582
		TIH	Toromont Industries Ltd.	0.776
		WJA	WestJet Airlines Ltd.	0.603
Consumer Discretionary	0.593	CTC	Canadian Tire Corporation	0.590
		FGL	The Forzani Group Ltd.	1.292
		RON	RONA Inc.	0.395
Consumer Staples	0.321	L	Loblaw Companies Limited	0.223
		MFI	Maple Leaf Foods Inc.	0.079
		SC	Shoppers Drug Mart Corporation	0.511
Health Care	0.489	BVF	Biovail Corporation	0.432
		MDS	MDS Inc.	0.847
Financials	0.595	AGF.B	AGF Management Limited	1.476
		MFC	Manulife Financial Corporation	0.934
		OCX	ONEX Corporation	0.998
		TD	The Toronto-Dominion Bank	0.442
Information Technology	1.47	RIM	Research In Motion Limited	1.714
Telecommunications Services	0.540	BCE	BCE Inc.	0.487
		MBT	Manitoba Telecom Services Inc.	0.252
		T	TELUS Corporation	0.512
Utilities	0.488	FTS	Fortis Inc.	0.136
		TA	TransAlta Corporation	0.888

1. What is the market portfolio?

2. Define the beta of a security.

10.8 BETA AND THE COST OF CAPITAL

Throughout this text, we have emphasized that financial managers should evaluate an investment opportunity based on its cost of capital, which is the expected return available on alternative investments in the market with comparable risk and term. For risky investments, this cost of capital corresponds to the risk-free interest rate, plus an appropriate risk premium. Now that we can measure the systematic risk of an investment according to its beta, we are in a position to estimate the risk premium investors will require.

ESTIMATING THE RISK PREMIUM

Before we can estimate the risk premium of an individual stock, we need a way to assess investors' appetite for risk. The size of the risk premium investors' will require to make a risky investment depends upon their risk aversion. Rather than attempt to measure this risk aversion directly, we can measure it indirectly by looking at the risk premium investors' demand for investing in systematic, or market, risk.

THE MARKET RISK PREMIUM. We can calibrate investors' appetite for market risk from the market portfolio.

The risk premium investors can earn by holding the market portfolio is the difference between the market portfolio's expected return and the risk-free interest rate:

$$\text{Market Risk Premium} = E[R_{Mkt}] - r_f$$

For example, if the risk-free rate is 5% and the expected return of the market portfolio is 11%, the market risk premium is 6%. In the same way that the market interest rate reflects investors' patience and determines the time value of money, the market risk premium reflects investors' risk tolerance and determines the market price of risk in the economy.

ADJUSTING FOR BETA. The market risk premium is the reward investors expect to earn for holding a portfolio with a beta of 1 – the market portfolio itself. Consider an investment opportunity with a beta of 2. This investment carries twice as much systematic risk as an investment in the S&P/TSX Composite Index. That is, for each dollar we invest in the opportunity, we could invest twice that amount in the S&P/TSX Composite Index and be exposed to the same amount of systematic risk. So, by the Law of One Price, to invest in the opportunity with a beta of 2, investors will require double the risk premium.

To summarize, we can use the beta of the investment to determine the scale of the investment in the S&P/TSX Composite Index that has equivalent systematic risk. Thus, to compensate

COMMON MISTAKE BETA VERSUS VOLATILITY

Recall that beta differs from volatility. Volatility measures total risk—that is, both market and firm-specific risks—so that there is no necessary relationship between volatility and beta. Consider that Biovail (a drug company) and RIM may have similar volatilities. Biovail, however, has a much lower beta. While drug companies face a great deal of risk related to the development and approval of new drugs, this risk is unrelated to the rest of the economy. And though health care expenditures do vary a little with the state of the economy, they vary much less than expenditures on technology. Thus, while their volatilities are similar, much more of the risk of Biovail's stock is diversifiable risk, whereas RIM's stock has a much greater proportion of systematic risk.

investors for the time value of their money as well as the systematic risk they are bearing, the cost of capital, r_i for an investment with β_i should satisfy the following general formula:

Estimating a Traded Security's Expected Return from Its Beta

$$E[R] = \text{Risk-Free Interest Rate} + \text{Risk Premium} \qquad (10.10)$$
$$= r_f + \beta \times (E[R_{Mkt}] - r_f)$$

As an example, suppose the market risk premium is 6% and the risk-free interest rate is 4%. According to Eq. 10.10, investors' expected return for Research In Motion Limited (ticker: RIM) and WestJet Airlines Ltd. (ticker: WJA) stocks is

$$E[R_{RIM}] = 0.04 + 1.196 \times 0.06 = 0.11176 = 11.176\%$$
$$E[R_{WJA}] = 0.04 + 0.470 \times 0.06 = 0.0682 = 6.82\%$$

Thus, investors in Research In Motion expect a much higher return on average to compensate them for Research In Motion's much higher systematic risk.

EXAMPLE 10.9
EXPECTED RETURNS AND BETA

Problem

Suppose the risk-free rate is 5% and the economy is equally likely to be strong or weak. Verify that Eq. 10.10 holds for the type S firms considered in Example 10.8. How does this cost of capital compare with the expected return for these firms?

Solution

If the economy is equally likely to be strong or weak, the expected return of the market is $E[R_{Mkt}] = 50\%(0.47) + 50\%(-0.25) = 11\%$, and the market risk premium is $E[R_{Mkt}] - r_f = 11\% - 5\% = 6\%$. Given the beta of 0.833 for type S firms that we calculated in Example 10.8, the estimate of the expected return for type S firms from Eq. 10.10 is

$$r_S = r_f + \beta_S \times (E[R_{Mkt}] - r_f) = 5\% + 0.833 \times (11\% - 5\%) = 10\%$$

This matches their expected return: $50\%(0.4) + 50\%(-0.2) = 10\%$.

What happens if a stock has a negative beta? According to Eq. 10.10, such a stock would have a negative risk premium—it would have an expected return below the risk-free rate. While this might seem unreasonable at first, note that a stock with a negative beta will tend to do well when times are bad, so owning it will provide insurance against the systematic risk of other stocks in the portfolio. (We saw an example of such a security in Example 3A.2 in Chapter 3.) Risk-averse investors are willing to pay for this insurance provided by negative beta stocks by accepting a return below the risk-free interest rate.

THE CAPITAL ASSET PRICING MODEL

Equation 10.10 for estimating the cost of capital is often referred to as the **Capital Asset Pricing Model (CAPM)**,[12] the most important method for estimating the cost of capital

---

12. The CAPM was first developed independently by Lintner and Sharpe. See L. Lintner "The Valuation of Risk Assets and the Selection of Risky Investments in Stock Portfolios and Capital Budgets," *Review of Economics and Statistics* 47 (1965): 13–37; and W. F. Sharpe, "Capital Asset Prices: A Theory of Market Equilibrium under Conditions of Risk," *Journal of Finance* 19 (1964): 425–442.

that is used in practice. In this chapter, we have provided an intuitive justification of the CAPM, and its use of the market portfolio as the benchmark for systematic risk. We provide a more complete development of the model and its assumptions in the next chapter, where we also detail the portfolio optimization process used by professional fund managers. Then, in Chapter 12, we look at the practicalities of implementing the CAPM, and develop statistical tools for estimating the betas of individual stocks, together with methods for estimating the beta and cost of capital of projects within these firms. Finally, in Chapter 13 we look at the empirical evidence for (and against) the CAPM, both as a model of investor behaviour and as forecast of expected returns, and introduce some proposed extensions to the CAPM.

INTERVIEW WITH RANDALL LERT

Prior to retiring in late 2008, Randall P. Lert was chief investment officer and chief portfolio strategist at Russell Investments, a global investment company with $136 billion in assets under management and the creator of the Russell 3000® Index. Randy formed RPL Consulting to advise clients on investment management and portfolio strategy.

QUESTION: How does diversification affect portfolio strategy and the risk-return tradeoff?

ANSWER: Holding a large, strategically allocated portfolio across many asset classes maximizes your return for a given level of risk, because different markets are not perfectly correlated to each other. The *number* of stocks per se does not drive diversification; *weighting* does. A 1000-stock portfolio with very divergent weightings from the market index will have more idiosyncratic risk than a 100-stock portfolio whose weights approximate the index. If I hold 100 stocks but underweight the 50 largest, which constitute half the market capitalization of the index, my portfolio will diverge more from the benchmark than a 100 stock portfolio holding the top 50 relatively close to market weight but scattering the other 50 stocks.

QUESTION: In the U.S., history shows a relatively large reward for taking systematic equity risk versus holding bonds. What is your view of this risk/reward tradeoff going forward in light of the current financial crisis?

ANSWER: In general, investment managers assume there is a premium for longer-maturity bonds and fixed income securities with credit risk relative to cash or the risk free rate. Currently the industry assigns a risk premium of about 2–3% for bonds relative to cash, and the risk premium of stocks relative to long-term bonds is another 2–3%, for a 4–6% equity risk premium. Clearly different firms and different forecasters will have somewhat different views but a 4–6% risk premium for stocks is about the industry average. This is a bit lower than has been realized historically. Until the capital market events that started in the fall of 2007, it was generally believed that what has come to be known as The Great Moderation (from roughly 1981–2007) was the new norm for developed economies. That idea suggested that the systematic risk of equity investing was lower due primarily to superior macroeconomic policy, resulting in most investment firms lowering the equity risk premium. However, the events of the fall of 2008 called that view into question. In the summer of 2009, it is too soon to determine the long-term impact, if any, of the financial crisis on long-term risk premium estimates. Nor have we seen how this crisis will really end. For the most part, at this point the crisis is not yet reflected in long-term risk premium estimates. It is therefore premature to make significant changes to the long-term forecast.

CONCEPT CHECK

1. How can you use a security's beta to estimate its cost of capital?

2. If a risky investment has a beta of zero, what should its cost of capital be according to the CAPM? How can you justify this?

SUMMARY

1. A probability distribution summarizes information about possible different returns and their likelihood of occurring.

   a. The expected, or mean, return is the return we expect to earn on average:

$$\text{Expected Return} = E[R] = \sum_R p_R \times R \tag{10.1}$$

   b. The variance or standard deviation measures the variability of the returns:

$$Var(R) = E[(R - E[R])^2] = \sum_R p_R \times (R - E[R])^2 \tag{10.2}$$

$$SD(R) = \sqrt{Var(R)}$$

   c. The standard deviation of a return is also called its volatility.

2. The realized or total return for an investment is the total of the dividend yield and the capital gain rate.

   a. Using the empirical distribution of realized returns, we can estimate the expected return and variance of the distribution of returns by calculating the average annual return and variance of realized returns:

$$\bar{R} = \frac{1}{T}(R_1 + R_2 + \cdots + R_T) = \frac{1}{T}\sum_{t=1}^{T} R_t \tag{10.6}$$

$$Var(R) = \frac{1}{T-1}\sum_{t=1}^{T}(R_t - \bar{R})^2 \tag{10.7}$$

   b. The square root of the estimated variance is an estimate of the volatility of returns.

   c. Because a security's historical average return is only an estimate of its true expected return, we use the standard error of the estimate to gauge the amount of estimation error:

$$SD(\text{Average of Independent, Identical Risks}) = \frac{SD(\text{Individual Risk})}{\sqrt{\text{Number of Observations}}} \tag{10.8}$$

3. Based on historical data, small stocks have had higher volatility and higher average returns than large stocks, which have had higher volatility and higher average returns than bonds.

4. There is no clear relationship between the volatility and return of individual stocks.

   a. Larger stocks tend to have lower overall volatility, but even the largest stocks are typically more risky than a portfolio of large stocks.

   b. All stocks seem to have higher risk and lower returns than would be predicted based on extrapolation of data for large portfolios.

5. The total risk of a security represents both idiosyncratic risk and systematic risk.

 a. Variation in a stock's return due to firm-specific news is called idiosyncratic risk. This type of risk is also called firm-specific, unsystematic, unique, or diversifiable risk.

 b. Systematic risk is risk due to market-wide news that affect all stocks simultaneously. Common risk is also called market or undiversifiable risk.

6. Diversification eliminates idiosyncratic risk but does not eliminate systematic risk.

 a. Because investors can eliminate idiosyncratic risk, they do not require a risk premium for taking it on.

 b. Because investors cannot eliminate systematic risk, they must be compensated for holding it. As a consequence, the risk premium for a stock depends on the amount of its systematic risk rather than its total risk.

7. An efficient portfolio is a portfolio that contains only systematic risk and cannot be diversified further—that is, there is no way to reduce the risk of the portfolio without lowering its expected return.

8. The market portfolio is a portfolio that contains all shares of all stocks and securities in the market. The market portfolio is often assumed to be efficient.

9. If the market portfolio is efficient, we can measure the systematic risk of a security by its beta (β). The beta of a security is the sensitivity of the security's return to the return of the overall market.

10. The market risk premium is the expected excess return of the market portfolio:

$$\text{Market Risk Premium} = E[R_{Mkt}] - r_f \qquad (10.9)$$

11. The cost of capital for a risky investment equals the risk-free rate plus a risk premium. The Capital Asset Pricing Model (CAPM) states that the risk premium equals the investment's beta times the market risk premium:

$$r = r_f + \beta \times (E[R_{Mkt}] - r_f) \qquad (10.10)$$

KEY TERMS

PROBLEMS

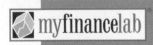

Common Measures of Risk and Return

EXCEL   1.   The figure below shows the one-year return distribution for RCS stock. Calculate

a. The expected return

b. The standard deviation of the return

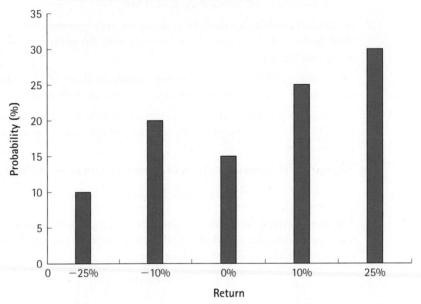

EXCEL   2.   The table below shows the one-year return distribution of Startup Inc. Calculate

a. The expected return

b. The standard deviation of the return

Return	Probability
−100%	40%
−75%	20%
−50%	20%
−25%	10%
1000%	10%

3.   Characterize the difference between the two stocks in Problems 1 and 2. What tradeoffs would you face in choosing one to hold?

Historical Returns of Stocks and Bonds

4.   You bought a stock one year ago for $50 per share and sold it today for $55 per share. It paid a $1 per share dividend today.

a. What was your realized return?

b. How much of the return came from dividend yield and how much came from capital gain?

5. Repeat Problem 4 assuming that the stock fell $5 to $45 instead.

    a. Is your capital gain different? Why or why not?

    b. Is your dividend yield different? Why or why not?

EXCEL   6. Using the data in the table below, calculate the return for investing in Boeing stock from January 2, 2003, to January 2, 2004, and also from January 2, 2008, to January 2, 2009, assuming all dividends are reinvested in the stock immediately.

Historical Stock and Dividend Data for Boeing

Date	Price	Dividend	Date	Price	Dividend
1/2/03	33.88		1/2/08	86.62	
2/5/03	30.67	0.17	2/6/08	79.91	0.40
5/14/03	29.49	0.17	5/7/08	84.55	0.40
8/13/03	32.38	0.17	8/6/08	65.40	0.40
11/12/03	39.07	0.17	11/5/08	49.55	0.40
1/2/04	41.99		1/2/09	45.25	

EXCEL   7. Download the spreadsheet from www.myfinancelab.com that contains historical monthly prices and dividends (paid at the end of the month) for Ford Motor Company stock (Ticker: F) from August 1994 to August 1998. Calculate the realized return over this period, expressing your answer in percent per month.

EXCEL   8. Using the same data as in Problem 7, compute the

    a. Average monthly return over this period

    b. Monthly volatility (or standard deviation) over this period

EXCEL   9. Explain the difference between the average return you calculated in Problem 8(a) and the realized return you calculated in Problem 7. Are both numbers useful? If so, explain why.

*10. Compute the 95% confidence interval of the estimate of the average monthly return you calculated in Problem 8(a).

The Historical Tradeoff between Risk and Return

11. How does the relationship between the average return and the historical volatility of individual stocks differ from the relationship between the average return and the historical volatility of large, well-diversified portfolios?

Common Versus Independent Risk

12. Consider two local banks. Bank A has 100 loans outstanding, each for $1 million, that it expects will be repaid today. Each loan has a 5% probability of default, in which case the bank is not repaid anything. The chance of default is independent across all the loans. Bank B has only one loan of $100 million outstanding, which it also expects will be repaid today. It also has a 5% probability of not being repaid. Explain the difference between the types of risk each bank faces. Which bank faces less risk? Why?

*13. Using the data in Problem 12, calculate

    a. The expected overall payoff of each bank.

    b. The standard deviation of the overall payoff of each bank.

Diversification in Stock Portfolios

14. You are a risk-averse investor who is considering investing in one of two economies. The expected return and volatility of all stocks in both economies is the same. In the first economy, all stocks move together: In good times all prices rise together and in bad times they all fall together. In the second economy, stock returns are independent: One stock increasing in price has no effect on the prices of other stocks. Which economy would you choose to invest in? Explain.

15. Consider an economy with two types of firms, S and I. S firms all move together. I firms move independently. For both types of firms, there is a 60% probability that the firms will have a 15% return and a 40% probability that the firms will have a −10% return. What is the volatility (standard deviation) of a portfolio that consists of an equal investment in 20
    a. Type S firms?
    b. Type I firms?

*16. Using the data in Problem 15, plot the volatility as a function of the number of firms in the two portfolios.

17. Explain why the risk premium of a stock does not depend on its diversifiable risk.

18. Identify each of the following risks as either systematic risk or diversifiable risk:
    a. The risk that the CEO of your firm is killed in a plane accident
    b. The risk that the economy slows, decreasing demand for your firm's products
    c. The risk that your best employees will be hired away
    d. The risk that the new product you expect your R&D division to produce will not materialize

 19. Suppose the risk-free interest rate is 5%, and the stock market will return either 40% or −20% each year, with each outcome equally likely. Compare the following two investment strategies: (i) invest for one year in the risk-free investment, and one year in the market or (ii) invest for both years in the market.
    a. Which strategy has the highest expected final payoff?
    b. Which strategy has the highest standard deviation for the final payoff?
    Does holding stocks for a longer period decrease your risk?

Measuring Systematic Risk

20. What is an efficient portfolio?

21. What does the beta of a stock measure?

22. Suppose the market portfolio is equally likely to increase by 30% or decrease by 10%.
    a. Calculate the beta of a firm that goes up on average by 43% when the market goes *up* and goes down by 17% when the market goes *down*.
    b. Calculate the beta of a firm that goes up on average by 18% when the market goes *down* and goes down by 22% when the market goes *up*.
    c. Calculate the beta of a firm that is expected to go up by 4% *independently* of the market.

Beta and the Cost of Capital

23. Suppose the risk-free interest rate is 4%.
    a. i. Use the beta you calculated for the stock in Problem 22 (a) to estimate its expected return.
       ii. How does this compare with the stock's actual expected return?
    b. i. Use the beta you calculated for the stock in Problem 22 (b) to estimate its expected return.
       ii. How does this compare with the stock's actual expected return?

EXCEL

24. Suppose the market risk premium is 6% and the risk-free interest rate is 4%. Using the data in Table 10.6, calculate the expected return of investing in

  a. Suncor Energy Inc.

  b. Bombardier Inc.

  c. Manulife Financial Corporation

25. Suppose the market risk premium is 6.5% and the risk-free interest rate is 5%. Calculate the cost of capital of investing in a project with a beta of 1.2.

26. State whether each of the following is inconsistent with an efficient capital market, the CAPM, or both:

  a. A security with only diversifiable risk has an expected return that exceeds the risk-free interest rate

  b. A security with a beta of 1 had a return last year of 15% when the market had a return of 9%

  c. Small stocks with a beta of 1.5 tend to have higher returns on average than large stocks with a beta of 1.5

DATA CASE

EXCEL

Today is May 21, 2010, and you have just started your new job with a financial planning firm. In addition to studying for all your license exams, you have been asked to review a portion of a client's stock portfolio to determine the risk/return profiles of 12 stocks in the portfolio. Unfortunately, your small firm cannot afford the expensive databases that would provide all this information with a few simple keystrokes, but that's why they have you. Specifically, you have been asked to determine the monthly average returns and standard deviations for the 12 stocks for the past five years. In the following chapters, you will be asked to do more extensive analyses on these same stocks.

The stocks (with their symbols in parentheses) are:

Apple Computer (AAPL)
Archer Daniels Midland (ADM)
Boeing (BA)
Citigroup (C)
Caterpillar (CAT)
Deere & Co. (DE)
Hershey (HSY)
Motorola (MOT)
Proctor and Gamble (PG)
Sirius Satellite Radio (SIRI)
Wal-Mart (WMT)
Yahoo! (YHOO)

1. Collect price information for each stock from Yahoo! Finance (http://finance.yahoo.com) as follows:

  a. Enter the stock symbol. On the page for that stock, click "Historical Prices" on the left side of the page.

  b. Enter the "start date" as May 21, 2004, and the "end date" as May 1, 2008, to cover the five-year period. Make sure you click "monthly" next to the date.

  c. After hitting "Get Prices," scroll to the bottom of the first page and click "Download to Spreadsheet." If you are asked if you want to open or save the file, click open.

    d. Copy the entire spreadsheet, open Excel, and paste the Web data into a spreadsheet. Delete all the columns except the date and the adjusted close (the first and last columns).

    e. Keep the Excel file open and go back to the Yahoo! Finance Web page and hit the back button. If you are asked if you want to save the data, click no.

    f. When you return to the prices page, enter the next stock symbol and hit "Get Prices" again. Do not change the dates or frequency, but make sure you have the same dates for all the stocks you will download. Again, click "Download to Spreadsheet" and then open the file. Copy the last column, "Adj. Close," paste it into the Excel file and change "Adj. Close" to the stock symbol. Make sure that the first and last prices are in the same rows as the first stock.

    g. Repeat these steps for the remaining ten stocks, pasting each closing price right next to the other stocks, again making sure that the correct prices on the correct dates all appear in the same rows.

2. Convert these prices to monthly returns as the percentage change in the monthly prices. (*Hint:* Create a separate worksheet within the Excel file.) Note that to compute a return for each month, you need a beginning and ending price, so you will not be able to compute the return for the first month.

3. Compute the mean monthly returns and standard deviations for the monthly returns of each of the stocks.[13] Convert the monthly statistics to annual statistics for easier interpretation (multiply the mean monthly return by 12, and multiply the monthly standard deviation by $\sqrt{12}$).

4. Add a column in your Excel worksheet with the average return across stocks for each month. This is the monthly return to an equally weighted portfolio of these 12 stocks. Compute the mean and standard deviation of monthly returns for the equally weighted portfolio. Double check that the average return on this equally weighted portfolio is equal to the average return of all of the individual stocks. Convert these monthly statistics to annual statistics (as described in step 3) for interpretation.

5. Using the annual statistics, create an Excel plot with standard deviation (volatility) on the *x*-axis and average return on the *y*-axis as follows:

    a. Create three columns on your spreadsheet with the statistics you created in questions 3 and 4 for each of the individual stocks and the equally weighted portfolio. The first column will have the ticker, the second will have annual standard deviation, and the third will have the annual mean return.

    b. Highlight the data in the last two columns (standard deviation and mean), choose >Insert>Chart>XY Scatter Plot. Complete the chart wizard to finish the plot.

6. What do you notice about the volatilities of the individual stocks, compared to the volatility of the equally weighted portfolio?

---

13. In Eq. 10.4, we showed how to compute returns with stock price and dividend data. The "adjusted close" series from Yahoo! Finance is already adjusted for dividends and splits, so we may compute returns based on the percentage change in monthly adjusted prices.

CHAPTER

11

Optimal Portfolio Choice and the Capital Asset Pricing Model

In this chapter, we quantify the ideas we introduced in Chapter 10, and explain how an investor can choose an efficient portfolio. In particular, we will see how to find the optimal portfolio for an investor who wants to earn the highest possible return given the level of volatility he or she is willing to accept by developing the statistical techniques of *mean-variance portfolio optimization*.[1] Both elegant and practical, these techniques are used routinely by professional investors, money managers, and financial institutions. We then introduce the assumptions of the Capital Asset Pricing Model (CAPM), the most important model of the relationship between risk and return.[2] Under these assumptions, the efficient portfolio is the market portfolio of all stocks and securities. As a result, the expected return of any security depends upon its beta with the market portfolio.

In the last chapter, we explained how to calculate the expected return and volatility of a single stock. To find the efficient portfolio, we must understand how to do the same thing for a portfolio of stocks. We begin this chapter by explaining how to calculate the expected return and volatility of a portfolio. With these statistical tools in hand, we then describe how an investor can create an efficient portfolio out of

---

1. The techniques of portfolio optimization were developed in a 1952 paper by Harry Markowitz, as well as in related work by Andrew Roy (1952) and Bruno de Finetti (1940) (see additional readings for this chapter in the Textbook Resources section on MyFinanceLab).

2. The CAPM was proposed as a model of risk and return by William Sharpe in a 1964 paper, as well as in related papers by Jack Treynor (1962), John Lintner (1965), and Jan Mossin (1966). For their contributions to the theory, Markowitz and Sharpe received the Nobel Prize in economics in 1990.

individual stocks, and consider the implications, if all investors attempt to do so, for an investment's expected return and cost of capital.

In our exploration of these concepts, we take the perspective of a stock market investor. These concepts, however, are also important for a corporate financial manager. After all, financial managers are also investors, investing money on behalf of their shareholders. When a company makes a new investment, financial managers must ensure that the investment has a positive NPV. Doing so requires knowing the cost of capital of the investment opportunity and, as we shall see in the next chapter, the CAPM is the main method used by most major corporations to calculate the cost of capital.

11.1 THE EXPECTED RETURN OF A PORTFOLIO

To find an optimal portfolio, we need a method to define a portfolio and analyze its return. We can describe a portfolio by its **portfolio weights**, the fraction of the total investment in the portfolio held in each individual investment in the portfolio:

$$x_i = \frac{\text{Value of investment } i}{\text{Total value of portfolio}} \tag{11.1}$$

These portfolio weights add up to 1 (that is, $\sum_i x_i = 1$), so that they represent the way we have divided our money between the different individual investments in the portfolio.

As an example, consider a portfolio with 200 shares of Barrick Gold Corp. worth $30 per share and 100 shares of WestJet worth $40 per share. The total value of the portfolio is $200 \times \$30 + 100 \times \$40 = \$10,000$, and the corresponding portfolio weights x_B and x_W are

$$x_B = \frac{200 \times \$30}{10,000} = 60\%$$

$$x_W = \frac{100 \times \$40}{10,000} = 40\%$$

Given the portfolio weights, we can calculate the return on the portfolio. Suppose $x_1, \ldots, x_n$ are the portfolio weights of the n investments in a portfolio, and these investments have returns $R_1, \ldots, R_n$. Then the return on the portfolio, R_P, is the weighted average of the returns on the investments in the portfolio, where the weights correspond to portfolio weights:

$$R_P = x_1 R_1 + x_2 R_2 + \cdots + x_n R_n = \sum_i x_i R_i \tag{11.2}$$

The return of a portfolio is straightforward to compute if we know the returns of the individual stocks and the portfolio weights.

EXAMPLE 11.1   CALCULATING PORTFOLIO RETURNS

Problem

Suppose you buy 200 shares of Barrick Gold Corp. at $30 per share and 100 shares of WestJet at $40 per share. If Barrick's share price goes up to $36 and WestJet's share price falls to $38, what is the new value of the portfolio, and what return did the portfolio earn? Show that Eq. 11.2 holds. After the price changes, what are the new portfolio weights?

Solution

The new value of the portfolio is $200 \times \$36 + 100 \times \$38 = \$11,000$, for a gain of $1000 or a 10% return on your initial $10,000 investment. The return on Barrick stock was $36/30 - 1 = 20\%$, and the return on WestJet stock was $38/40 - 1 = -5\%$. Given the initial portfolio weights of 60% Barrick and 40% WestJet, we can also compute the return of the portfolio from Eq. 11.2:

$$R_P = x_B R_B + x_W R_W = 60\% \times 0.2 + 40\% \times (-0.05) = 10\%$$

After the price change, the new portfolio weights are

$$x_B = \frac{200 \times \$36}{11,000} = 65.45\%$$

$$x_W = \frac{100 \times \$38}{11,000} = 34.55\%$$

Without trading, the weights will increase for those stocks in the portfolio whose returns exceed the portfolio's.

Equation 11.2 also allows us to compute the expected return of a portfolio. Using the facts that the expectation of a sum is just the sum of the expectations and that the expectation of a known multiple is just the multiple of its expectation, we arrive at the following formula for a portfolio's expected return:

$$E[R_P] = E\left[\sum_i x_i R_i\right] = \sum_i E[x_i R_i] = \sum_i x_i E[R_i] \tag{11.3}$$

That is, the expected return of a portfolio is simply the weighted average of the expected returns of the investments within it, using the portfolio weights.

EXAMPLE 11.2

PORTFOLIO EXPECTED RETURN

Problem

Suppose you invest $10,000 in The Forzani Group stock and $30,000 in TransCanada Corp. stock. You expect a return of 10% for The Forzani Group and 16% for TransCanada Corp. What is the expected return for your portfolio?

Solution

You have $40,000 invested in total, so your portfolio weights are $10,000/40,000 = 25\%$ in Forzani and $30,000/40,000 = 75\%$ in TransCanada. Therefore, the expected return on your portfolio is

$$E[R_P] = x_F E[R_F] + x_T E[R_T] = 25\% \times 0.10 + 75\% \times 0.16 = 14.5\%$$

CONCEPT CHECK

1. What is a portfolio weight?

2. How do we calculate the return on a portfolio?

11.2   THE VOLATILITY OF A TWO-STOCK PORTFOLIO

As we explained in Chapter 10, combining stocks in a portfolio eliminates some of their risk through diversification. The amount of risk that will remain depends on the degree to which the stocks are exposed to common risks. In this section we describe the statistical tools that we can use to quantify the risk stocks have in common and determine the volatility of a portfolio.

COMBINING RISKS

Let's begin with a simple example of how risk changes when stocks are combined in a portfolio. Table 11.1 shows returns for three hypothetical stocks, along with their average returns and volatilities. While the three stocks have the same volatility and average return, the pattern of their returns differs. When the airline stocks performed well, the oil stock tended to do poorly (see 2004–2005), and when the airlines did poorly, the oil stock tended to do well (2007–2008).

Table 11.1 also shows the returns for two portfolios of the stocks. The first portfolio consists of equal investments in the two airlines, NorthJet and SouthJet. The second portfolio includes equal investments in SouthJet and AlbertaOil. The average return of both portfolios is equal to the average return of the stocks, consistent with Eq. 11.3. However, their volatilities—12.1% for portfolio 1 and 5.1% for portfolio 2—are very different from the individual stocks *and* from each other.

This example demonstrates two important phenomena. First, by combining stocks into a portfolio, we reduce risk through diversification. Because the prices of the stocks do not move identically, some of the risk is averaged out in a portfolio. As a result, both portfolios have lower risk than the individual stocks. Second, the amount of risk that is eliminated in a portfolio depends on the degree to which the stocks face common risks and their prices move together. Because the two airline stocks tend to perform well or poorly at the same time, the portfolio of airline stocks has a volatility that is only slightly lower than that of the individual stocks. The airline and oil stocks, by contrast, do not move together; indeed, they tend to move in opposite directions. As a result, some risk is cancelled out, making that portfolio much less risky.

| TABLE **11.1** | RETURNS FOR THREE STOCKS, AND PORTFOLIOS OF PAIRS OF STOCKS |

	Stock Returns			Portfolio Returns	
				(1)	(2)
Year	NorthJet	SouthJet	AlbertaOil	$1/2R_N + 1/2R_S$	$1/2R_S + 1/2R_A$
2004	21%	9%	−2%	15.0%	3.5%
2005	30%	21%	−5%	25.5%	8.0%
2006	7%	7%	9%	7.0%	8.0%
2007	−5%	−2%	21%	−3.5%	9.5%
2008	−2%	−5%	30%	−3.5%	12.5%
2009	9%	30%	7%	19.5%	18.5%
Average Return	10.0%	10.0%	10.0%	10.0%	10.0%
Volatility	13.4%	13.4%	13.4%	12.1%	5.1%

DETERMINING COVARIANCE AND CORRELATION

To find the risk of a portfolio, we need to know more than the risk and return of the component stocks: We need to know the degree to which the stocks face common risks and their returns move together. In this section, we introduce two statistical measures, covariance and correlation, that allow us to measure the co-movement of returns.

Covariance is the expected product of the deviations of two returns from their means. The covariance between returns R_i and R_j is defined as follows:

Covariance between Returns R_i and R_j

$$Cov(R_i, R_j) = E[(R_i - E[R_i])(R_j - E[R_j])] \tag{11.4}$$

When estimating the covariance from historical data, we use the formula[3]

Estimate of the Covariance from Historical Data

$$Cov(R_i, R_j) = \frac{1}{T-1} \sum_t (R_{i,t} - \bar{R}_i)(R_{j,t} - \bar{R}_j) \tag{11.5}$$

Intuitively, if two stocks move together, their returns will tend to be above or below average at the same time, and the covariance will be positive. If the stocks move in opposite directions, one will tend to be above average when the other is below average, and the covariance will be negative.

CORRELATION.   While the sign of the covariance is easy to interpret, its magnitude is not. It will be larger if the stocks are more volatile (and so have larger deviations from their expected returns), and it will be larger the more closely the stocks move in relation to each other. In order to control for the volatility of each stock, and quantify the strength of the relationship between them, we can calculate the **correlation** between two stock returns, defined as the covariance of the returns divided by the standard deviation of each return:

$$Corr(R_i, R_j) = \frac{Cov(R_i, R_j)}{SD(R_i)\ SD(R_j)} \tag{11.6}$$

The correlation between two stocks has the same sign as their covariance, so it has a similar interpretation. Dividing by the volatilities ensures that correlation is always between -1 and $+1$, which allows us to gauge the strength of the relationship between the stocks. As Figure 11.1 shows, correlation is a barometer of the degree to which the

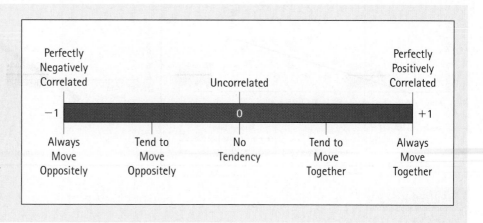

FIGURE 11.1

Correlation

Correlation measures how returns move in relation to each other. It is between $+1$ (returns always move together) and -1 (returns always move oppositely). Independent risks have no tendency to move together and have zero correlation.

3. As with Eq. 10.7 for historical volatility, we divide by $T-1$ rather than by T to make up for the fact that we have used the data to compute the average returns $\bar{R}$, eliminating a degree of freedom.

Each graph shows observations of Stock j's returns plotted against Stock i's returns. As you can see in Graph A, when there is perfect negative correlation, $\text{Corr}(R_i, R_j) = -1$, the plots all fall on a perfectly straight line that is downward sloping. In Graph B, there is negative correlation between the two stocks' returns, $\text{Corr}(R_i, R_j) = -0.5$, so we see a negative relationship as shown by the line of best fit, but because of the weaker relationship compared to Graph A, the points do not all fall on the regression line. With zero correlation, Graph C, there is no relationship between the two stocks' returns and there is no line that best describes the relationship. The two stocks' returns are independent of each other. Graph D shows the plots with positive correlation, $\text{Corr}(R_i, R_j) = +0.5$. The two stocks' returns tend to move together as shown by the line of best fit, but the relationship is not perfect so we see deviations from the line. Finally, in Graph E, we see the results if two stocks' returns are perfectly positively correlated, $\text{Corr}(R_i, R_j) = +1$. There is positive relationship between the two stocks' returns, and because the correlation is $+1$, their returns fall on a perfectly straight line that is upward sloping.

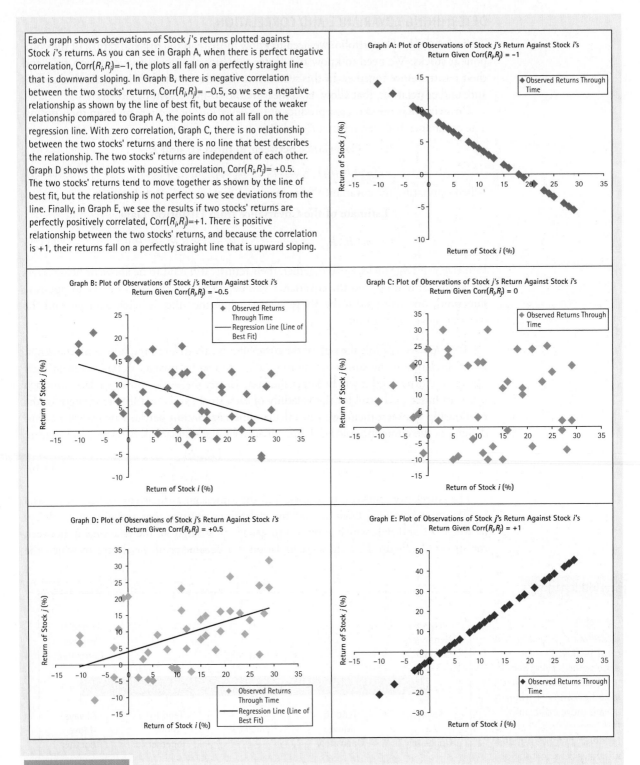

FIGURE 11.11

(Continued)

returns share common risk and tend to move together. The closer the correlation is to $+1$, the more two stocks' returns tend to move as a result of a common risk. When the correlation (and thus the covariance) equals 0, the returns are *uncorrelated*; that is, they have no tendency to move either together or in opposition to one another. Independent risks are uncorrelated. Finally, the closer the correlation is to -1, the more the two stocks' returns tend to move in opposite directions.

EXAMPLE 11.3	COMPUTING THE COVARIANCE AND CORRELATION

Problem

Using the data in Table 11.1, what are the covariance and the correlation between NorthJet and SouthJet? Between SouthJet and AlbertaOil?

Solution

First we compute the deviation of each return from its mean by subtracting the average return of each stock (10%) from the returns in Table 11.1. Then we compute the product of these deviations between the pairs of stocks, sum them, and divide by $T - 1 = 5$ to compute the covariance, as in Table 11.2.

From the table, we can see that NorthJet and SouthJet have a positive covariance (0.0112), indicating a tendency to move together, whereas SouthJet and AlbertaOil have a negative covariance (-0.0128), indicating a tendency to move oppositely. We can determine the strength of these tendencies by computing the correlation, which we obtain by dividing the covariance by the standard deviation of each stock (13.4%). The correlation for NorthJet and SouthJet is 62.4%; the correlation for SouthJet and AlbertaOil is -71.3%.

TABLE 11.2	COMPUTING THE COVARIANCE AND CORRELATION BETWEEN PAIRS OF STOCKS

Year	Deviation from Mean $(R_N - \bar{R}_N)$	$(R_S - \bar{R}_S)$	$(R_A - \bar{R}_A)$	NorthJet and SouthJet $(R_N - \bar{R}_N)(R_S - \bar{R}_S)$	SouthJet and AlbertaOil $(R_S - \bar{R}_S)(R_A - \bar{R}_A)$
2004	11%	-1%	-12%	-0.0011	0.0012
2005	20%	11%	-15%	0.0220	-0.0165
2006	-3%	-3%	-1%	0.0009	0.0003
2007	-15%	-12%	11%	0.0180	-0.0132
2008	-12%	-15%	20%	0.0180	-0.0300
2009	-1%	20%	-3%	-0.0020	-0.0060
Sum $= \sum_t (R_{i,t} - \bar{R}_i)(R_{j,t} - \bar{R}_j) =$				0.0558	-0.0642
Covariance: $Cov(R_i, R_j) = \dfrac{1}{T-1}$ Sum $=$				0.0112	-0.0128
Correlation: $Corr(R_i, R_j) = \dfrac{Cov(R_i, R_j)}{SD(R_i)\ SD(R_j)} =$				0.624	-0.713

EXAMPLE 11.4	THE COVARIANCE AND CORRELATION OF A STOCK WITH ITSELF

Problem

What are the covariance and the correlation of a stock's return with itself?

Solution

Let R_s be the stock's return. From the definition of the covariance,

$$Cov(R_s, R_s) = E[(R_s - E[R_s])(R_s - E[R_s])] = E[(R_s - E[R_s])^2]$$
$$= Var(R_s)$$

where the last equation follows from the definition of the variance. That is, the covariance of a stock with itself is simply its variance. Then,

$$Corr(R_s, R_s) = \frac{Cov(R_s, R_s)}{SD(R_s)\ SD(R_s)} = \frac{Var(R_s)}{SD(R_s)^2} = 1$$

where the last equation follows from the definition of the standard deviation. That is, a stock's return is perfectly positively correlated with itself, as it always moves together with itself in perfect synchronicity.

When will stock returns be highly correlated with each other? Stock returns will tend to move together if they are affected similarly by economic events. Thus stocks in the same industry tend to have more highly correlated returns than stocks in different industries. This tendency is illustrated in Table 11.3, which shows the volatility of individual stock returns and the correlation between them for several common stocks. General Mills, the only food

TABLE 11.3	HISTORICAL ANNUAL VOLATILITIES AND CORRELATIONS FOR SELECTED STOCKS (BASED ON MONTHLY RETURNS, 1996–2008)

	Microsoft	Dell	Alaska Air	Southwest Airlines	Ford Motor	General Motors	General Mills
Volatility (Standard Deviation)	37%	50%	38%	31%	42%	41%	18%
Correlation with							
Microsoft	1.00	0.62	0.25	0.23	0.26	0.23	0.10
Dell	0.62	1.00	0.19	0.21	0.31	0.28	0.07
Alaska Air	0.25	0.19	1.00	0.30	0.16	0.13	0.11
Southwest Airlines	0.23	0.21	0.30	1.00	0.25	0.22	0.20
Ford Motor	0.26	0.31	0.16	0.25	1.00	0.62	0.07
General Motors	0.23	0.28	0.13	0.22	0.62	1.00	0.02
General Mills	0.10	0.07	0.11	0.20	0.07	0.02	1.00

COMPUTING THE VARIANCE, COVARIANCE, AND CORRELATION IN MICROSOFT EXCEL

The computer spreadsheet program Excel does not compute the standard deviation, variance, covariance, and correlation consistently. The Excel functions STDEV and VAR correctly use Eq. 10.7 to estimate the standard deviation and variance from historical data. But the Excel function COVAR does *not* use Eq. 11.5; instead, Excel divides by T instead of $T - 1$. Therefore, to estimate the covariance from a sample of historical returns using COVAR, you must correct the inconsistency by multiplying by the number of data points and dividing by the number of data points minus one; that is, $COVAR * T/(T - 1)$. Alternatively, you can use the function CORREL to compute the correlation. Because the function CORREL is implemented in a way that is consistent with STDEV and VAR, you can estimate the covariance by multiplying the correlation by the standard deviation of each return.

processing firm, has the lowest correlation with all the stocks, whereas each of the other stocks is most highly correlated with the other firm in its industry. All of the correlations are positive, however, illustrating the general tendency of stocks to move together.

EXAMPLE 11.5

COMPUTING THE COVARIANCE FROM THE CORRELATION

Problem

Using the data from Table 11.3, what is the covariance between Microsoft and Dell?

Solution

We can rewrite Eq. 11.6 to solve for the covariance:

$$Cov(R_{MSFT}, R_{DELL}) = Corr(R_{MSFT}, R_{DELL})\, SD(R_{MSFT})\, SD(R_{DELL})$$
$$= (0.62)\,(0.37)\,(0.50) = 0.1147$$

COMPUTING A PORTFOLIO'S VARIANCE AND VOLATILITY

We now have the tools needed to compute the variance of a portfolio. Recall from Example 11.4 that the variance of a return is equal to the covariance of a return with itself. Therefore, for a two-stock portfolio with $R_P = x_1 R_1 + x_2 R_2$,

$$
\begin{aligned}
Var(R_P) &= Cov(R_P, R_P) \\
&= Cov(x_1 R_1 + x_2 R_2, x_1 R_1 + x_2 R_2) \qquad (11.7)\\
&= x_1 x_1 Cov(R_1, R_1) + x_1 x_2 Cov(R_1, R_2) + x_2 x_1 Cov(R_2, R_1) + x_2 x_2 Cov(R_2, R_2)
\end{aligned}
$$

In the last line of Eq. 11.7, we use the fact that, as with expectations, we can change the order of the covariance with sums and multiples.[4] By combining terms and recognizing

---

4. That is, $Cov(A + B, C) = Cov(A, C) + Cov(B, C)$ and $Cov(mA, B) = m\, Cov(A, B)$.

that $Cov(R_i, R_i) = Var(R_i)$, we arrive at our main result of this section:

The Variance of a Two-Stock Portfolio

$$Var(R_P) = x_1^2 Var(R_1) + x_2^2 Var(R_2) + 2x_1 x_2 Cov(R_1, R_2) \qquad (11.8)$$

As always, the volatility is the square root of the variance, $SD(R_P) = \sqrt{Var(R_P)}$.

Let's check this formula for the airline and oil stocks in Table 11.1. Consider the portfolio containing shares of SouthJet and AlbertaOil. The variance of each stock is equal to the square of its volatility, $0.134^2 = 0.018$. From Example 11.3, the covariance between the stocks is -0.0128. Therefore, the variance of a portfolio with 50% invested in each stock is

$$
\begin{aligned}
Var\left(\tfrac{1}{2}R_S + \tfrac{1}{2}R_A\right) &= x_S^2 Var(R_S) + x_A^2 Var(R_A) + 2x_S x_A Cov(R_S, R_A) \\
&= \left(\tfrac{1}{2}\right)^2 (0.018) + \left(\tfrac{1}{2}\right)^2 (0.018) + 2\left(\tfrac{1}{2}\right)\left(\tfrac{1}{2}\right)(-0.0128) \\
&= 0.0026
\end{aligned}
$$

The volatility of the portfolio is $\sqrt{0.0026} = 5.1\%$, which corresponds to the calculation in Table 11.1. If we repeat this calculation for the NorthJet and SouthJet portfolio, the calculation is the same except for the stocks' higher covariance of 0.112, which leads to a higher volatility of 12.1%.

As we saw in Table 11.1, Eq. 11.8 shows that the variance of the portfolio depends on the variance of the individual stocks *and* on the covariance between them. We can also rewrite Eq. 11.8 using the stocks' volatilities and calculating the covariance from the correlation as in Example 11.5:

$$Var(R_P) = x_1^2 SD(R_1)^2 + x_2^2 SD(R_2)^2 + 2x_1 x_2 Corr(R_1, R_2) SD(R_1) SD(R_2) \qquad (11.9)$$

Equations 11.8 and 11.9 demonstrate that with a positive amount invested in each stock, the more the stocks move together and the higher their covariance or correlation, the more variable the portfolio will be. The portfolio will have the greatest variance if the stocks have a perfect positive correlation of $+1$.

EXAMPLE 11.6   COMPUTING THE VOLATILITY OF A TWO-STOCK PORTFOLIO

Problem

Using the data from Table 11.3, what is the volatility of a portfolio with equal amounts invested in Microsoft and Dell stock? What is the volatility of a portfolio with equal amounts invested in Dell and Alaska Air stock?

Solution

With portfolio weights of 50% each in Microsoft and Dell stock, from Eq. 11.9, the portfolio's variance is

$$
\begin{aligned}
&= x_M^2 SD(R_M)^2 + x_D^2 SD(R_D)^2 + 2x_M x_D Corr(R_M, R_D) SD(R_M) SD(R_D) \\
Var(R_P) &= (0.50)^2 (0.37)^2 + (0.50)^2 (0.50)^2 + 2(0.50)(0.50)(0.62)(0.37)(0.50) \\
&= 0.1541
\end{aligned}
$$

The volatility is therefore $SD(R_P) = \sqrt{Var(R_P)} = \sqrt{0.1541} = 39.3\%$

For the portfolio of Dell and Alaska (ALK) stock,

$$= x_D^2 SD(R_D)^2 + x_A^2 SD(R_A)^2 + 2x_D x_A Corr(R_D, R_A) SD(R_D) SD(R_A)$$

$$= (0.50)^2(0.50)^2 + (0.50)^2(0.38)^2 + 2(0.50)(0.50)(0.19)(0.50)(0.38)$$

$$= 0.1167$$

The volatility in this case is $SD(R_P) = \sqrt{Var(R_P)} = \sqrt{0.1167} = 34.2\%$.

Note that the portfolio of Dell and Alaska Air stock is less volatile than either of the individual stocks. It is also less volatile than the portfolio of Dell and Microsoft stock. Even though Alaska Air's stock returns are more volatile than Microsoft's, its much lower correlation with Dell's returns leads to greater diversification in the portfolio.

CONCEPT CHECK

1. What is the correlation measure?

2. How does the correlation between the stocks affect the portfolio's volatility?

11.3 THE VOLATILITY OF A LARGE PORTFOLIO

We can gain additional benefits of diversification by holding more than two stocks in our portfolio. Let's consider how to calculate the volatility of a large portfolio, and determine the amount of diversification that is possible if we hold many stocks.

LARGE PORTFOLIO VARIANCE

Recall that the return on a portfolio of n stocks is simply the weighted average of the returns of the stocks in the portfolio:

$$R_P = x_1 R_1 + x_2 R_2 + \cdots + x_n R_n = \sum_i x_i R_i$$

Using the properties of the covariance, we can write the variance of a portfolio as follows:

$$Var(R_P) = Cov(R_P, R_P) = Cov(\textstyle\sum_i x_i R_i, R_P) = \sum_i x_i \, Cov(R_i, R_P) \quad (11.10)$$

This equation indicates that the *variance of a portfolio is equal to the weighted average covariance of each stock with the portfolio.* This expression reveals that the risk of a portfolio depends on how each stock's return moves in relation to it.

We can reduce the formula even further by replacing the second R_P with a weighted average and simplifying:

$$Var(R_P) = \sum_i x_i \, Cov(R_i, R_P) = \sum_i x_i \, Cov(R_i, \textstyle\sum_j x_j R_j)$$

$$= \sum_i \sum_j x_i x_j \, Cov(R_i, R_j) \quad (11.11)$$

This formula says that the variance of a portfolio is equal to the sum of the covariances of the returns of all pairs of stocks in the portfolio multiplied by each of their portfolio weights.[5] That is, the overall variability of the portfolio depends on the total co-movement of the stocks within it.

---

5. Looking back, we can see that Eq. 11.11 generalizes the case of two stocks in Eq. 11.7.

DIVERSIFICATION WITH AN EQUALLY WEIGHTED PORTFOLIO

We can use Eq. 11.11 to calculate the variance of an **equally weighted portfolio**, a portfolio in which the same amount is invested in each stock; thus, $x_i = 1/n$ for each stock. In this case, we have the following formula:[6]

Variance of an Equally Weighted Portfolio of n Stocks

$$Var(R_P) = \frac{1}{n}(\text{Average Variance of the Individual Stocks})$$

$$+ \left(1 - \frac{1}{n}\right)(\text{Average Covariance between the Stocks}) \quad (11.12)$$

Equation 11.12 demonstrates that as the number of stocks, n, grows large, the variance of the portfolio is determined primarily by the average covariance among the stocks. Consider a portfolio of stocks selected randomly from the stock market. The historical volatility of the return of a typical large firm in the stock market is about 40%, and the typical correlation between the returns of large firms is about 28%. Given these statistics, how does the volatility of an equally weighted portfolio vary with the number of stocks?

From Eq. 11.12, the volatility of an n-stock portfolio is given by

$$SD(R_P) = \sqrt{\frac{1}{n}(0.40^2) + \left(1 - \frac{1}{n}\right)(0.28 \times 0.40 \times 0.40)}$$

We graph the volatility for different numbers of stocks in Figure 11.2. Note that the volatility declines as the number of stocks in the portfolio grows. In fact, nearly half of the

FIGURE 11.2

Volatility of an Equally Weighted Portfolio Versus the Number of Stocks

The volatility declines as the number of stocks in the portfolio increases. Even in a very large portfolio, however, market risk remains.

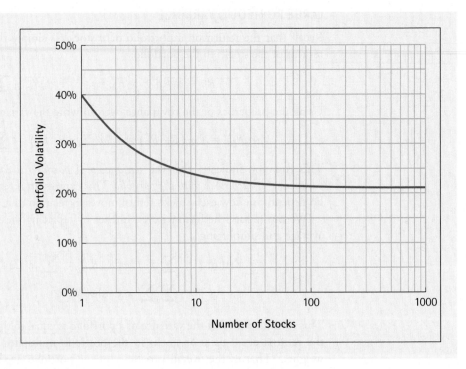

6. For an n-stock portfolio, there are n variance terms (anytime $i = j$ in Eq. 11.11) with weight $x_i^2 = 1/n^2$ on each, which implies a weight of $n/n^2 = 1/n$ on the average variance. There are $n^2 - n$ covariance terms (all the $n \times n$ pairs minus the n variance terms) with weight $x_i x_j = 1/n^2$ on each, which implies a weight of $(n^2 - n)/n^2 = 1 - 1/n$ on the average covariance.

volatility of the individual stocks is eliminated in a large portfolio as the result of diversification. The benefit of diversification is most dramatic initially: The decrease in volatility when going from one to two stocks is much larger than the decrease when going from 100 to 101 stocks—indeed, almost all of the benefit of diversification can be achieved with about 30 stocks. Even for a very large portfolio, however, we cannot eliminate all risk. The variance of the portfolio converges to the average covariance, so the volatility declines to $\sqrt{0.28 \times 0.4 \times 0.4} = 21.17\%$.[7]

EXAMPLE 11.7 DIVERSIFICATION USING DIFFERENT TYPES OF STOCKS

Problem

Stocks within a single industry tend to have a higher correlation than stocks in different industries. Likewise, stocks in different countries have lower correlation on average than stocks within Canada. What is the volatility of a very large portfolio of stocks within an industry in which the stocks have a volatility of 40% and a correlation of 60%? What is the volatility of a very large portfolio of international stocks with a volatility of 40% and a correlation of 10%?

Solution

From Eq. 11.12, the volatility of the industry portfolio as $n \to \infty$ is given by

$$\sqrt{\text{Average Covariance}} = \sqrt{0.60 \times 0.40 \times 0.40} = 31.0\%$$

This volatility is higher than when using stocks from different industries as in Figure 11.2. Combining stocks from the same industry that are more highly correlated therefore provides less diversification. We can achieve superior diversification using international stocks. In this case,

$$\sqrt{\text{Average Covariance}} = \sqrt{0.10 \times 0.40 \times 0.40} = 12.6\%$$

Equation 11.12 can also be used to derive one of the key results that we discussed in Chapter 10: When risks are independent, all of the risk can be diversified by holding a large portfolio.

EXAMPLE 11.8 VOLATILITY WHEN RISKS ARE INDEPENDENT

Problem

What is the volatility of an equally weighted average of n independent, identical risks?

---

7. You might wonder what happens if the average covariance is negative. It turns out that while the covariance between a pair of stocks can be negative, as the portfolio grows large the average covariance cannot be negative because the returns of all stocks cannot move in opposite directions simultaneously.

Solution

If risks are independent, they are uncorrelated and their covariance is zero. Using Eq. 11.12, the volatility of an equally weighted portfolio of the risks is

$$SD(R_P) = \sqrt{Var(R_P)} = \sqrt{\tfrac{1}{n} Var(\text{Individual Risk})} = \frac{SD(\text{Individual Risk})}{\sqrt{n}}$$

This result coincides with Eq. 10.8, which we used earlier to evaluate independent risks. Note that as $n \rightarrow \infty$, the volatility goes to 0, that is, a very large portfolio will have *no* risk. In this case, all risk can be eliminated because there is no common risk.

DIVERSIFICATION WITH GENERAL PORTFOLIOS

The results in the last section depend on the portfolio being equally weighted. For a portfolio with arbitrary weights, we can rewrite Eq. 11.10 in terms of the correlation as follows:

$$Var(R_P) = \sum_i x_i \, Cov(R_i, R_P) = \sum_i x_i \, SD(R_i) SD(R_P) Corr(R_i, R_P)$$

Dividing both sides of this equation by the standard deviation of the portfolio yields the following important decomposition of the volatility of a portfolio:

Volatility of a Portfolio with Arbitrary Weights

Security i's contribution to the
volatility of the portfolio

$$SD(R_P) = \sum_i \underbrace{x_i \times SD(R_i) \times Corr(R_i, R_P)}_{} \tag{11.13}$$

Amount of i held   Total Risk of i Fraction of i's risk that is common to P

Equation 11.13 states that each security contributes to the volatility of the portfolio according to its volatility, or total risk, scaled by its correlation with the portfolio, which adjusts for the fraction of the total risk that is common to the portfolio. Therefore, when combining stocks into a portfolio that puts positive weight on each stock, unless all of the stocks have a perfect positive correlation of $+1$ with the portfolio (and thus with one another), the risk of the portfolio will be lower than the weighted average volatility of the individual stocks:

$$SD(R_P) = \sum_i x_i SD(R_i) \, Corr(R_i, R_P) < \sum_i x_i SD(R_i) \tag{11.14}$$

Contrast Eq. 11.14 with Eq. 11.3 for the expected return. The expected return of a portfolio is equal to the weighted average expected return, but the volatility of a portfolio is *less than* the weighted average volatility: We can eliminate some volatility by diversifying.

CONCEPT CHECK

1. How does the volatility of an equally weighted portfolio change as more stocks are added to it?

2. How does the volatility of a portfolio compare with the weighted average volatility of the stocks within it?

11.4 RISK VERSUS RETURN: CHOOSING AN EFFICIENT PORTFOLIO

Now that we understand how to calculate the expected return and volatility of a portfolio, we can return to the main goal of the chapter: how an investor can create an efficient portfolio. Let's start with the simplest case—an investor who can choose between only two stocks.

EFFICIENT PORTFOLIOS WITH TWO STOCKS

Consider a portfolio of Intel and Coca-Cola stock. Suppose an investor believes these stocks will perform as follows:

| Stock | Expected Return | Volatility | Correlation with ... | |
			Intel	Coca-Cola
Intel	26%	50%	1.0	0.0
Coca-Cola	6%	25%	0.0	1.0

How should the investor choose a portfolio of these two stocks? Are some portfolios preferable to others?

Let's compute the expected return and volatility for different combinations of the stocks. Consider a portfolio with 40% invested in Intel stock and 60% invested in Coca-Cola stock. We can compute the expected return from Eq. 11.3 as

$$E[R_{40-60}] = x_I E[R_I] + x_C E[R_C] = 0.40(26\%) + 0.60(6\%) = 14\%$$

We can compute the variance using Eq. 11.9,

$$Var(R_{40-60}) = x_I^2 SD(R_I)^2 + x_C^2 SD(R_C)^2 + 2x_I x_C Corr(R_I, R_C) SD(R_I) SD(R_C)$$

$$= 0.40^2(0.50)^2 + 0.60^2(0.25)^2 + 2(0.40)(0.60)(0)(0.50)(0.25)$$

$$= 0.0625$$

so that the volatility is $SD(R_{40-60}) = \sqrt{0.0625} = 25\%$. Table 11.4 shows the results for different portfolio weights.

Due to diversification, it is possible to find a portfolio with even lower volatility than either stock: Investing 20% in Intel stock and 80% in Coca-Cola stock, for example, has a volatility of only 22.3%. But knowing that investors care about volatility *and* expected return, we must consider both simultaneously. To do so, we plot the volatility and expected return of each portfolio in Figure 11.3. We labelled the portfolios from Table 11.4 with the portfolio weights. The curve (a hyperbola) represents the set of portfolios that we can create using arbitrary weights.

Faced with the choices in Figure 11.3, which ones make sense for an investor who is concerned with both the expected return and the volatility of her portfolio? Suppose the investor considers investing 100% in Coca-Cola stock. As we can see from Figure 11.3, other portfolios—such as the portfolio with 20% in Intel stock and 80% in Coca-Cola stock—make the investor better off in *both* ways: (1) They have a higher expected return and (2) they have lower volatility. As a result, investing solely in Coca-Cola stock is not a good idea.

IDENTIFYING INEFFICIENT PORTFOLIOS. More generally, we say a portfolio is an **inefficient portfolio** whenever it is possible to find another portfolio that is better in

EXPECTED RETURNS AND VOLATILITY FOR DIFFERENT PORTFOLIOS OF TWO STOCKS

TABLE 11.4

Portfolio	Weights	Expected Return (%)	Volatility (%)
x_I	x_C	$E[R_P]$	$SD[R_P]$
1.00	0.00	26.0	50.0
0.80	0.20	22.0	40.3
0.60	0.40	18.0	31.6
0.40	0.60	14.0	25.0
0.20	0.80	10.0	22.3
0.00	1.00	6.0	25.0

FIGURE 11.3

Volatility Versus Expected Return for Portfolios of Intel and Coca-Cola Stock

Labels indicate portfolio weights (x_I, x_C) for Intel and Coca-Cola stocks. Portfolios on the red portion of the curve, with at least 20% invested in Intel stock, are efficient. Those on the blue portion of the curve, with less than 20% invested in Intel stock, are inefficient—an investor can earn a higher expected return with lower risk by choosing an alternative portfolio.

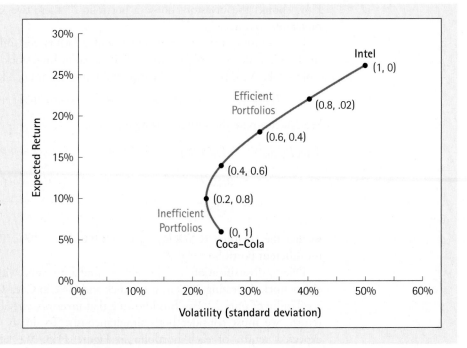

terms of both expected return and volatility. Looking at Figure 11.3, a portfolio is inefficient if there are other portfolios above and to the left—that is, to the northwest—of it. Investing solely in Coca-Cola stock is inefficient, and the same is true of all portfolios with more than 80% in Coca-Cola stock (the blue part of the curve). Inefficient portfolios are not optimal for an investor.

IDENTIFYING EFFICIENT PORTFOLIOS.   By contrast, portfolios with at least 20% in Intel stock are efficient (the red part of the curve): There is no other portfolio of the two stocks that offers a higher expected return with lower volatility. But while we can rule out inefficient portfolios as inferior investment choices, we cannot easily rank the efficient ones: investors will choose among them based on their own preferences for return versus risk. For example, an extremely conservative investor who cares only about minimizing risk would choose the lowest-volatility portfolio (20% Intel, 80% Coca-Cola). An aggressive investor might choose to invest 100% in Intel stock—even though that approach is riskier, the investor may be willing to take that chance to earn a higher expected return.

EXAMPLE 11.9

IMPROVING RETURNS WITH AN EFFICIENT PORTFOLIO

Problem

Sally Ferson has invested 100% of her money in Coca-Cola stock and is seeking investment advice. She would like to earn the highest expected return possible without increasing her volatility. Which portfolio would you recommend?

Solution

In Figure 11.3, we can see that Sally can invest up to 40% in Intel stock without increasing her volatility. Because Intel stock has a higher expected return than Coca-Cola stock, she will earn higher expected returns by putting more money in Intel stock. Therefore, you should recommend that Sally put 40% of her money in Intel stock, leaving 60% in Coca-Cola stock. This portfolio has the same volatility of 25%, but an expected return of 14% rather than the 6% she has now.

THE EFFECT OF CORRELATION

In Figure 11.3, we assumed that the returns of Intel and Coca-Cola stocks are uncorrelated. Let's consider how the risk and return combinations in the figure would change if the correlations were different.

Correlation has no effect on the expected return of a portfolio. For example, a 40–60 portfolio will still have an expected return of 14%. However, the volatility of the portfolio will differ depending on the correlation, as we saw in Section 11.2. In particular, the lower the correlation, the lower the volatility we can obtain. In terms of Figure 11.3, as we lower the correlation and therefore the volatility of the portfolios, the curve showing the portfolios will bend to the left to a greater degree. This effect is illustrated in Figure 11.4.

When the stocks are perfectly positively correlated, the set of portfolios is identified by the straight line between them. In this extreme case (the red line in Figure 11.4), the volatility of the portfolio is equal to the weighted average volatility of the two stocks—there is no diversification. When the correlation is less than 1, however, the volatility of the portfolios is reduced due to diversification, and the curve bends to the left. The reduction in risk (and the bending of the curve) becomes greater as the correlation decreases. At the other extreme of perfect negative correlation (blue line), the line again becomes straight, this time reflecting off the vertical axis. In particular, when the two stocks are perfectly negatively correlated, it becomes possible to hold a portfolio that bears absolutely no risk.

SHORT SALES

Thus far we have considered only portfolios in which we invest a positive amount in each stock. A positive investment in a security can be referred to as a **long position** in the security. But it is also possible to invest a *negative* amount in a stock, called a **short position**, by engaging in a **short sale**, a transaction in which you sell a stock that you do not own and then buy that stock back in the future. (For the mechanics of a short sale, see the box on page 373). As Example 11.10 shows, we can include a short position as part of a portfolio by assigning that stock a negative portfolio weight.

Effect on Volatility and Expected Return of Changing the Correlation between Intel and Coca-Cola Stock

This figure illustrates correlations of 1, 0.5, 0, −0.5, and −1. The lower the correlation, the lower the risk of the portfolios.

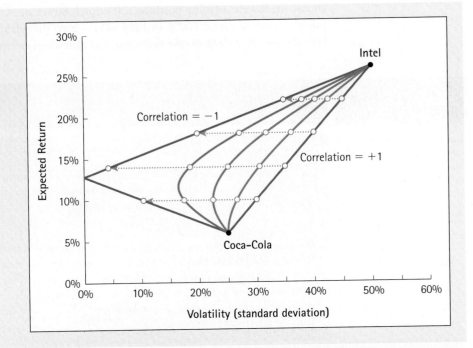

EXAMPLE **11.10**

EXPECTED RETURN AND VOLATILITY WITH A SHORT SALE

Problem

Suppose you have $20,000 in cash to invest. You decide to short sell $10,000 worth of Coca-Cola stock and invest the proceeds from your short sale, plus your $20,000, in Intel. What is the expected return and volatility of your portfolio?

Solution

We can think of our short sale as a negative investment of −$10,000 in Coca-Cola stock. We then invested $30,000 (the $10,000 proceeds from your short sale, plus your $20,000) in Intel stock. The corresponding portfolio weights are

$$x_I = \frac{\text{Value of Investment in Intel}}{\text{Total Value of Portfolio}} = \frac{30,000}{20,000} = 150\%$$

$$x_C = \frac{\text{Value of Investment in Coca-Cola}}{\text{Total Value of Portfolio}} = \frac{-10,000}{20,000} = -50\%$$

Note that the portfolio weights still add up to 100%. Using these portfolio weights, we can calculate the expected return and volatility of the portfolio using Eqs. 11.3 and 11.8 as before:

$$E[R_P] = X_I E[R_I] + x_C E[R_C] = 1.50 \times 26\% + (-0.50) \times 6\% = 36\%$$

$$SD(R_P) = \sqrt{Var(R_P)} = \sqrt{x_I^2 Var(R_I) + x_C^2 Var(R_C) + 2x_I x_C Cov(R_I, R_C)}$$

$$= \sqrt{1.5^2 \times 0.50^2 + (-0.5)^2 \times 0.25^2 + 2(1.5)(-0.5)(0)} = 76.0\%$$

Note that in this case, short selling increases the expected return of your portfolio, but also its volatility, above those of the individual stocks.

THE MECHANICS OF A SHORT SALE

At the end of 2007 it was becoming apparent that the Canadian Imperial Bank of Commerce (CIBC) had substantial exposure to the subprime mortgage crisis in the U.S. and problems in the market for asset-backed commercial paper in Canada. In early October 2007, CIBC's stock price was still about $100 per share. By February 26, 2008, its stock had fallen to $69.28 per share. CIBC was set to file its interim financial statements on February 28, 2008. On the day the statements were made public, CIBC's stock dropped to $67.07 per share but many investors felt it had further to fall. The **short interest** (number of shares sold short) in CIBC exceeded 12.6 million shares.

How do you sell CIBC stock if you do not own it? To short sell a stock, you must contact your broker. Your broker will try to borrow the stock from someone who currently owns it. Suppose John Doe currently holds CIBC stock in a brokerage account. Your broker can lend you shares from John Doe's account so that you can sell them in the market at the current stock price. Of course, at some point you must close the short sale and return the shares to John Doe. So, you will buy the shares in the market, and your broker will replace them in John Doe's account. In the meantime, you must also pay John Doe any dividends that CIBC would have paid him had you not borrowed his shares.*

The chart illustrates the cash flows from a short sale. First you receive the current price of the stock. Then you must pay any dividends. Finally you pay the future stock price. This is exactly the reverse of the cash flows you receive from buying a stock:

	Date 0	Date t	Date 1
Cash flows from buying a stock	$-P_0$	$+Div_t$	$+P_1$
Cash flows from short selling a stock	$+P_0$	$-Div_t$	$-P_1$

Because the cash flows are reversed, if you short sell a stock, rather than receiving its return, you must *pay* its return to the person from whom you borrowed the stock. In this way, short selling is like borrowing money at an interest rate equal to the return on the stock (which is unknown until the transaction is completed).[†] Investors who believed CIBC stock would have a low or negative return might therefore decide to short sell the stock. In fact, an investor who short sold 1000 CIBC shares on February 28, 2008, for $67.07 per share and closed the short position on March 17, 2008, at a price of $56.21 per share would have made $10,860.

The Cash Flows Associated with a Short Sale
P_0 is the initial price of the stock, P_1 is the price of the stock when the short sale is closed, and Div_t are dividends paid by the stock at any date t between 0 and 1.

---

*In practice, John Doe may not even know his shares of the stock have been borrowed. He continues to receive dividends as before and, should he need the shares for any reason, the broker will replace them by either (1) borrowing shares from someone else or (2) forcing the short-seller to close his position and buy the shares in the market.

[†]Typically, the broker will charge a fee for finding the shares to borrow, and require the short-seller to deposit collateral guaranteeing the short-seller's ability to buy the stock later. The fees and the opportunity cost of depositing collateral tend to be small, so we ignore them in our analysis.

FIGURE 11.5

Portfolios of Intel and Coca-Cola Allowing for Short Sales

Labels indicate portfolio weights (x_I, x_C) for Intel and Coca-Cola stocks. Red indicates efficient portfolios; blue indicates inefficient portfolios. The dashed curves indicate positions that require shorting either Coca-Cola (red) or Intel (blue). Shorting Intel to invest in Coca-Cola is inefficient. Shorting Coca-Cola to invest in Intel is efficient and might be attractive to an aggressive investor who is seeking high expected returns.

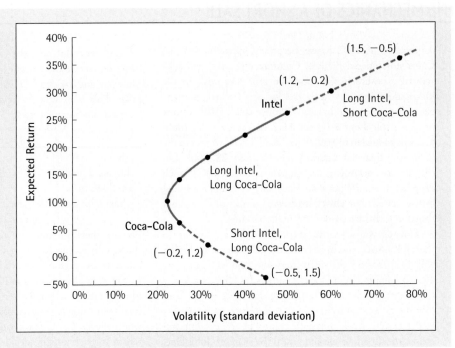

Short selling is clearly profitable if you expect a stock's price to decline in the future. When you borrow a stock to short sell it, you are obligated to buy and return it in the future. So when the stock price declines you receive more upfront for the shares than the cost to replace them in the future. But as the above example shows, it can be advantageous even if you expect the stock's price to rise, as long as you invest the proceeds in another stock with an even higher expected return. That said, as the example also shows, short selling can greatly increase the risk of the portfolio.

In Figure 11.5, we show the effect on the investor's choice set when we allow for short sales. Short selling Intel to invest in Coca-Cola is not efficient (blue dashed curve)—other portfolios exist that have a higher expected return *and* a lower volatility. However, because Intel is expected to outperform Coca-Cola, short selling Coca-Cola to invest in Intel is efficient in this case. While such a strategy leads to a higher volatility, it also provides the investor with a higher expected return. This strategy could be attractive to an aggressive investor. In general, short selling leads to higher expected returns if the stocks that are shorted are expected to have lower returns than the stocks in which the portfolio is long.

EFFICIENT PORTFOLIOS WITH MANY STOCKS

Recall from Section 11.3 that adding more stocks to a portfolio reduces risk through diversification. Let's consider the effect of adding a third stock to our portfolio, Bore Industries, which is uncorrelated with Intel and Coca-Cola but is expected to have a very low return of 2%, and the same volatility as Coca-Cola (25%). Figure 11.6 illustrates the portfolios that we can construct using these three stocks.

Because Bore stock is inferior to Coca-Cola stock—it has the same volatility but a lower return—you might guess that no investor would want to hold a long position in Bore. However, that conclusion ignores the diversification opportunities that Bore provides. Figure 11.6 shows the results of combining Bore with Coca-Cola or with Intel (light blue curves), or combining Bore with a 50–50 portfolio of Coca-Cola and Intel

FIGURE 11.6

Expected Return and Volatility for Selected Portfolios of Intel, Coca-Cola, and Bore Industries Stocks

By combining Bore (B) with Intel (I), Coca-Cola (C), and portfolios of Intel and Coca-Cola, we introduce new risk and return possibilities. We can also do better than with just Coca-Cola and Intel alone (the black curve). Portfolios of Bore and Coca-Cola (B + C) and Bore and Intel (B + I) are shown in light blue in the figure. The dark blue curve is a combination of Bore with a portfolio of Intel and Coca-Cola.

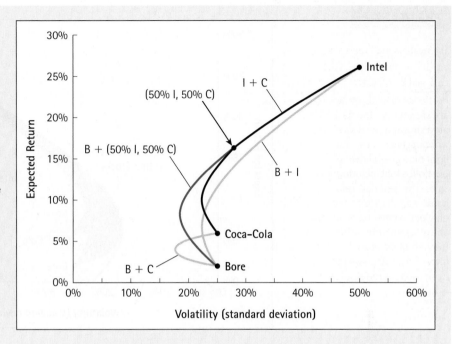

(dark blue curve).[8] Notice that some of the portfolios we obtained by combining only Intel and Coca-Cola (black curve) are inferior to these new possibilities.

When we combine Bore stock with every portfolio of Intel and Coca-Cola, and also allow for short sales, we get an entire region of risk and return possibilities rather than just a single curve. This region is depicted as the shaded area in Figure 11.7. But note that most of these portfolios are inefficient. The efficient portfolios—those offering the highest possible expected return for a given level of volatility—are those on the northwest edge of the shaded region, which we call the **efficient frontier** for these three stocks. In this case none of the stocks, on its own, is on the efficient frontier, so it would not be efficient to put all our money in a single stock.

When the set of investment opportunities increases from two to three stocks, the efficient frontier improves. Visually, the old frontier with any two stocks is located inside the new frontier. In general, adding new investment opportunities allows for greater diversification and improves the efficient frontier. Figure 11.8 shows the effect of increasing the set from three stocks (Bombardier, TD Bank, and Shoppers Drug Mart) to ten stocks. Even though the added stocks appear to offer inferior risk–return combinations on their own, because they allow for additional diversification, the efficient frontier improves with their inclusion. Thus, to arrive at the best possible set of risk and return opportunities, we should keep adding stocks until all investment opportunities are represented. Ultimately, based on our estimates of returns, volatilities, and correlations, we can construct the

---

8. When a portfolio includes another portfolio, we can compute the weight of each stock by multiplying the portfolio weights. For example, a portfolio with 30% in Bore stock and 70% in the *portfolio* of (50% Intel, 50% Coca-Cola) has 30% in Bore stock, 70% × 50% = 35% in Intel stock, and 70% × 50% = 35% in Coca-Cola stock.

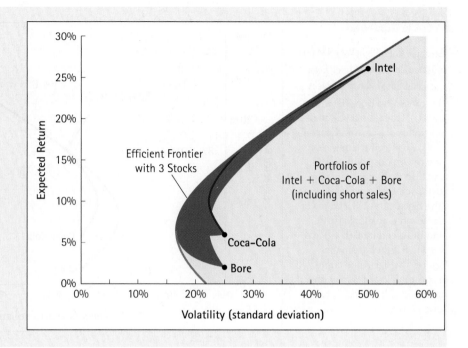

FIGURE 11.7

The Volatility and Expected Return for All Portfolios of Intel, Coca-Cola, and Bore Stock

Portfolios of all three stocks are shown, with the dark blue area showing portfolios without short sales, and the light blue area showing portfolios that include short sales. The best risk–return combinations are on the efficient frontier (red curve). The efficient frontier improves (has a higher return for each level of risk) when we move from two to three stocks.

FIGURE 11.8

Efficient Frontier with Ten Stocks Versus Three Stocks

The efficient frontier expands as new investments are added. (Based on monthly returns, 2002–2006.)

efficient frontier for *all* available risky investments showing the best possible risk and return combinations that can be obtained by optimal diversification.

CONCEPT CHECK

1. How does the correlation between two stocks affect the risk and return of portfolios that combine them?

2. What is the efficient frontier?

3. How does the efficient frontier change when we use more stocks to construct portfolios?

11.5 RISK-FREE SAVING AND BORROWING

Thus far, we have considered the risk and return possibilities that result from combining risky investments into portfolios. By including all risky investments in the construction of the efficient frontier, we achieve maximum diversification.

There is another way besides diversification to reduce risk that we have not yet considered: We can keep some of our money in a safe, no-risk investment like Treasury Bills. Of course, doing so will likely reduce our expected return. Conversely, if we are an aggressive investor who is seeking high expected returns, we might decide to borrow money to invest even more in the stock market. In this section we will see that the ability to choose the amount to invest in risky versus riskless securities allows us to determine the *optimal portfolio* of risky securities for an investor.

INVESTING IN RISK-FREE SECURITIES

Consider an arbitrary risky portfolio with returns R_P. Let's look at the effect on risk and return of putting a fraction x of our money in the portfolio, while leaving the remaining fraction $(1 - x)$ in risk-free Treasury Bills with a yield of r_f.

Using Eq. 11.3 and Eq. 11.8, we calculate the expected return and variance of this portfolio, whose return we will denote by R_{xP}. First, the expected return is

$$E[R_{xP}] = (1 - x)r_f + xE[R_P]$$

$$= r_f + x(E[R_P] - r_f) \tag{11.15}$$

The first equation simply states that the expected return is the weighted average of the expected returns of Treasury Bills and the portfolio. (Because we know upfront the current interest rate paid on Treasury Bills, we do not need to compute an expected return for them.) The second equation rearranges the first to give a useful interpretation: Our expected return is equal to the risk-free rate plus a fraction of the portfolio's risk premium, $(E[R_P] - r_f)$, based on the fraction x that we invest in it.

Next let's compute the volatility. Because the risk-free rate r_f is fixed and does not move with (or against) our portfolio, its volatility and covariance with the portfolio are both zero. Thus,

$$SD(R_{xP}) = \sqrt{(1 - x)^2 Var(r_f) + x^2 Var(R_P) + 2(1 - x)x\, Cov(r_f, R_P)}$$

$$= \sqrt{x^2 Var(R_P)}$$
$$= xSD(R_P) \tag{11.16}$$

That is, the volatility is only a fraction of the volatility of the portfolio, based on the amount we invest in it.

The blue line in Figure 11.9 illustrates combinations of volatility and expected return for different choices of x. Looking at Eq. 11.15 and Eq. 11.16, as we increase the fraction x invested in P, we increase both our risk and our risk premium proportionally. Hence the line is *straight* from the risk-free investment through P.

BORROWING AND BUYING STOCKS ON MARGIN

As we increase the fraction x invested in the portfolio P from 0 to 100%, we move along the line in Figure 11.9 from the risk-free investment to P. If we increase x beyond 100%, we get points beyond P in the graph. In this case, we are short selling the risk-free investment, so we

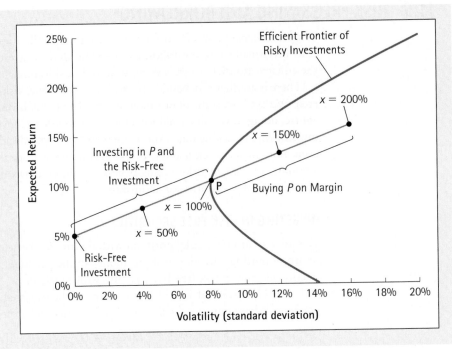

The Risk–Return Combinations from Combining a Risk-Free Investment and a Risky Portfolio

Given a risk-free rate of 5%, the risk-free investment is represented in the graph by the point with 0% volatility and an expected return of 5%. The blue line shows the portfolios obtained by investing x in portfolio P and $(1 - x)$ in the risk-free investment. Investments with weight $x > 100\%$ in portfolio P require borrowing at the risk-free interest rate.

must pay the risk-free return. That is, short selling the risk-free investment is equivalent to borrowing money at the risk-free interest rate through a standard loan.

Borrowing money to invest in stocks is referred to as **buying stocks on margin** or using leverage. A portfolio that consists of a short position in the risk-free investment is known as a *levered* portfolio. As you might expect, margin investing is a risky investment strategy. Note that the region of the blue line in Figure 11.9 with $x > 100\%$ has higher risk than the portfolio P itself. At the same time, margin investing can provide higher expected returns than investing in P using only the funds we have available.

EXAMPLE 11.11

MARGIN INVESTING

Problem

Suppose you have $10,000 in cash, and you decide to borrow another $10,000 at a 5% interest rate to invest $20,000 in a portfolio Q with a 10% expected return and a 20% volatility. What is the expected return and volatility of your investment? What is your realized return if Q goes up 30% over the course of the year? What if Q falls by 10%?

Solution

You have doubled your investment in Q by buying stocks on margin, so $x = 200\%$. From Eqs. 11.15 and 11.16, we see that you have increased both your expected return and your risk relative to the portfolio Q:

$$E[R_{xQ}] = r_f + x(E[R_Q] - r_f) = 5\% + 2 \times (10\% - 5\%) = 15\%$$
$$SD(R_{xQ}) = x \, SD(R_Q) = 2 \times (20\%) = 40\%$$

If Q goes up 30%, your investment will be worth $26,000. But you will owe $10,000 × 1.05 = $10,500 on your loan, for a net payoff of $15,500, or a 55% return on your $10,000 investment. If Q drops by 10%, you are left with $18,000 − $10,500 = $7500, and your return is −25%. Thus the use of margin doubled the range of your returns (55% − (−25%) = 80% versus 30% − (−10%) = 40%, corresponding to the doubling of the volatility of the portfolio.

IDENTIFYING THE TANGENT PORTFOLIO

Looking back at Figure 11.9, we can see that portfolio P is not the best portfolio to combine with the risk-free investment. By forming a portfolio out of the risk-free asset and a portfolio somewhat higher on the efficient frontier than portfolio P, we will get a line that is steeper than the line through P. If the line is steeper, then for any level of volatility, we will earn a higher expected return.

To earn the highest possible expected return for any level of volatility we must find the portfolio that generates the steepest possible line when combined with the risk-free investment. The slope of the line through a given portfolio P is often referred to as the **Sharpe ratio** of the portfolio:

$$\text{Sharpe Ratio} = \frac{\text{Portfolio Excess Return}}{\text{Portfolio Volatility}} = \frac{E[R_P] - r_f}{SD(R_P)} \qquad (11.17)$$

The Sharpe ratio measures the ratio of reward-to-volatility provided by a portfolio.[9] The optimal portfolio to combine with the risk-free asset will be the one with the highest Sharpe ratio, where the line with the risk-free investment just touches, and so is tangent to, the efficient frontier of risky investments, as shown in Figure 11.10. The portfolio that generates this tangent line is known as the **tangent portfolio**. All other portfolios of risky assets lie below this line. Because the tangent portfolio has the highest Sharpe ratio of any portfolio in the economy, the tangent portfolio provides the biggest reward per unit of volatility of any portfolio available.[10]

As is evident from Figure 11.10, combinations of the risk-free asset and the tangent portfolio provide the best risk and return tradeoff available to an investor. This observation has a striking consequence: The tangent portfolio is efficient and once we include the risk-free investment, all efficient portfolios are combinations of the risk-free investment and the tangent portfolio. Therefore, the optimal portfolio of *risky* investments no longer depends on how conservative or aggressive the investor is; every investor should invest in the tangent portfolio *independent of his or her taste for risk*. The investor's preferences will determine only *how much* to invest in the tangent portfolio versus the risk-free investment. Conservative investors will invest a small amount, choosing a portfolio on the line near the risk-free investment. Aggressive investors will invest more, choosing a portfolio that is near the tangent portfolio or even beyond it by buying stocks on margin. Both types of investors will choose to hold the *same* portfolio of risky assets, the tangent portfolio.

---

9. The Sharpe ratio was first introduced by William Sharpe as a measure to compare the performance of mutual funds. See William Sharpe, "Mutual Fund Performance," *Journal of Business* (January 1966): 119–138.

10. The Sharpe ratio can also be interpreted as the number of standard deviations the portfolio's return would have to fall to underperform the risk-free investment. Thus, if returns are normally distributed, the tangent portfolio is the portfolio with the greatest chance of earning a return above the risk-free rate.

FIGURE 11.10

FIGURE 11.10

The Tangent or Efficient Portfolio
The tangent portfolio is the portfolio with the highest Sharpe ratio. Investments on the green line connecting the risk-free investment and the tangent portfolio provide the best risk and return tradeoff available to an investor. As a result, the tangent portfolio is also referred to as the efficient portfolio.

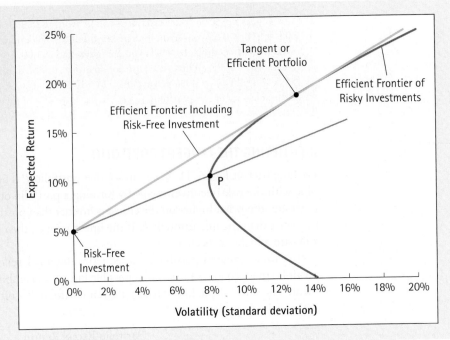

EXAMPLE 11.12   OPTIMAL PORTFOLIO CHOICE

Problem
Your uncle asks for investment advice. Currently, he has $100,000 invested in portfolio P as graphed in Figure 11.10, which has an expected return of 10.5% and a volatility of 8%. Suppose the risk-free rate is 5%, and the tangent portfolio has an expected return of 18.5% and a volatility of 13%. To maximize his expected return without increasing his volatility, which portfolio would you recommend? If your uncle prefers to keep his expected return the same but minimize his risk, which portfolio would you recommend?

Solution
In either case the best portfolios are combinations of the risk-free investment and the tangent portfolio. If we invest an amount x in the tangent portfolio T, using Eq. 11.15 and Eq. 11.16 the expected return and volatility are

$$E[R_{xT}] = r_f + x(E[R_T] - r_f) = 5\% + x(18.5\% - 5\%)$$

$$SD(R_{xT}) = x\, SD(R_T) = x(13\%)$$

So, to maintain the volatility at 8%, $x = 8\%/13\% = 61.5\%$. In this case, your uncle should invest $61,500 in the tangent portfolio, and the remaining $38,500 in the risk-free investment. His expected return will then be 5% + (61.5%)(13.5%) = 13.3%, the highest possible given his level of risk.

Alternatively, to keep the expected return equal to the current value of 10.5%, x must satisfy 5% + x(13.5%) = 10.5%, so x = 40.7%. Now your uncle should invest $40,700 in the tangent portfolio and $59,300 in the risk-free investment, lowering his volatility level to (40.7%)(13%) = 5.29%, the lowest possible given his expected return.

We have achieved one of the primary goals of this chapter and explained how to identify the efficient portfolio of risky assets. The **efficient portfolio** is the tangent portfolio, the portfolio with the highest Sharpe ratio in the economy. By combining it with the risk-free investment, an investor will earn the highest possible expected return for any level of volatility he or she is willing to bear.

CONCEPT CHECK

1. What do we know about the Sharpe ratio of the efficient portfolio?

2. If investors are holding optimal portfolios, how will the portfolios of a conservative and an aggressive investor differ?

11.6 THE EFFICIENT PORTFOLIO AND REQUIRED RETURNS

Thus far, we have evaluated the optimal portfolio choice for an investor, and concluded that the tangent or efficient portfolio in Figure 11.10 offers the highest Sharpe ratio and therefore the best risk–return tradeoff available. We now turn to the implications of this result for a firm's cost of capital. After all, if a firm wants to raise new capital, investors must find it attractive to increase their investment in it. In this section we derive a condition to determine whether we can improve a portfolio by adding more of a given security, and use it to calculate an investor's required return for holding an investment.

PORTFOLIO IMPROVEMENT: BETA AND THE REQUIRED RETURN

Take an arbitrary portfolio P, and let's consider whether we could raise its Sharpe ratio by selling some of our risk-free assets (or borrowing money) and investing the proceeds in an investment i. If we do so, there are two consequences:

1. Expected return: Because we are giving up the risk-free return and replacing it with i's return, our expected return will increase by i's excess return, $E[R_i] - r_f$.

2. Volatility: We will add the risk that i has in common with our portfolio (the rest of i's risk will be diversified). From Eq. 11.13, incremental risk is measured by i's volatility multiplied by its correlation with P: $SD(R_i) \times Corr(R_i, R_p)$.

Is the gain in return from investing in i adequate to make up for the increase in risk? Another way we could have increased our risk would have been to invest more in portfolio P itself. In that case, P's Sharpe ratio, $\dfrac{E[R_P] - r_f}{SD(R_P)}$, tells us how much the return would increase for a given increase in risk. Because the investment in i increases risk by $SD(R_i) \times Corr(R_i, R_p)$, it offers a larger increase in return than we could have gotten from P alone if [11]

$$\underbrace{E[R_i] - r_f}_{\substack{\text{Additional return} \\ \text{from investment } i}} > \overbrace{\underbrace{SD(R_i) \times Corr(R_i, R_p)}_{\substack{\text{Incremental volatility} \\ \text{from investment } i}} \times \underbrace{\frac{E[R_P] - r_f}{SD(R_P)}}_{\substack{\text{Return per unit of volatility} \\ \text{availiable from portfolio } P}}}^{\text{Additional return from taking the same risk investing in } P} \tag{11.18}$$

---

11. If $Corr(R_i, R_p)$ is positive, we can write Eq. 11.18 more intuitively as a comparison of the "incremental Sharpe ratio" of investment i (ratio of the gain in expected return to the incremental volatility) with the Sharpe ratio of the portfolio:

$$\frac{E[R_i] - r_f}{SD(R_i) \times Corr(R_i, R_p)} > \frac{E[R_P] - r_f}{SD(R_P)}$$

To provide a further interpretation for this condition, let's combine the volatility and correlation terms in Eq. 11.18 to define the *beta of investment i with portfolio P*:

Beta of Investment *i* with Portfolio *P*

$$\beta_i^P \equiv \frac{SD(R_i) \times Corr(R_i, R_P)}{SD(R_P)} = \frac{Cov(R_i, R_P)}{Var(R_P)} \qquad (11.19)$$

β_i^P measures the sensitivity of the investment *i* to the fluctuations of the portfolio *P*. That is, for each 1% change in the portfolio's excess return, the investment's excess return is expected to change by β_i^P% due to risks that *i* has in common with *P*. With this definition, we can restate Eq. 11.18 as follows:

$$E[R_i] > r_f + \beta_i^P \times (E[R_P] - r_f)$$

That is, *increasing the amount invested in i will increase the Sharpe ratio of portfolio P if its expected return E[R_i] exceeds the required return given portfolio P, defined as*

Required Return for Investment *i* Given Current Portfolio *P*

$$r_i = r_f + \beta_i^P \times (E[R_P] - r_f) \qquad (11.20)$$

The **required return** is the expected return that is necessary to compensate for the risk investment *i* will contribute to the portfolio. The required return for an investment *i* is equal to the risk-free interest rate plus a risk premium that is equal to the risk premium of the investor's current portfolio, *P*, scaled by *i*'s sensitivity to *P*, β_i^P. If *i*'s expected

---

EXAMPLE **11.13**   THE REQUIRED RETURN OF A NEW INVESTMENT

Problem
You are currently invested in the Omega Fund, a broad-based fund with an expected return of 15% and a volatility of 20%, as well as in risk-free Treasury Bills paying 3%. Your broker suggests that you add a real estate fund to your portfolio. The real estate fund has an expected return of 9%, a volatility of 35%, and a correlation of 0.10 with the Omega Fund. Will adding the real estate fund improve your portfolio?

Solution
Let R_{re} be the return of the real estate fund and R_O be the return of the Omega Fund. From Eq. 11.19, the beta of the real estate fund with the Omega Fund is

$$\beta_{re}^O = \frac{SD(R_{re}) Corr(R_{re}, R_O)}{SD(R_O)} = \frac{35\% \times 0.10}{20\%} = 0.175$$

We can then use Eq. 11.20 to determine the required return that makes the real estate fund an attractive addition to our portfolio:

$$r_{re} = r_f + \beta_{re}^O(E[R_O] - r_f) = 3\% + 0.175 \times (15\% - 3\%) = 5.1\%$$

Because its expected return exceeds the required return of 5.1%, investing some amount in the real estate fund will improve our portfolio's Sharpe ratio.

INTERVIEW WITH MANMEET BHATIA

Prior to becoming vice-president of OceanRock Investments, part of Qtrade Financial Group, Manmeet Bhatia worked as OceanRock's portfolio manager, launching high net worth individual and institutional wealth management for Canadian clients.

QUESTION: What does your company do?

ANSWER: Qtrade does several things. We're in wealth management, handling Canadian investors, approximately $5 billion of assets under administration. We have the online brokerage, which was the origin of the company. We partnered up with several credit unions with our online brokerage. We have a mutual funds company, an insurance division, a high net worth wealth management division, and a portfolio management company.

QUESTION: Can you comment on your investment philosophy?

ANSWER: We believe in taking clients who have invested with our mutual funds specifically or a high net worth investment program to the end goal and that they present with as little volatility as possible. A key ingredient in investing is ensuring that the client stays invested. Market timing represents a philosophy that is difficult to manage and nearly impossible to win in the long run. Having said that, staying invested over the course of time provides the best results from a long-term standpoint. So, what is the key ingredient to keeping a client invested? It is to minimize volatility for a given return. Client emotions play a significant role from a behavioural finance standpoint. You see emotions come at peaks and valleys for individual clients, causing them to conduct the absolute wrong action plan at the wrong time. People tend to buy high and sell low as greed and fear come into play. Our job is to minimize that greed and minimize the fear that a client may experience. We try to provide as smooth a ride as possible, reducing the significant ups and downs that cause these emotions to peak and valley, and we do that via downside risk protection via diversification. We believe in a strategic foundation, investing across several geographies in the world—global-based investments. Canada is a fantastic place to invest, but it represents 3% to 4% of the world's market capitalization. Opportunities exist around the world that we want to take advantage of.

QUESTION: Can you comment on the Canadian market as an investment opportunity?

ANSWER: One of the best places to invest is in Canada from a standpoint of opportunities that don't necessarily fall under market efficiencies. The United States is a great example of a very efficient market. Information on every company, especially for the large caps, is significant and the market is quite efficient. Canada represents an opportunity where there isn't as much coverage on the research side of Canadian companies and thus an opportunity for value-adding research may exist. Canada is still a relatively efficient market, but we believe there is an opportunity to gain some benefit on the Canadian equity side.

QUESTION: Can you offer some comments on exchange-traded funds?

ANSWER: Exchange-traded funds provide an efficient and effective way to gain exposure to specific markets or market areas. If I wanted to buy into China my options are individual research, take a chance on certain securities and hope they pay off based on my fundamental research, or if I believe China is a growth opportunity for the future, I can buy an ETF in China and gain exposure to that market. If I'm bullish on an entire sector, the ETF will give me exposure into that. Also with ETFs, there is a lot of flexibility. If I want to move from one market or sector to another, rather than making a determination which company to sell and how much of that company to sell, it's a simple task to sell out of an entire ETF and buy into another.

QUESTION: Can you offer any advice for new university graduates seeking careers as portfolio managers?

ANSWER: I think the portfolio management business is definitely a lucrative one, definitely satisfying, definitely interesting. If an individual wants to move in that direction one of the key elements is understanding the end user, whether it be an institutional client or an individual client. The best way to start out in that realm is to actually be client-facing. To be able to feel the empathy, the sympathy, for these individuals; they're not just numbers on a screen that go up and down, but they are individuals who hold these assets. Having said that, getting your feet wet in a situation working for a credit union, for example, dealing with the face-to-face client is often a great way to pick up experience that will help you later on as you move over into the institutional realm. In addition to that, computer skills are essential. Working with Excel, working with spreadsheets is highly valuable and I think any institution is going to take great consideration of someone with experience on that side.

return exceeds this required return, then adding more of it will improve the performance of the portfolio.

EXPECTED RETURNS AND THE EFFICIENT PORTFOLIO

If a security's expected return exceeds its required return, then we can improve the performance of portfolio P by adding more of the security. But how much more should we add? As we buy shares of security i, its correlation (and therefore its beta) with our portfolio will increase, ultimately raising its required return until $E[R_i] = r_i$. At this point our holdings of security i are optimal. Similarly, if security i's expected return is less than the required return r_i, we should reduce our holdings of i. As we do so the correlation and the required return r_i will fall until $E[R_i] = r_i$.

Thus, if we have no restrictions on our ability to buy or sell securities that are traded in the market, we will continue to trade until the expected return of each security equals its required return—that is, until $E[R_i] = r_i$ holds for all i. At this point, no trade can possibly improve the risk–reward ratio of the portfolio, and our portfolio is the optimal, efficient portfolio. That is,

A portfolio is efficient if and only if the expected return of every available security equals its required return.

From Eq. 11.20, this result implies the following relationship between the expected return of any security and its beta with the efficient portfolio:

Expected Return of a Security

$$E[R_i] = r_i \equiv r_f + \beta_i^{eff} \times (E[R_{eff}] - r_f) \tag{11.21}$$

where R_{eff} is the return of the efficient portfolio, the portfolio with the highest Sharpe ratio of any portfolio in the economy.

EXAMPLE 11.14   IDENTIFYING THE EFFICIENT PORTFOLIO

Problem
Consider the Omega Fund and real estate fund of Example 11.13. Suppose you have $100 million invested in the Omega Fund. In addition to this position, how much should you invest in the real estate fund to form an efficient portfolio of these two funds?

Solution
Suppose that for each $1 invested in the Omega Fund, we borrow x_{re} dollars (or sell x_{re} worth of Treasury Bills) to invest in the real estate fund. Then our portfolio has a return of $R_P = R_O + x_{re}(R_{re} - r_f)$, where R_O is the return of the Omega Fund and R_{re} is the return of the real estate fund. Table 11.5 shows the change to the expected return and volatility of our portfolio as we increase the investment x_{re} in the real estate fund, using the formulas

$$E[R_P] = E[R_O] + x_{re}(E[R_{re}] - r_f)$$

$$Var(R_P) = Var[R_O + x_{re}(R_{re} - r_f)] = Var(R_O) + x_{re}^2 Var(R_{re}) + 2x_{re}Cov(R_{re},R_O)$$

Adding the real estate fund initially improves the Sharpe ratio of the portfolio, as defined by Eq. 11.17. As we add more of the real estate fund, however, its correlation with our portfolio rises, computed as

$$Corr(R_{re}, R_P) = \frac{Cov(R_{re}, R_P)}{SD(R_{re})SD(R_P)} = \frac{Cov(R_{re}, R_O + x_{re}(R_{re} - r_f))}{SD(R_{re})SD(R_P)}$$

$$= \frac{x_{re}Var(R_{re}) + Cov(R_{re}, R_O)}{SD(R_{re})SD(R_P)}$$

The beta of the real estate fund—computed from Eq. 11.19—also rises, increasing the required return. The required return equals the 9% expected return of the real estate fund at about $x_{re} = 11\%$, which is the same level of investment that maximizes the Sharpe ratio. Thus the efficient portfolio of these two funds includes $0.11 in the real estate fund per $1 invested in the Omega Fund.

Before we move on, note the significance of Eq. 11.21. This equation establishes the relation between an investment's risk and its expected return. It states that *we can determine the appropriate risk premium for an investment from its beta with the efficient portfolio*. The efficient or tangent portfolio, which has the highest possible Sharpe ratio of any portfolio in the market, provides the benchmark that identifies the systematic risk present in the economy.

In Chapter 10 we argued that *market portfolio* of all risky securities should be well diversified, and therefore could be used as a benchmark to measure systematic risk. To understand the connection between the market portfolio and the efficient portfolio, we must consider the implications of the collective investment decisions of all investors, which we turn to next.

SHARPE RATIO AND REQUIRED RETURN FOR DIFFERENT INVESTMENTS IN THE REAL ESTATE FUND

TABLE 11.5

x_{re}	$E[R_P]$	$SD(R_P)$	Sharpe Ratio	$Corr(R_{re}, R_P)$	β_{re}^P	Required Return r_{re}
0%	15.00%	20.00%	0.6000	10.0%	0.18	5.10%
4%	15.24%	20.19%	0.6063	16.8%	0.29	6.57%
8%	15.48%	20.47%	0.6097	23.4%	0.40	8.00%
10%	15.60%	20.65%	0.6103	26.6%	0.45	8.69%
11%	15.66%	20.74%	0.6104	28.2%	0.48	9.03%
12%	15.72%	20.84%	0.6103	29.7%	0.50	9.35%
16%	15.96%	21.30%	0.6084	35.7%	0.59	10.60%

NOBEL PRIZE **HARRY MARKOWITZ AND JAMES TOBIN**

The techniques of mean-variance portfolio optimization, which allow an investor to find the portfolio with the highest expected return for any level of variance (or volatility), were developed in an article, "Portfolio Selection," published in the *Journal of Finance* in 1952 by Harry Markowitz. Markowitz's approach has evolved into one of the main methods of portfolio optimization used on Wall Street. In recognition for his contribution to the field, Markowitz was awarded the Nobel Prize for economics in 1990. The same ideas were developed concurrently by Andrew Roy in "Safety First and the Holding of Assets," published in *Econometrica* in the same year in which Markowitz's article appeared. In 1999, after winning the Nobel Prize, Markowitz wrote "I am often called the father of modern portfolio theory, but Roy can claim an equal share of this honor."[*] Ironically Mark Rubinstein[†] appears to have discovered another article that develops some of these ideas published twelve years earlier

in 1940 by Bruno de Finetti in the Italian journal *Giornale dell'Instituto Italiano degli Attuari*. It has remained in obscurity perhaps because it was first translated into English in 2004 (by Luca Barone).[‡]

James Tobin furthered this theory with the important insight that by combining risky securities with a risk-free investment, an optimal tangent portfolio could be found that does not depend on an investor's tolerance for risk. In his article "Liquidity Preference as Behavior Toward Risk" published in the *Review of Economic Studies* in 1958, Tobin proved a "Separation Theorem," which showed that Markowitz's techniques could be applied to find the tangent portfolio, and then investors could choose their exposure to risk by varying their investments in the tangent portfolio and the risk-free investment. Tobin was awarded the Nobel Prize for economics in 1981 for his contributions to finance and economics.

---

[*]H. M. Markowitz, "The Early History of Portfolio Theory: 1600–1960," *Financial Analysts Journal* 55 (1999): 5–16.

[†]M. Rubinstein, *A History of the Theory of Investments* (New Jersey: John Wiley & Sons, 2006), 349.

[‡]English translation in *Journal of Investment Management*, Third Quarter, 2006.

CONCEPT CHECK
1. When will a new investment improve the Sharpe ratio of a portfolio?

2. An investment's cost of capital is determined by its beta with what portfolio?

11.7   THE CAPITAL ASSET PRICING MODEL

As shown in the prior section, once we can identify the efficient portfolio, we can compute the expected return of any security based on its beta with the efficient portfolio according to Equation 11.6. But to implement this approach, we face an important practical problem: To identify the efficient portfolio we must know the expected returns, volatilities, and correlations between investments. These quantities are difficult to forecast. Under these circumstances, how do we put the theory into practice?

To answer this question we revisit the Capital Asset Pricing Model (CAPM), which we introduced in Chapter 10. This model allows us to identify the efficient portfolio of risky assets without having any knowledge of the expected return of each security. Instead, the CAPM uses the optimal choices investors make to identify the efficient portfolio as the market portfolio, the portfolio of all stocks and securities in the market. To obtain this remarkable result, we make three assumptions regarding the behaviour of investors.

THE CAPM ASSUMPTIONS

Three main assumptions underlie the CAPM. The first is a familiar one that we have adopted since Chapter 3:

1. *Investors can buy and sell all securities at competitive market prices (without incurring taxes or transactions costs) and can borrow and lend at the risk-free interest rate.*

The second assumption is that *all* investors behave as we have described thus far in this chapter, and choose a portfolio of traded securities that offers the highest possible expected return given the level of volatility they are willing to accept:

2. *Investors hold only efficient portfolios of traded securities—portfolios that yield the maximum expected return for a given level of volatility.*

Of course, there are many investors in the world, and each may have his or her own estimates of the volatilities, correlations, and expected returns of the available securities. But investors don't come up with these estimates arbitrarily; they base them on historical patterns and other information (including market prices) that is widely available to the public. If all investors use publicly available information sources, then their estimates are likely to be similar. Consequently, it is not unreasonable to consider a special case in which all investors have the same estimates concerning future investments and returns, called **homogeneous expectations**. Although investors' expectations are not completely identical in reality, assuming homogeneous expectations should be a reasonable approximation in many markets, and represents the third simplifying assumption of the CAPM:

3. *Investors have homogeneous expectations regarding the volatilities, correlations, and expected returns of securities.*

SUPPLY, DEMAND, AND THE EFFICIENCY OF THE MARKET PORTFOLIO

If investors have homogeneous expectations, then each investor will identify the same portfolio as having the highest Sharpe ratio in the economy. Thus all investors will demand the *same* efficient portfolio of risky securities—the tangent portfolio in Figure 11.10—adjusting only their investment in risk-free securities to suit their particular appetite for risk.

But if every investor is holding the tangent portfolio, then the combined portfolio of risky securities of *all* investors must also equal the tangent portfolio. Furthermore, because every security is owned by someone, the sum of all investors' portfolios must equal the portfolio of all risky securities available in the market, which we defined in Chapter 10 as the market portfolio. Therefore, *the efficient, tangent portfolio of risky securities (the portfolio that all investors hold) must equal the market portfolio.*

The insight that the market portfolio is efficient is really just the statement that *demand must equal supply.* All investors demand the efficient portfolio, and the supply of securities is the market portfolio; hence the two must coincide. If a security was not part of the efficient portfolio, then no investor would want to own it, and demand for this security would not equal its supply. This security's price would fall, causing its expected return to rise until it became an attractive investment. In this way, prices in the market will adjust so that the efficient portfolio and the market portfolio coincide, and demand equals supply.

EXAMPLE 11.15	PORTFOLIO WEIGHTS AND THE MARKET PORTFOLIO

Problem

Suppose that after much research, you have identified the efficient portfolio. As part of your holdings, you have decided to invest $10,000 in Microsoft and $5000 in Pfizer stock. Suppose your friend, who is a wealthier but more conservative investor, has $2000 invested in Pfizer. If your friend's portfolio is also efficient, how much has she invested in Microsoft? If all investors are holding efficient portfolios, what can you conclude about Microsoft's market capitalization, compared to Pfizer's?

Solution

Because all efficient portfolios are combination of the risk-free investment and the tangent portfolio, they share the same proportions of risky stocks. Thus, since you have invested twice as much in Microsoft as in Pfizer, the same must be true for your friend; therefore, she has invested $4000 in Microsoft stock. If all investors hold efficient portfolios, the same must be true of each of their portfolios. Because, collectively, all investors own all shares of Microsoft and Pfizer, Microsoft's market capitalization must therefore be twice that of Pfizer's.

OPTIMAL INVESTING: THE CAPITAL MARKET LINE

When the CAPM assumptions hold, the market portfolio is efficient, so the tangent portfolio in Figure 11.10 is actually the market portfolio. We illustrate this result in Figure 11.11. Recall that the tangent line graphs the highest possible expected return we can achieve for any level of volatility. When the tangent line goes through the market

---

FIGURE 11.11

The Capital Market Line
When investors have homogeneous expectations, the market portfolio and the efficient portfolio coincide. Therefore the capital market line (CML), which is the line from the risk-free investment through the market portfolio, represents the highest expected return available for any level of volatility.

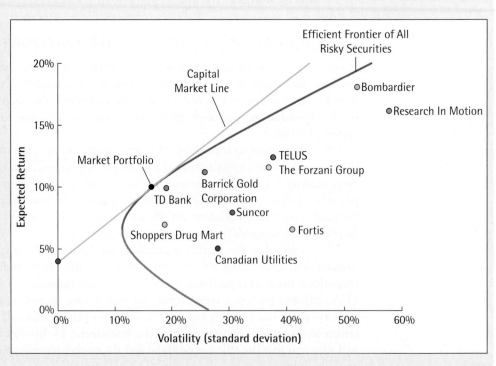

portfolio, it is called the **capital market line (CML)**. According to the CAPM, all investors should choose a portfolio on the capital market line, by holding some combination of the risk-free security and the market portfolio.

CONCEPT CHECK

1. Explain why the market portfolio is efficient according to the CAPM.
2. What is the capital market line (CML)?

11.8 DETERMINING THE RISK PREMIUM

MARKET RISK AND BETA

In Eq.11.21, we showed that the expected return of an investment is given by its beta with the efficient portfolio. But if the market portfolio is efficient, we can rewrite Eq. 11.21 as

The CAPM Equation for the Expected Return

$$E[R_i] = r_i = r_f + \underbrace{\beta_i \times (E[R_{Mkt}] - r_f)}_{\text{Risk premium for security } i}$$

(11.22)

where β_i is the beta of the security with respect to the market portfolio, defined as (using Eqs. 11.19 and 11.6)

$$\beta_i = \frac{\overbrace{SD(R_i) \times Corr(R_i, R_{Mkt})}^{\text{Volatility of } i \text{ that is common with the market}}}{SD(R_{Mkt})} = \frac{Cov(R_i, R_{Mkt})}{Var(R_{Mkt})}$$

(11.23)

The beta of a security measures its volatility due to market risk relative to the market as a whole, and thus captures the security's sensitivity to market risk.

Equation 11.22 is the same result that we derived intuitively at the conclusion of Chapter 10. It states that to determine the appropriate risk premium for any investment, we must rescale the market risk premium (the amount by which the market's expected return exceeds the risk-free rate) by the amount of market risk present in the security's returns, measured by its beta with the market.

We can interpret the CAPM equation as follows. Following the Law of One Price, in a competitive market, investments with similar risk should have the same expected return. Because investors can eliminate firm-specific risk by diversifying their portfolios, the right measure of risk is the investment's beta with the market portfolio, β_i. As the next example demonstrates, the CAPM Equation 11.22 states that the investment's expected return should therefore match the expected return of the capital market line portfolio with the same level of market risk.

EXAMPLE 11.16

COMPUTING THE EXPECTED RETURN FOR A STOCK

Problem

Suppose the risk-free return is 4% and the market portfolio has an expected return of 10% and a volatility of 16.4%. The Forzani Group stock has a 36.89% volatility and a correlation with the market of 0.56. What is The Forzani Group's beta with the market? What capital market line portfolio has equivalent market risk, and what is its expected return?

Solution

To compute beta using Eq. 11.23:

$$\beta_{FGL} = \frac{SD(R_{FGL})\,Corr(R_{FGL}, R_{Mkt})}{SD(R_{Mkt})} = \frac{36.89\% \times 0.56}{16.4\%} = 1.26$$

That is, for each 1% move of the market portfolio, Forzani stock tends to move about 1.26%. We could obtain the same sensitivity to market risk by investing 126% in the market portfolio, and taking a 26% short position in the risk-free security. Because it has the same market risk, Forzani's stock should have the same expected return as this portfolio, which is (using Eq. 11.15)

$$E[R_{FGL}] = r_f + \beta_{FGL}(E[R_{Mkt}] - r_f) = 4\% + 1.26(10\% - 4\%) = 11.56\%$$

This calculation is precisely the CAPM Equation 11.22. Thus, investors will require an expected return of 11.56% to compensate for the risk associated with The Forzani Group stock.

THE SECURITY MARKET LINE

Equation 11.22 implies that there is a linear relationship between a stock's beta and its expected return. Panel b of Figure 11.12 graphs this line through the risk-free investment (with a beta of 0) and the market (with a beta of 1); it is called the *security market line (SML)*. Under the CAPM assumptions, the **security market line (SML)** is the line along which all individual securities should lie when plotted according to their expected return and beta, as shown in panel b.

Contrast this result with the capital market line shown in panel a of Figure 11.12, where there is no clear relationship between an individual stock's volatility and its expected return. As we illustrate for Suncor Energy (SU), a stock's expected return is due only to the fraction of its volatility that is common with the market—$Corr(R_{SU}, R_{Mkt}) \times SD(R_{SU})$; the distance of each stock to the right of the capital market line is due to its diversifiable risk. The relationship between risk and return for individual securities becomes evident only when we measure market risk rather than total risk.

EXAMPLE 11.17	A NEGATIVE-BETA STOCK

Problem

Suppose the stock of SNC-Lavalin Group Inc. (SNC) has a negative beta of −0.17. How does its required return compare to the risk-free rate, according to the CAPM? Does this result make sense?

Solution

Because the expected return of the market is higher than the risk-free rate, Eq. 11.24 implies that the expected return of SNC will be *below* the risk-free rate. For example, if the risk-free rate is 4% and the expected return on the market is 10%,

$$E[R_{SNC}] = 4\% - 0.17(10\% - 4\%) = 2.98\%$$

(See Figure 11.12: The SML drops below r_f for $\beta < 0$.) This result seems odd: Why would investors be willing to accept a 2.98% expected return on this stock when they can invest in a safe investment and earn 4%? A savvy investor will not hold SNC alone; instead, she will hold it in combination with other securities as part of a well-diversified portfolio. Because SNC will tend to rise when the market and most other securities fall, SNC provides "recession insurance" for the portfolio, and investors will pay for this insurance by accepting an expected return below the risk-free rate.

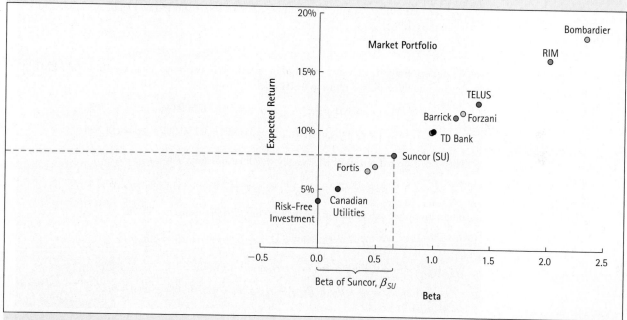

FIGURE 11.12

The Capital Market Line and the Security Market Line

(a) The CML depicts portfolios combining the risk-free investment and the efficient portfolio, and shows the highest expected return that we can attain for each level of volatility. According to the CAPM, the market portfolio is on the CML, and all other stocks and portfolios contain diversifiable risk and lie to the right of the CML, as illustrated for Suncor (SU).
(b) The SML shows the expected return for each security as a function of its beta with the market. According to the CAPM, the market portfolio is efficient, so all stocks and portfolios should lie on the SML.

BETA OF A PORTFOLIO

Because the security market line applies to all tradeable investment opportunities, we can apply it to portfolios as well. Consequently, the expected return of a portfolio is given by Eq. 11.24 and therefore depends on the portfolio's beta. We calculate the beta of a portfolio $R_p = \sum_i x_i R_i$ as follows:

$$
\beta_P = \frac{Cov(R_P, R_{Mkt})}{Var(R_{Mkt})} = \frac{Cov\left(\sum_i x_i R_i, R_{Mkt}\right)}{Var(R_{Mkt})} = \sum_i x_i \frac{Cov(R_i, R_{Mkt})}{Var(R_{Mkt})}
$$

$$
= \sum_i x_i \beta_i
$$

(11.24)

In other words, *the beta of a portfolio is the weighted average beta of the securities in the portfolio.*

EXAMPLE 11.18

THE EXPECTED RETURN OF A PORTFOLIO

Problem

Suppose Pfizer's stock has a beta of 0.50, whereas Home Depot's beta is 1.25. If the risk-free interest rate is 4%, and the expected return of the market portfolio is 10%, what is the expected return of an equally weighted portfolio of Pfizer and Home Depot stocks, according to the CAPM?

Solution

We can compute the expected return of the portfolio in two ways. First, we can use the SML to compute the expected return of each stock:

$$
E[R_{PFE}] = r_f + \beta_{PFE}(E[R_{Mkt}] - r_f) = 4\% + 0.50(10\% - 4\%) = 7.0\%
$$

$$
E[R_{HD}] = r_f + \beta_{HD}(E[R_{Mkt}] - r_f) = 4\% + 1.25(10\% - 4\%) = 11.5\%
$$

Then the expected return of the equally weighted portfolio P is

$$
E[R_P] = \tfrac{1}{2}E[R_{PFE}] + \tfrac{1}{2}E[R_{HD}] = \tfrac{1}{2}(7.0\%) + \tfrac{1}{2}(11.5\%) = 9.25\%
$$

Alternatively, we can compute the beta of the portfolio using Eq. 11.24:

$$
\beta_P = \tfrac{1}{2}\beta_{PFE} + \tfrac{1}{2}\beta_{HD} = \tfrac{1}{2}(0.50) + \tfrac{1}{2}(1.25) = 0.875
$$

We can then find the portfolio's expected return from the SML:

$$
E[R_P] = r_f + \beta_P(E[R_{Mkt}] - r_f) = 4\% + 0.875(10\% - 4\%) = 9.25\%
$$

SUMMARY OF THE CAPITAL ASSET PRICING MODEL

In these last two sections, we have explored the consequences of the CAPM assumptions that markets are competitive, investors choose efficient portfolios, and investors have homogeneous expectations. The CAPM leads to two major conclusions:

■ *The market portfolio is the efficient portfolio.* Therefore, the highest expected return for any given level of volatility is obtained by a portfolio on the capital market line, which combines the market portfolio with risk-free saving or borrowing.

NOBEL PRIZE WILLIAM SHARPE ON THE CAPM

William Sharpe received the Nobel Prize in 1990 for his development of the Capital Asset Pricing Model. Here are his comments on the CAPM from a 1998 interview with Jonathan Burton:*

Portfolio theory focused on the actions of a single investor with an optimal portfolio. I said, What if everyone was optimizing? They've all got their copies of Markowitz and they're doing what he says. Then some people decide they want to hold more IBM, but there aren't enough shares to satisfy demand. So they put price pressure on IBM and up it goes, at which point they have to change their estimates of risk and return, because now they're paying more for the stock. That process of upward and downward pressure on prices continues until prices reach an equilibrium and everyone collectively wants to hold what's available. At that point, what can you say about the relationship between risk and return? The answer is that expected return is proportionate to beta relative to the market portfolio.

The CAPM was and is a theory of equilibrium. Why should anyone expect to earn more by investing in one security as opposed to another? You need to be compensated for doing badly when times are bad. The security that is going to do badly just when you need money when times are bad is a security you have to hate, and there had better be some redeeming virtue or else who will hold it? That redeeming virtue has to be that in normal times you expect to do better. The key insight of the Capital Asset Pricing Model is that higher expected returns go with the greater risk of doing badly in bad times. Beta is a measure of that. Securities or asset classes with high betas tend to do worse in bad times than those with low betas.

The CAPM was a very simple, very strong set of assumptions that got a nice, clean, pretty result. And then almost immediately, we all said, Let's bring more complexity into it to try to get closer to the real world. People went on—myself and others—to what I call "extended" Capital Asset Pricing Models, in which expected return is a function of beta, taxes, liquidity, dividend yield, and other things people might care about.

Did the CAPM evolve? Of course. But the fundamental idea remains that there's no reason to expect reward just for bearing risk. Otherwise, you'd make a lot of money in Las Vegas. If there's reward for risk, it's got to be special. There's got to be some economics behind it or else the world is a very crazy place. I don't think differently about those basic ideas at all.

*Jonathan Burton, "Revisiting the Capital Asset Pricing Model," Dow Jones Asset Manager (May/June 1998): 20–28.

■ *The risk premium for any investment is proportional to its beta with the market.* Therefore, the relationship between risk and the required return is given by the security market line described by Eqs. 11.22 and 11.23.

The CAPM model is based on strong assumptions. Because some of these assumptions do not fully describe investors' behaviour, some of the model's conclusions are not completely accurate; it is certainly not the case that every investor holds the market portfolio, for instance. We will examine individual investor behaviour in more detail in Chapter 13, where we also consider proposed extensions to the CAPM. Nevertheless, financial economists find the qualitative intuition underlying the CAPM compelling, so it is still the most common and important model of risk and return. While not perfect, it is widely regarded as a very useful approximation and is used by firms and practitioners as a practical means to estimate a security's expected return and an investment's cost of capital. In the next chapter, we will explain in more detail how to implement the model, looking more closely at the construction of the market portfolio and developing a means to estimate the betas of firms' securities as well as their underlying investments.

CONCEPT CHECK

1. What is the security market line (SML)?

2. According to the CAPM, how can we determine a stock's expected return?

SUMMARY

1. The portfolio weight is the initial fraction x_i of an investor's money invested in each asset. Portfolio weights add up to 1.

$$x_i = \frac{\text{Value of Investment } i}{\text{Total Value of Portfolio}} \tag{11.1}$$

2. The expected return of a portfolio is the weighted average of the expected returns of the investments within it, using the portfolio weights.

$$E[R_p] = \sum_i x_i E[R_i] \tag{11.3}$$

3. To find the risk of a portfolio, we need to know the degree to which stock returns move together. Covariance and correlation measure the co-movement of returns.

   a. The covariance between returns R_i and R_j is defined by

   $$Cov(R_i, R_j) = E[(R_i - E[R_i])(R_j - E[R_j])] \tag{11.4}$$

   and is estimated from historical data using

   $$Cov(R_i, R_j) = \frac{1}{T-1} \sum_t (R_{i,t} - \bar{R}_i)(R_{j,t} - \bar{R}_j) \tag{11.5}$$

   b. The correlation is defined as the covariance of the returns divided by the standard deviation of each return. The correlation is always between -1 and $+1$. It represents the fraction of the volatility due to risk that is common to the securities.

   $$Corr(R_i, R_j) = \frac{Cov(R_i, R_j)}{SD(R_i) \; SD(R_j)} \tag{11.6}$$

4. The variance of a portfolio depends on the covariance of the stocks within it.

   a. For a portfolio with two stocks, the portfolio variance is

   $$Var(R_P) = x_1^2 Var(R_1) + x_2^2 Var(R_2) + 2x_1 x_2 Cov(R_1, R_2) \tag{11.8}$$

   $$Var(R_P) = x_1^2 SD(R_1)^2 + x_2^2 SD(R_2)^2 + 2x_1 x_2 Corr(R_1, R_2) SD(R_1) SD(R_2) \tag{11.9}$$

   b. If the portfolio weights are positive, as we lower the covariance between the two stocks in a portfolio, we lower the portfolio variance.

5. The variance of an equally weighted portfolio is

   $$Var(R_P) = \frac{1}{n}(\text{Average Variance of the Individual Stocks})$$

   $$+ \left(1 - \frac{1}{n}\right)(\text{Average Covariance Between the Stocks}) \tag{11.12}$$

6. Diversification eliminates independent risks. The volatility of a large portfolio results from the common risk between the stocks in the portfolio.

7. Each security contributes to the volatility of the portfolio according to its total risk scaled by its correlation with the portfolio, which adjusts for the fraction of the total risk that is common to the portfolio.

   $$SD(R_P) = \sum_i x_i \times SD(R_i) \times Corr(R_i, R_P) \tag{11.13}$$

8. Efficient portfolios offer investors the highest possible expected return for a given level of risk. The set of efficient portfolios is called the efficient frontier. As investors add stocks to a portfolio, the efficient portfolio improves.

   a. An investor seeking high expected returns and low volatility should invest only in efficient portfolios.

b. Investors will choose from the set of efficient portfolios based on their own preferences for return versus risk.

9. Investors may use short sales in their portfolios. A portfolio is short those stocks with negative portfolio weights. Short selling extends the set of possible portfolios.

10. Portfolios can be formed by combining the risk-free asset with a portfolio of risky assets.

   a. The expected return and volatility for this type of portfolio is

$$E[R_{xP}] = r_f + x(E[R_p] - r_f) \tag{11.15}$$

$$SD(R_{xP}) = xSD(R_P) \tag{11.16}$$

   b. The risk–return combinations of the risk-free investment and a risky portfolio lie on a straight line connecting the two investments.

11. The goal of an investor who is seeking to earn the highest possible expected return for any level of volatility is to find the portfolio that generates the steepest possible line when combined with the risk-free investment. The slope of this line is called the Sharpe ratio of the portfolio.

$$\text{Sharpe Ratio} = \frac{\text{Portfolio Excess Return}}{\text{Portfolio Volatility}} = \frac{E[R_P] - r_f}{SD(R_P)} \tag{11.17}$$

12. The risky portfolio with the highest Sharpe ratio is called the efficient portfolio. The efficient portfolio is the optimal combination of risky investments independent of the investor's appetite for risk. An investor can select a desired degree of risk by choosing the amount to invest in the efficient portfolio relative to the risk-free investment.

13. The beta of an investment with a portfolio is

$$\beta_i^P \equiv \frac{SD(R_i) \times Corr(R_i, R_P)}{SD(R_P)} = \frac{Cov(R_i, R_P)}{Var(R_P)} \tag{11.19}$$

Beta indicates the sensitivity of the investment's return to fluctuations in the portfolio's return.

14. Buying shares of security i improves the performance of a portfolio if its expected return exceeds the required return:

$$r_i = r_f + \beta_i^P \times (E[R_P] - r_f) \tag{11.20}$$

15. A portfolio is efficient when $E[R_i] = r_i$ for all securities. The following relationship therefore holds between beta and expected returns for traded securities:

$$E[R_i] = r_i \equiv r_f + \beta_i^{eff} \times (E[R_{eff}] - r_f) \tag{11.21}$$

16. Three main assumptions underlie the Capital Asset Pricing Model (CAPM):

   a. Investors trade securities at competitive market prices (without incurring taxes or transaction costs) and can borrow and lend at the risk-free rate.

   b. Investors choose efficient portfolios.

   c. Investors have homogeneous expectations regarding the volatilities, correlations, and expected returns of securities.

17. Because the supply of securities must equal the demand for securities, the CAPM implies that the market portfolio of all risky securities is the efficient portfolio.

18. Under the CAPM assumptions, the capital market line (CML), which is the set of portfolios obtained by combining the risk-free security and the market portfolio, is the set of portfolios with the highest possible expected return for any level of volatility.

19. The CAPM Equation states that the risk premium of any security is equal to the market risk premium multiplied by the beta of the security. This relationship is called the security market line (SML), and it determines the required return for an investment:

$$E[R_i] = r_i = r_f + \underbrace{\beta_i \times (E[R_{Mkt}] - r_f)}_{\text{Risk premium for security } i} \tag{11.22}$$

20. The beta of a security measures the amount of the security's risk that is common to the market portfolio or market risk. Beta is defined as follows:

$$\beta_i = \frac{\overbrace{SD(R_i) \times Corr(R_i, R_{Mkt})}^{\text{Volatility of } i \text{ that is common with the market}}}{SD(R_{Mkt})} = \frac{Cov(R_i, R_{Mkt})}{Var(R_{Mkt})} \tag{11.23}$$

21. The beta of a portfolio is the weighted-average beta of the securities in the portfolio.

KEY TERMS

buying stocks on margin *p. 378*
capital market line (CML) *p. 389*
correlation *p. 359*
covariance *p. 359*
efficient frontier *p. 375*
efficient portfolio *p. 381*
equally weighted portfolio *p. 366*
homogeneous expectations *p. 387*
inefficient portfolio *p. 369*

long position *p. 371*
portfolio weights *p. 356*
required return *p. 382*
security market line (SML) *p. 390*
Sharpe ratio *p. 379*
short interest *p. 373*
short position *p. 371*
short sale *p. 371*
tangent portfolio *p. 379*

PROBLEMS

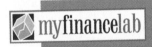 The problems marked in green can be found on MyFinanceLab at www.myfinancelab.com. An asterisk (*) indicates problems with a higher level of difficulty. Additional readings for this chapter may be found in the Textbook Resources section on MyFinanceLab.

The Expected Return of a Portfolio

1. You are considering how to invest part of your retirement savings. You have decided to put $200,000 into three stocks: 50% of the money in GoldFinger (currently $25/share), 25% of the money in Moosehead (currently $80/share), and the remainder in Venture Associates (currently $2/share). If GoldFinger stock goes up to $30/share, Moosehead stock drops to $60/share, and Venture Associates stock rises to $3 per share,
    a. What is the new value of the portfolio?
    b. What return did the portfolio earn?
    c. If you don't buy or sell shares after the price change, what are your new portfolio weights?

2. You own 3 stocks: 1,000 shares of Apple Computer, 10,000 shares of Cisco Systems, and 5,000 shares of Goldman Sachs Group. The current share prices and expected returns of Apple, Cisco, and Goldman are, respectively, $125, $19, $120 and 12%, 10%, 10.5%.
    a. What are the portfolio weights of the three stocks in your portfolio?
    b. What is the expected return of your portfolio?
    c. Assume that both Apple and Cisco go up by $5 and Goldman goes down by $10. What are the new portfolio weights?

d. Assuming the stocks' expected returns remain the same, what is the expected return of the portfolio at the new prices?

3. Consider a world that only consists of the three stocks shown in the following table:

Stock	Total Number of Shares Outstanding	Current Price per Share	Expected Return
First Bank	100 million	$100	18%
Fast Mover	50 million	$120	12%
Funny Bone	200 million	$30	15%

a. Calculate the total value of all shares outstanding currently.

b. What fraction of the total value outstanding does each stock make up?

c. You hold the market portfolio, that is, you have picked portfolio weights equal to the answer to part b (that is, each stock's weight is equal to its contribution to the fraction of the total value of all stocks). What is the expected return of your portfolio?

4. There are two ways to calculate the expected return of a portfolio: either calculate the expected return using the value and dividend stream of the portfolio as a whole, or calculate the weighted average of the expected returns of the individual stocks that make up the portfolio. Which return is higher?

The Volatility of a Two-Stock Portfolio

5. If the return of two stocks has a correlation of 1, what does this imply about the relative movements in the stock prices?

EXCEL
6. Using the data in the following table, estimate (a) the average return and volatility for each stock, (b) the covariance between the stocks, and (c) the correlation between these two stocks.

Year	Realized Returns	
	Stock A	Stock B
2004	−10%	21%
2005	20%	30%
2006	5%	7%
2007	−5%	−3%
2008	2%	−8%
2009	9%	25%

EXCEL
7. Use the data in Problem 6, consider a portfolio that maintains a 50% weight on stock A and a 50% weight on stock B.

a. What is the return each year of this portfolio?

b. Based on your results from part a, compute the average return and volatility of the portfolio.

c. Show that (i) the average return of the portfolio is equal to the average of the average returns of the two stocks and (ii) the volatility of the portfolio equals the same result as from the calculation in Eq. 11.9.

d. Explain why the portfolio has a lower volatility than the average volatility of the two stocks.

EXCEL
8. Using your estimates from Problem 6, calculate the volatility (standard deviation) of a portfolio that is 70% invested in stock A and 30% invested in stock B.

EXCEL
9. Using the data from Table 11.3, what is the covariance between the stocks of Alaska Air and Southwest Airlines?

10. Suppose two stocks have a correlation of 1. If the first stock has an above-average return this year, what is the probability that the second stock will have an above-average return?

11. Arbour Systems and Gencore stocks both have a volatility of 40%. Compute the volatility of a portfolio with 50% invested in each stock if the correlation between the stocks is (a) +1, (b) 0.50, (c) 0, (d) −0.50, and (e) −1.0. In which cases is the volatility lower than that of the original stocks?

12. Suppose Wesley Publishing's stock has a volatility of 60%, while Addison Printing's stock has a volatility of 30%. If the correlation between these stocks is 25%, what is the volatility of the following portfolios of Addison and Wesley: (a) 100% Addision, (b) 75% Addison and 25% Wesley, and (c) 50% Addison and 50% Wesley.

13. Suppose Avon and Nova stocks have volatilities of 50% and 25%, respectively, and they are perfectly negatively correlated. What portfolio of these two stocks has zero risk?

EXCEL

14. Suppose Tex stock has a volatility of 40%, and Mex stock has a volatility of 20%. If Tex and Mex are uncorrelated,

   a. What portfolio of the two stocks has the same volatility as Mex alone?

   b. What portfolio of the two stocks has the smallest possible volatility?

The Volatility of a Large Portfolio

15. Using the data from Table 11.3, what is the volatility of an equally weighted portfolio of Microsoft, Alaska Air, and Ford Motor stock?

16. Suppose that the average stock has a volatility of 50%, and that the correlation between pairs of stocks is 20%. Estimate the volatility of an equally weighted portfolio with (a) 1 stock, (b) 30 stocks, (c) 1000 stocks.

17. What is the volatility (standard deviation) of an equally weighted portfolio of stocks within an industry in which the stocks have a volatility of 50% and a correlation of 40% as the portfolio becomes arbitrarily large?

18. Consider an equally weighted portfolio of stocks in which each stock has a volatility of 40%, and the correlation between each pair of stocks is 20%.

   a. What is the volatility of the portfolio as the number of stocks becomes arbitrarily large?

   b. What is the average correlation of each stock with this large portfolio?

19. Stock A has a volatility of 65% and a correlation of 10% with your current portfolio. Stock B has a volatility of 30% and a correlation of 25% with your current portfolio. You currently hold both stocks. Which will increase the volatility of your portfolio: (i) selling a small amount of stock B and investing the proceeds in stock A, or (ii) selling a small amount of stock A and investing the proceeds in stock B?

20. You currently hold a portfolio of three stocks, Delta, Gamma, and Omega. Delta has a volatility of 60%, Gamma has a volatility of 30%, and Omega has a volatility of 20%. Suppose you invest ½ of your money in Delta, and 25% in each of Gamma and Omega.

   a. What is the highest possible volatility of your portfolio?

   b. If your portfolio has the volatility in part a, what can you conclude about the correlation between Delta and Omega?

Risk Versus Return: Choosing an Efficient Portfolio

21. Suppose Ford Motor stock has an expected return of 20% and a volatility of 40%, and Molson Coors Brewing has an expected return of 10% and a volatility of 30%. If the two stocks are uncorrelated,

   a. What is the expected return and volatility of an equally weighted portfolio of the two stocks?

   b. Given your answer to (a), is investing all of your money in Molson Coors stock an efficient portfolio of these two stocks?

   c. Is investing all of your money in Ford Motor an efficient portfolio of these two stocks?

22. Suppose Intel's stock has an expected return of 26% and a volatility of 50%, while Coca-Cola's has an expected return of 6% and a volatility of 25%. If these two stocks were perfectly negatively correlated (i.e., their correlation coefficient is -1),

    a. Calculate the portfolio weights that remove all risk.

    b. What is the risk-free rate of interest in this economy?

For problems 23–26, suppose Biovail and Shoppers Drug Mart have expected returns and volatilities shown below, with a correlation of 22%.

	$E[R]$	$SD[R]$
Biovail	7%	16%
Shoppers Drug Mart	10%	20%

23. Calculate (a) the expected return and (b) the volatility (standard deviation) of a portfolio that is equally invested in Biovail's and Shoppers Drug Mart's stock.

24. For the portfolio in Problem 23, if the correlation between Biovail's and Shoppers Drug Mart's stock were to increase,

    a. Would the expected return of the portfolio rise or fall?

    b. Would the volatility of the portfolio rise or fall?

25. Calculate (a) the expected return and (b) the volatility (standard deviation) of a portfolio that consists of a long position of $10,000 in Biovail and a short position of $2000 in Shoppers Drug Mart.

EXCEL   *26. Using the same data as for Problem 23, calculate the expected return and the volatility (standard deviation) of a portfolio consisting of Biovail's and Shoppers Drug Mart's stocks using a wide range of portfolio weights. Plot the expected return as a function of the portfolio volatility. Using your graph, identify the range of Biovail's portfolio weights that yield efficient combinations of the two stocks, rounded to the nearest percentage point.

27. A hedge fund has created a portfolio using just two stocks. It has shorted $35,000,000 worth of Oracle stock and has purchased $85,000,000 of Intel stock. The correlation between Oracle's and Intel's returns is 0.65. The expected returns and standard deviations of the two stocks are given in the table below:

	Expected Return	Standard Deviation
Oracle	12.00%	45.00%
Intel	14.50%	40.00%

    a. What is the expected return of the hedge fund's portfolio?

    b. What is the standard deviation of the hedge fund's portfolio?

28. Consider the portfolio in Problem 27. Suppose the correlation between Intel's and Oracle's stock increases, but nothing else changes. Would the portfolio be more or less risky with this change?

*29. Fred holds a portfolio with a 30% volatility. He decides short sell a stock with a 40% volatility and use the proceeds to invest more in his portfolio. If this transaction reduces the risk of his portfolio, what is the minimum possible correlation between the stock he shorted and his original portfolio?

30. Suppose Target's stock has an expected return of 20% and a volatility of 40%, Hershey's stock has an expected return of 12% and a volatility of 30%, and these two stocks are uncorrelated.

    a. What is the expected return and volatility of an equally weighted portfolio of the two stocks? Consider a new stock with an expected return of 16% and a volatility of 30%. Suppose this new stock is uncorrelated with Target's and Hershey's stock.

b. Is holding this stock alone attractive compared to holding the portfolio in part a?

c. Can you improve upon your portfolio in part a by adding this new stock to your portfolio? Explain.

31. You have $10,000 to invest. You decide to invest $20,000 in Google and short sell $10,000 worth of Yahoo! Google's expected return is 15% with a volatility of 30% and Yahoo!'s expected return is 12% with a volatility of 25%. The stocks have a correlation of 0.9. What is the expected return and volatility of the portfolio?

32. You expect HGH stock have a 20% return next year and a 30% volatility. You have $25,000 to invest, but plan to invest a total of $50,000 in HGH, raising the additional $25,000 by shorting *either* KBH or LWI stock. Both KBH and LWI have an expected return of 10% and a volatility of 20%. If KBH has a correlation of +0.5 with HGH, and LWI has a correlation of −0.50 with HGH, which stock should you short?

Risk-Free Saving and Borrowing

*33. Suppose you have $100,000 in cash and you decide to borrow another $15,000 at a 4% interest rate to invest in the stock market. You invest the entire $115,000 in a portfolio J with a 15% expected return and a 25% volatility.

a. What is the expected return and volatility (standard deviation) of your investment?

b. What is your realized return if J goes up 25% over the year?

c. What return do you realize if J falls by 20% over the year?

34. You have $100,000 to invest. You choose to put $150,000 into the market by borrowing $50,000.

a. If the risk-free interest rate is 5% and the market expected return is 10%, what is the expected return of your investment?

b. If the market volatility is 15%, what is the volatility of your investment?

35. You currently have $100,000 invested in a portfolio that has an expected return of 12% and a volatility of 8%. Suppose the risk-free rate is 5% and there is another portfolio that has an expected return of 20% and a volatility of 12%.

a. What portfolio has a higher expected return than your portfolio but with the same volatility?

b. What portfolio has a lower volatility than your portfolio but with the same expected return?

36. Assume the risk free rate is 4%. You are a financial advisor, and must choose *one* of the funds below to recommend to each of your clients. Whichever fund you recommend, your clients will then combine it with risk-free borrowing and lending depending on their desired level of risk.

	Expected Return	**Volatility**
Fund A	10%	10%
Fund B	15%	22%
Fund C	6%	2%

a. Which fund would you recommend to a client seeking the highest possible expected return with a maximum volatility of 22%?

b. Which fund would you recommend to a client seeking an expected return of 10% with the lowest possible volatility?

c. Which fund would you recommend without knowing your client's risk preference?

37. Assume all investors want to hold a portfolio that, for a given level of volatility, has the maximum possible expected return. Explain why, when a risk-free asset exists, all investors will choose to hold the same portfolio of risky stocks.

The Efficient Portfolio and Required Returns

38. In addition to risk-free securities, you are currently invested in the Maple Ridge Fund, a broad-based fund of stocks and other securities with an expected return of 12% and a volatility of 25%. Currently, the risk-free rate of interest is 4%. Your broker suggests that you add a venture capital fund to your current portfolio. The venture capital fund has an expected return of 20%, a volatility of 80%, and a correlation of 0.2 with the Maple Ridge Fund. Calculate the required return and use it to decide whether you should add the venture capital fund to your portfolio.

39. You have noticed a market investment opportunity that, given your current portfolio, has an expected return that exceeds your required return. What can you conclude about your current portfolio?

40. You are currently only invested in the Natasha Fund (aside from risk-free securities). It has an expected return of 14% with a volatility of 20%. Currently, the risk-free rate of interest is 3.8%. Your broker suggests that you add Hannah Corporation to your portfolio. Hannah Corporation has an expected return of 20%, a volatility of 60%, and a correlation of 0 with the Natasha Fund.

    a. Is your broker right?

    b. You follow your broker's advice and make a substantial investment in Hannah stock so that, considering only your risky investments, 60% is in the Natasha Fund and 40% is in Hannah stock. When you tell your finance professor about your investment, he says that you made a mistake and should reduce your investment in Hannah. Is your finance professor right?

    c. You decide to follow your finance professor's advice and reduce your exposure to Hannah. Now Hannah represents 15% of your risky portfolio, with the rest in the Natasha fund. Is this the correct amount of Hannah stock to hold?

41. Calculate the Sharpe ratio of each of the three portfolios in Problem 40. What portfolio weight in Hannah stock maximizes the Sharpe ratio?

42. Returning to Problem 38, assume you follow your broker's advice and put 50% of your money in the venture fund.

    a. What is the Sharpe ratio of the Maple Ridge Fund?

    b. What is the Sharpe ratio of your new portfolio?

    c. What is the optimal fraction of your wealth to invest in the venture fund? (*Hint:* Use Excel and round your answer to two decimal places.)

The Capital Asset Pricing Model

43. When the CAPM correctly prices risk, the market portfolio is an efficient portfolio. Explain why.

44. A big pharmaceutical company, DRIg, has just announced a potential cure for cancer. The stock price went from $5 to $100 in one day. A friend of yours calls you on the phone to tell you that he owns DRIg. You proudly reply that so do you. Since you have been friends for some time, you know that he holds the market, as do you, and so you both are invested in this stock. Both of you care only about expected return and volatility. The risk-free rate is 3%, quoted as an APR based on a 365-day year. DRIg made up 0.2% of the market portfolio before the news announcement.

    a. On the announcement your overall wealth went up by 1% (assume all other price changes cancelled out so that without DRIg, the market return would have been zero). How is your wealth invested?

    b. Your friend's wealth went up by 2%. How is he invested?

45. Your investment portfolio consists of $15,000 invested in only one stock—Microsoft. Suppose the risk-free rate is 5%, Microsoft stock has an expected return of 12% and a volatility of 40%,

and the market portfolio has an expected return of 10% and a volatility of 18%. Under the CAPM assumptions,

a. What alternative investment has the lowest possible volatility while having the same expected return as Microsoft? What is the volatility of this investment?

b. What investment has the highest possible expected return while having the same volatility as Microsoft? What is the expected return of this investment?

46. Suppose you group all the stocks in the world into two mutually exclusive portfolios (each stock is in only one portfolio): growth stocks and value stocks. Suppose the two portfolios have equal size (in terms of total value), a correlation of 0.5, and the following characteristics:

	Expected Return	Volatility
Value Stocks	13%	12%
Growth Stocks	17%	25%

The risk-free rate is 2%.

a. What is the expected return and volatility of the market portfolio (which is a 50-50 combination of the two portfolios)?

b. Does the CAPM hold in this economy? (*Hint:* Is the market porfolio efficient?)

Determining the Risk Premium

47. Suppose the risk-free return is 4% and the market portfolio has an expected return of 10% and a volatility of 16%. Johnson and Johnson Corporation (Ticker: JNJ) stock has a 20% volatility and a correlation with the market of 0.06.

a. What is Johnson and Johnson's beta with respect to the market?

b. Under the CAPM assumptions, what is its expected return?

EXCEL 48. Consider a portfolio consisting of the following three stocks:

	Portfolio Weight	Volatility	Correlation with the Market Portfolio
HEC Corp	0.25	12%	0.4
Green Midget	0.35	25%	0.6
AliveAndWell	0.4	13%	0.5

The volatility of the market portfolio is 10% and it has an expected return of 8%. The risk-free rate is 3%.

a. Compute the beta and expected return of each stock.

b. Using your answer from part a, calculate the expected return of the portfolio.

c. What is the beta of the portfolio?

d. Using your answer from part c, calculate the expected return of the portfolio and verify that it matches your answer to part b.

49. Suppose Intel stock has a beta of 2.16, whereas Boeing stock has a beta of 0.69. If the risk-free interest rate is 4% and the expected return of the market portfolio is 10%, what is the expected return of a portfolio that consists of 60% Intel stock and 40% Boeing stock, according to the CAPM?

*50. What is the risk premium of a zero-beta stock? Does this mean you can lower the volatility of a portfolio without changing the expected return by substituting out any zero-beta stock in a portfolio and replacing it with the risk-free asset?

DATA CASE

EXCEL

Your manager was so impressed with your work analyzing the return and standard deviations of the twelve stocks from Chapter 10 that he would like you to continue your analysis. Specifically, he wants you to update the stock portfolio by:

- Rebalancing the portfolio with the optimum weights that will provide the best risk and return combinations for the new 12-stock portfolio.

- Determining the improvement in the return and risk that would result from these optimum weights compared to the current method of equally weighting the stocks in the portfolio.

Use the Solver function in Excel to perform this analysis (the time-consuming alternative is to find the optimum weights by trial and error).

1. Begin with the equally weighted portfolio analyzed in Chapter 10. Establish the portfolio returns for the stocks in the portfolio using a formula that depends on the portfolio weights. Initially, these weights will all equal 1/12. You would like to allow the portfolio weights to vary, so you will need to list the weights for each stock in separate cells and establish another cell that sums the weights of the stocks. The portfolio returns for each month *must* reference these weights for Excel Solver to be of any use.

2. Compute the values for the monthly mean return and standard deviation of the portfolio. Convert these values to annual numbers (as you did in Chapter 10) for easier interpretation.

3. Compute the efficient frontier when short sales are not allowed. To activate the Solver function in Excel, click the "Tools," select "Add-Ins . . .," check "Solver Add-in" in the pop-up dialog box, and then click "OK." (*Note:* You may have to install the Solver function using the Microsoft Office Disk for the installation.) To set the Solver parameters:

    a. Set the target cell as the cell of interest, making it the cell that computes the (annual) portfolio standard deviation. Minimize this value.

    b. Establish the "By Changing Cells" by holding the control key and clicking in each of the 12 cells containing the weights of each stock.

    c. Add constraints by clicking on the add button next to the "Subject to the Constraints" box. One set of constraints will be the weight of each stock that is greater than or equal to zero. Calculate the constraints individually. A second constraint is that the weights will sum to one.

    d. Compute the portfolio with the lowest standard deviation for a given expected return. Start by finding this portfolio with an expected return of 5%. To do this, add a constraint that the (annual) portfolio return equals 0.05.

    e. If the parameters are set correctly, you should get a solution when you click "Solve." If there is an error, you will need to double-check the parameters, especially the constraints.

4. Record the resulting standard deviation for the "optimally weighted" portfolio with a return of 0.05 in a separate cell on the spreadsheet. Repeat step 3 to solve for the portfolio with the lowest standard deviation for several different choices of expected return: 0.1, 0.2, 0.3, and 0.4. Record these values. Plot the efficient frontier with the constraint of no short sales. To do this, create an XY Scatter Plot (similar to what you did in Chapter 10), with portfolio standard deviation on the *x*-axis and the return on the *y*-axis.

5. Redo your analysis to allow for short sales by removing the constraint that each portfolio weight is greater than or equal to zero. Use Solver to calculate the (annual) portfolio standard deviation when the annual portfolio returns are set to 0.05, 0.1, 0.2, 0.3, and 0.4. Plot the unconstrained efficient frontier on an XY Scatter Plot. How do these portfolios compare to the mean and standard deviation for the equally weighted portfolio analyzed in Chapter 10?

<table>
<tr><td>**CHAPTER 11**
APPENDIX</td><td># THE CAPM WITH DIFFERING INTEREST RATES</td></tr>
</table>

In this chapter, we assumed that investors faced the same risk-free interest rate whether they were saving or borrowing. In practice, investors receive a lower rate when they save than the rate they must pay when they borrow. For example, short-term margin loans from a broker are often 1% to 2% higher than the rates paid on short-term Treasury Bills. Banks, pension funds, and other investors with large amounts of collateral can borrow at rates that are generally within 1% of the rate on risk-free securities, but there is still a difference. Do these differences in interest rates affect the conclusions of the CAPM?

THE EFFICIENT FRONTIER WITH DIFFERING SAVING AND BORROWING RATES

Figure 11A.1 plots the risk and return possibilities when the saving and borrowing rates differ. In this graph, $r_S = 3\%$ is the rate earned on risk-free savings or lending, and $r_B = 6\%$ is the rate paid on borrowing. Each rate is associated with a different tangent portfolio, labelled T_S and T_B, respectively. A conservative investor who desires a low-risk portfolio can combine the portfolio T_S with saving at rate r_S to achieve risk and return combinations along the lower green line. An aggressive investor who desires high expected returns can invest in the portfolio T_B, using some amount of borrowed funds at rate r_B. By adjusting the amount of borrowing, the investor can achieve risk and return combinations on the upper green line. The combinations on the upper line are not as desirable as the combinations that would result if the investor could borrow at rate r_S, but the investor is unable to borrow at the lower rate. Finally, investors with intermediate preferences may choose portfolios on the red curve between T_S and T_B, which do not involve borrowing or lending.

FIGURE 11A.1

Tangent Portfolios with Different Saving and Borrowing Rates

Investors who save at rate r_s will invest in portfolio T_S, and investors who borrow at rate r_B will invest in portfolio T_B. Some investors may neither save nor borrow and invest in a portfolio on the efficient frontier between T_S and T_B.

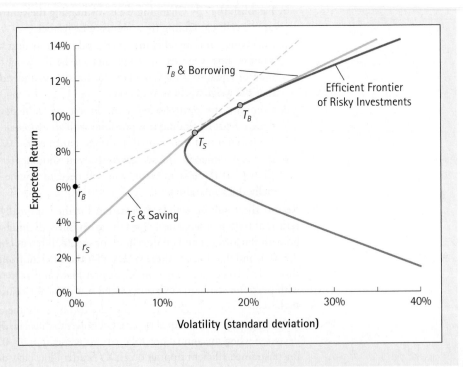

If borrowing and lending rates differ, then investors with different preferences will choose different portfolios of risky securities. Some will choose T_S combined with saving, some will choose T_B combined with borrowing, and some will choose portfolios on the curve between T_S and T_B. So, the first conclusion of the CAPM—that the market portfolio is the unique efficient portfolio of risky investments—is no longer valid.

THE SECURITY MARKET LINE WITH DIFFERING INTEREST RATES

The more important conclusion of the CAPM for corporate finance is the security market line, which relates the risk of an investment to its required return. It turns out that the SML is still valid when interest rates differ. To see why, we make use of the following result:

A combination of portfolios on the efficient frontier of risky investments is also on the efficient frontier of risky investments.[12]

Because all investors hold portfolios on the efficient frontier between T_S and T_B, and because all investors collectively hold the market portfolio, the market portfolio must lie on the frontier between T_S and T_B. As a result, the market portfolio will be tangent for some risk-free interest rate r^* between r_S and r_B, as illustrated in Figure 11A.2. Because our determination of the security market line depends only on the market portfolio being tangent for some interest rate, the SML still holds in the following form:

$$E[R_i] = r^* + \beta_i \ (E[R_{Mkt}] - r^*) \qquad (11A.1)$$

FIGURE 11A.2

Market Portfolio and Determination of r^* When Saving and Borrowing Rates Differ

Because all investors choose portfolios on the efficient frontier from T_S to T_B, the market portfolio is on the efficient frontier between them. The tangent line through the market portfolio determines the interest rate r^* that can be used in the SML.

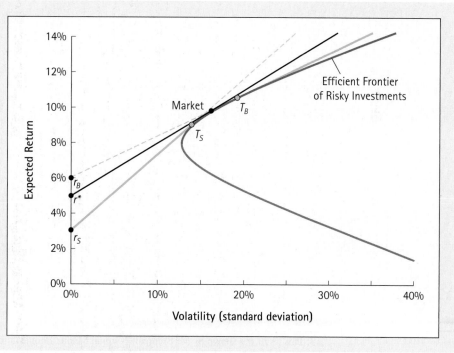

12. To understand this result intuitively, note that portfolios on the efficient frontier contain no diversifiable risk (otherwise we could reduce risk further without lowering the expected return). But a combination of portfolios that contain no diversifiable risk also contains no diversifiable risk, so it is also efficient.

That is, the SML holds with some rate r^* between r_S and r_B in place of r_f. The rate r^* depends on the proportion of savers and borrowers in the economy. But even without knowing those proportions, because saving and borrowing rates tend to be close to each other, r^* must be in a narrow range and we can use Eq. 11A.1 to provide reasonable estimates of expected returns.[13]

We can make a similar argument regarding the choice of which risk-free rate to use. As discussed in Chapter 8, the risk-free rate varies with the investment horizon according to the yield curve. When an investor chooses her optimal portfolio, she will do so by finding the tangent line using the risk-free rate that corresponds to her investment horizon. If all investors have the same horizon, then the risk-free rate corresponding to that horizon will determine the SML. If investors have different horizons (but still have homogeneous expectations), then the SML (Eq. 11A.1) will hold for some r^* on the current yield curve, with the rate depending on the proportion of investors with each investment horizon.[14]

---

13. This result was shown by M. Brennan, "Capital Market Equilibrium with Divergent Borrowing and Lending Rates," *Journal of Financial and Quantitative Analysis* 6 (1971): 1197–1205.

14. We can generalize the arguments in this section further to settings in which there is no risk-free asset; see Fischer Black, "Capital Market Equilibrium with Restricted Borrowing," *Journal of Business* 45 (1972): 444–455, and Mark Rubinstein, "The Fundamental Theorem of Parameter-Preference Security Valuation," *Journal of Financial and Quantitative Analysis* 1 (1973): 61–69.

Estimating the Cost of Capital

Evaluating investment opportunities requires financial managers to estimate the cost of capital. For example, when executives at Research In Motion Limited (RIM) evaluate a capital investment project, they must estimate the appropriate cost of capital in order to determine its NPV. The cost of capital should include a risk premium that compensates RIM's investors for taking on the risk of the new project. How can RIM executives estimate this risk premium and, therefore, the cost of capital?

In the last two chapters, we have developed a method to answer this question: the Capital Asset Pricing Model. In this chapter we will apply this knowledge to compute the cost of capital for an investment opportunity. We begin the chapter by focusing on an investment in the firm's stock. We show how to estimate the firm's equity cost of capital, including practical details of identifying the market portfolio and estimating equity betas. Next we develop methods to estimate the firm's debt cost of capital, based either on its yield or on its beta. Finally, we consider investing in a new project, and show how to estimate a project's cost of capital based on the unlevered cost of capital of comparable firms.

12.1 THE EQUITY COST OF CAPITAL

Recall that the cost of capital is the best expected return available in the market on investments with *similar* risk. The Capital Asset Pricing Model (CAPM) provides a practical way to determine this cost of capital. Under the CAPM, the market portfolio is a well-diversified, efficient portfolio representing the non-diversifiable risk in the economy. Investments therefore have similar risk if they have the same sensitivity to market risk, as measured by their beta with the market portfolio.

So, the cost of capital of any investment opportunity equals the expected return of available investments with the same beta. This estimate is provided by the Security Market Line equation of the CAPM, which states that, given the beta, β_i, of the investment opportunity:

The CAPM Equation for the Cost of Capital (Security Market Line)

$$r_i = r_f + \underbrace{\beta_i \times (E[R_{Mkt}] - r_f)}_{\text{Risk premium for security } i}$$

(12.1)

In other words, investors will require a risk premium comparable to what they would earn taking the same market risk through an investment in the market portfolio.

As our first application of the CAPM, consider an investment in the firm's stock. As we demonstrated in Chapter 9, to value a share of stock, we need to calculate the equity cost of capital. We can do so using Eq. 12.1 if we know the beta of the firm's stock.

EXAMPLE 12.1   COMPUTING THE EQUITY COST OF CAPITAL

Problem

Suppose you estimate that Google's stock has a volatility of 26% and a beta of 1.45. A similar process for UPS yields a volatility of 37% and a beta of 0.79. Which stock carries more total risk? Which has more market risk? If the risk-free interest rate is 3% and you estimate the market's expected return to be 8%, calculate the equity cost of capital for Google and UPS. Which company has a higher cost of equity capital?

Solution

Total risk is measured by volatility; therefore, UPS stock has more total risk than Google. Systematic risk is measured by beta. Google has a higher beta, so it has more market risk than UPS.

Given Google's estimated beta of 1.45, we expect the price for Google's stock to move by 1.45% for every 1% move of the market. Therefore, Google's risk premium will be 1.45 times the risk premium of the market, and Google's equity cost of capital (from Eq. 12.1) is

$$r_{GOOG} = 3\% + 1.45 \times (8\% - 3\%) = 4\% + 8.7\% = 10.25\%$$

UPS has a lower beta of 0.79. The equity cost of capital for UPS is

$$r_{UPS} = 3\% + 0.79 \times (8\% - 3\%) = 4\% + 4.74\% = 6.95\%$$

Because market risk cannot be diversified, it is market risk that determines the cost of capital; thus Google has a higher cost of equity capital than UPS, even though it is less volatile.

While the calculations in Example 12.1 are straightforward, to implement them we need a number of key inputs. In particular, we must

- Construct the market portfolio, and determine its expected excess return over the risk-free interest rate

- Estimate the stock's beta, or sensitivity to the market portfolio

We explain how to estimate these inputs in more detail in the next two sections.

CONCEPT CHECK

1. According to the CAPM, we can determine the cost of capital of an investment by comparing it to what portfolio?

2. What are the key inputs we need to estimate a firm's equity cost of capital using the CAPM?

12.2   THE MARKET PORTFOLIO

To estimate the equity cost of capital using the CAPM, the first thing we need to do is identify the market portfolio. While we have defined the market portfolio as the portfolio of *all* risky investments, what are the proportions of each? In this section we examine how the market portfolio is constructed, common proxies that are used to represent the market portfolio, and how we can estimate the market risk premium.

CONSTRUCTING THE MARKET PORTFOLIO

Because the market portfolio is defined as the total supply of securities, the proportions of each security should correspond exactly to the proportion of the total market that each security represents. Thus the market portfolio contains more of the largest stocks and less of the smallest stocks. Specifically, the investment in each security i is proportional to its **market capitalization**, which is the total market value of its outstanding shares:

$$MV_i = (\text{Number of Shares of } i \text{ Outstanding}) \times (\text{Price of } i \text{ per Share}) \qquad (12.2)$$

We then calculate the portfolio weights of each security as follows:

$$x_i = \frac{\text{Market Value of } i}{\text{Total Market Value of All Securities in the Portfolio}} = \frac{MV_i}{\sum_j MV_j} \qquad (12.3)$$

A portfolio like the market portfolio, in which each security is held in proportion to its market capitalization, is called a **value-weighted portfolio**. A value-weighted portfolio is also an **equal-ownership portfolio**: We hold an equal fraction of the total number of shares outstanding of each security in the portfolio. This last observation implies that even when market prices change, to maintain a value-weighted portfolio, we do not need to trade unless the number of shares outstanding of some security changes. Because very little trading is required to maintain it, a value-weighted portfolio is also a **passive portfolio**.

MARKET INDEXES

Rather than construct the market portfolio ourselves, if we focus our attention on Canadian stocks, we find two indexes that try to represent the performance of the Canadian stock market.

EXAMPLES OF MARKET INDEXES.   A **market index** reports the value of a particular portfolio of securities that make up the index. The most familiar index is the S&P/TSX Composite Index (formerly called the TSE 300 index). The original index was created in

VALUE-WEIGHTED PORTFOLIOS AND REBALANCING

As we pointed out in the text, value-weighted portfolios are very efficient from a transaction cost perspective because there is no need to rebalance the portfolio weights in the face of price changes. To see why, consider the following example.

Suppose we have $100,000 to invest in a value-weighted portfolio of TD Bank (TD), Suncor Energy (SU), Research In Motion (RIM), and Shoppers Drug Mart (SC). If the stock prices and number of shares outstanding are as shown in the table, what number of shares of each should we buy to construct a value-weighted portfolio?

Stock	Shares Outstanding (millions)	Stock Price ($)
TD	862.9	76.00
SU	1560.3	30.85
RIM	557.2	77.13
SC	217.4	43.59

Solution

First we compute the market capitalization for each stock by multiplying the number of shares outstanding by the current price per share. For example, TD Bank has a market capitalization of 862.9 million × $76.00 = $65.6 billion. Next we compute the total market capitalization for the four stocks and determine the percentage represented by each.

Stock	Market Cap (billions)	Percent of Total	Initial Investment	Shares Purchased	Ownership
TD	$ 65.6	39.47%	$ 39,470	519	0.000060%
SU	48.1	28.97%	28,970	939	0.000060%
RIM	43.0	25.86%	25,860	335	0.000060%
SC	9.5	5.70%	5700	131	0.000060%
Total	$166.2	100.00%	$100,000		

Based on the value weights, we can then determine the dollar amount to invest in each stock. For example, because TD Bank's market capitalization is about 39.47% of the total, we invest 39.47% × $100,000 = $39,470 in TD Bank stock. Given TD Bank's stock price of $76.00, investing $39,470 corresponds to purchasing $39,470/$76.00 = 519 shares of TD Bank stock. We compute the number of shares for each of the other stocks similarly.

In the last column of the table, we also compute the fraction of the total number of shares outstanding that we will purchase. For TD Bank, we are buying 519 of 862.9 million shares, or 0.000060% of the total outstanding. Note that the percentage is the same for each stock.

Now suppose that the price of TD Bank stock drops to $55 per share and Shoppers Drug Mart stock price rises to $70 per share. What trades are necessary to keep the portfolio value weighted?

Solution

Let's compute the value of each of the holdings:

Stock	Stock Price ($)	Shares Held	Value of Shares ($)	Percent of Portfolio
TD	55.00	519	28,563.81	30.9%
SU	30.85	939	28,970.00	31.3%
RIM	77.13	335	25,859.99	27.9%
SC	70.00	131	9,153.48	9.9%
Total			92,547.28	100.0%

The total value of the portfolio has dropped from $100,000 to $92,547.28, and each of the portfolio weights has changed. But compare the portfolio weights to the market value weights:

Stock	Shares Outstanding (millions)	Stock Price ($)	Market Cap (billions)	Percent of Total
TD	862.9	55.00	47.5	30.9%
SU	1560.3	30.85	48.1	31.3%
RIM	557.2	77.13	43.0	27.9%
SC	217.4	70.00	15.2	9.9%
Total			153.8	100.0%

The portfolio weights remain consistent with the market value weights. Therefore, no trades are necessary to keep the portfolio value weighted.

1977 with a base value of 1000 as of 1975. Since 2002, Standard & Poor's Corporation of New York has managed the index. The weights of the components of the index are determined by the market capitalization of the companies that comprise it (210 companies as of February 2010). The S&P/TSX Composite Index is a popular portfolio used to represent the market index when applying the CAPM to Canadian stocks, as it represents about 95% of Canada's equity market capitalization. Another popular index is the S&P/TSX 60 Index. The weights of the 60 companies' stocks are determined partially by their market values. They are also determined so the index reflects the relative values of the industry sectors that make up the broader composite index. The companies that make up the S&P/TSX 60 Index are large and very liquid. Because of the market capitalization and liquidity of the stocks, the S&P/TSX 60 Index is considered to be easier to replicate by investors and portfolio managers. The liquidity results in lower transaction costs (due to bid-ask spreads) and less price pressure (when trades occur) than for some of the smaller and more thinly traded stocks that are included in the S&P/TSX Composite Index. The S&P/TSX 60 Index is still quite representative of the overall Canadian market as it covers about 73% of the market value of Canadian equities traded.

Most Canadian media also report on the U.S. stock market. The most widely quoted stock index in the United States is the Dow Jones Industrial Average (DJIA), which consists of a portfolio of 30 large industrial stocks. While somewhat representative, the DJIA clearly does not represent the entire market. Also, the DJIA is a *price-weighted* (rather than value-weighted) *portfolio*. A **price-weighted portfolio** holds an equal number of shares of each stock, independent of their size. Despite being nonrepresentative of the entire market, the DJIA remains widely cited because it is one of the oldest stock market indexes (first published in 1884).

A better representation of the entire U.S. stock market is the S&P 500, a value-weighted portfolio of 500 of the largest U.S. stocks.[1] The S&P 500 was the first widely publicized value-weighted index in the U.S. (S&P began publishing its index in 1923, though it was based on a smaller number of stocks at that time), and it has become a

---

1. Standard & Poor's periodically replaces stocks in the index (on average about seven or eight stocks per year). While size is one criterion, Standard & Poor's also tries to maintain appropriate representation of different segments of the economy and chooses firms that are leaders in their industries. Also, from 2005, the value weights in the index are based on the number of shares available for public trading.

benchmark for professional investors. This index is the most commonly cited index when evaluating the overall performance of the U.S. stock market. It is also the standard portfolio used to represent "the market portfolio" when using the CAPM in practice. Even though the S&P 500 includes only 500 of the more than 7000 individual U.S. stocks in existence, because the S&P 500 includes the largest stocks, it represents more than 70% of the U.S. stock market in terms of market capitalization.

More recently created indexes, such as the Wilshire 5000, provide a value-weighted index of *all* U.S. stocks listed on the major stock exchanges.[2] While more complete than the S&P 500, and therefore more representative of the overall market, its returns are very similar; between 1990 and 2009, the correlation between their weekly returns was nearly 99%. Given this similarity, many investors view the S&P 500 as an adequate measure of overall U.S. stock market performance.

INVESTING IN A MARKET INDEX. The S&P/TSX Composite Index, S&P/TSX 60, and the S&P 500 indexes are all well-diversified indexes that roughly correspond to their respective markets. Not only are these indexes widely reported, but they are also easy to invest in. Many mutual fund companies offer funds, called **index funds**, that invest in one of these portfolios. In addition, *exchange-traded funds* represent these portfolios. An **exchange-traded fund (ETF)** is a security that trades directly on an exchange, like a stock, but represents ownership in a portfolio of stocks. For example, BlackRock Asset Management Canada Limited has several ETFs called iShares that trade on the TSX. Other subsidiaries of BlackRock Inc. have ETFs that trade on stock exchanges around the world. For Canadian investors, iShares are available that replicate the Canadian indexes and the different industry sector indexes for Canada. Also traded on the TSX are iShares that replicate the S&P 500 and other international stock indexes. By investing in an index or an exchange-traded fund, an individual investor with only a small amount to invest can easily achieve the benefits of broad diversification.

Although practitioners commonly use the S&P/TSX Composite in Canada and the S&P 500 in the United States as the market portfolio in the CAPM, no one does so because of a belief that these indexes are actually the market portfolio. Instead they view each of these indexes as a **market proxy**, a portfolio whose return they believe closely tracks the true market portfolio. Of course, how well the model works will depend on how closely the market proxy actually tracks the true market portfolio. We will return to this issue in Chapter 13.

CONCEPT CHECK   1. How is the weight of a stock in the market portfolio determined?

2. What is an exchange-traded fund (ETF)?

12.3   THE MARKET RISK PREMIUM

Recall that a key ingredient to the CAPM is the market risk premium, which is the expected excess return of the market portfolio: $E[R_{Mkt}] - r_f$. The market risk premium provides the benchmark by which we assess investors' willingness to hold market risk. Before we can estimate it, we must first discuss the choice of the risk-free interest rate to use in the CAPM.

---

2. The Wilshire 5000 began with approximately 5000 stocks when it was first published in 1974. While the name has not changed, the number of stocks in the index has grown with U.S. equity markets.

develop your financial plan, estimate the cost of capital of this opportunity assuming a risk-free rate of 3% and a market risk premium of 5%.

Solution

Checking google.com/finance, we find that Peet's has no debt and an estimated beta of 0.83. Using Peet's beta as the estimate of the project beta, we can apply Eq. 12.1 to estimate the cost of capital of this investment opportunity as

$$r_{project} = r_f + \beta_{PEET}\,(E[R_{Mkt}] - r) = 3\% + 0.83 \times 5\% = 7.15\%$$

Thus, assuming our coffee shop has a similar sensitivity to market risk as Peet's, we can estimate the appropriate cost of capital for our investment as 7.15%.

Let's review the intuition of Example 12.4. Rather than investing in the new coffee shop, you could invest in Peet's coffee shops simply by buying Peet's stock. Given this alternative, to be attractive the new investment must have an expected return at least equal to that of Peet's stock, which from the CAPM is 7.15%.

LEVERED FIRMS AS COMPARABLES

The situation is a bit more complicated if the comparable firm has debt. In that case, the cash flows generated by the firm's assets are used to pay both debt and equity holders. As a result, the returns of the firm's equity alone are not representative of the underlying assets; in fact, because of the firm's leverage, the equity will often be much riskier. Thus, the beta of a levered firm's equity will not be a good estimate of the beta of its assets and of our project.

How can we estimate the beta of the comparable firm's assets in this case? As shown in Figure 12.3 we can undo the effect of leverage and recreate a claim on the firm's assets by holding *both* its debt and equity simultaneously. Because the firm's cash flows will be used to pay either debt or equity holders, by holding both securities we are entitled to all of the cash flows generated by the firm's assets. The returns of the firm's assets must therefore match the returns of a portfolio of all of the firm's debt and equity combined. Similarly, the beta of the firm's assets will match the beta of this portfolio.

THE UNLEVERED COST OF CAPITAL

As we saw in Chapter 11, the expected return of a portfolio is equal to the weighted average of the expected returns of the securities in the portfolio, where the weights correspond to the relative market values of the different securities held. Thus, the firm's **asset cost of capital** or **unlevered cost of capital**, which is the expected return required by the firm's investors to hold the firm's underlying assets, is the weighted average of the firm's equity and debt costs of capital:

$$\binom{\text{Asset or Unlevered}}{\text{Cost of Capital}} = \binom{\text{Fraction of Firm Value}}{\text{Financed by Equity}}\binom{\text{Equity Cost}}{\text{of Capital}} + \binom{\text{Fraction of Firm Value}}{\text{Financed by Debt}}\binom{\text{Debt Cost}}{\text{of Capital}}$$

FIGURE 12.3

Using a Levered Firm as Comparable for a Project's Risk

If we identify a levered firm whose assets have comparable market risk to our project, then we can estimate the project's cost of capital based on a portfolio of the firm's debt and equity.

Writing this out, if we let E and D be the total market value of equity and debt of the comparable firm, with equity and debt costs of capital r_E and r_D, then we can estimate the firm's asset or unlevered cost of capital r_U as follows:[13]

Asset or Unlevered Cost of Capital

$$r_U = \frac{E}{E + D} r_E + \frac{D}{E + D} r_D \tag{12.8}$$

UNLEVERED BETA. Because the beta of a portfolio is the weighted average of the betas of the securities in the portfolio, we have a similar expression for the firm's **asset or unlevered beta**, which we can use to estimate the beta of our project:

Asset or Unlevered Beta

$$\beta_U = \frac{E}{E + D} \beta_E + \frac{D}{E + D} \beta_D \tag{12.9}$$

Let's apply these formulas in an example.

EXAMPLE 12.5   UNLEVERING THE COST OF CAPITAL

Problem

Your firm is considering expanding its household products division. You identify Procter & Gamble (PG) as a firm with comparable investments. Suppose PG's equity has a market capitalization of $144 billion and a beta of 0.57. PG also has $37 billion of debt outstanding, with a AA credit rating and an average yield of 3.1%. Estimate the beta of your firm's investment given a risk-free rate of 3% and a market risk premium of 5%.

Solution

Because investing in this division is like investing in PG's assets by holding its debt and equity, we can estimate our cost of capital based on PG's unlevered cost of capital. First we estimate PG's equity cost of capital using the CAPM as $r_E = 3\% + 0.57(5\%) = 5.85\%$. Because PG's debt is highly rated, we approximate its debt cost of capital using the debt yield of 3.1%. Thus, PG's unlevered cost of capital is

$$r_U = \frac{144}{144 + 37} 5.85\% + \frac{37}{144 + 37} 3.1\% = 5.29\%$$

Alternatively, we can estimate PG's unlevered beta. Given its high rating, if we assume PG's debt beta is zero, we have

$$\beta_U = \frac{144}{144 + 37} 0.57 + \frac{37}{144 + 37} 0 = 0.453$$

Taking this result as an estimate of the beta of our project, we can compute our project's cost of capital from the CAPM as $r_U = 3\% + 0.453(5\%) = 5.27\%$.

---

13. For simplicity, we assume here that the firm in question maintains a constant debt-equity ratio, so that the weights $E/(E + D)$ and $D/(E + D)$ are fixed. As a result, Eqs. 12.8 and 12.9 hold in the presence of taxes (if the project is equity financed). See Chapter 18 for details, and an analysis of settings with changing leverage.

The slight difference in r_U using the two methods arises because in the first case, we assumed the expected return of PG's debt is equal to its promised yield of 3.1%, while in the second case, we assumed the debt has a beta of zero, which implies an expected return equal to the risk-free rate of 3% according to the CAPM. The truth is somewhere between the two results, as PG's debt is not completely risk-free.

CASH AND NET DEBT. Sometimes firms maintain large cash balances in excess of their operating needs. This cash represents a risk-free asset on the firm's balance sheet, and reduces the average risk of the firm's assets. Often, we are interested in the risk of the firm's underlying business operations, separate from its cash holdings. That is, we are interested in the risk of the firm's enterprise value, which we defined in Chapter 2 as the combined market value of the firm's equity and debt, less any excess cash. In that case, we can measure the leverage of the firm in terms of its **net debt:**

$$\text{Net Debt} = \text{Debt} - \text{Excess Cash and Short-Term Investments} \quad (12.10)$$

The intuition for using net debt is that if the firm holds $1 in cash and $1 in risk-free debt, then the interest earned on the cash will equal the interest paid on the debt. The cash flows from each source cancel each other, just as if the firm held no cash and no debt.[14]

Note that if the firm has more cash than debt, its net debt will be negative. In this case, its unlevered beta and cost of capital will exceed its equity beta and cost of capital, as the risk of the firm's equity is mitigated by its cash holdings.

EXAMPLE 12.6

CASH AND BETA

Problem

In mid-2009, Apple had a market capitalization of $140 billion, no debt, and $24 billion in cash. If its estimated equity beta was 1.51, estimate the beta of Apple's underlying business enterprise.

Solution

Apple has net debt = −$24 billion. Therefore, Apple's enterprise value is $140 billion − $24 billion = $116 billion, which is the value of its underlying business excluding its

---

14. We can also think of the firm's enterprise value V in terms of a portfolio of equity and debt less cash: $V = E + D - C$, where C is excess cash. In that case, the natural extension of Eq. 12.9 is

$$\beta_U = \frac{E}{E + D - C}\beta_E + \frac{D}{E + D - C}\beta_D - \frac{C}{E + D - C}\beta_C$$

(and similarly for Eq. 12.8). The shortcut of using net debt is equivalent if the debt beta reflects the combined risk of the firm's debt and cash positions.

cash. Assuming Apple's cash investments are risk-free, we can estimate the beta of this enterprise value as

$$\beta_U = \frac{E}{E+D}\beta_E + \frac{D}{E+D}\beta_D = \frac{140}{140-24}1.51 + \frac{-24}{140-24}0 = 1.82$$

Note that in this case, Apple's equity is *less* risky than its underlying business activities due to its cash holdings.

INDUSTRY ASSET BETAS

Now that we can adjust for the leverage of different firms to determine their asset betas, it is possible to combine estimates of asset betas for multiple firms in the same industry or line of business. Doing so is extremely useful, as it will enable us to reduce our estimation error and improve the accuracy of the estimated beta for our project.

EXAMPLE 12.7   ESTIMATING AN INDUSTRY ASSET BETA

Problem

Consider the following data for U.S. department stores in mid-2009, showing the equity beta, ratio of net debt to enterprise value (D/V), and debt rating for each firm. Estimate the average and median asset beta for the industry.

Company	Ticker	Equity Beta	D/V	Debt Rating
Dillard's	DDS	2.38	0.59	B
J. C. Penney Company	JCP	1.60	0.17	BB
Kohl's	KSS	1.37	0.08	BBB
Macy's	M	2.16	0.62	BB
Nordstrom	JWN	1.94	0.35	BBB
Saks	SKS	1.85	0.50	CCC
Sears Holdings	SHLD	1.36	0.23	BB

Solution

Note that D/V provides the fraction of debt financing, and (1−D/V) the fraction of equity financing, for each firm. Using the data for debt betas from Table 12.3, we can apply Eq. 12.9 for each firm. For example, for Dillard's:

$$\beta_U = \frac{E}{E+D}\beta_E + \frac{D}{E+D}\beta_D = (1-0.59)2.38 + (0.59)0.26 = 1.13$$

Doing this calculation for each firm, we obtain the following estimates:

Ticker	Equity Beta	D/V	Debt Rating	Debt Beta	Asset Beta
DDS	2.38	0.59	B	0.26	1.13
JCP	1.60	0.17	BB	0.17	1.36
KSS	1.37	0.08	BBB	0.10	1.27

(*Continued*)

Ticker	Equity Beta	D/V	Debt Rating	Debt Beta	Asset Beta
M	2.16	0.62	BB	0.17	0.93
JWN	1.94	0.35	BBB	0.10	1.30
SKS	1.85	0.50	CCC	0.31	1.08
SHLD	1.36	0.23	BB	0.17	1.09
				Average	1.16
				Median	1.13

The large differences in the firms' equity betas are mainly due to differences in leverage. The firms' asset betas are much more similar, suggesting that the underlying businesses in this industry have similar market risk. By combining estimates from several closely related firms in this way, we can get a more accurate estimate of the beta for investments in this industry.

Figure 12.4 shows estimates of industry asset betas using global summary data. Note that businesses that are less sensitive to market and economic conditions, such as utilities and firms providing staples such as groceries, tend to have lower asset betas than more cyclical industries, such as high technology firms.

FIGURE 12.4

Global Industry Asset Betas (January 2010)

Betas are computed using 5 years of monthly returns for each stock and then averaged (simple). The unlevered betas are estimated using the average market debt/equity ratios by industrial sector. *Source:* Damodaran Online (April 2010).

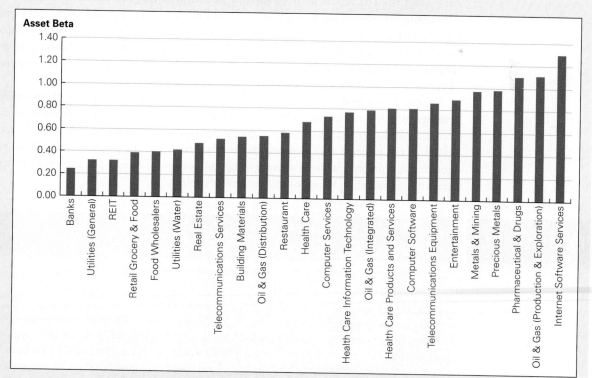

1. What data can we use to estimate the beta of a project?

2. Why does the equity beta of a levered firm differ from the beta of its assets?

12.7 PROJECT COST OF CAPITAL: RISK CHARACTERISTICS AND FINANCING

Thus far, we have evaluated a project's cost of capital by comparing it with the unlevered assets of firms in the same line of business. We have also assumed the project itself is unlevered; specifically, it is to be financed solely with equity. In this section we consider why and how we may need to adjust our analysis to account for differences between projects, in terms of both their risk and their mode of financing.

PROJECT RISK CHARACTERISTICS

Firm asset betas reflect the market risk of the *average* project in a firm. But individual projects may be more or less sensitive to market risk. A financial manager evaluating a new investment should try to assess how this project might compare with the average project.

As an example, conglomerate 3M has both a health care division and a computer display and graphics division. These divisions are likely to have very different market risks (note the difference in asset betas between healthcare supplies and computer peripherals in Figure 12.4). 3M's own asset beta will represent an average of the risk of these and 3M's other divisions, and would not be an appropriate measure of risk for projects in either division. Instead, financial managers should evaluate projects based on asset betas of firms that concentrate in a similar line of business. Thus, for multi-divisional firms, identifying a set of "pure play" comparables for each division is helpful in estimating appropriate divisional costs of capital.

Even within a firm with a single line of business, some projects obviously have different market risk characteristics from the firm's other activities. For example, if RIM were considering whether to buy or lease an office building to expand its headquarters, the cash flows associated with this decision are clearly very different from the cash flows associated with its typical project of developing mobile telecommunications hardware, and we should use a different cost of capital. (Indeed, we will discuss the risk and appropriate cost of capital associated with leasing in more detail in Chapter 25.)

Another factor that can affect the market risk of a project is its degree of **operating leverage**, which is the relative proportion of fixed versus variable costs. Holding fixed the cyclicality of the project's revenues, a higher proportion of fixed costs will increase the sensitivity of the project's cash flows to market risk and raise the project's beta. Thus, we should assign projects with an above-average proportion of fixed costs and thus greater-than-average operating leverage a higher cost of capital.

EXAMPLE 12.8

OPERATING LEVERAGE AND BETA

Problem

Consider a project that is expected to generate revenues each year of $120 with costs of $50. These costs are completely variable, so that the profit margin of the project will remain constant. Suppose the project has a beta of 1.0, the risk-free rate is 5%, and the expected return of the market is 10%. What is the value of this project? What would its value and beta be if the revenues continued to vary with a beta of 1.0, but the costs were instead completely fixed at $50 per year?

Solution

The expected cash flow of the project is $120 − $50 = $70 per year. Given a beta of 1.0, the appropriate cost of capital is $r = 5\% + 1.0(10\% − 5\%) = 10\%$. Thus, the value of the project if the costs are completely variable is $70/10% = $700.

If instead the costs are fixed, then we can compute the value of the project by discounting the revenues and costs separately. The revenues still have a beta of 1.0, and thus a cost of capital of 10%, for a present value of $120/10% = $1200. Because the costs are fixed, we should discount them at the risk-free rate of 5%, so their present value is $50/5% = $1000. Thus, with fixed costs the project has a value of only $1200 − $1000 = $200.

What is the beta of the project now? We can think of the project as a portfolio that is long the revenues and short the costs. The project's beta is the weighted average of the revenue and cost betas, or

$$\beta_P = \frac{R}{R-C}\beta_R - \frac{C}{R-C}\beta_C = \frac{1200}{1200-1000}1.0 - \frac{1000}{1200-1000}0 = 6.0$$

Given a beta of 6.0, the project's cost of capital with fixed costs is $r = 5\% + 6.0(10\% − 5\%) = 35\%$. To verify this result, note that the present value of the expected profits is then $70/35% = 200. As this example shows, increasing the proportion of fixed versus variable costs can significantly increase a project's beta (and reduce its value).

PROJECT FINANCING AND THE WEIGHTED AVERAGE COST OF CAPITAL

In Section 12.5, we presumed the project we are evaluating is all-equity financed; that is, the firm does not plan any additional borrowing as a result of the project. What is the importance of this financing assumption, and how might the project's cost of capital change if the firm does use leverage to finance the project?

The complete answer to this question will be the topic of Part 5 of the text, where we consider the many implications of the firm's choice of financing policy. We provide a quick preview here of some key results.

PERFECT CAPITAL MARKETS. Let's begin by recalling our discussion in Chapter 3 where we argued that with perfect capital markets—by which we mean no taxes, transactions costs, or other frictions—the choice of financing does not affect the cost of capital or NPV of a project. Rather, a project's cost of capital and NPV are solely determined by its free cash

COMMON MISTAKE   ADJUSTING FOR EXECUTION RISK

When a company launches a new product or makes some other type of new investment, it is often subject to a greater degree of **execution risk**, which is the risk that—due to missteps in the firm's execution—the project may fail to generate the forecasted cashflows. For example, there may be a greater chance of manufacturing delays or marketing mistakes.

Firms sometimes try to adjust for this risk by assigning a higher cost of capital to new projects. Such adjustments are generally incorrect, as execution risk is typically firm-specific risk, which is diversifiable. (Intuitively, as a shareholder investing in many firms, you can diversify the risk that some firms may suffer execution failures while others do not.) The cost of capital for the project should only depend on its sensitivity to market-wide risks.

Of course, this does not mean that we should ignore execution risk. We should capture this risk in the expected cash flows generated by the project. For example, if a project is expected to generate a free cash flow of $100 next year, but there is a 20% chance it might fail and generate nothing, than our expected free cash flow is only $80. Thus, the free cash flows that we discount will be lower the greater the degree of execution risk.

flows. In this setting then, our assumption regarding the project's financing is innocuous. Its cost of capital would be the same whether or not, and to what extent, it is financed in part with debt. The intuition for this result, which we gave in Chapter 3, is that in a competitive and perfect market, all financing transactions are zero-NPV transactions that do not affect value.

TAXES—A BIG IMPERFECTION. When market frictions do exist, the firm's decision regarding how to finance the project may have consequences that affect the project's value. Perhaps the most important example comes from the Income Tax Act, which allows the firm to deduct interest payments on debt when calculating its taxable income. As we saw in Chapter 5, if the firm pays interest rate r on its debt, then once the tax deduction is accounted for, the net cost to the firm is given by

$$\text{Effective After-Tax Interest Rate} = r(1 - \tau_C) \qquad (12.11)$$

where τ_C is the firm's corporate tax rate.

THE WEIGHTED AVERAGE COST OF CAPITAL. As we will see in Chapter 15, when the firm finances its own project using debt, it will benefit from the interest tax deduction. We can include this benefit by calculating the firm's effective after-tax cost of capital, called the **weighted average cost of capital**, or **WACC**, using its after-tax cost of debt:

Weighted Average Cost of Capital (WACC)

$$r_{wacc} = \frac{E}{E + D} r_E + \frac{D}{E + D} r_D (1 - \tau_C) \qquad (12.12)$$

Comparing the weighted average cost of capital, r_{wacc}, with the unlevered cost of capital, r_U, defined in Eq. 12.8, note that the WACC is based on the effective after-tax cost of debt, whereas the unlevered cost of capital is based on the firm's pretax cost of debt. The unlevered cost of capital is therefore also referred to as the **pretax WACC**. Let's review the key distinctions between them:

1. The unlevered cost of capital (or pretax WACC) is the expected return investors will earn holding the firm's assets (ignoring any taxes the investors might pay). In a world with taxes, it can be used to evaluate an *all-equity financed project* with the same risk as the firm.

2. The weighted average cost of capital (or WACC) is the effective after-tax cost of capital to the firm. Because interest expense is tax deductible, the WACC is less than the expected return of the firm's assets. In a world with taxes, the WACC can be used to evaluate a project with the same risk and *same financing as the firm itself.*

We'll return to consider the WACC in additional detail, as well other implications of the firm's financing decisions, in Part 5 of the text.

EXAMPLE 12.9

ESTIMATING THE WACC

Problem
Dunlap Corp. has a market capitalization of $100 million and $25 million in outstanding debt. Dunlap's equity cost of capital is 10%, and its debt cost of capital is 6%. What is Dunlap's unlevered cost of capital? If its corporate tax rate is 40%, what is Dunlap's weighted average cost of capital?

Solution

Dunlap's unlevered cost of capital, or pretax WACC, is given by

$$r_U = \frac{E}{E+D}r_E + \frac{D}{E+D}r_D = \frac{100}{125}10\% + \frac{25}{125}6\% = 9.2\%$$

Thus, we would use a cost of capital of 9.2% to evaluate all-equity financed projects with the same risk as Dunlap's assets.

Dunlap's weighted average cost of capital, or WACC, is given by

$$r_{wacc} = \frac{E}{E+D}r_E + \frac{D}{E+D}r_D(1-\tau_C) = \frac{100}{125}10\% + \frac{25}{125}6\%(1-40\%) = 8.72\%$$

The WACC of 8.72% can be used to evaluate projects with the same risk and the same mix of debt and equity financing as Dunlap's assets. It is a lower rate than the unlevered cost of capital to reflect the tax deductibility of interest expenses.

FINAL THOUGHTS ON USING THE CAPM

In this chapter, we have developed an approach to estimating a firm's or project's cost of capital using the CAPM. Along the way, we have had to make a number of practical choices, approximations, and estimations. And these decisions were on top of the assumptions of the CAPM itself, which are not completely realistic. At this point, you might be wondering: How reliable, and thus worthwhile, are the results that we can obtain following this approach?

While there is no definitive answer to this question, we offer several thoughts. First, the types of approximations that we used to estimate the cost of capital are no different from our other approximations throughout the capital budgeting process. In particular, the revenue and other cash flow projections we must make when valuing a stock or an investment in a new product are likely to be far more speculative than any we have made in estimating the cost of capital. Thus, the imperfections of the CAPM may not be critical in the context of capital budgeting and corporate finance, where errors in estimating project cash flows are likely to have a far greater impact than small discrepancies in the cost of capital.

Second, in addition to being very practical and straightforward to implement, the CAPM-based approach is very robust. While perhaps not perfectly accurate, the estimates tend to be in the ballpark. Other methods, such as relying on average historical returns, can lead to much larger errors. When the CAPM does generate errors, they are likely to be small.

Third, the CAPM imposes a disciplined process on managers to identify the cost of capital. There are few parameters available to adjust in order to achieve a desired result, and the assumptions made are straightforward to document. As a result, the CAPM may make the capital budgeting process less subject to managerial manipulation than if managers could set project costs of capital without clear justification.

Finally, and perhaps most importantly, even if the CAPM model is not perfectly accurate, *it gets managers to think about risk in the correct way.* Managers of widely held corporations should not worry about diversifiable risk, which shareholders can easily eliminate in their own portfolios. They should focus on, and be prepared to compensate investors for, the market risk in the decisions that they make.

Thus, despite its potential flaws, there are very good reasons to use the CAPM as a basis for calculating the cost of capital. In our view, the CAPM is viable, especially when measured relative to the effort required to implement a more sophisticated model (such as the one we will develop in Chapter 13). Consequently, it is no surprise that the CAPM remains the predominant model used in practice to determine the cost of capital.

While the CAPM is likely to be an adequate and practical approach for capital budgeting, you may still wonder how reliable its conclusions are for investors. For example, is holding the market index really the best strategy for investors, or can they do better by trading on news, or hiring a professional fund manager? And how do investors actually behave? We consider these questions in Chapter 13.

CONCEPT CHECK

1. Which errors in the capital budgeting process are likely to be more important than discrepancies in the cost of capital estimate?

2. Even if the CAPM is not perfect, why might we continue to use it in corporate finance?

SUMMARY

1. Given a security's beta, we can estimate its cost of capital using the CAPM equation for the security market line:

$$r_i = r_f + \underbrace{\beta_i \times (E[R_{Mkt}] - r_f)}_{\text{Risk premium for security } i} \qquad (12.1)$$

2. To implement the CAPM, we must (i) construct the market portfolio, and determine its expected excess return over the risk-free interest rate and (ii) estimate the stock's beta, or sensitivity to the market portfolio.

3. The market portfolio is a value-weighted portfolio of all securities traded in the market. According to the CAPM, the market portfolio is efficient.

4. In a value-weighted portfolio, the amount invested in each security is proportional to its market capitalization.

5. A value-weighted portfolio is also an equal-ownership portfolio. Thus it is a passive portfolio, meaning no rebalancing is necessary due to daily price changes.

6. Because the true market portfolio is difficult if not impossible to construct, in practice we use a proxy for the market portfolio, such as the S&P/TSX Composite Index in Canada and the S&P 500 or Wilshire 5000 indices in the United States.

7. The risk-free rate in the security market line should reflect an average of the risk-free borrowing and lending rates. Practitioners generally choose the risk-free rate from the yield curve based on the investment horizon.

8. While the historical return of the S&P/TSX Composite Index has been about 5.5% more than Canadian Treasury Bills since 1900, research suggests that future excess returns are likely to be lower. Since 1950, the average excess return of the S&P/TSX has been 3.6% over Canadian Treasury Bills.

9. Beta measures a security's sensitivity to market risk. Specifically, beta is the expected change (in %) in the return of a security given a 1% change in the return of the market portfolio.

10. To estimate beta, we often use historical returns. Beta corresponds to the slope of the best-fitting line in the plot of a security's excess returns versus the market's excess returns.

11. If we regress a stock's excess returns against the market's excess returns, the intercept is the stock's alpha. It measures how the stock has performed historically relative to the security market line.

12. Unlike estimating an average return, reliable beta estimates can be obtained with just a few years of data.

13. Betas tend to be stable over time, whereas alphas do not seem to be persistent.

14. Because of default risk, the debt cost of capital, which is its expected return to investors, is less than its yield to maturity, which is its promised return.

15. Given annual default and expected loss rates, the debt cost of capital can be estimated as

$$r_d = \text{Yield to Maturity} - \text{Prob(default)} \times \text{Expected Loss Rate} \qquad (12.7)$$

16. We can also estimate the expected return for debt based on its beta using the CAPM. However, beta estimates for individual debt securities are hard to obtain. In practice, estimates based on the debt's rating may be used.

17. We can estimate a project's cost of capital based on the asset or unlevered beta of comparable firms in the same line of business, based on the *market* value of the firm's equity and debt:

$$r_U = \frac{E}{E + D} r_E + \frac{D}{E + D} r_D \qquad (12.8)$$

18. We can also estimate the beta of a project as the unlevered beta of a comparable firm:

$$\beta_U = \frac{E}{E + D} \beta_E + \frac{D}{E + D} \beta_D \qquad (12.9)$$

19. Because cash holdings will reduce a firm's equity beta, when unlevering betas we can use the firm's net debt, which is debt less excess cash.

20. We can reduce estimation error by averaging unlevered betas for several firms in the same industry to determine an industry asset beta.

21. Firm or industry asset betas reflect the market risk of the average project in that firm or industry. Individual projects may be more or less sensitive to the overall market. Operating leverage is one factor that can increase a project's market risk.

22. We should not adjust the cost of capital for project-specific risks (such as execution risk). These risks should be reflected in the project's cash flow estimates.

23. An unlevered cost of capital can be used to evaluate an equity-financed project. If the project will be financed in part with debt, the firm's effective after-tax cost of debt is less than its expected return to investors. In that case, the weighted average cost of capital can be used:

$$r_{wacc} = \frac{E}{E + D} r_E + \frac{D}{E + D} r_D (1 - \tau_C) \qquad (12.12)$$

24. The CAPM is not perfect, and there are many estimates and approximations we must make to implement it. That said, it is straightforward to use, relatively robust, and hard to manipulate, and it correctly emphasizes the importance of market risk. As a result, it is the most popular and best available method to use for capital budgeting.

KEY TERMS

alpha *p. 419*
asset beta *p. 424*
asset cost of capital *p. 423*
characteristic line *p. 416*
equal-ownership portfolio *p. 409*
error (residual) term *p. 418*
exchange-traded fund *p. 412*
execution risk *p. 429*
index funds *p. 412*
linear regression *p. 417*
market capitalization *p. 409*
market index *p. 409*

market proxy *p. 412*
net debt *p. 425*
operating leverage *p. 428*
passive portfolio *p. 409*
pretax WACC *p. 430*
price-weighted portfolio *p. 411*
unlevered beta *p. 424*
unlevered cost of capital *p. 423*
value-weighted portfolio *p. 409*
weighted average cost of capital
    (WACC) *p. 430*

PROBLEMS

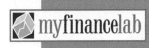 The problems marked in green can be found on MyFinanceLab at www.myfinancelab.com. Visit your MyFinanceLab for additional practice. An asterik (*) indicates problems with a higher level of difficulty. Additional readings for this chapter may be found in the Textbook Resources section on MyFinanceLab.

The Equity Cost of Capital

1. Suppose Pepsico's stock has a beta of 0.57. If the risk-free rate is 3% and the expected return of the market portfolio is 8%, what is Pepsico's equity cost of capital?

2. Suppose the market portfolio has an expected return of 10% and a volatility of 20%, while Microsoft's stock has a volatility of 30%.

    a. Given its higher volatility, should we expect Microsoft to have an equity cost of capital that is higher than 10%?

    b. What would have to be true for Microsoft's equity cost of capital to be equal to 10%?

3. Aluminum maker Alcoa has a beta of about 2.0, whereas Hormel Foods has a beta of 0.45. If the expected excess return of the marker portfolio is 5%, which of these firms has a higher equity cost of capital, and how much higher is it?

The Market Portfolio

 4. Suppose all possible investment opportunities in the world are limited to the five stocks listed in the table below. What does the market portfolio consist of?

Stock	Price/Share ($)	Number of Shares Outstanding (millions)
A	10	10
B	20	12
C	8	3
D	50	1
E	45	20

 5. Given $100,000 to invest, construct a value-weighted portfolio of the four stocks listed below.

Stock	Price/Share ($)	Number of Shares Outstanding (millions)
Grizzly Ltd.	13	1000
DAS	22	1.25
Polar Beer	43	30
PDJB	5	10

6. Using the data in Problem 4, suppose you are holding a market portfolio and have invested $12,000 in Stock C.

   a. How much have you invested in Stock A?

   b. How many shares of Stock B do you hold?

   c. If the price of Stock C suddenly drops to $4 per share, what trades would you need to make to maintain a market portfolio?

7. Suppose Best Buy stock is trading for $40 per share for a total market cap of $16 billion and Walt Disney has 1.8 billion shares outstanding. If you hold the market portfolio, and as part of it hold 100 shares of Best Buy, how many shares of Walt Disney do you hold?

8. Standard and Poor's also publishes the S&P Equal Weight Index, which is an equally weighted version of the S&P 500.

   a. To maintain a portfolio that tracks this index, what trades would need to be made in response to daily price changes?

   b. Explain why this index would not be suitable as a market proxy.

The Market Risk Premium

9. Suppose that in place of the S&P 500, you wanted to use a broader market portfolio of all U.S. stocks and bonds as the market proxy. Could you use the same estimate for the market risk premium when applying the CAPM? If not, how would you estimate the correct risk premium to use?

10. From the start of 1999 to the start of 2009, the S&P 500 had a negative return. Does this mean the market risk premium we should use in the CAPM is negative?

11. If one stock in a value-weighted portfolio goes up in price and all other stock prices remain the same, what trades are necessary to keep the portfolio value weighted?

Beta Estimation

12. You need to estimate the equity cost of capital for XYZ Corp. Unfortunately, you only have the following data available regarding past returns:

Year	Risk-free Return	Market Return	XYZ Return
2009	3%	6%	10%
2010	1%	−37%	−45%

   a. What was XYZ's average historical return?

   b. Compute the market's and XYZ's excess returns for each year. Estimate XYZ's beta.

   c. Estimate XYZ's historical alpha.

   d. Suppose the current risk-free rate is 3% and you expect the market's return to be 8%. Use the CAPM to estimate an expected return for XYZ Corp.'s stock.

   e. Would you base your estimate of XYZ's equity cost of capital on your answer in part a or in part d? How does your answer to part c affect your estimate? Explain.

EXCEL *13. Go to the Spreadsheet section on MyFinanceLab to get the Nike data Spreadsheet for Chapter 12 to estimate the beta of Nike and Dell stock based on their monthly returns from 2004–2008. (*Hint:* You can use the SLOPE() function in Excel.)

EXCEL *14. Using the same data as in Problem 13, estimate the alpha of Nike and Dell stock, expressed as % per month. (*Hint:* You can use the INTERCEPT( ) function in Excel.)

EXCEL *15. Using the same data as in Problem 13, estimate the 95% confidence interval for the alpha and beta of Nike and Dell stock using Excel's regression tool (from the data analysis menu).

The Debt Cost of Capital

16. In mid-2009, Ralston Purina had AA-rated, 6-year bonds outstanding with a yield to maturity of 3.75%. At the time, similar maturity Treasuries had a yield of 3%.

a. If Ralston Purina's bonds were risk-free, what is your estimate of the expected return for these bonds?

b. If you believe Ralston Purina's bonds have 1% chance of default per year and that expected loss rate in the event of default is 40%, what is your estimate of the expected return for these bonds?

17. In mid-2009, Rite Aid had CCC-rated, 6-year bonds outstanding with a yield to maturity of 17.3%. At the time, similar maturity Treasuries had a yield of 3%. Suppose the market risk premium is 5% and you believe Rite Aid's bonds have a beta of 0.31. If the expected loss rate of these bonds in the event of default is 60%, what annual probability of default would be consistent with the yield to maturity of these bonds?

18. The Dunley Corp. plans to issue 5-year bonds. It believes the bonds will have a BBB rating. Suppose AAA bonds with the same maturity have a 4% yield. If the market risk premium is 5%, using the data in Table 12.2 and Table 12.3:

a. Estimate the yield Dunley will have to pay, assuming an expected 60% loss rate in the event of default during average economic times. What spread over AAA bonds will it have to pay?

b. Estimate the yield Dunley would have to pay if it were a recession, assuming the expected loss rate is 80% at that time. What is Dunley's spread over AAA now?

c. In fact, one might expect risk premia and betas to increase in recessions. Redo part b assuming that the market risk premium and the beta of debt both increase by 20%; that is, they equal 1.2 times their value in recessions.

A Project's Cost of Capital

19. Your firm is planning to invest in an automated packaging plant. Harburtin Industries is an all-equity firm that specializes in this business. Suppose Harburtin's equity beta is 0.85, the risk-free rate is 4%, and the market risk premium is 5%. If your firm's project is all equity financed, estimate its cost of capital.

20. Consider the setting of Problem 19. You decided to look for other comparables to reduce estimation error in your cost of capital estimate. You find a second firm, Thurbinar Design, which is also engaged in a similar line of business. Thurbinar has a stock price of $20 per share, with 15 million shares outstanding. It also has $100 million in outstanding debt, with a yield on the debt of 4.5%. Thurbinar's equity beta is 1.00.

a. Assume Thurbinar's debt has a beta of zero. Estimate Thurbinar's unlevered beta. Use the unlevered beta and the CAPM to estimate Thurbinar's unlevered cost of capital.

b. Estimate Thurbinar's equity cost of capital, and assume its debt cost of capital equals its yield. Based on these results, estimate Thurbinar's unlevered cost of capital.

c. Explain the difference between your estimate in parts a and b.

d. You decide to average your results in parts a and b, and then average this result with your estimate from Problem 19. What is your estimate for the cost of capital of your firm's project?

21. IDX Tech is looking to expand its investment in advanced security systems. The project will be financed with equity. You are trying to assess the value of the investment, and must estimate its cost of capital. You find the following data for a publicly traded firm in the same line of business:

Debt outstanding (book value, AA-rated)	$400 million
Number of shares of common stock	80 million
Stock price per share	$15.00
Book value of equity per share	$6.00
Beta of equity	1.20

What is your estimate of the project's beta? What assumptions do you need to make?

22. In June 2009, Cisco Systems had a market capitalization of $115 billion. It had A-rated debt of $10 billion as well as cash and short-term investments of $34 billion, and its estimated equity beta at the time was 1.27.

    a. What is Cisco's enterprise value?

    b. Assuming Cisco's debt has a beta of zero, estimate the beta of Cisco's underlying business enterprise.

23. Consider the following airline industry data from mid-2009:

Company Name	Market Capitalization ($mm)	Total Enterprise Value ($mm)	Equity Beta	Debt Ratings
Delta Air Lines (DAL)	4,938.5	17,026.5	2.04	BB
Southwest Airlines (LUV)	4,896.8	6,372.8	0.966	A/BBB
JetBlue Airways (JBLU)	1,245.5	3,833.5	1.91	B/CCC
Continental Airlines (CAL)	1,124.0	4,414.0	1.99	B

    a. Use the estimates in Table 12.3 to estimate the debt beta for each firm (use an average if multiple ratings are listed).

    b. Estimate the asset beta for each firm.

    c. What is the average asset beta for the industry, based on these firms?

Project Cost of Capital: Risk Characteristics and Financing

24. Weston Enterprises is an all-equity firm with two divisions. The soft drink division has an asset beta of 0.60, expects to generate free cash flow of $50 million this year, and anticipates a 3% perpetual growth rate. The industrial chemicals division has an asset beta of 1.20, expects to generate free cash flow of $70 million this year, and anticipates a 2% perpetual growth rate. Suppose the risk-free rate is 4% and the market risk premium is 5%.

    a. Estimate the value of each division.

    b. Estimate Weston's current equity beta and cost of capital. Is this cost of capital useful for valuing Weston's projects? How is Weston's equity beta likely to change over time?

*25. Harrison Holdings Inc. (HHI) is publicly traded, with a current share price of $32 per share. HHI has 20 million shares outstanding, as well as $64 million in debt. The founder of HHI, Harry Harrison, made his fortune in the fast food business. He sold off part of his fast food empire and purchased a professional hockey team. HHI's only assets are the hockey team, together with 50% of the outstanding shares of Harry's Hotdogs restaurant chain. Harry's Hotdogs (HDG) has a market capitalization of $850 million and an enterprise value of $1.05 billion. After a little research, you find that the average asset beta of other fast food restaurant chains is 0.75. You also find that the debt of HHI and HDG is highly rated, and so you decide to estimate the beta of both firms' debt as zero. Finally, you do a regression analysis on HHI's historical stock returns in comparison to the S&P 500, and estimate an equity beta of 1.33. Given this information, estimate the beta of HHI's investment in the hockey team.

26. Your company operates a steel plant. On average, revenues from the plant are $30 million per year. All of the plant's costs are variable costs, and they are consistently 80% of revenues, including energy costs associated with powering the plant, which represents one-quarter of the plant's costs, or an average of $6 million per year. Suppose the plant has an asset beta of 1.25, the risk-free rate is 4%, and the market risk premium is 5%. The tax rate is 40%, and there are no other costs.

    a. Estimate the value of the plant today assuming no growth.

    b. Suppose you enter a long-term contract that will supply all of the plant's energy needs for a fixed cost of $3 million per year (before tax). What is the value of the plant if you take this contract?

    c. How would taking the contract in part b change the plant's cost of capital? Explain.

27. Unida Systems has 40 million shares outstanding trading for $10 per share. In addition, Unida has $100 million in outstanding debt. Suppose Unida's equity cost of capital is 15%, its debt cost of capital is 8%, and the corporate tax rate is 40%.

    a. What is Unida's unlevered cost of capital?

    b. What is Unida's after-tax debt cost of capital?

    c. What is Unida's weighted average cost of capital?

28. You would like to estimate the weighted average cost of capital for a new airline business. Based on its industry asset beta, you have already estimated an unlevered cost of capital for the firm of 9%. However, the new business will be 25% debt-financed, and you anticipate its debt cost of capital will be 6%. If its corporate tax rate is 40%, what is your estimate of its WACC?

DATA CASE

EXCEL

You work in Walt Disney Company's corporate finance and treasury department and have just been assigned to the team estimating Disney's WACC. You must estimate this WACC in preparation for a team meeting later today. You quickly realize that the information you need is readily available online.

1. Go to http://finance.yahoo.com. Under "Market Summary," you will find the yield to maturity for ten-year Treasury bonds listed as "10 Yr Bond(%)." Collect this number as your risk-free rate.

2. In the box next to the "Get Quotes" button, type Walt Disney's ticker symbol (DIS) and press enter. Once you see the basic information for Disney, find and click "Key Statistics" on the left side of the screen. From the key statistics, collect Disney's market capitalization (its market value of equity), enterprise value (market-value equity + net debt), cash, and beta.

3. To get Disney's cost of debt and the market value of its long-term debt, you will need the price and yield to maturity on the firm's existing long-term bonds. Go to http://cxa.marketwatch.com/finra/BondCenter/Default.aspx. Under "Quick Bond Search," click "Corporate" and type Disney's ticker symbol. A list of Disney's outstanding bond issues will appear. Assume that Disney's policy is to use the yield to maturity on non-callable ten-year obligations as its cost of debt. Find the non-callable bond issue that is as close to ten years from maturity as possible. (*Hint:* You will see a column titled "Callable"; make sure the issue you choose has "No" in this column.) Find the yield to maturity for your chosen bond issue (it is in the column titled "Yield"). Hold the mouse over the table of Disney's bonds and right-click. Select "Export to Microsoft Excel." An Excel spreadsheet with all of the data in the table will appear.

4. You now have the price for each bond issue, but you need to know the size of the issue. Returning to the Web page, click "Walt Disney Company" in the first row. This brings up a Web page with all of the information about the bond issue. Scroll down until you find "Amount Outstanding" on the right side. Noting that this amount is quoted in thousands of dollars (e.g., $60,000 means $60 million = $60,000,000), record the issue amount in the appropriate row of your spreadsheet. Repeat this step for all of the bond issues.

5. The price for each bond issue in your spreadsheet is reported as a percentage of the bond's par value. For example, 104.50 means that the bond issue is trading at 104.5% of its par value. You can calculate the market value of each bond issue by multiplying the amount outstanding by (Price ÷ 100). Do so for each issue and then calculate the total of all the bond issues. This is the market value of Disney's debt.

6. Compute the weights for Disney's equity and debt based on the market value of equity and Disney's market value of debt, computed in step 5.

7. Calculate Disney's cost of equity capital using the CAPM, the risk-free rate you collected in step 1, and a market risk premium of 5%.

8. Assuming that Disney has a tax rate of 35%, calculate its effective cost of debt capital.

9. Calculate Disney's WACC.

10. Calculate Disney's net debt by subtracting its cash (collected in step 2) from its debt. Recalculate the weights for the WACC using the market value of equity, net debt, and enterprise value. Recalculate Disney's WACC using the weights based on the net debt. How much does it change?

11. How confident are you of your estimate? Which implicit assumptions did you make during your data collection efforts?

CHAPTER 12 APPENDIX

PRACTICAL CONSIDERATIONS WHEN FORECASTING BETA

The CAPM is a significant and elegant theory of the relationship between risk and return. As discussed in Section 12.3, we can estimate stock betas in practice by regressing past stock returns on returns of the market portfolio. As with all theories, we must make a number of practical choices when using the CAPM. Important choices in estimating beta include (1) the time horizon used, (2) the index used as the market portfolio, and (3) the method used to extrapolate from past betas to future betas.

TIME HORIZON

When estimating beta by using past returns, there is a tradeoff regarding which time horizon to use to measure returns. If we use too short a time horizon, our estimate of beta will be unreliable. If we use very old data, they may be unrepresentative of the current market risk of the security. For stocks, common practice is to use at least two years of weekly return data or five years of monthly return data.[15]

THE MARKET PROXY

The CAPM predicts that a security's expected return depends on its beta with regard to the market portfolio of *all* risky investments available to investors. As mentioned earlier, in practice the S&P/TSX Composite Index is used as the market proxy in Canada and the S&P 500 is used in the United States. Other proxies may be used too; even a broader market index that includes both equities and fixed-income securities is sometimes used. When evaluating international stocks, it is common practice to use a specific country index or an international market index.

BETA VARIATION AND EXTRAPOLATION

When using historical data, there is always the possibility of estimation error. Thus we should be suspicious of estimates that are extreme relative to industry norms; in fact, many practitioners prefer to use average industry betas rather than individual stock betas. In addition, evidence suggests that betas tend to regress toward the average beta of 1.0 over time.[16] For both of these reasons, many practitioners use adjusted betas, which are calculated by averaging the estimated beta with 1.0. For example, Bloomberg computes adjusted betas using the following formula:

$$\text{Adjusted Beta of Security } i = \tfrac{2}{3}\beta_i + \tfrac{1}{3}(1.0) \tag{12A.1}$$

The estimation methodologies of three data providers appear in Table 12A.1. Each employs a unique methodology, which leads to differences in the reported betas.

---

15. While daily returns would provide even more sample points, we generally do not use them due to the concern—especially for smaller, less liquid stocks—that short-term factors might influence daily returns that are not representative of the longer-term risks affecting the security. Ideally, we should use a return interval equal to our investment horizon. The need for sufficient data, however, makes monthly returns the longest practical choice.

16. See M. Blume, "Betas and Their Regression Tendencies," *Journal of Finance* 30 (1975): 785–795.

FIGURE 13.1

An Inefficient Market Portfolio
If the market portfolio is not equal to the efficient portfolio, then the market is not in the CAPM equilibrium. The figure illustrates this possibility if news is announced that raises the expected return of TELUS and Suncor stocks and lowers the expected return of RIM and TD Bank stocks compared to the situation depicted in Figure 11.12.
Sources: **CFMRC and individual company Web sites.**

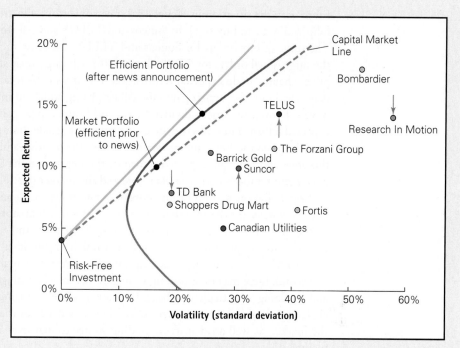

FIGURE 13.2

Deviations from the Security Market Line
If the market portfolio is not efficient, then stocks will not all lie on the security market line. The distance of a stock above or below the security market line is the stock's alpha. We can improve upon the market portfolio by buying stocks with positive alphas and selling stocks with negative alphas, but as we do so, prices will change and their alphas will shrink towards zero (i.e., they will move toward the Security Market Line).
Sources: **CFMRC and individual company Web sites.**

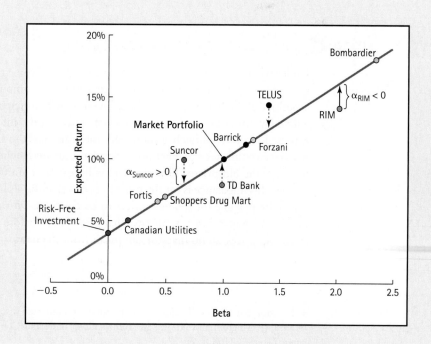

PROFITING FROM NON-ZERO ALPHA STOCKS

Faced with the situation in Figure 13.2, savvy investors who are holding the market portfolio will want to buy stock in Suncor and TELUS and sell stock in TD Bank and RIM. The surge of buy orders for Suncor and TELUS will cause their stock prices to rise, and the surge of sell orders for TD Bank and RIM will cause their stock prices to fall. As stock prices change, so do expected returns. Recall that a stock's total return is equal to its dividend yield plus the capital gain rate. All else being equal, an increase in the current stock price will lower the stock's dividend yield and future capital gain rate, thereby lowering its expected return. Thus, as savvy investors attempt to trade to improve their portfolios, they raise the price and lower the expected return of the positive-alpha stocks, and they depress the price and raise the expected return of the negative-alpha stocks, until the stocks are once again on the Security Market Line and the market portfolio is efficient.

Notice that the actions of investors have two important consequences. First, while the CAPM conclusion that the market is always efficient may not literally be true, competition among savvy investors who try to "beat the market" and earn a positive alpha should keep the market portfolio close to efficient much of the time. In that sense, we can view the CAPM as an approximate description of a competitive market.

Second, there exist trading strategies that take advantage of non-zero alpha stocks, and by doing so actually can beat the market. In the remainder of this chapter we will explore both of these consequences, looking at evidence of the approximate efficiency of the market, as well as identifying trading strategies that may actually do better than the market.

CONCEPT CHECK

1. If investors attempt to buy a stock with a positive alpha, what is likely to happen to its price and expected return? How will this affect its alpha?

2. What is the consequence of investors exploiting non-zero alpha stocks for the efficiency of the market portfolio?

13.2 INFORMATION AND RATIONAL EXPECTATIONS

Under what circumstances could an investor profit from trading a non-zero alpha stock? Consider the situation in Figure 13.2 after the news announcement. Because Suncor has a positive alpha before prices adjust, investors will anticipate that the price will rise and will likely put in buy orders at the current prices. If the information that altered Suncor's expected return is publicly announced, there are likely to be a large number of investors who receive this news and act on it. Similarly, anybody who hears the news will not want to sell at the old prices. That is, there will be a large order imbalance. The only way to remove this imbalance is for the price to rise so that the alpha is zero. Note that in this case it is quite possible for the new prices to come about *without trade*. That is, the competition between investors is so intense that prices move before any investor can actually trade at the old prices, so no investor can profit from the news.[3]

---

3. The idea that prices will adjust to information without trade is sometimes referred to as the *no-trade theorem*. (P. Milgrom and N. Stokey, "Information, Trade and Common Knowledge," *Journal of Economic Theory* 26 (1982): 17–27.)

INFORMED VERSUS UNINFORMED INVESTORS

As the above example makes clear, *in order to profit by buying a positive-alpha stock, there must be someone willing to sell it.* Under the CAPM assumption of homogeneous expectations, which states that all investors have the same information, it would seem that all investors would be aware that the stock had a positive alpha and none would be willing to sell.

Of course, the assumption of homogeneous expectations is not necessarily a good description of the real world. In reality, investors have different information and spend varying amounts of effort researching stocks. Consequently, we might expect that sophisticated investors would learn that Suncor has a positive alpha, and that they would be able to purchase shares from more naive investors.

However, even differences in the quality of investors' information will not necessarily be enough to generate trade in this situation. An important conclusion of the CAPM is that investors should hold the market portfolio (combined with risk-free investments), and this investment advice *does not depend on the quality of an investor's information or trading skill.* Even naive investors with no information can follow this investment advice, and as the following example shows, by doing so they can avoid being taken advantage of by more sophisticated investors.

EXAMPLE 13.1

HOW TO AVOID BEING OUTSMARTED IN FINANCIAL MARKETS

Problem

Suppose you are an investor without access to any information regarding stocks. You know that other investors in the market possess a great deal of information and are actively using that information to select an efficient portfolio. You are concerned that because you are less informed than the average investor, your portfolio will underperform the portfolio of the average investor. How can you prevent that outcome and guarantee that your portfolio will do as well as that of the average investor?

Solution

Even though you are not as well informed, you can guarantee yourself the same return as the average investor simply by holding the market portfolio. Because the aggregate of all investors' portfolios must equal the market portfolio (that is, demand must equal supply), if you hold the market portfolio then you must make the same return as the average investor.

On the other hand, suppose you don't hold the market portfolio, but instead hold less of Suncor stock than its market weight. This must mean that in aggregate all other investors have over-weighted Suncor relative to the market. Because other investors are more informed than you are, they must realize Suncor is a good deal, and so are happy to profit at your expense. You can prevent this by holding the market, which guarantees that informed traders will not make money at your expense.

What if all uninformed investors realized the point in this example and hold the market? In that case, by supply and demand, informed investors must also hold the market and so informed investors cannot exploit their informational advantage! All investors, regardless of their information, must make the same return. Thus, the only way informed investors can take advantage of less informed investors is if the less informed investors choose to depart from the strategy of holding the market portfolio. Even if they do, as an uninformed investor, you can always guarantee that informed investors' profits do not come at your expense by simply holding the market portfolio.

RATIONAL EXPECTATIONS

Example 13.1 is very powerful. It implies that every investor, regardless of how little information he or she has access to, can guarantee him- or herself the average return and earn an alpha of zero simply by holding the market portfolio. Thus no investor should choose a portfolio with a negative alpha. However, because the average portfolio of all investors is the market portfolio, the average alpha of all investors is zero. If no investor earns a negative alpha, then no investor can earn a positive alpha, and the market portfolio must be efficient. As a result, the CAPM does not depend on the assumption of homogeneous expectations. Rather it requires only that investors have **rational expectations**, which means that all investors correctly interpret and use their own information, as well as information that can be inferred from market prices or the trades of others.[4]

For an investor to earn a positive alpha and beat the market, some investors must hold portfolios with negative alphas. Because these investors could have earned a zero alpha by holding the market portfolio, we reach the following important conclusion:

The market portfolio can be inefficient (so it is possible to beat the market) only if a significant number of investors either

1. *Do not have rational expectations so that they misinterpret information and believe they are earning a positive alpha when they are actually earning a negative alpha, or*

2. *Care about aspects of their portfolios other than expected return and volatility, and so are willing to hold inefficient portfolios of securities.*

How do investors actually behave? Do the uninformed investors heed this advice and hold the market portfolio? To shed light on these questions, we review the evidence on individual investor behaviour next.

CONCEPT CHECK
1. How can uninformed or unskilled investors guarantee themselves a non-negative alpha?
2. Under what conditions will it be possible to earn a positive alpha and beat the market?

13.3   THE BEHAVIOUR OF INDIVIDUAL INVESTORS

In this section, we examine whether small, individual investors heed the advice of the CAPM and hold the market portfolio. As we will see, many investors do not appear to hold an efficient portfolio, but instead fail to diversify and trade too much. Given the results of the last section, these departures from the market create an opportunity for more sophisticated investors to profit at individual investors' expense. We then consider whether it is possible to exploit this opportunity by looking for predictable, systematic patterns in the types of errors individual investors make.

---

4. See, e.g., P. DeMarzo and C. Skiadas, "Aggregation, Determinacy, and Informational Efficiency for a Class of Economies with Asymmetric Information," *Journal of Economic Theory* 80 (1998): 123–152.

UNDERDIVERSIFICATION AND PORTFOLIO BIASES

One of the most important implications of our discussion of risk and return is the benefit of diversification. By appropriately diversifying their portfolios, investors can reduce risk without reducing their expected return. In that sense, diversification is a "free lunch" that all investors should take advantage of.

Despite this benefit, there is much evidence that individual investors fail to diversify their portfolios adequately. Evidence from the U.S. Survey of Consumer Finances shows that, for households that held stocks, the median number of stocks held by investors in 2001 was four, and 90% of investors held fewer than 10 different stocks.[5] Moreover, these investments are often concentrated in stocks of companies in the same industry, or which are geographically close, further limiting the degree of diversification attained. A related finding comes from studying how individuals allocate their retirement savings accounts (401K plans). A study of large plans found that employees invested close to a third of their assets in their employer's own stock.[6] These underdiversification results are not unique to U.S. investors: A comprehensive study of Swedish investors documents that approximately one-half of the volatility in investors' portfolios is due to firm-specific risk.[7]

There are a number of potential explanations for this behaviour. One is that investors suffer from a **familiarity bias**, so that they favour investments in companies they are familiar with.[8] Another is that investors have **relative wealth concerns** and care most about the performance of their portfolio relative to that of their peers. This desire to "keep up with the Joneses" can lead investors to choose undiversified portfolios that match those of their colleagues or neighbours.[9] In any case, this underdiversification is one important piece of evidence that individual investors may choose suboptimal portfolios.

EXCESSIVE TRADING AND OVERCONFIDENCE

According to the CAPM, investors should hold risk-free assets in combination with the market portfolio of all risky securities. In Chapter 12, we demonstrated that because the market portfolio is a value-weighted portfolio, it is also a passive portfolio in the sense that an investor does not need to trade in response to daily price changes in order to maintain it. Thus, if all investors held the market, we would see relatively little trading volume in financial markets.

In reality, a tremendous amount of trading occurs each day. In 2008, for example, annual turnover on the NYSE exceeded 135%, implying that each share of each stock was traded 1.35 times on average. Figure 13.3 shows the increase in share turnover in recent years.

In an influential study of the trading behaviour of individual investors that held accounts at a discount brokerage, researchers Brad Barber and Terrance Odean found that

---

5. V. Polkovnichenko, "Household Portfolio Diversification: A Case for Rank Dependent Preferences," *Review of Financial Studies* 18 (2005): 1467–1502.

6. S. Benartzi, "Excessive Extrapolation and the Allocation of 401(k) Accounts to Company Stock," *Journal of Finance* 56 (2001): 1747–1764.

7. J. Campbell, "Household Finance," *Journal of Finance,* 61 (2006): 1553–1604.

8. G. Huberman, "Familiarity Breeds Investment," *Review of Financial Studies* 14 (2001): 659–680.

9. P. DeMarzo, R. Kaniel, and I. Kremer, "Diversification as a Public Good: Community Effects in Portfolio Choice," *Journal of Finance* 59 (2004): 1677–1715.

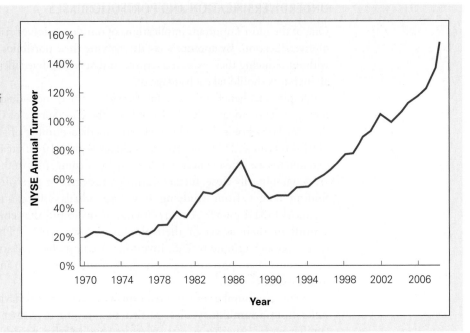

FIGURE 13.3

NYSE Annual Share Turnover, 1970–2008

The plot shows the annual share turnover (number of shares traded in the year/total number of shares). Note the increase in turnover in recent years. Such high turnover is difficult to reconcile with the CAPM, which implies that investors should hold passive market portfolios.
Source: **Data from** www.nyxdata. com.

individual investors tend to trade very actively, with average turnover almost 50% above the overall rates reported in Figure 13.3 during the time period of their study.[10]

What might explain this trading behaviour? Psychologists have known since the 1960s that uninformed individuals tend to overestimate the precision of their knowledge. For example, many sports fan sitting in the stands confidently second-guess the coaching decisions on the field, truly believing that they can do a better job. In finance we call this presumptuousness the **overconfidence hypothesis**. Barber and Odean hypothesized that this kind of behaviour also characterizes individual investment decision making. Like sports fans, individual investors believe they can pick winners and losers when, in fact, they cannot; this overconfidence leads them to trade too much.

An implication of this overconfidence hypothesis is that, assuming they have no true ability, investors who trade more will not earn higher returns. Instead, their performance will be worse once we take into account the costs of trading (due to both commissions and bid-ask spreads). Figure 13.4 documents precisely this result, showing that much investor trading appears not to be based on rational assessments of performance.

As additional evidence, Barber and Odean contrasted the behaviour and performance of men versus women.[11] Psychological studies have shown that, in areas such as finance, men tend to be more overconfident than women. Consistent with the overconfidence hypothesis, they documented that men tend to trade more than women, and that their portfolios have lower returns as a result. These differences are even more pronounced for single men and women.

---

10. B. Barber and T. Odean, "Trading Is Hazardous to Your Wealth: The Common Stock Investment Performance of Individual Investors," *Journal of Finance* 55 (2000): 773–806.

11. B. Barber and T. Odean, "Boys Will Be Boys: Gender, Overconfidence, and Common Stock Investment," *Quarterly Journal of Economics* 116 (2001): 261–292.

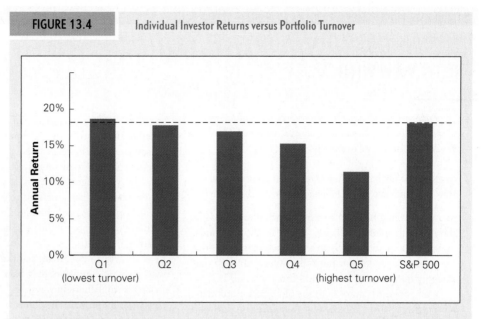

FIGURE 13.4   Individual Investor Returns versus Portfolio Turnover

The plot shows average annual return (net of commissions and trading costs) for individual investors at a large discount brokerage from 1991–1997. Investors are grouped into quintiles based on their average annual turnover. While the least-active investors had slightly (but not significantly) better performance than the S&P 500, performance declined with the rate of turnover.

Source: B. Barber and T. Odean, "Trading Is Hazardous to Your Wealth: The Common Stock Investment Performance of Individual Investors," *Journal of Finance* 55 (2000): 773–806.

Researchers have obtained similar results in an international context. Using an extraordinarily detailed database on Finnish investors, researchers Mark Grinblatt and Matti Keloharju found that trading activity increases with psychological measures of overconfidence. Interestingly, they also find that trading activity increases with the number of speeding tickets an individual receives, which they interpret as a measure of **sensation seeking**, or the individual's desire for novel and intense risk-taking experiences. In both cases, the increased trading does not appear to be profitable for investors.[12]

INDIVIDUAL BEHAVIOUR AND MARKET PRICES

Thus, in reality, individual investors are underdiversified and trade too much, violating a key prediction of the CAPM. But does this observation imply that the remaining conclusions of the CAPM are invalid?

The answer is, not necessarily. If individuals depart from the CAPM in random, idiosyncratic ways, then despite the fact that each individual doesn't hold the market, when we combine their portfolios together these departures will tend to cancel out just like any other idiosyncratic risk. In that case, individuals will hold the market portfolio *in aggregate*, and there will be no effect on market prices or returns. Intuitively, these uninformed

12. M. Grinblatt and M. Keloharju, "Sensation Seeking, Overconfidence, and Trading Activity," *Journal of Finance* 64 (2009): 549–578.

INTERVIEW WITH JONATHAN CLEMENTS

Jonathan Clements is the former personal finance columnist for the Wall Street Journal *and author of* The Little Book of Main Street Money *(Wiley, 2009).*

QUESTION: **You have written for years on personal finance. How has academic theory influenced investor behaviour?**

ANSWER: When I started writing about mutual funds in the 1980s, investors would ask, "What are the best funds?" Today, they are more likely to say, "I'm looking to add a foreign-stock fund to my portfolio. Which funds in that category do you like? Or should I index instead?"

We have gotten away from the blind pursuit of market-beating returns, and there is more focus on portfolio construction and a growing willingness to consider indexing. That reflects the impact of academic research.

What has really influenced investors has been the academic "grunt work" of the past four decades, which has given us a decent grasp of what historical market returns look like. Thanks to that research, many ordinary investors have a better understanding of how stocks have performed relative to bonds. They realize that most actively managed stock mutual funds don't beat the market, and thus there is a case for indexing. They appreciate that different market sectors perform well at different times, so there is a real value in diversifying.

QUESTION: **Some have critiqued the idea of holding a well-diversified portfolio, arguing that diversification hasn't worked in the 2008–2009 financial crisis. Is diversification still the best strategy?**

ANSWER: Yes, when markets collapse, pretty much every sector gets bludgeoned. But just because investments rise and fall in sync with one another doesn't mean they rise and fall by the same amount. You might have a portfolio where one sector falls 40 percent and another loses 20 percent. Sure, losing 20 percent stings. Still, holding that sector is reducing your portfolio's overall loss, so you are indeed benefiting from diversification.

QUESTION: **Academics talk about efficient frontiers and optimal portfolios. How does that translate into advice for someone looking to build a portfolio?**

ANSWER: While academic research has influenced ordinary investors, we shouldn't overstate the case. To some extent, the research has merely codified what investors already knew intuitively. For instance, investors have always thought about risk as well as return, and they have always been inclined to diversify. The academic research may have made investors a little more rigorous in their thinking, but it didn't radically change their behaviour.

Moreover, to the extent that the research doesn't fit with investors' intuition, they have clearly rejected it. Investors still behave in ways that academics would consider suboptimal. They don't build well-diversified portfolios and then focus on the risk and return of the overall portfolio. Instead, they build moderately diversified portfolios—and then pay a lot of attention to the risk and reward of each investment they own.

QUESTION: **How does risk tolerance affect the type of portfolio a person should build?**

ANSWER: In theory, investors should hold the globally diversified all-asset "market portfolio" and then, depending on their risk tolerance, either add risk-free assets to reduce volatility or use leverage to boost returns. But almost nobody invests that way. In fact, I once tried to find out what the market portfolio looks like—and discovered nobody knows for sure.

Among the vast majority of ordinary investors, the idea of using leverage to buy investments is an anathema. In practice, many are doing just that. They hold a portfolio of assets, including stocks, bonds, and real estate, and they have a heap of debt, including their mortgage, auto loans, and credit-card balances. But the implication—that they effectively have a leveraged stock market bet—would horrify most investors.

While nobody seems to know what the market portfolio looks like, investors have become willing to consider a broader array of assets, including foreign stocks, real estate investment trusts, and commodities. I think the trend will continue, as people come to realize that they can lower a portfolio's risk level by adding apparently risky investments.

investors may simply be trading with themselves, generating trading commissions for their brokers but without impacting the efficiency of the market.

So, in order for the behaviour of uninformed investors to have an impact on the market, there must be patterns to their behaviour that lead them to depart from the CAPM in systematic ways, thus imparting systematic uncertainty into prices. For investors' trades to be correlated in this way they must share a common motivation. Consequently, in the next section we will investigate what might motivate investors to depart from the market portfolio, and show that investors appear to suffer from some common, and predictable, biases.

CONCEPT CHECK

1. Do investors hold well-diversified portfolios?

2. Why is the high trading volume observed in markets inconsistent with the CAPM equilibrium?

3. In addition to departing from the market portfolio, what else must be true about the behaviour of small, uninformed investors for them to have an impact on market prices?

13.4 SYSTEMATIC TRADING BIASES

We begin our review of what researchers have discovered about investor behaviour with the disposition effect: the tendency to hold on to stocks that have lost value and sell stocks that have risen in value since the time of purchase.

HANGING ON TO LOSERS AND THE DISPOSITION EFFECT

Investors tend to hold on to stocks that have lost value and sell stocks that have risen in value since the time of purchase. We call this tendency to hang on to losers and sell winners the **disposition effect**. Researchers Hersh Shefrin and Meir Statman, building on the work of psychologists Daniel Kahneman and Amos Tversky, posited that this effect arises due to investors' increased willingness to take on risk in the face of possible losses.[13] It may also reflect a reluctance to "admit a mistake" by taking the loss.

Researchers have verified the disposition effect in many studies. For example, in a study of all trades in the Taiwanese stock market from 1995–1999, investors in aggregate were twice as likely to realize gains as they were to realize losses. Also, nearly 85% of individual investors were subject to this bias.[14] On the other hand, mutual funds and foreign investors did not exhibit the same tendency, and other studies have shown that more sophisticated investors appear to be less susceptible to the disposition effect.[15]

This behavioural tendency to sell winners and hang on to losers is costly from a tax perspective. Because capital gains are taxed only when the asset is sold, it is optimal for tax purposes to postpone taxable gains by continuing to hold profitable investments; delaying the tax payment reduces its present value. On the other hand, investors should capture tax

13. H. Shefrin and M. Statman, "The Disposition to Sell Winners Too Early and Ride Losers Too Long: Theory and Evidence," *Journal of Finance* 40 (1985): 777–790, and D. Kahneman and A. Tversky, "Prospect Theory: An Analysis of Decision Under Risk," *Econometrica* 47 (1979): 263–291.

14. B. Barber, Y. T. Lee, Y. J. Liu, and T. Odean, "Is the Aggregate Investor Reluctant to Realize Losses? Evidence from Taiwan," *European Financial Management* 13 (2007): 423–447.

15. R. Dhar and N. Zhu, "Up Close and Personal: Investor Sophistication and the Disposition Effect," *Management Science* 52 (2006): 726–740.

NOBEL PRIZE KAHNEMAN AND TVERSKY'S PROSPECT THEORY

In 2002, the Nobel Prize for Economics was awarded to Daniel Kahneman for his development of Prospect Theory with fellow psychologist Amos Tversky (who would have surely shared the prize if not for his death in 1996). Prospect Theory provides a descriptive model of the way individuals make decisions under uncertainty, predicting the choices people *do* make rather than the ones they *should* make. It posits that people evaluate outcomes relative to the status quo or similar reference point (the *framing effect*), will take on risk to avoid realizing losses, and put too much weight on unlikely events. The disposition effect follows from Prospect Theory by assuming investors frame their decisions by comparing the sale price with the purchase price for each stock. In a similar way, Prospect Theory provides an important foundation for much research in behavioural economics and finance.

losses by selling their losing investments, especially near the year's end, in order to accelerate the tax write-off.

Of course, hanging on to losers and selling winners might make sense if investors forecast that the losing stocks would ultimately "bounce back" and outperform the winners going forward. While investors may in fact have this belief, it does not appear to be justified; if anything, the losing stocks that investors continue to hold tend to *underperform* the winners that they sell. According to one study, losers underperformed winners by 3.4% over the year after the winners were sold.[16]

INVESTOR ATTENTION, MOOD, AND EXPERIENCE

Individual investors generally are not full-time traders. As a result, they have limited time and attention to spend on their investment decisions, and so may be influenced by attention-grabbing news stories or other events. Studies show that individuals are more likely to buy stocks that have recently been in the news, engaged in advertising, experienced exceptionally high trading volume, or had extreme (positive or negative) returns.[17]

Investment behaviour also seems to be affected by investors' moods. For example, sunshine generally has a positive effect on mood, and studies have found that stock returns tend to be higher when it is a sunny day at the location of the stock exchange. In New York City, the annualized market return on perfectly sunny days is approximately 24.8% per year versus 8.7% per year on perfectly cloudy days.[18] Further evidence of the link between investor mood and stock returns comes from the effect of major sports events on returns. One recent study estimates that a loss in the World Cup elimination stage lowers the next

---

16. T. Odean, "Are Investors Reluctant to Realize Their Losses?" *Journal of Finance* 53 (1998): 1775–1798.

17. See G. Grullon, G. Kanatas, and J. Weston, "Advertising, Breadth of Ownership, and Liquidity," *Review of Financial Studies* 17 (2004): 439–461; M. Seasholes and G. Wu, "Predictable Behavior, Profits, and Attention," *Journal of Empirical Finance* 14 (2007): 590–610; B. Barber and T. Odean, "All That Glitters: The Effect of Attention and News on the Buying Behavior of Individual and Institutional Investors," *Review of Financial Studies* 21 (2008): 785–818.

18. Based on data from 1982–1997; see D. Hirshleifer and T. Shumway, "Good Day Sunshine: Stock Returns and the Weather," *Journal of Finance* 58 (2003): 1009–1032.

day's stock returns in the losing country by about 0.50%, presumably due to investors' poor mood.[19]

Finally, investors appear to put too much weight on their own experience rather than considering all the historical evidence. As a result, people who grow up and live during a time of high stock returns are more likely to invest in stocks than people who grow up and live during a time of low stock returns.[20]

HERD BEHAVIOUR

Thus far, we have considered common factors that might lead to correlated trading behaviour by investors. An alternative reason why investors make similar trading errors is that they are actively *trying* to follow each other's behaviour. This phenomenon, in which individuals imitate each other's actions, is referred to as **herd behaviour.**

There are several reasons why traders might herd in their portfolio choices. First, they might believe others have superior information which they can take advantage of by copying their trades. This behaviour can lead to a **cascade effect** in which traders ignore their own information hoping to profit from the information of others.[21] A second possibility is that, due to relative wealth concerns, individuals choose to herd in order to avoid the risk of underperforming their peers.[22] Third, professional fund managers may face reputational risk if they stray too far from the actions of their peers.[23]

IMPLICATIONS OF BEHAVIOURAL BIASES

The insight that investors make mistakes is not news. What is, however, surprising is that these mistakes persist even though they may be economically costly and there is a relatively easy way to avoid them—buying and holding the market portfolio.

Regardless of why individual investors choose not to protect themselves by holding the market portfolio, the fact that they don't has potential implications for the CAPM. If individual investors are engaging in strategies that earn negative alphas, it may be possible for a few more sophisticated investors to take advantage of this behaviour and earn positive alphas. Is there evidence that such savvy investors exist? In the next section we examine evidence regarding this possibility.

CONCEPT CHECK

1. What are several systematic behavioural biases that individual investors fall prey to?

2. What implication might these behavioural biases have for the CAPM?

---

19. A. Edmans, D. Garcia, and O. Norli, "Sports Sentiment and Stock Returns," *Journal of Finance* 62 (2007): 1967–1998.

20. U. Malmendier and S. Nagel, "Depression Babies: Do Macroeconomic Experiences Affect Risk-Taking?," NBER working paper no. 14813.

21. See, e.g., S. Bikhchandani, D. Hirshleifer, and I. Welch, "A Theory of Fads, Fashion, Custom and Cultural Change as Informational Cascades," *Journal of Political Economy* 100 (1992): 992–1026; and C. Avery and P. Zemsky, "Multidimensional Uncertainty and Herd Behavior in Financial Markets," *American Economic Review* 88 (1998): 724–48.

22. P. DeMarzo, R. Kaniel, and I. Kremer, "Relative Wealth Concerns and Financial Bubbles," *Review of Financial Studies* 21 (2008): 19–50.

23. D. Scharfstein and J. Stein, "Herd Behavior and Investment," *American Economic Review* 80 (1990): 465–79.

13.5   THE EFFICIENCY OF THE MARKET PORTFOLIO

When individual investors make mistakes, can sophisticated investors easily profit at their expense? In order for sophisticated investors to profit from investor mistakes, two conditions must hold. First, the mistakes must be sufficiently pervasive and persistent to affect stock prices. That is, investor behaviour must push prices so that non-zero alpha trading opportunities become apparent, as in Figure 13.2. Second, there must be limited competition to exploit these non-zero alpha opportunities. If competition is too intense, these opportunities will be quickly eliminated before any trader can take advantage of them in a significant way. In this section, we examine whether there is any evidence that individual or professional investors can outperform the market without taking on additional risk.

TRADING ON NEWS OR RECOMMENDATIONS

A natural place to look for profitable trading opportunities is in reaction to big news announcements or analysts' recommendations. If enough other investors are not paying attention, perhaps one can profit from these public sources of information.

TAKEOVER OFFER.   One of the biggest news announcements for a firm, in terms of stock price impact, is when it is the target of a takeover offer. Typically, the offer is for a significant premium to the target's current stock price, and while the target's stock price typically jumps on the announcement, it often does not jump completely to the offer price. While it might seem that this difference creates a profitable trading opportunity, it most cases there is usually remaining uncertainty regarding whether the deal will occur at the initially offered price, at a higher price, or fail to occur at all. Figure 13.5 shows the average

FIGURE 13.5

Returns to Holding Target Stocks Subsequent to Takeover Announcements

After the initial jump in the stock price at the time of the announcement, target stocks do not appear to earn abnormal subsequent returns on average. However, stocks that are ultimately acquired tend to appreciate and have positive alphas, while those that are not acquired have negative alphas. Thus, an investor could profit from correctly predicting the outcome.

Source: Adapted from M. Bradley, A. Desai, and E. H. Kim, "The Rationale Behind Interfirm Tender Offers: Information or Synergy?" *Journal of Financial Economics* **11** (1983): 183–206.

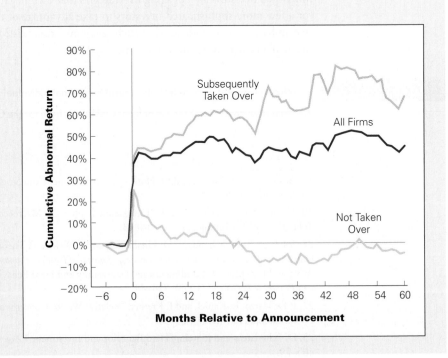

response to many such takeover announcements, showing the target stock's **cumulative abnormal return**, which measures the stock's return relative to that predicted based on its beta, at the time of the event. Figure 13.5 reveals that the initial jump in the stock price is high enough so that the stock's future returns do not outperform the market, on average. However, if we *could* predict whether the firm would ultimately be acquired or not, we could earn profits trading on that information.

STOCK RECOMMENDATIONS.   We could also consider stock recommendations. For example, popular commentator Jim Cramer makes numerous stock recommendations on his evening television show, *Mad Money*. Do investors profit from following these recommendations? Figure 13.6 shows the results of a recent study that analyzed the average stock price reaction to these recommendations, based on whether the recommendation coincided with a news story about the company. In the case where there is news, it appears that the stock price correctly reflects this information the next day, and stays flat (relative to the market) subsequently. On the other hand, for the stocks without news, there appears to be a significant jump in the stock price the next day, but the stock price then tends to fall relative to the market, generating a negative alpha, over the next several weeks. The authors of the study found that the stocks without news tended to be smaller, less liquid stocks; it appears that the individual investors who buy these stocks based on the recommendation push the price too high. They appear to be subject to an overconfidence bias, trusting too much in Cramer's recommendation and not adequately taking into account the behaviour of their fellow investors. The more interesting question is, why don't smart investors short these stocks and prevent the overreaction? In fact they do (the amount of short interest rises for these stocks), but because these small stocks are difficult to locate and borrow and therefore costly to short, the price does not correct immediately.

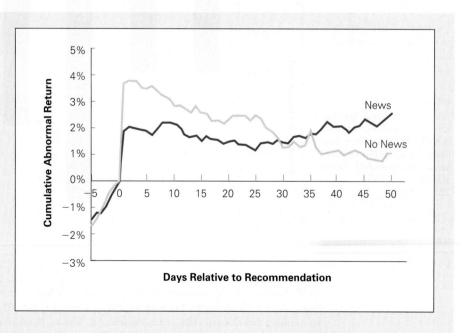

FIGURE 13.6

Stock Price Reactions to Recommendations on *Mad Money*

When recommendations coincide with news, the initial stock price reaction appears correct and future alphas are not significantly different from zero. Without news, the stock price appears to overreact. While sophisticated investors gain by shorting these stocks, costs of shorting limit their ability to do so.

Source: Adapted from J. Engelberg, C. Sasseville, and J. Williams, "Market Madness? The Case of Mad Money," SSRN working paper, 2009.

THE PERFORMANCE OF FUND MANAGERS

The previous results suggest that though it may not be easy to profit simply by trading on news, more sophisticated investors might be able to do so (for example, by being better able to predict takeover outcomes, or short small stocks). Presumably, professional fund managers, such as those who manage mutual funds, should be in the best position to take advantage of such opportunities. Interestingly, numerous studies report that the actual returns to investors of the average mutual fund have a negative alpha, as shown in Figure 13.7.[24]

Of course, the fact that the average mutual fund has a negative alpha does not imply that all mutual funds do. Some funds may have exceptional managers who consistently deliver positive alphas to their investors. How can we identify such superior funds? A natural place to start would be to look at funds that have been highly ranked based on their historical performance. Indeed organizations such as Morningstar rank managers each year. For example, Legg Mason's William Miller, whose performance we highlighted in the introduction to this chapter, was not only named by Morningstar as manager of the year in 1998, but he was named manager of the decade the following year. As we have already noted, investors who were motivated to invest based on these awards would have seen poor performance over the next 10 years. Miller's experience is not exceptional. At the end of each year Forbes publishes an Honor Roll of top mutual funds based on an analysis of the past performance and riskiness of the fund. In a 1994 study, Vanguard CEO John Bogle compared the returns from investing in the market index with the returns from investing each year in the newly announced Honor Roll funds. Over a 19-year period, the Honor Roll portfolio had an annual return of 11.2%, whereas the market index fund had an

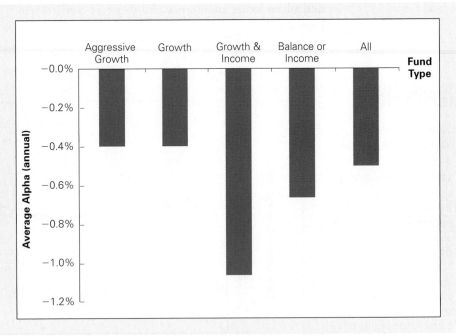

FIGURE 13.7

Estimated Alphas for U.S. Mutual Funds (1975–2002)

The figure shows average annual alphas for mutual funds by fund type. For each category, the average fund has a negative estimated alpha.

Source: Adapted from R. Kosowski, A. Timmermann, R. Wermers, and H. White, "Can Mutual Fund 'Stars' Really Pick Stocks? New Evidence from a Bootstrap Analysis," *Journal of Finance* 61 (2006): 2551–2596.

---

24. R. Kosowski, A. Timmermann, R. Wermers, and H. White, "Can Mutual Fund 'Stars' Really Pick Stocks? New Evidence from a Bootstrap Analysis," *Journal of Finance* 61 (2006): 2551–2596; for similar results using data through 2006, see E. Fama and K. French, "Luck versus Skill in the Cross Section of Mutual Fund Alpha Estimates," Tuck School of Business Working Paper No. 2009–56.

annual return of 13.1%.[25] Thus, the superior past performance of these funds was not a good predictor of their future ability to outperform the market. Other studies have confirmed this result, and found little predictability in fund performance.[26]

While these results regarding mutual fund performance may seem surprising, they are nevertheless consistent with a competitive capital market. Suppose investors could predict that a skilled manager would generate a positive alpha in the future. As with any other profitable trading opportunity, investors would rush to invest with this manager, who would then be flooded with capital. For example, during his meteoric rise, Legg Mason manager William Miller saw his capital under management grow from about $700 million in 1992 to $28 billion in 2007. But the more capital the manager has to invest, the harder it is to find profitable trading opportunities. If these opportunities are exhausted, the manager can no longer produce better-than-average performance. Ultimately, the fund's returns should fall until its alpha is no longer positive.[27] The fact that alphas are somewhat negative could reflect other benefits these funds provide, or could result from overconfidence. Investors put too much confidence in their ability to select fund managers and thus commit too much capital to them.[28]

Researchers have obtained similar results when evaluating institutional fund managers responsible for managing retirement plans, pension funds, and endowment assets. A study investigating the hiring decisions of plan sponsors found that sponsors picked managers that had significantly outperformed their benchmarks historically (see Figure 13.8). Once these new managers were hired, however, their performance looked very similar to the average fund, with returns exceeding their benchmarks by an amount roughly equal to their management fees.

THE WINNERS AND LOSERS

The evidence in this section suggests that while it may be possible to improve on the market portfolio, it isn't easy. This result is perhaps not so surprising, for as we noted in Section 13.2, the average investor (on a value-weighted basis) earns an alpha of zero, *before* including trading costs. So beating the market should require special skills, such as better analysis of information, or lower trading costs.

Because individual investors are likely to be at a disadvantage on both counts, as well as subject to behavioural biases, the CAPM wisdom that investors should "hold the market"

---

25. J. Bogle, *Bogle on Mutual Funds: New Perspectives for the Intelligent Investor* (Burr Ridge, Illinois: Irwin Professional Publishing, 1994).

26. One possible exception is fund fees; ironically, funds with higher fees seem to generate *lower* returns for their investors. See M. Carhart, "On Persistence in Mutual Fund Performance," *Journal of Finance* 52 (1997): 57–82.

27. This mechanism was proposed by J. B. Berk and R. C. Green, "Mutual Fund Flows in Rational Markets," *Journal of Political Economy* 112 (2004): 1269–1295. The following studies all find that new capital flows into funds that do well and out of funds that do poorly: M. J. Gruber, "Another Puzzle: The Growth in Actively Managed Mutual Funds," *Journal of Finance* 51 (1996): 783–810; E. R. Sirri and P. Tufano, "Costly Search and Mutual Fund Flows," *Journal of Finance* 53 (1998): 1589–1622; J. Chevalier and G. Ellison, "Risk Taking by Mutual Funds as a Response to Incentives," *Journal of Political Economy* 105 (1997): 1167–1200.

28. In Miller's case most investors paid dearly for their confidence in him—although his losses post-2007 equalled his gains from 1992, most investors were not invested in 1992, and so they experienced overall performance that lagged the S&P 500. Not surprisingly, after 2007 he experienced large capital outflows, so by the end of 2008 he had only about $1.2 billion under management.

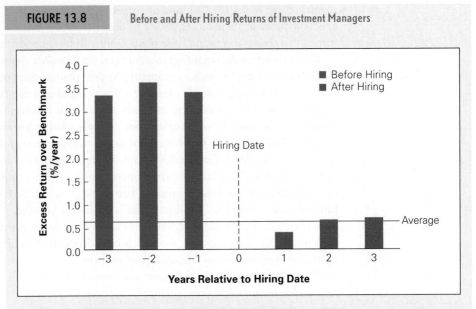

FIGURE 13.8   Before and After Hiring Returns of Investment Managers

While plan sponsors tend to hire managers who have significantly outperformed their benchmarks historically, after-hiring performance is similar to the excess return of the average fund (0.64% on a value-weighted basis). Data are based on 8,755 hiring decisions of 3,400 plan sponsors from 1994–2003, and returns are gross of management fees (which tend to range from 0.5%–0.7%/year).

Sources: A. Goyal and S. Wahal, "The Selection and Termination of Investment Management Firms by Plan Sponsors," *Journal of Finance* 63 (2008): 1805–1847, and with J. Busse, "Performance and Persistence in Institutional Investment Management," *Journal of Finance,* forthcoming.

is probably the best advice for most people. Indeed, a comprehensive study of the Taiwan stock market found that individual investors there lose an average of 3.8% per year by trading, with roughly 1/3 of the losses due to poor trades and the remaining 2/3 due to transactions costs.[29]

The same study reported that institutions earn 1.5% per year on average from their trades. But while professional fund managers may profit due to their talent, information, and superior trading infrastructure, the results in this section suggest that little of those profits goes to the investors who invest with them. If investors do not benefit from the skills of fund managers, who does? The answer is the managers themselves. Almost all **money managers** charge investors a fee based on the amount of capital they have under management. Because investors compete with each other to find successful managers, better managers manage larger funds and these managers earn larger fees.

CONCEPT CHECK

1. Should uninformed investors expect to make money by trading based on news announcements?

2. If fund managers are talented, why do the returns of their funds to investors not have positive alphas?

---

29. Taiwan provides a unique opportunity to study how profits are distributed, because unlike in the U.S., the identity of buyers and sellers is tracked for all trades. See B. Barber, Y. T. Lee, Y. J. Liu, and T. Odean, "Just How Much Do Individual Investors Lose by Trading?" *Review of Financial Studies* 22 (2009): 609–632.

INTERVIEW WITH JOHN BOGLE

John C. Bogle founded The Vanguard Group in 1974 and created the first index mutual fund, the Vanguard 500 Index Fund, in 1975. He served as Vanguard's chairman and chief executive officer until 1996 and senior chairman until 2000. He is currently president of the Bogle Financial Markets Research Center.

QUESTION: **Vanguard is known for its index funds. Why is indexing as popular as it is?**

ANSWER: Indexing is popular because it works. The average mutual fund manager cannot beat the market. All fund managers like to say they will beat the market; over a decade, almost 80 percent are wrong. It's the triumph of hope over experience. Over the last 20 years, the average annual return of the S&P 500 was about 13.2%. The average equity mutual fund returned several percentage points less because of expenses, turnover costs, and initial sales charges.

To make matters worse, many fund investors also incur timing and selection penalties. They invest very little when the market's low and a lot when it is high. They buy the wrong funds—telecommunications funds, technology funds, new economy funds—at the market's high. History has shown that after costs and penalties, most mutual fund investors earned returns considerably below returns earned by the average fund. An index fund has no sales charges and an all-in cost of 0.15%, versus an all-in cost of about 3% for active equity funds. Indexing wins, only because it can't lose.

QUESTION: **As a pioneer of indexing, can you explain how theory and evidence came together in the 1970s to suggest that indexing was a smart investment strategy?**

ANSWER: The seed was planted in the 1950s when I was writing my senior thesis at Princeton on mutual funds and did studies showing that funds couldn't outperform market averages. Opportunity and motive came together when I started Vanguard in 1974. We had a company to run, and the only way to beat the market was to remove costs from the equation. I told Vanguard's directors that I wanted to start an index fund as a way to put Vanguard on the map. Paul Samuelson recently described that creation as the equivalent of the alphabet and the wheel.

We can argue about efficient markets forever. I would say they are strongly efficient, but not perfectly so. Indexing is a smart investment strategy because it's based on the "Cost Matters Hypothesis": gross return – costs = net return to investors. We took the costs out of the equation. Beating the market is a zero sum game on average. Subtract intermediation costs, and it becomes a losing game. Indexing is not magic. It's infinite diversification, infinitely small costs, tiny portfolio turnover, and therefore high tax efficiency. But it took a long while for people to accept this idea.

QUESTION: **Exchange Traded Funds (ETFs) are growing rapidly. What are the tradeoffs between an ETF and a traditional index fund?**

ANSWER: The two are essentially the same. ETFs come in two distinct types. One is all-stock-market ETFs, like VIPERs and SPDRs (based on the S&P 500), and the others are sector funds—European, Asian, technology, energy sectors. I don't believe in sectors. I believe in owning the whole market. We pay selection and timing penalties when we buy sectors. ETFs also charge commissions, so the costs mount up if you want to invest a small amount each month or trade them.

There is nothing wrong with buying a SPDR or VIPER, or buying a Vanguard S&P Index fund or total stock market index fund, and holding it forever. However, people tend to hold their index funds for a long time and use ETFs largely as trading vehicles. Long-term investing and short-term speculation are opposite sides of the same coin. I believe in ETFs for buying and holding purposes—which they are rarely used for—and I don't believe in them for speculative and trading purposes.

13.6   STYLE-BASED TECHNIQUES AND THE MARKET EFFICIENCY DEBATE

In the previous section we looked for evidence that professional investors could profit at small investors' expense and outperform the market. In this section we will take a different tack. Rather than looking at managers' profits, we will look at possible *trading strategies*. In particular, many fund managers distinguish their trading strategies based on the types of stocks they tend to hold; specifically, small versus large stocks, and value versus growth stocks. In this section, we will consider these alternative investment styles, and see whether some strategies have generated higher returns historically than the CAPM predicts.

SIZE EFFECTS

Small stocks (those with smaller market capitalizations) have historically earned higher average returns than the market portfolio. Moreover, while small stocks do tend to have high market risk, their returns appear high even accounting for their higher beta, an empirical result we call the **size effect**.

EXCESS RETURN AND MARKET CAPITALIZATIONS.   To compare the performance of portfolios formed based on size, researchers Eugene Fama and Kenneth French[30] divided stocks each year into 10 portfolios by ranking them each year based on their market capitalizations, and collecting the smallest 10% of stocks into the first portfolio, the next 10% into the second portfolio, up to the biggest 10% into the tenth portfolio. They then recorded the monthly excess returns of each decile portfolio over the following year. After repeating this process for each year, they calculated the average excess return of each portfolio and the beta of the portfolio; Figure 13.9 shows the result. As you can see, although the portfolios with higher betas yield higher returns, most portfolios plot above the security market line (SML); all except one portfolio had a positive alpha. The smallest deciles exhibit the most extreme effect.

As is evident from Figure 13.9, even these portfolios have large standard errors—none of the alpha estimates is significantly different from zero. However, 9 of the 10 portfolios plot above the SML. If the positive alphas were due purely to statistical error, we would expect as many portfolios to appear above the line as below it. Consequently, a test of whether the alphas of all 10 portfolios are jointly all equal to zero can be statistically rejected.

EXCESS RETURN AND BOOK-TO-MARKET RATIO.   Researchers have found similar results using the **book-to-market ratio**, the ratio of the book value of equity to the market value of equity, to form stocks into portfolios. Recall from Chapter 2 that practitioners refer to stocks with high book-to-market ratios as value stocks, and to those with low book-to-market ratios as growth stocks. Figure 13.10 demonstrates that value stocks tend to have positive alphas, and growth stocks tend to have low or negative alphas. Once again, a joint test of whether all 10 portfolios have an alpha of zero is rejected.

SIZE EFFECTS AND EMPIRICAL EVIDENCE.   The size effect—the observation that small stocks (or stocks with a high book-to-market ratio) have positive alphas—was first discovered in 1981 by Rolf Banz.[31] At the time, researchers did not find the evidence

---

30. See E. Fama and K. French, "The Cross-Section of Stock Returns," *Journal of Finance* 47 (1992): 427–465.

31. See R. Banz, "The Relationship Between Return and Market Values of Common Stock," *Journal of Financial Economics* 9 (1981): 3–18. A similar relation between stock price (rather than size) and future returns was found by M. E. Blume and F. Husic, "Price, Beta and Exchange Listing," *Journal of Finance* 28 (1973): 283–299.

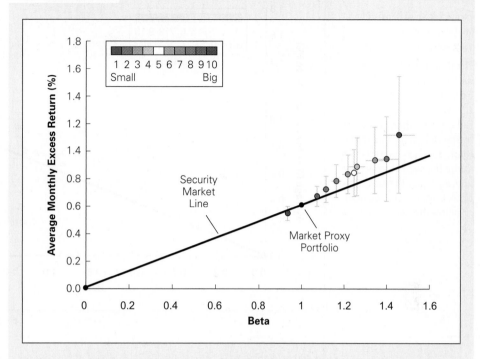

FIGURE 13.9 Excess Return of Size Portfolios, 1926–2008

The plot shows the average monthly excess return (the return minus the one-month risk-free rate) for 10 portfolios formed in each year based on firms' market capitalizations, plotted as a function of the portfolio's estimated beta. The black line is the security market line. If the market portfolio is efficient and there is no measurement error, all portfolios would plot along this line. The error bars mark the 95% confidence bands of the beta and expected excess return estimates. Note the tendency of small stocks to be above the security market line.
Source: Data courtesy of Kenneth French.

to be convincing because financial economists had been *searching* the data, looking for stocks with positive alphas. Because of estimation error, it is always possible to find stocks with estimated positive alphas; indeed, if we look hard enough, it is also always possible to find something these stocks have in common. As a consequence, many researchers were inclined to view Banz's findings as due to a **data snooping bias**, which is the idea that given enough characteristics, it will always be possible to find some characteristic that by pure chance happens to be correlated with the estimation error of average returns.[32]

After the publication of Banz's study, however, a theoretical reason emerged that explained the relationship between market capitalization and expected returns. Financial economists realized that as long as beta is not a *perfect* measure of risk—either due to estimation error, or because the market portfolio is not efficient—we should *expect* to observe the size effect.[33] To understand why, consider a stock with a positive alpha. All else being

---

32. David Leinweber, in his book *Nerds on Wall Street* (Wiley Financial, 2008), illustrates this point by searching the data for a patently absurd characteristic that is correlated with returns. He found that over a 13-year period annual butter production in Bangladesh can "explain" annual variation in S&P 500 returns!

33. See J. B. Berk, "A Critique of Size Related Anomalies," *Review of Financial Studies* 8 (1995): 275–286.

FIGURE 13.10

Excess Return of Book-
to-Market Portfolios,
1926–2008

The plot shows the same
data as Figure 13.9, with
portfolios formed based on
stocks' book-to-market
ratios rather than size. Note
the tendency of value stocks
(high book-to-market) to be
above the security market
line, and growth stocks (low
book-to-market) to be near
or below the line.

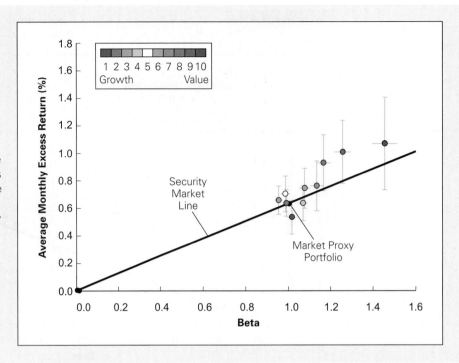

equal, a positive alpha implies that the stock also has a relatively high expected return. A
higher expected return implies a lower price; the only way to offer a higher expected
return is for investors to buy the stock's dividend stream at a lower price. A lower price
means a lower market capitalization (and similarly a higher book-to-market ratio—market capitalization is in the *denominator* of the book-to-market ratio). Thus, when a
financial economist forms a portfolio of stocks with low market capitalizations (or high
book-to-market ratios), that collection contains stocks that will likely have higher
expected returns and, if the market portfolio is not efficient, positive alphas. Similarly, a
stock that plots below the security market line will have a lower expected return and, all
else being equal, a higher price, implying that it has a higher market capitalization and
lower book-to-market ratio. Hence a portfolio of stocks with high market capitalizations
or low book-to-market ratios will have negative alphas if the market portfolio is not efficient. Let's illustrate with a simple example.

EXAMPLE 13.2   RISK AND THE MARKET VALUE OF EQUITY

Problem
Consider two firms, SM Industries and BiG Corporation, which are expected to pay dividends of $1 million per year in perpetuity. SM's dividend stream is riskier than BiG's, so its
cost of capital is 14% per year. BiG's cost of capital is 10%. Which firm has the higher market value? Which firm has the higher expected return? Now assume both stocks have the
same estimated beta, either because of estimation error, or because the market portfolio is

not efficient. Based on this beta, the CAPM would assign an expected return of 12% to both stocks. How do the market values of the firms relate to their alphas?

Solution

The timeline of dividends is the same for both firms:

To calculate the market value of SM, we calculate the present value of its future expected dividends using the perpetuity formula and a cost of capital of 14%:

$$\text{Market Value of SM} = \frac{1}{0.14} = \$7.143 \text{ million}$$

Similarly, the market value of BiG is

$$\text{Market Value of BiG} = \frac{1}{0.10} = \$10 \text{ million}$$

SM has the lower market value, and a higher expected return (14% vs. 10%). It also has the higher alpha:

$$\alpha_{SM} = 0.14 - 0.12 = 2\%$$
$$\alpha_{BiG} = 0.10 - 0.12 = -2\%$$

Consequently, the firm with the lower market value has the higher alpha.

When the market portfolio is not efficient, theory predicts that stocks with low market capitalizations or high book-to-market ratios will have positive alphas. In light of this observation, the size effect is, indeed, potential evidence against the efficiency of the market portfolio.

MOMENTUM

Researchers have also used past stock returns to form portfolios with positive alphas. For example, for the years 1965 to 1989, Narishiman Jegadeesh and Sheridan Titman[34] ranked stocks each month by their realized returns over the prior 6 to 12 months. They found that the best-performing stocks had positive alphas over the next 3 to 12 months. This evidence goes against the CAPM: When the market portfolio is efficient, past returns should not predict alphas.

Investors can exploit this result by buying stocks that have had past high returns and (short) selling stocks that have had past low returns, which is called a **momentum strategy**. Jegadeesh and Titman showed that over the period 1965–1989, this strategy would have produced an alpha of over 12% per year.

IMPLICATIONS OF POSITIVE-ALPHA TRADING STRATEGIES

Over the years since the discovery of the CAPM, it has become increasingly clear to researchers and practitioners alike that by forming portfolios based on market capitalization,

---

34. See N. Jegadeesh and S. Titman, "Returns to Buying Winners and Selling Losers: Implications for Market Efficiency," *Journal of Finance* 48 (1993): 65–91.

book-to-market ratios, and past returns, investors can construct trading strategies that have a positive alpha. Given these results, we are left to draw one of two conclusions:

1. Investors are systematically ignoring positive-NPV investment opportunities. That is, the CAPM correctly computes required risk premiums, but investors are ignoring opportunities to earn extra returns without bearing any extra risk, either because they are unaware of them or because the costs to implement the strategies are larger than the NPV of undertaking them.

2. The positive-alpha trading strategies contain risk that investors are unwilling to bear but the CAPM does not capture. That is, a stock's beta with the market portfolio does not adequately measure a stock's systematic risk, and so the CAPM does not correctly compute the risk premium.

The only way a positive-NPV opportunity can persist in a market is if some barrier to entry restricts competition. In this case, it is very difficult to identify what these barriers might be. The existence of these trading strategies has been widely known for more than 15 years. Not only is the information required to form the portfolios readily available, but many mutual funds follow momentum-based and market capitalization/book-to-market–based strategies. Hence, the first conclusion does not seem likely.

That leaves the second possibility: The market portfolio is not efficient, and therefore a stock's beta with the market is not an adequate measure of its systematic risk. Stated another way, the profits (positive alphas) from the trading strategy are really returns for bearing risk that investors are averse to and the CAPM does not capture. There are several reasons why the market portfolio might not be efficient. Let's examine each possibility in turn.

PROXY ERROR. The true market portfolio may be efficient, but the proxy we have used for it may be inaccurate. The true market portfolio consists of all traded investment wealth in the economy, including bonds, real estate, art, precious metals, and so on. We cannot include most of these investments in the market proxy because competitive price data is not available. Consequently, standard proxies like the S&P TSX Composite in Canada or the S&P 500 in the U.S. may be inefficient compared with the true market, and stocks will have non-zero alphas.[35] In this case, the alphas merely indicate that the wrong proxy is being used; they do not indicate forgone positive-NPV investment opportunities.[36]

BEHAVIOURAL BIASES. As we discussed in Section 13.4, some investors may be subject to systematic behavioural biases. For example, they may be attracted to large growth stocks that receive greater news coverage. Or they may sell winners and hang on to losers, following a contrarian strategy. By falling prey to these biases, these investors are holding inefficient portfolios. More sophisticated investors hold an efficient portfolio, but because supply must equal demand, this efficient portfolio must include more small, value, and momentum stocks to offset the trades of biased investors. While alphas are zero with

---

35. When the true market portfolio is efficient, even a small difference between the proxy and true market portfolio can lead to an insignificant relation between beta and returns. See R. Roll and S. Ross, "On the Cross-Sectional Relation between Expected Returns and Beta," *Journal of Finance* 49(1) (1994): 101–121.

36. Because we cannot actually construct the *true* market portfolio of *all* risky investments, the CAPM theory is in some sense untestable (see R. Roll, "A Critique of the Asset Pricing Theory's Tests," *Journal of Financial Economics* 4 (1977): 129–176). Of course, from a corporate manager's perspective, whether the CAPM is testable is irrelevant—as long as an efficient portfolio can be identified, he or she can use it to compute the cost of capital.

respect to this efficient portfolio, they are positive when compared with the market portfolio (which is the combined holdings of the biased and sophisticated investors).

ALTERNATIVE RISK PREFERENCES AND NON-TRADEABLE WEALTH. Investors may also choose inefficient portfolios because they care about risk characteristics other than the volatility of their traded portfolio. For example, they may be attracted to investments with skewed distributions that have a small probability of an extremely high payoff. As a result, they might be willing to hold some diversifiable risk in order to obtain such a payoff. In addition, investors are exposed to other significant risks outside their portfolio that are not tradeable, the most important of which is due to their human capital.[37] For example, a banker at Goldman Sachs is exposed to financial sector risk, while a software engineer is exposed to risk in the high-tech sector. When choosing a portfolio, investors may deviate from the market portfolio to offset these inherent exposures.[38]

It is important to appreciate that just because the market portfolio is not efficient, this does not rule out the possibility of *another* portfolio being efficient. In fact, as we pointed out in Chapter 11, the CAPM pricing relationship holds with *any* efficient portfolio. Consequently, in light of the evidence against the efficiency of the market portfolio, researchers have developed alternative models of risk and return that do not rely on the efficiency of the market portfolio in particular. In the next section we develop such a model.

CONCEPT CHECK

1. What does the existence of a positive-alpha trading strategy imply?

2. If investors have a significant amount of non-tradeable (but risky) wealth, why might the market portfolio not be efficient?

13.7 MULTIFACTOR MODELS OF RISK

In Chapter 11, we presented the expected return of any marketable security as a function of the expected return of the efficient portfolio:

$$E[R_s] = r_f + \beta_s^{eff} \times (E[R_{eff}] - r_f) \qquad (13.3)$$

When the market portfolio is not efficient, to use Eq. 13.3 we need to find an alternative method to identify an efficient portfolio.

As a practical matter, it is extremely difficult to identify portfolios that are efficient because we cannot measure the expected return and the standard deviation of a portfolio with great accuracy. Yet, although we might not be able to identify the efficient portfolio itself, we do know some characteristics of the efficient portfolio. First, any efficient portfolio will be well diversified. Second, we can construct an efficient portfolio from other well-diversified portfolios. This latter observation may seem trivial, but it is actually quite useful: It implies that *it is not actually necessary to identify the efficient portfolio itself.* As long as we can identify a *collection* of well-diversified portfolios from which an efficient portfolio can be constructed, we can use the collection itself to measure risk.

---

37. Although rare, there are innovative new markets that allow people to trade their human capital to finance their education; see M. Palacios, *Investing in Human Capital: A Capital Markets Approach to Student Funding* (Cambridge, U.K.: Cambridge University Press, 2004).

38. Indeed, human capital risk can explain some of the inefficiency of common market proxies. See R. Jagannathan and Z. Wang, "The Conditional CAPM and the Cross-Sections of Expected Returns," *Journal of Finance* 51 (1996): 3–53; and I. Palacios-Huerta, "The Robustness of the Conditional CAPM with Human Capital," *Journal of Financial Econometrics* 1 (2003): 272–289.

USING FACTOR PORTFOLIOS

Assume that we have identified portfolios that we can combine to form an efficient portfolio; we call these portfolios **factor portfolios**. Then, as we show in the appendix, if we use N factor portfolios with returns $R_{F1}, ..., R_{FN}$, the expected return of asset s is given by

Multifactor Model of Risk

$$E[R_s] = r_f + \beta_s^{F1}(E[R_{F1}] - r_f) + \beta_s^{F2}(E[R_{F2}] - r_f) + \cdots + \beta_s^{FN}(E[R_{FN}] - r_f)$$

$$= r_f + \sum_{n=1}^{N} \beta_s^{Fn}(E[R_{Fn}] - r_f) \tag{13.4}$$

Here $\beta_s^{F1}, ..., \beta_s^{FN}$ are the **factor betas**, one for each risk factor, and have the same interpretation as the beta in the CAPM. Each factor beta is the expected percent change in the excess return of a security for a 1% change in the excess return of the factor portfolio.

Eq.13.4 says that we can write the risk premium of any marketable security as the sum of the risk premium of each factor multiplied by the sensitivity of the stock with that factor—the factor betas. There is nothing inconsistent between Eq. 13.4, which gives the expected return in terms of multiple factors, and Eq. 13.3, which gives the expected return in terms of just the efficient portfolio. *Both* equations hold; the difference between them is simply the portfolios that we use. When we use an efficient portfolio, it alone will capture all systematic risk. Consequently, we often refer to this model as a **single-factor model**. If we use more than one portfolio as factors, then together these factors will capture all systematic risk, but note that each factor in Eq. 13.4 captures different components of the systematic risk. When we use more than one portfolio to capture risk, the model is known as a **multifactor model**. Each portfolio can be interpreted as either a risk factor itself or a portfolio of stocks correlated with an unobservable risk factor.[39] The model is also referred to as the **Arbitrage Pricing Theory (APT)**.

We can simplify Eq. 13.4 a bit further. Think of the expected excess return of each factor, $E[R_{Fn}] - r_f$, as the expected return of a portfolio in which we borrow the funds at rate r_f to invest in the factor portfolio. Because this portfolio costs nothing to construct (we are borrowing the funds to invest), it is called a **self-financing portfolio**. We can also construct a self-financing portfolio by going long some stocks, and going short other stocks with equal market value. In general, a self-financing portfolio is any portfolio with portfolio weights that sum to zero rather than one. If we require that all factor portfolios are self-financing (either by borrowing funds or shorting stocks), then we can rewrite Eq. 13.4 as

Multifactor Model of Risk with Self-Financing Portfolios

$$E[R_s] = r_f + \beta_s^{F1}E[R_{F1}] + \beta_s^{F2}E[R_{F2}] + \cdots + \beta_s^{FN}E[R_{FN}]$$

$$= r_f + \sum_{n=1}^{N} \beta_s^{Fn}E[R_{Fn}] \tag{13.5}$$

To recap, it is possible to calculate the cost of capital without actually identifying the efficient portfolio using a multifactor risk model. Rather than relying on the efficiency of

---

39. This form of the multifactor model was originally developed by Stephen Ross, although Robert Merton had developed an alternative multifactor model earlier. See S. Ross, "The Arbitrage Theory of Capital Asset Pricing," *Journal of Economic Theory* 13 (1976): 341–360; and R. Merton, "An Intertemporal Capital Asset Pricing Model," *Econometrica* 41 (1973): 867–887.

a single portfolio (such as the market), multifactor models rely on the weaker condition that we can construct an efficient portfolio from a collection of well-diversified portfolios or factors. We next explain how to select the factors.

SELECTING THE PORTFOLIOS

The most obvious portfolio to use when identifying a collection of portfolios that contain the efficient portfolio is the market portfolio itself. Historically, the market portfolio has commanded a large premium over short-term risk-free investments, such as Treasury Bills. Even if the market portfolio is not efficient, it still captures many components of systematic risk. As Figures 13.1 and 13.2 demonstrate, even when the model fails, portfolios with higher average returns *do* tend to have higher betas. Thus the first portfolio in the collection is a self-financing portfolio that consists of a long position in the market portfolio that is financed by a short position in the risk-free security.

How do we go about picking the other portfolios? As we pointed out earlier, trading strategies based on market capitalization, book-to-market ratios, and momentum appear to have positive alphas, meaning that the portfolios that implement the trading strategy capture risk that is not captured by the market portfolio. Hence these portfolios are good candidates for the other portfolios in a multifactor model. We will construct three additional portfolios out of these trading strategies: The first trading strategy selects stocks based on their market capitalization, the second uses the book-to-market ratio, and the third uses past returns.

MARKET CAPITALIZATION STRATEGY.   Each year, we place firms into one of two portfolios based on their market value of equity: Firms with market values below the median of NYSE firms form an equally weighted portfolio, S, and firms above the median market value form an equally weighted portfolio, B. We use NYSE firms because of their availability and high degree of liquidity. A trading strategy that each year buys portfolio S (small stocks) and finances this position by short selling portfolio B (big stocks) has produced positive risk-adjusted returns historically. This self-financing portfolio is widely known as the **small-minus-big (SB) portfolio**.

BOOK-TO-MARKET RATIO STRATEGY.   A second trading strategy that has produced positive risk-adjusted returns historically uses the book-to-market ratio to select stocks. Each year firms with book-to-market ratios less than the 30th percentile of NYSE firms form an equally weighted portfolio called the low portfolio, L. Firms with book-to-market ratios greater than the 70th percentile of NYSE firms form an equally weighted portfolio called the high portfolio, H. A trading strategy that each year takes a long position in portfolio H, which it finances with a short position in portfolio L, has produced positive risk-adjusted returns. We add this self-financing portfolio (high minus low book-to-market stocks) to our collection and call it the **high-minus-low (HML) portfolio** (we can also think of this portfolio as long value stocks, and short growth stocks).

PAST RETURNS STRATEGY.   The third trading strategy is a momentum strategy. Each year we rank stocks by their return over the last one year,[40] and construct a portfolio that goes long the top 30% of stocks and short the bottom 30%. This trading strategy requires holding this portfolio for a year; we then form a new self-financing portfolio and hold it

---

40. Because of short-term trading effects, the most recent month's return is often dropped, so we actually use an 11-month return.

for another year. We repeat this process annually. The resulting self-financing portfolio is known as the **prior one-year momentum (PR1YR) portfolio.**

FAMA-FRENCH-CARHART FACTOR SPECIFICATION. The collection of these four portfolios—the excess return of the market ($Mkt - r_f$), SMB, HML, and PR1YR—is currently the most popular choice for the multifactor model. Using this collection, the expected return of security s is given by:

Fama-French-Carhart Factor Specification

$$E[R_s] = r_f + \beta_s^{Mkt}(E[R_{Mkt}] - r_f) + \beta_s^{SMB} E[R_{SMB}]$$
$$+ \beta_s^{HML} E[R_{HML}] + \beta_s^{PR1YR} E[R_{PR1YR}] \tag{13.6}$$

where β_s^{Mkt}, β_s^{SMB}, β_s^{HML}, and β_s^{PR1YR} are the factor betas of stock s and measure the sensitivity of the stock to each portfolio. Because the four portfolios in Eq. 13.6 were identified by Eugene Fama, Kenneth French, and Mark Carhart, we will refer to this collection of portfolios as the **Fama-French-Carhart (FFC) factor specification.**

THE COST OF CAPITAL WITH FAMA-FRENCH-CARHART FACTOR SPECIFICATION

Multifactor models have a distinct advantage over single-factor models in that it is much easier to identify a collection of portfolios that captures systematic risk than just a single portfolio. They also have an important disadvantage, however: We must estimate the expected return of *each* portfolio. Because expected returns are not easy to estimate, each portfolio we add to the collection increases the difficulty of implementing the model. This task is especially complex because it is unclear *which* economic risk the portfolios capture, so we cannot hope to come up with a reasonable estimate of what the return should be (as we did with the CAPM) based on an economic argument. To implement the model, we have little choice other than to use historical average returns on the portfolios.[41]

Because the returns on the FFC portfolios are so volatile, we use over 80 years of data to estimate the expected return. Table 13.1 shows the monthly average return as well as the

FFC PORTFOLIO AVERAGE MONTHLY RETURNS, 1926–2008

TABLE 13.1			
Factor Portfolio	**Average Monthly Return (%)**		**95% Confidence Band (%)**
Mkt – r_f	0.59		±0.34
SMB	0.23		±0.21
HML	0.41		±0.22
PR1YR	0.77		±0.29

Data Source: Kenneth French http://mba.tuck.dartmouth.edu/pages/faculty/ken.french/data_library.html.

---

41. There is a second, more subtle disadvantage to most factor models. Because factor models are designed to price traded securities, there is no guarantee that they will accurately price risks that are not currently traded (e.g., the risk associated with a new technology). In practice, it is assumed that any non-traded risk is idiosyncratic, and therefore does not command a risk premium.

95% confidence bands of the FFC portfolios (we use a value-weighted portfolio of all NYSE, AMEX, and NASDAQ stocks as the proxy for the market portfolio). Even with 80 years of data, however, all of the estimates of the expected returns are imprecise.

EXAMPLE 13.3

USING THE FFC FACTOR SPECIFICATION TO CALCULATE THE COST OF CAPITAL

Problem

You are considering making an investment in a project in the fast food industry. You determine that the project has the same level of non-diversifiable risk as investing in McDonald's stock. Determine the cost of capital by using the FFC factor specification.

Solution

You decide to use data over the past nine years to estimate the factor betas of McDonald's stock (ticker: MCD). Therefore, you regress the monthly excess return (the realized return in each month minus the risk-free rate) of McDonald's stock on the return of each portfolio. The coefficient estimates are the factor betas. Here are the estimates of the four factor betas and their 95% confidence interval based on data from years 2000 through 2008:

Factor	Beta Estimate	Lower 95%	Upper 95%
Mkt	0.974	0.699	1.249
SMB	-0.412	-0.729	-0.096
HML	0.543	0.194	0.892
PR1YR	0.052	-0.153	0.257

Using these estimates and the current risk-free monthly rate of 3%/12 = 0.25%, you calculate the monthly expected return of investing in McDonald's stock:

$$E[R_{MCD}] = r_f + \beta_{MCD}^{Mkt}(E[R_{Mkt}] - r_f) + \beta_{MCD}^{SMB} E[R_{SMB}] + \beta_{MCD}^{HML} E[R_{HML}] + \beta_{MCD}^{PR1YR} E[R_{PR1YR}]$$

$$= 0.25\% + 0.974 \times 0.59\% - 0.412 \times 0.23\% + 0.543 \times 0.41\% + 0.052 \times 0.77\%$$

$$= 0.993\%$$

Expressed as an APR, the expected return is 0.993% × 12 = 11.916%. The annual cost of capital of the investment opportunity is about 11.9%. (Note, however, the substantial uncertainty both in the factor betas and their expected returns.)

The FFC factor specification was identified a little more than fifteen years ago. Although it is widely used in academic literature to measure risk, much debate persists about whether it really is a significant improvement over the CAPM.[42] The one area where researchers have found that the FFC factor specification does appear to do better than the CAPM is measuring the risk of actively managed mutual funds. Researchers have

---

42. See M. Cooper, R. Gutierrez, Jr., and B. Marcum, "On the Predictability of Stock Returns in Real Time," *Journal of Business* 78 (2005): 469–500.

found that funds with high returns in the past have positive alphas under the CAPM.[43] When Mark Carhart repeated the same test using the FFC factor specification to compute alphas, he found no evidence that mutual funds with high past returns had future positive alphas.[44]

CONCEPT CHECK

1. What is the advantage of a multifactor model over a single-factor model?

2. How can you use the Fama-French-Carhart factor specification to estimate the cost of capital?

13.8 METHODS USED IN PRACTICE

Given the evidence for and against the efficiency of the market portfolio, what method do managers actually use to calculate the cost of capital? In fact, a survey of 392 CFOs conducted by John Graham and Campbell Harvey found that 73.5% of the firms that they questioned use the CAPM to calculate the cost of capital, as indicated in Figure 13.11. They also found that larger firms were more likely to use the CAPM than were smaller firms.

What about the other methods? Among the firms Graham and Harvey surveyed, only about one-third reported using a multifactor model to calculate the cost of capital. Two other methods that some firms in the survey reported using are historical average returns (40%) and the dividend discount model (16%). By dividend discount model, practitioners mean Eq. 9.7 in Chapter 9: They estimate the firm's expected future growth rate and add the current dividend yield to determine the stock's expected total return.

In short, there is no clear answer to the question of which technique is used to measure risk in practice—it very much depends on the organization and the sector. It is not difficult

FIGURE 13.11

How Firms Calculate the Cost of Capital

The figure shows the percentage of firms that use the CAPM, multifactor models, the historical average return, and the dividend discount model. The dividend discount model was presented in Chapter 9.

Source: J. R. Graham and C. R. Harvey, "The Theory and Practice of Corporate Finance: Evidence from the Field," *Journal of Financial Economics* 60 (2001): 187–243.

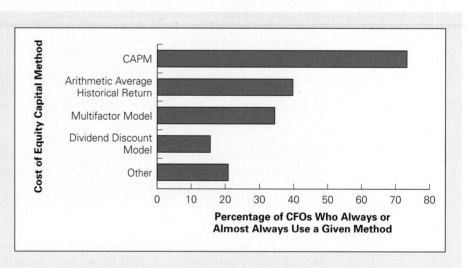

43. See M. Grinblatt and S. Titman, "The Persistence of Mutual Fund Performance," *Journal of Finance* 47 (1992): 1977–1984; and D. J. Hendricks, J. Patel, and R. Zeckhauser, "Hot Hands in Mutual Funds: Short-Run Persistence of Performance 1974–1988," *Journal of Finance* 4 (1993): 93–130.

44. See M. Carhart, "On Persistence in Mutual Fund Performance," *Journal of Finance* 52 (1997): 57–82.

to see why there is so little consensus in practice about which technique to use. *All the techniques we covered are imprecise.* Financial economics has not yet reached the point where we can provide a theory of expected returns that gives a precise estimate of the cost of capital. Consider, too, that all techniques are not equally simple to implement. Because the tradeoff between simplicity and precision varies across sectors, practitioners apply the techniques that best suit their particular circumstances.

When making a capital budgeting decision, the cost of capital is just one of several imprecise estimates that go into the NPV calculation. Indeed, in many cases the imprecision in the cost of capital estimate is less important than the imprecision in the estimate of future cash flows. Often the least complicated models to implement are used most often. In this regard, the CAPM has the dual virtues of being both simple to implement and reasonably reliable.

CONCEPT CHECK

1. Which is the most popular method used by corporations to calculate the cost of capital?

2. What other techniques do corporations use to calculate the cost of capital?

SUMMARY

1. The difference between a stock's expected return and its required return according to the security market line is the stock's alpha:

$$\alpha_s = E[R_s] - r_s \tag{13.2}$$

2. While the CAPM conclusion that the market is always efficient may not literally be true, competition among savvy investors who try to "beat the market" and earn a positive alpha should keep the market portfolio close to efficient much of the time.

3. If all investors have homogeneous expectations, which states that all investors have the same information, all investors would be aware that the stock had a positive alpha and none would be willing to sell. The only way to restore the equilibrium in this case is for the price to rise so that the alpha is zero.

4. An important conclusion of the CAPM is that investors should hold the market portfolio (combined with risk-free investments), and this investment advice *does not depend on the quality of an investor's information or trading skill.* By doing so they can avoid being taken advantage of by more sophisticated investors.

5. The CAPM requires only that investors have rational expectations, which means that all investors correctly interpret and use their own information, as well as information that can be inferred from market prices or the trades of others.

6. The market portfolio can be inefficient only if a significant number of investors either do not have rational expectations or care about aspects of their portfolios other than expected return and volatility.

7. There is evidence that individual investors fail to diversify their portfolios adequately (underdiversification bias) and favour investments in companies they are familiar with (familiarity bias).

8. Investors appear to trade too much. This behaviour stems, at least in part, from investor overconfidence: the tendency of uninformed individuals to overestimate the precision of their knowledge.

9. In order for the behaviour of uninformed investors to have an impact on the market, there must be patterns to their behaviour that lead them to depart from the CAPM in systematic ways, thus imparting systematic uncertainty into prices.

10. Examples of behaviour that could be systematic across investors is the disposition effect (the tendency to hang on to losers and sell winners), investor moods swings that result from common events like weather, and putting too much weight on their own experience. Investors could also herd, actively trying to follow each other's behaviour.

11. It is not easy to profit simply by trading on news, but professional investors might be able to do so by, for example, being better able to predict takeover outcomes. However, in equilibrium, individual investors should not expect to share any of the benefit of this skill by investing with such professional investors. The empirical evidence supports this: On average, investors earn negative alphas when they invest in managed mutual funds.

12. Because beating the market requires enough trading skill to overcome transaction costs as well as behavioural biases, CAPM wisdom that investors should "hold the market" is probably the best advice for most people.

13. The size effect refers to the observation that historically stocks with low market capitalizations have had positive alphas compared to the predictions of the CAPM. The size effect is evidence that the market portfolio is not efficient, which suggests that the CAPM does not accurately model expected returns. Researchers find similar results using the book-to-market ratio instead of firm size (market capitalization).

14. A momentum trading strategy that goes long stocks with high past risk-adjusted returns and short stocks with low past returns also generates positive CAPM alphas, providing further evidence that the market portfolio is not efficient and that the CAPM does not accurately model expected returns.

15. Securities may have non-zero alphas if the market portfolio that is used is not a good proxy for the true market portfolio.

16. The market portfolio will be inefficient if some investors' portfolio holdings are subject to systematic behavioural biases.

17. The market portfolio will be inefficient either if investors care about risk characteristics other than the volatility of their traded portfolio or if investors are exposed to other significant risks outside their portfolio that are not tradeable, the most important of which is due to their human capital.

18. When more than one portfolio is used to capture risk, the model is known as a multifactor model. This model is also sometimes called the Arbitrage Pricing Theory (APT). Using a collection of N well-diversified portfolios, the expected return of stock s is

$$E[R_s] = r_f + \beta_s^{F1}(E[R_{F1}] - r_f) + \beta_s^{F2}(E[R_{F2}] - r_f) + \cdots + \beta_s^{FN}(E[R_{FN}] - r_f)$$

$$= r_f + \sum_{n=1}^{N} \beta_s^{Fn}(E[R_{Fn}] - r_f) \tag{13.4}$$

19. A simpler way to write multifactor models is to express risk premiums as the expected return on a self-financing portfolio. A self-financing portfolio is a portfolio that costs nothing to construct. By using the expected returns of self-financing portfolios, the expected return of a stock can be expressed as

$$E[R_s] = r_f + \beta_s^{F1} E[R_{F1}] + \beta_s^{F2} E[R_{F2}] + \cdots + \beta_s^{FN} E[R_{FN}]$$

$$= r_f + \sum_{n=1}^{N} \beta_s^{Fn} E[R_{Fn}] \tag{13.5}$$

20. The portfolios that are most commonly used in a multifactor model are the market port-folio (Mkt), small-minus-big (SMB) portfolio, high-minus-low (HML) portfolio, and prior one-year momentum (PR1YR) portfolio. This model is known as the Fama-French-Carhart factor specification:

$$E[R_s] = r_f + \beta_s^{Mkt}(E[R_{Mkt}] - r_f) + \beta_s^{SMB}E[R_{SMB}]$$
$$+ \beta_s^{HML}E[R_{HML}] + \beta_s^{PR1YR}E[R_{PR1YR}] \qquad (13.6)$$

KEY TERMS

alpha *p. 444*
Arbitrage Pricing Theory (APT) *p. 468*
book-to-market ratio *p. 462*
cascade effect *p. 455*
cumulative abnormal return *p. 457*
data snooping bias *p. 463*
disposition effect *p. 453*
factor betas *p. 468*
factor portfolios *p. 468*
familiarity bias *p. 449*
Fama-French-Carhart (FFC) factor
  specification *p. 470*
herd behaviour *p. 455*
high-minus-low (HML) portfolio *p. 469*

momentum strategy *p. 465*
money manager *p. 460*
multifactor model *p. 468*
multiple regression *p. 480*
overconfidence hypothesis *p. 450*
prior one-year momentum (PR1YR)
  portfolio *p. 470*
rational expectations *p. 448*
relative wealth concerns *p. 449*
self-financing portfolio *p. 468*
sensation seeking *p. 451*
single-factor model *p. 468*
size effect *p. 462*
small-minus-big (SMB) portfolio *p. 469*

PROBLEMS

The problems marked in green can be found on MyFinanceLab at www.myfinancelab.com. Visit your MyFinanceLab for additional practice. An asterisk (*) indicates problems with a higher level of difficulty. Additional readings for this chapter may be found in the Textbook Resources section on MyFinanceLab.

Competition and Capital Markets

1. Assume that all investors have the same information and care only about expected return and volatility. If new information arrives about one stock, can this information affect the price and return of other stocks? If so, explain why.

EXCEL

2. Assume that the CAPM is a good description of stock price returns. The market expected return is 7% with 10% volatility, and the risk-free rate is 3%. New news arrives that does not change any of these numbers but it does change the expected return of the following stocks:

	Expected Return	**Volatility**	**Beta**
Green Leaf	12%	20%	1.5
NatSam	10%	40%	1.8
HanBel	9%	30%	0.75
Rebecca Automobile	6%	35%	1.2

a. At current market prices, which stocks represent buying opportunities?

b. On which stocks should you put a sell order in?

3. Suppose the CAPM equilibrium holds perfectly. Then the risk-free interest rate increases, *and nothing else changes.*

   a. Is the market portfolio still efficient?

   b. If your answer to part a is yes, explain why. If not, describe which stocks would be buying opportunities and which stocks would be selling opportunities.

Information and Rational Expectations

4. You know that there are informed traders in the stock market and you are uninformed. Describe an investment strategy that guarantees that you will not lose money to the informed traders and explain why it works.

5. What are the only conditions under which the market portfolio might not be an efficient portfolio?

6. Explain what the following sentence means: The market portfolio is a fence that protects the sheep from the wolves, but the nothing can protect the sheep from themselves.

7. You are trading in a market in which you know there are a few highly skilled traders who are better informed than you are. There are no transaction costs. Each day you randomly choose 5 stocks to buy and 5 stocks to sell (by, perhaps, throwing darts at a dartboard).

   a. Over the long run will your strategy outperform, underperform, or have the same return as a buy and hold strategy of investing in the market portfolio?

   b. Would your answer to part a change if all traders in the market were equally well informed and were equally skilled?

The Behaviour of Individual Investors

8. Why does the CAPM imply that investors should trade very rarely?

9. Your brother Joe is a surgeon who suffers badly from the overconfidence bias. He loves to trades stocks and believes his predictions with 100% confidence. In fact, he is uninformed like most investors. Rumours are that Vital Signs (a startup that makes warning labels in the medical industry) will receive a takeover offer at $20 per share. Absent the takeover offer, the stock will trade at $15 per share. The uncertainty will be resolved in the next few hours. Your brother believes that the takeover will occur with certainty and has instructed his broker to buy the stock at any price less than $20. In fact the true probability of a takeover is 50%, but a few people are informed and know whether the takeover will actually occur. They also have submitted orders. Nobody else is trading in the stock.

   a. Describe what will happen to the market price if in fact the takeover will occur. What will your brother's profits be: positive, negative, or zero?

   b. Describe what will happen to the market if the takeover will not occur. What will your brother's profits be: positive, negative, or zero?

   c. What are your brother's expected profits?

10. To put the turnover of Figure 13.3 into perspective, let's do a back of the envelope calculation of what an investor's average turnover per stock would be were he or she to follow a policy of investing in the S&P 500 portfolio. Because the portfolio is value weighted, the trading would be required when Standard and Poor's changes the constituent stocks. Let's ignore additional but less important reasons like new share issuances and repurchases. Assuming they change 23 stocks a year (the historical average since 1962) what would you estimate the investor's per stock share turnover to be? Assume that the average total number of shares outstanding for the stocks that are added or deleted from the index is the same as the average number of shares outstanding for S&P 500 stocks.

11. How does the disposition effect impact investors' tax obligations?

12. Consider the price paths of the following two stocks over six time periods:

	1	2	3	4	5	6
Stock 1	10	12	14	12	13	16
Stock 2	15	11	8	16	15	18

Neither stock pays dividends. Assume you are an investor with the disposition effect and you bought at time 1 and right now it is time 3. Assume throughout this question that you do no trading (other than what is specified) in these stocks.

   a. Which stock(s) would you be inclined to sell? Which would you be inclined to hold on to?

   b. How would your answer change if right now is time 6?

   c. What if you bought at time 3 instead of 1 and today is time 6?

   d. What if you bought at time 3 instead of 1 and today is time 5?

13. Suppose that all investors have the disposition effect. A new stock has just been issued at a price of $50, so all investors in this stock purchased the stock today. A year from now the stock will be taken over, for a price of $60 or $40 depending on the news that comes out over the year. The stock will pay no dividends. Investors will sell the stock whenever the price goes up by more than 10%.

   a. Suppose good news comes out in 6 months (implying the takeover offer will be $60). What equilibrium price will the stock trade for after the news comes out, that is, the price that equates supply and demand?

   b. Assume that you are the only investor who does not suffer from the disposition effect and your trades are small enough to not affect prices. Without knowing what will actually transpire, what trading strategy would you instruct your broker to follow?

The Efficiency of the Market Portfolio

14. Davita Spencer is a manager at Half Dome Asset Management. She can generate an alpha of 2% a year up to $100 million. After that her skills are spread too thin, so cannot add value, and her alpha is zero. Half Dome charges a fee of 1% of per year on the total amount of money under management (at the beginning of each year). Assume that there are always investors looking for positive alpha and no investor would invest in a fund with a negative alpha. In equilibrium, that is, when no investor either takes out money or wishes to invest new money,

   a. What alpha do investors in Davita's fund expect to receive?

   b. How much money will Davita have under management?

   c. How much money will Half Dome generate in fee income?

15. Assume the economy consisted of 3 types of people: 50% are fad followers; 45% are passive investors, they have read this book and so hold the market portfolio; and 5% are informed traders. The portfolio consisting of all the informed traders has a beta of 1.5 and an expected return of 15%. The market expected return is 11%. The risk-free rate is 5%.

   a. What alpha do the informed traders make?

   b. What is the alpha of the passive investors?

   c. What is the expected return of the fad followers?

   d. What alpha do the fad followers make?

16. Explain what the size effect is.

*17. Assume all firms have the same expected dividends. If they have different expected returns, how will their market values and expected returns be related? What about the relation between their dividend yields and expected returns?

EXCEL   18. Each of the six firms in the table below is expected to pay the listed dividend payment every year in perpetuity.

Firm	Dividend ($ million)	Cost of Capital (%/Year)
S1	10	8
S2	10	12
S3	10	14
B1	100	8
B2	100	12
B3	100	14

a. Using the cost of capital in the table, calculate the market value of each firm.

b. Rank the three S firms by their market values and look at how their cost of capital is ordered. What would be the expected return for a self-financing portfolio that went long on the firm with the largest market value and shorted the firm with the lowest market value? (The expected return of a self-financing portfolio is the weighted average return of the constituent securities.) Repeat using the B firms.

c. Rank all six firms by their market values. How does this ranking order the cost of capital? What would be the expected return for a self-financing portfolio that went long on the firm with the largest market value and shorted the firm with the lowest market value?

d. Repeat part c but rank the firms by the dividend yield instead of the market value. What can you conclude about the dividend yield ranking compared to the market value ranking?

EXCEL   19. Consider the following stocks, all of which will pay a liquidating dividend in a year and nothing in the interim:

	Market Capitalization ($ million)	Expected Liquidating Dividend ($ million)	Beta
Stock A	800	1000	0.77
Stock B	750	1000	1.46
Stock C	950	1000	1.25
Stock D	900	1000	1.07

a. Calculate the expected return of each stock.

b. What is the sign of correlation between the expected return and market capitalization of the stocks?

EXCEL   20. In problem 19, assume the risk-free rate is 3% and the market risk premium is 7%.

a. What does the CAPM predict the expected return for each stock should be?

b. Clearly, the CAPM predictions are not equal to the actual expected returns, so the CAPM does not hold. You decide to investigate this further. To see what kind of mistakes the CAPM is making, you decide to regress the actual expected return onto the expected return predicted by the CAPM.[45] What is the intercept and slope coefficient of this regression?

  c. What are the residuals of the regression in part b? That is, for each stock compute the difference between the actual expected return and the best fitting line given by the intercept and slope coefficient in part b.

  d. What is the sign of the correlation between the residuals you calculated in part c and market capitalization?

  e. What can you conclude from your answers to part b of the previous problem and part d of this problem about the relation between firm size (market capitalization) and returns? (The results do not depend on the particular numbers in this problem. You are welcome to verify this for yourself by redoing the problems with another value for the market risk premium, and by picking the stock betas and market capitalizations randomly.[46])

21. Explain how to construct a positive-alpha trading strategy if stocks that have had relatively high returns in the past tend to have positive alphas and stocks that have had relatively low returns in the past tend to have negative alphas.

*22. If you can use past returns to construct a trading strategy that makes money (has a positive alpha), it is evidence that the market portfolio is not efficient. Explain why.

23. Explain why you might expect stocks to have non-zero alphas if the market proxy portfolio is not highly correlated with the true market portfolio, even if the true market portfolio is efficient.

24. Explain why, if some investors are subject to systematic behavioural biases, while others pick efficient portfolios, the market portfolio will not be efficient.

25. Explain why an employee who cares only about expected return and volatility will likely underweight the amount of money he or she invests in his own company's stock relative to an investor who does not work for his or her company.

Multifactor Models of Risk

EXCEL 26. Using the factor beta estimates in Table 13.2 below and the expected return estimates in Table 13.1, calculate the risk premium of General Electric stock (ticker: GE) using the FFC factor specification.

EXCEL 27. You are currently considering an investment in a project in the energy sector. The investment has the same riskiness as Exxon Mobil stock (ticker: XOM). Using the data in Figure 13.9 and Table 13.2, calculate the cost of capital using the FFC factor specification if the current risk-free rate is 6% per year.

EXCEL 28. You work for Microsoft Corporation (ticker: MSFT), and you are considering whether to develop a new software product. The risk of the investment is the same as the risk of the company. Using the data in Table 13.1 and Table 13.2, calculate the cost of capital using the FFC factor specification if the current risk-free rate is 5.5% per year.

ESTIMATED FACTOR BETAS

TABLE 13.2

Factor	MSFT	XOM	GE
MKT	1.068	0.243	0.747
SMB	−0.374	0.125	−0.478
HML	−0.814	0.144	−0.232
PR1YR	−0.226	−0.185	−0.147

45. The Excel function SLOPE will produce the desired answers.

46. The Excel command RAND will produce a random number between 0 and 1.

CHAPTER 13 APPENDIX

BUILDING A MULTIFACTOR MODEL

In this appendix we show that if an efficient portfolio can be constructed out of a collection of well-diversified portfolios, the collection of portfolios will correctly price assets. To keep things simple, assume that we have identified two portfolios that we can combine to form an efficient portfolio; we call these portfolios **factor portfolios** and denote their returns by R_{F1} and R_{F2}. The efficient portfolio consists of some (unknown) combination of these two factor portfolios, represented by portfolio weights x_1 and x_2:

$$R_{eff} = x_1 R_{F1} + x_2 R_{F2} \tag{13A.1}$$

To see that we can use these factor portfolios to measure risk, consider regressing the excess returns of some stock s on the excess returns of *both* factors:

$$R_s - r_f = \alpha_s + \beta_s^{F1}(R_{F1} - r_f) + \beta_s^{F2}(R_{F2} - r_f) + \varepsilon_s \tag{13A.2}$$

This statistical technique is known as a **multiple regression**—it is exactly the same as the linear regression technique we described in Chapter 12, except now we have two regressors, $R_{F1} - r_f$ and $R_{F2} - r_f$, whereas in Chapter 12 we only had one regressor, the excess return of the market portfolio. Otherwise the interpretation is the same. We write the excess return of stock s as the sum of a constant, α_s, plus the variation in the stock that is related to each factor, and an error term ε_s that has an expectation of zero and is uncorrelated with either factor. The error term represents the risk of the stock that is unrelated to either factor.

If we can use the two factor portfolios to construct the efficient portfolio, as in Eq. 13A.1, then the constant term α_s in Eq. 13A.2 is zero (up to estimation error). To see why, consider a portfolio in which we buy stock s, then sell a fraction β_s^{F1} of the first factor portfolio and β_s^{F2} of the second factor portfolio, and invest the proceeds from these sales in the risk-free investment. This portfolio, which we call P, has return

$$\begin{aligned} R_P &= R_s - \beta_s^{F1} R_{F1} - \beta_s^{F2} R_{F2} + (\beta_s^{F1} + \beta_s^{F2}) r_f \\ &= R_s - \beta_s^{F1}(R_{F1} - r_f) - \beta_s^{F2}(R_{F2} - r_f) \end{aligned} \tag{13A.3}$$

Using Eq. 13A.2 to replace R_s and simplifying, the return of this portfolio is

$$R_P = r_f + \alpha_s + \varepsilon_s \tag{13A.4}$$

That is, portfolio P has a risk premium of α_s and risk given by ε_s. Now, because ε_s is uncorrelated with each factor, it must be uncorrelated with the efficient portfolio; that is,

$$\begin{aligned} Cov(R_{eff}, \varepsilon_s) &= Cov(x_1 R_{F1} + x_2 R_{F2}, \varepsilon_s) \\ &= x_1 Cov(R_{F1}, \varepsilon_s) + x_2 Cov(R_{F2}, \varepsilon_s) = 0 \end{aligned} \tag{13A.5}$$

But recall from Chapter 11 that *risk that is uncorrelated with the efficient portfolio is firm-specific risk that does not command a risk premium.* Therefore, the expected return of portfolio P is r_f, which means α_s must be zero.[47]

Setting α_s equal to zero and taking expectations of both sides of Eq. 13A.2, we get the following two-factor model of expected returns:

$$E[R_s] = r_f + \beta_s^{F1}(E[R_{F1}] - r_f) + \beta_s^{F2}(E[R_{F2}] - r_f) \tag{13A.6}$$

---

47. That is, Eq. 13.6 implies $\beta_P^{eff} = \dfrac{Cov(R_{eff}, \varepsilon_s)}{Var(R_{eff})} = 0$. Substituting this result into Eq. 13.3 gives

$E[R_P] = r_f$. But from Eq. 13A.4, $E[R_P] = r_f + \alpha_s$, and hence $\alpha_s = 0$.

Capital Structure and Dividend Policy

THE LAW OF ONE PRICE CONNECTION. One of the fundamental questions of corporate finance is how a firm should choose the set of securities it will issue to raise capital from investors. This decision determines the firm's capital structure, which is the total amount of debt, equity, and other securities that a firm has outstanding. Does the choice of capital structure affect the value of the firm? In Chapter 14 we consider this question in a perfect capital market. There we apply the Law of One Price to show that as long as the cash flows generated by the firm's assets are unchanged, then the value of the firm—which is the total value of its outstanding securities—does not depend on its capital structure. Therefore, if capital structure has a role in determining the firm's value, it must come from important market imperfections that we explore in subsequent chapters. In Chapter 15, we analyze the role of debt in reducing the taxes a firm or its investors will pay, while in Chapter 16 we consider the costs of financial distress and changes to managerial incentives that result from leverage. Finally, in Chapter 17, we consider the firm's choice of payout policy and ask: Which is the best method for the firm to return capital to its investors? Again, the Law of One Price implies that the firm's choice to pay dividends or repurchase its stock will not affect its value in a perfect capital market. We then examine how market imperfections affect this important insight and shape the firm's optimal payout policy.

Capital Structure in a Perfect Market

When a firm needs to raise new funds to undertake its investments, it must decide which type of security it will issue to investors. Even absent a need for new funds, firms can issue new securities and use the funds to repay debt or repurchase shares. What considerations should guide these decisions?

Consider the case of Dan Harris, chief financial officer of Electronic Business Services (EBS), who has been reviewing plans for a major expansion of the firm. To pursue the expansion, EBS plans to raise $50 million from outside investors. One possibility is to raise the funds by selling shares of EBS stock. Due to the firm's risk, Dan estimates that equity investors will require a 10% risk premium over the 5% risk-free interest rate. That is, the company's equity cost of capital is 15%.

Some senior executives at EBS, however, have argued that the firm should consider borrowing the $50 million instead. EBS has not borrowed previously and, given its strong balance sheet, it should be able to borrow at a 6% interest rate. Does the low interest rate of debt make borrowing a better choice of financing for EBS? If EBS does borrow, will this choice affect the NPV of the expansion, and therefore change the value of the firm and its share price?

We explore these questions in this chapter in a setting of **perfect capital markets**, in which all securities are fairly priced, there are no taxes or transaction costs, and the total cash flows of the firm's projects are not affected by how the firm finances them. Although in reality capital markets are not perfect, this setting provides an important benchmark. Perhaps surprisingly, with perfect capital markets, the Law of One Price implies that the choice of debt or equity financing will *not* affect the total value of a firm, its share price, or its cost of capital. Thus, in a perfect world, EBS will be indifferent regarding the choice of financing for its expansion.

14.1 EQUITY VERSUS DEBT FINANCING

The relative proportions of debt, equity, and other securities that a firm has outstanding constitute its **capital structure**. When corporations raise funds from outside investors, they must choose which type of security to issue. The most common choices are financing through equity alone and financing through a combination of debt and equity. We begin our discussion by considering both of these options.

FINANCING A FIRM WITH EQUITY

Consider an entrepreneur with the following investment opportunity. For an initial investment of $800 this year, a project will generate cash flows of either $1400 or $900 next year. The cash flows depend on whether the economy is strong or weak, respectively. Both scenarios are equally likely, and are shown in Table 14.1.

Because the project cash flows depend on the overall economy, they contain market risk. As a result, suppose that, to invest in this project, investors demand a risk premium over the current risk-free interest rate of 5%. Suppose that, given the market risk of the investment, the appropriate risk premium is 10%.

What is the NPV of this investment opportunity? Given a risk-free interest rate of 5% and a risk premium of 10%, the cost of capital for this project is 15%. Because the expected cash flow in one year is $\frac{1}{2}(\$1400) + \frac{1}{2}(\$900) = \$1150$, we get

$$NPV = -\$800 + \frac{\$1150}{1.15} = -\$800 + \$1000$$
$$= \$200$$

Thus the investment has a positive NPV.

If this project is financed using equity alone, how much would investors be willing to pay for the firm's shares? Recall from Chapter 3 that, in the absence of arbitrage, the price of a security equals the present value of its cash flows. Because the firm has no other liabilities, equity holders will receive all of the cash flows generated by the project on date 1. Hence the market value of the firm's equity today will be

$$PV(\text{equity cash flows}) = \frac{\$1150}{1.15} = \$1000$$

THE PROJECT CASH FLOWS

TABLE 14.1

Date 0	Date 1	
	Strong Economy	**Weak Economy**
−$800	$1400	$900

TABLE 14.2	CASH FLOWS AND RETURNS FOR UNLEVERED EQUITY

| | Date 0 | Date 1: Cash Flows | | Date 1: Returns | |
	Initial Value	Strong Economy	Weak Economy	Strong Economy	Weak Economy
Unlevered equity	$1000	$1400	$900	40%	−10%

So, the entrepreneur can raise $1000 by selling the equity in the firm. After paying the investment cost of $800, the entrepreneur can keep the remaining $200—the project NPV—as a profit. In other words, the project's NPV represents the value to the initial owners of the firm (in this case, the entrepreneur) created by the project.

What are the cash flows and returns for the shareholders who purchase the firm's equity? Equity in a firm with no debt is called **unlevered equity**. Because there is no debt, the date 1 cash flows of the unlevered equity are equal to those of the project. Given equity's initial value of $1000, a shareholder's returns are either 40% or −10% as shown in Table 14.2.

The strong and weak economy outcomes are equally likely, so the expected return on the unlevered equity is (40%) + (−10%) = 15%. Because the risk of unlevered equity equals the risk of the project, shareholders are earning an appropriate return for the risk they are taking.

FINANCING A FIRM WITH DEBT AND EQUITY

Financing the firm exclusively with equity is not the entrepreneur's only option. She can also raise part of the initial capital using debt. Suppose she decides to borrow $500 initially, in addition to selling equity. Because the project's cash flow will always be enough to repay the debt, the debt is risk free. Thus the firm can borrow at the risk-free interest rate of 5%, and it will owe the debt holders $500 \times 1.05 = \$525$ in one year.

Equity in a firm that also has debt outstanding is called **levered equity**. Promised payments to debt holders must be made before any payments to equity holders are distributed. Given the firm's $525 debt obligation, the shareholders will receive only $1400 − $525 = $875 if the economy is strong and $900 − $525 = $375 if the economy is weak. Table 14.3 shows the cash flows of the debt, the levered equity, and the total cash flows of the firm.

What price E should the levered equity sell for, and which is the best capital structure choice for the entrepreneur? In an important paper, researchers Franco Modigliani and Merton Miller proposed an answer to this question that surprised researchers and practitioners at the time.[1] They argued that with perfect capital markets, the total value of a firm should not depend on its capital structure. Their reasoning: The firm's total cash flows still equal the cash flows of the project, and therefore have the same present value of $1000 calculated earlier (see the last line in Table 14.3). Because the cash flows of the debt and equity sum to the cash flows of the project, by the Law of One Price the combined values of debt and equity must be $1000. Therefore, if the value of the debt is $500, the value of the levered equity must be $E = \$1000 − \$500 = \$500$.

---

1. F. Modigliani and M. Miller, "The Cost of Capital, Corporation Finance and the Theory of Investment," *American Economic Review* 48:3 (1958): 261–297.

are consistent with MM Proposition I. While EPS increases on average, this increase is necessary to compensate shareholders for the additional risk they are taking, so LVI's share price does not increase as a result of the transaction. Let's check this result in an example.

EXAMPLE 14.9

THE MM PROPOSITIONS AND EARNINGS PER SHARE

Problem

Assume that LVI's EBIT is not expected to grow in the future and that all earnings are paid as dividends. Use MM Propositions I and II to show that the increase in expected EPS for LVI will not lead to an increase in the share price.

Solution

Without leverage, expected earnings per share and therefore dividends are $1 each year, and the share price is $7.50. Let r_U be LVI's cost of capital without leverage. Then we can value LVI as a perpetuity:

$$P = \$7.50 = \frac{Div}{r_U} = \frac{EPS}{r_U} = \frac{\$1.00}{r_U}$$

Therefore, LVI's current share price implies $r_U = 1/7.50 = 13.33\%$.

The market value of LVI stock without leverage is $7.50 per share × 10 million shares = $75 million. If LVI uses debt to repurchase $15 million worth of the firm's equity (that is, 2 million shares), then the remaining equity will be worth $75 million − $15 million = $60 million according to MM Proposition I. After the transaction, LVI's debt-equity ratio is $15 million ÷ $60 million =1/4. Using MM Proposition II, LVI's equity cost of capital with leverage will be

$$r_E = r_U + \frac{D}{E}(r_U - r_D) = 13.33\% + \frac{1}{4}(13.33\% - 8\%) = 14.66\%$$

Given that expected EPS is now $1.10 per share, the new value of the shares equals

$$P = \frac{\$1.10}{r_E} = \frac{\$1.10}{14.66\%} = \$7.50 \text{ per share}$$

Thus, even though EPS is higher, due to the additional risk, shareholders will demand a higher return. These effects cancel out, so the price per share is unchanged.

Because the firm's earnings per share and price-earnings ratio are affected by leverage, we cannot reliably compare these measures across firms with different capital structures. For this reason, most analysts prefer to use performance measures and valuation multiples that are based on the firm's earnings before interest has been deducted. For example, the ratio of enterprise value to EBIT (or EBITDA) is more useful when analyzing firms with very different capital structures than is comparing their P/E ratios.

EQUITY ISSUANCES AND DILUTION

Another often-heard fallacy is that issuing equity will dilute existing shareholders' ownership, so debt financing should be used instead. By **dilution**, the proponents of this fallacy mean that if the firm issues new shares, the cash flows generated by the firm must be divided among a larger number of shares, thereby reducing the value of each individual share. The problem with this line of reasoning is that it ignores the fact that the cash raised by issuing new shares will increase the firm's assets. Let's consider an example.

Suppose Jet Set Airlines (JSA) is a highly successful discount airline serving the Toronto-Montreal-Ottawa triangle. It currently has no debt and 500 million shares outstanding. These shares are currently trading at a price of $16. Last month the firm announced that it would expand its operations by adding Vancouver, Calgary, and Edmonton flights. The expansion will require the purchase of $1 billion of new planes, which will be financed by issuing new equity. How will the share price change when the new equity is issued today?

Based on the current share price of the firm (prior to the issue), the equity and therefore the assets of the firm have a market value of 500 million shares × $16 per share = $8 billion. Because the expansion decision has already been made and announced, in perfect capital markets this value incorporates the NPV associated with the expansion.

Suppose JSA sells 62.5 million new shares at the current price of $16 per share to raise the additional $1 billion needed to purchase the planes.

Assets ($ million)	Before Equity Issue	After Equity Issue
Cash		1000
Existing assets	8000	8000
	8000	9000
Shares outstanding (million)	500	562.5
Value per share	$16.00	$16.00

Two things happen when JSA issues equity. First, the market value of its assets grows because of the additional $1 billion in cash the firm has raised. Second, the number of shares increases. Although the number of shares has grown to 562.5 million, the value per share is unchanged: $9 billion ÷ 562.5 million shares = $16 per share.

In general, as long as the firm sells the new shares of equity *at a fair price*, there will be no gain or loss to shareholders associated with the equity issue itself. The money taken in by the firm as a result of the share issue exactly offsets the dilution of the shares. *Any gain or loss associated with the transaction will result from the NPV of the investments the firm makes with the funds raised.*

CONCEPT CHECK

1. If a change in leverage raises a firm's earnings per share, should this cause its share price to rise in a perfect market?

2. True or false: When a firm issues equity, it increases the supply of its shares in the market, which should cause its share price to fall.

14.5   MM: BEYOND THE PROPOSITIONS

Since the publication of their original paper, Modigliani and Miller's ideas have greatly influenced finance research and practice. Perhaps more important than the specific propositions themselves is the approach that MM took to derive them. Proposition I was one of the first arguments to show that the Law of One Price could have strong implications for security prices and firm values in a competitive market; it marks the beginning of the modern theory of corporate finance.

Modigliani and Miller's work formalized a new way of thinking about financial markets that was first put forth by John Burr Williams in his 1938 book, *The Theory of Investment Value*. In it Williams argues:

If the investment value of an enterprise as a whole is by definition the present worth of all its future distributions to security holders, whether on interest or dividend account, then this value in no wise depends on what the company's capitalization is. Clearly, if a single individual or a single institutional investor owned all of the bonds, stocks and warrants issued by the corporation, it would not matter to this investor what the company's capitalization was (except for details concerning the income tax). Any earnings collected as interest could not be collected as dividends. To such an individual it would be perfectly obvious that total interest- and dividend-paying power was in no wise dependent on the kind of securities issued to the company's owner. Furthermore no change in the investment value of the enterprise as a whole would result from a change in its capitalization. Bonds could be retired with stock issues, or two classes of junior securities could be combined into one, without changing the investment value of the company as a whole. Such constancy of investment value is analogous to the indestructibility of matter or energy: it leads us to speak of the Law of the Conservation of Investment Value, just as physicists speak of the Law of the Conservation of Matter, or the Law of the Conservation of Energy.

Thus, the results in this chapter can be interpreted more broadly as the **conservation of value principle** for financial markets: *With perfect capital markets, financial transactions neither add nor destroy value, but instead represent a repackaging of risk (and therefore return).*

The conservation of value principle extends far beyond questions of debt versus equity or even capital structure. It implies that any financial transaction that appears to be a good deal in terms of adding value either is too good to be true or is exploiting some type of market imperfection. To make sure the value is not illusory, it is important to identify the market imperfection that is the source of value. In the next several chapters we will examine different types of market imperfections and the potential sources of value that they introduce for the firm's capital structure choice and other financial transactions.

NOBEL PRIZE FRANCO MODIGLIANI AND MERTON MILLER

Franco Modigliani and Merton Miller, the authors of the Modigliani-Miller Propositions, have each won the Nobel Prize in economics for their work in financial economics, including their capital structure propositions. Modigliani won the Nobel Prize in 1985 for his work on personal savings and for his capital structure theorems with Miller. Miller earned his prize in 1990 for his analysis of portfolio theory and capital structure.

Miller once described the MM propositions in an interview this way:

People often ask: Can you summarize your theory quickly? Well, I say, you understand the M&M theorem if you know why this is a joke: The pizza delivery man comes to Yogi Berra after the game and says, "Yogi, how do you want this pizza cut, into quarters or eighths?" And Yogi says, "Cut it in eight pieces. I'm feeling hungry tonight."

Everyone recognizes that's a joke because obviously the number and shape of the pieces don't affect the size of the

pizza. And similarly, the stocks, bonds, warrants, et cetera, issued don't affect the aggregate value of the firm. They just slice up the underlying earnings in different ways.[*]

Modigliani and Miller each won the Nobel Prize in large part for their observation that the value of a firm should be unaffected by its capital structure in perfect capital markets. While the intuition underlying the MM propositions may be as simple as slicing pizza, their implications for corporate finance are far-reaching. The propositions imply that the true role of a firm's financial policy is to deal with (and potentially exploit) financial market imperfections such as taxes and transaction costs. Modigliani and Miller's work began a long line of research into these market imperfections, which we look at over the next several chapters.

___

[*]Peter J. Tanous, *Investment Gurus* (New York: Institute of Finance, 1997).

INTERVIEW WITH PAUL JEWER

Paul Jewer, BBA, CA, is senior vice-president, finance, and treasurer at Sobeys Inc., one of Canada's leading grocery retailers. Sobeys operates stores across Canada in all 10 provinces.

QUESTION: **What is the role of a treasurer?**

ANSWER: A treasurer helps an organization finance its opportunities and manage its risks. To finance opportunities, a treasurer can lead relations with investors and key lending partners, and arrange financing with various financial providers. A treasurer helps manage risk by providing overall financial advice on the use of capital in an organization and through the use of products that include derivatives and insurance.

QUESTION: **How is your company financed?**

ANSWER: Sobeys is financed with equity and debt. The important thing is to find the appropriate mix. Sobeys recently went through a privatization transaction. Currently all Sobeys shares are held by the Empire Company Limited, which is a family-controlled but publicly listed company on the TSX. Our debt is held by investors across Canada and we also finance the company with an appropriate level of bank debt.

QUESTION: **What factors affect a company like yours in choosing the level of leverage?**

ANSWER: Overall the leverage decision is made by balancing the return to equity holders with an appropriate amount of risk. We need an appropriate economic return while ensuring that there is sufficient liquidity for the organization to continue to do its business and to grow. We look for a level of leverage that allows us quick access to the capital markets should a significant opportunity arise, and we balance our funding opportunities across a series of partners to ensure that we have those important relationships developed so that we can crystallize on opportunities as they present themselves.

QUESTION: **Finance theory indicates leverage can have positive or negative impacts. Can you comment on whether these factors are important in your company's leverage choice?**

ANSWER: Positives include interest tax shields and a reduction of financial slack. Negatives include financial distress costs. Clearly debt has the lowest cost of capital after tax; therefore, in order to be competitive from an overall cost perspective, Sobeys needs to have a sufficient level of debt to finance its operations. We manage our debt-equity mix based on the opportunities that we have as an organization, the risk profile we are willing to accept, and the outlook for the economic environment. We also balance our cash flow requirements over an extended period of time so that we are prepared to deal with any temporary disruptions or challenges and prepared to capitalize on larger opportunities should they present themselves.

QUESTION: **Are there any other factors that affect your leverage decision?**

ANSWER: From a debt perspective, we look for an appropriate balance of fixed-rate and floating-rate debt to appropriately manage risk and exposure to interest rates. From an equity perspective, we have always had the benefit of having a significant majority shareholder, and now a sole shareholder (the Empire Company). It is important to generate an appropriate return on capital for our equity holders and to have an appropriate balance of debt and equity so that our bond holders and our debt holders feel very comfortable that we will generate the financial return to repay our indebtedness.

We focus on the long term. We are prepared to leverage the company for significant transactions. In 1998, for example, we leveraged up so we could acquire the Oshawa Group; that was really transformational from a company perspective. More recently, we leveraged up the company to privatize it. Following these leveraging up events we usually focus on paying down some of that temporary debt to get to a more appropriate long-term balance between debt and equity.

QUESTION: **What are some of the risks specific to the grocery retail industry? Do these risks impact your capital structure?**

ANSWER: Clearly there is competitive risk. This includes the risk of entry of new competitors and the pricing pressures that we may face as our competitors continue to try to grow their business in Canada. There is also commodity risk. The cost of inputs into products, of products that we buy inside Canada, and of products we import can change significantly as the underlying commodity prices change. There is some foreign currency risk because we purchase significant amounts outside Canada. The risk of inflation is certainly always present. Some of this risk is mitigated by the fact that some of the costs can be passed on to the consumers. In terms of our capital structure, we choose our debt and equity levels so that we can handle these risks should negative outcomes occur.

 Visit MyFinanceLab at www.myfinancelab.com to see the accompanying video for this interview.

CONCEPT CHECK

1. Consider the questions facing Dan Harris, CFO of EBS, at the beginning of this chapter. What answers would you give based on the Modigliani-Miller Propositions? What considerations should the capital structure decision be based on?

2. State the conservation of value principle for financial markets.

SUMMARY

1. The collection of securities a firm issues to raise capital from investors is called the firm's capital structure. Equity and debt are the securities most commonly used by firms. When equity is used without debt, the firm is said to be unlevered. Otherwise, the amount of debt determines the firm's leverage.

2. The owner of a firm should choose the capital structure that maximizes the total value of the securities issued.

3. Capital markets are said to be perfect if they satisfy three conditions:

   a. Investors and firms can trade the same set of securities at competitive market prices equal to the present value of their future cash flows.

   b. There are no taxes, transaction costs, or issuance costs associated with security trading.

   c. A firm's financing decisions do not change the cash flows generated by its investments, nor do they reveal new information about them.

4. According to MM Proposition I, with perfect capital markets the value of a firm is independent of its capital structure.

   a. With perfect capital markets, homemade leverage is a perfect substitute for firm leverage.

   b. If otherwise identical firms with different capital structures have different values, the Law of One Price would be violated and an arbitrage opportunity would exist.

5. The market value balance sheet shows that the total market value of a firm's assets equals the total market value of the firm's liabilities, including all securities issued to investors. Changing the capital structure therefore alters how the value of the assets is divided across securities, but not the firm's total value.

6. A firm can change its capital structure at any time by issuing new securities and using the funds to pay its existing investors. An example is a leveraged recapitalization in which the firm borrows money (issues debt) and repurchases shares (or pays a dividend). MM Proposition I implies that such transactions will not change the share price.

7. According to MM Proposition II, the cost of capital for levered equity is

$$r_E = r_U + \frac{D}{E}(r_U - r_D) \tag{14.5}$$

8. Debt is less risky than equity, so it has a lower cost of capital. Leverage increases the risk of equity, however, raising the equity cost of capital. The benefit of debt's lower cost of capital is offset by the higher equity cost of capital, leaving a firm's weighted average cost of capital (WACC) unchanged with perfect capital markets:

$$r_{wacc} = \frac{E}{E+D}r_E + \frac{D}{E+D}r_D = r_U = r_A \qquad (14.6, 14.7)$$

9. The market risk of a firm's assets can be estimated by its unlevered beta:

$$\beta_U = \frac{E}{E+D}\beta_E + \frac{D}{E+D}\beta_D \qquad (14.8)$$

10. Leverage increases the beta of a firm's equity:

$$\beta_E = \beta_U + \frac{D}{E}(\beta_U - \beta_D) \qquad (14.9)$$

11. A firm's net debt is equal to its debt less its holdings of cash and other risk-free securities. We can compute the cost of capital and the beta of the firm's business assets, excluding cash, by using its net debt when calculating its WACC or unlevered beta.

12. Leverage can raise a firm's expected earnings per share, but it also increases the volatility of earnings per share. As a result, shareholders are not better off and the value of equity is unchanged.

13. As long as shares are sold to investors at a fair price, there is no cost of dilution associated with issuing equity. While the number of shares increases when equity is issued, the firm's assets also increase because of the cash raised, and the per-share value of equity remains unchanged.

14. With perfect capital markets, financial transactions are a zero-NPV activity that neither add nor destroy value on their own, but rather repackage the firm's risk and return. Capital structure—and financial transactions more generally—affect a firm's value only because of its impact on some type of market imperfection.

KEY TERMS

capital structure *p. 483*
conservation of value principle *p. 503*
debt-to-value ratio *p. 494*
dilution *p. 501*
homemade leverage *p. 488*
leveraged recapitalization *p. 491*
levered equity *p. 484*

market value balance sheet *p. 490*
net debt *p. 498*
perfect capital markets *p. 482*
unlevered beta *p. 497*
unlevered equity *p. 484*
weighted average cost of capital
  (WACC) *p. 494*

PROBLEMS

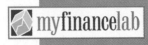

The problems marked in green can be found on MyFinanceLab at www.myfinancelab.com. Visit your MyFinanceLab for additional practice. An asterisk (*) indicates problems with a higher level of difficulty. Additional readings for this chapter may be found in the Textbook Resources section on MyFinanceLab.

Equity Versus Debt Financing

1. Consider a project with free cash flows in one year of $130,000 or $180,000, with each outcome being equally likely. The initial investment required for the project is $100,000, and the project's cost of capital is 20%. The risk-free interest rate is 10%.

    a. What is the NPV of this project?

b. Suppose that to raise the funds for the initial investment, the project is sold to investors as an all-equity firm. The equity holders will receive the cash flows of the project in one year. How much money can be raised in this way—that is, what is the initial market value of the unlevered equity?

c. Suppose the initial $100,000 is instead raised by borrowing at the risk-free interest rate. What are the cash flows of the levered equity, and what is its initial value according to MM?

2. You are an entrepreneur starting a biotechnology firm. If your research is successful, the technology can be sold for $30 million. If your research is unsuccessful, it will be worth nothing. To fund your research, you need to raise $2 million. Investors are willing to provide you with $2 million in initial capital in exchange for 50% of the unlevered equity in the firm.

a. What is the total market value of the firm without leverage?

b. Suppose you borrow $1 million. According to MM, what fraction of the firm's equity will you need to sell to raise the additional $1 million you need?

c. What is the value of your share of the firm's equity in parts a and b?

3. Starpack Industries owns assets that will have an 80% probability of having a market value of $50 million in one year. There is a 20% chance that the assets will be worth only $20 million. The current risk-free rate is 5%, and Starpack's assets have a cost of capital of 10%.

a. If Starpack is unlevered, what is the current market value of its equity?

b. Suppose instead that Starpack has debt with a face value of $20 million due in one year. According to MM, what is the value of Starpack's equity in this case?

c. What is the expected return of Starpack's equity without leverage? What is the expected return of Starpack's equity with leverage?

d. What is the lowest possible realized return of Starpack's equity with and without leverage?

4. Wolfrum Technology (WT) has no debt. Its assets will be worth $450 million in one year if the economy is strong, but only $200 million in one year if the economy is weak. Both events are equally likely. The market value today of its assets is $250 million.

a. What is the expected return of WT stock without leverage?

b. Suppose the risk-free interest rate is 5%. If WT borrows $100 million today at this rate and uses the proceeds to pay an immediate cash dividend, what will be the market value of its equity just after the dividend is paid, according to MM?

c. What is the expected return of MM stock after the dividend is paid in part b?

Modigliani-Miller I: Leverage, Arbitrage, and Firm Value

5. Suppose there are no taxes. Firm ABC has no debt, and firm XYZ has debt of $5000 on which it pays interest of 10% each year. Both companies have identical projects that generate free cash flows of $800 or $1000 each year. After paying any interest on debt, both companies use all remaining free cash flows to pay dividends each year.

a. Fill in the table below showing the payments debt and equity holders of each firm will receive given each of the two possible levels of free cash flows.

| | ABC | | XYZ | |
FCF	Debt Payments	Equity Dividends	Debt Payments	Equity Dividends
$ 800				
$1000				

b. Suppose you hold 10% of the equity of ABC. What is another portfolio you could hold that would provide the same cash flows?

c. Suppose you hold 10% of the equity of XYZ. If you can borrow at 10%, what is an alternative strategy that would provide the same cash flows?

6. Suppose Alpha Industries and Omega Technology have identical assets that generate identical cash flows. Alpha Industries is an all-equity firm, with 10 million shares outstanding that trade for a price of $22 per share. Omega Technology has 20 million shares outstanding as well as debt of $60 million.

   a. According to MM Proposition 1, what is the stock price for Omega Technology?

   b. Suppose Omega Technology stock currently trades for $11 per share. What arbitrage opportunity is available? What assumptions are necessary to exploit this opportunity?

7. Cisoft is a highly profitable technology firm that currently has $5 billion in cash. The firm has decided to use this cash to repurchase shares from investors, and it has already announced these plans to investors. Currently, Cisoft is an all-equity firm with 5 billion shares outstanding. These shares currently trade for $12 per share. Cisoft has issued no other securities except for stock options given to its employees. The current market value of these options is $8 billion.

   a. What is the market value of Cisoft's non-cash assets?

   b. With perfect capital markets, what is the market value of Cisoft's equity after the share repurchase? What is the value per share?

8. Schwartz Industry is an industrial company with 100 million shares outstanding and a market capitalization (equity value) of $4 billion. It has $2 billion of debt outstanding. Management have decided to delever the firm by issuing new equity to repay all outstanding debt.

   a. How many new shares must the firm issue?

   b. Suppose you are a shareholder holding 100 shares, and you disagree with this decision. Assuming a perfect capital market, describe what you can do to undo the effect of this decision.

9. Magma International is an all-equity firm with 100 million shares outstanding, which are currently trading for $7.50 per share. A month ago, Magma announced it will change its capital structure by borrowing $100 million in short-term debt, borrowing $100 million in long-term debt, and issuing $100 million of preferred stock. The $300 million raised by these issues, plus another $50 million in cash that Magma already has, will be used to repurchase existing shares of stock. The transaction is scheduled to occur today. Assume perfect capital markets.

   a. What is the market value balance sheet for Magma

      i. Before this transaction?

      ii. After the new securities are issued but before the share repurchase?

      iii. After the share repurchase?

   b. At the conclusion of this transaction, how many shares outstanding will Magma have, and what will the value of those shares be?

Modigliani-Miller II: Leverage, Risk, and the Cost of Capital

10. Explain what is wrong with the following argument: "If a firm issues debt that is risk free, because there is no possibility of default, the risk of the firm's equity does not change. Therefore, risk-free debt allows the firm to get the benefit of a low cost of capital of debt without raising its cost of capital of equity."

11. Consider the entrepreneur described in Section 14.1 (and referenced in Tables 14.1 to 14.3). Suppose she funds the project by borrowing $750 rather than $500.

   a. According to MM Proposition I, what is the value of the equity? What are its cash flows if the economy is strong? What are its cash flows if the economy is weak?

   b. What is the return of the equity in each case? What is its expected return?

c. What is the risk premium of equity in each case? What is the sensitivity of the levered equity return to systematic risk? How does its sensitivity compare to that of unlevered equity? How does its risk premium compare to that of unlevered equity?

d. What is the debt-equity ratio of the firm in this case?

e. What is the firm's WACC in this case?

12. Hardmon Enterprises is currently an all-equity firm with an expected return of 12%. It is considering a leveraged recapitalization in which it would borrow and repurchase existing shares.

   a. Suppose Hardmon borrows to the point that its debt-equity ratio is 0.50. With this amount of debt, the debt cost of capital is 6%. What will the expected return of equity be after this transaction?

   b. Suppose instead Hardmon borrows to the point that its debt-equity ratio is 1.50. With this amount of debt, Hardmon's debt will be much riskier. As a result, the debt cost of capital will be 8%. What will the expected return of equity be in this case?

   c. A senior manager argues that it is in the best interest of the shareholders to choose the capital structure that leads to the highest expected return for the stock. How would you respond to this argument?

13. Suppose Microsoft has no debt and an equity cost of capital of 9.2%. The average debt-to-value ratio for the software industry is 13%. What would its cost of equity be if it took on the average amount of debt for its industry at a cost of debt of 6%?

14. Global Pistons (GP) has common stock with a market value of $200 million and debt with a value of $100 million. Investors expect a 15% return on the stock and a 6% return on the debt. Assume perfect capital markets.

   a. Suppose GP issues $100 million of new stock to buy back the debt. What is the expected return of the stock after this transaction?

   b. Suppose instead GP issues $50 million of new debt to repurchase stock.

      i. If the risk of the debt does not change, what is the expected return of the stock after this transaction?

      ii. If the risk of the debt increases, would the expected return of the stock be higher or lower than in part i?

15. Hubbard Industries is an all-equity firm whose shares have an expected return of 10%. Hubbard does a leveraged recapitalization, issuing debt and repurchasing stock, until its debt-equity ratio is 0.60. Due to the increased risk, shareholders now expect a return of 13%. Assuming there are no taxes and Hubbard's debt is risk free, what is the interest rate on the debt?

16. Yellowknife Mining has 50 million shares that are currently trading for $4 per share and $200 million worth of debt. The debt is risk free and has an interest rate of 5%, and the expected return of Yellowknife stock is 11%. Suppose a mining strike causes the price of Yellowknife stock to fall 25% to $3 per share. The value of the risk-free debt is unchanged. Assuming there are no taxes and the unlevered beta of Yellowknife's assets is unchanged, what happens to Yellowknife's equity cost of capital?

17. Mercer Corp. is an all-equity firm with 10 million shares outstanding and $100 million worth of debt outstanding. Its current share price is $75. Mercer's equity cost of capital is 8.5%. Mercer has just announced that it will issue $350 million worth of debt. It will use the proceeds from this debt to pay off its existing debt, and use the remaining $250 million to pay an immediate dividend. Assume perfect capital markets.

   a. Estimate Mercer's share price just after the recapitalization is announced, but before the transaction occurs.

   b. Estimate Mercer's share price at the conclusion of the transaction. (*Hint:* Use the market value balance sheet.)

c. Suppose Mercer's existing debt was risk free with a 4.25% expected return, and its new debt is risky with a 5% expected return. Estimate Mercer's equity cost of capital after the transaction.

18. In June 2009, Apple Computer had no debt, total equity capitalization of $128 billion, and a (equity) beta of 1.7 (as reported on Google Finance). Included in Apple's assets was $25 billion in cash and risk-free securities. Assume that the risk-free rate of interest is 5% and the market risk premium is 4%.

a. What is Apple's enterprise value?

b. What is the beta of Apple's business assets?

c. What is Apple's WACC?

*19. Indell stock has a current market value of $120 million and a beta of 1.50. Indell currently has risk-free debt as well. The firm decides to change its capital structure by issuing $30 million in additional risk-free debt, and then using this $30 million plus another $10 million in cash to repurchase stock. With perfect capital markets, what will the beta of Indell stock be after this transaction?

Capital Structure Fallacies

20. Salish Industries is an all-equity firm whose stock has a beta of 1.2 and an expected return of 12.5%. Suppose it issues new risk-free debt with a 5% yield and repurchases 40% of its stock. Assume perfect capital markets.

a. What is the beta of Salish stock after this transaction?

b. What is the expected return of Salish stock after this transaction?

Suppose that prior to this transaction, Salish had expected earnings per share this coming year of $1.50, with a forward P/E ratio (that is, the share price divided by the expected earnings for the coming year) of 14.

c. What is Salish's expected earnings per share after this transaction? Does this change benefit shareholders? Explain.

d. What is Salish's forward P/E ratio after this transaction? Is this change in the P/E ratio reasonable? Explain.

21. You are CEO of a high-growth technology firm. You plan to raise $180 million to fund an expansion by issuing either new shares or new debt. With the expansion, you expect earnings next year of $24 million. The firm currently has 10 million shares outstanding, with a price of $90 per share. Assume perfect capital markets.

a. If you raise the $180 million by selling new shares, what will the forecast for next year's earnings per share be?

b. If you raise the $180 million by issuing new debt with an interest rate of 5%, what will the forecast for next year's earnings per share be?

c. What is the firm's forward P/E ratio (that is, the share price divided by the expected earnings for the coming year) if it issues equity? What is the firm's forward P/E ratio if it issues debt? How can you explain the difference?

22. Yukon Ltd. is an all-equity firm with 100 million shares outstanding currently trading for $8.50 per share. Suppose Yukon decides to grant a total of 10 million new shares to employees as part of a new compensation plan. The firm argues that this new compensation plan will motivate employees and is a better strategy than giving salary bonuses because it will not cost the firm anything.

a. If the new compensation plan has no effect on the value of Yukon's assets, what will the share price of the stock be once this plan is implemented?

b. What is the cost of this plan for Yukon's investors? Why is issuing equity costly in this case?

DATA CASE

You work in the corporate finance division of The Home Depot and your boss has asked you to review the firm's capital structure. Specifically, your boss is considering changing the firm's debt level. Your boss remembers something from his MBA program about capital structure being irrelevant, but isn't quite sure what that means. You know that capital structure is irrelevant under the conditions of perfect markets and will demonstrate this point for your boss by showing that the weighted average cost of capital remains constant under various levels of debt. So, for now, suppose that capital markets are perfect as you prepare responses for your boss.

You would like to analyze relatively modest changes to Home Depot's capital structure. You would like to consider two scenarios: the firm issues $1 billion in new debt to repurchase stock, and the firm issues $1 billion in new stock to repurchase debt. Use Excel to answer the following questions using Eq. 14.5 and Eq. 14.6 from this chapter, and assuming a cost of unlevered equity (r_U) of 12 percent.

1. Obtain the financial information you need for Home Depot.

   a. Go to Nasdaq.com (www.nasdaq.com), click on "Summary Quotes" on the left-hand side, and enter Home Depot's stock symbol (HD). Click on Go. From the Summary Quotes page, get the current stock price and number of shares outstanding.

   b. Click on "Company Financials" and the annual income statement should appear. Put the cursor in the middle of the statement, right-click your mouse, and select "Export to Microsoft Excel." (You will not need the income statement until Chapter 15, but collect all of the background data in one step.) Go back to the NASDAQ Web page and select the balance sheet. Export that to Excel as well and then cut and paste the balance sheet to the same worksheet as the income statement.

   c. To get the cost of debt for Home Depot, go to NASD BondInfo (http://cxa. marketwatch.com/finra/BondCenter/Default.aspx). Select the corporate toggle, search by symbol and enter Home Depot's symbol. The next page will contain information for all of Home Depot's outstanding and recently matured bonds. Select the latest yield on an outstanding bond with the shortest remaining maturity (the maturity date is on the line describing each issue; sometimes the list also contains recently retired bonds, so make sure not to use one of those).

2. Compute the market D/E ratio for Home Depot. Approximate the market value of debt by the book value of net debt; include both Long-Term Debt and Short-Term Debt/Current Portion of Long-Term Debt from the balance sheet and subtract any cash holdings. Use the stock price and number of shares outstanding to calculate the market value of equity.

3. Compute the cost of levered equity (r_E) for Home Depot using their current market debt-to-equity ratio and Eq. 14.5 from the chapter.

4. Compute the current weighted average cost of capital (WACC) for Home Depot using Eq. 14.6 and the existing yield on the outstanding bonds as r_D given their current debt-to-equity ratio.

5. Repeat steps 3 and 4 for the two scenarios you would like to analyze, issuing $1 billion in debt to repurchase stock, and issuing $1 billion in stock to repurchase debt. (Although you realize that the cost of debt capital (r_D) may change with changes in leverage, for these modestly small changes you decide to assume that r_D remains constant. We will explore the relation between changing leverage and changing r_D more fully in Chapter 16.) What is the market D/E ratio in each of these cases?

6. Prepare a written explanation for your boss explaining the relationship between capital structure and the cost of capital in this exercise.

7. What implicit assumptions in this exercise generate the results found in Question 5? How might your results differ in the "real world"?

Debt and Taxes

In a perfect capital market, the Law of One Price implies that all financial transactions have an NPV of zero and neither create nor destroy value. Consequently, in the previous chapter we found that the choice of debt versus equity financing does not affect the value of a firm: The funds raised from issuing debt equal the present value of the future interest and principal payments the firm will make. While leverage increases the risk and cost of capital of the firm's equity, the firm's weighted average cost of capital (WACC), total value, and share price are unaltered by a change in leverage. That is, *in a perfect capital market, a firm's choice of capital structure is unimportant.*

This statement is at odds, however, with the observation that firms invest significant resources, both in terms of managerial time and effort and investment banking fees, in managing their capital structures. In many instances, the choice of leverage is of critical importance to a firm's value and future success. As we will show, there are large and systematic variations in the typical capital structures for different industries. For example, Microsoft has essentially had negative debt for many years as it had significant cash balances combined with no or low amounts of borrowings. At the end of the 2008 fiscal year (June 30, 2008), Microsoft had no long-term debt and it had cash and short-term investments on hand of over $23 billion. Through the worst of the financial crisis Microsoft was actually able to raise capital and its long-term debt rose to $3.7 billion by fiscal year-end 2009; Microsoft's cash and short-term investments also rose to almost $31.5 billion. In contrast, Canadian Pacific Railway (CP) carries significant debt in excess of cash and short-term investments. At the end of 2008, CP had long-term debt of almost 4.7 billion while cash and short-term investments were only 117.6 million. CP's debt-to-equity ratio at the end of 2008 was 0.78. Railways in general have higher debt ratios than software companies. If capital structure is unimportant, why do we see such consistent differences in capital structures across firms and industries? Why do managers dedicate so much time, effort, and expense to the capital structure choice?

As Modigliani and Miller made clear in their original work, capital structure does not matter in *perfect* capital markets.[1] Recall from Chapter 14 that a perfect capital market exists under the following assumptions:

1. Investors and firms can trade the same set of securities at competitive market prices equal to the present value of their future cash flows.
2. There are no taxes, transaction costs, or issuance costs associated with security trading.
3. A firm's financing decisions do not change the cash flows generated by its investments, nor do they reveal new information about them.

Thus, if capital structure *does* matter, then it must stem from a market *imperfection*. In this chapter, we focus on one such imperfection—taxes. Corporations and investors must pay taxes on the income they earn from their investments. As we will see, a firm can enhance its value by using leverage to minimize the taxes it, and its investors, pay.

15.1   THE INTEREST TAX DEDUCTION

Corporations must pay taxes on the income that they earn. Because they pay taxes on their profits after interest payments are deducted, interest expenses reduce the amount of corporate tax firms must pay. This feature of tax law creates an incentive to use debt.

Let's consider the impact of interest expenses on the taxes paid by The Forzani Group Ltd., a sporting goods store chain. Forzani had earnings before interest and taxes of approximately $77.6 million in 2008, and interest expenses of about $5.8 million. Given Forzani's marginal corporate tax rate of about 34%,[2] the effect of leverage on Forzani's earnings is shown in Table 15.1.

As we can see from Table 15.1, Forzani's net income in 2008 was lower with leverage than it would have been without leverage. Thus Forzani's debt obligations reduced the

---

1. See F. Modigliani and M. H. Miller, "The Cost of Capital, Corporation Finance and the Theory of Investment," *American Economic Review* 48 (June 1958): 261–297. In their 1963 paper, "Corporate Income Taxes and the Cost of Capital: A Correction," *American Economic Review* 53 (June 1963): 433–443, Modigliani and Miller adjusted their analysis to incorporate taxes.

2. Forzani paid an average tax rate of approximately 38% in 2008, after accounting for other credits and deferrals and, in particular, future tax assets created by deferred lease inducements. Because we are interested in the impact of a change in leverage, Forzani's marginal tax rate—the tax rate that would apply to additional taxable income—is relevant to our discussion.

FORZANI'S INCOME WITH AND WITHOUT LEVERAGE, 2008 ($ THOUSANDS)

TABLE 15.1

	With Leverage	Without Leverage
Earnings Before Interest and Taxes (EBIT)	77,600	77,600
Interest Expense	−5,800	0
Earnings Before Taxes (EBT)	71,800	77,600
Taxes @ 34%	−24,412	−26,384
Net Income	47,388	51,216

Source: The Forzani Group Ltd. 2008 Annual Report.

value of its equity. But more importantly, the *total* amount available to *all* investors was higher with leverage:

	With Leverage	Without Leverage
Interest paid to debt holders	5800	0
Income available to equity holders	47,388	51,216
Total available to all investors	53,188	51,216

With leverage, Forzani was able to pay out $53.188 million in total to its investors, versus only $51.216 million without leverage, representing an increase of $1.972 million.

It might seem odd that a firm can be better off with leverage even though its earnings are lower. But recall from Chapter 14 that the value of a firm is the total amount it can raise from all investors, not just equity holders. So, if the firm can pay out more in total with leverage (including interest payments to debt holders), it will be able to raise more total capital initially.

Where does the additional $1.972 million come from? Looking at Table 15.1, we can see that this gain is equal to the reduction in taxes with leverage: $26.384 million − $24.412 million = $1.972 million. Because Forzani does not owe taxes on the $5.8 million of earnings it used to make interest payments, this $5.8 million is *shielded* from the corporate tax, providing the tax savings of 34% × $5.8 million = $1.972 million.

In general, the gain to investors from the tax deductibility of interest payments is referred to as the **interest tax shield**. The interest tax shield is the additional amount that a firm would have paid in taxes if it did not have leverage. We can calculate the amount of the interest tax shield each year as follows:

$$\text{Interest Tax Shield} = \text{Corporate Tax Rate} \times \text{Interest Payments} \tag{15.1}$$

EXAMPLE 15.1

COMPUTING THE INTEREST TAX SHIELD

Problem

Shown below is the income statement for D. S. Builders (DSB). Given its marginal corporate tax rate of 35%, what is the amount of the interest tax shield for DSB in years 2008 through 2011?

DSB Income Statement ($ million)	2008	2009	2010	2011
Total sales	$3369	$3706	$4077	$4432
Cost of sales	−2359	−2584	−2867	−3116
Selling, general, and administrative expense	−226	−248	−276	−299
Depreciation	−22	−25	−27	−29
Operating income	762	849	907	988
Other income	7	8	10	12
EBIT	769	857	917	1000
Interest expense	−50	−80	−100	−100
Income before tax	719	777	817	900
Taxes (35%)	−252	−272	−286	−315
Net income	$467	$505	$531	$585

Solution

From Eq. 15.1, the interest tax shield is the tax rate of 35% multiplied by the interest payments in each year:

($ million)	2008	2009	2010	2011
Interest payment	50	80	100	100
Interest tax shield (35% × interest expense)	17.5	28	35	35

CONCEPT CHECK

1. With corporate income taxes, explain why a firm's value can be higher with leverage even though its earnings are lower.

2. What is the interest tax shield?

15.2 VALUING THE INTEREST TAX SHIELD

When a firm uses debt, the interest tax shield provides a corporate tax benefit each year. To determine the benefit of leverage for the value of the firm, we must compute the present value of the stream of future interest tax shields the firm will receive.

THE INTEREST TAX SHIELD AND FIRM VALUE

Each year a firm makes interest payments, the cash flows it pays to investors will be higher than they would be without leverage by the amount of the interest tax shield:

$$\begin{pmatrix} \text{Cash Flows to Investors} \\ \text{with Leverage} \end{pmatrix} = \begin{pmatrix} \text{Cash Flows to Investors} \\ \text{without Leverage} \end{pmatrix} + (\text{Interest Tax Shield})$$

Figure 15.1 illustrates this relationship. Here you can see how each dollar of pretax cash flows is divided. The firm uses some fraction to pay taxes, and it pays the rest to investors. By increasing the amount paid to debt holders through interest payments, the amount of the pretax cash flows that must be paid as taxes decreases. The gain in total cash flows to investors is the interest tax shield.

The Cash Flows of the Unlevered and Levered Firm

By increasing the cash flows paid to debt holders through interest payments, a firm reduces the amount paid in taxes. The increase in total cash flows paid to investors is the interest tax shield. (The figure assumes a 40% marginal corporate tax rate.)

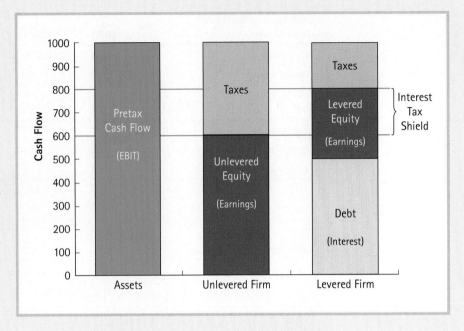

Because the cash flows of the levered firm are equal to the sum of the cash flows from the unlevered firm plus the interest tax shield, by the Law of One Price the same must be true for the present values of these cash flows. Thus, letting V^L and V^U represent the value of the firm with and without leverage, respectively, we have the following change to MM Proposition I in the presence of taxes:

The total value of the levered firm exceeds the value of the firm without leverage due to the present value of the tax savings from debt:

$$V^L = V^U + PV(\text{Interest Tax Shield}) \tag{15.2}$$

Clearly, there is an important tax advantage to the use of debt financing. But how large is this tax benefit? To compute the increase in the firm's total value associated with the interest tax shield, we need to forecast how a firm's debt—and therefore its interest payments—will vary over time. Given a forecast of future interest payments, we can determine the interest tax shield and compute its present value by discounting it at a rate that corresponds to its risk.

EXAMPLE 15.2   **VALUING THE INTEREST TAX SHIELD WITHOUT RISK**

Problem

Suppose DSB plans to pay $100 million in interest each year for the next 10 years, and then repay the principal of $2 billion in year 10. These payments are risk free, and DSB's marginal tax rate will remain 35% throughout this period. If the risk-free interest rate is 5%, by how much does the interest tax shield increase the value of DSB?

Solution

In this case, the interest tax shield is 35% $\times$ \$100 million = \$35 million each year for the next 10 years. Therefore, we can value it as a 10-year annuity. Because the tax savings are known and not risky, we can discount them at the 5% risk-free rate:

$$PV(\text{Interest Tax Shield}) = \$35 \text{ million} \times \frac{1}{0.05}\left(1 - \frac{1}{1.05^{10}}\right)$$

$$= \$270 \text{ million}$$

The final repayment of principal in year 10 is not deductible, so it does not contribute to the tax shield.

THE INTEREST TAX SHIELD WITH PERMANENT DEBT

In Example 15.2 we know with certainty the firm's future tax savings. In practice, this case is rare. Typically, the level of future interest payments varies due to changes the firm makes in the amount of debt outstanding, changes in the interest rate on that debt, and the risk that the firm may default and fail to make an interest payment. In addition, the firm's marginal tax rate may fluctuate due to changes in the tax law and changes in the firm's income bracket.

Rather than attempting to account for all possibilities here, we will consider the special case in which the firm issues debt and plans to keep the dollar amount of debt constant forever.[3] For example, the firm might issue a perpetual consol bond, making only interest payments but never repaying the principal. More realistically, suppose the firm issues short-term debt, such as a five-year coupon bond. When the principal is due, the firm raises the money needed to pay it by issuing new debt. In this way, the firm never pays off the principal but simply refinances it whenever it comes due. In this situation, the debt is effectively permanent.

Many large firms have a policy of maintaining a certain amount of debt on their balance sheets. As old bonds and loans mature, new borrowing takes place. What is special here is that we are considering the value of the interest tax shield with a *fixed* dollar amount of outstanding debt, rather than an amount that changes with the size of the firm.

PIZZA AND TAXES

In Chapter 14, we mentioned the pizza analogy that Merton Miller once used to describe the MM Propositions with perfect capital markets: No matter how you slice it, you still have the same amount of pizza.

We can extend this analogy to the setting with taxes, but the story is a bit different. In this case, every time the owner sells a slice of pizza to equity holders, he must give a slice to the Canada Revenue Agency (CRA) as a tax payment. But if the owner sells a slice to debt holders, there is no tax. Thus, by selling more slices to debt holders than to equity holders, the revenues from a single pizza are increased. While the total amount of pizza does not change, the owner will give less away in taxes, leaving more pizza to sell to customers.

---

3. We discuss how to value the interest tax shield with more complicated leverage policies, such as maintaining a constant debt-equity or interest coverage ratio, in Chapter 18.

Suppose a firm borrows debt D and keeps the debt permanently. If the firm's marginal tax rate is τ_c, and if the debt is riskless with a risk-free interest rate r_f, then the interest tax shield each year is $\tau_c \times r_f \times D$, and we can value the tax shield as a perpetuity:

$$PV(\text{Interest Tax Shield}) = \frac{\tau_c \times \text{Interest}}{r_f} = \frac{\tau_c \times (r_f \times D)}{r_f}$$
$$= \tau_c \times D$$

This calculation assumes the debt is risk free and the risk-free interest rate is constant. These assumptions are not necessary, however. If the debt is fairly priced, no arbitrage implies that its market value must equal the present value of the future interest payments:[4]

$$\text{Market Value of Debt} = D = PV(\text{Future Interest Payments}) \qquad (15.3)$$

If the firm's marginal tax rate is constant,[5] then we have the following general formula:

Value of the Interest Tax Shield of Permanent Debt

$$PV(\text{Interest Tax Shield}) = PV(\tau_c \times \text{Future Interest Payments})$$
$$= \tau_c \times PV(\text{Future Interest Payments})$$
$$= \tau_c \times D \qquad (15.4)$$

This formula shows the magnitude of the interest tax shield. Given a 35% corporate tax rate, it implies that for every \$1 in new permanent debt that the firm issues, the value of the firm increases by \$0.35.

THE WEIGHTED AVERAGE COST OF CAPITAL WITH TAXES

The tax benefit of leverage can also be expressed in terms of the weighted average cost of capital. When a firm uses debt financing, the cost of the interest it must pay is offset to some extent by the tax savings from the interest tax shield. For example, suppose a firm with a 35% tax rate borrows \$100,000 at 10% interest per year. Then its net cost at the end of the year is

		Year-End
Interest expense	$r \times \$100,000 =$	10,000
Tax savings	$-\tau_c \times r \times \$100,000 =$	−3,500
Effective after-tax cost of debt	$r \times (1 - \tau_c) \times \$100,000 =$	\$6,500

The effective cost of the debt is only \$6,500/\$100,000 = 6.50% of the loan amount, rather than the full 10% interest. Thus, the tax deductibility of interest lowers the effective cost of debt financing for the firm. More generally,[6]

With tax-deductible interest, the effective after-tax borrowing rate is $r(1 - \tau_c)$.

In Chapter 14, we showed that without taxes, the firm's WACC was equal to its unlevered cost of capital, which is the average return that the firm must pay to its investors

4. Equation 15.3 holds even if interest rates fluctuate and the debt is risky, as long as any new debt is also fairly priced. It requires only that the firm never repay the principal on the debt (it either refinances or defaults on the principal). The result follows by the same argument that we used in Chapter 9 to show that the price of equity should equal the present value of the future dividends.

5. The tax rate may not be constant if the firm's taxable income fluctuates sufficiently to change the firm's tax bracket (we discuss this possibility further in Section 15.5). If the firm's taxable income were to fall into a lower tax bracket for an extended period, the value of the tax shield would be reduced.

6. In Chapter 5, we derived this same result for the effective after-tax interest earned from non-tax-sheltered investments.

The WACC with and without Corporate Taxes

We compute the WACC as a function of the firm's target debt-to-value ratio using Eq. 15.5. As in Figure 14.1, the firm's unlevered cost of capital or pretax WACC is constant, reflecting the required return of the firm's investors based on the risk of the firm's assets. However, the (effective after-tax) WACC, which represents the after-tax cost to the firm, declines with leverage as the interest tax shield grows. The figure assumes a marginal corporate income tax rate of $\tau_c = 35\%$.

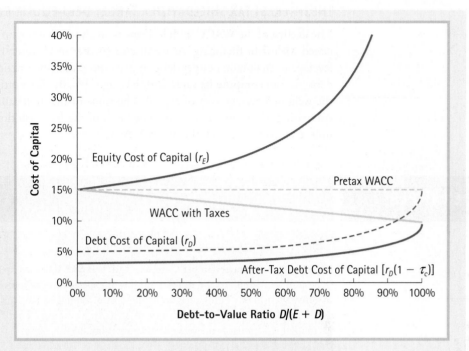

(equity holders and debt holders). The tax-deductibility of interest payments, however, lowers the effective after-tax cost of debt *to the firm*. We account for the benefit of the interest tax shield by calculating the WACC using the effective after-tax cost of debt:

Weighted Average Cost of Capital (After Tax)[7]

$$r_{wacc} = \frac{E}{E + D} r_E + \frac{D}{E + D} r_D (1 - \tau_c) \tag{15.5}$$

The WACC represents the effective cost of capital to the firm, after including the benefits of the interest tax shield. From Eq. 15.5, we have the following relationship between the WACC and the firm's pretax WACC:

$$r_{wacc} = \underbrace{\frac{E}{E + D} r_E + \frac{D}{E + D} r_D}_{\text{Pretax WACC}} - \underbrace{\frac{D}{E + D} r_D \tau_c}_{\substack{\text{Reduction Due} \\ \text{to Interest Tax Shield}}} \tag{15.6}$$

As we will show in Chapter 18, even in the presence of taxes, a firm's target leverage ratio does not affect the firm's pretax WACC, which equals its unlevered cost of capital and depends only on the risk of the firm's assets.[8] Thus, the higher the firm's leverage, the more the firm exploits the tax advantage of debt, and the lower its WACC. Figure 15.2 illustrates this decline in the WACC with the firm's leverage ratio.

---

7. Appendix 18A.1 of Chapter 18 contains a formal derivation of this formula. Equation 15.5 assumes the interest on debt and its expected return r_D are equal, which is a reasonable approximation if the debt has very low risk and is trading near par. If not, the more precise expression for the after-tax debt cost of capital is $(r_D - \tau_c \bar{r}_D)$, where $\bar{r}_D = $ (current interest expense)/(market value of debt).

8. Specifically, if the firm adjusts its leverage to maintain a target debt-equity ratio or interest coverage ratio, then its pretax WACC remains constant and equal to its unlevered cost of capital. See Chapter 18 for a full discussion of the relationship between the firm's levered and unlevered costs of capital.

THE INTEREST TAX SHIELD WITH A TARGET DEBT-EQUITY RATIO

The decline of the WACC with leverage is an alternative way to view the tax benefits associated with debt financing. As we discuss further in Chapter 18, when a firm adjusts its leverage to maintain a target debt-equity ratio rather than maintain a permanent level of debt, we can compute its value with leverage, V^L, by discounting its free cash flow using the weighted average cost of capital. The value of the interest tax shield can be found by comparing V^L to the unlevered value, V^U, of the free cash flow discounted at the firm's unlevered cost of capital, the pretax WACC.

EXAMPLE 15.3   **VALUING THE INTEREST TAX SHIELD WITH A TARGET DEBT-EQUITY RATIO**

Problem

Suppose West Fraser Timber Company Ltd. is expected to have free cash flow in the coming year of $4.25 million and its free cash flow is expected to grow at a rate of 4% per year thereafter. West Fraser Timber has an equity cost of capital of 10% and a debt cost of capital of 6%, and it pays a corporate tax rate of 35%. If West Fraser Timber maintains a debt-equity ratio of 0.50, what is the value of its interest tax shield?

Solution

We can estimate the value of West Fraser Timber's interest tax shield by comparing its value with and without leverage. We compute its unlevered value by discounting its free cash flow at its pretax WACC:

$$\text{Pretax WACC} = \frac{E}{E+D}r_E + \frac{D}{E+D}r_D = \frac{1}{1+0.5}10\% + \frac{0.5}{1+0.5}6\% = 8.67\%$$

Because West Fraser Timber's free cash flow is expected to grow at a constant rate, we can value it as a constant growth perpetuity:

$$V^U = \frac{4.25}{8.67\% - 4\%} = \$91 \text{ million}$$

To compute West Fraser Timber's levered value, we calculate its WACC:

$$\text{WACC} = \frac{E}{E+D}r_E + \frac{D}{E+D}r_D(1-\tau_c)$$

$$= \frac{1}{1+0.5}10\% + \frac{0.5}{1+0.5}6\%(1-0.35) = 7.97\%$$

Thus, West Fraser Timber's value including the interest tax shield is

$$V^L = \frac{4.25}{7.97\% - 4\%} = \$107 \text{ million}$$

The value of the interest tax shield is therefore

$$PV(\text{Interest Tax Shield}) = V^L - V^U = 107 - 91 = \$16 \text{ million}$$

CONCEPT CHECK
1. With corporate taxes as the only market imperfection, how does the value of the firm with leverage differ from its value without leverage?

2. How does leverage affect a firm's weighted average cost of capital?

15.3 RECAPITALIZING TO CAPTURE THE TAX SHIELD

When a firm makes a significant change to its capital structure, the transaction is called a recapitalization (or simply a "recap"). In Chapter 14, we introduced a leveraged recapitalization in which a firm issues a large amount of debt and uses the proceeds to pay a special dividend or to repurchase shares. Leveraged recaps were especially popular in the mid- to late-1980s, when many firms found that these transactions could reduce their tax payments.

Let's see how such a transaction might benefit current shareholders. Midco Industries has 20 million shares outstanding with a market price of $15 per share and no debt. Midco has had consistently stable earnings, and pays a 35% tax rate. Management plans to borrow $100 million on a permanent basis through a leveraged recap in which they would use the borrowed funds to repurchase outstanding shares. Their expectation is that the tax savings from this transaction will boost Midco's stock price and benefit shareholders. Let's see if this expectation is realistic.

THE TAX BENEFIT

First, we examine the tax consequences of Midco's leveraged recap. Without leverage, Midco's total market value is the value of its unlevered equity. Assuming the current stock price is the fair price for the shares without leverage:

$$V^U = (20 \text{ million shares}) \times (\$15/\text{share}) = \$300 \text{ million}$$

With leverage, Midco will reduce its annual tax payments. If Midco borrows $100 million using permanent debt, the present value of the firm's future tax savings is

$$PV(\text{interest tax shield}) = \tau_c D = 35\% \times \$100 \text{ million} = \$35 \text{ million}$$

Thus the total value of the levered firm will be

$$V^L = V^U + \tau_c D = \$300 \text{ million} + \$35 \text{ million} = \$335 \text{ million}$$

This total value represents the combined value of the debt and the equity after the recapitalization. Because the value of the debt is $100 million, the value of the equity is

$$E = V^L - D = \$335 \text{ million} - \$100 \text{ million} = \$235 \text{ million}$$

While total firm value has increased, the value of equity dropped after the recap. How do shareholders benefit from this transaction?

Even though the value of the shares outstanding drops to $235 million, don't forget that shareholders will also receive the $100 million that Midco will pay out through the share repurchase. In total, they will receive the full $335 million, a gain of $35 million over the value of their shares without leverage. Let's trace the details of the share repurchase and see how it leads to an increase in the stock price.

THE SHARE REPURCHASE

Suppose Midco repurchases its shares at their current price of $15 per share. The firm will repurchase $100 million ÷ $15 per share = 6.67 million shares, and it will then have 20 − 6.67 = 13.33 million shares outstanding. Because the total value of equity is $235 million, the new share price is

$$\frac{\$235 \text{ million}}{13.33 \text{ million shares}} = \$17.625$$

The shareholders who keep their shares earn a capital gain of $17.625 − $15 = $2.625 per share, for a total gain of

$$\$2.625/\text{share} \times 13.33 \text{ million shares} = \$35 \text{ million}$$

In this case, the shareholders who remain after the recap receive the benefit of the tax shield. However, you may have noticed something odd in the previous calculations. We assumed that Midco was able to repurchase the shares at the initial price of $15 per share, and then demonstrated that the shares would be worth $17.625 after the transaction. Why would a shareholder agree to sell the shares for $15 when they are worth $17.625?

NO ARBITRAGE PRICING

The previous scenario represents an arbitrage opportunity. Investors could *buy* shares for $15 immediately before the repurchase, and they could sell these shares immediately afterward at a higher price. But this activity would raise the share price above $15 even before the repurchase: Once investors know the recap will occur, the share price will rise immediately to a level that reflects the $35 million value of the interest tax shield that the firm will receive. That is, the value of the Midco's equity will rise *immediately* from $300 million to $335 million. With 20 million shares outstanding, the share price will rise to

$$\$335 \text{ million} \div 20 \text{ million shares} = \$16.75 \text{ per share}$$

Midco must offer at least this price to repurchase the shares.

With a repurchase price of $16.75, the shareholders who tender their shares and the shareholders who hold their shares both gain $16.75 − $15 = $1.75 per share as a result of the transaction. The benefit of the interest tax shield goes to all 20 million of the original shares outstanding for a total benefit of $1.75/share × 20 million shares = $35 million. In other words,

When securities are fairly priced, the original shareholders of a firm capture the full benefit of the interest tax shield from an increase in leverage.

ANALYZING THE RECAP: THE MARKET VALUE BALANCE SHEET

We can analyze the recapitalization using the market value balance sheet, a tool we developed in Chapter 14. It states that the total market value of a firm's securities must equal the total market value of the firm's assets. In the presence of corporate taxes, *we must include the interest tax shield as one of the firm's assets.*

| EXAMPLE 15.4 | ALTERNATIVE REPURCHASE PRICES |

Problem

Suppose Midco announces a price at which it will repurchase $100 million worth of its shares. Show that $16.75 is the lowest price it could offer and expect shareholders to tender their shares. How will the benefits be divided if Midco offers more than $16.75 per share?

Solution

For each repurchase price, we can compute the number of shares Midco will repurchase, as well as the number of shares that will remain after the share repurchase. Dividing the $235 million total value of equity by the number of remaining shares gives Midco's new share price after the transaction. No shareholders will be willing to sell their shares unless the repurchase price is at least as high as the share price after the transaction; otherwise, they would be better off waiting to sell their shares. As the table shows, the repurchase price must be at least $16.75 for shareholders to be willing to sell rather than waiting to receive a higher price.

Repurchase Price ($/share)	Shares Repurchased (million)	Shares Remaining (million)	New Share Price ($/share)
P_R	$R = 100/P_R$	$N = 20 - R$	$P_N = 235/N$
15.00	6.67	13.33	$17.63
16.25	6.15	13.85	16.97
16.75	5.97	14.03	16.75
17.25	5.80	14.20	16.55
17.50	5.71	14.29	16.45

If Midco offers a price above $16.75, then all existing shareholders will be eager to sell their shares, because the shares will have a lower value after the transaction is completed. In this case, Midco's offer to repurchase shares will be oversubscribed and Midco will need to use a lottery or some other rationing mechanism to choose from whom it will repurchase shares. In that case, more of the benefits of the recap will go to the shareholders who are lucky enough to be selected for the repurchase.

We analyze the leveraged recap by breaking this transaction into steps, as shown in Table 15.2. First, the recap is announced. At this point, investors anticipate the future interest tax shield, raising the value of Midco's assets by $35 million. Next, Midco issues $100 million in new debt, increasing both Midco's cash and liabilities by that amount. Finally, Midco uses the cash to repurchase shares at their market price of $16.75. In this step, Midco's cash declines, as does the number of shares outstanding.

Note that the share price rises at the announcement of the recap. This increase in the share price is due solely to the present value of the (anticipated) interest tax shield. Thus, even though leverage reduces the total value of equity, shareholders capture the benefits of the interest tax shield upfront.[9]

---

9. We are ignoring other potential side effects of leverage, such as costs of future financial distress. We discuss such costs in Chapter 16.

TABLE 15.2	MARKET VALUE BALANCE SHEET FOR THE STEPS IN MIDCO'S LEVERAGED RECAPITALIZATION

Market Value Balance Sheet ($ million)	Initial	Step 1: Recap Announced	Step 2: Debt Issuance	Step 3: Share Repurchase
Assets				
Cash	0	0	100	0
Original assets (V^U)	300	300	300	300
Interest tax shield	0	35	35	35
Total assets	300	335	435	335
Liabilities				
Debt	0	0	100	100
Equity = Assets − Liabilities	300	335	335	235
Shares outstanding (million)	20	20	20	14.03
Price per share	$15.00	$16.75	$16.75	$16.75

CONCEPT CHECK

1. How can shareholders benefit from a leveraged recap when it reduces the total value of equity?

2. How does the interest tax shield enter into the market value balance sheet?

15.4 PERSONAL TAXES

So far, we have looked at the benefits of leverage with regard to the taxes a corporation must pay. By reducing a firm's corporate tax liability, debt allows the firm to pay more of its cash flows to investors.

Unfortunately for investors, after they receive the cash flows, they are generally taxed again. For individuals, interest payments received from debt are taxed as regular income. Equity investors also must pay taxes on dividends and capital gains. What are the consequences to firm value of these additional taxes?

INCLUDING PERSONAL TAXES IN THE INTEREST TAX SHIELD

The value of a firm is equal to the amount of money the firm can raise by issuing securities. The amount of money an investor will pay for a security ultimately depends on the benefits the investor will receive—namely, the cash flows the investor will receive *after all taxes have been paid*. Thus, just like corporate taxes, personal taxes reduce the cash flows to investors and diminish firm value. As a result, the actual interest tax shield depends on the reduction in the total taxes (both corporate and personal) that are paid.[10]

---

10. This point was made most forcefully in yet another pathbreaking article by Merton Miller, "Debt and Taxes," *Journal of Finance* 32 (1977): 261–275. See also Merton H. Miller and Myron S. Scholes, "Dividends and Taxes," *Journal of Financial Economics* (December 1978): 333–364.

TABLE 15.3   2008 CANADIAN TAX RATES FOR THE TOP TAX BRACKET

| | Corporate Income Tax | | Personal Income Tax | | | |
| | Small Businesses | Other Businesses | Ordinary Income including Interest Income | Equity Income | | |
				Capital Gains	Eligible Dividends*	Average
Federal Tax Only	11.0%	19.5%	29.0%	14.5%	14.6%	14.5%
Combined Federal and Provincial Taxes:						
Alberta	14.0%	29.5%	39.0%	19.5%	16.0%	17.8%
British Columbia	14.5%	30.5%	43.7%	21.9%	18.5%	20.2%
Manitoba	13.0%	32.5%	46.4%	23.2%	23.8%	23.5%
New Brunswick	16.0%	32.5%	47.0%	23.5%	23.2%	23.3%
Newfoundland and Labrador	14.2%	35.5%	45.0%	22.5%	28.1%	25.3%
Northwest Territories	15.0%	31.0%	43.1%	21.5%	18.3%	19.9%
Nova Scotia	16.0%	35.5%	48.3%	24.1%	28.4%	26.2%
Nunavut	15.0%	31.5%	40.5%	20.3%	22.2%	21.2%
Ontario	16.5%	33.5%†	46.4%	23.2%	24.0%	23.6%
Prince Edward Island	14.2%	35.5%	47.4%	23.7%	24.4%	24.1%
Quebec	19.0%	30.9%	48.2%	24.1%	29.7%	26.9%
Saskatchewan	15.5%	31.5%†	44.0%	22.0%	20.4%	21.2%
Yukon	15.0%†	34.5%‡	42.4%	21.2%	17.2%	19.2%
Average	15.22%	32.6%	44.7%	22.4%	22.6%	22.5%

*Rates shown are for the actual dividend amount, not the grossed up amount.
†Deduct 2% for manufacturing and processing business income.
‡Deduct 12.5% for manufacturing and processing business income.
Sources: Canada Revenue Agency, www.taxtips.ca, Ernst & Young (various reports).

Personal taxes have the potential to offset some of the corporate tax benefits of leverage that we have described. In particular, in Canada and many other countries, interest income has historically been taxed more heavily than dividends or capital gains from equity. Table 15.3 shows the 2008 top federal tax rates in Canada.

To determine the true tax benefit of leverage, we need to evaluate the combined effect of both corporate and personal taxes. Consider a firm with $1 of earnings before interest and taxes. The firm can either pay this $1 to debt holders as interest, or it can pay the $1 to equity holders directly, as a dividend, or indirectly, by retaining it so that shareholders receive the $1 through a capital gain. Figure 15.3 shows the tax consequences of each option.

Using average 2008 tax rates across all provinces and territories (the last row of Table 15.3), debt offers a clear tax advantage. With respect to corporate taxes, for every $1 in pretax cash

FIGURE 15.3

After-Tax Investor Cash Flows Resulting from $1 in EBIT
Interest income is taxed at rate τ_i for the investor. Dividend or capital gain income is taxed at rate τ_c for the corporation, and again at rate τ_e for the investor.

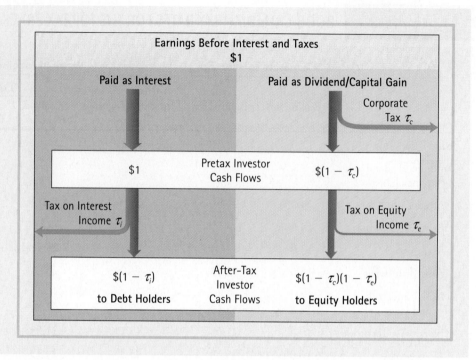

flows that debt holders receive, equity holders receive $\tau_c = 32.6\%$ less. But at the personal level, the income tax rate on interest income is $\tau_i = 44.7\%$, whereas the tax rate on equity income is only $\tau_e = 22.5\%$ (the average of the capital gains rate and dividend rate). Combining corporate and personal rates leads to the following comparison:

	After-Tax Cash Flows	**Using Average Federal/Provincial Combined Rates for 2008**
To debt holders	$(1 - \tau_i)$	$(1 - 0.447) = 0.553$
To equity holders	$(1 - \tau_c)(1 - \tau_e)$	$(1 - 0.326)(1 - 0.225) = 0.52235$

While a tax advantage to debt remains, it is not as large as we calculated based on corporate taxes alone. To express the comparison in relative terms, note that equity holders receive

$$\tau^* = \frac{0.553 - 0.55235}{0.553} = 5.54\%$$

less after taxes than debt holders. In this case, personal taxes reduce the tax advantage of debt from 32.6% to 5.54%.

In general, every $1 received after taxes by debt holders from interest payments costs equity holders $(1 - \tau^*)$ on an after-tax basis, where

Effective Tax Advantage of Debt

$$\tau^* = \frac{(1 - \tau_i) - (1 - \tau_c)(1 - \tau_e)}{(1 - \tau_i)} = 1 - \frac{(1 - \tau_c)(1 - \tau_e)}{(1 - \tau_i)} \quad (15.7)$$

When there are no personal taxes, or when the personal tax rates on debt and equity income are the same ($\tau_i = \tau_e$), this formula reduces to $\tau^* = \tau_c$. But when equity income is taxed less heavily ($\tau_i > \tau_e$), then τ^* is less than τ_c.

EXAMPLE 15.5	CALCULATING THE EFFECTIVE TAX ADVANTAGE OF DEBT

Problem

What is the effective tax advantage of debt in British Columbia? In Newfoundland and Labrador?

Solution

Using Eq. 15.7 and the tax rates in Table 15.3, we can calculate

$$\tau_{BC}^* = 1 - \frac{(1 - 0.305)(1 - 0.202)}{(1 - 0.437)} = 1.49\%$$

$$\tau_{NL}^* = 1 - \frac{(1 - 0.355)(1 - 0.253)}{(1 - 0.45)} = 12.4\%$$

Given the greater difference between personal tax rates on debt versus equity income in B.C., the effective tax advantage of debt is much lower than it is in Newfoundland and Labrador.

Figure 15.4 depicts the effective tax advantage of debt across each province and territory in Canada. Shown is the effective tax advantage of debt for investments held in tax-exempt accounts and investments held in taxable accounts. In tax-exempt accounts, such as RRSPs, RRIFs, and Tax-Free Savings Accounts (TFSAs), there is no personal tax and thus no personal tax disadvantage to earning debt income relative to equity income.

VALUING THE INTEREST TAX SHIELD WITH PERSONAL TAXES

How does the foregoing analysis of personal taxes affect our valuation of the debt tax shield? We postpone a detailed answer to this question until Chapter 18, and limit our discussion here to a few important observations. First, as long as $\tau^* > 0$, then despite any

FIGURE 15.4

The Effective Tax Advantage of Debt Across Provinces and Territories, 2008

After adjusting for personal taxes, the tax advantage of debt τ^* is relatively low when investments are held in taxable accounts. When investments are held in accounts exempt from personal taxes, $\tau^* = \tau_c$.

Sources: Canada Revenue Agency, www.taxtips.ca, and Ernst & Young (various reports).

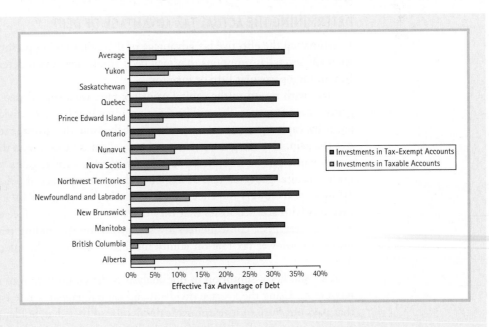

tax disadvantage of debt at the personal level, a net tax advantage for leverage remains. In the case of permanent debt, the value of the firm with leverage becomes

$$V^L = V^U + \tau^* D \tag{15.8}$$

Because the personal tax disadvantage of debt generally implies $\tau^* < \tau_c$, comparing Eq. 15.8 with Eq. 15.4 we see that the benefit of leverage is reduced.

Personal taxes have a similar, but indirect, effect on the firm's weighted average cost of capital. While we still compute the WACC using the corporate tax rate τ_c as in Eq. 15.5, with personal taxes the firm's equity and debt costs of capital will adjust to compensate investors for their respective tax burdens. The net result is that a personal tax disadvantage for debt causes the WACC to decline more slowly with leverage than it otherwise would.

EXAMPLE 15.6	ESTIMATING THE INTEREST TAX SHIELD WITH PERSONAL TAXES

Problem

Estimate the value of Midco after its $100 million leveraged recap, accounting for personal taxes in 2008.

Solution

Given $\tau^* = 5.54\%$ in 2008, and given Midco's current value $V^U = \$300$ million, we estimate $V^L = V^U + \tau^* D = \$300$ million $+ 5.54\%(\$100$ million$) = \$305.54$ million. With 20 million original shares outstanding, the stock price would increase by $5.54 million ÷ 20 million shares = $0.28 per share.

DETERMINING THE ACTUAL TAX ADVANTAGE OF DEBT

In estimating the effective tax advantage of debt after taking personal taxes into account, we made several assumptions that may need adjustment when determining the actual tax benefit for a particular firm or investor.

First, with regard to the capital gains tax rate, we assumed that investors paid capital gains taxes every year. But unlike taxes on interest income or dividends, which are paid annually, capital gains taxes are paid only at the time the investor sells the stock and realizes the gain. Deferring the payment of capital gains taxes lowers the present value of the taxes, which can be interpreted as a lower *effective* capital gains tax rate. For example, given a capital gains tax rate of 22.4% and an interest rate of 6%, holding the asset for 10 more years lowers the effective tax rate this year to $(22.4\%)/1.06^{10} = 12.5\%$. Also, investors with accrued losses that they can use to offset gains face a zero effective capital gains tax rate. As a consequence, investors with longer holding periods or with accrued losses face a lower tax rate on equity income, decreasing the effective tax advantage of debt.

A second key assumption in our analysis is the computation of the tax rate on equity income τ_e. Using the average dividend and capital gains tax rate is reasonable for a firm that pays out 50% of its earnings as dividends, so that shareholder gains from additional earnings were evenly split between dividends and capital gains. For firms with much

CUTTING PERSONAL TAXES ON INVESTMENT INCOME

On February 26, 2008, Finance Minister James Flaherty presented the 2008 budget for the Government of Canada. In that budget was the introduction of a new savings vehicle called the Tax-Free Savings Account (TFSA). The TFSA, subsequently introduced in 2009, allows investors to add $5000 per year into an account where investment income would not be taxed. For many investors, the TFSA and their RRSPs would shelter all of their investment income from taxes. The net effect of this is that the effective tax advantage of debt would be the full

corporate tax rate, $\tau^* = \tau_C$. Time will tell how this affects Canadian corporations' capital structure decisions. If Canadian debt and equity investments are revalued to reflect a move toward zero personal tax rates on investment income, what will happen? The personal tax disadvantage of debt income will be reduced. This should increase the value of debt securities and decrease corporations' cost of debt. Overall, we should expect to see a greater use of debt financing.

higher or much lower payout ratios, however, this average would not be accurate. For example, for firms that do not pay dividends, the capital gains tax rate should be used as the tax rate on equity income.

What is the bottom line? Calculating the effective tax advantage of debt accurately is extremely difficult, and this advantage will vary across firms (and from investor to investor). A firm must consider the tax bracket of its typical debt holders to estimate τ_i, and the tax bracket and holding period of its typical equity holders to determine τ_e.

If, for instance, a firm's investors hold shares primarily through their retirement accounts, or a new TFSA, $\tau^* < t_c$. While t* is likely to be somewhat below t_c for the typical firm, exactly how much lower is open to debate. Our calculation of τ^* in Figure 15.4 should be interpreted as a very rough guide at best.[11]

CONCEPT CHECK
1. Why is there a personal tax disadvantage of debt?
2. How does the personal tax disadvantage of debt change the value of leverage for the firm?

15.5 OPTIMAL CAPITAL STRUCTURE WITH TAXES

In Modigliani and Miller's setting of perfect capital markets, firms could use any combination of debt and equity to finance their investments without changing the value of the firm. In effect, any capital structure was optimal. In this chapter we have seen that taxes change that conclusion because interest payments create a valuable tax shield. Even after adjusting for personal taxes, the value of a firm with leverage exceeds the value of an unlevered firm, and there is a tax advantage to using debt financing.

DO FIRMS PREFER DEBT?

Do firms show a preference for debt in practice? Figure 15.5 illustrates the net new issues of equity and debt by corporations in Canada. For equity, the figure shows the total amount of new equity issued, less the amount retired through share repurchases

---

11. For a discussion of methods of estimating τ^* and the need to include personal taxes, see John R. Graham, "Do Personal Taxes Affect Corporate Financing Decisions?" *Journal of Public Economics* 73 (August 1999): 147–185.

FIGURE 15.5

Net External Financing of Corporations in Canada, 1977–2007

Sources: Bank of Canada (Net Issuances) and Statistic Canada (Capital Expenditures).

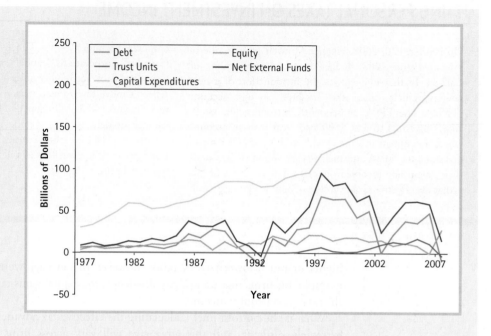

and acquisitions. For debt, it shows the total amount of new borrowing less the amount of loans repaid and includes bonds, commercial paper, and bankers' acceptances. The latter two debt securities are short-term instruments that are defined in Chapter 26. Net issuances of income trust units are also shown. Recall from Chapter 1 that income trusts essentially hold all the equity and debt of a corporation and allow the firm's income to flow through to investors without any tax at the business level (much like interest payments).

Over the 31-year period shown in Figure 15.5, Canadian corporations issued, on average, $21.1 billion of debt per year compared to $11.7 billion of equity per year. Over the past 20 years, the tendency to use debt instead of equity is more pronounced but there are some notable exceptions. During the recession of 1991–1992, more debt was redeemed than issued. In the early 2000s, the issuance of income trust units surpassed debt and equity issuances, but this ended in the last quarter of 2006 following the government's pronouncement that income trusts would lose their preferential tax treatment. In 2001–2003, there were net redemptions of short-term debt amid fears of a recession following the collapse of the market for high-tech stocks, several corporate accounting scandals (such as Enron), and the events of September 11, 2001. These redemptions pushed the overall debt issuance slightly negative in 2002. In the latter half of 2007, a crisis occurred in Canadian short-term debt markets related to asset-backed commercial paper. This crisis led to very few new issues of commercial paper and many redemptions, as rolling over the commercial paper was often not possible. Thus for 2007 we see an overall negative net issuance of debt. This pattern continued into 2008 as the financial crisis deepened but should reverse and see greater debt issuances as credit becomes less tight.

While firms seem to prefer debt when raising external funds, not all investment is externally funded. As Figure 15.5 also shows, capital expenditures greatly exceed firms' external financing, implying that most investment and growth is supported by internally generated

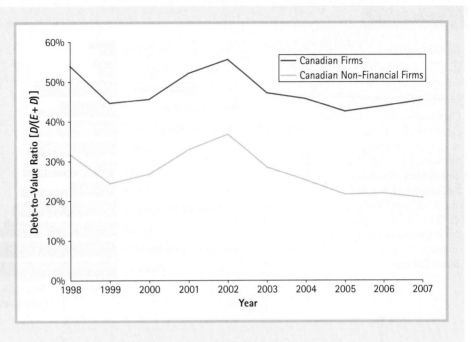

FIGURE 15.6

Debt-to-Value Ratio
[$D/(E + D)$] of
Canadian Firms,
1998–2007

Although firms have
primarily issued debt rather
than equity, the average
proportion of debt in their
capital structures has not
increased due to the overall
growth in the value of
existing equity.
Source: **Compustat.**

funds, such as retained earnings. Thus, even though firms have not issued as much new equity as new debt, the market value of equity has risen over time as firms have grown. In fact, as shown in Figure 15.6, debt as a fraction of firm value has varied in a range from 42% to 56% for the average firm. The average debt-to-value ratio is higher in times when the stock market is lower. This is evident in 1998 as the Canadian market was affected by financial crises in Asia and Russia, and in 2001–2002 as the TSX fell substantially with other world markets. A lower trend for the debt-to-value ratio is evident in the years following 2002 and is due to two factors: the rebound of the TSX and the increasing use of income trusts. The use of debt also varies greatly by industry. Figure 15.7 shows debt as a fraction of firm value for a number of industry sectors and the overall market.

Clearly, there are large differences across industries. Firms in growth industries like health care and information technology carry very little debt, whereas utilities and financial firms have high leverage ratios. Thus the differences in the leverage ratios of Microsoft and Canadian Pacific Railway noted in the introduction to this chapter are not unique to these firms, but rather are typical of their respective industries. You may notice in Figure 15.7 that some industries appear to have a dramatic drop in their leverage ratios between 1998 and 2007. The materials and energy sectors are two that stand out. The materials sector primarily includes mining companies that produce commodities such as gold, platinum, other metals, coal, diamonds, and other minerals. The energy sector is primarily related to oil and natural gas. For both of these sectors, the dramatic increases in the prices of their commodities have resulted in rapidly rising equity prices and thus lower debt-to-value [$D/(E + D)$] ratios. In addition, the conversion to income trusts had been extensive in the energy sector.

These data raise important questions. If debt provides a tax advantage that lowers a firm's weighted average cost of capital and increases firm value, why does debt make up less than half of the capital structure of most firms? And why does the leverage choice vary

Debt-to-Value Ratio [$D/(E + D)$] for Select Industry Sectors in Canada, 1998 and 2007 Debt levels are determined by book values, and equity by market values. The average debt financing for Canadian firms was about 54% in 1998 and 45% in 2007, but note the large differences by industry.
Source: Compustat.

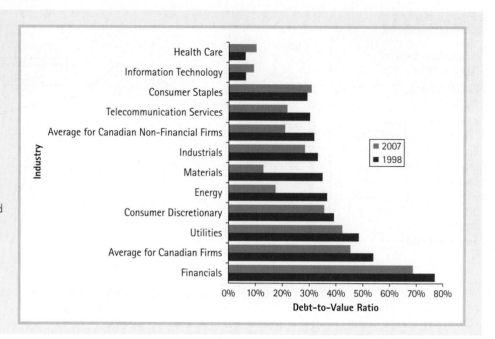

so much across industries? To begin to answer these questions, let's consider a bit more carefully what the optimal capital structure is from a tax perspective.

LIMITS TO THE TAX BENEFIT OF DEBT

To receive the full tax benefits of leverage, a firm need not use 100% debt financing. A firm receives a tax benefit only if it is paying taxes in the first place. That is, the firm must have taxable earnings. This constraint may limit the amount of debt needed as a tax shield.

To determine the optimal level of leverage, compare the three leverage choices shown in Table 15.4 for a firm with earnings before interest and taxes (EBIT) equal to $1000 and a corporate tax rate of $\tau_c = 35\%$. With no leverage, the firm owes tax of $350 on the full $1000 of EBIT. If the firm has high leverage with interest payments equal to $1000, then it can shield its earnings from taxes, thereby saving the $350 in taxes. Now consider a third case, in which the firm has excess leverage so that interest payments exceed EBIT. In this case, the firm has a net operating loss, but there is no increase in the tax savings. Because the firm is paying no taxes already, there is no immediate tax shield from the excess leverage.[12]

Thus no corporate tax benefit arises from incurring interest payments that regularly exceed EBIT. And, because interest payments constitute a tax disadvantage at the investor

---

12. Recall from Chapter 7 that if the firm paid taxes during the prior three years, it could "carry back" the current year's net operating loss to apply for a refund of some of those taxes. Alternatively, the firm could "carry forward" the net operating loss up to 20 years to shield future income from taxes (although waiting to receive the credit reduces its present value). Thus there can be a tax benefit from interest in excess of EBIT if it does not occur on a regular basis. For simplicity, we ignore tax-loss carrybacks and carryforwards in this discussion.

TAX SAVINGS WITH DIFFERENT AMOUNTS OF LEVERAGE

TABLE 15.4

	No Leverage	High Leverage	Excess Leverage
EBIT	$1,000	$1,000	$1,000
Interest expense	0	−1,000	−1,100
Income before tax	1,000	0	0
Taxes (35%)	−350	0	0
Net income	650	0	−100
Tax savings from leverage	$0	$350	$350

level as discussed in Section 15.4, investors will pay higher personal taxes with excess leverage, making them worse off.[13] We can quantify the tax disadvantage for excess interest payments by setting $\tau_c = 0$ (assuming there is no reduction in the corporate tax for excess interest payments) in Eq. 15.7 for τ^*:

$$\tau^*_{ex} = 1 - \frac{(1 - \tau_e)}{(1 - \tau_i)} = \frac{\tau_e - \tau_i}{(1 - \tau_i)} < 0 \qquad (15.9)$$

Note that τ^*_{ex} is negative because equity is taxed less heavily than interest for investors ($\tau_e < \tau_i$). From Table 15.3, using average 2008 tax rates, this disadvantage is

$$\tau^*_{ex} = \frac{22.5\% - 44.7\%}{(1 - 44.7\%)} = -40.1\%$$

Therefore, the optimal level of leverage from a tax saving perspective is the level such that interest equals EBIT. The firm shields all of its taxable income, and it does not have any tax-disadvantaged excess interest. Figure 15.8 shows the tax savings at different levels of interest payments when EBIT equals $1000 with certainty. In this case, an interest payment of $1000 maximizes the tax savings.

Of course, it is unlikely that a firm can predict its future EBIT precisely. If there is uncertainty regarding EBIT, then with a higher interest expense there is a greater risk that interest will exceed EBIT. As a result, the tax savings for high levels of interest fall, possibly reducing the optimal level of the interest payment, as shown in Figure 15.8.[14] In general, as a firm's interest expense approaches its expected taxable earnings, the marginal tax advantage of debt declines, limiting the amount of debt the firm should use.

---

13. Of course, another problem can arise from having excess leverage: The firm may not be able to afford the excess interest and could be forced to default on the loan. We discuss financial distress (and its potential costs) in Chapter 16.

14. Details of how to compute the optimal level of debt when earnings are risky can be found in a paper by John Graham, "How Big Are the Tax Benefits of Debt?" *Journal of Finance* 55:5 (October 2000): 1901–1941.

FIGURE 15.8

Tax Savings for Different Levels of Interest

When EBIT is known with certainty, the tax savings is maximized if the interest expense is equal to EBIT. When EBIT is uncertain, the tax savings decline for high levels of interest because of the risk that the interest payment will be in excess of EBIT.

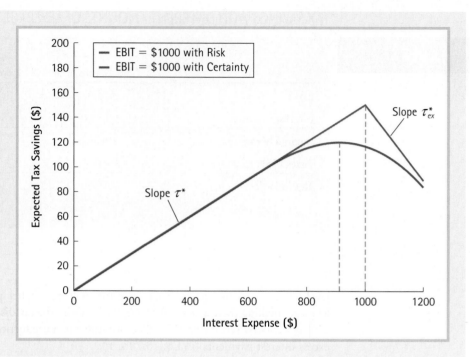

GROWTH AND DEBT

In a tax-optimal capital structure, the level of interest payments depends on the level of EBIT. What does this conclusion tell us about the optimal fraction of debt in a firm's capital structure?

If we examine young technology or biotechnology firms, we often find that these firms do not have any taxable income. Their value comes mainly from the prospect that they will produce high future profits. A biotech firm might be developing drugs with tremendous potential, but it has yet to receive any revenue from these drugs. Such a firm will not have taxable earnings. In that case, a tax-optimal capital structure does not include debt. We would expect such a firm to finance its investments with equity alone. Only later, when the firm matures and becomes profitable, will it have taxable cash flows. At that time it should add debt to its capital structure.

Even for a firm with positive earnings, growth will affect the optimal leverage ratio. To avoid excess interest, this type of firm should have debt with interest payments that are below its expected taxable earnings:

$$\text{Interest} = r_D \times \text{Debt} \leq \text{EBIT} \quad \text{or} \quad \text{Debt} \leq \frac{\text{EBIT}}{r_D}$$

That is, from a tax perspective, the firm's optimal level of debt is proportional to its current earnings. However, the value of the firm's equity will depend on the growth rate of earnings: The higher the growth rate, the higher the value of equity (and equivalently, the higher the firm's price-earnings multiple). As a result, *the optimal proportion of debt in the firm's capital structure* $[D/(E + D)]$ *will be lower, the higher the firm's growth rate.*[15]

---

15. This explanation for the low leverage of high growth firms is developed in a paper by J. L. Berens and C. J. Cuny, "The Capital Structure Puzzle Revisited," *Review of Financial Studies* 8:4 (Winter 1995): 1185–1208.

FIGURE 15.9

Interest Payments as a Percentage of EBIT for Canadian Firms, 1988–2007
Source: Compustat.

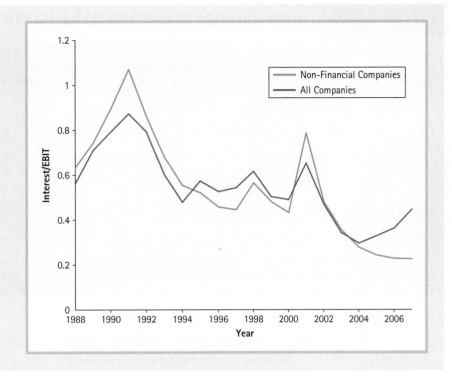

OTHER TAX SHIELDS

Up to this point, we have assumed that interest is the only means by which firms can shield earnings from corporate taxes. But there are numerous other provisions in the tax laws for deductions and tax credits, such as Capital Cost Allowance (CCA), investment tax credits, carryforwards of past operating losses, and the like. To the extent that a firm has other tax shields, its taxable earnings will be reduced and it will rely less heavily on the interest tax shield.[16]

THE LOW LEVERAGE PUZZLE

Do firms choose capital structures that fully exploit the tax advantages of debt? The results of this section imply that to evaluate this question, we should compare the level of firms' interest payments to their taxable income, rather than simply consider the fraction of debt in their capital structures. Figure 15.9 compares interest expenses and EBIT for Canadian firms. It reveals two important patterns. First, firms appear to shield a greater percentage of their earnings from taxes in recessions (the early 1990s) and economic slowdowns (the early 2000s) than in other years. The reason for this is that during tough economic times, EBIT drops, but firms must still make their debt payments. Second, as the use of income trusts grew in the 2000s, firms relied on less debt as the income trust structure fully shielded them

---

16. See H. DeAngelo and R. Masulis, "Optimal Capital Structure Under Corporate and Personal Taxation," *Journal of Financial Economics* 8 (March 1980): 3–27. For a discussion of methods to estimate a firm's marginal tax rate to account for these effects, see John R. Graham, "Proxies for the Corporate Marginal Tax Rate," *Journal of Financial Economics* 42 (April 1996): 187–221.

TABLE 15.5	INTERNATIONAL LEVERAGE AND TAX RATES (1990)

Country	$D/(E + D)$	Net of Cash $D/(E + D)$	Interest/EBIT	τ_c	τ^*
United States	28%	23%	41%	34.0%	34.0%
Japan	29%	17%	41%	37.5%	31.5%
Germany	23%	15%	31%	50.0%	3.3%
France	41%	28%	38%	37.0%	7.8%
Italy	46%	36%	55%	36.0%	18.6%
United Kingdom	19%	11%	21%	35.0%	24.2%
Canada	35%	32%	65%	38.0%	28.9%

Source: R. Rajan and L. Zingales, "What Do We Know About Capital Structure? Some Evidence from International Data," *Journal of Finance* 50:5 (December 1995): 1421–1460. Data are for median firms and top marginal tax rates.

from corporate tax. The drop in the use of debt seems to have levelled off by 2007 and we should expect it to reverse given the government's announced cancellation of income trusts' preferential tax treatment. In addition, with greater opportunities for individuals to hold investments in tax-free accounts, the effective tax advantage of debt, τ^*, should be higher and we should expect to see firms move toward a greater reliance on debt.

Table 15.5 shows international leverage levels from a 1995 study by Raghuram Rajan and Luigi Zingales using 1990 data. Note that firms in many countries have similar low proportions of debt financing, with firms in the United Kingdom exhibiting especially low leverage. Also, with the exception of Canada and Italy, firms shield less than half of their taxable income using interest payments. The corporate tax laws are similar across all countries in terms of the tax advantage of debt. Personal tax rates vary more significantly, however, leading to greater variation in τ^*.[17] In addition, the industrial makeup of corporations across countries varies significantly. In Canada, for instance, the corporate sector is more highly weighted by financial, energy, and mining companies than in the other countries shown in Table 15.5.

Are firms under-leveraged? They seem to have excess EBIT to cover additional interest payments and their leverage ratios do not look excessive.[18] Either firms are content to pay more taxes than necessary rather than maximize shareholder value, or there is more to the capital structure story than we have uncovered so far. While some firms may deliberately choose a suboptimal capital structure, it is hard to accept that most firms are acting suboptimally. The consensus of so many managers in choosing low levels of leverage suggests that debt financing has other costs that prevent firms from using the interest tax shield fully.

---

17. Similar low leverage results continue to hold using more recent data from 2006; see J. Fan, S. Titman, and G. Twite, "An International Comparison of Capital Structure and Debt Maturity Choices," SSRN working paper, 2008.

18. Additional evidence is provided by John Graham in "How Big Are the Tax Benefits of Debt?" *Journal of Finance* 55:5 (October 2000): 1901–1941, where he estimates that the typical firm exploits less than half of the potential tax benefits of debt.

INTERVIEW WITH GERRY SCHWARTZ

Gerry Schwartz, MBA, LLB, BComm, is the founder, chairman, and CEO of Onex Corporation. Prior to founding Onex, Mr. Schwartz was also co-founder and president of what is now CanWest Global Communications.

QUESTION: How do you classify Onex Corporation?

ANSWER: Onex is a private equity firm with a substantial difference, in that the majority of the money we invest is ours rather than third-party capital. We invest in the equity of companies and supplement our investment with leverage. We only buy controlling positions in the companies in which we invest.

QUESTION: What sort of companies do you look for?

ANSWER: We look for a business in which we can change something to create value. This usually means changing the cost structure (an efficiency gain) or changing the customer base (expanding the market). Once we determine what we think should be changed, we manage that change after we are involved with the company.

QUESTION: Some of the companies that you're involved with right now are in the areas of health care and aircraft. How do you pick your acquisitions? Do you look at specific industries?

ANSWER: No, we don't restrict ourselves to specific industries. We just look for companies where we think we can grow the business or make a significant value-increasing difference in the way it's operated.

QUESTION: What are some of the factors to consider when deciding how much leverage to use for a company?

ANSWER: Leverage is an effective tax shield. It is quite common that some companies are under leveraged, so you might want to increase the amount of leverage. But you need to be careful. Leverage is a double-edged sword. If you have any difficulty down the road with the company, high leverage can make things really oppressive.

QUESTION: What do you mean?

ANSWER: Leverage magnifies the outcomes that equity holders see. That means it magnifies both good times and bad times. In the bad times you might want to have more flexibility than a highly leveraged structure will allow.

QUESTION: So you need to balance tax shields with other effects of leverage like flexibility and growth?

ANSWER: Exactly. The leverage that we typically employ is about half of what is typical in the private equity industry. It's hard to grow a business when it's over-leveraged, so we try to leverage prudently.

QUESTION: Are there other aspects of leverage that are important?

ANSWER: Using leverage can help to create a more efficient environment. When you're highly leveraged you've got to look at ways to reduce it quickly, so private equity owners will often be more efficient in the use of working capital. But Onex does not try to maximize leverage for its risk-reward aspects. We need to build the business and grow it.

QUESTION: Can you share any other insights about your strategy at Onex?

ANSWER: We own a number of different businesses, often in different fields. But sometimes we'll own more than one company in the same field. Take our health care companies as an example. We keep each one separate. We have management as partial owners in the particular business with us, and we don't act as a conglomerate. We don't move capital from one to another. We don't move management teams from one to another. And that's been a pretty effective way for us to do business.

When we get involved with a new company, we hope to keep the senior management team. Some are receptive; some aren't. We are really making a sort of partnership with the pre-Onex senior management.

We have been able to grow at least half a dozen businesses from the relatively modest beginnings of a couple hundred million in revenues to between three and eight billion in revenues.

Our biggest failures have been from over-leveraging and trying to grow the business at the same time. And our biggest successes have been when we could change the customer base of the business. Overall, it's about identifying some way that we can increase value through our involvement in another company, and we've had some nice successes.

Talk to financial managers and they will quickly point out a key cost of debt missing from our analysis: Increasing the level of debt increases the probability of bankruptcy. Aside from taxes, another important difference between debt and equity financing is that debt payments *must* be made to avoid bankruptcy, whereas firms have no similar obligation to pay dividends or realize capital gains. If bankruptcy is costly, these costs might offset the tax advantages of debt financing. Bankruptcy costs might also vary across industries and thus help to explain the different usage of debt across industries and countries. We explore the role of financial bankruptcy costs and other market imperfections in Chapter 16.

CONCEPT CHECK

1. How does the growth rate of a firm affect the optimal fraction of debt in the capital structure?

2. Do firms choose capital structures that fully exploit the tax advantages of debt?

SUMMARY

1. Because interest expense is tax deductible, leverage increases the total amount of income available to all investors.

2. The gain to investors from the tax deductibility of interest payments is called the interest tax shield.

$$\text{Interest Tax Shield} = \text{Corporate Tax Rate} \times \text{Interest Payments} \quad (15.1)$$

3. When we consider corporate taxes, the total value of a levered firm equals the value of an unlevered firm plus the present value of the interest tax shield.

$$V^L = V^U + PV(\text{Interest Tax Shield}) \quad (15.2)$$

4. When a firm's marginal tax rate is constant and there are no personal taxes, the present value of the interest tax shield from permanent debt equals the tax rate times the value of the debt, $\tau_c D$.

5. The firm's pretax WACC measures the required return to the firm's investors. Its effective after-tax WACC, or simply the WACC, measures the cost to the firm after including the benefit of the interest tax shield. The two notions are related as follows:

$$r_{wacc} = \frac{E}{E + D} r_E + \frac{D}{E + D} r_D (1 - \tau_c) \quad (15.5)$$

$$r_{wacc} = \underbrace{\frac{E}{E + D} r_E + \frac{D}{E + D} r_D}_{\text{Pretax WACC}} - \underbrace{\frac{D}{E + D} r_D \tau_c}_{\substack{\text{Reduction Due} \\ \text{to Interest Tax Shield}}} \quad (15.6)$$

Absent other market imperfections, the WACC declines with a firm's leverage.

6. When the firm maintains a target leverage ratio, we compute its levered value V^L as the present value of its free cash flows using the WACC, whereas its unlevered value V^U is the present value of its free cash flows using its unlevered cost of capital or pretax WACC.

7. When securities are fairly priced, the original shareholders of a firm capture the full benefit of the interest tax shield from an increase in leverage.

8. Personal taxes offset some of the corporate tax benefits of leverage. Every $1 received after taxes by debt holders from interest payments costs equity holders $(1 − τ^*)$ on an after-tax basis, where

$$\tau^* = \frac{(1 - \tau_i) - (1 - \tau_c)(1 - \tau_e)}{(1 - \tau_i)} = 1 - \frac{(1 - \tau_c)(1 - \tau_e)}{(1 - \tau_i)} \qquad (15.7)$$

9. The optimal level of leverage from a tax saving perspective is the level such that interest equals EBIT. In this case, the firm takes full advantage of the corporate tax deduction of interest, but avoids the tax disadvantage of excess leverage at the personal level.

10. The optimal fraction of debt, as a proportion of a firm's capital structure, declines with the growth rate of the firm.

11. The interest expense of the average firm is well below its taxable income, implying that firms do not fully exploit the tax advantages of debt.

KEY TERM

interest tax shield *p. 514*

PROBLEMS

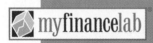

The Interest Tax Deduction

1. Pelamed Pharmaceuticals has EBIT of $325 million in 2011. In addition, Pelamed has interest expenses of $125 million and a corporate tax rate of 40%.
   a. What is Pelamed's 2011 net income?
   b. What is the total of Pelamed's 2011 net income and interest payments?
   c. If Pelamed had no interest expenses, what would its 2011 net income be? How does it compare to your answer in part b?
   d. What is the amount of Pelamed's interest tax shield in 2011?

2. Grommit Engineering expects to have net income next year of $20.75 million and free cash flow of $22.15 million. Grommit's marginal corporate tax rate is 35%.
   a. If Grommit increases leverage so that its interest expense rises by $1 million, how will its net income change?
   b. For the same increase in interest expense, how will free cash flow change?

3. Suppose the corporate tax rate is 40%. Consider a firm that earns $1000 before interest and taxes each year with no risk. The firm's capital expenditures equal its depreciation expenses (assumed to equal CCA) each year, and it will have no changes to its net working capital. The risk-free interest rate is 5%.
   a. Suppose the firm has no debt and pays out its net income as a dividend each year. What is the value of the firm's equity?
   b. Suppose instead the firm makes interest payments of $500 per year. What is the value of equity? What is the value of debt?

c. What is the difference between the total value of the firm with leverage and without leverage?

d. The difference in part c is equal to what percentage of the value of the debt?

EXCEL   4. Braxton Enterprises currently has debt outstanding of $35 million and an interest rate of 8%. Braxton plans to reduce its debt by repaying $7 million in principal at the end of each year for the next five years. If Braxton's marginal corporate tax rate is 40%, what is the interest tax shield from Braxton's debt in each of the next five years?

Valuing the Interest Tax Shield

EXCEL   5. Your firm currently has $100 million in debt outstanding with a 10% interest rate. The terms of the loan require the firm to repay $25 million of the balance each year. Suppose that the marginal corporate tax rate is 40%, and that the interest tax shields have the same risk as the loan. What is the present value of the interest tax shields from this debt?

6. Arnell Industries has just issued $10 million in debt (at par). The firm will pay interest only on this debt. Arnell's marginal tax rate is expected to be 35% for the foreseeable future.

   a. Suppose Arnell pays interest of 6% per year on its debt. What is its annual interest tax shield?

   b. What is the present value of the interest tax shield, assuming its risk is the same as the loan?

   c. Suppose instead that the interest rate on the debt is 5%. What is the present value of the interest tax shield in this case?

EXCEL   7. Ten years have passed since Arnell issued $10 million in debt that pays perpetual interest with a 6% annual coupon, as in Problem 6. Tax rates have remained the same at 35% but interest rates have dropped so Arnell's current cost of debt capital is 4%.

   a. What is Arnell's annual interest tax shield?

   b. What is the present value of the interest tax shield today?

8. Bay Transport Systems (BTS) currently has $30 million in debt outstanding. In addition to 6.5% interest, it plans to repay 5% of the remaining balance each year. If BTS has a marginal corporate tax rate of 40%, and if the interest tax shields have the same risk as the loan, what is the present value of the interest tax shield from the debt?

9. Safeco Inc. has no debt, and maintains a policy of holding $10 million in excess cash reserves, invested in risk-free government securities. If Safeco pays a corporate tax rate of 35%, what is the cost of permanently maintaining this $10 million reserve? (*Hint:* What is the present value of the additional taxes that Safeco will pay?)

10. Rogot Instruments makes fine violins and cellos. It has $1 million in debt outstanding, equity valued at $2 million and pays corporate income tax at a rate of 35%. Its cost of equity is 12% and its cost of debt is 7%.

    a. What is Rogot's pretax WACC?

    b. What is Rogot's (effective after-tax) WACC?

11. Rumolt Motors has 30 million shares outstanding with a price of $15 per share. In addition, Rumolt has issued bonds with a total current market value of $150 million. Suppose Rumolt's equity cost of capital is 10% and its debt cost of capital is 5%.

    a. What is Rumolt's pretax weighted average cost of capital?

    b. If Rumolt's corporate tax rate is 35%, what is its after-tax weighted average cost of capital?

12. Summit Builders has a market debt-equity ratio of 0.65, a corporate tax rate of 40%, and it pays 7% interest on its debt. The interest tax shield from its debt lowers Summit's WACC by what amount?

13. NatNah, a builder of acoustic accessories, has no debt and an equity cost of capital of 15%. Suppose NatNah decides to increase its leverage and maintain a market debt-to-value ratio of 0.5. Suppose its debt cost of capital is 9% and its corporate tax rate is 35%. If NatNah's pretax

WACC remains constant, what will its (effective after-tax) WACC be with the increase in leverage?

14. Restex maintains a debt-equity ratio of 0.85, and has an equity cost of capital of 12% and a debt cost of capital of 7%. Restex's corporate tax rate is 40%, and its market capitalization is $220 million.

    a. If Restex's free cash flow is expected to be $10 million in one year, what constant expected future growth rate is consistent with the firm's current market value?

    b. Estimate the value of Restex's interest tax shield.

15. Acme Storage has a market capitalization of $100 million and debt outstanding of $40 million. Acme plans to maintain this same debt-equity ratio in the future. The firm pays an interest rate of 7.5% on its debt and has a corporate tax rate of 35%.

    a. If Acme's free cash flow is expected to be $7 million next year and is expected to grow at a rate of 3% per year, what is Acme's WACC?

    b. What is the value of Acme's interest tax shield?

Recapitalizing to Capture the Tax Shield

16. Milton Industries expects free cash flow of $5 million each year. Milton's corporate tax rate is 35%, and its unlevered cost of capital is 15%. The firm also has outstanding debt of $19.05 million, and it expects to maintain this level of debt permanently.

    a. What is the value of Milton Industries without leverage?

    b. What is the value of Milton Industries with leverage?

17. Suppose Microsoft has 8.75 billion shares outstanding and pays a marginal corporate tax rate of 35%. If Microsoft announces that it will pay out $50 billion in cash to investors through a combination of a special dividend and a share repurchase, and if investors had previously assumed Microsoft would retain this excess cash permanently, by how much will Microsoft's share price change upon the announcement?

18. Kurz Manufacturing is currently an all-equity firm with 20 million shares outstanding and a stock price of $7.50 per share. Although investors currently expect Kurz to remain an all-equity firm, Kurz plans to announce that it will borrow $50 million and use the funds to repurchase shares. Kurz will pay interest only on this debt, and it has no further plans to increase or decrease the amount of debt. Kurz is subject to a 40% corporate tax rate.

    a. What is the market value of Kurz's existing assets before the announcement?

    b. What is the market value of Kurz's assets (including any tax shields) just after the debt is issued, but before the shares are repurchased?

    c. What is Kurz's share price just before the share repurchase? How many shares will Kurz repurchase?

    d. What are Kurz's market value balance sheet and share price after the share repurchase?

19. Rally Inc. is an all-equity firm with assets worth $25 billion and 10 billion shares outstanding. Rally plans to borrow $10 billion and use these funds to repurchase shares. The firm's corporate tax rate is 35%, and Rally plans to keep its outstanding debt equal to $10 billion permanently.

    a. Without the increase in leverage, what would Rally's share price be?

    b. Suppose Rally offers $2.75 per share to repurchase its shares. Would shareholders sell for this price?

    c. Suppose Rally offers $3.00 per share, and shareholders tender their shares at this price. What will Rally's share price be after the repurchase?

d. What is the lowest price Rally can offer and have shareholders tender their shares? What will its stock price be after the share repurchase in that case?

Personal Taxes

20. Suppose the corporate tax rate is 40% and investors pay a tax rate of 15% on income from dividends or capital gains and a tax rate of 33.3% on interest income. Your firm decides to add debt so it will pay an additional $15 million in interest each year. It will pay this interest expense by cutting its dividend.

    a. How much will debt holders receive after paying taxes on the interest they earn?

    b. By how much will the firm need to cut its dividend each year to pay this interest expense?

    c. By how much will this cut in the dividend reduce equity holders' annual after-tax income?

    d. How much less will the government receive in total tax revenues each year?

    e. What is the effective tax advantage of debt τ^*?

21. Apple Corporation had no debt on its balance sheet in 2008 but paid $2 billion in taxes. Suppose Apple were to issue sufficient debt to reduce its taxes by $1 billion per year permanently. Assume Apple's marginal corporate tax rate is 35% and its borrowing cost is 7.5%.

    a. If Apple's investors do not pay personal taxes (because they hold their Apple stock in tax-free retirement accounts), how much value would be created (what is the value of the tax shield)?

    b. How does your answer change if instead you assume that Apple's investors pay a 15% tax rate on income from equity and a 35% tax rate on interest income?

22. Markum Enterprises is considering permanently adding $100 million of debt to its capital structure. Markum's corporate tax rate is 35%.

    a. Absent personal taxes, what is the value of the interest tax shield from the new debt?

    b. If investors pay a tax rate of 40% on interest income and a tax rate of 20% on income from dividends and capital gains, what is the value of the interest tax shield from the new debt?

*23. Garnet Corporation is considering issuing risk-free debt or risk-free preferred stock. The tax rate on interest income is 35%, and the tax rate on dividends or capital gains from preferred stock is 15%. However, the dividends on preferred stock are not deductible for corporate tax purposes, and the corporate tax rate is 40%.

    a. If the risk-free interest rate for debt is 6%, what is cost of capital for risk-free preferred stock?

    b. What is the after-tax debt cost of capital for the firm? Which security is cheaper for the firm?

    c. Show that the after-tax debt cost of capital is equal to the preferred stock cost of capital multiplied by $(1 - \tau^*)$.

*24. Suppose the tax rate on interest income is 35% and the average tax rate on capital gains and dividend income is 10%. How high must the marginal corporate tax rate be for debt to offer a tax advantage?

Optimal Capital Structure with Taxes

25. With its current leverage, Impi Corporation will have net income next year of $4.5 million. If Impi's corporate tax rate is 35% and it pays 8% interest on its debt, how much additional debt can Impi issue this year and still receive the benefit of the interest tax shield next year?

*26. Colt Systems will have EBIT this coming year of $15 million. It will also spend $6 million on total capital expenditures and increases in net working capital, and have $3 million in depreciation expenses (assume CCA = depreciation). Colt is currently an all-equity firm with a corporate tax rate of 35% and a cost of capital of 10%.

a. If Colt is expected to grow by 8.5% per year, what is the market value of its equity today?

b. If the interest rate on its debt is 8%, how much can Colt borrow now and still have non-negative net income this coming year?

c. Is there a tax incentive for Colt to choose a debt-to-value ratio that exceeds 50%? Explain.

EXCEL *27. PMF Inc. is equally likely to have EBIT this coming year of $10 million, $15 million, or $20 million. Its corporate tax rate is 35%, and investors pay a 15% tax rate on income from equity and a 35% tax rate on interest income.

a. What is the effective tax advantage of debt if PMF has interest expenses of $8 million this coming year?

b. What is the effective tax advantage of debt for interest expenses in excess of $20 million? (Ignore carryforwards.)

c. What is the expected effective tax advantage of debt for interest expenses between $10 million and $15 million? (Ignore carryforwards.)

d. What level of interest expense provides PMF with the greatest tax benefit?

DATA CASE

EXCEL Your boss was impressed with your presentation regarding the irrelevance of capital structure from the previous chapter but, as expected, has realized that market imperfections like taxes must be accounted for. You have now been asked to include taxes in your analysis. Your boss knows that interest is deductible and has decided that the stock price of Home Depot should increase if the firm increases its use of debt. Thus, your boss wants to propose a share repurchase program using the proceeds from a new debt issue and wants to present this plan to the CEO and perhaps to the board of directors.

Your boss would like you to examine the impact of two different scenarios, adding a modest level of debt and adding a higher level of debt. In particular, your boss would like to consider issuing $1 billion in new debt or $5 billion in new debt. In either case, Home Depot would use the proceeds to repurchase stock.

1. Using the financial statements for Home Depot that you downloaded in Chapter 14, determine the average corporate tax rate for Home Depot over the last four years by dividing Income Tax by Earnings before Tax for each of the last four years.

2. Begin by analyzing the scenario with $1 billion in new debt. Assuming the firm plans to keep this new debt outstanding forever, determine the present value of the tax shield of the new debt. What additional assumptions did you need to make for this calculation?

3. Determine the new stock price if the $1 billion in debt is used to repurchase stock.
   a. Use the current market value of Home Depot's equity that you calculated in Chapter 14.
   b. Determine the new market value of the equity if the repurchase occurs.
   c. Determine the new number of shares and the stock price after the repurchase is announced.

4. What will Home Depot's D/E ratio based on book values be after it issues new debt and repurchases stock? What will its market value D/E ratio be?

5. Repeat steps 2–4 for the scenario in which Home Depot issues $5 billion in debt and repurchases stock.

6. Based on the stock price, does the debt increase and stock repurchase appear to be a good idea? Why or why not? What issues might the executives of Home Depot raise that aren't considered in your analysis?

NOTATION

β_D debt beta

β_E equity beta

E market value of equity

D market value of debt

I the amount invested in a new project

NPV net present value

PV present value

V^U value of the unlevered firm

V^L value of the firm with leverage

τ^* effective tax advantage of debt

Financial Distress, Managerial Incentives, and Information

Modigliani and Miller demonstrated that capital structure does not matter in a perfect capital market. In Chapter 15, we found a tax benefit of leverage, at least up to the point that a firm's EBIT exceeds the interest payments on the debt. Yet we saw that the average Canadian firm shields only about 65% of its earnings in this way and the numbers are even lower in other developed countries. Why don't firms use more debt?

We can gain some insight by looking at Air Canada. For the six-year period 1994 through 1999, Air Canada paid interest expenses of $1 billion, relative to EBIT of more than $1.4 billion. During this period, it reported a total provision for taxes on its income statement exceeding $175 million. In 2000, Air Canada took on extra debt as it merged with Canadian Airlines. In July 2000, the company appeared to have a level of debt that was high but well matched to its assets and the EBIT produced. Even so, as a result of rising fuel and labour costs, and a decline in travel following the terrorist attacks of September 11, 2001, Air Canada filed for bankruptcy protection on April 1, 2003. It only got worse for Air Canada as the SARS outbreak hit its main hub of Toronto and further reduced revenue in 2003. As this case demonstrates, firms such as airlines whose future cash flows are unstable and highly sensitive to shocks in the economy run the risk of bankruptcy if they use too much leverage. The costs of bankruptcy may at least partially offset the benefits of the interest tax shield, prompting firms to use less leverage than if they were motivated by tax savings alone.

When a firm has trouble meeting its debt obligations we say the firm is in **financial distress**. In this chapter, we consider how a firm's choice of capital structure can, due to market imperfections, affect its costs of financial distress, alter managers' incentives, and signal information to investors. Each of these consequences of the capital structure decision can be significant, and each may offset the tax benefits of leverage when leverage is high. Thus these imperfections may help to explain the levels of debt that we generally observe. In addition, because their effects are likely to vary widely across different types of firms, they may help to explain the large discrepancies in leverage choices that exist across industries and countries, as documented in the previous chapter in Figure 15.7 and Table 15.5.

16.1 DEFAULT AND BANKRUPTCY IN A PERFECT MARKET

Debt financing puts an obligation on a firm. A firm that fails to make the required interest or principal payments on the debt is in **default**. After the firm defaults, debt holders are given certain rights to the assets of the firm. In the extreme case, the debt holders take legal ownership of the firm's assets through a process called bankruptcy. Recall that equity financing does not carry this risk. While equity holders hope to receive dividends, the firm is not legally obligated to pay them.

Thus it seems that an important consequence of leverage is the risk of bankruptcy. Does this risk represent a disadvantage to using debt? Not necessarily. As we pointed out in Chapter 14, Modigliani and Miller's results continue to hold in a perfect market even when debt is risky and the firm may default. Let's review that result by considering a hypothetical example.

ARMIN INDUSTRIES: LEVERAGE AND THE RISK OF DEFAULT

Armin Industries faces an uncertain future in a challenging business environment. Due to increased competition from foreign imports as the Canadian dollar rose, its revenues have fallen dramatically in the past years. Armin's managers hope that a new product in the company's pipeline will restore its fortunes. While the new product represents a significant advance over Armin's competitors' products, whether that product will be a hit with consumers remains uncertain. If it is a hit, revenues and profits will grow, and Armin will be worth $150 million at the end of the year. If it fails, Armin will be worth only $80 million.

Armin Industries may employ one of two alternative capital structures: (1) It can use all-equity financing or (2) it can use debt that matures at the end of the year with a total of $100 million due. Let's look at the consequences of these capital structure choices when the new product succeeds, and when it fails, in a setting of perfect capital markets.

SCENARIO 1: NEW PRODUCT SUCCEEDS.   If the new product is successful, Armin is worth $150 million. Without leverage, equity holders own the full amount. With leverage, Armin must make the $100 million debt payment, and Armin's equity holders will own the remaining $50 million.

But what if Armin does not have $100 million in cash available at the end of the year? Even though its assets will be worth $150 million, much of that value may come from anticipated *future* profits from the new product, rather than cash in the bank. In that case, if Armin has debt, will it be forced to default?

With perfect capital markets, the answer is no. As long as the value of the firm's assets exceeds its liabilities, Armin will be able to repay the loan. Even if it does not have the cash immediately available, it can raise the cash by obtaining a new loan or by issuing new shares.

For example, suppose Armin currently has 10 million shares outstanding. Because the value of its equity is $50 million, these shares are worth $5 per share. At this price, Armin can raise $100 million by issuing 20 million new shares and use the proceeds to pay off the debt. After the debt is repaid, the firm's equity is worth $150 million. Because there is now a total of 30 million shares, the share price remains $5 per share.

This scenario shows that if a firm has access to capital markets and can issue new securities at a fair price, *then it need not default as long as the market value of its assets exceeds its liabilities.* That is, whether default occurs depends on the relative values of the firm's assets and liabilities, not on its cash flows. Many firms experience years of negative cash flows yet remain solvent.

SCENARIO 2: NEW PRODUCT FAILS. If the new product fails, Armin is worth only $80 million. If the company has all-equity financing, equity holders will be unhappy but there is no immediate legal consequence for the firm. In contrast, if Armin has $100 million in debt due, it will experience financial distress. The firm will be unable to make its $100 million debt payment and will have no choice except to default. In bankruptcy, debt holders will receive legal ownership of the firm's assets, leaving Armin's shareholders with nothing. Because the assets the debt holders receive have a value of $80 million, they will suffer a loss of $20 million relative to the $100 million they were owed. Equity holders in a corporation have limited liability, so the debt holders cannot sue Armin's shareholders for this $20 million—they must accept the loss.

COMPARING THE TWO SCENARIOS. Table 16.1 compares the outcome of each scenario without leverage and with leverage. Both debt and equity holders are worse off if the product fails rather than succeeds. Without leverage, if the product fails equity holders lose $150 million − $80 million = $70 million. With leverage, equity holders lose $50 million, and debt holders lose $20 million, *but the total loss is the same—$70 million.* Overall, *if the new product fails, Armin's investors are equally unhappy whether the firm is levered and declares bankruptcy or whether it is unlevered and the share price declines.*[1]

VALUE OF DEBT AND EQUITY WITH AND WITHOUT LEVERAGE ($ MILLION)

TABLE 16.1

	Without Leverage		With Leverage	
	Success	Failure	Success	Failure
Debt value	—	—	100	80
Equity value	150	80	50	0
Total to all investors	150	80	150	80

1. There is a temptation to look only at shareholders and to say they are worse off when Armin has leverage because their shares are worthless. In fact, shareholders are worse off by $50 million relative to success when the firm is levered, versus $70 million without leverage. What really matters is the total value to all investors, which will determine the total amount of capital the firm can raise initially.

This point is an important one. When a firm declares bankruptcy, the news often makes headlines. Much attention is paid to the firm's poor results and the loss to investors. But the decline in value is not *caused* by bankruptcy: The decline is the same whether or not the firm has leverage. That is, if the new product fails, Armin will experience **economic distress**, which is a significant decline in the value of a firm's assets, whether or not it experiences financial distress due to leverage.

BANKRUPTCY AND CAPITAL STRUCTURE

With perfect capital markets, Modigliani-Miller (MM) Proposition I applies: The total value to all investors does not depend on the firm's capital structure. Investors as a group are *not* worse off because a firm has leverage. While it is true that bankruptcy results from a firm having leverage, bankruptcy alone does not lead to a greater reduction in the total value to investors. Thus there is no disadvantage to debt financing, and a firm will have the same total value and will be able to raise the same amount initially from investors with either choice of capital structure.

EXAMPLE 16.1

BANKRUPTCY RISK AND FIRM VALUE

Problem

Suppose the risk-free rate is 5% and Armin's new product is equally likely to succeed or to fail. For simplicity, suppose that Armin's cash flows are unrelated to the state of the economy (i.e., the risk is diversifiable), so that the project has a beta of 0 and the cost of capital is the risk-free rate. Compute the value of Armin's securities at the beginning of the year with and without leverage, and show that MM Proposition I holds.

Solution

Without leverage, the equity is worth either $150 million or $80 million at year-end. Because the risk is diversifiable, no risk premium is necessary and we can discount the expected value of the firm at the risk-free rate to determine its value without leverage at the start of the year:[2]

$$\text{Equity (unlevered)} = V^U = \frac{\frac{1}{2}(150) + \frac{1}{2}(80)}{1.05} = \$109.52 \text{ million}$$

With leverage, equity holders receive $50 million or nothing, and debt holders receive $100 million or $80 million. Thus

$$\text{Equity (levered)} = \frac{\frac{1}{2}(50) + \frac{1}{2}(0)}{1.05} = \$23.81 \text{ million}$$

$$\text{Debt} = \frac{\frac{1}{2}(100) + \frac{1}{2}(80)}{1.05} = \$85.71 \text{ million}$$

Therefore, the value of the levered firm is $V^L = E + D = 23.81 + 85.71 = \$109.52$ million. With or without leverage, the total value of the securities is the same, verifying MM Proposition I. The firm is able to raise the same amount from investors using either capital structure.

---

2. If the risk were not diversifiable and a risk premium were needed, the calculations here would become more complicated but the end result would not change.

CONCEPT CHECK
1. With perfect capital markets, under what conditions will a levered firm default?
2. Does the risk of default reduce the value of the firm?

16.2 THE COSTS OF BANKRUPTCY AND FINANCIAL DISTRESS

With perfect capital markets, the *risk* of bankruptcy is not a disadvantage of debt; bankruptcy simply shifts the ownership of the firm from equity holders to debt holders without changing the total value available to all investors.

Is this description of bankruptcy realistic? No. Bankruptcy is rarely simple and straightforward—equity holders don't just "hand the keys" to debt holders the moment the firm defaults on a debt payment. Rather, bankruptcy is a long and complicated process that imposes both direct and indirect costs on the firm and its investors that the assumption of perfect capital markets ignores.

BANKRUPTCY LAW

We know that when a firm fails to make a required payment to debt holders, it is in default. Debt holders can then take legal action against the firm to collect payment by seizing the firm's assets. Because most firms have multiple creditors, without coordination it is difficult to guarantee that each creditor will be treated fairly. Moreover, because the assets of the firm might be more valuable if kept together, creditors seizing assets in a piecemeal fashion might destroy much of the remaining value of the firm.

Canadian bankruptcy law was created to organize this process so that creditors are treated fairly and the value of the assets is not needlessly destroyed. There are two relevant acts for financially distressed firms in Canada: the **Bankruptcy and Insolvency Act (BIA)** and the **Companies' Creditors Arrangement Act (CCAA)**.

The BIA applies to businesses and individuals. Usually smaller companies use the BIA and liquidation is often the result. Under the BIA, a firm may put forth a proposal that can be either accepted or rejected by its creditors. To be accepted, each class of creditor must vote and pass the proposal and the court must also give its approval. A creditor class is said to pass the proposal if at least a majority of the creditors in number and two-thirds in value agree to the proposal. If a proposal does not pass, a trustee is appointed to oversee the liquidation of the firm's assets through an auction. The proceeds from the liquidation are used to pay the firm's creditors, and the firm ceases to exist.

The CCAA applies to firms that owe $5 million or more to creditors. It allows a company to pre-empt going into formal bankruptcy under the BIA and, instead, propose a formal **plan of arrangement** (or reorganization). Once the company has applied to the court for protection against its creditors, a **stay**, under the CCAA, all pending collection attempts are automatically suspended, and the firm's existing management is given the opportunity to propose a reorganization plan. While developing the plan, management continues to operate the business under the watch of a **monitor** (often the company's auditor). The plan of arrangement specifies the treatment of each creditor of the firm. In addition to cash payment, creditors may receive new debt or equity securities of the firm. The value of cash and securities is generally less than the amount each creditor is owed, but more than the creditors would receive if the firm were shut down immediately and liquidated. The creditors must vote to accept the plan, and it must be approved by the court.[3] If an acceptable plan is not put forth, the company loses its protection under the CCAA and the stay is lifted. The company is not automatically forced to enter into bankruptcy but will likely do so under the BIA, either voluntarily or by petition of its creditors. At this point, liquidation is the likely eventual outcome.

In the U.S., firms may file for bankruptcy protection under the provisions of the 1978 Bankruptcy Reform Act. The main bankruptcy laws for corporations in the U.S. fall under two chapters. **Chapter 7** is for liquidation of firms. **Chapter 11** is for reorganization and is similar to the CCAA in Canada. A notable difference between the CCAA and Chapter 11 is that under Chapter 11 the bankruptcy court can impose a plan (in a process commonly known as a "cram down") even if not all creditor classes approve it.

DIRECT COSTS OF BANKRUPTCY

Bankruptcy law is designed to provide an orderly process for settling a firm's debts. However, the process is still complex, time-consuming, and costly. When a corporation becomes financially distressed, outside professionals, such as legal and accounting experts, consultants, appraisers, auctioneers, and others with experience selling distressed assets, are generally hired. Investment bankers may also assist with a potential financial restructuring.

These outside experts are costly. At the time Enron entered Chapter 11 bankruptcy, it reportedly spent a record $30 million per month on legal and accounting fees, and the total cost ultimately exceeded $750 million. WorldCom paid its advisors $657 million as part of its reorganization to become MCI. Between 2003 and 2005, United Airlines paid a team of over 30 advisory firms an average of $8.6 million per month for legal and professional services related to its Chapter 11 reorganization. Air Canada's professional fees related to its restructuring in 2003 and 2004 totalled $215 million. The largest bankruptcy in history, Lehman Brother's 2008 filing, is expected to entail fees of over $900 million.[4]

In addition to the money spent by the firm, the creditors may incur costs during the bankruptcy process. In the case of Chapter 11 reorganization in the U.S., creditors must often wait several years for a reorganization plan to be approved and to receive payment. Proceedings under the BIA or CCAA in Canada are usually shorter than those in the United States, but the delays are still significant for creditors, as they do not have access to their money. To ensure that their rights and interests are respected, and to assist in valuing their claims in a proposed reorganization, creditors may seek separate legal representation and professional advice; these services are costly too.

Whether paid by the firm or its creditors, these direct costs of bankruptcy reduce the value of the assets that the firm's investors will ultimately receive. In the case of Enron, reorganization costs were expected to approach 10% of the value of the assets. Studies

---

3. Specifically, management holds the exclusive right to propose a plan of arrangement during the initial stay (which is 30 days), and the stay may be extended indefinitely by the court. Thereafter, any interested party may propose a plan. Creditors who will receive full payment or have their claims fully reinstated under the plan are deemed unimpaired, and do not vote on the plan of arrangement. All impaired creditors are grouped according to the nature of their claims. If the plan is approved by creditors holding two-thirds of the claim amount in each group and a majority in the number of the claims in each group, the court may sanction the plan. If a class of creditors or the court does not approve the plan of arrangement, the stay is lifted.

4. For further information on the UAL and Lehman bankruptcies, see Julie Johnsson, "UAL a Ch. 11 Fee Machine," *Crain's Chicago Business,* June 27, 2005, and A. Jones, "Lawyers Set to Profit on Lehman," *Wall Street Journal,* April 16, 2009.

typically report that the average direct costs of bankruptcy are approximately 3% to 4% of the pre-bankruptcy market value of total assets.[5] The costs are likely to be higher for firms with more complicated business operations and for firms with larger numbers of creditors, because it may be more difficult to reach agreement among many creditors regarding the final disposition of the firm's assets. Because many aspects of the bankruptcy process are independent of the size of the firm, the costs are typically higher, in percentage terms, for smaller firms. A study of Chapter 7 liquidations of small businesses in the United States found that the average direct costs of bankruptcy were 12% of the value of the firm's assets.[6]

Given the substantial legal and other direct costs of bankruptcy, firms in financial distress can avoid filing for bankruptcy by first negotiating directly with creditors. When a financially distressed firm is successful at reorganizing outside of bankruptcy, it is called a **workout**. Consequently, the direct costs of bankruptcy should not substantially exceed the cost of a workout. Another approach is a **prepackaged bankruptcy** (or "prepack"), in which a firm will *first* develop a reorganization plan with the agreement of its main creditors, and *then* file under the CCAA (or Chapter 11 in the United States) to implement the plan (and pressure any creditors who attempt to hold out for better terms). With a prepack, the firm emerges from bankruptcy quickly and with minimal direct costs.[7]

INDIRECT COSTS OF FINANCIAL DISTRESS

Aside from the direct legal and administrative costs of bankruptcy, many other *indirect* costs are associated with financial distress (whether or not the firm has formally filed for bankruptcy). While these costs are difficult to measure accurately, they are often much larger than the direct costs of bankruptcy.

Loss of Customers. Because bankruptcy may enable firms to walk away from future commitments to their customers, customers may be unwilling to purchase products whose value depends on future support or service from the firm. This problem affects many technology firms because customers may hesitate to commit to a hardware or software platform that may not be supported or upgraded in the future. Airlines face similar problems: Tickets are sold in advance, so customers will be reluctant to buy tickets if they believe the airline may cease operations or fail to honour their

5. See Jerold Warner, "Bankruptcy Costs: Some Evidence," *Journal of Finance* 32 (1977): 337–347; Lawrence Weiss, "Bankruptcy Resolution: Direct Costs and Violation of Priority of Claims," *Journal of Financial Economics* 27 (1990): 285–314; Edward Altman, "A Further Empirical Investigation of the Bankruptcy Cost Question," *Journal of Finance* 39 (1984): 1067–1089; and Brian Betker, "The Administrative Costs of Debt Restructurings: Some Recent Evidence," *Financial Management* 26 (1997): 56–68. Lynn LoPucki and Joseph Doherty report that direct costs of bankruptcy may have fallen by more than 50% during the 1990s, due to a reduction in the length of time spent in bankruptcy; these authors estimate them at approximately 1.5% of firm value ("The Determinants of Professional Fees in Large Bankruptcy Reorganization Cases," *Journal of Empirical Legal Studies* 1 (2004): 111–141).

6. See Robert Lawless and Stephen Ferris, "Professional Fees and Other Direct Costs in Chapter 7 Business Liquidations," *Washington University Law Quarterly* (Fall 1997): 1207–1236. For comparative international data, see K. Thorburn, "Bankruptcy Auctions: Costs, Debt Recovery and Firm Survival," *Journal of Financial Economics* 58 (2000): 337–368, and A. Raviv and S. Sundgren, "The Comparative Efficiency of Small-Firm Bankruptcies: A Study of the U.S. and the Finnish Bankruptcy Codes," *Financial Management* 27 (1998): 28–40.

7. See E. Tashjian, R. C. Lease, and J. J. McConnell, "An Empirical Analysis of Prepackaged Bankruptcies," *Journal of Financial Economics* 40 (1996): 135–162.

accumulated frequent-flyer mileage. Manufacturers of durable goods may lose potential customers who are worried that warranties will not be honoured or replacement parts will not be available; this was a particular problem in 2009 for General Motors and Chrysler when they went bankrupt, but the worries were reduced when the Canadian and U.S. governments came to the companies' rescue. In contrast, the loss of customers is likely to be small for producers of raw materials (such as sugar or aluminum), as the value of these goods, once delivered, does not depend on the seller's continued success.[8]

Loss of Suppliers. Customers are not the only ones who retreat from a firm in financial distress. Suppliers may be unwilling to provide a firm with inventory if they fear they will not be paid. For example, Kmart Corporation filed for bankruptcy protection in January 2002 in part because the decline in its stock price scared suppliers, which then refused to ship goods. Eaton's faced a similar fate. In 1997 the company restructured under the CCAA but its fortunes waned. By 1999, suppliers were reluctant to deliver to Eaton's stores and customers found sparsely filled racks of clothes and old stock. In 1999, Eaton's attempted another restructuring, was bought by Sears Canada, and eventually closed completely. Swissair faced problems with suppliers too. It was forced to shut down because its suppliers refused to fuel its planes. This type of disruption is an important financial distress cost for firms that rely heavily on trade credit. In many cases, the bankruptcy filing itself can alleviate these problems through **debtor-in-possession financing (DIP)**. DIP financing is new debt issued by a bankrupt firm. Because this kind of debt is senior to all existing creditors, DIP financing, if it can be arranged, may allow a firm that has filed for bankruptcy renewed access to financing to keep operating.

Loss of Employees. Because firms in distress cannot offer job security with long-term employment contracts, they may have difficulty hiring new employees, and existing employees may quit or be hired away. Retaining key employees may be costly: Pacific Gas and Electric Corporation implemented a retention program costing over $80 million to retain 17 key employees while in bankruptcy.[9] This type of financial distress cost is likely to be high for firms whose value is derived largely from their human resources. Even more tragic for these firms is that their best employees will be the most marketable to other employers and may be the first to leave or most costly to keep when a company is perceived to become financially distressed.

Loss of Receivables. Firms in financial distress tend to have difficulty collecting money that is owed to them. According to one of Enron's bankruptcy lawyers, "Many customers who owe smaller amounts are trying to hide from us. They must believe that Enron will never bother with them because the amounts are not particularly large in any individual case."[10] Knowing that the firm's resources are already spread thinly, debtors assume they may have an opportunity to avoid their obligations to the firm.

---

8. This argument was put forth by Sheridan Titman, "The Effect of Capital Structure on a Firm's Liquidation Decision," *Journal of Financial Economics* 13 (1984): 137–151. Timothy Opler and Sheridan Titman report 17.7% lower sales growth for highly leveraged firms compared to their less leveraged competitors in R&D-intensive industries during downturns ("Financial Distress and Corporate Performance," *Journal of Finance* 49 (1994): 1015–1040).

9. Rick Jurgens, "PG&E to Review Bonus Program," *Contra Costa Times,* December 13, 2003.

10. Kristen Hays, "Enron Asks Judge to Get Tough on Deadbeat Customers," *Associated Press,* August 19, 2003.

Fire Sales of Assets. Companies in distress may be forced to sell assets quickly to raise cash. Of course, selling assets quickly may not be optimal, which means accepting a lower price than the assets are actually worth. A study of airlines by Todd Pulvino shows that companies in bankruptcy or financial distress sell their aircraft at prices that are 15% to 40% below the prices received by financially healthy firms.[11] Discounts are also observed when distressed firms attempt to sell subsidiaries. The costs of selling assets below their value are greatest for firms with assets that lack competitive, liquid markets.

Delayed Liquidation. Bankruptcy protection can be used by management to delay the liquidation of a firm that should be shut down. A study by Lawrence Weiss and Karen Wruck estimates that Eastern Airlines lost more than 50% of its value while in bankruptcy because management was allowed to continue making negative-NPV investments.[12]

Costs to Creditors. Aside from the direct legal costs that creditors may incur when a firm defaults, there may be other, indirect costs to creditors. If the loan to the firm was a significant asset for the creditor, default of the firm may lead to costly financial distress *for the creditor.*[13] For example, in 1998 Russia's default on its bonds led to the collapse of Long Term Capital Management (LTCM), and fears arose that some of LTCM's creditors might become distressed as well. The collapse of the subprime mortgage market in the U.S. in 2008 led to the demise of Bear Stearns, a prominent Wall Street financial institution. In both the LTCM and Bear Stearns cases, the U.S. Federal Reserve Board stepped in to orchestrate bailouts so a ripple effect through the financial industry would be avoided.

OVERALL IMPACT OF INDIRECT COSTS.   In total, the indirect costs of financial distress may be substantial. When estimating them, however, we must remember two important points. First, we need to identify losses to total firm value (and not solely losses to equity holders or debt holders, or transfers between them). Second, we need to identify the incremental losses that are associated with financial distress, above and beyond any losses that would occur due to the firm's economic distress.[14] A study of highly levered firms by Gregor Andrade and Steven Kaplan estimated a potential loss due to financial distress of 10% to 20% of firm value.[15] We next consider the consequences of these potential costs of leverage for firm value.

---

11. "Do Asset Fire-Sales Exist? An Empirical Investigation of Commercial Aircraft Transactions," *Journal of Finance* 53 (1998): 939–978, and "Effects of Bankruptcy Court Protection on Asset Sales," *Journal of Financial Economics* 52 (1999): 151–186. For examples from other industries, see Timothy Kruse, "Asset Liquidity and the Determinants of Asset Sales by Poorly Performing Firms," *Financial Management* 31 (2002): 107–129.

12. "Information Problems, Conflicts of Interest, and Asset Stripping: Ch. 11's Failure in the Case of Eastern Airlines," *Journal of Financial Economics* 48, 55–97.

13. While these costs are borne by the creditor and not by the firm, the creditor will consider these potential costs when setting the rate of the loan.

14. For an insightful discussion of this point, see Robert Haugen and Lemma Senbet, "Bankruptcy and Agency Costs: Their Significance to the Theory of Optimal Capital Structure," *Journal of Financial and Quantitative Analysis* 23 (1988): 27–38, where they also point out that the magnitude of financial distress costs can be no larger than the costs of restructuring the firm before the costs are incurred.

15. Gregor Andrade and Steven Kaplan, "How Costly Is Financial (Not Economic) Distress? Evidence from Highly Leveraged Transactions That Became Distressed," *Journal of Finance* 53 (1998): 1443–1493.

CONCEPT CHECK

1. If a firm files for protection under the CCAA in Canada or Chapter 11 of the U.S. bankruptcy code, which party gets the first opportunity to propose a plan for the firm's reorganization?

2. Why are the losses of debt holders whose claims are not fully repaid not a cost of financial distress, whereas the loss of customers who fear the firm will stop honouring warranties is?

16.3 FINANCIAL DISTRESS COSTS AND FIRM VALUE

The costs of financial distress described in the previous section represent an important departure from Modigliani and Miller's assumption of perfect capital markets. MM assumed that the cash flows of a firm's assets do not depend on its choice of capital structure. As we have discussed, however, levered firms risk incurring financial distress costs that reduce the cash flows available to investors.

ARMIN INDUSTRIES: THE IMPACT OF FINANCIAL DISTRESS COSTS

To illustrate how these financial distress costs affect firm value, consider again the example of Armin Industries. With all-equity financing, Armin's assets will be worth $150 million if its new product succeeds and $80 million if the new product fails. In contrast, with debt of $100 million, Armin will be forced into bankruptcy if the new product fails. In this case, some of the value of Armin's assets will be lost to bankruptcy and financial distress costs. As a result, debt holders will receive less than $80 million. We show the impact of these costs in Table 16.2, where we assume debt holders receive only $60 million after accounting for the costs of financial distress.

As Table 16.2 shows, the total value to all investors is now less with leverage than it is without leverage when the new product fails. The difference of $80 million − $60 million = $20 million is due to financial distress costs. These costs will lower the total value of the firm with leverage, and MM's Proposition I will no longer hold, as illustrated in Example 16.2.

WHO PAYS FOR FINANCIAL DISTRESS COSTS?

The financial distress costs in Table 16.2 reduce the payments to the debt holders when the new product has failed. In that case, the equity holders have already lost their investment and have no further interest in the firm. It might seem as though these costs are irrelevant from the shareholders' perspective. Why should equity holders care about costs borne by debt holders?

It is true that after a firm is in bankruptcy, equity holders care little about bankruptcy costs. But debt holders are not foolish—they recognize that when the firm defaults, they will not be able to get the full value of the assets. As a result, they will pay less for the debt

VALUE OF DEBT AND EQUITY WITH AND WITHOUT LEVERAGE ($ MILLION)

TABLE 16.2

	Without Leverage		With Leverage	
	Success	**Failure**	**Success**	**Failure**
Debt value	—	—	100	60
Equity value	150	80	50	0
Total to all investors	150	80	150	60

EXAMPLE 16.2   **FIRM VALUE WHEN FINANCIAL DISTRESS IS COSTLY**

Problem

Compare the current value of Armin Industries with and without leverage, given the data in Table 16.2. Assume that the risk-free rate is 5%, the new product is equally likely to succeed or fail, and the risk is diversifiable.

Solution

With and without leverage, the payments to equity holders are the same as in Example 16.1. There we computed the value of unlevered equity as $109.52 million and the value of levered equity as $23.81 million. But due to bankruptcy costs, the value of the debt is now

$$\text{Debt} = \frac{\frac{1}{2}(100) + \frac{1}{2}(60)}{1.05} = \$76.19 \text{ million}$$

The value of the levered firm is $V^L = E + D = 23.81 + 76.19 = \$100$ million, which is less than the value of the unlevered firm, $V^U = \$109.52$ million. Thus, due to bankruptcy costs, the value of the levered firm is $9.52 million less than its value without leverage. This loss equals the present value of the $20 million in financial distress costs the firm will pay if the product fails:

$$PV(\text{Financial Distress Costs}) = \frac{\frac{1}{2}(0) + \frac{1}{2}(20)}{1.05} = \$9.52 \text{ million}$$

---

initially. How much less? Precisely the amount they will ultimately give up—the present value of the bankruptcy costs.

But if the debt holders pay less for the debt, there is less money available for the firm to pay dividends, repurchase shares, and make investments. That is, this difference is money out of the equity holders' pockets. This logic leads to the following general result:

When securities are fairly priced, the original shareholders of a firm pay the present value of the costs associated with bankruptcy and financial distress.

EXAMPLE 16.3   **FINANCIAL DISTRESS COSTS AND THE STOCK PRICE**

Problem

Suppose that at the beginning of the year, Armin Industries has 10 million shares outstanding and no debt. Armin then announces plans to issue one-year debt with a face value of $100 million and to use the proceeds to repurchase shares. Given the data in Table 16.2, what will the new share price be? As in the previous examples, assume the risk-free rate is 5%, the new product is equally likely to succeed or fail, and this risk is diversifiable.

Solution

From Example 16.1, the value of the firm without leverage is $109.52 million. With 10 million shares outstanding, this value corresponds to an initial share price of $10.952 per share. In Example 16.2, we saw that with leverage, the total value of the firm is only $100 million. In anticipation of this decline in value, the price of the stock should fall to $100 million ÷ 10 million shares = $10 per share on announcement of the recapitalization.

Let's check this result. From Example 16.2, due to bankruptcy costs, the new debt is worth $76.19 million. Thus, at a price of $10 per share, Armin will repurchase 7.619 million shares, leaving 2.381 million shares outstanding. In Example 16.1, we computed the value of levered equity as $23.81 million. Dividing by the number of shares gives a share price after the transaction of

$$\$23.81 \text{ million} \div 2.381 \text{ million shares} = \$10 \text{ per share}$$

Thus the recapitalization will cost shareholders $0.952 per share or $9.52 million in total. This cost matches the present value of financial distress costs computed in Example 16.2. Thus, although debt holders bear these costs in the end, shareholders pay the present value of the costs of financial distress upfront.

CONCEPT CHECK

1. In Examples 16.1 through 16.3, Armin incurred financial distress costs only in the event that the new product failed. Why might Armin incur financial distress costs even *before* the success or failure of the new product is known?

2. Why should shareholders be concerned about financial distress costs that will be borne by debt holders?

3. True or False: Bankruptcy costs only occur in bankruptcy when the equity is worthless anyway. Hence equity holders do not bear the costs of bankruptcy.

16.4 OPTIMAL CAPITAL STRUCTURE: THE TRADEOFF THEORY

We can now combine our knowledge of the benefits of leverage from the interest tax shield (discussed in Chapter 15) with the costs of financial distress to determine the amount of debt that a firm should issue to maximize its value. The analysis presented in this section is called the **tradeoff theory** because it weighs the benefits of debt that result from shielding cash flows from taxes against the costs of financial distress associated with leverage.

According to this theory, *the total value of a levered firm equals the value of the firm without leverage plus the present value of the tax savings from debt, less the present value of financial distress costs:*

$$V^L = V^U + PV(\text{Interest Tax Shield}) - PV(\text{Financial Distress Costs}) \quad (16.1)$$

Equation 16.1 shows that leverage has costs as well as benefits. Firms have an incentive to increase leverage to exploit the tax benefits of debt. But with too much debt, they are more likely to risk default and incur financial distress costs.

THE PRESENT VALUE OF FINANCIAL DISTRESS COSTS

Aside from simple examples, calculating the precise present value of financial distress costs is quite complicated. Three key factors determine the present value of financial distress costs: (1) the probability of financial distress, (2) the magnitude of the costs if the firm is in distress, and (3) the appropriate discount rate for the distress costs. In Example 16.3, when Armin is levered, the present value of its financial distress costs depends on the probability that the new product will fail (50%), the magnitude of the costs if it does fail ($20 million), and the discount rate (5%).

What determines each of these factors? The probability of financial distress depends on the likelihood that a firm will be unable to meet its debt commitments and therefore default. This probability increases with the amount of a firm's liabilities (relative to its assets). It also increases with the volatility of a firm's cash flows and asset values. Thus firms with steady, reliable cash flows, such as utility companies, are able to use high levels of debt and still have a very low probability of default. Firms whose value and cash flows are very volatile (for example, semiconductor firms) must have much lower levels of debt to avoid a significant risk of default.

The magnitude of the financial distress costs will depend on the relative importance of the sources of these costs discussed in Section 16.2 and is likely to vary by industry. For example, technology firms are likely to incur high costs when they are in financial distress, due to the potential for loss of customers and key personnel, as well as a lack of tangible assets that can be easily liquidated. In contrast, real estate firms are likely to have low costs of financial distress, as much of their value derives from assets that can be sold relatively easily.

OPTIMAL LEVERAGE

Figure 16.1 shows how the value of a levered firm, V^L, varies with the level of permanent debt, D, according to Eq. 16.1. With no debt, the value of the firm is V^U. For low levels of debt, the risk of default remains low and the main effect of an increase in leverage is an increase in the interest tax shield, which has present value $\tau^* D$, where τ^* is the effective tax advantage of debt calculated in Chapter 15. If there were no costs of financial distress, the value would continue to increase at this rate until the interest on the debt exceeds the firm's earnings before interest and taxes and the tax shield is exhausted.

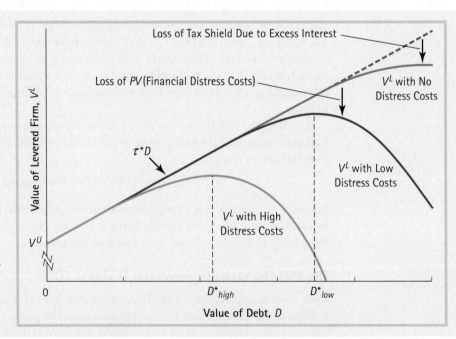

FIGURE 16.1

Optimal Leverage with Taxes and Financial Distress Costs

As the level of debt, D, increases, the tax benefits of debt increase by $\tau^* D$ until the interest expense exceeds the firm's EBIT. The probability of default, and hence the present value of financial distress costs, also increase with D. The optimal level of debt, D^*, occurs when these effects balance out and V^L is maximized. D^* will be lower for firms with higher costs of financial distress.

The costs of financial distress reduce the value of the levered firm, V^L. The amount of the reduction increases with the probability of default, which in turn increases with the level of the debt, D. The tradeoff theory states that firms should increase their leverage until it reaches the level D^* for which V^L is maximized. At this point, the tax savings that result from increasing leverage are just offset by the increased probability of incurring the costs of financial distress.

Figure 16.1 also illustrates the optimal debt choices for two types of firms. The optimal debt choice for a firm with low costs of financial distress is indicated by D^*_{low}, and the optimal debt choice for a firm with high costs of financial distress is indicated by D^*_{high}. Not surprisingly, with higher costs of financial distress, it is optimal for the firm to choose lower leverage.

The tradeoff theory helps to resolve two puzzles regarding leverage that arose in Chapter 15. First, the presence of financial distress costs can explain why firms choose debt levels that are too low to fully exploit the interest tax shield. Second, differences in the magnitude of financial distress costs and the volatility of cash flows can explain the differences in the use of leverage across industries. Since the weighting of industry sectors differs across countries, this also explains some of the differences in leverage observed across countries. That said, bankruptcy costs alone may not be sufficient to explain all of the variation observed. Fortunately, the tradeoff theory can be easily extended to include other effects of leverage—which may be even more important than financial distress costs—that we discuss next.

EXAMPLE 16.4

CHOOSING AN OPTIMAL DEBT LEVEL

Problem

Mapleleaf Industries is considering adding leverage to its capital structure. Mapleleaf's managers believe they can add as much as $35 million in debt and exploit the benefits of the tax shield (for which they estimate $\tau^* = 15\%$). However, they also recognize that higher debt increases the risk of financial distress. Based on simulations of the firm's future cash flows, the CFO has made the following estimates (in millions of dollars):[16]

Debt	0	10	20	25	30	35
PV(Interest tax shield)	0.00	1.50	3.00	3.75	4.50	5.25
PV(Financial distress costs)	0.00	0.00	0.38	1.62	4.00	6.38

What is the optimal debt choice for Mapleleaf?

Solution

From Eq. 16.1, the net benefit of debt is determined by subtracting PV(Financial distress costs) from PV(Interest tax shield). The net benefit for each level of debt is

Debt	0	10	20	25	30	35
Net benefit	0.00	1.50	2.62	2.13	0.50	21.13

The level of debt that leads to the highest net benefit is $20 million. Mapleleaf will gain $3 million due to tax shields, and lose $0.38 million due to the present value of distress costs, for a net gain of $2.62 million.

---

16. The PV of the interest tax shield is computed as $\tau^* D$. The PV of financial distress costs is difficult to estimate and requires option valuation techniques we introduce in Part 7 of the text.

CONCEPT CHECK   1. Describe the tradeoff theory.

2. According to the tradeoff theory, all else being equal, which type of firm has a higher optimal level of debt: a firm with very volatile cash flows or a firm with very safe, predictable cash flows?

16.5 EXPLOITING DEBT HOLDERS: THE AGENCY COSTS OF LEVERAGE

In this section, we consider another way that capital structure can affect a firm's cash flows: It can alter managers' incentives and change their investment decisions. If these changes have a negative NPV, they will be costly for the firm.

The type of costs we describe in this section are examples of **agency costs**—costs that arise when there are conflicts of interest between stakeholders. Because top managers often hold shares in the firm and are hired and retained with the approval of the board of directors, which itself is elected by shareholders, managers will generally make decisions that increase the value of the firm's equity. When a firm has leverage, a conflict of interest exists if investment decisions have different consequences for the value of equity and the value of debt. Such a conflict is most likely to occur when the risk of financial distress is high. In some circumstances, managers may take actions that benefit shareholders but harm the firm's creditors and lower the total value of the firm.

We illustrate this possibility by considering a firm that is facing financial distress, Poisson Ltd. Poisson has a loan of $1 million due at the end of the year. Without a change in its strategy, the market value of its assets will be only $900,000 at that time, and Poisson will default on its debt. In this situation, let's consider several types of agency costs that might arise.

EXCESSIVE RISK-TAKING AND ASSET SUBSTITUTION

Poisson executives are considering a new strategy that seemed promising initially but appears risky after closer analysis. The new strategy requires no upfront investment, but it has only a 50% chance of success. If it succeeds, it will increase the value of the firm's assets to $1.3 million. If it fails, the value of the firm's assets will fall to $300,000. Therefore, the expected value of the firm's assets under the new strategy is 50% × $1.3 million + 50% × $300,000 = $800,000, a decline of $100,000 from their value of $900,000 under the old strategy. Despite the negative expected payoff, some within the firm have suggested that Poisson should go ahead with the new strategy, in the interest of better serving its shareholders. How can shareholders benefit from this decision?

As Table 16.3 shows, if Poisson does nothing, it will ultimately default and equity holders will get nothing with certainty. Thus equity holders have nothing to lose if Poisson tries the risky strategy. If the strategy succeeds, equity holders will receive $300,000 after paying off the debt. Given a 50% chance of success, the equity holders' expected payoff is $150,000.

Clearly, equity holders gain from this strategy, even though it has a negative expected payoff. Who loses? The debt holders: If the strategy fails, they bear the loss. As shown in Table 16.3, if the project succeeds, debt holders are fully repaid and receive $1 million. If the project fails, they receive only $300,000. Overall, the debt holders' expected payoff is $650,000, a loss of $250,000 relative to the $900,000 they would have received under the old strategy. This loss corresponds to the $100,000 expected loss of the risky strategy and the $150,000 gain of the equity holders. Effectively, the equity holders are gambling with the debt holders' money.

OUTCOMES FOR POISSON'S DEBT AND EQUITY UNDER EACH STRATEGY ($ THOUSAND)

TABLE 16.3

	Old Strategy	New Risky Strategy		
		Success	Failure	Expected
Value of assets	900	1300	300	800
Debt	900	1000	300	650
Equity	0	300	0	150

This example illustrates a general point: *When a firm faces financial distress, shareholders can gain by making sufficiently risky investments, even if they have negative NPV.*[17] Because leverage gives shareholders an incentive to replace low-risk assets with riskier ones, this result is often referred to as the **asset substitution problem**. It can also lead to overinvestment, as shareholders may gain by the firm undertaking negative-NPV, but sufficiently risky, projects that it would otherwise reject. If the firm increases risk through a negative-NPV decision or investment, the total value of the firm will be reduced. This cost is likely to be highest for firms that can easily increase the risk of their investments.

DEBT OVERHANG AND UNDER-INVESTMENT

Suppose Poisson does not pursue the risky strategy. Instead, the firm's managers consider an attractive investment opportunity that requires an initial investment of $100,000 and will generate a risk-free return of 50%. That is, it has the following cash flows (in thousands of dollars):

If the current risk-free rate is 5%, this investment clearly has a positive NPV. The only problem is that Poisson does not have the cash on hand to make the investment.

Could Poisson raise the $100,000 by issuing new equity? Unfortunately, it cannot. Suppose equity holders were to contribute the $100,000 in new capital required. Their payoff at the end of the year is shown in Table 16.4.

Thus, if equity holders contribute $100,000 to fund the project, they get back only $50,000. The other $100,000 from the project goes to the debt holders, whose payoff increases from $900,000 to $1 million. Because the debt holders receive most of the benefit, this project is a negative-NPV investment opportunity for equity holders, even though it offers a positive NPV for the firm.

This example illustrates another general point: *When a firm faces financial distress, it may choose not to finance new, positive-NPV projects.*[18] In this case, there is an **debt overhang** or **under-investment problem**: Shareholders choose to not invest in a positive-NPV

---

17. For more on this problem see Michael Jensen and William Meckling, "Theory of the Firm: Managerial Behavior, Agency Costs and Ownership Structure," *Journal of Financial Economics* (1976): 305–360.

18. For more on debt overhang, see Stewart Myers, "Determinants of Corporate Borrowing," *Journal of Financial Economics* (1977): 147–175.

OUTCOMES FOR POISSON'S DEBT AND EQUITY WITH AND WITHOUT THE NEW PROJECT ($ THOUSAND)

TABLE 16.4

	Without New Project	**With New Project**
Existing assets	900	900
New project		150
Total firm value	900	1050
Debt	900	1000
Equity	0	50

project. This failure to invest is costly for debt holders and for the overall value of the firm, because it is giving up the NPV of the missed opportunities. The cost is highest for firms that are likely to have profitable future growth opportunities requiring large investments.

CASHING OUT

When a firm faces financial distress, shareholders have an incentive not to invest and to withdraw money from the firm if possible. As an example, suppose Poisson has equipment it can sell for $25,000 at the beginning of the year. It will need this equipment to continue normal operations during the year; without it, Poisson will have to shut down some operations and the firm will be worth only $800,000 at year-end. Although selling the equipment reduces the value of the firm by $100,000, if it is likely that Poisson will default at year-end, this cost would be borne by the debt holders. So, equity holders gain if Poisson sells the equipment and uses the $25,000 to pay an immediate cash dividend. This incentive to liquidate assets at prices below their actual value is another form of under-investment that results from debt.

ESTIMATING THE DEBT OVERHANG.   How much leverage must a firm have for there to be a significant debt overhang problem? While difficult to estimate precisely, we can use a useful approximation. Suppose equity holders invest an amount I in a new investment project. Let D and E be the market value of the firm's debt and equity, and let β_D and β_E

FINANCIAL **CRISIS**
BAILOUTS, DISTRESS COSTS, AND DEBT OVERHANG

Firms and financial institutions in or near financial distress in the midst of the 2008 financial crisis experienced many of the costs associated with financial distress that we have described, creating further negative consequences for the real economy.

Of particular concern was the seeming unwillingness of banks to make loans to borrowers at reasonable terms. One possible explanation was that the borrowers were not creditworthy and so lending to them was a negative NPV invest-

ment. But many, including the banks themselves, pointed to another culprit: some banks were subject to debt overhang that made it extremely difficult to raise the capital needed to make positive-NPV loans. Government bailouts (such as the U.S. government purchases of bank stock or the Canadian government purchases of bank mortgages) provided banks with capital, alleviating their debt overhang and increasing the availability of credit to the rest of the economy.

be their respective betas. Then the following approximate rule (which we later derive in Chapter 21) applies: equity holders will benefit from the new investment if

$$\frac{NPV}{I} > \frac{\beta_D D}{\beta_E E} \tag{16.2}$$

That is, the project's profitability index (NPV/I) must exceed a cutoff equal to the relative riskiness of the firm's debt (β_D/β_E) times its debt-equity ratio (D/E). Note that if the firm has no debt ($D = 0$) or its debt is risk free ($\beta_D = 0$), then Eq. 16.2 is equivalent to $NPV > 0$. But if the firm's debt is risky, the required cutoff is positive and increases with the firm's leverage. Equity holders will reject positive-NPV projects with profitability indices below the cutoff, leading to under-investment and reduction in firm value.

EXAMPLE 16.5

ESTIMATING THE DEBT OVERHANG

Problem

In Chapter 12 we estimated that Sears had an equity beta of 1.36, a debt beta of 0.17, and a debt-equity ratio of 0.30, while Saks had an equity beta of 1.85, a debt beta of 0.31, and a debt-equity ratio of 1.0. For both firms, estimate the minimum NPV such that a new $100,000 investment (which does not change the volatility of the firm) will benefit shareholders. Which firm has the more severe debt overhang?

Solution

We can use Eq. 16.2 to estimate the cutoff level of the profitability index for Sears as $(0.17/1.36) \times 0.30 = 0.0375$. Thus, the NPV would need to equal at least $3,750 for the investment to benefit shareholders. For Saks, the cutoff is $0.31/1.85 = 0.1675$. Thus, the minimum NPV for Saks is $16,750. Saks has the more severe debt overhang, as its shareholders will reject projects with positive NPVs up to this higher cutoff. Similarly, Saks shareholders would benefit if the firm liquidated up to $116,750 worth of assets to pay out an additional $100,000 in dividends.

AGENCY COSTS AND THE VALUE OF LEVERAGE

These examples illustrate how leverage can encourage managers and shareholders to take actions that reduce firm value. At the time the action is taken, the equity holders benefit at the expense of the debt holders. But, as with financial distress costs, it is the shareholders of the firm who ultimately bear these agency costs. When a firm *initially* chooses to add leverage to its capital structure, what happens to the share price? At first glance, perhaps the share price should rise due to the expectation of equity holders' ability to exploit debt holders in times of distress. However, the debt holders recognize this possibility and pay less for the debt when it is issued. This increases the cost of debt (or the cash flows that must be promised to debt holders for a given amount of debt issued) and leaves less cash available to be paid to equity holders. So the expected benefit to shareholders is more than offset by the depressed price received for the debt when it is issued. The net effect is a reduction in the initial share price of the firm. The amount of this reduction will correspond to the expectation of negative NPV decisions or investments if the firm does go into financial distress.

These agency costs of debt can arise only if there is some chance the firm will default and impose losses on its debt holders. The magnitude of the agency costs increases with the risk, and therefore the amount, of the firm's debt. Agency costs, therefore, represent another cost of increasing the firm's leverage that will affect the firm's optimal capital structure choice.

EXAMPLE 16.6   **AGENCY COSTS AND THE AMOUNT OF LEVERAGE**

Problem

Would the agency costs described previously arise if Poisson had less leverage and owed $400,000 rather than $1 million?

Solution

If Poisson makes no new investments or changes to its strategy, the firm will be worth $900,000. Thus the firm will remain solvent and its equity will be worth $900,000 − $400,000 = $500,000.

If Poisson takes the risky strategy, its assets will be worth either $1.3 million or $300,000, so equity holders will receive $900,000 or $0. In this case, the equity holders' expected payoff with the risky project is only $450,000. Thus equity holders will reject the risky strategy.

What about under-investment? If Poisson raises $100,000 from equity holders to fund a new investment that increases the value of assets by $150,000, the equity will be worth

$$\$900,000 + \$150,000 - \$400,000 = \$650,000$$

This is a gain of $150,000 over the $500,000 equity holders would receive without the investment. Because their payoff has gone up by $150,000 for a $100,000 investment, they will be willing to invest in the new project.

Similarly, Poisson has no incentive to cash out and sell equipment to pay a dividend. If the firm pays the dividend, equity holders receive $25,000 today. But their future payoff declines to $800,000 − $400,000 = $400,000. Thus they give up $100,000 in one year for a $25,000 gain today. For any reasonable discount rate, this is a bad deal and shareholders will reject the dividend.

DEBT MATURITY AND COVENANTS

Several things can be done to mitigate the agency costs of debt. First, note that the magnitude of agency costs likely depends on the maturity of debt. With long-term debt, equity holders have more opportunities to profit at the debt holders' expense before the debt matures. Thus agency costs are smallest for short-term debt.[19] For example, if Poisson's debt were due today, the firm would be forced to default or renegotiate with debt holders before it could increase risk, fail to invest, or cash out. However, by relying on short-term debt the firm will be obligated to repay or refinance its debt more frequently. Short-term debt may also increase the firm's risk of financial distress and its associated costs.

---

19. See Shane Johnson, "Debt Maturity and the Effects of Growth Opportunities and Liquidity on Leverage," *Review of Financial Studies* 16 (March 2003): 209–236, for empirical evidence supporting this hypothesis.

Second, as a condition of making a loan, creditors often place restrictions on the actions that the firm can take. Such restrictions are referred to as **debt covenants**. Covenants may limit the firm's ability to pay large dividends or the types of investments that the firm can make. These covenants are often designed to prevent management from exploiting debt holders, so they may help to reduce agency costs. Conversely, because covenants hinder management flexibility, they have the potential to get in the way of positive NPV opportunities and so can have costs of their own.[20]

CONCEPT CHECK

1. Why do firms have an incentive to both take excessive risk and under-invest when they are in financial distress?

2. Why would debt holders desire covenants that restrict the firm's ability to pay dividends, and why might shareholders also benefit from this restriction?

16.6 MOTIVATING MANAGERS: THE AGENCY BENEFITS OF LEVERAGE

In Section 16.5, we took the view that managers act in the interests of the firm's equity holders, and we considered the potential conflicts of interest between debt holders and equity holders when a firm has leverage. Of course, managers also have their own personal interests, which may differ from those of both equity holders and debt holders. Although managers often do own shares of the firm, in most large corporations they own only a very small fraction of the outstanding shares. And while the shareholders, through the board of directors, have the power to fire managers, they rarely do so unless the firm's performance is exceptionally poor.[21]

This separation of ownership and control creates the possibility of **management entrenchment**; facing little threat of being fired and replaced, managers are free to run the firm in their own best interests. As a result, managers may make decisions that benefit themselves at investors' expense. In this section, we consider how leverage can provide incentives for managers to run the firm more efficiently and effectively. The benefits we describe in this section, in addition to the tax benefits of leverage, give the firm an incentive to use debt rather than equity financing.

CONCENTRATION OF OWNERSHIP

One advantage of using leverage is that it allows the original owners of the firm to maintain their equity stake. As major shareholders, they will have a strong interest in doing what is best for the firm. Next we consider an example of such a situation.

Manmeet Bhatia is the owner of a successful furniture store. He plans to expand by opening several new stores. Manmeet can either borrow the funds needed for expansion or raise the money by selling shares in the firm. If he issues equity, he will need to sell 40% of the firm to raise the necessary funds.

If Manmeet uses debt, he retains ownership of 100% of the firm's equity. As long as the firm does not default, any decision Manmeet makes that increases the value of the firm by $1 increases the value of his own stake by $1. But if Manmeet issues equity, he

---

20. For an analysis of the costs and benefits of bond covenants, see C. W. Mazurek and J. B. Warner, "On Financial Contracting: An Analysis of Bond Covenants," *Journal of Financial Economics* (June 1979): 117–161.

21. See, for example, Jerold Warner, Ross Watts, and Karen Wruck, "Stock Prices and Top Management Changes," *Journal of Financial Economics* 20 (1988): 461–492.

retains only 60% of the equity. Thus Manmeet gains only $0.60 for every $1 increase in firm value.

The difference in Manmeet's ownership stake changes his incentives in running the firm. Suppose the value of the firm depends largely on Manmeet's personal effort. Manmeet is then likely to work harder, and the firm will be worth more, if he receives 100% of the gains rather than only 60%.

Another effect of issuing equity is Manmeet's temptation to enjoy corporate perks, such as a large office with fancy artwork, a corporate limo and driver, a corporate jet, or a large expense account. With leverage, Manmeet is the sole owner and will bear the full cost of these perks. But with equity, Manmeet bears only 60% of the cost; the other 40% will be paid for by the new equity holders. Thus, with equity financing, it is more likely that Manmeet will overspend on these luxuries.

The costs of reduced effort and excessive spending on perks are another form of agency cost. These agency costs arise in this case due to the dilution of ownership that occurs when equity financing is used. Who pays these agency costs? As always, if securities are fairly priced, the original owners of the firm pay the cost. In our example, Manmeet will find that if he chooses to issue equity, the new investors will discount the price they will pay to reflect Manmeet's lower effort and increased spending on perks. In this case, using leverage can benefit the firm by preserving ownership concentration and avoiding these agency costs.[22]

REDUCTION OF WASTEFUL INVESTMENT

While ownership is often concentrated for small, young firms, ownership typically becomes more diluted over time as a firm grows. First, the original owners of the firm may retire, and the new managers likely will not hold as large an ownership stake. Second, firms often need to raise more capital for investment than can be sustained using debt alone (recall the discussion of debt capacity and growth in Chapter 15). Third, owners will often choose to sell off their stakes and invest in a well-diversified portfolio to reduce risk. For firms in the U.S. and U.K., the predominant ownership structure is for large firms to be widely held by the public. Most U.S. CEOs own less than 1% of their firm's shares. In most other countries, including Canada, the widely held firm is not the norm. In many cases the actual ownership and exposure to the resources of the firm is small while the voting control is large. This is accomplished by dominant shareholders (usually controlling families) that utilize super-voting shares, cross ownership, or pyramidal ownership structures.[23]

---

22. This potential benefit of leverage is discussed by Michael Jensen and William Meckling, "Theory of the Firm: Managerial Behavior, Agency Costs and Ownership Structure," *Journal of Financial Economics* 3 (1976): 305–360. Note also that because managers who own a large block of shares are more difficult to replace, increased ownership concentration may also lead to increased entrenchment and reduce incentives; see Randall Morck, Andrei Shleifer, and Robert W. Vishny, "Management Ownership and Market Valuation," *Journal of Financial Economics* 20 (1988): 293–315.

23. Randall Morck, David Stangeland, and Bernard Yeung ("Inherited Wealth, Corporate Control and Economic Growth: The Canadian Disease?" in *Concentrated Corporate Ownership*, National Bureau of Economic Research, University of Chicago Press, 2000) find that over 40% of the largest publicly traded firms in Canada are controlled by an individual or family group. For a good summary of the divergence between asset ownership and voting control and the issues surrounding it internationally, see the paper by Randall Morck, Daniel Wolfenzon, and Bernard Yeung, "Corporate Governance, Economic Entrenchment and Growth," *Journal of Economic Literature* 43 (2005): 655–720.

EXCESSIVE PERKS AND CORPORATE SCANDALS

While most CEOs and managers exercise proper restraint when spending shareholders' money, there have been some highly publicized exceptions in the corporate scandals that have come to light.

Former Enron CFO Andrew Fastow reportedly used complicated financial transactions to enrich himself with at least $30 million of shareholder money. Tyco Corporation's ex-CEO Dennis Kozlowski will be remembered for his $6000 shower curtain, $6300 sewing basket, and $17 million Fifth Avenue condo, all paid for with Tyco funds. In total, he and former CFO Mark Swartz were convicted of pilfering $600 million from company coffers.[*] Former WorldCom CEO Bernie Ebbers, who was convicted for his role in the firm's $11 billion accounting scandal, borrowed more than $400 million from the company at favourable terms from late 2000 to early 2002. Among other things, he used the money from these loans to give gifts to friends and family, as well as build a house.[†] Former Canadian and then British lord Conrad

Black owned Hollinger International (a newspaper company and the founder of the *National Post*) through holding companies and super-voting stock.[‡] Many allegations were made against him, including diverting $60 million to himself and close colleagues and their companies that should have gone to Hollinger International from the sale of its newspaper assets. Other excesses that were noted in Black's trial and by the media were that Hollinger paid two-thirds of the $62,000 cost of Black's party for his wife's birthday in 2000 and Hollinger paid $565,000 for Black and his wife to holiday on the island of Bora Bora in the South Pacific in 2001.[§] Lord Black stands convicted on fraud and obstruction of justice charges.

But these are certainly exceptional cases. And they were not, in and of themselves, the cause of all the firms' problems, but rather a symptom of a broader problem of a lack of oversight and accountability within these firms, together with an opportunistic attitude of the managers involved.

[*]Melanie Warner, "Exorcism at Tyco," *Fortune Magazine,* April 28, 2003, p. 106.
[†]Andrew Backover, "Report Slams Culture at WorldCom," *USA Today*, November 5, 2002, p. 1B.
[‡]Floyd Norris, "Panel Says Conrad Black Ran a 'Corporate Kleptocracy,'" *New York Times*, August 31, 2004.
[§]CBC, June 27, 2007, www.cbc.ca/news/background/black_conrad/trial-glance.html.

With such low stakes in the ownership of the cash flows produced by the firm's assets, the potential for a conflict of interest between managers and equity holders is high. Appropriate monitoring and standards of accountability are required to prevent abuse. While most successful firms have implemented appropriate mechanisms to protect shareholders, each year scandals are revealed in which managers have acted against shareholders' interests.

While overspending on personal perks may be a problem for large firms, these costs are likely to be small relative to the overall value of the firm. A more serious concern for large corporations is that managers may make large, unprofitable investments: Bad investment decisions have destroyed many otherwise successful firms. But what would motivate managers to make negative-NPV investments?

Some financial economists explain a manager's willingness to engage in negative-NPV investments as *empire building*. According to this view, managers prefer to run large firms rather than small ones, so they will take on investments that increase the size—rather than the profitability—of the firm. One potential reason for this preference is that managers of large firms tend to earn higher salaries, and they may also have more prestige and garner greater publicity than managers of small firms. As a result, managers may expand (or fail to shut down) unprofitable divisions, pay too much for acquisitions, make unnecessary capital expenditures, or hire unnecessary employees.

Another reason that managers may over-invest is that they are overconfident. Even when managers attempt to act in shareholders' interests, they may make mistakes. Managers tend to be bullish on the firm's prospects and so may believe that new opportunities

FINANCIAL **CRISIS**
MORAL HAZARD AND THE GOVERNMENT BAILOUT

The term **moral hazard** refers to the idea that individuals will change their behaviour if they are not fully exposed to its consequences. Discussion of moral hazard's role in the 2008 financial crisis has centred on mortgage brokers, investment bankers, and corporate managers who earned large bonuses when their businesses did well, but did not need to repay these bonuses later if things turned sour. The agency costs described in this chapter represent another form of moral hazard, as equity holders may take excessive risk or pay excessive dividends if the negative consequences will be borne by bondholders.

How are such abuses by equity holders normally held in check? Bondholders will either charge equity holders for the risk of this abuse by increasing the cost of debt, or, more likely, equity holders will credibly commit not to take on excessive

risk by, for example, agreeing to very strong bond covenants and other monitoring.

Ironically, despite the potential immediate benefits of the government bailouts in response to the 2008 financial crisis, by protecting the bondholders of many large corporations, the governments may have simultaneously weakened this disciplining mechanism and thereby increased the likelihood of future crises. With this precedent in place, all lenders to corporations deemed "too big to fail" may presume they have an implicit government guarantee, thus lowering their incentives to insist on strong covenants and to monitor whether those covenants are being satisfied. Without this monitoring the probability of future abuses by equity holders and managers has likely been increased, as has the government's liability.

---

are better than they actually are. They may also become committed to investments the firm has already made and continue to invest in projects that should be cancelled.[24]

For managers to engage in wasteful investment, they must have the cash to invest. This observation is the basis of the **free cash flow hypothesis**, the view that wasteful spending is more likely to occur when firms have high levels of cash flow in excess of what is needed to make all positive-NPV investments and payments to debt holders.[25] Only when cash is tight will managers be motivated to run the firm as efficiently as possible. According to this hypothesis, leverage increases firm value because it commits the firm to making future interest payments, thereby reducing excess cash flows and wasteful investment by managers.[26]

A related idea is that leverage can reduce the degree of managerial entrenchment because managers are more likely to be fired when a firm faces financial distress. Managers who are less entrenched may be more concerned about their performance and less likely to engage in wasteful investment. In addition, when the firm is highly levered, creditors themselves will closely monitor the actions of managers, providing an additional layer of management oversight.[27]

---

24. For evidence of the relationship between CEO overconfidence and investment distortions, see Ulrike Malmendier and Geoffrey Tate, "CEO Overconfidence and Corporate Investment," *Journal of Finance* 60 (2005): 2661–2700. See also J. B. Heaton, "Managerial Optimism and Corporate Finance," *Financial Management* 31 (2002): 33–45, and Richard Roll, "The Hubris Hypothesis of Corporate Takeovers," *Journal of Business* 59 (1986): 197–216.

25. The hypothesis that excess cash flow induces empire building was put forth by M. Jensen, "Agency Costs of Free Cash Flow, Corporate Finance, and Takeovers," *American Economic Review* 76 (1986): 323–329.

26. Of course, if the firm did not generate sufficient free cash flow, managers could also raise new capital for wasteful investment. But new investors would be reluctant to contribute to such an endeavour and would offer unfavourable terms. In addition, raising external funds would likely attract greater scrutiny and public criticism regarding the investment.

27. See, for example, M. Harris and A. Raviv, "Capital Structure and the Informational Role of Debt," *Journal of Finance* 45:2 (1990): 321–349.

LEVERAGE AND COMMITMENT

Leverage may also tie managers' hands and commit them to pursue strategies with greater vigour than they would without the threat of financial distress. For example, when Air Canada was in the process of reorganizing under the CCAA in 2003–2004, it was able to win wage concessions from its powerful unions by explaining that the high cost structure, if continued, would push Air Canada into bankruptcy and liquidation. Without the threat of bankruptcy, Air Canada's managers might not have reached such an agreement with its unions as quickly or achieved the same wage concessions.[28]

In effect, leverage forces managers to create and maintain competitive advantages because the firm cannot afford to fall behind as that would put the firm at risk of bankruptcy.[29]

CONCEPT CHECK

1. In what ways might managers benefit by overspending on acquisitions?

2. How might shareholders use the firm's capital structure to prevent this problem?

16.7   AGENCY COSTS AND THE TRADEOFF THEORY

We can now adjust Eq. 16.1 for the value of the firm to include the costs and benefits of the incentives that arise when the firm has leverage. This more complete equation is shown below:

$$V^L = V^U + PV(\text{Interest Tax Shield}) - PV(\text{Financial Distress Costs})$$
$$- PV(\text{Agency Costs of Debt}) + PV(\text{Agency Benefits of Debt}) \quad (16.3)$$

The net effect of the costs and benefits of leverage on the value of a firm is illustrated in Figure 16.2. With no debt, the value of the firm is V^U. As the debt level increases, the firm benefits from the interest tax shield (which has present value $\tau^* D$). The firm also benefits from improved incentives for management, which reduce wasteful investment and perks. If the debt level is too large, however, firm value is reduced due to the loss of tax benefits (when interest exceeds EBIT), financial distress costs, and the agency costs of leverage. The optimal level of debt, D^*, balances the costs and benefits of leverage.

---

28. See E. C. Perotti and K. E. Spier, "Capital Structure as a Bargaining Tool: The Role of Leverage in Contract Renegotiation," *American Economic Review* (December 1993): 1131–1141. Debt can also affect a firm's bargaining power with its suppliers; see S. Dasgupta and K. Sengupta, "Sunk Investment, Bargaining and Choice of Capital Structure," *International Economic Review* (February 1993): 203–220, and O. H. Sarig, "The Effect of Leverage on Bargaining with a Corporation," *Financial Review* 33 (February 1998): 1–16. Debt may also enhance a target's bargaining power in a control contest; see M. Harris and A. Raviv, "Corporate Control Contests and Capital Structure," *Journal of Financial Economics* (March 1988): 55–86, and R. Israel, "Capital Structure and the Market for Corporate Control: The Defensive Role of Debt Financing," *Journal of Finance* (September 1991): 1391–1409.

29. Note that a firm weakened by too much leverage might become so financially fragile that it crumbles in the face of competition, allowing other firms to erode its markets; see James Brander and Tracy Lewis, "Oligopoly and Financial Structure: The Limited Liability Effect," *American Economic Review* 76 (1986): 956–970. Judy Chevalier finds that leverage reduces the competitiveness of supermarket firms ("Capital Structure and Product-Market Competition: Empirical Evidence from the Supermarket Industry," *American Economic Review* 85 (1995): 415–435. Patric Bolton and David Scharfstein discuss the effects of not having deep pockets in "A Theory of Predation Based on Agency Problems in Financial Contracting," *American Economic Review* 80 (1990): 93–106.

Optimal Leverage with Taxes, Financial Distress, and Agency Costs

As the level of debt, D, increases, the value of the firm increases from the interest tax shield as well as improvements in managerial incentives. If leverage is too high, however, the present value of financial distress costs, as well as the agency costs from debt holder–equity holder conflicts, dominates and reduces firm value. The optimal level of debt, D^*, balances these benefits and costs of leverage.

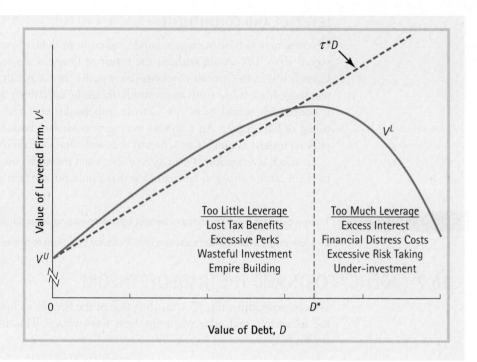

THE OPTIMAL DEBT LEVEL

It is important to note that the relative magnitudes of the different costs and benefits of debt vary with the characteristics of the firm. Likewise, the optimal level of debt varies. As an example, let's contrast the optimal capital structure choice for two types of firms.[30]

R&D-INTENSIVE FIRMS.   Firms with high R&D costs and future growth opportunities typically maintain low debt levels. These firms tend to have low current free cash flows, so they need little debt to provide a tax shield or to control managerial spending. In addition, they tend to have high human capital, so there will be large costs as a result of financial distress. Also, these firms may find it easy to increase the risk of their business strategy (by pursuing a riskier technology) and often need to raise additional capital to fund new investment opportunities. Thus their agency costs of debt are also high. Biotechnology and technology firms often maintain less than 10% leverage.

LOW-GROWTH, MATURE FIRMS.   Mature, low-growth firms with stable cash flows and tangible assets often fall into the high-debt category. These firms tend to have high free cash flows with few good investment opportunities. Thus the tax shield and incentive benefits of leverage are likely to be high. With tangible assets, the financial distress costs of leverage are likely to be low, as the assets can be liquidated for close to their full value. Examples of low-growth industries in which firms typically maintain greater than 20% leverage include real estate, utilities, and supermarket chains.

DEBT LEVELS IN PRACTICE

The tradeoff theory explains how firms *should* choose their capital structures to maximize value to current shareholders. Evaluating whether they actually do so is not so straightforward, however, as many of the costs of leverage are hard to measure.

Why might firms *not* choose an optimal capital structure? Capital structure decisions, like investment decisions, are made by managers who have their own incentives. Proponents of the **management entrenchment theory** of capital structure believe that managers choose a capital structure to avoid the discipline of debt and maintain their own entrenchment. Thus managers seek to *minimize* leverage to prevent the job loss that would accompany financial distress. Managers are constrained from using too little debt, however, to keep shareholders happy. If managers sacrifice too much firm value, disgruntled shareholders may try to replace them or sell the firm to an acquirer. Under this hypothesis, firms will have leverage that is less than the optimal level D^* in Figure 16.2, and increase it toward D^* only in response to a takeover threat or the threat of shareholder activism.[31]

CONCEPT CHECK

1. Describe how management entrenchment can affect the value of the firm.

2. Coca-Cola Enterprises is almost 50% debt-financed, while Biovail, a pharmaceutical firm, has no long-term debt. Why might these firms choose such different capital structures?

16.8   ASYMMETRIC INFORMATION AND CAPITAL STRUCTURE

Throughout this chapter, we have assumed that managers, shareholders, and creditors have the same information. We have also assumed that securities are fairly priced: The firm's shares and debt are priced according to their true underlying value. These assumptions may not always be accurate in practice. Managers' information about the firm and its future cash flows is likely to be superior to that of outside investors—there is **asymmetric information** between managers and investors. In this section, we consider how asymmetric information may motivate managers to alter a firm's capital structure.

LEVERAGE AS A CREDIBLE SIGNAL

Consider the plight of Monika Mazurek, CEO of Beltran International, who believes her company's stock is undervalued. Market analysts and investors are concerned that several of Beltran's key patents will expire soon, and that new competition will force Beltran to cut prices or lose customers. Mazurek believes that new product innovations and soon-to-be-introduced manufacturing improvements will keep Beltran ahead of its competitors and enable it to sustain its current profitability well into the future. She seeks to convince investors of Beltran's promising future and to increase Beltran's current stock price.

One potential strategy is to launch an investor relations campaign. Mazurek can issue press releases, describing the merits of the new innovations and the manufacturing improvements. But Mazurek knows that investors may be skeptical of these press releases

---

31. See Jeffrey Zwiebel, "Dynamic Capital Structure Under Managerial Entrenchment," *American Economic Review* 86 (1996): 1197–1215; Luigi Zingales and Walter Novaes, "Capital Structure Choice When Managers are in Control: Entrenchment versus Efficiency," *Journal of Business* 76 (2002): 49–82; and Erwan Morellec, "Can Managerial Discretion Explain Observed Leverage Ratios," *Review of Financial Studies* 17 (2004): 257–294. Jonathan Berk, Richard Stanton, and Josef Zechner, "Human Capital, Bankruptcy and Capital Structure," working paper, 2006.

if their claims cannot be verified. After all, managers, much like politicians, have an incentive to sound optimistic and confident about what they can achieve.

Because investors expect her to be biased, to convince the market Mazurek must take actions that give credible signals of her knowledge of the firm. That is, she must take actions that the market understands she would be unwilling to do unless her statements were true. This idea is more general than manager–investor communication; it is at the heart of much human interaction. We call it the **credibility principle**:

Claims in one's self-interest are credible only if they are supported by actions that would be too costly to take if the claims were untrue.

This principle is the essence behind the adage "Actions speak louder than words."

One way a firm can credibly convey its strength to investors is by making statements about its future prospects that investors and analysts can ultimately verify. If the penalties for intentionally deceiving investors are large, investors will generally believe such statements.[32]

For example, suppose Mazurek announces that pending long-term contracts from the Canadian, U.S., British, and Japanese governments will increase revenues for Beltran by 30% next year. Because this statement can be verified after the fact, it would be costly to make it if untrue. For deliberate misrepresentation, the Ontario Securities Commission (OSC) would likely fine the firm and file charges against Mazurek. The firm could also be sued by its investors. If Beltran is also listed on a U.S. stock exchange, the U.S. Securities and Exchange Commission (SEC) may also pursue charges and fines, which are generally larger than what is assessed in Canada. These large costs would likely outweigh any potential benefits to Mazurek and Beltran for temporarily misleading investors and boosting the share price. Thus investors will likely view the announcement as credible.

But what if Beltran cannot yet reveal specific details regarding its future prospects? Perhaps the contracts for the government orders have not yet been signed or cannot be disclosed for other reasons. How can Mazurek credibly communicate her positive information regarding the firm?

One strategy is to commit the firm to large future debt payments. If Mazurek is right, then Beltran will have no trouble making the debt payments. But if Mazurek is making false claims and the firm does not grow, Beltran will have trouble paying its creditors and will experience financial distress. This distress will be costly for the firm and also for Mazurek, who will likely lose her job. Thus Mazurek can use leverage as a way to convince investors that she does have information that the firm will grow, even if she cannot provide verifiable details about the sources of growth. Investors know that Beltran would be at risk of defaulting without growth opportunities, so they will interpret the additional leverage as a credible signal of the CEO's confidence. The use of leverage as a way to signal good information to investors is known as the **signalling theory of debt**.[33]

32. In the United States, the Sarbanes-Oxley Act of 2002 increased the penalties for securities fraud to include up to 10 years of imprisonment. The SEC and U.S. prosecutors have been diligent in pursuing such actions. Unfortunately, enforcement and penalties in Canada are often seen to be lacking. See the article by Tyler Hamilton, "Why the OSC So Rarely Gets Its Man" in the *Toronto Star*, December 1, 2007, for discussion of enforcement in Canada and the U.S. and examples of many Canadian cases that end with no conviction or minimal fines.

33. Such a theory is developed by Stephen Ross, "The Determination of Financial Structure: The Incentive-Signaling Approach," *Bell Journal of Economics* 8 (1977): 23–40.

EXAMPLE 16.6	DEBT SIGNALS STRENGTH

Problem

Suppose that Beltran currently uses all-equity financing, and that Beltran's market value in one year's time will be either $100 million or $50 million depending on the success of the new strategy. Currently, investors view the outcomes as equally likely, but Mazurek has information that success is virtually certain. Will leverage of $25 million make Mazurek's claims credible? How about leverage of $55 million?

Solution

If leverage is substantially less than $50 million, Beltran will have no risk of financial distress regardless of the outcome. As a result, there is no cost of leverage even if Mazurek does not have positive information. Thus leverage of $25 million would not be a credible signal of strength to investors.

However, leverage of $55 million is likely to be a credible signal. If Mazurek has no positive information, there is a significant chance that Beltran will face bankruptcy under this burden of debt. Thus Mazurek would be unlikely to agree to this amount of leverage unless she is certain about the firm's prospects.

ISSUING EQUITY AND ADVERSE SELECTION

Suppose a used-car dealer tells you he is willing to sell you a nice-looking sports car for $5000 less than its typical price. Rather than feel lucky, perhaps you should react with skepticism: If the dealer is willing to sell it for such a low price, there must be something wrong with the car—it is probably a "lemon."

The idea that buyers will be skeptical of a seller's motivation for selling was formalized by George Akerlof.[34] Akerlof showed that if the seller has private information about the quality of the car, then his *desire to sell* reveals the car is probably of low quality. Buyers are therefore reluctant to buy except at heavily discounted prices. Owners of high-quality cars

NOBEL PRIZE THE 2001 NOBEL PRIZE IN ECONOMICS

In 2001, George Akerlof, Michael Spence, and Joseph Stiglitz jointly received the Nobel Prize in economics for their analyses of markets with asymmetric information and adverse selection. In this chapter, we discuss the implications of their theory for firm capital structure. This theory, however, has much broader applications. As described on the Nobel Prize Web site (http://nobelprize.org):

Many markets are characterized by asymmetric information: Actors on one side of the market have much better information than those on the other. Borrowers know more than lenders about their repayment prospects, man-

agers and boards know more than shareholders about the firm's profitability, and prospective clients know more than insurance companies about their accident risk. During the 1970s, this year's Laureates laid the foundation for a general theory of markets with asymmetric information. Applications have been abundant, ranging from traditional agricultural markets to modern financial markets. The Laureates' contributions form the core of modern information economics.

© The Nobel Foundation

---

34. "The Market for Lemons: Quality, Uncertainty, and the Market Mechanism," *Quarterly Journal of Economics* 84 (1970): 488–500.

are reluctant to sell because they know buyers will think they are selling a lemon and offer only a low price. Consequently, the quality and prices of cars sold in the used-car market are both low. This result is referred to as **adverse selection**: The selection of cars sold in the used-car market is worse than average.

Adverse selection extends beyond the used-car market. In fact, it applies in any setting in which the seller has more information than the buyer. Adverse selection leads to the **lemons principle**:

When a seller has private information about the value of a good, buyers will discount the price they are willing to pay due to adverse selection.

We can apply this principle to the market for equity.[35] Suppose the owner of a start-up company tells you that his firm is a wonderful investment opportunity and then offers to sell you 70% of his stake in the firm. He states that he is selling *only* because he wants to diversify. Although you appreciate this desire, you also suspect the owner may be eager to sell such a large stake because he has negative information about the firm's future prospects. That is, he may be trying to cash out before the bad news becomes known.[36]

As with the used-car dealer, a firm owner's desire to sell equity may lead you to question how good an investment opportunity it really is. Based on the lemons principle, you therefore reduce the price you are willing to pay. This discount of the price due to adverse selection is a potential cost of issuing equity, and it may make owners with good information refrain from issuing equity.

EXAMPLE **16.7**	ADVERSE SELECTION IN EQUITY MARKETS

Problem

Puchatek stock is worth either $100 per share, $80 per share, or $60 per share. Investors believe each case is equally likely, and the current share price is equal to the average value of $80.

Suppose the CEO of Puchatek announces he will sell most of his holdings of the stock to diversify. Diversifying is worth 10% of the share price—that is, the CEO would be willing to receive 10% less than the shares are worth to achieve the benefits of diversification. If investors believe the CEO knows the true value, how will the share price change if he tries to sell? Will the CEO sell at the new share price?

Solution

If the true value of the shares were $100, the CEO would not be willing to sell at the market price of $80 per share, which would be 20% below their true value. So, if the CEO tries to sell, shareholders can conclude the shares are worth either $80 or $60. In that case, the share price should fall to the average value of $70. But again, if the true value were $80, the CEO would be willing to sell for $72, but not $70 per share. So, if he still tries to sell, investors will know the true value is $60 per share. Thus the CEO will sell only if the true value is the lowest possible price, $60 per share. If the CEO knows the firm's stock is worth $100 or $80 per share, he will not sell.

---

35. See Hayne Leland and David Pyle, "Information Asymmetries, Financial Structure and Financial Intermediation," *Journal of Finance* 32 (1977): 371–387.

36. Again, if the owner of the firm (or the car, in the earlier example) has very specific information that can be verified ex-post, there are potential legal consequences for not revealing that information to a buyer. Generally, however, there is a great deal of subtle information the seller might have that would be impossible to verify.

In explaining adverse selection, we considered an owner of a firm selling his or her *own* shares. What if a manager of the firm decides to sell securities on the *firm's* behalf? If the securities are sold at a price below their true value, the buyer's windfall represents a cost for the firm's current shareholders. Acting on behalf of the current shareholders, the manager may be unwilling to sell.[37]

Let's consider a simple example. Gentec is a biotech firm with no debt, and its 20 million shares are currently trading at $10 per share, for a total market value of $200 million. Based on the prospects for one of Gentec's new drugs, management believes the true value of the company is $300 million, or $15 per share. Management believes the share price will reflect this higher value after the clinical trials for the drug are concluded next year.

Gentec has already announced plans to raise $60 million from investors to build a new research lab. It can raise the funds today by issuing 6 million new shares at the current price of $10 per share. In that case, after the good news comes out, the value of the firm's assets will be $300 million (from the existing assets) plus $60 million (new lab), for a total value of $360 million. With 26 million shares outstanding, the new share price will be $360 million ÷ 26 million shares = $13.85 per share.

But suppose Gentec waits for the good news to come out and the share price to rise to $15 *before* issuing the new shares. At that time, the firm will be able to raise the $60 million by selling 4 million shares. The firm's assets will again be worth a total of $360 million, but Gentec will have only 24 million shares outstanding, which is consistent with the share price of $360 million ÷ 24 million shares = $15 per share.

Thus issuing new shares when management knows they are underpriced is costly for the original shareholders. Their shares will be worth only $13.85 rather than $15. As a result, if Gentec's managers care primarily about the firm's current shareholders, they will be reluctant to sell securities at a price that is below their true value. If they believe the shares are underpriced, managers will prefer to wait until after the share price rises to issue equity.

This preference not to issue equity that is underpriced leads us to the same lemons problem we had before: Managers who know securities have a high value will not sell, and those who know they have a low value will sell. Due to this adverse selection, investors will be willing to pay only a low price for the securities. The lemons problem creates a cost for firms that need to raise capital from investors to fund new investments. If they try to issue equity, investors will discount the price they are willing to pay to reflect the possibility that managers are privy to bad news.

IMPLICATIONS FOR EQUITY ISSUANCE

Adverse selection has a number of important implications for equity issuance. First and foremost, the lemons principle directly implies that

1. *The stock price declines on the announcement of an equity issue.*

When a firm issues equity, it signals to investors that its equity may be overpriced. As a result, investors are willing to pay less for the equity and the stock price declines. Numerous studies on U.S. companies have confirmed this result, finding that the stock price

---

37. Stewart Myers and Nicholas Majluf demonstrated this result, and a number of its implications for capital structure, in an influential paper, "Corporate Financing and Investment Decisions When Firms Have Information that Investors Do Not Have," *Journal of Financial Economics* 13 (1984): 187–221.

falls about 3% on average on the announcement of an equity issue by a publicly traded firm.[38]

As was true for Gentec, managers issuing equity have an incentive to delay the issue until any news that might positively affect the stock price becomes public. In contrast, there is no incentive to delay the issue if managers expect negative news to come out. These incentives lead to the following pattern:

2. *The stock price tends to rise prior to the announcement of an equity issue.*

This result is also supported empirically, as illustrated in Figure 16.3 using data from a study by Deborah Lucas and Robert McDonald. They found that stocks with equity issues outperformed the market by almost 50% in the year and a half prior to the announcement of the issue.

Managers may also try to avoid the price decline associated with adverse selection by issuing equity at times when they have the smallest informational advantage over investors. For example, because a great deal of information is released to investors at the time of earnings announcements, equity issues are often timed to occur immediately after these announcements. That is,

3. *Firms tend to issue equity when information asymmetries are minimized, such as immediately after earnings announcements.*[39]

IMPLICATIONS FOR CAPITAL STRUCTURE

Because managers find it costly to issue equity that is underpriced, they may seek alternative forms of financing. While debt issues may also suffer from adverse selection, because the value of low-risk debt is not very sensitive to managers' private information about the firm (but is instead determined mainly by interest rates), the degree of underpricing will tend to be smaller for debt than for equity. Of course, a firm can avoid underpricing altogether by financing investment using its cash (retained earnings) when possible. Thus

Managers who perceive the firm's equity is underpriced will have a preference to fund investment using retained earnings or debt, rather than equity.

The converse to this statement is also true: Managers who perceive the firm's equity to be overpriced will prefer to issue equity, as opposed to issuing debt or using retained earnings, to fund investment. However, due to the negative stock price reaction when issuing equity, it is less likely that equity will be overpriced. In fact, absent other motives to issue equity, if both managers and investors behave rationally, the price drop upon announcement may be sufficient to deter managers from issuing equity except as a last resort.

The idea that managers will prefer to use retained earnings first, and will issue new equity only as a last resort, is often referred to as the **pecking order hypothesis**, put forth

---

38. See Paul Asquith and David Mullins, "Equity Issues and Offering Dilution," *Journal of Financial Economics* 15 (1986): 61–89; Ronald Masulis and Ashok Korwar, "Seasoned Equity Offerings: An Empirical Investigation," *Journal of Financial Economics* 15 (1986): 91–118; and Wayne Mikkelson and Megan Partch, "Valuation Effects of Security Offerings and the Issuance Process," *Journal of Financial Economics* 15 (1986): 31–60.

39. In a 1991 study, Robert Korajczyk, Deborah Lucas, and Robert McDonald confirmed this timing and reported that the negative stock price reaction is smallest immediately after earnings announcements, and becomes larger as the amount of time since the last earnings announcement increases ("The Effect of Information Releases on the Pricing and Timing of Equity Issues," *Review of Financial Studies* 4 (1991): 685–708).

FIGURE 16.3

Stock Returns Before and After an Equity Issue

Stocks tend to rise (relative to the market) before an equity issue is announced. Upon announcement, stock prices fall on average. This figure shows the average return relative to the market before and after announcements using data from Deborah Lucas and Robert McDonald, "Equity Issues and Stock Price Dynamics," *Journal of Finance* 45 (1990): 1019–1043.

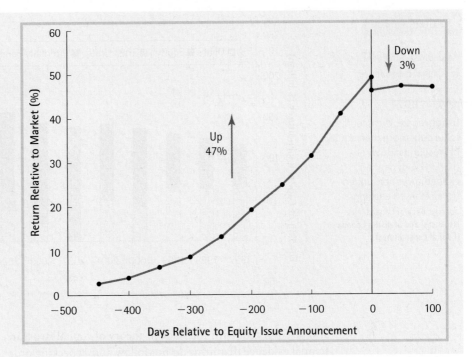

by Stewart Myers.[40] While difficult to test directly, this hypothesis is consistent with the aggregate data on corporate financing in Figure 16.4, which shows that firms tend to be net repurchasers (rather than issuers) of equity, whereas they are issuers of debt. Moreover, the vast majority of investment is funded by retained earnings, with net external financing amounting to less than 30% of capital expenditures in most years. These observations can

EXAMPLE 16.8

THE PECKING ORDER OF FINANCING ALTERNATIVES

Problem

Axon Industries needs to raise $10 million for a new investment project. If the firm issues one-year debt, it may have to pay an interest rate of 7%, although Axon's managers believe that 6% would be a fair rate given the level of risk. However, if the firm issues equity, they believe the equity may be underpriced by 5%. What is the cost to current shareholders of financing the project out of retained earnings, debt, and equity?

Solution

If the firm spends $10 million out of retained earnings, rather than paying that money out to shareholders as a dividend, the cost to shareholders is $10 million. Using debt costs the firm $10 × (1.07) = $10.7 million in one year, which has a present value based on management's view of the firm's risk of $10.7 ÷ (1.06) = $10.094 million. Finally, if equity is underpriced by 5%, then to raise $10 million the firm will need to issue $10.5 million in new equity. Thus, the cost to existing shareholders will be $10.5 million. Comparing the three, retained earnings are the cheapest source of funds, followed by debt, and finally by equity.

---

40. Stewart Myers, "The Capital Structure Puzzle," *Journal of Finance* 39 (1984): 575–592.

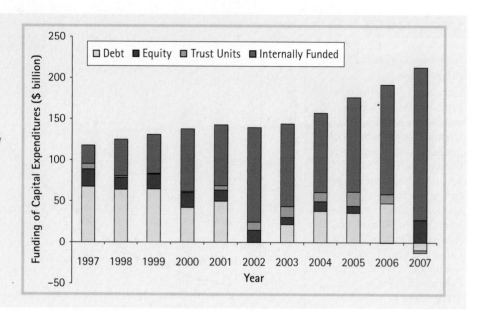

FIGURE 16.4

Aggregate Sources of Funding for Capital Expenditures, Canadian Corporations, 1997–2007

In aggregate, firms tend to issue debt more than equity or trust units. But more than 60% of capital expenditures are funded from retained earnings.

Sources: Bank of Canada (Net Issuances) and Statistics Canada (Capital Expenditures).

also be consistent with the tradeoff theory of capital structure, however, and there is substantial evidence that firms do not follow a *strict* pecking order, as firms often issue equity even when borrowing is possible.[41]

Aside from a general preference for using retained earnings or debt as a source of funding rather than equity, adverse selection costs do not lead to a clear prediction regarding a firm's overall capital structure. Instead, these costs imply that managers' choice of financing will depend, in addition to the other costs and benefits discussed in this chapter, on whether they believe the firm is currently underpriced or overpriced by investors. This dependence is sometimes referred to as the **market timing** view of capital structure: The firm's overall capital structure depends in part on the market conditions that existed when it sought funding in the past. As a result, similar firms in the same industry might end up with very different, but nonetheless optimal, capital structures.[42]

Indeed, even the pecking order hypothesis does not provide a clear prediction regarding capital structure on its own. While it argues that firms should prefer to use retained earnings, then debt, and then equity as funding sources, retained earnings are merely another form of equity financing (they increase the value of equity while the value of debt remains unchanged). Therefore, firms might have low leverage either because they are unable to issue additional debt and are forced to rely on equity financing or because they are sufficiently profitable to finance all investment using retained earnings.

CONCEPT CHECK

1. How does asymmetric information explain the negative stock price reaction to the announcement of an equity issue?

2. Why might firms prefer to fund investments using retained earnings or debt rather than issuing equity?

---

41. See Mark Leary and Michael Roberts, "Financial Slack and Tests of the Pecking Order's Financing Hierarchy," *Journal of Financial Economics*, forthcoming.

42. For evidence suggestive of the idea that firms' capital structures result from past attempts to time the equity market, see Jeffrey A. Wurgler and Malcolm P. Baker, "Market Timing and Capital Structure," *Journal of Finance* 57 (2002): 1–32.

16.9   CAPITAL STRUCTURE: THE BOTTOM LINE

Over the past three chapters, we have examined a number of factors that might influence a firm's choice of capital structure. What is the bottom line for a financial manager?

The most important insight regarding capital structure goes back to Modigliani and Miller: With perfect capital markets, a firm's security choice alters the risk of the firm's equity, but it does not change its value or the amount it can raise from outside investors. Thus the optimal capital structure depends on market imperfections, such as taxes, financial distress costs, agency costs, and asymmetric information.

Of all the different possible imperfections that drive capital structure, the most clear-cut, and possibly the most significant, is taxes. The interest tax shield allows firms to repay investors and avoid the corporate tax. Each dollar of permanent debt financing provides the firm with a tax shield worth τ^* dollars, where τ^* is the effective tax advantage of debt. For firms with consistent taxable income, this benefit of leverage is important to consider.

While firms should use leverage to shield their income from taxes, how much of their income should they shield? If leverage is too high, there is an increased risk that a firm may not be able to meet its debt obligations and will be forced to default. While the risk of default is not itself a problem, financial distress may lead to other consequences that reduce the value of the firm. Firms must, therefore, balance the tax benefits of debt against the costs of financial distress.

Agency costs and benefits of leverage are also important determinants of capital structure. Too much debt can motivate managers and equity holders to take excessive risks or under-invest in a firm. When free cash flows are high, too little leverage may encourage wasteful spending. This effect may be especially important for firms in countries lacking strong protections for investors against self-interested managers.[43] When agency costs are significant, short-term debt may be the most attractive form of external financing. This may help explain the higher use of debt in Canada than in the United States. Also, different industry sectors are predominant in the Canadian economy.

A firm must also consider the potential signalling and adverse selection consequences of its financing choice. Because bankruptcy is costly for managers, increasing leverage can signal managers' confidence in the firm's ability to meet its debt obligations. When managers have different views regarding the value of securities, managers can benefit current shareholders by issuing securities that are the most overpriced. However, investors will respond to this incentive by lowering the price they are willing to pay for securities that the firm issues, leading to negative price reaction when a new issue is announced. This effect is most pronounced for equity issues, because the value of equity is most sensitive to the managers' private information. To avoid this "lemons cost," firms should rely first on retained earnings, then debt, and finally equity. This pecking order of financing alternatives will be most important when managers are likely to have a great deal of private information regarding the value of the firm.

Finally, it is important to recognize that because actively changing a firm's capital structure (for example, by selling or repurchasing shares or bonds) entails transaction costs, firms may be unlikely to change their capital structures unless they depart significantly from the optimal level. As a result, most changes to a firm's debt-equity ratio are likely to occur passively, as the market value of the firm's equity fluctuates with changes in the firm's stock price.[44]

---

43. See Joseph Fan, Sheridan Titman, and Garry Twite, "An International Comparison of Capital Structure and Debt Maturity Choices," working paper, University of Texas–Austin, 2003.

44. See I. Strebulaev, "Do Tests of Capital Structure Theory Mean What They Say?," *Journal of Finance* 62 (2007): 1747–1787.

CONCEPT CHECK

1. Consider the differences in leverage across industries shown in Figure 15.7. To what extent can you account for these differences?

2. What are some reasons firms might depart from their optimal capital structure, at least in the short run?

SUMMARY

1. In the Modigliani-Miller setting, leverage may result in bankruptcy, but bankruptcy alone does not reduce the value of the firm. With perfect capital markets, bankruptcy shifts ownership from the equity holders to debt holders without changing the total value available to all investors.

2. Large Canadian firms can file for protection under the Companies' Creditors Arrangement Act (CCAA) or for bankruptcy under the Bankruptcy and Insolvency Act (BIA). U.S. firms can file for bankruptcy protection under the provisions of the 1978 Bankruptcy Reform Act.
   a. Under BIA (or U.S. Chapter 7 liquidation), a trustee oversees the liquidation of the firm's assets.
   b. Under a CCAA filing (or U.S. Chapter 11 reorganization), management attempts to develop a plan of arrangement that will improve operations and maximize value to investors. If the firm cannot successfully reorganize, it may be liquidated under the BIA (or Chapter 7 in the United States).

3. Bankruptcy is a costly process that imposes both direct and indirect costs on a firm and its investors.
   a. Direct costs include the costs of experts and advisors such as lawyers, accountants, appraisers, and investment bankers hired by the firm or its creditors during the bankruptcy process.
   b. Indirect costs include the loss of customers, suppliers, employees, or receivables during bankruptcy. Firms also incur indirect costs when they need to sell assets at distressed prices.

4. When securities are fairly priced, the original shareholders of a firm pay the present value of the costs associated with bankruptcy and financial distress.

5. According to the tradeoff theory, the total value of a levered firm equals the value of the firm without leverage plus the present value of the tax savings from debt minus the present value of financial distress costs:

$$V^L = V^U + PV(\text{Interest Tax Shield}) - PV(\text{Financial Distress Costs}) \qquad (16.1)$$

   Optimal leverage is the level of debt that maximizes V^L.

6. Agency costs arise when there are conflicts of interest between stakeholders. When a firm faces financial distress, the following may occur.
   a. Asset Substitution: Shareholders can gain by undertaking a negative-NPV project if it is sufficiently risky.
   b. Debt Overhang: A firm may be unable to finance new positive-NPV projects.
   c. Cashing Out: Shareholders have an incentive to liquidate assets at prices below their market values and distribute the proceeds as a dividend.

7. Leverage has agency benefits and can improve incentives for managers to run a firm more efficiently and effectively due to
   a. Increased ownership concentration: Managers with higher ownership concentration are more likely to work hard and less likely to avail themselves of corporate perks.

b. Reduced free cash flow: Firms with less free cash flow are less likely to pursue wasteful investments.

c. Reduced managerial entrenchment and increased commitment: The threat of financial distress and being fired may commit managers more fully to pursue strategies that improve operations.

8. The tradeoff theory may be extended to include agency costs. The value of a firm, including agency costs and benefits, is:

$$V^L = V^U + PV(\text{Interest Tax Shield}) - PV(\text{Financial Distress Costs})$$
$$- PV(\text{Agency Costs of Debt}) + PV(\text{Agency Benefits of Debt}) \qquad (16.3)$$

Optimal leverage is the level of debt that maximizes V^L.

9. When managers have better information than investors, there is asymmetric information. Given asymmetric information, managers may use leverage as a credible signal to investors of the firm's ability to generate future free cash flow.

10. According to the lemons principle, when managers have private information about the value of a firm, investors will discount the price they are willing to pay for a new equity issue due to adverse selection.

11. Managers are more likely to sell equity when they know a firm is overvalued. As a result,

a. The stock price declines when a firm announces an equity issue.

b. The stock price tends to rise prior to the announcement of an equity issue because managers tend to delay equity issues until after good news becomes public.

c. Firms tend to issue equity when information asymmetries are minimized.

d. Managers who perceive that the firm's equity is underpriced will have a preference to fund investment using retained earnings or debt, rather than equity. This result is called the pecking order hypothesis.

12. There are numerous frictions that drive the firm's optimal capital structure. But if there are substantial transactions costs to changing the firm's capital structure, most changes in the firm's leverage are likely to occur passively, based on fluctuations in the firm's stock price.

KEY TERMS

adverse selection *p. 572*
agency costs *p. 558*
asset substitution problem *p. 559*
asymmetric information *p. 569*
Bankruptcy and Insolvency Act (BIA)
  p. 548
Chapter 7 *p. 549*
Chapter 11 *p. 549*
Companies' Creditors Arrangement Act
  (CCAA) *p. 548*
credibility principle *p. 570*
debt covenants *p. 563*
debt overhang *p. 559*
debtor-in-possession financing (DIP) *p. 551*
default *p. 545*
economic distress *p. 547*

financial distress *p. 545*
free cash flow hypothesis *p. 566*
lemons principle *p. 572*
management entrenchment *p. 563*
management entrenchment theory *p. 569*
market timing *p. 576*
monitor *p. 548*
moral hazard *p. 566*
pecking order hypothesis *p. 574*
plan of arrangement *p. 548*
prepackaged bankruptcy *p. 550*
signalling theory of debt *p. 570*
stay *p. 548*
tradeoff theory *p. 555*
under-investment problem *p. 559*
workout *p. 550*

PROBLEMS

The problems marked in green can be found on MyFinanceLab at www.myfinancelab.com. Visit your MyFinanceLab for additional practice. An asterisk (*) indicates problems with a higher level of difficulty. Additional readings for this chapter may be found in the Textbook Resources section on MyFinanceLab.

Default and Bankruptcy in a Perfect Market

1. Gladstone Corporation is about to launch a new product. Depending on the success of the new product, Gladstone may have one of four values next year: $150 million, $135 million, $95 million, and $80 million. These outcomes are all equally likely, and this risk is diversifiable. Gladstone will not make any payouts to investors during the year. Suppose the risk-free interest rate is 5% and assume perfect capital markets.

    a. What is the initial value of Gladstone's equity without leverage?

    Now suppose Gladstone has zero-coupon debt with a $100 million face value due next year.

    b. What is the initial value of Gladstone's debt?

    c. What is the yield-to-maturity of the debt? What is its expected return?

    d. What is the initial value of Gladstone's equity? What is Gladstone's total value with leverage?

2. Bartek Industries has no cash and a debt obligation of $36 million that is now due. The market value of Bartek's assets is $81 million, and the firm has no other liabilities. Assume perfect capital markets.

    a. Suppose Bartek has 10 million shares outstanding. What is Bartek's current share price?

    b. How many new shares must Bartek issue to raise the capital needed to pay its debt obligation?

    c. After repaying the debt, what will Bartek's share price be?

The Costs of Bankruptcy and Financial Distress

3. When a firm defaults on its debt, debt holders often receive less than 50% of the amount they are owed. Is the difference between the amount debt holders are owed and the amount they receive a *cost* of bankruptcy?

4. Which type of firm is more likely to experience a loss of customers in the event of financial distress:

    a. Campbell Soup Company or Intuit Inc. (a maker of accounting software)?

    b. Allstate Corporation (an insurance company) or Reebok International (a footwear and clothing firm)?

5. Which type of asset is more likely to be liquidated for close to its full market value in the event of financial distress:

    a. An office building or a brand name?

    b. Product inventory or raw materials?

    c. Patent rights or engineering "know-how"?

6. Suppose Tefco Corp. has a value of $100 million if it continues to operate, but has outstanding debt of $120 million that is now due. If the firm declares bankruptcy, bankruptcy costs will equal $20 million, and the remaining $80 million will go to creditors. Instead of declaring bankruptcy, management proposes to exchange the firm's debt for a fraction of its equity in a workout. What fraction of the firm's equity would it need to offer to creditors for the workout to be successful?

7. You have received two job offers. Firm A offers to pay you $85,000 per year for two years. Firm B offers to pay you $90,000 per year for two years. Both jobs are equivalent.

    a. If both contracts are certain, which is more attractive?

    Suppose that firm A's contract is certain, but that firm B has a 50% chance of going bankrupt next year. In that event, it will cancel your contract and pay you the lowest amount possible for you not to quit. If you did quit, you expect you could find a new job paying $85,000 per year, but you would be unemployed for 3 months while you search for it.

    b. What is the least firm B can pay you next year in order to match what you would earn if you quit?

    c. Given your answer to part b, and assuming your cost of capital is 5%, which offer pays you a higher present value of your expected wage?

    d. Based on this example, discuss one reason why firms with a higher risk of bankruptcy may need to offer higher wages to attract employees.

Financial Distress Costs and Firm Value

8. As in Problem 1, Gladstone Corporation is about to launch a new product. Depending on the success of the new product, Gladstone may have one of four values next year: $150 million, $135 million, $95 million, and $80 million. These outcomes are all equally likely, and this risk is diversifiable. Suppose the risk-free interest rate is 5% and that, in the event of default, 25% of the value of Gladstone's assets will be lost to bankruptcy costs. (Ignore all other market imperfections, such as taxes.)

    a. What is the initial value of Gladstone's equity without leverage?

    Now suppose Gladstone has zero-coupon debt with a $100 million face value due next year.

    b. What is the initial value of Gladstone's debt?

    c. What is the yield-to-maturity of the debt? What is its expected return?

    d. What is the initial value of Gladstone's equity? What is Gladstone's total value with leverage?

    Suppose Gladstone has 10 million shares outstanding and no debt at the start of the year.

    e. If Gladstone does not issue debt, what is its share price?

    f. If Gladstone issues debt of $100 million due next year and uses the proceeds to repurchase shares, what will its share price be? Why does your answer differ from that in part e?

9. Richmond Industries issued 1.5 million new shares of equity to raise $50 million to finance a new investment. The equity just started trading on the stock market and investors have learned that Richmond expects to earn free cash flows of $10 million each year in perpetuity. Richmond has 5 million shares outstanding, and it has no other assets or opportunities. Suppose the appropriate discount rate for Richmond's future free cash flows is 8% and the only capital market imperfections are corporate taxes and financial distress costs.

    a. What is the NPV of Richmond's investment?

    b. What is Richmond's share price today?

    Suppose Richmond borrows the $50 million instead and thus there are only 3.5 million shares outstanding. The firm will pay interest only on this loan each year, and it will maintain an outstanding balance of $50 million on the loan. Suppose that Richmond's corporate tax rate is 40% and expected free cash flows are still $10 million each year.

    c. What is Richmond's share price today if the investment is financed with debt?

    Now suppose that with leverage, Richmond's expected free cash flows will decline to $9 million per year due to reduced sales and other financial distress costs. Assume that the appropriate discount rate for Richmond's future free cash flows is still 8%.

    d. What is Richmond's share price today given the financial distress costs of leverage?

10. You work for a large car manufacturer that is currently financially healthy. Your manager feels that the firm should take on more debt because it can thereby reduce the expense of car warranties. To quote your manager, "If we go bankrupt, we don't have to service the warranties. We therefore have lower bankruptcy costs than most corporations, so we should use more debt." Is he right?

Optimal Capital Structure: The Tradeoff Theory

11. Apple Computer has no debt. As Problem 15.21 makes clear, by issuing debt Apple can generate a very large tax shield potentially worth over $10 billion. Given Apple's success, one would be hard pressed to argue that Apple's management are naive and unaware of this huge potential to create value. A more likely explanation is that issuing debt would entail other costs. What might these costs be?

12. Hawar International is a shipping firm with a current share price of $5.50 and 10 million shares outstanding. Suppose Hawar announces plans to lower its corporate taxes by borrowing $20 million and repurchasing shares.

    a. With perfect capital markets, what will the share price be after this announcement?

    Suppose that Hawar pays a corporate tax rate of 30% and that shareholders expect the change in debt to be permanent.

    b. If the only imperfection is corporate taxes, what will the share price be after this announcement?

    c. Suppose the only imperfections are corporate taxes and financial distress costs. If the share price rises to $5.75 after this announcement, what is the PV of financial distress costs Hawar will incur as the result of this new debt?

13. Your firm is considering issuing one-year debt, and has come up with the following estimates of the value of the interest tax shield and the probability of distress for different levels of debt:

	Debt Level ($ million)						
	0	**40**	**50**	**60**	**70**	**80**	**90**
PV(interest tax shield, $ million)	0.00	0.76	0.95	1.14	1.33	1.52	1.71
Probability of Financial Distress	0%	0%	1%	2%	7%	16%	31%

Suppose the firm has a beta of zero, so that the appropriate discount rate for financial distress costs is the risk-free rate of 5%. Which level of debt above is optimal if, in the event of distress, the firm will have distress costs equal to

    a. $2 million?   b. $5 million?   c. $25 million?

14. Marpor Industries has no debt and expects to generate free cash flows of $16 million each year. Marpor believes that if it permanently increases its level of debt to $40 million, the risk of financial distress may cause it to lose some customers and receive less favourable terms from its suppliers. As a result, Marpor's expected free cash flows with debt will be only $15 million per year. Suppose Marpor's tax rate is 35%, the risk-free rate is 5%, the expected return of the market is 15%, and the beta of Marpor's free cash flows is 1.10 (with or without leverage).

    a. Estimate Marpor's value without leverage.

    b. Estimate Marpor's value with the new leverage.

15. Real estate purchases are often financed with at least 80% debt. Most corporations, however, have less than 50% debt financing. Provide an explanation for this difference using the tradeoff theory.

16. On May 14, 2008, General Motors paid a dividend of 25¢ per share. During the same quarter GM lost a staggering $15.5 billion, or $27.33 per share. Seven months later the company asked for billions of dollars of government aid and ultimately declared bankruptcy just over a year later, on June 1, 2009. At that point a share of GM was worth only a little more than a dollar.

    a. If you ignore the possibility of a government bailout, the decision to pay a dividend, given how close the company was to financial distress, is an example of what kind of cost?

    *b. How would your answer to part a change if GM executives anticipated that there was a possibility of a government bailout should the firm be forced to declare bankruptcy?

17. Dynron Corporation's primary business is natural gas transportation using its vast gas pipeline network. Dynron's assets currently have a market value of $150 million. The firm is exploring the possibility of raising $50 million by selling part of its pipeline network and investing the $50 million in a fibre optic network to generate revenues by selling high-speed network bandwidth. While this new investment is expected to increase profits, it will also substantially increase Dynron's risk. If Dynron is levered, would this investment be more or less attractive to equity holders than if Dynron had no debt?

18. Consider a firm whose only asset is a plot of vacant land, and whose only liability is debt of $15 million due in one year. If left vacant, the land will be worth $10 million in one year. Alternatively, the firm can develop the land at an upfront cost of $20 million. The developed land will be worth $35 million in one year. Suppose the risk-free interest rate is 10%, assume all cash flows are risk free, and assume there are no taxes.

    a. If the firm chooses not to develop the land, what is the value of the firm's equity today? What is the value of the debt today?

    b. What is the NPV of developing the land?

    c. Suppose the firm raises $20 million from equity holders to develop the land. If the firm develops the land, what is the value of the firm's equity today? What is the value of the firm's debt today?

    d. Given your answer to part c, would equity holders be willing to provide the $20 million needed to develop the land?

EXCEL

19. Sarvon Systems has a debt-equity ratio of 1.2, an equity beta of 2.0, and a debt beta of 0.30. It currently is evaluating the following projects, none of which would change the firm's volatility (amounts in $ millions):

Project	A	B	C	D	E
Investment	100	50	85	30	75
NPV	20	6	10	15	18

    a. Which project will equity holders agree to fund?

    b. What is the cost to the firm of the debt overhang?

20. Zymase is a biotechnology start-up firm. Researchers at Zymase must choose one of three different research strategies. The payoffs (after-tax) and their likelihood for each strategy are shown below. The risk of each project is diversifiable.

Strategy	Probability	Payoff ($ million)
A	100%	75
B	50%	140
	50%	0
C	10%	300
	90%	40

a. Which project has the highest expected payoff?

b. Suppose Zymase has debt of $40 million due at the time of the project's payoff. Which project has the highest expected payoff for equity holders?

c. Suppose Zymase has debt of $110 million due at the time of the project's payoff. Which project has the highest expected payoff for equity holders?

d. If management chooses the strategy that maximizes the payoff to equity holders, what is the expected agency cost to the firm from having $40 million in debt due? What is the expected agency cost to the firm from having $110 million in debt due?

Motivating Managers:
The Agency
Benefits of Leverage

21. You own your own firm, and you want to raise $30 million to fund an expansion. Currently, you own 100% of the firm's equity, and the firm has no debt. To raise the $30 million solely through equity, you will need to sell two-thirds of the firm. However, you would prefer to maintain at least a 50% equity stake in the firm to retain control.

a. If you borrow $20 million, what fraction of the equity will you need to sell to raise the remaining $10 million? (Assume perfect capital markets.)

b. What is the smallest amount you can borrow to raise the $30 million without giving up control? (Assume perfect capital markets.)

EXCEL   22. Empire Industries forecasts net income this coming year as shown below (in thousands of dollars):

EBIT	$1,000
Interest expense	0
Income before tax	1,000
Taxes	−350
Net income	$650

Approximately $200,000 of Empire's earnings will be needed to make new, positive-NPV investments. Unfortunately, Empire's managers are expected to waste 10% of its net income on needless perks, pet projects, and other expenditures that do not contribute to the firm. All remaining income will be returned to shareholders through dividends and share repurchases.

a. What are the two benefits of debt financing for Empire?

b. By how much would each $1 of interest expense reduce Empire's dividend and share repurchases?

c. What is the increase in the *total* funds Empire will pay to investors for each $1 of interest expense?

23. Ralston Enterprises has assets that will have a market value in one year as shown below:

Probability	1%	6%	24%	38%	24%	6%	1%
Value ($ million)	70	80	90	100	110	120	130

That is, there is a 1% chance the assets will be worth $70 million, a 6% chance the assets will be worth $80 million, and so on. Suppose the CEO is contemplating a decision that will benefit her personally but will reduce the value of the firm's assets by $10 million. The CEO is likely to proceed with this decision unless it substantially increases the firm's risk of bankruptcy.

    a. If Ralston has debt due of $75 million in one year, the CEO's decision will increase the probability of bankruptcy by what percentage?

    b. What level of debt provides the CEO with the biggest incentive not to proceed with the decision?

Agency Costs and the Tradeoff Theory

24. Although the major benefit of debt financing—the tax shield—is easy to observe, many of the indirect costs of debt financing can be quite subtle and difficult to observe. Describe some of these costs.

25. If it is managed efficiently, Remel Inc. will have assets with a market value of $50 million, $100 million, or $150 million next year, with each outcome being equally likely. However, managers may engage in wasteful empire building, which will reduce the firm's market value by $5 million in all cases. Managers may also increase the risk of the firm, changing the probability of each outcome to 50%, 10%, and 40%, respectively.

    a. What is the expected value of Remel's assets if it is run efficiently?

Suppose managers will engage in empire building unless that behaviour increases the likelihood of bankruptcy. They will choose the risk of the firm to maximize the expected payoff to equity holders.

    b. Suppose Remel has debt due in one year as shown below. For each case, indicate whether managers will engage in empire building, and whether they will increase risk. What is the expected value of Remel's assets in each case?

        i. $44 million   iii. $90 million

        ii. $49 million   iv. $99 million

    c. Suppose the tax savings from the debt, after including investor taxes, is equal to 10% of the expected payoff of the debt. The proceeds from the debt, as well as the value of any tax savings, will be paid out to shareholders immediately as a dividend when the debt is issued. Which debt level in part b is optimal for Remel?

26. Which of the following industries have low optimal debt levels according to the tradeoff theory? Which have high optimal levels of debt?

    a. Tobacco firms

    b. Accounting firms

    c. Mature restaurant chains

    d. Lumber companies

    e. Cell phone manufacturers

27. According to the managerial entrenchment theory, managers choose capital structure so as to preserve their control of the firm. On the one hand, debt is costly for managers because they risk losing control in the event of default. On the other hand, if they do not take advantage of the tax shield provided by debt, they risk losing control through a hostile takeover.

Suppose a firm expects to generate free cash flows of $90 million per year and the discount rate for these cash flows is 10%. The firm pays a tax rate of 40%. A raider is poised to take over the firm and finance it with $750 million in permanent debt. The raider will generate the same free cash flows, and the takeover attempt will be successful if the raider can offer a premium of 20% over the current value of the firm. What level of permanent debt will the firm choose, according to the managerial entrenchment hypothesis?

28. Info Systems Technology (IST) manufactures microprocessor chips for use in appliances and other applications. IST has no debt and 100 million shares outstanding. The correct price for these shares is either $14.50 or $12.50 per share. Investors view both possibilities as equally likely, so the shares currently trade for $13.50.

    IST must raise $500 million to build a new production facility. Because the firm would suffer a large loss of both customers and engineering talent in the event of financial distress, managers believe that if IST borrows the $500 million, the present value of financial distress costs will exceed any tax benefits by $20 million. At the same time, because investors believe that managers know the correct share price, IST faces a lemons problem if it attempts to raise the $500 million by issuing equity.

    a. Suppose that if IST issues equity, the share price will remain $13.50. To maximize the long-term share price of the firm once its true value is known, would managers choose to issue equity or borrow the $500 million if

        i. They know the correct value of the shares is $12.50?

        ii. They know the correct value of the shares is $14.50?

    b. Given your answer to part a, what should investors conclude if IST issues equity? What will happen to the share price?

    c. Given your answer to part a, what should investors conclude if IST issues debt? What will happen to the share price in that case?

    d. How would your answers change if there were no distress costs, but only tax benefits of leverage?

29. During the dot-com boom of the late 1990s, the stock prices of many Internet firms soared to extreme heights. As CEO of such a firm, if you believed your stock was significantly overvalued, would using your stock to acquire non-Internet stocks be a wise idea, even if you had to pay a small premium over their fair market value to make the acquisition?

*30. "We R Toys" (WRT) is considering expanding into new geographic markets. The expansion will have the same business risk as WRT's existing assets. The expansion will require an initial investment of $50 million and is expected to generate perpetual EBIT of $20 million per year. After the initial investment, future capital expenditures are expected to equal depreciation (assumed equal to CCA charges), and no further additions to net working capital are anticipated.

    WRT's existing capital structure is composed of $500 million in equity and $300 million in debt (market values), with 10 million equity shares outstanding. The unlevered cost of capital is 10%, and WRT's debt is risk free with an interest rate of 4%. The corporate tax rate is 35%, and there are no personal taxes.

    a. WRT initially proposes to fund the expansion by issuing equity. If investors were not expecting this expansion, and if they share WRT's view of the expansion's profitability, what will the share price be once the firm announces the expansion plan?

    b. Suppose investors think that the EBIT from WRT's expansion will be only $4 million. What will the share price be in this case? How many shares will the firm need to issue?

    c. Suppose WRT issues equity as in part b. Shortly after the issue, new information emerges that convinces investors that management was, in fact, correct regarding the cash flows from the expansion. What will the share price be now? Why does it differ from that found in part a?

    d. Suppose WRT instead finances the expansion with a $50 million issue of permanent risk-free debt. If WRT undertakes the expansion using debt, what is its new share price once the new information comes out? Comparing your answer with that in part c, what are the two advantages of debt financing in this case?

CHAPTER

17

Payout Policy

For many years, Microsoft Corporation chose to distribute cash to investors primarily by repurchasing its own stock. During the five fiscal years ending June 2004, for example, Microsoft spent an average of $5.4 billion per year on share repurchases. Microsoft began paying dividends to investors in 2003, with what CFO John Connors called "a starter dividend" of $0.08 per share. Then, on July 20, 2004, Microsoft stunned financial markets by announcing plans to pay the largest single cash dividend payment in history, a one-time dividend of $32 billion, or $3 per share, to all shareholders of record on November 17, 2004. In addition to this dividend, Microsoft announced plans to repurchase up to $30 billion of its stock over the next four years and pay regular quarterly dividends at an annual rate of $0.32 per share.

When a firm's investments generate free cash flow, the firm must decide how to use that cash. If the firm has new positive-NPV investment opportunities, it can reinvest the cash and increase the value of the firm. Many young, rapidly growing firms reinvest 100% of their cash flows in this way. But mature, profitable firms such as Microsoft often find that they generate more cash than they need to fund all of their attractive investment opportunities. When a firm has excess cash, it can hold those funds as part of its cash reserves or pay the cash out to shareholders. If the firm decides to follow the latter approach, it has two choices: It can pay a dividend or it can repurchase shares from current owners. These decisions represent the firm's payout policy.

In this chapter, we show that, as with capital structure, a firm's payout policy is shaped by market imperfections, such as taxes, agency costs, transaction costs, and asymmetric information between managers and investors. We look at why some firms prefer to pay dividends, whereas others pay no dividends at all and rely exclusively on share repurchases. In addition, we explore why some firms retain cash and build up large reserves, while others tend to pay out their excess cash.

17.1   DISTRIBUTIONS TO SHAREHOLDERS

Figure 17.1 illustrates the alternative uses of free cash flow.[1] The way a firm chooses between these alternatives is referred to as its **payout policy**. We begin our discussion of a firm's payout policy by considering the choice between paying dividends and repurchasing shares. In this section, we examine the details of these methods of paying cash to shareholders.

DIVIDENDS

A public company's board of directors determines the amount of the firm's dividend. The board sets the amount per share that will be paid and decides when the payment will occur. The date on which the board authorizes the dividend is the **declaration date**. After the board declares the dividend, the firm is legally obligated to make the payment.

The firm will pay the dividend to all shareholders of record on a specific date, set by the board, called the **record date**. Because it takes three business days for shares to be registered, only shareholders who purchase the stock at least three days prior to the record date receive the dividend. As a result, the date two business days prior to the record date is known as the **ex-dividend date**; anyone who purchases the stock on or after the ex-dividend date will not receive the dividend. Finally, on the **payable date** (or **distribution date**), which is generally about a month after the record date, the firm mails dividend cheques to the registered shareholders. Figure 17.2 shows these dates for Microsoft's $3 dividend.

Most companies that pay dividends pay them at regular, quarterly intervals. Companies typically adjust the amount of their dividends gradually, with little variation in the amount of the dividend from quarter to quarter. Occasionally, a firm may pay a one-time, **special dividend** that is usually much larger than a regular dividend, as was Microsoft's $3 dividend in 2004. Figure 17.3 shows the dividends paid by GM from 1983 to 2006. In addition to regular dividends, GM paid special dividends in December 1997 and again in May 1999 (associated with spin-offs of subsidiaries, discussed further in Section 17.7).

FIGURE 17.1

Uses of Free Cash Flow

A firm can retain its free cash flow, either investing or accumulating it, or pay out its free cash flow through a dividend or share repurchase. The choice between these options is determined by the firm's payout policy.

---

1. Strictly speaking, Figure 17.1 is for an all-equity firm. For a levered firm, we would begin with the firm's free cash flow to equity, which we define in Chapter 18 as free cash flow less (after-tax) payments to debt holders.

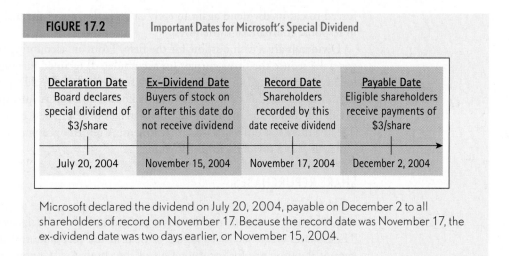

FIGURE 17.2   Important Dates for Microsoft's Special Dividend

Declaration Date	Ex-Dividend Date	Record Date	Payable Date
Board declares special dividend of $3/share	Buyers of stock on or after this date do not receive dividend	Shareholders recorded by this date receive dividend	Eligible shareholders receive payments of $3/share
July 20, 2004	November 15, 2004	November 17, 2004	December 2, 2004

Microsoft declared the dividend on July 20, 2004, payable on December 2 to all shareholders of record on November 17. Because the record date was November 17, the ex-dividend date was two days earlier, or November 15, 2004.

Notice that GM split its stock in March 1989 so that each owner of one share received a second share. This kind of transaction is called a 2-for-1 stock split. More generally, in a **stock split** or **stock dividend**, the company issues additional shares rather than cash to its shareholders. In the case of GM's stock split, the number of shares doubled, but the dividend per share was cut in half (from $1.50 per share to $0.75 per share), so that the total amount GM paid out as a dividend was the same just before and just after the split. (We discuss stock splits and stock dividends further in Section 17.7.) While GM raised its dividends throughout the 1980s, it cut its dividend during the recession in the early 1990s. GM raised its dividends again in the late 1990s, but was

FIGURE 17.3

Dividend History for GM Stock, 1983–2008

Until suspending its dividends in July 2008, GM had paid a regular dividend each quarter since 1983. GM paid additional special dividends in December 1997 and May 1999, and had a 2-for-1 stock split in March 1989. GM ultimately filed for bankruptcy in June 2009.

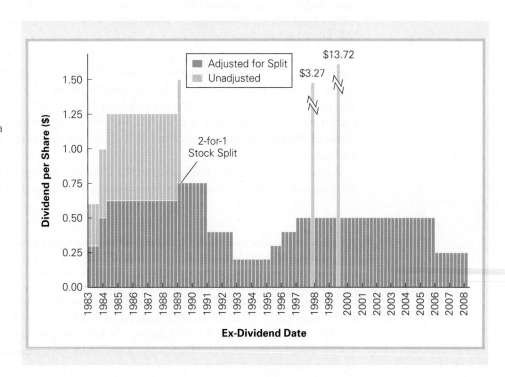

forced to cut its dividend again in early 2006 and suspend them altogether in July 2008 in response to financial difficulties.

Dividends are a cash outflow for the firm. From an accounting perspective, dividends generally reduce the firm's current (or accumulated) retained earnings. In some cases, dividends are attributed to other accounting sources, such as paid-in capital or the liquidation of assets. In this case the dividend is known as a **return of capital** or a **liquidating dividend**. While the source of the funds makes little difference to a firm or to investors directly, there is a difference in tax treatment: A return of capital is taxed as a capital gain rather than as a dividend for the investor.[2]

SHARE REPURCHASES

An alternative way to pay cash to investors is through a share repurchase or buyback. In this kind of transaction, the firm uses cash to buy shares of its own outstanding stock. These shares are generally cancelled or held in the corporate treasury depending on the laws of the province for incorporation of the company. We now examine three possible transaction types for a share repurchase.

OPEN MARKET REPURCHASE.   An **open market repurchase** is the most common way that firms repurchase shares. A firm announces its intention to buy its own shares in the open market, and then proceeds to do so over time like any other investor. The firm may take a year or more to buy the shares, and it is not obligated to repurchase the full amount it originally stated. Also, the firm must not buy its shares in a way that might appear to manipulate the price. For example, both TSX and SEC guidelines recommend that the firm not purchase more than 25% of the average daily trading volume in its shares on a single day, nor make purchases at the market open or within 30 minutes of the close of trade.[3]

While open market share repurchases represent about 95% of all repurchase transactions,[4] other methods are available to a firm that wants to buy back its stock. These methods are used when a firm wishes to repurchase a substantial portion of its shares, often as part of a recapitalization.

TENDER OFFER.   A firm can repurchase shares through a **tender offer** in which it offers to buy shares at a prespecified price during a short time period—generally within 20 days. The price is usually set at a substantial premium (10% to 20% is typical) to the current market price. The offer often depends on shareholders tendering a sufficient number of shares. If shareholders do not tender enough shares, the firm may cancel the offer and no buyback occurs.

A related method is the **Dutch auction** share repurchase, in which the firm lists different prices at which it is prepared to buy shares, and shareholders in turn indicate how

---

2. The return on capital reduces an investor's adjusted cost base for the shares. When the shares are eventually sold, the difference between the sale price and the adjusted cost base is treated as a capital gain (or capital loss if negative) and taxed accordingly. There is also a difference in the accounting treatment. A cash dividend reduces the cash and retained earnings shown on the balance sheet, whereas a return of capital reduces paid-in capital. This accounting difference has no direct economic consequence, however.

3. SEC Rule 10b-18, introduced in 1983, defines guidelines for open market share repurchases in the U.S. The TSX Company Manual, Part VI, Section 629 defines the guidelines in Canada.

4. G. Grullon and D. Ikenberry, "What Do We Know About Stock Repurchases?" *Journal of Applied Corporate Finance* 13:1 (2000): 31–51.

many shares they are willing to sell at each price. The firm then pays the lowest price at which it can buy back its desired number of shares.

TARGETED REPURCHASE. A firm may also purchase shares directly from a major shareholder in a **targeted repurchase**. In this case the purchase price is negotiated directly with the seller. A targeted repurchase may occur if a major shareholder desires to sell a large number of shares but the market for the shares is not sufficiently liquid to sustain such a large sale without severely affecting the price. Under these circumstances, the shareholder may be willing to sell shares back to the firm at a discount to the current market price. Alternatively, if a major shareholder is threatening to take over the firm and remove its management, the firm may decide to eliminate the threat by buying out the shareholder—often at a large premium over the current market price. This type of transaction is called **greenmail**.

CONCEPT CHECK

1. How is a stock's ex-dividend date determined, and what is its significance?

2. What is a Dutch auction share repurchase?

17.2 COMPARISON OF DIVIDENDS AND SHARE REPURCHASES

If a corporation decides to pay cash to shareholders, it can do so through either dividend payments or share repurchases. How do firms choose between these alternatives? In this section, we show that in the perfect capital markets setting of Modigliani and Miller, the method of payment does not matter.

Consider the case of Genron Corporation, a hypothetical firm. Genron has $20 million in excess cash and no debt. The firm expects to generate additional free cash flows of $48 million per year in subsequent years. If Genron's unlevered cost of capital is 12%, then the enterprise value of its ongoing operations is

$$\text{Enterprise Value} = PV(\text{Future FCF}) = \frac{\$48 \text{ million}}{12\%} = \$400 \text{ million}$$

Including the cash, Genron's total market value is $420 million.

Genron's board is meeting to decide how to pay out its $20 million in excess cash to shareholders. Some board members have advocated using the $20 million to pay a $2 cash dividend for each of Genron's 10 million outstanding shares. Others have suggested repurchasing shares instead of paying a dividend. Still others have proposed that Genron raise additional cash and pay an even larger dividend today, in anticipation of the high future free cash flows it expects to receive. Will the amount of the current dividend affect Genron's share price? Which policy would shareholders prefer?

Let's analyze the consequences of each of these three alternative policies and compare them in a setting of perfect capital markets.

ALTERNATIVE POLICY 1: PAY DIVIDEND WITH EXCESS CASH

Suppose the board opts for the first alternative and uses all excess cash to pay a dividend. With 10 million shares outstanding, Genron will be able to pay a $2 dividend immediately. Because the firm expects to generate future free cash flows of $48 million per year, it anticipates paying a dividend of $4.80 per share each year thereafter. The board declares the dividend and sets the record date as December 14, so that the ex-dividend date is December 12. Let's compute Genron's share price just before and after the stock goes ex-dividend.

The fair price for the shares is the present value of the expected dividends given Genron's equity cost of capital. Because Genron has no debt, its equity cost of capital equals its unlevered cost of capital of 12%. Just before the ex-dividend date, the stock is said to trade **cum-dividend** ("with the dividend") because anyone who buys the stock will be entitled to the dividend. In this case,

$$P_{cum} = \text{Current Dividend} + PV(\text{Future Dividends}) = 2 + \frac{4.80}{0.12} = 2 + 40 = \$42$$

After the stock goes ex-dividend, new buyers will not receive the current dividend. At this point the share price will reflect only the dividends in subsequent years:

$$P_{ex} = PV(\text{Future Dividends}) = \frac{4.80}{0.12} = \$40$$

The share price will drop on the ex-dividend date, December 12. The amount of the price drop is equal to the amount of the current dividend, $2. We can also determine this change in the share price using the market value balance sheet (values in millions of dollars):

	December 11 (cum-dividend)	December 12 (ex-dividend)
Cash	20	0
Other assets	400	400
Total market value	420	400
Shares (millions)	10	10
Share price	$42	$40

As the market value balance sheet shows, the share price falls when a dividend is paid because the reduction in cash decreases the market value of the firm's assets. Although the stock price falls, holders of Genron stock do not incur a loss overall. Before the dividend, their stock was worth $42. After the dividend, their stock is worth $40 and they hold $2 in cash from the dividend, for a total value of $42.[5]

The fact that the stock price falls by the amount of the dividend also follows from the assumption that no opportunity for arbitrage exists. If it fell by less than the dividend, an investor could earn a profit by buying the stock just before it goes ex-dividend and selling it just after, as the dividend would more than cover the capital loss on the stock. Similarly, if the stock price fell by more than the dividend, an investor could profit by selling the stock just before it goes ex-dividend and buying it just after. Therefore, no arbitrage implies:

In a perfect capital market, when a dividend is paid, the share price drops by the amount of the dividend when the stock begins to trade ex-dividend.

---

5. For simplicity, we have ignored the short delay between the ex-dividend date and the payable date of the dividend. In reality, the shareholders do not receive the dividend immediately, but rather the *promise* to receive it within several weeks. The stock price adjusts by the present value of this promise, which is effectively equal to the amount of the dividend unless interest rates are extremely high.

ALTERNATIVE POLICY 2: SHARE REPURCHASE (NO DIVIDEND)

Suppose that Genron does not pay a dividend this year, but instead uses the $20 million to repurchase its shares on the open market. How will the repurchase affect the share price?

With an initial share price of $42, Genron will repurchase $20 million ÷ $42 per share = 0.476 million shares, leaving only $10 - 0.476 = 9.524$ million shares outstanding. Once again, we can use Genron's market value balance sheet to analyze this transaction:

	December 11 (before repurchase)	December 12 (after repurchase)
Cash	20	0
Other assets	400	400
Total market value of assets	420	400
Shares (millions)	10	9.524
Share price	$42	$42

In this case, the market value of Genron's assets falls when the company pays out cash, but the number of shares outstanding also falls. The two changes offset each other, so the share price remains the same.

GENRON'S FUTURE DIVIDENDS.   We can also see why the share price does not fall after the share repurchase by considering the effect on Genron's future dividends. In future years, Genron expects to have $48 million in free cash flow, which can be used to pay a dividend of $48 million ÷ 9.524 million shares = $5.04 per share each year. Thus, with a share repurchase, Genron's share price today is

$$P_{rep} = \frac{5.04}{0.12} = \$42$$

In other words, by not paying a dividend today and repurchasing shares instead, Genron is able to raise its dividends *per share* in the future. The increase in future dividends compensates shareholders for the dividend they give up today. This example illustrates the following general conclusion about share repurchases:

In perfect capital markets, an open market share repurchase has no effect on the stock price, and the stock price is the same as the cum-dividend price if a dividend were paid instead.

INVESTOR PREFERENCES.   Would an investor prefer that Genron issue a dividend or repurchase its stock? Both policies lead to the same *initial* share price of $42. But is there a difference in shareholder value *after* the transaction? Consider an investor who currently holds 2000 shares of Genron stock. Assuming the investor does not trade the stock, the investor's holdings after a dividend or share repurchase are as follows:

Dividend	Repurchase
$40 × 2000 = $80,000 stock	$42 × 2000 = $84,000 stock
$2 × 2000 = $4000 cash	

In either case, the value of the investor's portfolio is $84,000 immediately after the transaction. The only difference is the distribution between cash and stock holdings.

COMMON MISTAKE REPURCHASES AND THE SUPPLY OF SHARES

There is a misconception that when a firm repurchases its own shares, the price rises due to the decrease in the supply of shares outstanding. This intuition follows naturally from the standard supply and demand analysis taught in microeconomics. Why does that analysis not apply here?

When a firm repurchases its own shares, two things happen. First, the supply of shares is reduced. At the same time, however, the value of the firm's assets declines when it spends its cash to buy the shares. If the firm repurchases its shares at their market price, these two effects offset each other, leaving the share price unchanged.

This result is similar to the dilution fallacy discussed in Chapter 14: When a firm issues shares at their market price, the share price does not fall due to the increase in supply. The increase in supply is offset by the increase in the firm's assets that results from the cash it receives from the issuance.

Thus it might seem the investor would prefer one approach or the other based on whether she needs the cash.

But if Genron repurchases shares and the investor wants cash, she can raise cash by selling shares. For example, she can sell $4000 \div $42 per share = 95 shares to raise about $4000 in cash. She will then hold 1905 shares, or $1905 \times $42 \approx $80,000$ in stock. Thus, in the case of a share repurchase, by selling shares an investor can create a *homemade dividend*.

Similarly, if Genron pays a dividend and the investor does not want the cash, she can use the $4000 proceeds of the dividend to purchase 100 additional shares at the ex-dividend share price of $40 per share. As a result she will hold 2100 shares, worth $2100 \times $40 = $84,000$.[6]

We summarize these two cases below:

Dividend + Buy 100 shares	Repurchase + Sell 95 shares
$40 × 2100 = $84,000 stock	$42 × 1905 ≈ $80,000 stock
	$42 × 95 ≈ $ 4000 cash

By selling shares or reinvesting dividends, the investor can create any combination of cash and stock desired. As a result, the investor is indifferent between the various payout methods the firm might employ:

In perfect capital markets, investors are indifferent between the firm distributing funds via dividends or share repurchases. By reinvesting dividends or selling shares, they can replicate either payout method on their own.

ALTERNATIVE POLICY 3: HIGH DIVIDEND (EQUITY ISSUE)

Let's look at a third possibility for Genron. Suppose the board wishes to pay an even larger dividend than $2 per share right now. Is that possible and, if so, will the higher dividend make shareholders better off?

Genron plans to pay $48 million in dividends starting next year. Suppose the firm wants to start paying that amount today. Because it has only $20 million in cash today, Genron needs an additional $28 million to pay the larger dividend now. It could raise cash by scaling back its investments. But if the investments have positive NPV, reducing them would lower firm value. An alternative way to raise more cash is to borrow money or

---

6. In fact, many firms allow investors to register for a dividend reinvestment program, or DRIP, which automatically reinvests any dividends into new shares of the stock.

sell new shares. Let's consider an equity issue. Given a current share price of $42, Genron could raise $28 million by selling $28 million ÷ $42 per share = 0.67 million shares. Because this equity issue will increase Genron's total number of shares outstanding to 10.67 million, the amount of the dividend per share each year will be

$$\frac{\$48 \text{ million}}{10.67 \text{ million shares}} = \$4.50 \text{ per share}$$

Under this new policy, Genron's cum-dividend share price is

$$P_{cum} = 4.50 + \frac{4.50}{0.12} = 4.50 + 37.50 = \$42$$

As in the previous examples, the initial share value is unchanged by this policy, and increasing the dividend has no benefit to shareholders.

EXAMPLE 17.1

HOMEMADE DIVIDENDS

Problem

Suppose Genron does not adopt the third alternative policy, and instead pays a $2 dividend per share today. Show how an investor holding 2000 shares could create a homemade dividend of $4.50 per share × 2000 shares = $9000 per year on her own.

Solution

If Genron pays a $2 dividend, the investor receives $4000 in cash and holds the rest in stock. To receive $9000 in total today, she can raise an additional $5000 by selling 125 shares at $40 per share just after the dividend is paid. In future years, Genron will pay a dividend of $4.80 per share. Because she will own 2000 − 125 = 1875 shares, the investor will receive dividends of 1875 × $4.80 = $9000 per year from then on.

MODIGLIANI-MILLER AND DIVIDEND POLICY IRRELEVANCE

In our analysis we considered three possible dividend policies for the firm: (1) pay out all cash as a dividend, (2) pay no dividend and use the cash instead to repurchase shares, or (3) issue equity to finance a larger dividend. These policies are illustrated in Table 17.1.

GENRON'S DIVIDENDS PER SHARE EACH YEAR UNDER THE THREE ALTERNATIVE POLICIES

TABLE 17.1

	Initial Share Price	Dividend Paid ($ per share)			
		Year 0	Year 1	Year 2	...
Policy 1:	$42.00	2.00	4.80	4.80	...
Policy 2:	$42.00	0	5.04	5.04	...
Policy 3:	$42.00	4.50	4.50	4.50	...

COMMON MISTAKE   THE BIRD IN THE HAND FALLACY

"A bird in the hand is worth two in the bush."

The **bird in the hand hypothesis** states that firms choosing to pay higher current dividends will enjoy higher stock prices because shareholders prefer current dividends to future ones (with the same present value). According to

this view, alternative policy 3 would lead to the highest share price for Genron.

Modigliani and Miller's response to this view is that with perfect capital markets, shareholders can generate an equivalent homemade dividend at any time by selling shares. Thus the dividend choice of the firm should not matter.[*]

---

[*]The bird in the hand hypothesis is proposed in Lintner and Gordon's early studies of dividend policy. See M. J. Gordon, "Optimal Investment and Financing Policy," *Journal of Finance* 18:2 (1963): 264–272, and J. Lintner, "Dividends, Earnings, Leverage, Stock Prices and the Supply of Capital to Corporations," *Review of Economics and Statistics* 44:3 (1962): 243–269.

Table 17.1 shows an important tradeoff: If Genron pays a higher *current* dividend per share, it will pay lower *future* dividends per share. For example, if the firm raises the current dividend by issuing equity, it will have more shares and therefore smaller free cash flows per share to pay dividends in the future. If the firm lowers the current dividend and repurchases its shares, it will have fewer shares in the future, so it will be able to pay a higher dividend per share. The net effect of this tradeoff is to leave the total present value of all future dividends, and hence the current share price, unchanged.

The logic of this section matches that in our discussion of capital structure in Chapter 14. There we explained that in perfect capital markets, buying and selling equity and debt are zero-NPV transactions that do not affect firm value. Moreover, any choice of leverage by a firm could be replicated by investors using homemade leverage. As a result, the firm's choice of capital structure is irrelevant.

Here we have established the same principle for a firm's choice of a dividend. Regardless of the amount of cash the firm has on hand, it can pay a smaller dividend (and use the remaining cash to repurchase shares) or a larger dividend (by selling equity to raise cash). Because buying or selling shares is a zero-NPV transaction, such transactions have no effect on the initial share price. Furthermore, shareholders can create a homemade dividend of any size by buying or selling shares themselves.

Modigliani and Miller developed this idea in another influential paper published in 1961.[7] As with their result on capital structure, it went against the conventional wisdom that dividend policy could change a firm's value and make its shareholders better off even absent market imperfections. We state here their important proposition.

MM Dividend Irrelevance: *In perfect capital markets, holding fixed the investment policy of a firm, the firm's choice of dividend policy is irrelevant and does not affect the initial share price.*

DIVIDEND POLICY WITH PERFECT CAPITAL MARKETS

The examples in this section illustrate the idea that by using share repurchases or equity issues a firm can easily alter its dividend payments. Because these transactions do not alter the value of the firm, neither does dividend policy.

---

7. See M. Modigliani and M. Miller, "Dividend Policy, Growth, and the Valuation of Shares," *Journal of Business* 34:4 (1961): 411–433. See also J. B. Williams, *The Theory of Investment Value* (Cambridge, MA: Harvard University Press, 1938).

This result may at first seem to contradict the idea that the price of a share should equal the present value of its future dividends. As our examples have shown, however, a firm's choice of dividend today affects the dividends it can afford to pay in the future in an offsetting fashion. Thus, while dividends *do* determine share prices, a firm's choice of dividend policy does not.

As Modigliani and Miller make clear, the value of a firm ultimately derives from its underlying free cash flow. A firm's free cash flow determines the level of payouts that it can make to its investors. In a perfect capital market, whether these payouts are made through dividends or share repurchases does not matter. Of course, in reality capital markets are not perfect. As with capital structure, it is the imperfections in capital markets that should determine the firm's payout policy.

CONCEPT CHECK

1. True or False: When a firm repurchases its own shares, the price rises due to the decrease in the supply of shares outstanding.

2. In a perfect capital market, how important is the firm's decision to pay dividends versus repurchase shares?

17.3 THE TAX DISADVANTAGE OF DIVIDENDS

As with capital structure, taxes are an important market imperfection that influence a firm's decision to pay dividends or repurchase shares.

TAXES ON DIVIDENDS AND CAPITAL GAINS

Shareholders typically must pay taxes on the dividends they receive. They must also pay capital gains taxes when they sell their shares. Historically, the taxes applied to dividend income have been higher than taxes applied to capital gains income. The actual difference in tax rates on dividend income and capital gains income has changed over the years in both Canada and the United States. (From 2003–2010 they were equal in the U.S., but the law specifying these rates was set to expire in 2010.) However, taxes on capital gains income are deferred until the stock is sold; thus the present value of the taxes on capital gains is usually substantially less than the taxes on dividends (that occur in the year of the dividend payment).

Do taxes affect investors' preferences for dividends versus share repurchases? When a firm pays a dividend, shareholders are taxed according to the dividend tax rate. If the firm repurchases shares instead, and shareholders sell shares to create a homemade dividend, the homemade dividend will be taxed according to the capital gains tax rate. If dividends are taxed at a higher rate than capital gains, which is the case in Canada, shareholders will prefer share repurchases to dividends.[8]

The higher tax rate on dividends also makes it undesirable for a firm to raise funds to pay a dividend. Absent taxes and issuance costs, if a firm raises money by issuing shares and then gives that money back to shareholders as a dividend, shareholders are no better or worse off—they get back the money they put in. When dividends are taxed at a higher rate than capital gains, however, this transaction hurts shareholders because they will receive less than their initial investment.

---

8. Not all countries tax dividends at a higher rate than capital gains. In Germany, for example, dividends are taxed at a lower rate than capital gains for most classes of investors.

EXAMPLE **17.2**	ISSUING EQUITY TO PAY A DIVIDEND

Problem

Suppose a firm raises $10 million from shareholders and uses this cash to pay them $10 million in dividends. If the dividend is taxed at a 40% rate, and if capital gains are taxed at a 15% rate, how much will shareholders receive after taxes?

Solution

Shareholders will owe 40% of $10 million, or $4 million in dividend taxes. Because the value of the firm will fall when the dividend is paid, shareholders' capital gain on the stock will be $10 million less when they sell, lowering their capital gains taxes by 15% of $10 million, or $1.5 million. Thus, in total, shareholders will pay $4 million − $1.5 million = $2.5 million in taxes, and they will receive back only $7.5 million of their $10 million investment.

OPTIMAL DIVIDEND POLICY WITH TAXES

When the tax rate on dividends exceeds the tax rate on capital gains, shareholders will pay lower taxes if a firm uses share repurchases for all payouts rather than dividends. This tax savings will increase the value of a firm that uses share repurchases rather than dividends. We can also express the tax savings in terms of a firm's equity cost of capital. Firms that use dividends will have to pay a higher pre-tax return to offer their investors the same after-tax return as firms that use share repurchases.[9] As a result, the optimal dividend policy when the dividend tax rate exceeds the capital gain tax rate is to *pay no dividends at all.*

While firms still do pay dividends, substantial evidence shows that many firms have recognized their tax disadvantage. For example, prior to 1980, most U.S. firms used dividends exclusively to distribute cash to shareholders (see Figure 17.4). But by 2000, only 23% of firms relied on dividends. At the same time, 17% of all firms used share repurchases exclusively or in combination with dividends. The trend away from dividends has noticeably reversed, however, since the 2003 reduction in the U.S. dividend tax rate.[10]

We see a more dramatic trend if we consider the relative magnitudes of both forms of corporate payouts. Figure 17.5 shows the relative importance of share repurchases as a proportion of total payouts to shareholders. While dividends accounted for more than 80% of corporate payouts until the early 1980s, the importance of share repurchases grew dramatically in the mid-1980s. Repurchase activity slowed during the 1990–1991 U.S. recession, but by the end of the 1990s repurchases exceeded the value of dividend

---

9. For an extension of the CAPM that includes investor taxes, see M. Brennan, "Taxes, Market Valuation and Corporation Financial Policy," *National Tax Journal* 23:4 (1970): 417–427.

10. See G. Grullon and R. Michaely, "Dividends, Share Repurchases, and the Substitution Hypothesis," *Journal of Finance* 57:4 (2002): 1649–1684, and E. Fama and K. French, "Disappearing Dividends: Changing Firm Characteristics or Lower Propensity to Pay?" *Journal of Financial Economics* 60:3 (2001): 3–43. For an examination of the changing trend since 2000, see B. Julio and D. Ikenberry, "Reappearing Dividends," *Journal of Applied Corporate Finance* 16:4 (2004): 89–100.

FIGURE 17.4

The Decline in Payouts and the Use of Dividends

This figure shows the percentage of publicly traded U.S. industrial firms each year that made payouts to shareholders. The shaded regions show the firms that used dividends exclusively, repurchases exclusively, or both. Note the trend away from the use of dividends over time, with firms that made payouts showing a greater reliance on share repurchases, together with a sharp decrease in the percentage of firms making payouts of any kind.

Source: Compustat.

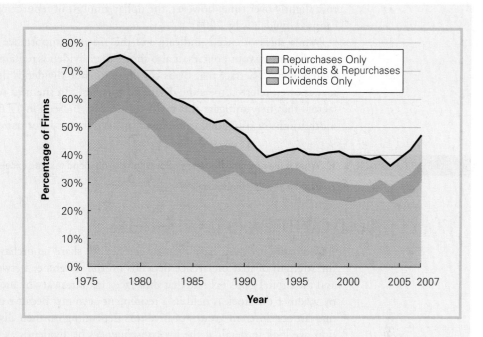

payments for U.S. industrial firms. A similar pattern is found for Canadian firms. Luke Schmidt, in his 2006 Master's thesis at the University of Saskatchewan, found that in 1995 the dollar amount of dividends was more than four times the dollar amount of share repurchases by Canadian corporations. The dollar amount of dividends fluctuated and

FIGURE 17.5

The Changing Composition of Shareholder Payouts

This figure shows the value of share repurchases as a percentage of total payouts to shareholders (dividends and repurchases). Although initially small, the total dollar amount of share repurchases has grown faster than dividends, so that by the late 1990s share repurchases surpassed dividends to become the largest form of corporate payouts for U.S. industrial firms.

Source: Compustat data for U.S. firms, excluding financial firms and utilities.

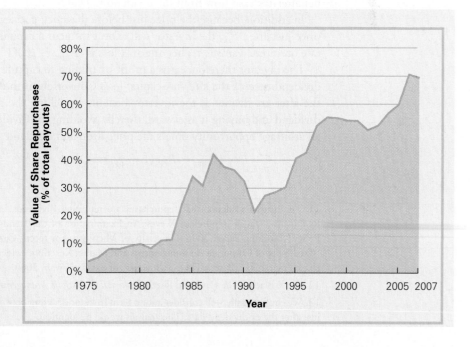

rose slightly over time; however, the dollar amount of repurchases grew substantially and eclipsed dividends by 2004.[11]

While this evidence is indicative of the growing importance of share repurchases as a part of firms' payout policies, it also shows that dividends remain a key form of payouts to shareholders. The fact that firms continue to issue dividends despite their tax disadvantage is often referred to as the **dividend puzzle**.[12] In the next section, we consider some factors that may mitigate this tax disadvantage. In Section 17.6, we examine alternative motivations for using dividends based on asymmetric information.

CONCEPT CHECK
1. What is the optimal dividend policy when the dividend tax rate exceeds the capital gain tax rate?
2. What is the dividend puzzle?

17.4   DIVIDEND CAPTURE AND TAX CLIENTELES

While many investors have a tax preference for share repurchases rather than dividends, the strength of that preference depends on the difference between the dividend tax rate and the capital gains tax rate that they face. Tax rates vary by income, by jurisdiction, and by whether the stock is held in a retirement account. Because of these differences, firms may attract different groups of investors depending on their dividend policy. In this section, we look in detail at the tax consequences of dividends as well as investor strategies that may reduce the impact of dividend taxes on firm value.

THE EFFECTIVE DIVIDEND TAX RATE

To compare investor preferences, we must quantify the combined effects of dividend and capital gains taxes to determine an effective dividend tax rate for an investor. For simplicity, consider an investor who buys a stock today just before it goes ex-dividend and sells the stock just after.[13] By doing so, the investor will qualify for, and capture, the dividend. If the stock pays a dividend of amount Div, and the investor's dividend tax rate is τ_d, then her after-tax cash flow from the dividend is $Div(1 - \tau_d)$.

In addition, because the price just before the stock goes ex-dividend, P_{cum}, exceeds the price just after, P_{ex}, the investor will expect to incur a capital loss on her trade. If her tax rate on capital gains is τ_g, her after-tax loss is $(P_{cum} - P_{ex})(1 - \tau_g)$.

The investor therefore earns a profit by trading to capture the dividend if the after-tax dividend exceeds the after-tax capital loss. Conversely, if the after-tax capital loss exceeds the after-tax dividend, the investor benefits by selling the stock just before it goes ex-dividend and buying it afterward, thereby avoiding the dividend. In other words, there is an arbitrage opportunity unless the price drop and dividend are equal after taxes:

$$(P_{cum} - P_{ex})(1 - \tau_g) = Div(1 - \tau_d) \tag{17.1}$$

---

11. For further evidence that repurchases are replacing dividends in the U.S., see A. Dittmar and R. Dittmar, "Stock Repurchase Waves: An Examination of the Trends in Aggregate Corporate Payout Policy," Working Paper, 2006, University of Michigan. For recent Canadian evidence, see L. Schmidt, "Credibility of Corporate Announcements and Market Reaction: Evidence from Canadian Share Repurchase Programs," Master's Thesis, University of Saskatchewan, 2006.

12. See F. Black, "The Dividend Puzzle," *Journal of Portfolio Management* 2 (1976): 5–8.

13. We could equally well consider a long-term investor deciding between selling the stock just before or just after the ex-dividend date. The analysis would be identical.

We can write Eq. 17.1 in terms of the share price drop as

$$P_{cum} - P_{ex} = Div \times \left(\frac{1 - \tau_d}{1 - \tau_g} \right) = Div \times \left(1 - \frac{\tau_d - \tau_g}{1 - \tau_g} \right) = Div \times (1 - \tau_d^*) \qquad (17.2)$$

where we define τ_d^* to be the **effective dividend tax rate**:

$$\tau_d^* = \left(\frac{\tau_d - \tau_g}{1 - \tau_g} \right) \qquad (17.3)$$

The effective dividend tax rate τ_d^* measures the additional tax paid by the investor per dollar of after-tax capital gains income that is instead received as a dividend.[14]

EXAMPLE 17.3	CHANGES IN THE EFFECTIVE DIVIDEND TAX RATE

Problem

According to Ernst & Young the marginal tax rates for an Ontario investor in the highest Canadian tax bracket were 23.21% for capital gains and 31.34% for dividends in 2003. In 2008, this same Ontario investor faced marginal tax rates of 23.21% for capital gains and 23.96% for dividends. Assume the investor plans to hold a stock for one year. What was the effective dividend tax rate for this investor in 2003? How did the effective dividend tax rate change in 2008?

Solution

In 2003 we have $\tau_d = 31.34\%$ and $\tau_g = 23.21\%$. Thus

$$\tau_d^* = \frac{.3134 - .2321}{1 - .2321} = 10.59\%$$

This indicates a significant tax disadvantage of dividends; each $1 of dividends is worth only $0.8941 in capital gains. However, after the tax revisions that occurred by 2008, $\tau_d = 23.96\%$, $\tau_g = 23.21\%$, and

$$\tau_d^* = \frac{.2396 - .2321}{1 - .2321} = 0.98\%$$

Therefore, by 2008 the tax disadvantage of dividends had almost disappeared for a one-year investor in Ontario. In Alberta, British Columbia, New Brunswick, the Northwest Territories, and Yukon, by 2008 there was actually a tax advantage for dividends for a one-year investor.

---

14. Elton and Gruber first identified and found empirical support for Eq. 17.2. See E. Elton and M. Gruber, "Marginal Stockholder Tax Rates and the Clientele Effect," *Review of Economics and Statistics* 52:1 (1970): 68–74. For investor reaction to major U.S. tax code changes, see J. L. Koski, "A Micro-structure Analysis of Ex-Dividend Stock Price Behavior Before and After the 1984 and 1986 Tax Reform Acts," *Journal of Business* 69 (1996): 313–338.

TAX DIFFERENCES ACROSS INVESTORS

The effective dividend tax rate τ_d^* for an investor depends on the tax rates the investor faces on dividends and capital gains. These rates differ across investors for a variety of reasons.

Income Level. Investors with different levels of income fall into different tax brackets and face different tax rates.

Investment Horizon. Long-term investors can defer the payment of capital gains taxes (lowering their effective capital gains tax rate even further). An investor who never intends to sell her shares effectively pays no capital gains tax. For example, an investor who holds her shares for a long time period and then plans to donate her shares to a Canadian charity will not have to pay any capital gains tax and the full amount of the donation will be eligible for a charitable tax credit.

Tax Jurisdiction. Canadian investors are subject to provincial taxes that differ by province. U.S. investors in Canadian stocks and Canadian investors in U.S. stocks are subject to a 15% withholding tax for dividends they receive. Other foreign investors may be subject to a higher withholding tax on dividends they receive. There is no similar withholding for capital gains.

Type of Investor or Investment Account. Stocks held by individual investors in a registered retirement savings plan (RRSP), registered retirement income fund (RRIF), or tax-free savings account (TFSA) are not subject to taxes on dividends or capital gains.[15] Similarly, stocks held through pension funds or nonprofit endowment funds are not subject to dividend or capital gains taxes. Corporations that hold stocks are able to exclude 100% of dividends they receive from corporate taxes, but are unable to exclude capital gains.

To illustrate, consider four different investors: (1) a "buy and hold" Ontario investor who holds the stock in a taxable account and plans to eventually donate the stock to a registered Canadian charity, (2) an Ontario investor who holds the stock in a taxable account but plans to sell it in one year, (3) a pension fund or RRSP, and (4) an Ontario corporation. Under the maximum 2008 combined Ontario and federal tax rates, the effective dividend tax rate for each would be

1. Buy and hold and donate individual investor: $\tau_d = 23.96\%$, $\tau_g = 0$, and $\tau_d^* = 23.96\%$
2. One-year individual investor: $\tau_d = 23.96\%$, $\tau_g = 23.21\%$, and $\tau_d^* = 0.98\%$
3. Pension fund or RRSP: $\tau_d = 0$, $\tau_g = 0$, and $\tau_d^* = 0$
4. Corporation: Given a corporate tax rate of 34%, $\tau_d = 0$, $\tau_g = 17\%$, and $\tau_d^* = -20.48\%$

As a result of their different tax rates, these investors have varying preferences regarding dividends. Long-term investors are more heavily taxed on dividends, so they would prefer share repurchases to dividend payments. One-year investors, pension funds, and other non-taxed investors have little or no tax preference for share repurchases over dividends; they would prefer a payout policy that most closely matches their cash needs. For example, a non-taxed investor who desires current income would prefer high dividends so as to avoid the brokerage fees and other transaction costs of selling the stock.

Finally, the negative effective dividend tax rate for corporations implies that corporations enjoy a tax *advantage* associated with dividends. For this reason, a corporation that chooses to invest its cash will prefer to hold stocks with high dividend yields.

---

15. While taxes may be owed when the money is withdrawn from the retirement account, these taxes do not depend on whether the money came from dividends or capital gains.

DIFFERING DIVIDEND POLICY PREFERENCES ACROSS INVESTOR GROUPS

TABLE 17.2

Investor Group	Dividend Policy Preference	Proportion of Investors
Individual investors	Tax disadvantage for dividends Prefer share repurchase	~52%
Institutions, pension funds, retirement accounts	No tax preference Prefer dividend policy that matches income needs	~47%
Corporations	Tax advantage for dividends	~1%

Source: Proportions based on *Federal Reserve Flow of Funds Accounts.*

CLIENTELE EFFECTS

Table 17.2 summarizes the different preferences across investor groups. The proportions are based on investors in the United States. These differences in tax preferences create **clientele effects**, in which the dividend policy of a firm is optimized for the tax preference of its investor clientele. Individuals in the highest tax brackets have a preference for stocks that pay no or low dividends, whereas tax-free investors and corporations have a preference for stocks with high dividends. In this case, a firm's dividend policy is optimized for the tax preference of its investor clientele.

Evidence supports the existence of tax clienteles. For example, Franklin Allen and Roni Michaely[16] report that in 1996 individual investors held 54% of all stocks by market value, yet received only 35% of all dividends paid, indicating that individuals tend to hold stocks with low dividend yields. Of course, the fact that high-tax investors receive any dividends at all implies that the clienteles are not perfect—dividend taxes are not the only determinants of investors' portfolios.

Another clientele strategy is a dynamic clientele effect, also called the **dividend-capture theory**.[17] This theory states that absent transaction costs, investors can trade shares at the time of the dividend so that non-taxed investors receive the dividend. That is, non-taxed investors need not hold the high-dividend-paying stocks all the time; it is necessary only that they hold them when the dividend is actually paid.

An implication of this theory is that we should see large volumes of trade in a stock around the ex-dividend day, as high-tax investors sell and low-tax investors buy the stock in anticipation of the dividend, and then reverse those trades just after the ex-dividend date. Consider Figure 17.6, which illustrates the price and volume for the stock of Value Line, Inc., during 2004. On April 23, Value Line announced it would use its accumulated cash to pay a special dividend of $17.50 per share, with an ex-dividend date of May 20. Note the substantial increase in the volume of trade around the time of the special dividend. The volume of trade in the month following the special dividend announcement was more than 25 times the volume in the month prior to the announcement. In the three months following the announcement of the special dividend, the cumulative volume exceeded 65% of the total shares available for trade.

16. F. Allen and R. Michaely, "Payout Policy," in *Handbook of the Economics of Finance: Corporate Finance Volume 1A*, Chapter 7 (Amsterdam: Elsevier, 2003) (ed: G. M. Constantinides, M. Harris, and R. M. Stulz).

17. This idea is developed by A. Kalay, "The Ex-Dividend Day Behavior of Stock Prices: A Re-Examination of the Clientele Effect," *Journal of Finance* 37:4 (1982): 1059–1070. See also J. Boyd and R. Jagannathan, "Ex-Dividend Price Behavior of Common Stocks," *Review of Financial Studies* 7:4 (1994): 711–741, who discuss the complications that arise with multiple tax clienteles.

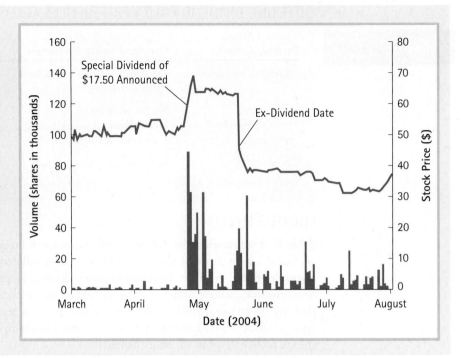

Volume and Share Price Effects of Value Line's Special Dividend

On announcement of the special dividend of $17.50 per share, Value Line's share price (shown in blue) rose, as did the volume of trades (shown in red). The share price dropped by $17.91 on the ex-dividend date, and the volume gradually declined over the following weeks. This pattern of volume is consistent with non-taxed investors buying the stock before the ex-dividend date and selling it afterward. (We consider reasons for the jump in the stock price on the announcement of the dividend in Sections 17.5 and 17.6.)

While this evidence supports the dividend-capture theory, it is also true that many high-tax investors continue to hold stocks even when dividends are paid. For a small ordinary dividend, the transaction costs and risks of trading the stock probably offset the benefits associated with dividend capture.[18] Large increases in volume, as in the case of Value Line, tend to be associated with large special dividends. Thus, while clientele effects and dividend-capture strategies reduce the relative tax disadvantage of dividends, they do not eliminate it.[19]

CONCEPT CHECK

1. Under what conditions will investors have a tax preference for share repurchases rather than dividends?

2. What does the dividend-capture theory imply about the volume of trade in a stock around the ex-dividend day?

---

18. The risk of the dividend-capture strategy is that the stock price may fluctuate for reasons unrelated to the dividend before the transaction can be completed. See J. Koski and R. Michaely, "Prices, Liquidity, and the Information Content of Trades," *Review of Financial Studies* 13:3 (2000): 659–696, who demonstrate that in some cases the risk can be eliminated by negotiating a purchase and sale simultaneously, but with settlement dates before and after the ex-dividend date. In this case the amount of dividend-related volume is greatly increased.

19. These effects are one reason it is difficult to find evidence that the equity cost of capital increases with dividend yields as one would expect if long-term investors are an important clientele. While evidence was found by R. Litzenberger and K. Ramaswamy ("The Effects of Personal Taxes and Dividends on Capital Asset Prices: Theory and Empirical Evidence," *Journal of Financial Economics* 7:2 (1979): 163–195), this evidence is contradicted by the results of F. Black and M. Scholes ("The Effects of Dividend Yield and Dividend Policy on Common Stock Prices and Returns," *Journal of Financial Economics* 1:1 (1974): 1–22). A. Kalay and R. Michaely provide an explanation for the differing results of these studies and do not find a significant impact of dividend yields on expected returns ("Dividends and Taxes: A Reexamination," *Financial Management* 29:2 (2000): 55–75).

17.5 PAYOUT VERSUS RETENTION OF CASH

Looking back at Figure 17.1, we have thus far considered only one aspect of a firm's payout policy: the choice between paying dividends and repurchasing shares. But how should a firm decide the amount it should pay out to shareholders and the amount it should retain?

To answer this question, we must first consider what the firm will do with cash that it retains. It can invest the cash in new projects or in financial instruments. We will demonstrate that in the context of perfect capital markets, once a firm has taken all positive-NPV investments, it is indifferent between saving excess cash and paying it out. But once we consider market imperfections, there is a tradeoff: Retaining cash can reduce the costs of raising capital in the future, but it can also increase taxes and agency costs.

RETAINING CASH WITH PERFECT CAPITAL MARKETS

If a firm retains cash, it can use those funds to invest in new projects. If new positive-NPV projects are available, this decision is clearly the correct one. Making positive-NPV investments will create value for the firm's investors, whereas saving the cash or paying it out will not. However, once the firm has already taken all positive-NPV projects, any additional projects it takes on are zero- or negative-NPV investments. Taking on negative-NPV investments will reduce shareholder value, as the benefits of such investments do not exceed their costs.

Of course, rather than waste excess cash on negative-NPV projects, a firm can hold the cash in the bank or use it to purchase financial assets. The firm can then pay the money to shareholders at a future time or invest it when positive-NPV investment opportunities become available.

What are the advantages and disadvantages of retaining cash and investing in financial securities? In perfect capital markets, buying and selling securities is a zero-NPV transaction, so it should not affect firm value. Shareholders can make any investment a firm makes on their own if the firm pays out the cash. Thus it should not be surprising that with perfect capital markets, the retention versus payout decision—just like the dividend versus share repurchase decision—is irrelevant to total firm value.

As Example 17.4 illustrates, there is no difference for shareholders if the firm pays the cash immediately or retains the cash and pays it out at a future date. This example

---

EXAMPLE 17.4

DELAYING DIVIDENDS WITH PERFECT MARKETS

Problem

Yellowknife Mining has $100,000 in excess cash. Yellowknife is considering investing the cash in one-year Treasury Bills paying 6% interest, and then using the cash to pay a dividend next year. Alternatively, the firm can pay a dividend immediately and shareholders can invest the cash on their own. In a perfect capital market, which option will shareholders prefer?

Solution

If Yellowknife pays an immediate dividend, the shareholders receive $100,000 today. If Yellowknife retains the cash, at the end of one year the company will be able to pay a dividend of

$$\$100{,}000 \times (1.06) = \$106{,}000$$

This payoff is the same as if shareholders had invested the $100,000 in Treasury Bills themselves. In other words, the present value of this future dividend is exactly $106,000 ÷ (1.06) = $100,000. Thus shareholders are indifferent about whether the firm pays the dividend immediately or retains the cash.

provides yet another illustration of Modigliani and Miller's fundamental insight regarding financial policy irrelevance in perfect capital markets:

MM Payout Irrelevance: *In perfect capital markets, if a firm invests excess cash flows in financial securities, the firm's choice of payout versus retention is irrelevant and does not affect the initial value of the firm.*

Thus, the decision of whether to retain cash depends on market imperfections, which we turn to next.

TAXES AND CASH RETENTION

Example 17.4 assumed perfect capital markets, and so ignored the effect of taxes. How would our result change with taxes?

EXAMPLE 17.5	RETAINING CASH WITH CORPORATE TAXES

Problem

Suppose Yellowknife must pay corporate taxes at a 35% rate on the interest it will earn from the one-year Treasury Bill paying 6% interest. Would pension fund investors (who do not pay taxes on their investment income) prefer that Yellowknife use its excess cash to pay the $100,000 dividend immediately or retain the cash for one year?

Solution

If Yellowknife pays an immediate dividend, shareholders receive $100,000 today. If Yellowknife retains the cash for one year, it will earn an after-tax return on the Treasury Bills of

$$6\% \times (1 - 0.35) = 3.90\%$$

Thus, at the end of the year, Yellowknife will pay a dividend of $100,000 \times (1.039) = $103,900.

This amount is less than the $106,000 the investors would have earned if they had invested the $100,000 in Treasury Bills themselves. Because Yellowknife must pay corporate taxes on the interest it earns, there is a tax disadvantage to retaining cash. Pension fund investors will therefore prefer that Yellowknife pay the dividend now.

As Example 17.5 shows, corporate taxes make it costly for a firm to retain excess cash. This effect is the very same effect we identified in Chapter 15 with regard to leverage: When a firm pays interest, it receives a tax deduction for that interest, whereas when a firm receives interest, it owes taxes on the interest. As we discussed in Chapter 14, cash is equivalent to *negative* leverage, so the tax advantage of leverage implies a tax disadvantage to holding cash.

ADJUSTING FOR INVESTOR TAXES

The decision to pay out versus retain cash may also affect the taxes paid by shareholders. While pension and retirement fund investors are tax exempt, most individual investors must pay taxes on interest, dividends, and capital gains. How do investor taxes affect the tax disadvantage of retaining cash?

We illustrate the tax impact with a simple example. Consider a firm whose only asset is $100 in cash, and suppose all investors face identical tax rates. Let's compare the option of

EXAMPLE 17.6

MICROSOFT'S SPECIAL DIVIDEND

Problem

In the introduction to this chapter, we described Microsoft's special dividend of $3 per share, or $32 billion, during late 2004. If Microsoft had instead retained that cash permanently, what would the present value of the additional taxes paid be?

Solution

If Microsoft retained the cash, the interest earned on it would be subject to a 35% corporate tax rate. Because the interest payments are risk free, we can discount the tax payments at the risk-free interest rate under the assumption that Microsoft's marginal corporate tax rate will remain constant (or that any changes to it have a beta of zero). Thus, the present value of the tax payments on Microsoft's additional interest income would be

$$\frac{\$32 \text{ billion} \times r_f \times 35\%}{r_f} = \$32 \text{ billion} \times 35\% = \$11.2 \text{ billion}$$

So, on a per-share basis, Microsoft's tax savings from paying out the cash rather than retaining it is $3 \times 35\% = \$1.05$ per share.

paying out this cash as an immediate dividend of $100 with the option of retaining the $100 permanently and using the interest earned to pay dividends.

Suppose the firm pays out its cash immediately as a dividend and shuts down. Because the ex-dividend price of the firm is zero (it has shut down), using Eq. 17.2 we find that before the dividend is paid the firm has a share price of

$$P_{cum} = P_{ex} + Div_0 \times \left(\frac{1-\tau_d}{1-\tau_g}\right) = 0 + 100 \times \left(\frac{1-\tau_d}{1-\tau_g}\right) \tag{17.4}$$

This price reflects the fact that the investor will pay tax on the dividend at rate τ_d, but will receive a tax credit (at capital gains tax rate τ_g) for the capital loss when the firm shuts down.

Alternatively, the firm can retain the cash and invest it in Treasury Bills, earning interest at rate r_f each year. After paying corporate taxes on this interest at rate τ_c, the firm can pay a perpetual dividend of

$$Div = 100 \times r_f \times (1 - \tau_c)$$

each year and retain the $100 in cash permanently. What price will an investor pay for the firm in this case? The investor's cost of capital is the after-tax return that she could earn by investing in Treasury Bills on her own: $r_f \times (1 - \tau_i)$, where τ_i is the investor's tax rate on interest income. Because the investor must pay taxes on the dividends as well, the value of the firm if it retains the $100 is[20]

$$P_{retain} = \frac{Div \times (1-\tau_d)}{r_f \times (1-\tau_i)} = \frac{100 \times r_f \times (1-\tau_c) \times (1-\tau_d)}{r_f \times (1-\tau_i)}$$

$$= 100 \times \frac{(1-\tau_c)(1-\tau_d)}{(1-\tau_i)} \tag{17.5}$$

---

20. There is no capital gains tax consequence in this case because the share price will remain the same each year.

Comparing Eqs. 17.5 and 17.4,

$$P_{retain} = P_{cum} \times \frac{(1-\tau_c)(1-\tau_g)}{(1-\tau_i)} = P_{cum} \times (1-\tau^*_{retain}) \tag{17.6}$$

where τ^*_{retain} measures the effective tax disadvantage of retaining cash:

$$\tau^*_{retain} = \left[1 - \frac{(1-\tau_c)(1-\tau_g)}{(1-\tau_i)} \right] \tag{17.7}$$

Because the dividend tax will be paid whether the firm pays the cash immediately or retains the cash and pays the interest over time, the dividend tax rate does not affect the cost of retaining cash in Eq. 17.7.[21] The intuition for Eq. 17.7 is that when a firm retains cash, it must pay corporate tax on the interest it earns. In addition, the investor will owe capital gains tax on the increased value of the firm. In essence, the interest on retained cash is taxed twice. If the firm paid the cash to its shareholders instead, they could invest it and be taxed only once on the interest that they earn. The cost of retaining cash therefore depends on the combined effect of the corporate and capital gains taxes, compared to the single tax on interest income. Using average 2008 tax rates (see Table 15.3), $\tau_c = 32.6\%$, $\tau_i = 44.7\%$, and $\tau_g = 22.4\%$, we get an effective tax disadvantage of retained cash of $\tau^*_{retain} = 5.4\%$. Thus, after adjusting for investor taxes, there remains over a 5% tax *disadvantage* for the firm to retaining excess cash.

ISSUANCE AND DISTRESS COSTS

If there is a tax disadvantage to retaining cash, why do some firms accumulate large cash balances? Generally, they retain cash balances to cover potential future cash shortfalls. For example, if there is a reasonable likelihood that future earnings will be insufficient to fund future positive-NPV investment opportunities, a firm may start accumulating cash to make up the difference. This motivation is especially relevant for firms that may need to fund large-scale research and development projects or large acquisitions.

The advantage of holding cash to cover future potential cash needs is that this strategy allows a firm to avoid the transaction costs of raising new capital (through new debt or equity issues). The direct costs of issuance range from 1% to 3% for debt issues and from 3.5% to 7% for equity issues. There can also be substantial indirect costs of raising capital due to the agency and adverse selection (lemons) costs discussed in Chapter 16.

---

21. Equation 17.7 also holds if the firm uses any (constant) mix of dividends and share repurchases. However, if the firm initially retains cash by cutting back only on share repurchases, and then later uses the cash to pay a mix of dividends and repurchases, then we would replace τ_g in Eq. 17.7 with the average tax rate on dividends and capital gains, $\tau_e = \alpha\tau_d + (1-\alpha)\tau_g$, where α is the proportion of dividends versus repurchases. In that case, τ^*_{retain} equals the effective tax disadvantage of debt τ^* we derived in Eq. 15.7, where we implicitly assumed that debt was used to fund a share repurchase (or to avoid an equity issue), and that the future interest payments displaced a mix of dividends and share repurchases. Using τ_g here is sometimes referred to as the "new view" or "trapped-equity" view of retained earnings; see, for example, A. J. Auerbach, "Tax Integration and the 'New View' of the Corporate Tax: A 1980s Perspective," *Proceedings of the National Tax Association—Tax Institute of America* (1981): 21–27. Using τ_e corresponds to the "traditional view"; see, for example, J. M. Poterba and L. H. Summers, "Dividend Taxes, Corporate Investment, and 'Q,'" *Journal of Public Economics* 22 (1983): 135–167.

A firm must therefore balance the tax costs of holding cash with the potential benefits of not having to raise external funds in the future. Firms with very volatile earnings may also build up cash reserves to enable them to weather temporary periods of operating losses. By holding sufficient cash, these firms can avoid financial distress and its associated costs.

AGENCY COSTS OF RETAINING CASH

There is no benefit to shareholders when a firm holds cash above and beyond its future investment or liquidity needs, however. In fact, in addition to the tax cost, there are likely to be agency costs associated with having too much cash in the firm. As discussed in Chapter 16, when firms have excessive cash, managers may use the funds inefficiently by continuing money-losing pet projects, paying excessive executive perks, or over-paying for acquisitions. Leverage is one way to reduce a firm's excess cash; dividends and share repurchases perform a similar role by taking cash out of the firm. (See also the discussion on page 572 of equity holders' incentive to "cash out" when the firm is in or near financial distress.)

Thus paying out excess cash through dividends or share repurchases can boost the stock price by reducing managers' ability and temptation to waste resources and increasing managers' ability to negotiate, on the firm's behalf, with other stakeholders. For example, the roughly $10 increase in Value Line's stock price on the announcement of its special dividend, shown in Figure 17.6, likely corresponds to the perceived tax benefits and reduced agency costs that would result from the transaction.

EXAMPLE 17.7

CUTTING NEGATIVE-NPV GROWTH

Problem

Alsand Oil is an all-equity firm with 100 million shares outstanding. Alsand has $150 million in cash and expects future free cash flows of $65 million per year. Management plans to use the cash to expand the firm's operations, which will in turn increase future free cash flows by 12%. If the cost of capital of Alsand's investments is 10%, how would a decision to use the cash for a share repurchase rather than the expansion change the share price?

Solution

If Alsand uses the cash to expand, its future free cash flows will increase by 12% to $65 million × 1.12 = $72.8 million per year. Using the perpetuity formula, its market value will be $72.8 million ÷ 10% = $728 million, or $7.28 per share.

If Alsand does not expand, the value of its future free cash flows will be $65 million ÷ 10% = $650 million. Adding the cash, Alsand's market value is $800 million, or $8.00 per share. If Alsand repurchases shares, there will be no change to the share price: It will repurchase $150 million ÷ $8.00/share = 18.75 million shares, so it will have assets worth $650 million with 81.25 million shares outstanding, for a share price of $650 million ÷ 81.25 million shares = $8.00/share.

In this case, cutting investment and growth to fund a share repurchase increases the share price by $0.72 per share. The reason is the expansion has a negative NPV: It costs $150 million, but increases future free cash flows by only $7.8 million per year, for an NPV of

$$-\$150 \text{ million} + \$7.8 \text{ million}/10\% = -\$72 \text{ million, or } -\$0.72 \text{ per share}$$

FIRMS WITH LARGE CASH BALANCES (APRIL 2009)

TABLE 17.3

Ticker	Company	Cash ($ billion)	Percentage of Market Capitalization
MSFT	Microsoft	25.3	16%
PFE	Pfizer	34.9	38%
CSCO	Cisco Systems	33.5	32%
APPL	Apple	25.0	26%
INTC	Intel	10.6	12%
HPQ	Hewlett-Packard	12.9	15%

Source: Google Finance, April 2009.

Ultimately, firms should choose to retain cash for the same reasons they would use low leverage[22]—to preserve financial slack for future growth opportunities and to avoid financial distress costs. These needs must be balanced against the tax disadvantage of holding cash and the agency cost of wasteful investment. It is not surprising, then, that high-tech and biotechnology firms, which typically choose to use little debt, also tend to retain and accumulate large amounts of cash. See Table 17.3 for a list of some firms with large cash balances.

As with capital structure decisions, however, payout policies are generally set by managers, whose incentives may differ from those of shareholders. Managers may prefer to retain and maintain control over the firm's cash rather than pay it out. The retained cash can be used to fund investments that are costly for shareholders but have benefits for managers (for instance, pet projects and excessive salaries), or it can simply be held as a means to reduce leverage and the risk of financial distress that could threaten managers' job security. According to the managerial entrenchment theory of payout policy, managers pay out cash only when pressured to do so by the firm's investors.[23]

CONCEPT CHECK

1. Is there an advantage for a firm to retain its cash instead of paying it out to shareholders in perfect capital markets?

2. How do corporate taxes affect the decision of a firm to retain excess cash?

17.6 SIGNALLING WITH PAYOUT POLICY

One market imperfection that we have not yet considered is asymmetric information. When managers have better information than investors regarding the future prospects of the firm, their payout decisions may signal this information. In this section, we look at managers' motivations when setting a firm's payout policy, and we evaluate what these decisions may communicate to investors.

---

22. As discussed in Chapter 14, we can view excess cash as negative debt. As a consequence, the tradeoffs from holding excess cash are very similar to those involved in the capital structure decision.

23. Recall from Section 16.7 that the managerial entrenchment theory of capital structure argued that managers choose low leverage to avoid the discipline of debt and preserve their job security. Applied to payout policy, the same theory implies that managers will reduce leverage further by choosing to hold too much cash.

FIGURE 17.7

GM's Earnings and Dividends per Share, 1985–2008

Compared to GM's earnings, its dividend payments have remained relatively stable. (Data adjusted for splits, earnings exclude extraordinary items.)

Sources: Compustat, CapitalIQ, and GM.

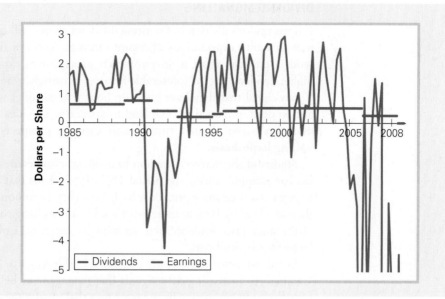

DIVIDEND SMOOTHING

Firms can change dividends at any time, but in practice they vary the sizes of their dividends relatively infrequently. For example, General Motors (GM) has changed the amount of its regular dividend only eight times over a 20-year period. Yet during that same period, GM's earnings varied widely, as shown in Figure 17.7.

The pattern seen with GM is typical of most firms that pay dividends. Firms adjust dividends relatively infrequently, and dividends are much less volatile than earnings. This practice of maintaining relatively constant dividends is called **dividend smoothing**. Firms also increase dividends much more frequently than they cut them. For example, from 1971 to 2001, only 5.4% of dividend changes were decreases.[24] In a classic survey of corporate executives, John Lintner[25] suggested that these observations resulted from (1) management's belief that investors prefer stable dividends with sustained growth and (2) management's desire to maintain a long-term target level of dividends as a fraction of earnings. Thus firms raise their dividends only when they perceive a long-term sustainable increase in the expected level of future earnings, and cut them only as a last resort.[26]

How can firms keep dividends smooth as earnings vary? As we have already discussed, firms can maintain almost any level of dividend in the short run by adjusting the number of shares they repurchase or issue and the amount of cash they retain. However, due to the tax and transaction costs of funding a dividend with new equity issues, managers do not wish to commit to a dividend that the firm cannot afford to pay out of regular earnings. For this reason, firms generally set dividends at a level they expect to be able to maintain based on the firm's earnings prospects.

---

24. F. Allen and R. Michaely, "Payout Policy," in G. M. Constantinides, M. Harris, and R. M. Stulz, eds., *Handbook of the Economics of Finance* (2003).

25. J. Lintner, "Distribution of Incomes of Corporations Among Dividends, Retained Earnings and Taxes," *American Economic Review* 46 (1956): 97–113.

26. While perhaps a good description of how firms *do* set their dividends, as we have shown in this chapter there is no clear reason why firms *should* smooth their dividends, nor convincing evidence that investors prefer this practice.

DIVIDEND SIGNALLING

If firms smooth dividends, the firm's dividend choice will contain information regarding management's expectations of future earnings. When a firm increases its dividend, it sends a positive signal to investors that management expects to be able to afford the higher dividend for the foreseeable future. Conversely, when managers cut the dividend, it may signal that they have given up hope that earnings will rebound in the near term and so need to reduce the dividend to save cash. The idea that dividend changes reflect managers' views about a firm's future earnings prospects is called the **dividend signalling hypothesis**.

Studies of the market's reaction to dividend changes are consistent with this hypothesis. For example, during the period 1967–1993, firms that raised their dividend by 10% or more saw their stock prices rise by 1.34% after the announcement, while those that cut their dividend by 10% or more experienced a price change of -3.71%.[27] The average size of the stock price reaction increases with the magnitude of the dividend change, and is larger for dividend cuts.[28]

Dividend signalling is similar to the use of leverage as a signal that we discussed in Chapter 16. Increasing debt signals that management believes the firm can afford the future interest payments, in the same way that raising the dividend signals the firm can afford to maintain the dividends in the future. However, while cutting the dividend is costly for managers in terms of their reputation and the reaction of investors, it is by no means as costly as failing to make debt payments. As a consequence, we would expect dividend changes to be a somewhat weaker signal than leverage changes. Indeed, empirical studies have found average stock price increases of more than 10% when firms replace equity with debt, and decreases of 4% to 10% when firms replace debt with equity.[29]

While an increase of a firm's dividend may signal management's optimism regarding its future cash flows, it might also signal a lack of investment opportunities. For example, Microsoft's move to initiate dividends in 2003 was largely seen to be a result of its declining growth prospects as opposed to a signal about its increased future profitability.[30] Conversely, a firm might cut its dividend to exploit new positive-NPV investment opportunities. In this case, the dividend decrease might lead to a positive—rather than negative—stock price reaction (see the box on Royal and SunAlliance's dividend cut, on next page). In general, we must interpret dividends as a signal in the context of the type of new information managers are likely to have.

---

27. See G. Grullon, R. Michaely, and B. Swaminathan, "Are Dividend Changes a Sign of Firm Maturity?" *Journal of Business* 75:3 (2002): 387–424. The effects are even larger for dividend initiations (13.4%) and omissions (27%), according to studies by R. Michaely, R. Thaler, and K. Womack, "Price Reactions to Dividend Initiations and Omissions: Overreaction or Drift?" *Journal of Finance* 50:2 (1995): 573–608, and similar results by P. Healy and K. Palepu, "Earnings Information Conveyed by Dividend Initiations and Omissions," *Journal of Financial Economics* 21:2 (1988): 149–176.

28. Not all of the evidence is consistent with dividend signalling, however. For example, it has been difficult to document a relationship between dividend changes and realized future earnings (S. Benartzi, R. Michaely and R. Thaler, "Do Changes in Dividends Signal the Future or the Past?" *Journal of Finance* 52:3 (1997): 1007–1034).

29. C. Smith, "Raising Capital: Theory and Evidence," in D. Chew, ed., *The New Corporate Finance* (McGraw-Hill, 1993).

30. See "An End to Growth?" *The Economist* (July 22, 2004): 61.

ROYAL & SUNALLIANCE'S DIVIDEND CUT

In some quarters, Julian Hance must have seemed like a heretic. On November 8, 2001, the finance director of Royal & SunAlliance, a U.K.-based insurance group with £12.6 billion (€20.2 billion) in annual revenue, did the unthinkable—he announced that he would cut the firm's dividend.

Many observers gasped at the decision. Surely, they argued, cutting the dividend was a sign of weakness. Didn't companies only cut their dividend when profits were falling?

Quite the contrary, countered Hance. With insurance premiums rising around the world, particularly following the World Trade Center tragedy, Royal & SunAlliance believed that its industry offered excellent growth opportunities.

"The outlook for business in 2002 and beyond makes a compelling case for reinvesting capital in the business rather than returning it to shareholders," explains Hance.

The stock market agreed with him, sending Royal & SunAlliance's shares up 5% following its dividend news. "Cutting the dividend is a positive move," observes Matthew Wright, an insurance analyst at Credit Lyonnais. "It shows the company expects future profitability to be good."

Source: Justin Wood, CFO Europe, December 2001.

SIGNALLING AND SHARE REPURCHASES

Share repurchases, like dividends, may also signal managers' information to the market. However, several important differences distinguish share repurchases and dividends. First, managers are much less committed to share repurchases than to dividend payments. As we noted earlier, when firms announce authorization for an open market share repurchase, they generally announce the maximum amount they plan to spend on repurchases. The actual amount spent, however, may be far less. Also, it may take several years to complete the share repurchase.[31] Second, unlike with dividends, firms do not smooth their repurchase activity from year to year. As a result, announcing a share repurchase today does not necessarily represent a long-term commitment to repurchase shares. In this regard, share repurchases may be less of a signal than dividends about future earnings of a firm.

A third key difference between dividends and share repurchases is that the cost of a share repurchase depends on the market price of the stock. If managers believe the stock is currently overvalued, a share repurchase will be costly to the firm. That is, buying the stock at its current (overvalued) price is a negative-NPV investment. By contrast, repurchasing shares when managers perceive the stock to be undervalued is a positive-NPV investment. Managers will clearly be more likely to repurchase shares if they believe the stock to be undervalued.

Thus share repurchases may signal that managers believe the firm to be undervalued (or at least not severely overvalued). Share repurchases are a credible signal that the shares are under-priced, because if they are over-priced a share repurchase is costly for current shareholders (and particularly for long-term investors who do not sell during the share repurchase). If investors believe that managers have better information regarding the firm's prospects and act on behalf of current shareholders, then investors will react favourably to share repurchase announcements.

---

31. See C. Stephens and M. Weisbach, "Actual Share Reacquisitions in Open-Market Repurchase Programs," *Journal of Finance* 53:1 (1998): 313–333, for an analysis of how firms' actual repurchases compare to their announced plans. For details of how share repurchase programs are implemented, see D. Cook, L. Krigman, and J. Leach, "On the Timing and Execution of Open Market Repurchases," *Review of Financial Studies* 17:2 (2004): 463–498.

| EXAMPLE **17.8** | SHARE REPURCHASES AND MARKET TIMING |

Problem

Clark Industries has 200 million shares outstanding, a current share price of $30, and no debt. Clark's management believes that the shares are under-priced, and that the true value is $35 per share. Clark plans to pay $600 million in cash to its shareholders by repurchasing shares at the current market price. Suppose that soon after the transaction is completed, new information comes out that causes investors to revise their opinion of the firm and agree with management's assessment of Clark's value. What is Clark's share price after the new information comes out? How would the share price differ if Clark waited until after the new information came out to repurchase the shares?

Solution

Clark's initial market cap is $30/share × 200 million shares = $6 billion, of which $600 million is cash and $5.4 billion corresponds to other assets. At the current share price, Clark will repurchase $600 million ÷ $30/share = 20 million shares. The market value balance sheet before and after the transaction is shown below (in millions of dollars):

	Before Repurchase	After Repurchase	After New Information
Cash	600	0	0
Other assets	5400	5400	6400
Total market value of assets	6000	5400	6400
Shares (millions)	200	180	180
Share Price	**$30**	**$30**	**$35.56**

According to management, Clark's initial market capitalization should be $35/share × 200 million shares = $7 billion, of which $6.4 billion would correspond to other assets. As the market value balance sheet shows, after the new information comes out Clark's share price will rise to $35.56.

If Clark waited for the new information to come out before repurchasing the shares, it would buy shares at a market price of $35 per share. Thus it would repurchase only 17.1 million shares. The share price after the repurchase would be $6.4 billion ÷ 182.9 shares = $35.

By repurchasing shares while the stock is under-priced, the ultimate share price will be $0.56 higher, for a total gain of $0.56 × 180 million shares = $100 million for long-term shareholders. Note, this gain equals the loss to the selling shareholders from selling 20 million shares at a price that is $5 below their true value.

As this example shows, the gain from buying shares when the stock is under-priced leads to an increase in the firm's long-run share price. The firm may therefore try to time its repurchases appropriately. Anticipating this strategy, shareholders may interpret a share repurchase as a signal that the firm is undervalued.

In a 2004 survey, 87% of CFOs agreed that firms should repurchase shares when their stock price is a good value relative to its true value,[32] implicitly indicating that most CFOs believe that they should act in the interests of the long-term shareholders. Thus, if investors

---

32. A. Brav, J. Graham, C. Harvey, and R. Michaely, "Payout Policy in the 21st Century," *Journal of Financial Economics* 77:3 (2005): 483–527.

believe that managers have better information regarding the firm's prospects than they do, then investors should react favourably to share repurchase announcements. Indeed they do: The average market price reaction to the announcement of an open market share repurchase program is about 3% (with the size of the reaction increasing in the portion of shares outstanding sought).[33] The reaction is much larger for fixed-price tender offers (12%) and Dutch auction share repurchases (8%).[34] Recall that these methods of repurchase are generally used for very large repurchases conducted in a very short timeframe and are often part of an overall recapitalization. Also, the shares are repurchased at a premium to the current market price. Thus tender offers and Dutch auction repurchases are even stronger signals than open market repurchases that management views the current share price as undervalued.

CONCEPT CHECK

1. What possible signals does a firm give when it cuts its dividend?

2. Would managers be more likely to repurchase shares if they believe the stock is undervalued or overvalued?

17.7   STOCK DIVIDENDS, SPLITS, AND SPIN-OFFS

In this chapter, we have focused on a firm's decision to pay cash to its shareholders. But a firm can pay another type of dividend that does not involve cash: a stock dividend. In this case, each shareholder who owns the stock before it goes ex-dividend receives additional shares of stock of the firm itself (a stock split) or of a subsidiary (a spin-off). Here we briefly review these two types of transactions.

STOCK DIVIDENDS AND SPLITS

If a company declares a 10% stock dividend, each shareholder will receive one new share of stock for every 10 shares already owned. Stock dividends of 50% or higher are generally referred to as stock splits. For example, with a 50% stock dividend, each shareholder will receive one new share for every two shares owned. Because a holder of two shares will end up holding three new shares, this transaction is also called a 3:2 ("3-for-2") stock split. Similarly, a 100% stock dividend is equivalent to a 2:1 stock split.

With a stock dividend, a firm does not pay out any cash to shareholders. As a result, the total market value of the firm's assets and liabilities, and therefore of its equity, is unchanged. The only thing that is different is the number of shares outstanding. The stock price will therefore fall because the same total equity value is now divided over a larger number of shares.

Let's illustrate a stock dividend for Genron. Suppose Genron paid a 50% stock dividend (a 3:2 stock split) rather than a cash dividend. Table 17.4 shows the market value balance sheet and the resulting share price before and after the stock dividend.

A shareholder who owns 100 shares before the dividend has a portfolio worth $42 \times 100 = \$4200$. After the dividend, the shareholder owns 150 shares worth $28, giving a portfolio value of $\$28 \times 150 = \$4200$. (Note the important difference between a stock split and a share issuance: When the company issues shares, the number of shares increases,

---

33. See D. Ikenberry, J. Lakonishok, and T. Vermaelen, "Market Underreaction to Open Market Share Repurchases," *Journal of Financial Economics* 39:2 (1995): 181–208, and G. Grullon and R. Michaely, "Dividends, Share Repurchases, and the Substitution Hypothesis," *Journal of Finance* 57:4 (2002): 1649–1684.

34. R. Comment and G. Jarrell, "The Relative Signaling Power of Dutch-Auction and Fixed-Price Self-Tender Offers and Open-Market Share Repurchases," *Journal of Finance* 46:4 (1991): 1243–1271.

INTERVIEW WITH JOHN CONNORS

John Connors was senior vice-president and chief financial officer of Microsoft. He retired in 2005 and is now a partner at Ignition Partners, a Seattle venture capital firm.

QUESTION: Microsoft declared a dividend for the first time in 2003. What goes into the decision of a company to initiate a dividend?

ANSWER: Microsoft was in a unique position. The company had never paid a dividend and was facing shareholder pressure to do something with its $60 billion cash buildup. The company considered five key questions in developing its distribution strategy:

1. Can the company sustain payment of a cash dividend in perpetuity and increase the dividend over time? Microsoft was confident it could meet that commitment and raise the dividend in the future.

2. Is a cash dividend a better return to stockholders than a stock buyback program? These are capital structure decisions: Do we want to reduce our shares outstanding? Is our stock attractively priced for a buyback, or do we want to distribute the cash as a dividend? Microsoft had plenty of capacity to issue a dividend and continue a buyback program.

3. What is the tax effect of a cash dividend versus a buyback to the corporation and to shareholders? From a tax perspective to shareholders, it was largely a neutral decision in Microsoft's case.

4. What is the psychological impact on investors, and how does it fit the story of the stock for investors? This is a more qualitative factor. A regular ongoing dividend put Microsoft on a path to becoming an attractive investment for income investors.

5. What are the public relations implications of a dividend program? Investors don't look to Microsoft to hold cash but to be a leader in software development and provide equity growth. So they viewed the dividend program favourably.

QUESTION: How does a company decide whether to increase its dividend, have a special dividend, or repurchase its stock to return capital to investors?

ANSWER: The decision to increase the dividend is a function of cash flow projections. Are you confident that you have adequate cash flow to sustain this and future increases? Once you increase the dividend, investors expect future increases as well. Some companies establish explicit criteria for dividend increases. In my experience as a CFO, the analytic framework involves a set of relative comparables. What are the dividend payouts and dividend yields of the market in general and of your peer group, and where are we relative to them? We talk to significant investors and consider what is best for increasing shareholder value long term.

A special dividend is a very efficient form of cash distribution that generally involves a nonrecurring situation, such as the sale of a business division or a cash award from a legal situation. Also, companies without a comprehensive distribution strategy use special dividends to reduce large cash accumulations. For Microsoft, the 2004 special dividend and announcement of the stock dividend and stock buyback program resolved the issue of what to do with all the cash and clarified our direction going forward.

QUESTION: What other factors go into dividend decisions?

ANSWER: Powerful finance and accounting tools help us to make better and broader business decisions. But these decisions involve as much psychology and market thinking as math. You have to consider non-quantifiable factors such as the psychology of investors. Not long ago, everyone wanted growth stocks; no one wanted dividend-paying stocks. Now dividend stocks are in vogue. You must also take into account your industry and what the competition is doing. In many tech companies, employee ownership in the form of options programs represents a fairly significant percentage of fully diluted shares. Dividend distributions reduce volatility of stock and hence the value of options.

At the end of the day, you want to be sure that your cash distribution strategy helps your overall story with investors.

CUM- AND EX-DIVIDEND SHARE PRICE FOR GENRON WITH A 50% STOCK DIVIDEND ($ MILLION)

TABLE 17.4

	December 11 (cum-dividend)	December 12 (ex-dividend)
Cash	20	20
Other assets	400	400
Total market value of assets	420	420
Shares (millions)	10	15
Share price	$42	$28

but the firm also raises cash to add to its existing assets. If the shares are sold at a fair price, the stock price should not change.)

Unlike cash dividends, stock dividends are not taxed. Thus, from both the firm's and shareholders' perspectives, there is no real consequence to a stock dividend. The number of shares is proportionally increased and the price per share is proportionally reduced so that there is no change in value.

Why, then, do companies pay stock dividends or split their stock? The typical motivation for a stock split is to keep the share price in a range thought to be attractive to small investors. Stocks generally trade in lots of 100 shares, and in any case do not trade in units less than one share. As a result, if the share price rises significantly, it might be difficult for small investors to afford one share, let alone 100. Making the stock more attractive to small investors can increase the demand for and the liquidity of the stock, which may in turn boost the stock price. On average, announcements of stock splits are associated with a 2% increase in the stock price.[35]

Most firms use splits to keep their share prices from exceeding $100. From 1990 to 2000, Cisco Systems split its stock nine times, so that one share purchased at the IPO split into 288 shares. Had it not split, Cisco's share price at the time of its March 2000 split would have been 288 × $72.19, or $20,790.72.

Firms also do not want their stock prices to fall too low. First, a stock price that is very low raises transaction costs for investors. For example, the spread between the bid and ask price for a stock has a minimum size of one tick, which is $0.01 (for the NYSE and NASDAQ exchanges and for TSX stocks with stock prices greater than $0.50). In percentage terms, the tick size is larger for stocks with a low price than for stocks with a high price. Also, many exchanges require stocks to maintain a minimum price to remain

35. S. Nayak and N. Prabhala, "Disentangling the Dividend Information in Splits: A Decomposition Using Conditional Event-Study Methods," *Review of Financial Studies* 14:4 (2001): 1083–1116. For evidence that stock splits are successful at attracting individual investors, see R. Dhar, W. Goetzmann, and N. Zhu, "The Impact of Clientele Changes: Evidence from Stock Splits," *Yale ICF Working Paper no. 03-14* (2004). While splits seem to increase the number of shareholders, evidence of their impact on liquidity is mixed; see, for example, T. Copeland, "Liquidity Changes Following Stock Splits," *Journal of Finance* 34:1 (1979): 115–141, and J. Lakonishok and B. Lev, "Stock Splits and Stock Dividends: Why, Who and When," *Journal of Finance* 42:4 (1987): 913–932.

BERKSHIRE HATHAWAY'S A & B SHARES

Many managers split their stock to keep the price affordable for small investors, making it easier for them to buy and sell the stock. Warren Buffett, chairman and chief executive of Berkshire Hathaway, disagrees. As he commented in Berkshire's 1983 annual report: "We are often asked why Berkshire does not split its stock . . . we want [shareholders] who think of themselves as business owners with the intention of staying a long time. And, we want those who keep their eyes focused on business results, not market prices." In its 40-year history, Berkshire Hathaway has never split its stock.

As a result of Berkshire Hathaway's strong performance and the lack of stock splits, the stock price climbed. By 1996, it exceeded $30,000 per share. Because this price was much too expensive for some small investors, several financial intermediaries created unit investment trusts whose only investment was Berkshire shares. (Unit investment trusts are similar to mutual funds, but their

investment portfolio is fixed.) Investors could buy smaller interests in these trusts, effectively owning Berkshire stock with a much lower initial investment.

In response, in February 1996 Buffett announced the creation of a second class of Berkshire Hathaway stock, the Class B shares. Each owner of the original shares (now called Class A shares) was offered the opportunity to convert each A share into 30 B shares. "We're giving shareholders a do-it-yourself split, if they care to do it," Buffett said. Through the B shares, investors could own Berkshire stock with a smaller investment, and they would not have to pay the extra transaction costs required to buy stock through the unit trusts.

Meanwhile the value of the A shares has continued to do well. After reaching a peak of $148,000 in late 2007 and dropping to below $75,000 in March 2009 (at the bottom of the financial crisis), the price of one share of Berkshire Hathaway Class A shares was more than $120,000 per share in October 2010.*

*We should note that Buffett's logic for not splitting the stock is a bit puzzling. Why should letting the stock price rise to a very high level attract a "better" investor clientele compared to splitting the stock and keeping its price in a more typical range? And if an extremely high stock price were advantageous, Buffett could have obtained it much sooner through a reverse split of the stock.

listed on an exchange. (For example, the NYSE and NASDAQ require listed firms to maintain a price of at least $1 per share. The TSX has no such requirement.)

If the price of the stock falls too low, a company can engage in a **reverse split** and reduce the number of shares outstanding. For example, in a 1:10 reverse split, every 10 shares of stock are replaced with a single share. As a result, the share price increases tenfold. Reverse splits became necessary for many dot-coms after the dot-com bust in 2000. Infospace.com, for instance, split 2:1 three times in 1999 through 2000, but was forced to implement a 1:10 reverse split in 2002 when its share price dropped below $0.40.

Through a combination of splits and reverse splits, firms on major exchanges (like the NYSE) can keep their share prices in any range they desire. As Figure 17.8 shows, almost all firms on major exchanges (like the NYSE) have stock prices below $100 per share, with most firms' prices being between $5 and $60 per share. In January 2010, the average price for shares traded on the TSX was about $11.62 per share. For exchanges like the TSX Venture Exchange, it is more common for firms to have lower stock prices, including many with prices below $1 per share. In January 2010, the average price for shares traded on the TSX Venture Exchange was about $0.46 per share.

SPIN-OFFS

Rather than pay a dividend using cash or shares of its own stock, a firm can also distribute shares of a subsidiary in a transaction referred to as a **spin-off**. Non-cash special dividends are commonly used to spin off assets or a subsidiary as a separate company. For example, after selling 10% of Northern Electric stock in an initial public offering in 1973, and

FIGURE 17.8

Distribution of Share Prices on the NYSE (June 2009)
By using splits and reverse splits, most firms keep their share prices between $2.50 and $60 to reduce transaction costs for investors. The median share price is $13.55.

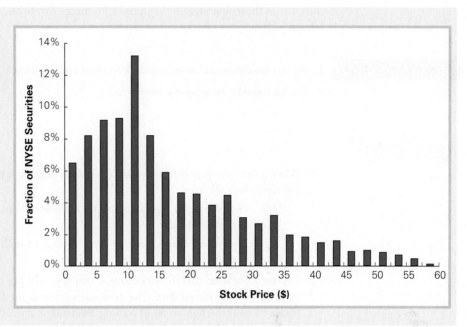

further reductions in ownership over the years, Bell Canada Enterprises (BCE) announced it would spin off its 35% ownership of Nortel in May 2000. The spin-off was accomplished through a special dividend in which each BCE shareholder received 1.570386 shares of Nortel per share of BCE owned. After receiving the Nortel shares, BCE shareholders could trade them separately from the shares of the parent firm.

On the effective date of the arrangement, May 1, 2000, Nortel shares had an average price of $86.49. Thus the value of the special dividend was

$$1.570386 \text{ Nortel shares} \times \$86.49 \text{ per share} = \$135.82 \text{ per share}$$

A shareholder who initially owned 100 shares of BCE stock would receive 157 shares of Nortel stock, plus cash of $0.0386 \times \$86.49 = \$3.34$ in place of the fractional shares.

Alternatively, BCE could have sold the shares of Nortel and distributed the cash to shareholders as a cash dividend. The transaction BCE chose offers two advantages over that strategy: (1) it avoids the transaction costs associated with such a sale and (2) the special dividend is not taxed as a cash distribution. Instead, BCE shareholders who received Nortel shares are liable for capital gains tax only at the time they sell the Nortel shares.[36]

Here we have considered only the methods of distributing the shares of the firm that has been spun off, either by paying a stock dividend or by selling the shares directly and then distributing (or retaining) the cash. The decision of whether to do the spin-off in the first place raises a new question: When is it better for two firms to operate as separate entities, rather than as a single combined firm? The issues that arise in addressing this question are

---

36. The capital gain is computed by allocating a fraction of the adjusted cost basis (ACB) of the BCE shares to the Nortel shares received. Because of the relative values of BCE shares and Nortel shares on the ex-dividend date, BCE advised that 30.79% of the original BCE shares' ACB should be allocated to the post–spin-off BCE shares ACB and that 69.21% of the original BCE shares' ACB should be allocated to the ACB of the new Nortel shares.

the same as those that arise in the decision to merge two firms, which we discuss further in Chapter 28.

CONCEPT CHECK

1. What is the difference between a stock dividend and a stock split?

2. What is the main purpose of a reverse split?

SUMMARY

1. When a firm wants to distribute cash to its shareholders, it can pay a cash dividend or it can repurchase shares.

   a. Most companies pay regular, quarterly dividends. Sometimes firms announce one-time, special dividends.

   b. Firms repurchase shares using an open market repurchase, a tender offer, a Dutch auction repurchase, or a targeted repurchase.

2. On the declaration date, firms announce that they will pay dividends to all shareholders of record on the record date. The ex-dividend date is the first day on which the stock trades without the right to an upcoming dividend; it is usually two trading days prior to the record date. Dividend cheques are mailed on the payment date.

3. In a stock split or a stock dividend, a company distributes additional shares rather than cash to shareholders.

4. In perfect capital markets, the stock price falls by the amount of the dividend when a dividend is paid. An open market share repurchase has no effect on the stock price, and the stock price is the same as the cum-dividend price if a dividend were paid instead.

5. The Modigliani-Miller dividend irrelevance proposition states that in perfect capital markets, holding fixed the investment policy of a firm, the firm's choice of dividend policy is irrelevant and does not affect the initial share price.

6. In reality, capital markets are not perfect, and market imperfections affect firm dividend policy.

7. Taxes are an important market friction that affects dividend policy.

   a. Considering taxes as the only market imperfection, when the tax rate on dividends exceeds the tax rate on capital gains, the optimal dividend policy is for firms to pay no dividends. Firms should use share repurchases for all payouts.

   b. The effective dividend tax rate, τ_d^*, measures the net tax cost to the investor per dollar of dividend income received.

$$\tau_d^* = \left(\frac{\tau_d - \tau_g}{1 - \tau_g} \right) \tag{17.3}$$

   The effective dividend tax rate varies across investors for several reasons, including income level, investment horizon, tax jurisdiction, and type of investment account.

   c. Different investor taxes create clientele effects, in which the dividend policy of a firm suits the tax preference of its investor clientele.

8. Modigliani-Miller payout policy irrelevance says that, in perfect capital markets, if a firm invests excess cash flows in financial securities, the firm's choice of payout versus retention is irrelevant and does not affect the initial share price.

9. Corporate taxes make it costly for a firm to retain excess cash. Even after adjusting for investor taxes, retaining excess cash brings a substantial tax disadvantage for a firm. The effective tax disadvantage of retaining cash is given by

$$\tau_{retain}^* = \left[1 - \frac{(1-\tau_c)(1-\tau_g)}{(1-\tau_i)} \right] \qquad (17.7)$$

10. Even though there is a tax disadvantage to retaining cash, some firms accumulate cash balances. Cash balances help firms minimize the transaction costs of raising new capital when they have future potential cash needs. However, there is no benefit to shareholders from firms holding cash in excess of future investment needs.

11. In addition to the tax disadvantage of holding cash, agency costs may arise, as managers may be tempted to spend excess cash on inefficient investments and perks. Without pressure from shareholders, managers may choose to hoard cash to spend in this way or as a means of reducing a firm's leverage and increasing their job security.

12. Dividends and share repurchases help minimize the agency problem of wasteful spending when a firm has excess cash. They also reduce the transfer of value to debt holders or other stakeholders.

13. Firms typically maintain relatively constant dividends. This practice is called dividend smoothing.

14. The idea that dividend changes reflect managers' views about firms' future earnings prospects is called the dividend signalling hypothesis.

    a. Managers usually increase dividends only when they are confident the firm will be able to afford higher dividends for the foreseeable future.

    b. When managers cut the dividend, it may signal that they have lost hope that earnings will improve.

15. Share repurchases may be used to signal positive information, as repurchases are more attractive if management believes the stock is undervalued at its current price.

16. With a stock dividend, shareholders receive either additional shares of stock of the firm itself (a stock split) or shares of a subsidiary (a spin-off). The stock price generally falls proportionally with the size of the split.

17. A reverse split decreases the number of shares outstanding, and therefore results in a higher share price.

KEY TERMS

bird in the hand hypothesis *p. 596*
clientele effect *p. 603*
cum-dividend *p. 592*
declaration date *p. 588*
dividend puzzle *p. 600*
dividend signalling hypothesis *p. 612*
dividend smoothing *p. 611*
dividend-capture theory *p. 603*
Dutch auction *p. 590*
effective dividend tax rate *p. 601*
ex-dividend date *p. 588*
greenmail *p. 591*
liquidating dividend *p. 590*

open market repurchase *p. 590*
payable date (distribution date) *p. 588*
payout policy *p. 588*
record date *p. 588*
return of capital *p. 590*
reverse split *p. 618*
special dividend *p. 588*
spin-off *p. 618*
stock dividend *p. 589*
stock split *p. 589*
targeted repurchase *p. 591*
tender offer *p. 590*

PROBLEMS

Distributions to Shareholders

1. What options does a firm have to spend its free cash flow (after it has satisfied all interest obligations)?

2. ABC Corporation announced that it will pay a dividend to all shareholders of record as of Monday, April 3, 2009. It takes three business days after a purchase for the new owners of a share of stock to be registered.

    a. When is the last day an investor can purchase ABC stock and still get the dividend payment?

    b. When is the ex-dividend date?

3. Describe the different mechanisms available to a firm to repurchase shares.

Comparison of Dividends and Share Repurchases

4. RFC Corp. has announced a $1 dividend. If RFC's last cum-dividend price is $50, what should its first ex-dividend price be (assuming perfect capital markets)?

5. EJH Company has a market capitalization of $1 billion and 20 million shares outstanding. It plans to distribute $100 million through an open market repurchase. Assuming perfect capital markets,

    a. What will the price per share of EJH be right before the repurchase?

    b. How many shares will be repurchased?

    c. What will the price per share of EJH be right after the repurchase?

6. KMS Corporation has assets with a market value of $500 million, $50 million of which are cash. It has debt of $200 million, and 10 million shares outstanding. Assume perfect capital markets.

    a. What is its current stock price?

    b. If KMS distributes $50 million as a dividend, what will its share price be after the dividend is paid?

    c. If instead KMS distributes $50 million as a share repurchase, what will its share price be once the shares are repurchased?

    d. What will its new market debt-equity ratio be after either transaction?

7. Natsam Corporation has $250 million of excess cash. The firm has no debt and 500 million shares outstanding with a current market price of $15 per share. Natsam's board has decided to pay out this cash as a one-time dividend.

    a. What is the ex-dividend price of a share in a perfect capital market?

    b. If the board instead decided to use the cash to do a one-time share repurchase, in a perfect capital market what is the price of the shares once the repurchase is complete?

    c. In a perfect capital market, which policy (in part a or b) makes investors in the firm better off?

8. Suppose the board of Natsam Corporation decided to do the share repurchase in Problem 7b, but you, as an investor, would have preferred to receive a dividend payment. How can you leave yourself in the same position as if the board had elected to make the dividend payment instead?

9. Suppose you work for Oracle Corporation, and part of your compensation takes the form of stock options. The value of the stock option is equal to the difference between Oracle's stock price and an exercise price of $10 per share at the time that you exercise the option. As an option holder, would you prefer that Oracle use dividends or share repurchases to pay out cash to shareholders? Explain.

The Tax Disadvantage of Dividends

10. The HNH Corporation will pay a constant dividend of $2 per share, per year, in perpetuity. Assume all investors pay a 20% tax on dividends and that there is no capital gains tax. The cost of capital for investing in HNH stock is 12%.
    a. What is the price of a share of HNH stock?
    b. Assume that management makes a surprise announcement that HNH will no longer pay dividends but will use the cash to repurchase stock instead. What is the price of a share of HNH stock now?

Dividend Capture and Tax Clienteles

11. What was the effective dividend tax rate for a Quebec investor in the highest tax bracket who planned to hold a stock for one year in 2008? How did this compare to an Alberta investor in the highest tax bracket who planned to hold a stock for one year in 2008? (See Table 15.3 for data.)

12. Suppose that all capital gains are taxed at a 25% rate and that the dividend tax rate is 50%. Arbuckle Corp. is currently trading for $30, and is about to pay a $6 special dividend.
    a. Absent any other trading frictions or news, what will its share price be just after the dividend is paid?

    Suppose Arbuckle made a surprise announcement that it would do a share repurchase rather than pay a special dividend.
    b. What net tax savings per share for an investor would result from this decision?
    c. What would happen to Arbuckle's stock price upon the announcement of this change?

13. An investor bought 500 shares in West Coast Hydro for $100 per share. The shares are currently trading for $105 and tomorrow they go ex-dividend. The dividend that was declared was for $5 per share and is to be paid shortly. The investor would like to sell the shares either today or tomorrow. When should the investor sell? Show the after-tax cash flows to the investor of the two alternatives assuming the investor is a Quebec resident. How would this change if the investor was an Alberta resident? How would this change if the investor held the shares within an RRSP and did not plan to withdraw from the RRSP?

14. On Monday, November 15, 2004, TheStreet.Com reported: "An experiment in the efficiency of financial markets will play out Monday following the expiration of a $3.08 dividend privilege for holders of Microsoft." The story went on: "The stock is currently trading ex-dividend both the special $3 payout and Microsoft's regular 8-cent quarterly dividend, meaning a buyer doesn't receive the money if he acquires the shares now." Microsoft stock ultimately opened for trade at $27.34 on the ex-dividend date (November 15), down $2.63 from its previous close.
    a. Assuming that this price drop resulted only from the dividend payment (no other information affected the stock price that day), what does this decline in price imply about the effective dividend tax rate for Microsoft?
    b. Based on this information, which investors are most likely to be the marginal investors (the ones who determine the price) in Microsoft stock? (Assume U.S. investors are taxed on both dividends and capital gains at a rate of 15%.)
        i. Long-term individual investors
        ii. One-year individual investors

      iii. Pension funds

      iv. Corporations

15. At current tax rates, which investors are most likely to hold a stock that has a high dividend yield?

    a. Individual investors

    b. Pension funds

    c. Mutual funds

    d. Corporations

16. Que Corp. pays a regular dividend of $1 per share. Typically, the stock price drops by $0.80 per share when the stock goes ex-dividend. Suppose the capital gains tax rate is 20%, but investors pay different tax rates on dividends. Absent transactions costs, what is the highest dividend tax rate of an investor who could gain from trading to capture the dividend?

17. A stock that you know is held by long-term individual investors paid a large one-time dividend. You notice that the price drop on the ex-dividend date is about the size of the dividend payment. You find this relationship puzzling given the tax disadvantage of dividends. Explain how the dividend-capture theory might account for this behaviour.

Payout Versus Retention of Cash

18. Clovix Corp. has $50 million in cash, 10 million shares outstanding, and a current share price of $30. Clovix is deciding whether to use the $50 million to pay an immediate special dividend of $5 per share, or to retain and invest it at the risk-free rate of 10% and use the $5 million in interest earned to increase its regular annual dividend of $0.50 per share. Assume perfect capital markets.

    a. Suppose Clovix pays the special dividend. How can a shareholder who would prefer an increase in the regular dividend create it on her own?

    b. Suppose Clovix increases its regular dividend. How can a shareholder who would prefer the special dividend create it on her own?

EXCEL 19. Assume capital markets are perfect. Kay Industries currently has $100 million invested in short-term Treasury securities paying 7%, and it pays out the interest payments on these securities as a dividend. The board is considering selling the Treasury securities and paying out the proceeds as a one-time dividend payment.

    a. If the board went ahead with this plan, what would happen to the value of Kay stock upon the announcement of a change in policy?

    b. What would happen to the value of Kay stock on the ex-dividend date of the one-time dividend?

    c. Given these price reactions, will this decision benefit investors?

EXCEL 20. Redo Problem 19 but assume that Kay must pay a corporate tax rate of 35%, and investors pay no taxes.

EXCEL 21. Re-do Problem 19 but assume that

    a. Investors pay a 15% tax on dividends but no capital gains taxes or taxes on interest income, and Kay does not pay corporate taxes.

    b. Investors pay a 15% tax on dividends and capital gains and a 35% tax on interest income, while Kay pays a 35% corporate tax rate.

22. Harris Corp. has $250 million in cash, and 100 million shares outstanding. Suppose the corporate tax rate is 35% and investors pay no taxes on dividends, capital gains, or interest income. Investors had expected Harris to pay out the $250 million through a share repurchase. Suppose instead that Harris announces it will permanently retain the cash and use the

interest on the cash to pay a regular dividend. If there are no other benefits of retaining the cash, how will Harris's stock price change upon this announcement?

23. Raviv Industries has $100 million in cash that it can use for a share repurchase. Suppose instead Raviv invests the funds in an account paying 10% interest for one year.

    a. If the corporate tax rate is 40%, how much additional cash will Raviv have at the end of the year net of corporate taxes?

    b. If investors pay a 20% tax rate on capital gains, by how much will the value of their shares have increased, net of capital gains taxes?

    c. If investors pay a 30% tax rate on interest income, how much would they have had if they invested the $100 million on their own?

    d. Suppose Raviv retained the cash so that it would not need to raise new funds from outside investors for an expansion it has planned for next year. If it did raise new funds, it would have to pay issuance fees. How much does Raviv need to save in issuance fees to make retaining the cash beneficial for its investors? (Assume fees can be expensed for corporate tax purposes.)

24. Use the data in Table 15.3 to calculate the tax disadvantage of retained cash (assume firms are not small businesses).

    a. Assume the firm and investors were taxed in Alberta.

    b. Assume the firm and investors were taxed in Quebec.

Signalling with Payout Policy

25. Explain under which conditions an increase in the dividend payment can be interpreted as a signal of

    a. Good news

    b. Bad news

26. Why is an announcement of a share repurchase considered a positive signal?

EXCEL *27. AMC Corporation currently has an enterprise value of $400 million and $100 million in excess cash. The firm has 10 million shares outstanding and no debt. Suppose AMC uses its excess cash to repurchase shares. After the share repurchase, news will come out that will change AMC's enterprise value to either $600 million or $200 million.

    a. What is AMC's share price prior to the share repurchase?

    b. What is AMC's share price after the repurchase if its enterprise value goes up? What is AMC's share price after the repurchase if its enterprise value declines?

    c. Suppose AMC waits until after the news comes out to do the share repurchase. What is AMC's share price after the repurchase if its enterprise value goes up? What is AMC's share price after the repurchase if its enterprise value declines?

    d. Suppose AMC management expects good news to come out. Based on your answers to parts b and c, if management desires to maximize AMC's ultimate share price, will they undertake the repurchase before or after the news comes out? When would management undertake the repurchase if they expect bad news to come out?

    e. Given your answer to part d, what effect would you expect an announcement of a share repurchase to have on the stock price? Why?

Stock Dividends, Splits, and Spin-offs

28. Berkshire Hathaway's A shares are trading at $120,000 per share. What split ratio would it need to bring its stock price down to $50 per share?

EXCEL 29. Suppose the stock of Host Hotels & Resorts is currently trading for $20 per share.

    a. If Host issued a 20% stock dividend, what will its new share price be?

    b. If Host does a 3:2 stock split, what will its new share price be?

    c. If Host does a 1:3 reverse split, what will its new share price be?

30. Explain why most companies choose to pay stock dividends (split their stock).

31. When might it be advantageous to undertake a reverse stock split?

32. After the market close on May 11, 2001, Adaptec, Inc., distributed a dividend of shares of its software division, Roxio, Inc. Each Adaptec shareholder received 0.1646 share of Roxio stock per share of Adaptec stock owned. At the time, Adaptec stock was trading at a price of $10.55 per share (cum-dividend), and Roxio's share price was $14.23 per share. In a perfect market, what would Adaptec's ex-dividend share price be after this transaction?

DATA CASE

In your role as a consultant at a wealth management firm, you have been assigned a very powerful client who holds 1 million shares of Amazon.com purchased on February 28, 2003. In researching Amazon, you discovered that they are holding a large amount of cash, which was surprising since the firm has only relatively recently begun operating at a profit. Additionally, your client is upset that the Amazon stock price has been somewhat stagnant as of late. The client is considering approaching the board of directors with a plan for half of the cash the firm has accumulated, but can't decide whether a share repurchase or a special dividend would be best. You have been asked to determine which initiative would generate the greatest amount of money after taxes, assuming that with a share repurchase your client would keep the same proportion of ownership. Because both dividends and capital gains are taxed at the same rate (15%), your client has assumed that there is no difference between the repurchase and the dividend. To confirm, you need to "run the numbers" for each scenario.

1. Go to the NASDAQ homepage (www.nasdaq.com), enter the symbol for Amazon (AMZN), and click "Summary Quote."

   a. Record the current price and the number of shares outstanding.

   b. Click on company financials and then select the balance sheet. Right-click with the cursor in the middle of the balance sheet and select "Export to Microsoft Excel."

2. Using one-half of the most recent cash and cash equivalents reported on the balance sheet (in thousands of dollars), compute the following:

   a. The number of shares that would be repurchased given the current market price.

   b. The dividend per share that could be paid given the total number of shares outstanding.

3. Go to Yahoo! Finance (http://finance.yahoo.com) to obtain the price at which your client purchased the stock on February 28, 2003.

   a. Enter the symbol for Amazon and click "Get Quotes."

   b. Click "Historical Prices," enter the date your client purchased the stock as the start date and the end date, and hit Enter. Record the adjusted closing price.

4. Compute the total cash that would be received by your client under the repurchase and the dividend both before and after taxes.

5. The calculation in the last step reflects your client's immediate cash flow and tax liability, but it does not consider the final payoff for the client after any shares not sold in a repurchase are liquidated. To incorporate this feature, you first decide to see what happens if the client sells all remaining shares of stock immediately after the dividend or the repurchase. Assume that the stock price will fall by the amount of the dividend if a dividend is paid. What are the client's total after-tax cash flows (considering both the payout and the capital gain) under the repurchase of the dividend in this case?

6. Under which program would your client be better off before taxes? Which program is better after taxes, assuming the remaining shares are sold immediately after the dividend is paid?

7. Because your client is unlikely to sell all 1 million shares today, at the time of dividend/repurchase, you decide to consider two longer holding periods. Assume that under both plans the client sells all remaining shares of stock 5 years later, or the client sells 10 years later. Assume that the stock will return 10% per year going forward. Also assume that Amazon will pay no other dividends over the next 10 years.

   a. What would the stock price be after 5 years or 10 years if a dividend is paid now?

   b. What would the stock price be after 5 years or 10 years if Amazon repurchases shares now?

   c. Calculate the total after-tax cash flows at both points in time (when the dividend payment or the share repurchase takes place, and when the rest of the shares are sold) for your client if the remaining shares are sold in 5 years under both initiatives. Compute the difference between the cash flows under both initiatives at each point in time. Repeat assuming the shares are sold in 10 years.

8. Repeat Question 7 assuming the stock will return 20% per year going forward. What do you notice about the difference in the cash flows under the two initiatives when the return is 20% and 10%?

9. Calculate the NPV of the difference in the cash flows under both holding period assumptions for a range of discount rates. Based on your answer to Question 8, what is the correct discount rate to use?

THE LAW OF ONE PRICE CONNECTION. In this part of the text we return to the topic of valuation and integrate our understanding of risk, return, and the firm's choice of capital structure. Chapter 18 combines the knowledge of the first five parts of the text and develops the three main methods for capital budgeting with leverage and market imperfections: The weighted average cost of capital (WACC) method, the adjusted present value (APV) method, and the flow-to-equity (FTE) method. While the Law of One Price guarantees that all three methods ultimately lead to the same assessment of value, we will identify conditions that can make one method easiest to apply. Chapter 19 applies Chapter 18's methods of valuation to value a corporation in the context of a leveraged acquisition. Chapter 19 thus serves as a capstone case that illustrates how all the concepts developed to date in the text are used to make complex, real-world financial decisions.

CHAPTER

18

NOTATION

FCF_t	free cash flows at date t
r_{wacc}	weighted average cost of capital
r_E, r_D	equity and debt costs of capital
r_D^*	equity-equivalent debt cost of capital
E	market value of equity
D	market value of debt (net of cash)
τ_c	marginal corporate tax rate
D_t	incremental debt of project on date t
V_t^L	value of a levered investment on date t
d	debt-to-value ratio
r_U	unlevered cost of capital
V^U	unlevered value of investment
T^s	value of predetermined tax shields
k	interest coverage ratio
Int_t	interest expense on date t
D^s	debt net of predetermined tax shields
ϕ	permanence of the debt level
τ_e, τ_i	tax rate on equity and interest income
τ^*	effective tax advantage of debt

Capital Budgeting and Valuation with Leverage

In early 2009, General Electric Company (GE) had a market capitalization of approximately $107 billion. With debt of close to $457 billion, GE's total enterprise value was $564 billion, making it the most valuable business in the world, with almost twice the value of its closest rival. GE's businesses include power generation and air transportation equipment, health care and medical equipment, consumer appliances, consumer and commercial financing and insurance, as well as entertainment through its affiliate, NBC Universal. With a debt-equity ratio exceeding 80%, leverage is clearly part of GE's business strategy. How should a firm that uses leverage, like GE, incorporate the costs and benefits associated with leverage into its capital budgeting decisions? And how should a firm adjust for the differences in risk, and debt capacity, associated with its different business activities?

We introduced capital budgeting in Chapter 7. There we outlined the following basic procedure: First we estimate the incremental free cash flow generated by the project; then we discount the free cash flow based on the project's cost of capital to determine the NPV. Thus far, we have focused on all-equity financed projects. In this chapter we integrate lessons from Parts 4 and 5 of the text into our capital budgeting framework and consider alternative financing arrangements. In particular, we address how the financing decision of the firm can affect both the cost of capital and the set of cash flows that we ultimately discount.

We begin by introducing the three main methods for capital budgeting with leverage and market imperfections: the weighted average cost of capital (WACC) method, the adjusted present value (APV) method, and the flow-to-equity (FTE) method. While their details differ, when appropriately applied each method produces the same estimate of an investment's (or firm's) value. The choice of method is thus guided by which is the simplest to use in a given setting. Ultimately, we will develop recommendations regarding the best method to use depending on the firm's financing policy.

Throughout this chapter, we focus on the intuition and implementation of the main capital budgeting methods. The appendix to the chapter provides additional details about the justification for and assumptions behind some of the results we use in the chapter. It also introduces advanced computational techniques that can be used in Excel to solve for leverage and value simultaneously.

18.1 OVERVIEW

We introduce the three main methods of capital budgeting in Sections 18.2 through 18.4.

ASSUMPTIONS IN VALUATION EXAMPLE

To illustrate these methods and the relationships between them most clearly, we apply each method to a single example in which we have made a number of simplifying assumptions:

1. *The project has average risk.* We assume initially that the market risk of the project is equivalent to the average market risk of the firm's investments. In that case, the project's cost of capital can be assessed based on the risk of the firm.

2. *The firm's debt-equity ratio is constant.* We initially consider a firm that adjusts its leverage continuously to maintain a constant debt-equity ratio in terms of market values. This policy determines the amount of debt the firm will take on when it accepts a new project. It also implies that the risk of the firm's equity and debt, and therefore its weighted average cost of capital, will not fluctuate due to leverage changes.

3. *Corporate taxes are the only imperfection.* We assume initially that at the firm's debt-equity ratio the main effect of leverage on valuation is due to the corporate tax shield. We ignore personal taxes and issuance costs, and we assume that other imperfections (such as financial distress or agency costs) are not significant at the level of debt chosen.

While these assumptions are restrictive, they are also a reasonable approximation for many projects and firms. The first assumption is likely to fit typical projects of firms with investments concentrated in a single industry. In that case, the market risk of both the project and the firm will primarily depend on the sensitivity of the industry to the overall economy. The second assumption, while unlikely to hold exactly, reflects the fact that firms tend to increase their levels of debt as they grow larger; some may even have an explicit target for their debt-equity ratio. Finally, for firms without very high levels of debt, the interest tax shield is likely to be the most important market imperfection affecting the capital budgeting decision. Hence, the third assumption is a reasonable starting point to begin our analysis.

Of course, while these three assumptions may be a reasonable approximation in many situations, there are certainly projects and firms for which they do not apply. The remainder of the chapter therefore relaxes these assumptions and shows how to generalize the methods to more complicated settings. In Section 18.5, we adjust these methods for projects whose risk or debt capacity is substantially different from the rest of the firm. These adjustments are especially important for multidivisional firms, such as GE. In Section 18.6, we consider alternative leverage policies for the firm (rather than maintaining a constant debt-equity ratio) and adapt the APV method to handle such cases. We consider the consequence of other market imperfections, such as issuance, distress, and agency costs, on valuation in Section 18.7. Finally, in Section 18.8, we investigate a number of advanced topics, including periodically adjusted leverage policies and the effect of investor taxes.

RECAP: KEY VALUATION CONCEPTS

Before we turn to the specifics, we will revisit some important ideas we encountered earlier in the text that underpin the valuation methods.

Chapter 15 demonstrated that because interest payments are deductible as an expense for the corporation, debt financing creates a valuable interest tax shield for the firm. We can include the value of this tax shield in the capital budgeting decision in two ways. First, we can use the effective after-tax interest rate as the cost of debt when computing the project's weighted average cost of capital, or WACC using the *WACC method*, which we explain in the next section. Alternatively, we can value the project's free cash flows using the pretax WACC (which is based on the pretax cost of debt), and value the interest tax shields separately. This approach is the *adjusted present value (APV) method*, which we explain in Section 18.3.

Our third method makes use of the observation in Chapter 9 that rather than value the firm based on its free cash flows, we can also value based on the total payouts to shareholders. The *flow-to-equity (FTE) method*, introduced in Section 18.4, applies this idea to value the incremental payouts to equity associated with a project.

CONCEPT CHECK

1. Describe three simplifying assumptions that we make in valuing a project.

2. What are the three methods we can use to include the value of the interest tax shield in the capital budgeting decision?

18.2 THE WEIGHTED AVERAGE COST OF CAPITAL METHOD

The WACC method takes the interest tax shield into account by using the after-tax cost of capital as the discount rate. When the market risk of the project is similar to the average market risk of the firm's investments, then its cost of capital is equivalent to the firm's WACC. As we showed in Chapter 15, the WACC incorporates the benefit of the interest tax shield by using the firm's *after-tax* cost of capital for debt:

$$r_{wacc} = \frac{E}{E + D} r_E + \frac{D}{E + D} r_D (1 - \tau_c) \tag{18.1}$$

In this formula,

E = market value of equity	r_E = equity cost of capital
D = market value of debt (net of cash)	r_D = debt cost of capital
τ_c = marginal corporate tax rate	

For now, we assume that the firm maintains a constant debt-equity ratio and that the WACC calculated in Eq. 18.1 remains constant over time.[1] Because the WACC

---

1. In Section 18.8 we consider the case in which the WACC changes over time due to changes in leverage.

incorporates the tax savings from debt, we can compute the *levered value* of an investment, which is its value including the benefit of interest tax shields given the firm's leverage policy, by discounting its future free cash flow using the WACC. Specifically, if FCF_t is the expected free cash flow of an investment at the end of year t, then the investment's initial levered value, V_0^L, is[2]

$$V_0^L = \frac{FCF_1}{1 + r_{wacc}} + \frac{FCF_2}{(1 + r_{wacc})^2} + \frac{FCF_3}{(1 + r_{wacc})^3} + \cdots \tag{18.2}$$

USING THE WACC TO VALUE A PROJECT

Let's apply the WACC method to value a project. Avco Inc. is a manufacturer of custom packaging products. Avco is considering introducing a new line of packaging, the RFX series, that will include an embedded radio-frequency identification (RFID) tag, which is a miniature radio antenna and transponder that allows a package to be tracked much more efficiently and with fewer errors than standard bar codes.

Avco engineers expect the technology used in these products to become obsolete after four years. During the next four years, however, the marketing group expects annual sales of $60 million per year for this product line. Manufacturing costs and operating expenses are expected to be $25 million and $9 million, respectively, per year. Developing the product will require upfront R&D and marketing expenses of $6.67 million, together with a $24 million investment in equipment. The equipment will be obsolete in four years and will be depreciated via the straight-line method over that period. Avco bills the majority of its customers in advance, and it expects no net working capital requirements for the project. Avco pays a corporate tax rate of 40%. Using this information, the spreadsheet in Table 18.1 projects the project's expected free cash flow.

EXPECTED FREE CASH FLOW FROM AVCO'S RFX PROJECT*

TABLE 18.1

SPREADSHEET

	Year	0	1	2	3	4
Incremental Earnings Forecast ($ million)						
1 Sales		—	60.00	60.00	60.00	60.00
2 Cost of Goods Sold		—	(25.00)	(25.00)	(25.00)	(25.00)
3 **Gross Profit**		—	35.00	35.00	35.00	35.00
4 Operating Expenses		(6.67)	(9.00)	(9.00)	(9.00)	(9.00)
5 Depreciation		—	(6.00)	(6.00)	(6.00)	(6.00)
6 **EBIT**		(6.67)	20.00	20.00	20.00	20.00
7 Income Tax at 40%		2.67	(8.00)	(8.00)	(8.00)	(8.00)
8 **Unlevered Net Income**		(4.00)	12.00	12.00	12.00	12.00
Free Cash Flow						
9 Plus: Depreciation		—	6.00	6.00	6.00	6.00
10 Less: Capital Expenditures		(24.00)	—	—	—	—
11 Less: Increases in NWC		—	—	—	—	—
12 **Free Cash Flow**		(28.00)	18.00	18.00	18.00	18.00

*For simplicity we are assuming the straight-line depreciation will replace CCA for tax purposes. A full discussion of CCA is found in Chapter 7.

---

2. See Appendix Section 18A.1 for a formal justification of this result.

AVCO'S CURRENT MARKET VALUE BALANCE SHEET ($ MILLION) AND COST OF CAPITAL WITHOUT THE RFX PROJECT

TABLE 18.2

Assets		Liabilities		Cost of Capital	
Cash	20	Debt	320	Debt	6%
Existing Assets	600	Equity	300	Equity	10%
Total Assets	620	Total Liabilities and Equity	620		

The market risk of the RFX project is expected to be similar to that for the company's other lines of business. Thus we can use Avco's equity and debt to determine the weighted average cost of capital for the new project. Table 18.2 shows Avco's current market value balance sheet and equity and debt costs of capital. Avco has built up $20 million in cash for investment needs, so that its *net* debt is $D = 320 - 20 = \$300$ million. Avco's enterprise value, which is the market value of its non-cash assets, is $E + D = \$600$ million. Avco intends to maintain a similar (net) debt-equity ratio for the foreseeable future, including any financing related to the RFX project.

With this capital structure, Avco's weighted average cost of capital is

$$r_{wacc} = \frac{E}{E+D}r_E + \frac{D}{E+D}r_D(1-\tau_c) = \frac{300}{600}(10.0\%) + \frac{300}{600}(6.0\%)(1-0.40)$$
$$= 6.8\%$$

We can determine the value of the project, including the tax shield from debt, by calculating the present value of its future free cash flows, V_0^L, using the WACC:

$$V_0^L = \frac{18}{1.068} + \frac{18}{1.068^2} + \frac{18}{1.068^3} + \frac{18}{1.068^4} = \$61.25 \text{ million}$$

Because the upfront cost of launching the product line is only $28 million, this project is a good idea—taking the project results in an NPV of $61.25 - 28 = \$33.25$ million for the firm.

SUMMARY OF THE WACC METHOD

To summarize, the key steps in the WACC valuation method are as follows:

1. Determine the free cash flow of the investment.

2. Compute the weighted average cost of capital using Eq. 18.1.

3. Compute the value of the investment, including the tax benefit of leverage, by discounting the free cash flow of the investment using the WACC.

In many firms, the corporate treasurer performs the second step, calculating the firm's WACC. This rate can then be used throughout the firm as the companywide cost of capital for new investments *that are of comparable risk to the rest of the firm and that will not alter the firm's debt-equity ratio.* Employing the WACC method in this way is very simple and straightforward. As a result, it is the method that is most commonly used in practice for capital budgeting purposes.

EXAMPLE 18.1

VALUING AN ACQUISITION USING THE WACC METHOD

Problem

Suppose Avco is considering the acquisition of another firm in its industry that specializes in custom packaging. The acquisition is expected to increase Avco's free cash flow by $3.8 million the first year, and this contribution is expected to grow at a rate of 3% per year from then on. Avco has negotiated a purchase price of $80 million. After the transaction, Avco will adjust its capital structure to maintain its current debt-equity ratio. If the acquisition has similar risk to the rest of Avco, what is the value of this deal?

Solution

The free cash flows of the acquisition can be valued as a growing perpetuity. Because its risk matches the risk for the rest of Avco, and because Avco will maintain the same debt-equity ratio going forward, we can discount these cash flows using the WACC of 6.8%. Thus the value of the acquisition is

$$V^L = \frac{3.8}{6.8\% - 3\%} = \$100 \text{ million}$$

Given the purchase price of $80 million, the acquisition has an NPV of $20 million.

IMPLEMENTING A CONSTANT DEBT-EQUITY RATIO

Thus far we have simply assumed the firm adopted a policy of keeping its debt-equity ratio constant. In fact, an important advantage of the WACC method is that you do not need to know how this leverage policy is implemented to make the capital budgeting decision. Nevertheless, keeping the debt-equity ratio constant has implications for how the firm's total debt will change with new investment. For example, Avco currently has a debt-equity ratio of 300/300 = 1 or, equivalently, a debt-to-value ratio $[D/(E + D)]$ of 50%. To maintain this ratio, the firm's new investments must be financed with debt equal to 50% of their market value.

By undertaking the RFX project, Avco adds new assets to the firm with initial market value $V_0^L = \$61.25$ million. Therefore, to maintain its debt-to-value ratio, Avco must add 50% × 61.25 = $30.625 million in new debt.[3] Avco can add this debt either by reducing cash or by borrowing and increasing debt. Suppose Avco decides to spend its $20 million in cash and borrow an additional $10.625 million. Because only $28 million is required to fund the project, Avco will pay the remaining 30.625 − 28 = $2.625 million to shareholders through a dividend (or share repurchase). Table 18.3 shows Avco's market value balance sheet with the RFX project in this case.

This financing plan maintains Avco's 50% debt-to-value ratio. The market value of Avco's equity increases by 330.625 − 300 = $30.625 million. Adding the dividend of

---

3. We can also evaluate the project's debt as follows: Of the $28 million upfront cost of the project, 50% ($14 million) will be financed with debt. In addition, the project generates an NPV of $33.25 million, which will increase the market value of the firm. To maintain a debt-equity ratio of 1, Avco must add debt of 50% × 33.25 = $16.625 million at the time when the NPV of the project is anticipated (which could occur before the new investment is made). Thus the total new debt is 14 + 16.625 = $30.625 million.

AVCO'S CURRENT MARKET VALUE BALANCE SHEET ($ MILLION) WITH THE RFX PROJECT

TABLE 18.3

Assets		Liabilities	
Cash	—	Debt	330.625
Existing Assets	600.00		
RFX Project	61.25	Equity	330.625
Total Assets	661.25	Total Liabilities and Equity	661.25

$2.625 million, the shareholders' total gain is $30.625 + 2.625 = \$33.25$ million, which is exactly the NPV we calculated for the RFX project.

What happens over the life of the project? First, define an investment's **debt capacity**, D_t, as the amount of debt at date t that is required to maintain the firm's target debt-to-value ratio, d. If V_t^L, is the project's levered continuation value on date t—that is, the levered value of its free cash flow after date t—then

$$D_t = d \times V_t^L \tag{18.3}$$

We compute the debt capacity for the RFX project in the spreadsheet in Table 18.4. Starting with the project's free cash flow, we compute its levered continuation value at each date (line 2) by discounting the future free cash flow at the WACC as in Eq. 18.2. Because the continuation value at each date includes the value of all subsequent cash flows, it is even simpler to compute the value at each date by working backward from period 4, discounting next period's free cash flow and continuation value:

$$V_t^L = \frac{FCF_{t+1} + \overbrace{V_{t+1}^L}^{\substack{\text{Value of FCF in year} \\ t+2 \text{ and beyond}}}}{1 + r_{wacc}} \tag{18.4}$$

Once we have computed the project's value V_t^L at each date, we apply Eq. 18.3 to compute the project's debt capacity at each date (line 3). As the spreadsheet shows, the project's debt capacity declines each year, and falls to zero by the end of year 4.

CONTINUATION VALUE AND DEBT CAPACITY OF THE RFX PROJECT OVER TIME

TABLE 18.4

SPREADSHEET

	Year	0	1	2	3	4
Project Debt Capacity ($ million)						
1 **Free Cash Flow**		(28.00)	18.00	18.00	18.00	18.00
2 Levered Value, V^L (at r_{wacc} = 6.8%)		61.25	47.41	32.63	16.85	—
3 **Debt Capacity (at d = 50%)**		**30.62**	**23.71**	**16.32**	**8.43**	**—**

EXAMPLE 18.2	DEBT CAPACITY FOR AN ACQUISITION

Problem

Suppose Avco proceeds with the acquisition described in Example 18.1. How much debt must Avco use to finance the acquisition and still maintain its debt-to-value ratio? How much of the acquisition cost must be financed with equity?

Solution

From the solution to Example 18.2, the market value of the assets acquired in the acquisition, V^L, is \$100 million. Thus, to maintain a 50% debt-to-value ratio, Avco must increase its debt by \$50 million. The remaining \$30 million of the \$80 million acquisition cost will be financed with new equity. In addition to the \$30 million in new equity, the value of Avco's existing shares will increase in value by the \$20 million NPV of the acquisition, so in total the market value of Avco's equity will rise by \$50 million.

CONCEPT CHECK

1. Describe the key steps in the WACC valuation method.

2. How does the WACC method take into account the tax shield?

18.3 THE ADJUSTED PRESENT VALUE METHOD

The **adjusted present value (APV)** method is an alternative valuation method in which we determine the levered value V^L of an investment by first calculating its *unlevered value* V^U, which is its value without any leverage, and then adding the value of the interest tax shield. That is, we showed in Chapter 15,[4]

The APV Formula

$$V^L = APV = V^U + PV(\text{Interest Tax Shield}) \qquad (18.5)$$

As we did with the WACC method, we focus solely on the corporate tax benefits of debt for now and defer the discussion of other consequences of leverage to Section 18.7. As Eq. 18.5 shows, the APV method incorporates the value of the interest tax shield directly, rather than by adjusting the discount rate as in the WACC method. Let's demonstrate the APV method by returning to Avco's RFX project.

THE UNLEVERED VALUE OF THE PROJECT

From the free cash flow estimates in Table 18.1, the RFX project has an upfront cost of \$28 million, and it generates \$18 million per year in free cash flow for the next four years. The first step in the APV method is to calculate the value of these free cash flows using the project's cost of capital if it were financed without leverage.

What is the project's unlevered cost of capital? Because the RFX project has similar risk to Avco's other investments, its unlevered cost of capital is the same as for the firm as a

---

4. Stewart Myers developed the application of APV to capital budgeting, see "Interactions of Corporate Financing and Investment Decisions—Implications for Capital Budgeting," *Journal of Finance* 29:1 (1974): 1–25.

whole. That is, the **unlevered cost of capital** is equal to Avco's pretax WACC, the average return the firm's investors expect to earn:

Unlevered Cost of Capital with a Target Leverage Ratio

$$r_U = \frac{E}{E + D} r_E + \frac{D}{E + D} r_D = \text{Pretax WACC} \tag{18.6}$$

To understand why the firm's unlevered cost of capital equals its pretax WACC, note that the pretax WACC represents investors' required return for holding the entire firm (equity and debt). Thus, it will depend only on the firm's overall risk. So long as the firm's leverage choice does not change the overall risk of the firm, the pretax WACC must be the same whether the firm is levered or unlevered—recall Figure 15.2 on page 519.

Of course this argument relies on the assumption that the overall risk of the firm is independent of the choice of leverage. As we showed in Chapter 14 this assumption always holds in a perfect market. It will also hold in a world with taxes whenever the risk of the tax shield is the same as the risk of the firm (so the size of the tax shield will not change the overall riskiness of the firm). In Appendix Section 18A.2, we show that the tax shield will have the same risk as the firm if the firm maintains a *target leverage ratio*. A **target leverage ratio** means that the firm adjusts its debt proportionally to the project's value or its cash flows, so that a constant debt-equity ratio is a special case.[5]

Applying Eq. 18.6 to Avco, we find its unlevered cost of capital to be

$$r_U = 0.50 \times 10.0\% + 0.50 \times 6.0\% = 8.0\%$$

Avco's unlevered cost of capital is less than its equity cost of capital of 10.0% (which includes the financial risk of leverage), but is more than its WACC of 6.8% (which incorporates the tax benefit of leverage).

Given our estimate of the unlevered cost of capital r_U and the project's free cash flows, we calculate the project's value without leverage:

$$V^U = \frac{18}{1.08} + \frac{18}{1.08^2} + \frac{18}{1.08^3} + \frac{18}{1.08^4} = \$59.62 \text{ million}$$

VALUING THE INTEREST TAX SHIELD

The value of the unlevered project, V^U, calculated above does not include the value of the tax shield provided by the interest payments on debt; it is the value of the project were it purely equity-financed. Given the project's debt capacity from Table 18.4, we can estimate the expected interest payments and the tax shield as shown in the spreadsheet in Table 18.5. The interest paid in year t is estimated based on the amount of debt outstanding at the end of the prior year:

$$\text{Interest paid in year } t = r_D \times D_{t-1} \tag{18.7}$$

The interest tax shield is equal to the interest paid multiplied by the corporate tax rate τ_c.

To compute the present value of the interest tax shield, we need to determine the appropriate cost of capital. As we have already discussed, *because Avco maintains a fixed debt-equity ratio*, the risk of the tax shield is the same as the risk of the project. The interest tax shields shown in Table 18.5 are expected values, and the true amount of

---

5. See Appendix Section 18A.2 for further details.

EXPECTED DEBT CAPACITY, INTEREST PAYMENTS, AND INTEREST TAX SHIELD FOR AVCO'S RFX PROJECT

TABLE 18.5

SPREADSHEET

	Year	0	1	2	3	4
Interest Tax Shield ($ million)						
1 **Debt Capacity, D_t**		30.62	23.71	16.32	8.43	—
2 Interest Paid (at $r_D = 6\%$)			1.84	1.42	0.98	0.51
3 **Interest Tax Shield (at $\tau_c = 40\%$)**			0.73	0.57	0.39	0.20

the interest tax shield each year will vary with the cash flows of the project. If the project does well, its value will be higher, it will support more debt, and the interest tax shield will be higher. If the project goes poorly, its value will fall, Avco will reduce its debt level, and the interest tax shield will be lower. Because the tax shield will fluctuate with the growth of the project:

When the firm maintains a target leverage ratio, its future interest tax shields have similar risk to the project's cash flows, so they should be discounted at the project's unlevered cost of capital.

For Avco's RFX project, we have

$$PV(\text{interest tax shield}) = \frac{0.73}{1.08} + \frac{0.57}{1.08^2} + \frac{0.39}{1.08^3} + \frac{0.20}{1.08^4} = \$1.63 \text{ million}$$

While we have used the unlevered cost of capital r_U to discount the tax shield in this case, the correct discount rate for the interest tax shield depends critically on the firm's leverage policy. In Section 18.5 we consider the case in which the debt levels are fixed in advance (and so do not fluctuate with the cash flows of the project), which implies that the tax shield has a lower risk than the project itself.

To determine the value of the project with leverage, we add the value of the interest tax shield to the unlevered value of the project:[6]

$$V^L = V^U + PV(\text{interest tax shield}) = 59.62 + 1.63 = \$61.25 \text{ million}$$

Again, given the $28 million initial investment required, the RFX project has an NPV with leverage of $61.25 - 28 = \$33.25$ million, which matches precisely the value we computed in Section 18.2 using the WACC approach.

SUMMARY OF THE APV METHOD

To determine the value of a levered investment using the APV method, we proceed as follows:

1. Determine the investment's value without leverage, V^U, by discounting its free cash flows at the unlevered cost of capital, r_U. With a constant debt-equity ratio, r_U may be estimated using Eq. 18.6.

---

6. Because we are using the same discount rate for the free cash flow and the tax shield, the cash flows of the project and the tax shield can be combined first and then discounted at the rate r_U. The combined cash flows are also referred to as the capital cash flows (CCF): CCF = FCF + Interest Tax Shield. This method is known as the CCF or "compressed APV" method; see S. Kaplan and R. Ruback, "The Valuation of Cash Flow Forecasts: An Empirical Analysis," *Journal of Finance* 50:4 (1995): 1059–1093, and R. Ruback, "Capital Cash Flows: A Simple Approach to Valuing Risky Cash Flows," *Financial Management* 31:2 (2002): 85–103.

2. Determine the present value of the interest tax shield.

   a. Determine the expected interest tax shield: Given expected debt D_t on date t, the interest tax shield on date $t + 1$ is $\tau_c\, r_D\, D_t$.[7]

   b. Discount the interest tax shield. If a constant debt-equity ratio is maintained, using r_U is appropriate.

3. Add the unlevered value, V^U, to the present value of the interest tax shield to determine the value of the investment with leverage, V^L.

The APV method is more complicated than the WACC method because we must compute two separate valuations: the unlevered project and the interest tax shield. Furthermore, in this example, to determine the project's debt capacity for the interest tax shield calculation, we relied on the calculation in Table 18.4, *which depended on the value of the project.* Thus, we need to know the debt level to compute the APV, but with a constant debt-equity ratio we need to know the project's value to compute the debt level. As a result, implementing the APV approach with a constant debt-equity ratio requires solving for the project's debt and value *simultaneously.* (See Appendix Section 18A.3 for an example of this calculation.)

Despite its complexity, the APV method has some advantages. As we shall see in Section 18.6, it can be easier to apply than the WACC method when the firm does not maintain a constant debt-equity ratio. The APV approach also provides managers with an explicit valuation of the tax shield itself. In the case of Avco's RFX project, the benefit of the interest tax shield is relatively small. Even if tax rates were to change, or if Avco decided for other reasons not to increase its debt, the profitability of the project would not be jeopardized. However, this need not always be the case. Consider again the acquisition in Example 18.1, where the APV method makes clear that the gain from the acquisition crucially depends on the interest tax shield.

EXAMPLE 18.3

USING THE APV METHOD TO VALUE AN ACQUISITION

Problem

Consider again Avco's acquisition from Examples 18.1 and 18.2. The acquisition will contribute $3.8 million in free cash flows the first year, which will grow by 3% per year thereafter. The acquisition cost of $80 million will be financed with $50 million in new debt initially. Compute the value of the acquisition using the APV method, assuming Avco will maintain a constant debt-equity ratio for the acquisition.

Solution

First, we compute the value without leverage. Given Avco's unlevered cost of capital of $r_U = 8\%$, we get

$$V^U = 3.8/(8\% - 3\%) = \$76 \text{ million}$$

---

7. The return on the debt need not come solely from interest payments, so this value is an approximation. The same approximation is implicit in the definition of the WACC (see also footnote 26 in Appendix Section 18A.1).

Avco will add new debt of $50 million initially to fund the acquisition. At a 6% interest rate, the interest expense the first year is 6% × 50 = $3 million, which provides an interest tax shield of 40% × 3 = $1.2 million. Because the value of the acquisition is expected to grow by 3% per year, the amount of debt the acquisition supports—and, therefore, the interest tax shield—is expected to grow at the same rate. The present value of the interest tax shield is

$$PV(\text{interest tax shield}) = 1.2/(8\% - 3\%) = \$24 \text{ million}$$

The value of the acquisition with leverage is given by the APV:

$$V^L = V^U + PV(\text{interest tax shield}) = 76 + 24 = \$100 \text{ million}$$

This value is identical to the value computed in Example 18.1 and implies an NPV of 100 − 80 = $20 million for the acquisition. Without the benefit of the interest tax shield, the NPV would be 76 − 80 = −$4 million.

We can easily extend the APV approach to include other market imperfections such as financial distress, agency, and issuance costs. We discuss these complexities further in Section 18.7.

CONCEPT CHECK

1. Describe the adjusted present value (APV) method.

2. At what rate should we discount the interest tax shield when a firm maintains a target leverage ratio?

18.4 THE FLOW-TO-EQUITY METHOD

In the WACC and APV methods, we value a project based on its free cash flow, which is computed ignoring interest and debt payments. Some students find these methods confusing because, if the goal is to determine the benefit of the project to shareholders, it seems to them that we should focus on the cash flows that *shareholders* will receive.

In the **flow-to-equity (FTE)** valuation method, we explicitly calculate the free cash flow available to equity holders *taking into account all payments to and from debt holders.* The cash flows to equity holders are then discounted using the *equity* cost of capital.[8] Despite this difference in implementation, the FTE method produces the same assessment of the project's value as the WACC or APV methods.

CALCULATING THE FREE CASH FLOW TO EQUITY

The first step in the FTE method is to determine the project's **free cash flow to equity (FCFE)**. The FCFE is the free cash flow that remains after adjusting for interest payments, debt issuance, and debt repayment. The spreadsheet shown in Table 18.6 calculates the FCFE for Avco's RFX project.

Comparing the FCFE estimates in Table 18.6 with the free cash flow estimates in Table 18.1, we notice two changes. First, we deduct interest expenses (computed in Table 18.5) on line 7, before taxes. As a consequence, we compute the incremental net

---

8. The FTE approach is very similar to the total payout method for valuing the firm described in Chapter 9. In that method, we value the total dividends and repurchases that the firm pays to shareholders.

EXPECTED FREE CASH FLOWS TO EQUITY FROM AVCO'S RFX PROJECT

TABLE 18.6

SPREADSHEET

Year	0	1	2	3	4
Incremental Earnings Forecast ($ million)					
1 Sales	—	60.00	60.00	60.00	60.00
2 Cost of Goods Sold	—	(25.00)	(25.00)	(25.00)	(25.00)
3 **Gross Profit**	—	35.00	35.00	35.00	35.00
4 Operating Expenses	(6.67)	(9.00)	(9.00)	(9.00)	(9.00)
5 Depreciation	—	(6.00)	(6.00)	(6.00)	(6.00)
6 **EBIT**	(6.67)	20.00	20.00	20.00	20.00
7 Interest Expense	—	(1.84)	(1.42)	(0.98)	(0.51)
8 **Pretax Income**	(6.67)	18.16	18.58	19.02	19.49
9 Income Tax at 40%	2.67	(7.27)	(7.43)	(7.61)	(7.80)
10 **Net Income**	(4.00)	10.90	11.15	11.41	11.70
Free Cash Flow to Equity					
11 Plus: Depreciation	—	6.00	6.00	6.00	6.00
12 Less: Capital Expenditures	(24.00)	—	—	—	—
13 Less: Increases in NWC	—	—	—	—	—
14 Plus: Net Borrowing	30.62	(6.92)	(7.39)	(7.89)	(8.43)
15 **Free Cash Flow to Equity**	**2.62**	**9.98**	**9.76**	**9.52**	**9.27**

income of the project on line 10, rather than its *unlevered* net income as we do when computing free cash flows. The second change appears on line 14, where we add the proceeds from the firm's net borrowing activity. These proceeds are positive when the firm issues debt; they are negative when the firm reduces its debt by repaying principal. For the RFX project, Avco issues $30.62 million in debt initially. At date 1, however, the debt capacity of the project falls to $23.71 million (see Table 18.4), so that Avco must repay $30.62 - 23.71 = \$6.91$ million of the debt.[9] In general, given the project's debt capacity D_t,

$$\text{Net Borrowing at Date } t = D_t - D_{t-1} \tag{18.8}$$

As an alternative to Table 18.6, we can compute a project's FCFE directly from its free cash flow. Because interest payments are deducted before taxes in line 7, we adjust the firm's FCF by their after-tax cost. We then add net borrowing to determine FCFE:

Free Cash Flow to Equity

$$FCFE = FCF - \underbrace{(1 - \tau_c) \times (\text{Interest Payments})}_{\text{After-tax interest expense}} + (\text{Net Borrowing}) \tag{18.9}$$

We illustrate this alternative calculation for Avco's RFX project in Table 18.7. Note that the project's FCFE is lower than its FCF in years 1 through 4 due to the interest and principal payments on the debt. In year 0, however, the proceeds from the loan more than offset the negative free cash flow, so FCFE is positive (and equal to the dividend we calculated in Section 18.2).

VALUING EQUITY CASH FLOWS

The project's free cash flow to equity shows the expected amount of additional cash the firm will have available to pay dividends (or conduct share repurchases) each year. Because

---

9. The $0.01 million difference in the spreadsheet is due to rounding.

COMPUTING FCFE FROM FCF FOR AVCO'S RFX PROJECT

TABLE 18.7

SPREADSHEET

Free Cash Flow to Equity ($ million)	Year	0	1	2	3	4
1	Free Cash Flow	(28.00)	18.00	18.00	18.00	18.00
2	After-tax Interest Expense	—	(1.10)	(0.85)	(0.59)	(0.30)
3	Net Borrowing	30.62	(6.92)	(7.39)	(7.89)	(8.43)
4	Free Cash Flow to Equity	2.62	9.98	9.76	9.52	9.27

these cash flows represent payments to equity holders, they should be discounted at the project's equity cost of capital. Given that the risk and leverage of the RFX project are the same as for Avco overall, we can use Avco's equity cost of capital of $r_E = 10.0\%$ to discount the project's FCFE:

$$NPV(FCFE) = 2.62 + \frac{9.98}{1.10} + \frac{9.76}{1.10^2} + \frac{9.52}{1.10^3} + \frac{9.27}{1.10^4} = \$33.25 \text{ million}$$

The value of the project's FCFE represents the gain to shareholders from the project. It is identical to the NPV we computed using the WACC and APV methods.

Why isn't the project's NPV lower now that we have deducted interest and debt payments from the cash flows? Recall that these costs of debt are offset by cash received when the debt is issued. Looking back at Table 18.6, the cash flows from debt in lines 7 and 14 have an NPV of zero assuming the debt is fairly priced.[10] In the end, the only effect on value comes from a reduction in the tax payments, leaving the same result as with the other methods.

SUMMARY OF THE FLOW-TO-EQUITY METHOD

The key steps in the flow-to-equity method for valuing a levered investment are as follows:

1. Determine the free cash flow to equity of the investment using Eq. 18.9.

2. Determine the equity cost of capital, r_E.

3. Compute the equity value, E, by discounting the free cash flow to equity using the equity cost of capital.

---

10. The interest and principal payments for the RFX project are as follows:

	Year	0	1	2	3	4
1	Net Borrowing	30.62	(6.92)	(7.39)	(7.89)	(8.43)
2	Interest Expense	—	(1.84)	(1.42)	(0.98)	(0.51)
3	Cash Flow from Debt	30.62	(8.76)	(8.81)	(8.87)	(8.93)

Because these cash flows have the same risk as the debt, we discount them at the debt cost of capital of 6% to compute their NPV:

$$30.62 + \frac{-8.76}{1.06} + \frac{-8.81}{1.06^2} + \frac{-8.87}{1.06^3} + \frac{-8.93}{1.06^4} = 0.$$

Applying the FTE method was simplified in our example because the project's risk and leverage matched the firm's, and the firm's equity cost of capital was expected to remain constant. Just as with the WACC, however, this assumption is reasonable only if the firm maintains a constant debt-equity ratio. If the debt-equity ratio changes over time, the risk of equity—and, therefore, its cost of capital—will change as well.

In this setting, the FTE approach has the same disadvantage associated with the APV approach: We need to compute the project's debt capacity to determine interest and net borrowing before we can make the capital budgeting decision. For this reason, in most settings the WACC is easier to apply. The FTE method can offer an advantage when calculating the value of equity for the entire firm if the firm's capital structure is complex and the market values of other securities in the firm's capital structure are not known. In that case the FTE method allows us to compute the value of equity directly. In contrast, the WACC and APV methods compute the firm's enterprise value, so that a separate valuation of the other components of the firm's capital structure is needed to determine the value of equity. Finally, by emphasizing a project's implication for equity, the FTE method may be viewed as a more transparent method for discussing a project's benefit to shareholders—a managerial concern.

EXAMPLE 18.4   USING THE FTE METHOD TO VALUE AN ACQUISITION

Problem

Consider again Avco's acquisition from Examples 18.1 through 18.3. The acquisition will contribute $3.8 million in free cash flows the first year, growing by 3% per year thereafter. The acquisition cost of $80 million will be financed with $50 million in new debt initially. What is the value of this acquisition using the FTE method?

Solution

Because the acquisition is being financed with $50 million in new debt, the remaining $30 million of the acquisition cost must come from equity:

$$FCFE_0 = -80 + 50 = -\$30 \text{ million}$$

In one year, the interest on the debt will be $6\% \times 50 = \$3$ million. Because Avco maintains a constant debt-equity ratio, the debt associated with the acquisition is also expected to grow at a 3% rate: $50 \times 1.03 = \$51.5$ million. Therefore, Avco will borrow an additional $51.5 - 50 = \$1.5$ million in one year.

$$FCFE_1 = +3.8 - (1 - 0.40) \times 3 + 1.5 = \$3.5 \text{ million}$$

After year 1, FCFE will also grow at a 3% rate. Using the cost of equity $r_E = 10\%$, we compute the NPV:

$$NPV(FCFE) = -30 + 3.5/(10\% - 3\%) = \$20 \text{ million}$$

This NPV matches the result we obtained with the WACC and APV methods.

WHAT COUNTS AS "DEBT"?

Firms often have many types of debt as well as other liabilities, such as leases. Practitioners use different guidelines to determine which to include as debt when computing the WACC. Some use only long-term debt. Others use both long-term and short-term debt, plus lease obligations. Students are often confused by these different approaches and are left wondering: Which liabilities should be included as debt?

In fact, any choice will work if done correctly. We can view the WACC and FTE methods as special cases of a more general approach in which we *value the after-tax cash flows from a set of the firm's assets and liabilities by discounting them at the after-tax weighted average cost of capital of the firm's remaining assets and liabilities.* In the WACC method, the FCF does not include the interest and principal payments on debt, so debt is included in the calculation of the weighted average cost of capital. In the FTE method, the FCFE incorporates the after-tax cash flows to and from debt holders, so debt is excluded from the weighted average cost of capital (which is simply the equity cost of capital).

Other combinations are also possible. For example, long-term debt can be included in the weighted average cost of capital, and short-term debt can be included as part of the cash flows. Similarly, other assets (such as cash) or liabilities (such as leases) can be included either in the weighted average cost of capital or as part of the cash flow. All such methods, if applied consistently, will lead to an equivalent valuation. Typically, the most convenient choice is the one for which the assumption of a constant debt-to-value ratio is a reasonable approximation.

CONCEPT CHECK

1. Describe the key steps in the flow-to-equity method for valuing a levered investment.

2. Why does the assumption that the firm maintains a constant debt-equity ratio simplify the flow-to-equity calculation?

18.5 PROJECT-BASED COSTS OF CAPITAL

Up to this point we have assumed that both the risk and the leverage of the project under consideration matched those characteristics for the firm as a whole. This assumption allowed us, in turn, to assume that the cost of capital for a project matched the cost of capital of the firm.

In the real world, specific projects often differ from the average investment made by the firm. Consider General Electric Company, discussed in the introduction to this chapter. Projects in its health care division are likely to have different market risk than projects in air transportation equipment or at NBC Universal. Projects may also vary in the amount of leverage they will support—for example, acquisitions of real estate or capital equipment are often highly levered, whereas investments in intellectual property are not. In this section, we show how to calculate the cost of capital for the project's cash flows when a project's risk and leverage differ from those for the firm overall.

ESTIMATING THE UNLEVERED COST OF CAPITAL

We begin by explaining how to calculate the unlevered cost of capital of a project with market risk that is very different from the rest of the firm. Suppose Avco launches a new plastics manufacturing division that faces different market risks than its main packaging business. What unlevered cost of capital would be appropriate for this division?

We can estimate r_U for the plastics division by looking at other single-division plastics firms that have similar business risks. For example, suppose two firms are comparable to the plastics division and have the following characteristics:

Firm	Equity Cost of Capital	Debt Cost of Capital	Debt-to-Value Ratio, $D/(E + D)$
Comparable #1	12.0%	6.0%	40%
Comparable #2	10.7%	5.5%	25%

Assuming that both firms maintain a target leverage ratio, we can estimate the unlevered cost of capital for each competitor by using the pretax WACC from Eq. 18.6:

$$\text{Competitor 1:} \quad r_U = 0.60 \times 12.0\% + 0.40 \times 6.0\% = 9.6\%$$

$$\text{Competitor 2:} \quad r_U = 0.75 \times 10.7\% + 0.25 \times 5.5\% = 9.4\%$$

Based on these comparable firms, we estimate an unlevered cost of capital for the plastics division of about 9.5%.[11] With this rate in hand, we can use the APV approach to calculate the value of Avco's investment in plastic manufacturing. To use either the WACC or FTE method, however, we need to estimate the project's equity cost of capital, which will depend on the incremental debt the firm will take on as a result of the project.

PROJECT LEVERAGE AND THE EQUITY COST OF CAPITAL

Suppose the firm will fund the project according to a target leverage ratio. This leverage ratio may differ from the firm's overall leverage ratio, as different divisions or types of investments may have different optimal debt capacities. We can rearrange terms in Eq. 18.6 to get the following expression for the equity cost of capital:[12]

$$r_E = r_U + \frac{D}{E}(r_U - r_D) \tag{18.10}$$

Equation 18.10 shows that the project's equity cost of capital depends on its unlevered cost of capital, r_U, and the debt-equity ratio of the incremental financing that will be put in place to support the project. For example, suppose that Avco plans to maintain an equal mix of debt and equity financing as it expands into plastics manufacturing and it expects its borrowing cost to remain at 6%. Given its 9.5% unlevered cost of capital, the plastics division's equity cost of capital is

$$r_E = 9.5\% + \frac{0.50}{0.50}(9.5\% - 6\%) = 13.0\%$$

Once we have the equity cost of capital, we can use Eq. 18.1 to determine the division's WACC:

$$r_{wacc} = 0.50 \times 13.0\% + 0.50 \times 6.0\% \times (1 - 0.40) = 8.3\%$$

Based on these estimates, Avco should use a WACC of 8.3% for the plastics division, compared to the WACC of 6.8% for the packaging division that we calculated in Section 18.2.

---

11. If we are using the CAPM to estimate expected returns, this procedure is equivalent to unlevering the betas of comparable firms using Eq. 12.9:

$$\beta_U = [E/(E + D)]\, \beta_E + [D/(D + E)]\, \beta_D.$$

12. In a CAPM setting, Eq. 18.10 is equivalent to relevering the beta according to Eq. 12.9.

Solution

Using the APV method, the unlevered value of the land is $V^U = FCF/r_U = 4.5/0.07 = 64.29 million. Because the debt is permanent, the value of the tax shield is $\tau_c D = 0.35(30) = 10.50$. Therefore, $V^L = 64.29 + 10.50 = \$74.79$ million.

To use the WACC method, we apply Eq. 18.21 with $\phi = T^s/(\tau_c D) = 1$ and $d = 30/74.79 = 40.1\%$. Therefore, the WACC for the investment is

$$r_{wacc} = r_U = d\,\tau_c r_U = 7\% - 0.401 \times 0.35 \times 7\% = 6.017\%$$

and $V^L = 4.5/0.06017 = \$74.79$ million.

THE WACC OR FTE METHOD WITH CHANGING LEVERAGE

When a firm does not maintain a constant debt-equity ratio for a project, the APV method is generally the most straightforward method to apply. The WACC and FTE methods become more difficult to use because when the proportion of debt financing changes, the project's equity cost of capital and WACC will not remain constant over time. With a bit of care, however, these methods can still be used (and, of course, will lead to the same result as the APV method).

As an example, the spreadsheet in Table 18.10 computes the equity cost of capital and WACC for the RFX project each year given the fixed debt schedule shown in line 3. The value of the project with leverage using the APV method is computed in line 7 as the total of the unlevered value and the value of the tax shield. With the project's equity value and net debt D^s in hand, we can use Eq. 18.20 to calculate the project's equity cost of capital each year (line 11). Note that the equity cost of capital declines over time as the project's leverage ratio D^s/E declines. By year 3, the debt is fully repaid and the equity cost of capital equals the unlevered cost of capital of 8%.

ADJUSTED PRESENT VALUE AND COST OF CAPITAL FOR AVCO'S RFX PROJECT WITH A FIXED DEBT SCHEDULE

TABLE 18.10

SPREADSHEET

	Year	0	1	2	3	4
Unlevered Value ($ million)						
1 Free Cash Flow		(28.00)	18.00	18.00	18.00	18.00
2 Unlevered Value, V^U (at $r_u = 8.0\%$)		59.62	46.39	32.10	16.67	—
Interest Tax Shield						
3 Debt Schedule, D_t		30.62	20.00	10.00	—	—
4 Interest Paid (at $r_d = 6\%$)		—	1.84	1.20	0.60	—
5 Interest Tax Shield (at $\tau_c = 40\%$)		—	0.73	0.48	0.24	—
6 Tax Shield Value, T^s (at $r_D = 6.0\%$)		1.32	0.67	0.23	—	—
Adjusted Present Value						
7 **Levered Value, $V^L = V^U + T^s$**		**60.94**	**47.05**	**32.33**	**16.67**	**—**
Effective Leverage and Cost of Capital						
8 Equity, $E = V^L - D$		30.32	27.05	22.33	16.67	—
9 Effective Debt, $D^s = D - T^s$		29.30	19.33	9.77	—	—
10 Effective Debt-Equity Ratio, D^s/E		0.966	0.715	0.438	0.000	
11 **Equity Cost of Capital, r_E**		**9.93%**	**9.43%**	**8.88%**	**8.00%**	
12 WACC, r_{wacc}		6.75%	6.95%	7.24%	8.00%	

Given the project's equity cost of capital, we compute its WACC using Eq. 18.1 in line 12. For example, at the beginning of the project,

$$r_{wacc} = \frac{E}{E + D} r_E + \frac{D}{E + D} r_D (1 - \tau_c)$$

$$= \frac{30.32}{60.94} 9.93\% + \frac{30.62}{60.94} 6\%(1 - 0.40) = 6.75\%$$

Note that as the leverage of the project falls, its WACC rises, until it eventually equals the unlevered cost of capital of 8% when the project debt is fully repaid at year 3.

Once we have computed the WACC or the equity cost of capital, we can value the project using the WACC or FTE method. Because the cost of capital changes over time, we must use a different discount rate each year when applying these methods. For example, using the WACC method, the levered value each year is computed as

$$V_t^L = \frac{FCF_{t+1} + V_{t+1}^L}{1 + r_{wacc}(t)} \qquad (18.22)$$

where $r_{wacc}(t)$ is the project's WACC in year t. This calculation is shown in Table 18.11. Note that the levered value matches the result from the APV method (line 7 in Table 18.10). The same approach can be used when applying the FTE method.[24]

PERSONAL TAXES

As we discussed in Chapter 15, leverage has tax consequences for both investors and corporations. For individuals, interest income from debt is generally taxed more heavily than income from equity (capital gains and dividends). So how do personal taxes affect our valuation methods?

If investors are taxed on the income they receive from holding equity or debt, it will raise the return they require to hold those securities. That is, the equity and debt cost of capital in the market *already* reflects the effects of investor taxes. As a result, *the WACC method does not change in the presence of investor taxes*; we can continue to compute the WACC according to Eq. 18.1 and compute the levered value as in Section 18.2.

The APV approach, however, requires modification in the presence of investor taxes because it requires that we compute the unlevered cost of capital. This computation *is* affected by the presence of investor taxes. Let τ_e be the tax rate investors pay on equity

WACC METHOD FOR AVCO'S RFX PROJECT WITH A FIXED DEBT SCHEDULE

TABLE 18.11

SPREADSHEET

	Year	0	1	2	3	4
WACC Method ($ million)						
1 Free Cash Flow		(28.00)	18.00	18.00	18.00	18.00
2 WACC, r_{wacc}		6.75%	6.95%	7.24%	8.00%	
3 **Levered Value V^L (at r_{wacc})**		60.94	47.05	32.33	16.67	—

---

24. You will notice, however, that we used the APV to compute the debt-equity ratio each period, which we needed to calculate r_E and r_{wacc}. If we had not already solved for the APV, we would need to determine the project's value and WACC simultaneously, using the approach described in Appendix Section 18A.3.

income (dividends) and τ_i be the tax rate investors pay on interest income. Then, given an expected return on debt r_D, define r_D^* as the expected return on equity income that would give investors the same after-tax return: $r_D^* (1 - \tau_e) = r_D (1 - \tau_i)$. So

$$r_D^* \equiv r_D \frac{(1 - \tau_i)}{(1 - \tau_e)} \tag{18.23}$$

Because the unlevered cost of capital is for a hypothetical firm that is all equity, investors' tax rates on income for such a firm are the equity rates, so we must use the rate r_D^* when computing the unlevered cost of capital. Therefore, Eq. 18.20 becomes

Unlevered Cost of Capital with Personal Taxes

$$r_U = \frac{E}{E + D^s} r_E + \frac{D^s}{E + D^s} r_D^* \tag{18.24}$$

Next, we must compute the interest tax shield using the effective tax advantage of debt, τ^*, in place of τ_c. The effective tax rate τ^* incorporates the investors' tax rate on equity income, τ_e, and on interest income, τ_i, and was defined in Chapter 15 as follows:

$$\tau^* = 1 - \frac{(1 - \tau_c)(1 - \tau_e)}{(1 - \tau_i)} \tag{18.25}$$

We then calculate the interest tax shield using tax rate τ_c^* and interest rate r_D^*:

$$\text{Interest Tax Shield in Year } t = \tau^* \times r_D^* \times D_{t-1} \tag{18.26}$$

Finally we discount the interest tax shields at rate r_U if the firm maintains a target leverage ratio or at rate r_D^* if the debt is set according to a predetermined schedule.[25]

EXAMPLE 18.12

USING THE APV METHOD WITH PERSONAL TAXES

Problem

Apex Corporation has an equity cost of capital of 14.4% and a debt cost of capital of 6%, and the firm maintains a debt-equity ratio of 1. Apex is considering an expansion that will contribute $4 million in free cash flows the first year, growing by 4% per year thereafter. The expansion will cost $60 million and will be financed with $40 million in new debt initially with a constant debt-equity ratio maintained thereafter. Apex's corporate tax rate is 40%; the tax rate on interest income is 40%; and the tax rate on equity income is 20%. Compute the value of the expansion using the APV method.

---

25. If the debt is permanent, for example, the value of the tax shield is $\tau^* r_D^* D / r_D^* = \tau^* D$, as shown in Chapter 15.

Solution

First, we compute the value without leverage. From Eq. 18.23, the debt cost of capital of 6% is equivalent to an equity rate of

$$r_D^* = r_D \frac{1 - \tau_i}{1 - \tau_e} = 6\% \times \frac{1 - 0.40}{1 - 0.20} = 4.5\%$$

Because Apex maintains a constant debt-equity ratio, $D^s = D$ and Apex's unlevered cost of capital is, using Eqs. 18.23 and 18.24,

$$r_U = \frac{E}{E + D^s} r_E + \frac{D^s}{E + D^s} r_D^* = 0.50 \times 14.4\% + 0.50 \times 4.5\% = 9.45\%$$

Therefore, $V^U = 4/(9.45\% - 4\%) = \$73.39$ million.

From Eq. 18.25, the effective tax advantage of debt is

$$\tau^* = 1 - \frac{(1 - \tau_c)(1 - \tau_e)}{(1 - \tau_i)} = 1 - \frac{(1 - 0.40)(1 - 0.20)}{(1 - 0.40)} = 20\%$$

Apex will add new debt of $40 million initially, so from Eq. 18.26 the interest tax shield is $20\% \times 4.5\% \times 40 = \$0.36$ million the first year (note that we use r_D^* here). With a growth rate of 4%, the present value of the interest tax shield is

$$PV(\text{Interest Tax Shield}) = 0.36/(9.45\% - 4\%) = \$6.61 \text{ million}$$

Therefore the value of the expansion with leverage is given by the APV:

$$V^L = V^U + PV(\text{Interest Tax Shield}) = 73.39 + 6.61 = \$80 \text{ million}$$

Given the cost of $60 million, the expansion has an NPV of $20 million.

Let's check this result using the WACC method. Note that the expansion has the same debt-to-value ratio of 40/80 = 50% as the firm overall. Thus its WACC is equal to the firm's WACC:

$$r_{wacc} = \frac{E}{E + D} r_E + \frac{D}{E + D} r_D (1 - \tau_c)$$

$$= 0.50 \times 14.4\% + 0.50 \times 6\% \times (1 - 0.40) = 9\%$$

Therefore, $V^L = 4/(9\% - 4\%) = \$80$ million, as before.

As Example 18.12 illustrates, the WACC method is much simpler to apply than the APV method in the case with investor taxes. More significantly, the WACC approach does not require knowledge of investors' tax rates. This fact is important because in practice, estimating the marginal tax rate of the investor can be very difficult.

If the investment's leverage or risk does not match the firm's, then investor tax rates are required even with the WACC method, as we must unlever and/or re-lever the firm's cost of capital using Eq. 18.24. When the investor's tax rate on interest income exceeds that on equity income, an increase in leverage will lead to a smaller reduction in the WACC (see Problem 25).

CONCEPT CHECK

1. When a firm has predetermined tax shields, how do we measure its net debt when calculating its unlevered cost of capital?

2. If the firm's debt-equity ratio changes over time, can the WACC method still be applied?

SUMMARY

1. The key steps in the WACC valuation method are as follows:

    a. Determine the unlevered free cash flows of the investment.

    b. Compute the weighted average cost of capital:

    $$r_{wacc} = \frac{E}{E + D} r_E + \frac{D}{E + D} r_D (1 - \tau_c) \tag{18.1}$$

    c. Compute the value with leverage, V^L, by discounting the free cash flows of the investment using the WACC.

2. To determine the value of a levered investment using the APV method, proceed as follows:

    a. Determine the investment's value without leverage, V^U, by discounting its free cash flows at the unlevered cost of capital, r_U.

    b. Determine the present value of the interest tax shield.

        i. Given debt D_t on date t, the tax shield on date $t + 1$ is $\tau_c r_D D_t$.

        ii. If the debt level varies with the investment's value or free cash flow, use discount rate r_U. If the debt is predetermined, discount the tax shield at rate r_D.

    c. Add the unlevered value V^U to the present value of the interest tax shield to determine the value of the investment with leverage, V^L.

3. The key steps in the flow-to-equity method for valuing a levered investment are as follows:

    a. Determine the free cash flow to equity of the investment:

    $$FCFE = FCF - (1 - \tau_c) \times (\text{Interest Payments}) + (\text{Net Borrowing}) \tag{18.9}$$

    b. Compute the equity value, E, by discounting the free cash flow to equity using the equity cost of capital.

4. If a project's risk is different from that of the firm as a whole, we must estimate its cost of capital separately from the firm's cost of capital. We estimate the project's unlevered cost of capital by looking at the unlevered cost of capital for other firms with similar market risk as the project.

5. With a target leverage ratio, the unlevered, equity, and weighted average costs of capital are related as follows:

    $$r_U = \frac{E}{E + D} r_E + \frac{D}{E + D} r_D = \text{Pretax WACC} \tag{18.6}$$

    $$r_E = r_U + \frac{D}{E} (r_U - r_D) \tag{18.10}$$

    $$r_{wacc} = r_U - d\tau_c r D, \tag{18.11}$$

    where $d = D/(D + E)$ is the project's debt-to-value ratio.

6. When assessing the leverage associated with a project, we must consider its incremental impact on the debt, net of cash balances, of the firm overall and not just the specific financing used for that investment.

7. A firm has a constant interest coverage policy if it sets debt to maintain its interest expenses as a fraction, k, of free cash flow. The levered value of a project with such a leverage policy is $V^L = (1 + \tau_c k) V^U$.

8. If a firm chooses to keep the level of debt at a constant level, D, permanently, then the levered value of a project with such a leverage policy is $V^L = V^U + \tau_c \times D$.

9. In general, the WACC method is the easiest to use when a firm has a target debt-equity ratio that it plans to maintain over the life of the investment. For other leverage policies, the APV method is usually the most straightforward method.

10. Issuance costs and any costs or gains from mispricing of issued securities should be included in the assessment of a project's value.

11. Financial distress costs are likely to (1) lower the expected free cash flow of a project and (2) raise its unlevered cost of capital. Taking these effects into account, together with other agency and asymmetric information costs, may limit a firm's use of leverage.

12. If a firm adjusts its debt annually to a target leverage ratio, the value of the interest tax shield is enhanced by the factor $(1 + r_U)/(1 + r_D)$.

13. If the firm does not adjust leverage continuously, so that some of the tax shields are predetermined, the unlevered, equity, and weighted average costs of capital are related as follows:

$$r_U = \frac{E}{E + D^s} r_E + \frac{D^s}{E + D^s} r_D \text{ or, equivalently, } r_E = r_U + \frac{D^s}{E}(r_U - r_D) \quad (18.20)$$

$$r_{wacc} = r_U - d\tau_c \left[r_D + \phi(r_U - r_D) \right] \quad (18.21)$$

where $d = D/(D + E)$ is the debt-to-value ratio of the project, $D^s = D - T^s$, and T^s is the value of predetermined interest tax shields, and $\phi = T^s/(\tau_c D)$ reflects the permanence of the debt level.

14. The WACC method does not need to be modified to account for investor taxes. For the APV method, we use the interest rate

$$r_D^* \equiv r_D \frac{(1 - \tau_i)}{(1 - \tau_e)} \quad (18.23)$$

in place of r_D and we replace τ_c with the effective tax rate:

$$\tau^* = 1 - \frac{(1 - \tau_c)(1 - \tau_e)}{(1 - \tau_i)} \quad (18.25)$$

KEY TERMS

adjusted present value (APV) *p. 637*
constant interest coverage ratio *p. 650*
debt capacity *p. 636*
flow to equity (FTE) *p. 641*

free cash flow to equity (FCFE) *p. 641*
target leverage ratio *p. 638*
unlevered cost of capital *p. 638*

PROBLEMS

Overview

1. Explain whether each of the following projects is likely to have risk similar to the average risk of the firm.

   a. The Clorox Company considers launching a new version of Armor All designed to clean and protect notebook computers.

   b. Google Inc. plans to purchase real estate to expand its headquarters.

   c. London Drugs decides to expand the number of stores it has in western Canada.

   d. GE decides to open a new Universal Studios theme park in China.

2. Suppose Caterpillar Inc. has 665 million shares outstanding with a share price of $74.77 and $25 billion in debt. If in three years, Caterpillar has 700 million shares outstanding trading for $83 per share, how much debt will Caterpillar have if it maintains a constant debt-equity ratio?

3. In 2006, Intel Corporation had a market capitalization of $112 billion, debt of $2.2 billion, cash of $9.1 billion, and EBIT of more than $11 billion. If Intel were to increase its debt by $1 billion and use the cash for a share repurchase, which market imperfections would be most relevant for understanding the consequence for Intel's value? Why?

The Weighted Average Cost of Capital Method

4. Suppose Goodyear Tire and Rubber Company is considering divesting one of its manufacturing plants. The plant is expected to generate free cash flows of $1.5 million per year, growing at a rate of 2.5% per year. Goodyear has an equity cost of capital of 8.5%, a debt cost of capital of 7%, a marginal corporate tax rate of 35%, and a debt-equity ratio of 2.6. If the plant has average risk and Goodyear plans to maintain a constant debt-equity ratio, what after-tax amount must it receive for the plant for the divestiture to be profitable?

5. Suppose Lucent Technologies has an equity cost of capital of 10%, market capitalization of $10.8 billion, and an enterprise value of $14.4 billion. Suppose Lucent's debt cost of capital is 6.1% and its marginal tax rate is 35%.

   a. What is Lucent's WACC?

   b. If Lucent maintains a constant debt-equity ratio, what is the value of a project with average risk and the following expected free cash flows?

Year	0	1	2	3
FCF	−100	50	100	70

   c. If Lucent maintains its debt-equity ratio, what is the debt capacity of the project in part b?

6. Acort Industries has 10 million shares outstanding and a current share price of $40 per share. It also has long-term debt outstanding. This debt is risk free, is four years away from maturity, has annual coupons with a coupon rate of 10%, and a $100 million face value. The first of the remaining coupon payments will be due in exactly one year. The riskless interest rates for all

maturities are constant at 6%. Acort has EBIT of $106 million, which is expected to remain constant each year. New capital expenditures are expected to equal depreciation (assumed to equal CCA) and equal $13 million per year, while no changes to net working capital are expected in the future. The corporate tax rate is 40%, and Acort is expected to keep its debt-equity ratio constant in the future (by either issuing additional new debt or buying back some debt as time goes on).

    a. Based on this information, estimate Acort's WACC.

    b. What is Acort's equity cost of capital?

The Adjusted Present Value Method

7. Suppose Goodyear Tire and Rubber Company has an equity cost of capital of 8.5%, a debt cost of capital of 7%, a marginal corporate tax rate of 35%, and a debt-equity ratio of 2.6. Suppose Goodyear maintains a constant debt-equity ratio.

    a. What is Goodyear's WACC?

    b. What is Goodyear's unlevered cost of capital?

    c. Explain, intuitively, why Goodyear's unlevered cost of capital is less than its equity cost of capital and higher than its WACC.

8. You are a consultant who was hired to evaluate a new product line for Gupta Enterprises. The upfront investment required to launch the product line is $10 million. The product will generate free cash flow of $750,000 the first year, and this free cash flow is expected to grow at a rate of 4% per year. Gupta has an equity cost of capital of 11.3%, a debt cost of capital of 5%, and a tax rate of 35%. Gupta maintains a debt-equity ratio of 0.40.

    a. What is the NPV of the new product line (including any tax shields from leverage)?

    b. How much debt will Gupta initially take on as a result of launching this product line?

    c. How much of the product line's value is attributable to the present value of interest tax shields?

9. Consider Lucent's project in Problem 5.

    a. What is Lucent's unlevered cost of capital?

    b. What is the unlevered value of the project?

    c. What are the interest tax shields from the project? What is their present value?

    d. Show that the APV of Lucent's project matches the value computed using the WACC method.

The Flow-to-Equity Method

10. Consider Lucent's project in Problem 5.

    a. What is the free cash flow to equity for this project?

    b. What is its NPV computed using the FTE method? How does it compare with the NPV based on the WACC method?

11. In year 1, AMC will earn $2000 before interest and taxes. The market expects these earnings to grow at a rate of 3% per year. The firm will make no net investments (i.e., capital expenditures will equal depreciation and, for simplicity, we will assume depreciation is equal to the CCA amount) or changes to net working capital. Assume that the corporate tax rate equals 40%. Right now, the firm has $5000 in risk-free debt. It plans to keep a constant ratio of debt to equity every year, so that on average the debt will also grow by 3% per year. Suppose the risk-free rate equals 5% and the expected return on the market equals 11%. The asset beta for this industry is 1.11.

    a. If AMC were an all-equity (unlevered) firm, what would its market value be?

    b. Assuming the debt is fairly priced, what is the amount of interest AMC will pay next year? If AMC's debt is expected to grow by 3% per year, at what rate are its interest payments expected to grow?

c. Even though AMC's debt is *riskless* (the firm will not default), the future growth of AMC's debt is uncertain, so the exact amount of the future interest payments is risky. Assuming the future interest payments have the same beta as AMC's assets, what is the present value of AMC's interest tax shield?

d. Using the APV method, what is AMC's total market value, V^L? What is the market value of AMC's equity?

e. What is AMC's WACC? (*Hint:* Work backward from the FCF and V^L.)

f. Using the WACC method, what is the expected return for AMC's equity?

g. Show that the following holds for AMC: $\beta_A = \dfrac{E}{D+E}\beta_E + \dfrac{D}{D+E}\beta_D.$

h. Assuming that the proceeds from any increases in debt are paid out to equity holders, what cash flows do the equity holders expect to receive in one year? At what rate are those cash flows expected to grow? Use that information plus your answer to part f to derive the market value of equity using the FTE method. How does that compare to your answer in part d?

Project-Based Costs of Capital

12. Donnelly Ocean Group (DOG) has historically maintained a debt-equity ratio of approximately 0.20. Its current stock price is $50 per share, with 2.5 billion shares outstanding. The firm enjoys very stable demand for its products, and consequently it has a low equity beta of 0.50 and can borrow at 4.20%, just 20 basis points over the risk-free rate of 4%. The expected return of the market is 10%, and DOG's tax rate is 35%.

   a. This year, DOG is expected to have free cash flows of $6.0 billion. What constant expected growth rate of free cash flow is consistent with its current stock price?

   b. DOG believes it can increase debt without any serious risk of distress or other costs. With a higher debt-equity ratio of 0.50, it believes its borrowing costs will rise only slightly to 4.5%. If DOG announces that it will raise its debt-equity ratio to 0.5 through a leveraged recap, determine the increase in the stock price that would result from the anticipated tax savings.

13. Cozens Cosmetics Corp. (CCC) is a newly public firm with 10 million shares outstanding. You are doing a valuation analysis of CCC. You estimate its free cash flow in the coming year to be $15 million, and you expect the firm's free cash flows to grow by 4% per year in subsequent years. Because the firm has only been listed on the stock exchange for a short time, you do not have an accurate assessment of CCC's equity beta. However, you do have beta data for UAL, another firm in the same industry:

	Equity Beta	Debt Beta	Debt-Equity Ratio
UAL	1.5	0.30	1

   CCC has a much lower debt-equity ratio of 0.30, which is expected to remain stable, and its debt is risk free. CCC's corporate tax rate is 40%, the risk-free rate is 5%, and the expected return on the market portfolio is 11%.

   a. Estimate CCC's equity cost of capital.

   b. Estimate CCC's share price.

EXCEL 14. Zhou Enterprises (ZE) currently has no debt in its capital structure. The beta of its equity is 1.50. For each year into the indefinite future, Zhou's free cash flow is expected to equal $25 million. Zhou is considering changing its capital structure by issuing debt and using the proceeds to buy back stock. It will do so in such a way that it will have a 30% debt-equity ratio after the change, and it will maintain this debt-equity ratio forever. Assume that Zhou's debt cost of capital will be 6.5%. Zhou faces a corporate tax rate of 35%. Except for the corporate tax rate of 35%, there are no market imperfections. Assume that the CAPM holds, the risk-free rate of interest is 5%, and the expected return on the market is 11%.

a. Using the information provided, fill in the table below:

	Debt-Equity Ratio	Debt Cost of Capital	Equity Cost of Capital	Weighted Average Cost of Capital
Before change in capital structure	0	N/A		
After change in capital structure	0.30	6.5%		

b. Using the information provided and your calculations in part a, determine the value of the tax shield acquired by Zhou if it changes its capital structure in the way it is considering.

APV with Other Leverage Policies

 15. You are evaluating a project that requires an investment of $90 today and provides a single cash flow of $115 for sure one year from now. You decide to use 100% debt financing, that is, you will borrow $90. The risk-free rate is 5% and the tax rate is 40%. Assume that the investment is fully depreciated at the end of the year, so without leverage you would owe taxes on the difference between the project cash flow and the investment, that is, $15.

  a. Calculate the NPV of this investment opportunity using the APV method.

  b. Using your answer to part a, calculate the WACC of the project.

  c. Verify that you get the same answer using the WACC method to calculate NPV.

  d. Finally, show that flow-to-equity also correctly gives the NPV of this investment opportunity.

16. Whistler Corporation adjusts its debt so that its interest expenses are 20% of its free cash flow. Whistler is considering an expansion that will generate free cash flows of $2.5 million this year and is expected to grow at a rate of 4% per year from then on. Suppose Whistler's marginal corporate tax rate is 40%.

  a. If the unlevered cost of capital for this expansion is 10%, what is its unlevered value?

  b. What is the levered value of the expansion?

  c. If Whistler pays 5% interest on its debt, what amount of debt will it take on initially for the expansion?

  d. What is the debt-to-value ratio for this expansion? What is its WACC?

  e. What is the levered value of the expansion using the WACC method?

17. You are on your way to an important budget meeting. In the elevator, you review the project valuation analysis you had your summer associate prepare for one of the projects to be discussed:

	0	1	2	3	4
EBIT		10.0	10.0	10.0	10.0
Interest (5%)		−4.0	−4.0	−3.0	−2.0
Earnings Before Taxes		6.0	6.0	7.0	8.0
Taxes		−2.4	−2.4	−2.8	−3.2
Depreciation		25.0	25.0	25.0	25.0
Cap Ex	−100.0				
Additions to NWC	−20.0				20.0
Net New Debt	80.0	0.0	−20.0	−20.0	−40.0
FCFE	−40.0	28.6	8.6	9.2	9.8
NPV at 11% Equity Cost of Capital		5.9			

Looking over the spreadsheet, you realize that while all of the cash flow estimates are correct, your associate used the flow-to-equity valuation method and discounted the cash flows using the *company's* equity cost of capital of 11%. However, the project's incremental leverage is very different from the company's historical debt-equity ratio of 0.20. For this project, the company will instead borrow $80 million upfront and repay $20 million in year 2, $20 million in year 3, and $40 million in year 4. Thus the *project's* equity cost of capital is likely to be higher than the firm's, not constant over time—invalidating your associate's calculation.

Clearly, the FTE approach is not the best way to analyze this project. Fortunately, you have your calculator with you, and with any luck you can use a better method before the meeting starts.

a. What is the present value of the interest tax shield associated with this project?

b. What are the free cash flows of the project?

c. What is the best estimate of the project's value from the information given?

18. Your firm is considering building a $600 million plant to manufacture HDTV circuitry. You expect operating profits (EBITDA) of $145 million per year for the next ten years. Assume that for tax purposes, the plant will be depreciated (i.e., have CCA calculated) on a straight-line basis over ten years (assuming no salvage value for tax purposes). After ten years, the plant will have a salvage value of $300 million (which, since it will be fully depreciated, is then taxable). The project requires $50 million in working capital at the start, which will be recovered in year 10 when the project shuts down. The corporate tax rate is 35%. All cash flows occur at the end of the year.

a. If the risk-free rate is 5%, the expected return of the market is 11%, and the asset beta for the consumer electronics industry is 1.67, what is the NPV of the project?

b. Suppose that you can finance $400 million of the cost of the plant using ten-year, 9% coupon bonds sold at par. This amount is incremental new debt associated specifically with this project and will not alter other aspects of the firm's capital structure. What is the value of the project, including the tax shield of the debt?

Other Effects of Financing

19. DAS Corporation is currently an all-equity firm, with assets with a market value of $100 million and 4 million shares outstanding. DAS is considering a leveraged recapitalization to boost its share price. The firm plans to raise a fixed amount of permanent debt (i.e., the outstanding principal will remain constant) and use the proceeds to repurchase shares. DAS pays a 35% corporate tax rate, so one motivation for taking on the debt is to reduce the firm's tax liability. However, the upfront investment banking fees associated with the recapitalization will be 5% of the amount of debt raised. Adding leverage will also create the possibility of future financial distress or agency costs; shown below are DAS's estimates for different levels of debt:

Debt amount ($ million):	0	10	20	30	40	50
Present value of expected distress and agency costs ($ million):	0.0	−0.3	−1.8	−4.3	−7.5	−11.3

a. Based on this information, which level of debt is the best choice for DAS?

b. Estimate the stock price once this transaction is announced.

20. Your firm is considering a $150 million investment to launch a new product line. The project is expected to generate a free cash flow of $20 million per year, and its unlevered cost of capital is 10%. To fund the investment, your firm will take on $100 million in permanent debt.

a. Suppose the marginal corporate tax rate is 35%. Ignoring issuance costs, what is the NPV of the investment, including any tax benefits of leverage?

b. Suppose your firm will pay a 2% underwriting fee when issuing the debt. It will raise the remaining $50 million by issuing equity. In addition to the 5% underwriting fee for the equity issue, you believe that your firm's current share price of $40 is $5 per share less than its true value. What is the NPV of the investment in this case (including any tax benefits of leverage)? (Assume all fees are on an after-tax basis.)

21. Consider Avco's RFX project from Section 18.3. Suppose that Avco is receiving government loan guarantees that allow it to borrow at the 6% rate. Without these guarantees, Avco would pay 6.5% on its debt.

    a. What is Avco's unlevered cost of capital given its true debt cost of capital of 6.5%?

    b. What is the unlevered value of the RFX project in this case? What is the present value of the interest tax shield?

    c. What is the NPV of the loan guarantees? (*Hint*: Because the actual loan amounts will fluctuate with the value of the project, discount the expected interest savings at the unlevered cost of capital.)

    d. What is the levered value of the RFX project, including the interest tax shield and the NPV of the loan guarantees?

Advanced Topics in Capital Budgeting

22. Arden Corporation is considering an investment in a new project with an unlevered cost of capital of 9%. Arden's marginal corporate tax rate is 40%, and its debt cost of capital is 5%.

    a. Suppose Arden adjusts its debt continuously to maintain a constant debt-equity ratio of 50%. What is the appropriate WACC for the new project?

    b. Suppose Arden adjusts its debt once per year to maintain a constant debt-equity ratio of 50%. What is the appropriate WACC for the new project now?

    c. Suppose the project has free cash flows of $10 million per year, which are expected to decline by 2% per year. What is the value of the project in parts a and b now?

23. XL Sports is expected to generate free cash flows of $10.9 million per year. XL has permanent debt of $40 million, a tax rate of 40%, and an unlevered cost of capital of 10%.

    a. What is the value of XL's equity using the APV method?

    b. What is XL's WACC? What is XL's equity value using the WACC method?

    c. If XL's debt cost of capital is 5%, what is XL's equity cost of capital?

    d. What is XL's equity value using the FTE method?

EXCEL *24. Propel Corporation plans to make a $50 million investment, initially funded completely with debt. The free cash flows of the investment and Propel's incremental debt from the project are shown below:

Year	0	1	2	3
Free cash flows	−50	40	20	25
Debt	50	30	15	0

Propel's incremental debt for the project will be paid off according to the predetermined schedule shown. Propel's debt cost of capital is 8%, and its tax rate is 40%. Propel also estimates an unlevered cost of capital for the project of 12%.

    a. Use the APV method to determine the levered value of the project at each date and its initial NPV.

    b. Calculate the WACC for this project at each date. How does the WACC change over time? Why?

    c. Compute the project's NPV using the WACC method.

    d. Compute the equity cost of capital for this project at each date. How does the equity cost of capital change over time? Why?

    e. Compute the project's equity value using the FTE method. How does the initial equity value compare with the NPV calculated in parts a and c?

*25. Gartner Systems has no debt and an equity cost of capital of 10%. Gartner's current market capitalization is $100 million, and its free cash flows are expected to grow at 3% per year. Gartner's corporate tax rate is 35%. Investors pay tax rates of 40% on interest income and 20% on equity income.

    a. Suppose Gartner adds $50 million in permanent debt and uses the proceeds to repurchase shares. What will Gartner's levered value be in this case?

    b. Suppose instead Gartner decides to maintain a 50% debt-to-value ratio going forward. If Gartner's debt cost of capital is 6.67%, what will Gartner's levered value be in this case?

EXCEL   ***26.** Revtek Inc. has an equity cost of capital of 12% and a debt cost of capital of 6%. Revtek maintains a constant debt-equity ratio of 0.5, and its tax rate is 35%.

    a. What is Revtek's WACC given its current debt-equity ratio?

    b. Assuming no personal taxes, how will Revtek's WACC change if it increases its debt-equity ratio to 2 and its debt cost of capital remains at 6%?

    c. Now suppose investors pay tax rates of 40% on interest income and 15% on income from equity. How will Revtek's WACC change if it increases its debt-equity ratio to 2 in this case?

    d. Provide an intuitive explanation for the difference in your answers to parts b and c.

DATA CASE

EXCEL

Toyota Motor Company is expanding the production of their gas-electric hybrid drive systems and plans to begin production in the United States. To enable the expansion they are contemplating investing $1.5 billion in a new plant with an expected 10-year life. The anticipated free cash flows from the new plant would be $220 million the first year of operation and grow by 10% for each of the next two years and then 5% per year for the remaining seven years. As a newly hired MBA in the capital budgeting division you have been asked to evaluate the new project using the WACC, adjusted present value, and flow-to-equity methods. You will compute the appropriate costs of capital and the net present values with each method. Because this is your first major assignment with the firm, they want you to demonstrate that you are capable of handling the different valuation methods. You must seek out the information necessary to value the free cash flows but will be provided some directions to follow. (This is an involved assignment, but at least you don't have to come up with the actual cash flows for the project!)

1. Go to MarketWatch.com (www.marketwatch.com) and get the quote for Toyota (symbol: TM).

    a. Click on "Financials." The income statements for the last four fiscal years will appear. Place the cursor in the middle of the statements and right-click the mouse. Select "Export to Microsoft Excel."

    b. Go back to the Web page and select "Balance Sheets" from the top of the page. Repeat the download procedure for the balance sheets, then copy and paste them into the same worksheet as the income statements.

    c. Click on "Historical Quote" in the left column, and find Toyota's stock price for the last day of the month at the end of each of the past four fiscal years. Record the stock price on each date in your spreadsheet.

2. Create a timeline in Excel with the free cash flows for the ten years of the project.

3. Determine the WACC using Eq. 18.1.

    a. For the cost of debt, r_D:

      i. Go to NASD BondInfo (http://cxa.marketwatch.com/finra/BondCenter/Default.aspx) and click to search by symbol. Enter Toyota's symbol and press enter.

    ii. Find the yield for the Toyota Motor Credit Corp. bond with a maturity of 1/12/2021. Enter the yield on your spreadsheet as an estimate of Toyota's debt cost of capital.

  b. For the cost of equity, r_E:

    i. Get the yield on the ten-year U.S. Treasury Bond from Yahoo! Finance (http://finance.yahoo.com). Scroll down to the Market Summary. Enter that yield as the risk-free rate.

    ii. Find the beta for Toyota from Nasdaq.com. Enter the symbol for Toyota and click on "Summary Quote." The beta for Toyota will be listed there.

    iii. Use a market risk premium of 4.50% to compute r_E using the CAPM.

  c. Determine the values for E and D from Eq. 18.1 for Toyota and the debt-to-value and equity-to-value ratios.

    i. To compute the net debt for Toyota add the long-term debt and the short-term debt and subtract cash and cash equivalents for each year on the balance sheet.

    ii. Multiply the historical stock prices by the "Basic Weighted Shares Outstanding" data in the income statement to compute Toyota's market capitalization at the end of each fiscal year.

    iii. Compute Toyota's enterprise value at the end of each fiscal year by combining the values obtained for its equity market capitalization and its net debt.

    iv. Compute Toyota's debt-to-value ratio at the end of each year by dividing its net debt by its enterprise value. Use the average ratio from the last four years as an estimate for Toyota's target debt-to-value ratio.

  d. Determine Toyota's tax rate by dividing the income tax by earnings before tax for each year. Take the average of the four rates as Toyota's marginal corporate tax rate.

  e. Compute the WACC for Toyota using Eq. 18.1.

4. Compute the NPV of the hybrid engine expansion given the free cash flows you calculated using the WACC method of valuation.

5. Determine the NPV using the adjusted present value method, and also using the flow-to-equity method. In both cases, assume Toyota maintains the target leverage ratio you computed in Question 3c.

6. Compare the results under the three methods and explain how the resulting NPVs are achieved under each of the three different methods.

FOUNDATIONS AND FURTHER DETAILS

**CHAPTER 18
APPENDIX**

In this appendix we look at the foundations for the WACC method, and for the relationship between a firm's levered and unlevered costs of capital. We also address how we can solve for a firm's leverage policy and value simultaneously.

18A.1   DERIVING THE WACC METHOD

The WACC can be used to value a levered investment, as in Eq. 18.2 on page 633. Consider an investment that is financed by both debt and equity. Because equity holders require an expected return of r_E on their investment and debt holders require a return of r_D, the firm will have to pay investors a total of

$$E(1 + r_E) + D(1 + r_D) \tag{18A.1}$$

next year. What is the value of the investment next year? The project generates free cash flows of FCF_1 at the end of the year. In addition, the interest tax shield of the debt provides a tax savings of $\tau_c \times$ (interest on debt) $< \tau_c\, r_D\, D$.[26] Finally, if the investment will continue beyond next year, it will have a continuation value of V_1^L. Thus, to satisfy investors, the project cash flows must be such that

$$E(1 + r_E) + D(1 + r_D) = FCF_1 + \tau_c r_D D + V_1^L \tag{18A.2}$$

Because $V_0^L = E + D$, we can write the WACC definition in Eq. 18.1 as

$$r_{wacc} = \frac{E}{V_0^L} r_E + \frac{D}{V_0^L} r_D (1 - \tau_c) \tag{18A.3}$$

If we move the interest tax shield to the left side of Eq. 18A.2, we can use the definition of the WACC to rewrite Eq. 18A.2 as follows:

$$\underbrace{E(1 + r_E) + D[1 + r_D(1 - \tau_c)]}_{V_0^L(1 + r_{wacc})} = FCF_1 + V_1^L \tag{18A.4}$$

Dividing by $(1 + r_{wacc})$, we can express the value of the investment today as the present value of next period's free cash flows and continuation value:

$$V_0^L = \frac{FCF_1 + V_1^L}{1 + r_{wacc}} \tag{18A.5}$$

---

26. The return on the debt r_D need not come solely from interest payments. If C_t is the coupon paid and D_t is the market value of the debt in period t, then in period t, r_D is defined as

$$r_D = \frac{E[\text{Coupon Payment} + \text{Capital Gain}]}{\text{Current Price}} = \frac{E[C_{t+1} + D_{t+1} - D_t]}{D_t}$$

The return that determines the firm's interest expense is

$$\bar{r}_D = \frac{E[C_{t+1} + \bar{D}_{t+1} - \bar{D}_t]}{D_t}$$

where $\bar{D}_t$ is the value of the debt on date t according to a fixed schedule set by the tax law based on the difference between the bond's initial price and its face value, which is called the bond's *original issue discount* (OID). (If the bond is issued at par and the firm will not default on the next coupon, then $\bar{D}_t = \bar{D}_{t+1}$ and $\bar{r}_D = C_{t+1}/D_t$, which is the bond's *current yield*.) Thus the true after-tax cost of debt is $(r_D - \tau_c \bar{r}_D)$. In practice, the distinction between r_D and $\bar{r}_D$ is often ignored, and the after-tax cost of debt is computed as $r_D(1 - \tau_c)$. Also, the debt's yield to maturity is often used in place of r_D. Because the yield to maturity ignores default risk, it generally overstates r_D and therefore the WACC.

In the same way, we can write the value in one year, V_1^L, as the discounted value of the free cash flows and continuation value of the project in year 2. If the WACC is the same next year, then

$$V_0^L = \frac{FCF_1 + V_1^L}{1 + r_{wacc}} = \frac{FCF_1 + \dfrac{FCF_2 + V_2^L}{1 + r_{wacc}}}{1 + r_{wacc}} = \frac{FCF_1}{1 + r_{wacc}} + \frac{FCF_2 + V_2^L}{(1 + r_{wacc})^2} \quad (18A.6)$$

By repeatedly replacing each continuation value, and *assuming the WACC remains constant*, we can derive Eq. 18.2:[27]

$$V_0^L = \frac{FCF_1}{1 + r_{wacc}} + \frac{FCF_2}{(1 + r_{wacc})^2} + \frac{FCF_3}{(1 + r_{wacc})^3} + \cdots \quad (18A.7)$$

That is, *the value of a levered investment is the present value of its future free cash flows using the weighted average cost of capital.*

18A.2   THE LEVERED AND UNLEVERED COST OF CAPITAL

In this appendix, we derive the relationship between the levered and unlevered cost of capital for the firm. Suppose an investor holds a portfolio of all of the equity and debt of the firm. Then the investor will receive the free cash flows of the firm plus the tax savings from the interest tax shield. These are the same cash flows an investor would receive from a portfolio of the unlevered firm (which generates the free cash flows) and a separate "tax shield" security that paid the investor the amount of the tax shield each period. Because these two portfolios generate the same cash flows, by the Law of One Price they have the same market values:

$$V^L = E + D = V^U + T \quad (18A.8)$$

where T is the present value of the interest tax shield. Equation 18A.8 is the basis of the APV method. Because these portfolios have equal cash flows, they must also have identical expected returns, which implies

$$E\, r_E + D\, r_D = V^U r_U + T r_T \quad (18A.9)$$

where r_T is the expected return associated with the interest tax shields. The relationship between r_E, r_D, and r_U will depend on the expected return r_T, which is determined by the risk of the interest tax shield. Let's consider the two cases discussed in the text.

TARGET LEVERAGE RATIO

Suppose the firm adjusts its debt continuously to maintain a target debt-to-value ratio, or a target ratio of interest to free cash flow. Because the firm's debt and interest payments will vary with the firm's value and cash flows, it is reasonable to expect the risk of the interest tax shield will equal that of the firm's free cash flow, so $r_T = r_U$. Making this assumption, which we return to below, Eq. 18A.9 becomes

$$E\, r_E + D\, r_D = V^U r_U + T\, r_U = (V^U + T) r_U$$
$$= (E + D) r_U \quad (18A.10)$$

Dividing by $(E + D)$ leads to Eq. 18.6.

---

27. This expansion is the same approach we took in Chapter 9 to derive the discounted dividend formula for the stock price.

IDEKO'S PLANNED DEBT AND INTEREST PAYMENTS

TABLE 19.5

SPREADSHEET

Year	2010	2011	2012	2013	2014	2015
Debt and Interest Table ($ 000)						
1 Outstanding Debt		100,000	100,000	100,000	115,000	120,000	120,000
2 Interest on Term Loan	6.80%		(6,800)	(6,800)	(6,800)	(7,820)	(8,160)

Given Ideko's outstanding debt, its interest expense each year is computed as[2]

$$\text{Interest in Year } t = \text{Interest Rate} \times \text{Ending Balance in Year } (t-1) \qquad (19.2)$$

The interest on the debt will provide a valuable tax shield to offset Ideko's taxable income.

In addition to the tax benefit, the loan will allow PKK to limit its investment in Ideko and preserve its capital for other investments and acquisitions. The sources and uses of funds for the acquisition are shown in the Table 19.6 spreadsheet. In addition to the $150 million purchase price for Ideko's equity, $4.5 million will be used to repay Ideko's existing debt. With $5 million in advisory and other fees associated with the transaction, the acquisition will require $159.5 million in total funds. PKK's sources of funds include the new loan of $100 million as well as Ideko's own excess cash (which PKK will have access to). Thus PKK's required equity contribution to the transaction is $159.5 - 100 - 6.5 = $53 million.

SOURCES AND USES OF FUNDS FOR THE IDEKO ACQUISITION

TABLE 19.6

SPREADSHEET

Acquisition Financing ($ 000)				
Sources		**Uses**	
1 New Term Loan	100,000	Purchase Ideko Equity	150,000
2 Excess Ideko Cash	6,500	Repay Existing Ideko Debt	4,500
3 PKK Equity Investment	53,000	Advisory and Other Fees	5,000
4 Total Sources of Funds	159,500	Total Uses of Funds	159,500

CONCEPT CHECK

1. What are the different operational improvements PKK plans to make?

2. Why is it necessary to consider these improvements to assess whether the acquisition is attractive?

19.3 BUILDING THE FINANCIAL MODEL

The value of any investment opportunity arises from the future cash flows it will generate. To estimate the cash flows resulting from the investment in Ideko, we begin by projecting Ideko's future earnings. We then consider Ideko's working capital and investment needs and estimate its free cash flow. With these data in hand, we can forecast Ideko's balance sheet and statement of cash flows.

---

2. Equation 19.2 assumes that changes in debt occur at the end of the year. If debt changes during the year, it is more accurate to compute interest expenses based on the average level of debt during the year.

FORECASTING EARNINGS

We can forecast Ideko's income statement for the five years following the acquisition based on the operational and capital structure changes proposed. This income statement is often referred to as a **pro forma** income statement, because it is not based on actual data but rather depicts the firm's financials under a given set of hypothetical assumptions. The pro forma income statement translates our expectations regarding the operational improvements PKK can achieve at Ideko into consequences for the firm's earnings.

To build the pro forma income statement, we begin with Ideko's sales. Each year, sales can be calculated from the estimates in Table 19.3 as follows:

$$\text{Sales} = \text{Market Size} \times \text{Market Share} \times \text{Average Sales Price} \qquad (19.3)$$

For example, in 2011, Ideko has projected sales of 10.5 million $\times$ 11% $\times$ 76.5 = $88.358 million. The spreadsheet in Table 19.7 shows Ideko's current (2010) sales as well as projections for five years after the acquisition (2011–2015).

The next items in the income statement detail the cost of goods sold. The raw materials cost can be calculated from sales as

$$\text{Raw Materials} = \text{Market Size} \times \text{Market Share} \times \text{Raw Materials per Unit} \qquad (19.4)$$

In 2011, the cost of raw materials is 10.5 million $\times$ 11% $\times$ 16.16 = $18.665 million. The same method can be applied to determine the direct labour costs. Sales, marketing, and administrative costs can be computed directly as a percentage of sales. For example:

$$\text{Sales and Marketing} = \text{Sales} \times (\text{Sales and Marketing \% of Sales}) \qquad (19.5)$$

Therefore, sales and marketing costs are forecast to be $88.358 million $\times$ 16.5% = $14.579 million in 2011.

Deducting these operating expenses from Ideko's sales, we can project EBITDA over the next five years as shown in Table 19.7. Subtracting the depreciation expenses we estimated in Table 19.4, we arrive at Ideko's earnings before interest and taxes. We next

TABLE 19.7

SPREADSHEET

PRO FORMA INCOME STATEMENT FOR IDEKO, 2010–2015

	Year	2010	2011	2012	2013	2014	2015
Income Statement ($ 000)							
1 Sales		75,000	88,358	103,234	119,777	138,149	158,526
2 Cost of Goods Sold							
3 Raw Materials		(16,000)	(18,665)	(21,593)	(24,808)	(28,333)	(32,193)
4 Direct Labour Costs		(18,000)	(21,622)	(25,757)	(30,471)	(35,834)	(41,925)
5 **Gross Profit**		41,000	48,071	55,883	64,498	73,982	84,407
6 Sales and Marketing		(11,250)	(14,579)	(18,582)	(23,356)	(27,630)	(31,705)
7 Administrative		(13,500)	(13,254)	(15,485)	(16,769)	(17,959)	(20,608)
8 **EBITDA**		16,250	20,238	21,816	24,373	28,393	32,094
9 Depreciation		(5,500)	(5,450)	(5,405)	(6,865)	(7,678)	(7,710)
10 **EBIT**		10,750	14,788	16,411	17,508	20,715	24,383
11 Interest Expense (net)		(75)	(6,800)	(6,800)	(6,800)	(7,820)	(8,160)
12 **Pretax Income**		10,675	7,988	9,611	10,708	12,895	16,223
13 Income Tax		(3,736)	(2,796)	(3,364)	(3,748)	(4,513)	(5,678)
14 **Net Income**		6,939	5,193	6,247	6,960	8,382	10,545

deduct interest expenses according to the schedule given in Table 19.5.[3] The final expense is the corporate income tax, which we computed using the tax rate in Table 19.3 as

$$\text{Income Tax} = \text{Pretax Income} \times \text{Tax Rate} \qquad (19.6)$$

After income taxes, we are left with Ideko's projected pro forma net income as the bottom line in Table 19.7. Based on our projections, net income will rise by 52% from $6.939 million to $10.545 million at the end of five years, though it will drop in the near term due to the large increase in interest expense from the new debt.

EXAMPLE 19.3	FORECASTING INCOME

Problem

By what percentage is Ideko's EBITDA expected to grow over the five-year period? By how much would it grow if Ideko's market share remained at 10%?

Solution

EBITDA will increase from $16.25 million to $32.09 million, or $(32.09/16.25) - 1 = 97\%$, over the five years. With a 10% market share rather than a 15% market share, sales will be only $(10\%/15\%) = 66.7\%$ of the forecast in Table 19.7. Because Ideko's operating expenses are proportional to its sales, its expenses and EBITDA will also be 66.7% of the current estimates. Thus EBITDA will grow to $66.7\% \times 32.09 = \$21.40$ million, which is an increase of only $(21.40/16.25) - 1 = 32\%$.

WORKING CAPITAL REQUIREMENTS

The spreadsheet in Table 19.8 lists Ideko's current working capital requirements and forecasts the firm's future working capital needs. (See Chapter 26 for a further discussion of working capital requirements and their determinants.) This forecast includes the plans to tighten Ideko's credit policy, speed up customer payments, and reduce Ideko's inventory of raw materials.

TABLE 19.8	IDEKO'S WORKING CAPITAL REQUIREMENTS
SPREADSHEET	

	Year	2010	>2010
Working Capital Days			
Assets	Based on:	Days	Days
1 Accounts Receivable	Sales Revenue	90	60
2 Raw Materials	Raw Materials Costs	45	30
3 Finished Goods	Raw Materials + Labour Costs	45	45
4 Minimum Cash Balance	Sales Revenue	30	30
Liabilities			
5 Wages Payable	Direct Labour + Admin Costs	15	15
6 Other Accounts Payable	Raw Materials + Sales and Marketing	45	45

---

3. This interest expense should be offset by any interest earned on investments. As we discuss later in this chapter, we assume that Ideko does not invest its excess cash balances, but instead pays them out to its owner, PKK. Thus net interest expenses are solely due to Ideko's outstanding debt.

TABLE 19.9
SPREADSHEET

IDEKO'S NET WORKING CAPITAL FORECAST

	Year	2010	2011	2012	2013	2014	2015
Working Capital ($ 000)							
Assets							
1 Accounts Receivable		18,493	14,525	16,970	19,689	22,709	26,059
2 Raw Materials		1,973	1,534	1,775	2,039	2,329	2,646
3 Finished Goods		4,192	4,967	5,838	6,815	7,911	9,138
4 Minimum Cash Balance		6,164	7,262	8,485	9,845	11,355	13,030
5 Total Current Assets		30,822	28,288	33,067	38,388	44,304	50,872
Liabilities							
6 Wages Payable		1,294	1,433	1,695	1,941	2,211	2,570
7 Other Accounts Payable		3,360	4,099	4,953	5,938	6,900	7,878
8 Total Current Liabilities		4,654	5,532	6,648	7,879	9,110	10,448
Net Working Capital							
9 Net Working Capital (5 − 8)		26,168	22,756	26,419	30,509	35,194	40,425
10 Increase in Net Working Capital			(3,412)	3,663	4,089	4,685	5,231

Based on these working capital requirements, the spreadsheet in Table 19.9 forecasts Ideko's net working capital (NWC) over the next five years. Each line item in the spreadsheet is found by computing the appropriate number of day's worth of the corresponding revenue or expense from the income statement (Table 19.7). For example, accounts receivable in 2011 is calculated as[4]

$$\text{Accounts Receivable} = \text{Days Required} \times \frac{\text{Annual Sales}}{365 \text{ days/yr}}$$

$$= 60 \text{ days} \times \frac{\$88.358 \text{ million/yr}}{365 \text{ days/yr}} = \$14.525 \text{ million} \qquad (19.7)$$

Similarly, Ideko's inventory of finished goods will be $45 \times (18.665 + 21.622)/365 = \$4.967$ million.

Table 19.9 also lists Ideko's minimum cash balance each year. This balance represents the minimum level of cash needed to keep the business running smoothly, allowing for the daily variations in the timing of income and expenses. Firms generally earn little or no interest on these balances, which are held in cash or in chequing or short-term savings accounts. As a consequence, we account for this opportunity cost by including the minimal cash balance as part of the firm's working capital.

We assume that Ideko will earn no interest on this minimal balance. (If it did, this interest would reduce the firm's net interest expense in the income statement.) We also assume that Ideko will pay out as dividends all cash not needed as part of working capital. Therefore, Ideko will hold no excess cash balances or short-term investments above the minimal level reported in Table 19.9. If Ideko were to retain excess funds,

---

4. If products are highly seasonal, large fluctuations in working capital may occur over the course of the year. When these effects are important, it is best to develop forecasts on a quarterly or monthly basis so that the seasonal effects can be tracked.

these balances would be included as part of its financing strategy (reducing its net debt), and not as part of working capital.[5]

Ideko's net working capital for each year is computed in Table 19.9 as the difference between the forecasted current assets and current liabilities. Increases in net working capital represent a cost to the firm. Note that as a result of the improvements in accounts receivable and inventory management, Ideko will reduce its net working capital by more than $3.4 million in 2011. After this initial savings, working capital needs will increase in conjunction with the growth of the firm.

FORECASTING FREE CASH FLOW

We now have the data needed to forecast Ideko's free cash flows over the next five years. Ideko's earnings are available from the income statement (Table 19.7), as are its depreciation and interest expenses. Capital expenditures are available from Table 19.4, and changes in net working capital can be found in Table 19.9. We combine these items to estimate the free cash flows in the spreadsheet in Table 19.10.

To compute Ideko's free cash flow, which excludes cash flows associated with leverage, we first adjust net income by adding back the after-tax interest payments associated with the net debt in its capital structure:[6]

$$\text{After-Tax Interest Expense} =$$
$$(1 - \text{Tax Rate}) \times (\text{Interest on Debt} - \text{Interest on Excess Cash}) \qquad (19.8)$$

Because Ideko has no excess cash, its after-tax interest expense in 2011 is $(1 - 35\%) \times 6.8 = \$4.42$ million, providing unlevered net income of $5.193 + 4.42 = \$9.613$ million. We could also compute the unlevered net income in Table 19.10 by starting with EBIT and deducting taxes. In 2011, for example, EBIT is forecasted as $14.788 million, which amounts to $14.788 \times (1 - 35\%) = \$9.613$ million after taxes.

TABLE 19.10

SPREADSHEET

IDEKO'S FREE CASH FLOW FORECAST

	Year	2010	2011	2012	2013	2014	2015
Free Cash Flow ($ 000)							
1 Net Income			5,193	6,247	6,960	8,382	10,545
2 Plus: After-Tax Interest Expense			4,420	4,420	4,420	5,083	5,304
3 Unlevered Net Income			9,613	10,667	11,380	13,465	15,849
4 Plus: Depreciation			5,450	5,405	6,865	7,678	7,710
5 Less: Increases in NWC			3,412	(3,663)	(4,089)	(4,685)	(5,231)
6 Less: Capital Expenditures			(5,000)	(5,000)	(20,000)	(15,000)	(8,000)
7 **Free Cash Flow of Firm**			13,475	7,409	(5,845)	1,458	10,328
8 Plus: Net Borrowing			—	—	15,000	5,000	—
9 Less: After-Tax Interest Expense			(4,420)	(4,420)	(4,420)	(5,083)	(5,304)
10 **Free Cash Flow to Equity**			9,055	2,989	4,735	1,375	5,024

---

5. Firms often hold excess cash in anticipation of future investment needs or possible cash shortfalls. Because Ideko can rely on PKK to provide needed capital, excess cash reserves are unnecessary.

6. If Ideko had some interest income or expenses from working capital, we would *not* include that interest here. We adjust only for interest that is related to the firm's *financing*—that is, interest associated with debt and *excess* cash (cash not included as part of working capital).

To compute Ideko's free cash flow from its unlevered net income, we add back depreciation (which is not a cash expense), and deduct Ideko's increases in net working capital and capital expenditures. The free cash flow on line 7 of Table 19.10 shows the cash the firm will generate for its investors, both debt and equity holders. While Ideko will generate substantial free cash flow over the next five years, the level of free cash flow varies substantially from year to year. It is highest in 2011 (due mostly to the large reduction in working capital) and is forecasted to be negative in 2013 (when the plant expansion will begin).

To determine the free cash flow to equity, we first add Ideko's net borrowing (that is, increases to net debt):

$$\text{Net Borrowing in Year } t = \text{Net Debt in Year } t - \text{Net Debt in Year } (t - 1) \qquad (19.9)$$

Ideko will borrow in 2013 and 2014 as part of its expansion. We then deduct the after-tax interest payments that were added in line 2.

As shown in the last line of Table 19.10, during the next five years Ideko is expected to generate a positive free cash flow to equity, which will be used to pay dividends to PKK. The free cash flow to equity will be highest in 2011; by 2015, PKK will recoup a significant fraction of its initial investment.

EXAMPLE 19.4

LEVERAGE AND FREE CASH FLOW

Problem

Suppose Ideko does not add leverage in 2013 and 2014, but instead keeps its debt fixed at $100 million until 2015. How would this change in its leverage policy affect its expected free cash flow? How would it affect the free cash flow to equity?

Solution

Because free cash flow is based on unlevered net income, it will not be affected by Ideko's leverage policy. Free cash flow to equity will be affected, however. Net borrowing will be zero each year, and the firm's after-tax interest expense will remain at the 2011 level of $4.42 million:

Year	2010	2011	2012	2013	2014	2015
Free Cash Flow ($ 000)						
1 Free Cash Flow of Firm		13,475	7,409	(5,845)	1,458	10,328
2 Plus: Net Borrowing		—	—	—	—	—
3 Less: After-Tax Interest Expense		(4,420)	(4,420)	(4,420)	(4,420)	(4,420)
4 Free Cash Flow to Equity		9,055	2,989	(10,265)	(2,962)	5,908

In this case, Ideko will have a negative free cash flow to equity in 2013 and 2014. That is, without additional borrowing, PKK will have to invest additional capital in the firm to fund the expansion.

THE BALANCE SHEET AND STATEMENT OF CASH FLOWS (OPTIONAL)

The information we have calculated so far can be used to project Ideko's balance sheet and statement of cash flows through 2015. While these statements are not critical for our valuation, they often prove helpful in providing a more complete picture of how a firm will

TABLE 19.11

SPREADSHEET

PRO FORMA BALANCE SHEET FOR IDEKO, 2010–2015

Year	2010	2011	2012	2013	2014	2015
Balance Sheet ($ 000)						
Assets						
1 Cash and Cash Equivalents	6,164	7,262	8,485	9,845	11,355	13,030
2 Accounts Receivable	18,493	14,525	16,970	19,689	22,709	26,059
3 Inventories	6,165	6,501	7,613	8,854	10,240	11,784
4 **Total Current Assets**	30,822	28,288	33,067	38,388	44,304	50,873
5 Property, Plant, and Equipment	49,500	49,050	48,645	61,781	69,102	69,392
6 Goodwill	72,332	72,332	72,332	72,332	72,332	72,332
7 **Total Assets**	152,654	149,670	154,044	172,501	185,738	192,597
Liabilities						
8 Accounts Payable	4,654	5,532	6,648	7,879	9,110	10,448
9 Debt	100,000	100,000	100,000	115,000	120,000	120,000
10 **Total Liabilities**	104,654	105,532	106,648	122,879	129,110	130,448
Shareholders' Equity						
11 Starting Shareholders' Equity		48,000	44,138	47,396	49,621	56,628
12 Net Income		5,193	6,247	6,960	8,382	10,545
13 Dividends	(2,000)	(9,055)	(2,989)	(4,735)	(1,375)	(5,024)
14 Capital Contributions	50,000	—	—	—	—	—
15 **Shareholders' Equity**	48,000	44,138	47,396	49,621	56,628	62,149
16 **Total Liabilities and Equity**	152,654	149,670	154,044	172,501	185,738	192,597

grow during the forecast period. These statements for Ideko are shown in the spreadsheets in Tables 19.11 and 19.12.

On the balance sheet (Table 19.11), current assets and liabilities come from the net working capital spreadsheet (Table 19.9). The inventory entry on the balance sheet includes both raw materials and finished goods. Property, plant, and equipment information comes from the capital expenditure spreadsheet (Table 19.4), and the debt comes from Table 19.5. The goodwill entry arises from the difference in the acquisition price and Ideko's initial book value of equity in Table 19.1:

$$\text{New Goodwill} = \text{Acquisition Price} - \text{Fair Market Value of Net Assets Acquired} \quad (19.10)$$

Given the acquisition price of $150 million, and using Ideko's existing book value of equity of $77.668 million in Table 19.1 as an approximation of the fair market value of net assets acquired, the new goodwill is $150 - 77.668 = \$72.332$ million.[7] The shareholders' equity of $48 million in 2010 arises from PKK's initial equity contribution of $53 million less $5 million in advisory fee expenses.[8] The shareholders' equity increases each year through retained earnings (net income less dividends) and new capital contributions. Dividends

---

7. We have simplified somewhat the balance sheet adjustments and goodwill calculation. In particular, the book values of Ideko's assets and liabilities may be "stepped up" to reflect current fair values.

8. Under Canadian GAAP, the transaction cost of the purchase includes the direct costs of the business combination (including, for example, advisory fees). Going forward under IFRS, transaction costs of a business combination will be expensed as incurred. For simplicity, any tax consequences of the advisory fees have been ignored.

TABLE 19.12

SPREADSHEET

PRO FORMA STATEMENT OF CASH FLOWS FOR IDEKO, 2010–2015

	Year	2010	2011	2012	2013	2014	2015
	Statement of Cash Flows ($ 000)						
1	Net Income		5,193	6,247	6,960	8,382	10,545
2	Depreciation		5,450	5,405	6,865	7,678	7,710
3	Changes in Working Capital						
4	Accounts Receivable		3,968	(2,445)	(2,719)	(3,020)	(3,350)
5	Inventory		(336)	(1,112)	(1,242)	(1,385)	(1,544)
6	Accounts Payable		878	1,116	1,231	1,231	1,338
7	**Cash from Operating Activities**		15,153	9,211	11,095	12,885	14,699
8	Capital Expenditures		(5,000)	(5,000)	(20,000)	(15,000)	(8,000)
9	Other Investment		–	–	–	–	–
10	**Cash from Investing Activities**		(5,000)	(5,000)	(20,000)	(15,000)	(8,000)
11	Net Borrowing		–	–	15,000	5,000	–
12	Dividends		(9,055)	(2,989)	(4,735)	(1,375)	(5,024)
13	Capital Contributions		–	–	–	–	–
14	**Cash from Financing Activities**		(9,055)	(2,989)	10,265	3,625	(5,024)
15	**Change in Cash** (7 + 10 + 14)		1,098	1,223	1,360	1,510	1,675

after 2010 are taken from the free cash flow to equity given in Table 19.10. (If free cash flow to equity were negative in any year, it would appear as a capital contribution in line 14 of the balance sheet.) As a check on the calculations, note that the balance sheet does, indeed, balance: Total assets equal total liabilities and equity.[9]

Ideko's book value of equity will decline in 2011, as Ideko reduces its working capital and pays out the savings as part of a large dividend. The firm's book value will then rise as it expands. Ideko's book debt-equity ratio will decline from $100,000/48,000 = 2.1$ to $120,000/62,149 = 1.9$ during the five-year period.

The statement of cash flows in Table 19.12 starts with net income. Cash from operating activities includes depreciation as well as changes to working capital items (other than cash) from Table 19.9. Cash from investing activities includes the capital expenditures in Table 19.4. Cash from financing activities includes net borrowing from Table 19.10 and dividends or capital contributions determined by the free cash flow to equity in Table 19.10. As a final check on the calculations, note that the change in cash and cash equivalents on line 15 equals the change in the minimum cash balance shown on the balance sheet (Table 19.11).

CONCEPT CHECK

1. What is a pro forma income statement?

2. How do we calculate the firm's free cash flow and the free cash flow to equity?

---

9. In Table 19.11, goodwill is assumed to remain constant. For financial accounting purposes, goodwill is not amortized but is subject to an impairment test at least once a year as specified in the Canadian Institute of Chartered Accountants (CICA) Handbook, Section 3062, so the amount of goodwill may change over time (though any changes in goodwill due to impairment have no tax accounting consequences).

19.4 ESTIMATING THE COST OF CAPITAL

To value PKK's investment in Ideko, we need to assess the risk associated with Ideko and estimate an appropriate cost of capital. Because Ideko is a private firm, we cannot use its own past returns to evaluate its risk, but must instead rely on comparable publicly traded firms. In this section, we use data from the comparable firms identified earlier to estimate a cost of capital for Ideko.

Our approach is as follows. First, we use the techniques developed in Part 4 of the text to estimate the equity cost of capital for Oakley, Luxottica Group, and Nike. We then estimate the unlevered cost of capital for each firm based on its capital structure. The unlevered costs of capital of the comparable firms are next used to estimate Ideko's unlevered cost of capital. Once we have this estimate, we can use Ideko's capital structure to determine its equity cost of capital or WACC, depending on the valuation method employed.

CAPM-BASED ESTIMATION

To determine an appropriate cost of capital, we must first determine the appropriate measure of risk. PKK's investment in Ideko will represent a large fraction of its portfolio. As a consequence, PKK itself is not well diversified. But PKK's investors are primarily pension funds and large institutional investors which are themselves well diversified and which evaluate their performance relative to the market as a benchmark. Thus you decide that estimating market risk using the CAPM approach is justified.

Using the CAPM, we can estimate the equity cost of capital for each comparable firm based on the beta of its equity. As outlined in Chapter 12, the standard approach to estimating an equity beta is to determine the historical sensitivity of the stock's returns to the market's returns by using linear regression to estimate the slope coefficient in the equation:

$$\underbrace{R_s - r_f}_{\substack{\text{Excess return} \\ \text{of stock } s}} = \alpha_s + \beta_s \underbrace{\left(R_{mkt} - r_f\right)}_{\substack{\text{Excess return} \\ \text{of market portfolio}}} + \varepsilon_s \tag{19.11}$$

As a proxy for the market portfolio, we will use a value-weighted portfolio of all NYSE, AMEX, and NASDAQ stocks because our comparable firms all trade in the U.S. With data from 2005 to 2009, we calculate the excess return—the realized return minus the yield on a one-month U.S. Treasury security—for each firm and for the market portfolio. We then estimate the equity beta for each firm by regressing its excess return onto the excess return of the market portfolio. We perform the regression for both monthly returns and ten-day returns. The estimated equity betas, together with their 95% confidence intervals, are shown in Table 19.13.

While we would like to assess risk and, therefore, estimate beta based on longer horizon returns (consistent with our investors' investment horizon), the confidence intervals we obtain using monthly data are extremely wide. These confidence intervals narrow

EQUITY BETAS WITH CONFIDENCE INTERVALS FOR COMPARABLE FIRMS

TABLE 19.13

Firm	Monthly Returns		Ten-Day Returns	
	Beta	95% C.I.	Beta	95% C.I.
Oakley	1.99	1.2 to 2.8	1.37	0.9 to 1.9
Luxottica	0.56	0.0 to 1.1	0.86	0.5 to 1.2
Nike	0.48	−0.1 to 1.0	0.69	0.4 to 1.1

CAPITAL STRUCTURE AND UNLEVERED BETA ESTIMATES FOR COMPARABLE FIRMS

TABLE 19.14

Firm	$\dfrac{E}{E+D}$	$\dfrac{D}{E+D}$	β_E	β_D	β_U
Oakley	1.00	0.00	1.50	—	1.50
Luxottica	0.83	0.17	0.75	0	0.62
Nike	1.05	−0.05	0.60	0	0.63

somewhat when we use ten-day returns. In any case, the results make clear that a fair amount of uncertainty persists when we estimate the beta for an individual firm.

UNLEVERING BETA

Given an estimate of each firm's equity beta, we next "unlever" the beta based on the firm's capital structure. Here we use Eq. 12.9 (which is equivalent, in terms of returns, to calculating the pretax WACC as in Eq. 18.6):

$$\beta_U = \left(\frac{\text{Equity Value}}{\text{Enterprise Value}} \right) \beta_E + \left(\frac{\text{Net Debt Value}}{\text{Enterprise Value}} \right) \beta_D \qquad (19.12)$$

Recall that we must use the *net* debt of the firm—that is, we must subtract any cash from the level of debt—so we use the enterprise value of the firm as the sum of debt and equity in the formula.[10] Table 19.14 shows the capital structure for each comparable firm. Oakley has no debt, while Luxottica has about 17% debt in its capital structure. Nike holds cash that exceeds its debt, leading to a negative net debt in its capital structure.

Table 19.14 also estimates the unlevered beta of each firm. Here we have used an equity beta for each firm within the range of the results from Table 19.13. Given the low or negative debt levels for each firm, assuming a beta for debt of zero is a reasonable approximation. We then compute an unlevered beta for each firm according to Eq. 19.12.

The range of the unlevered betas for these three firms is large. Both Luxottica and Nike have relatively low betas, presumably reflecting the relative noncyclicality of their core businesses (prescription eyewear for Luxottica and athletic shoes for Nike). Oakley has a much higher unlevered beta, perhaps because the high-end specialty sports eyewear it produces is a discretionary expense for most consumers.

IDEKO'S UNLEVERED COST OF CAPITAL

The data from the comparable firms provides guidance to us for estimating Ideko's unlevered cost of capital. Ideko's products are not as high end as Oakley's eyewear, so their sales are unlikely to vary as much with the business cycle as Oakley's sales do. However, Ideko does not have a prescription eyewear division, as Luxottica does. Ideko's products are also fashion items rather than exercise items, so we expect Ideko's cost of capital to be closer to Oakley's than to Nike's or Luxottica's. We therefore use 1.20 as our preliminary

---

10. Recall from Chapter 18 that Eq. 19.12 assumes that the firm will maintain a target leverage ratio. If the debt is expected to remain fixed for some period, we should also deduct the value of the predetermined tax shields from the firm's net debt.

estimate for Ideko's unlevered beta, which is somewhat above the average of the comparables in Table 19.14.

We use the security market line of the CAPM to translate this beta into a cost of capital for Ideko. We assume that in 2010 the one-year Canadian Treasury Bill rates are approximately 4%; we use this rate for the risk-free interest rate. We also need an estimate of the market risk premium. Since 1960, the average annual return of the value-weighted market portfolio of U.S. stocks has exceeded that of one-year Treasuries by approximately 5%. In Canada, this number has been about 6%. However, these estimates are backward-looking numbers. As we mentioned in Chapter 12, some researchers believe that future stock market excess returns are likely to be lower than this historical average. In our valuation of Ideko, we will use 5% as the expected market risk premium.

Based on these choices, our estimate of Ideko's unlevered cost of capital is

$$r_U = r_f + \beta_U (E[R_{mkt}] - r_f) = 4\% + 1.20(5\%)$$
$$= 10\%$$

Of course, as our discussion has made clear, this estimate contains a large amount of uncertainty. Thus we will include sensitivity analysis with regard to the unlevered cost of capital in our analysis.

EXAMPLE 19.5

ESTIMATING THE UNLEVERED COST OF CAPITAL

Problem

Using the monthly equity beta estimates for each firm in Table 19.13, what range of unlevered cost of capital estimates is possible?

Solution

Oakley has the highest equity beta of 1.99, which is also its unlevered beta (it has no debt). With this beta, the unlevered cost of capital would be $r_U = 4\% + 1.99(5\%) = 13.95\%$. At the other extreme, given its capital structure, Luxottica's equity beta of 0.56 implies an unlevered beta of $(0.56)(0.83) = 0.46$. With this beta, the unlevered cost of capital would be $r_U = 4\% + 0.46(5\%) = 6.3\%$.

Note: We have assumed the same risk-free rate and market risk premium in the U.S. for our comparables as we did for Ideko in Canada. If conditions are different, we should use the relevant numbers from each of the two countries.

As with any analysis based on comparables, experience and judgment are necessary to come up with a reasonable estimate of the unlevered cost of capital. In this case, our choice would be guided by industry norms, an assessment of which comparable is closest in terms of market risk, and possibly knowledge of how cyclical Ideko's revenues have been historically.

CONCEPT CHECK

1. What is a standard approach to estimate an equity beta?

2. How do we estimate a firm's unlevered cost of capital using data from comparable publicly traded firms?

19.5 VALUING THE INVESTMENT

Thus far, we have forecasted the first five years of cash flows from PKK's investment in Ideko, and we have estimated the investment's unlevered cost of capital. In this section, we combine these inputs to estimate the value of the opportunity. The first step is to develop an estimate of Ideko's value at the end of our five-year forecast horizon. To do so, we consider both a multiples approach and a discounted cash flow (DCF) valuation using the WACC method. Given Ideko's free cash flow and continuation value, we then estimate its total enterprise value in 2010 using the APV method. Deducting the value of debt and PKK's initial investment from our estimate of Ideko's enterprise value gives the NPV of the investment opportunity. In addition to NPV, we look at some other common metrics, including IRR and cash multiples.

THE MULTIPLES APPROACH TO CONTINUATION VALUE

Practitioners generally estimate a firm's continuation value (also called the terminal value) at the end of the forecast horizon using a valuation multiple. While forecasting cash flows explicitly is useful in capturing those specific aspects of a company that distinguish the firm from its competitors in the short run, in the long run firms in the same industry typically have similar expected growth rates, profitability, and risk. As a consequence, multiples are likely to be relatively homogeneous across firms. Thus applying a multiple is potentially as reliable as estimating the value based on an explicit forecast of distant cash flows.

Of the different valuation multiples available, the EBITDA multiple is most often used in practice. In most settings, the EBITDA multiple is more reliable than sales or earnings multiples because it accounts for the firm's operating efficiency and is not affected by leverage differences between firms. We estimate the continuation value using an EBITDA multiple as follows:

$$\text{Continuation Enterprise Value at Forecast Horizon} = \text{EBITDA at Horizon} \times \text{EBITDA Multiple at Horizon} \quad (19.13)$$

From the income statement in Table 19.7, Ideko's EBITDA in 2015 is forecast to be $32.09 million. If we assume its EBITDA multiple in 2015 is unchanged from the value of 9.1 that we calculated at the time of the original purchase, then Ideko's continuation value in 2015 is $32.09 \times 9.1 = \$292.05$ million. This calculation is shown in the spreadsheet in Table 19.15. Given Ideko's outstanding debt of $120 million in 2015, this estimate corresponds to an equity value of $172.05 million.

Table 19.15 also shows Ideko's sales and P/E multiples based on this continuation value. The continuation value is 1.8 times Ideko's 2015 sales, and the equity value is 16.3 times Ideko's 2015 earnings. Because the P/E multiple is affected by leverage, we also report Ideko's **unlevered P/E ratio**, which is calculated as its continuing enterprise value divided by its unlevered net income in 2015 (listed in Table 19.10). Ideko would have this P/E

TABLE 19.15

SPREADSHEET

CONTINUATION VALUE ESTIMATE FOR IDEKO

Continuation Value: Multiples Approach ($ 000)			Common Multiples	
1	EBITDA in 2015	32,094	Common Multiples	
2	EBITDA multiple	9.1×	EV/Sales	1.8×
3	Continuation Enterprise Value	292,052	P/E (levered)	16.3×
4	Debt	(120,000)	P/E (unlevered)	18.4×
5	Continuation Equity Value	172,052		

ratio if it had no debt in 2015, so this information is useful when comparing Ideko to unlevered firms in the industry.

We can use the various multiples to assess the reasonableness of our estimated continuation value. While the value-to-sales ratio is high compared to the overall sporting goods industry, these multiples are otherwise low relative to the comparables in Table 19.2, and we would consider this estimate of Ideko's continuation value as reasonable (if not relatively conservative).

THE DISCOUNTED CASH FLOW APPROACH TO CONTINUATION VALUE

One difficulty with relying solely on comparables when forecasting a continuation value is that we are comparing *future* multiples of the firm with *current* multiples of its competitors. In 2015, the multiples of Ideko and the comparables we have chosen may all be very different, especially if the industry is currently experiencing abnormal growth. To guard against such a bias, it is wise to check our estimate of the continuation value based on fundamentals using a discounted cash flow approach.

To estimate a continuation value in year T using discounted cash flows, we assume a constant expected growth rate, g, and a constant debt-equity ratio. As explained in Chapter 18, when the debt-equity ratio is constant, the WACC valuation method is the simplest to apply:

$$\text{Enterprise Value in Year } T = V_T^L = \frac{FCF_{T+1}}{r_{wacc} - g} \qquad (19.14)$$

To estimate free cash flow in year $T + 1$, recall that free cash flow is equal to unlevered net income plus depreciation, less capital expenditures and increases in net working capital (see Table 19.10):

$$FCF_{T+1} = \text{Unlevered Net Income}_{T+1} + \text{Depreciation}_{T+1}$$
$$- \text{Increases in NWC}_{T+1} - \text{Capital Expenditures}_{T+1} \qquad (19.15)$$

Suppose the firm's sales are expected to grow at a nominal rate g. If the firm's operating expenses remain a fixed percentage of sales, then its unlevered net income will also grow at rate g. Similarly, the firm's receivables, payables, and other elements of net working capital will grow at rate g.

What about capital expenditures? The firm will need new capital to offset depreciation; it will also need to add capacity as its production volume grows. Given a sales growth rate g, we may expect that the firm will need to expand its investment in fixed assets at the same rate. In that case,[11]

$$\text{Capital Expenditures}_{T+1} = \text{Depreciation}_{T+1} + g \times \text{Fixed Assets}_T$$

---

11. Here, fixed assets are measured according to their book value net of accumulated depreciation. This level of capital expenditures is required to maintain the firm's ratio of sales to fixed assets (also called its fixed asset turnover ratio). However, a number of factors could affect the required level of capital expenditures needed to sustain a given growth rate. For example, some amount of revenue growth may be accommodated through productivity gains (or be the result of inflation), rather than an increase in fixed assets. Also, the book value of the firm's fixed assets may misrepresent the cost of adding new assets (one could consider market value instead). Absent knowledge of these details, the approach taken here provides a reasonable estimate.

Thus, given a growth rate of g for the firm, we can estimate its free cash flow as

$$FCF_{T+1} = (1 + g) + \text{Unlevered Net Income}_T - g \times \text{Net Working Capital}_T$$
$$- g \times \text{Fixed Assets}_T \qquad (19.16)$$

Together, Eqs. 19.14 and 19.16 allow us to estimate a firm's continuation value based on its long-run growth rate.

EXAMPLE 19.6

A DCF ESTIMATE OF THE CONTINUATION VALUE

Problem

Estimate Ideko's continuation value in 2015 assuming a future expected growth rate of 5%, a future debt-to-value ratio of 40%, and a debt cost of capital of 6.8%.

Solution

In 2015, Ideko's unlevered net income is forecasted to be $15.849 million (Table 19.10), with working capital of $40.425 million (Table 19.9). It has fixed assets of $69.392 million (Table 19.4). From Eq. 19.16, we can estimate Ideko's free cash flow in 2016:

$$FCF_{2016} = (1.05)(15.849) - (5\%)(40.425) - (5\%)(69.392) = \$11.151 \text{ million}$$

This estimate represents nearly an 8% increase over Ideko's 2015 free cash flow of $10.328 million. It exceeds the 5% growth rate of sales due to the decline in the required additions to Ideko's net working capital as its growth rate slows.

With a debt-to-value ratio of 40%, Ideko's WACC can be calculated from Eq. 18.11:

$$r_{wacc} = r_U - d\tau_c r_D = 10\% - 0.40(0.35)\,6.8\% = 9.05\%$$

Given the estimate of Ideko's free cash flow and WACC, we can estimate Ideko's continuation value in 2015:

$$V_{2015}^L = \frac{11.151}{9.05\% - 5\%} = \$275.33 \text{ million}$$

This continuation value represents a terminal EBITDA multiple of $275.33/32.09 = 8.6$.

Both the multiples approach and the discounted cash flow approach are useful in deriving a realistic continuation value estimate. Our recommendation is to combine both approaches, as we do in Table 19.16. As shown in the spreadsheet, our projected EBITDA multiple of 9.1 can be justified according to the discounted cash flow method with a nominal long-term growth rate of about 5.3%.[12] Given an inflation rate of 2%, this nominal rate represents a real growth rate of about 3.3%. This implied growth rate is another important reality check for our continuation value estimate. If it is much higher than our expectations of long-run growth for the industry as a whole, we should be more skeptical of the estimate being used.

---

12. The exact nominal growth rate needed to match an EBITDA multiple of 9.1 is 5.33897%, which can be found using Solver in Excel.

TABLE 19.16
SPREADSHEET

DISCOUNTED CASH FLOW ESTIMATE OF CONTINUATION VALUE, WITH IMPLIED EBITDA MULTIPLE

Continuation Value: DCF and EBITDA Multiple ($ 000)			
1 Long-Term Growth Rate	5.3%		
2 Target $D/(E + D)$	40.0%		
3 Projected WACC	9.05%		
Free Cash Flow in 2016			
4 Unlevered Net Income	16,695	Continuation Enterprise Value	292,052
5 Less: Increase in NWC	(2,158)		
6 Less: Increase in Fixed Assets*	(3,705)	Implied EBITDA Multiple	9.1×
7 Free Cash Flow	10,832		

*The increase in fixed assets equals the difference between capital expenditures and depreciation, and so subtracting this amount is equivalent to adding back depreciation and subtracting capital expenditures.

APV VALUATION OF IDEKO EQUITY

Our estimate of Ideko's continuation value summarizes the value of the firm's free cash flow beyond the forecast horizon. We can combine it with our forecast for free cash flow through 2015 (Table 19.10, line 7) to estimate Ideko's value today. Recall from Chapter 18 that because the debt is paid on a fixed schedule during the forecast period, the APV method is the easiest valuation method to apply.

The steps to estimate Ideko's value using the APV method are shown in the spreadsheet in Table 19.17. First, we compute Ideko's unlevered value V^U, which is the firm's value if we were to operate the company without leverage during the forecast period and sell it for its continuation value at the end of the forecast horizon. Thus the final value in 2015 would be the continuation value we estimated in Table 19.15. The value in earlier periods

COMMON MISTAKE CONTINUATION VALUES AND LONG-RUN GROWTH

The continuation value is one of the most important estimates when valuing a firm. A common mistake is to use an overly optimistic continuation value, which will lead to an upward bias in the estimated current value of the firm. Here are several pitfalls to beware of:

Using multiples based on current high growth rates. Continuation value estimates are often based on current valuation multiples of existing firms. But if these firms are currently experiencing high growth that will eventually slow down, their multiples can be expected to decline over time. In this scenario, if we estimate a continuation value based on today's multiples without accounting for this decline as growth slows, the estimate will be biased upward.

Ignoring investment necessary for growth. When using the discounted cash flow method, we cannot assume that

$FCF_{T+1} = FCF_T (1 + g)$ if the firm's growth rate has changed between T and $T + 1$. Whenever the growth rate changes, expenditures on working and fixed capital will be affected, and we must take this effect into account as we do in Eq. 19.16.

Using unsustainable long-term growth rates. When using the discounted cash flow method, we must choose a long-term growth rate for the firm. By choosing a high rate, we can make the continuation value estimate extremely high. In the long run, however, firms cannot continue to grow faster than the overall economy. Thus we should be suspicious of long-term growth rates that exceed the expected rate of GDP growth, which has averaged between 2.5% and 3.5% in *real* terms (that is, not including inflation) over the past several decades.

includes the free cash flows paid by the firm (from Table 19.10) discounted at the unlevered cost of capital r_U that we estimated in Section 19.4:

$$V_{t-1}^{U} = \frac{FCF_t + V_t^U}{1 + r_U} \qquad (19.17)$$

Next, we incorporate Ideko's interest tax shield during the forecast horizon. The interest tax shield equals the tax rate of 35% (Table 19.3) multiplied by Ideko's scheduled interest payments (see Table 19.5). Because the debt levels are predetermined, we compute the value T^s of the tax shield by discounting the tax savings at the debt interest rate, $r_D = 6.80\%$:

$$T_{t-1}^s = \frac{\text{Interest Tax Shield}_t + T_t^s}{1 + r_D} \qquad (19.18)$$

Combining the unlevered value and the tax shield value gives the APV, which is Ideko's enterprise value given the planned leverage policy. By deducting debt, we obtain our estimate for the value of Ideko's equity during the forecast period.

Thus our estimate for Ideko's initial enterprise value is $213 million, with an equity value of $113 million. As PKK's initial cost to acquire Ideko's equity is $53 million (see Table 19.6), based on these estimates the deal looks attractive, with an NPV of $113 million − $53 million = $60 million.

A REALITY CHECK

At this point, it is wise to step back and assess whether our valuation results make sense. Does an initial enterprise value of $213 million for Ideko seem reasonable compared to the values of other firms in the industry?

Here again, multiples are helpful. Let's compute the initial valuation multiples that would be implied by our estimated enterprise value of $213 million and compare them to Ideko's closest competitors as we did in Table 19.2. Table 19.18 provides our results.

TABLE 19.17	**APV ESTIMATE OF IDEKO'S INITIAL EQUITY VALUE**
SPREADSHEET	

	Year	2010	2011	2012	2013	2014	2015
APV Method ($ 000)							
1 Free Cash Flow			13,475	7,409	(5,845)	1,458	10,328
2 Unlevered Value V^u		202,732	209,530	223,075	251,227	274,891	292,052
3 Interest Tax Shield			2,380	2,380	2,380	2,737	2,856
4 Tax Shield Value T^s		10,428	8,757	6,972	5,067	2,674	–
5 APV: $V^L = V^u + T^s$		213,160	218,287	230,047	256,294	277,566	292,052
6 Debt		(100,000)	(100,000)	(100,000)	(115,000)	(120,000)	(120,000)
7 Equity Value		113,160	118,287	130,047	141,294	157,566	172,052

COMMON MISTAKE MISSING ASSETS OR LIABILITIES

When computing the enterprise value of a firm from its free cash flows, remember that we are valuing only those assets and liabilities whose cash flow consequences are included in our projections. Any "missing" assets or liabilities must be added to the APV estimate to determine the value of equity. In this case, we deduct the firm's debt and add any excess cash or other marketable securities that have not been included (for Ideko, excess cash has already been paid out and will remain at zero, so no adjustment is needed). We also adjust for any other assets or liabilities that have not been explicitly considered. For example, if a firm owns vacant land, or if it has patents or other rights whose potential cash flows were not included in the projections, the value of these assets must be accounted for separately. The same is true for liabilities such as stock option grants, potential legal liabilities, leases (if the lease payments were not included in earnings), or underfunded pension liabilities.

Naturally, the valuation multiples based on the estimated enterprise value of $213 million, which would correspond to a purchase price of $215 million given Ideko's existing debt and excess cash, are higher than those based on a purchase price of $150 million. They are now at the top end or somewhat above the range of the values of the other firms that we used for comparison. While these multiples are not unreasonable given the operational improvements that PKK plans to implement, they indicate that our projections may be somewhat optimistic and depend critically on PKK's ability to achieve the operational improvements it plans.

Our estimated initial EBITDA multiple of 13.1 also exceeds the multiple of 9.1 that we assumed for the continuation value. Thus our estimate forecasts a decline in the EBITDA multiple, which is appropriate given our expectation that growth will be higher in the short run. If the multiple did not decline, we should question whether our continuation value is too optimistic.

IRR AND CASH MULTIPLES

While the NPV method is the most reliable method when evaluating a transaction like PKK's acquisition of Ideko, real-world practitioners often use IRR and the *cash multiple* (or multiple of money) as alternative valuation metrics. We discuss both of these methods in this section.

To compute the IRR, we must compute PKK's cash flows over the life of the transaction. PKK's initial investment in Ideko, from Table 19.6, is $53 million. PKK will then receive cash dividends from Ideko based on the free cash flow to equity reported in Table 19.10. Finally, we assume that PKK will sell its equity share in Ideko at the end of

| TABLE 19.18 | IDEKO FINANCIAL RATIOS COMPARISON, MID-2010, BASED ON DISCOUNTED CASH FLOW ESTIMATE VERSUS PROPOSED PURCHASE PRICE |

Ratio	Ideko (estimated value)	Ideko (purchase price)	Oakley Inc.	Luxottica Group	Nike Inc.	Sporting Goods
P/E	31.0×	21.6×	24.8×	28.0×	18.2×	20.3×
EV/Sales	2.8×	2.0×	2.0×	2.7×	1.5×	1.4×
EV/EBITDA	13.1×	9.1×	11.6×	14.4×	9.3×	11.4×

INTERVIEW WITH JOSEPH L. RICE, III

Joseph L. Rice, III is a founding partner and chairman of Clayton, Dubilier & Rice (CD&R). Since its formation in 1978, the firm has invested more than $6 billion in 38 businesses with an aggregate transaction value in excess of $40 billion.

QUESTION: How has private equity business changed since you began in the industry?

ANSWER: The term "private equity" is very broad and today can cover virtually every kind of investing, short of investing in the stock or bond markets. The buyout business represents a significant component of the private equity market. Since I started in 1966, I've seen many changes as the asset class has matured. In the 1960s and 1970s, the buyout business had relatively little following. Limited capital availability kept transactions small, and we relied on unconventional funding sources. The total purchase price of my first transaction was approximately $3 million, financed through a secured bank line and from individuals contributing amounts ranging from $25,000 to $50,000. In contrast, recently we bought Hertz from Ford for approximately $15 billion.

As the industry has evolved, the attractive returns generated from buyout investments have attracted broader interest from both institutions and high net worth individuals. Buyout firms apply a variety of value creation models, including financial engineering, multiple arbitrage, and industry sector bets, such as technology or healthcare. Today there is more focus on generating returns from improving business performance—which has always been CD&R's underlying investment approach. The character of the businesses that we buy has also changed. Traditionally, this was an asset-heavy business, with much of the financing coming from banks that lent against percentages of inventory and receivables and the liquidation value of hard assets. Now it's become more of a cash flow business.

QUESTION: What makes a company a good buyout candidate?

ANSWER: We look to acquire good businesses at fair prices. Acquiring non-core, underperforming divisions of large companies and making them more effective has been a fertile investment area for CD&R. These divestiture buyouts tend to be complex and require experience and patience to execute. For example, we were in discussions with Ford management for three years prior to leading the Hertz division acquisition.

After running a series of projections based on information from management, we develop a capital structure designed to ensure the viability of the acquisition candidate. We are relatively unconcerned with EPS but are very return conscious, focusing on cash and creating long-term shareholder value. We must also believe that we can generate a return on equity that meets our standards and justifies our investors' commitments to us.

We also acquire businesses confronting strategic issues where our operating expertise can bring value, such as Kinko's, a great brand franchise that we reorganized and expanded. We prefer service and distribution businesses to large manufacturers because of the wage differential between Asia and the United States and Europe. We also prefer businesses with a diversity of suppliers and customers and where there are multiple levers under our control to improve operating performance.

QUESTION: Post-acquisition, what is the role of the private equity firm?

ANSWER: CD&R brings both a hands-on ownership style and capital. After closing a transaction, we assess current management's capability to do the job our investment case calls for. If necessary, we build and strengthen the management team. Then we work with them to determine the appropriate strategy to produce outstanding results. Finally, we aggressively pursue productivity, cost reduction, and growth initiatives to enhance operating and financial performance. At Kinko's, we restructured 129 separate S-corporations into one centralized corporation and installed a new management team. Our key strategic decision was transforming Kinko's from a loose confederation of consumer and small business–oriented copy shops into a highly networked company serving major corporations. In the end, that is what made the company an attractive acquisition for FedEx in 2004.

TABLE 19.19	**IRR AND CASH MULTIPLE FOR PKK'S INVESTMENT IN IDEKO**
SPREADSHEET	

	Year	2010	2011	2012	2013	2014	2015
IRR and Cash Multiple							
1 Initial Investment		(53,000)					
2 Free Cash Flow to Equity			9,055	2,989	4,735	1,375	5,024
3 Continuation Equity Value							172,052
4 PKK Cash Flows		(53,000)	9,055	2,989	4,735	1,375	177,077
5 IRR		33.3%					
6 Cash Multiple		3.7×					

five years, receiving the continuation equity value. We combine these data to determine PKK's cash flows in the spreadsheet in Table 19.19. Given the cash flows, we compute the IRR of the transaction, which is 33.3%.

While an IRR of 33.3% might sound attractive, it is not straightforward to evaluate in this context. To do so, we must compare it to the appropriate cost of capital for PKK's investment. Because PKK holds an equity position in Ideko, we should use Ideko's equity cost of capital. Of course, Ideko's leverage ratio changes over the five-year period, which will change the risk of its equity. Thus there is no single cost of capital to compare to the IRR.[13]

The spreadsheet in Table 19.19 also computes the cash multiple for the transaction. The **cash multiple** (also called the **multiple of money** or **absolute return**) is the ratio of the total cash received to the total cash invested. The cash multiple for PKK's investment in Ideko is

$$\text{Cash Multiple} = \frac{\text{Total Cash Received}}{\text{Total Cash Invested}}$$
$$= \frac{9055 + 2989 + 4735 + 1375 + 177{,}077}{53{,}000} = 3.7 \qquad (19.19)$$

That is, PKK expects to receive a return that is 3.7 times its investment in Ideko. The cash multiple is a common metric used by investors in transactions such as this one. It has an obvious weakness: The cash multiple does not depend on the amount of time it takes to receive the cash, nor does it account for the risk of the investment. It is therefore useful only for comparing deals with similar time horizons and risk.

CONCEPT CHECK

1. What are the main methods of estimating the continuation value of the firm at the end of the forecast horizon?

2. What are the potential pitfalls of analyzing a transaction like this one based on its IRR or cash multiple?

---

13. See the appendix to this chapter for a calculation of Ideko's annual equity cost of capital.

19.6   SENSITIVITY ANALYSIS

Any financial valuation is only as accurate as the estimates on which it is based. Before concluding our analysis, it is important to assess the uncertainty of our estimates and to determine their potential impact on the value of the deal.

Once we have developed the spreadsheet model for PKK's investment in Ideko, it is straightforward to perform a sensitivity analysis to determine the impact of changes in different parameters on the deal's value. For example, the spreadsheet in Table 19.20 shows the sensitivity of our estimates of the value of PKK's investment to changes in our assumptions regarding the exit EBITDA multiple that PKK obtains when Ideko is sold, as well as Ideko's unlevered cost of capital.

In our initial analysis, we assumed an exit EBITDA multiple of 9.1. Table 19.20 shows that each 1.0 increase in the multiple represents about $20 million in initial value.[14] PKK will break even on its $53 million investment in Ideko with an exit multiple of slightly more than 6.0. The table also shows, however, that an exit multiple of 6.0 is consistent with a future growth rate for Ideko of less than 2%, which is even less than the expected rate of inflation and perhaps unrealistically low.

Table 19.20 also illustrates the effect of a change to our assumption about Ideko's unlevered cost of capital. A higher unlevered cost of capital reduces the value of PKK's investment; yet, even with a rate as high as 14%, the equity value exceeds PKK's initial investment. However, if the unlevered cost of capital exceeds 12%, the implied long-term growth rate that justifies the assumed exit EBITDA multiple of 9.1 is probably unrealistically high. Thus, if we believe the unlevered cost of capital falls within this range, we should lower our forecast for the exit EBITDA multiple, which will further reduce the value of PKK's equity. Conversely, if we are confident in our estimate of the exit multiple, this analysis lends further support to our choice for the unlevered cost of capital.

The exercises at the end of this chapter continue the sensitivity analysis by considering different levels of market share growth and changes to working capital management.

TABLE 19.20

SPREADSHEET

SENSITIVITY ANALYSIS FOR PKK'S INVESTMENT IN IDEKO

Exit EBITDA Multiple		6.0	7.0	8.0	9.1	10.0	11.0
Implied Long-Run Growth Rate		1.60%	3.43%	4.53%	**5.34%**	5.81%	6.21%
Ideko Enterprise Value	($ million)	151.4	171.3	191.2	**213.2**	231.1	251.0
PKK Equity Value	($ million)	51.4	71.3	91.2	**113.2**	131.1	151.0
PKK IRR		14.8%	22.1%	28.0%	**33.3%**	37.1%	40.8%

Unlevered Cost of Capital		9.0%	10.0%	11.0%	12.0%	13.0%	14.0%
Implied Long-Run Growth Rate		3.86%	**5.34%**	6.81%	8.29%	9.76%	11.24%
Ideko Enterprise Value	($ million)	222.1	**213.2**	204.7	196.7	189.1	181.9
PKK Equity Value	($ million)	122.1	**113.2**	104.7	96.7	89.1	81.9

---

14. In fact, we can calculate this directly as the present value of Ideko's projected EBITDA in 2015: ($32.094 million)/$(1.10^5)$ = $19.928 million.

1. What is the purpose of the sensitivity analysis?

2. Table 19.20 shows the sensitivity analysis for PKK's investment in Ideko. Based on the exit EBITDA multiple, do you recommend the acquisition of Ideko?

SUMMARY

1. Valuation using comparables may be used as a preliminary way to estimate the value of a firm.

2. The value of an investment ultimately depends on the firm's future cash flows. To estimate cash flows, it is first necessary to look at a target firm's operations, investments, and capital structure to assess the potential for improvements and growth.

3. A financial model may be used to project the future cash flows from an investment.

   a. A pro forma income statement projects the firm's earnings under a given set of hypothetical assumptions.

   b. The financial model should also consider future working capital needs and capital expenditures to estimate future free cash flows.

   c. Based on these estimates, we can forecast the balance sheet and statement of cash flows.

4. To value an investment, we need to assess its risk and estimate an appropriate cost of capital. One method for doing so is to use the CAPM.

   a. Use the CAPM to estimate the equity cost of capital for comparable firms, based on their equity betas.

   b. Given an estimate of each comparable firm's equity beta, unlever the beta based on the firm's capital structure.

   c. Use the CAPM and the estimates of unlevered betas for comparable firms to estimate the unlevered cost of capital for the investment.

5. In addition to forecasting cash flows for a few years, we need to estimate the firm's continuation value at the end of the forecast horizon.

   a. One method is to use a valuation multiple based on comparable firms.

   b. To estimate a continuation value in year T using discounted cash flows, it is common practice to assume a constant expected growth rate g and a constant debt-equity ratio:

$$\text{Enterprise Value in Year } T = V_T^L = \frac{FCF_{T+1}}{r_{wacc} - g} \tag{19.14}$$

6. Given the forecasted cash flows and an estimate of the cost of capital, the final step is to combine these inputs to estimate the value of the opportunity. We may use the valuation methods described in Chapter 18 to calculate firm value.

7. While the NPV method is the most reliable approach for evaluating an investment, practitioners often use the IRR and cash multiple as alternative valuation metrics.

   a. We use the cash flows over the lifetime of the investment to calculate the IRR.

b. The cash multiple for an investment is the ratio of the total cash received to the total cash invested:

$$\text{Cash Multiple} = \frac{\text{Total Cash Received}}{\text{Total Cash Invested}} \tag{19.19}$$

8. Sensitivity analysis is useful for evaluating the uncertainty of estimates used for valuation and the impact of this uncertainty on the value of the deal.

KEY TERMS

cash multiple (multiple of money, absolute
    return) *p. 703*

pro forma *p. 686*
unlevered P/E ratio *p. 696*

PROBLEMS

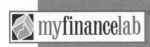 The problems marked in green can be found on MyFinanceLab at www.myfinancelab.com. Visit your MyFinanceLab for additional practice. An asterisk (*) indicates problems with a higher level of difficulty. Additional readings for this chapter may be found in the Textbook Resources section on MyFinanceLab.

Valuation Using Comparables

1. You would like to compare Ideko's profitability to its competitors' profitability using the EBITDA/sales multiple. Given Ideko's current sales of $75 million, use the information in Table 19.2 to compute a range of EBITDA for Ideko assuming it is run as profitably as its competitors.

The Business Plan

2. Assume that Ideko's market share will increase by 0.5% per year rather than the 1% used in the chapter. What production capacity will Ideko require each year? When will an expansion become necessary (when production volume will exceed the current level by 50%)?

3. Under the assumption that Ideko market share will increase by 0.5% per year, you determine that the plant will require an expansion in 2015. The cost of this expansion will be $15 million. Assuming the financing of the expansion will be delayed accordingly, calculate the projected interest payments and the amount of the projected interest tax shields (assuming that the interest rates on the term loans remain the same as in the chapter) through 2015.

Building the Financial Model

4. Under the assumption that Ideko's market share will increase by 0.5% per year (and the investment and financing will be adjusted as described in Problem 3), you project the following depreciation:

	Year	2010	2011	2012	2013	2014	2015
Fixed Assets and Capital Investment ($ 000)							
2	New Investment	5,000	5,000	5,000	5,000	5,000	20,000
3	Depreciation	(5,500)	(5,450)	(5,405)	(5,365)	(5,328)	(6,795)

Using this information, project net income through 2015 (that is, reproduce Table 19.7 under the new assumptions).

EXCEL   **5.** Under the assumptions that Ideko's market share will increase by 0.5% per year (implying that the investment, financing, and depreciation will be adjusted as described in Problems 3 and 4) and that the forecasts in Table 19.8 remain the same, calculate Ideko's working capital requirements though 2015 (that is, reproduce Table 19.9 under the new assumptions).

EXCEL   **6.** Under the assumptions that Ideko's market share will increase by 0.5% per year (implying that the investment, financing, and depreciation will be adjusted as described in Problems 3 and 4) but that the projected improvements in net working capital do not transpire (so the numbers in Table 19.8 remain at their 2010 levels through 2015), calculate Ideko's working capital requirements though 2015 (that is, reproduce Table 19.9 under these assumptions).

EXCEL   **7.** Forecast Ideko's free cash flow (reproduce Table 19.10), assuming Ideko's market share will increase by 0.5% per year; investment, financing, and depreciation will be adjusted accordingly; and the projected improvements in working capital occur (that is, under the assumptions in Problem 5).

EXCEL   **8.** Forecast Ideko's free cash flow (reproduce Table 19.10), assuming Ideko's market share will increase by 0.5% per year; investment, financing, and depreciation will be adjusted accordingly; and the projected improvements in working capital do *not* occur (that is, under the assumptions in Problem 6).

EXCEL   ***9.** Reproduce Ideko's balance sheet and statement of cash flows, assuming Ideko's market share will increase by 0.5% per year; investment, financing, and depreciation will be adjusted accordingly; and the projected improvements in working capital occur (that is, under the assumptions in Problem 5).

EXCEL   ***10.** Reproduce Ideko's balance sheet and statement of cash flows, assuming Ideko's market share will increase by 0.5% per year; investment, financing, and depreciation will be adjusted accordingly; and the projected improvements in working capital do *not* occur (that is, under the assumptions in Problem 6).

Estimating the Cost of Capital

11. Calculate Ideko's unlevered cost of capital when Ideko's unlevered beta is 1.1 rather than 1.2 and all other required estimates are the same as in the chapter.

12. Calculate Ideko's unlevered cost of capital when the market risk premium is 6% rather than 5%, the risk-free rate is 5% rather than 4%, and all other required estimates are the same as in the chapter.

Valuing the Investment

EXCEL   **13.** Using the information produced in the income statement in Problem 4, use EBITDA as a multiple to estimate the continuation value in 2015, assuming the current value remains unchanged (reproduce Table 19.15). Infer the EV/sales and the unlevered and levered P/E ratios implied by the continuation value you calculated.

14. How does the assumption on future improvements in working capital affect your answer to Problem 13?

EXCEL   **15.** Approximately what expected future long-run growth rate would provide the same EBITDA multiple in 2015 as Ideko has today (i.e., 9.1)? Assume that the future debt-to-value ratio is held constant at 40%; the debt cost of capital is 6.8%; Ideko's market share will increase by 0.5% per year until 2015; investment, financing, and depreciation will be adjusted accordingly; and the projected improvements in working capital occur (that is, the assumptions in Problem 5).

EXCEL   **16.** Approximately what expected future long-run growth rate would provide the same EBITDA multiple in 2015 as Ideko has today (i.e., 9.1)? Assume that the future debt-to-value ratio is held constant at 40%; the debt cost of capital is 6.8%; Ideko's market share will increase by 0.5% per year; investment, financing, and depreciation will be adjusted accordingly; and the projected improvements in working capital do *not* occur (that is, the assumptions in Problem 6).

EXCEL **17.** Using the APV method, estimate the value of Ideko and the NPV of the deal using the continuation value you calculated in Problem 13 and the unlevered cost of capital estimate in Section 19.4. Assume that the debt cost of capital is 6.8%; Ideko's market share will increase by 0.5% per year until 2015; investment, financing, and depreciation will be adjusted accordingly; and the projected improvements in working capital occur (that is, the assumptions in Problem 5).

EXCEL **18.** Using the APV method, estimate the value of Ideko and the NPV of the deal using the continuation value you calculated in Problem 13 and the unlevered cost of capital estimate in Section 19.4. Assume that the debt cost of capital is 6.8%; Ideko's market share will increase by 0.5% per year; investment, financing, and depreciation will be adjusted accordingly; and the projected improvements in working capital do *not* occur (that is, the assumptions in Problem 6).

EXCEL **19.** Use your answers from Problems 17 and 18 to infer the value today of the projected improvements in working capital under the assumptions that Ideko's market share will increase by 0.5% per year and that investment, financing, and depreciation will be adjusted accordingly.

CHAPTER 19 APPENDIX

notation

r_E equity cost of capital

COMPENSATING MANAGEMENT

The success of PKK's investment critically depends on its ability to execute the operational improvements laid out in its business plan. PKK has learned from experience that it is much more likely to achieve its goals if the management team responsible for implementing the changes is given a strong incentive to succeed. PKK therefore considers allocating 10% of Ideko's equity to a management incentive plan. This equity stake would be vested over the next five years, and it would provide Ideko's senior executives with a strong financial interest in the success of the venture. What is the cost to PKK of providing this equity stake to the management team? How will this incentive plan affect the NPV of the acquisition?

To determine the value of the acquisition to PKK, we must include the cost of the 10% equity stake granted to management. Because the grant vests after five years, management will not receive any of the dividends paid by Ideko during that time. Instead, management will receive the equity in five years time, at which point we have estimated the value of Ideko's equity to be $172 million (see Table 19.15). Thus the cost of management's stake in 2015 is equal to 10% × $172 million = $17.2 million according to our estimate. We must determine the present value of this amount today.

Because the payment to the managers is an equity claim, to compute its present value we must use an equity cost of capital. We take an FTE valuation approach to estimate the cost of management's share in Ideko, shown in the spreadsheet in Table 19A.1.

To compute Ideko's equity cost of capital r_E, we use Eq. 18.20, which applies when the debt levels of the firm follow a known schedule:

$$\text{Cost of Management's Share}_t = \frac{\text{Cost of Management's Share}_{t+1}}{1+r_E(t)}$$

Using the debt, equity, and tax shield values from the spreadsheet in Table 19.17 to compute the effective leverage ratio $(D - T^s)/E$, we compute r_E each year as shown in the spreadsheet.

TABLE 19A.1 SPREADSHEET

FTE ESTIMATE OF THE COST OF MANAGEMENT'S SHARE AND PKK'S EQUITY VALUE

	Year	2010	2011	2012	2013	2014	2015
Management/PKK Share ($ 000)							
1	Management Payoff (10% share)						17,205
2	Effective Leverage $(D - T^s)/E$	0.792	0.771	0.715	0.778	0.745	
3	Equity Cost of Capital r_E	12.53%	12.47%	12.29%	12.49%	12.38%	
4	Cost of Management's Share	(9,576)	(10,777)	(12,120)	(13,610)	(15,309)	(17,205)
5	Ideko Equity Value	113,160	118,287	130,047	141,294	157,566	172,052
6	PKK Equity	103,583	107,511	117,927	127,684	142,256	154,847

We then compute the cost of management's equity share by discounting at this rate:

$$r_E = r_U + \frac{D - T^s}{E}(r_U - r_D)$$

(19A.1)

Once we have determined the cost of management's equity share, we deduct it from the total value of Ideko's equity (from Table 19.17) to determine the value of PKK's share of Ideko's equity, shown as the last line of the spreadsheet. Given the initial cost of the acquisition to PKK of $53 million, PKK's NPV from the investment, including the cost of management's compensation, is $103.58 million $-$ $53 million $=$ $50.58 million.

Options

THE LAW OF ONE PRICE CONNECTION. Having developed the tools to make current investment decisions, we turn to settings in which the firm or an investor has the option to make a future investment decision. Chapter 20 introduces financial options, which give investors the right to buy or sell a security in the future. Financial options are an important tool for corporate financial managers seeking to manage or evaluate risk. Options are an example of a derivative security. In the last 30 years there has been enormous growth in the derivative securities markets in general and options markets in particular. This growth can be traced directly to the discovery of methods for valuing options, which we derive in Chapter 21 using the Law of One Price. An important corporate application of option theory is in the area of real investment decision making. Future investment decisions within the firm are known as real options and Chapter 22 applies real option theory to corporate decision making.

Financial Options

NOTATION

PV	present value
Div	dividend
C	call option price
P	put option price
S	stock price
K	strike price
dis	discount from face value
r_f	risk-free interest rate
NPV	net present value

In this chapter we introduce the **financial option**, a financial contract between two parties. Since the introduction of publicly traded options on the Chicago Board Options Exchange (CBOE) in 1973, financial options have become one of the most important and actively traded financial assets. The Montreal Exchange was the first to trade stock options in Canada in 1975. Over time the Montreal Exchange added options on other products: fixed income securities (1991), stock indexes (1999), exchange-traded funds (2000), and the U.S. dollar (2005). In May 2008, the Montreal Exchange merged with the TSX Group to become the TMX Group. Options have become important tools for corporate financial managers. For example, many large corporations have operations in different parts of the world, so they face exposure to exchange rate risk and other types of business risk. To control this risk, they use options as part of their corporate risk management practices. In addition, the capitalization of the firm itself—that is, its mix of debt and equity—can be thought of as options on the underlying assets of the firm. As we will see, viewing the firm's capitalization in this way yields important insights into the firm's capital structure as well as the conflicts of interests that arise between equity investors and debt investors.

Before we can discuss the corporate applications of options, we first need to understand what options are and what factors affect their value. In this chapter, we provide an overview of the basic types of financial options, introduce important terminology, and describe the payoffs to various option-based strategies. We next discuss the factors that affect option prices. Finally, we model the equity and debt of the firm as options to gain insight into the conflicts of interest between equity and debt holders, as well as the pricing of risky debt.

20.1 OPTION BASICS

A financial option contract gives its owner the right (but not the obligation) to purchase or sell an asset at a fixed price at some future date. Two distinct kinds of option contracts exist: call options and put options. A **call option** gives the owner the right to *buy* the asset; a **put option** gives the owner the right to *sell* the asset. Because an option is a contract between two parties, for every owner of a financial option, there is also an **option writer**, the person who takes the other side of the contract.

The most commonly encountered option contracts are options on shares of stock. A stock option gives the holder the option to buy or sell a share of stock on or before a given date for a given price. For example, a call option on Telus Corp. stock might give the holder the right to purchase a share of TELUS for $50 per share at any time up to, for example, June 17, 2011. Similarly, a put option on TELUS stock might give the holder the right to sell a share of TELUS stock for $49 per share at any time up to, say, January 20, 2012.

UNDERSTANDING OPTION CONTRACTS

Practitioners use specific words to describe the details of option contracts. When a holder of an option enforces the agreement and buys or sells a share of stock at the agreed-upon price, he or she is **exercising** the option. The price at which the holder buys or sells the share of stock when the option is exercised is called the **strike price** or **exercise price**.

There are two kinds of options. **American options**, the most common kind, allow their holders to exercise the option on any date up to and including a final date called the **expiration date**. **European options** allow their holders to exercise the option *only* on the expiration date—holders cannot exercise before the expiration date. The names *American* and *European* have nothing to do with the location where the options are traded: Both types are traded worldwide.

An option contract is a contract between two parties. The option buyer, also called the option holder, holds the right to exercise the option and has a *long* position in the contract. The option seller, also called the option writer, sells (or writes) the option and has a *short* position in the contract. Because the long side has the option to exercise, the short side has an *obligation* to fulfill the contract. For example, suppose you own a call option on Bombardier stock with an exercise price of $5. Bombardier stock is currently trading for $9, so you decide to exercise the option. The person holding the short position in the contract is obligated to sell you a share of Bombardier stock for $5. Your $4 gain—the difference between the price you pay for the share of stock and the price at which you can sell the share in the market—is the short position's loss.

Investors exercise options only when they stand to gain something. Consequently, whenever an option is exercised, the person holding the short position funds the gain. That is, the obligation will be costly. Why, then, do people write options? The answer is that when you sell an option you get paid for it—options always have non-negative prices. The market price of the option is called the **option premium**. This upfront payment compensates the seller for the risk of loss in the event that the option holder chooses to exercise the option.

INTERPRETING STOCK OPTION QUOTATIONS

Stock options are traded on organized exchanges. The oldest and largest is the Chicago Board Options Exchange (CBOE). By convention, all traded options expire on the Saturday following the third Friday of the month. The same convention is used in the Montreal Exchange.

TABLE 20.1

OPTION QUOTES FOR BOW.COM STOCK

BOW   48.35 —

Nov 24, 2009 @ 11:35 ET (Data 15 Minutes Delayed)   Bid 48.35   Ask 48.37   Vol 3831766

Calls	Last Sale	Net	Bid	Ask	Vol	Open Int	Puts	Last Sale	Net	Bid	Ask	Vol	Open Int
09 Dec 45.00 (BQW LI-E)	4.00	pc	3.70	3.90	0	16021	09 Dec 45.00 (BQW XI-E)	0.30	−0.05	0.30	0.40	30	20788
09 Dec 47.50 (BQW LW-E)	2.20	−0.25	1.90	2.00	86	18765	09 Dec 47.50 (BQW XW-E)	0.75	−0.15	0.95	1.05	292	13208
09 Dec 50.00 (BQW LJ-E)	0.80	−	0.75	0.85	144	9491	09 Dec 50.00 (BQW XJ-E)	2.30	+0.20	2.30	2.40	177	5318
09 Dec 55.00 (BQW LK-E)	0.15	pc	0.05	0.10	0	2497	09 Dec 55.00 (BQW XK-E)	6.10	pc	6.60	6.80	0	895
10 Jan 45.00 (BQW AI-E)	4.93	pc	4.80	5.00	0	18765	10 Jan 45.00 (BQW MI-E)	1.20	−0.10	1.20	1.30	8	29717
10 Jan 47.50 (BQW AW-E)	3.70	+0.10	3.20	3.30	5	8068	10 Jan 47.50 (BQW MW-E)	1.95	+0.15	2.05	2.15	10	6632
10 Jan 50.00 (BQW AJ-E)	2.15	+0.15	1.95	2.05	208	27416	10 Jan 50.00 (BQW MJ-E)	3.30	+0.20	3.30	3.50	162	6668
10 Jan 55.00 (BQW AK-E)	0.70	+0.10	0.60	0.70	65	8475	10 Jan 55.00 (BQW MK-E)	6.90	−2.50	7.00	7.10	67	5621

Source: Bow.com is a hypothetical stock but the quotes are based on those from the Chicago Board Options Exchange at www.cboe.com.

Table 20.1 shows near-term options on Bow.com as though they were taken from the CBOE Web site (www.cboe.com) on November 24, 2009. Call options are listed on the left and put options on the right. Each line corresponds to a particular option. The first two digits in the option name refer to the year of expiration. The option name also includes the month of expiration, the strike or exercise price, and the ticker symbol of the individual option (in parentheses). Looking at Table 20.1, the first line of the left column is a call option with an exercise price of $45 that expires on the Saturday following the third Friday of December 2009 (December 19, 2009). The columns to the right of the name display market data for the option. The first of these columns shows the last sales price, followed by the net change from the previous day's last reported sales price ("pc" indicates that no trade has occurred on this day, so the last sales price is the previous day's last reported sales price), the current bid and ask prices, and the daily volume. The final column is the **open interest**, the total number of contracts of that particular option that have been written.

Above the table we find information about the stock itself. In this case, Bow.com's stock last traded at a price of $48.35 per share. We also see the current bid and ask prices for the stock, as well as the volume of trade.

When the exercise price of an option is equal to the current price of the stock, the option is said to be **at-the-money**. Notice that much of the trading occurs in options that are closest to being at-the-money—that is, calls and puts with exercise prices of either $47.50 or $50. Notice how the December 50.00 calls have high volume. They last traded for 80¢, midway between the current bid price (75¢) and the ask price (85¢), which indicates that the trade likely occurred recently because the last traded price is a current market price.

Stock option contracts are always written on 100 shares of stock. If, for instance, you decided to purchase one December 47.50 call contract, you would be purchasing an option to buy 100 shares at $47.50 per share. Option prices are quoted on a per-share basis, so the ask price of $2.00 implies that you would pay $100 \times 2 = \$200$ for the contract. Similarly, if you decide to buy a December 45 put contract, you would pay $100 \times 0.40 = \$40$ for the option to sell 100 shares of Bow.com stock for $45 per share.

Note from Table 20.1 that for each expiration date, call options with lower strike prices have higher market prices—the right to buy the stock at a lower price is more valuable than the right to buy it for a higher price. Conversely, because the put option gives the holder the right to sell the stock at the strike price, for the same expiration puts with higher strikes are more valuable. On the other hand, holding fixed the strike price, both calls and puts are more expensive for a longer time to expiration. Because these options are American-style options that can be exercised at any time, having the right to buy or sell for a longer period is more valuable.

If the payoff from exercising an option immediately is positive, the option is said to be **in-the-money**. Call options with strike prices below the current stock price are in-the-money, as are put options with strike prices above the current stock price. Conversely, if the payoff from exercising the option immediately is negative, the option is **out-of-the-money**. Call options with strike prices above the current stock price are out-of-the-money, as are put options with strike prices below the current stock price. Of course, a holder would not exercise an out-of-the-money option. Options where the strike price and the stock price are very far apart are referred to as **deep in-the-money** or **deep out-of-the-money**.

EXAMPLE 20.1

PURCHASING OPTIONS

Problem
It is midday on November 24, 2009, and you have decided to purchase 10 January call contracts on Bow.com stock with an exercise price of $50. Because you are buying, you must pay the ask price. How much money will this purchase cost you? Is this option in-the-money or out-of-the-money?

Solution
From Table 20.1, the ask price of this option is $2.05. You are purchasing 10 contracts and each contract is on 100 shares, so the transaction will cost $2.05 \times 10 \times 100 = \$2050$ (ignoring any commission fees). Because this is a call option and the exercise price is above the current stock price ($48.35), the option is currently out-of-the-money.

OPTIONS ON OTHER FINANCIAL SECURITIES

Although the most commonly traded options are written on stocks, options on other financial assets do exist. Perhaps the most well known are options on stock indexes in the United States such as the S&P 100 index, the S&P 500 index, the Dow Jones Industrial index, and the NYSE index. These options have become very popular because they allow investors to protect the value of their investments from adverse market changes. In Canada, the Montreal Exchange's only broad index option is on the S&P TSX 60. In addition, Montreal offers options on exchange-traded funds (such as iShares) that track the S&P TSX 60, various industry sectors, fixed income products, and selected commodity prices.

As we will see shortly, a stock index put option can be used to offset the losses on an investor's portfolio in a market downturn. Using an option to reduce risk in this way is called **hedging**. Options also allow investors to **speculate**, or place a bet on the direction in which they believe the market is likely to move. By purchasing a call, for example, investors can bet on a market rise with a much smaller investment than investing in the market index itself.

Options are also traded on fixed-income securities. These options allow investors to bet on or hedge interest rate risk. Montreal offers options on futures of three-month Bankers' Acceptances and 10-year Government of Canada Bonds. Similarly, options on currencies and commodities allow investors to hedge or speculate on risks in these markets. In Montreal, there is an option contract on 10,000 U.S. dollars. On the ICE Futures Canada exchange, headquartered in Winnipeg, options on canola, feed wheat, and western barley are traded. The main markets for options on other agricultural commodities, metals, and energy are in either Chicago or New York.

CONCEPT CHECK

1. What is the difference between an American option and a European option?

2. Does the holder of an option have to exercise it?

3. Why does an investor who writes (shorts) an option have an obligation?

20.2 OPTION PAYOFFS AT EXPIRATION

From the Law of One Price, the value of any security is determined by the future cash flows an investor receives from owning it. Therefore, before we can assess what an option is worth, we must determine an option's payoff at the time of expiration.

LONG POSITION IN AN OPTION CONTRACT

Assume you own an option with a strike price of $20. If, on the expiration date, the stock price is greater than the strike price, say $30, you can make money by exercising the call (by paying $20, the strike price, for the stock) and immediately selling the stock in the open market for $30. The $10 difference is what the option is worth. Consequently, when the stock price on the expiration date exceeds the strike price, the value of the call is the difference between the stock price and the strike price. When the stock price is less than the strike price at expiration, the holder will not exercise the call, so the option is worth nothing. These payoffs are plotted in Figure 20.1.[1]

Thus, if S is the stock price at expiration, K is the exercise price, and C is the value of the call option, the value of the call at expiration is

Call Value at Expiration
$$C = max(S - K, 0) \tag{20.1}$$

where *max* is the maximum of the two quantities in the parentheses. The call's value is the maximum of the difference between the stock price and the strike price, $S - K$, and zero.

The holder of a put option will exercise the option if the stock price S is below the strike price K. Because the holder receives K when the stock is worth S, the holder's gain is equal to $K - S$. Thus, the value of a put at expiration is

Put Price at Expiration
$$P = max(K - S, 0) \tag{20.2}$$

---

1. Payoff diagrams like the ones in this chapter seem to have been introduced by Louis Bachelier in 1900 in his book, *Theorie de la Speculation* (Paris: Villars, 1900). Reprinted in English in P. H. Cootner (ed.), *The Random Character of Stock Market Prices* (Cambridge, MA: M.I.T. Press, 1964).

FIGURE 20.1

Payoff of a Call Option with a Strike Price of $20 at Expiration

If the stock price is greater than the strike price ($20), the call will be exercised, and the holder's payoff is the difference between the stock price and the strike price. If the stock price is less than the strike price, the call will not be exercised, and so has no value.

EXAMPLE 20.2

PAYOFF OF A PUT OPTION AT MATURITY

Problem

You own a put option on Onex Corp. stock with an exercise price of $20 that expires today. Plot the value of this option as a function of the stock price.

Solution

Let S be the stock price and P be the value of the put option. The value of the option is

$$P = max(20 - S, 0)$$

Plotting this function gives

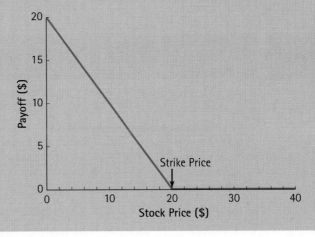

Short Position in a Call Option at Expiration

If the stock price is greater than the strike price, the call will be exercised, so a person on the short side of a call will lose the difference between the stock price and the strike price. If the stock price is less than the strike price, the call will not be exercised, and the seller will have no obligation.

SHORT POSITION IN AN OPTION CONTRACT

An investor holding a short position in an option has an obligation: This investor takes the opposite side of the contract to the investor who is long. Thus the short position's cash flows are the negative of the long position's cash flows. Because an investor who is long an option can only receive money at expiration—that is, the investor will not exercise an option that is out-of-the-money—a short investor can only pay money.

To demonstrate, assume you have a short position in a call option with an exercise price of $20. If the stock price is greater than the strike price of a call—for example, $25—the holder will exercise the option. You then have the obligation to sell the stock for the strike price of $20. Because you must purchase the stock at the market price of $25, you lose the difference between the two prices, or $5. However, if the stock price is less than the strike price at the expiration date, the holder will not exercise the option, so in this case you lose nothing; you have no obligation. These payoffs are plotted in Figure 20.2.

EXAMPLE 20.3   **PAYOFF OF A SHORT POSITION IN A PUT OPTION**

Problem
You are short a put option on Bombardier stock with an exercise price of $20 that expires today. What is your payoff at expiration as a function of the stock price?

Solution
If S is the stock price, your cash flows will be

$$-max(20 - S, 0)$$

If the current stock price is $30, then the put will not be exercised and you will owe nothing. If the current stock price is $15, the put will be exercised and you will lose $5. The figure plots your cash flows:

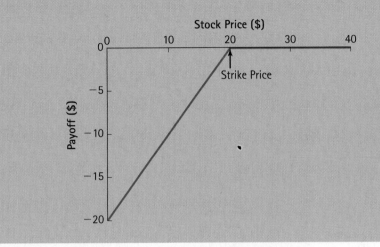

Notice that because the stock price cannot fall below zero, the downside for a short position in a put option is limited to the strike price of the option. A short position in a call, however, has no limit on the downside (see Figure 20.2).

PROFITS FOR HOLDING AN OPTION TO EXPIRATION

Although payouts on a long position in an option contract are never negative, the profit from purchasing an option and holding it to expiration could well be negative because the payout at expiration might be less than the initial cost of the option.

To see how this works, let's consider the potential profits from purchasing the 10 January 50.00 call option on Bow.com stock quoted in Table 20.1. The option costs $2.05 and expires in 52 days. Assume you choose to finance the purchase by borrowing $2.05 at an interest rate of 3% per year. If the stock price at expiration is S, then the profit is the call payoff minus the amount owed on the loan: $max(S - 50, 0) - 2.05 \times 1.03^{52/365}$, shown as the red curve in Figure 20.3. Once the cost of the position is taken into account, you make a positive profit only if the stock price exceeds $52.06. As we can see from Table 20.1, the further in-the-money the option is, the higher its initial price and so the larger your potential loss. An out-of-the-money option has a smaller initial cost and hence a smaller potential loss, but the probability of a gain is also smaller because the point where profits become positive is higher.

Because a short position in an option is the other side of a long position, the profits from a short position in an option are just the negative of the profits of a long position. For example, a short position in an out-of-the-money call like the 10 January 55 Bow.com call in Figure 20.3 produces a small positive profit if Bow.com's stock is below $55.70, but leads to losses if the stock price is above $55.70.

| EXAMPLE 20.4 | PROFIT ON HOLDING A POSITION IN A PUT OPTION UNTIL EXPIRATION |

Problem

Assume you decided to purchase each of the January put options quoted in Table 20.1 on November 24, 2009, and you financed each position by shorting a two-month bond with a yield of 3%. Plot the profit of each position as a function of the stock price on expiration.

Solution

Suppose S is the stock price on expiration, K is the strike price, and P is the price of each put option on November 24. Then your cash flows on the expiration date will be

$$\max(K - S, 0) - P \times 1.03^{52/365}$$

Plotting is shown below. Note the same tradeoff between the maximum loss and the potential for profit as for the call options.

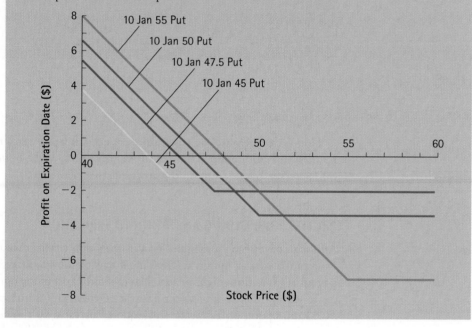

RETURNS FOR HOLDING AN OPTION TO EXPIRATION

We can also compare options based on their potential returns. Figure 20.4 shows the return from purchasing one of the January 2010 options in Table 20.1 on November 24, 2009, and holding it until the expiration date. Let's begin by focusing on call options, shown in panel (a). In all cases, the maximum loss is 100%—the option may expire worthless. Notice how the curves change as a function of the strike price—the distribution of returns for out-of-the-money call options are more extreme than those for in-the-money calls. That is, an out-of-the money call option is more likely to have a −100% return, but if the stock goes up sufficiently it will also have a much higher return than an in-the-money call option. Similarly, all call options have more extreme returns than the stock itself (given Bow.com's initial price of $48.35, the range of stock prices shown in the plot represent

FIGURE 20.3

Profit from Holding a Call Option to Expiration

The curves show the profit per share from purchasing the January call options in Table 20.1 on November 24, 2009, financing this purchase by borrowing at 3%, and holding the position until the expiration date.

returns from -17% to $+24\%$). As a consequence, the risk of a call option is amplified relative to the risk of the stock, and the amplification is greater for deeper out-of-the-money calls. Thus, if a stock had a positive beta, call options written on the stock would have even higher betas and expected returns than the stock itself.[2]

FIGURE 20.4   Option Returns from Purchasing an Option and Holding It to Expiration

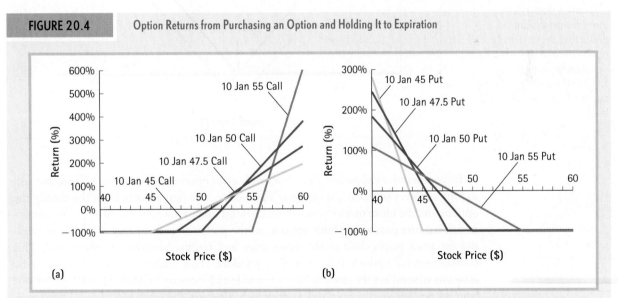

(a) The return on the expiration date from purchasing one of the January call options in Table 20.1 on November 24, 2009, and holding the position until the expiration date; (b) the same return for the January put options in the table.

---

2. In Chapter 21, we explain how to calculate the expected return and risk of holding an option. In doing so, we will derive these relations rigorously.

Now consider the returns for put options. Look carefully at panel (b) in Figure 20.4. The put position has a higher return in states with *low* stock prices; that is, if the stock has a positive beta, the put has a negative beta. Hence, put options on positive beta stocks have lower expected returns than the underlying stock. The deeper out-of-the-money the put option is, the more negative its beta, and the lower its expected return. As a result, put options are generally not held as an investment, but rather as insurance to hedge other risk in a portfolio.

COMBINATIONS OF OPTIONS

Sometimes investors combine option positions by holding a portfolio of options. In this section, we describe the most common combinations.

STRADDLE. What would happen at expiration if you were long both a put option and a call option with the same strike price? Figure 20.5 shows the payout on the expiration date of both options.

FIGURE 20.5

Payoff and Profit from a Straddle

A combination of a long position in a put and a call with the same strike price and expiration date provides a positive payoff (solid line) so long as the stock price does not equal the strike price. After deducting the cost of the options, the profit is negative for stock prices close to the strike price and positive elsewhere (dashed line).

By combining a call option (blue line) with a put option (red line), you will receive cash so long as the options do not expire at-the-money. The farther away from the money the options are, the more money you will make (solid line). However, to construct the combination requires purchasing both options, so the profits after deducting this cost are negative for stock prices close to the strike price and positive elsewhere (dashed line). This combination of options is known as a **straddle**. This strategy is sometimes used by investors who expect the stock to be very volatile and move up or down a large amount, but who do not necessarily have a view on which direction the stock will move. Conversely, investors who expect the stock to end up near the strike price may choose to sell a straddle.

BUTTERFLY SPREAD. The combination of options in Figure 20.5 makes money when the stock and strike prices are far apart. It is also possible to construct a combination of options that has the opposite exposure: It pays off when the stock price is close to the strike price.

FIGURE 20.6

Butterfly Spread
The yellow line represents the payoff from a long position in a $20 call. The red line represents the payoff from a long position in a $40 call. The blue line represents the payoff from a short position in two $30 calls. The black line shows the payoff of the entire combination, called a butterfly spread, at expiration.

Suppose you are long two call options with the same expiration date on NOVA Chemicals Corp. stock: one with an exercise price of $20 and the other with an exercise price of $40. In addition, suppose you are short two call options on NOVA Chemicals stock, both with an exercise price of $30. Figure 20.6 plots the value of this combination at expiration.

The yellow line in Figure 20.6 represents the payoff at expiration from the long position in the $20 call. The red line represents the payoff from the long position in the $40 call. The blue line represents the payoff from the short position in the two $30 calls. The black line shows the payoff of the entire combination. For stock prices less than $20, all options are out-of-the-money, so the payoff is zero. For stock prices greater than $40, the losses from the short position in the $30 calls exactly offset the gain from the $20 and $40 options, and the value of the entire portfolio of options is zero.[3] Between $20 and $40, however, the payoff is positive. It reaches a maximum at $30. Practitioners call this combination of options a **butterfly spread**.

Because the payoff of the butterfly spread is positive, it must have a positive initial cost. (Otherwise, it would be an arbitrage opportunity.) Therefore, the cost of the $20 and $40 call options must exceed the proceeds from selling two $30 call options.

PORTFOLIO INSURANCE.   Let's see how we can use combinations of options to insure a stock against a loss. Assume you currently own Bow.com stock and would like to insure the stock against the possibility of a price decline. To do so, you could simply sell the stock, but you would also give up the possibility of making money if the stock price increases. How can you insure against a loss without relinquishing the upside? You can purchase a put option, sometimes known as a **protective put**.

For example, suppose you want to insure against the possibility that the price of Bow.com stock will drop below $45. You decide to purchase a January 45 European put option. The orange line in Figure 20.7(a) shows the value of the combined position on the expiration

---

3. To see this, note that $(S - 20) + (S - 40) - 2(S - 30) = 0$.

EXAMPLE 20.5   STRANGLE

Problem

You are long both a call option and a put option on Onex Corp. stock with the same expiration date. The exercise price of the call option is $40; the exercise price of the put option is $30. Plot the payoff of the combination at expiration.

Solution

The red line represents the put's payouts and the blue line represents the call's payouts. In this case, you do not receive money if the stock price is between the two strike prices. This option combination is known as a **strangle**.

FIGURE 20.7   Portfolio Insurance

The plots show two different ways to insure against the possibility of the price of Bow.com stock falling below $45. The orange line in (a) indicates the value on the expiration date of a position that is long one share of Bow.com stock and one European put option with a strike of $45 (the blue dashed line is the payoff of the stock itself). The orange line in (b) shows the value on the expiration date of a position that is long a zero-coupon risk-free bond with a face value of $45 and a European call option on Bow.com with a strike price of $45 (the green dashed line is the bond payoff).

date of the option. If Bow.com stock is above $45 in January, you keep the stock, but if it is below $45 you exercise your put and sell it for $45. Thus, you get the upside, but are insured against a drop in the price of Bow.com's stock.

You can use the same strategy to insure against a loss on an entire portfolio of stocks by using put options on the portfolio of stocks as a whole rather than just a single stock. Consequently, holding stocks and put options in this combination is known as **portfolio insurance**.

Purchasing a put option is not the only way to buy portfolio insurance. You can achieve exactly the same effect by purchasing a bond and a call option. Let's return to the insurance we purchased on Bow.com stock. Bow.com stock does not pay dividends, so there are no cash flows before the expiration of the option. Thus, instead of holding a share of Bow.com stock and a put, you could get the same payoff by purchasing a risk-free zero-coupon bond with a face value of $45 and a European call option with a strike price of $45. In this case, if Bow.com is below $45, you receive the payoff from the bond. If Bow.com is above $45, you can exercise the call and use the payoff from the bond to buy the stock for the strike price of $45. The orange line in Figure 20.7(b) shows the value of the combined position on the expiration date of the option; it achieves exactly the same payoffs as owning the stock itself and a put option.

CONCEPT CHECK
1. What is a straddle?

2. Explain how you can use put options to create portfolio insurance. How can you create portfolio insurance using call options?

20.3 PUT-CALL PARITY

Consider the two different ways to construct portfolio insurance illustrated in Figure 20.7: (1) purchase the stock and a put or (2) purchase a bond and a call. Because both positions provide exactly the same payoff, the Law of One Price requires that they must have the same price.

Let's write this concept more formally. Let K be the strike price of the option (the price we want to ensure that the stock will not drop below), C the call price, P the put price, and S the stock price. Then, if both positions have the same price,

$$S + P = PV(K) + C$$

The left side of this equation is the cost of buying the stock and a put (with a strike price of K); the right side is the cost of buying a zero-coupon bond with face value K and a call option (with a strike price of K). Recall that the price of a zero-coupon bond is just the present value of its face value, which we have denoted by $PV(K)$. Rearranging terms gives an expression for the price of a European call option for a non-dividend-paying stock:

$$C = P + S - PV(K) \tag{20.3}$$

This relationship between the value of the stock, the bond, and call and put options is known as **put-call parity**. It says that the price of a European call equals the price of the stock plus an otherwise identical put minus the price of a bond that matures on the expiration date of the option. In other words, you can think of a call as a combination of a levered position in the stock, $S - PV(K)$, plus insurance against a drop in the stock price, the put P.

EXAMPLE **20.6**	USING PUT-CALL PARITY

Problem

You are an options dealer who deals in non-publicly traded options. One of your clients wants to purchase a one-year European call option on HAL Computer Systems stock with a strike price of $20. Another dealer is willing to write a one-year European put option on HAL stock with a strike price of $20, and sell you the put option for a price of $1.50 per share. If HAL pays no dividends and is currently trading for $18 per share, and if the risk-free interest rate is 6%, what is the lowest price you can charge for the option and guarantee yourself a profit?

Solution

Using put-call parity, we can replicate the payoff of the one-year call option with a strike price of $20 by holding the following portfolio: Buy the one-year put option with a strike price of $20 from the dealer, buy the stock, and sell a one-year risk-free zero-coupon bond with a face value of $20. With this combination, we have the following final payoff depending on the final price of HAL stock in one year, S_1:

	Final HAL Stock Price	
	$S_1 < \$20$	$S_1 > \$20$
Buy Put Option	$20 - S_1$	0
Buy Stock	S_1	S_1
Sell Bond	-20	-20
Portfolio	0	$S_1 - 20$
Sell Call Option	0	$-(S_1 - 20)$
Total Payoff	0	0

Note that the final payoff of the portfolio of the three securities matches the payoff of a call option. Therefore, we can sell the call option to our client and have future payoff of zero no matter what happens. Doing so is worthwhile as long as we can sell the call option for more than the cost of the portfolio, which is

$$P + S - PV(K) = \$1.50 + \$18 - \$20/1.06 = \$0.632$$

What happens if the stock pays a dividend? In that case, the two different ways to construct portfolio insurance do not have the same payout because the stock will pay a dividend while the zero-coupon bond will not. Thus the two strategies will cost the same to implement only if we add the present value of future dividends to the combination of the bond and the call:

$$S + P = PV(K) + PV(Div) + C$$

The left side of this equation is the value of the stock and a put; the right side is the value of a zero-coupon bond, a call option, and the future dividends paid by the stock during the life of the options, denoted by Div. Rearranging terms gives the general put-call parity formula:

Put-Call Parity

$$C = P + S - PV(K) - PV(Div) \tag{20.4}$$

In this case, the call is equivalent to having a levered position in the stock without dividends plus insurance against a fall in the stock price.

1. Explain put-call parity.
2. If a put option trades at a higher price from the value indicated by the put-call parity equation, what action should you take?

20.4 FACTORS AFFECTING OPTION PRICES

Put-call parity gives the price of a European call option in terms of the price of a European put, the underlying stock, and a zero-coupon bond. Therefore, to compute the price of a call using put-call parity, you have to know the price of the put. In Chapter 21, we explain how to calculate the price of a call without knowing the price of the put. Before we get there, let's first investigate the factors that affect option prices.

STRIKE PRICE AND STOCK PRICE

As we noted earlier for the Bow.com option quotes in Table 20.1, the value of an otherwise identical call option is higher if the strike price the holder must pay to buy the stock is lower. Because a put is the right to sell the stock, puts with a lower strike price are less valuable.

For a given strike price, the value of a call option is higher if the current price of the stock is higher, as there is a greater likelihood the option will end up in-the-money. Conversely, put options increase in value as the stock price falls.

ARBITRAGE BOUNDS ON OPTION PRICES

We have already seen that an option's price cannot be negative. Furthermore, because an American option carries all the same rights and privileges as an otherwise equivalent European option, it cannot be worth less than a European option. If it were, you could make arbitrage profits by selling a European call and using part of the proceeds to buy an otherwise equivalent American call option. Thus *an American option cannot be worth less than its European counterpart.*

The maximum payoff for a put option occurs if the stock becomes worthless (if, say, the company files for bankruptcy). In that case, the put's payoff is equal to the strike price. Because this payoff is the highest possible, *a put option cannot be worth more than its strike price.*

For a call option, the lower the strike price, the more valuable the call option. If the call option had a strike price of zero, the holder would always exercise the option and receive the stock at no cost. This observation gives us an upper bound on the call price: *A call option cannot be worth more than the stock itself.*

The **intrinsic value** of an option is the value it would have if it expired immediately. Therefore, the intrinsic value is the amount by which the option is currently in-the-money, or 0 if the option is out-of-the-money. If an American option is worth less than its intrinsic value, you could make arbitrage profits by purchasing the option and immediately exercising it. Thus *an American option cannot be worth less than its intrinsic value.*

The **time value** of an option is the difference between the current option price and its intrinsic value. Because an American option cannot be worth less than its intrinsic value, it cannot have a negative time value.

OPTION PRICES AND THE EXPIRATION DATE

For American options, the longer the time to the expiration date, the more valuable the option. To see why, let's consider two options: an option with one year until the expiration date and an option with six months until the expiration date. The holder of the one-year option can turn her option into a six-month option by simply exercising it early. That is, the one-year option has all the same rights and privileges as the six-month option, so by the Law of One Price, it cannot be worth less than the six-month option: *An American option with a later expiration date cannot be worth less than an otherwise identical American option with an earlier expiration date.* Usually the right to delay exercising the option is worth something, so the option with the later expiration date will be more valuable.

What about European options? The same argument will not work for European options, because a one-year European option cannot be exercised early at six months. As a consequence, a European option with a later expiration date may potentially trade for less than an otherwise identical option with an earlier expiration date. For example, think about a European call on a stock that pays a liquidating dividend in six months (a liquidating dividend is paid when a corporation chooses to go out of business, sells off all of its assets, and pays out the proceeds as a dividend). A one-year European call option on this stock would be worthless, but a six-month call would be worth something. Now think about a European put option on the stock of a company that has gone bankrupt (and will not be reorganized). The stock price, S, is effectively zero and will not change. With a three-month European put, you would exercise in three months and get the exercise price, K, at that time. Since there is no risk, the current value to you of that put is the present value of K determined using the risk-free interest rate, r_f and discounting for one-quarter of a year.

Current Value of a Three-Month European Put Given $S = 0$: $PV = \dfrac{K}{(1 + r_f)^{0.25}}$

With a one-year European put, you cannot exercise and receive K for one whole year, thus the value to you now from holding the put is less than that for the three-month European put.

Current Value of a One-Year European Put Given $S = 0$: $PV = \dfrac{K}{(1 + r_f)^1}$

Had you been holding an American put, you could exercise it now and get the full amount of K now. Thus, when $S = 0$, the value to you now of the American put would be K (as long as you have time to exercise it before it expires).

OPTION PRICES AND VOLATILITY

An important criterion that determines the price of an option is the volatility of the underlying stock. Consider the following simple example.

EXAMPLE 20.7   OPTION VALUE AND VOLATILITY

Problem

Two European call options with a strike price of $50 are written on two different stocks. Suppose that tomorrow the *low-volatility* stock will have a price of $50 for certain. The *high-volatility* stock will be worth either $60 or $40, with each price having equal probability. If the expiration date of both options is tomorrow, which option will be worth more today?

> ### Solution
>
> The expected value of *both* stocks tomorrow is $50—the low-volatility stock will be worth this amount for sure, and the high-volatility stock has an expected value of 40\left(\frac{1}{2}\right)$ + 60\left(\frac{1}{2}\right)$ = $50. However, the options have very different values. The option on the low-volatility stock is worth nothing because there is no chance it will expire in-the-money (the low-volatility stock will be worth $50 and the strike price is $50). The option on the high-volatility stock is worth a positive amount because there is a 50% chance that it will be worth $60 − $50 = $10 and a 50% chance that it will be worthless. The value today of a 50% chance of a positive payoff (with no chance of a loss) is positive.

Example 20.7 illustrates an important principle: *The value of an option generally increases with the volatility of the stock.* The intuition for this result is that an increase in volatility increases the likelihood of very high and very low returns for the stock. The holder of a call option benefits from a higher payoff when the stock goes up and the option is in-the-money, but earns the same (zero) payoff no matter how far the stock drops once the option is out-of-the-money. Because of this asymmetry of the option's payoff, an option holder gains from an increase in volatility.

Recall that adding a put option to a portfolio is akin to buying insurance against a decline in value. Insurance is more valuable when there is higher volatility—hence put options on more volatile stocks are also worth more.

CONCEPT CHECK

1. What is the intrinsic value of an option?

2. Can a European option with a later expiration date be worth less than an identical European option with an earlier expiration date?

3. How does the volatility of a stock affect the value of puts and calls written on the stock?

20.5 EXERCISING OPTIONS EARLY

One might guess that the ability to exercise the American option early would make an American option more valuable than an equivalent European option. Surprisingly, this is not always the case—sometimes, they have equal value. Let's see why.

NON-DIVIDEND-PAYING STOCKS

Let's consider first options on a stock that will not pay any dividends prior to the expiration date of the options. In that case, the put-call parity formula for the value of the call option is (see Eq. 20.3):

$$C = P + S − PV(K)$$

We can write the price of the zero-coupon bond as $PV(K) = K − dis(K)$, where $dis(K)$ is the amount of the discount from face value. Substituting this expression into put-call parity gives

$$C = \underbrace{S − K}_{\text{Intrinsic value}} + \underbrace{dis(K) + P}_{\text{Time value}} \tag{20.5}$$

In this case, both terms that make up the time value of the call option are positive before the expiration date: As long as interest rates remain positive, the discount on a zero-coupon bond before the maturity date is positive, and the put price is also positive, so a European call always has a positive time value. Because an American option is worth at least as much as a European option, it must also have a positive time value before expiration. Hence, *the price of any call option on a non-dividend-paying stock always exceeds its intrinsic value.*

This result implies that it is *never* optimal to exercise a call option on a non-dividend-paying stock early—you are always better off just selling the option. It is straightforward to see why. When you exercise an option, you get its intrinsic value. But as we have just seen, the price of a call option on a non-dividend-paying stock always exceeds its intrinsic value. Thus, if you want to liquidate your position in a call on a non-dividend-paying stock, you will get a higher price if you sell it rather than exercise it. Because it is never optimal to exercise an American call on a non-dividend-paying stock early, the right to exercise the call early is worthless. For this reason, *an American call on a non-dividend-paying stock has the same price as its European counterpart.*

Intuitively, there are two benefits to delaying the exercise of a call option. First, the holder delays paying the strike price, and second, by retaining the right not to exercise, the holder's downside is limited. (These benefits are represented by the discount and put values in Eq. 20.5.)

In the case of a non-dividend-paying stock, there is an important implication that we can draw from the fact that the American call will have the same price as the European call. Earlier we found that American calls with later expiration dates are more valuable than their equivalent American calls with earlier expiration dates. Thus, for *non-dividend-paying* stocks, European calls with later expiration dates will also be more valuable than their equivalent European call options with earlier expiration dates.

What about an American put option on a non-dividend-paying stock? Does it ever make sense to exercise it early? The answer is yes, under certain circumstances. To see why, note that we can rearrange the put-call parity relationship as expressed in Eq. 20.5 to get the price of a European put option:

$$P = \underbrace{K - S}_{\text{Intrinsic value}} \underbrace{- \, dis(K) + C}_{\text{Time value}} \tag{20.6}$$

In this case, the time value of the option includes a negative term, the discount on a bond with face value K. When the put option is sufficiently deep in-the-money, this discount will be large relative to the value of the call, and the time value of a European put option will be negative. In that case, the European put will sell for less than its intrinsic value. However, its American counterpart cannot sell for less than its intrinsic value (because otherwise arbitrage profits would be possible by immediately exercising it), which implies that the American option can be worth more than an otherwise identical European option. Because the only difference between the two options is the right to exercise the option early, this right must be valuable—there must be states in which it is optimal to exercise the American put early.

Let's examine an extreme case to illustrate when it is optimal to exercise an American put early: Suppose the firm goes bankrupt and the stock is worth nothing. In such a case, the value of the put equals its upper bound—the strike price—so its price cannot go any higher. Thus no future appreciation is possible. However, if you exercise the put early, you can get the strike price today and earn interest on the proceeds in the interim. Hence it makes sense to exercise this option early. Although this example is extreme, it illustrates that it is often optimal to exercise deep in-the-money put options early. This is the same situation described earlier that shows that for European puts, a later expiration date may actually decrease the put's value.

*14. A forward contract is a contract to purchase an asset at a fixed price on a particular date in the future. Both parties are obligated to fulfill the contract. Explain how to construct a forward contract on a share of stock from a position in options.

15. You own a share of Costco stock. You are worried that its price will fall and would like to insure yourself against this possibility. How can you purchase insurance against this possibility?

16. It is July 13, 2009, and you own IBM stock. You would like to ensure that the value of your holdings will not fall significantly. Using the data in Problem 3, and expressing your answer in terms of a percentage of the current value of your portfolio,

   a. What will it cost to ensure that the value of your holdings will not fall below $95 share between now and the third Friday in July?

   b. What will it cost to ensure that the value of your holdings will not fall below $95 share between now and the third Friday in August?

   c. What will it cost to ensure that the value of your holdings will not fall below $100 share between now and the third Friday in August?

Put-Call Parity

17. Dynamic Energy Systems stock is currently trading for $33 per share. The stock pays no dividends. A one-year European put option on Dynamic with a strike price of $35 is currently trading for $2.10. If the risk-free interest rate is 10% per year, what is the price of a one-year European call option on Dynamic with a strike price of $35?

18. You happen to be checking the newspaper and notice an arbitrage opportunity. The current stock price of Intrawest is $20 per share and the one-year risk-free interest rate is 8%. A one-year put on Intrawest with a strike price of $18 sells for $3.33, while the identical call sells for $7. Explain what you must do to exploit this arbitrage opportunity.

19. Consider the July 2009 IBM call and put options in Problem 3. Ignoring the negligible interest you might earn on T-Bills over the remaining few days of life of the options, show that there is no arbitrage opportunity using put-call parity for the options with a $100 strike price. Specifically,

   a. What is your profit/loss if you buy a call and T-Bills, and sell IBM stock and a put option?

   b. What is your profit/loss if you buy IBM stock and a put option, and sell a call and T-Bills?

   c. Explain why your answers to parts a and b are not both zero.

Factors Affecting Option Prices

20. Suppose Amazon stock is trading for $70 per share and Amazon pays no dividends.

   a. What is the maximum possible price of a call option on Amazon?

   b. What is the maximum possible price of a put option on Amazon with a strike price of $100?

   c. What is the minimum possible value of a call option on Amazon stock with a strike price of $50?

   d. What is the minimum possible value of an American put option on Amazon stock with a strike price of $100?

21. Consider the data for IBM options in Problem 3. Suppose a new American-style put option on IBM is issued with a strike price of $110 and an expiration date of August 1.

   a. What is the maximum possible price for this option?

   b. What is the minimum possible price for this option?

22. You are watching the option quotes for your favourite stock, when suddenly there is a news announcement. Explain what type of news would lead to the following effects:

   a. Call prices increase, and put prices fall.

   b. Call prices fall, and put prices increase.

   c. Both call and put prices increase.

Exercising Options Early

*23. Why is it *never* optimal to exercise an American call option on a non-dividend-paying stock early?

*24. Explain why an American call option on a non-dividend-paying stock always has the same price as its European counterpart.

25. Consider an American put option on XAL stock with a strike price of $55 and one year to expiration. Assume XAL pays no dividends, XAL is currently trading for $10 per share, and the one-year interest rate is 10%. If it is optimal to exercise this option early,

    a. What is the price of a one-year American put option on XAL stock with a strike price of $60 per share?

    b. What is the maximum price of a one-year American call option on XAL stock with a strike price of $55 per share?

26. The stock of Harford Inc. is about to pay a $0.30 dividend. It will pay no more dividends for the next month. Consider call options that expire in one month. If the interest rate is 6% APR (monthly compounding), for what range of strike prices could early exercise of the call option be optimal? (Round to the nearest $1.)

27. Suppose the S&P 500 is at 900 and a one-year European call option with a strike price of $400 has a negative time value. If the interest rate is 5%, what can you conclude about the dividend yield of the S&P 500 (assume all dividends are paid at the end of the year)?

28. Suppose the S&P 500 is at 900 and it will pay a dividend of $30 at the end of the year. Suppose the interest rate is 2%. If a one-year European put option has a negative time value, what is the lowest possible strike price it could have?

Options and Corporate Finance

29. Wesley Corp. stock is trading for $25/share. Wesley has 20 million shares outstanding and a market debt-equity ratio of 0.5. Wesley's debt is zero coupon debt with a 5-year maturity and a yield to maturity of 10%.

    a. Describe Wesley's equity as a call option. What is the maturity of the call option? What is the market value of the asset underlying this call option? What is the strike price of this call option?

    b. Describe Wesley's debt using a call option.

    c. Describe Wesley's debt using a put option.

*30. Express the position of an equity holder in terms of put options.

31. Use the data in Table 20.5 to determine the rate Buffin would pay if it issued $105 billion in zero-coupon debt due in January 2012. Suppose Buffin currently has 300 million shares outstanding, implying a market value of $121.8 billion. The current two-year risk-free rate is 4.5%. (Assume perfect capital markets.)

*32. Suppose Buffin were to issue $93 billion in zero-coupon senior debt and another $12 billion in zero-coupon junior debt, both due in January 2012. Suppose Buffin currently has 300 million shares outstanding, implying a market value of $121.8 billion. The current two-year risk-free rate is 4.5% per year. Use the option data in Table 20.5 to determine the rate Buffin would pay on the junior debt issue. (Assume perfect capital markets.)

DATA CASE

Your uncle owns 10,000 shares of Wal-Mart stock. He is concerned about the short-term outlook for Wal-Mart's stock due to an impending "major announcement." This announcement has received much attention in the press so he expects the stock price will change significantly in the next month, but is unsure whether it will be a profit or a loss. He hopes the price will increase, but he also doesn't want to suffer if the price were to fall in the short term.

His broker recommended he buy a "protective put" on the stock, but your uncle has never traded options before and is not much of a risk taker. He wants you to devise a plan for him to capitalize if the announcement is positive but still be protected if the news causes the price to drop. You realize that a protective put will protect him from the downside risk, but you think a straddle may offer similar downside protection, while increasing the upside potential. You decide to show him both strategies and the resulting profits and returns he could face from each.

1. Download option quotes on options that expire in approximately one month on Wal-Mart from the Chicago Board Options Exchange (www.cboe.com) into an Excel spread-sheet. If you choose to download "near-term at-the-money" options you will get a range of options expiring in about a month. You can only get active quotes while the exchange is open; bid or ask prices are not available when it is closed.

2. Determine your uncle's profit and return using the protective put.
   a. Identify the expiring put with an exercise price closest to, but not below, the current stock price. Determine the investment required to protect all 10,000 shares.
   b. Determine the put price at expiration for each stock price at $5 increments from $25 to $65 using Eq. 20.2.
   c. Compute the profit (or loss) on the put for each stock price used in part b.
   d. Compute the profit on the stock from the current price for each stock price used in part b.
   e. Compute his overall profit (or loss) of the protective put, that is, combining the put and his stock for each price used in parts c and d.
   f. Compute the overall return of the protective put.

3. Determine your uncle's profit and return using the straddle.
   a. Compute the investment your uncle would have to make to purchase the call and put with the same exercise price and expiration as the put option in Question 2, to cover all 10,000 of his shares.
   b. Determine the value at expiration of the call and the put options at each $5 incre-ment of stock prices from $25 to $65 using Eqs. 20.1 and 20.2.
   c. Determine the profit (or loss) on the options at each stock price used in part b.
   d. Determine the profit (or loss) on the stock from the current price for each stock price used in part b.
   e. Compute his overall profit (or loss) of the stock plus straddle, that is, combining the position in both options and his stock for each price used in parts c and d.
   f. Compute the overall return of this position.

4. Was the broker correct that the protective put would prevent your uncle from losing if the announcement caused a large decrease in the stock value? What is your uncle's maximum possible loss using the protective put?

5. What is the maximum possible loss your uncle could experience using the straddle?

6. Which strategy, the protective put or the straddle, provides the maximum upside poten-tial for your uncle? Why does this occur?

CHAPTER

21

Option Valuation

Robert Merton and Myron Scholes were awarded the 1997 Nobel Prize in economics for their 1973 discovery, together with Fischer Black,[1] of a formula to calculate the price of an option: the *Black-Scholes Option Pricing Model*. Although the formula itself represented an enormous contribution to economics, even more important were the techniques that Black, Scholes, and Merton developed to value options. These techniques changed the course of financial economics and gave birth to a new profession: financial engineering. Financial engineers routinely use formulas to price financial securities in much the same way as mechanical engineers use Newton's laws to build bridges. The most important factor contributing to the huge growth in the types of financial securities that are available today are the techniques financial engineers use to price them. All of these techniques can be traced back to the Black-Scholes formula. Today, most large corporations rely on these financial securities to manage risk. Without the Black-Scholes formula, the job of corporate managers would be very different: many corporations would be forced to bear much more risk than they now do.

These formulas rely primarily on the Law of One Price. That is, they do not depend on knowing unobservable parameters such as investor tastes and beliefs. It is the need, in most applications, to model human preferences that makes economics an inexact science. The great insight that Merton, Black, and Scholes brought to economics is that in the case of options it is not necessary to model preferences. As we will explain in this chapter, their work demonstrated how to apply the Law of One Price to value a vast new range of financial securities based on the current market prices of stocks and bonds.

---

1. The Black-Scholes formula was derived in a paper jointly written by Fischer Black and Myron Scholes ("The Pricing of Options and Corporate Liabilities," *Journal of Political Economy* 81 (1973)), which relied on earlier work by Robert Merton. Unfortunately, Black died two years before the prize was awarded (Nobel Prizes are not awarded posthumously).

With the importance of the Black-Scholes formula kept firmly in mind, our objective in this chapter is to explain the most commonly used techniques (all of which derive from Black and Scholes' insights) for calculating the price of an option: the *Binomial Option Pricing Model*, the *Black-Scholes formula*, and *risk-neutral probabilities*. We apply these techniques to show how to value stock options and quantify their risk and return. We then show how to use the Black-Scholes formula to estimate the beta of risky debt. With this foundation in place, we will be able to cover important applications of option pricing for corporate managers in subsequent chapters.

21.1 THE BINOMIAL OPTION PRICING MODEL

We begin our study of option pricing with the **Binomial Option Pricing Model**.[2] This model prices options by making the simplifying assumption that at the end of the next period, the stock price has only two possible values. This assumption allows us to demonstrate the key insight of Black and Scholes—that option payoffs can be replicated exactly by constructing a portfolio out of a risk-free bond and the underlying stock. Furthermore, we will see that the model can be quite realistic if we consider stock price movements over very short time intervals.

A TWO-STATE SINGLE-PERIOD MODEL

Let's start by calculating the price of a single-period option in a very simple world. We will value the option by first constructing a **replicating portfolio**, a portfolio of other securities that has exactly the same value in one period as the option. Then, because they have the same payoffs, the Law of One Price implies that the current value of the call and the replicating portfolio must be equal.

Consider a European call option that expires in one period and has an exercise price of $50. Assume that the stock price today is equal to $50. We also assume here and throughout the chapter that the stock pays no dividends (unless explicitly indicated). In one period, the stock price will either rise by $10 or fall by $10. The one-period risk-free rate is 6%. We can summarize this information on a **binomial tree**—a timeline with two branches at every date representing the possible events that could happen at those times:

The binomial tree contains all the information we currently know: the value of the stock, bond, and call options in each state in one period, as well as the price of the stock and bond today (for simplicity, we assume the bond price today is $1, so in one period it

2. See J. Cox, S. Ross, and M. Rubinstein, "Option Pricing, A Simplified Approach," *Journal of Financial Economics* 7:3 (1979): 229–263. In a concurrent paper, J. R. Rendleman and B. J. Bartter ("Two-State Option Pricing," *Journal of Finance* 34:5 (December 1979): 1093–1110) develop the same technique.

will be worth $1.06). We define the state in which the stock price goes up (to $60) as the *up* state and the state in which the stock price goes down (to $40) as the *down* state.

In order to determine the value of the option using the Law of One Price, we must show that we can replicate its payoffs using a portfolio of the stock and the bond. Let Δ be the number of shares of stock we purchase, and let B be our initial investment in bonds. To create a call option using the stock and the bond, the value of the portfolio consisting of the stock and bond must match the value of the option in every possible state. Thus, in the up state, the value of the portfolio must be $10 (the value of the call in that state):

$$60\Delta + 1.06B = 10 \tag{21.1}$$

In the down state, the value of the portfolio must be zero (the value of the call in that state):

$$40\Delta + 1.06B = 0 \tag{21.2}$$

Equations 21.1 and 21.2 are two simultaneous equations with two unknowns, Δ and B. We'll write down the general formula to solve these equations shortly, but in this case we can check that the solution is

$$\Delta = 0.5$$

$$B = -18.8679$$

A portfolio that is long 0.5 share of stock and short approximately $18.87 worth of bonds (i.e., we have borrowed $18.87 at a 6% interest rate) will have a value in one period that exactly matches the value of the call. Let's verify this explicitly:

$$60 \times 0.5 - 1.06 \times 18.87 = 10$$

$$40 \times 0.5 - 1.06 \times 18.87 = 0$$

Therefore, by the Law of One Price, the price of the call option today must equal the current market value of the replicating portfolio. The value of the portfolio today is the value of 0.5 shares at the current share price of $50, less the amount borrowed:

$$50\Delta + B = 50(0.5) - 18.87 = 6.13 \tag{21.3}$$

Thus the price of the call today is $6.13.[3]

Figure 21.1 illustrates how we can use the stock and the bond to replicate the payoff of the call option in this case. As a function of the future stock price, the payoff of the replicating portfolio is a line with a slope of $\Delta = 0.5$, and an intercept of $1.06 B = 1.06(-18.87) = -20$. This line is very different from the line showing the payoff of the call option, which is zero below the strike price of $50 and increases 1:1 with the stock price above $50. The secret of the binomial model is that, while the option and the replicating portfolio do not have the same payoffs in general, they have the same payoffs given the only two outcomes we have assumed possible for the stock price: $40 and $60.

---

3. If the call's price were different, there would be an arbitrage opportunity. For example, if the call price were $6.50, we could earn a profit by buying the replicating portfolio for $6.13 and selling the call option for $6.50. Because they have the same future payoff, we have taken no risk, and earn an immediate profit of $6.50 - 6.13 = $0.37 per option sold.

FIGURE 21.1

Replicating an Option in the Binomial Model

The red line shows the payoff of the replicating portfolio and the blue line shows the payoff of the call option, as a function of next period's stock price. While they do not match everywhere, they do match for the two possible outcomes of the stock price next period, $40 and $60.

Note that by using the Law of One Price, we are able to solve for the price of the option *without knowing the probabilities of the states in the binomial tree.* That is, we did not need to specify the likelihood that the stock would go up versus down. This remarkable result was a very important discovery because the probabilities of future states are part of investor beliefs, so they are very difficult to estimate. The preceding argument shows that we do not need to know these probabilities to value options. It also means that we do not need to know the expected return of the stock, which will depend on these probabilities.

THE BINOMIAL PRICING FORMULA

Now that we have seen the basic idea, let's consider a more general example. Suppose the current stock price is S, and the stock price will either go up to S_u or down to S_d next period. The risk-free interest rate is r_f. Let's determine the price of an option that has a value of C_u if the stock goes up, and C_d if the stock goes down:

Note that in the depiction of the binomial tree above, for simplicity we did not write down the bond payoff since it earns a return of r_f in either case.

What is the value of the option today? Again, we must determine the number of shares of stock, Δ, and the position in the bond, B, such that the payoff of the replicating portfolio matches the payoff of the option if the stock goes up or down:

$$S_u \Delta + (1 + r_f)B = C_u \quad \text{and} \quad S_d \Delta + (1 + r_f)B = C_d \qquad (21.4)$$

Solving these two equations for the two unknowns Δ and B we get the general formula for the replicating formula in the binomial model:

Replicating Portfolio in the Binomial Model

$$\Delta = \frac{C_u - C_d}{S_u - S_d} \quad \text{and} \quad B = \frac{C_d - S_d \Delta}{1 + r_f} \tag{21.5}$$

Note that the formula for Δ in Eq. 21.5 can be interpreted as the sensitivity of the option's value to changes in the stock price. It is equal to the slope of the line showing the payoff of the replicating portfolio in Figure 21.1.

Once we know the replicating portfolio, we can calculate the value C of the option today as the cost of this portfolio:

Option Price in the Binomial Model

$$C = S\Delta + B \tag{21.6}$$

Equations 21.5 and 21.6 summarize the Binomial Option Pricing Model. Though they are relatively simple, by applying them in different ways we will see that they are quite powerful. For one thing, they do not require that the option we are valuing is a call option—we can use them to value *any* security whose payoff depends on the stock price. For example, we can use them to price a put, as in the next example.

EXAMPLE 21.1

VALUING A PUT OPTION

Problem

Suppose a stock is currently trading for $60, and in one period will either go up by 20% or fall by 10%. If the one-period risk-free rate is 3%, what is the price of a European put option that expires in one period and has an exercise price of $60?

Solution

We begin by constructing a binomial tree:

Thus, we can solve for the value of the put by using Eqs. 21.5 and 21.6 with $C_u = 0$ (the value of the put when the stock goes up) and $C_d = 6$ (the value of the put when the stock goes down). Therefore,

$$\Delta = \frac{C_u - C_d}{S_u - S_d} = \frac{0 - 6}{72 - 54} = -0.3333 \quad \text{and} \quad B = \frac{C_d - S_d \Delta}{1 + r_f} = \frac{6 - 54(-0.3333)}{1.03} = 23.30$$

This portfolio is short 0.3333 shares of the stock, and has $23.30 invested in the risk-free bond. Let's check that it replicates the put if the stock goes up or down:

$$72(-0.3333) + 1.03(23.30) = 0 \quad \text{and} \quad 54(-0.3333) + 1.03(23.30) = 6$$

Thus, the value of the put is the initial cost of this portfolio. Using Eq. 21.6:

$$\text{Put value} = C = S\Delta + B$$
$$= 60(-0.3333) + 23.30 = \$3.30$$

You might be skeptical at this point. Showing that we can value call and put options in a simple two-state one-period example is one thing; pricing real-world options is another matter altogether. Yet, as we show in the next section, this simple two-state model is easily generalized.

A MULTIPERIOD MODEL

The problem with the simple two-state example is that there are many more than two possible outcomes for the stock price in the real world. To make the model more realistic, we must allow for the possibility of many states and periods.

Let's consider a two-period binomial tree for the stock price:

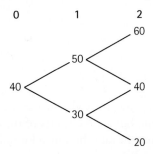

The key property of the binomial model is that in each period, there are only two possible outcomes—the stock goes either up or down. But by adding an additional period, the number of possible stock prices at the end has increased. Let's assume again that the risk-free rate of interest is 6% per period and consider how to price a call option with a strike price of $50 that expires in two periods.

To calculate the value of an option in a multiperiod binomial tree, we start at the end of the tree and work backwards. At time 2, the option expires, so its value is equal to its intrinsic value. In this case, the call will be worth $10 if the stock price goes up to $60, and will be worth zero otherwise.

Next let's determine the value of the option in each possible state at time 1. What is the value of the option if the stock price has gone up to $50 at time 1? In this case, because the option expires next period, the remaining part of the binomial tree is as follows:

This binomial tree is exactly the same tree that we considered in the one-period model at the start of this section. There we computed the replicating portfolio as having $\Delta = 0.5$

shares of stock and a bond position of $B = -\$18.87$, for an initial call value of $6.13 (see Eq. 21.3).

What if the stock price has dropped to $30 at time 1? In that case the binomial tree for the next period is

The option is worthless in both states at time 2, so the value of the option in the down state at time 1 must also be zero (and the replicating portfolio is simply $\Delta = 0$ and $B = 0$).

Given the value of the call option in either state at time 1, we can now work backwards and determine the value of the call at time 0. In that case, we can write the binomial tree over the next period as follows:

In this case, the call values at the end of the tree (time 1) are not the final payoffs of the option, but are the values of the option one period prior to expiration. Nonetheless, we can use the same binomial formulas to calculate the replicating portfolio at time 0, which is a portfolio whose value will match the value of the option at time 1. From Eq. 21.5:

$$\Delta = \frac{C_u - C_d}{S_u - S_d} = \frac{6.13 - 0}{50 - 30} = 0.3065 \quad \text{and}$$

$$B = \frac{C_d - S_d \Delta}{1 + r_f} = \frac{0 - 30(0.3065)}{1.06} = -8.67$$

From Eq. 21.6, the initial value of the call option is equal to the initial cost of this portfolio:

$$C = S\Delta + B = 40(0.3065) - 8.67 = \$3.59$$

Therefore, the initial value of the call option at time 0 is $3.59.

For this two-period call option, while we can still construct the option out of the stock and the bond, we now need to adjust our replicating portfolio at the end of each period. That is, we start off long 0.3065 shares of stock and borrow $8.67 (for an initial cost of $3.59). If the stock price drops to $30, our shares are worth $30 × 0.3065 = $9.20, and our debt has grown to $8.67 × 1.06 = $9.20. Thus, the net value of the portfolio is worthless (matching the option value), and we can liquidate the portfolio (at no cost). If the stock price rises to $50, the net value of the portfolio rises to $6.13. In that case, the new Δ of the replicating portfolio is 0.5. We therefore buy 0.50 − 0.3065 = 0.1935 more shares of stock and pay for it by borrowing 0.1935 × $50 = $9.67. This retrading requires no new money; at the end our total debt will be $8.67 \times 1.06 + 9.67 = \$18.87$, which matches the value for B we calculated earlier. Therefore, on the expiration date at time 2, the value of the portfolio is $10 if the stock goes up to $60, and is zero otherwise.

The idea that you can replicate the option payoff by dynamically trading in a portfolio of the underlying stock and a risk-free bond was one of the most important contributions of the original Black-Scholes paper. Today, this kind of replication strategy is called a **dynamic trading strategy**.

EXAMPLE 21.2

USING THE BINOMIAL OPTION PRICING MODEL TO VALUE A PUT OPTION

Problem

Suppose the current price of Narver Network Systems stock is $50 per share. In each of the next two years, the stock price will either increase by 20% or decrease by 10%. The 3% one-year risk-free rate of interest will remain constant. Calculate the price of a two-year European put option on Narver Network Systems stock with a strike price $60.

Solution

Here is the binomial tree for the stock price, together with the final payoffs of the put option:

If the stock goes up to $60 at time 1, we are in exactly the same situation as in Example 21.1. Using our result there, we see that if the stock is worth $60 at time 1, the value of the put option is $3.30.

If the stock goes down to $45 at time 1, then at time 2 the put option will be worth either $6 if the stock goes up, or $19.50 if the stock goes down. Using Eq. 21.5:

$$\Delta = \frac{C_u - C_d}{S_u - S_d} = \frac{6 - 19.5}{54 - 40.5} = -1 \text{ and } B = \frac{C_d - S_d\Delta}{1 + r_f} = \frac{19.5 - 40.5(-1)}{1.03} = 58.25$$

This portfolio is short 1 share of the stock, and has $58.25 invested in the risk-free bond. Because the value of the bond will grow to $58.25 \times 1.03 = \$60$ at time 2, the value of the replicating portfolio will be $60 less the final price of the stock, matching the payoff of the put option. Thus, the value of the put is the cost of this portfolio. Using Eq. 21.6:

$$\text{Put value} = C = S\Delta + B = 45(-1) + 58.25 = \$13.25$$

Now consider the value of the put option at time 0. In period 1, we have calculated that the put will be worth $3.30 if the stock goes up to $60, and $13.25 if the stock falls to $45. The binomial tree at time 0 is

Using Eq. 21.5 and Eq. 21.6, the replicating portfolio and put value at time 0 are

$$\Delta = \frac{C_u - C_d}{S_u - S_d} = \frac{3.30 - 13.25}{60 - 45} = -0.6633,$$

$$B = \frac{C_d - S_d \Delta}{1 + r_f} = \frac{13.25 - 45(-0.6633)}{1.03} = 41.84, \quad \text{and}$$

$$\text{Put value} = C = S\Delta + B = 50(-0.6633) + 41.84 = \$8.68$$

Thus, the value of European put option at time 0 is $8.68.

MAKING THE MODEL REALISTIC

Using the methods of the previous section, we can value options given any number of periods in the binomial stock price tree. But of course, to price an option for an actual stock, the binomial tree must be a realistic model of the way the stock is likely to evolve in the future.

While binary up or down movements are not the way stock prices behave on an annual or even daily basis, they are a much more reasonable description of stock prices over very short time periods, such as the time between trades. By decreasing the length of each period, and increasing the number of periods in the stock price tree, we can construct a realistic model for the stock price. Figure 21.2 shows an example of a stock price path in

FIGURE 21.2

A Binomial Stock Price Path

The figure depicts a stock price path with 900 periods during the year, and a random stock return of +1% or −1% each period. With a large number of periods, and small movements in the stock price each period, the binomial model is a realistic model of stock price behaviour.

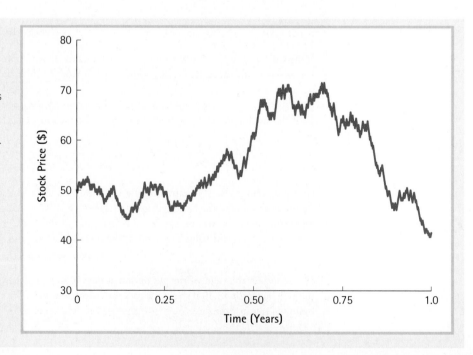

which the stock price moves up or down by 1% each of 900 periods over the year. With many short periods, these stock price paths look very similar to the price charts for real stocks. Practitioners routinely use this method to calculate the prices of options and other types of derivative securities. With a fast computer, prices can be computed very quickly even with thousands of periods.[4]

As we mentioned earlier, the techniques of the Binomial Option Pricing Model are not specific to European call and put options. We can use it to price any security whose payoff depends on the stock price. But for the special case of European call and put options, there is an alternative approach. If we let the length of each period shrink to zero, and the number of periods per year grows to infinity, the results of the Binomial Option Pricing Model can be calculated using a single, simple formula: The Black-Scholes formula. We consider it next.

CONCEPT CHECK
1. What is the key assumption of the Binomial Option Pricing Model?
2. Why don't we need to know the probabilities of the states in the binominal tree in order to solve for the price of the option?
3. What is a replicating portfolio?

21.2   THE BLACK-SCHOLES OPTION PRICING MODEL

Although Black and Scholes did not originally derive it that way, the **Black-Scholes Option Pricing Model** can be derived from the Binomial Option Pricing Model by making the length of each period, and the movement of the stock price per period, shrink to zero and letting the number of periods grow infinitely large. Rather than derive the formula here, we will state it and focus on its applications.

THE BLACK-SCHOLES FORMULA

Before stating the Black-Scholes formula for the price of an option, it is necessary to introduce some terminology. Let S be the current price of the stock, T be the number of years left to expiration, K be the exercise price, and σ be the annual volatility (standard deviation) of the stock's return. Then the value, at time t, of a call option on a stock that does not pay dividends prior to the option's expiration date is given by

Black-Scholes Price of a Call Option on a Non-Dividend-Paying Stock

$$C = S \times N(d_1) - PV(K) \times N(d_2) \tag{21.7}$$

where $N(d)$ is the **cumulative normal distribution**—that is, the probability, as shown in Figure 21.3, that a normally distributed variable is less than d—and

$$d_1 = \frac{\ln[S/PV(K)]}{\sigma\sqrt{T}} + \frac{\sigma\sqrt{T}}{2} \quad \text{and} \quad d_2 = d_1 - \sigma\sqrt{T} \tag{21.8}$$

$PV(K)$ is the present value (price) of a risk-free zero-coupon bond that pays K on the expiration date of the option.

---

4. There is a question of how to calibrate the up or down movements each period. A standard approach is to assume the stock's return each period is $\pm\sigma/\sqrt{n}$, where σ is the stock's volatility and n is the number of periods per year.

FIGURE 21.3

Normal Distribution

$N(d)$, the cumulative normal distribution, is the probability that a normally distributed random variable will take on a value less than d. This probability is equal to the area under the normal distribution (bell curve) to the left of the point d—the shaded area in the figure. Because it is a probability, $N(d)$ has a minimum value of 0 and a maximum value of 1. It can be calculated using the function NORMSDIST(d) in Excel.

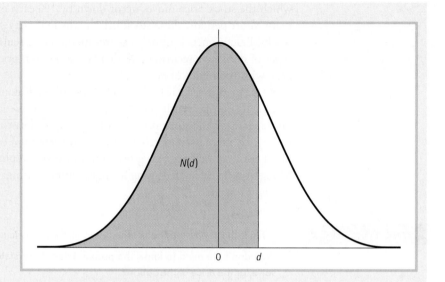

We need only five input parameters to price the call: the stock price, the strike price, the exercise date, the risk-free interest rate (to compute the present value of the strike price), and the volatility of the stock. What is equally notable is what we do *not* need. Just as we do not need to know the probabilities in the Binomial Option Pricing Model, we do not need to know the expected return on the stock to calculate the option price in the Black-Scholes Option Pricing Model. The expected return of the stock is difficult to measure with great accuracy, as we learned in Part 4 of the text; if it were a required input, we could not expect the formula to deliver the option price with much accuracy. Indeed, the only parameter in the Black-Scholes formula that we need to forecast is the stock's volatility. Because a stock's volatility is much easier to measure (and forecast) than its expected return, the Black-Scholes formula can be very precise.

You might wonder how it is possible to compute the value of a security like an option that appears to depend critically on the future stock price without knowing the expected return of the stock. In fact, the expected return of the stock is already incorporated into the current stock price (which is the discounted value of its future payoffs). The Black-Scholes formula depends on the stock's current price, and so, in a sense, uses this information implicitly.

The Black-Scholes formula is derived assuming that the call is a European option. Recall from Chapter 20 that an American call option on a non-dividend-paying stock always has the same price as its European counterpart. Thus the Black-Scholes formula can be used to price American or European call options on non-dividend-paying stocks.

EXAMPLE 21.3

VALUING A CALL OPTION WITH THE BLACK-SCHOLES FORMULA

Problem

JetBlue Airways does not pay dividends. Using the data in Table 21.1, compare the price on July 24, 2009, for the December 2009 American call option on JetBlue with a strike price of $6.00 to the price predicted by the Black-Scholes formula. Assume that the volatility of Jet-Blue is 65% per year and that the risk-free rate of interest is 1% per year.

Solution

We use $5.03 (the closing price) for the per-share price of JetBlue stock. Because the December contract expires on the Saturday following the third Friday of December (December 19), there are 148 days left until expiration. The present value of the strike price is $PV(K) = 6.00/(1.01)^{148/365} = \$5.976$. Calculating d_1 and d_2 from Eq. 21.8 gives

$$d_1 = \frac{\ln[S/PV(K)]}{\sigma\sqrt{T}} + \frac{\sigma\sqrt{T}}{2}$$

$$= \frac{\ln(5.03/5.976)}{0.65\sqrt{\frac{148}{365}}} + \frac{0.65\sqrt{\frac{148}{365}}}{2} = -0.209$$

$$d_2 = d_1 - \sigma\sqrt{T} = -0.209 - 0.65\sqrt{\frac{148}{365}} = -0.623$$

Substituting d_1 and d_2 into the Black-Scholes formula given by Eq. 21.7 results in

$$C = S \times N(d_1) - PV(K) \times N(d_2)$$
$$= 5.03 \times 0.417 - 5.976 \times 0.267$$
$$= \$0.50$$

In Table 21.1, the bid and ask prices for this option are $0.45 and $0.55.

Figure 21.4 plots the value of the call option in Example 21.3 as a function of JetBlue's current stock price. Notice how the value of the option always lies above its intrinsic value.

EUROPEAN PUT OPTIONS. We can use the Black-Scholes formula to compute the price of a European put option on a non-dividend-paying stock by using the put-call parity

TABLE 21.1   JETBLUE OPTION QUOTES

| JBLU | | | | | | | | | | 5.03 +0.11 |
| Jul 24 2009 @ 17:17 ET | | | | **Bid** 5.03 | **Ask** 5.04 | | **Size** 168 × 96 | | | **Vol** 7335887 |

Calls	Bid	Ask	Vol	Open Int	Puts	Bid	Ask	Vol	Open Int
09 Dec 5.00 (JGQ LA)	0.80	0.90	47	5865	09 Dec 5.00 (JGQ XA)	0.80	0.90	6	1000
09 Dec 6.00 (JGQ LF)	0.45	0.55	2	259	09 Dec 6.00 (JGQ XF)	1.40	1.50	0	84
10 Jan 5.00 (JGQ AA)	0.85	1.00	125	6433	10 Jan 5.00 (JGQ MA)	0.85	0.95	10	14737
10 Jan 6.00 (JGQ AF)	0.50	0.60	28	0	10 Jan 6.00 (JGQ MF)	1.45	1.55	0	22
10 Jan 9.00 (JGQ AI)	0.05	0.15	0	818	10 Jan 9.00 (JGQ MI)	4.00	4.10	0	0
10 Mar 5.00 (JGQ CA)	1.05	1.15	0	50	10 Mar 5.00 (JGQ OA)	1.00	1.10	0	40
10 Mar 6.00 (JGQ CF)	0.65	0.75	0	146	10 Mar 6.00 (JGQ OF)	1.60	1.70	10	41
10 Mar 7.00 (JGQ CG)	0.40	0.50	5	3	10 Mar 7.00 (JGQ OG)	2.30	2.45	10	0

Source: Chicago Board Options Exchange at www.cboe.com.

FIGURE 21.4

Black-Scholes Value on July 24, 2009, of the December 2009 $6.00 Call on JetBlue Stock

The red curve shows the Black-Scholes value of the call option as a function of JetBlue's stock price. The circle shows the value at JetBlue's current price of $5.03. The black line is the intrinsic value of the call.

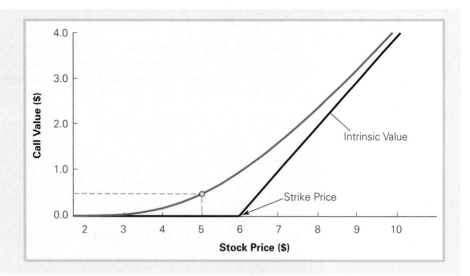

formula we derived in Chapter 20 (see Eq. 20.3). The price of a European put from put-call parity is

$$P = C - S + PV(K)$$

Substituting for C using the Black-Scholes formula gives

Black-Scholes Price of a European Put Option on a Non-Dividend-Paying Stock

$$P = PV(K)\,[1 - N(d_2)] - S\,[1 - N(d_1)] \tag{21.9}$$

EXAMPLE 21.4

VALUING A PUT OPTION WITH THE BLACK-SCHOLES FORMULA

Problem

Using the Black-Scholes formula and the data in Table 21.1, compute the price of a January 2010 $5 put option and compare it to the price in the market. Is the Black-Scholes formula the correct way to price these options? (As before, assume that the volatility of JetBlue is 65% per year and that the risk-free rate of interest is 1% per year.)

Solution

The contract expires on January 16, 2010, or 176 days from the quote date. The present value of the strike price is $PV(K) = 5.00/(1.01)^{176/365} = \$4.976$. Calculating d_1 and d_2 from Eq. 21.8 gives

$$d_1 = \frac{\ln[S/PV(K)]}{\sigma\sqrt{T}} + \frac{\sigma\sqrt{T}}{2}$$

$$= \frac{\ln(5.03/4.976)}{0.65\sqrt{\frac{176}{365}}} + \frac{0.65\sqrt{\frac{176}{365}}}{2} = 0.250$$

$$d_2 = d_1 - \sigma\sqrt{T} = 0.250 - 0.65\sqrt{\frac{176}{365}} = -0.201$$

Substituting d_1 and d_2 into the Black-Scholes formula for a put option, using Eq. 21.9, gives

$$P = PV(K)\,[1 - N(d_2)] - S[1 - N(d_1)]$$
$$= 4.976 \times (1 - 0.420) - 5.03 \times (1 - 0.599)$$
$$= \$0.87$$

Given the bid and ask prices of \$0.85 and \$0.95, respectively, for the option, this estimate is within the bid-ask spread. But the Black-Scholes formula for puts is valid for European options, and the quotes are for American options. Hence, in this case, the Black-Scholes option price is a lower bound on the actual value of the put, as an American put might be exercised early to benefit from interest on the strike price. However, given that interest on the \$5 strike price is less than \$0.03, in this case the approximation is a close one.

Figure 21.5 plots the value of the European put option in Example 21.4 as a function of JetBlue's stock price. Notice how the value of the option can lie below its intrinsic value (though the effect is slight given low current interest rates). The Black-Scholes formula prices European puts, and, as you will recall from Chapter 20, the time value of deep-in-the-money puts can be negative.

DIVIDEND-PAYING STOCKS. The Black-Scholes formula applies to call options on non-dividend-paying stocks. However, we can easily adjust the formula for European options on dividend-paying stocks.

The holder of a European call option does not receive the benefit of any dividends that will be paid prior to the expiration date of the option. Indeed, as we saw in Chapter 17, the stock price tends to drop by the amount of the dividend when the stock goes ex-dividend. Because the final stock price will be lower, dividends decrease the value of a call option.

FIGURE 21.5

Black-Scholes Value on July 24, 2009, of the January 2010 \$5 Put on JetBlue Stock

The red curve shows the Black-Scholes value of the put option as a function of JetBlue's stock price. The circle shows the value at JetBlue's current price of \$5.03. The black line is the intrinsic value of the put. For stock prices below \$2.25, the European put's value is slightly less than its intrinsic value.

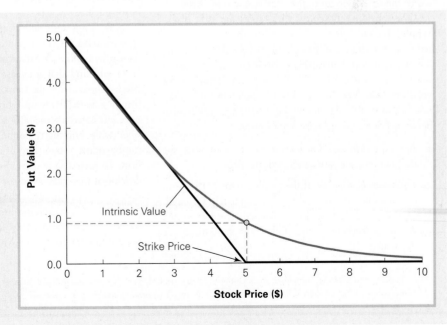

COMMON MISTAKE VALUING EMPLOYEE STOCK OPTIONS

In the last 20 years, it has become common practice to compensate executives by granting them **executive stock options (ESOs)**—call options on their company's stock. Until 2005, Canadian accounting standards did not require firms to include stock option grants as part of their compensation expense. Now, under the Canadian Institute of Chartered Accountants (CICA) Handbook, Section 3870, firms are required to expense these options when calculating their earnings. Regardless of the accounting requirement, both firms and employees would like to know the value of this compensation. While it is tempting to use the Black-Scholes formula to value an ESO, there are several important pitfalls to be aware of when doing so.

To understand the difficulties of using the Black-Scholes formula to value ESOs, it is important to appreciate how they are usually granted. ESOs are typically American-style options with exercise dates up to ten years in the future. However, there is usually a vesting period (often as long as five years) during which the employee does not actually own the option. Instead, he or she owns a right to the option at the end of the vesting period. If the employee leaves the firm during this period, the individual forfeits this right and so does not get the option. Once the vesting period has passed, the employee owns the option but *it is not tradeable*—the only way the employee can liquidate the option is by exercising it. Furthermore, most executives face restrictions in trading their own company stock, so they effectively cannot construct a replicating portfolio. Because of these restrictions, ESOs are not worth the same amount to the employee and the firm.

One obvious difficulty with applying the Black-Scholes formula to such options is that the formula requires an estimate of the volatility of the stock over the life of the option. Forecasting volatility up to ten years in the future is extremely difficult. But even if the stock's volatility were known, the Black-Scholes formula does not account for the following important differences between ESOs and ordinary stock options:

1. *ESOs are dilutive.* When exercised, they increase the number of shares outstanding of the firm.

2. *ESOs may be forfeited.* If the employee leaves the firm, options that are not vested are immediately forfeited. Options already vested are forfeited if not exercised within a certain period following the employee's departure.

3. *ESOs may be exercised early.* Once vested, the employee can exercise the options at any time.

Unless the number of options is large relative to the total number of shares outstanding, the first difference is not that important. The second difference is important for employees and firms with high employee turnover.

The third difference is very important for employees and all firms. Employees are risk averse, but are not permitted to hedge the risk of the option by trading the replicating portfolio. As a consequence, the employee's preferences and beliefs matter in computing the ESO's value: A more risk-averse employee will attach a lower value to the option than a less risk-averse employee. Furthermore, the only way an employee can eliminate his or her risk from the option is to exercise it and sell the stock. *Hence most employees choose to exercise early.** In this case, employees are forfeiting the (often substantial) remaining time value of their options in exchange for a reduction in their risk.

Thus the Black-Scholes formula (which assumes no early exercise) overestimates the cost of the option to the firm and its benefit to the employee. Because the firm can hedge its option liabilities, risk is not an issue when evaluating the cost of the option to the firm. Thus, the Black-Scholes formula overstates the cost by not accounting for forfeitures and early exercise. Because the employee cannot sell or hedge the risk of the option, the Black-Scholes formula overstates the value of the option to the employee even further by not accounting for the personal cost of bearing risk.

How important are these differences? The answer appears to be, very important. In a recent paper, Professors Ashish Jain and Ajay Subramanian adjust for these differences and find that for reasonable parameter values, the Black-Scholes formula can overestimate the cost to the firm of a vested five-year option by as much as 40%.† And once one considers the personal cost of being under-diversified while holding the option, its value to the employee can be as low as one-third of the cost of the option to the firm. To account for these discrepancies, researchers have developed methods based on the binomial model in Section 21.1 that incorporate the probability and effect of forfeiture and early exercise directly into the binomial tree (see the additional readings for this chapter in the Textbook Resources section on MyFinanceLab).

---

*See S. Huddart and M. Lang, "Employee Stock Option Exercises: An Empirical Analysis," *Journal of Accounting and Economics* 21:1 (1996): 5–43.
†The Intertemporal Exercise and Valuation of Employee Options," *Accounting Review* 79:3 (2004): 705–743.

Let $PV(Div)$ be the present value of any dividends paid prior to the expiration date of the option. Then a security that is identical to the stock, but did not pay any of the these dividends, would have a current market price of

$$S^x = S - PV(Div) \qquad (21.10)$$

The value S^x is the current price of the stock excluding any dividends prior to expiration. *Because a European call option is the right to buy the stock without these dividends, we can evaluate it using the Black-Scholes formula with S^x in place of S.*

A useful special case is when the stock will pay a dividend that is proportional to its stock price at the time the dividend is paid. If q is the stock's (compounded) dividend yield until the expiration date, then[5]

$$S^x = S/(1 + q) \qquad (21.11)$$

EXAMPLE 21.5

VALUING A DIVIDEND-PAYING EUROPEAN CALL OPTION WITH THE BLACK-SCHOLES FORMULA

Problem

World Wide Plants will pay an annual dividend yield of 5% on its stock. Plot the value of a one-year European call option with a strike price of $20 on World Wide Plants stock as a function of the stock price. Assume that the volatility of World Wide Plants stock is 20% per year and that the one-year risk-free rate of interest is 4%.

Solution

The price of the call is given by the standard Black-Scholes formula, Eq. 21.7, but with the stock price replaced throughout with $S^x = S/(1.05)$. For example, with a stock price of $30, $S^x = 30/(1.05) = 28.57$, $PV(K) = 20/1.04 = 19.23$, and

$$d_1 = \frac{\ln[S^x/PV(K)]}{\sigma\sqrt{T}} + \frac{\sigma\sqrt{T}}{2}$$

$$= \frac{\ln(28.57/19.23)}{0.2} + 0.1 = 2.08$$

$$d_2 = d_1 - \sigma\sqrt{T} = 2.08 - 0.2 = 1.88$$

so

$$C(S) = S^x N(d_1) - PV(K)N(d_2) = 28.57(0.981) - 19.23(0.970) = 9.37$$

---

5. To see why, suppose that whenever the dividend is paid, we reinvest it. Then if we buy $1/(1 + q)$ shares today, at expiration we will own $[1/(1 + q)] \times (1 + q) = 1$ share. Thus, by the Law of One Price, the value today of receiving one share at expiration is $S/(1 + q)$.

Plotting this function (in red) gives

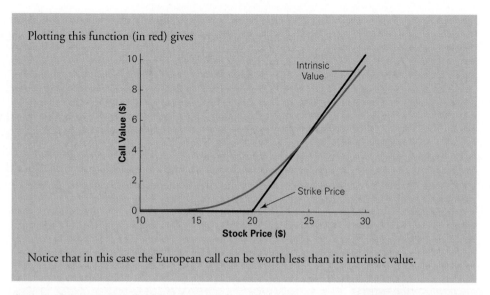

Notice that in this case the European call can be worth less than its intrinsic value.

IMPLIED VOLATILITY

Of the five required inputs in the Black-Scholes formula, four are directly observable: S, K, T, and the risk-free interest rate. Only one parameter, σ, the volatility of the stock price, is not observable directly. Practitioners use two strategies to estimate the value of this variable. The first, most straightforward approach is to use historical data. The second approach is to "back out" the volatility using the Black-Scholes formula itself. That is, you can take the option price quoted in the market as an input and solve for the volatility. This estimate of a stock's volatility is known as the **implied volatility**. The implied volatility from one option can be used to estimate the value of other options on the stock with the same expiration date (as well as those with different expiration dates if the stock's volatility is not expected to change over time).

EXAMPLE 21.6	COMPUTING THE IMPLIED VOLATILITY FROM AN OPTION PRICE

Problem

Use the price of the March 2010 call on JetBlue with a strike price of $5.00 in Table 21.1 to calculate the implied volatility for JetBlue from July 2009 to March 2010. Assume the risk-free rate of interest is 1% per year.

Solution

The call expires on March 20, 2010, or 239 days after the quote date. The stock price is $5.03, and $PV(K) = 5.00/(1.01)^{239/365} = \$4.968$. Substituting these values into the Black-Scholes formula, Eq. 21.7, gives

$$C = 5.03 N(d_1) - 4.968 N(d_2)$$

where

$$d_1 = \frac{\ln(5.03/4.968)}{\sigma\sqrt{\frac{239}{365}}} + \frac{\sigma\sqrt{\frac{239}{365}}}{2} \quad \text{and} \quad d_2 = d_1 - \sigma\sqrt{\frac{239}{365}}$$

We can compute the Black-Scholes option value C for different volatilities using this equation. The option value C increases with σ, and is equal $1.10 (average bid and ask price for the call) when $\sigma \approx 67\%$. (You can find this value by trial and error or by using Excel's Solver tool.) If we look at the bid price of $1.05, the implied volatility is about 64%, and at the ask price of $1.15, the implied volatility is about 70%. Thus the 65% volatility we used in Example 21.3 and Example 21.4 is within the range of implied volatilities calculated using the option's bid and ask prices.

THE REPLICATING PORTFOLIO

Although we introduced the concept of the replicating portfolio in the discussion of the Binomial Option Pricing Model, it was actually Black and Scholes who discovered this important insight while deriving their model. To see how the replicating portfolio is constructed in the Black-Scholes model, recall from the Binomial Option Pricing Model that the price of a call option is given by the price of the replicating portfolio, as shown in Eq. 21.6:

$$C = S\Delta + B$$

FINANCIAL CRISIS
THE VIX INDEX

The use of the Black-Scholes option pricing formula to compute implied volatility has become so ubiquitous that the Chicago Board Options Exchange introduced an index in January 1990 that tracked the one-month implied volatility of options written on the S&P 500 Index. Quoted in percent per annum, this index has since become one of the most-cited measures of market volatility. Because it characterizes the level of investor uncertainty, it is often referred to as the "fear index."

As the figure below shows, before the 2008 financial crisis the index had averaged about 20% since its inception and had never been over 46%. It was just 16% as recently as May 2008.

But the VIX jumped dramatically in the wake of Lehman Brothers default on September 15, and by the end of October 2008 it had quadrupled, reaching an intraday high of nearly 90%, almost twice its previous all-time high. The index remained at these historically high levels for several months, reflecting the unprecedented uncertainty that accompanied the financial crisis. As this uncertainty dissipated in 2009, the index began to drop. By mid-June 2009 it was around 25%, reflecting renewed investor confidence in markets. However, as turmoil in European markets (in particular Greece) increased, the VIX again rose above 40% in May 2010.

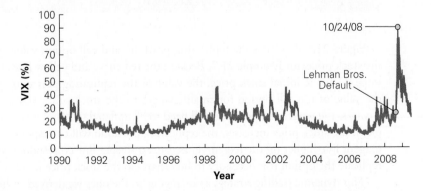

Source: Yahoo! Finance (http://finance.yahoo.com/q/bc?s=%5Evix).

Comparing this expression to the Black-Scholes formula from Eq. 21.7 gives the amount of stock and bonds in the Black-Scholes replicating portfolio:

Black-Scholes Replicating Portfolio of a Call Option

$$\Delta = N(d_1)$$
$$B = -PV(K)N(d_2) \tag{21.12}$$

Recall that $N(d)$ is the cumulative normal distribution function; that is, it has a minimum value of 0 and a maximum value of 1. So Δ is between 0 and 1, and B is between $-K$ and 0. The **option delta**, Δ, has a natural interpretation: It is the change in the price of the option given a $1 change in the price of the stock. Because Δ is always less than 1, the change in the call price is always less than the change in the stock price.

EXAMPLE 21.7

COMPUTING THE REPLICATING PORTFOLIO

Problem

PNA Systems pays no dividends and has a current stock price of $10 per share. If its returns have a volatility of 40% and the risk-free rate is 5%, what portfolio would you hold today to replicate a one-year at-the-money call option on the stock?

Solution

We can apply the Black-Scholes formula with $S = 10$, $PV(K) = 10/1.05 = 9.524$, and

$$d_1 = \frac{\ln[S/PV(K)]}{\sigma\sqrt{T}} + \frac{\sigma\sqrt{T}}{2} = \frac{\ln(10/9.524)}{40\%} + \frac{40\%}{2} = 0.322$$

$$d_2 = d_1 - \sigma\sqrt{T} = 0.322 - 0.40 = -0.078$$

From Eq. 21.12, the replicating portfolio for the option is

$$\Delta = N(d_1) = N(0.322) = 0.626$$

$$B = -PV(K)N(d_2) = -9.524 \times N(-0.078) = -4.47$$

That is, we should buy 0.626 shares of the PNA stock, and borrow $4.47, for a total cost of $10(0.626) - 4.47 = $1.79, which is the Black-Scholes value of the call option.

Figure 21.6 illustrates the replicating portfolio and call option value, as a function of the stock price, for Example 21.7. Because the red curve and yellow line are tangent (with slope Δ) at the initial stock price, the value of the replicating portfolio will approximate the value of the call option for small changes to the stock price. But as the stock price changes, the replicating portfolio will need to be updated to maintain accuracy. For example, if the stock price increases, the replicating portfolio will correspond to a new, steeper tangent line higher on the red curve. Because a steeper line corresponds to a higher Δ, to replicate the option it is necessary to buy shares as the stock price increases.

This dynamic trading strategy is analogous to the ones we derived earlier for the Binomial Option Pricing Model. In the binomial model, we were able to replicate the payoff

FIGURE 21.6

Replicating Portfolio for the Call Option in Example 21.7
The replicating portfolio has the same initial value as the call option, and the same initial sensitivity to the stock price (given by Δ). Because the red curve and yellow line are tangent, the value of the replicating portfolio will approximate the value of the call option for small changes to the stock price. But to maintain accuracy, the replicating portfolio must be updated as the stock price changes.

of an option because we only needed to match two of its payoffs at any time. The great insight of Black, Scholes, and Merton was that if we can update our portfolio continuously, we can replicate an option on the stock by constantly adjusting our portfolio to remain on a line that is tangent to the value of the option.

Notice that the replicating portfolio of a call option always consists of a long position in the stock and a short position in the bond; in other words, the replicating portfolio is a leveraged position in the stock. Because a leveraged position in a stock is riskier than the stock itself, this implies that call options on a positive-beta stock are *more* risky than the underlying stock and therefore have higher returns and higher betas.

We can also derive the replicating portfolio for a put option. Comparing the Black-Scholes price of a put from Eq. 21.9 with Eq. 21.6 gives

Black-Scholes Replicating Portfolio of a Put Option

$$\Delta = -[1 - N(d_1)]$$
$$B = PV(K)[1 - N(d_2)] \tag{21.13}$$

In this case, Δ is between -1 and 0, and B is between 0 and K. Thus the replicating portfolio of a put option always consists of a long position in the bond and a short position in the stock, implying that put options on a positive-beta stock will have a negative beta.

CONCEPT CHECK

1. What are the inputs of the Black-Scholes option pricing formula?

2. What is the implied volatility of a stock?

3. How does the delta of a call option change as the stock price increases?

21.3 RISK-NEUTRAL PROBABILITIES

In both the binomial and Black-Scholes pricing models, we do not need to know the probability of each possible future stock price to calculate the option price. But what if we did know these probabilities? In that case we could calculate the price of the option as we have done for other financial assets: We could calculate the expected payoff of the option and discount it at the appropriate cost of capital. The drawback of this approach is that even if we know the probabilities, it is very difficult to estimate the cost of capital for a particular asset, and options are no exception. There is, however, one case in which the cost of capital can be precisely estimated. If all market participants were risk neutral, then *all* financial assets (including options) would have the same cost of capital—the risk-free rate of interest. Let's consider that scenario and see its implications for option prices.

A RISK-NEUTRAL TWO-STATE MODEL

Imagine a world consisting of only risk-neutral investors, and consider the two-state example in Section 21.1 in the risk-neutral world. Recall that the stock price today is equal to $50. In one period it will either go up by $10 or go down by $10, and the one-period risk-free rate of interest is 6%. Let ρ be the probability that the stock price will increase, which means $(1 - \rho)$ is the probability that it will go down. The value of the stock today must equal the present value of the expected price next period discounted at the risk-free rate:

$$50 = \frac{60\rho + 40(1 - \rho)}{1.06} \tag{21.14}$$

This equation is solved with $\rho = 65\%$. Because we now know the probability of each state, we can price the call by calculating the present value of its expected payoff next period. Recall that the call option had an exercise price of $50, so it will be worth either $10 or nothing at expiration. The present value of the expected payouts is

$$\frac{10(0.65) + 0(1 - 0.65)}{1.06} = 6.13 \tag{21.15}$$

This is precisely the value we calculated in Section 21.1 using the Binomial Option Pricing Model where we did *not* assume that investors were risk neutral. It is not a coincidence. Because no assumption on the risk preferences of investors is necessary to calculate the option price using either the binomial model or the Black-Scholes formula, the models must work for any set of preferences, *including* risk-neutral investors.

IMPLICATIONS OF THE RISK-NEUTRAL WORLD

Let's take a step back and consider the importance of the conclusion that if we use the binomial model or Black-Scholes model to price options, we do not need to make any assumption regarding investor risk preferences, the probability of each state, or the stock's expected return. These models *give the same option price no matter what the actual risk preferences and expected stock returns are.* To understand how these two settings can be consistent with the same prices for securities note that,

- In the real world, investors are risk averse. Thus, the expected return of a typical stock includes a positive risk premium to compensate investors for risk.
- In the hypothetical risk-neutral world, investors do not require compensation for risk. So for the stock price to be the same as in the real world, investors must be more pessimistic. Thus, stocks that in reality have expected returns above the risk-free rate, when evaluated using these more pessimistic probabilities have expected returns that equal the risk-free rate.

In other words, the ρ in Eqs. 21.14 and 21.15 is not the actual probability of the stock price increasing. Rather, it represents how the actual probability would have to be adjusted to keep the stock price the same in a risk-neutral world. For this reason, we refer to ρ and $(1 - \rho)$ as **risk-neutral probabilities**. These risk-neutral probabilities are known by other names as well: **state-contingent prices**, **state prices**, or **martingale prices**.

To illustrate, suppose the stock considered above, with a current price of $50, will increase to $60 with a true probability of 75%, or fall to $40 with a true probability of 25%:

This stock's true expected return is therefore

$$\frac{60 \times 0.75 + 40 \times 0.25}{50} - 1 = 10\%$$

Given the risk-free interest rate of 6%, this stock has a 4% risk premium. But as we calculated earlier in Eq. 21.14, the risk-neutral probability that the stock will increase is $\rho = 65\%$, which is less than the true probability. Thus the expected return of the stock in the risk-neutral world is $(60 \times 0.65 + 40 \times 0.35)/50 - 1 = 6\%$ (equal to the risk-free rate). To ensure that all assets in the risk-neutral world have an expected return equal to the risk-free rate, relative to the true probabilities, the risk-neutral probabilities overweight the bad states and underweight the good states.

RISK-NEUTRAL PROBABILITIES AND OPTION PRICING

We can exploit the insight that if the stock price dynamics are the same in the risk-neutral and risk-averse worlds, the option prices must be the same, to develop another technique for pricing options. Consider again the general binomial stock price tree:

First we can compute the risk-neutral probability that makes the stock's expected return equal to the risk-free interest rate:

$$\frac{\rho S_u + (1-\rho)S_d}{S} - 1 = r_f$$

Solving this equation for the risk-neutral probability ρ we get

$$\rho = \frac{(1+r_f)S - S_d}{S_u - S_d} \tag{21.16}$$

We can then compute the value of the option by computing its expected payoff using the risk-neutral probabilities, and discount the expected payoff at the risk-free interest rate.

EXAMPLE 21.8 | **OPTION PRICING WITH RISK-NEUTRAL PROBABILITIES**

Problem

Using Narver Network Systems stock from Example 21.2, imagine all investors are risk neutral and calculate the probability of every state in the next two years. Use these probabilities to calculate the price of a two-year call option on Narver Network Systems stock with a strike price $60. Then price a two-year European put option with the same strike price.

Solution

The binomial tree in the three-state example is

First we use Eq. 21.16 to compute the risk-neutral probability that the stock price will increase. At time 0 we have

$$\rho = \frac{(1+r_f)S - S_d}{S_u - S_d} = \frac{(1.03)50 - 45}{60 - 45} = 0.433$$

Because the stock has the same returns (up 20% or down 10%) at each date, we can check that the risk-neutral probability is the same at each date as well.

Consider the call option with a strike price of $60. This call pays $12 if the stock goes up twice, and zero otherwise. The risk-neutral probability that the stock will go up twice is 0.433×0.433, so the call option has an expected payoff of

$$0.433 \times 0.433 \times \$12 = \$2.25$$

We compute the current price of the call option by discounting this expected payoff at the risk-free rate: $C = \$2.25/1.03^2 = \$2.12$.

Consider next the European put option with a strike price of $60. The put ends up in-the-money if the stock goes down twice, if it goes up and then down, or if it goes down and then up. Because the risk-neutral probability of a drop in the stock price is $1 - 0.433 = 0.567$, the expected payoff of the put option is

$$0.567 \times 0.567 \times \$19.5 + 0.433 \times 0.567 \times \$6 + 0.567 \times 0.433 \times \$6 = \$9.21$$

The value of the put today is therefore $P = \$9.21/1.03^2 = \$8.68$, which is the price we calculated in Example 21.2.

As the calculation of the put price in Example 21.8 makes clear, by using the probabilities in the risk-neutral world we can price any **derivative security**—that is, any security whose payoff depends solely on the prices of other marketed assets. After we have constructed the tree and calculated the probabilities in the risk-neutral world, we can use them to price the derivative by simply discounting its expected payoff (using the risk-neutral probabilities) at the risk-free rate.

The risk-neutral pricing method is the basis for a common technique for pricing derivative securities called **Monte Carlo simulation**. In this approach, the expected payoff of the derivative security is estimated by calculating its average payoff after simulating many random paths for the underlying stock price. In the randomization, the risk-neutral probabilities are used, and so the average payoff can be discounted at the risk-free rate to estimate the derivative security's value.

CONCEPT CHECK
1. What are risk-neutral probabilities?

2. Does the binominal model or Black-Scholes model assume that investors are risk neutral?

21.4 RISK AND RETURN OF AN OPTION

To measure the risk of an option, we must compute the option beta. The simplest way to do so is to compute the beta of the replicating portfolio. Recall that the beta of a portfolio is just the weighted average beta of the constituent securities that make up the portfolio. In this case the portfolio consists of $S \times \Delta$ dollars invested in the stock and B dollars invested in the bond, so the beta of an option is

$$\beta_{option} = \frac{S\Delta}{S\Delta + B}\beta_S + \frac{B}{S\Delta + B}\beta_B$$

where β_S is the stock's beta and β_B is the bond's beta. In this case the bond is riskless, so $\beta_B = 0$. Thus the option beta is

Beta of an Option

$$\beta_{option} = \frac{S\Delta}{S\Delta + B}\beta_S \qquad (21.17)$$

Recall that for a call option, Δ is greater than zero and B is less than zero. Thus, for a call written on a stock with positive beta, the beta of the call always exceeds the beta of the stock. For a put option, Δ is less than zero and B is greater than zero; thus the beta of a put option written on a positive-beta stock is always negative. This result should not be surprising. A put option is a hedge, so its price goes up when the stock price goes down.

EXAMPLE 21.9

BETA OF AN OPTION

Problem

Calculate the betas of the JetBlue call and put options in Example 21.3 and Example 21.4, assuming JetBlue's stock has a beta of 0.85.

Solution

From Example 21.3, the December 2009 $6 call option has a value of $C = \$0.50$ and a delta of $N(d_1) = 0.417$. Thus its beta is given by

$$\beta_{Call} = \frac{S\Delta}{S\Delta + B}\beta_{Stock} = \frac{S \times N(d_1)}{C}\beta_{Stock}$$

$$= \frac{5.03 \times 0.417}{0.50} \times 0.85 = 3.57$$

Similarly, the beta of the January 2010 $5 put option is given by

$$\beta_{Put} = \frac{S\Delta}{S\Delta + B}\beta_{Stock} = \frac{-S[1 - N(d_1)]}{P}\beta_{Stock}$$

$$= \frac{-5.03[1 - 0.599]}{0.87} \times 0.85 = -1.97$$

The expression $S\Delta/(S\Delta + B)$ is the ratio of the amount of money in the stock position in the replicating portfolio to the value of the replicating portfolio (or the option price); it is known as the **leverage ratio**. Figure 21.7 shows how the leverage ratio changes for puts and calls. As the figure shows, the magnitude of the leverage ratio for options can be very large, especially for out-of-the-money options. Thus, calls and puts on a positive-beta stock have very large positive and negative betas, respectively. Note also that as the stock price changes, the beta of an option will change, with its magnitude falling as the option goes in-the-money.

Recall that expected returns and beta are linearly related. Hence, out-of-the-money calls have the highest expected returns and out-of-the-money puts have the lowest

FIGURE 21.7

Leverage Ratios of Options
The leverage ratio for a call option is always greater than 1, but out-of-the-money calls have higher leverage ratios than in-the-money calls. Put leverage ratios are always negative, and out-of-the-money puts have more negative leverage ratios than in-the-money puts. Data shown are for one-year options on a stock with a 30% volatility, given a risk-free interest rate of 5%.

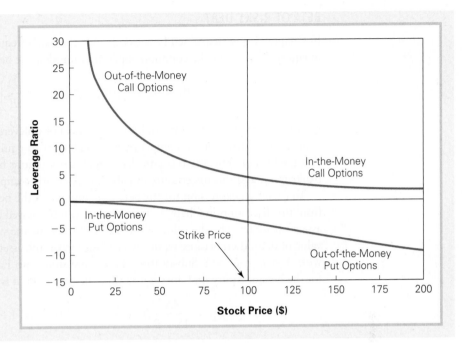

FIGURE 21.8

Security Market Line and Options
The figure shows how the expected return of different options are related.

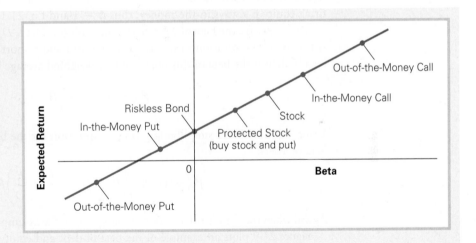

expected returns. The expected returns of different options are plotted on the security market line in Figure 21.8.

CONCEPT CHECK

1. Is the beta of a call greater or smaller than the beta of the underlying stock?

2. What is the leverage ratio of a call?

21.5 CORPORATE APPLICATIONS

We close this chapter by developing two important corporate applications of option pricing: unlevering the beta of equity and calculating the beta of risky debt, and deriving the approximation formula to value debt overhang that we introduced in Chapter 16.

BETA OF RISKY DEBT

In Chapter 14, we explained how to calculate the beta of equity from the unlevered beta of equity. If we make the common approximation that the beta of debt is zero, then

$$\beta_E = \beta_U + \frac{D}{E}(\beta_U - \beta_D) \approx \left(1 + \frac{D}{E}\right)\beta_U \qquad (21.18)$$

where β_E is the beta of equity and β_U is the beta of unlevered equity (or the beta of the firm's assets). However, for companies with high debt-to-equity ratios, the approximation that the beta of debt is zero is unrealistic; such corporations have a positive probability of bankruptcy, and this uncertainty usually has systematic components.

   To derive an expression for the beta of equity when the beta of debt is not zero, recall from the discussion in Chapter 20 that equity can be viewed as a call option on the firm's assets.[6] If we let A be the value of the firm's assets, E be the value of equity, and D be the value of debt, then because equity is a call option on the assets of the firm, $E = \Delta D + B$ with $A = E + D = S$. Substituting these expressions into Eq. 21.17 gives an expression for the beta of equity that does not assume the beta of debt is zero:

$$\beta_E = \frac{A\Delta}{A\Delta + B}\beta_U = \frac{(E + D)\Delta}{E}\beta_U = \Delta\left(1 + \frac{D}{E}\right)\beta_U \qquad (21.19)$$

where we have used the fact that $A = D + E$. Note that when the debt is risk free, the firm's equity is always in-the-money; thus $\Delta = 1$ and Eq. 21.19 reduces to Eq. 21.18.

   We can derive the beta of debt in a similar fashion. Debt, D, is equal to a portfolio consisting of a long position in the assets of the firm and a short position in its equity. The beta of debt is the beta of this portfolio (the weighted average beta):

$$\beta_D = \frac{A}{D}\beta_U - \frac{E}{D}\beta_E$$

Using Eq. 21.19 and simplifying gives an expression for the beta of debt in terms of the beta of assets:

$$\beta_D = (1 - \Delta)\frac{A}{D}\beta_U = (1 - \Delta)\left(1 + \frac{E}{D}\right)\beta_U \qquad (21.20)$$

Again, when the debt is riskless, $\Delta = 1$ and $\beta_D = 0$, the assumption we made in Eq. 21.18.

   Figure 21.9 plots an example of the beta of debt and equity as a function of the firm's leverage using Eq. 21.12. For simplicity, we have assumed that the firm's beta of assets is 1. For low levels of debt, the approximation that the beta of debt is zero works reasonably well. As the debt-to-equity ratio becomes larger, however, the beta of debt begins to rise above zero and the beta of equity no longer increases proportionally with the debt-equity ratio.

   In most applications, the beta of equity can be estimated. Using the beta of equity, we can calculate the beta of debt and the unlevered beta. For example, to unlever the beta, we can solve Eq. 21.19 for β_U:

$$\beta_U = \frac{\beta_E}{\Delta\left(1 + \dfrac{D}{E}\right)} \qquad (21.21)$$

---

6. The idea to view debt and equity as options was first developed by R. C. Merton in "On the Pricing of Corporate Debt: The Risk Structure of Interest Rates," *Journal of Finance* 29 (1974): 449–470.

FIGURE 21.9

Beta of Debt and Equity
The blue curve is the beta of equity and the red curve is the beta of debt as a function of the firm's debt-to-equity ratio. The black line shows the beta of equity when the beta of debt is assumed to be zero. The firm is assumed to hold five-year zero-coupon debt and reinvest all its earnings. (The firm's beta of assets is 1, the risk-free interest rate is 3% per year, and the volatility of assets is 30% per year.)

EXAMPLE 21.10

COMPUTING THE BETA OF DEBT

Problem

You would like to know the beta of debt for BB Industries. The value of BB's outstanding equity is $40 million, and you have estimated its beta to be 1.2. However, you cannot find enough market data to estimate the beta of its debt, so you decide to use the Black-Scholes formula to find an approximate value for the debt beta. BB has four-year zero-coupon debt outstanding with a face value of $100 million that currently trades for $75 million. BB pays no dividends and reinvests all of its earnings. The four-year risk-free rate of interest is currently 5.13%. What is the beta of BB's debt?

Solution

We can interpret BB's equity as a four-year call option on the firm's assets with a strike price of $100 million. The present value of the strike price is $100 million$/(1.0513)^4 = 81.86 million. The current market value of BB's assets is $40 + $75 = 115 million. Therefore, the implied volatility of BB's assets is equal to the implied volatility of a call option whose price is 40 when the stock price is 115 and the present value of the strike price is 81.86. Using trial and error, we find an implied volatility of about 25%. With this volatility, the delta of the call option is

$$\Delta = N(d_1) = N\left(\frac{\ln(115/81.86)}{0.25(2)} + 0.25\right) = 0.824$$

First we use Eq. 21.21 to solve for BB's unlevered beta:

$$\beta_U = \frac{\beta_E}{\Delta\left(1 + \dfrac{D}{E}\right)} = \frac{1.2}{0.824\left(1 + \dfrac{75}{40}\right)} = 0.51$$

We can then use Eq. 21.20 to estimate the beta of BB's debt:

$$\beta_D = (1 - \Delta)\left(1 + \frac{E}{D}\right)\beta_U = (1 - 0.824)\left(1 + \frac{40}{75}\right)0.51 = 0.14$$

DEBT OVERHANG

Recall, from Chapter 16, how the effect of debt overhang impacts investment policy. When a levered firm makes an investment financed entirely with equity, the equity holders incur the initial investment, I, but must share the benefits of the investment with debt holders. Consequently, equity holders might choose to turn down positive NPV investments. We can use option theory to measure the extent of this problem.

Assume that taking on the investment does not increase the volatility of the firm's assets. Recall that the option delta, δ, measures the change in the value of the option for a $1 change in the value of the underlying security. The investment opportunity will increase the value of the firm's assets by the amount of the investment plus the NPV of the opportunity: $I + NPV$. So because equity is an option on the assets of the firm, the value of equity will go up by $\Delta(I + NPV)$. Thus equity holders will only undertake the investment if

$$\Delta(I + NPV) - I > 0$$

Simplifying this expression gives

$$\frac{NPV}{I} > \frac{1 - \Delta}{\Delta} \tag{21.22}$$

Notice that when debt is riskless, $\Delta = 1$, equity holders invest whenever the NPV is positive. Alternatively, when there is no possibility of avoiding bankruptcy $\Delta = 0$, and equity holders choose never to invest.

We can calculate the ratio $(1 - \Delta)/\Delta$ explicitly as we did in Example 21.10, by using the Black-Scholes formulae. Alternatively, we could also calculate this ratio from the beta of debt and equity. Note that Eqs 21.19 and 21.20 can be used to provide

$$\frac{1 - \Delta}{\Delta} = \frac{\dfrac{D}{A}\dfrac{\beta_D}{\beta_U}}{\dfrac{E}{A}\dfrac{\beta_E}{\beta_U}} = \frac{D}{E}\frac{\beta_D}{\beta_E} \tag{21.23}$$

Combining Eqs. 21.22 and 21.23 gives the approximation we introduced in Chapter 16:

$$\frac{NPV}{I} > \frac{D}{E}\frac{\beta_D}{\beta_E}$$

Equity holders will only invest if the profitability index exceeds the ratio of the riskiness of debt to equity multiplied by the debt to equity ratio.

CONCEPT CHECK

1. How can we estimate the beta of debt?

2. Can the beta of debt exceed the beta of the firm's assets?

SUMMARY

1. An option can be valued using a portfolio that replicates the payoffs of the option in different states. The Binomial Option Pricing Model assumes two possible states for the next time period, given today's state.

2. The value of an option is the value of the portfolio that replicates its payoffs. The replicating portfolio will hold the underlying asset and risk-free debt, and will need to be rebalanced over time.

3. The replicating portfolio for the Binomial Option Pricing Model is

$$\Delta = \frac{C_u - C_d}{S_u - S_d} \quad \text{and} \quad B = \frac{C_d - S_d\Delta}{1 + r_f} \tag{21.5}$$

4. Given the replicating portfolio, the value of the option is

$$C = S\Delta + B \tag{21.6}$$

5. The Black-Scholes option pricing formula for the price of a call option on a non-dividend-paying stock is

$$C = S \times N(d_1) - PV(K) \times N(d_2) \tag{21.7}$$

where $N(d)$ is the cumulative normal distribution and

$$d_1 = \frac{\ln[S/PV(K)]}{\sigma\sqrt{T}} + \frac{\sigma\sqrt{T}}{2}$$

$$d_2 = d_1 - \sigma\sqrt{T} \tag{21.8}$$

6. Only five input parameters are required to price a call: the stock price, the strike price, the exercise date, the risk-free rate, and the volatility of the stock. We do not need to know the expected return on the stock to calculate the option price.

7. The Black-Scholes option pricing formula for the price of a European put option on a non-dividend-paying stock is

$$P = PV(K)[1 - N(d_2)] - S[1 - N(d_1)] \tag{21.9}$$

8. We can evaluate a European option on a stock that pays dividends using the Black-Scholes formula with S^x in place of S where

$$S^x = S - PV(Div) \tag{21.10}$$

If the stock pays a (compounded) dividend yield of q prior to the expiration date, then

$$S^x = S/(1 + q) \tag{21.11}$$

9. The Black-Scholes replicating portfolio is
   a. For a call option on a non-dividend-paying stock

$$\Delta = N(d_1) \quad \text{and} \quad B = -PV(K)N(d_2) \tag{21.12}$$

   b. For a European put option on a non-dividend-paying stock

$$\Delta = -[1 - N(d_1)] \quad \text{and} \quad B = PV(K)[1 - N(d_2)] \tag{21.13}$$

   c. The replicating portfolio must be continuously updated to remain tangent to the option value

10. Risk-neutral probabilities are the probabilities under which the expected return of all securities equals the risk-free rate. These probabilities can be used to price any other asset for which the payoffs in each state are known.

11. In a binomial tree, the risk-neutral probability r that the stock price will increase is given by

$$\rho = \frac{(1 + r_f)S - S_d}{S_u - S_d} \qquad (21.16)$$

12. The price of any derivative security can be obtained by discounting the expected cash flows computed using the risk-neutral probabilities at the risk-free rate.

13. The beta of an option can also be calculated by computing the risk of its replicating portfolio. For stocks with positive betas, calls will have larger betas than the underlying stock, while puts will have negative betas. The magnitude of the option beta is higher for options that are further out-of-the-money.

14. When debt is risky, the beta of equity increases with leverage according to

$$\beta_E = \frac{A\Delta}{A\Delta + B}\beta_U = \frac{(E + D)\Delta}{E}\beta_U = \Delta\left(1 + \frac{D}{E}\right)\beta_U \qquad (21.19)$$

We can also use Eq. 21.19 to solve for the firm's unlevered beta and debt beta, given an estimate of the beta and delta of the firm's equity.

KEY TERMS

Binomial Option Pricing Model *p. 747*
binomial tree *p. 747*
Black-Scholes Option Pricing
    Model *p. 755*
cumulative normal distribution *p. 755*
derivative security *p. 769*
dynamic trading strategy *p. 753*
executive stock option (ESO) *p. 760*
implied volatility *p. 762*

leverage ratio *p. 770*
martingale prices *p. 767*
Monte Carlo simulation *p. 769*
option delta *p. 764*
replicating portfolio *p. 747*
risk-neutral probabilities *p. 767*
state prices *p. 767*
state-contingent prices *p. 767*

PROBLEMS

The problems marked in green can be found on MyFinanceLab at www.myfinancelab.com. Visit your MyFinanceLab for additional practice. An asterisk (*) indicates problems with a higher level of difficulty. Additional readings for this chapter may be found in the Textbook Resources section on MyFinanceLab.

The Binomial Option Pricing Model

1. The current price of Estelle Corporation stock is $25. In each of the next two years, this stock price will either go up by 20% or go down by 20%. The stock pays no dividends. The one-year risk-free interest rate is 6% and will remain constant. Using the binomial model, calculate the price of a one-year call option on Estelle stock with a strike price of $25.

2. Using the information in Problem 1, use the binomial model to calculate the price of a one-year put option on Estelle stock with a strike price of $25.

3. The current price of Natasha Corporation stock is $6. In each of the next two years, this stock price can either go up by $2.50 or go down by $2. The stock pays no dividends. The one-year risk-free interest rate is 3% and will remain constant. Using the binomial model, calculate the price of a two-year call option on Natasha stock with a strike price of $7.

4. Using the information in Problem 3, use the binomial model to calculate the price of a two-year European put option on Natasha stock with a strike price of $7.

5. Suppose the option in Example 21.1 actually sold in the market for $8.00. Describe a trading strategy that yields arbitrage profits.

*6. Suppose the option in Example 21.2 actually sold today for $5.00. You do not know what the option will trade for next period. Describe a trading strategy that will yield arbitrage profits.

7. Eagletron's current stock price is $10. Suppose that over the current year, the stock price will either increase by 100 percent or decrease by 50 percent. Also, the risk-free rate is 25 percent (EAR).

    a. What is the value today of a one-year at-the-money European put option on Eagletron stock?

    b. What is the value today of a one-year European put option on Eagletron stock with a strike price of $20?

    c. Suppose the put options in parts a and b could be exercised either immediately or in one year. What would their values be in this case?

8. What is the highest possible value for the delta of a call option? What is the lowest possible value? (*Hint:* See Figure 21.1.)

*9. Hema Corp. is an all-equity firm with a current market value of $1,000 million (i.e., $1 billion) and will be worth $900 million or $1,400 million in one year. The risk-free interest rate is 5% (EAR). Suppose Hema Corp. issues zero-coupon, one-year debt with a face value of $1,050 million, and uses the proceeds to pay a special dividend to shareholders. Assuming perfect capital markets, use the binomial model to answer the following:

    a. What are the payoffs of the firm's debt in one year?

    b. What is the value today of the debt today?

    c. What is the yield on the debt (EAR)?

    d. Using Modigliani-Miller: What is the value of Hema's equity before the dividend is paid? What is the value of equity just after the dividend is paid?

    e. Show that the ex-dividend value of Hema's equity is consistent with the binomial model. What is the Δ of the equity, when viewed as a call option on the firm's assets?

*10. Consider the setting of Problem 9. Suppose that in the event Hema Corp. defaults, $90 million of its value will be lost to bankruptcy costs. Assume there are no other market imperfections.

    a. What is the present value of these bankruptcy costs, and what is their delta with respect to the firm's assets?

    b. In this case, what is the value and yield of Hema's debt?

    c. In this case, what is the value of Hema's equity before the dividend is paid? What is the value of equity just after the dividend is paid?

The Black-Scholes Option Pricing Model

11. Roslin Robotics stock has a volatility of 30% and a current stock price of $60 per share. Roslin pays no dividends. The risk-free interest rate is 5% (EAR). Determine the Black-Scholes value of a one-year, at-the-money call option on Roslin stock.

12. Rebecca is interested in purchasing a European call on a hot new stock, Up Inc. The call has a strike price of $100 and expires in 90 days. The current price of Up stock is $120, and the stock has a standard deviation of 40% per year. The risk-free interest rate is 6.38% (EAR).

   a. Using the Black-Scholes formula, compute the price of the call.

   b. Use put-call parity to compute the price of the put with the same strike and expiration date.

13. Using the data in Table 21.1, compare the price on July 24, 2009, of the following options on JetBlue stock to the price predicted by the Black-Scholes formula. Assume that the standard deviation of JetBlue stock is 65% per year and that the short-term risk-free rate of interest is 1% (EAR).

   a. December 2009 call option with a $5.00 strike price

   b. December 2009 put option with a $6.00 strike price

   c. March 2010 put option with a $7.00 strike price

14. Using the market data in Table 20.5 and a risk-free rate of 4.5% (EAR), calculate the two-year implied volatility of Buffin stock in December 2009, using the 310 January 2012 call option.

15. Using the implied volatility you calculated in Problem 14 and the information in that problem, use the Black-Scholes option pricing formula to calculate the value of the 340 January 2012 call option.

16. Plot the value of a two-year European put option with a strike price of $20 on World Wide Plants as a function of the stock price. Recall that World Wide Plants has a constant dividend yield of 5% per year and that its volatility is 20% per year. The two-year risk-free rate of interest is 4% (EAR). Explain why there is a region where the option trades for less than its intrinsic value.

17. Consider the at-the-money call option on Roslin Robotics evaluated in Problem 11. Suppose the call option is not available for trade in the market. You would like to replicate a long position in 1000 call options.

   a. What portfolio should you hold today?

   b. Suppose you purchase the portfolio in part a. If Roslin stock goes up in value to $62 per share today, what is the value of this portfolio now? It is within what % of the value of 1000 call options?

   c. After the stock price change in part b, how should you adjust your portfolio to continue to replicate the options?

18. Consider again the at-the-money call option on Roslin Robotics evaluated in Problem 11. What is the impact on the value of this call option of each of the following changes (evaluated separately)?

   a. The stock price increases by $1 to $61.

   b. The volatility of the stock goes up by 1% to 31%.

   c. Interest rates go up by 1% to 6%.

   d. One month elapses, with no other change.

   e. The firm announces a $1 dividend, paid immediately.

Risk-Neutral Probabilities

19. Harbin Manufacturing has 10 million shares outstanding with a current share price of $20 per share. In one year, the share price is equally likely to be $30 or $18. The risk-free interest rate is 5% (EAR).

   a. What is the expected return on Harbin stock?

   b. What is the risk-neutral probability that Harbin's stock price will increase?

in the context of a few stylized examples, the three most common options that occur in capital budgeting: the option to wait for the optimal time to invest, the option to grow in the future, and the option to abandon a poorly performing project. We then consider two important applications: deciding the order in which to complete a staged investment opportunity and deciding which of two mutually exclusive projects of different lengths is the wisest investment. Finally, we explain rules of thumb that managers often use to account for real options in the capital budgeting decision.

22.1 REAL VERSUS FINANCIAL OPTIONS

The financial options we have studied in the previous two chapters give their holders the right to buy, or sell, a traded asset such as a stock. Amgen's option to invest in research and development for new products is an example of a different type of option, called a **real option**. A real option is the right to take a particular business decision, such as make a capital investment. A key distinction between a real option and a financial option is that real options, and the underlying assets on which they are based, are often not traded in competitive markets; for example, there is no market for Amgen's R&D in a particular drug.

Despite this distinction, many of the principles that we developed in the last two chapters for financial options also apply to real options. In particular, because real options allow a decision maker to choose the most attractive alternative after new information has been learned, the presence of real options adds value to an investment opportunity. This value can be substantial, especially in environments with a great deal of uncertainty. Thus, to make an investment decision correctly, the value of these options must be included in the decision-making process.

Our approach to capital budgeting thus far has focused on the initial investment decision without explicitly considering future decisions that may need to be made over the life of a project. Rather, we assumed that our forecast of the project's expected future cash flows already incorporated the effect of future decisions that would be made. In this chapter, we take a closer look at how these cash flows, and therefore the NPV of a project, are determined when a firm must react to changing business conditions over the life of a project. To do so, we begin by introducing a new analytical tool called a decision tree.

CONCEPT CHECK

1. What is the difference between a real option and a financial option?
2. Why does a real option add value to an investment decision?

22.2 DECISION TREE ANALYSIS

Most investment projects allow for the possibility of reevaluating the decision to invest at a later point in time. Let's illustrate with a simple example. Suppose Anjali is financing part of her MBA education by running a small business. She purchases goods on eBay and resells the merchandise at farmers' markets and swap meets. Anjali would like to run her business more efficiently, so she decides to use some of the knowledge she has gained in graduate school. Swap meets and farmers' markets typically charge her $500 in advance to set up her small booth. Ignoring the cost of the booth, if she goes to every meet, her average profit on the goods that she sells is $1100 per meet. Let's represent Anjali's options

FIGURE 22.1

FIGURE 22.1

Anjali's Choices
The optimal decision appears in blue.

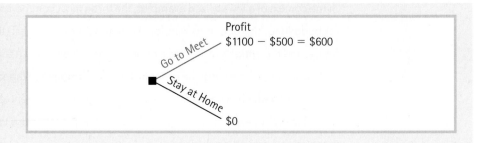

Profit
$1100 − $500 = $600

Go to Meet

Stay at Home

$0

with regard to setting up her booth on a **decision tree**, a graphical representation of future decisions and uncertainty resolution.

Figure 22.1 represents Anjali's initial decision tree. The box at the node (represented by a square) indicates that Anjali must decide which branch to follow. Note that there is an important difference between the decision tree in Figure 22.1 and the binomial trees in Chapter 21. There, the uncertainty was not under the control of the decision maker. Here, Anjali decides how the uncertainty is resolved. Because the NPV of setting up a booth is $1100 − $500 = $600, the optimal decision (shown in blue) would be to set up the booth.

MAPPING UNCERTAINTIES ON A DECISION TREE

While going to the swap meet appears to be the optimal decision, Anjali is aware that attendance at swap meets and farmer's markets is weather dependent: In good weather her profits are much higher (usually around $1500); in bad weather, which occurs about 25% of the time, business is so slow that she usually drops her prices and, including her setup costs, averages a small loss of about $100. This adds another element of uncertainty for Anjali's consideration. Figure 22.2 represents this uncertainty on a decision tree.

Notice that the decision tree now contains two kinds of nodes: **decision nodes** that are marked with square boxes (pay the fee and go to the meet versus do nothing) and **information nodes** in which uncertainty is involved that is out of the control of the decision maker (rain or sunshine) that are marked with circles. Figure 22.2 also indicates the point at which each cash flow is committed. Because the booth fee is paid in advance, the cash flow is incurred before Anjali finds out about the weather.

Notice, however, that the decision tree in Figure 22.2 is not a full description of Anjali's alternatives. Although the fee for the booth is sunk once Anjali finds out about the weather, she is not forced to go to the meet, sit in the booth, and lose the additional $100. That is, it does not make sense for her to commit to go to the swap meet *before* she finds

FIGURE 22.2

Effect of the Weather on Anjali's Options
The optimal decision appears in blue.

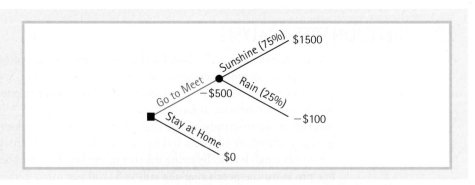

Sunshine (75%) $1500

Go to Meet
−$500

Rain (25%)

−$100

Stay at Home

$0

FIGURE 22.3

Anjali's Decision Tree When She Can Observe the Weather Before She Makes the Decision to Go to the Meet

Her optimal decisions are shown in blue.

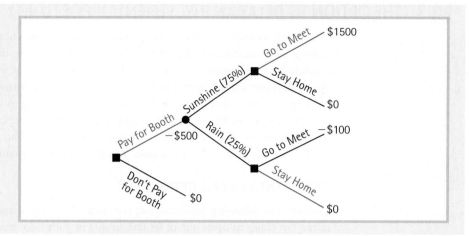

REAL OPTIONS

out what the weather is like. Figure 22.3 represents her decision tree when Anjali optimally chooses to wait until the day of the meet to decide whether she will go: If it rains, she optimally chooses to stay at home. The $500 loss for the booth is unavoidable, but in bad weather she does not incur the additional $100 loss at the meet.

The difference between the decision trees in Figures 22.2 and 22.3 is an example of a real option. Anjali has the option to wait until she finds out what the weather is like before she decides whether she should go to the meet. This flexibility has value (she can avoid a further $100 loss). By committing ahead of time, she gives up this value.

How valuable is the real option to Anjali? Let's assume for simplicity that Anjali is risk neutral about the risk from the weather, and that the time delays are short so that we can ignore discounting. We can compute the value of the real option by comparing her expected profit *without the real option* to wait until the weather is revealed (Figure 22.1 or 22.2) to the value *with the option* to wait (Figure 22.3). If Anjali commits to go regardless of the weather, her expected profit is $0.75 \times \$1500 + 0.25 \times (-\$100) = \$1100$, her average profit if she goes to every meet. However, if she goes only when the weather is good, her profit is $0.75 \times \$1500 = \$1125$. The value of the real option is the difference, $\$1125 - \$1100 = \$25$.

Should Anjali pay for the booth? Let's assume she has to pay for the booth only the day before the meet, so we can ignore the time value of money. Then the NPV of paying for the booth is $\$1125 - \$500 = \$625$, which is positive. Thus Anjali should always pay for the booth.

Many corporate investment decisions contain real options like Anjali's. Unfortunately, in most cases these options are investment specific, so it is impossible to present a general theory of real options. Instead, we will concentrate on the three kinds of real options that are most frequently encountered in practice: (1) the option to delay an investment opportunity, (2) the option to grow, and (3) the option to abandon an investment opportunity.

CONCEPT CHECK

1. What is the difference between an information node and a decision node on a decision tree?

2. What makes a real option valuable?

22.3 THE OPTION TO DELAY AN INVESTMENT OPPORTUNITY

The simple example of Anjali's swap meet illustrates how choosing the optimal time to commit to an investment opportunity has value. In this case the decision about when to commit (go to the swap meet) is easy: Once the booth is paid for, there is no cost to waiting to find out about the weather. In the real world, of course, there is often a cost to delaying an investment decision. For example, by choosing to wait for more information you give up any profits the project might generate in the interim. In addition, a competitor could use the delay to develop a competing product. The decision to wait therefore involves a tradeoff between these costs and the benefit of remaining flexible.

INVESTMENT AS A CALL OPTION

Consider the following investment opportunity. You have negotiated a deal with a major restaurant chain to open one of its restaurants in your hometown. The terms of the contract specify that you must open the restaurant either immediately or in exactly one year. If you do neither, you lose the right to open the restaurant at all. Figure 22.4 shows these choices on a decision tree.

You are wondering how much you should pay for this opportunity. It will cost you $5 million to open the restaurant, whether you open it now or in one year. If you open the restaurant immediately, you expect it to generate $600,000 in free cash flow the first year. While future cash flows will vary with the consumer tastes and the state of the economy, on average these cash flows are expected to grow at a rate of 2% per year. The appropriate cost of capital for this investment is 12%, so that you estimate the value of the restaurant, if it were open today, would be

$$V = \frac{\$600{,}000}{12\% - 2\%} = \$6 \text{ million} \tag{22.1}$$

You also double-check this value using comparables. Suppose there exists a publicly traded firm operating equivalent franchises elsewhere in the province, and this firm provides an essentially perfect comparable for your investment. This firm has an enterprise value equal to 10 times its free cash flow, leading to an equivalent valuation.

Thus, the NPV of opening the restaurant immediately is $1 million, implying that the contract is worth at least $1 million. But given the flexibility you have to delay opening for one year, should you be willing to pay more? And when should you open the restaurant?

FIGURE 22.4

Restaurant Investment Opportunity

The restaurant must be opened either immediately or in exactly one year.

If we wait to open the restaurant, our decision can be based on new information about the restaurant's value, which can take on many values.

BLACK-SCHOLES OPTION VALUE PARAMETERS FOR EVALUATING A REAL OPTION TO INVEST

TABLE 22.1

Financial Option		Real Option	Example
Stock Price	S	Current Market Value of Asset	$6 million
Strike Price	K	Upfront Investment Required	$5 million
Expiration Date	T	Final Decision Date	1 year
Risk-Free Rate	r_f	Risk-Free Rate	5%
Volatility of Stock	σ	Volatility of Asset Value	40%
Dividend	Div	FCF Lost from Delay	$0.6 million

To answer these questions, we need to evaluate the NPV from waiting to open the restaurant. If we wait, then one year from now we will have the choice to invest $5 million to open the restaurant, or lose our right to open it and receive nothing. Thus, at that time, the decision is easy—we will open the restaurant if its value at that time, based on any new information about the economy and consumer tastes and trends, is above $5 million. But because trends in this industry can change quickly, there is a great deal of uncertainty as to what the expected cash flows and the value of the restaurant will be at that time.

We can incorporate this uncertainty into our estimate of the contract's value by recognizing that our payoff if we delay is equivalent to the payoff of a one-year European call option on the restaurant with a strike price of $5 million. Because the final payoff in one year is equivalent to a call option, we can use the techniques of Chapter 21 to value it. Suppose that the risk-free interest rate is 5%. We can estimate the volatility of the value of the restaurant by looking at the return volatility of the publicly traded comparable firm; suppose this volatility is 40%. Finally, if we wait to open the restaurant we will lose out on the $600,000 in free cash flow we would have earned in the first year. In terms of a financial option, this free cash flow is equivalent to a dividend paid by a stock—the holder of a call option does not receive the dividend until the option is exercised. Let's assume for now this cost is the only cost of delay—there are no additional costs in terms of lost growth of the restaurant cash flows, for example.

Table 22.1 shows how we can reinterpret the parameters for the Black-Scholes formula for financial options to evaluate this real option to invest in the restaurant. To apply the Black-Scholes formula, recall from Eq. 21.10 that we must compute the current value of the asset *without* the dividends that will be missed:

$$S^x = S - PV(Div) = \$6 \text{ million} - \frac{\$0.6 \text{ million}}{1.12} = \$5.46 \text{ million}$$

Note that we compute the present value of the lost cash flow using the project's cost of capital of 12%. Next we need to compute the present value of the cost to open the restaurant in one year. Because this cash flow is certain, we discount it at the risk-free rate:

$$PV(K) = \frac{\$5 \text{ million}}{1.05} = \$4.76 \text{ million}$$

Now we can compute the value of the call option to open the restaurant using Eqs. 21.7 and 21.8:

$$d_1 = \frac{\ln[S^x/PV(K)]}{\sigma\sqrt{T}} + \frac{\sigma\sqrt{T}}{2} = \frac{\ln(5.46/4.76)}{0.40} + 0.20 = 0.543$$

$$d_2 = d_1 - \sigma\sqrt{T} = 0.543 - 0.40 = 0.143$$

and therefore,

$$\begin{aligned}
C &= S^x N(d_1) - PV(K)N(d_2) \\
&= (\$5.46 \text{ million}) \times (0.706) - (\$4.76 \text{ million}) \times (0.557) \\
&= \$1.20 \text{ million}
\end{aligned} \tag{22.2}$$

The result in Eq. 22.2 states that the value today from waiting to invest in the restaurant next year, and only opening it if it is profitable to do so, is $1.20 million. This value exceeds the NPV of $1 million from opening the restaurant today. Thus, we are better off waiting to invest, and the value of the contract is $1.20 million.

What is the advantage of waiting in this case? If we wait, we will learn more about the likely success of the business by observing the performance of the comparable firm. Because our investment in the restaurant is not yet committed, we can cancel our plans if the popularity of the restaurant should decline. By opening the restaurant today, we give up this option to "walk away."[1]

Of course, there is a trade-off—if we wait to invest we give up the profits the restaurant will generate the first year. Whether it is optimal to invest today will depend on the magnitude of these lost profits, compared to the benefit of preserving our right to change our decision. To see this trade-off, suppose instead that the first-year free cash flow of the restaurant is projected to be $700,000, so that the current value of the restaurant is $7 million (using the $10\times$ multiple of the comparable, or a similar calculation to Eq. 22.1). In this case, the same analysis shows that the value of the call option would be $1.91 million. Because the value of opening the restaurant today is $7 million − $5 million = $2 million, in this case it would not be optimal to wait, and we would open the restaurant immediately.

Figure 22.5 plots the NPV of investing today (red line) and the value of waiting (yellow curve) as a function of today's value of the restaurant. As the figure makes clear, you should invest today (and give up the option to wait) only if the current value of the restaurant exceeds $6.66 million. Thus your optimal investment strategy is to invest today only if the NPV of the investment opportunity exceeds 6.66 − 5 = $1.66 million.

FACTORS AFFECTING THE TIMING OF INVESTMENT

This example illustrates how the real option to wait affects the capital budgeting decision. Without the option to choose the time when to invest, it is optimal to invest as long as NPV > 0. *But when you have the option of deciding when to invest, it is usually optimal to invest only when the NPV is substantially greater than zero.*

To understand this result, think of the timing decision as a choice between two mutually exclusive projects: (1) invest today or (2) wait. Faced with mutually exclusive choices, we should choose the project with the higher NPV. That is, we should invest today only if the NPV of investing today exceeds the value of the option of waiting. If we can always walk away from the project, the value of the option of waiting will be positive, and so the NPV of investing today must be even higher for us to choose not to wait.

---

1. A second benefit from waiting is that the cost of opening the restaurant is assumed to stay the same ($5 million), so the present value of this cost declines if we wait. This benefit is specific to the example. Depending on the scenario, the cost of investing may rise or fall over time.

FIGURE 22.5

The Decision to Invest in the Restaurant

The red line denotes the NPV of investing today. The yellow curve shows the value today of waiting one year to make the decision (i.e., the value of the call option). The black curve indicates the value of the contract, which gives us the option to invest today, in one year, or not at all. The optimal investment strategy is to invest today only if the value of the operating restaurant exceeds $6.66 million.

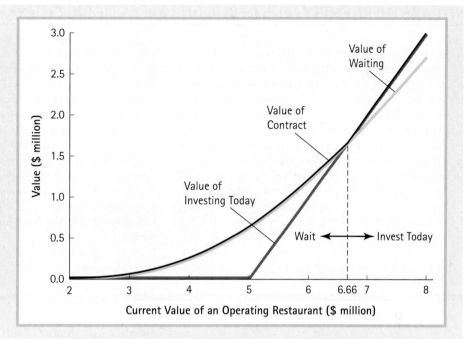

An interesting aspect of the restaurant investment opportunity is the value of the deal when the ongoing value of a restaurant is less than $5 million. In this case the NPV of opening a restaurant is negative, so without the option to wait the investment opportunity is worthless. But from Figure 22.5 we see that, with the option to wait, the investment opportunity is clearly not worthless. Even if the current value of the restaurant is $4 million (which means the NPV of investing today is −$1 million), the value of the opportunity is still worth about $248,000. That is, you would still be willing to pay up to $248,000 to sign the deal. Thus, given the option to wait, an investment that currently has a negative NPV can have a positive value.

Aside from the current NPV of the investment, what other factors affect the value of an investment and the decision to wait? From Figure 22.5 we can see that factors that increase the value of the call option will increase the benefit of waiting. Recall from our study of financial options in Chapters 20 and 21 that both the volatility and the dividends of the stock affect the value of a call option and the optimal time to exercise the call. These factors have their counterparts for real options:

- *Volatility:* By delaying an investment, we can base our decision on additional information. The option to wait is most valuable when there is a great deal of uncertainty regarding what the value of the investment will be in the future. If there is little uncertainty, the benefit of waiting is diminished.

- *Dividends:* Recall that absent dividends, it is not optimal to exercise a call option early. In the real option context, the dividends correspond to any value from the investment that we give up by waiting. It is always better to wait unless there is a cost to doing so. The greater the cost, the less attractive the option to delay becomes.[2]

---

2. Randall Morck, Eduardo Schwartz, and David Stangeland modelled the valuation of forestry resources using a real options framework. In their paper, they essentially had a negative dividend because the forest kept growing as long as the option to cut it was not exercised. Interested readers can consult R. Morck, E. Schwartz, and D. Stangeland, "The Valuation of Forestry Resources Under Stochastic Prices and Inventories," *Journal of Financial and Quantitative Analysis* 24:4 (1989): 473–488.

WHY ARE THERE EMPTY LOTS IN BUILT-UP AREAS OF BIG CITIES?

Have you ever wondered why there are empty lots (for example, a parking lot) right next to a multi-storey building in a city? After all, if it was optimal for the next-door neighbour to build a multi-storey building, why would someone choose to leave the lot empty? In many cases, the property taxes exceed the revenue generated by the empty lot, so by putting a revenue-producing building on the lot, the owner could turn a negative cash flow into a positive cash flow. However, by building on the lot, the owner gives up the option to construct a different building in the future. If there is a large amount of uncertainty about the kind of building to put on the lot, and if this uncertainty might be resolved in the future, it might

make sense to wait for additional information before breaking ground on a building. The value of waiting might exceed the net present value of building today.*

Notice a similar effect in the price of agricultural land that is close to big cities. Even though the land might produce the same agricultural revenue as similar land 100 kilometres away, the price of the land closer to the city is higher because the price reflects the possibility that the city might grow to the point that it becomes economical to put the land to non-agricultural use—that is, subdivide it and build single-family housing. The option to one day use the land in this way is reflected in the current price of the land.

*S. Titman, "Urban Land Prices Under Uncertainty," *American Economic Review* 75 (1985): 505–514, develops this idea.

EXAMPLE 22.1   EVALUATING THE DECISION TO WAIT

Problem

Suppose your current estimate of the restaurant's value is $6 million. What would be the value of the restaurant contract if the volatility of the restaurant's value were 25% rather than 40%? Alternatively, suppose the volatility is 40%, but waiting would lead competitors to expand and reduce the future free cash flows of the restaurant by 10%. What is the value of the contract in this case?

Solution

With a lower volatility of 25%, we have

$$d_1 = \frac{\ln[S^x/PV(K)]}{\sigma\sqrt{T}} + \frac{\sigma\sqrt{T}}{2} = \frac{\ln(5.46/4.76)}{0.25} + 0.125 = 0.674$$

$$d_2 = d_1 - \sigma\sqrt{T} = 0.674 - 0.25 = 0.424$$

The value of the call option is

$$C = S^x N(d_1) - PV(K)N(d_2)$$
$$= (\$5.46 \text{ million}) \times (0.750) - (\$4.76 \text{ million}) \times (0.664)$$
$$= \$0.93 \text{ million}$$

Therefore, it is better to invest immediately and get an NPV of $1 million, rather than wait. With the lower volatility, not enough information will be learned over the next year to justify the cost of waiting.

Now let's suppose the volatility is 40%, but waiting leads to increased competition. In this case, we should deduct the loss from increased competition as an additional "dividend" that we forgo by waiting. Thus,

$$S^x = S - PV(\text{First-Year FCF}) - PV(\text{Lost FCF from Competition})$$

$$= \left(\$6 \text{ million} - \frac{\$0.6 \text{ million}}{1.12} \right) \times (1 - 0.10) = \$4.92 \text{ million}$$

Now,

$$d_1 = \frac{\ln[S^x / PV(K)]}{\sigma \sqrt{T}} + \frac{\sigma \sqrt{T}}{2} = \frac{\ln(4.92/4.76)}{0.40} + 0.20 = 0.283$$

$$d_2 = d_1 - \sigma \sqrt{T} = 0.283 - 0.40 = -0.117$$

The value of the call option in this case is

$$C = S^x N(d_1) - PV(K)N(d_2)$$

$$= (\$4.92 \text{ million}) \times (0.611) - (\$4.76 \text{ million}) \times (0\ 453) = \$0.85 \text{ million}$$

Again, it would not be optimal to wait. In this case, despite the information to be gained, the costs associated with waiting are too high.

CONCEPT CHECK

1. What is the economic tradeoff between investing immediately or waiting?

2. How does the option to wait affect the capital budgeting decision?

FINANCIAL CRISIS
UNCERTAINTY, INVESTMENT, AND THE OPTION TO DELAY

In mid-September 2008, with the markets for investment capital frozen, the U.S. Treasury announced an unprecedented program to help unfreeze credit markets and stave off a deep recession. The well-founded worry was that the dysfunctional financial markets would effectively cut off business activity and thus precipitate a crash in the real economy. Despite the passage of a $750 billion relief program (the Troubled Asset Relief Program—TARP), the economy in the U.S. (and many economies around the world) plunged into the deepest recession in at least 20 years. What went wrong?

One likely factor was lawmakers' insensitivity to the effect of uncertainty on the real option to delay investment. Ironically, the original idea behind TARP was to reduce uncertainty by making a huge capital commitment to buy troubled assets and effectively signal the U.S. government's intention to stabilize markets. The hoped-for result was an increase in investment. Although interest rates did drop, markets failed to stabilize and an increase in investment did not materialize.

TARP failed in its primary mission to decrease uncertainty. Indeed, concerns about whether the program would be implemented and how it would be implemented contributed significantly to overall uncertainty in the economy, making the option to delay investment until the uncertainty was resolved more valuable. In the end, the combination of this increased uncertainty together with a gloomy economic forecast led to a 19.1% decline in business investment in the fourth quarter of 2008, the largest decline since 1975.

22.4 GROWTH AND ABANDONMENT OPTIONS

Imagine that you formed a corporation. Acting on behalf of this corporation, you signed the restaurant contract described in the last section. Assume the current value of an operating restaurant is $4 million, so the NPV of investing today is negative. If the corporation has no other assets, what is the value of the corporation? As we have already seen, even though it does not make sense to invest today, the value of the *contract* is $248,000 because it gives the corporation the option to open the restaurant in a year. Because the corporation owns this contract, it is worth $248,000. Even though the corporation produces no cash flows and owns only a right to invest in a project that has a negative NPV, the corporation is worth a positive amount.

When a firm has a real option to invest in the future, as in the restaurant example, it is known as a **growth option**. In other situations, the firm may have the option to reduce the scale of its investment in the future; the option to disinvest is known as an **abandonment option**. Because these options have value, they contribute to the value of any firm that has future possible investment opportunities.

VALUING GROWTH POTENTIAL

Future growth opportunities can be thought of as a collection of real call options on potential projects. Out-of-the-money calls are riskier than in-the-money calls, and because most growth options are likely to be out-of-the-money, the growth component of firm value is likely to be riskier than the ongoing assets of the firm. This observation might explain why young firms (and small firms) have higher returns than older, established firms. It also explains why R&D-intensive firms often have high costs of capital even when most of the R&D risk is idiosyncratic.[3]

It is tempting to use the Black-Scholes formula to value future growth options, but often there are good reasons why this formula might not price these options correctly. For example, the Black-Scholes formula values European options, whereas most growth options can be exercised at any time. Black-Scholes also assumes a particular distribution (log normal) for the future value of the assets. As we explained in Chapter 21, an alternative to using the Black-Scholes formula is to compute the value of growth options using risk-neutral probabilities. Let's demonstrate how to go about valuing real options in this way with a simplified example.

StartUp Incorporated is a new company whose only asset is a patent it purchased on a new drug. If produced, the drug will generate certain profits of $1 million per year for the remaining life of the patent, which is 17 years (after then, competition will drive profits to zero). It will cost $10 million today to produce the drug. Assume that the yield on a 17-year risk-free annuity is currently 8% per year. What is the value of the patent?

Using the formula for the present value of an annuity, the NPV of investing today in the drug is

$$NPV = \frac{1 \text{ million}}{0.08}\left(1 - \frac{1}{1.08^{17}}\right) - 10 \text{ million} = -\$878,362$$

Based on this calculation, it does not make sense to invest in the drug today. But what if interest rates change? Let's assume that interest rates will change in exactly one year. At

---

3. Readers interested in a more in-depth discussion of the relation between R&D risk and returns can consult J. B. Berk, R. C. Green, and V. Naik, "The Valuation and Return Dynamics of New Ventures," *Review of Financial Studies* 17 (2004): 1–35.

that time, all risk-free interest rates in the economy will be either 10% per year or 5% per year, and then will remain at that level forever. Clearly, an increase in interest rates will make matters worse. Because interest rates will remain at the new, higher level forever, it will never be optimal to invest. Thus the value of this growth option is zero in that state. However, if rates drop, the NPV of undertaking the investment, given that the patent will have a remaining life of 16 years, is

$$NPV = \frac{1 \text{ million}}{0.05}\left(1 - \frac{1}{1.05^{16}}\right) - 10 \text{ million} = \$837,770$$

In this case it is optimal to invest. We can put this information on a decision tree, as shown in Figure 22.6.

Recall from Chapter 21 that to find risk-neutral probabilities, we solve for the probabilities so that the expected return of all financial assets is equal to the current risk-free rate. In Chapter 21, we used stock as the financial asset; in this case, we use the 17-year risk-free annuity that pays $1000 per year as the financial asset. The value today of this annuity is

$$S = \frac{1000}{0.08}\left(1 - \frac{1}{1.08^{17}}\right) = \$9122$$

A year from now, the annuity will pay $1000, and it will have 16 years left to maturity. Therefore, including the payment, it will be worth either

$$S_u = 1000 + \frac{1000}{0.1}\left(1 - \frac{1}{1.1^{16}}\right) = \$8824$$

if interest rates go up, or, if interest rates fall,

$$S_d = 1000 + \frac{1000}{0.05}\left(1 - \frac{1}{1.05^{16}}\right) = \$11,838$$

Suppose the current one-year risk-free interest rate is equal to 6%. (Note that this rate is below the current 17-year annuity rate of 8%; thus, the current yield curve is upward

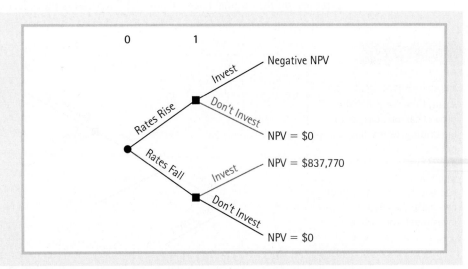

FIGURE 22.6

StartUp's Decision to Invest in the Drug
If interest rates rise, it does not make sense to invest. If rates fall, it is optimal to develop the drug.

sloping.) We can calculate the risk-neutral probability of interest rates increasing, which we denote by ρ, using Eq. 21.16,

$$\rho = \frac{(1 + r_f)S - S_d}{S_u - S_d} = \frac{1.06 \times 9122 - 11{,}838}{8824 - 11{,}838} = 71.95\%$$

That is, a risk-neutral probability of 71.95% that interest rates will rise is required for the annuity to have an expected return equal to the risk-free rate of 6% over the next year.

Now that we have calculated the risk-neutral probabilities for the interest rate movements, we can use them to value StartUp's patent. The value today of the investment opportunity is the present value of the expected cash flows (using risk-neutral probabilities) discounted at the risk-free rate:

$$PV = \frac{837{,}770 \times (1 - 0.7195) + 0 \times 0.7195}{1.06} = \$221{,}693$$

In this example, even though the cash flows of the project are known with certainty, the uncertainty regarding future interest rates creates substantial option value for the firm. The firm's ability to use the patent and grow should interest rates fall is worth close to a quarter of a million dollars.

STAGED INVESTMENT: THE OPTION TO EXPAND

Future growth options are not only important to firm value, but can also be important in the value of an individual project. By undertaking a project, a firm often gets the opportunity to invest in new projects to which firms outside the industry do not have easy access. For example, a fashion designer might introduce a new line of clothes knowing that if the line proves popular, he has the option to launch a new line of accessories based on those clothes.

Consider an investment opportunity with an option to grow that requires a $10 million investment today. In one year we will find out whether the project, which entails introducing a new product into the business machines market, is successful. The risk-neutral probability that the project will generate $1 million per year in perpetuity is 50%; otherwise, the project will generate nothing. At any time we can double the size of the project on the original terms. Figure 22.7 represents these decisions on a decision tree.

FIGURE 22.7

Staged Investment Opportunity
At any time the size of the project can be doubled on the original terms. It is optimal to make this decision after we find out whether the project is a success. This growth option can make the initial investment worthwhile.

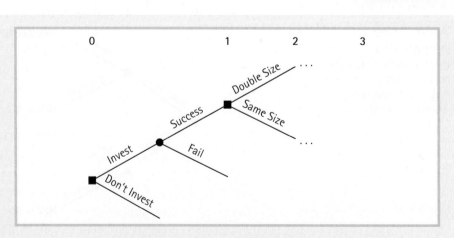

INTERVIEW WITH SCOTT MATHEWS

Scott Mathews is associate technical fellow with the computational finance and stochastic modelling team within Boeing's advanced research and development division. He has expertise in business engineering, a technology that features complex financial and investment risk models applying real asset option pricing for new products and strategically significant projects. Mr. Mathews has a number of patents in the field of real options.

QUESTION: How can real options be used to manage projects?

ANSWER: High-potential projects typically have substantial uncertain cash flows owing to technology and market uncertainties, and therefore your corporate finance team has to be more active in managing these projects. Essentially they act as internal venture capitalists, seeking high payoffs from risky projects. We use real options to evaluate these types of investment opportunities. With real options, we can answer the questions: Given the technical and market risks of the project, how much should we spend at the early stages? Does each incremental investment increase my return opportunities or decrease risk, and how? What amount of technology and market "learning" must be accomplished to merit a follow-on investment?

Real options are call options on an opportunity, giving you the right to stop, start, or modify a project at some future date. They are contingent, so you can make a strategic, rather than tactical, investment. By investing a small amount at each stage, you can gather enough information to decide what to do next. This limits your losses but still lets you capitalize on opportunities that arise. You don't reject (or approve) the project outright, but make incremental investments in the technology or market to gather sufficient information to determine whether this investment optimizes the company's strategy and produces positive returns over the long term.

QUESTION: Explain the concepts of "pilot" and "commercial" stages.

ANSWER: The "pilot" stage refers to the incremental, staged investments we make to move projects through "decision gates," investing a small and appropriate amount to gather information about the technology and the market, while driving down the project risks. At the end of each decision gate the project is re-evaluated. If there is a reasonable weighted probability of a successful outcome, we invest again and continue to the next decision gate. Projects go through several gates, and at each one we focus on reducing uncertainty, until arriving at a decision point of whether to make a large, discretionary, one-time investment (the "strike price") that launches the "piloted" concepts into production—the "commercial" stage—or terminate the project.

QUESTION: How does staging development create a real option with value?

ANSWER: Staging development is how we use real options to manage projects. By staging development we are buying knowledge, especially about the project risks and opportunities. As a project moves through gates, projects compete for funding, and we use this knowledge to decide which projects should proceed and which ones should be deferred. The approach brings together the engineering, marketing, and finance disciplines to give a uniform look at risks and investment opportunities. This is one of the huge powers of the technique.

Boeing's ability to solve aviation challenges with a high degree of efficiency is our competitive advantage and allows us to "buy" these options at below their market value through investments (the "premium") in our engineering processes. Buying an option for less provides direct value to shareholders. We can leverage our internal knowledge with a relatively small amount of money and hedge the risks. It's a tricky process, and is not completely financial. It often requires judgment as well.

Assume that risk-free rates are constant at 6% per year. If we ignore the option to double the size of the project and we invest today, then the expected cash flows are $1 million $\times$ 0.5 = $500,000 per year. Computing the NPV gives

$$NPV_{\text{without growth option}} = \frac{500,000}{0.06} - 10,000,000 = -\$1.667 \text{ million}$$

Based on this analysis, it appears that it is not optimal to undertake the project today. Of course, that also means we will never find out whether the project is successful.

Consider undertaking the project and exercising the growth option to double the size in a year if the product takes off. The NPV of doubling the size of the project in a year in this state is

$$NPV_{\text{doubling after a year}} = \frac{1,000,000}{0.06} - 10,000,000 = \$6.667 \text{ million}$$

The risk-neutral probability that this state will occur is 50%, so the expected value of this growth option is 6.667 $\times$ 0.5 = $3.333 million. The present value of this amount today is

$$PV_{\text{growth option}} = \frac{3.333}{1.06} = \$3.145 \text{ million}$$

We have this option only if we choose to invest today (otherwise, we never find out how the product performs), so the NPV of undertaking this investment is the NPV we calculated above plus the value of the growth option we obtain by undertaking the project:

$$NPV = NPV_{\text{without growth option}} + PV_{\text{growth option}}$$
$$= -1.667 + 3.145 = \$1.478 \text{ million}$$

Our analysis shows that the NPV of the investment opportunity is positive and the firm should undertake it.

Notice that it is optimal to undertake the investment today only because of the existence of the future expansion option. If we could find out how well the product would sell without actually producing it, then it would not make sense to invest until we found out this information. Because the only way to find out if the product is successful is to make and market it, it is optimal to proceed. In this case the project is viable because we can experiment at a low scale and preserve the option to grow later.

This project is an example of a strategy that many firms use when they undertake big projects. Rather than commit to the entire project initially, a firm experiments by undertaking the project in stages. It implements the project on a smaller scale first; if the small-scale project proves successful, the firm then exercises the option to grow the project.

THE OPTION TO ABANDON

The previous two examples consider cases in which the firm has the option to grow or expand if the project proves successful. Alternatively, when a project is unsuccessful, the firm may be able to mitigate its loss by abandoning the project. An abandonment option is the option to walk away. Abandonment options can add value to a project because a firm can drop a project if it turns out to be unsuccessful.

THE OPTION TO SHUT DOWN

To illustrate, assume you are the CFO of a publicly traded multinational chain of gourmet food stores. Your company is considering opening a new store in the recently renovated Ferry Building in New York. If you do not sign the lease on the store today, someone else will, so you will not have the opportunity to open a store later. There is a clause in the lease that allows you to break the lease at no cost in two years.

Including the lease payments, the new store will cost $10,000 per month to operate. Because the building has just reopened, you do not know what the pedestrian traffic will be. If your customers are mainly limited to morning and evening commuters, you expect to generate $8000 per month in revenue in perpetuity. If, however, the building follows the lead of the Ferry Building in San Francisco and becomes a tourist attraction, you believe that your revenue will be double that amount. You estimate there is a 50% probability that the Ferry Building will become a tourist attraction. The costs to set up the store will be $400,000. Assume that the risk-free interest rate is constant at 7% per year.

The number of tourists visiting the New York Ferry Building represents idiosyncratic uncertainty (recall that this is the kind of uncertainty investors in your company can cost-lessly diversify). Hence the appropriate cost of capital is the risk-free rate of 7% per year. Note that

$$1.07^{1/12} = 1.00565$$

This means the monthly discount rate is 0.565%. If you were forced to operate the store under all circumstances, then the expected revenue will be $8000 \times 0.5 + $16,000 \times 0.5 = $12,000. The NPV of the investment is the present value of the revenues minus the costs:

$$NPV = \frac{12,000}{0.00565} - \frac{10,000}{0.00565} - 400,000 = -\$46,018$$

It would not make sense to open the store.

Of course, you do not have to keep operating the store. You have an option to get out of the lease after two years at no cost, and after the store is open it will be immediately obvious whether the Ferry Building is a tourist attraction. In this case, the decision tree looks like Figure 22.8.

FIGURE 22.8

Decision to Open a Store in the New York Ferry Building
You must decide now whether to sign the lease and open the store, but you have an option to abandon the lease in 24 months (2 years). The profitability of the store depends on whether the Ferry Building becomes a tourist attraction.

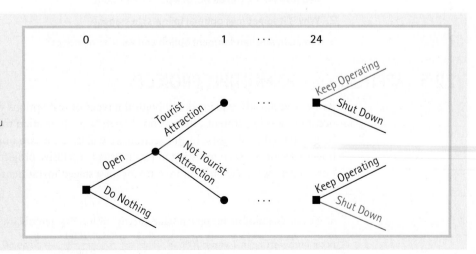

If the Ferry Building is a tourist attraction, the NPV of the investment opportunity is

$$NPV = \frac{16,000}{0.00565} - \frac{10,000}{0.00565} - 400,000 = \$661,947$$

If the Ferry Building does not become a tourist attraction, you will close the store after two years. The NPV of the investment opportunity in this state is just the NPV of operating for two years:

$$NPV = \frac{8000}{0.00565}\left(1 - \frac{1}{1.00565^{24}}\right) - \frac{10,000}{0.00565}\left(1 - \frac{1}{1.00565^{24}}\right) - 400,000$$
$$= -\$444,770$$

There is an equal probability of each state and, because the risk is idiosyncratic, the actual and risk-neutral probabilities are the same. Thus the NPV of opening the store is just the expected value using the actual probabilities:

$$\$661,947 \times 0.5 - \$444,770 \times 0.5 = \$108,589$$

By exercising the option to abandon the venture, you limit your losses and so the NPV of undertaking the investment is positive. The value of the option to abandon is the difference between the NPV with and without the option: $108,589 - (-46,018) = \$154,607$.[4]

It is easy to ignore or understate the importance of the option to abandon. In many applications killing an economically unsuccessful venture can add more value than starting a new venture. Often, however, managers focus on the value created by starting new ventures and deemphasize the value created by abandoning old ventures. Some of this behaviour undoubtedly results from the same behavioural biases that we discussed in Chapter 13 that cause individual investors to hold on to losers. It is also closely tied to the sunk cost fallacy, the idea that once a manager makes a large investment, he or she should not abandon a project. As we pointed out in Chapter 7, sunk costs should have no bearing on an investment decision. If continuing a project is a negative-NPV undertaking, you can create value by abandoning, regardless of how much investment has already been sunk into the project.

CONCEPT CHECK

1. Why can a firm with no ongoing projects, and investment opportunities that currently have negative NPVs, still be worth a positive amount?

2. Why is it sometimes optimal to invest in stages?

3. How can an abandonment option add value to a project?

22.5 APPLICATIONS TO MULTIPLE PROJECTS

As we have already explained, although the types of real options we have discussed thus far occur in most investments, there is no "boilerplate" application that we can present that can be generalized to all cases. In this section we will describe two important new applications: how to decide between investing in two mutually exclusive projects of different lengths, and how to determine the order of investment for a staged investment opportunity.

---

4. We can also calculate the option value directly; with a 50% probability, we avoid the losses of $2000 per month starting in 2 years: $50\% \times \dfrac{1}{1.00565^{24}} \times \dfrac{2000}{0.00656} = \$154,607$.

COMPARING MUTUALLY EXCLUSIVE INVESTMENTS WITH DIFFERENT LIVES

Consider the following problem faced by a financial analyst at Canadian Motors. Last year, an engineering firm named Advanced Mechanics was asked to design a new machine that will attach car chassis to bodies. The firm has produced two designs. The cheaper design will cost $10 million to implement and last 5 years. The more expensive design will cost $16 million and last 10 years. In both cases, the machines are expected to save Canadian Motors $3 million per year. If the cost of capital is 10%, which design should Canadian Motors approve?

STANDALONE NPV OF EACH DESIGN.   Let's first calculate the NPV of each decision on a standalone basis. The NPV of adopting the 5-year machine is

$$NPV_{5yr} = \frac{3}{0.1}\left(1 - \frac{1}{1.1^5}\right) - 10 = \$1.37 \text{ million}$$

The NPV of the 10-year machine is

$$NPV_{10yr} = \frac{3}{0.1}\left(1 - \frac{1}{1.1^{10}}\right) - 16 = \$2.43 \text{ million}$$

If the analyst simply picked the design with the higher standalone NPV, he would choose the longer-lived design. However, the preceding NPV calculation ignores the difference in these projects' life spans. The longer-lived design embodies a 10-year production plan. The shorter-lived design only captures what will happen over the next 5 years. To truly compare the two options, we must consider what will happen once the shorter-lived equipment wears out. Let's consider three possibilities: 1) the technology is not replaced, 2) it is replaced at the same terms, or 3) technological advances allow us to replace it at improved terms.

NO REPLACEMENT.   If the shorter-lived technology is not replaced (and the firm reverts to its old production process), there will be no additional benefits once its 5-year life ends. In that case, the original comparison is correct, and the 10-year machine will increase firm value by $2.43 - 1.37 = \$1.06$ million more than the shorter-lived design.

One reason we might not replace the technology is if we expect its cost to increase. For example, suppose its cost in five years' time will be $11.37 million or higher (an increase of 2.6% per year). In that case, because the cost of the machine has gone up by more than its current NPV of $1.37 million, replacement will not be optimal. Thus, the prior comparison is correct and the longer-lived design should be implemented.

REPLACEMENT AT THE SAME TERMS.   Suppose that we expect the costs and benefits of the shorter-lived design to be the same in five years. In that case it will be optimal to replace it, in which case we will again earn its NPV of $1.37 million. We should include this benefit when we evaluate the NPV of the 5-year design, leading to a total NPV over the 10-year horizon of

$$NPV_{5yr, \text{ with replacement}} = 1.37 + \frac{1.37}{1.10^5} = \$2.22 \text{ million}$$

Allowing for replacement at the same terms substantially increases the NPV we calculated for the 5-year design. However, it is still inferior to the $2.43 million NPV from the 10-year design.

REPLACEMENT AT IMPROVED TERMS.   In reality, the future cost of a machine is uncertain. Because of technological advances, machines may become less expensive rather than more expensive (think about the steadily declining prices of computers). Suppose we expect the cost of the new technology to fall to $7 million at the end of five years. Because the cost has declined by $3 million, its NPV will rise to 3 + 1.37 = $4.37 million. In that case the NPV of the 5-year design over a 10-year horizon is

$$NPV_{5 \text{ yr, with improved replacement}} = 1.37 + \frac{4.37}{1.10^5} = \$4.08 \text{ million}$$

Thus, if terms are expected to improve in this way, the 5-year design is optimal for the firm, increasing firm value by 4.08 − 2.43 = $1.65 million compared to the 10-year machine.

VALUING THE REPLACEMENT OPTION.   As the above analysis reveals, adopting 5-year machine provides the firm with a replacement option in 5 years' time. In order to compare the two designs correctly, we must determine the value of this replacement option, which will depend on the likelihood that the cost of the machine will decrease or increase.

EXAMPLE 22.2   **VALUING THE REPLACEMENT OPTION**

Problem
Suppose the cost of the shorter-lived machine is equally likely to rise to $12 million, stay equal to $10 million, or fall to $7 million, and suppose this risk does not change the project's cost of capital. Which machine should the firm choose?

Solution
If the cost rises to $12 million, the firm will choose not to replace the machine and get an NPV of 0. If the cost stays the same or falls, the firm will replace the machine and get an NPV of $1.37 million or $4.37 million, respectively. Given the probabilities, the NPV of the 5-year machine over the 10-year horizon is

$$NPV_{5 \text{ yr, with uncertain replacement}} = 1.37 + \frac{\frac{1}{3}(0) + \frac{1}{3}(1.37) + \frac{1}{3}(4.37)}{1.10^5} = \$2.56 \text{ million}$$

Thus, given this uncertainty, the shorter-lived machine offers a higher NPV over 10 years than the $2.43 million NPV of the longer-lived machine. By committing to the longer-lived project, the firm would give up its real option to react to technological and market changes.

STAGING MUTUALLY DEPENDENT INVESTMENTS

In analyzing the value of the option to grow, we considered the real option value of a staged investment opportunity. The advantage of staging is that it allows us to postpone investment until after we learn important new information. We can avoid making the investment unless the new information suggests it is worthwhile.

In many applications the stages have a natural order; e.g., investing in a prototype before developing on a large scale. But in some situations we can choose the order of the development stages. In that case, how can we do so to maximize the value of the real options that we create?

EQUIVALENT ANNUAL BENEFIT METHOD

Traditionally, managers have accounted for the difference in project lengths by calculating the **equivalent annual benefit (EAB)** of each project, which is the constant annuity payment over the life of the project that is equivalent to receiving its NPV today. The **equivalent annual benefit method** then selects the project with the higher equivalent annual benefit.

For example, in the case of Canadian Motors, the equivalent annual benefit of each machine is

$$EAB_{5\,yr} = \frac{1.37}{\dfrac{1}{0.10}\left(1 - \dfrac{1}{1.10^5}\right)} = \$0.361 \text{ million},$$

$$EAB_{10\,yr} = \frac{2.43}{\dfrac{1}{0.10}\left(1 - \dfrac{1}{1.10^{10}}\right)} = \$0.395 \text{ million}$$

Thus, the 10-year machine has the higher equivalent annual benefit and would be chosen under this method.

The equivalent annual benefit method assumes that we earn the project's EAB over the entire forecast horizon. For the 5-year machine, this assumption means that we would earn an NPV over 10 years of

$$NPV_{5\,yr\,EAB} = \frac{0.361}{0.10}\left(1 - \frac{1}{1.10^{10}}\right) = \$2.22 \text{ million}$$

Comparing this result with our earlier analysis, we see that using the EAB method is equivalent to assuming that we can replace the project at identical terms over the entire horizon. While this assumption may be correct, in most instances there is significant uncertainty regarding the project terms in the future. In that case, real option methods must be used to determine the correct choice.

AN EXAMPLE: ECLECTIC MOTORS. Eclectic Motors is considering developing an electric car that would compete directly with gasoline-powered cars. They must overcome three technological hurdles to produce a successful car:

1. Significantly reduce the weight of the body of the car without compromising strength and safety using improved material technology.

2. Develop a method to rapidly recharge the batteries.

3. Advance battery technology to reduce weight and increase storage capacity.

Though Eclectic's engineers have already made significant breakthroughs on aspects of each hurdle, further research and substantial risk remain, as shown in the following estimates regarding the time and cost required, as well as the likelihood of success, for each task:

REQUIRED TIME, COST, AND LIKELIHOOD OF SUCCESS FOR ECLECTIC'S PROJECT

TABLE 22.2

Technology	Cost	Time	Probability of Success
Materials	$100 million	1 year	50%
Recharger	$400 million	1 year	50%
Battery	$100 million	4 years	25%

Suppose all three risks are idiosyncratic and the risk-free interest rate is 6%. Given Eclectic's resources, it can only work on one technology at a time. Eclectic's managers know that by appropriately staging these investments, they can enhance the firm's value. The question is, assuming that it makes sense to proceed, which technology should they tackle first?

MUTUALLY DEPENDENT INVESTMENTS.   Eclectic's electric car project represents a situation with **mutually dependent investments**, a situation in which the value of one project depends upon the outcome of the others. In this case, we assume that all three challenges must be overcome, or there will be no benefit. Thus, the optimal order is to proceed with the challenge which will minimize the expected cost of development.

INVESTMENT SCALE.   Consider first the materials and recharger technologies. These two are identical except for the upfront investment cost. Let's compare the expected cost of completing them in different orders. If we begin with the materials technology, the expected cost to complete both is

$$\underbrace{100}_{\substack{\text{Investment} \\ \text{in materials}}} + \underbrace{0.50}_{\substack{\text{Probability} \\ \text{materials} \\ \text{technology} \\ \text{succeeds}}} \times \underbrace{\frac{1}{1.06}}_{\substack{\text{PV of} \\ \text{delay}}} \times \underbrace{400}_{\substack{\text{Investment} \\ \text{in recharger}}} = \quad \$288.7 \text{ million}$$

If we begin with the recharger technology, the expected cost is

$$\underbrace{400}_{\substack{\text{Investment} \\ \text{in recharger}}} + \underbrace{0.50}_{\substack{\text{Probability} \\ \text{recharger} \\ \text{technology} \\ \text{succeeds}}} \times \underbrace{\frac{1}{1.06}}_{\substack{\text{PV of} \\ \text{delay}}} \times \underbrace{100}_{\substack{\text{Investment} \\ \text{in materials}}} = \quad \$447.2 \text{ million}$$

Thus it is clear that Eclectic should invest in the materials technology before working on the recharger. Because the cost of the recharger is greater, we don't want to waste our investment in it if the materials technology fails. As this example shows, other things being equal, it is beneficial to make the least costly investments first, delaying more expensive investments until it is clear they are warranted.

INVESTMENT TIME AND RISK.   Next let's compare the materials and battery technologies. These projects have the same cost, but the battery technology will take longer and has a greater chance of failure. Considering only these two projects, if we begin with the materials technology, the expected cost of completing both is

$$\underbrace{100}_{\substack{\text{Investment} \\ \text{in materials}}} + \underbrace{0.50}_{\substack{\text{Probability} \\ \text{materials} \\ \text{technology} \\ \text{succeeds}}} \times \underbrace{\frac{1}{1.06}}_{\substack{\text{PV of} \\ \text{delay}}} \times \underbrace{100}_{\substack{\text{Investment} \\ \text{in battery}}} = \quad \$147.2 \text{ million}$$

If we begin with the battery technology, the expected cost is

$$\underbrace{100}_{\substack{\text{Investment} \\ \text{in battery}}} + \underbrace{0.25}_{\substack{\text{Probability} \\ \text{battery} \\ \text{technology} \\ \text{succeeds}}} \times \underbrace{\frac{1}{1.06^4}}_{\substack{\text{PV of} \\ \text{delay}}} \times \underbrace{100}_{\substack{\text{Investment} \\ \text{in battery}}} = \quad \$119.80 \text{ million}$$

Thus, Eclectic should work on the battery technology before working on the materials. Given its greater risk, we will learn more if the battery project succeeds regarding the viability of the overall project. Due to its longer time requirement, we also benefit from the time value of postponing the following investments further. In general, other things equal, it is beneficial to invest in riskier and lengthier projects first, delaying future investments until the most information is learned.

A GENERAL RULE. As we have seen, the cost, time, and risk of each project will determine the optimal order to invest. Intuitively, by making smaller, riskier investments first, we gain the most additional information at the lowest cost. (Thus, the battery project should definitely come before the recharger project.) In general, we can find the optimal order to stage mutually dependent projects by ranking each, from highest to lowest, according to

$$\frac{1 - PV(\text{success})}{PV(\text{investment})} \tag{22.3}$$

where $PV(\text{success})$ is the value at the start of the project of receiving \$1 if the project succeeds (i.e., the present value of the (risk-neutral) probability of success) and PV (Investment) is the project's required investment, again expressed as a present value at the project's start.

EXAMPLE 22.3	DECIDING THE ORDER OF INVESTMENT WITH MULTIPLE STAGES

Problem

Use Eq. 22.3 to rank the stages of Eclectic's electric care project and determine the optimal order.

Solution

Evaluating Eq. 22.3 for each stage, we have

Materials: $[1 - (0.50/1.06)]/100 = 0.00528$

Recharger: $[1 - (0.50/1.06)]/400 = 0.00132$

Battery: $[1 - (0.25/1.06^4)]/100 = 0.00802$

So, Eclectic should develop the batteries first, then the body materials, and finally the charger, matching our earlier analysis.

Until now we have ignored the decision on whether it is optimal to develop at all. In evaluating the overall investment decision, the first step is to decide on the optimal order of investment in each stage. Once that order has been determined, we can calculate the overall NPV of the opportunity and reach a decision on whether to proceed.

| EXAMPLE **22.4** | DECIDING WHETHER TO INVEST IN A PROJECT WITH MULTIPLE STAGES |

Problem

Eclectic's managers estimate that once they make these technological breakthroughs, they can develop the electric car, and the present value of all future profits will be $4 billion. Does the decision to develop the car make sense?

Solution

To decide whether development makes sense we must compute the NPV given the optimal order from Example 22.3:

$$NPV = -100 - 0.25\frac{100}{1.06^4} - 0.25 \times 0.5\frac{400}{1.06^5} + 0.25 \times 0.5 \times 0.5\frac{4000}{1.06^6} = \$19.1 \text{ million}$$

Thus, it is profitable to develop the electric car. However, this result crucially depends on the optimal staging—the NPV would be negative if Eclectic chose any other order!

CONCEPT CHECK

1. Why is it inappropriate to simply pick the higher NPV project when comparing mutually exclusive investment opportunities with different lives?

2. What is a major shortcoming of the equivalent annual benefit method?

3. How can you decide the order of investment in a staged investment decision?

22.6   RULES OF THUMB

One of the major drawbacks of using the concepts introduced in this chapter is that they are difficult to implement. In practice, correctly modelling the sources of uncertainty and the appropriate dynamic decisions usually requires an extensive amount of time and financial expertise. Furthermore, in most cases, the solutions are problem specific, so the time and expertise spent on one problem are not transferable to other problems. Consequently, many firms resort to different rules of thumb.[5] Here we examine two commonly used rules of thumb: the profitability index and hurdle rates.

THE PROFITABILITY INDEX RULE

As we explained in Section 22.1, when an investment opportunity can be delayed, it is optimal to invest only when the NPV of the investment project is sufficiently high. In most applications, it is quite difficult to calculate precisely how high the NPV must be to trigger investment. As a result, some firms use the following rule of thumb: Invest whenever the profitability index exceeds a specified level.

Recall from Chapter 6 that in the simple case of a project where the only resource is the upfront investment, the profitability index is

$$\text{Profitability Index} = \frac{\text{NPV}}{\text{Initial Investment}}$$

---

5. See Robert McDonald, "Real Options and Rules of Thumb in Capital Budgeting," in M. J. Brennan and L. Trigeorgis (eds.), *Project Flexibility, Agency, and Competition* (London: Oxford University Press, 2000), for a detailed analysis of the performance of different rules of thumb.

The **profitability index rule** directs you to invest whenever the profitability index exceeds some predetermined number. When the investment cannot be delayed, the optimal rule is to invest whenever the profitability index is greater than zero. When there is an option to delay, a common rule of thumb is to invest only when the index is at least 1. Often, firms set high thresholds because the cost of investing at the wrong time is usually asymmetric. It is often better to wait too long (use a profitability index criterion that is too high) than to invest too soon (use a profitability index criterion that is too low).

THE HURDLE RATE RULE

The profitability index rule of thumb raises the bar on the NPV to take into account the option to wait. Rather than invest when the NPV is zero, you wait until the NPV is a multiple of the initial investment. Instead of raising the bar on the NPV, the **hurdle rate rule** raises the discount rate. The hurdle rate rule uses a higher discount rate than the cost of capital to compute the NPV, but then applies the regular NPV rule: Invest whenever the NPV calculated using this higher discount rate is positive. This higher discount rate is known as the **hurdle rate** because if the project can jump this hurdle—that is, have a positive NPV at this higher discount rate—then it should be undertaken.

When the source of uncertainty that creates a motive to wait is interest rate uncertainty, there is a natural way to approximate the optimal hurdle rate. In this case, the rule of thumb is to multiply the cost of capital by the ratio of the **callable annuity rate**, which is the rate on a risk-free annuity that can be repaid (or *called*) at any time, to the risk-free riskless rate:

$$\text{Hurdle Rate} = \text{Cost of Capital} \times \frac{\text{Callable Annuity Rate}}{\text{Risk-Free Rate}} \qquad (22.4)$$

We should then invest whenever the NPV of the project is positive using this hurdle rate as the discount rate.

What is the intuition for this rule? Let's assume you have a risk-free project that you can delay. It currently has a positive NPV. You intend to borrow the initial investment but you are unsure whether you should wait in the hope that interest rates will fall. If you take out a regular loan and interest rates decrease, you will be stuck paying a higher rate. However, if you take out a callable loan and interest rates fall, then you can refinance and take advantage of the lower rates. So, if the project has a positive NPV using the callable annuity rate as the discount rate, you can have your cake and eat it too: You can immediately get the benefits of the investment by undertaking it and still take advantage of a lower rate if rates fall. Thus it makes sense to invest immediately. The rule of thumb approximately implements this decision rule.

How large is the difference between the hurdle rate and the cost of capital? One way to tell is to look at the difference in the interest rate of a government-guaranteed mortgage that is prepayable and the interest rate on a similar non-prepayable equal maturity government bond. As can be seen in Figure 22.9, in Canada, 5-year mortgage rates have averaged about 33% higher than similar 5-year Government of Canada Bonds (e.g., 4% versus 3%). In the U.S. the difference is about 20%. A reason for the difference is that the Canadian data also includes uninsured mortgages whereas the U.S. data does not. Therefore, using a hurdle rate 20% higher than the firm's cost of capital might be a reasonable adjustment to account for the firm's ability to wait until interest rates are sufficiently favourable to invest.

FIGURE 22.9

FIGURE 22.9

Historical Ratio of Mortgage Rates to Risk-free Rates, December 1980 to July 2007

The graph shows the ratio of the 5-year fixed-rate mortgage yield to the yield on the 5-year Government of Canada bond. Historically, mortgage rates have generally been 33% higher than long-term risk-free rates.

Source: Bank of Canada.

EXAMPLE **22.5**

USING THE HURDLE RATE RULE FOR THE OPTION TO DELAY

Problem

You have the opportunity to invest in a risk-free technology. The investment will require an upfront payment of $1 million and will provide a constant annual cash flow of $90,000 every year in perpetuity. Suppose all interest rates will either be 10% or 5% in one year and remain there forever. The risk-neutral probability interest rates will drop to 5% is 90%. The one-year risk-free interest rate is 8%, and today's rate on a risk-free perpetual bond is 5.4%. The rate on an equivalent perpetual bond that is repayable at any time (the callable annuity rate) is 9%.[6] Should you invest in the technology today, or wait and see if rates drop and then invest?

Solution

Because the investment is risk free, the cost of capital is the risk-free rate. Thus, Eq. 22.4 suggests using a hurdle rate equal to the callable annuity rate of 9%. With that rate,

$$NPV = \frac{90,000}{0.09} - 1,000,000 = 0$$

The hurdle rate rule implies that you are indifferent. Let's see if this is correct. The actual cost of capital is 5.4% (the rate offered on a risk-free perpetuity), so the investment opportunity clearly has a positive NPV:

$$NPV = \frac{90,000}{0.054} - 1,000,000 = \$666,667$$

---

6. To check that these rates make sense, note that a $1000 perpetual bond paying $54 per year would be worth $54 + 54/.05 = $1134 if interest rates fall and $54 + 54/.10 = 594 if rates rise, for a (risk-neutral) expected payoff of 0.9 × 1134 + 0.1 × 594 = $1080, for an expected return equal to the one-year risk-free rate of 8%. Similarly, a $1000 callable bond with a coupon of $90 would be worth $90 + 1000 = $1090 if rates fall and the bond is prepaid and $90 + 90/.10 = $990 if rates rise, again for a risk-neutral expected payoff of 0.9 × 1090 + 0.1 × 990 = $1080.

Let's see what the NPV of waiting is. If we delay the investment, it makes sense to invest only if rates drop to 5%, in which case

$$NPV_{\text{rates go down}} = \frac{90,000}{0.05} - 1,000,000 = \$800,000$$

The present value today of the expected NPV using risk-neutral probabilities is therefore

$$\frac{800,000 \times 0.90}{1.08} = \$666,667$$

The hurdle rate rule is correct: You really are indifferent between investing today and waiting.

In situations like Example 22.5, when the cash flows are constant and perpetual, and the reason to wait derives solely from interest rate uncertainty, the rule of thumb is always exact.[7] However, when these conditions are not satisfied, the rule of thumb merely approximates the correct decision.

While using a hurdle rate rule for deciding when to invest might be a cost-effective way to make investment decisions, it is important to remember that this rule does not provide an accurate measure of *value*. The value of making an investment is the NPV calculated using the cost of capital as the discount rate, not the hurdle rate. Thus, while the rule of thumb provides the correct time to invest in Example 22.5, the actual value of undertaking the investment is $666,666.67—the NPV when the correct cost of capital is used as the discount rate.

APPLYING HURDLE RATES AND THE PROFITABILITY INDEX SIMULTANEOUSLY

Potentially there could be an advantage to using both rules of thumb simultaneously. That is, the decision when to invest can be made by first computing the NPV using the hurdle rate in Eq. 22.4 to account for interest rate uncertainty. The profitability index can then be calculated using this NPV, with the firm accepting the project only if the profitability index exceeds a threshold that accounts for cash flow uncertainty.

CONCEPT CHECK

1. Explain the profitability index rule of thumb.

2. What is the hurdle rate rule?

22.7 KEY INSIGHTS FROM REAL OPTIONS

Although a simple rule on how to account for all real options does not exist, there are a few simple principles that we have covered in this chapter. In closing, it is worth restating these principles:

OUT-OF-THE-MONEY REAL OPTIONS HAVE VALUE. Even if an investment opportunity currently has negative NPV, it does not imply that the opportunity is worthless. So long as there is a chance that the investment opportunity could have positive NPV in the future, the opportunity is worth something today.

---

7. See Jonathan B. Berk, "A Simple Approach for Deciding When to Invest," *American Economic Review* 89 (1999): 1319–1326.

IN-THE-MONEY REAL OPTIONS NEED NOT BE EXERCISED IMMEDIATELY.   You should not necessarily take on an investment opportunity that has positive NPV today. If you can delay the investment opportunity, the option to delay might be worth more than the NPV of undertaking the investment now. In this case you should not undertake the investment and instead delay it.

WAITING IS VALUABLE.   Value can be created by waiting for uncertainty to resolve because once uncertainty is resolved, you can make better decisions with better information. Thus, if there is no cost to waiting, investing early never makes sense. If there is a cost, always weigh the benefits of waiting for resolution of uncertainty against the costs of waiting.

DELAY INVESTMENT EXPENSES AS MUCH AS POSSIBLE.   Because waiting is valuable, you should only incur investment expenses at the last possible moment. Committing capital before it is absolutely necessary reduces value because it gives up the option to make a better decision once uncertainty has been resolved.

Combining these insights, we find that by staging investments, and using clear, valuation-based methods to determine at each stage if the firm should abandon, defer, continue, or grow an investment opportunity, managers can substantially increase firm value.

SUMMARY

1. A real option is an option where the underlying asset is a physical, rather than a financial, asset.

2. A decision tree is a graphical way to represent alternative decisions and potential outcomes in an uncertain economy. It contains decision nodes and information nodes.

3. By waiting before committing to an investment, a firm can obtain more information about the investment's returns. By correctly choosing the time to invest, it can add value.

4. When you have the option of deciding when to invest, it is usually optimal to invest only when the NPV is substantially greater than zero.

5. Given the option to wait, an investment that currently has a negative NPV can have a positive value.

6. The option to wait is most valuable when there is a great deal of uncertainty regarding what the value of the investment will be in the future.

7. In the real option context, the dividends correspond to any value from the investment that we give up by waiting. Absent dividends, a call option should not be exercised early.

8. By undertaking a project, a firm often gets the opportunity to make investments that it would not have otherwise. The opportunity to invest in projects in the future—that is, the firm's growth options—is worth something today.

9. When firms find themselves involved in a project that is losing money, with little prospect of turning things around in the future, they can exercise their abandonment option and walk away.

10. In choosing between investments with different lives, a firm must take into account its option to replace or extend the life of the shorter-lived project at the end of its original life.

11. Managers sometimes use the equivalent annual benefit method to compare projects of different lengths. It implicitly assumes that the projects can be replaced at their original terms. Using the equivalent annual benefit method might produce different recommendations than when future uncertainty is taken into account.

12. When deciding the order of investment for a multi-stage investment decision, there is a benefit to taking smaller and riskier investments first in order to gain additional information at low cost. If the projects are mutually dependent so that all projects must succeed for the firm to realize any benefit, the optimal order can be determined by ranking the projects according to Eq. 22.4.

13. The profitability index rule of thumb calls for investing whenever the profitability index exceeds some predetermined number. It is a way of accounting for the option to wait when there is cash flow uncertainty.

14. The hurdle rate rule of thumb computes the NPV using the hurdle rate, a discount rate higher than the cost of capital, and specifies that the investment should be undertaken only when the NPV computed this way is positive. It is a way of accounting for the option to wait when there is interest rate uncertainty.

KEY TERMS

abandonment option *p. 790*
callable annuity rate *p. 803*
decision node *p. 782*
decision tree *p. 782*
equivalent annual benefit (EAB) *p. 799*
equivalent annual benefit method,
  p. 799

growth option *p. 790*
hurdle rate *p. 803*
hurdle rate rule *p. 803*
information node *p. 782*
mutually dependent investments *p. 800*
profitability index rule *p. 803*
real option *p. 781*

PROBLEMS

The problems marked in green can be found on MyFinanceLab at www.myfinancelab.com. Visit your MyFinanceLab for additional practice. An asterisk (*) indicates problems with a higher level of difficulty. Additional readings for this chapter may be found in the Textbook Resources section on MyFinanceLab.

Decision Tree Analysis

1. Your company is planning on opening an office in Japan. Profits depend on how fast the economy in Japan recovers from its current recession. There is a 50% chance of recovery this year. You are trying to decide whether to open the office now or in a year. Construct the decision tree that shows the choices you have to open the office either today or one year from now.

EXCEL

2. You are trying to decide whether to make an investment of $500 million in a new technology to produce Everlasting Gobstoppers. There is a 60% chance that the market for these candies will produce profits of $100 million annually, a 20% chance the market will produce profits of $50 million, and a 20% chance that there will be no profits. The size of the market will become clear one year from now. Currently, the cost of capital of the project is 11% per year. There is a 20% chance that the cost of capital will drop to 9% in a year and stay at that level forever and an 80% chance that it will stay at 11% forever. Movements in the cost of capital are unrelated to the size of the candy market. Construct the decision tree that shows the choices you have to make the investment either today or one year from now.

3. Using the information in Problem 2, rework the problem assuming you find out the size of the Everlasting Gobstopper market one year *after you make the investment.* That is, if you do not make the investment, you do not find out the size of the market. Construct the decision tree that shows the choices you have under these circumstances.

4. Describe the benefits and costs of delaying an investment opportunity.

5. You are a financial analyst at Global Conglomerate and are considering entering the shoe business. You believe that you have a very narrow window for entering this market. Because of Christmas demand, the time is right today and you believe that exactly a year from now would also be a good opportunity. Other than these two opportunities, you do not think another opportunity will exist to break into this business. It will cost you $35 million to enter the market. Because other shoe manufacturers exist and are public companies, you can construct a perfectly comparable company. Hence you have decided to use the Black-Scholes formula to decide when and if you should enter the shoe business. Your analysis implies that the current value of an operating shoe company is $40 million. However, the flow of customers is uncertain, so the value of the company is volatile—your analysis indicates that the volatility is 25% per year. Fifteen percent of the value of the company is attributable to the value of the free cash flows (cash available to you to spend how you wish) expected in the first year. If the one-year risk-free rate of interest is 4%,

   a. Should Global enter this business and, if so, when?

   b. How will the decision change if the current value of a shoe company is $36 million instead of $40 million?

   c. Plot the value of your investment opportunity as a function of the current value of a shoe company.

6. It is the beginning of September and you have been offered the following deal to go heli-skiing. If you pick the first week in January and pay for your vacation now, you can get a week of heli-skiing for $2500. However, if you cannot ski because the helicopters cannot fly due to bad weather, there is no snow, or you get sick, you do not get a refund. There is a 40% probability that you will not be able to ski. If you wait until the last minute and go only if you know that the conditions are perfect and you are well, the vacation will cost $4000. You estimate that the pleasure you get from heli-skiing is worth $6000 per week to you (if you had to pay any more than that, you would choose not to go). If your cost of capital is 8% per year, should you book ahead or wait?

7. A professor in the computer science department at the Northern Atlantic Institute of Technology has a patent on a search engine technology and would like to sell it to you, an interested venture capitalist. The patent has a remaining life of 17 years. The technology will take a year to implement (thus there will be no cash inflow in the first year) and has an upfront cost of $100 million. You believe this technology will be able to capture 1% of the Internet search market, and currently this market generates profits of $1 billion per year. Over the next five years, the risk-neutral probability that profits will grow at 10% per year is 20% and the risk-neutral probability that profits will grow at 5% per year is 80%. This growth rate will become clear one year from now (after the first year of growth). After five years, profits are expected to decline 2% annually. No profits are expected after the patent runs out. Assume that all risk-free interest rates are constant (regardless of the term) at 10% per year.

   a. Calculate the NPV of undertaking the investment today.

   b. Calculate the NPV of waiting a year to make the investment decision.

   c. What is your optimal investment strategy?

*8. The management of Western Express Corporation is considering investing 10% of all future earnings in growth. The company has a single growth opportunity that it can take either now or in one period. Although the managers do not know the return on investment with certainty, they know it is equally likely to be either 10% or 14% per year. In one period they will find out which state will occur. Currently the firm pays out all earnings as a dividend of $10 million; if it does not make the investment, dividends are expected to remain at this level forever. If Western Express undertakes the investment, the new dividend will reflect the realized return on investment and will grow at the realized rate forever. Assuming the opportunity cost of capital is 10.1%, what is the value of the company just before the current dividend is paid (the cum-dividend value)?

*9.   What decision should you make in Problem 2 if the one-year cost of capital is 15.44% and the profits last forever?

Growth And Abandonment Options

10.   Your R&D division has just synthesized a material that will superconduct electricity at room temperature; you have given the go-ahead to try to produce this material commercially. It will take five years to find out whether the material is commercially viable, and you estimate that the probability of success is 25%. Development will cost $10 million per year, paid at the beginning of each year. If development is successful and you decide to produce the material, the factory will be built immediately. It will cost $1 billion to put in place, and will generate profits of $100 million at the end of every year in perpetuity. Assume that the current five-year risk-free interest rate is 10% per year and the yield on a perpetual risk-free bond will be either 12%, 10%, 8%, or 5% in five years. Assume that the risk-neutral probability of each possible rate is the same. What is the value today of this project?

*11.   You are an analyst working for Scotia Capital, and you are trying to value the growth potential of a large, established company, Big Industries. Big Industries has a thriving R&D division that has consistently turned out successful products. You estimate that, on average, the division launches two projects every three years, so you estimate that there is a 66% chance that a project will be produced every year. Typically, the investment opportunities the R&D division produces require an initial investment of $10 million and yield profits of $1 million per year that grow at one of three possible growth rates in perpetuity: 3%, 0%, and 23%. All three growth rates are equally likely for any given project. These opportunities are always "take it or leave it" opportunities: If they are not undertaken immediately, they disappear forever. Assume that the cost of capital will always remain at 12% per year. What is the present value of all future growth opportunities Big Industries will produce?

*12.   Repeat Problem 11, but this time assume that all the probabilities are risk-neutral probabilities, which means the cost of capital is always the risk-free rate. The current interest rate for a risk-free perpetuity is 8%; in one year, there is a 64.375% chance that all risk-free interest rates will be 10% and stay there forever and a 35.625% chance that they will be 6% and stay there forever. The current one-year risk-free rate is 7%.

13.   You own a small networking startup. You have just received an offer to buy your firm from a large, publicly traded firm, JCH Systems. Under the terms of the offer, you will receive 1 million shares of JCH. JCH stock currently trades for $25 per share. You can sell the shares of JCH that you will receive in the market at any time. But as part of the offer, JCH also agrees that at the end of the next year, it will buy the shares back from you for $25 per share if you desire. Suppose the current one-year risk-free rate is 6.18%, the volatility of JCH stock is 30%, and JCH does not pay dividends.

   a. Is this offer worth more than $25 million? Explain.

   b. What is the value of the offer?

14.   You own a wholesale plumbing supply store. The store currently generates revenues of $1 million per year. Next year, revenues will either decrease by 10% or increase by 5%, with equal probability, and then stay at that level as long as you operate the store. You own the store outright. Other costs run $900,000 per year. There are no costs to shutting down; in that case you

can always sell the store for $500,000. What is the business worth today if the cost of capital is fixed at 10%?

EXCEL   *15. You own a copper mine. The price of copper is currently $1.50 per pound. The mine produces 1 million pounds of copper per year and costs $2 million per year to operate. It has enough copper to operate for 100 years. Shutting the mine down would entail bringing the land up to environmental standards and is expected to cost $5 million. Reopening the mine once it is shut down would be an impossibility given current environmental standards. The price of copper has an equal (and independent) probability of going up or down by 25% each year for the next two years and then will stay at that level forever. Calculate the NPV of continuing to operate the mine if the cost of capital is fixed at 15%. Is it optimal to abandon the mine or keep it operating?

16. An original silver dollar from the late eighteenth century consists of approximately 24 grams of silver. At a price of 19¢ per gram ($6 per troy ounce), the silver content of the coin is currently worth about $4.50. Assume that these coins are in plentiful supply and are not collector's items, so they have no numismatic value. If the current price of silver is 19¢ per gram, will the price of the coin be greater than, less than, or equal to $4.50? Justify your answer.

Applications to Multiple Projects

17. What implicit assumption is made when managers use the equivalent annual benefit method to decide between two projects with different lives that use the same resource?

18. You own a cab company and are evaluating two options to replace your fleet. Either you can take out a five-year lease on the replacement cabs for $500 per month per cab, or you can purchase the cabs outright for $30,000, in which case the cabs will last eight years. You must return the cabs to the leasing company at the end of the lease. The leasing company is responsible for all maintenance costs, but if you purchase the cabs, you will buy a maintenance contract that will cost $100 per month for the life of each cab. Each cab will generate revenues of $1000 per month. Assume the cost of capital is fixed at 12%.

a. Calculate the NPV per cab of both possibilities: purchasing the cabs or leasing them.

b. Calculate the equivalent monthly annual benefit of both opportunities.

c. If you are leasing a cab, you have the opportunity to buy the used cab after five years. Assume that in five years a five-year-old cab will cost either $10,000 or $16,000, with equal likelihood; will have maintenance costs of $500 per month; and will last three more years. Which option should you take?

*19. You own a piece of raw land in an up-and-coming area in Gotham City. The costs to construct a building increase disproportionately with the size of the building. A building of q square feet costs $0.1 \times q^2$ to build. After you construct a building on the lot, it will last forever but you are committed to it: You cannot put another building on the lot. Buildings currently rent at $100 per square foot per month. Rents in this area are expected to increase in five years. There is a 50% chance that they will rise to $200 per square foot per month and stay there forever and a 50% chance that they will stay at $100 per square foot per month forever. The cost of capital is fixed at 12% per year.

a. Should you construct a building on the lot right away? If so, how large should the building be?

b. If you choose to delay the decision, how large a building will you construct in each possible state in five years?

20. Genenco is developing a new drug that will slow the aging process. In order to succeed, two breakthroughs are needed, one to increase the potency of the drug, and the second to eliminate toxic side effects. Research to improve the drug's potency is expected to require an upfront investment of $10 million and take two years; the drug has a 5% chance of success.

Reducing the drug's toxicity will require a $30 million upfront investment, take four years, and has a 20% chance of success. If both efforts are successful, Genenco can sell the patent for the drug to a major drug company for $2 billion. All risk is idiosyncratic, and the risk-free rate is 6%.

    a. What is the NPV of launching both research efforts simultaneously?

    b. What is the optimal order to stage the investments?

    c. What is the NPV with the optimal staging?

21. Your engineers are developing a new product to launch next year that will require both software and hardware innovations. The software team requests a budget of $5 million and forecasts an 80% chance of success. The hardware team requests a $10 million budget and forecasts a 50% chance of success. Both teams will need 6 months to work on the product, and the risk-free interest rate is 4% APR with semiannual compounding.

    a. Which team should work on the project first?

    b. Suppose that before anyone has worked on the project, the hardware team comes back and revises their proposal, changing the estimated chance of success to 75% based on new information. Will this affect your decision in part a?

Rules of Thumb

22. Your firm is thinking of expanding. If you invest today, the expansion will generate $10 million in FCF at the end of the year, and will have a continuation value of either $150 million (if the economy improves) or $50 million (if the economy does not improve). If you wait until next year to invest, you will just receive the continuation value. Suppose the risk-free rate is 5% and the risk-neutral probability that the economy improves is 45%. Assume the cost of expanding is the same this year or next year.

    a. If the cost of expanding is $80 million, should you do so today, or wait until next year to decide?

    b. At what cost of expanding would you be indifferent between expanding now and waiting? What profitability index does this correspond to?

23. Assume that the project in Example 22.5 pays an annual cash flow of $100,000 (instead of $90,000).

    a. What is the NPV of investing today?

    b. What is the NPV of waiting and investing tomorrow?

    c. Verify that the hurdle rate rule of thumb gives the correct time to invest in this case.

24. Assume that the project in Example 22.5 pays an annual cash flow of $80,000 (instead of $90,000).

    a. What is the NPV of investing today?

    b. What is the NPV of waiting and investing tomorrow?

    c. Verify whether the hurdle rate rule of thumb (based on the data in the example) gives the correct time to invest in this case.

Long-Term Financing

THE LAW OF ONE PRICE CONNECTION. How should a firm raise the funds it needs to undertake its investments? In the capital structure part of the text, we discussed the financial manager's choice among the major categories of financing, debt, and equity. In this part of the book, we explain the mechanics of implementing these decisions. Chapter 23 describes the process a company goes through when it raises equity capital. In Chapter 24, we review firms' use of debt markets to raise capital. Chapter 25 introduces an alternative to long-term debt financing, leasing. By presenting leasing as a financing alternative, we apply the Law of One Price to determine that the benefits of leasing must derive from tax differences, incentive effects, or other market imperfections.

CHAPTER 23

The Mechanics of Raising Equity Capital

As we pointed out in Chapter 1, most businesses in Canada are small sole proprietorships and partnerships. That said, as a whole, these firms generate only 30% of total Canadian business income before tax. One limitation of a sole proprietorship is that it does not allow access to outside equity capital, so the business has relatively little capacity for growth. Another limitation is that the sole proprietor is forced to hold a large fraction of his or her wealth in a single asset—the company—and therefore is likely to be undiversified. By incorporating, businesses can gain access to capital and founders can reduce the risk of their portfolios by selling some of their equity and diversifying. Consequently, even though corporations make up the minority of Canadian businesses, they account for 70% of business income before tax in the Canadian economy. A similar situation is found in most developed countries. For example, in the U.S., over 80% of businesses are either sole proprietorships or partnerships, but nearly 85% of sales are generated by businesses organized as corporations.

In this chapter, we discuss how companies raise equity capital. To illustrate this concept, we follow the case of a real company, RealNetworks, Inc. (ticker: RNWK). RealNetworks is a leading creator of digital media services and software. Customers use RealNetworks products to find, play, purchase, and manage digital music, videos, and games. RealNetworks was founded in 1993 and incorporated in 1994. Using the example of RealNetworks, we first discuss the alternative ways new companies can raise capital and then examine the impact of these funding alternatives on current and new investors.

23.1 EQUITY FINANCING FOR PRIVATE COMPANIES

The initial capital that is required to start a business is usually provided by the entrepreneur herself and her immediate family. Few families, however, have the resources to finance a growing business, so growth almost always requires outside capital. A private company must seek sources that can provide this capital, but it must also understand how the infusion of outside capital will affect the control of the company, particularly when outside investors decide to cash out their investments in the company.

SOURCES OF FUNDING

When a private company decides to raise outside equity capital, it can seek funding from several potential sources: angel investors, venture capital firms, private equity firms, institutional investors, sovereign wealth funds, and corporate investors.

ANGEL INVESTORS. Individual investors who buy equity in small private firms are called **angel investors**. For many start-ups, the first round of outside private equity financing is often obtained from angels. These investors are frequently friends or acquaintances of the entrepreneur. Because their capital investment is often large relative to the amount of capital already in place at the firm, they typically receive a sizeable equity share in the business in return for their funds. As a result, these investors may have substantial influence in the business decisions of the firm. Angels may also bring expertise to the firm that the entrepreneur lacks.

Although in some cases the capital available from angel investors is sufficient, in most cases firms need more capital than what a few angels can provide. Finding angels is difficult—often it is a function of how well connected the entrepreneur is in the local community. Most entrepreneurs, especially those launching their first start-up company, have few relationships with people with substantial capital to invest. At some point, many firms that require equity capital for growth must turn to the venture capital industry.

VENTURE CAPITAL FIRMS. A **venture capital firm** is a limited partnership that specializes in raising money to invest in the private equity of young firms. Table 23.1 lists the 10 largest venture capital funds raised in Canada between 2002 and 2006.

Typically, institutional investors, such as pension funds, are the limited partners. The general partners work for the venture capital firm and run the venture capital firm; they are called **venture capitalists**. Venture capital firms offer limited partners a number of advantages over investing directly in start-ups themselves. Venture firms invest in many start-ups, so limited partners get the benefit of this diversification. More importantly, limited partners also benefit from the expertise of the general partners. However, these advantages come at a cost—general partners charge substantial fees to run the firm. In addition to an annual management fee of about 1.5% to 2.5% of the fund's committed capital, general partners also take a share of any positive return generated by the fund in a fee referred to as **carried interest**. Most firms charge 20%, but the successful firms may take more than 30% of any profits as carried interest.

Venture capital firms can provide substantial capital for young companies. For example, Thomson Reuters reports that, in 2007, the private equity market devoted to venture capital totalled over $22 billion in Canada. Over $16 billion was raised between 2001 and 2007 by venture capital funds in Canada. In 2007, Canadian venture capital funds did 520 deals providing funding of $1.5 billion, or about $2.9 million per deal. In return, venture capitalists often demand a great deal of control. Paul Gompers and Josh Lerner[1]

---

1. Paul A. Gompers and Josh Lerner, *The Venture Capital Cycle* (Cambridge, MA: M.I.T. Press, 1999).

THE 10 LARGEST VENTURE CAPITAL FUNDS RAISED IN CANADA BETWEEN 2002 AND 2006

TABLE 23.1

Venture Capital Fund	Amount Raised ($ million)
Celtic House Venture Partners Fund III	280
Ventures West 8	250
MDS Life Sciences Technology Fund	211
Jefferson Partners Fund IV LP	150
Celtic House Venture Partners Fund II	135
Skypoint Telecom Fund II	130
J.L. Albright IV Venture Fund	121
MMV Financial	112
EdgeStone Capital Venture Fund II LP	108
CTI Life Sciences Fund	100

Source: Private Equity Canada 2006, © 2007 McKinsey & Company and Thomson Financial Canada.

report that venture capitalists typically control about one-third of the seats on a start-up's board of directors, and often represent the single largest voting block on the board. Although entrepreneurs generally view this control as a necessary cost of obtaining venture capital, it can actually be an important benefit of accepting venture financing. Venture capitalists use their control to protect their investments, so they may therefore perform a key nurturing and monitoring role for the firm.

The importance of the venture capital sector has grown enormously in the last 50 years. It peaked at the height of the dot-com boom in 2000–2001. As Figure 23.1 shows, the sector declined and then levelled off in the following years.

PRIVATE EQUITY FIRMS.   A **private equity firm** is organized very similarly to venture capital firms, but these firms invest in the equity of existing privately held firms rather than start-up companies. Often private equity firms initiate their investment by finding a publicly traded firm and purchasing all the outstanding equity, thereby taking the company private in a transaction called a **leveraged buyout (LBO)** because in most cases the private equity firms use debt as well as equity to finance the purchase.

Private equity firms share the advantages of venture capital firms, and also charge similar fees. One key difference between private equity and venture capital is the magnitude invested. Because private equity firms are buying existing mature businesses, the investment size is often over 100 times the size of a typical venture capital investment. Table 23.2 lists the top 10 private equity funds in the world in 2009 based on the total amount of investment capital each firm raised over the last five years.

INSTITUTIONAL INVESTORS.   Institutional investors such as pension funds, insurance companies, endowments, and foundations manage large quantities of money. They are major investors in many different types of assets, so, not surprisingly, they are also active investors in private companies. Institutional investors may invest directly in private firms, or they may invest indirectly by becoming limited partners in venture capital firms. Institutional interest

FIGURE 23.1

Venture Capital Funding in Canada

Panel (a) indicates the total number of venture capital deals by year. Panel (b) shows the total dollar amount of venture capital funds raised.

Sources: Canadian Venture Capital Association, Macdonald and Associates Ltd., McKinsey & Company, Thomson Reuters Canada, and Industry Canada.

(a)

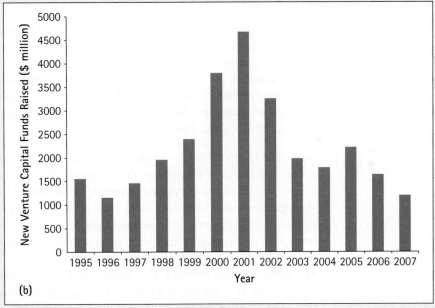

(b)

in private equity has grown dramatically in recent years. For example, McKinsey & Company reported that in Canada, institutional investors accounted for 32% (or $24 billion) of private equity funds under management in 2007, up from 28% (or $18 billion) in 2006.

SOVEREIGN WEALTH FUNDS. **Sovereign wealth funds (SWFs)** are pools of money controlled by a government. They are usually raised from royalty, resource revenue, or taxes that have been collected. SWFs have existed for many years. For example, the Kuwait Investment Board was founded in 1953 and is now called the Kuwait Reserve for Future Generations. The Alberta Heritage Savings Trust Fund, founded in 1976, is

TOP 10 PRIVATE EQUITY FUNDS IN THE WORLD IN 2009

TABLE 23.2

Rank	Firm Name	Headquarters	Five-Year Fundraising Total ($ millions)
1	TPG	Fort Worth	$52,352
2	Goldman Sachs Principal Investment Area	New York	$48,993
3	The Carlyle Group	Washington DC	$47,732
4	Kohlberg Kravis Roberts	New York	$40,460
5	Apollo Global Management	New York	$35,183
6	Bain Capital	Boston	$34,949
7	CVC Capital Partners	London	$33,726
8	The Blackstone Group	New York	$30,800
9	Warburg Pincus	New York	$23,000
10	Apax Partners	London	$21,336

Source: Private Equity International, www.peimedia.com/pei300.

another example. In 2007, SWFs became increasingly newsworthy as they invested in troubled financial institutions. SWFs also play an active role in the private equity market and are the largest limited partners in global private equity markets. According to the SWF Institute (www.swfinstitute.org), as of June 30, 2008, the largest SWF was the Abu Dhabi Investment Authority with assets of $875 billion. In 2008, the top 10 SWFs in terms of assets came from Abu Dhabi, China (three funds), Singapore (two funds), Norway, Saudi Arabia, Kuwait, and Russia.

CORPORATE INVESTORS. Many established corporations purchase equity in younger, private companies. A corporation that invests in private companies is called many different names, including **corporate investor**, **corporate partner**, **strategic partner**, and **strategic investor**. Most of the other types of investors in private firms that we have considered so far are primarily interested in the financial return that they will earn on their investments. Corporate investors, by contrast, might invest for corporate strategic objectives in addition to the desire for investment returns. For example, in May 2009 automaker Daimler invested $50 million for a 10% equity stake in electric car maker Tesla as part of a strategic collaboration on the development of lithium-ion battery systems, electric drive systems, and individual vehicle projects.

OUTSIDE INVESTORS

When a company founder decides to sell equity to outside investors for the first time, it is common practice for private companies to issue preferred stock rather than common stock to raise capital. **Preferred stock** issued by mature companies such as banks usually has a preferential dividend and seniority in any liquidation and sometimes special voting rights. Conversely, the preferred stock issued by young companies typically does not pay regular cash dividends. However, this preferred stock usually gives the owner an option to convert it into common stock on some future date, so it is often called **convertible preferred stock**. In short, it will have all of the future rights and benefits of common stock if things go well. Of course, if the company runs into financial difficulties, the preferred stockholders have a senior claim on the assets of the firm relative to any common stockholders (who are often the employees of the firm).

RealNetworks, which was founded by Robert Glaser in 1993, was initially funded with an investment of approximately $1 million by Glaser. As of April 1995, Glaser's $1 million initial investment in RealNetworks represented 13,713,439 shares of Series A preferred stock, implying an initial purchase price of about $0.07 per share. RealNetworks needed more capital, and management decided to raise this money by selling equity in the form of convertible preferred stock.

The company's first round of outside equity funding was Series B preferred stock. RealNetworks sold 2,686,567 shares of Series B preferred stock at $0.67 per share in April 1995.[2] After this funding round the distribution of ownership was

	Number of Shares	Price per Share ($)	Total Value ($ million)	Percentage Ownership
Series A	13,713,439	0.67	9.2	83.6%
Series B	2,686,567	0.67	1.8	16.4%
	16,400,006		11.0	100.0%

The Series B preferred shares were new shares of stock being sold by RealNetworks. At the price the new shares were sold for, Glaser's shares were worth $9.2 million and represented 83.6% of the outstanding shares. The value of the prior shares outstanding at the price in the funding round ($9.2 million in this example) is called the **pre-money valuation**. The value of the whole firm (old plus new shares) at the funding round price ($11.0 million) is known as the **post-money valuation**.

EXAMPLE 23.1

FUNDING AND OWNERSHIP

Problem
You founded your own firm two years ago. You initially contributed $100,000 of your money and in return received 1,500,000 shares of stock. Since then, you have sold an additional 500,000 shares to angel investors. You are now considering raising even more capital from a venture capitalist. This venture capitalist would invest $6 million and would receive 3,000,000 newly issued shares. What is the post-money valuation? Assuming that this is the venture capitalist's first investment in your company, what percentage of the firm will she end up owning? What percentage will you own? What is the value of your shares?

Solution
After this funding round, there will be a total of 5,000,000 shares outstanding:

Your shares	1,500,000
Angel investors' shares	500,000
Newly issued shares	3,000,000
Total	5,000,000

---

2. The number of shares of RealNetworks preferred stock given here for this and subsequent funding comes from the IPO prospectus (available on EDGAR at www.sec.gov/edgar/searchedgar/webusers. htm). For simplicity, we have ignored warrants to purchase additional shares that were also issued and a small amount of employee common stock that existed.

The venture capitalist would be paying $6,000,000/3,000,000 = $2 per share. Therefore, the post-money valuation would be 5,000,000($2) = $10 million. Because she is buying 3,000,000 shares, and there will be 5,000,000 total shares outstanding after the funding round, the venture capitalist will end up owning 3,000,000/5,000,000 = 60% of the firm. You will own 1,500,000/5,000,000 = 30% of the firm, and the post-money valuation of your shares is 1,500,000($2) = $3,000,000.

Over the next few years, RealNetworks raised three more rounds of outside equity in addition to the Series B funding round:

Series	Date	Number of Shares	Share Price ($)	Capital Raised ($ million)
B	April 1995	2,686,567	0.67	1.8
C	Oct. 1995	2,904,305	1.96	5.7
D	Nov. 1996	2,381,010	7.53	17.9
E	July 1997	3,338,374	8.99	30.0

In each case, investors bought preferred stock in the private company. These investors were very similar to the profile of typical investors in private firms that we described earlier. Angel investors purchased the Series B stock. The investors in Series C and D stock were primarily venture capital funds. Microsoft purchased the Series E stock as a corporate investor.

EXITING AN INVESTMENT IN A PRIVATE COMPANY

Over time, the value of a share of RealNetworks' stock and the size of its funding rounds increased. Because investors in Series E were willing to pay $8.99 for a share of preferred stock with equivalent rights in July 1997, the post-money valuation of existing preferred stock was $8.99 per share. Because RealNetworks was still a private company, however, investors could not liquidate their investment by selling their stock in the public stock markets.

An important consideration for investors in private companies is their **exit strategy**— how they will eventually realize the return from their investment. Investors exit in two main ways: through an acquisition or through an initial public offering (IPO). Often large corporations purchase successful start-up companies. In such a case, the acquiring company purchases the outstanding stock of the private company, allowing all investors to cash out. Roughly 81% of Canadian venture capital–backed exits from 2003–2007 occurred through mergers or acquisitions.[3]

The alternative way to provide liquidity to its investors is for the company to become a publicly traded company. From 2003–2007, there were 42 IPOs of Canadian venture capital–backed companies.

CONCEPT CHECK

1. What are the main sources of funding for private companies to raise outside equity capital?

2. What is a venture capital firm?

---

3. Thomson Financial, *Canada's Venture Capital Industry in 2007*.

INTERVIEW WITH DAN MACDONALD

Dan MacDonald is president and CEO of InNOVAcorp. Based in Halifax, InNOVAcorp is an early stage venture capital firm, focusing on high-potential venture-grade companies in the areas of information technology, life sciences, and clean technology.

QUESTION: Can you describe InNOVAcorp's business model?

ANSWER: InNOVAcorp is a venture capital company. We identify high-potential start-up companies and work with them, invest in them, and ultimately bring them to market. Our business model is centred on the success of the companies in which we invest. We provide equity funding, and for that we get shares in the companies. As these companies progress and make revenues and profits, we get revenues from dividends. We get a financial exit when a company is acquired or merged with another, larger company. From time to time these companies go public in initial public offerings; we make money and are able to exit that way too.

QUESTION: What are some of the challenges facing InNOVAcorp in its venture capital operations?

ANSWER: There are three main challenges we face working with start-up companies. One is skill sets. Most start-up companies have very strong and deep skills in a particular area of business but lack other skills like marketing and business development. We can help through our business incubation and mentoring services. The second challenge we face is market validation. Many companies really struggle to validate the marketability or the addressable market of their product. Our expert staff and advisors and our extensive network allow us to help our companies with competitive analysis, business planning, and business counselling. Third is the challenge of raising money. It is always difficult to raise money for start-up companies. With the market turmoil and contractions in the credit market in 2008, this challenge is especially important.

QUESTION: Can you discuss InNOVAcorp's successes and opportunities?

ANSWER: From an opportunity point of view there are many high-tech companies starting in the area that we serve. That is good news. Our pipeline in 2005 was 85 prospect companies; in 2007 it was 258. There is a lot of buzz around start-up companies, so there is an opportunity for us to seize the best and brightest of those. InNOVAcorp has had a lot of recent successes. As of 2007, we have helped raise over $95 million in venture capital for our companies. For every dollar that we invest, we look to leverage at least three other dollars. We have been able to raise that $95 million alongside our own monies. In 2007, the companies that came through our business model generated over $205 million of export revenue. That is a significant success. Some of the companies that we have invested in over the last couple of years have gained significant traction and are taking on the world in the areas of medical devices, information technology, and clean technology.

A key success factor for our business model, and more specifically for our investee companies, is the ability to raise money by syndicating venture deals. In other words, it is not good enough for InNOVAcorp to invest in a high-potential company; we need to attract other syndicated investors from the region, nationally, and even internationally. That is a key success factor for InNOVAcorp.

QUESTION: Why are venture capital firms like InNOVAcorp important for the Canadian economy?

ANSWER: Firms like InNOVAcorp help to renew the Canadian economy. The economies of the world are changing very rapidly. There is definitely a tilt in momentum from resource-based industries toward knowledge-based industries. InNOVAcorp is an organization looking for, helping, mentoring, and building knowledge-based companies. That is very important for the Canadian economy.

For more on the Dan MacDonald interview, see his discussion of mergers and acquisitions in Chapter 28.

23.2 THE INITIAL PUBLIC OFFERING

The process of selling stock to the public for the first time is called an **initial public offering (IPO)**. In this section we look at the mechanics of IPOs and discuss some related puzzles.

ADVANTAGES AND DISADVANTAGES OF GOING PUBLIC

The two advantages of going public are greater liquidity and better access to capital. By going public, companies give their private equity investors the ability to diversify. In addition, public companies typically have access to much larger amounts of capital through the public markets, both in the initial public offering and in subsequent offerings. The Canadian IPO market was hot from 2004 to 2006. According to PricewaterhouseCoopers, over $6.3 billion of equity was issued, on average, per year. In 2007, this number dropped to only $3.4 billion as equity markets contracted due to the global credit crisis. Ernst & Young reported that 2008 IPO activity globally was down more than 60% compared to 2007 and continued to drop in the first half of 2009.

The average size of an IPO in Canada in 2007 was only $34.5 million, which is quite small compared to IPOs in other countries. In the U.S. in 2007, the average IPO was for $220 million. According to Ernst & Young, in 2006 the ten largest equity issues in the world each raised more than $2 billion (see Table 23.3). In RealNetworks' case, its last round of private equity funding raised about $30 million in July 1997. The firm raised $43 million when it went public in November of the same year; less than two years later, it raised an additional $267 million by selling more stock to the public. As a public company, RealNetworks was able to raise substantially more money.

The major advantage of undertaking an IPO is also one of the major disadvantages of an IPO: When investors diversify their holdings, the equity holders of the corporation become more widely dispersed. This undermines investors' ability to monitor the company's management and thus represents a loss of control. Furthermore, once a company goes public, it

THE 10 LARGEST GLOBAL EQUITY ISSUES, 2006

TABLE 23.3

Rank	Issuer Company Name	Country	Amount ($US billion)
1	Industrial & Commercial Bank of China-ICBC	China	21.929
2	Bank of China Ltd	China	11.186
3	Rosneft	Russian Federation	10.656
4	Natixis	France	5.296
5	Standard Life Assurance Co	United Kingdom	4.444
6	Lotte Shopping Ltd	South Korea	3.738
7	Aozora Bank Ltd	Japan	3.218
8	Saras Spa	Italy	2.637
9	Mastercard Inc	United States	2.579
10	China Communications Construction Co Ltd	China	2.379

Source: Ernst & Young, *Globalization Global IPO Trends Report 2007.*

must satisfy all of the requirements of public companies. Several high-profile corporate scandals during the early part of the twenty-first century prompted tougher regulations designed to address corporate abuses. Organizations such as the Securities and Exchange Commission (SEC) in the United States, the provincial securities commissions in Canada, the securities exchanges (including the TSX, New York Stock Exchange, and NASDAQ), the U.S. Congress (through the Sarbanes-Oxley Act of 2002), and the Parliament of Canada adopted new standards that focused on more thorough financial disclosure, greater accountability, and more stringent requirements for the board of directors. These standards, in general, were designed to provide better protection for investors. However, compliance with the new standards is costly and time-consuming for public companies.

TYPES OF OFFERINGS

After deciding to go public, managers of the company work with an **underwriter**, an investment banking firm that manages the offering and designs its structure. Choices include the type of shares to be sold and the mechanism the financial advisor will use to sell the stock.

PRIMARY AND SECONDARY OFFERINGS. At an IPO, a firm offers a large block of shares for sale to the public for the first time. The shares that are sold in the IPO may be either new shares that raise new capital, known as a **primary offering**, or existing shares that are sold by current shareholders (as part of their exit strategy), known as a **secondary offering**.

BEST-EFFORTS, FIRM COMMITMENT, AND AUCTION IPOs. For smaller IPOs, the underwriter commonly accepts the deal on a **best-efforts** basis. In this case, the underwriter does not guarantee that the stock will be sold, but instead tries to sell the stock for the best possible price. Often such deals have an all-or-none clause: Either all of the shares are sold in the IPO, or the deal is called off.

More commonly, an underwriter and an issuing firm agree to a **firm commitment** IPO, in which the underwriter guarantees that it will sell all of the stock at the offer price. The underwriter purchases the entire issue (at a slightly lower price than the offer price) and then resells it at the offer price. If the entire issue does not sell out, the underwriter is on the hook: The remaining shares must be sold at a lower price and the underwriter must take the loss. The most notorious loss in the industry happened when the British government privatized British Petroleum. In a highly unusual deal, the company was taken public gradually. The British government sold its final stake in British Petroleum at the time of the October 1987 stock market crash. The offer price was set just before the crash, but the offering occurred after the crash.[4] At the end of the first day's trading, the underwriters were facing a loss of $1.29 billion. The price then fell even further, until the Kuwaiti Investment Office stepped in and started purchasing a large stake in the company.

In recent years, the investment banking firm of W.R. Hambrecht and Company has attempted to change the IPO process by selling new issues directly to the public using an online **auction IPO** mechanism called OpenIPO. Rather than setting the price itself in the traditional way, Hambrecht lets the market determine the price of the stock by auctioning off the company.[5] Investors place bids over a set period of time. An auction IPO then sets

---

4. This deal was exceptional in that the offer price was determined more than a week before the issue date. In the United States, the underwriter usually sets the final offer price within a day of the IPO date.

5. You can find details about Hambrecht's auction IPO process at www.wrhambrecht.com/ind/auctions/openipo/index.html.

the highest price such that the number of bids at or above that price equals the number of offered shares. All winning bidders pay this price, even if their bid was higher. The first OpenIPO was the $11.55 million IPO for Ravenswood Winery, completed in 1999.

EXAMPLE 23.2   **AUCTION IPO PRICING**

Problem

Fleming Educational Software Inc. is selling 500,000 shares of stock in an auction IPO. At the end of the bidding period, Fleming's investment bank has received the following bids:

Price ($)	Number of Shares Bid
8.00	25,000
7.75	100,000
7.50	75,000
7.25	150,000
7.00	150,000
6.75	275,000
6.50	125,000

What will the offer price of the shares be?

Solution

First, we compute the total number of shares demanded at or above any given price:

Price ($)	Cumulative Demand
8.00	25,000
7.75	125,000
7.50	200,000
7.25	350,000
7.00	500,000
6.75	775,000
6.50	900,000

For example, the company has received bids for a total of 125,000 shares at $7.75 per share or higher (25,000 + 100,000 = 125,000).

Fleming is offering a total of 500,000 shares. The winning auction price would be $7.00 per share, because investors have placed orders for a total of 500,000 shares at a price of $7.00 or higher. All investors who placed bids of at least this price will be able to buy the stock for $7.00 per share, even if their initial bid was higher.

In this example, the cumulative demand at the winning price exactly equals the supply. If total demand at this price were greater than supply, all auction participants who bid prices higher than the winning price would receive their full bid (at the winning price). Shares would be awarded on a pro rata basis to bidders who bid exactly the winning price.

GOOGLE'S IPO

On April 29, 2004, Google Inc. announced plans to go public. Breaking with tradition, Google startled Wall Street by declaring its intention to rely heavily on the auction IPO mechanism for distributing its shares. Google had been profitable since 2001, so, according to Google executives, access to capital was not the only motive to go public. The company also wanted to provide employees and private equity investors with liquidity.

One of the major attractions of the auction mechanism was the possibility of allocating shares to more individual investors. Google also hoped to discourage short-term speculation by letting market bidders set the IPO price. After the Internet stock market boom, there were many lawsuits related to the way underwriters allocated shares. Google hoped to avoid the allocation scandals by letting the auction allocate shares.

Investors who wanted to bid opened a brokerage account with one of the deal's underwriters and then placed their bids with the brokerage house. Google and its underwriters identified the highest bid that allowed the company to sell all of the shares being offered. They also had the flexibility to choose to offer shares at a lower price.

On August 18, 2004, Google sold 19.6 million shares at $85 per share. The $1.67 billion raised was easily the largest auction IPO ever. Google stock (ticker: GOOG) opened trading on the NASDAQ market the next day at $100 per share. Although the Google IPO sometimes stumbled along the way, it represents the most significant example of the use of the auction mechanism as an alternative to the traditional IPO mechanism.

Sources: Kevin Delaney and Robin Sidel, "Google IPO Aims to Change the Rules," *The Wall Street Journal,* April 30, 2004, p. C1; Ruth Simon and Elizabeth Weinstein, "Investors Eagerly Anticipate Google's IPO," *The Wall Street Journal,* April 30, 2004, p. C1; Gregory Zuckerman, "Google Shares Prove Big Winners—for a Day," *The Wall Street Journal,* August 20, 2004, p. C1.

In 2004 Google went public using the auction mechanism, which generated some interest in this alternative. In May 2005, Morningstar raised $140 million in its IPO using a Hambrecht OpenIPO auction.[6] Although the auction IPO mechanism seemed to represent an alternative to traditional IPO procedures, it has not been widely adopted in Canada, the United States, or abroad. Between 1999 and 2008, Hambrecht completed fewer than eighteen auction IPOs.

THE MECHANICS OF AN IPO

The traditional IPO process follows a standardized form. In this section, we explore the steps that underwriters go though during an IPO.

UNDERWRITERS AND THE SYNDICATE. Many IPOs, especially the larger offerings, are managed by a group of underwriters. The **lead underwriter** is the primary investment banking firm responsible for managing the deal. The lead underwriter provides most of the advice and arranges for a group of other underwriters, called the **syndicate**, to help market and sell the issue. Table 23.4 shows the top investment bankers ranked by proceeds raised through equity-related issues (including IPOs) for all Canadian issues and all global issues during 2007. As you can see, the Canadian banks dominate the Canadian market but the major U.S. investment and commercial banks dominate the global underwriting business.

6. Interested readers can find more about auction and traditional IPOs in A. E. Sherman, "Global Trends in IPO Methods: Book Building versus Auctions with Endogenous Entry," *Journal of Financial Economics* 78:3 (2005): 615–649.

2007 TOP 10 CANADIAN EQUITY AND EQUITY-RELATED ISSUERS

TABLE 23.4

Rank	Investment Banking Firm	Proceeds from All Canadian Issues (CAD billion)	Number of Deals
1	RBC Capital Markets	6.3	56
2	BMO Capital Markets	4.5	39
3	Canaccord Capital Corp	4.1	100
4	CIBC World Markets Inc	3.9	58
5	TD Securities Inc	3.7	36
6	GMP Capital Corp	3.5	58
7	Scotia Capital	1.9	24
8	National Bank Financial Inc	1.2	24
9	Genuity Capital Markets	1.2	16
10	UBS	1.1	4

2007 TOP 10 INTERNATIONAL EQUITY AND EQUITY-RELATED ISSUERS

Rank	Investment Banking Firm	Proceeds from All International Issues (USD billion)	Number of Deals
1	UBS	81.2	365
2	JPMorgan	77.8	312
3	Citi	71.1	309
4	Goldman Sachs & Co	70.1	233
5	Morgan Stanley	64.7	271
6	Merrill Lynch	60.6	260
7	Credit Suisse	54.6	235
8	Deutsche Bank AG	52.2	214
9	Lehman Brothers	29.4	153
10	China International Capital Co	20.2	12

Source: Thomson Reuters, Fourth Quarter 2007 *Equity Capital Markets Review* and Fourth Quarter 2007 *Canadian Equity Capital Markets Review.*

Underwriters market the IPO, and they help the company with all the necessary filings. More importantly, they actively participate in determining the offer price. In many cases, the underwriter will also commit to making a market in the stock after the issue, thereby guaranteeing that the stock will be liquid.

REGULATORY FILINGS.   The relevant securities commissions (each provincial securities commission in Canada and the SEC in the United States) require that companies file certain legal documents that provide financial and other information about the company to investors, prior to an IPO. In the U.S., this step is the preparation of the **registration statement**. Company managers work closely with the underwriters to prepare this registration statement and submit it to the SEC. Part of the registration statement, called the **preliminary prospectus** or **red herring**, circulates to investors before the stock is offered. In Canada, the first step is the preparation of the preliminary prospectus; there is no separate registration statement. The reason a preliminary prospectus is also called a red herring is because of the red writing on the prospectus indicating that the prospectus is not yet final, the information may not be complete, and the securities may not be sold until a receipt for the final prospectus is obtained from the relevant securities regulators.

The securities regulators review the preliminary prospectus to make sure that the company has disclosed all of the information necessary for investors to decide whether to purchase the stock. Once the company has satisfied the regulators' disclosure requirements, the regulators approve the stock for sale to the general public. In Canada, the Ontario Securities Commission (OSC) usually takes the lead in reviewing and approving the preliminary prospectus. The other provincial securities commissions usually follow Ontario's decision. The company prepares the **final prospectus** containing all the details of the IPO, including the number of shares offered and the offer price.[7]

To illustrate this process, let's return to RealNetworks. Figure 23.2 shows the cover page for the final prospectus for RealNetworks' IPO. This cover page includes the name of the company, the list of lead underwriters, and summary information about the pricing of the deal. The offering was a primary offering of 3 million shares.

VALUATION. Before the offer price is set, the underwriters work closely with the company to come up with a price range that they believe provides a reasonable valuation for the firm using the techniques described in Chapter 9. As we pointed out in that chapter, there are two ways to value a company: estimate the future cash flows and compute the present value, or estimate the value by examining comparable companies. Most underwriters use both techniques. However, when these techniques give substantially different answers, they often rely on comparables based on recent IPOs.

Once an initial price range is established, the underwriters try to determine what the market thinks of the valuation. They begin by arranging a **road show**, in which senior management and the lead underwriters travel around the country (and sometimes around the world) promoting the company and explaining their rationale for the offer price to the underwriters' largest customers—mainly institutional investors such as mutual funds and pension funds.

At the end of the road show, customers inform the underwriters of their interest by telling the underwriters how many shares they may want to purchase. Although these commitments are non-binding, the underwriters' customers value their long-term relationships with the underwriters, so they rarely go back on their word. The underwriters then add up the total demand and adjust the price until it is unlikely that the issue will fail. This process for coming up with the offer price based on customers' expressions of interest is called **book building**. Because no offer price is set in an auction IPO, book building is not as important in that venue as it is in traditional IPOs. In a recent paper, Professors Ravi Jagannathan and Ann Sherman examine why auctions have failed to become a popular

---

7. Canadian prospectuses may be found at SEDAR, the Web site for Canadian Securities Administrators: www.sedar.com. For U.S. registration statements you can check at EDGAR, the SEC Web site providing registration information to investors: www.sec.gov/edgar/searchedgar/webusers.htm.

The Cover Page of
RealNetworks' IPO Prospectus
The cover page includes the
name of the company, a list
of lead underwriters, and
summary information
about the pricing of the
deal.
Source: Courtesy of RealNetworks,
Inc.

3,000,000 Shares

RealNetworks, Inc.
(formerly "Progressive Networks, Inc.")

Common Stock
(par value $.001 per share)

All of the 3,000,000 shares of Common Stock offered hereby are being sold by RealNetworks, Inc. Prior to the offering, there has been no public market for the Common Stock. For factors considered in determining the initial public offering price, see "Underwriting".

The Common Stock offered hereby involves a high degree of risk. See "Risk Factors" beginning on page 6.

The Common Stock has been approved for quotation on the Nasdaq National Market under the symbol "RNWK," subject to notice of issuance.

THESE SECURITIES HAVE NOT BEEN APPROVED OR DISAPPROVED BY THE SECURITIES AND EXCHANGE COMMISSION OR ANY STATE SECURITIES COMMISSION NOR HAS THE SECURITIES AND EXCHANGE COMMISSION OR ANY STATE SECURITIES COMMISSION PASSED UPON THE ACCURACY OR ADEQUACY OF THIS PROSPECTUS. ANY REPRESENTATION TO THE CONTRARY IS A CRIMINAL OFFENSE.

	Initial Public Offering Price(1)	Underwriting Discount(2)	Proceeds to Company(3)
Per Share	$12.50	$0.875	$11.625
Total(4)	$37,500,000	$2,625,000	$34,875,000

(1) In connection with the offering, the Underwriters have reserved up to 300,000 shares of Common Stock for sale at the initial public offering price to employees and friends of the Company.

(2) The Company has agreed to indemnify the Underwriters against certain liabilities, including liabilities under the Securities Act of 1933, as amended. See "Underwriting".

(3) Before deducting estimated expenses of $950,000 payable by the Company.

(4) The Company has granted the Underwriters an option for 30 days to purchase up to an additional 450,000 shares at the initial public offering price per share, less the underwriting discount, solely to cover over-allotments. If such option is exercised in full, the total initial public offering price, underwriting discount and proceeds to Company will be $43,125,000, $3,018,750 and $40,106,250, respectively. See "Underwriting".

The shares offered hereby are offered severally by the Underwriters, as specified herein, subject to receipt and acceptance by them and subject to their right to reject any order in whole or in part. It is expected that certificates for the shares will be ready for delivery in New York, New York on or about November 26, 1997, against payment therefor in immediately available funds.

Goldman, Sachs & Co.
BancAmerica Robertson Stephens
NationsBanc Montgomery Securities, Inc.

The date of this Prospectus is November 21, 1997.

IPO method and have been plagued by inaccurate pricing and poor aftermarket performance. They suggest that, since auctions do not use the book building process which aids in price discovery, investors are discouraged from participating in auctions.[8]

---

8. "Why Do IPO Auctions Fail?" NBER working paper 12151, March 2006.

| EXAMPLE 23.3 | VALUING AN IPO USING COMPARABLES |

Problem

Wagner Inc. is a private company that designs, manufactures, and distributes branded consumer products. During the most recent fiscal year, Wagner had revenues of $325 million and earnings of $15 million. Wagner has filed a registration statement with the SEC for its IPO. Before the stock is offered, Wagner's investment bankers would like to estimate the value of the company using comparable companies. The investment bankers have assembled the following information based on data for other companies in the same industry that have recently gone public. In each case, the ratios are based on the IPO price.

Company	Price/Earnings	Price/Revenues
Ray Products Corp.	18.8×	1.2×
Byce-Frasier Inc.	19.5×	0.9×
Fashion Industries Group	24.1×	0.8×
Recreation International	22.4×	0.7×
Mean	21.2×	0.9×

After the IPO, Wagner will have 20 million shares outstanding. Estimate the IPO price for Wagner using the price/earnings ratio and the price/revenues ratio.

Solution

If the IPO price of Wagner is based on a price/earnings ratio that is similar to those for recent IPOs, then this ratio will equal the mean of recent deals, or 21.2. Given earnings of $15 million, the total market value of Wagner's stock will be ($15 million)(21.2) = $318 million. With 20 million shares outstanding, the price per share should be $15.90.

Similarly, if Wagner's IPO price implies a price/revenues ratio equal to the recent average of 0.9, then using its revenues of $325 million, the total market value of Wagner will be ($325 million)(0.9) = $292.5 million, or ($292.5/20) = $14.63 per share.

Based on these estimates, the underwriters will probably establish an initial price range for Wagner stock of $13 to $17 per share to take on the road show.

PRICING THE DEAL AND MANAGING RISK. In the RealNetworks' IPO, the final offer price was $12.50 per share.[9] Also, the company agreed to pay the underwriters a fee, called an **underwriting spread**, of $0.875 per share—exactly 7% of the issue price. Because this was a firm commitment deal, the underwriters bought the stock from RealNetworks for $12.50 − $0.875 = $11.625 per share and then resold it to their customers for $12.50 per share.

Recall that when an underwriter provides a firm commitment, it is potentially exposing itself to the risk that the investment banking firm might have to sell the shares at less than the offer price and take a loss. However, according to Tim Loughran and Jay Ritter, between 1990 and 1998, just 9% of U.S. IPOs experienced a fall in share price on the first

---

9. Stock prices for RealNetworks throughout this chapter have not been adjusted for two subsequent stock splits.

day.[10] For another 16% of firms, the price at the end of the first day was the same as the offer price. Therefore, the vast majority of IPOs experienced a price increase on the first day of trading, indicating that the initial offer price was generally lower than the price that stock market investors were willing to pay.

Underwriters appear to use the information they acquire during the book-building stage to intentionally underprice the IPO, thereby reducing their exposure to losses. Furthermore, once the issue price (or offer price) is set, underwriters may invoke another mechanism to protect themselves against a loss—the **over-allotment allocation**, or **greenshoe provision**.[11] This option allows the underwriter to issue more stock, amounting to 15% of the original offer size, at the IPO offer price. Look at footnote 4 on the front page of the RealNetworks prospectus in Figure 23.2. This footnote is a greenshoe provision.

Let's illustrate how underwriters use the greenshoe provision to protect themselves against a loss and thereby manage risk. The RealNetworks prospectus specified that 3 million shares would be offered at $12.50 per share. In addition, the greenshoe provision allowed for the issue of an additional 450,000 shares at $12.50 per share. Underwriters initially market both the initial allotment and the allotment in the greenshoe provision—in RealNetworks' case, all 3.45 million shares (the $12.50 per share price is set so that all 3.45 million shares are expected to sell)—by short selling the greenshoe allotment. Then, if the issue is a success, the underwriter exercises the greenshoe option, thereby covering its short position. If the issue is not a success, the underwriter covers the short position by repurchasing the greenshoe allotment (450,000 shares in the RealNetworks IPO) in the aftermarket, thereby supporting the price.[12]

Once the IPO process is complete, the company's shares trade publicly on an exchange. The lead underwriter usually makes a market in the stock and assigns an analyst to cover it. By doing so, the underwriter increases the liquidity of the stock in the secondary market. This service is of value to both the issuing company and the underwriter's customers. A liquid market ensures that investors who purchased shares via the IPO are able to easily trade those shares. If the stock is actively traded, the issuer will have continued access to the equity markets in the event that the company decides to issue more shares in a new offering. In most cases, the pre-existing shareholders are subject to a 180-day **lockup**; they cannot sell their shares for 180 days after the IPO. Once the lockup period expires, they are free to sell their shares.

IPO PUZZLES

Four characteristics of IPOs puzzle financial economists and are relevant for the financial manager:

1. On average, IPOs appear to be underpriced. The price at the end of trading on the first day is often substantially higher than the IPO price.

2. The number of issues is highly cyclical. When times are good, the market is flooded with new issues; when times are bad, the number of issues dries up.

---

10. "Why Don't Issuers Get Upset About Leaving Money on the Table in IPOs?" *Review of Financial Studies* 15:2 (2002): 413–443.

11. The name derives from the Green Shoe Company, the first issuer to have an over-allotment option in its IPO.

12. Reena Aggarwal, "Stabilization Activities by Underwriters After IPOs," *Journal of Finance* 55:3 (2000): 1075–1103, finds that underwriters initially oversell by an average 10.75% and then cover themselves if necessary using the greenshoe option.

FINANCIAL **CRISIS**
IPO DEALS IN 2008-09

The drop in IPO issues during the 2008 financial crisis was both global and dramatic. The figure below shows the total worldwide dollar volume of IPO proceeds in billions of dollars (blue bars) and number of deals (red line) by quarter, from the last quarter of 2006 to the first quarter of 2009. Comparing the fourth quarter of 2007 (a record quarter for IPO issues) to the fourth quarter of 2008, dollar volume dropped a stunning 97% from $102 billion to just $3 billion. Things got even worse in the first quarter of 2009 with just

$1.4 billion raised. The market for IPOs essentially dried up altogether.

During the 2008 financial crisis, IPO markets were not the only equity issue markets that saw a collapse in volume. The extreme market uncertainty at the time created a "flight to quality." Investors, wary of taking risk, sought to move their capital into risk-free investments like U.S. Treasury securities. The result was a crash in existing equity prices and a greatly reduced supply of new capital to risky asset classes.

Source: Ernst & Young, "Shifting Landscape—Are You Ready?" *Global IPO Trends Report 2009.*

drastically between 2000 and 2001 as to cause a decline of 48% in the dollar volume of new issues. It appears that the number of IPOs is not solely driven by the demand for capital. Sometimes firms and investors seem to favour IPOs; at other times firms appear to rely on alternative sources of capital, and financial economists are not sure why.

COST OF AN IPO

A typical spread—that is, the discount below the issue price at which the underwriter purchases the shares from the issuing firm—is 7% of the issue price for U.S. IPOs. For an issue size of $50 million, this amounts to $3.5 million. By most standards this fee is large, especially considering the additional cost to the firm associated with underpricing. As Figure 23.5 shows, compared to other security issues, the total cost of issuing stock for the first time is substantially larger than the costs for other securities.

Even more puzzling is the seeming lack of sensitivity of fees to issue size. Although a large issue requires some additional effort, one would not expect the increased effort to be rewarded as lucratively. For example, Hsuan-Chi Chen and Jay Ritter found that almost all issues ranging in size from $20 million to $80 million paid fees of about 7%. It is difficult to understand how a $20 million issue can be profitably done for "only" $1.4 million, while an $80 million issue requires paying fees of $5.6 million. Maher Kooli and Jean-Marc Suret found that the fees for Canadian IPOs are less than those for *similar-sized* IPOs in the U.S. For a $50 million IPO, the Canadian spread is only about 6%, compared to 7% in the U.S. However, most Canadian IPOs are much smaller than U.S.

FIGURE 23.5

Relative Costs of Issuing Securities

This figure shows the total direct costs (all underwriting, legal, and auditing costs) of issuing securities as a percentage of the amount of money raised. The figure reports results for IPOs, seasoned equity offerings (subsequent equity offerings), convertible bonds, and straight bonds, for issues of different sizes from 1990–1994.

Source: Adapted from I. Lee, S. Lochhead, J. Ritter, and Q. Zhao, "The Costs of Raising Capital," *Journal of Financial Research* 19:1 (1996): 59–74.

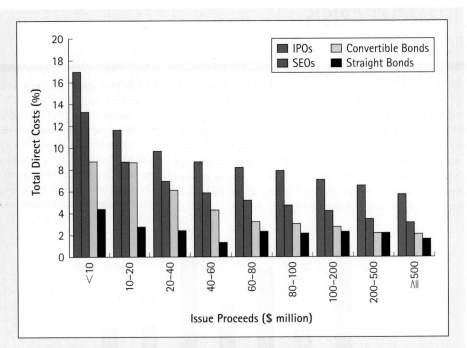

IPOs. The average Canadian IPO is only about one-fifteenth as large as the average U.S. IPO. For very small IPOs there is sensitivity of fees to issue size. The total fee, as a percent of the IPO size, is substantially higher than for large IPOs. As a result, Kooli and Suret also found that when the total fee as a percent of the IPO size is calculated for every IPO, the average percentage spread across all IPOs in Canada is higher than the average percentage spread across all IPOs in the U.S.[15]

No researcher has provided a satisfactory answer to this puzzle. Chen and Ritter argue for implicit collusion by the underwriters, but in response to their paper Robert Hansen finds no evidence of any such collusion.[16] He shows that there is low underwriting industry concentration, that there have been significant new entrants in the IPO-underwriting market, and that a 7% spread is less profitable than normal investment banking activities.

One possible explanation is that by attempting to undercut its rivals, an underwriter may risk signalling that it is not the same quality as its higher-priced competitors, making firms less likely to select that underwriter. Craig Dunbar examined this hypothesis.[17] He found that underwriters charging slightly lower fees appear to enjoy a greater market share, but those charging significantly lower fees have smaller market shares. Indeed, in support of the idea that the quality of the underwriter is important, underwriters that charge very high fees gain market share.

---

15. See Hsuan-Chi Chen and Jay R. Ritter, "The Seven Percent Solution," *Journal of Finance* 55:3 (2000): 1105–1131. See also Maher Kooli and Jean-Marc Suret, "How Cost-Effective Are Canadian IPO Markets?" *Canadian Investment Review* (Winter 2003): 20–28.

16. Robert S. Hansen, "Do Investment Banks Compete in IPOs?: The Advent of the '7% Plus Contract,'" *Journal of Financial Economics* 59:3 (2001): 313–346.

17. Craig G. Dunbar, "Factors Affecting Investment Banks Initial Public Offering Market Share," *Journal of Financial Economics* 55:1 (2000): 3–41.

LONG-RUN UNDERPERFORMANCE

We know that the shares of IPOs generally perform very well immediately following the public offering. It's perhaps surprising, then, that Jay Ritter found that newly listed firms subsequently appear to perform relatively poorly over the following three to five years after their IPOs.[18] In follow-up studies, Alon Brav, Christopher Geczy, and Paul Gompers found that IPOs between 1975 and 1992 underperformed by an average of 44% relative to the S&P 500 over the subsequent five years. Vijay Jog and A. Srivastava found similar results in Canada. Between 1972 and 1993 IPOs underperformed the TSE 300 market index by 17.9%.[19] Jay Ritter and Ivo Welch found that IPOs between 1980 and 2001 underperformed the market by an average of 23.4% during the subsequent three years.[20]

As we will see in the next section, underperformance is not unique to an initial public issuance of equity: It is associated with subsequent issuances as well. Recently, researchers have begun to explore the possibility that underperformance might not result from the issue of equity itself, but rather from the conditions that motivated the equity issuance in the first place. We will explain this idea in more detail in the next section after we explain how a public company issues additional equity.

CONCEPT CHECK

1. Explain the mechanics of an auction IPO.
2. List and discuss four characteristics about IPOs that financial economists find puzzling.

23.3 THE SEASONED EQUITY OFFERING

A firm's need for outside capital rarely ends at the IPO. Usually, profitable growth opportunities occur throughout the life of the firm, and in some cases it is not feasible to finance these opportunities out of retained earnings. Thus, more often than not, firms return to the equity markets and offer new shares for sale, a type of offering called a **seasoned equity offering (SEO)**.

THE MECHANICS OF AN SEO

When a firm issues stock using an SEO, it follows many of the same steps as for an IPO. The main difference is that a market price for the stock already exists, so the price-setting process is not necessary.

RealNetworks has conducted several SEOs since its IPO in 1997. On June 17, 1999, the firm offered 4 million shares in an SEO at a price of $58 per share. Of these shares, 3,525,000 were **primary shares**—new shares issued by the company. The remaining 475,000 shares were **secondary shares**—shares sold by existing shareholders, including the company's founder, Robert Glaser, who sold 310,000 of his shares. Most of the rest of RealNetworks' SEOs occurred between 1999 and 2004 and included secondary shares sold by existing shareholders rather than directly by RealNetworks.

---

18. Jay R. Ritter, "The Long-Run Performance of Initial Public Offerings," *Journal of Finance* 46:1 (1991): 3–27.

19. See Alon Brav, Christopher Geczy, and Paul Gompers, "Is the Abnormal Return Following Equity Issuances Anomalous?" *Journal of Financial Economics* 56 (2000): 209–249, and Vijay Jog and Ashwani Srivastava, "Underpricing of Canadian Initial Public Offerings 1971–1992—An Update," *FINECO* 4 (1994): 81–89.

20. "A Review of IPO Activity, Pricing, and Allocations," *Journal of Finance* 57:4 (2002): 1795–1828.

Historically, intermediaries would advertise the sale of stock (both IPOs and SEOs) by taking out advertisements in newspapers called **tombstones**. Through these ads, investors would know who to call to buy stock. Today, investors become informed about the impending sale of stock by the news media, via a road show, or through the book-building process, so these tombstones are purely ceremonial. Figure 23.6 shows the tombstone advertisement for one RealNetworks SEO.

Two kinds of seasoned equity offerings exist: a cash offer and a rights offer. In a **cash offer**, the firm offers the new shares to investors at large. In a **rights offer**, the firm offers the new shares only to existing shareholders. In Canada and the United States, most offers are cash offers, but the same is not true elsewhere. For example, in the United Kingdom, most seasoned offerings of new shares are rights offers.

Rights offers protect existing shareholders from underpricing. To see how, suppose a company holds $100 in cash and has 50 shares outstanding. Each share is worth $2. The company announces a cash offer for 50 shares at $1 per share. Once this offer is complete,

---

FIGURE 23.6

Tombstone Advertisement for a RealNetworks SEO

This tombstone appeared in *The Wall Street Journal* and advertised the underwriters' participation in this RealNetworks SEO.

Source: Courtesy of RealNetworks, Inc.

4,600,000 Shares

RealNetworks, Inc.

Common Stock

———

Price $58 Per Share

———

Upon request, a copy of the Prospectus describing these securities and the business of the Company may be obtained within any State from any Underwriter who may legally distribute it within such State. The securities are offered only by means of the Prospectus, and this announcement is neither an offer to sell nor a solicitation of an offer to buy.

Goldman, Sachs & Co.

BancBoston Robertson Stephens

Donaldson, Lufkin & Jenrette

Lehman Brothers

Thomas Weisel Partners LLC

Bear, Stearns & Co. Inc.	**Credit Suisse First Boston**	**Ragen MacKenzie** Incorporated
Warburg Dillon Read LLC	**Wasserstein Perella Securities, Inc.**	
Friedman Billings Ramsey	**Pacific Crest Securities Inc.**	

July 7, 1999

the company will have $150 in cash and 100 shares outstanding. The price per share is now $1.50 to reflect the fact that the new shares were sold at a discount. The new shareholders therefore receive a $0.50 windfall at the expense of the old shareholders.

The old shareholders would be protected if, instead of a cash offer, the company did a rights offer. In this case, rather than offer the new shares for general sale, every shareholder would have the right to purchase an additional share for $1 per share. If all shareholders chose to exercise their rights, then after the sale the value of the company would be the same as with a cash offer: It would be worth $150 with 100 shares outstanding and a price of $1.50 per share. In this case, however, the $0.50 windfall accrues to existing shareholders, which exactly offsets the drop in the stock price. Thus, if a firm's management is concerned that its equity may be underpriced in the market, by using a rights offering the firm can continue to issue equity without imposing a loss on its current shareholders.

EXAMPLE 23.5	RAISING MONEY WITH RIGHTS OFFERS

Problem

You are the CFO of a company that is currently worth $1 billion. The firm has 100 million shares outstanding, so the shares are trading at $10 per share. You need to raise $200 million and have announced a rights issue. Each existing shareholder is sent one right for every share he or she owns. You have not decided how many rights you will require to purchase a share of new stock. You will require either four rights to purchase one share at a price of $8 per share, or five rights to purchase two new shares at a price of $5 per share. Which approach will raise more money?

Solution

If all shareholders exercise their rights, then in the first case, 25 million new shares will be purchased at a price of $8 per share, raising $200 million. In the second case, 40 million new shares will be purchased at a price of $5 per share, also raising $200 million. If all shareholders exercise their rights, both approaches will raise the same amount of money.

In both cases, the value of the firm after the issue is $1.2 billion. In the first case, there are 125 million shares outstanding, so the price per share after the issue is $9.60. This price exceeds the issue price of $8, so the shareholders will exercise their rights. In the second case, the number of shares outstanding will grow to 140 million, resulting in a post-issue stock price of $1.2 billion for 140 million shares = $8.57 per share (also higher than the issue price). Again, the shareholders will exercise their rights. In both cases, the same amount of money is raised.

PRICE REACTION

Researchers have found that, on average, the market greets the news of an SEO with a price decline. Often the value destroyed by the price decline can be a significant fraction of the new money raised. This price decline is consistent with the adverse selection we discussed in Chapter 16. Because a company concerned about protecting its existing shareholders will tend to sell only at a price that correctly values or overvalues the firm, investors infer from the decision to sell that the company is likely to be overvalued; hence the price drops with the announcement of the SEO.

FIGURE 23.7

Post-SEO Performance
The figure plots the risk-adjusted return (realized alpha using the Fama-French-Carhart factor specification) of a portfolio made up of seasoned equity offerings between 1976 and 1996. The long-run underperformance appears much more pronounced among smaller firms.

Source: Adapted from A. Brav, C. Geczy, and P. Gompers, "Is the Abnormal Return Following Equity Issuances Anomalous?," *Journal of Financial Economics* 56 (2000): 209–249, Figure 3.

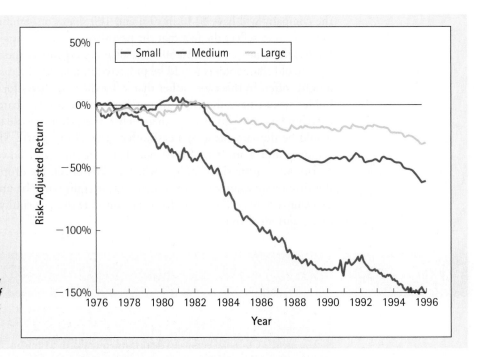

Although adverse selection is a plausible explanation for SEO price reaction, some puzzles remain unexplained. First, by offering a rights issue, a company can mitigate the adverse selection. It is not clear, then, at least in Canada and the United States, why companies do not initiate more rights issues. Second, as with IPOs, evidence suggests that companies underperform following a seasoned offering (see Figure 23.7). At first glance, this underperformance appears to suggest that the stock price decrease is not large enough, because underperformance implies that the price following the issue was too high.

A possible explanation for SEO subsequent underperformance, put forward by Murray Carlson, Adlai Fisher, and Ron Giammarino of the University of British Columbia, is that this outcome might not have to do with the SEO announcement itself, but rather with the conditions that led the firm to choose a SEO.[21] The decision to raise financing externally usually implies that a firm plans to pursue an investment opportunity. As explained in Chapter 22, when a firm invests, it is exercising its growth options. Growth options are riskier than projects themselves, so upon exercise the firm's beta decreases, which explains the post-SEO lower returns. Researchers have found empirical support for this hypothesis.[22]

---

21. Murray Carlson, Adlai Fisher, and Ronald Giammarino, "Corporate Investment and Asset Price Dynamics: Implications for the Cross-Section of Returns," *Journal of Finance* 59:6 (2004): 2577–2603.

22. Alon Brav, Christopher Geczy, and Paul Gompers (referenced in footnote 19); Espen Eckbo, Ronald Masulis, and Oyvind Norli, "Seasoned Public Offerings: Resolution of the New Issues Puzzle," *Journal of Financial Economics* 56:2 (2000): 251–291; Evgeny Lyandres, Le Sun, and Lu Zhang, "Investment-Based Underperformance Following Seasoned Equity Offerings" NBER working paper no. W11459, July 2005, http://ssrn.com/abstract=755695; and Murray Carlson, Adlai Fisher, and Ronald Giammarino, "SEOs, Real Options, and Risk Dynamics: Empirical Evidence," University of British Columbia working paper (2006).

ISSUANCE COSTS

Although not as costly as IPOs, as Figure 23.5 shows, seasoned offerings are still expensive. Underwriting fees amount to 5% of the proceeds of the issue and, as with IPOs, the variation of total costs across issues of different sizes is relatively small. Furthermore, rights offers have lower costs than cash offers.[23] Given the other advantages of a rights offer, it is a puzzle why the majority of offers in Canada and the United States are cash offers. The one advantage of a cash offer is that the underwriter takes on a larger role and, therefore, can credibly certify the issue's quality. If there is a large amount of asymmetric information and a large proportion of existing shareholders are buying the offering anyway, the benefits of certification might overcome the cost difference. Espen Eckbo and Ronald Masulis have found empirical support for this hypothesis.[24]

CONCEPT CHECK

1. What is the difference between a cash offer and a rights offer for a seasoned equity offering?

2. What is the average stock price reaction to an SEO?

SUMMARY

1. Private companies can raise outside equity capital from angel investors, venture capital firms, institutional investors, sovereign wealth funds, or corporate investors.

2. When a company founder sells stock to an outsider to raise capital, the founder's ownership share and control over the company are reduced.

3. Equity investors in private companies plan to sell their stock eventually through one of two main exit strategies: an acquisition or a public offering.

4. An initial public offering (IPO) is the first time a company sells its stock to the public.

5. The main advantages of going public are greater liquidity and better access to capital. Disadvantages include regulatory and financial reporting requirements and the undermining of the investors' ability to monitor the company's management.

6. During an IPO, the shares sold may represent either a primary offering (if the shares are being sold to raise new capital) or a secondary offering (if the shares are sold by earlier investors).

7. Stock may be sold during an IPO on a best-efforts basis, as a firm commitment IPO, or using an auction IPO. The firm commitment process is the most common practice for large firms in Canada and the United States.

8. An underwriter is an investment bank that manages the IPO process and helps the company sell its stock.

   a. The lead underwriter is responsible for managing the IPO.

   b. The lead underwriter forms a group of underwriters, called the investment syndicate, to help sell the stock.

---

23. In the United Kingdom, Myron Slovin, Marie Sushka, and Kam Wah Lai [*Journal of Financial Economics* 57:2 (2000)] found that the average fee for a cash offer is 6.1% versus 4.6% for an underwritten rights offer.

24. "Adverse Selection and the Rights Offer Paradox," *Journal of Financial Economics* 32 (1992): 293–332.

9. The securities regulators require that a company file a preliminary prospectus (in Canada) or a registration statement (in the U.S.) prior to an IPO. The preliminary prospectus (which is part of the registration statement in the U.S.) circulates to investors before the stock is offered. After the deal is completed, the company files a final prospectus and the shares can be sold to the public.

10. Underwriters value a company before an IPO using valuation techniques and by book building.

11. Underwriters face risk during an IPO. A greenshoe provision is one way underwriters manage the risk associated with IPOs.

12. Several puzzles are associated with IPOs.

   a. IPOs are underpriced on average.

   b. New issues are highly cyclical.

   c. The transaction costs of an IPO are very high.

   d. Long-run performance after an IPO is poor on average.

13. A seasoned equity offering (SEO) is the sale of stock by a company that is already publicly traded.

14. Two kinds of SEOs exist: a cash offer (when new shares are sold to investors at large) and a rights offer (when new shares are offered only to existing shareholders).

15. The stock price reaction to an SEO is negative on average.

KEY TERMS

PROBLEMS

The problems marked in green can be found on MyFinanceLab at www.myfinancelab.com. Visit your MyFinanceLab for additional practice. Additional readings for this chapter may be found in the Textbook Resources section on MyFinanceLab.

Equity Financing for Private Companies

1. What are some of the alternative sources from which private companies can raise equity capital?

2. What are the advantages and the disadvantages to a private company of raising money from a corporate investor?

3. Starware Software was founded last year to develop software for gaming applications. The founder initially invested $800,000 and received 8 million shares of stock. Starware now needs to raise a second round of capital, and it has identified a venture capitalist who is interested in investing. This venture capitalist will invest $1 million and wants to own 20% of the company after the investment is completed.

   a. How many shares must the venture capitalist receive to end up with 20% of the company? What is the implied price per share of this funding round?

   b. What will the value of the whole firm be after this investment (the post-money valuation)?

EXCEL

4. Suppose venture capital firm GSB partners raised $100 million to invest in a new fund. GSB charges a 2% management fee each year over the 10-year life of the fund. At the end of 10 years, the investments made by the fund are worth $400 million. GSB also charges 20% carried interest on the profits of the fund (net of management fees).

   a. Assuming all funds were invested immediately (except for aggregate management fees) and all proceeds were received at the end of 10 years, what is the IRR of the investments GSB partners made?

   b. What is the IRR for GSB's limited partners?

EXCEL

5. Three years ago, you founded your own company. You invested $100,000 of your money and received 5 million shares of Series A preferred stock. Your company has since been through three additional rounds of financing.

Round	Price ($)	Number of Shares
Series B	0.50	1,000,000
Series C	2.00	500,000
Series D	4.00	500,000

   a. What is the pre-money valuation for the Series D funding round?

   b. What is the post-money valuation for the Series D funding round?

   c. Assuming that you own only the Series A preferred stock (and that each share of all series of preferred stock is convertible into one share of common stock), what percentage of the firm do you own after the last funding round?

The Initial Public Offering

6. What are the main advantages and disadvantages of going public?

7. Do underwriters face the most risk from a best-efforts IPO, a firm commitment IPO, or an auction IPO? Why?

8. Roundtree Software is going public using an auction IPO. The firm has received the following bids:

Price ($)	Number of Shares
14.00	100,000
13.80	200,000
13.60	500,000
13.40	1,000,000
13.20	1,200,000
13.00	800,000
12.80	400,000

Assuming Roundtree would like to sell 1.8 million shares in its IPO, what will the winning auction offer price be?

EXCEL

9. Three years ago, you founded Outdoor Recreation Inc., a retailer specializing in the sale of equipment and clothing for recreational activities such as camping, skiing, and hiking. So far, your company has gone through three funding rounds:

Round	Date	Investor	Shares	Share Price ($)
Series A	Feb. 2008	You	500,000	1.00
Series B	Aug. 2009	Angels	1,000,000	2.00
Series C	Sept. 2010	Venture capital	2,000,000	3.50

It is now 2011 and you need to raise additional capital to expand your business. You have decided to take your firm public through an IPO. You would like to issue an additional 6.5 million new shares through this IPO. Assuming that your firm successfully completes its IPO, you forecast that 2011 net income will be $7.5 million.

a. Your investment banker advises you that the prices of other recent IPOs have been set such that the P/E ratios based on 2011 forecasted earnings average 20.0. Assuming that your IPO is set at a price that implies a similar multiple, what will your IPO price per share be?

b. What percentage of the firm will you own after the IPO?

10. What is IPO underpricing? If you decide to try to buy shares in every IPO, will you necessarily make money from the underpricing?

11. Margoles Publishing recently completed its IPO. The stock was offered at a price of $14 per share. On the first day of trading, the stock closed at $19 per share. What was the initial return on Margoles? Who benefited from this underpricing? Who lost, and why?

12. Chen Brothers Inc. sold 4 million shares in its IPO, at a price of $18.50 per share. Management negotiated a fee (the underwriting spread) of 7% on this transaction. What was the dollar cost of this fee?

13. Your firm has 10 million shares outstanding, and you are about to issue 5 million new shares in an IPO. The IPO price has been set at $20 per share, and the underwriting spread is 7%. The IPO is a big success with investors, and the share price rises to $50 the first day of trading.

a. How much did your firm raise from the IPO?

b. What is the market value of the firm after the IPO?

c. Suppose your firm could have issued shares directly to investors at their fair market value, in a perfect market with no underwriting spread and no underpricing. What would the share price have been in this case, if you raised the same amount as in part a?

d. Comparing parts b and c, what is the total cost to the firm's original investors due to market imperfections from the IPO?

14. You have an arrangement with your broker to request 1000 shares of all available IPOs. Suppose that 10% of the time, the IPO is "very successful" and appreciates by 100% on the first day, 80% of the time it is "successful" and appreciates by 10%, and 10% of the time it "fails" and falls by 15%.

   a. By what amount does the average IPO appreciate the first day; i.e., what is the average IPO underpricing?

   b. Suppose you expect to receive 50 shares when the IPO is very successful, 200 shares when it is successful, and 1000 shares when it fails. Assume the average IPO price is $15. What is your expected one-day return on your IPO investments?

The Seasoned Equity Offering

15. On January 20, Metropolitan Inc. sold 8 million shares of stock in an SEO. The current market price of Metropolitan at the time was $42.50 per share. Of the 8 million shares sold, 5 million shares were primary shares being sold by the company, and the remaining 3 million shares were being sold by the venture capital investors. Assume the underwriter charges 5% of the gross proceeds as an underwriting fee (which is shared proportionately between primary and secondary shares).

   a. How much money did Metropolitan raise?

   b. How much money did the venture capitalists receive?

16. What are the advantages to a company of selling stock in an SEO using a cash offer? What are the advantages of a rights offer?

17. MacKenzie Corporation currently has 10 million shares of stock outstanding at a price of $40 per share. The company would like to raise money and has announced a rights issue. Every existing shareholder will be sent one right per share of stock that he or she owns. The company plans to require 5 rights to purchase one share at a price of $40 per share.

   a. Assuming the rights issue is successful, how much money will it raise?

   b. What will the share price be after the rights issue? (Assume perfect capital markets.)

   Suppose instead the firm changes the plan so that *each* right gives the holder the right to purchase one share at $8 per share.

   c. How much money will the new plan raise?

   d. What will the share price be after the rights issue?

   e. Which plan is better for the firm's shareholders? Which is more likely to raise the full amount of capital?

CHAPTER

24

NOTATION

YTC   yield to call on a callable bond

YTM   yield to maturity on a bond

PV   present value

Debt Financing

In 2005, Ford Motor Company decided to put one of its subsidiaries, Hertz Corporation, up for competitive bid. On September 13, 2005, *The Wall Street Journal* reported that a group of private investors led by Clayton, Dubilier & Rice (CDR), a private equity firm, had reached a deal with Ford to purchase Hertz's outstanding equity for $5.6 billion. In addition, Hertz had $9.1 billion in existing debt that needed to be refinanced as part of the deal. CDR planned to finance the transaction in part by raising over $11 billion in new debt. Using this Hertz deal as an illustrative example, in this chapter we examine how corporations use the debt markets to raise capital.

When companies raise capital by issuing debt, they have several potential sources from which to seek funds. To complete the Hertz purchase, the group led by CDR ended up relying on at least four different kinds of debt: domestic- and foreign-denominated high-yield bonds, bank loans, and asset-backed securities. In addition, each debt issue has its own specific terms, determined at the time of issue. We therefore begin our exploration of debt financing by explaining the process of issuing debt.

Corporations are not the only entities that use debt financing. Governments, municipalities, and other local entities as well as quasi-government entities (such as Crown corporations) also use the debt markets to raise capital. Hence the scope of this chapter is necessarily broader than that of the last chapter. Here, we introduce all of the important types of debt that exist—not just corporate debt. Finally, we discuss some of the more advanced features of bonds, such as the call provision.

24.1 CORPORATE DEBT

Recall from Chapter 23 our discussion of how private companies become public companies. The deal in which CDR bought Hertz is an example of the opposite transition—a public company becoming private, in this case through a leveraged buyout. In a **leveraged buyout (LBO)**, a group of private investors purchases all the equity of a public corporation.[1] With a total value of $15.2 billion,[2] the leveraged buyout of Hertz was the second largest transaction of its kind at the time of its announcement (the largest LBO at the time was the $31.3 billion takeover of RJR-Nabisco in 1989, surpassed by a $33 billion buyout of hospital owner HCA in 2006 and a $33 billion buyout of Bell Canada announced in 2008 but subsequently cancelled in December of that year). Taking a public corporation private in this way requires issuing large amounts of corporate debt. Table 24.1 shows the debt that was issued to finance the Hertz LBO. Using these debt issues as an example, let's begin by explaining how corporations issue debt.

NEW DEBT ISSUED AS PART OF THE HERTZ LBO

TABLE 24.1

Type of Debt	Amount ($ million)
Public debt	
Junk bond issues	2,668.9
Private debt	
Term loan	1,707.0
Asset-backed revolving line of credit	400.0
Asset-backed "fleet" debt	6,348.0
Total	**$11,123.9**

PUBLIC DEBT

Corporate bonds are securities issued by corporations. They account for a significant amount of invested capital. At the end of 2007, the value of outstanding Canadian corporate bonds was about $452 billion.

THE PROSPECTUS.   A public bond issue is similar to a stock issue. A prospectus or offering memorandum must be produced that describes the details of the offering (Figure 24.1). In addition, for public offerings, the prospectus must include an **indenture**, a formal contract between the bond issuer and a trust company. The trust company represents the bondholders and makes sure that the terms of the indenture are enforced. In the case of default, the trust company represents the bondholders' interests.

---

1. At the time of the deal, Hertz was a wholly owned subsidiary of Ford Motor Company, which itself is a public company. Prior to Ford's acquisition of Hertz's outstanding shares in 2001, Hertz was publicly traded.

2. The total value includes $5.6 billion in equity, $9.1 billion in debt, and $0.5 billion in fees and expenses. In addition to $11.1 billion in new debt, the transaction was financed using $1.8 billion of Hertz's own cash and securities (including a $1.2 billion obligation from Ford, which was forgiven as part of the payment to Ford). The remaining $2.3 billion in private equity was contributed by Clayton, Dubilier & Rice; The Carlyle Group; and Merrill Lynch Global Private Equity.

FIGURE 24.1

Front Cover of the Offering
Memorandum of the Hertz
Junk Bond Issue
Source: Courtesy of Hertz
Corporation.

OFFERING MEMORANDUM   CONFIDENTIAL

CCMG Acquisition Corporation
to be merged with and into The Hertz Corporation
$1,800,000,000 8.875% Senior Notes due 2014
$600,000,000 10.5% Senior Subordinated Notes due 2016
€225,000,000 7.875% Senior Notes due 2014

The Company is offering $1,800,000,000 aggregate principal amount of its 8.875% Senior Notes due 2014 (the "Senior Dollar Notes"), $600,000,000 aggregate principal amount of its 10.5% Senior Subordinated Notes due 2016 (the "Senior Subordinated Notes" and, together with the Senior Dollar Notes, the "Dollar Notes"), and €225,000,000 aggregate principal amount of its 7.875% Senior Notes due 2014 (the "Senior Euro Notes"). The Senior Dollar Notes and the Senior Euro Notes are collectively referred to as the "Senior Notes," and the Dollar Notes and the Senior Euro Notes are collectively referred to as the "Notes."

The Senior Notes will mature on January 1, 2014 and the Senior Subordinated Notes will mature on January 1, 2016. Interest on the Notes will accrue from December 21, 2005. We will pay interest on the Notes on January 1 and July 1 of each year, commencing July 1, 2006.

We have the option to redeem all or a portion of the Senior Notes and the Senior Subordinated Notes at any time (1) before January 1, 2010 and January 1, 2011, respectively, at a redemption price equal to 100% of their principal amount plus the applicable make-whole premium set forth in this offering memorandum and (2) on or after January 1, 2010 and January 1, 2011, respectively, at the redemption prices set forth in this offering memorandum. In addition, on or before January 1, 2009, we may, on one or more occasions, apply funds equal to the proceeds from one or more equity offerings to redeem up to 35% of each series of Notes at the redemption prices set forth in this offering memorandum. If we undergo a change of control or sell certain of our assets, we may be required to offer to purchase Notes from holders.

The Senior Notes will be senior unsecured obligations and will rank equally with all of our senior unsecured indebtedness. The Senior Subordinated Notes will be unsecured obligations and subordinated in right of payment to all of our existing and future senior indebtedness. Each of our domestic subsidiaries that guarantees specified bank indebtedness will guarantee the Senior Notes with guarantees that will rank equally with all of the senior unsecured indebtedness of such subsidiaries and the Senior Subordinated Notes with guarantees that will be unsecured and subordinated in right of payment to all existing and future senior indebtedness of such subsidiaries.

We have agreed to make an offer to exchange the Notes for registered, publicly tradable notes that have substantially identical terms as the Notes. The Dollar Notes are expected to be eligible for trading in the Private Offering, Resale and Trading Automated Linkages (PORTAL™) market. This offering memorandum includes additional information on the terms of the Notes, including redemption and repurchase prices, covenants and transfer restrictions.

Investing in the Notes involves a high degree of risk. See "Risk Factors" beginning on page 23.

We have not registered the Notes under the federal securities laws of the United States or the securities laws of any other jurisdiction. The Initial Purchasers named below are offering the Notes only to qualified institutional buyers under Rule 144A and to persons outside the United States under Regulation S. See "Notice to Investors" for additional information about eligible offerees and transfer restrictions.

Price for each series of Notes: 100%

We expect that (i) delivery of the Dollar Notes will be made to investors in book-entry form through the facilities of The Depository Trust Company on or about December 21, 2005 and (ii) delivery of the Senior Euro Notes will be made to investors in book-entry form through the facilities of the Euroclear System and Clearstream Banking, S.A. on or about December 21, 2005.

Joint Book-Running Managers

Deutsche Bank Securities   **Lehman Brothers**

Merrill Lynch & Co.   **Goldman, Sachs & Co.**   **JPMorgan**

Co-Lead Managers

BNP PARIBAS   **RBS Greenwich Capital**   **Calyon**

The date of this offering memorandum is December 15, 2005.

While corporate bonds almost always pay coupons semiannually, a few corporations (for instance, Coca-Cola) have issued zero-coupon bonds. Corporate bonds have historically been issued with a wide range of maturities. Most corporate bonds have maturities of 30 years or less, although in the past there have even been perpetual bonds (that never mature). In July 1993, for example, the Walt Disney Company issued $150 million in bonds with a maturity of 100 years; these bonds soon became known as the "Sleeping Beauty" bonds. Air Canada had several issues of perpetual bonds; however, these defaulted when the company went bankrupt in 2003.

The face value or principal amount of the bond is denominated in standard increments, most often $1000. The face value does not always correspond to the actual money raised because of underwriting fees and the possibility that the bond might not actually sell for its face value when it is offered for sale initially. If a coupon bond is issued at a discount, it is called an **original issue discount (OID)** bond.

BEARER BONDS AND REGISTERED BONDS.   In a public offering, the indenture lays out the terms of the bond issue. Most corporate bonds are coupon bonds, and coupons are paid in one of two ways. Historically, most bonds were **bearer bonds**, like the one pictured in Figure 24.2. Bearer bonds are like currency: Whoever physically holds the bond certificate owns the bond. To receive a coupon payment, the holder of a bearer bond must provide explicit proof of ownership. The holder does so by literally clipping a coupon off the bond certificate and remitting it to the paying agent. Anyone producing such a coupon is entitled to the payment—hence the name "coupon" payment. Besides the obvious hassles associated with clipping coupons and mailing them in, there are serious security concerns with bearer bonds. Losing such a bond certificate is like losing currency.

Consequently, almost all bonds that are issued today are **registered bonds**. The issuer maintains a list of all holders of its bonds. Brokers keep issuers informed of any changes in ownership. On each coupon payment date, the bond issuer consults its list of registered owners and mails each owner a cheque (or directly deposits the coupon payment into the owner's brokerage account). This system also facilitates tax collection because the government can easily keep track of all interest payments made.

TYPES OF CORPORATE DEBT.   Four types of corporate debt are typically issued: **notes**, **debentures**, **mortgage bonds**, and **asset-backed bonds** (Table 24.2). Debentures and notes are **unsecured debt**, which means that in the event of a bankruptcy bondholders have a claim to only the assets of the firm that are not already pledged as collateral on other debt. Notes typically have shorter maturities (less than ten years) than debentures.

FIGURE 24.2

A Bearer Bond and Its Unclipped Coupons Issued by the Elmira and Williamsport Railroad Company for $500
Source: Courtesy of Heritage Auctions, Inc. © 1999–2006.

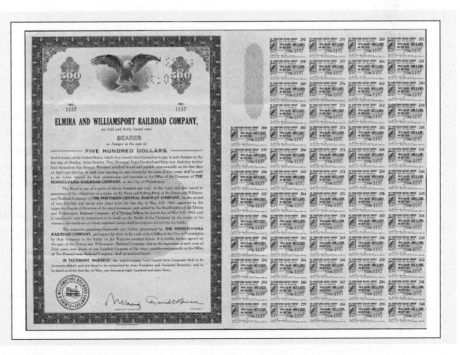

TYPES OF CORPORATE DEBT

TABLE 24.2

Secured	Unsecured
Mortgage bonds (secured with property)	Notes (original maturity less than 10 years)
Asset-backed bonds (secured with any asset)	Debentures

Asset-backed bonds and mortgage bonds are **secured debt**: Specific assets are pledged as collateral that bondholders have a direct claim to in the event of bankruptcy. Mortgage bonds are secured by real property, whereas asset-backed bonds can be secured by any kind of asset. Although the word "bond" is commonly used to mean any kind of debt security, technically a corporate bond must be secured.

Let's illustrate these concepts by returning to the Hertz LBO. Recall that CDR intended to refinance approximately $9 billion of existing Hertz corporate debt. So, subsequent to the agreement, Hertz made a tender offer—a public announcement of an offer to all existing bondholders to buy back its existing debt. This debt repurchase was financed by issuing several kinds of new debt (both secured and unsecured), all of which were claims on Hertz's corporate assets.

As part of the financing, CDR planned to issue $2.7 billion worth of unsecured debt[3]—in this case, high-yield notes known as junk bonds (bonds rated below investment grade).[4] The high-yield issue was divided into three kinds of debt or **tranches** (Table 24.3), all of which made semiannual coupon payments and were issued at par. The largest tranche was a $1.8 billion face-value note maturing in eight years. It paid a coupon of 8.875%, which at the time represented a 4.45% spread over U.S. Treasuries. The rest of the debt financing was made up of asset-backed debt that was sold privately and bank loans.

SENIORITY.   Recall that debentures and notes are unsecured. Because more than one debenture might be outstanding, the bondholder's priority in claiming assets in the event of default, known as the bond's **seniority**, is important. As a result, most debenture issues contain clauses restricting the company from issuing new debt with equal or higher priority than existing debt.

When a firm conducts a subsequent debenture issue that has lower priority than its outstanding debt, the new debt is known as a **subordinated debenture**. In the event of default, the assets not pledged as collateral for outstanding bonds cannot be used to pay off the holders of subordinated debentures until all more senior debt has been paid off. In Hertz's case, one tranche of the junk bond issue is a note that is subordinated to the other two tranches. In the event of bankruptcy, this note has a lower-priority claim on the firm's assets. Because holders of this tranche are likely to receive less in the event of a Hertz default, the yield on this debt is higher than that of the other tranches—10.5% compared to 8.875% for the first tranche.

---

3. In the end, the firm issued only $2 billion in debt because fewer existing bondholders tendered their bonds than expected ($1.6 billion of existing debt remained on the balance sheet after the LBO was completed).

4. A description of corporate credit ratings can be found in Chapter 8 (see Table 8.4).

TABLE 24.3	HERTZ'S DECEMBER 2005 JUNK BOND ISSUES		

	Senior Dollar-Denominated Note	Senior Euro-Denominated Note	Subordinated Dollar-Denominated Note
Face value	$1.8 billion	€225 million	$600 million
Maturity	December 1, 2014	December 1, 2014	December 1, 2016
Coupon	8.875%	7.875%	10.5%
Issue price	Par	Par	Par
Yield	8.875%	7.875%	10.5%
Call features	Up to 35% of the outstanding principal callable at 108.875% in the first three years.	Up to 35% of the outstanding principal callable at 107.875% in the first three years.	Up to 35% of the outstanding principal callable at 110.5% in the first three years.
	After four years, fully callable at:	After four years, fully callable at:	After five years, fully callable at
	• 104.438% in 2010	• 103.938% in 2010	• 105.25% in 2011
	• 102.219% in 2011	• 101.969% in 2011	• 103.50% in 2012
	• Par thereafter	• Par thereafter	• 101.75% in 2013
			• Par thereafter
Settlement	December 21, 2005	December 21, 2005	December 21, 2005
Rating Standard & Poor's	B	B	B
Moody's	B1	B1	B3
Fitch	BB–	BB–	B+

BOND MARKETS. The third tranche of Hertz's junk bond issue is a note that is denominated in euros rather than U.S. dollars—it is an international bond. International bonds are classified into four broadly defined categories. **Domestic bonds** are bonds issued by a local entity and traded in a local market, but purchased by foreigners. They are denominated in the local currency. **Foreign bonds** are bonds issued by a foreign company in a local market and are intended for local investors. They are also denominated in the local currency. Foreign bonds in Canada and the United States are known as **Maple bonds** and **Yankee bonds**, respectively. In other countries, foreign bonds also have special names. For example, in Japan they are called **Samurai bonds**; in the United Kingdom, they are known as **Bulldogs**.

Eurobonds are international bonds that are not denominated in the local currency of the country in which they are issued. Consequently, there is no connection between the physical location of the market on which they trade and the location of the issuing entity. They can be denominated in any number of currencies that might or might not be connected to the location of the issuer. The trading of these bonds is not subject to any particular nation's regulations. **Global bonds** combine the features of domestic, foreign, and Eurobonds, and are offered for sale in several different markets simultaneously. The Hertz junk bond issue is an example of a global bond issue: It was simultaneously offered for sale in the United States and Europe.

A bond that makes its payments in a foreign currency contains the risk of holding that currency and, therefore, is priced off the yields of similar bonds in that currency. Hence the euro-denominated note of the Hertz junk bond issue has a different yield from the dollar-denominated note, even though both bonds have the same seniority and maturity. While they have the same default risk, they differ in their exchange rate risk—the risk that the foreign currency will change in value relative to the local currency.

PRIVATE DEBT

In addition to the junk bond issue, Hertz took out more than $2 billion in bank loans. Bank loans are an example of **private debt**, debt that is not publicly traded. The private debt market is larger than the public debt market. Private debt has the advantage that it avoids the cost of registration but has the disadvantage of being illiquid.

There are two segments of the private debt market: term loans and private placements.

TERM LOANS.   Hertz negotiated a $1.7 billion **term loan**, a bank loan that lasts for a specific term. The term of the Hertz loan was seven years. This particular loan is an example of a **syndicated bank loan**: a single loan that is funded by a group of banks rather than just a single bank. Usually, one member of the syndicate (the lead bank) negotiates the terms of the bank loan. In the Hertz case, Deutsche Bank AG negotiated the loan with CDR and then sold portions of it off to other banks—mostly smaller regional banks that had excess cash but lacked the resources to negotiate a loan of this magnitude by themselves.

Most syndicated loans are rated as investment grade. However, Hertz's term loan is an exception. Term loans such as Hertz's that are associated with LBOs are known as leveraged syndicated loans and are rated as speculative grade; in Hertz's case, Standard & Poor's rated the term loan as BB and Moody's rated it as Ba2.

In addition to the term loan, Dow Jones reported that Hertz negotiated an asset-backed revolving line of credit. A **revolving line of credit** is a credit commitment for a specific time period up to some limit (five years and $1.6 billion in Hertz's case), which a company can use as needed. Hertz's initial draw on the line of credit was $400 million. Because the line of credit is backed by specific assets, it is more secure than the term loan, so Standard & Poor's gave it a BB+ rating.

PRIVATE PLACEMENTS.   A **private placement** is a bond issue that does not trade on a public market but rather is sold to a small group of investors. Because a private placement does not need to be registered, it is less costly to issue. Instead of an indenture, often a simple promissory note is sufficient. Privately placed debt also need not conform to the same standards as public debt; as a consequence, it can be tailored to the particular situation.

Returning to the Hertz deal, CDR privately placed an additional $4.2 billion of U.S. asset-backed securities and $2.1 billion of international asset-backed securities. In this case, the assets backing the debt were the fleet of rental cars Hertz owned; hence this debt was termed "Fleet Debt" in the offering memorandum.

In 1990, the U.S. Securities and Exchange Commission (SEC) issued Rule 144A, which significantly increased the liquidity of certain privately placed debt. Private debt issued under this rule can be traded by large financial institutions among themselves. The rule was motivated by a desire to increase the access of foreign corporations to U.S.

debt markets. Bonds that are issued under this rule are nominally private debt, but because they are tradeable between financial institutions they are only slightly less liquid than public debt. In fact, the $2.8 billion Hertz junk bond issue in Table 24.3 is actually debt issued under Rule 144A (which explains why the offering document in Figure 24.1 is called an "offering memorandum" rather than a "prospectus," because the latter term is reserved for public offerings). As part of the offering, however, the issuers agreed to publicly register the bonds within 390 days.[5] Because the debt was marketed and sold with the understanding that it would become public debt, we classified that issue as public debt.

CONCEPT CHECK
1. List four types of corporate debt that are typically issued.
2. What are the four categories of international bonds?

24.2 OTHER TYPES OF DEBT

Corporations are not the only entities that use debt. We begin with the largest debt sector, loans to government entities.

SOVEREIGN DEBT

Sovereign debt is debt issued by national governments. In 1998, the Government of Canada had about $360 billion of bonds outstanding. By the end of 2007, this amount dropped to only $267 billion following several years of budget surpluses being used to pay down the federal government debt (since that time, the amount has risen as Canada ran deficits in order to attempt to mitigate the economic downturn resulting from the global economic crisis).

The Canadian government sells its domestic debt to financial market distributors and dealers through auctions run by the Bank of Canada. Four kinds of domestic debt securities and three types of foreign debt securities are used by the Government of Canada (see Table 24.4). In addition to these tradeable securities, the government also borrows directly from individuals through Canada Savings Bonds and Canada Premium Bonds (available through financial institutions). **Cash management bills** are pure discount bonds that are issued with very short maturities: as short as one day and less than three months. Treasury Bills are the most common form of pure discount bonds and they are issued with original maturities of either three, six, or twelve months. Fixed-coupon marketable bonds (more commonly known as Government of Canada bonds) are semiannual coupon bonds with original maturities of between 2 and 40 years.

The last type of domestic security that the Government of Canada is currently issuing is the **real return bond** with maturities of up to 30 years. These bonds are standard coupon bonds with one difference: The outstanding principal is adjusted for inflation. Thus, although the coupon *rate* is fixed, the dollar coupon varies because the semiannual coupon payments are a fixed rate of the inflation-adjusted principal. Thus the dollar amounts of both the coupons and the final repayment are adjusted for the effects of inflation.

---

5. If Hertz failed to fulfill this commitment, the interest rate on all the outstanding bonds would increase by 0.5%.

TABLE **24.4**	EXISTING GOVERNMENT OF CANADA SECURITIES

Security Name	Type	Currency of Denomination*	Original Maturity
Cash Management Bills	Discount	CAD	1 day to less than 3 months
Treasury Bills	Discount	CAD	3, 6, or 12 months
Fixed-Coupon Marketable Bonds (Government of Canada Bonds)	Coupon	CAD	2 to 40 years
Real Return Bonds	Coupon	CAD	up to 30 years
Canada Bills	Discount	USD	up to 270 days
Canada Notes	Coupon	USD	up to 5 years
Euro Medium-Term Notes	Coupon	Various (not CAD or USD)	up to 5 years

*CAD refers to the Canadian dollar; USD refers to the U.S. dollar.
Sources: Bank of Canada, Government of Canada (Department of Finance), and Investopedia.com.

EXAMPLE **24.1**	COUPON PAYMENTS ON REAL RETURN BONDS

Problem

Suppose that in January 2000 the Government of Canada issued a 30-year real return bond with a coupon rate of 4%. On the date of issue, the consumer price index (CPI) was 93.5. In July 2008, the CPI had increased to 116.1. What coupon payment was made in July 2008?

Solution

Between the issue date and July 2008, the CPI appreciated by a factor of 116.1/93.5 = 1.24171. Consequently, the principal amount of the bond increased by this amount; that is, the original face value of $1000 increased to $1241.71. Because the bond pays semiannual coupons, the coupon payment was $1241.17 × 0.04/2 = $24.83.

Government of Canada securities are initially sold to the public by auction. Two kinds of auctions are used by the Bank of Canada. For Treasury Bills and fixed-coupon marketable bonds, a multiple-price auction (also called a discriminatory price auction) is used. In this type of auction, the Bank of Canada receives bids from government securities distributors and sells the securities to these dealers at their bid prices. Starting with the highest bidder (in dollar terms) or lowest bidder (in yield terms) the securities are allocated until all are sold. The result is that each successful bidder may pay a different price for the security being sold. The second type of auction is the Dutch auction (or single-price auction), which is used for real return bonds. In this system, bidders submit their bid prices and the number of securities they desire. The bids are ranked from the highest price down. The lowest price that results in all securities being sold becomes the price charged to all bidders.[6] All income from Government of Canada securities is taxable at the federal

---

6. See the Bank of Canada's glossary for further information: www.bankofcanada.ca/en/glossary/.

and provincial levels. If an investor sells a security before it matures, there may be taxes on both interest income and capital gains.[7]

Zero-coupon government securities with maturities longer than one year also trade in the bond market. They are called **STRIP bonds** (Separate Trading of Registered Interest and Principal). The Government of Canada itself does not issue STRIP bonds. Instead, investors (or, more usually, investment banks) purchase fixed-coupon notes and bonds and then resell each coupon and principal payment separately as a zero-coupon bond.

AGENCY SECURITIES

Agency securities are issued by Crown corporations of the Canadian federal government. Canada Mortgage and Housing Corporation (CMHC) bonds are an example, as are Business Development Bank of Canada (BDC) bonds, and Export Development Canada (EDC) bonds. These bonds are either a direct obligation of the Government of Canada (this is the case for the BDC) or are fully guaranteed by the Government of Canada (e.g., the CMHC's bonds).

Agency securities are issued in a variety of types and maturities. By far, the largest fraction of the issues consists of **mortgage-backed securities (MBS)**. Mortgage-backed securities, such as those guaranteed by the CMHC, are one type of **asset-backed securities**. In the case of an MBS, each security is backed by an underlying portfolio or **pool** of mortgages. (Other asset-backed securities may be backed by a portfolio of credit card receivables, consumer loans, car loans, etc.—these would not be considered agency securities if they were created by financial institutions rather than government agencies.) When homeowners in the pool make their mortgage payments, this cash is passed through (minus servicing fees) to the holders of the mortgage-backed securities. Consequently, the cash flows of mortgage-backed securities mirror the cash flows of home mortgages: They are annuities that pay fixed monthly payments over the term of the mortgages in the pool (the most common term is five years) plus a final principal repayment at the end of the term. As most Canadian mortgages have an amortization period longer than the mortgage term, there is normally a substantial amount of principal outstanding at the end of the term. As with most mortgages, the entire principal is not returned at maturity; instead, part of it is also paid back gradually over the life of the bond.

As discussed in Chapter 22, a mortgage borrower usually has an option to repay some or all of the mortgage loan early and this early repayment of principal is also passed through to owners of mortgage-backed securities. Thus holders of CMHC guaranteed mortgage-backed securities face prepayment risk—the risk that the bond will be partially (or wholly) repaid earlier than expected.

PROVINCIAL AND MUNICIPAL BONDS

Provincial and **municipal bonds** are issued by provincial and local governments and their Crown corporations (e.g., Manitoba Hydro or Hydro Quebec). Their interest is treated as taxable income by the Canada Revenue Agency. In the United States, so-called "**munis**" (issued by U.S. states or municipalities) are not taxable at the federal level and some are also exempt from state and local taxes.

---

7. See the Canada Revenue Agency for more information on the taxation of interest and capital gains: www.cra.gc.ca.

FINANCIAL CRISIS
SUBPRIME MORTGAGE-BACKED SECURITIES

The Canada Mortgage and Housing Corporation (CMHC) restricts the types of mortgages that it is prepared to securitize into mortgage-backed securities. For example, CMHC will only securitize mortgages below a certain face value and, more importantly, that meet certain credit criteria. Mortgages that have a high default probability are known as **subprime mortgages**, and the CMHC will not insure these. Nevertheless, subprime mortgages do get written by financial institutions and they are often pooled into mortgage-backed securities and sold to other investors. We can attribute part of the U.S. housing boom in the mid-2000s to the increased availability of subprime mortgages. As the number of subprime mortgages exploded so, too, did the incentives to securitize them.

Unlike the CMHC, private organizations do not carry a government guarantee. Investors looked to credit rating agencies to assess the credit worthiness of the privately issued subprime mortgage-backed securities.* While housing prices in the U.S. rose, default rates on subprime mortgages remained low and the credit rating agencies came under intense pressure to issue the highest credit ratings to subprime mortgage-backed securities. Issuers naturally wanted the high ratings to be able to sell the bonds for high prices, but regulated investors

such as banks also wanted the bonds highly rated so that they would be able to hold them as reserve capital.

When the U.S. housing market turned for the worse in 2007, increased default rates on mortgages resulted in defaults of the securities backed by these mortgages—the subprime mortgage-backed securities did not live up to their high credit rating. A vicious cycle ensued as the credit rating companies dropped the ratings on the bonds, forcing the banks to sell them at a loss (the prices of the bonds dropped as their ratings dropped). As more and more holders of these bonds moved to sell them, the prices dropped further. These losses ate away at the banks' capital base, causing them to pull back from lending. The end result was a near collapse of the financial system and a severe lack of credit availability.

*In addition, private asset-backed securities can be backed by other asset-backed securities. When banks re-securitize other asset-backed securities the new asset-backed security is known as a **collateralized debt obligation (CDO)**. CDO cash flows are usually divided into different tranches that are assigned different priority. For example, investors in the junior tranche of a CDO do not receive any cash flows until investors in the senior tranche have received their promised cash flows.

Most provincial and municipal bonds pay semiannual coupons. A single issue will sometimes contain a number of different maturity dates. Such issues are often called **serial bonds** because the bonds are scheduled to mature serially over a number of years. The coupons on municipal bonds can be either *fixed* or *floating*. A fixed-coupon bond has the same coupon over the life of the bond. In a floating-rate issue, the coupon of the bond is adjusted periodically. The reset formula is a spread over a reference rate like the rate on Treasury Bills that is established when the bond is first issued.

Bonds backed by the full faith and credit of a local government are known as **general obligation bonds** and are not as secure as bonds backed by the full faith and credit of the federal government. Sometimes local governments strengthen the commitment further by tying the promise to a particular revenue source, such as a special fee. Because a local government can always use its general revenue to repay such bonds, this commitment is over and above the usual commitment, so these bonds are called **double-barrelled**. Not all municipal bonds are backed by the full faith and credit of the local government, however. Instead, the local government can pledge specific revenues generated by projects that were initially financed by the bond issue. These bonds are called **revenue bonds**.

CONCEPT CHECK

1. What are the seven kinds of securities issued by the Canadian government?

2. What is an asset-backed security?

3. What is the major difference between U.S. municipal bonds and Canadian municipal bonds?

24.3 BOND COVENANTS

Covenants are restrictive clauses in a bond contract that limit the issuer from taking actions that may undercut its ability to repay the bonds. One might guess that such covenants would not be necessary—after all, why would managers voluntarily take actions that increase the firm's default risk? However, recall from Chapter 16 that when a firm is levered, managers may have an incentive to take actions that benefit equity holders at the expense of debt holders.

For example, once bonds are issued, equity holders have an incentive to increase dividends at the expense of debt holders. Think of an extreme case in which a company issues a bond, and then immediately liquidates its assets, pays out the proceeds (including those from the bond issue) in the form of a dividend to equity holders, and declares bankruptcy. In this case, the equity holders receive the value of the firm's assets plus the proceeds from the bond, while bondholders are left with nothing. Consequently, bond agreements often contain covenants that restrict the ability of management to pay dividends. Other covenants may restrict the level of further indebtedness and specify that the issuer must maintain a minimum amount of working capital. If the issuer fails to live up to any covenant, the bond goes into default. Covenants in the Hertz junk bond issue limited Hertz's ability to incur more debt, make dividend payments, redeem stock, make investments, create liens, transfer or sell assets, and merge or consolidate. They also included a requirement to offer to repurchase the bonds at 101% of face value if the corporation experiences a change in control.

Recall that CDR made a tender offer to repurchase all of Hertz's outstanding debt. CDR made this offer because the outstanding debt had a restrictive covenant that made it difficult to complete a merger or takeover of Hertz. Once the group led by CDR owned more than 50% of this debt, the terms of the prospectus gave CDR the ability to unilaterally change any covenant, thus allowing them to proceed with the LBO.

You might expect that equity holders would try to include as few covenants as possible in a bond agreement. In fact, this is not necessarily the case. The stronger the covenants in the bond contract, the less likely the issuer will default on the bond, and so the lower the interest rate investors will require to buy the bond. That is, by including more covenants, issuers can reduce their costs of borrowing. As discussed in Chapter 16, if the covenants are designed to reduce agency costs by restricting management's ability to take negative-NPV actions that exploit debt holders, then the reduction in the firm's borrowing cost can more than outweigh the cost of the loss of flexibility associated with covenants.

CONCEPT CHECK

1. What happens if an issuer fails to live up to a bond covenant?

2. Why can bond covenants reduce a firm's borrowing cost?

24.4 REPAYMENT PROVISIONS

A bond issuer repays its bonds by making coupon and principal payments as specified in the bond contract. However, this is not the only way an issuer can repay bonds. For example, the issuer can repurchase a fraction of the outstanding bonds in the market, or it can make a tender offer for the entire issue, as Hertz did on its existing bonds. Another way issuers repay bonds is to exercise a *call* provision that allows the issuer to repurchase the bonds at a predetermined price. Bonds that contain such a provision are known as **callable bonds**.

CALL PROVISIONS

Hertz's junk bonds are examples of callable bonds. Table 24.3 lists the call features in each tranche. A call feature allows the issuer of the bond the right (but not the obligation) to retire all outstanding bonds on (or after) a specific date (the **call date**), for the **call price**. The call price is generally set at or above, and expressed as a percentage of, the bond's face value. In Hertz's case, the call dates of the two senior tranches are at the end of the fourth year. For the duration of 2010, the $1.8 billion issue has a call price of 104.438% of the face value of the bond. In the following years, the call price is gradually reduced until in 2012 the bond becomes callable at par. The euro-denominated bond has similar terms at slightly different call prices. The subordinated tranche's call date is a year later and has a different call price structure.

The Hertz bonds are also partially callable in the first three years. Hertz has the option to retire up to 35% of the outstanding principal at the call prices listed in Table 24.3, as long as the funds needed to repurchase the bonds are derived from the proceeds of an equity issuance.

To understand how call provisions affect the price of a bond, we first need to consider when an issuer will exercise its right to call the bond. An issuer can always retire one of its bonds early by repurchasing the bond in the open market. If the call provision offers a cheaper way to retire the bonds, however, the issuer will forgo the option of purchasing the bonds in the open market and call the bonds instead.

Let's examine a more concrete example. Consider a case in which an issuer has issued two bonds that are identical in every respect except that one is callable at par (redeemable at face value) and the other is not callable. This issuer wants to retire one of the two bonds. How does it decide which bond to retire? If bond yields have dropped since the issue date, the non-callable bond will be trading at a premium. Thus, if the issuer wished to retire this bond (by repurchasing it in the open market), it would have to repay more than the outstanding principal. If it chose to call the callable bond instead, the issuer

NEW YORK CITY CALLS ITS MUNICIPAL BONDS

In November 2004, New York City announced plans to call $430 million of its municipal bonds. New York City was an AAA-rated borrower, and these bonds paid relatively high interest rates of 6% to 8%. The city would be refinancing the bonds with new bonds that paid interest rates between 3% and 5%. In total, New York City called 63 individual bond issues with original maturities between 2012 and 2019.

Investors were attracted to the older municipal bonds because of their higher yields. Despite these yields, they did not expect New York City to call these bonds, so the market price for these bonds earlier in the year was 10% to 20% higher than their face value. When New York City announced its plans to call the bonds at prices slightly higher than the face value investors were caught off guard and the market value of the bonds fell accordingly. Investors suffered losses of 15% or more on their AAA-rated investment.

Investors did not expect New York City to call these bonds because it had already refinanced the debt in the early 1990s. According to Internal Revenue Service rules, the city could not refinance again with another tax-exempt issue. However, New York City surprised the market when it decided to refinance the bonds by issuing taxable bonds instead. Although it happens rarely, this example illustrates that investors are sometimes surprised by issuer call strategies.

Source: Aaron Lucchetti, "Municipal-Bond Bans Get a Rude Awakening—Call Feature Can Catch Investors and Money Managers Off Guard," *The Wall Street Journal,* February 8, 2005, p. C1.

would simply pay the outstanding principal. Hence, if yields have dropped, it is cheaper to retire the callable bond. Note that because bond yields have dropped, by exercising the call on the callable bond and then immediately refinancing, the issuer can lower its borrowing costs. Conversely, if yields increased after the issue date, there is no reason to refinance. In addition, both bonds would be trading at a discount. Even if the issuer wished to retire some bonds, it would be better off by repurchasing either bond at less than par in the market than by calling the callable bond for par. Thus when yields have risen, the issuer will not choose to exercise the call on the callable bond.

Let's consider this scenario from the perspective of a bondholder. As we have seen, the issuer will exercise the call option only when the coupon rate of the bond exceeds the prevailing market rate. Therefore, the only time the call is exercised, the bondholder finds herself in the position of looking for an alternative investment when market rates are lower than the bond's coupon rate. That is, the holder of a callable bond faces reinvestment risk precisely when it hurts: when market rates are lower than the coupon rate she is currently receiving. This makes the callable bond relatively less attractive to the bondholder than the identical non-callable bond. Consequently, a callable bond will trade at a lower price (and therefore a higher yield) than an otherwise equivalent non-callable bond.

To understand the relationship between the prices of otherwise identical callable and non-callable bonds, first consider what happens to a bond that is callable at par on only one specific date. Figure 24.3 plots the price of a callable bond and an otherwise identical non-callable bond on the call date as a function of the yield on the non-callable bond. When the yield of the non-callable bond is less than the coupon, the callable bond will be called, so its price is $100. If this yield is greater than the coupon, then the callable bond will not be called, so it has the same price as the non-callable bond. Note that the callable bond price is capped at par: The price can be low when yields are high, but does not rise above the par value when the yield is low.

Before the call date, investors anticipate the optimal strategy that the issuer will follow, and the bond price reflects this strategy, as Figure 24.4 illustrates. When market yields are

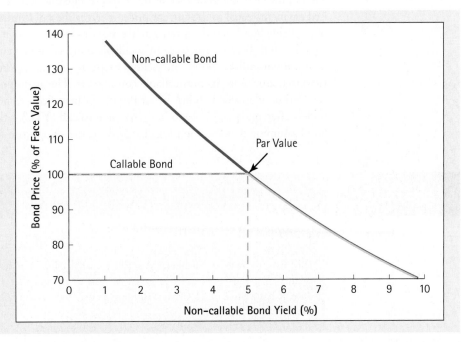

FIGURE 24.3

Prices of Callable and Non-callable Bonds on the Call Date
This figure shows the prices of a callable bond (gold line) and an otherwise identical non-callable bond (blue line) on the call date as a function of the yield on the non-callable bond. Both bonds have a 5% coupon rate. (The callable bond is assumed to be callable at par on one date only.)

Prices of Callable and Non-callable Bonds Prior to the Call Date

When non-callable bond yields are high relative to the callable bond coupon, investors anticipate that the likelihood of exercising the call is low and the callable bond price is similar to that of an otherwise identical non-callable bond. When market yields are low relative to the bond coupon, investors anticipate that the bond will likely be called, so its price is close to the price of a non-callable bond that matures on the call date.

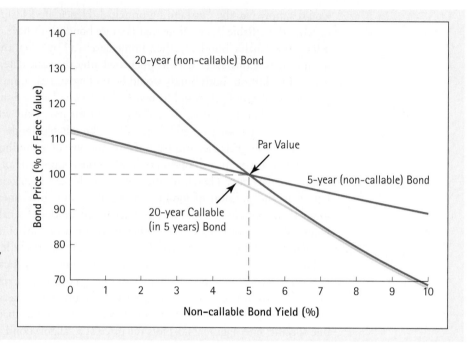

high relative to the bond coupon, investors anticipate that the likelihood of exercising the call is low and the bond price is similar to an otherwise identical non-callable bond. On the other hand, when market yields are low relative to the bond coupon, investors anticipate that the bond will likely be called, so its price is close to the price of a non-callable bond that matures on the call date.

The yield to maturity of a callable bond is calculated as if the bond were not callable. That is, the yield is still defined as the discount rate that sets the present value of the promised payments equal to the current price, *ignoring* the call feature. We can think of the yield of a callable bond as the interest rate the bondholder receives if the bond is not called and repaid in full. Because the price of a callable bond is lower than the price of an otherwise identical non-callable bond, the yield to maturity of a callable bond will be higher than the yield to maturity for its non-callable counterpart. The assumption that underlies the yield calculation of a callable bond—that it will not be called—is not always realistic, so bond traders often quote the yield to call. The **yield to call (YTC)** is the annual yield of a callable bond assuming that the bond is called at the earliest opportunity.

EXAMPLE 24.2

CALCULATING THE YIELD TO CALL

Problem

IBM has just issued a callable (at par) five-year, 8% coupon bond with annual coupon payments. The bond can be called at par in one year or anytime thereafter on a coupon payment date. It has a price of $103 per $100 face value. What is the bond's yield to maturity and yield to call?

Solution

The timeline of the promised payments for this bond (if it is not called) is

Setting the present value of the payments equal to the current price gives

$$103 = \frac{8}{(YTM)}\left(1 - \frac{1}{(1 + YTM)^5}\right) + \frac{100}{(1 + YTM)^5}$$

Solving for YTM (using the annuity spreadsheet) gives the bond's yield to maturity:

	NPER	RATE	PV	PMT	FV	Excel Formula
Given	5		−103	8	100	
Solve for Rate		7.26%				=RATE(5,8,−103,100)

The bond has a yield to maturity of 7.26%.

The timeline of the payments if the bond is called at the first available opportunity is

Setting the present value of these payments equal to the current price gives

$$103 = \frac{108}{(1 + YTC)}$$

Solving for YTC gives the yield to call:

$$YTC = \frac{108}{103} - 1 = 4.85\%$$

The annuity spreadsheet can be used to derive the same result:

	NPER	RATE	PV	PMT	FV	Excel Formula
Given	1		−103	8	100	
Solve for Rate		4.85%				=RATE(1,8,−103,100)

Rather than a standard call provision as just described, many companies have adopted the "**Canada call**" or "**make-whole call**" provision instead. This call provision sets the call price as the present value of the remaining coupons, which is calculated using a rate that adjusts with changes in prevailing interest rates in the economy. Thus, if interest rates fall, the call price rises and the incentive to call the bond in order to refinance at lower rates is eliminated due to the higher call price that would need to be paid. Gady Jacoby and David Stangeland describe how, in 1993, 41% of Canadian corporate bonds had the standard call provision while only 23% had the Canada call provision, but by 1999 only 8% of Canadian corporate bonds had the standard call provision while 47% had the Canada call provision. Why do corporations bother with the Canada call provision instead of just leaving the bonds as noncallable? Perhaps management would like to retire a bond issue for reasons other than a drop in interest rates. For example, if a change in capital structure is desired (see Chapters 14–16) or if a bond covenant becomes troublesome, management may prefer retiring the bond issue. It may be less costly to call the bond than to repurchase it on the open market through a tender offer. This benefit may outweigh the fact that, under a Canada call provision, the call price is greater than the present value of the remaining coupons.[8]

SINKING FUNDS

Another way bonds are repaid is through a **sinking fund**. Instead of repaying the entire principal balance on the maturity date, the company makes regular payments into a sinking fund administered by a trustee over the life of the bond. These payments are then used to repurchase bonds. In this way, the company can reduce the amount of outstanding debt without affecting the cash flows of the remaining bonds.

How does the trustee decide which bonds to repurchase? If the bonds are trading at below their face value, the company simply repurchases the bonds in the market. But if a bond is trading at above its face value, because the bonds are repurchased at par the decision is made by lottery.

Sinking fund provisions usually specify a minimum rate at which the issuer must contribute to the fund. In some cases, the issuer has the option to accelerate these payments. Because the sinking fund allows the issuer to repurchase the bonds at par, the option to accelerate the payments is another form of call provision.

The manner in which an outstanding balance is paid off using a sinking fund depends on the issue. Some issues specify equal payments over the life of the bond, ultimately retiring the issue on the maturity date of the bond. In other cases, the sinking fund payments are not sufficient to retire the entire issue and the company must make a large payment on the maturity date, known as a **balloon payment**. Often, sinking fund payments start only a few years after the bond issue. Bonds can be issued with both a sinking fund and call provision.

CONVERTIBLE PROVISIONS

Another way bonds are retired is by converting them into equity. Some corporate bonds have a provision that gives the bondholder an option to convert each bond owned into a fixed number of shares of common stock at a ratio called the **conversion ratio**. Such bonds are called **convertible bonds**. The provision usually gives bondholders the right to convert the bond into stock at any time up to the maturity date for the bond.[9]

To understand how a conversion feature changes the value of a bond, note that this provision gives a call option to the holder of a bond. Thus a convertible bond can be thought of as a regular bond plus a special type of call option called a **warrant**. A warrant is a call option written by the company itself on *new* stock (whereas a regular call option is written on existing stock). That is, when a holder of a warrant exercises it and thereby purchases stock, the company delivers this stock by issuing new stock. In all other respects, a warrant is identical to a call option.[10]

---

8. See Gady Jacoby and David Stangeland's article, "The Make-Whole, Doomsday, and Canada Call Provisions" in the *Northern Finance Association Conference Proceedings*, September 2004.

9. Some convertible bonds do not allow conversion for a specified amount of time after the issue date.

10. When a regular call is exercised, the loss incurred by the writer of the call accrues to an unknown third party. However, when a warrant is exercised, the loss accrues to the equity holders of the firm (because they are forced to sell new equity at below-market value), which *includes* the holder of the warrant (upon exercise, the warrant holder becomes an equity holder). This dilution effect implies that the gain from exercising a warrant is less than that from a call, so warrants are worth less than calls.

FIGURE 24.5

Convertible Bond Value
At maturity, the value of a convertible bond is the maximum of the value of a $1000 straight bond and 15 shares of stock, and will be converted if the stock is above the conversion price. Prior to maturity, the value of the convertible bond will depend upon the likelihood of conversion, and will be above that of a straight bond or 15 shares of stock.

On the maturity date of the bond, the strike price of the embedded warrant in a convertible bond is equal to the face value of the bond divided by the conversion ratio—that is, the **conversion price**. So, on the maturity date of a convertible bond with a $1000 face value and a conversion ratio of 15, if you converted the bond into stock, you would receive 15 shares. If you did not convert, you would receive $1000. Hence by converting you essentially "paid" $1000 for 15 shares, implying a price per share of $1000/15 = $66.67. If the price of the stock exceeds $66.67, you would choose to convert; otherwise, you would take the cash. At maturity, you will choose to convert whenever the stock price exceeds the conversion price. As shown in Figure 24.5, the value of the bond is the maximum of its face value ($1000) and the value of 15 shares of stock.

What about prior to the maturity date? If the stock does not pay a dividend, then we know from our discussion of call options in Chapter 20 that it is never optimal to exercise a call early. Hence, the holder of a convertible bond should wait until the maturity date of the bond before deciding whether to convert. The value of the bond prior to maturity is plotted in Figure 24.5. If the stock price is low so that the embedded warrant is deep out-of-the-money, the conversion provision is not worth much and the bond's value is close to the value of a straight bond—an otherwise identical bond without the conversion provision. When the stock price is high and the embedded warrant is deep in-the-money, then the convertible bond trades close to—but higher than (to reflect the time value of the option)—the value of the bond if converted.

Often companies issue convertible bonds that also have a standard call feature. With these bonds, if the issuer calls them, the holder can choose to convert rather than let the bonds be called. When the bonds are called, the holder faces exactly the same decision as he would on the maturity date of the bonds: He will choose to convert if the stock price exceeds the conversion price and let the bonds be called otherwise. Thus, by calling the bonds, a company can force bondholders to make their decision to exercise the conversion option earlier than they would otherwise like. Calling a convertible bond therefore transfers the remaining time value of the conversion option from bondholders to shareholders.

When a corporation issues convertible debt, it is giving the holder an option—a warrant, in this case. As we learned in Chapter 20, options always have a positive value; hence a convertible bond is worth more than an otherwise identical straight bond. Consequently, if both bonds are issued at par, the non-convertible bond must offer a higher interest rate. Many people point to the lower interest rates of convertible bonds and argue that therefore convertible debt is cheaper than straight debt.

As we learned in Chapter 14, in a perfect market the choice of financing cannot affect the value of a firm. Hence the argument that convertible debt is cheaper because it has a lower interest rate is fallacious. Convertible debt carries a lower interest rate because it has an embedded warrant. If the price of a firm were subsequently to rise so that the bondholders choose to convert, the current shareholders will have to sell an equity stake in their firm for below-market value. The lower interest rate is compensation for the possibility that this event will occur. Why would managers choose to use convertible bonds? If management and investors had different perceptions about the riskiness of the firm, then a convertible bond might be priced to satisfy both management and investors. Consider the case where investors' assessment of the firm's risk was higher than management's assessment. With a straight bond, investors would give a lower valuation than what management considers fair; thus managers would not use the bond to finance the firm. However, with a convertible bond, investors will place a higher value on the option component (as, from Chapter 20, we know options are more valuable when the underlying asset is riskier) and a lower value on the straight bond component. Management will place a lower value on the option component and a higher value on the straight bond component. Overall, though, both investors and managers may agree that the total price of the convertible bond is fair, so the convertible bond can be used to finance the firm.

CONCEPT CHECK

1. What is a sinking fund?

2. Do callable bonds have a higher or lower yield than otherwise identical bonds without a call feature? Why?

3. Why does a convertible bond have a lower yield than an otherwise identical bond without the option to convert?

SUMMARY

1. Companies can raise debt using different sources. Typical types of debt are public debt, which trades in a public market, and private debt, which is negotiated directly with a bank or a small group of investors. The securities that companies issue when raising debt are called corporate bonds.

2. For public offerings, the bond agreement takes the form of an indenture, a formal contract between the bond issuer and a trust company. The indenture lays out the terms of the bond issue.

3. Four types of corporate bonds are typically issued: notes, debentures, mortgage bonds, and asset-backed bonds. Notes and debentures are unsecured.

4. Corporate bonds differ in their level of seniority. In case of bankruptcy, senior debt is paid in full first before subordinated debt is paid.

5. International bonds are classified into four broadly defined categories: domestic bonds that trade in foreign markets, foreign bonds that are issued in a local market by foreign entity, Eurobonds that are not denominated in the local currency of the country in which they are issued, and global bonds that trade in several markets simultaneously.

6. Private debt can be in the form of term loans or private placements. A term loan is a bank loan that lasts for a specific term. A private placement is a bond issue that is sold to a small group of investors.

7. Governments, provinces, and other government-sponsored enterprises issue bonds too.

8. The Government of Canada has issued four kinds of domestic securities: cash management bills, Treasury Bills, fixed-coupon marketable bonds (also known as Government of Canada bonds), and real return bonds.

9. Agency securities are issued by agencies of the Canadian government or by Canadian government Crown corporations. Examples include bonds issued by the Canada Mortgage and Housing Corporation (CMHC), Business Development Bank of Canada (BDC), and Export Development Canada (EDC).

10. An asset-backed security (ABS) is a security that is made up of other financial securities, that is, the security's cash flows come from the cash flows of the underlying financial securities that "back" it. The underlying financial securities could be mortgages, credit card receivables, consumer loans, etc.

11. Holders of mortgage-backed securities (MBS) guaranteed by the CMHC face prepayment risk, which is the risk that they will find that the bond will be partially (or wholly) repaid earlier than expected. However, an MBS issued by the CMHC does not have default risk, unlike an MBS issued by a financial institution.

12. A collateralized debt obligation is an asset-backed security that is backed by other asset-backed securities.

13. Provincial and municipal bonds are issued by Canadian provinces, their Crown corporations, and municipalities. In the U.S., "munis" are issued by state and local governments. U.S. munis have a distinguishing characteristic in that the income on municipal bonds is not taxable at the federal level in the U.S.

14. Covenants are restrictive clauses in the bond contract that help investors by limiting the issuer's ability to take actions that will increase the default risk and reduce the value of the bonds.

15. A call provision gives the issuer of the bond the right (but not the obligation) to retire the bond after a specific date (but before maturity).

16. A callable bond will generally trade at a lower price than an otherwise equivalent non-callable bond.

17. The yield to call is the yield of a callable bond assuming that the bond is called at the earliest opportunity.

18. Another way in which a bond is repaid before maturity is by periodically repurchasing part of the debt through a sinking fund.

19. Some corporate bonds, known as convertible bonds, have a provision that allows the holder to convert them into equity.

20. Convertible debt carries a lower interest rate than other comparable non-convertible debt.

KEY TERMS

agency securities *p. 855*
asset-backed bonds *p. 849*
asset-backed security (ABS) *p. 855*
balloon payment *p. 862*

bearer bonds *p. 849*
Bulldogs *p. 851*
call date *p. 858*
call price *p. 858*

PROBLEMS

The problems marked in green can be found on MyFinanceLab at www.myfinancelab.com. Visit your MyFinanceLab for additional practice. Additional readings for this chapter may be found in the Textbook Resources section on MyFinanceLab.

Corporate Debt

1. Explain some of the differences between a public debt offering and a private debt offering.

2. Why do bonds with lower seniority have higher yields than equivalent bonds with higher seniority?

3. Explain the difference between a secured corporate and an unsecured corporate bond.

4. What is the difference between a foreign bond and a Eurobond?

Other Types of Debt

5. Describe the kinds of domestic securities the Canadian government uses to finance the federal debt.

6. On January 15, 2010, the Canadian government issued a five-year inflation-indexed note with a coupon of 3%. On the date of issue, the consumer price index (CPI) was 250. By January 15, 2015, the CPI had increased to 300. What principal and coupon payment was made on January 15, 2015?

7. On January 15, 2020, the Canadian government issued a ten-year inflation-indexed note with a coupon of 6%. On the date of issue, the CPI was 400. By January 15, 2030, the CPI had decreased to 300. What principal and coupon payment was made on January 15, 2030? Assume that the principal payment is protected against falling below par value (but the coupon payment is not similarly protected).

8. Describe what prepayment risk is in a mortgage-backed bond guaranteed by the CMHC.

9. What is the distinguishing feature of how U.S. municipal bonds are taxed?

Bond Covenants

10. Explain why bond issuers might voluntarily choose to put restrictive covenants into a new bond issue.

Repayment Provisions

 11. General Electric has just issued a callable ten-year, 6% coupon bond with annual coupon payments. The bond can be called at par in one year or anytime thereafter on a coupon payment date. It has a price of $102. What is the bond's yield to maturity and yield to call?

 12. Boeing Corporation has just issued a callable (at par) three-year, 5% coupon bond with semi-annual coupon payments. The bond can be called at par in two years or anytime thereafter on a coupon payment date. It has a price of $99. What is the bond's yield to maturity and yield to call?

13. Explain why the yield on a convertible bond is lower than the yield on an otherwise identical bond without a conversion feature.

 14. You own a bond with a face value of $10,000 and a conversion ratio of 450. What is the conversion price?

DATA CASE

You are still employed at The Home Depot. Recall the presentation of Chapter 15's plan to increase leverage to the board of directors. The idea of changing Home Depot's capital structure stirred some conversations among top executives. The CFO and other top managers in the finance division are all aware that increasing the debt load will have ramifications in the credit markets. Specifically, they realize that the firm's debt rating could change, which will raise the cost of borrowing as well as possibly lower the value of the existing debt. No one is exactly sure what the impact will be, but they all agree that it deserves investigation.

Because you prepared the spreadsheet data, you have been summoned to an executive-level meeting and asked to estimate the impact of increasing the debt of the firm. Use the spreadsheet from Chapter 15's Data Case as a starting point. You are to consider four different scenarios: issuing $1 billion, $10 billion, $20 billion, and $30 billion in new debt. In each case, proceeds from the debt will be used to repurchase stock. The CFO believes that the $1 billion level will not affect the firm's credit rating. However, each larger increase in debt will cause the debt to be downgraded one level. For example, the $10 billion scenario will lower the current debt rating one level, the $20 billion scenario would lower the rating still another level, and so on. Your job is to determine the impact of additional debt on borrowing costs at each debt level. Assume the new debt will be raised by issuing 10-year bonds.

1. Determine the current debt rating for The Home Depot.
   a. Research the current bond rating at NASD BondInfo (http://cxa.marketwatch.com/finra/BondCenter/Default.aspx). Click the Bond Type to be Corporate, and then enter the symbol for Home Depot (HD). (By the way, well done on being savvy enough not to ask the executives for Home Depot's bond rating!)

b. What is the Moody's bond rating on the Home Depot bond with the maturity closest to ten years from today? What is the yield on this bond?

2. Because lower bond ratings will lead to higher interest costs, you will need to determine those costs. Go to Bonds Online (www.bondsonline.com) and click on "Today's Market." Next, click on "U.S. Corporate Bond Spreads." You will see a table of bond spreads prepared by Reuters and the date the table was prepared right below it. These spreads represent the increased yield a bond must pay over the U.S. Treasury of the same maturity. Choose the 10-year spread for Home Depot's current rating and the three ratings below it. The spreads are in basis points; a basis point is 1/100th of a percentage point (thus, 50 basis points is 0.5%). We will adjust these old spreads to estimate the current spread.

   a. Because these spreads are dated, you will need to create new yield spreads for the various ratings. Use the current difference between the Home Depot bond's yield and the 10-year Treasury as the true spread for the rating. Using Excel, compute the spreads for the other ratings, by adding the *difference* in spreads from the table to the new true spread for Home Depot's rating. Finally, determine the yield for each rating by adding the new spread to the yield on the 10-year Treasury bond.

   b. Compute the required yields on 10-year bonds at each of the new debt levels requested.

3. What factors cause the bond rating to fall, and the bond yields to increase, as Home Depot increases its debt levels?

CHAPTER

25

NOTATION

L lease payments

PV present value

r_D debt cost of capital

τ_c marginal corporate income tax rate

r_U unlevered cost of capital

$_{vacc}$ weighted average cost of capital

Leasing

To implement an investment project, a firm must acquire the necessary property, plant, and equipment. As an alternative to purchasing these assets outright, the firm can lease them. You are probably familiar with leases if you have leased a car or rented an apartment. These consumer rentals are similar to the leases used by businesses: The owner retains title to the asset, and the firm pays for its use of the asset through regular lease payments. When firms lease property, plant, or equipment, the leases generally exceed one year. This chapter focuses on such long-term leases.

If you can purchase an asset, you can probably lease it. Commercial real estate, computers, trucks, copy machines, airplanes, and even power plants are all examples of assets that firms can lease rather than buy. Equipment leasing is a rapidly growing industry, with more than one-half of the world's leasing now being done by companies in Europe and Japan. More than 25% of the world's jet fleet, by dollar value, is leased.[1] The top aircraft leasing company by fleet size at the start of 2009 was GE Commercial Aviation Services. GE owns approximately 1845 aircraft, the world's largest commercial airplane fleet.[2] GE leases these commercial aircraft to some 250 airline customers in 70 countries.

As you will learn, leases are not merely an alternative to purchasing; they also function as an important financing method for tangible assets. In fact, long-term leasing is the most common method of equipment financing. How do companies such as GE Commercial Aviation Services set the terms for their leases? How do their

---

1. beaconfunding (www.beaconfunding.com/vendor_programs/statistics.aspx).
2. GE Capital Aviation Services Global Fact Sheet (www.gecas.com/News/GECAS_Fact_Sheet.pdf).

customers the commercial airlines evaluate and negotiate these leases? In this chapter, we first discuss the basic types of leases and provide an overview of the accounting and tax treatment of leases. We next show how to evaluate the lease-versus-buy decision. Firms often cite various benefits to leasing as compared to purchasing property and equipment, and we conclude the chapter with an evaluation of their reasoning.

25.1   THE BASICS OF LEASING

A lease is a contract between two parties: the lessee and the lessor. The **lessee** is liable for periodic payments in exchange for the right to use the asset. The **lessor** is the owner of the asset, who is entitled to the lease payments in exchange for lending the asset.

Most leases involve little or no upfront payment. Instead, the lessee commits to make regular lease (or rental) payments for the term of the contract. At the end of the contract term, the lease specifies who will retain ownership of the asset and at what terms. The lease also specifies any cancellation provisions, the options for renewal and purchase, and the obligations for maintenance and related servicing costs.

EXAMPLES OF LEASE TRANSACTIONS

Many types of lease transactions are possible based on the relationship between the lessee and the lessor. In a **sales-type lease**, the lessor is the manufacturer (or a primary dealer) of the asset. For example, IBM both manufactures and leases computers. Similarly, Xerox leases its copy machines. Ford Credit Canada leases the vehicles sold by Ford. Manufacturers generally set the terms of these leases as part of a broader sales and pricing strategy, and they may bundle other services or goods (such as software, maintenance, or product upgrades) as part of the lease.

In a **direct lease**, the lessor is not the manufacturer, but is often an independent company that specializes in purchasing assets and leasing them to customers. For example, Ryder Systems, Inc., owns more than 135,000 commercial trucks, tractors, and trailers, which it leases to small businesses and large enterprises throughout Canada, the United States, and the United Kingdom. In many instances of direct leases, the lessee identifies the equipment it needs first and then finds a leasing company to purchase the asset.

If a firm already owns an asset it would prefer to lease, it can arrange a **sale and lease-back** transaction. In this type of lease, the lessee receives cash from the sale of the asset and then makes lease payments to retain the use of the asset. In 2002, San Francisco Municipal Railway (Muni) used the $35 million in proceeds from the sale and leaseback of 118 of its light-rail vehicles to offset a large operating budget deficit. The purchaser, CIBC World Markets, received a tax benefit from depreciating the rail cars, something Muni could not do as a public transit agency.

With many leases, the lessor provides the initial capital necessary to purchase the asset, and then receives and retains the lease payments. In a **leveraged lease**, however, the lessor borrows from a bank or other lender to obtain the initial capital for the purchase, using the lease payments to pay interest and principal on the loan. Also, in some circumstances, the lessor is not an independent company but rather a separate business partnership, called a **special-purpose entity (SPE)**, which is created by the lessee for the sole purpose of obtaining the lease. SPEs are commonly used in **synthetic leases**, which are designed to obtain specific accounting and tax treatment (discussed further in Section 25.2). Their use is diminishing in Canada as accounting moves to international financial reporting standards. Under these standards, if the purpose of the SPE is solely to benefit the related company, the SPE must be consolidated with its related company.

LEASE PAYMENTS AND RESIDUAL VALUES

Suppose your business needs a new $20,000 electric forklift for its warehouse operations and you are considering leasing the forklift for four years. In this case, the lessor will purchase the forklift and allow you to use it for four years. At that point, you will return the forklift to the lessor. How much should you expect to pay for the right to use the forklift for the first four years of its life?

The cost of the lease will depend on the asset's **residual value**, which is its market value at the end of the lease. Suppose the residual value of the forklift in four years will be $6000. If lease payments of amount L are made monthly, then the lessor's cash flows from the transaction are as follows (note that lease payments are typically made at the beginning of each payment period):

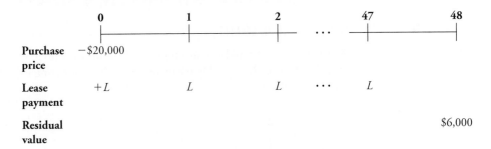

In a perfect capital market (where lessors compete with one another in initiating leases), the lease payment should be set so that the NPV of the transaction is zero and the lessor breaks even:

$$PV(\text{Lease Payments}) = \text{Purchase Price} - PV(\text{Residual Value}) \qquad (25.1)$$

In other words, *in a perfect market, the cost of leasing is equivalent to the cost of purchasing and reselling the asset.*

Thus the amount of the lease payment will depend on the purchase price, the residual value, and the appropriate discount rate for the cash flows.

EXAMPLE 25.1   **LEASE TERMS IN A PERFECT MARKET**

Problem
Suppose the purchase price of the forklift is $20,000, its residual value in four years is certain to be $6000, and there is no risk that the lessee will default on the lease. If the risk-free interest rate is a 6% APR with monthly compounding, what would be the monthly lease payment for a four-year lease in a perfect capital market?

Solution

Because all cash flows are risk free, we can discount them using the risk-free interest rate of $6\%/12 = 0.5\%$ per month. From Eq. 25.1,

$$PV(\text{Lease Payments}) = \$20,000 - \$6000/1.005^{48} = \$15,277.41$$

What monthly lease payment L has this present value? We can interpret the lease payments as an annuity. Because the first lease payment starts today, we can view the lease as an initial payment of L plus a 47-month annuity of L. Thus, using the annuity formula, we need to find L so that

$$15,277.41 = L + L \times \frac{1}{0.005}\left(1 - \frac{1}{1.005^{47}}\right) = L \times \left[1 + \frac{1}{0.005}\left(1 - \frac{1}{1.005^{47}}\right)\right]$$

Solving for L, we get

$$L = \frac{15,277.41}{1 + \dfrac{1}{0.005}\left(1 - \dfrac{1}{1.005^{47}}\right)} = \$357.01 \text{ per month}$$

LEASES VERSUS LOANS

Alternatively, you could obtain a four-year loan for the purchase price and buy the forklift outright. If M is the monthly payment for a fully amortizing loan, the lender's cash flows will be as follows:

Assuming the loan is fairly priced, the loan payments would be such that

$$PV(\text{Loan Payments}) = \text{Purchase Price} \qquad (25.2)$$

Comparing Eq. 25.2 with Eq. 25.1, we see that while with a standard loan we are financing the entire cost of the asset, with a lease we are financing only the cost of the economic depreciation of the asset during the term of the lease. Because we are getting the entire asset when we purchase it with the loan, the loan payments are higher than the lease payments.

EXAMPLE 25.2

LOAN PAYMENTS IN A PERFECT MARKET

Problem

Suppose that you purchase the forklift for $20,000 by borrowing the purchase price using a four-year annuity loan. What would the monthly loan payment be in a perfect capital

If Spafax's borrowing rate is 8%, the cost of buying the office computers has present value

$$PV(\text{Buy}) = -50,000 + \frac{3938}{1.08} + \frac{6103}{1.08^2} + \frac{3357}{1.08^3} + \frac{1846}{1.08^4}$$

$$+ \frac{1015}{1.08^5} - \frac{1241}{1.08^6} = -\$35,627$$

The cost of leasing the computers has present value

$$PV(\text{Lease}) = -12,000 - \frac{7800}{1.08} - \frac{7800}{1.08^2} - \frac{7800}{1.08^3} - \frac{7800}{1.08^4} + \frac{4200}{1.08^5} = -\$34,976$$

Thus leasing is cheaper than buying, with a net savings of $35,627 - \$34,976 = \$651$.

The preceding analysis ignores an important point, however. When a firm enters into a lease, it is committing to lease payments that are a fixed future obligation of the firm. If the firm is in financial distress and cannot make the lease payments, the lessor can seize the computers. Moreover, the lease obligations themselves could trigger financial distress. Therefore, when a firm leases an asset, it is effectively adding leverage to its capital structure (whether or not the lease appears on the balance sheet for accounting purposes).

Because leasing is a form of financing, we should compare it to other financing options that Spafax may have. Rather than buy the asset outright, Spafax could borrow funds to finance the purchase of the computers, thus matching the leverage of the lease. If Spafax does borrow, it will also benefit from the interest tax shield provided by leverage. This tax advantage may make borrowing to buy the office computers more attractive than leasing. Thus, to evaluate a lease correctly, we should compare it to purchasing the asset using an equivalent amount of leverage. In other words, the appropriate comparison is not lease versus buy, but rather lease versus borrow.

LEASE VERSUS BORROW (THE RIGHT COMPARISON)

To compare leasing to borrowing, we must determine the amount of the loan that leads to the same level of fixed obligations that Spafax would have with the lease. We call this loan the **lease-equivalent loan**. That is, the lease-equivalent loan is the loan that is required on the purchase of the asset that leaves the purchaser with the same obligations as the lessee would have.[11]

THE LEASE-EQUIVALENT LOAN. To compute the lease-equivalent loan in Spafax's case, we first compute the difference between the cash flows from leasing versus buying, which we refer to as the incremental free cash flow of leasing. As Table 25.2 shows, relative to buying, leasing saves cash upfront but generally results in lower future cash flows. The incremental free cash flow in years 1 through 6 represents the effective leverage the firm takes on by leasing. Alternatively, Spafax could take on this same leverage by purchasing the office computers and taking on a loan with these same after-tax debt payments. How much could Spafax borrow by taking on such a loan? Because the future incremental cash flows are the after-tax payments Spafax will make on the loan, the initial balance on the lease-equivalent loan is the present value of these cash flows using Spafax's after-tax cost of debt:

$$\text{Loan Balance} = PV[\text{Future FCF of Lease Versus Buy at } r_D(1 - \tau_c)] \tag{25.4}$$

---

11. See Stewart Myers, David Dill, and Alberto Bautista, "Valuation of Financial Lease Contracts," *Journal of Finance* 31:3 (1976): 799–819, for a development of this method.

INCREMENTAL FREE CASH FLOWS OF LEASING VERSUS BUYING

TABLE 25.2

SPREADSHEET

	Year	0	1	2	3	4	5	6
1	FCF Lease (Line 7, Table 25.1)	(12,000)	(7,800)	(7,800)	(7,800)	(7,800)	4,200	—
2	Less: FCF Buy (Line 4, Table 25.1)	50,000	(3,938)	(6,103)	(3,357)	(1,846)	(1,015)	(1,241)
3	**Lease–Buy**	38,000	(11,738)	(13,903)	(11,157)	(9,646)	3,185	(1,241)

Using Spafax's after-tax borrowing cost of 8% $(1 - 35\%) = 5.2\%$, the initial loan balance is

$$\text{Loan Balance} = \frac{11{,}738}{1.052} + \frac{13{,}903}{1.052^2} + \frac{11{,}157}{1.052^3} + \frac{9646}{1.052^4}$$
$$- \frac{3185}{1.052^5} + \frac{1241}{1.052^6} = \$39{,}622 \qquad (25.5)$$

Equation 25.5 implies that if Spafax is willing to take on the future obligations implied by leasing, it could instead buy the office computers and borrow $39,622. This exceeds the savings in year 0 from leasing of $38,000 shown in Table 25.2. Thus, by buying and borrowing using the lease-equivalent loan, Spafax saves an additional $39,622 − 38,000 = $1622 initially, and so leasing the computers is unattractive relative to this alternative.

We verify this result explicitly in the spreadsheet in Table 25.3. There we compute the cash flows that result from buying the computers and borrowing using the lease-equivalent loan. Line 1 shows the lease-equivalent loan balance, which we compute at each date by applying Eq. 25.4. Line 2 shows the initial borrowing and principal payments of the loan (computed as the change in the loan balance from the prior year). Line 3 shows the interest due each year (8% of the prior loan balance), and line 4 computes the interest tax shield (35% of the interest amount). Line 4 then totals the after-tax cash flows of the loan, which we combine with the free cash flow from buying the office computers, to compute the total cash flow from buying and borrowing on line 7.

Comparing the cash flows from buying the office computers and financing them with the lease-equivalent loan (line 7 of Table 25.3) with the cash flows of the lease (e.g., line 1 of Table 25.2), we see that in both cases Spafax has a net future obligation of $7800 per year for four years followed by an inflow of $4200 in year 5. But while the leverage is the same for the two strategies, the initial cash flow is not. With the lease, Spafax will pay

CASH FLOWS FROM BUYING AND BORROWING USING THE LEASE-EQUIVALENT LOAN

TABLE 25.3

SPREADSHEET

	Year	0	1	2	3	4	5	6
	Lease–Equivalent Loan							
1	Loan Balance (PV at 5.2%)	39,622	29,945	17,599	7,358	(1,906)	1,180	—
	Buy with Lease–Equivalent Loan							
2	Net Borrowing (Repayment)	39,622	(9,677)	(12,346)	(10,242)	(9,264)	3,085	(1,180)
3	Interest (at 8%)		(3,170)	(2,396)	(1,408)	(589)	152	(94)
4	Interest Tax Shield at 35%		1,109	838	493	206	(53)	33
5	Cash Flows of Loan (After-tax)	39,622	(11,738)	(13,903)	(11,157)	(9,646)	3,185	(1,241)
6	FCF Buy	(50,000)	3,938	6,103	3,357	1,846	1,015	1,241
7	Cash Flows of Borrow + Buy	(10,378)	(7,800)	(7,800)	(7,800)	(7,800)	4,200	—

$12,000 initially; with the loan, Spafax will pay the purchase price of the office computers minus the amount borrowed, or $50,000 − $39,622 = $10,378. Again we see that borrowing to buy the computers is cheaper than the lease, with a savings of $12,000 − $10,378 = $1622. For Spafax, the lease is not attractive. If Spafax is willing to take on that much leverage, it would be better off doing so by borrowing to purchase the office computers, rather than leasing them.

A DIRECT METHOD.   Now that we have seen the role of the lease-equivalent loan, we can use the tools of Chapter 18 to directly compare leasing with an equivalent debt-financed purchase. Recall from Chapter 18 that when the cash flows of an investment will be offset completely with leverage, the appropriate weighted average cost of capital is given by $r_U − \tau_c r_D$, where r_U is the unlevered cost of capital for the investment (see Eq. 18.11 and the discussion on pages 647–649). Because the incremental cash flows from leasing versus borrowing are relatively safe, $r_U = r_D$ and so $r_{wacc} = r_D(1 − \tau_c)$. Thus, *we can compare leasing to buying the asset using equivalent leverage by discounting the incremental cash flows of leasing versus buying using the after-tax borrowing rate.*

In Spafax's case, discounting the incremental free cash flow in Table 25.2 at Spafax's after-tax borrowing cost of 8% × (1 − 35%) = 5.2%, we get

$$NPV(\text{Lease Versus Borrow}) = 38,000 − \frac{11,738}{1.052} − \frac{13,903}{1.052^2} − \frac{11,157}{1.052^3} − \frac{9646}{1.052^4}$$

$$+ \frac{3185}{1.052^5} − \frac{1241}{1.052^6} = −\$1622$$

Notice this is precisely the difference we calculated earlier.

THE EFFECTIVE AFTER-TAX LEASE BORROWING RATE.   We can also compare leasing and buying in terms of an effective after-tax borrowing rate associated with the lease. This is given by the IRR of the incremental lease cash flows in Table 25.2, which we can calculate as 7.17%:

$$38,000 − \frac{11,738}{1.0717} − \frac{13,903}{1.0717^2} − \frac{11,157}{1.0717^3} − \frac{9646}{1.0717^4} + \frac{3185}{1.0717^5} − \frac{1241}{1.0717^6} = 0$$

Thus the lease is equivalent to borrowing at an after-tax rate of 7.17%. This option is not attractive compared to the after-tax rate of only 8% × (1 − 35%) = 5.2% that Spafax pays on its debt. Because we are borrowing (positive followed by negative cash flows), a lower IRR is better. But be careful with this approach—as discussed in Chapter 6, if the cash flows alternate signs more than once, the IRR method cannot always be relied upon.

EVALUATING A TRUE TAX LEASE

In sum, when evaluating a true tax lease, we should compare leasing to a purchase that is financed with equivalent leverage. We suggest the following approach:

1. Compute the *incremental cash flows* for leasing versus buying, as we did in Table 25.2. Include the CCA tax shield (if buying) and the tax deductibility of the lease payments if leasing.

2. Compute the NPV of leasing versus buying using equivalent leverage by discounting the incremental cash flows at the *after-tax borrowing rate.*

If the NPV computed in step 2 is negative, then leasing is unattractive compared to traditional debt financing. In this case, the firm should not lease, but rather should acquire the asset using an optimal amount of leverage (based on the tradeoffs and techniques discussed in Parts 5 and 6 of the text).

If the NPV computed in step 2 is positive, then leasing does provide an advantage over traditional debt financing and should be considered. Management should recognize, however, that while it may not be listed on the balance sheet, the lease increases the firm's effective leverage by the amount of the lease-equivalent loan.[12]

EXAMPLE 25.6	EVALUATING NEW LEASE TERMS

Problem

Suppose Spafax rejects the lease we analyzed and the lessor agrees to lower the lease rate to $11,400 per year. Does this change make the lease attractive?

Solution

The incremental cash flows are shown in the following table:

Year	0	1	2	3	4	5	6
Buy							
1 Capital Expenditures	(50,000)	—	—	—	—	—	—
2 CCA Deduction	—	11,250	17,438	9,591	5,275	2,901	3,546
3 CCA Tax Shield	—	3,938	6,103	3,357	1,846	1,015	1,241
4 Free Cash Flow (Buy)	(50,000)	3,938	6,103	3,357	1,846	1,015	1,241
Lease							
5 Lease Payments	(11,400)	(11,400)	(11,400)	(11,400)	(11,400)	—	—
6 Income Tax Savings	—	3,990	3,990	3,990	3,990	3,990	—
7 Free Cash Flow (Lease)	(11,400)	(7,410)	(7,410)	(7,410)	(7,410)	3,990	—
Lease vs. Buy							
8 Lease–Buy	38,600	(11,348)	(13,513)	(10,767)	(9,256)	2,975	(1,241)

Note: The following data were used to create this table: Asset cost = 50,000; Lease payments = 11,400; CCA rate $d = 45\%$; $\tau_c = 35\%$.

Using Spafax's after-tax borrowing cost of 5.2%, the gain from leasing versus an equivalently leveraged purchase is

$$NPV(\text{Lease Versus Borrow}) = 38,600 - \frac{11,348}{1.052} - \frac{13,513}{1.052^2} - \frac{10,767}{1.052^3}$$

$$- \frac{9256}{1.052^4} + \frac{2975}{1.052^5} - \frac{1241}{1.052^6}$$

$$= 38,600 - 38,409$$

$$= \$191$$

Therefore, the lease is attractive at the new terms.

---

12. If financial distress or other costs of leverage are large, the firm may wish to offset some of this increase in leverage by reducing other debt of the firm.

9. Good reasons for leasing include tax differences, reduced resale costs, efficiency gains from specialization, reduced bankruptcy costs, risk transfer, and improved incentives.

10. Suspect reasons for leasing include avoiding capital expenditure controls, preserving capital, and reducing leverage through off-balance-sheet financing.

KEY TERMS

$1.00 out lease *p. 874*
capital (finance) lease *p. 876*
direct lease *p. 870*
fair market value cap lease *p. 874*
fair market value (FMV) lease *p. 873*
fixed price lease *p. 874*
lease-equivalent loan *p. 883*
lessee *p. 870*
lessor *p. 870*
leveraged lease *p. 870*

non-tax lease *p. 879*
operating lease *p. 876*
residual value *p. 871*
sale and leaseback *p. 870*
sales-type lease *p. 870*
security interest *p. 879*
special-purpose entity (SPE) *p. 870*
synthetic lease *p. 870*
true lease *p. 879*
true tax lease *p. 879*

PROBLEMS

The problems marked in green can be found on MyFinanceLab at www.myfinancelab.com. Visit your MyFinanceLab for additional practice. An asterisk (*) indicates problems with a higher level of difficulty. Additional readings for this chapter may be found in the Textbook Resources section on MyFinanceLab.

The Basics of Leasing

1. Suppose an H1200 supercomputer has a cost of $200,000 and will have a residual market value of $60,000 in five years. The risk-free interest rate is 5% APR with monthly compounding.
   a. What is the risk-free monthly lease rate for a five-year lease in a perfect market?
   b. What would be the monthly payment for a five-year $200,000 risk-free loan to purchase the H1200?

2. Suppose the risk-free interest rate is 5% APR with monthly compounding. If a $2 million MRI machine can be leased for seven years for $22,000 per month, what residual value must the lessor recover to break even in a perfect market with no risk?

3. Consider a five-year lease for a $400,000 bottling machine, with a residual market value of $150,000 at the end of the five years. If the risk-free interest rate is 6% APR with monthly compounding, compute the monthly lease payment in a perfect market for the following leases:
   a. A fair market value lease
   b. A $1.00 out lease
   c. A fixed price lease with an $80,000 final price

Accounting, Tax, and Legal Consequences of Leasing

 4. Acme Distribution currently has the following items on its balance sheet:

Assets		Liabilities	
Cash	20	Debt	70
Property, Plant, and Equipment	175	Equity	125

How will Acme's balance sheet change if it enters into an $80 million capital lease for new warehouses? What will its book debt-equity ratio be? How will Acme's balance sheet and debt-equity ratio change if the lease is an operating lease?

5. Your firm is considering leasing a $50,000 copier. The copier has an estimated economic life of eight years. Suppose the appropriate discount rate is 9% APR with monthly compounding. Classify each lease below as a capital lease or operating lease, and explain why.

    a. A four-year fair market value lease with payments of $1150 per month

    b. A six-year fair market value lease with payments of $790 per month

    c. A five-year fair market value lease with payments of $925 per month

    d. A five-year fair market value lease with payments of $1000 per month and an option to cancel after three years with a $9000 cancellation penalty

The Leasing Decision

6. Craxton Engineering will either purchase or lease a new $756,000 fabricator. If purchased, the fabricator will be depreciated for tax purposes on a straight-line basis over seven years. Craxton can lease the fabricator for $130,000 per year for seven years. Craxton's tax rate is 35%. (Assume the fabricator has no residual value at the end of the seven years and the lease will be deemed a true tax lease.)

    a. What are the free cash flow consequences of buying the fabricator?

    b. What are the free cash flow consequences of leasing the fabricator?

    c. What are the incremental free cash flows of leasing versus buying?

EXCEL 7. Riverton Mining plans to purchase or lease $220,000 worth of excavation equipment. If purchased, the equipment will be depreciated for tax purposes on a straight-line basis over five years, after which it will be worthless. If leased, the annual lease payments will be $55,000 per year for five years and the lease will be deemed a true tax lease. Riverton's borrowing cost is 8%, and its tax rate is 35%.

    a. If Riverton purchases the equipment, what is the amount of the lease-equivalent loan?

    b. Is Riverton better off leasing the equipment or financing the purchase using the lease-equivalent loan?

    c. What is the effective after-tax lease borrowing rate? How does this compare to Riverton's actual after-tax borrowing rate?

EXCEL 8. Suppose Clorox can lease a new computer data processing system for $975,000 per year for five years under a true tax lease. Alternatively, it can purchase the system for $4.25 million. Assume Clorox has a borrowing cost of 7% and a tax rate of 35% and the system will be obsolete at the end of five years.

    a. If Clorox is able to depreciate (for tax purposes) the computer equipment on a straight-line basis over the next five years, and if the lease qualifies as a true tax lease, is it better to lease or finance the purchase of the equipment?

    b. Suppose that if Clorox buys the equipment, it will use accelerated depreciation (i.e., CRA's CCA) for tax purposes. Specifically, the CCA rate will be 45% and any undepreciated capital cost in year 6 will be taken as a terminal loss. Compare leasing with purchase in this case.

EXCEL *9. Suppose Procter and Gamble (P&G) is considering purchasing $15 million in new manufacturing equipment. If it purchases the equipment, it will depreciate it for tax purposes on a straight-line basis over the five years, after which the equipment will be worthless. It will also be responsible for maintenance expenses of $1 million per year, paid in each of years + through 5. Alternatively, it can also lease the equipment under a true tax lease for $4.2 million per year for the five years, in which case the lessor will provide necessary maintenance. Assume P&G's tax rate is 35% and its borrowing cost is 7%.

a. What is the NPV associated with leasing the equipment (assuming it is a true tax lease) versus financing it with the lease-equivalent loan?

b. What is the break-even lease rate—that is, what lease amount could P&G pay each year and be indifferent between leasing and financing a purchase?

Reasons for Leasing

   *10. Suppose Netflix is considering the purchase of special software to facilitate its move into video-on-demand services. In total, it will purchase $48 million in new software. This software will qualify for CCA deductions at a rate of 100%. However, because of the firm's substantial loss carryforwards, Netflix estimates its marginal tax rate to be 10% over the next five years, so it will get very little tax benefit from the CCA deductions. Thus Netflix considers leasing the software instead. Suppose Netflix and the lessor face the same 8% borrowing rate, but the lessor has a 40% tax rate. For the purpose of this question, assume the software is worthless after five years, the lease term is five years, and the lease qualifies as a true tax lease.

a. What is the lease rate for which the lessor will break even?

b. What is the gain to Netflix with this lease rate?

c. What is the source of the gain in this transaction?

be charged an additional fee for paying late or may be required to pay cash before delivery (CBD) or to pay cash on delivery (COD) for future purchases. In some cases, the supplier may refuse to do business in the future with the delinquent firm.

ELECTRONIC CHEQUE PROCESSING. Firms can employ several methods to reduce their collection and disbursement floats. In addition, many countries have streamlined the way cheques are handled. In the 1980s, Singapore began making electronic images of cheques. By 2001, the cheque-clearing systems in Singapore, Spain, the United Kingdom, and Australia allowed for the clearing of cheques through the use of image transmissions rather than physically moving actual paper cheques. In 2004, the United States adopted such a system. In Canada, the Canadian Payments Association had been working on the "Truncation and Electronic Cheque Presentment" system, with a goal of implementation by 2009. The 11-year-old project was scrapped in October of 2008, and banks have developed and implemented their own imaging projects to try to gain efficiencies. These systems allow for cheques to clear more quickly. As the efficiency increases, it may be possible for financial institutions to reduce the hold period that is sometimes applied when a cheque is deposited. If this occurs, then a firm's collection float would be reduced. So far, though, evidence from the United States shows that even though the funds are taken out of the cheque writer's account almost immediately, the cheque recipient's account is not credited as quickly.

There are, however, several ways that a firm *can* reduce its collection float. For example, the firm may streamline its in-house cheque-processing procedures. In addition, with electronic collection, funds are automatically transferred from the customer's bank account to the firm's bank account on the payment date, reducing the collection float to zero. The methods a firm employs to reduce its collection float are not without costs, of course. Therefore, to decide which, if any, to employ, the firm must compare the costs and benefits of systems that allow it to use its cash for a longer period.

CONCEPT CHECK
1. What does the term "2/10, net 30" mean?
2. Why do companies provide trade credit?

26.3 RECEIVABLES MANAGEMENT

So far, we have discussed the costs and benefits of trade credit in general. Next, we look at some issues that arise specifically from the management of a firm's accounts receivable. In particular, we focus on how a firm adopts a policy for offering credit to its customers and how it monitors its accounts receivable on an ongoing basis.

DETERMINING THE CREDIT POLICY

Establishing a credit policy involves three steps that we will discuss in turn:

1. Establishing credit standards
2. Establishing credit terms
3. Establishing a collection policy

ESTABLISHING CREDIT STANDARDS. Management must first decide on its credit standards. Will it extend credit to anyone who applies for it? Or will it be selective and extend credit only to those customers who have very low credit risk? Unless the firm adopts the former policy, it will need to assess the credit risk of each customer before deciding whether to grant credit. Large firms perform this analysis in-house with their own credit departments. Small firms purchase credit reports from credit rating agencies such as Dun & Bradstreet.

The decision of how much credit risk to assume plays a large role in determining how much money a firm ties up in its receivables. While a restrictive policy can result in a lower sales volume, the firm will have a smaller investment in receivables. Conversely, a less selective policy will produce higher sales, but the level of receivables will also rise.

ESTABLISHING CREDIT TERMS.   After a firm decides on its credit standards, it must next establish its credit terms. The firm decides on the length of the period before payment must be made (the "net" period) and chooses whether to offer a discount to encourage early payments. If it offers a discount, it must also determine the discount percentage and the discount period. If the firm is relatively small, it will probably follow the lead of other firms in the industry in establishing these terms.

ESTABLISHING A COLLECTION POLICY.   The last step in the development of a credit policy is to decide on a collection policy. The content of this policy can range from doing nothing if a customer is paying late (generally not a good choice), to sending a polite letter of inquiry, to charging interest on payments extending beyond a specified period, to threatening legal action at the first late payment.

MONITORING ACCOUNTS RECEIVABLE

After establishing a credit policy, a firm must monitor its accounts receivable to analyze whether its credit policy is working effectively. Two tools that firms use to monitor the accounts receivable are the accounts receivable days (or average collection period) and the aging schedule.

ACCOUNTS RECEIVABLE DAYS.   The accounts receivable days is the average number of days that it takes a firm to collect on its sales. A firm can compare this number to the payment policy specified in its credit terms to judge the effectiveness of its credit policy. If the credit terms specify "net 30" and the accounts receivable days outstanding is 50 days, the firm can conclude that its customers are paying 20 days late, on average.

The firm should also look at the trend in the accounts receivable days over time. If the accounts receivable days ratio of a firm has been approximately 35 days for the past few years and it is 43 days this year, the firm may want to re-examine its credit policy. Of course, if the economy is sluggish, the entire industry may be affected. Under these circumstances, the increase might have little to do with the firm itself.

Because accounts receivable days can be calculated from the firm's financial statements, outside investors commonly use this measure to evaluate a firm's credit management policy. A major weakness of the accounts receivable days is that it is merely one number and conceals much useful information. Seasonal sales patterns may cause the number calculated for the accounts receivable days to change depending on when the calculation takes place. The number can also look reasonable even when a substantial percentage of the firm's customers are paying late.

AGING SCHEDULE.   An **aging schedule** categorizes accounts by the number of days they have been on the firm's books. It can be prepared using either the number of accounts or the dollar amount of the accounts receivable outstanding. For example, assume that a firm selling on terms of 2/15, net 30, has $530,000 in accounts receivable that has been on the

AGING SCHEDULES

TABLE 26.2

(a) Number of Accounts

Days Outstanding	Number of Accounts	Percentage of Accounts (%)
1–15	220	38.6
16–30	190	33.3
31–45	80	14.0
46–60	60	10.5
60+	20	3.5
	570	100.0

(b) Dollar Amounts Outstanding

Days Outstanding	Amount Outstanding ($)	Percentage Outstanding (%)
1–15	530,000	33.1
16–30	450,000	28.1
31–45	350,000	21.9
46–60	200,000	12.5
60+	70,000	4.4
	1,600,000	100.0

books for 15 or fewer days in 220 accounts. Another $450,000 has been on the books for 16 to 30 days and is made up of 190 accounts, and $350,000 has been on the books for 31 to 45 days and represents 80 accounts. The firm has $200,000 that has been on the books for 46 to 60 days in 60 accounts. Yet another $70,000 has been on the books for more than 60 days and is made up of 20 accounts. Table 26.2 includes aging schedules based on the number of accounts and dollar amounts outstanding.

In this case, if the firm's average daily sales is $65,000, its accounts receivable days is $1,600,000/$65,000 = 25 days. But on closer examination, using the aging schedules in Table 26.2, we can see that 28% of the firm's credit customers (and 39% by dollar amounts) are paying late.

EXAMPLE 26.3   **AGING SCHEDULES**

Problem

Financial Training Systems (FTS) bills its accounts on terms of 3/10, net 30. The firm's accounts receivable include $100,000 that has been outstanding for 10 or fewer days, $300,000 outstanding for 11 to 30 days, $100,000 outstanding for 31 to 40 days, $20,000 outstanding for 41 to 50 days, $10,000 outstanding for 51 to 60 days, and $2000 outstanding for more than 60 days. Prepare an aging schedule for FTS.

Solution

With the available information, we can calculate the aging schedule based on dollar amounts outstanding.

Days Outstanding	Amount Outstanding ($)	Percentage Outstanding (%)
1–10	100,000	18.8
11–30	300,000	56.4
31–40	100,000	18.8
41–50	20,000	3.8
51–60	10,000	1.9
60+	2,000	0.3
	532,000	100.0

If the aging schedule gets "bottom-heavy"—that is, if the percentages in the lower half of the schedule begin to increase—the firm will likely need to revisit its credit policy. The aging schedule is also sometimes augmented by analysis of the **payments pattern**, which provides information on the percentage of monthly sales that the firm collects in each month after the sale. By examining past data, a firm may observe that 10% of its sales are usually collected in the month of the sale, 40% in the month following the sale, 25% two months after the sale, 20% three months after the sale, and 5% four months after the sale. Management can compare this normal payments pattern to the current payments pattern. Knowledge of the payments pattern is also useful for forecasting the firm's working capital requirements.

CONCEPT CHECK

1. Describe three steps in establishing a credit policy.

2. What is the difference between accounts receivable days and an aging schedule?

26.4 PAYABLES MANAGEMENT

A firm should choose to borrow using accounts payable only if trade credit is the cheapest source of funding. The cost of the trade credit depends on the credit terms. The higher the discount percentage offered, the greater the cost of forgoing the discount. The cost of forgoing the discount is also higher with a shorter loan period. When a company has a choice between trade credit from two different suppliers, it should take the least-expensive alternative.

In addition, a firm should always pay on the latest day allowed. For example, if the discount period is 10 days and the firm is taking the discount, payment should be made on day 10, not on day 2. If the discount is not taken and the terms are 2/10, net 30, the full payment should be made on day 30, not on day 16. A firm should strive to keep its money working for it as long as possible without developing a bad relationship with its suppliers or engaging in unethical practices. In this section, we examine two techniques that firms use to monitor their accounts payable.

DETERMINING ACCOUNTS PAYABLE DAYS OUTSTANDING

Similar to the situation with its accounts receivable, a firm should monitor its accounts payable to ensure that it is making its payments at an optimal time. One method is to calculate the accounts payable days outstanding and compare it to the credit terms. The accounts payable days outstanding is the accounts payable balance expressed in terms of the number of days of cost of goods sold. If the accounts payable outstanding is 40 days and the terms are 2/10, net 30, the firm can conclude that it generally pays late and may be risking supplier difficulties. Conversely, if the accounts payable days outstanding is 25 days and the firm has not been taking the discount, the firm is paying too early. It could be earning another five days' interest on its money.

EXAMPLE 26.4

ACCOUNTS PAYABLE MANAGEMENT

Problem

The Rowd Company has an average accounts payable balance of $250,000. Its average daily cost of goods sold is $14,000, and it receives terms of 2/15, net 40, from its suppliers. Rowd chooses to forgo the discount. Is the firm managing its accounts payable well?

Solution

The firm is not managing its accounts payable well. Rowd's accounts payable days outstanding is $250,000/$14,000 = 17.9$ days. If Rowd made payment three days earlier, it could take advantage of the 2% discount. If for some reason it chooses to forgo the discount, it should not be paying the full amount until the fortieth day.

STRETCHING ACCOUNTS PAYABLE

Some firms ignore the payment due period and pay later, in a practice referred to as **stretching the accounts payable**. Given terms of 2/10, net 30, for example, a firm may choose to not pay until 45 days have passed. Doing so reduces the direct cost of trade credit because it lengthens the time that a firm has use of the funds. While the interest rate per period remains the same—$2/$98 = 2.04\%$—the firm is now using the $98 for 35 days beyond the discount period, rather than 20 days as provided by the trade credit terms.

EXAMPLE 26.5

COST OF TRADE CREDIT WITH STRETCHED ACCOUNTS PAYABLE

Problem

What is the effective annual cost of credit terms of 1/15, net 40, if the firm stretches the accounts payable to 60 days?

Solution

The interest rate per period is $1/$99 = 1.01\%$. If the firm delays payment until the sixtieth day, it has use of the funds for 45 days beyond the discount period. There are $365/45 = 8.11$ 45-day periods in one year. Thus the effective annual cost is $(1.0101)^{8.11} - 1 = 8.49\%$.

Firms may also make a payment on the thirtieth day but pay only the discounted price. Some may pay only the discounted price and pay even later than the thirtieth day. While all of these actions will reduce the effective annual rate associated with the trade credit, the firm may incur costs as a result of these actions. Suppliers may react to a firm whose payments are always late by imposing terms of cash on delivery (COD) or cash before delivery (CBD). The delinquent firm then bears the additional costs associated with these terms and may have to negotiate a bank loan to have the cash available to pay. The supplier may also discontinue business with the delinquent customer, leaving the customer to find another source, which may be more expensive or of lower quality. Alternatively, the supplier may anticipate that a delinquent firm will stretch its payments in the future and, to compensate, quote higher prices to that firm. A poor credit rating might also result, making it difficult for the delinquent firm to obtain good terms with any other supplier. Moreover, when a firm explicitly agrees to the terms of the sale, violating these terms constitutes unethical business behaviour in most people's minds.

CONCEPT CHECK

1. What is accounts payable days outstanding?
2. What are the costs of stretching accounts payable?

26.5 INVENTORY MANAGEMENT

As we discussed earlier, in a perfect markets setting, firms would not need to have accounts payable or receivable. Interest rates on trade credit would be competitive, and firms could use alternative sources of financing. However, unlike trade credit, inventory represents one of the required factors of production. Therefore, even in a perfect markets setting in which the Modigliani-Miller propositions hold, firms still need inventory.

Inventory management receives extensive coverage in a course on operations management. Nevertheless, it is the firm's financial manager who must arrange for the financing necessary to support the firm's inventory policy and who is responsible for ensuring the firm's overall profitability. Therefore, the role of the inventory manager is to balance the costs and benefits associated with inventory. Because excessive inventory uses cash, efficient management of inventory increases firm value.

BENEFITS OF HOLDING INVENTORY

A firm needs its inventory to operate for several reasons. First, inventory helps minimize the risk that the firm will not be able to obtain an input it needs for production. If a firm holds too little inventory, **stock-outs**, the situation when a firm runs out of money, may occur, leading to lost sales. Disappointed customers may switch to one of the firm's competitors.

Second, firms may hold inventory because such factors as seasonality in demand mean that customer purchases do not perfectly match the most efficient production cycle. Consider the case of the Sandpoint Toy Company. As is typical for many toy manufacturers, 80% of Sandpoint's annual sales occur between September and December, in anticipation of the holiday gift season. It is more efficient for Sandpoint to manufacture toys at relatively constant levels throughout the year. If Sandpoint produces its toys at a constant rate, its inventory levels will increase to very high levels by August, in anticipation of the increase in sales beginning in September. In contrast, Sandpoint may consider a seasonal manufacturing strategy, producing more toys between September and December when sales are high. Under this strategy, inventory would not accumulate, freeing up cash flow from working capital and reducing the costs of inventory. However, seasonal manufacturing incurs additional costs, such as increased wear and tear on the manufacturing equipment during peak demand and the need to hire and train seasonal workers. Sandpoint must weigh the costs of the inventory buildup under constant production against the benefits of more efficient production. The optimal choice is likely to involve a compromise between the two extremes, so that Sandpoint will carry some inventory.

COSTS OF HOLDING INVENTORY

As suggested by the Sandpoint Toy example, tying up capital in inventory is costly for a firm. We can classify the direct costs associated with inventory into three categories:

- *Acquisition costs* are the costs of the inventory itself over the period being analyzed (usually one year).

- *Order costs* are the total costs of placing an order over the period being analyzed.

- *Carrying costs* include storage costs, insurance, taxes, spoilage, obsolescence, and the opportunity cost of the funds tied up in the inventory.

Minimizing these total costs involves some tradeoffs. For example, if we assume no quantity discounts are available, the lower the level of inventory a firm carries, the lower its carrying cost, but the higher its annual order costs because it needs to place more orders during the year.

In 2003, the apparel chain GAP reduced its investment in inventory significantly by reducing its inventory days outstanding by 24%. This change freed up $344 million for other purposes. GAP invested some of this cash in short-term securities—primarily in U.S. government and agency securities and in bank certificates of deposits with maturities between three months and one year. The firm reported an increase of *$1.2 million* in interest income in fiscal year 2003 compared with fiscal year 2002. It attributed the increase to increases in the average cash balances available for investment.[4]

Some firms seek to reduce their carrying costs as much as possible. With "**just-in-time**" **(JIT) inventory management**, a firm acquires inventory precisely when needed so that its inventory balance is always zero, or very close to it. This technique requires exceptional coordination with suppliers as well as a predictable demand for the firm's products. In addition, there may be a trickle-down effect when one firm in an industry adopts JIT. For example, in 1999, Toys "R" Us instituted JIT, which caused one of its suppliers, toy manufacturer Hasbro, to make changes in its production schedule.[5]

CONCEPT CHECK
1. What are the benefits and costs of holding inventory?
2. Describe "just-in-time" inventory management.

26.6 CASH MANAGEMENT

In the Modigliani-Miller setting, the level of cash is irrelevant. With perfect capital markets, a firm is able to raise new money instantly at a fair rate, so it can never be short of cash. Similarly, the firm can invest excess cash at a fair rate to earn an NPV of zero.

In the real world, of course, markets are not perfect. Liquidity has a cost; for example, holding liquid assets may earn a below-market return, and a firm may face transaction costs if it needs to raise cash quickly. Similarly, recall from Chapter 16 that holding excess cash has a tax disadvantage. In these cases, the optimal strategy for a firm is to hold cash in anticipation of seasonalities in demand for its products and random shocks that affect

---

4. GAP 2003 annual report.

5. Hasbro 1999 annual report.

its business. Risky firms and firms with high-growth opportunities tend to hold a relatively high percentage of assets as cash. Firms with easy access to capital markets (for which the transaction costs of accessing cash are therefore lower) tend to hold less cash.[6] In this section, we examine the firm's motivation for holding cash, tools for managing cash, and the short-term securities in which firms invest.

MOTIVATION FOR HOLDING CASH

There are three reasons why a firm holds cash:

- To meet its day-to-day needs
- To compensate for the uncertainty associated with its cash flows
- To satisfy bank requirements

In this section, we examine each of these motivations for holding cash in detail.

TRANSACTIONS BALANCE.   Just like you, a firm must hold enough cash to pay its bills. The amount of cash a firm needs to be able to pay its bills is sometimes referred to as a **transactions balance**. The amount of cash a firm needs to satisfy the transactions balance requirement depends on both the average size of the transactions made by the firm and the firm's cash cycle, discussed earlier in the chapter. Retail firms also need cash to facilitate transactions with their customers (for example, the "float" required to be kept in cash registers).

PRECAUTIONARY BALANCE.   The amount of cash a firm holds to counter the uncertainty surrounding its future cash needs is known as a **precautionary balance**. The size of this balance depends on the degree of uncertainty surrounding a firm's cash flows. The more uncertain future cash flows are, the harder it is for a firm to predict its transactions need, so the larger the precautionary balance must be.

COMPENSATING BALANCE.   A firm's bank may require it to hold a **compensating balance** in an account at the bank as compensation for services that the bank performs. Compensating balances are typically deposited in accounts that either earn no interest or pay a very low interest rate. This arrangement is similar to a bank offering individuals free chequing so long as their balances do not fall below a certain level—say, $1000. Essentially, the customer has $1000 cash that he cannot use unless he is willing to pay a service charge. Similarly, the cash that a firm has tied up to meet a compensating balance requirement is unavailable for other uses.

ALTERNATIVE INVESTMENTS

In our discussion of collection and disbursement floats, we assumed that the firm will invest any cash in short-term securities. In fact, the firm may choose from a variety of short-term securities that differ somewhat with regard to their default risk and liquidity risk. The greater the risk, the higher the expected return on the investment. The financial manager must decide how much risk she is willing to accept in return for a higher yield. If her firm expects to need the funds within the next 30 days, the manager will probably avoid the less liquid options. Table 26.3 briefly describes the most frequently used short-term investments; these short-term debt securities are collectively referred to as money market securities.

---

6. See T. Opler, L. Pinkowitz, R. Stulz, and R. Williamson, "The Determinants and Implications of Corporate Cash Holdings," *Journal of Financial Economics* 52:1 (1999): 3–46.

TABLE 26.3   MONEY MARKET INVESTMENT OPTIONS

Investment	Description	Maturity	Risk	Liquidity
Cash Management Bills	Very-short-term debt of the Canadian government.	One day up to less than three months when newly issued.	Default risk free.	Very liquid and marketable.
Treasury Bills	Short-term debt of the Canadian government. Provincial governments also issue their own T-bills.	Three, six, or twelve months when newly issued.	Default risk free.	Very liquid and marketable.
Term Deposits, Certificates of Deposit (CDs), Guaranteed Investment Certificate (GIC)	Short-term debt issued by banks.	Term deposits have maturities up to one year. CDs maturities are 30 days to five years. GICs maturities are one to five years.	If the issuing bank is insured by the CDIC, any amount up to $100,000 is free of default risk because it is covered by the insurance. Any amount in excess of $100,000 is not insured and is subject to default risk.	These are generally not liquid. CDs from U.S. banks do have a liquid secondary market.
Repurchase Agreements	Essentially a loan arrangement wherein a securities dealer is the "borrower" and the investor is the "lender." The investor buys securities, such as treasury bills, from the securities dealer, with an agreement to sell the securities back to the dealer at a later date for a specified higher price.	Very short term, ranging from overnight to approximately three months in duration.	The security serves as collateral for the loan, and therefore the investor is exposed to very little risk. However, the investor needs to consider the creditworthiness of the securities dealer when assessing the risk.	No secondary market for repurchase agreements.
Banker's Acceptances	Drafts written by the borrower and guaranteed by the bank on which the draft is drawn. Typically used in international trade transactions. The borrower is an importer who writes the draft in payment for goods.	Typically one to six months.	Because both the borrower and a bank have guaranteed the draft, there is very little risk.	When the exporter receives the draft, he may hold it until maturity and receive its full value or he may sell the draft at a discount prior to maturity.
Bearer Deposit Note	Short-term discount notes issued by banks.	Up to one year.	Guaranteed by the issuing bank, but not by the CDIC, there is very little risk.	Secondary market exists.
Commercial Paper	Short-term, unsecured debt issued by large corporations. The minimum denomination is $25,000, but most commercial paper has a face value of $100,000 or more.	Typically one to six months.	Default risk depends on the creditworthiness of the issuing corporation.	Secondary market exists.

FINANCIAL CRISIS
CASH BALANCES

Corporate liquidity is measured as corporate investments in short-term, marketable securities. In the United States, it rose from $3.6 trillion in 1999 to $5.6 trillion in 2007, for an increase of almost 55%. According to a 2004 survey of more than 360 companies conducted by Treasury Strategies Inc., a Chicago consultant, more than half of those firms consider themselves to be net investors, having more short-term investments than short-term debt outstanding.

Why have companies been accumulating more cash? Factors include a shift away from industries such as manufacturing that spend heavily on plant and equipment, strength in sectors such as financial services that have low capital expenditures and high cash flows, and reluctance by companies to invest heavily after the technology spending spree in the late 1990s. As a result, corporate savings have reached an all-time high.

How are companies investing their cash? A 2007 survey by Treasury Strategies indicated that 20% is invested in money market funds and accounts, 18% is invested in bonds and notes, and the remainder is invested directly in commercial paper, CDs, repurchase agreements, and other investments.

During the 2008 financial crisis, short-term credit markets froze and many businesses that relied on short-term credit found themselves unable to conduct business. You might expect that businesses that held a lot of cash were in good shape. However, cash-holding firms during the crisis did not know what to do with the cash. Before it became clear that governments were going to bail out large banks, firms had to worry about how secure their cash was. In the event of a bank bankruptcy, the firm risked losing access to its cash in the short term and perhaps ultimately losing the cash altogether. For firms that relied on cash balances to conduct business, the impact of the breakdown in financial markets was potentially as big as for firms that relied on credit.

Thus a financial manager who wants to invest the firm's funds in the least risky security will choose to invest in Treasury Bills. However, if the financial manager wishes to earn a higher return on the firm's short-term investments, she may opt to invest some or all of the firm's excess cash in a riskier alternative, such as commercial paper.

CONCEPT CHECK

1. List three reasons why a firm holds cash.

2. What tradeoff does a firm face when choosing how to invest its cash?

SUMMARY

1. Working capital management involves managing the firm's short-term assets and short-term liabilities.

2. A firm's cash cycle is the length of time between when the firm pays cash to purchase its initial inventory and when it receives cash from the sale of the output produced from that inventory. The operating cycle is the average length of time between when a firm originally purchases its inventory and when it receives the cash back from selling its product.

3. Trade credit is effectively a loan from the selling firm to its customer. The cost of trade credit depends on the credit terms. The cost of not taking a discount that is offered by a supplier implies an interest rate for the loan.

4. Companies provide trade credit to their customers for two reasons: (a) as an indirect way to lower prices and (b) because they may have advantages in making loans to their customers relative to other potential sources of credit.

5. A firm should compare the cost of trade credit with the cost of alternative sources of financing in deciding whether to use the trade credit offered.

6. Establishing a credit policy involves three steps: establishing credit standards, establishing credit terms, and establishing a collection policy.

7. The days sales outstanding ratio and aging schedule are two methods used to monitor the effectiveness of a firm's credit policy.

8. Firms should monitor accounts payable to ensure that they are making payments at an optimal time.

9. Firms hold inventory to avoid lost sales due to stock-outs and because of such factors as seasonal demand.

   a. Because excessive inventory uses cash, efficient inventory management increases the firm's free cash flow and thus increases firm value.

   b. The costs of inventory include acquisition costs, order costs, and carrying costs.

10. If a firm's need to hold cash is reduced, the funds can be invested in a number of different short-term securities, including Treasury Bills, certificates of deposit, commercial paper, repurchase agreements, banker's acceptances, and bearer deposit notes.

KEY TERMS

aging schedule *p. 906*
availability float *p. 904*
cash conversion cycle (CCC) *p. 900*
cash cycle *p. 899*
collection float *p. 904*
compensating balance *p. 912*
disbursement float *p. 904*
"just-in-time" (JIT) inventory
    management *p. 911*

mail float *p. 904*
operating cycle *p. 900*
payments pattern *p. 908*
precautionary balance *p. 912*
processing float *p. 904*
stock-out *p. 910*
stretching the accounts payable *p. 909*
trade credit *p. 902*
transactions balance *p. 912*

PROBLEMS

The problems marked in green can be found on MyFinanceLab at www.myfinancelab.com. An asterisk (*) indicates problems with a higher level of difficulty. Additional readings for this chapter may be found in the Textbook Resources section on MyFinanceLab.

Overview of Working Capital

1. Answer the following:

   a. What is the difference between a firm's cash cycle and its operating cycle?

   b. How will a firm's cash cycle be affected if a firm increases its inventory, all else being equal?

   c. How will a firm's cash cycle be affected if a firm begins to take the discounts offered by its suppliers, all else being equal?

2. Does an increase in a firm's cash cycle necessarily mean that a firm is managing its cash poorly?

3. Aberdeen Outboard Motors is contemplating building a new plant. The company anticipates that the plant will require an initial investment of $2 million in net working capital today. The plant will last 10 years, at which point the full investment in net working capital will be recovered. Given an annual discount rate of 6%, what is the net present value of this working capital investment?

4. The Greek Connection had sales of $32 million in 2009, and a cost of goods sold of $20 million. A simplified balance sheet for the firm appears below:

THE GREEK CONNECTION
Balance Sheet
As of December 31, 2009
(thousands of dollars)

Assets		Liabilities and Equity	
Cash	$ 2,000	Accounts payable	$ 1,500
Accounts receivable	3,950	Notes payable	1,000
Inventory	1,300	Accruals	1,220
Total current assets	7,250	Total current liabilities	3,720
Net plant, property		Long-term debt	3,000
and equipment	8,500	Total liabilities	6,720
Total assets	$15,750	Common equity	9,030
		Total liabilities and equity	$15,750

a. Calculate The Greek Connection's net working capital in 2009.

b. Calculate the cash conversion cycle of The Greek Connection in 2009.

c. The industry average accounts receivable days is 30 days. What would the cash conversion cycle for The Greek Connection have been in 2009 had it met the industry average for accounts receivable days?

Trade Credit

5. Assume the credit terms offered to your firm by your suppliers are 3/5, net 30. Calculate the cost of the trade credit if your firm does not take the discount and pays on day 30.

6. Your supplier offers terms of 1/10, net 45. What is the effective annual cost of trade credit if you choose to forgo the discount and pay on day 45?

7. The Fast Reader Company supplies bulletin board services to numerous hotel chains nationwide. The owner of the firm is investigating the desirability of employing a billing firm to do her billing and collections. Because the billing firm specializes in these services, collection float will be reduced by 20 days. Average daily collections are $1200, and the owner can earn 8% annually (expressed as an APR with monthly compounding) on her investments. If the billing firm charges $250 per month, should the owner employ the billing firm?

8. The Saban Corporation is trying to decide whether to switch to a bank that will accommodate electronic funds transfers from Saban's customers. Saban's financial manager believes the new system would decrease its collection float by as much as five days. The new bank would require a compensating balance of $30,000, whereas its present bank has no compensating balance requirement. Saban's average daily collections are $10,000, and it can earn 8% on its short-term investments. Should Saban make the switch? (Assume the compensating balance at the new bank will be deposited in a non-interest-earning account.)

Receivables Management

9. What are the three steps involved in establishing a credit policy?

10. The Manana Corporation had sales of $60 million this year. Its accounts receivable balance averaged $2 million. How long, on average, does it take the firm to collect on its sales?

11. The Mighty Power Tool Company has the following accounts on its books:

Customer	Amount Owed ($)	Age (days)
ABC	50,000	35
DEF	35,000	5
GHI	15,000	10
KLM	75,000	22
NOP	42,000	40
QRS	18,000	12
TUV	82,000	53
WXY	36,000	90

The firm extends credit on terms of 1/15, net 30. Develop an aging schedule using 15-day increments through 60 days, and then indicate any accounts that have been outstanding for more than 60 days.

Payables Management

12. What is meant by "stretching the accounts payable"?

*13. Simple Simon's Bakery purchases supplies on terms of 1/10, net 25. If Simple Simon's chooses to take the discount offered, it must obtain a bank loan to meet its short-term financing needs. A local bank has quoted Simple Simon's owner an interest rate of 12% on borrowed funds. Should Simple Simon's enter the loan agreement with the bank and begin taking the discount?

14. Your firm purchases goods from its supplier on terms of 3/15, net 40.

   a. What is the effective annual cost to your firm if it chooses not to take the discount and makes its payment on day 40?

   b. What is the effective annual cost to your firm if it chooses not to take the discount and makes its payment on day 50?

*15. Use the financial statements supplied below for International Motor Corporation (IMC) to answer the following questions.

   a. Calculate the cash conversion cycle for IMC for both 2009 and 2010. What change has occurred, if any? All else being equal, how does this change affect IMC's need for cash?

   b. IMC's suppliers offer terms of net 30. Does it appear that IMC is doing a good job of managing its accounts payable?

INTERNATIONAL MOTOR CORPORATION
Income Statement ($ million)
for the years ended December 31

	2009	2010
Sales	$60,000	$75,000
Cost of goods sold	52,000	61,000
Gross profit	$ 8,000	$ 14,000
Selling and general and administrative expenses	6,000	8,000
Operating profit	$ 2,000	$ 6,000
Interest expense	1,400	1,300
Earnings before tax	$ 600	$ 4,700
Taxes	300	2,350
Earnings after tax	$ 300	$ 2,350

INTERNATIONAL MOTOR CORPORATION
Balance Sheet ($ million)
as of December 31

	2009	2010		2009	2010
Assets			**Liabilities**		
Cash	$ 3,080	$ 6,100	Accounts payable	$ 3,600	$ 4,600
Accounts			Notes payable	1,180	1,250
receivable	2,800	6,900	Accruals	5,600	6,211
Inventory	6,200	6,600	Total current		
Total current assets	12,080	19,600	liabilities	10,380	12,061
Net plant, property,			Long-term debt	6,500	7,000
and equipment	23,087	20,098	Total liabilities	16,880	19,061
Total assets	$35,167	$39,698	**Equity**		
			Common stock	2,735	2,735
			Retained earnings	15,552	17,902
			Total equity	18,287	20,637
			Total liabilities and		
			equity	$35,167	$39,698

Inventory Management

16. Ontario Valley Homecare Suppliers Inc. (OVHS) had $20 million in sales in 2008. Its cost of goods sold was $8 million, and its average inventory balance was $2,000,000.

   a. Calculate the average number of days, inventory outstanding for OVHS.

   b. The average days of inventory in the industry is 73 days. By how much would OVHS reduce its investment in inventory if it could improve its inventory days to meet the industry average?

Cash Management

17. Which of the following short-term securities would you expect to offer the highest before-tax return: Treasury Bills, certificates of deposit, bearer deposit notes, or commercial paper? Why?

DATA CASE

You are the chief financial officer (CFO) of BP. This afternoon you played golf with a member of the company's board of directors. Somewhere during the back nine, the board member enthusiastically described a recent article she had read in a leading management journal. This article noted several companies that had improved their stock price performance through effective working capital management, and the board member was intrigued. She wondered whether BP was managing its working capital effectively and, if not, whether BP could accomplish something similar. How was BP managing its working capital, and how does it compare to its competitors?

Upon returning home, you decide to do a quick preliminary investigation using information freely available on the Internet.

1. Obtain BP's financial statements for the past four years from NASDAQ's Web site (www.nasdaq.com).

    a. Enter the stock symbol (BP) in the box and click on "Summary Quotes."

    b. Next click on "Company Financials" below the stock price near the middle of the screen.

    c. The income statements will come up first. Place the cursor in the statement and right-click the mouse. Select "Export to Microsoft Excel" from the menu.

    d. Go back to the Web page and click on "Balance Sheets" from the top of the page; repeat the download procedure for the balance sheets.

    e. Copy and paste the balance sheet so that it is on the same worksheet as the income statement.

2. Obtain the industry ratios for comparison from the Reuters Web site (http://www.reuters.com/finance/stocks/).

    a. Enter the stock symbol (BP.n) in the box at the top and click "Search."

    b. Click on the "Financials" tab. from the menu on the left side of the page. You will have to register (it's free) or use the username and password supplied by your instructor.

    c. Copy and paste the efficiency ratios onto your spreadsheet where BP's financial statements are located.

3. Compute the cash conversion cycle for BP for each of the last four years.

    a. Compute the Inventory Days using "Cost of Revenue" as cost of goods sold and a 365-day year.

    b. Compute Accounts Receivable Days using a 365-day year.

    c. Compute Accounts Payable Days.

    d. Compute the cash conversion cycle for each year.

4. How has BP's CCC changed over the last few years?

5. Compare BP's inventory and receivables turnover ratios for the most recent year to the industry average.

    a. Compute the inventory turnover ratio as Cost of Revenue/Inventory.

    b. Compute the receivable turnover ratio as Total Revenue/Net Receivables.

    c. How do BP's numbers compare to the industry averages? Do they confirm or refute your answer to Question 4?

6. Determine how BP's free cash flow would change if BP's inventory and accounts receivable balances were adjusted to meet the industry averages.

7. Determine the amount of additional free cash flow that would be available if BP adjusted its Accounts Payable Days to 75 days.

8. Determine the net amount of additional free cash flow and BP's cash conversion cycle if its inventory and receivables turnover ratios were at the industry average and its payable days were 75 days.

9. What are your impressions regarding BP's working capital management based on this preliminary analysis? Discuss any advantages and disadvantages of bringing the cash conversion cycle more in line with the industry averages.

10. You are somewhat concerned about the reliability of financial data from the Internet, and decide to check the data versus BP's SEC filings. To obtain these filings, go to MSN (http://moneycentral.msn.com/home.asp). Type BP into the "Name or Symbol" box and click Go. Once BP comes up, select "SEC Filings" from the vertical menu on the left-hand side. Scroll through the filings to find the latest 20-F, Foreign Annual Reports. Download the PDF version of this report and expand the document bookmarks on the left-hand side. Select Base, then Financial Statements, and then either the Balance Sheet or Income Statement to find the numbers you need. Is there any discrepancy between these numbers and the data you downloaded originally?

Short-Term Financial Planning

Mattel Inc. is a multinational company with year-end 2007 assets of over $4.8 billion. Mattel designs and manufactures toys throughout the world; its major product lines include the Barbie, Hot Wheels, Fisher-Price, and American Girl brands. The demand for toys is typically highly seasonal, with demand peaking during the fall in anticipation of December's holiday retailing season. As a result, Mattel's revenues vary dramatically throughout the calendar year. For example, revenues during the fourth quarter of the calendar year are typically more than twice as high as revenues in the first quarter.

Mattel's varying business revenues cause its cash flows to be highly cyclical. The firm generates surplus cash during some months; it has a great demand for capital during other months. These seasonal financing requirements are quite different from its ongoing, long-term demand for permanent capital. How does a company such as Mattel manage its short-term cash needs within each calendar year?

In this chapter, we analyze short-term financial planning. We begin by showing how companies forecast their cash flows to determine their short-term financing needs, and we explore reasons why firms use short-term financing. We next discuss financing policies that guide these financing decisions. Finally, we compare alternative ways a company can finance a shortfall during periods when it is not generating enough cash, including short-term financing with bank loans, commercial paper, and secured financing.

27.1 FORECASTING SHORT-TERM FINANCING NEEDS

The first step in short-term financial planning is to forecast the company's future cash flows. This exercise has two distinct objectives. First, a company forecasts its cash flows to determine whether it will have surplus cash or a cash deficit for each period. Second, management needs to decide whether that surplus or deficit is temporary or permanent. If it is permanent, it may affect the firm's long-term financial decisions. For example, if a company anticipates an ongoing surplus of cash, it may choose to increase its dividend payout. Deficits resulting from investments in long-term projects are often financed using long-term sources of capital, such as equity or long-term bonds.

In this chapter, we focus specifically on short-term financial planning. With this perspective, we are interested in analyzing the types of cash surpluses or deficits that are temporary and, therefore, short-term in nature. When a company analyzes its short-term financing needs, it typically examines cash flows at quarterly intervals. To illustrate, let's assume that it is currently December 2012 and consider the case of Springfield Snow boards Inc. Springfield manufactures snowboarding equipment, which it sells primarily to sports retailers. Springfield anticipates that in 2013 its sales will grow by 10%, to $20 million, and its total net income will be $1,950,000. Assuming that both sales and production will occur uniformly throughout the year, management's forecast of its quarterly net income and statement of cash flows for 2013 is presented in the spreadsheet in Table 27.1 (also shown, in grey, is the income statement from the fourth quarter of 2012).[1]

From this forecast, we see that Springfield is a profitable company. Its quarterly net income is almost $500,000. Springfield's capital expenditures are equal to depreciation, and while Springfield's working capital requirements increase in the first quarter due to the increase in sales, they remain constant thereafter and so have no further cash flow consequence. Based on these projections, Springfield will be able to fund projected sales growth from its operating profit and, in fact, will accumulate excess cash on an ongoing basis. Given similar growth forecasts for next year and beyond, this surplus is likely to be long term. Springfield could reduce the surplus by paying some of it out as a dividend or by repurchasing shares.

Let's now turn to Springfield's potential short-term financing needs. Firms require short-term financing for three reasons: seasonalities, negative cash flow shocks, and positive cash flow shocks.

SEASONALITIES

For many firms, sales are seasonal. When sales are concentrated during a few months, sources and uses of cash are also likely to be seasonal. Firms in this position may find themselves with a surplus of cash during some months that is sufficient to compensate for a shortfall during other months. However, because of timing differences, such firms often have short-term financing needs.

To illustrate, let's return to the example of Springfield Snowboards. In Table 27.1, management assumed that Springfield's sales occur uniformly throughout the year. In reality, for a snowboard manufacturer, sales are likely to be highly seasonal. Assume that 20% of sales occur during the first quarter, 10% during each of the second and third quarters (largely Southern Hemisphere sales), and 60% of sales during the fourth quarter,

---

1. Given the extensive coverage we have provided in Chapters 2 and 19 on how to construct pro forma financial statements, we do not rehash those details here. For simplicity, we have assumed Springfield has no debt, and earns no interest on retained cash.

PROJECTED FINANCIAL STATEMENTS FOR SPRINGFIELD SNOWBOARDS, 2013, ASSUMING LEVEL SALES

TABLE 27.1

SPREADSHEET

Quarter	2012Q4	2013Q1	2013Q2	2013Q3	2013Q4
Income Statement ($000)					
1 Sales	4,545	5,000	5,000	5,000	5,000
2 Cost of Goods Sold	(2,955)	(3,250)	(3,250)	(3,250)	(3,250)
3 Selling, General, and Administrative	(455)	(500)	(500)	(500)	(500)
4 EBITDA	1,136	1,250	1,250	1,250	1,250
5 Depreciation	(455)	(500)	(500)	(500)	(500)
6 EBIT	682	750	750	750	750
7 Taxes	(239)	(263)	(263)	(263)	(263)
8 Net Income	443	488	488	488	488
Statement of Cash Flows					
9 Net Income		488	488	488	488
10 Depreciation		500	500	500	500
11 Changes in Working Capital					
12 Accounts Receivable		(136)	–	–	–
13 Inventory		–	–	–	–
14 Accounts Payable		48	–	–	–
15 Cash from Operating Activities		899	988	988	988
16 Capital Expenditures		(500)	(500)	(500)	(500)
17 Other Investment		–	–	–	–
18 Cash from Investing Activities		(500)	(500)	(500)	(500)
19 Net Borrowing		–	–	–	–
20 Dividends		–	–	–	–
21 Capital Contributions		–	–	–	–
22 Cash from Financing Activities		–	–	–	–
23 Change in Cash and Equivalents (15 + 18 + 22)		399	488	488	488

in anticipation of the (Northern Hemisphere) winter snowboarding season. The spreadsheet in Table 27.2 presents the resulting statement of cash flows. These forecasts continue to assume production occurs uniformly throughout the year.

From Table 27.2, we see that Springfield is still a profitable company, and its annual net income still totals $1,950,000. However, the introduction of seasonal sales creates some dramatic swings in Springfield's short-term cash flows. There are two effects of seasonality on cash flows. First, while cost of goods sold fluctuates proportionally with sales, other costs (such as administrative overhead and depreciation) do not, leading to large changes in the firm's net income by quarter. Second, net working capital changes are more pronounced. In the first quarter, Springfield receives cash by collecting the receivables from last year's high fourth quarter sales. During the second and third quarters, the company's inventory balance increases. Given capacity constraints in its manufacturing equipment, Springfield produces snowboards throughout the year, even though sales during the summer are low. Because production occurs uniformly, accounts payable do not vary over the year. Inventory, however, builds up in anticipation of fourth quarter sales—and increases in inventory use cash. As a consequence, Springfield has negative net cash flows during the second and third quarters, primarily to fund its inventory. By the fourth quarter, high sales recover cash for the company.

Seasonal sales create large short-term cash flow deficits and surpluses. During the second and third quarters, the company will need to find additional short-term sources of cash to fund inventory. During the fourth quarter, Springfield will have a large short-term surplus. Given that its seasonal cash flow needs are likely to recur next year, Springfield

PROJECTED FINANCIAL STATEMENTS FOR SPRINGFIELD SNOWBOARDS, 2013, ASSUMING SEASONAL SALES

TABLE 27.2

SPREADSHEET

Quarter	2012Q4	2013Q1	2013Q2	2013Q3	2013Q4
Income Statement ($000)					
1 Sales	10,909	4,000	2,000	2,000	12,000
2 Cost of Goods Sold	(7,091)	(2,600)	(1,300)	(1,300)	(7,800)
3 Selling, General, and Administrative	(773)	(450)	(350)	(350)	(850)
4 EBITDA	3,045	950	350	350	3,350
5 Depreciation	(455)	(500)	(500)	(500)	(500)
6 EBIT	2,591	450	(150)	(150)	2,850
7 Taxes	(907)	(158)	53	53	(998)
8 Net Income	1,684	293	(98)	(98)	1,853
Statement of Cash Flows					
9 Net Income		293	(98)	(98)	1,853
10 Depreciation		500	500	500	500
11 Changes in Working Capital					
12 Accounts Receivable		2,073	600	—	(3,000)
13 Inventory		(650)	(1,950)	(1,950)	4,550
14 Accounts Payable		48	—	—	—
15 Cash from Operating Activities		2,263	(948)	(1,548)	3,903
16 Capital Expenditures		(500)	(500)	(500)	(500)
17 Other Investment		—	—	—	—
18 Cash from Investing Activities		(500)	(500)	(500)	(500)
19 Net Borrowing		—	—	—	—
20 Dividends		—	—	—	—
21 Capital Contributions		—	—	—	—
22 Cash from Financing Activities		—	—	—	—
23 Change in Cash and Equivalents (15 + 18 + 22)		1,763	(1,448)	(2,048)	3,403

may choose to invest this cash in one of the short-term investment options discussed in Chapter 26. Management can then use this cash to fund some of its short-term working capital needs during the following year.

NEGATIVE CASH FLOW SHOCKS

Occasionally, a company will encounter circumstances in which cash flows are temporarily negative for an unexpected reason. We refer to such a situation as a negative cash flow shock. Like seasonalities, negative cash flow shocks can create short-term financing needs.

Returning to the Springfield Snowboards example, assume that during April 2013, management learns that some manufacturing equipment has broken unexpectedly. It will cost an additional $1,000,000 to replace the equipment.[2] To illustrate the effect of this negative cash flow shock, we return to the base case in which Springfield's sales are level rather than seasonal. (The marginal impact of this negative shock given seasonal sales would be similar.) The spreadsheet in Table 27.3 presents cash flows with level sales and the broken equipment.

In this case, the one-time expenditure of $1 million to replace equipment results in a negative net cash flow of $513,000 during the second quarter of 2013. If its cash reserves

---

2. For simplicity, assume that the book value of the replaced equipment is zero, so that the equipment change does not have any immediate tax consequences. Also, assume that Springfield obtains the replacement equipment quickly, so that any interruption in production is negligible. The general results contained in the discussion still hold if we relax these assumptions, although the calculations are somewhat more complex.

PROJECTED FINANCIAL STATEMENTS FOR SPRINGFIELD SNOWBOARDS, 2013, ASSUMING LEVEL SALES AND A NEGATIVE CASH FLOW SHOCK

TABLE 27.3

SPREADSHEET

Quarter	2012Q4	2013Q1	2013Q2	2013Q3	2013Q4
Income Statement ($000)					
1 Sales	4,545	5,000	5,000	5,000	5,000
2 Cost of Goods Sold	(2,955)	(3,250)	(3,250)	(3,250)	(3,250)
3 Selling, General, and Administrative	(455)	(500)	(500)	(500)	(500)
4 EBITDA	1,136	1,250	1,250	1,250	1,250
5 Depreciation	(455)	(500)	(500)	(525)	(525)
6 EBIT	682	750	750	725	725
7 Taxes	(239)	(263)	(263)	(254)	(254)
8 Net Income	443	488	488	471	471
Statement of Cash Flows					
9 Net Income		488	488	471	471
10 Depreciation		500	500	525	525
11 Changes in Working Capital					
12 Accounts Receivable		(136)	–	–	–
13 Inventory		–	–	–	–
14 Accounts Payable		48	–	–	–
15 **Cash from Operating Activities**		899	988	996	996
16 Capital Expenditures		(500)	(1,500)	(525)	(525)
17 Other Investment		–	–	–	–
18 **Cash from Investing Activities**		(500)	(1,500)	(525)	(525)
19 Net Borrowing		–	–	–	–
20 Dividends		–	–	–	–
21 Capital Contributions		–	–	–	–
22 **Cash from Financing Activities**		–	–	–	–
23 **Change in Cash and Equivalents** (15 + 18 + 22)		399	(513)	471	471

are insufficient, Springfield will have to borrow (or arrange for another financing source) to cover the $513,000 shortfall. However, the company continues to generate positive cash flow in subsequent quarters, and by the fourth quarter it will have generated enough in cumulative cash flow to repay any loan. Therefore, this negative cash flow shock has created the need for short-term financing.

POSITIVE CASH FLOW SHOCKS

We next analyze a case in which a positive cash flow shock affects short-term financing needs. Although this surprise is good news, it still creates demand for short-term financing.

During the first quarter of 2013, the director of marketing at Springfield Snowboards announces a deal with a chain of outdoor sporting goods stores located in Alberta and British Columbia. Springfield will be the exclusive supplier to this customer, leading to an overall sales increase of 20% for the firm. The increased sales will begin in the second quarter. As part of the deal, Springfield has agreed to a one-time expense of $500,000 for marketing in areas where the stores are located. An extra $1 million in capital expenditures is also required during the first quarter to increase production capacity. Likewise, sales growth will affect required working capital.

Managers at Springfield prepared the cash flow forecasts in the spreadsheet in Table 27.4 to reflect this new business. Notice that net income is lower during the first quarter, reflecting the $500,000 increase in marketing expenses. By contrast, net income in subsequent quarters is higher, reflecting the higher sales. Sales increases in each of the first two quarters result in increases in accounts receivable and accounts payable.

PROJECTED FINANCIAL STATEMENTS FOR SPRINGFIELD SNOWBOARDS, 2013, ASSUMING LEVEL SALES AND A GROWTH OPPORTUNITY

TABLE 27.4

SPREADSHEET

Quarter	2012Q4	2013Q1	2013Q2	2013Q3	2013Q4
Income Statement ($000)					
1 Sales	4,545	5,000	6,000	6,000	6,000
2 Cost of Goods Sold	(2,955)	(3,250)	(3,900)	(3,900)	(3,900)
3 Selling, General, and Administrative	(455)	(1,000)	(600)	(600)	(600)
4 EBITDA	1,136	750	1,500	1,500	1,500
5 Depreciation	(455)	(500)	(525)	(525)	(525)
6 EBIT	682	250	975	975	975
7 Taxes	(239)	(88)	(341)	(341)	(341)
8 Net Income	443	163	634	634	634
Statement of Cash Flows					
9 Net Income		163	634	634	634
10 Depreciation		500	525	525	525
11 Changes in Working Capital					
12 Accounts Receivable		(136)	(300)	–	–
13 Inventory		–	–	–	–
14 Accounts Payable		48	105	–	–
15 Cash from Operating Activities		574	964	1,159	1,159
16 Capital Expenditures		(1,500)	(525)	(525)	(525)
17 Other Investment		–	–	–	–
18 Cash from Investing Activities		(1,500)	(525)	(525)	(525)
19 Net Borrowing		–	–	–	–
20 Dividends		–	–	–	–
21 Capital Contributions		–	–	–	–
22 Cash from Financing Activities		–	–	–	–
23 Change in Cash and Equivalents (15 + 18 + 22)		(926)	439	634	634

Even though the unexpected event in this case—the opportunity to grow more rapidly—is positive, it results in a negative net cash flow during the first quarter, due primarily to the new marketing expenses and capital expenditures. However, because the company will be even more profitable in subsequent quarters, this financing need is temporary.

Now that we have explained how a company determines its short-term needs, let's explore how these needs are financed.

CONCEPT CHECK

1. How do we forecast the firm's future cash requirements?

2. What is the effect of seasonalities on short-term cash flows?

27.2 THE MATCHING PRINCIPLE

In a perfect capital market, the choice of financing is irrelevant; thus how the firm chooses to finance its short-term cash needs cannot affect value. In reality, important market frictions exist, including transaction costs. For example, one transaction cost is the opportunity cost of holding cash in accounts that pay little or no interest. Firms also face high transaction costs if they need to negotiate a loan on short notice to cover a cash shortfall. Firms can increase their value by adopting a policy that minimizes these kinds of costs. One such policy is known as the matching principle. The **matching principle** states that short-term needs should be financed with short-term debt and long-term needs should be financed with long-term sources of funds.

PERMANENT WORKING CAPITAL

Permanent working capital is the amount that a firm must keep invested in its short-term assets to support its continuing operations. Because this investment in working capital is required so long as the firm remains in business, it constitutes a long-term investment. The matching principle indicates that the firm should finance this permanent investment in working capital with long-term sources of funds. Such sources have lower transaction costs than short-term sources of funds, which would have to be replaced more often.

TEMPORARY WORKING CAPITAL

Another portion of a firm's investment in its accounts receivable and inventory is temporary and results from seasonal fluctuations in the firm's business or unanticipated shocks. This **temporary working capital** is the difference between the actual level of investment in short-term assets and the permanent working capital investment. Because temporary working capital represents a short-term need, the firm should finance this portion of its investment with short-term financing.

To illustrate the distinction between permanent and temporary working capital, we return to the Springfield Snowboards example. Table 27.2 presented cash flow forecasts assuming seasonal sales. In the spreadsheet in Table 27.5, we report the underlying levels of working capital that correspond to these forecasts.

In Table 27.5, we see that working capital for Springfield varies from a minimum of $2,125,000 in the first quarter of 2013 to $5,425,000 in the third quarter. The minimum level of working capital, or $2,125,000, can be thought of as the firm's permanent working capital. The difference between this minimum level and the higher levels in subsequent quarters (for example, $5,425,000 − $2,125,000 = $3,300,000 in the third quarter) reflects Springfield's temporary working capital requirements.

FINANCING POLICY CHOICES

Following the matching principle should, in the long run, help minimize a firm's transaction costs.[3] But what if, instead of using the matching principle, a firm financed its permanent working capital needs with short-term debt? When the short-term debt comes due, the

PROJECTED LEVELS OF WORKING CAPITAL FOR SPRINGFIELD SNOWBOARDS, 2013, ASSUMING SEASONAL SALES

TABLE 27.5

SPREADSHEET

Quarter	2012Q4	2013Q1	2013Q2	2013Q3	2013Q4
Net Working Capital Requirements ($000)					
1 Minimum Cash Balance	500	500	500	500	500
2 Accounts Receivable	3,273	1,200	600	600	3,600
3 Inventory	300	950	2,900	4,850	300
4 Accounts Payable	(477)	(525)	(525)	(525)	(525)
5 **Net Working Capital**	3,595	2,125	3,475	5,425	3,875

---

3. Some evidence indicates that most firms appear to follow the matching principle. See W. Beranek, C. Cornwell, and S. Choi, "External Financing, Liquidity, and Capital Expenditures," *Journal of Financial Research* (Summer 1995): 207–222, and M. H. Stohs and D. C. Mauer, "The Determinants of Corporate Debt Maturity Structure," *Journal of Business* 69:3 (1996): 279–312.

c. an electric utility

d. a company that operates toll roads

e. a restaurant chain

2. Sailboats Etc. is a retail company specializing in sailboats and other sailing-related equipment. The following table contains financial forecasts as well as current (month 0) working capital levels. During which months are the firm's seasonal working capital needs the greatest? When does it have surplus cash?

($000)	Month						
	0	1	2	3	4	5	6
Net Income		$10	$12	$15	$25	$30	$18
Depreciation		2	3	3	4	5	4
Capital Expenditures		1	0	0	1	0	0
Levels of Working Capital							
Accounts Receivable	$2	3	4	5	7	10	6
Inventory	3	2	4	5	5	4	2
Accounts Payable	2	2	2	2	2	2	2

The Matching Principle

3. What is the difference between permanent working capital and temporary working capital?

4. Quarterly working capital levels for your firm for the next year are included in the following table. What are the permanent working capital needs of your company? What are the temporary needs?

($000)	Quarter			
	1	2	3	4
Cash	$100	$100	$100	$100
Accounts Receivable	200	100	100	600
Inventory	200	500	900	50
Accounts Payable	100	100	100	100

5. Why might a company choose to finance permanent working capital with short-term debt?

Short-Term Financing with Bank Loans

6. The Hand-to-Mouth Company needs a $10,000 loan for the next 30 days. It is trying to decide which of three alternatives to use:

Alternative A: Forgo the discount on its trade credit agreement that offers terms of 2/10, net 30.

Alternative B: Borrow the money from Bank A, which has offered to lend the firm $10,000 for 30 days at an APR of 12%. The bank will require a (no-interest) compensating balance of 5% of the face value of the loan and will charge a $100 loan origination fee, which means Hand-to-Mouth must borrow even more than the $10,000.

Alternative C: Borrow the money from Bank B, which has offered to lend the firm $10,000 for 30 days at an APR of 15%. The loan has a 1% loan origination fee.

Which alternative is the cheapest source of financing for Hand-to-Mouth?

7. Consider two loans with a one-year maturity and identical face values: an 8% loan with a 1% loan origination fee and an 8% loan with a 5% (no-interest) compensating balance requirement. Which loan would have the higher effective annual rate? Why?

8. What is the difference between evergreen credit and a revolving line of credit?

9. Which of the following one-year, $1000 bank loans offers the lowest effective annual rate?
    a. a loan with an APR of 6%, compounded monthly
    b. a loan with an APR of 6%, compounded annually, that also has a compensating balance requirement of 10% (on which no interest is paid)
    c. a loan with an APR of 6%, compounded annually, that has a 1% loan origination fee

10. The Needy Corporation borrowed $10,000 from Bank Ease. According to the terms of the loan, Needy must pay the bank $400 in interest every three months for the three-year life of the loan, with the principal to be repaid at the maturity of the loan. What effective annual rate is Needy paying?

Short-Term Financing with Commercial Paper

11. The Treadwater Bank wants to raise $1 million using three-month commercial paper. The net proceeds to the bank will be $985,000. What is the effective annual rate of this financing for Treadwater?

12. Magna Corporation has an issue of commercial paper with a face value of $1,000,000 and a maturity of six months. Magna received net proceeds of $973,710 when it sold the paper. What is the effective annual rate of the paper to Magna?

13. What is the difference between direct paper and dealer paper?

14. The Signet Corporation has issued four-month commercial paper with a $6 million face value. The firm netted $5,870,850 on the sale. What effective annual rate is Signet paying for these funds?

Short-Term Financing with Secured Financing

15. What is the difference between pledging accounts receivable to secure a loan and factoring accounts receivable?

16. Stelco has borrowed $5 million for one month at a stated annual rate of 9%, using inventory stored in a field warehouse as collateral. The warehouser charges a $5000 fee, payable at the end of the month. What is the effective annual rate of this loan?

17. Discuss the three different arrangements under which a firm may use inventory to secure a loan.

18. The Rasputin Brewery is considering using a public warehouse loan as part of its short-term financing. The firm will require a loan of $500,000. Interest on the loan will be 10% (APR, annual compounding) to be paid at the end of the year. The warehouse charges 1% of the face value of the loan, payable at the beginning of the year. What is the effective annual rate of this warehousing arrangement?

PART

10

Special Topics

THE LAW OF ONE PRICE CONNECTION. In Part 10, the final section of the text, we address special topics in corporate financial management. The Law of One Price continues to provide a unifying framework as we consider these topics. Chapter 28 discusses mergers and acquisitions and Chapter 29 provides an overview of corporate governance. In Chapter 30, we focus on corporations' use of derivatives to manage risk. We use the Law of One Price to evaluate the costs and benefits of risk management. Chapter 31 introduces the issues a firm faces when making a foreign investment and addresses the valuation of foreign projects. We value foreign currency cash flows in the context of internationally integrated capital markets, a condition that we demonstrate with the Law of One Price.

CHAPTER

28

NOTATION

EPS	earnings per share
P/E	price-earnings ratio
A	premerger total value of acquirer
T	premerger total value of target
S	value of all synergies
N_A	premerger number of shares of acquirer outstanding
x	number of new shares issued by acquirer to pay for target
P_T	premerger share price of target
P_A	premerger share price of acquirer
N_T	premerger number of shares of target outstanding

Mergers and Acquisitions

On July 14, 2008, St. Louis–based Anheuser-Busch agreed to be acquired by Belgian-based beer giant InBev for $70 per share in cash. The agreement ended 150 years of independence for the brewer of iconic Budweiser beer. In fact, Anheuser-Busch's board flatly rejected InBev's initial $65 per share offer, preferring to remain independent. However, the sweetened offer, valuing the company at $60 billion, was too compelling a deal for shareholders for Anheuser's board to pass up. Next, InBev's managers faced the daunting task of integrating Anheuser's organization and brands into their global company and generating enough value from the transaction to justify the price they paid. Given the complexity and potential sums of money at stake, it is clear that some of the most important decisions financial managers make concern mergers and acquisitions.

In this chapter, we first provide some historical background about the market for mergers and acquisitions. Next, we discuss some of the reasons why a corporate financial manager may decide to pursue an acquisition. We then review the takeover process. Finally, we address the question of who gets the value that is added when a takeover occurs.

28.1 BACKGROUND AND HISTORICAL TRENDS

Mergers and acquisitions are part of what is often referred to as "the market for corporate control." When one firm acquires another, there is typically a buyer, the **acquirer** or **bidder**, and a seller, the **target** firm. There are two primary mechanisms by which ownership and control of a public corporation can change: Either another corporation or group of individuals can acquire the target firm, or the target firm can merge with another firm. In both cases, the acquiring entity must purchase the stock or existing assets of the target either for cash or for something of equivalent value (such as shares in the acquiring or newly merged corporation). For simplicity, we refer to either mechanism as a **takeover**.

The global takeover market is highly active, averaging more than $1 trillion per year in transaction value. Table 28.1 lists the 10 largest transactions completed during the 13-year period from 1995 through 2008. As the table indicates, takeovers happen between well-known companies, and individual transactions can involve huge sums of money.

MERGER WAVES

The takeover market is also characterized by **merger waves**—peaks of heavy activity followed by quiet troughs of few transactions. Figure 28.1 displays the time series of takeover activity from 1926 to 2008. Merger activity is greater during economic expansions than during contractions and correlates with bull markets. Many of the same technological and economic conditions that lead to bull markets also motivate managers to reshuffle assets

| TABLE 28.1 | THE 10 LARGEST MERGER TRANSACTIONS, 1995–2008 |

Date				
Announced	**Completed**	**Target Name**	**Acquirer Name**	**Value ($US billion)**
Nov. 1999	June 2000	Mannesmann AG	Vodafone AirTouch PLC	203
Oct. 2004	Dec. 2004	Shell Transport and Trading	Royal Dutch Petroleum	185
Jan. 2000	Jan. 2001	Time Warner	America Online Inc.	182
Apr. 2007	Oct. 2007	ABN-AMRO Holding NV	RFS Holdings BV	99
Mar. 2006	Dec. 2006	Bell South	AT&T	89
Nov. 1999	June 2000	Warner-Lambert Co.	Pfizer Inc.	89
Dec. 1998	Nov. 1999	Mobil Corp.	Exxon Corp.	86
Jan. 2000	Dec. 2000	SmithKline Beecham PLC	Glaxo Wellcome PLC	79
Apr. 1998	Oct. 1998	Citicorp	Travelers Group Inc.	73
July 2001	Nov. 2002	AT&T Broadband & Internet Services Inc.	Comcast Corp.	72

Sources: Thomson Reuters, Thomson Financial's SDC M&A database.

Percentage of Public
Companies Taken Over Each
Quarter, 1926–2008

Mergers appear to occur
in distinct waves, with the
most recent waves
occurring in the 1960s,
1980s, 1990s, and
2000s.

Source: Authors' calculations
based on Center for Research in
Securities Prices data.

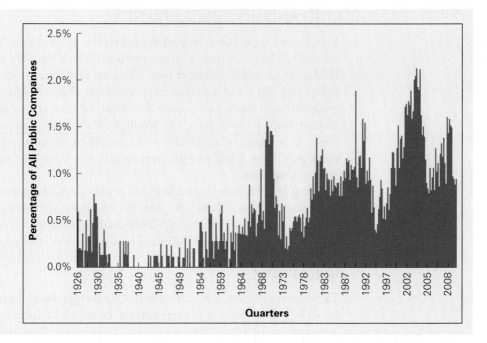

through mergers and acquisitions. Thus most likely the same economic activities that drive expansions also drive peaks in merger activity.[1]

Figure 28.1 shows that the periods of the greatest takeover activity occurred in the 1960s, 1980s, 1990s, and 2000s. Each merger wave was characterized by a typical type of deal. The increase in activity in the 1960s is known as the conglomerate wave because firms typically acquired firms in unrelated businesses. At the time, it was thought that managerial expertise was portable across business lines and that the conglomerate business form offered great financial advantages. This conglomerate fad eventually fell out of favour, and the 1980s were known for hostile, "bust-up" takeovers, in which the acquirer purchased a poorly performing conglomerate and sold off its individual business units for more than the purchase price. The 1990s, in contrast, were known for "strategic" or "global" deals that were more likely to be friendly and to involve companies in related businesses; these mergers often were designed to create strong firms on a scale that would allow them to compete globally. At the end of 2004, takeover activity began to pick up again, starting what many expect to be the next big merger wave, marked by consolidation in many industries, such as telecommunications and software. This wave also saw private equity playing a larger role than it had in the past, with some private equity groups, such as KKR, TPG, Blackrock, and Cerberus, taking ever-larger firms such as Hertz (see Chapter 24), Chrysler, and Harrah's private. According to Thomson Reuters, 2007 saw the value of merger and acquisition activity hit an all-time high, with over $4.5 trillion worth of deals announced globally. Almost 30% of these transactions involved consolidation in the materials, energy, and power sectors. The latest merger wave came to a crashing end, though, as the credit crisis of late 2007 and 2008 curtailed the ability to finance mergers.

---

1. See J. Harford, "What Drives Merger Waves," *Journal of Financial Economics* 77 (2005): 529–560, for an analysis of why these waves occur.

TYPES OF MERGERS

While we tend to talk about merger waves and mergers in general, the term "merger," as commonly used, encompasses several types of transactions that vary by the relation between the target and the acquirer and by the method of payment used in the transaction. If the target and acquirer are in the same industry, the merger is typically called a **horizontal merger**, whereas if the target's industry buys or sells to the acquirer's industry, it is called a **vertical merger**. Finally, if the target and acquirer operate in unrelated industries, the deal is a **conglomerate merger**. Conglomerate mergers, while popular in the 1960s, have generally fallen out of favour with shareholders because of the difficulty in creating value when combining two unrelated businesses.

Deals also vary based on whether the target shareholders receive stock or cash as payment for target shares. When they receive stock, the deal is often called a **stock swap**, because target shareholders are swapping their old stock for new stock in either the acquirer or a newly created merged firm. The consideration paid to target shareholders can be very complex, including debt instruments, options, and mixes of any of these with cash and/or stock. Commonly, however, target shareholders receive stock, cash, or a mix of the two.

While news reports understandably focus on the price and method of payment, the structure of a merger transaction, summarized in a **term sheet**, can be simple or incredibly complex. The items to negotiate include, among other things, who will run the new company, the size and composition of the new board, the location of the headquarters, and even the name of the new company.

CONCEPT CHECK

1. What are merger waves?

2. What types of deals were associated with the last three merger waves?

28.2 MARKET REACTION TO A TAKEOVER

In Canada and most U.S. states, the law requires that when existing shareholders of a target firm are forced to sell their shares, they receive a fair value for their shares. Typically, this concept is interpreted as the value exclusive of any value that arises because of the merger itself. For practical purposes, this principle translates into the share price prior to the merger. As a consequence, a bidder is unlikely to acquire a target company for less than its current market value. In practice, most acquirers pay a substantial **acquisition premium**, which is the percentage difference between the acquisition price and the premerger price of the target firm.

Table 28.2 lists the average historical premium and market reaction to a takeover.[2] As the table shows, acquirers pay an average premium of 43% over the premerger price of the

---

2. The original research done in the 1970s and 1980s documented that shareholders experience significant gains (between 20% and 30%) upon a successful takeover of their firms. See G. Mandelker, "Risk and Return: The Case of the Merging Firm," *Journal of Financial Economics* 1:4 (1974): 303–335; M. C. Jensen and R. S. Ruback, "The Market for Corporate Control: The Scientific Evidence," *Journal of Financial Economics* 11:1 (1983): 5–50; and M. Bradley, A. Desai, and E. H. Kim, "The Rationale Behind Interfirm Tender Offers: Information or Synergy," *Journal of Financial Economics* 11:1 (1983): 183–206. More recent papers have found combined losses on the order of $240 billion in capitalization at the announcement of takeover bids. This finding appears to be driven by spectacular losses from some large takeovers of public targets, especially in the late 1990s. See T. Loughran and A. Vijh, "Do Long-Term Shareholders Benefit from Corporate Acquisitions?" *Journal of Finance* 52:5 (1997): 1765–1790, and S. Moeller, R. Stulz, and F. Schlingemann, "Wealth Destruction on a Massive Scale: A Study of Acquiring Firm Returns in the Recent Merger Wave," *Journal of Finance* 60:2 (2005): 757–782.

AVERAGE ACQUISITION PREMIUM AND STOCK PRICE REACTIONS TO MERGERS

TABLE 28.2

Premium Paid over Premerger Price	Announcement Price Reaction	
	Target	Acquirer
43%	15%	1%

Source: Data based on all U.S. deals from 1980 to 2005 as reported in *Handbook of Corporate Finance: Empirical Corporate Finance*, Vol. 2, Chapter 15, pp. 291–430, B. E., Eckbo, ed., Elsevier/North-Holland Handbook of Finance Series, 2008.

target. When a bid is announced, the target shareholders enjoy a gain of 15% on average in their stock price. Although acquirer shareholders see an *average* gain of 1%, in half of the transactions, the bidder price *decreases*. These facts raise three important questions that we answer in this chapter:

1. Why do acquirers pay a premium over the market value for a target company?

2. Although the price of the target company rises on average upon the announcement of the takeover, why does it rise less than the premium offered by the acquirer?

3. If the transaction is a good idea, why does the acquirer not consistently experience a large price increase?

Let's start with the first question—why do acquirers pay a premium over market value? In fact, this question has two parts: (1) Why is the target worth a premium over the current market value? and (2) Even if the target is worth more than its premerger value, why do acquirers pay more than the premerger market price? In the next section, we answer the first part of this question. We delay the discussion of the second part until the end of the chapter, when we fully understand the mechanics of the takeover process.

CONCEPT CHECK

1. On average, what happens to the target share price on the announcement of a takeover?

2. On average, what happens to the acquirer share price on the announcement of a takeover?

28.3 REASONS TO ACQUIRE

For most investors an investment in the stock market is a zero-NPV investment. How, then, can an acquirer pay a premium for a target and still satisfy the requirement that the investment is a positive-NPV investment opportunity? The answer is that an acquirer might be able to add economic value, as a result of the acquisition, that an individual investor cannot add.

Large synergies are by far the most common justification that bidders give for the premium they pay for a target. An extreme example is SBC's acquisition of AT&T in 2005 for more than $15 billion. In interviews immediately after the announcement, SBC's chairman Ed Whitacre was quick to point out that the projected synergies of $15 billion alone could justify the price SBC agreed to pay for AT&T, let alone AT&T's assets.

Such synergies usually fall into two categories: cost reductions and revenue enhancements. Cost-reduction synergies are more common and easier to achieve because they generally translate into layoffs of overlapping employees and elimination of redundant resources. This was the case in the SBC/AT&T acquisition, which forecasted 13,000 layoffs in the first year. If the merger will create possibilities to expand into new markets or gain more customers, then the merger partners will predict synergies that enhance their revenue. For example, when Delta and Northwest airlines announced their merger agreement in April 2008, they forecasted $200–$300 million per year in revenue-enhancement synergies because their expanded network and flight options would bring in more customers and increase customer loyalty.

Let's examine in detail the synergies most often cited by acquirers to justify takeovers.

ECONOMIES OF SCALE AND SCOPE

A large company can enjoy **economies of scale**, or savings from producing goods in high volume, that are not available to a small company. Larger firms can also benefit from **economies of scope**, which are savings that come from combining the marketing and distribution of different types of related products (e.g., soft drinks and snack foods). In some cases, these economies are clear. For example, consider the wave of bank mergers that followed the federal government's relaxation of Depression-era banking laws. Today, customers of large banks benefit from other financial services besides traditional services such as loans, chequing and savings accounts, and the convenience of branches across the country.

There may also be costs associated with size. Chief among these is that larger firms are more difficult to manage. In a small firm, the CEO is often close to the firm's operations. He or she can keep in touch with the firm's largest customers and most important personnel, thereby keeping abreast of changing market conditions and potential problems. Because they receive information so quickly, small firms are often able to react in a timely way to changes in the economic environment.

VERTICAL INTEGRATION

Vertical integration refers to the merger of two companies in the same industry that make products required at different stages of the production cycle. A company might conclude that it can enhance its product if it has direct control of the inputs required to make the product. Similarly, another company might not be happy with how its products are being distributed, so it might decide to take control of its distribution channels.

The principal benefit of vertical integration is coordination. By putting two companies under central control, management can ensure that both companies work toward a common goal. For example, oil companies are often vertically integrated. They generally own all stages of the production process, from the oil fields, to the refineries, and so on, even down to the gas stations that distribute their primary product—gasoline. Many also have divisions that prospect for new oil.

Vertically integrated companies are large, and as we have already pointed out, large corporations are more difficult to run. Consequently not all successful corporations are vertically integrated. A good example is Microsoft Corporation. Microsoft has chosen to make the operating system that the vast majority of computers use, but not the computers themselves. Rival Apple Computers makes both. Although both companies are successful, over the long run Microsoft has been more successful than Apple. Some experts have argued that this is due to Microsoft's decision to not integrate vertically.

EXPERTISE

Firms often need expertise in particular areas to compete more efficiently. Faced with this situation, a firm can enter the labour market and attempt to hire personnel with the required skills. However, consider a case in which a new, more efficient technology has been developed to produce a firm's primary output. Hiring experienced workers directly might be very difficult in this scenario. If the firm is unfamiliar with the new technology, it could be difficult for existing managers to identify the talent they need. Even if such people are identified and hired, they must be supervised. In addition, without an in-depth understanding of the production process, effectively managing the process could pose problems.

A more efficient solution may be to purchase the talent as an already functioning unit by acquiring an existing firm. For example, in 2000 Paris-based AXA bought Sanford C. Bernstein, a Wall Street private partnership, to gain expertise and a preexisting client base in the huge U.S. asset management market. Similarly, U.K. builder Amec bought a large stake in Spie Batignolles, a French contractor, to gain local contacts and expertise in the French building industry. Such mergers are common in high-tech industries. Networking firm Cisco Systems is known for its strategy of buying young startup firms that have developed promising new networking technologies.

MONOPOLY GAINS

It is often argued that merging with or acquiring a major rival enables a firm to substantially reduce competition within the industry and thereby increase profits. Society as a whole bears the cost of monopoly strategies, so most countries have antitrust laws that limit such activity.

The extent to which these laws are enforced tends to vary across countries and over time depending on the policy of current leaders. When General Electric (GE) agreed to buy Honeywell in October 2000, the U.S. Justice Department approved the deal with limited conditions. However, the European Commission (EC) determined that putting GE's aircraft leasing division and Honeywell's extensive avionics product line under the same management would lead to unacceptable anticompetitive effects in the avionics market. Despite substantial concessions by GE and top-level political lobbying by U.S. officials, the EC refused to approve the deal, and it was eventually called off. The GE/Honeywell deal was the first time a merger of two U.S. companies that had been approved by U.S. authorities was blocked by European authorities. The EC had no direct jurisdiction over the merger of the companies, but it was in the position to impose crippling restrictions on sales inside the European Union.

Monopoly power could be very valuable, and we would expect that in the absence of strong antitrust laws, companies would merge. However, while all companies in an industry benefit when competition is reduced, only the merging company pays the associated costs (from, for instance, managing a larger corporation). Perhaps this reason, along with existing antitrust regulation, accounts for the lack of convincing evidence that monopoly gains result from the reduction of competition following takeovers. For example, financial researchers have found that the share prices of other firms in the same industry did not significantly increase following the announcement of a merger within the industry.[3]

EFFICIENCY GAINS

Another justification acquirers cite for paying a premium for a target is efficiency gains, which are often achieved through an elimination of duplication—for example, as in the SBC/AT&T merger mentioned earlier. Acquirers also often argue that they can run the target organization more efficiently than existing management could.

---

3. See B. E. Eckbo, "Horizontal Mergers, Collusion and Stockholder Wealth," *Journal of Financial Economics* 11:1 (1983): 241–273, and R. Stillman, "Examining Antitrust Policy Toward Horizontal Mergers," *Journal of Financial Economics* 11:1 (1983): 225–240.

Although in theory a chief executive of an inefficiently run corporation can be ousted by current shareholders voting to replace the board of directors, very few managers are replaced in this way. Instead, unhappy investors typically sell their stock, so the stock of a corporation with an inept chief executive trades at a discount relative to the price at which it would trade if it had a more capable chief executive. In such a situation, an acquirer could purchase shares at the discounted price to take control of the corporation and replace the chief executive with a more effective one. Once the benefits of the new management team become obvious to investors, the discount for the old management will likely disappear and the acquirer could resell its shares for a profit.

Although identifying poorly performing corporations is relatively easy, fixing them is another matter entirely. As any sports fan knows, replacing a manager of a team with a weak record is no guarantee that the team will start winning more games. Improving the performance of a public company is not a dissimilar problem. Takeovers relying on the improvement of target management are difficult to complete, and post-takeover resistance to change can be great. Thus not all inefficiently run organizations are necessarily more efficient following a takeover.

OPERATING LOSSES

When a firm makes a profit, it must pay taxes on the profit. However, when it makes a loss, the government does not rebate taxes. Thus it might appear that a conglomerate has a tax advantage over a single-product firm simply because losses in one division can offset profits in another division. Let's illustrate this scenario with an example.

EXAMPLE 28.1   TAXES FOR A MERGED CORPORATION

Problem

Consider two firms, Ying Corporation and Yang Corporation. Both corporations will either make $50 million or lose $20 million every year with equal probability. The only difference is that the firms' profits are perfectly negative correlated. That is, any year Yang Corporation earns $50 million, Ying Corporation loses $20 million, and vice versa. Assume that the corporate tax rate is 34%. What are the total expected after-tax profits of both firms when they are two separate firms? What are the expected after-tax profits if the two firms are combined into one corporation called Ying-Yang Corporation, but are run as two independent divisions? (Assume it is not possible to carry back or carry forward losses.)

Solution

Let's start with Ying Corporation. In the profitable state, the firm must pay corporate taxes, so after-tax profits are $50 \times (1 - 0.34) = \$33$ million. No taxes are owed when the firm reports losses, so the expected after-tax profits of Ying Corporation are $33(0.5) - 20(0.5) = \$6.5$ million.

Because Yang Corporation has identical expected profits, its expected profits are also $6.5 million. Thus the expected profit of both companies operated separately is just the sum of the expected profits of each company—$13 million.

The merged corporation, Ying-Yang Corporation, always makes a pretax profit equal to $50 - 20 = \$30$ million. After taxes, expected profits are therefore $30 \times (1 - 0.34) = \$19.8$ million. So Ying-Yang Corporation has significantly higher after-tax profits than the combined after-tax profits of Ying Corporation and Yang Corporation.

Although Example 28.1 is an extreme case, it illustrates the benefits of conglomeration. In Canada and the United States, however, these benefits are mitigated because the tax authorities allow companies to carry losses forward up to 20 years. That is, a company can use losses to offset earnings up to 20 years in the future. Furthermore, companies with current-year losses can also use them to offset earnings for the three prior years in Canada and the two prior years in the U.S. These carryback and carryforward provisions essentially deliver the benefits of conglomeration to a small firm with volatile earnings.

To justify a takeover based on operating losses, management would have to argue that the tax savings are over and above what the firm would save using carryback and carryforward provisions. In addition, the CRA in Canada and the IRS in the United States will disallow a tax break if it can show that the principal reason for a takeover is tax avoidance, so it is unlikely that the tax advantage could, by itself, be a valid reason to acquire another firm.

DIVERSIFICATION

The benefits of diversification are frequently cited as a reason for a conglomerate merger. The justification for these benefits comes in three forms: direct risk reduction, lower cost of debt or increased debt capacity, and liquidity enhancement. We discuss each in turn.

RISK REDUCTION.   Like a large portfolio, large firms bear less idiosyncratic risk, so often mergers are justified on the basis that the combined firm is less risky. The problem with this argument is that it ignores the fact that investors can achieve the benefits of diversification themselves by purchasing shares in the two separate firms. Because most stockholders will already be holding a well-diversified portfolio, they get no further benefit from the firm diversifying through acquisition. Moreover, as we have already pointed out, there are costs associated with merging and with running a large diversified firm. Because it may be harder to measure performance accurately in a conglomerate, agency costs may increase and resources may be inefficiently allocated across divisions.[4] As a result, it is cheaper for investors to diversify their own portfolios than to have the corporation do it through acquisition.

The only class of stockholders who can benefit from the diversification a merger generates are stockholders who do not hold well-diversified portfolios. Some employees, for instance, hold a large fraction of their wealth in shares of the corporation for which they work and are prevented from selling those shares because of stock and option compensation schemes intended as employee motivation. Because these employees are obligated to hold idiosyncratic risk, they benefit when the firm reduces that risk by conglomerating. Consequently, such employees have a self-interested incentive to have their own employer take over other firms. To the extent that these takeovers impose costs, they are not in the interests of most other shareholders.

DEBT CAPACITY AND BORROWING COSTS.   All else being equal, larger firms, because they are more diversified, have a lower probability of bankruptcy. Consequently, they have a higher debt capacity; in other words, they can increase leverage and thereby lower their costs of capital. This is often voiced as a good reason to engage in diversifying mergers.

We know from the discussion in Chapter 14 that in perfect capital markets, the financial decisions of a firm cannot affect its value. For the preceding argument to be correct, it must therefore rely on some *market imperfection*. The market imperfections cited most

---

4. See, e.g., A. M. Goel, V. Nanda, and M. P. Narayanan, "Career Concerns and Resource Allocation in Conglomerates," *Review of Financial Studies* 17:1 (2004): 99–128.

often by proponents of this line of reasoning are tax benefits and the costs associated with bankruptcy, such as those we discussed in Chapter 16. By diversifying, a firm may be able to increase its debt and enjoy greater tax savings without incurring significant costs of financial distress. For the increased tax benefits and reduction in bankruptcy costs to justify a merger, the gains must be large enough to offset any disadvantages of running a large firm.

LIQUIDITY.   As we have noted, shareholders of private companies are often under-diversified: They have a disproportionate share of their wealth invested in the private company. Consequently, when an acquirer buys a private target, it provides the target's owners with a way to reduce their risk exposure by cashing out their investment in the private target and reinvesting in a diversified portfolio. This liquidity that the bidder provides to the owners of a private firm can be valuable and often is an important incentive for the target shareholders to agree to the takeover.

EARNINGS GROWTH

It is possible to combine two companies with the result that the earnings per share of the merged company exceed the premerger earnings per share of either company, *even when the merger itself creates no economic value.* Let's look at how this can happen.

EXAMPLE 28.2   MERGERS AND EARNINGS PER SHARE

Problem

Consider two corporations that both have earnings of $5 per share. The first firm, Upper-Canada Enterprises, is a mature company with few growth opportunities. It has 1 million shares that are currently outstanding priced at $60 per share. The second company, Lower-Canada Corporation, is a young company with much more lucrative growth opportunities. Consequently, it has a higher value: Although it has the same number of shares outstanding, its stock price is $100 per share. Assume LowerCanada acquires UpperCanada using its own stock and the takeover adds no value. In a perfect market, what is the value of LowerCanada after the acquisition? At current market prices, how many shares must LowerCanada offer to UpperCanada's shareholders in exchange for their shares? Finally, what are LowerCanada's earnings per share after the acquisition?

Solution

Because the takeover adds no value, the post-takeover value of LowerCanada is just the sum of the values of the two separate companies: 100×1 million $+ 60 \times 1$ million $= \$160$ million. To acquire UpperCanada, LowerCanada must pay $60 million. At its pre-takeover stock price of $100 per share, the deal requires issuing 600,000 shares. As a group, UpperCanada's shareholders will then exchange 1 million shares in UpperCanada for 600,000 shares in Lower-Canada, or each shareholder will get 0.6 share in LowerCanada for each 1 share in UpperCanada. Notice that the price per share of LowerCanada stock is the same after the takeover: The new value of LowerCanada is $160 million and there are 1.6 million shares outstanding, giving it a stock price of $100 per share.

However, LowerCanada's earnings per share have changed. Prior to the takeover, both companies earned $5/share $\times$ 1 million shares $= \$5$ million. The combined corporation thus earns $10 million. There are 1.6 million shares outstanding after the takeover, so LowerCanada's post-takeover earnings per share are

$$EPS = \frac{\$10 \text{ million}}{1.6 \text{ million shares}} = \$6.25/\text{share}$$

By taking over UpperCanada, LowerCanada has raised its earnings per share by $1.25.

As Example 28.2 demonstrates, merging a company with little growth potential and a company with high growth potential (and thus low earnings per share) can raise earnings per share. In the past, people have cited this increase as a reason to merge. Of course, a savvy shareholder will see that the merger *adds no economic value*. All that has happened is that the high-growth company, whose value lies in its potential to generate earnings in the future, has purchased a company for which most of the value lies in its current ability to generate earnings. The price-earnings ratio reflects this reality.

EXAMPLE 28.3	MERGERS AND THE PRICE-EARNINGS RATIO

Problem

Calculate LowerCanada's price-earnings ratio, before and after the takeover described in Example 28.2.

Solution

Before the takeover, LowerCanada's price-earnings ratio is

$$P/E = \frac{\$100/\text{share}}{\$5/\text{share}} = 20$$

After the takeover, LowerCanada's price-earnings ratio is

$$P/E = \frac{\$100/\text{share}}{\$6.25/\text{share}} = 16$$

The price-earnings ratio has dropped to reflect the fact that after taking over UpperCanada, more of the value of LowerCanada comes from earnings from current projects than from its future growth potential.

MANAGER-DRIVEN REASONS TO MERGE

Most of the reasons given so far are economically motivated, shareholder-driven reasons to merge. However, managers sometimes have their own reasons to merge, due to either overconfidence or incentive conflicts with their shareholders. Studies have consistently found that the stock price of large bidders drops on average when a bid is announced, especially when the target is publicly traded. One possible explanation might be conflicts of interest and overconfidence.

CONFLICTS OF INTEREST

Managers may prefer to run a larger company due to the additional pay and prestige it brings. Because most CEOs hold only a small fraction of their firm's stock, they may not bear enough of the cost of an otherwise bad merger that increases their personal benefits.[5] For example, a CEO who owns 1% of her firm's stock bears 1% of every dollar lost on a bad acquisition, but enjoys 100% of the gains in compensation and prestige that come with being the CEO of a larger company. If the acquisition destroys $100 million in shareholder value, but increases the present value of her compensation by more than $1 million, she will prefer to execute the merger anyway. Why would the board of directors create these incentives? Due to either poor monitoring of the manager, or belief that the strategy is correct even if the stock market disagrees, boards typically increase the pay of CEOs along with the size of the firm, even if the size comes at the expense of poorly performing acquisitions.[6] We will discuss corporate governance further in the next chapter.

OVERCONFIDENCE

As we explained in Chapter 13, people in general tend to be overconfident in their abilities. Psychology research has shown that it takes repeated failures for a person to change his belief that he is above-average at some activity. Most CEOs perform at most one large acquisition during their tenure as CEO. In a well-known 1986 paper,[7] Richard Roll proposed the "**hubris hypothesis**" to explain takeovers, which maintains that overconfident CEOs pursue mergers that have a low chance of creating value because they truly believe that their ability to manage is great enough to succeed. The critical distinction between this hypothesis and the incentive conflict reason discussed above is that the overconfident managers believe they are doing the right thing for their shareholders, but are irrationally overestimating their own ability. Under the incentive conflict explanation, managers know they are destroying shareholder value, but personally gain from doing so.

CONCEPT CHECK

1. What are the reasons most often cited for a takeover?

2. Explain why diversification benefits and earnings growth are not good justifications for a takeover intended to increase shareholder wealth.

28.4 THE TAKEOVER PROCESS

In this section, we explore how the takeover process works. We begin by establishing how a bidder determines the initial offer. We then review the tax and accounting issues specific to a takeover and explain the regulatory approval process. We end by discussing board approval, including defensive strategies that boards implement to discourage takeovers.

---

5. Michael Jensen highlighted the agency conflict in acquisition decisions in his 1986 paper, "Agency Costs of Free Cash Flow, Corporate Finance and Takeovers" *American Economic Review* 76 (1986), 323–329.

6. J. Harford and K. Li, "Decoupling CEO Wealth and Firm Performance: The Case of Acquiring CEOs," *Journal of Finance* 62 (2007), 917–949, shows that in 75% of mergers where the acquiring shareholders lose money, acquiring CEOs are financially better off.

7. R. Roll, "The Hubris Hypothesis of Corporate Takeovers," *Journal of Business* 59:2 (1986): 197–216.

VALUATION

In Chapter 19, we demonstrated how a bidder values a target company. Recall that we explained, in the context of a single case study, how an acquirer values a target by using two different approaches. The first—and simplest—approach compares the target to other comparable companies. Although this approach is easy to implement, it gives at best a rough estimate of value. Valuing the target using a multiple based on comparable firms does not directly incorporate the operational improvements and other synergistic efficiencies that the acquirer intends to implement. Purchasing a corporation usually constitutes a very large capital investment decision, so it requires a more accurate estimate of value that includes careful analysis of both operational aspects of the firm and the ultimate cash flows the deal will generate. Thus the second approach to valuation requires making a projection of the expected cash flows that will result from the deal and valuing those cash flows.

A key issue for takeovers is quantifying and discounting the value added as a result of the merger. In Chapter 19, the acquirer was expected to implement operational improvements and make adjustments to the target's capital structure, thereby shielding additional income from taxes. As we showed in Section 28.3, a takeover can generate other sources of value. For simplicity, in this section we refer to any additional value created as the *takeover synergies*.

We know that the price paid for a target is equal to the target's pre-bid market capitalization plus the premium paid in the acquisition. If we view the pre-bid market capitalization as the stand-alone value of the target,[8] then from the bidder's perspective, the takeover is a positive-NPV project only if the premium it pays does not exceed the synergies created. Although the premium that is offered is a concrete number, the synergies are not—investors might well be skeptical of the acquirer's estimate of their magnitude. The bidder's stock price reaction to the announcement of the merger is one way to gauge investors' assessments of whether the bidder overpaid or underpaid for the target. As Table 28.2 shows, the average stock price reaction is 1%, but this amount is not statistically significantly different from zero. Thus the market, on average, believes that the premium is approximately equal to the synergies. Nonetheless, there is large variation in the premium across deals. One recent large-scale study of the value effects of mergers found that positive reactions to bids are concentrated in smaller bidders. In fact, during the 1990s, 87 large public acquirers announced bids that resulted in $1 billion or more in value reduction at announcement.[9] This finding is likely related to some of the managerial motives we discussed in the previous section.

THE OFFER

Once the acquirer has completed the valuation process, it is in the position to make a tender offer—that is, a public announcement of its intention to purchase a large block of shares for a specified price. There is no guarantee that, in fact, the takeover will take place at this price. Often acquirers have to raise the price to consummate the deal.

---

8. Rumours about a potential bid for the target will often push its share price up in anticipation of the premium offer. Practitioners refer to the "unaffected" target price, meaning the target's share price before it was affected by rumours of a takeover. This price would be used to compute the stand-alone value of the target.

9. S. Moeller, R. Stulz, and F. Schlingemann, "Wealth Destruction on a Massive Scale: A Study of Acquiring Firm Returns in the Recent Merger Wave," *Journal of Finance* 60:2 (2005): 757–782.

Not all tender offers are successful. When an acquirer bids for a target, the target firm's board may not accept the bid and recommend that existing shareholders not tender their shares, even when the acquirer offers a significant premium over the pre-offer share price. Even if the target board supports the deal, there is also the possibility that regulators might not approve the takeover. Because of this uncertainty about whether a takeover will succeed, the market price does not rise by the amount of the premium when the takeover is announced.

A bidder can use either of two methods to pay for a target: cash or stock. In a cash transaction, the bidder simply pays for the target, including any premium, in cash. In a stock-swap transaction, the bidder pays for the target by issuing new stock and giving it to the target shareholders; that is, the bidder offers to swap target stock for acquirer stock. The "price" offered is determined by the **exchange ratio**—the number of bidder shares received in exchange for each target share—multiplied by the market price of the acquirer's stock.

A stock-swap merger is a positive-NPV investment for the acquiring shareholders if the share price of the merged firm (the acquirer's share price after the takeover) exceeds the premerger price of the acquiring firm. We can write this condition as follows. Let A be the premerger, or standalone, value of the acquirer, and T be the premerger (standalone) value of the target. Let S be the value of the synergies created by the merger. If the acquirer has N_A shares outstanding before the merger, and issues x new shares to pay for the target, then the acquirer's share price should increase post-acquisition if

$$\frac{A + T + S}{N_A + x} > \frac{A}{N_A} \tag{28.1}$$

The left side of Eq. 28.1 is the share price of the merged firm. The numerator indicates the total value of the merged firm: the stand-alone value of the acquirer and target plus the value of the synergies created by the merger. The denominator represents the total number of shares outstanding once the merger is complete. The ratio is the postmerger share price. The right side of Eq. 28.1 is the premerger share price of the acquirer, the total premerger value of the acquirer divided by the premerger number of shares outstanding.

Solving Eq. 28.1 for x gives the maximum number of new shares the acquirer can offer and still achieve a positive NPV:

$$x < \left(\frac{T + S}{A}\right) N_A \tag{28.2}$$

We can express this relationship as an exchange ratio by dividing by the premerger number of target shares outstanding, N_T:

$$\text{Exchange ratio} = \frac{x}{N_T} < \left(\frac{T + S}{A}\right) \frac{N_A}{N_T} \tag{28.3}$$

We can also rewrite Eq. 28.3 in terms of the *premerger* target and acquirer share prices, $P_T = T/N_T$ and $P_A = A/N_A$:

$$\text{Exchange ratio} < \frac{P_T}{P_A}\left(1 + \frac{S}{T}\right) \tag{28.4}$$

EXAMPLE 28.4	MAXIMUM EXCHANGE RATIO IN A STOCK TAKEOVER

Problem

At the time Sprint announced plans to acquire Nextel in December 2004, Sprint stock was trading for $25 per share and Nextel stock was trading for $30 per share, implying a premerger value of Nextel of approximately $31 billion. If the projected synergies were $12 billion, what is the maximum exchange ratio Sprint could offer in a stock swap and still generate a positive NPV?

Solution

Using Eq. 28.4,

$$\text{Exchange ratio} < \frac{P_T}{P_A}\left(1 + \frac{S}{T}\right) = \frac{30}{25}\left(1 + \frac{12}{31}\right) = 1.665$$

MERGER "ARBITRAGE"

Once a tender offer is announced, the uncertainty about whether the takeover will succeed adds volatility to the stock price. This uncertainty creates an opportunity for investors to speculate on the outcome of the deal. Traders known as **risk-arbitrageurs**, who believe that they can predict the outcome of a deal, take positions based on their beliefs. While the strategies these traders use are sometimes referred to as arbitrage, they are actually quite risky, so they do not represent a true arbitrage opportunity in the sense we have defined in this book. Let's illustrate the strategy using the 2002 stock-swap merger of Hewlett-Packard (HP) and Compaq.

In September 2001, HP announced that it would purchase Compaq by swapping 0.6325 share of HP stock for each share of Compaq stock. After the announcement, HP traded for $18.87 per share, while the price of Compaq was $11.08 per share. Thus, Compaq's share price after the announcement was $0.8553 below the implied value of HP's offer, $18.87 × 0.6325 = $11.9353. It follows that if, just after the announcement, a risk-arbitrageur simultaneously purchased 10,000 Compaq shares and short sold 6325 HP shares, he would net 6325 × $18.87 − 10,000 × $11.08 = $8553. If the takeover was successfully completed on the original terms, the 10,000 Compaq shares would convert into 6325 HP shares; the risk-arbitrageur could then use those shares to cover the short position in HP and be left with no net exposure. Thus the risk-arbitrageur would pocket the original $8553 as a profit.[10] This potential profit arises from the difference between the target's stock price and the implied offer price, and is referred to as the **merger-arbitrage spread**. However, it is not a true arbitrage opportunity because there is a risk that the deal will not go through. If the takeover did not ultimately succeed, the risk-arbitrageur would eventually have to unwind his position at whatever market prices prevailed. Usually these prices would have moved against him (in particular, the price of Compaq would be likely to decline if the takeover did not occur), so he would face losses on the position.

The HP–Compaq takeover was distinctive in that the uncertainty about the success of the deal stemmed largely from acquirer discomfort with the deal rather than from target

---

10. For simplicity, we are ignoring dividend payments that were made during the period.

FIGURE 28.2

Merger-Arbitrage Spread for the Merger of HP and Compaq

The plot shows the potential profit, given that the merger was ultimately successfully completed, from purchasing 10,000 Compaq shares and short selling 6325 HP shares on the indicated date. A risk-arbitrageur who expects the deal to go through can profit by opening the position when the spread is large, and closing the position after it declines.

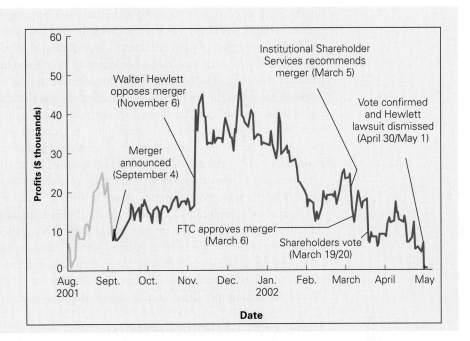

shareholder discomfort. Although initially supportive of the merger, the Hewlett family got cold feet. About two months after the deal was announced, Walter Hewlett disclosed his family's opposition to it. On the day of Walter Hewlett's announcement, the price of HP stock rose to $19.81, while Compaq's stock price fell to $8.50, causing the merger-arbitrage spread to widen to $19.81 × 6325 − $8.5 × 10,000 = $40,298. We plot the merger-arbitrage spread for the HP–Compaq merger in Figure 28.2. The risk-arbitrage strategy outlined above is effectively a short position on this spread, which pays off if the spread declines. Thus, an arbitrageur who opened the strategy when the deal was announced and closed it after Walter Hewlett announced his opposition would face a loss of $40,298 − $8553 = $31,745.

Although the Hewlett family members were large shareholders of HP, they were not controlling shareholders; they did not have enough shares to block the deal single-handedly. Hence a battle for control of HP ensued between the Hewlett family and CEO Carly Fiorina, the driving force behind the acquisition of Compaq. This conflict was only resolved months later when HP shareholders, by a slim margin, voted in favour of issuing new shares, thereby effectively approving the merger and netting a profit for any risk-arbitrageur who stayed the course. As is clear from Figure 28.2, risk-arbitrageurs who did not have the stomach to hold on would have faced large losses at several points during the roller-coaster ride. And while HP CEO Carly Fiorina survived this early challenge to her authority, the performance of HP following the merger vindicated Hewlett's position. HP's board ultimately fired Fiorina in 2005.

TAX AND ACCOUNTING ISSUES

Once the terms of trade have been decided, the tax and accounting implications of a merger can be determined. How the acquirer pays for the target affects the taxes of both the target shareholders and the combined firm. Any cash received in full or partial exchange for shares triggers an immediate tax liability for target shareholders. They will have to pay a capital gains tax on the difference between the price paid for their shares in the takeover and the price they paid when they first bought the shares. If the acquirer pays for the takeover entirely by exchanging bidder stock for target stock, then the tax liability is deferred until the target shareholders actually sell their new shares of bidder stock.

While the method of payment (cash or stock) affects how the value of the target's assets is recorded for tax purposes, it does not affect the combined firm's financial statements for financial reporting. The combined firm must mark up the value assigned to the target's assets on the financial statements by allocating the purchase price to target assets according to their fair market value. If the purchase price exceeds the fair market value of the target's identifiable assets, then the remainder is recorded as goodwill and is examined annually by the firm's accountants to determine whether its value has decreased. For example, in HP's takeover of Compaq, HP recorded more than $10 billion in goodwill. The footnotes to the statements attributed the goodwill to the value of the Compaq brand name, which is assumed to have an indefinite life.

Even when a merger has a positive NPV, bidding managers are typically very concerned with the effect of the merger on earnings. This is the other side of the earnings-growth argument as a reason to merge. Just as merging two companies can increase earnings without affecting economic value, it can also decrease earnings without affecting economic value. Nevertheless, acquirers are hesitant to commit to a deal that would be dilutive to earnings per share, even if only in the short run.

BOARD AND SHAREHOLDER APPROVAL

For a merger to proceed, both the target and the acquiring board of directors must approve the deal and put the question to a vote of the shareholders of the target (and, in some cases, the shareholders of the acquiring firm as well).

In a **friendly takeover**, the target board of directors supports the merger, negotiates with potential acquirers, and agrees on a price that is ultimately put to a shareholder vote. Although it is rare for acquiring boards to oppose a merger, target boards sometimes do not support the deal even when the acquirer offers a large premium. In a **hostile takeover**, the board of directors (together with upper-level management) fights the takeover attempt. To succeed, the acquirer must garner enough shares to take control of the target and replace the board of directors. When a takeover is hostile, the acquirer is often called a **raider**.

If the shareholders of a target company receive a premium over the current market value of their shares, why would a board of directors ever oppose a takeover? There are a number of reasons. The board might legitimately believe that the offer price is too low. In this case, a suitor that is willing to pay more might be found or the original bidder might be persuaded to raise its offer. Alternatively, if the offer is a stock-swap, target management may oppose the offer because they feel the acquirer's shares are over-valued, and therefore that the value of the offer is actually less than the standalone value of the target. Finally, managers (and the board) might oppose a takeover because of their own self-interests, especially if the primary motivation for the takeover is efficiency gains. In this case, the acquirer most likely plans to undertake a complete change of leadership of the corporation. Upper-level managers could view opposing the merger as a way of protecting their jobs (and the jobs of their employees). In fact, this concern is perhaps the single biggest reason for the negative associations that hostile takeovers generate. Bear in mind that if substantial efficiency gains are indeed possible, current management is not doing an effective job. A takeover, or threat thereof, might be the only recourse investors have to fix the problem.

In theory, the duty of the target board of directors is to choose the course of action that is in the best interests of the target shareholders. In practice, the courts have given target directors wide latitude under what is called the *business judgment rule* to determine the best course for their companies, including spurning a premium offer if the directors can reasonably argue that more value will eventually be realized for their shareholders by remaining independent. The premise of this rule is that absent evidence of misconduct or self-dealing, the court will not substitute its judgment for that of the elected, informed directors.

In merger transactions, however, there is heightened judicial scrutiny under what is commonly referred to as the "Revlon duties" and "Unocal case," named after the cases in which they were established. The **Revlon duties** state that if a change of control is going to occur, then directors must seek the highest value (they cannot favour one controlling entity over another based on anything other than value to shareholders). The **Unocal case** established that when the board takes actions deemed as defensive (we discuss these in detail in the next section), its actions are subject to extra scrutiny to ensure that they are not coercive or designed simply to preclude a deal. The board must believe that there is a threat to its corporate strategy and its defences must be proportional to the magnitude of the threat.

CONCEPT CHECK

1. What are the steps in the takeover process?

2. What do risk-arbitrageurs do?

28.5 TAKEOVER DEFENCES

For a hostile takeover to succeed, the acquirer must go around the target board and appeal directly to the target shareholders. The acquirer can do this by making an unsolicited offer to buy target stock directly from the shareholders (a **tender offer**). The acquirer will usually couple this with a **proxy fight**: The acquirer attempts to convince target shareholders to unseat the target board by using their proxy votes to support the acquirers' candidates for election to the target board. Target companies have a number of strategies available to them to stop this process. These strategies can force a bidder to raise its bid or entrench management more securely, depending on the independence of the target board. We begin with the most effective defensive strategy, the poison pill.

POISON PILLS

A **poison pill** is a rights offering that gives existing target shareholders the right to buy shares in either the target or the acquirer at a deeply discounted price once certain conditions are met. The acquirer is specifically excluded from this right. Because target shareholders can purchase shares at less than the market price, existing shareholders of the acquirer effectively subsidize their purchases. This subsidization makes the takeover so expensive for the acquiring shareholders that they choose to pass on the deal.

The poison pill was invented in 1982 by a takeover lawyer, Martin Lipton, who successfully warded off a takeover attempt of El Paso Electric by General American Oil.[11] Because the original poison pill goes into effect only in the event of a complete takeover (that is, a purchase of 100% of the outstanding shares), one way to circumvent it is to not do a complete takeover. The first time this work-around was used was by Sir James Goldsmith, who took control of Crown Zellerbach by purchasing slightly more than 50% of the outstanding stock. Because he did not purchase the rest, Crown Zellerbach's poison pill was ineffective.

In response to the takeover of Crown Zellerbach, corporate lawyers have perfected the original poison pill. Instead of giving existing shareholders the right to acquire shares in an acquiring company, most poison pills now specify that if a raider acquires more than a trigger amount (typically 20%) of the target shares (but chooses not to execute a complete

---

11. For a brief history, see Len Costa, "The Perfect Pill," *Legal Affairs* (March 2005), www.legalaffairs.org.

takeover by purchasing all outstanding shares), existing shareholders—with the exception of the acquirer—have the right to buy more shares in the target at a discounted price.

The name *poison pill* comes from the world of espionage. Once caught, a spy is supposed to take his own life by swallowing a poison pill rather than give up important secrets. Poison pills are very effective in stopping takeovers, but where is the suicide analogy? The answer is that by adopting a poison pill, a company effectively entrenches its management by making it much more difficult for shareholders to replace bad managers, thereby potentially destroying value. Financial research has verified this effect. A firm's stock price typically drops when it adopts a poison pill. Furthermore, once adopted, firms with poison pills have below-average financial performance.[12]

Not surprisingly, companies with poison pills are harder to take over, and when they are taken over, the premium that existing shareholders receive for their stock is higher. That is, because a poison pill increases the cost of a takeover, all else being equal, a target company must be in worse shape (there must be a greater opportunity for profit) to justify the expense of waging a takeover battle.

Poison pills also increase the bargaining power of the target firm when negotiating with the acquirer because poison pills make it difficult to complete the takeover without the cooperation of the target board. If used effectively, this bargaining power can allow target shareholders to capture more of the takeover gains by negotiating a higher premium than they would get if no pill existed. Numerous studies on the impact of anti-takeover provisions on takeovers have found that such provisions result in higher premiums accruing to existing shareholders of the target company.[13]

STAGGERED BOARDS

A determined bidder in the face of a poison pill has another option available to it: Get its own slate of directors elected to the target board, which it can submit at the next annual shareholders meeting. If the target shareholders elect those candidates, then the new directors can cancel the poison pill and accept the bidder's offer. To prevent such a coup from happening, about two-thirds of public companies have a **staggered** (or **classified**) **board**. In a typical staggered board, every director serves a three-year term and the terms are staggered so that only one-third of the directors are up for election each year. Thus, even if the bidder's candidates win board seats, it will control only a minority of the target board. A bidder's candidate would have to win a proxy fight two years in a row before the bidder had a majority presence on the target board. The length of time required to execute this manoeuvre can deter a bidder from making a takeover attempt when the target board is staggered. Most experts consider a poison pill combined with a staggered board to be the most effective defence available to a target company.

---

12. P. H. Malatesta and R. A. Walking, "Poison Pills Securities: Stockholder Wealth, Profitability and Ownership Structure," *Journal of Financial Economics* 20:1 (1988): 347–376; M. Ryngaert, "The Effects of Poison Pills Securities on Stockholder Wealth," *Journal of Financial Economics* 20:1 (1988): 377–417; and D. Stangeland, "Why Are Anti-Takeover Devices Being Used?" *Business Quarterly* 60:1 (1995): 35–41.

13. Georgeson and Company (1988) study; R. Comment and G. W. Schwert, "Poison or Placebo: Evidence on the Deterrence and Wealth Effects of Modern Antitakeover Measures," *Journal of Financial Economics* 39:1 (1995): 3–43; N. P. Varaiya, "Determinants of Premiums in Acquisition Transactions," *Managerial and Decision Economics* 8(3) (1987): 175–184; and R. Heron and E. Lie, "On the Use of Poison Pills and Defensive Payouts by Takeover Targets," *Journal of Business* 79:4 (2006): 1783–1807.

WHITE KNIGHTS

When a hostile takeover appears to be inevitable, a target company will sometimes look for another, friendlier company to acquire it. This company that comes charging to the target's rescue is known as a **white knight**. The white knight will make a more lucrative offer for the target than the hostile bidder. Incumbent managers of the target maintain control by reaching an agreement with the white knight to retain their positions.

One variant on the white knight defence is the **white squire** defence. In this case, a large investor or firm agrees to purchase a substantial block of shares in the target with special voting rights. This action prevents a hostile raider from acquiring control of the target. The idea is that the white squire itself will not choose to exercise its control rights.

GOLDEN PARACHUTES

A **golden parachute** is an extremely lucrative severance package that is guaranteed to a firm's senior managers in the event that the firm is taken over and the managers are let go. For example, when Ronald Perelman successfully acquired Revlon Corporation, the firm's former chairman, Michael Bergerac, was reported to have received a golden parachute compensation package worth in excess of $35 million.

Golden parachutes have been criticized because they are seen as both excessive and a misuse of shareholder wealth. In fact, the empirical evidence does not support this view.[14] If anything, it supports the view that an adoption of a golden parachute actually creates value. If a golden parachute exists, management will be more likely to be receptive to being taken over. This means the existence of golden parachutes lessens the likelihood of managerial entrenchment. Researchers have found that stock prices rise on average when companies announce that they plan to implement a golden parachute policy, and that the number of firms bidding against one another for the target and the size of the takeover premium are higher if a golden parachute agreement exists.

RECAPITALIZATION

Another defence against a takeover is a recapitalization, in which a company changes its capital structure to make itself less attractive as a target. For example, a company with a lot of cash might choose to pay out a large dividend. Companies without a lot of cash might instead choose to issue debt and then use the proceeds to pay a dividend or repurchase stock.

Why does increasing leverage make a firm less attractive as a target? In many cases, a substantial portion of the synergy gains that an acquirer anticipates from a takeover are from tax savings from an increase in leverage as well as other cost reductions. By increasing leverage on its own, the target firm can reap the benefit of the interest tax shields. In addition, the need to generate cash to meet the debt service obligations provides a powerful motivation to managers to run a corporation efficiently. In effect, the restructuring itself can produce efficiency gains, often removing the principal motivation for the takeover in the first place.

OTHER DEFENSIVE STRATEGIES

Corporate managers and defence advisors have devised other mechanisms to forestall a takeover. A corporation's charter can require a supermajority (sometimes as much as 80%) of votes to approve a merger. It can also restrict the voting rights of very large shareholders. Finally, a firm can require that a "fair" price be paid for the company, where the

---

14. M. Narayanan and A. Sundaram, "A Safe Landing? Golden Parachutes and Corporate Behavior," *University of Michigan Business School Working Paper No. 98015* (1998).

determination of what is "fair" is up to the board of directors or senior management. Beauty is always in the eye of the beholder, so "fair" in this case usually implies an optimistic determination of value.

We might expect the presence of defensive strategies to reduce firm value. However, Gregg Jarrell and Annette Poulsen[15] found that, on average, the public announcement of anti-takeover amendments by 600 firms in the period 1979–1985 had an insignificant effect on the value of announcing firms' shares.

REGULATORY APPROVAL

All mergers must be approved by regulators. In Section 28.2, we discussed monopoly gains from takeovers and the use of antitrust regulations to limit them. In Canada, the Competition Bureau monitors potential monopoly combinations and the Investment Canada Act governs takeovers by foreigners of Canadian corporations (the latter was used to block the takeover of Potash Corporation by BHP Billiton of Australia on November 3, 2010, on the grounds there was not a net benefit to Canada). In addition to the defensive strategies discussed above, management of a takeover target often will appeal directly to regulatory authorities with the hope that the regulators will block the hostile takeover.

In the United States, antitrust enforcement is governed by three main statutes: the Sherman Act, the Clayton Act, and the Hart-Scott-Rodino Act. The Sherman Act of 1890, which was passed in response to the formation of huge oil trusts such as Standard Oil, prohibits mergers that would create a monopoly or undue market control. The Clayton Act, enacted in 1914, strengthened the government's hand by prohibiting companies from acquiring the stock (or, as later amended, the assets) of another company if it would adversely affect competition. Under both the Sherman and Clayton acts, the government had to sue to block a merger. Often by the time a decision was rendered, the merger had taken place and it was difficult to undo it. The Hart-Scott-Rodino (HSR) Act of 1976 put the burden of proof on the merging parties. Under HSR, all mergers above a certain size (the formula for determining whether a transaction qualifies is complicated, but it comes out to approximately $60 million) must be approved by the government before the proposed takeovers occur. The government cannot delay the deal indefinitely, however, because it must respond with approval or a request for additional information within 20 days of receiving notification of the proposed merger. The U.S. government has been very active in enforcing competition policy and is rated by the Global Competition Review in the "elite" category for enforcement. (The United Kingdom and European Union competition commissions are also rated elite.) Some criticisms have been made regarding Canada's Competition Bureau because it does not appear to act as vigorously. Canada's Competition Bureau was rated in the "good" category by the Global Competition Review.

The European Commission has established a process similar to the HSR process, which requires merging parties to notify the EC, provide additional information if requested about the proposed merger, and wait for approval before proceeding. As discussed in the Honeywell/GE example, even though the EC technically lacks legal authority to block a merger of foreign companies, it can stop a takeover by imposing restrictions on the combined firm's operations and sales in Europe. Although globally, a proposed takeover might have to satisfy antitrust rules in more than 80 jurisdictions, practically the most important jurisdictions besides the home jurisdiction of the firm are Europe and the United States.

---

15. G. A. Jarrell and A. B. Poulsen, "Shark Repellents and Stock Prices: The Effects of Antitakeover Amendments Since 1980," *Journal of Financial Economics* 19 (1988): 127–168.

WEYERHAEUSER'S HOSTILE BID FOR WILLAMETTE INDUSTRIES

In November 2000, Weyerhaeuser, a forest products company based in Federal Way, Washington, announced a hostile bid of $48 per share for its smaller neighbour, Willamette Industries, based in Portland, Oregon. Weyerhaeuser had been pursuing Willamette in private since 1998, when Steve Rogel unexpectedly resigned as CEO of Willamette to become CEO of Weyerhaeuser. Each time Rogel approached his old employer in private, he was rebuffed. The response to the hostile tender offer was no different. Despite the fact that the bid represented a substantial premium to the firm's pre-bid stock price, the Willamette board rejected the offer and urged its shareholders not to tender their shares to Weyerhaeuser.

Willamette's defences included a staggered board and a poison pill, so Weyerhaeuser made its tender offer conditional on Willamette's board cancelling the poison pill. Consequently, Weyerhaeuser initiated a proxy fight at the next annual shareholders' meeting in June 2001. One of the directors up for reelection at that time was Duane McDougall, Willamette's CEO. One month before the meeting, Weyerhaeuser increased its offer to $50 per share, but Willamette's board still believed that the offer was too low and worried that too many of its long-time employees would face layoffs after the merger. Nonetheless, at the annual meeting, Weyerhaeuser's slate received 1.4% more votes than Willamette's, thereby removing Willamette's CEO from its board.

The loss of the board seats did not change Willamette's position. Willamette unsuccessfully searched for a white knight to generate a bidding contest that would force Weyerhaeuser to up its bid. It also entered into talks to buy Georgia-Pacific's building products division. Such a deal would have increased its size and added enough debt to its balance sheet to render the firm unattractive to Weyerhaeuser.

In the end, Weyerhaeuser increased its offer to $55.50 per share in January 2002, and Willamette finally agreed to a deal and called off its negotiations with Georgia-Pacific. Even without the presence of other bidders, Willamette's board was able to get what it considered to be a fair price from Weyerhaeuser.

CONCEPT CHECK

1. What defensive strategies are available to help target companies resist an unwanted takeover?

2. How can a hostile acquirer get around a poison pill?

28.6 WHO GETS THE VALUE ADDED FROM A TAKEOVER?

Now that we have explained the takeover process, we can return to the remaining questions we posed at the beginning of this chapter: why the price of the acquiring company does not rise at the announcement of the takeover and why the bidder is forced to pay a premium for the target.

You might imagine that the people who do the work of acquiring the corporation and replacing its management will capture the value created by the merger. Based on the average stock price reaction, it does not appear that the acquiring corporation generally captures this value. Instead, the premium the acquirer pays is approximately equal to the value it adds, which means the *target* shareholders ultimately capture the value added by the acquirer. To see why, we need to understand how market forces react to a takeover announcement.

THE FREE RIDER PROBLEM

Assume you are one of the 1 million shareholders of HighLife Corporation, all of whom own 1 share of stock. HighLife has no debt. Its chief executive is not doing a good job, preferring to spend his time using the company's jets to fly to the corporate condo in Whistler, B.C., rather than running the company in Regina. As such, the shares are trading at a substantial discount. They currently have a price of $45 per share, giving HighLife a market value of $45 million. Under a competent manager, the company would be worth

$75 million. HighLife's corporate charter specifies that a simple majority is required to make all decisions, so to take control of HighLife a shareholder must purchase half the outstanding shares.

T. Boone Icon decides to fix the situation (and make a profit at the same time) by making a tender offer to buy half the outstanding shares for $60 per share in cash. If fewer than 50% of the shareholders tender their shares, the deal is off.

In principle, this idea could land T. Boone a handsome profit. If 50% of shareholders tender their shares, those shares will cost him $60 × 500,000 = $30 million. Once he has control of the firm, he can replace the managers. When the executive jets and the Whistler condo are sold and the market realizes that the new managers are serious about improving performance, the market value of the firm will rise to $75 million. Hence T. Boone's shares will be worth $75 per share, netting him a profit of $15 × 500,000 = $7.5 million. But will 50% of the shareholders tender their shares?

The offer price of $60 per share exceeds the value of the firm if the takeover does not go through ($45 per share). Hence, the offer is a good deal for shareholders overall. But if all shareholders tender their shares, as an individual shareholder you could do better by not tendering your share. Then if T. Boone takes control, each of your shares will be worth $75 rather than the $60 you would get by tendering. Thus it is wiser to not tender. Of course, if all shareholders think this way no one will tender their shares, and T. Boone's deal will not get off the ground. The only way to persuade shareholders to tender their shares is to offer them at least $75 per share, which removes any profit opportunity for T. Boone. The problem here is that existing shareholders do not have to invest time and effort, but still participate in all the gains from the takeover that T. Boone Icon generates—hence the term "free rider problem." By sharing the gains in this way, T. Boone Icon is forced to give up substantial profits and thus will likely choose not to bother at all.[16]

TOEHOLDS

One way for T. Boone to get around the problem of shareholders' reluctance to tender their shares is to buy the shares secretly in the market. However, Canadian securities laws and the SEC rules in the U.S. make it difficult for investors to buy much more than about 10% of a firm in secret.[17] After T. Boone acquires such an initial stake in the target, called a **toehold**, he would have to make his intentions public by informing investors of his large stake. To successfully gain control of HighLife, he would have to announce a tender offer to buy an additional 40% of the shares for $75 per share. Once in control, he would be able to sell his stake for $75 per share. Assuming he accumulated the first 10% for $50 per share, his profits in this case will be $25 × 100,000 = $2.5 million. Not bad, but substantially less than the value he is adding.

Why should investors care whether T. Boone's profits are substantially lower than the value he is adding? The answer is that people like T. Boone perform an important service. Because of the threat that such a person might attempt to take over their company and

---

16. A rigorous analysis of the free rider problem in mergers can be found in S. Grossman and O. D. Hart, "Takeover Bids, the Free-Rider Problem, and the Theory of the Corporation," *Bell Journal of Economics* 11:1 (1980): 42–64.

17. In Canada, the rules require an investor to issue a press release once the 10% threshold is reached. If a takeover bid is already outstanding, a 5% threshold triggers the requirement for a press release. In the U.S., the rules require that any shareholder who owns more than 5% of a firm publicly disclose this fact, but the time delays in the disclosure process allow investors to accumulate more than 5% of the firm before this information is made public.

More recently, Erik Lie has found evidence suggesting that many executives have engaged in a more direct form of manipulating their stock option compensation: backdating their option grants.[8] **Backdating** refers to the practice of choosing the grant date of a stock option retroactively, so that the date of the grant would coincide with a date when the stock price was at its low for the quarter or for the year. By backdating the option in this way, the executive receives a stock option that is already in the money, with a strike price equal to the lower price on the supposed grant date.

The use of backdating suggests that some executive stock option compensation may not truly have been earned as the result of good *future* performance of the firm. Furthermore, unless it is reported in a timely manner to the tax authority and to shareholders, and reflected in the firm's financial statements, backdating is illegal. In mid-2006, the SEC and U.S. Justice Department investigations into alleged backdating were ongoing for more than 70 firms. New SEC rules require firms to report option grants within two days of the grant date, which may help prevent further abuses. Canadian rules require firms to report option grants within ten days of the end of the month the options were granted; this rule is similar to the prior rules in the U.S. and allows more time for backdating should the share price increase during the time since the option grant. In February 2009, executives at Research In Motion (RIM) agreed to pay about $77 million in penalties to settle an options-backdating investigation carried out by the Ontario Securities Commission.

CONCEPT CHECK

1. What is the main reason for tying managers' compensation to firm performance?
2. What is the negative effect of increasing the sensitivity of managerial pay to firm performance?

29.4 MANAGING AGENCY CONFLICT

Even with the risk benefits of separating ownership and control, there are still examples of corporations in which the top managers have substantial ownership interests (for example, Microsoft Corporation). One might conjecture that such corporations have suffered less from the conflict of interest between managers and shareholders.

Academic studies have supported the notion that greater managerial ownership is associated with fewer value-reducing actions by managers.[9] But while increasing managerial ownership may reduce perquisite consumption, it also makes managers harder to fire— thus reducing the incentive effect of the threat of dismissal. Thus, the relationship between managerial ownership and firm value is unlikely to be the same for every firm, or even for different executives of the same firm. Shareholders will use all of the tools at their disposal to manage the agency conflict. Thus, if managers have small ownership stakes, shareholders may use compensation policies or a stronger board to create the desired incentives. Harold Demsetz and Kenneth Lehn argue that if you look at a group of firms

---

8. See E. Lie, "On the Timing of CEO Stock Option Awards," *Management Science* 51 (2005): 802–812. Also, R. Heron and E. Lie show that new rules enacted as part of the Sarbanes-Oxley legislation in 2002 that require grants to be reported within two business days have curbed the practice of backdating ("Does Backdating Explain the Stock Price Pattern Around Executive Stock Option Grants?" *Journal of Financial Economics* 83:2 (2007): 271–295).

9. See, for example, R. Walkling and M. Long, "Agency Theory, Managerial Welfare, and Takeover Bid Resistance," *Rand Journal of Economics* 15:1 (1984): 54–68.

at any point in time, you should not necessarily see any relationship between ownership and value, unless you are able to control for all of the other, sometimes unobservable, parts of the governance system, including the risk aversion of the manager.[10] More recent studies have supported their position.[11]

DIRECT ACTION BY SHAREHOLDERS

If all else fails, the shareholders' last line of defence against expropriation by self-interested managers is direct action. Recall that shareholders elect the board of directors. Typically, these elections look like those in the former Soviet Union—there is only one slate of candidates and you vote "yes" or "no" for the slate as a whole. When shareholders are angry about the management of the company and frustrated by a board unwilling to take action, however, they have a variety of options for expressing that displeasure at their disposal.

SHAREHOLDER VOICE.   First, any shareholder can submit a resolution that is put to a vote at the annual meeting. A resolution could direct the board to take a specific action, such as discontinue investing in a particular line of business or country, or remove a poison pill. Such resolutions rarely receive majority support, but if large shareholders back them, they can be embarrassing for the board. Some large public pension funds, one of the first being CalPERS (the California Public Employees Retirement System), take an activist role in corporate governance. Typically these funds target firms that are taking actions without considering the concerns of the stockholders; for example, they may privately approach the board of the firm and ask it to reverse its course. The explicit threat at that stage is that if the board fails to comply, the pension fund will put the issue to a shareholder vote. Studies have reported that such activist investors are usually successful in achieving their goals without having to take matters public.[12]

Recently, shareholders have started organizing "no" votes. That is, when they are dissatisfied with a board, they simply refuse to vote to approve the slate of nominees for the board. The most high-profile example of this type of action occurred in 2004 with the Walt Disney Company. Major shareholders were dissatisfied with the recent performance of Disney under long-time CEO and chairman Michael Eisner. They began an organized campaign to persuade the majority of Disney shareholders to withhold their approval of the re-election of Eisner as director and chairman of the board. When the votes were counted, 45% of Disney's shareholders had voted to withhold approval of Eisner. While Eisner technically had won re-election, a 45% "no" vote is practically unprecedented in large public companies. The signal was clear, and an embarrassed Eisner and the Disney board decided that Eisner would remain CEO, but relinquish the chairman title. Shortly thereafter, Eisner announced plans to retire completely in 2006.

---

10. H. Demsetz and K. Lehn, "The Structure of Corporate Ownership: Causes and Consequences," *Journal of Political Economy* 93:6 (1985): 1155–1177.

11. C. Himmelberg, R. G. Hubbard, and D. Palia, "Understanding the Determinants of Managerial Ownership and the Link Between Ownership and Performance," *Journal of Financial Economics* 53:3 (1999): 353–384, and J. Coles, M. Lemmon, and J. F. Meschke, "Structural Models and Endogeneity in Finance," working paper, Arizona State University, 2004.

12. W. Carleton, J. Nelson, and M. Weisbach, "The Influence of Institutions on Corporate Governance Through Private Negotiations: Evidence from TIAA-CREF," *Journal of Finance* 53:4 (1998): 1335–1362.

SHAREHOLDER ACTIVISM AT *THE NEW YORK TIMES*

New York Times Co., publisher of *The New York Times*, is closely controlled by the Ochs-Sulzberger family, which owns most of the Class B voting shares, allowing it to elect 70% of the board members. However, in December 2007 and January 2008, two hedge funds working together started acquiring a large stake in the publicly traded Class A shares. The two funds, Harbinger Capital Partners and Firebrand Partners, initially acquired 5% of the shares, subsequently raising the stake to 19%. The funds also filed to nominate four dissident directors to the NYT Co. board, arguing that the Times was moving too slowly to develop digital content and should shed non-core assets. After initially resisting, the company agreed to accept two of the funds' nominees and the funds withdrew their competing proxy statement. Over the two-month period starting when the funds began their activism, the stock price of the company increased by close to 30%. This episode is indicative of two emerging trends in investor activism: hedge funds taking a more activist role and working in concert to effect change at a company, and an increased willingness of targeted companies to negotiate a settlement with activists (see Figure 29.2).

Source: Merissa Marr, "New York Times Co. Relents on Board Seats—Dissident Group Secures 2 on Expanded Panel; Dual-Stock Handcuffs," *The Wall Street Journal*, March 18, 2003, p. B3.

SHAREHOLDER APPROVAL. In addition to electing the directors of the company, shareholders must approve many major actions taken by the board. For example, target shareholders must approve merger agreements and, in some cases, so must bidder shareholders. Even in cases where bidder shareholders are not required to directly approve a merger, listing requirements on some exchanges, such as the NYSE, demand that shareholders approve any large issue of new shares, such as might be necessary in a stock-swap merger. Normally, approval is perfunctory, but it cannot be taken for granted. As we saw in Chapter 28, after Hewlett-Packard (HP) CEO Carly Fiorina negotiated the merger of HP and Compaq, the Hewlett family used their board seats and voting block to oppose the deal.

A recent movement, which gained momentum and regulators' interest during the 2008 financial crisis, is to let shareholders have a "say on pay," vote. Typically, this is a non-binding vote to approve or disapprove of the compensation plan for senior executives each year. In 2009, the SEC moved to require recipients of federal bailout money to give shareholders an advisory say on pay vote and some legislators planned bills extending this requirement to all public companies. Despite shareholder anger over losses at U.S. corporations during the financial crisis, surprisingly, it was not until May 2010 that the first two rejections of executives' pay packages occurred in the U.S. (at Motorola and Occidental Petroleum). In February 2010, CIBC became the first Canadian financial firm to conduct a say on pay vote. Its proposed compensation package passed with over 90% of shareholders approving it.

PROXY CONTESTS. Perhaps the most extreme form of direct action that disgruntled shareholders can take is to hold a proxy contest and introduce a rival slate of directors for election to the board. This action gives shareholders an actual choice between the nominees put forth by management and the current board and a completely different slate of nominees put forth by dissident shareholders. One early study of proxy contests found that the announcement of a contest increased firm stock price by 8% on average, even if the challenge was eventually unsuccessful and the incumbents won reelection.[13]

---

13. P. Dodd and J. Warner, "On Corporate Governance: A Study of Proxy Contests," *Journal of Financial Economics* 11:1 (1983): 401–438.

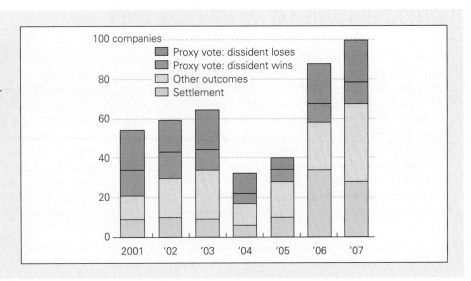

FIGURE 29.2

Recent Proxy Contest
Outcomes
Source: Phred Dvorak and Joann S.
Lublin, "Boards Give Up Taming
Act—Activist Investors Take Seats
Increasingly Without Fight," *The
Wall Street Journal*, April 7,
2008, p. C1.

MANAGEMENT ENTRENCHMENT

Given the importance of shareholder action in corporate governance, researchers and large investors alike have become increasingly interested in measuring the balance of power between shareholders and managers in a firm. Over time, the tools that managers can use to entrench themselves have evolved, including antitakeover protections such as those discussed in Chapter 28. The Investor Responsibility Research Center (IRRC) in the U.S. has collected information on 24 different characteristics that can entrench, or give more power to, managers vis-à-vis shareholders. These provisions include antitakeover statutes, poison pills, staggered boards, and restrictions on the ability of shareholders to call special meetings themselves.

Researchers have begun using data from the IRRC as a way to measure how entrenched managers are. One study found that firms with more restrictions on shareholder power performed worse than firms with less restrictions during the 1990s.[14] Other studies have found connections between the degree of entrenchment and the compensation offered to managers, and even to the value of acquisitions made.[15] While the index offered by the IRRC does not capture every aspect of corporate governance, many practitioners are finding it to be a useful summary measure of the degree to which managers are entrenched and less likely to have their actions checked by shareholders.

THE THREAT OF TAKEOVER

Many of the provisions listed in the IRRC index concern protection from takeovers. As we discussed in Chapter 28, one motivation for a takeover can be to replace poorly performing management. When internal governance systems such as ownership,

---

14. P. Gompers, J. Ishii, and A. Metrick, "Corporate Governance and Equity Prices," *Quarterly Journal of Economics* 118:1 (2003): 107–155. The cause of this effect, however, is not clear; see J. Core, W. Guay, and T. Rusticus, "Does Weak Governance Cause Weak Stock Returns? An Examination of Firm Operating Performance and Investors' Expectations," *Journal of Finance* 61:2 (2006): 655–687.

15. G. Garvey, and T. Milbourn, "Asymmetric Benchmarking in Compensation: Executives Are Paid for Good Luck but Not Punished for Bad," *Journal of Financial Economics* 82:1 (2006): 197–225, and R. Masulis, C. Wang, and F. Xie, "Corporate Governance and Acquirer Returns," *Journal of Finance* 62:4 (2007): 1851–1889.

compensation, board oversight, and shareholder activism fail, the one remaining way to remove poorly performing managers is by mounting a hostile takeover. Thus the effectiveness of the corporate governance structure of a firm depends on how well protected its managers are from removal in a hostile takeover.

An active takeover market is part of the system through which the threat of dismissal is maintained. In fact, some research has suggested that an active takeover market complements a board's own vigilance in dismissing incompetent managers. That research found that boards are actually more likely to fire managers for poor performance during active takeover markets than they are during lulls in takeover activity.[16] This finding also has implications internationally because some countries have much more active takeover markets than others. In particular, hostile takeovers are far more common in the United States than in other economies.

CONCEPT CHECK

1. Describe and explain a proxy contest.
2. What is the role of takeovers in corporate governance?

29.5   REGULATION

So far we've focused on those parts of the corporate governance system that have evolved over time as economic responses to the need for shareholders to mitigate the conflict of interest between themselves and managers. For example, boards of directors came into being long before there was any regulation of the governance of a company, and CEOs have long appointed independent directors to their boards without being required to do so. Nonetheless, from time to time, government has added to existing requirements by passing laws that force minimum standards of governance. A recent significant example is the Sarbanes-Oxley Act of 2002 (SOX) in the United States. (In the years that followed, similar regulations were enacted in some countries, including Canada.)

In the wake of the massive failures of large public companies and corporate fraud scandals mentioned in the introduction to this chapter, U.S. Congress rushed to enact legislation to fix what it saw as inadequate safeguards against malfeasance by managers of public corporations. The result was the Sarbanes-Oxley Act. Prior to SOX, the largest overhaul of securities markets and introduction of regulation came in response to the stock market crash of 1929 and the Great Depression that followed. The Exchange Acts of 1933 and 1934, among other things, established the Securities and Exchange Commission (SEC) and prohibited trading on private information gained as an insider of a firm.

THE SARBANES-OXLEY ACT

One of the most critical inputs to the monitoring process is accurate information. If a board of directors has inaccurate information, it cannot do its job. While SOX contains many provisions, the overall intent of the legislation was to improve the accuracy of information given to both boards and shareholders. SOX attempted to achieve this goal in three ways: (1) by overhauling incentives and independence in the auditing process, (2) by stiffening penalties for providing false information, and (3) by forcing companies to validate their internal financial control processes.

---

16. W. Mikkelson and M. Partch, "The Decline of Takeovers and Disciplinary Managerial Turnover," *Journal of Financial Economics* 44:2 (1997): 205–228.

INTERVIEW WITH LAWRENCE E. HARRIS

As chief economist of the U.S. Securities and Exchange Commission from 2002 to 2004, Dr. Lawrence E. Harris was the primary advisor to the SEC on all economic issues. He participated extensively in the development of Sarbanes-Oxley (SOX) regulations. Currently Dr. Harris holds the Fred V. Keenan Chair in Finance at the University of Southern California's Marshall School of Business.

QUESTION: Why is legislation such as Sarbanes-Oxley necessary to protect shareholders?

ANSWER: Public investors will supply capital to entrepreneurs seeking to fund new business ventures only if they believe it will be used wisely. Regrettably, history has shown that management too often has violated that trust.

The interests of managers and shareholders often conflict. To solve this agency problem, shareholders rely upon information produced by corporate accounting systems. Sarbanes-Oxley mandated accounting and audit standards to improve the quality of corporate financial disclosure.

Opponents of governance regulation believe that shareholders can—and should—take care of themselves. Unfortunately, shareholders often cannot exercise the control necessary to solve agency problems that they could not have anticipated when the firm was first founded. The firm's governance structure, which may have been sensible when the firm was a small company funded primarily by its founders, may no longer be appropriate for a large, widely held corporation operating in the modern economy. Management with little ownership stake may be entrenched, and the directors may be conflicted. When shareholders cannot solve their agency problems, the government must intervene with the lightest possible hand.

QUESTION: What are the costs and benefits of Sarbanes-Oxley?

ANSWER: Good corporate disclosure is essential to public finance. SOX improved the quality of disclosure by strengthening accounting and auditing standards. By requiring the CEO and CFO to sign accounts and attest to their accuracy, SOX also put teeth into enforcement if fraud is discovered.

What many people perceive as costs of SOX are really expenditures that weak firms avoided. All well-managed firms must ensure the integrity of their accounting. SOX merely requires that people adopt *existing* best practice. Many companies were already fully compliant with SOX in most essential respects.

Critics claim that SOX made going public more difficult for small firms by increasing the cost of being a public firm. But a public firm *must* have secure control mechanisms to protect shareholders. SOX may decrease the number of firms that go public, but it will also decrease the losses suffered by public investors.

SOX established the Public Corporation Auditing Oversight Board to regulate auditors. Previous efforts at self-regulation failed because accountants would not discipline their peers. Following numerous notable failures, Congress stepped in and created the PCAOB.

QUESTION: Is SOX a good law?

ANSWER: Regulators are blamed for failing to regulate when crises occur, but they do not bear the costs of their regulations. This asymmetry often causes them to underestimate the costs of their regulations and thus adopt unnecessary regulations. The problem is greatest when political considerations force Congress to write regulations that would be better written by well-informed specialists in regulatory agencies such as the SEC.

Congress wrote SOX in response to the financial accounting crises that greatly offended the public. Although SOX permits the SEC to essentially rewrite any provision that it determines not to be in the public interest, under the circumstances, it could not do so.

SOX is generally good regulation, but it has some notable unintended consequences. The power it gives audit firms over their corporate clients allows them to interpret SOX to their advantage and thereby increase the work necessary to comply with SOX. SOX also imposes unnecessary costs upon mutual funds. Investment companies are subject to SOX because they are public corporations, but they do not face the same accounting problems that operating companies face. In its haste to appease the public, Congress failed to be as discriminating as it could have been.

Many of the problems at Enron, WorldCom, and elsewhere were kept hidden from boards and shareholders until it was too late. In the wake of these scandals, many people felt that the accounting statements of these companies, while often remaining true to the letter of GAAP, did not present an accurate picture of the financial health of a company.

Auditing firms are supposed to ensure that a company's financial statements accurately reflect the financial state of the firm. In reality, most auditors have a longstanding relationship with their audit clients; this extended relationship and the auditors' desire to keep the lucrative auditing fees makes auditors less willing to challenge management. More important perhaps, most accounting firms have developed large and extremely profitable consulting divisions. Obviously, if an audit team refuses to accommodate a request by a client's management, that client will be less likely to choose the accounting firm's consulting division for its next consulting contract. SOX addressed this concern by putting strict limits on the amount of non-audit fees (consulting or otherwise) that an accounting firm can earn from the same firm that it audits. It also required that audit partners rotate every five years to limit the likelihood that auditing relationships become too cozy over long periods of time. Finally, SOX called on the SEC to force companies to have audit committees that are dominated by outside directors and required that at least one outside director have a financial background.

SOX also stiffened the criminal penalties for providing false information to shareholders. It required both the CEO and the CFO to personally attest to the accuracy of the financial statements presented to shareholders and to sign a statement to that effect. Penalties for providing false or misleading financial statements were increased under SOX—fines of as much as $5 million and imprisonment of a maximum of 20 years are permitted. Further, CEOs and CFOs must return bonuses or profits from the sale of stock or the exercise of options during any period covered by statements that are later restated.

Finally, Section 404 of SOX requires senior management and the boards of public companies to be comfortable enough with the process through which funds are allocated and controlled, and outcomes monitored throughout the firm, to be willing to attest to their effectiveness and validity. Section 404 has arguably garnered more attention than any other section in SOX because of the potentially enormous burden it places on every firm to validate its entire financial control system. When the SEC estimated the cost of implementing Section 404, its staff economists put the total cost at $1.24 billion. Recent estimates based on surveys by Financial Executives International and the American Electronics Association predict that the actual cost will be between $20 billion and $35 billion.[17] The burden of complying with this provision is greater, as a fraction of revenue, for smaller companies. The surveys cited earlier found that multi-billion-dollar companies will pay less than 0.05% of their revenues to comply, whereas small companies with less than $20 million in revenues will pay more than 3% of their revenues to comply.

THE CADBURY COMMISSION

It is difficult to determine definitively whether the costs of SOX outweigh its benefits: Even if we could measure the total direct and indirect costs of a law, we could never accurately estimate how much fraud is deterred by that law. One place to turn to for guidance

---

17. American Electronics Association, *Sarbanes-Oxley Section 404: The "Section" of Unintended Consequences and Its Impact on Small Business,* 2005.

is the experiences of other countries. The following quote from *The Independent*[18] sounds like it was written to describe the motivation behind the Sarbanes-Oxley legislation:

> Prompted by public concern over a string of unexpected collapses of recently audited firms and over big rises in executive pay, exchanges and public officials rode a wave of public outrage to institute corporate governance reforms to strengthen the independence of the board and address the conflicts of interest in the auditing process.

In actuality, this passage was written in 1992, and it described what happened in the United Kingdom in 1991. Following the collapse of some large public companies, the U.K. government commissioned Sir Adrian Cadbury to form a committee to develop a code of best practices in corporate governance. Sir Cadbury, in introducing his recommendations, reportedly said the following:

> The fundamental issue is one of pressure. There is pressure on the company to show the results that the market expects. There is pressure on the auditors who don't want to lose their jobs. The question is whether a structure can emerge out of the dialogue which is robust enough to give the shareholders what they ought to get and what they can rely upon. Internal controls are a part of the legitimate expectations of those who receive accounts.[19]

The problems that the Cadbury Commission identified are the same as those that SOX attempted to address in the United States ten years later. Perhaps not surprisingly, the resulting recommendations were quite similar as well. According to the commission's findings, audit and compensation committees should be made up entirely of independent directors or, at least, have a majority of them. The CEO should not be chairperson of the board, and at the very least there should be a lead independent director with similar agenda-setting powers. Auditors should be rotated, and there should be fuller disclosure of non-audit work. Unlike SOX, these recommendations were not backed up by the force of law. Rather, companies could adopt them or instead explain why they chose not to adopt them in their annual reports. Some researchers have studied firms that adopted the Cadbury recommendations versus those that did not. The results are mixed. While one study found that those firms that separated the position of CEO and chairman performed

MARTHA STEWART AND IMCLONE

The most famous recent insider trading case, which was widely reported in the media, involved Martha Stewart, self-made billionaire and CEO of a media empire built around her name. Stewart sold 3928 shares of ImClone Systems in December 2001, just before the Food and Drug Administration announced that it was rejecting ImClone's application to review a new cancer drug. The SEC investigated, alleging that Stewart sold the shares after receiving a tip from her broker that the ImClone founder and his family had been selling shares. Even though Stewart was not an employee of ImClone, insider trading laws prohibited her from trading on information gained through a tip, as the origin of the information violated the duty of trust. Nonetheless, in the end, Stewart was charged only with lying to a federal officer and conspiracy to obstruct justice (the investigation of her trades). She was convicted and served five months in prison and an additional five months of home confinement. In addition, she was fined $30,000.

Source: L. A. Times, July 16, 2004.

18. S. Pincombe, "Accountancy and Management: Auditors Look to Pass the Buck as Pressure for Reform Increases," *The Independent* (London), November 12, 1991, p. 21.

19. Ibid.

in particular, rank-and-file employees. As noted earlier, countries such as Germany give employees board representation. Others have mandated works councils, local versions of labour unions that are to be informed and consulted on major corporate decisions. Finally, some countries mandate employee participation in decision making in their constitutions. Table 29.1 summarizes employee standing in the governance of firms in OECD (Organisation for Economic Co-operation and Development) countries.

TABLE 29.1 EMPLOYEE PARTICIPATION IN CORPORATE GOVERNANCE IN OECD COUNTRIES

Country	Employees Appoint Some Board Members	Works Councils Mandated by Law	Constitutional Reference to Employee Participation in the Management of the Company
Australia	No	No	No
Austria	Yes	Yes	No
Belgium	No	Yes	No
Canada	No	No	No
Czech Republic	Yes	No	No
Denmark	Yes	Yes	No
Finland	No	Yes	No
France	No	Yes	Constitutional right
Germany	Yes	Yes	No
Greece	No	Yes	No
Hungary	No	Yes	No
Ireland	No	No	No
Italy	No	No	Constitutional right
Japan	No	No	No
Mexico	No	No	No
Netherlands	No	Yes	No
New Zealand	No	No	No
Norway	Yes	No	Constitutional right
Poland	No	No	No
Portugal	No	Yes	No
Slovak Republic	No	No	No
South Korea	No	Yes	No
Spain	No	Yes	No
Sweden	Yes	No	No
Switzerland	No	No	No
Turkey	No	No	No
United Kingdom	No	No	No
United States	No	No	No

Source: Organisation for Economic Co-operation and Development, *Survey of Corporate Governance Developments in OECD Countries* (2004).

CROSS-HOLDINGS

While in the United States it is rare for one company's largest shareholder to be another company, it is the norm in many countries, such as Germany, Japan, and South Korea. In Japan, groups of firms connected through cross-holdings and a common relation to a bank are known as *keiretsu*. Monitoring of each company comes from others in the group holding blocks of its stock and primarily from the main bank of the group, which as a creditor monitors the financial well-being of the group companies closely. In South Korea, huge conglomerate groups such as Hyundai, Samsung, LG, and SK comprise companies in widely diversified lines of business and are known as *chaebol*. For example, SK Corporation has subsidiary and group companies in energy, chemicals, pharmaceuticals, and telecommunications. An important difference between the Korean chaebol and the Japanese keiretsu is that in South Korea the firms do not share a common relationship with a single bank.

CONCEPT CHECK

1. How does shareholder protection vary across countries?

2. How can a minority owner in a business gain a controlling interest?

29.7   THE TRADEOFF OF CORPORATE GOVERNANCE

Corporate governance is a system of checks and balances that trades off costs and benefits. As this chapter makes clear, this tradeoff is very complicated. No one structure works for all firms. For example, it would be hard to argue that having Bill Gates as a controlling shareholder of Microsoft was bad for minority investors. For Microsoft, the alignment of incentives that Gates's large stake in Microsoft assured appeared to outweigh the costs of having such a large shareholder. In other cases, however, this is unlikely to be true.

The costs and benefits of a corporate governance system also depend on cultural norms. Acceptable business practice in one culture is unacceptable in another culture, and thus it is not surprising that there is such wide variation in governance structures across countries.[26]

It is important to keep in mind that good governance is value-enhancing and so, in principle, is something investors in the firm should strive for. Because there are many ways to implement good governance, one should expect firms to display—and firms do display—wide variation in their governance structures.

SUMMARY

1. Corporate governance refers to the system of controls, regulations, and incentives designed to prevent fraud from happening.

2. The conflicts between those who control the operations of a firm and those who supply capital to the firm are as old as the corporate organizational structure. Shareholders use a combination of incentives and threats of dismissal to mitigate this conflict.

---

26. Resources that detail how governance differs across the world include J. Charkham, *Keeping Good Company: A Study of Corporate Governance in Five Countries* (Oxford: Clarendon Press, 1994); J. Franks and C. Mayer, "Corporate Ownership and Control in the U.K., Germany and France," *Journal of Applied Corporate Finance* 9:4 (1997): 30–45; R. La Porta, F. Lopez-de-Silanes, and A. Shleifer, "Corporate Ownership Around the World," *Journal of Finance* 54:4 (1999): 471–517; and D. K. Denis and J. J. McConnell, "International Corporate Governance," *Journal of Financial and Quantitative Analysis* 38:1 (2003): 1–38.

3. The board of directors hires managers, sets their compensation, and fires them if necessary. Some boards become captured, meaning that they act in the interests of managers rather than shareholders. Boards with strong, outside directors who were nominated before the current CEO took the helm of the firm are the least likely to be captured.

4. Ownership of a company's stock by management can reduce managers' perquisite consumption. However, moderate holdings of shares can have a negative effect by making the managers harder to fire (reducing the threat of dismissal), without fully aligning their interests with those of shareholders.

5. By tying managers' compensation to firm performance, boards can better align managers' interests with shareholders' interests. Care must be taken to make sure managers do not have incentives to try to manipulate the firm's stock price to garner a big compensation payout.

6. If a board fails to act, shareholders are not without recourse. They can propose an alternate slate of directors or vote not to ratify certain actions of the board.

7. A board and management can adopt provisions, such as staggered boards and limitations on special shareholder meetings, that serve to entrench them. These provisions also have the effect of limiting the efficacy of a hostile takeover bid.

8. Despite the defences that a determined management can erect, one source of the threat of dismissal comes from a hostile acquirer, which can take over a firm and fire the management, even if the board fails to do so.

9. Regulation is an important piece of the total corporate governance environment. Regulation can be beneficial by reducing asymmetric information between managers and capital providers and thus reducing the overall cost of capital. Regulation also carries with it costs of compliance and enforcement. Good regulation balances these forces to produce a net benefit for society.

10. A recent and significant change to governance regulation came with the U.S. Sarbanes-Oxley Act of 2002. The act was intended to improve shareholder monitoring of managers by increasing the accuracy of their information.
    a. It overhauls incentives and independence in the auditing process.
    b. It stiffens the penalties for providing false information.
    c. It forces companies to validate their internal financial control process.

11. The Exchange Acts of 1933 and 1934 in the U.S. are the basis of insider trading regulation. Over time, the SEC and the courts have developed interpretations of the law that
    a. Prohibit insiders with a fiduciary duty to their shareholders from trading on material nonpublic information in that stock.
    b. Prohibit anyone with nonpublic information about a pending or ongoing tender offer from trading on that information or revealing it to someone who is likely to trade on it.

12. Corporate governance, regulations, and practices vary widely across countries.
    a. Some studies suggest that countries with common-law roots generally provide better shareholder protection than countries with civil-law origin.
    b. Ownership structures in Canada, Europe, and Asia often involve pyramidal control of a group of companies by a single family. In these situations, the controlling family has many opportunities for expropriation of minority shareholders through tunnelling.

    c. Dual class shares with differential voting rights allow a controlling shareholder or family to maintain control of a company or group even if their cash flow rights are relatively small. Dual class shares are common in Canada and other countries except the United States.

    d. Most countries give employees some role in governing a firm. Employee involvement usually takes the form of board seats or works councils that are consulted before major decisions.

    e. It is common outside the United States for a company's largest shareholder to be another company. These cross-holdings create incentives for firms to monitor each other.

KEY TERMS

backdating *p. 979*
captured *p. 976*
corporate governance *p. 973*
dual class shares *p. 988*
grey directors *p. 974*
inside directors *p. 974*

insider trading *p. 987*
outside (independent) directors *p. 975*
pyramid structure *p. 989*
stakeholder model *p. 990*
tunnelling *p. 990*

PROBLEMS

The problems marked in green can be found on MyFinanceLab at www.myfinancelab.com. Visit your MyFinanceLab for additional practice. Additional readings for this chapter may be found in the Textbook Resources section on MyFinanceLab.

Corporate Governance and Agency Costs

1. What inherent characteristic of corporations creates the need for a system of checks on manager behaviour?

2. What are some examples of agency problems?

3. What are the advantages and disadvantages of the corporate organizational structure?

Monitoring by the Board of Directors and Others

4. What is the role of the board of directors in corporate governance?

5. How does a board become captured by a CEO?

6. What role do security analysts play in monitoring?

7. How are lenders part of corporate governance?

8. What is a whistleblower?

Compensation Policies

9. What are the advantages and disadvantages of increasing the options granted to CEOs?

Managing Agency Conflict

10. Is it necessarily true that increasing managerial ownership stakes will improve firm performance?

11.   How can proxy contests be used to overcome a captured board?

12.   What is a say-on-pay vote?

13.   What are a board's options when confronted with dissident shareholders?

Regulation

14.   What is the essential tradeoff faced by government in designing regulation of public firms?

15.   Many of the provisions of the Sarbanes-Oxley Act of 2002 were aimed at auditors. How does this affect corporate governance?

16.   What are the costs and benefits of prohibiting insider trading?

17.   How do the laws on insider trading differ for merger- versus non-merger-related trading?

Corporate Governance Around the World

18.   Are the rights of shareholders better protected in the United States or in Canada?

19.   How can a controlling family use a pyramidal control structure to benefit itself at the expense of other shareholders?

Risk Management

All firms are subject to risk from a variety of sources: changes in consumer tastes and demand for their products, fluctuations in the cost of raw materials, employee turnover, the entry of new competitors, terrorist attacks, and countless other uncertainties. Entrepreneurs and corporate managers willingly take on these risks in the pursuit of high returns and accept them as part of the cost of doing business. But as with any other cost, firms should manage risk to minimize the effect on the value of the firm.

The primary method of risk management is prevention. For example, firms can avoid or at least reduce many potential risks by increasing safety standards in the workplace, by making prudent investment decisions, and by conducting appropriate due diligence when entering into new relationships. But some risks are too costly to prevent and are inevitable consequences of running a business. As discussed in Part 5 of the text, the firm shares these business risks with its investors through its capital structure. Some of the risk is passed on to debt holders, who bear the risk that the firm will default. Most of the risk is held by equity holders, who are exposed to the volatility of the stock's realized return. Both types of investors can reduce their risk by holding the firm's securities in a well-diversified portfolio.

Not all risks need to be passed on to the firm's debt and equity holders. Insurance and financial markets allow firms to trade risk and shield their debt and equity holders from some types of risk. For example, after a fire shut down its processing plant in January 2005, Suncor Energy received more than $200 million in settlements from insurance contracts covering both the damage to the plant and the lost business while the plant was being repaired. Much of the loss from the fire was thus borne by Suncor's insurers rather than by its investors. In 2004, Southwest Airlines received $455 million from financial contracts that compensated it for the rise in the cost of jet fuel. Air Canada received $31 million from financial contracts that protected its fuel prices in 2007 and had contracts that protected 28% of its 2008 fuel needs in the price range of $61–$68 per barrel while world oil prices surpassed $130 per barrel. In April 2009, Cisco held contracts to protect more than $5 billion worth of projected foreign revenues from fluctuations in exchange rates, and General Electric held contracts, with a total market value exceeding $15 billion, designed to reduce its exposure to interest rate fluctuations.

In this chapter, we consider the strategies that firms use to manage and reduce the risk borne by their investors. We begin with the most common form of risk management, insurance. After carefully considering the costs and benefits of insurance, we look at the ways firms can use financial markets to offload the risks associated with changes in commodity prices, exchange rate fluctuations, and interest rate movements.

30.1 INSURANCE

Insurance is the most common method firms use to reduce risk. Many firms purchase **property insurance** to insure their assets against hazards such as fire, storm damage, vandalism, earthquakes, and other natural and environmental risks. Other common types of insurance include:

- **Business liability insurance**, which covers the costs that result if some aspect of the business causes harm to a third party or someone else's property
- **Business interruption insurance**, which protects the firm against the loss of earnings if the business is interrupted due to fire, accident, or some other insured peril
- **Key personnel insurance**, which compensates for the loss or unavoidable absence of crucial employees in the firm

In this section, we illustrate the role of insurance in reducing risk and examine its pricing and potential benefits and costs for a firm.

THE ROLE OF INSURANCE: AN EXAMPLE

To understand the role of insurance in reducing risk, consider an oil refinery with a 1-in-5000, or 0.02%, chance of being destroyed by a fire in the next year. If it is destroyed, the firm estimates that it will lose $150 million in rebuilding costs and lost business. We can summarize the risk from fire with a probability distribution:

Event	Probability	Loss ($ million)
No fire	99.98%	0
Fire	0.02%	150

Given this probability distribution, the firm's expected loss from fire each year is

$$99.98\% \times (\$0) + 0.02\% \times (\$150 \text{ million}) = \$30,000$$

While the expected loss is relatively small, the firm faces a large downside risk if a fire does occur. If the firm could eliminate completely the chance of fire for less than the present value of $30,000 per year, it would do so; such an investment would have a positive NPV. But avoiding *any* chance of a fire is probably not feasible with current technology (or at least would cost far more than $30,000 per year). Consequently, the firm can manage the risk by instead purchasing insurance to compensate its loss of $150 million. In exchange, the firm will pay an annual fee, called an **insurance premium**, to the insurance company. In this way, insurance allows the firm to exchange a random future loss for a certain upfront expense.

INSURANCE PRICING IN A PERFECT MARKET

When a firm buys insurance, it transfers the risk of the loss to an insurance company. The insurance company charges an upfront premium to take on that risk. At what price will the insurance company be willing to bear the risk in a perfect market?

In a perfect market without other frictions, insurance companies should compete until they are just earning a fair return and the NPV from selling insurance is zero. The NPV is zero if the price of insurance equals the present value of the expected payment; in that case, we say the price is **actuarially fair**. If r_L is the appropriate cost of capital given the risk of the loss, we can calculate the actuarially fair premium as follows:[1]

Actuarially Fair Insurance Premium

$$\text{Insurance Premium} = \frac{\Pr(\text{Loss}) \times E[\text{Payment in the Event of Loss}]}{1 + r_L} \qquad (30.1)$$

The cost of capital r_L used in Eq. 30.1 depends on the risk being insured. Consider again the oil refinery. The risk of fire is surely unrelated to the performance of the stock market or the economy. Instead, this risk is specific to this firm and, therefore, diversifiable in a large portfolio. As we discussed in Chapter 10, by pooling together the risks from many policies, insurance companies can create very-low-risk portfolios whose annual claims are relatively predictable. In other words, the risk of fire has a beta of zero, so it will not command a risk premium. In this case, $r_L = r_f$, the risk-free interest rate.

Not all insurable risks have a beta of zero. Some risks, such as hurricanes and earthquakes, create losses of tens of billions of dollars and may be difficult to diversify completely.[2] Other types of losses may be correlated across firms. Increases in the cost of health care or more stringent environmental regulations raise the potential claims from health insurance and liability insurance for all firms. Finally, some risks can have a causal effect on the stock market: The September 11, 2001, terrorist attacks cost insurers

---

1. Equation 30.1 assumes insurance premiums are paid at the start of the year, and payments in the event of loss are made at the end of the year. It is straightforward to extend it to alternative timing assumptions.

2. For example, insured losses from hurricanes Katrina, Rita, and Wilma, which pummelled the southeastern United States in 2005, exceeded $40 billion, with total economic losses topping $100 billion. When insuring large risks like these, many insurance companies buy insurance on their own portfolios from *reinsurance companies*. Reinsurance firms pool risks globally from different insurance companies worldwide. For natural disasters, typically one-fourth to one-third of the insured losses is passed on to reinsurers.

actuarially fair premium to cover administrative expenses. To account for adverse selection, the insurance company estimates a 5% probability of loss for the $55 million policy and a 6% probability of loss for the $100 million policy.

Suppose the beta of the risk is zero and the risk-free rate is 5%. Which policy should the firm choose if its risk of loss is 5%? Which should it choose if its risk of loss is 6%?

Solution

The premium charged for each policy is

$$\text{Premium(\$55 million policy)} = \frac{5\% \times \$55 \text{ million}}{1.05} \times 1.20 = \$3.14 \text{ million}$$

$$\text{Premium(\$100 million policy)} = \frac{6\% \times \$100 \text{ million}}{1.05} \times 1.20 = \$6.86 \text{ million}$$

If the risk of a loss is 5%, the NPV of each policy is

$NPV(\$55 \text{ million policy})$

$$= -\$3.14 \text{ million} + \frac{5\% \times \$55 \text{ million}}{1.05} \times 1.50 = \$0.79 \text{ million}$$

$NPV(\$100 \text{ million policy})$

$$= -\$6.86 \text{ million} + \frac{5\% \times \$100 \text{ million}}{1.05} \times 1.50 = \$0.29 \text{ million}$$

Thus, with a 5% risk, the firm should choose the policy with lower coverage. If the risk of a loss is 6%, the policy with higher coverage is superior:

$NPV(\$55 \text{ million policy})$

$$= -\$3.14 \text{ million} + \frac{6\% \times \$55 \text{ million}}{1.05} \times 1.50 = \$1.57 \text{ million}$$

$NPV(\$100 \text{ million policy})$

$$= -\$6.86 \text{ million} + \frac{6\% \times \$100 \text{ million}}{1.05} \times 1.50 = \$1.71 \text{ million}$$

Note that the insurance company's concerns regarding adverse selection are justified: Firms that are riskier will choose the higher-coverage policy.

THE INSURANCE DECISION

In a perfect capital market, purchasing insurance does not add value to the firm. It can add value in the presence of market imperfections, but market imperfections are also likely to raise the premiums charged by insurers. For insurance to be attractive, the benefit to the firm must exceed the additional premium charged by the insurer.

For these reasons, insurance is most likely to be attractive to firms that are currently financially healthy, do not need external capital, and are paying high current tax rates. They will benefit most from insuring risks that can lead to cash shortfalls or financial distress, and that insurers can accurately assess and monitor to prevent moral hazard.

Full insurance is unlikely to be attractive for risks about which firms have a great deal of private information or that are subject to severe moral hazard. Also, firms that are already in financial distress have a strong incentive not to purchase insurance—they need cash today and have an incentive to take risk because future losses are likely to be borne by their debt holders.

1. How can insurance add value to a firm?

2. Identify the costs of insurance that arise due to market imperfections.

30.2 COMMODITY PRICE RISK

Firms use insurance to protect against the unlikely event that their real assets are damaged or destroyed by hazards such as fire, hurricane, accident, or other catastrophes that are outside their normal course of business. At the same time, many risks that firms face arise naturally as part of their business operations. For many firms, changes in the market prices of the raw materials they use and the goods they produce may be the most important source of risk to their profitability. In the airline industry, for example, the second largest expense after labour is jet fuel. With oil prices rising by a factor of 8 between 1999 and 2008, most major carriers have struggled to remain profitable. Industry analysts estimate that each $1 per barrel increase in the price of oil equates to a $425 million increase in the industry's annual jet fuel expenses. For an airline, the risk from increases in the price of oil is clearly one of the most important risks that it faces.

In this section, we discuss ways firms can reduce, or *hedge*, their exposure to commodity price movements. Like insurance, hedging involves contracts or transactions that provide the firm with cash flows that offset its losses from price changes.

HEDGING WITH VERTICAL INTEGRATION AND STORAGE

Firms can hedge risk by making real investments in assets with offsetting risk. The most common strategies are vertical integration and storage.

Vertical integration entails the merger of a firm and its supplier (or a firm and its customer). Because an increase in the price of the commodity raises the firm's costs and the supplier's revenues, these firms can offset their risks by merging. For example, in 2005 Japanese tire maker Bridgestone purchased a large Indonesian rubber plantation to control its costs. As the price of rubber increases, so will the profits of the rubber plantation, offsetting the higher costs of making tires. Similarly, airlines could offset their oil price risk by merging with an oil company.

While vertical integration can reduce risk, it does not always increase value. Recall the key lesson of Modigliani and Miller: Firms add no value by doing something investors can do for themselves. Investors concerned about commodity price risk can diversify by "vertically integrating" their portfolios and buying shares of the firm and its supplier. Because the acquiring firm often pays a substantial premium over the current share price of the firm being acquired, the shareholders of the acquiring firm would generally find it cheaper to diversify on their own.

Vertical integration can add value if combining the firms results in important synergies. For example, Boeing ultimately decided to purchase a number of its suppliers involved in its 787 "Dreamliner" to improve quality control and coordination, and reduce production delays. In many instances, however, diseconomies would be the more likely outcome of vertical integration, as the combined firm would lack a strategic focus (e.g., airlines and oil producers). Finally, vertical integration is not a perfect hedge: A firm's supplier is exposed to many other risks besides commodity prices. By integrating vertically, the firm eliminates one risk but acquires others.

A related strategy is the long-term storage of inventory. An airline concerned about rising fuel costs could purchase a large quantity of fuel today and store the fuel until it is needed. By doing so, the firm locks in its cost for fuel at today's price plus storage costs.

But for many commodities, storage costs are much too high for this strategy to be attractive. Such a strategy also requires a substantial cash outlay upfront. If the firm does not have the required cash, it would need to raise external capital—and consequently would suffer issuance and adverse selection costs. Finally, maintaining large amounts of inventory would dramatically increase working capital requirements, a cost for the firm.

HEDGING WITH LONG-TERM CONTRACTS

An alternative to vertical integration or storage is a long-term supply contract. Firms routinely enter into long-term lease contracts for real estate, fixing the price at which they will obtain office space many years in advance. Similarly, U.S. utility companies sign long-term supply contracts with Canadian power generators, and steelmakers sign long-term contracts with mining firms for iron ore. Through these contracts, both parties can achieve price stability for their product or input.

A good example is provided by Southwest Airlines. In early 2000, when oil prices were close to $20 per barrel, Chief Financial Officer Gary Kelly developed a strategy to protect the airline from a surge in oil prices. By the time oil prices soared above $30 per barrel later that year and put the airline industry into a financial crisis, Southwest had signed contracts guaranteeing a price for its fuel equivalent to $23 per barrel. The savings from its fuel hedge amounted to almost 50% of Southwest's earnings that year, as shown in Figure 30.1. Kelly went on to become Southwest's CEO, and Southwest has continued this strategy to hedge fuel costs. Between 1998 and 2008, Southwest saved $3.5 billion over what it would have spent if it had paid the industry's average price for jet fuel, accounting for 83% of the company's profits during that period.[10]

Of course, like insurance, commodity hedging does not always boost a firm's profits. Had oil prices fallen below $23 per barrel in the fall of 2000, Southwest's hedging

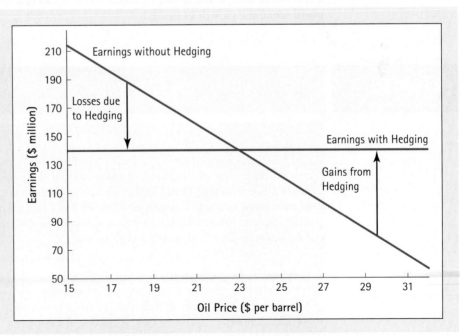

FIGURE 30.1

Commodity Hedging Smoothes Earnings

By locking in its fuel costs in 2000 through long-term supply contracts, Southwest Airlines kept its earnings stable in the face of fluctuating fuel prices. With a long-term contract at a price of $23 per barrel, Southwest gains by buying at this price if oil prices go above $23 per barrel. If oil prices fall below $23 per barrel, Southwest loses from its commitment to buy at a higher price.

10. www.usatoday.com/money/industries/travel/2008-07-23-southwest-jet-fuel_N.htm.

policy would have *reduced* the firm's earnings by obligating it to pay $23 per barrel for its oil (and perhaps Kelly might not have gone on to be CEO). Presumably, Southwest felt that it could afford to pay $23 per barrel for oil even if the price fell. While the long-term contracts would have been costly, they would not have led to financial distress. In other words, the long-term contracts stabilized Southwest's earnings at an acceptable level, no matter what happened to oil prices. Figure 30.1 illustrates how hedging stabilizes earnings.

Air Canada also has a history with fuel hedging. From 1994 to 1996, oil prices had increased by about 33%. In 1997, Air Canada signed contracts locking in about one-half of its anticipated 1998 fuel needs at an oil price of $19 per barrel. Unfortunately, in 1998, oil prices dropped to about $12 per barrel and Air Canada lost the equivalent of $89 million because of these contracts. Southwest increased its fuel hedges in the years that followed, but Air Canada hedged a lower proportion of its fuel costs. At the end of 2007, Air Canada had hedges for its anticipated fuel needs of about 20% for 2008, 3% for 2009, and 2% for 2010. At the beginning of 2007, Southwest had 100% of its fuel costs hedged. At the beginning of 2008, Southwest had its anticipated fuel costs hedged as follows: 70% for 2008 at $51 per barrel, 55% for 2009 at $51 per barrel, 30% for 2010 at $63 per barrel, and 15% for each of 2011 and 2012 at $63–$64 per barrel. Which strategy will be better depends on oil prices. By early July 2008, oil was over $145 per barrel, so Southwest's strategy looked better. An alternative strategy was followed by WestJet; at the end of 2007, WestJet had no outstanding fuel hedges. Certainly, the hedging strategy of Southwest helped its earnings in mid-2008, but as oil prices dropped rapidly with the onset of the world financial crisis and fell below $40 per barrel by the end of 2008, Southwest's hedging strategy hurt its earnings. Was WestJet the winner in terms of these hedged or unhedged strategies? Again, time will tell. By the end of April 2010, oil prices again were over $85 per barrel but quickly dropped below $70 per barrel a few weeks later as the Greek financial crisis threatened the Euro Zone recovery and world economic growth in general.

EXAMPLE 30.4   HEDGING WITH LONG-TERM CONTRACTS

Problem

Consider a chocolate maker that will need 10,000 tons of cocoa beans next year. The current market price of cocoa beans is $1400 per ton. At this price, the firm expects earnings before interest and taxes of $22 million next year. What will the firm's EBIT be if the price of cocoa beans rises to $1950 per ton? What will EBIT be if the price of cocoa beans falls to $1200 per ton? What will EBIT be in each scenario if the firm enters into a supply contract for cocoa beans for a fixed price of $1450 per ton?

Solution

If the price of cocoa beans increases to $1950 per ton, the firm's costs will increase by $(1950 - 1400) \times 10,000 = \$5.5$ million. Other things equal, EBIT will decline to $22 million − $5.5 million = $16.5 million. If the price of cocoa beans falls to $1200 per ton, EBIT will rise to $22 million − $(1200 - 1400) \times 10,000 = \$24$ million. Alternatively, the firm can avoid this risk by entering into the supply contract that fixes the price in either scenario at $1450 per ton, for an EBIT of $22 million − $(1450 - 1400) \times 10,000 = \$21.5$ million.

Often, long-term supply contracts are bilateral contracts negotiated by a buyer and a seller. Such contracts have several potential disadvantages. First, they expose each party to the risk that the other party may default and fail to live up to the terms of the contract. Thus, while they insulate the firms from commodity price risk, they expose them to credit risk. Second, such contracts cannot be entered into anonymously; the buyer and seller know each other's identity. This lack of anonymity may have strategic disadvantages. Finally, the market value of the contract at any point in time may not be easy to determine, making it difficult to track gains and losses, and it may be difficult or even impossible to cancel the contract if necessary.

An alternative strategy that avoids these disadvantages is to hedge with futures contracts. In the next section we investigate this strategy.

HEDGING WITH FUTURES CONTRACTS

A commodity futures contract is a type of long-term contract designed to avoid the disadvantages cited above. A **futures contract** is an agreement to trade an asset on some future date, at a price that is locked in today. Futures contracts are traded anonymously on an exchange at a publicly observed market price and are generally very liquid. Both the buyer and the seller can get out of the contract at any time by selling it to a third party at the current market price. Finally, through a mechanism we will describe shortly, futures contracts are designed to eliminate credit risk.

Figure 30.2 shows the prices in August 2005 of futures contracts for light, sweet crude oil traded on the New York Mercantile Exchange (NYMEX). Each contract represents a commitment to trade 1000 barrels of oil at the futures price on its delivery date. For example, by trading the June 2008 contract, buyers and sellers agreed in August 2005 to exchange 1000 barrels of oil in June 2008 at a price of $61 per barrel. By doing so, they are able to lock in the price they will pay or receive for oil almost three years in advance.

FIGURE 30.2

Historical Futures Prices for Light, Sweet Crude Oil, August 2005

Each point represents the futures price per barrel in August 2005 for the delivery of oil in the month indicated.

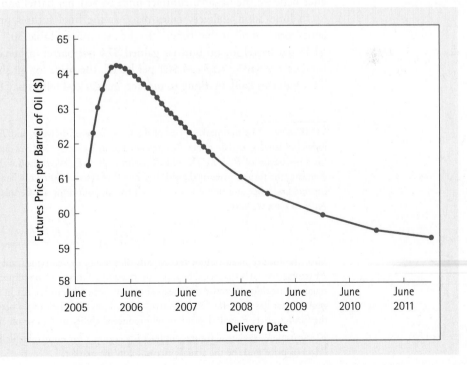

A futures price is not a price that is paid today. Rather, futures prices are prices *agreed to* today, to be paid in the future. The futures prices are determined in the market based on supply and demand for each delivery date. They depend on expectations of future oil prices, adjusted by an appropriate risk premium.[11]

ELIMINATING CREDIT RISK.   If a seller in 2005 commits to sell crude oil in June 2008 for $61 per barrel, how can the buyer be assured that the seller will honour that commitment? Consider what actually happened: By June of 2008, oil was trading at $135 per barrel. The seller would have a strong incentive to default if the original agreement was to sell at $61 per barrel. Similarly, if oil had dropped in price, say to $30 per barrel, the buyer would have had a strong incentive to default on the contract.

Futures exchanges use two mechanisms to prevent buyers or sellers from defaulting. First, traders are required to post collateral, called **margin**, when buying or selling commodities using futures contracts. This collateral serves as a guarantee that traders will meet their obligations. In addition, cash flows are exchanged on a daily basis, rather than waiting until the end of the contract, through a procedure called **marking to market**. That is, gains and losses are computed each day based on the change in the price of the futures contract.

MARKING TO MARKET: AN EXAMPLE.   Suppose that the price of the June 2008 futures contract varies as shown in Table 30.1 over the 700 remaining trading days between August 2005 and the delivery date in June 2008. A buyer who enters into the contract on date 0 has committed to pay the futures price of $61 per barrel for oil. If the next day the futures price is only $59 per barrel, the buyer has a loss of $2 per barrel on her position. This loss is settled immediately by deducting $2 from the buyer's margin account. If the price rises to $60 per barrel on day 2, the gain of $1 is added to the buyer's margin account. This process continues until the contract delivery date, with the daily gains and losses shown. The buyer's cumulative loss is the sum of these daily amounts and always equals the difference between the original contract price of $61 per barrel and the current contract price.

In June 2008, delivery takes place at the final futures price, which is equal to the actual price of oil at that time.[12] In the example in Table 30.1, the buyer ultimately pays $135 per barrel for oil but has gained $74 per barrel in her margin account. Thus, her total cost is $135 − $74 = $61 per barrel, the price for oil she originally committed to. Through this daily marking to market, buyers and sellers pay for any losses as they occur,

---

11. If we let P_t be the market price of oil at the time of delivery, and F_t be the futures price agreed to today for delivery on date t, then the buyer of a futures contract receives oil worth P_t and pays F_t at delivery, for a net payoff of $P_t - F_t$. The seller's payoff is $F_t - P_t$. We compute the NPV of the contract by discounting the futures price at the risk-free rate (because it is known when we enter the contract) and the expected oil price at a rate r_o that reflects a risk premium for oil. Because competition should drive the NPV to zero, we have

$$0 = \frac{E[P_t]}{(1 + r_o)^t} - \frac{F_t}{(1 + r_f)^t} \quad \text{or} \quad F_t = E[P_t]\frac{(1 + r_f)^t}{(1 + r_o)^t}$$

Also, the futures price cannot exceed cost of storing, or "carrying," oil for the future: $P_0 (1 + r_f)^t + FV(\text{storage costs})$. Otherwise, buying, storing, and selling oil using futures contracts would offer an arbitrage opportunity. (Because the cheapest way to store oil is to leave it in the ground, the futures price is generally far less than this "cost-of-carry" price. Thus the relationship between the current price, P_0, and the futures price, F_t, will depend on oil producers' ability to shift production across time.)

12. At its delivery date, a futures contract is a contract for immediate delivery. Thus, by the Law of One Price, its price must be the actual price of oil in the market.

TABLE 30.1	EXAMPLE OF MARKING TO MARKET AND DAILY SETTLEMENT FOR THE JUNE 2008 LIGHT, SWEET CRUDE OIL FUTURES CONTRACT ($/BBL)

Trading Day	August 05 0	1	2	3	4	...	698	699	June 08 700
Futures price	61	59	60	63	70	...	120	130	135
Daily marked to market profit/loss		−2	1	3	7	...	...	10	5
Cumulative profit/loss		−2	−1	2	9	...	59	69	74

rather than waiting until the final delivery date. In this way, the firm avoids the risk of default.[13]

In essence, the June 2008 futures contract is the same as a long-term supply contract with a set price of $61 per barrel of oil.[14] But unlike a bilateral contract, the buyer and the seller can close their positions at any time (and accept the cumulative losses or gains in their margin accounts), and the contract will then be reassigned to a new buyer or seller at its current price. Because of this liquidity and the lack of credit risk, commodity futures contracts are the predominant method by which many firms hedge oil price risk. Similar futures contracts exist for many other commodities, including natural gas, coal, electricity, silver, gold, aluminum, soybeans, corn, wheat, rice, cattle, pork bellies, cocoa, sugar, carbon dioxide emissions, and even frozen orange juice. During the financial crisis, there were defaults on many derivatives that were not traded through exchanges and not protected with the marking to market process. Since then, governments and regulators have been pushing for more transparency in these derivatives including the requirement for them to be traded on exchanges and for there to be margin requirements and marking to market processes in place.

DECIDING TO HEDGE COMMODITY PRICE RISK

In a perfect market, commodity supply contracts and futures contracts are zero-NPV investments that do not change the value of the firm. But hedging commodity price risk can benefit the firm by reducing the costs of other frictions. Just as with insurance, the potential benefits include reduced financial distress and issuance costs, tax savings, increased debt capacity, and improved managerial incentives and risk assessment. Commodity futures markets, in particular, provide valuable information to commodity producers and users. For example, an oil firm can lock in the future price of oil before it

---

13. For this system to work, the buyer's margin account must always have a sufficient balance to cover one day's loss. If a buyer's remaining margin in the account is too low, the exchange will require the buyer to replenish the account in a *margin call*. If the buyer fails to do so, the account will be closed and the buyer's contract will be assigned to a new buyer.

14. Because the daily marked-to-market gains and losses occur over the life of the contract rather than at the end, after we account for interest, the correct future value is actually somewhat higher than $61 per barrel. To account for this effect, which can be sizable for a multiyear contract, practitioners generally reduce the magnitude of their initial position to reflect the interest earned over the life of the contract. This adjustment is called *tailing the hedge*.

COMMON MISTAKE HEDGING RISK

There are several common mistakes to be avoided when hedging risk:

Account for Natural Hedges. Even though purchases of a commodity may be a firm's largest expense, they may not be a source of risk if the firm can pass along those costs to its customers. For example, gas stations do not need to hedge their cost of oil, because the price of gasoline—and thus their revenues—fluctuate with it. When a firm can pass on cost increases to its customers or revenue decreases to its suppliers, it has a **natural hedge** for these risks. A firm should hedge risks to its profits only after such natural hedges are accounted for, lest it overhedge and increase risk. In the case of Air Canada and WestJet, WestJet may not be able to pass on the full increase in its fuel cost if, because of Air Canada's hedges, Air Canada does not increase ticket prices. Thus, a requirement for being able to pass through price changes to customers is that your competitors will do so too.

Liquidity Risk. When hedging with futures contracts, the firm stabilizes its earnings by offsetting business losses with gains on the futures contracts and by offsetting business gains with losses on the futures contracts. In the latter scenario, the firm runs the risk of receiving margin

calls on its futures positions before it realizes the cash flows from the business gains. To effectively hedge, the firm must have, or be able to raise, the cash required to meet these margin calls or it may be forced to default on its positions. Hence, when hedging with future contracts the firm is exposed to **liquidity risk.** Such was the case for Metallgesellschaft Refining and Marketing (MGRM), which shut down in 1993 with more than $1 billion in losses in the oil futures market. MGRM had written long-term contracts to supply oil to its customers and hedged its risk that oil prices might rise by buying oil futures. When oil prices subsequently dropped, MGRM faced a cash flow crisis and could not meet the margin calls on its futures positions.

Basis Risk. Futures contracts are available only for a set of standardized commodities, with specific delivery dates and locations. Thus, while a futures contract that promises to deliver crude oil in Oklahoma in June 2013 is a reasonable hedge for the cost of jet fuel in Dallas in July 2013, it will not be a perfect match. **Basis risk** is the risk that arises because the value of the futures contract will not be perfectly correlated with the firm's actual exposure (recall the price drop of oil between April 30, 2010, and May 25, 2010, when it dropped from $86 to $68).

spends millions of dollars on drilling a new well. A farmer unsure of future crop prices can lock in the futures price of wheat when deciding the quantity to plant.

But while hedging commodity price risk has similar potential benefits as buying insurance, it does not have the same costs. In comparison to the market for hazard insurance, the commodity markets are less vulnerable to the problems of adverse selection and moral hazard. Firms generally do not possess better information than outside investors regarding the risk of future commodity price changes, nor can they influence that risk through their actions. Also, futures contracts are very liquid and do not entail large administrative costs.

Trading in these contracts carries other costs, however. First, as Figure 30.1 illustrates, when a firm hedges it will sometimes lose money. These losses will be offset by other gains or savings, but the firm must be sure it can weather the losses until it realizes the offsetting gains. Second, the firm may **speculate** by entering into contracts that do not offset its actual risks. Speculating increases the firm's risk rather than reducing it. When a firm authorizes managers to trade contracts to hedge, it opens the door to the possibility of speculation. The firm must guard against the potential to speculate and add risk to the firm through appropriate governance procedures.

CONCEPT CHECK
1. Discuss risk management strategies that firms use to hedge commodity price risk.
2. What are the potential risks associated with hedging using futures contracts?

30.3 EXCHANGE RATE RISK

Multinational firms face the risk of exchange rate fluctuations. In this section, we consider two strategies that firms use to hedge this risk: currency forward contracts and currency options.

EXCHANGE RATE FLUCTUATIONS

Recall from Chapter 3 that an exchange rate is the market rate at which one currency can be exchanged for another currency. Consider the relationship between the Canadian dollar (CAD) and the U.S. dollar (USD).[15] On January 18, 2002, the value of the CAD relative to the USD reached a new low of about 0.6202 USD/CAD or, equivalently,

$$\frac{1}{0.6202\ USD/CAD} = \frac{1.6124\ CAD}{USD}$$

On November 7, 2007, the CAD reached an all-time high, trading at over 1.10 USD at one point. Like most foreign exchange rates, the CAD/USD rate is a **floating rate**, which means it changes constantly depending on the quantity supplied and demanded for each currency in the market. The supply and demand for each currency is driven by three factors:

- *Firms trading goods:* A U.S. automaker exchanges USD for CAD to buy auto parts from a Canadian manufacturer.

- *Investors trading securities:* A Japanese investor exchanges yen (JPY) for USD to purchase U.S. bonds.

- *The actions of central banks in each country:* The British central bank may exchange pounds (GBP) for euros (EUR) in an attempt to keep down the value of the pound.

Because the supply and demand for currencies varies with global economic conditions, exchange rates are volatile. Figure 30.3 shows the USD end-of-year price of one CAD from 1948 through 2009. Notice that the value of the CAD fluctuates greatly over time. From 2002 to 2007, the value of the CAD climbed more than 77% relative to the USD. Also note the sharp drop off at the end of 2008 in the midst of the financial crisis.

Fluctuating exchanges rates cause a problem known as the *importer–exporter dilemma* for firms doing business in international markets. This is particularly important to Canada–U.S. trade, as our two countries are each other's biggest trading partners. To illustrate, consider the problem faced by Modern Bathrooms, a bathroom renovation company. Modern Bathrooms needs to import steam generators from a U.S. supplier, ThermaSol, so it can install steam rooms in customers' homes. If ThermaSol sets the price of its parts in USD, then Modern Bathrooms faces the risk that the CAD may fall, making the USD, and therefore the steam generators, more expensive. If ThermaSol sets its prices in CAD for its Canadian customers, then ThermaSol faces the risk that the CAD may fall and it will receive fewer USD for the steam generators it sells to Canadians.

---

15. Since many countries use the same currency symbols (e.g., $), in this chapter we will adopt the convention of using standardized three-letter currency codes. The first two letters of the code are from the country name and the third letter is from its currency. Thus, we have CAD for the **CA**NADIAN **D**OLLAR, USD for the **U**NITED **S**TATES **D**OLLAR, GBP for the **G**REAT **B**RITAIN **P**OUND, etc. Some currency codes are not so obvious because the country name is very different from its English name (e.g., the Swiss franc is CHF). Some currencies have also been replaced with new versions after the old version became too devalued (e.g., the Polish zloty is actually the **P**olish **N**ew **Z**loty and the code is PLN).

End-of-Year Values of One Canadian Dollar (CAD) in Terms of U.S. Dollars (USD) 1948–2009

Note the dramatic changes in the exchange rate over short periods.

Sources: Statistics Canada and Bank of Canada.

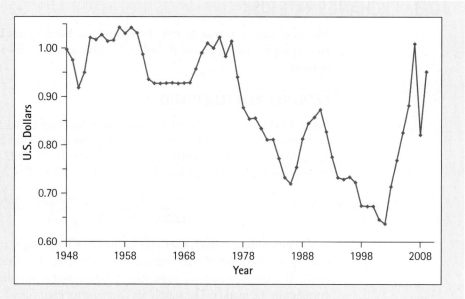

The problem of exchange rate risk is a general problem in any import–export relationship. If neither company will accept the exchange rate risk, the transaction may be difficult or impossible to negotiate. Example 30.5 demonstrates the potential magnitude of the problem.

EXAMPLE 30.5

THE EFFECT OF EXCHANGE RATE RISK

Problem

In late 2006, Whole Foods Market in the U.S. ordered its 2007 shipment of shampoos from Avalon Natural Products' Canadian manufacturing facility when the exchange rate was 0.85 USD per CAD. It agreed to a price of 500,000 CAD, to be paid when the shampoos were delivered in one year's time. One year later, the exchange rate was 1.05 USD per CAD. What was the actual cost in USD for Whole Foods Market when the payment was due? If the price had instead been set at 425,000 USD (which had equivalent value at the time of the agreement), how many CAD would Avalon have received?

Solution

With the price set at 500,000 CAD, Whole Foods Market had to pay (1.05 USD/CAD) × (500,000 CAD) = 525,000 USD. This cost is $100,000, or 24%, higher than it would have been if the price had been set in USD.

If the price had been set in USD, Whole Foods Market would have paid 425,000 USD, which would have been worth only 425,000 USD ÷ (1.05 USD/CAD) = 404,762 CAD to Avalon, or more than 19% less. Whether the price was set in CAD or USD, one of the parties would have suffered a substantial loss.

HEDGING WITH FORWARD CONTRACTS

Exchange rate risk naturally arises whenever transacting parties use different currencies: One of the parties will be at risk if exchange rates fluctuate. The most common method firms use to reduce the risk that results from changes in exchange rates is to hedge the transaction using currency forward contracts.

A **currency forward contract** is a contract that sets the exchange rate in advance. It is usually written between a firm and a bank, and it fixes a currency exchange rate for a transaction that will occur at a future date. A currency forward contract specifies (1) an exchange rate, (2) an amount of currency to exchange, and (3) a delivery date on which the exchange will take place. The exchange rate set in the contract is referred to as the **forward exchange rate**, because it applies to an exchange that will occur in the future. By entering into a currency forward contract, a firm can lock in an exchange rate in advance and reduce or eliminate its exposure to fluctuations in a currency's value.

EXAMPLE 30.6

USING A FORWARD CONTRACT TO LOCK IN AN EXCHANGE RATE

Problem

In late 2006, banks were offering one-year currency forward contracts with a forward exchange rate of 0.87 USD/CAD. Suppose that at that time, Whole Foods Market placed the order with Avalon's Canadian manufacturing facility with a price of 500,000 CAD and simultaneously entered into a forward contract to purchase 500,000 CAD at a forward exchange rate of 0.87 USD/CAD in one year. What payment would Whole Foods Market be required to make when the shampoos shipment took place in 2007?

Solution

Even though the exchange rate rose to 1.05 USD/CAD in 2007, making the CAD more expensive, Whole Foods Market would obtain the 500,000 CAD using the forward contract at the forward exchange rate of 0.87 USD/CAD. Thus, Whole Foods Market must pay

$$500{,}000 \text{ CAD} \times 0.87 \text{ USD/CAD} = 435{,}500 \text{ USD in 2007}$$

Whole Foods Market would pay this amount to the bank in exchange for 500,000 CAD, which are then paid to Avalon.

This forward contract would have been a good deal for Whole Foods Market because without the hedge, it would have had to exchange USD for CAD at the prevailing rate of 1.05 USD/CAD, raising its cost to 525,000 USD. However, the exchange rate could have moved the other way. If the exchange rate had fallen to 0.75 USD/CAD, the forward contract still commits Whole Foods Market to pay 0.87 USD/CAD. In other words, the forward contract locks in the exchange rate and eliminates the risk—whether the movement of the exchange rate is favourable or unfavourable.

If the forward contract allows the importer to eliminate the risk of a stronger CAD, where does the risk go? At least initially, the risk passes to the bank that has written the forward contract. Because the bank agrees to exchange USD for CAD at a fixed rate, it will experience a loss if the CAD increases in value. In Example 30.6, the bank receives only 435,000 USD in the forward contract, but gives up CAD worth 525,000 USD.

Why is the bank willing to bear this risk? First, the bank is much larger and has more capital than a small importer, so it can bear the risk without being in jeopardy of financial distress. More importantly, in most settings the bank will not even hold the risk. Instead, the bank will find another party willing to trade CAD for USD (like Modern Bathrooms in Canada that needs to import from ThermaSol, its U.S. supplier). By entering into a second forward contract with offsetting risk, the bank can eliminate its own risk altogether.

The Use of Currency Forwards to Eliminate Exchange Rate Risk

In this example, the Canadian importer and the U.S. importer both hedge their exchange rate risk by using currency forward contracts at 0.87 USD/CAD (shown in red). By writing offsetting contracts, the bank bears no exchange rate risk and earns a fee from each transaction.

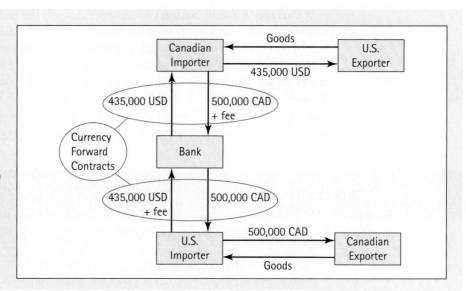

This situation is illustrated in Figure 30.4. A U.S. importer, who must pay for goods with CAD, purchases CAD from the bank through a forward contract with a forward exchange rate of 0.87 USD per CAD. This transaction locks in the U.S. importer's cost at 435,000 USD. Similarly, a Canadian importer, who must pay for goods in USD, uses a forward contract to sell the CAD to the bank, locking in the Canadian importer's cost at 500,000 CAD. The bank holds both forward contracts—the first to exchange USD for CAD and the second to exchange CAD for USD. The bank bears no exchange rate risk and earns fees from both the U.S. and Canadian importers. Most of the large Canadian banks offer services in both Canada and the U.S., so they are able to accommodate clients (such as these importers) in both countries.

CASH-AND-CARRY AND THE PRICING OF CURRENCY FORWARDS

An alternative method, the cash-and-carry strategy, also enables a firm to eliminate exchange rate risk. Because this strategy provides the same cash flows as the forward contract, we can use it to determine the forward exchange rate using the Law of One Price. Let's begin by considering the different ways investors can exchange foreign currency in the future for dollars in the future.

THE LAW OF ONE PRICE AND THE FORWARD EXCHANGE RATE.   Currency forward contracts allow investors to exchange a foreign currency in the future for dollars in the future at the forward exchange rate. We illustrate such an exchange in the **currency timeline** in Figure 30.5, which indicates time horizontally by dates (as in a standard timeline) and currencies vertically (CAD and USD). Thus "CAD in one year" corresponds to the lower-right point in the timeline and "USD in one year" corresponds to the upper-right point in the timeline. To convert cash flows between points, we must convert them at an appropriate rate. The forward exchange rate, indicated by $F_{USD/CAD}$, tells us the rate at which we can exchange CAD for USD in one year using a forward contract.

Figure 30.5 also illustrates other transactions that we can use to move between dates or currencies in the timeline. We can convert CAD to USD today at the current exchange rate, also referred to as the **spot exchange rate**, $S_{USD/CAD}$. By borrowing or

FIGURE 30.5

Currency Timeline Showing Forward Contract and Cash-and-Carry Strategy

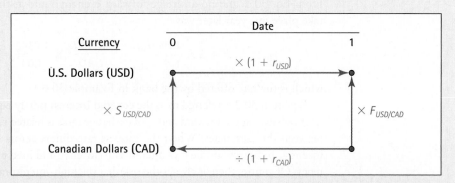

The cash-and-carry strategy (3 transactions in red) replicates the forward contract (in blue) by borrowing in one currency, converting to the other currency at the spot exchange rate, and investing in the new currency.

lending at the CAD interest rate r_{CAD}, we can exchange CAD today for CAD in one year. Finally, we can convert USD today for USD in one year at the USD interest rate r_{USD}, which is the rate at which banks will borrow or lend on USD-denominated accounts.

As Figure 30.5 shows, combining these other transactions provides an alternative way to convert CAD to USD in one year. The **cash-and-carry strategy** consists of the following three simultaneous trades:

1. Borrow CAD today using a one-year loan with the interest rate r_{CAD}.

2. Exchange the CAD for USD today at the spot exchange rate $S_{USD/CAD}$.

3. Invest the USD today for one year at the interest rate r_{USD}.

In one year's time, we will owe CAD (from the loan in transaction 1) and receive USD (from the investment in transaction 3). That is, we have converted CAD in one year to USD in one year, just as with the forward contract. This method is called a cash-and-carry strategy because we borrow cash that we then carry (invest) in the future.

Because the forward contract and the cash-and-carry strategy accomplish the same conversion, by the Law of One Price they must do so at the same rate. Combining the rates used in the cash-and-carry strategy leads to the following no-arbitrage formula for the forward exchange rate:

Covered Interest Parity

$$\underbrace{F}_{\substack{\text{USD in one year} \\ \text{CAD in one year}}} = \underbrace{S}_{\substack{\text{USD today} \\ \text{CAD today}}} \times \underbrace{\frac{1 + r_{USD}}{1 + r_{CAD}}}_{\substack{\text{USD in one year/USD today} \\ \text{CAD in one year/CAD today}}} \qquad (30.2)$$

Equation 30.2 expresses the forward exchange rate in terms of the spot exchange rate and the interest rates in each currency. Note that on both sides of the equation, the ultimate units are USD/CAD in one year.

Let's evaluate Eq. 30.2 for an example. Suppose in late 2006 the spot exchange rate was 0.85 USD/CAD, while one-year interest rates were 5.42% for USD and 3.00% for CAD.

From Eq. 30.2, the no-arbitrage forward exchange rate at that time for an exchange to take place one year later was

$$F = S \times \frac{1 + r_{USD}}{1 + r_{CAD}} = \frac{0.85\,USD}{CAD} \times \frac{1.0542}{1.03} = \frac{0.87\,USD}{CAD}$$

which is the rate offered by the bank in Example 30.6.

Equation 30.2 is referred to as the **covered interest parity equation**; it states that the difference between the forward and spot exchange rates is related to the interest rate differential between the currencies. When the interest rate differs across countries, investors have an incentive to borrow in the low-interest rate currency and invest in the high-interest rate currency. Of course, there is always the risk that the high-interest rate currency could depreciate while the investment is held. If you try to avoid this risk by locking in the future exchange rate using a forward contract, Eq. 30.2 implies that the forward exchange rate will exactly offset any benefit from the higher interest rate, eliminating any arbitrage opportunity.

EXAMPLE 30.7   COMPUTING THE NO-ARBITRAGE FORWARD EXCHANGE RATE

Problem

Suppose that in December 2012, the spot exchange rate for the Japanese yen is 116 JPY/USD. At the same time, the one-year interest rate in the United States is 4.85% and the one-year interest rate in Japan is 0.10%. Based on these rates, what one-year forward exchange rate is consistent with no arbitrage?

Solution

We can compute the forward exchange rate using Eq. 30.2. Because the exchange rate is in terms of JPY/USD, we need to ensure the interest rates are positioned properly in the formula:

$$F = S \times \frac{1 + r_{JPY}}{1 + r_{USD}} = \frac{116\,JPY}{USD} \times \frac{1.001}{1.0485} = \frac{110.7\,JPY}{USD}$$

This would be the forward rate observed in December 2012 for the currency exchange to occur in December 2013. (A useful rule to remember is that the ratio of interest rates must match the units of the exchange rate. Because the exchange rate is JPY/USD, we multiply with the JPY interest rate and divide with the USD interest rate. Of course, we could also solve the problem by converting all the rates to USD/JPY.) The forward exchange rate is lower than the spot exchange rate, offsetting the higher interest rate on dollar investments.

ADVANTAGES OF FORWARD CONTRACTS.   Why do firms use forward contracts rather than the cash-and-carry strategy? First, the forward contract is simpler, requiring one transaction rather than three, so it may have lower transaction fees. Second, many firms are not able to borrow easily in different currencies and may pay a higher interest rate if their credit quality is poor. Generally speaking, cash-and-carry strategies are used primarily by large banks, which can borrow easily and face low transaction costs. Banks use such a strategy to hedge their currency exposures that result from commitments to forward contracts.

EXAMPLE 30.8

USING THE CASH-AND-CARRY STRATEGY

Problem

Suppose it is now December 2012 and a Japanese bank enters into a forward contract with Japanese exporter Shimano, in which Shimano agrees to exchange 100 million USD for JPY in December 2013 at the forward exchange rate of 110.7 JPY/USD. If the current exchange rate is 116 JPY/USD, and one-year interest rates are 4.85% in the United States and 0.10% in Japan, how can the bank hedge its risk if it has no other clients interested in currency forward contracts?

Solution

The forward contract specifies that Shimano will pay 100 million USD to the bank in exchange for 100 million USD × 110.7 JPY/USD = 11.07 billion JPY. To hedge its risk, the bank may find another client or clients who would like to exchange yen for U.S. dollars. When no such clients can be found, the bank can still hedge its risk using a cash-and-carry strategy:

1. Borrow USD now at the USD interest rate of 4.85%. The bank can borrow 100 million USD/1.0485 = 95.37 million USD today and repay the loan using the cash received from Shimano.

2. Convert USD to JPY now at the spot exchange rate of 116 JPY/USD. The bank can convert the USD borrowed to 95.37 million USD × 116 JPY/USD = 11.06 billion JPY.

3. Invest the JPY now at the JPY interest rate of 0.10%. By depositing the JPY for one year, the bank will have 11.06 billion × 1.001 = 11.07 billion JPY in one year.

Through this combination of transactions, the bank can lock in its ability to convert U.S. dollars to yen at the rate agreed upon in the forward contract with Shimano.

Equation 30.2 easily generalizes to a forward contract longer than one year. Using the same logic, but investing or borrowing for T years rather than one year, the no-arbitrage forward rate for an exchange that will occur T years in the future is

$$F_T = S \times \frac{(1 + r_{USD})^T}{(1 + r_{CAD})^T} \tag{30.3}$$

where the spot and forward rates are in units of USD/CAD, and the interest rates are the current risk-free T-year rates from the yield curve for each currency.

HEDGING WITH OPTIONS

Currency options are another method that firms commonly use to manage exchange rate risk. Currency options, like the stock options introduced in Chapter 20, give the holder the right—but not the obligation—to exchange currency at a given exchange rate. Currency forward contracts allow firms to lock in a future exchange rate; currency options allow firms to insure themselves against the exchange rate moving beyond a certain level.

To demonstrate the difference between hedging with forward contracts and hedging with options, let's examine a specific situation. In June 2008, the one-year forward exchange rate was 1.00 CAD per USD. Instead of locking in this exchange rate using a forward contract, a firm that will need USD in one year can buy a call option on the

COST OF USD (CAD/USD) WHEN HEDGING WITH A CURRENCY OPTION WITH A STRIKE PRICE OF 1.00 CAD/USD AND AN INITIAL PREMIUM OF 0.05 CAD/USD

TABLE 30.2

Possible June 2009 Spot Exchange Rate	Exercise Option?	Exchange Rate Taken	+	Cost of Option	=	Total Cost
0.75 CAD/USD	No	0.75		0.05		0.80
0.90 CAD/USD	No	0.90		0.05		0.95
1.05 CAD/USD	Yes	1.00		0.05		1.05
1.20 CAD/USD	Yes	1.00		0.05		1.05

USD, giving it the right to buy USD at a maximum price.[16] Suppose a one-year European call option on the USD with a strike price of 1.00 CAD per USD trades for 0.05 CAD. That is, for a cost of 0.05 CAD, the firm can buy the right—but not the obligation—to purchase 1 USD for 1.00 CAD in one year's time. By doing so, the firm protects itself against a large increase in the value of the USD but still benefits if the USD declines.

Table 30.2 shows the outcome from hedging with a call option if the actual exchange rate in one year is one of the possible values listed in the first column. If the spot exchange rate is less than the 1.00 CAD per USD strike price of the option, then the firm will not exercise the option and will convert CAD to USD at the spot exchange rate. If the spot exchange rate is more than 1.00 CAD per USD, the firm will exercise the option and convert CAD to USD at the rate of 1.00 CAD per USD (see the second and third columns). We then add the initial cost of the option (fourth column) to determine the total dollar cost per USD paid by the firm (fifth column).[17]

We plot the data from Table 30.2 in Figure 30.6, where we compare hedging with options to the alternative of hedging with a forward contract or not hedging at all. If the firm does not hedge at all, its cost for USD is simply the spot exchange rate. If the firm hedges with a forward contract, it locks in the cost of USD at the forward exchange rate and the firm's cost is fixed. As Figure 30.6 shows, hedging with options represents a middle ground: The firm puts a *cap* on its potential cost, but will benefit if the USD depreciates in value.

OPTIONS VERSUS FORWARD CONTRACTS.   Why might a firm choose to hedge with options rather than forward contracts? Many managers want the firm to benefit if the exchange rate moves in their favour, rather than being stuck paying an above-market rate. Firms also prefer options to forward contracts if the transaction they are hedging might not take place. In this case, a forward could commit them to making an exchange at an unfavourable rate for currency they do not need, whereas an option allows them to walk away from the exchange.

---

16. Currency options can be purchased over the counter from a bank or on an exchange. The Montreal Exchange offers options on USD. The Philadelphia stock exchange is one exchange offering options between the USD and various currencies.

17. In computing the total cost, we have ignored the small amount of interest that could be earned on the option premium.

<table>
<tr><td>EXAMPLE 30.9</td><td>USING OPTIONS TO HEDGE A CONDITIONAL EXPOSURE</td></tr>
</table>

Problem

ICTV is a U.S. company that develops software for cable television networks. Executives at ICTV have just negotiated a 20 million British pound (GBP) deal with British cable operator Telewest. ICTV will receive the payment in six months' time, after ICTV demonstrates a prototype proving the viability of its technology. If Telewest is not satisfied with the technology, it can cancel the contract at that time and pay nothing. ICTV executives have two major concerns: (1) their engineers may not be able to meet Telewest's technology requirements and (2) even if the deal succeeds, the GBP may fall, reducing the USD value of the 20 million GBP payment.

Suppose the current exchange rate is 1.752 USD/GBP, the six-month forward exchange rate is 1.75 USD/GBP, and a six-month put option on the GBP with a strike price of 1.75 USD/GBP is trading for 0.05 USD/GBP. Compare ICTV's outcomes if it does not hedge, hedges using a forward contract, or hedges using the put option.

Solution

First, let's plot ICTV's revenue if it chooses not to hedge (the red lines in the plot):

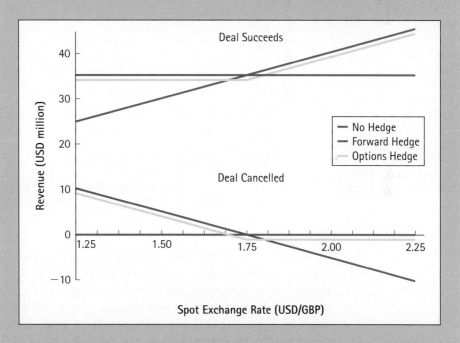

Suppose ICTV does not hedge and the British pound falls to 1.50 USD/GBP. Then ICTV's USD revenue from the deal will be only 20 million GBP × 1.50 USD/GBP = 30 million USD. However, if ICTV hedges the 20 million GBP payment using a forward contract, it will be guaranteed revenue of 20 million GBP × 1.75 USD/GBP = 35 million USD if the deal succeeds (the upper blue line). But if Telewest cancels the deal, ICTV will still be obligated by the forward contract to pay the bank 20 million GBP in exchange for 35 million USD. If the spot exchange rate rises to 2.00 USD/GBP, then the 20 million GBP will be worth 20 million GBP × 2.00 USD/GBP = 40 million USD, and ICTV will have a loss of 40 − 35 = 5 million USD on its forward contract (see the lower blue line).

Thus, if ICTV does not hedge or hedges with a forward contract, there are scenarios that lead to large losses. Now consider hedging with the put option. The upfront cost of the put option is 20 million GBP × 0.05 USD/GBP = 1 million USD, and the results of this hedge are plotted as the yellow curves. For example, if the deal succeeds and the GBP falls below 1.75 USD/GBP, ICTV can exercise the put and receive, net of the cost of the put,

$$20 \text{ million GBP} \times 1.75 \text{ USD/GBP} - 1 \text{ million USD} = 35 \text{ million USD} - 1 \text{ million USD}$$
$$= 34 \text{ million USD}$$

(We have ignored the small amount of interest on the cost of the put over six months.) If Telewest cancels the deal and the spot exchange rate rises, ICTV will lose the 1 million USD cost of the put. In either case, Telewest has limited its potential losses.

FIGURE 30.6

Comparison of Hedging the Exchange Rate Using a Forward Contract at 1.00 CAD/USD, an Option (Strike = 1.00 CAD/USD, Premium = 0.05 CAD/USD), or No Hedge

The forward hedge locks in an exchange rate and so eliminates all risk. Not hedging leaves the firm fully exposed. Hedging with an option allows the firm to benefit if the exchange rate falls and protects the firm from a very large increase.

CURRENCY OPTION PRICING.   In the preceding example, we assumed that ICTV could purchase a currency option at a price of 0.05 USD/GBP. But how do we determine the price of a currency option? Just as we determined the forward exchange rate by assessing banks' ability to replicate a forward contract using a cash-and-carry strategy, the prices of currency options are determined by identifying banks' ability to replicate them using dynamic trading strategies of the type introduced in Chapter 21 for stock options. In fact, we can apply the same pricing methodologies discussed in Chapter 21, such as the Black-Scholes formula or the binomial model, to currency options. In this case, the underlying asset is the currency, so we use the spot exchange rate in place of the stock price. The foreign interest rate you earn while holding the currency is analogous to the dividend yield for a stock. Recall that to price a European option on a dividend-paying stock, you simply replace the stock price, S, in the Black-Scholes formula with S^x, the current value of the stock excluding any dividends paid during the life of the option. In the case of a currency option, we can interpret the interest earned on the foreign currency as a dividend. For example, if the current spot exchange rate is S CAD per USD and the USD and CAD interest rates are r_{USD} and r_{CAD}, respectively, then from Eq. 21.11, $S^x = S/(1 + r_{USD})^T$, and the price of a European call option on the USD that expires in T years with a strike price of K CAD per USD is[18]

Price of a Call Option on a Currency

$$C = \frac{S}{(1 + r_{USD})^T} N(d_1) - \frac{K}{(1 + r_{CAD})^T} N(d_2) \tag{30.4}$$

where $N()$ is the normal distribution function and d_1 and d_2 are calculated using the fact that $S^x / PV(K) = F_T / K$ where F_T is the forward exchange rate from Eq. 30.3:

$$d_1 = \frac{\ln(F_T/K)}{\sigma\sqrt{T}} + \frac{\sigma\sqrt{T}}{2} \quad \text{and} \quad d_2 = d_1 - \sigma\sqrt{T} \tag{30.5}$$

We can also use option pricing techniques to estimate the implied volatility of the exchange rate.

EXAMPLE 30.10

IMPLIED VOLATILITY OF EXCHANGE RATES

Problem

Suppose the current exchange rate is 1.752 USD/GBP, the interest rate in the United States is 4.25%, the interest rate in the United Kingdom is 4.5%, and a six-month European call option on the British pound with a strike price of 1.75 USD/GBP trades for a price of 0.05 USD/GBP. Use the Black-Scholes formula to determine the implied volatility of the USD/GBP exchange rate.

Solution

We can use Eqs. 30.4 and 30.5 to compute the Black-Scholes price of a call option on the British pound. The inputs are $S =$ spot exchange rate $= 1.752$, $K = 1.75$, $T = 0.5$, $r_{USD} = 4.25\%$, and the U.K. interest rate $r_{GBP} = 4.5\%$. The forward exchange rate is $F_{0.5} = 1.752 \times (1.0425)^{1/2}/(1.045)^{1/2} = 1.75$. With a volatility of 10.3%, we have $d_1 = 0.036$ and $d_2 = 20.036$, with $N(d_1) = 0.514$ and $N(d_2) = 0.486$, and so the Black-Scholes value of the call is 0.048 USD/GBP. With a volatility of 10.4%, the Black-Scholes value is 0.051 USD/GBP. Thus the implied volatility of the USD/GBP exchange rate is between 10.3% and 10.4% per year.

CONCEPT CHECK

1. How can firms hedge exchange rate risk?

2. Why may a firm prefer to hedge exchange rate risk with options rather than forward contracts?

30.4 INTEREST RATE RISK

Firms that borrow must pay interest on their debt. An increase in interest rates raises firms' borrowing costs and can reduce their profitability. In addition, many firms have fixed long-term future liabilities, such as capital leases or pension fund liabilities. A decrease in interest

---

18. This formula for the price of a currency option was first derived by M. B. Garman and S. W. Kohlhagen, "Foreign-Currency Option Values," *Journal of International Money and Finance* 2 (1983): 231–237. Note, in the case where we are looking at an option on USD priced in CAD/USD, the spot and forward rates and Eq. 30.3 need to be stated as follows:

$$\underset{CAD/USD}{\underbrace{F_r}} = \underset{CAD/USD}{\underbrace{S}} \times \frac{(1 + r_{CAD})^T}{(1 + r_{USD})^T}$$

rates raises the present value of these liabilities and can lower the value of the firm. Thus, when interest rates are volatile, interest rate risk is a concern for many firms.

In this chapter, we have considered several methods that firms use to manage interest rate risk. Before firms can manage it, however, they must be able to measure it. Thus we begin by discussing the primary tool used to measure interest rate risk, duration. We will then see how firms can use *duration-hedging* to minimize their interest rate risk.

INTEREST RATE RISK MEASUREMENT: DURATION

In Chapter 8, we informally introduced the notion of a bond's duration as a measure of its sensitivity to interest rate changes. There we saw that the sensitivity of zero-coupon bonds to interest rates increases with their maturity. For example, for a ten-year, zero-coupon bond, an increase of one percentage point in the yield to maturity from 5% to 6% causes the bond price per $100 face value to fall from

$$\frac{100}{1.05^{10}} = \$61.39 \quad \text{to} \quad \frac{100}{1.06^{10}} = \$55.84$$

or a price change of $(55.84 - 61.39)/61.39 = -9.0\%$. The price of a five-year bond drops only 4.6% for the same yield change. The interest rate sensitivity of a *single* cash flow is roughly proportional to its maturity. The farther away the cash flow is, the larger the effect of interest rate changes on its present value.

Now consider a bond or portfolio with *multiple* cash flows. How will its value change if interest rates rise? As we saw in Chapter 11, the return of a portfolio is the value-weighted average of the returns of the elements of the portfolio. Because the interest rate sensitivity of a cash flow depends on its maturity, the interest rate sensitivity of a security with multiple cash flows depends on their value-weighted maturity. Thus, we formally define a security's duration as follows:[19]

Duration of a Security

$$\text{Duration} \equiv \sum_t \frac{PV(C_t)}{P} \times t \qquad (30.6)$$

where C_t is the cash flow on date t, $PV(C_t)$ is its present value (evaluated at the bond's yield), and $P = \sum_t PV(C_t)$ is the total present value of the cash flows, which is equal to the bond's current price. Therefore, the duration weights each maturity t by the percentage contribution of its cash flow to the total present value, $PV(C_t)/P$.

EXAMPLE 30.11	THE DURATION OF A COUPON BOND

Problem
What is the duration of a ten-year, zero-coupon bond? What is the duration of a ten-year bond with 10% annual coupons trading at par?

Solution
For a zero-coupon bond, there is only a single cash flow. Thus, in Eq. 30.6, $PV(C_{10}) = P$ and the duration is equal to the bond's maturity of ten years.

---

19. This measure is also called the *Macaulay duration*.

CASH FLOWS ($ MILLION) FOR A $100 MILLION FIXED-FOR-FLOATING INTEREST RATE SWAP

TABLE 30.6

Year	Six-Month LIBOR	Fixed Coupon	Floating-Rate Coupon	New Swap Cash Flow: Fixed–Floating
0.0	6.8%			0.0
0.5	7.2%	3.9	3.4	0.5
1.0	8.0%	3.9	3.6	0.3
1.5	7.4%	3.9	4.0	−0.1
2.0	7.8%	3.9	3.7	0.2
2.5	8.6%	3.9	3.9	0.0
3.0	9.0%	3.9	4.3	−0.4
3.5	9.2%	3.9	4.5	−0.6
4.0	8.4%	3.9	4.6	−0.7
4.5	7.6%	3.9	4.2	−0.3
5.0		3.9	3.8	0.1

contracts—is typically structured as a "zero-cost" security. The fixed rate of the swap contract is set based on current market conditions so that the swap is a fair deal (i.e., has an NPV of zero) for both sides.

COMBINING SWAPS WITH STANDARD LOANS. Corporations use interest rate swaps routinely to alter their exposure to interest rate fluctuations. The interest rate a firm pays on its loans can fluctuate for two reasons. First, the risk-free interest rate in the market may change. Second, the firm's credit quality, which determines the spread the firm must pay over the risk-free interest rate, can vary over time. By combining swaps with loans, firms can choose which of these sources of interest rate risk they will tolerate and which they will eliminate. Let's consider a typical example.

Alloy Cutting Corporation (ACC), a manufacturer of machine tools, is in the process of expanding its operations. It needs to borrow $10 million to fund this expansion. Currently, the six-month interest rate (LIBOR) is 4% and the ten-year interest rate is 6%—but these rates are for AA-rated firms. Given ACC's low current credit rating, the bank will charge the firm a spread of 1% above these rates.

ACC's managers are considering whether they should borrow on a short-term basis and then refinance the loan every six months or whether they should borrow using a long-term, ten-year loan. If they borrow for the short term, they worry that if interest rates rise substantially, the higher interest rates they will have to pay when they refinance the debt could lead to financial distress for ACC. They can avoid this risk if they borrow for the long term and lock in the interest rate for ten years. But long-term borrowing also has a downside. ACC's managers believe that their firm's credit rating will improve over the next few years as the expansion generates additional revenue. If they borrow using a ten-year loan, ACC will be stuck paying a spread based on its current credit quality.

TRADEOFFS OF LONG-TERM VERSUS SHORT-TERM BORROWING FOR ACC

TABLE 30.7

Strategy	Pro	Con
Borrow long term at $6\% + 1\% = 7\%$ fixed rate	Lock in current low interest rates at 6%	Lock in current high spread of 1% given low initial credit rating
Borrow short term at $\tilde{r}_t + \delta_t$	Get benefit of spread δ_t falling below 1% as credit rating improves	Risk of an increase in interest rates $\tilde{r}_t$ above 6%

Note: $\tilde{r}_t$ is the six-month interest rate (LIBOR) on date t. δ_t is the spread ACC must pay based on its credit rating on date t.

Table 30.7 highlights these tradeoffs. Borrowing long term has the advantage of locking in interest rates, but the disadvantage of not allowing ACC to get the benefit of its improving credit quality. Borrowing short term enables ACC to benefit as its credit quality improves, but it risks an increase in interest rates.

In this situation, ACC can use an interest rate swap to combine the best of both strategies. First, ACC can borrow the $10 million it needs for expansion using a short-term loan that is rolled over every six months. The interest rate on each loan will be $\tilde{r}_t + \delta_t$, where $\tilde{r}_t$ is the new (LIBOR) market rate and δ_t is the spread ACC must pay based on its credit rating at the time. Given ACC's belief that its credit quality will improve over time, δ_t should decline from its current 1% level.

Next, to eliminate the risk of an increase in the interest rate it will pay in the future, $\tilde{r}_t$, ACC can enter into a ten-year interest rate swap in which it agrees to pay a fixed rate of 6% per year in exchange for receiving the floating rate $\tilde{r}_t$.[25] Combining the cash flows from the swap with ACC's short-term borrowing, we can compute ACC's net borrowing cost as follows:

Short-Term Loan Rate	+	Fixed Rate Due on Swap	−	Floating Rate Received from Swap	=	Net Borrowing Cost
$\tilde{r}_t + \delta_t$	+	6%	−	$\tilde{r}_t$	=	$6\% + \delta_t$

That is, ACC will have an initial net borrowing cost of 7% (given its current credit spread of 1%), but this cost will decline in the future as its credit rating improves and the spread δ_t declines. At the same time, this strategy protects ACC from an increase in interest rates.

EXAMPLE 30.13

USING INTEREST RATE SWAPS

Problem

Bolt Industries is facing increased competition and wants to borrow $10 million in cash to protect against future revenue shortfalls. Currently, long-term AA rates are 10%. Bolt can borrow at 10.5% given its credit rating. The company is expecting interest rates to fall over

---

25. The fixed rate on the swap corresponds to the 10-year market rate for an AA-rated borrower. ACC would be able to get this rate on a swap, even though it is not AA-rated, because there is very little credit risk in a swap (because there is no exchange of the $10 million principal associated with a swap contract). As a result, swap rates are relatively independent of the user's credit quality.

the next few years, so it would prefer to borrow at short-term rates and refinance after rates drop. However, Bolt's management is afraid that its credit rating may deteriorate as competition intensifies, which may greatly increase the spread the firm must pay on a new loan. How can Bolt benefit from declining interest rates without worrying about changes in its credit rating?

Solution

Bolt can borrow at the long-term rate of 10.5% and then enter into a swap in which it *receives* a fixed rate of 10% and *pays* the short-term rate $\tilde{r}_t$. Its net borrowing cost will then be

Long-Term Loan Rate	+	Floating Rate Due on Swap	−	Fixed Rate Received from Swap	=	Net Borrowing Cost
10.5%	+	$\tilde{r}_t$	−	10%	=	$\tilde{r}_t + 0.5\%$

In this way, Bolt locks in its current credit spread of 0.5% but gets the benefit of lower rates as rates decline.

USING A SWAP TO CHANGE DURATION. Firms can also use interest rate swaps with duration-hedging strategies. The value of a swap, while initially zero, will fluctuate over time as interest rates change. When interest rates rise, the swap's value will fall for the party receiving the fixed rate; conversely, it will rise for the party paying the fixed rate.

For the party receiving the fixed rate, we can calculate the interest rate sensitivity of a swap by thinking of it as a portfolio that is long a long-term bond and short a short-term bond, each with a face value equal to the notional principal. Thus a ten-year, $10 million interest swap with a 6% fixed rate is equivalent to a portfolio that is long a ten-year, $10 million bond with a 6% coupon rate, and short a six-month, $10 million bond at the current short-term rate. Likewise, the party paying the fixed rate is short the ten-year bond and long a six-month bond.

A swap contract will therefore alter the duration of a portfolio according to the difference in the duration of the corresponding long-term and short-term bonds. We can apply Eq. 30.10 to compute the notional principal required to achieve a particular change in duration. Used in this way, swaps are a convenient way to alter the duration of a portfolio without buying or selling assets.

EXAMPLE 30.14   USING A SWAP TO IMMUNIZE A PORTFOLIO

Problem

How can Northland Bank use a swap to hedge its interest rate exposure rather than sell its mortgages?

Solution

Northland needs to reduce the duration of its $15 million in equity from 40.7 to 0. To compute the correct notional amount of the swap, we must first compute the duration of a current ten-year bond. Suppose the duration is 6.76. The duration of a six-month bond is 0.5. Then from Eq. 30.10,

$$N = \frac{40.7 \times 15}{(6.76 - 0.5)} = \$97.5 \text{ million}$$

Northland should enter into a swap with notional amount of $97.5 million. Because Northland would like to reduce the duration of its equity, it should enter into a swap of this size in which it *pays* fixed and receives floating, as this swap will increase in value if interest rates rise, **immunizing** its balance sheet.

CONCEPT CHECK

1. How do we calculate the duration of a portfolio?

2. How do firms manage interest rate risk?

SUMMARY

1. Insurance is a common method firms use to reduce risk. In a perfect market, the price of insurance is actuarially fair. An actuarially fair insurance premium is equal to the present value of the expected loss:

$$\frac{\Pr(\text{Loss}) \times E[\text{Payment in the Event of Loss}]}{1 + r_L} \tag{30.1}$$

2. Insurance for large risks that cannot be well diversified has a negative beta, which raises its cost.

3. The value of insurance comes from its ability to reduce the cost of market imperfections for the firm. Insurance may be beneficial to a firm because of its effects on bankruptcy and financial distress costs, issuance costs, taxes, debt capacity, and risk assessment.

4. The costs of insurance include administrative and overhead costs, adverse selection, and moral hazard.

5. Firms use several risk management strategies to hedge their exposure to commodity price movements.

    a. Firms can make real investments in assets with offsetting risk using such techniques as vertical integration and storage.

    b. Firms can enter into long-term contracts with suppliers or customers to achieve price stability.

    c. Firms can hedge risk by trading commodity futures contracts in financial markets.

6. Firms can manage exchange rate risk in financial markets using currency forward contracts to lock in an exchange rate in advance and currency options contracts to protect against an exchange rate moving beyond a certain level.

7. The cash-and-carry strategy is an alternative strategy that provides the same cash flows as the currency forward contract. By the Law of One Price, we determine the forward exchange rate by the cost-of-carry formula, called the covered interest parity equation. For an exchange that will take place in T years, the corresponding forward exchange rate is

$$F_T = S \times \frac{(1 + r_{USD})^T}{(1 + r_{CAD})^T} \quad \text{where } F_T \text{ and } S \text{ are quoted as USD/CAD} \tag{30.3}$$

8. Currency options allow firms to insure themselves against the exchange rate moving beyond a certain level. A firm may choose to use options rather than forward contracts if
   a. It would like to benefit from favourable exchange rate movements but not be obligated to make an exchange at unfavourable rates.
   b. There is some chance that the transaction it is hedging will not take place.

9. Currency options can be priced using the Black-Scholes formula, with the foreign interest rate as a dividend yield:

$$C = \frac{S}{(1 + r_{USD})^T} N(d_1) - \frac{K}{(1 + r_{CAD})^T} N(d_2) \tag{30.4}$$

where

$$d_1 = \frac{\ln(F_T/K)}{\sigma\sqrt{T}} + \frac{\sigma\sqrt{T}}{2} \quad \text{and} \quad d_2 = d_1 - \sigma\sqrt{T} \tag{30.5}$$

10. Firms face interest rate risk when exchange rates are volatile. The primary tool they use to measure interest rate risk is duration. Duration measures the value-weighted maturity of an asset.

$$\text{Duration} \equiv \sum_t \frac{PV(C_t)}{P} \times t \tag{30.6}$$

11. The interest rate sensitivity of a stream of cash flows increases with its duration. For a small change ε in the interest rate, the change in the present value of a stream of cash flows is given by

$$\text{Percent Change in Value} \approx -\text{Duration} \times \frac{\varepsilon}{1 + r/k} \tag{30.7}$$

where r is the current interest rate, expressed as an APR with k compounding periods per year.

12. The duration of a portfolio is equal to the value-weighted average duration of each security in the portfolio. The duration of a firm's equity is determined from the duration of its assets and liabilities:

$$D_E = D_{A-L} = \frac{A}{A - L} D_A - \frac{L}{A - L} D_L \tag{30.9}$$

13. Firms manage interest rate risk by buying or selling assets to make their equity duration neutral.

14. Interest rate swaps allow firms to separate the risk of interest rate changes from the risk of fluctuations in the firm's credit quality.
    a. By borrowing long term and entering into an interest rate swap in which the firm receives a fixed coupon and pays a floating-rate coupon, the firm will pay a floating interest rate plus a spread that is fixed based on its initial credit quality.
    b. By borrowing short term and entering into an interest rate swap in which the firm receives a floating-rate coupon and pays a fixed coupon, the firm will pay a fixed interest rate plus a spread that will float with its credit quality.

15. Firms use interest rate swaps to modify their interest rate risk exposure without buying or selling assets.

KEY TERMS

PROBLEMS

The problems marked in green can be found on MyFinanceLab at www.myfinancelab.com Visit your MyFinanceLab for additional practice. Additional readings for this chapter may be found in the Textbook Resources section on MyFinanceLab.

Insurance

1. The William Companies (WMB) owns and operates natural gas pipelines that deliver 12% of the natural gas consumed in the United States. WMB is concerned that a major hurricane could disrupt its Gulfstream pipeline, which runs 691 miles through the Gulf of Mexico. In the event of a disruption, the firm anticipates a loss of profits of $65 million. Suppose the likelihood of a disruption is 3% per year, and the beta associated with such a loss is −0.25. If the risk-free interest rate is 5% and the expected return of the market is 10%, what is the actuarially fair insurance premium?

2. Genentech's main facility is located in South San Francisco. Suppose that Genentech would experience a direct loss of $450 million in the event of a major earthquake that disrupted its operations. The chance of such an earthquake is 2% per year, with a beta of −0.5.

    a. If the risk-free interest rate is 5% and the expected return of the market is 10%, what is the actuarially fair insurance premium required to cover Genentech's loss?

    b. Suppose the insurance company raises the premium by an additional 15% over the amount calculated in part a to cover its administrative and overhead costs. What amount of financial distress or issuance costs would Genentech have to suffer if it were not insured to justify purchasing the insurance?

3. Your firm imports manufactured goods from China. You are worried that Canada–China trade negotiations could break down next year, leading to a moratorium on imports. In the event of a moratorium, your firm expects its operating profits to decline substantially and its marginal tax rate to fall from its current level of 40% to 10%.

    An insurance firm has agreed to write a trade insurance policy that will pay $500,000 in the event of an import moratorium. The chance of a moratorium is estimated to be 10%, with a beta of −1.5. Suppose the risk-free interest rate is 5% and the expected return of the market is 10%.

    a. What is the actuarially fair premium for this insurance?

    b. What is the NPV of purchasing this insurance for your firm? What is the source of this gain?

4. Your firm faces a 9% chance of a potential loss of $10 million next year. If your firm implements new policies, it can reduce the chance of this loss to 4%, but these new policies have an upfront cost of $100,000. Suppose the beta of the loss is 0 and the risk-free interest rate is 5%.

    a. If the firm is uninsured, what is the NPV of implementing the new policies?

    b. If the firm is fully insured, what is the NPV of implementing the new policies?

c. Given your answer to part b, what is the actuarially fair cost of full insurance?

d. What is the minimum-size deductible that would leave your firm with an incentive to implement the new policies?

e. What is the actuarially fair price of an insurance policy with the deductible in part d?

Commodity Price Risk

5. BHP Billiton is the world's largest mining firm. BHP expects to produce 2 billion pounds of copper next year, with a production cost of $0.90 per pound.

a. What will be BHP's operating profit from copper next year if the price of copper is $1.25, $1.50, or $1.75 per pound, and the firm plans to sell all of its copper next year at the going price?

b. What will be BHP's operating profit from copper next year if the firm enters into a contract to supply copper to end users at an average price of $1.45 per pound?

c. What will be BHP's operating profit from copper next year if copper prices are described as in part a, and the firm enters into supply contracts as in part b for only 50% of its total output?

d. Describe situations for which each of the strategies a, b, and c might be optimal.

EXCEL

6. Your utility company will need to buy 100,000 barrels of oil in ten days' time, and it is worried about fuel costs. Suppose you go long 100 oil futures contracts, each for 1000 barrels of oil, at the current futures price of $130 per barrel. Suppose futures prices change each day as follows:

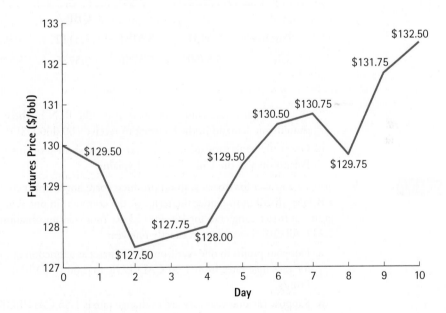

a. What is the mark-to-market profit or loss (in dollars) that you will have on each date?

b. What is your total profit or loss after ten days? Have you been protected against a rise in oil prices?

c. What is the largest cumulative loss you will experience over the ten-day period? In what case might this be a problem?

7. Suppose Starbucks consumes 100 million pounds of coffee beans per year. As the price of coffee rises, Starbucks expects to pass along 60% of the cost to its customers through higher prices

per cup of coffee. To hedge its profits from fluctuations in coffee prices, Starbucks should lock in the price of how many pounds of coffee beans using supply contracts?

Exchange Rate Risk

EXCEL   8.   Your start-up company has negotiated a contract to provide a database installation for a manufacturing company in Poland. That firm has agreed to pay you $100,000 in three months' time when the installation will occur. However, it insists on paying in Polish zloty (PLN). You don't want to lose the deal (the company is your first client!), but are worried about the exchange rate risk. In particular, you are worried the zloty could depreciate relative to the dollar. You contact Fortis Bank in Poland to see if you can lock in an exchange rate for the zloty in advance.

a. You find the following table posted on the bank's Web site, showing PLN per USD, per EUR, and per GBP:

	1 Week	2 Weeks	1 Month	2 Months	3 Months
USD					
Purchase	3.1433	3.1429	3.1419	3.1390	3.1361
Sale	3.1764	3.1761	3.1755	3.1735	3.1712
EUR					
Purchase	3.7804	3.7814	3.7836	3.7871	3.7906
Sale	3.8214	3.8226	3.8254	3.8298	3.8342
GBP					
Purchase	5.5131	5.5131	5.5112	5.5078	5.5048
Sale	5.5750	5.5750	5.5735	5.5705	5.5681

What exchange rate could you lock in for the PLN in three months? How many PLN should you demand in the contract to receive 100,000 USD?

b. Given the bank forward rates in part a, were short-term interest rates higher or lower in Poland than in the United States? Explain.

EXCEL   9.   You are a broker for frozen seafood products for Choyce Products. You just signed a deal with a Belgian distributor. Under the terms of the contract, in one year you will deliver 4000 kilograms of frozen king crab for 100,000 EUR. Your cost for obtaining the king crab is 110,000 CAD. All cash flows occur in exactly one year.

a. Plot your profits in one year from the contract as a function of the exchange rate in one year, for exchange rates from 1.00 CAD/EUR to 2.00 CAD/EUR. Label this line "Unhedged Profits."

b. Suppose the one-year forward exchange rate is 1.55 CAD/EUR. Suppose you enter into a forward contract to sell the euros you will receive at this rate. In the figure from part a, plot your combined profits from the crab contract and the forward contract as a function of the exchange rate in one year. Label this line "Forward Hedge."

c. Suppose that instead of using a forward contract, you consider using options. A one-year call option to buy EUR at a strike price of 1.55 CAD/EUR is trading for 0.10 CAD/EUR. Similarly, a one-year put option to sell euros at a strike price of 1.55 CAD/EUR is trading for 0.10 CAD/EUR. To hedge the risk of your profits, should you buy or sell the call or the put?

d. In the figure from parts a and b, plot your "all in" profits using the option hedge (combined profits of crab contract, option contract, and option price) as a function of the exchange rate in one year. Label this line "Option Hedge." (*Note:* You can ignore the effect of interest on the option price.)

e. Suppose that by the end of the year, a trade war erupts, leading to a European embargo on Canadian food products. As a result, your deal is cancelled, and you don't receive the euros or incur the costs of procuring the crab. However, you still have the profits (or losses) associated with your forward or options contract. In a new figure, plot the profits associated with the forward hedge and the options hedge (labelling each line). When there is a risk of cancellation, which type of hedge has the least downside risk? Explain briefly.

10. Suppose the current exchange rate is 1.80 USD/GBP, the interest rate in the United States is 5.25%, the interest rate in Great Britain is 4.0%, and the volatility of the USD/GBP exchange rate is 10%. Use the Black-Scholes formula to determine the price of a six-month European call option on the GBP with a strike price of 1.80 USD/GBP.

Interest Rate Risk

11. Assume each of the following securities has the same yield-to-maturity: a five-year, zero-coupon bond; a nine-year, zero-coupon bond; a five-year annuity; and a nine-year annuity. Rank these securities from lowest to highest duration.

12. You have been hired as a risk manager for Northland Bank. Currently, Northland's balance sheet is as follows (in millions of dollars):

Assets		Liabilities	
Cash Reserves	50	Chequing and Savings	80
Auto Loans	100	Guaranteed Investment Certificates	100
Mortgages	150	Long-Term Financing	100
Total Assets	300	Total Liabilities	280
		Owners' Equity	20
		Total Liabilities and Equity	300

When you analyze the duration of loans, you find that the duration of the auto loans is two years, while the mortgages have a duration of seven years. Both the cash reserves and the chequing and savings accounts have a zero duration. The GICs have a duration of two years and the long-term financing has a ten-year duration.

a. What is the duration of Northland's equity?

b. Suppose Northland experiences a rash of mortgage prepayments, reducing the size of the mortgage portfolio from $150 million to $100 million, and increasing cash reserves to $100 million. What is the duration of Northland's equity now? If interest rates are currently 4% but fall to 3%, estimate the approximate change in the value of Northland's equity.

c. Suppose that after the prepayments in b, but before a change in interest rates, Northland considers managing its risk by selling mortgages and/or buying ten-year Government of Canada STRIPs (zero coupon bonds). How many should the firm buy or sell to eliminate its current interest rate risk?

13. The Citrix Fund has invested in a portfolio of government bonds that has a current market value of $44.8 million. The duration of this portfolio of bonds is 13.5 years. The fund has borrowed to purchase these bonds, and the current value of its liabilities (i.e., the current value of the bonds it has issued) is $39.2 million. The duration of these liabilities is 4 years. The equity in the Citrix Fund (or its net worth) is obviously $5.6 million. The market-value balance sheet below summarizes this information:

Assets		Liabilities (Debt) and Equity	
Portfolio of Government Bonds (duration = 13.5)	$44,800,000	Short- and Long-Term Debt (duration = 4.0)	$39,200,000
		Equity	$5,600,000
Total	$44,800,000	Total	$44,800,000

Assume that the current yield curve is flat at 5.5%. You have been hired by the board of directors to evaluate the risk of this fund.

a. Consider the effect of a surprise increase in interest rates, such that the yields rise by 50 basis points (i.e., the yield curve is now flat at 6%). What would happen to the value of the assets in the Citrix Fund? What would happen to the value of the liabilities? What can you conclude about the change in the value of the equity under these conditions?

b. What is the initial duration of the Citrix Fund (i.e., the duration of the equity)?

c. As a result of your analysis, the board of directors fires the current manager of the fund. You are hired and given the objective of minimizing the fund's exposure to interest rate fluctuations. You are instructed to do so by liquidating a portion of the fund's assets and reinvesting the proceeds in short-term Treasury Bills and notes with an average duration of two years. How many dollars do you need to liquidate and reinvest to minimize the fund's interest rate sensitivity?

d. Rather than immunizing the fund using the strategy in part c, you consider using a swap contract. If the duration of a ten-year, fixed-coupon bond is seven years, what is the notational amount of the swap you should enter into? Should you receive or pay the fixed rate portion of the swap?

14. Your firm needs to raise $100 million in funds. You can borrow short term at a spread of 1.00% over LIBOR. Alternatively, you can issue ten-year, fixed-rate bonds at a spread of 2.50% over ten-year Government of Canada bonds, which currently yield 7.60%. Current ten-year interest rate swaps are quoted at LIBOR versus the 8.00% fixed rate.

Management believes that the firm is currently "under-rated" and that its credit rating is likely to improve in the next year or two. Nevertheless, the managers are not comfortable with the interest rate risk associated with using short-term debt.

a. Suggest a strategy for borrowing the $100 million. What is your effective borrowing rate?

b. Suppose the firm's credit rating does improve three years later. It can now borrow at a spread of 0.50% over Government of Canada bonds, which now yield 9.10% for a seven-year maturity. Also, seven-year interest rate swaps are quoted at LIBOR versus 9.50%. How would you lock in your new credit quality for the next seven years? What is your effective borrowing rate now?

CHAPTER
31

NOTATION

C_{FOC}	foreign currency cash flow
S	spot exchange rate
F	forward exchange rate
r^*_{HOC}	home currency cost of capital
r_{HOC}	home currency risk-free interest rate
r^*_{FOC}	foreign currency cost of capital
r_{FOC}	foreign currency risk-free interest rate
r_{wacc}	weighted average cost of capital
D	market value of debt
E	market value of equity
r_E	required return on equity
r_D	required return on debt
τ_C	corporate tax rate

International Corporate Finance

In the 1990s, Starbucks Coffee Company identified Japan as a potentially lucrative new market for its coffee products and decided to invest as much as $10 million in fiscal year 1996 to begin operations there. Because Starbucks realized it needed specialized knowledge of the Japanese market, it established a joint venture with Sazaby Inc., a Japanese retailer and restaurateur. This venture, called Starbucks Coffee Japan Ltd., intended to open as many as 12 stores in this initial phase. Although stores opened more slowly than expected, the venture had more than 200 stores and sales of 29 billion JPY (252 million USD) by 2001, and it opened its 500th store in November 2003.[1] To finance this growth, Starbucks Coffee Japan Ltd. used the Japanese capital markets. It held an initial public offering of shares on the Osaka Stock Exchange in October 2001 with a market capitalization of 90.88 billion JPY (756 million USD), raising 18.8 billion JPY (156 million USD) in additional capital for expansion. How did Starbucks' managers decide to undertake this investment opportunity? Why did they decide to use the Japanese domestic market to finance it rather than the home markets in the U.S.?

This chapter focuses on some of the factors a firm faces when making a foreign investment that it does not face when making a domestic investment. There are

---

1. Recall from Chapter 30 that we will use a three-digit currency code to indicate a country's currency: JPY = Japanese yen, USD = U.S. dollar. Using the currency codes avoids the confusion caused by the fact that many countries use the same symbol for their currency (e.g., $ is used in Canada, the U.S., and several other countries). For a list of countries, their three-digit currency codes, and their symbols, see the Web site maintained by Professor Werner Antweiler at the University of British Columbia's Sauder School of Business: http://fx.sauder.ubc.ca/currencies.html.

three key issues that arise when considering an investment in a foreign project like Starbucks Coffee Japan Ltd.:

- The project will most likely generate foreign currency cash flows, although the firm cares about the home currency value of the project.

- Interest rates and costs of capital will likely be different in the foreign country as a result of the macroeconomic environment.

- The firm will probably face a different tax rate in the foreign country and will be subject to both foreign and domestic tax laws.

As a first step toward evaluating foreign projects, this chapter discusses international capital markets. We begin by examining internationally integrated capital markets, which provide a useful benchmark for comparing different methods of valuing a foreign project. We next explain how to value a foreign project and address the three key issues mentioned previously. We then value foreign currency cash flows using two valuation methodologies and consider the implications of foreign and domestic tax codes. Finally, we explore the implications of internationally segmented capital markets.

31.1 INTERNATIONALLY INTEGRATED CAPITAL MARKETS

We begin our examination of valuing foreign projects by developing a conceptual benchmark based on the integration of capital markets across currencies and borders. In this framework, capital markets are internationally integrated when the value of a foreign investment does not depend on the currency (home or foreign) we use in the analysis.

Consider a risky foreign asset that is expected to pay the cash flow, C_{FOC}, in one period.[2] In a normal market, the price of this asset in a foreign market is the present value of this cash flow using the cost of capital of an investor local to that market:

$$PV_{FOC} = \frac{C_{FOC}}{(1 + r^*_{FOC})} \tag{31.1}$$

A Canadian investor who wants to purchase this asset in Canadian dollars (CAD) will have to pay

$$PV_{CAD} = S \times \frac{C_{FOC}}{(1 + r^*_{FOC})} \tag{31.2}$$

where S is the current spot exchange rate in CAD per FOC (foreign currency). Now any Canadian investor who actually purchased this security would have to convert the future cash flow into CAD so the payoff to such an investor is the CAD cash flow it produces. To value this cash flow, assume that the Canadian investor contracts today to convert the *expected* cash flow in one period at the forward rate, F, quoted as CAD per FOC. If we assume that spot exchange rates and the foreign currency cash flows of the security are

---

2. We will use FOC as the hypothetical code for the foreign currency.

uncorrelated, then this Canadian investor's expected CAD cash flow is $F \times C_{FOC}$.[3] If r^*_{CAD} is the appropriate cost of capital from the standpoint of a Canadian investor, the present value of this expected cash flow is

$$PV_{CAD} = \frac{F \times C_{FOC}}{(1 + r^*_{CAD})} \tag{31.3}$$

By the Law of One Price, this value must be equal to what the Canadian investor paid for the security:

$$S \times \frac{C_{FOC}}{(1 + r^*_{FOC})} = \frac{F \times C_{FOC}}{(1 + r^*_{CAD})}$$

Rearranging terms gives

$$\underset{CAD/FOC}{\underline{F}} = \frac{(1 + r^*_{CAD})}{(1 + r^*_{FOC})} \times \underset{CAD/FOC}{\underline{S}} \tag{31.4}$$

This condition ought to look familiar from Chapter 30, because Eq. 31.4 is simply covered interest parity, here derived for risky cash flows rather than riskless cash flows.

At this point, it is worth taking a step back and considering the assumptions specific to the international context that we needed to derive Eq. 31.4. Recall from Chapter 3 that in a normal market, prices are competitive. In this context, this concept means, among other things, that any investor can exchange either currency in any amount at the spot rate or forward rates and is free to purchase or sell any security in any amount in either country at their current market prices. Under these conditions, which we term **internationally integrated capital markets**, the value of an investment does not depend on the currency we use in the analysis.

EXAMPLE 31.1	**PRESENT VALUES AND INTERNATIONALLY INTEGRATED CAPITAL MARKETS**

Problem

You are a Canadian who is trying to calculate the present value of a 10 million JPY cash flow that will occur one year in the future. You know that the spot exchange rate is $S = 110$ JPY/CAD and the one-year forward rate is $F = 105.8095$ JPY/CAD. You also know that the appropriate CAD cost of capital for this cash flow is $r^*_{CAD} = 5\%$ and that the appropriate JPY cost of capital for this cash flow is $r^*_{JPY} = 1\%$. What is the present value of the 10 million JPY cash flow from the standpoint of a Japanese investor, and what is the CAD equivalent of this amount? What is the present value of the 10 million JPY cash flow from the standpoint of a Canadian investor who first converts the 10 million JPY into CAD and then applies the CAD discount rate?

---

3. The actual cash flow in foreign currency will be $C_{FOC} + \varepsilon$, where ε is the uncertainty in the cash flow and has an expected value of zero. In CAD terms, this cash flow is $F \times C_{FOC} + S_1 \times \varepsilon$ because the forward contract is only for the amount C_{FOC}; the rest must be converted at the prevailing spot rate in one period, S_1. Taking expectations, $E[S_1 \times \varepsilon] = E[S_1] \times E[\varepsilon] = 0$ because spot rates are uncorrelated with the project cash flows and $E[\varepsilon] = 0$.

> Solution
>
> The present value of the JPY cash flow is 10,000,000 JPY/(1.01) = 9,900,990 JPY, and the CAD equivalent is 9,900,990/110 = 90,009 CAD. (Note that we adjusted the formula in Eq. 31.2 because the exchange rate is expressed as JPY per CAD rather than CAD per JPY.) The present value from the standpoint of a Canadian investor who first converts the 10 million JPY into CAD using the forward rate and then applies the CAD cost of capital is (10,000,000 JPY/105.8095)/1.05 = 90,009 CAD. (Again, we have adjusted the formula in Eq. 31.3 because the exchange rate is expressed as JPY per CAD.) Because the Canadian and Japanese capital markets are internationally integrated, both methods produce the same result.

CONCEPT CHECK

1. What assumptions are needed to have internationally integrated capital markets?

2. What implication does internationally integrated capital markets have for the value of the same asset in different countries?

31.2   VALUATION OF FOREIGN CURRENCY CASH FLOWS

The most obvious difference between a domestic project and a foreign project is that the foreign project will most likely generate cash flows in a foreign currency. If the foreign project is owned by a domestic corporation, managers and shareholders need to determine the home currency value of the foreign currency cash flows.

In an internationally integrated capital market, two equivalent methods are available for calculating the NPV of a foreign project: Either we can calculate the NPV in the foreign country and convert it to the local currency at the spot rate, or we can convert the cash flows of the foreign project into the local currency and then calculate the NPV of these cash flows. The first method is essentially what we have done throughout this book (calculating the NPV of a project in a single currency) with the added step at the end of converting the NPV into the local currency using spot rates. Because this method should be familiar to you at this stage, we will instead concentrate on the second method.

WACC VALUATION METHOD IN DOMESTIC CURRENCY

The second valuation method requires converting the expected dollar value of the foreign currency cash flows and then proceeding to value the project as if it were a domestic project.

APPLICATION: ITYESI INC.   Ityesi Inc., a manufacturer of custom packaging products headquartered in Canada, wants to apply the weighted average cost of capital (WACC) technique to value a project in the United Kingdom. Ityesi is considering introducing a new line of packaging in the United Kingdom that will be its first foreign project. The project will be completely self-contained in the United Kingdom, such that all revenues are generated and all costs are incurred there.

Engineers expect the technology used in the new products to be obsolete after four years. The marketing group expects annual sales of 37.5 million GBP per year for this product line. Manufacturing costs and operating expenses are expected to total 15.625 million GBP and 5.625 million GBP per year, respectively. Developing the product will require an upfront investment of 15 million GBP in capital equipment that will be obsolete in four years and an initial marketing expense of 4.167 million GBP. Ityesi pays a corporate tax rate of 40% no matter in which country it manufactures its products. The expected GBP free cash flows of the proposed project are projected in the spreadsheet in Table 31.1.

Ityesi's managers have determined that there is no correlation between the uncertainty in these cash flows and the uncertainty in the spot CAD/GBP exchange rate. As we

EXPECTED FOREIGN FREE CASH FLOWS FROM ITYESI'S U.K. PROJECT

TABLE 31.1

SPREADSHEET

Year	0	1	2	3	4
Incremental Earnings Forecast (million GBP)					
1 Sales	—	37.500	37.500	37.500	37.500
2 Cost of Goods Sold	—	(15.625)	(15.625)	(15.625)	(15.625)
3 Gross Profit	—	21.875	21.875	21.875	21.875
4 Operating Expenses	(4.167)	(5.625)	(5.625)	(5.625)	(5.625)
5 Depreciation	—	(3.750)	(3.750)	(3.750)	(3.750)
6 EBIT	(4.167)	12.500	12.500	12.500	12.500
7 Income Tax at 40%	1.667	(5.000)	(5.000)	(5.000)	(5.000)
8 Unlevered Net Income	(2.500)	7.500	7.500	7.500	7.500
Free Cash Flow					
9 Plus: Depreciation	—	3.750	3.750	3.750	3.750
10 Less: Capital Expenditures	(15.000)	—	—	—	—
11 Less: Increases in NWC	—	—	—	—	—
12 Pound Free Cash Flow	(17.500)	11.250	11.250	11.250	11.250

explained in the last section, under this condition, the expected value of the future cash flows in CAD is the expected value in GBP multiplied by the forward exchange rate. Obtaining forward rate quotes for as long as four years in the future is difficult, so Ityesi's managers have decided to use the covered interest rate parity formula (Eq. 30.3, in Chapter 30) to compute the forward rates.

FORWARD EXCHANGE RATES.   The current spot exchange rate, S, is 2.00 CAD/GBP. Suppose that the yield curve in both countries is flat: The risk-free rate on CAD, r_{CAD}, is 4%, and the risk-free interest rate on pounds, r_{GBP}, is 7%. Using the covered interest parity condition for a multiyear forward exchange rate (Eq. 30.3):

$$F_1 = S \times \frac{(1 + r_{CAD})}{(1 + r_{GBP})} = (2.00 \ CAD/GBP)\frac{(1.04)}{(1.07)} = 1.9439 \ CAD/GBP$$

$$F_2 = S \times \frac{(1 + r_{CAD})^2}{(1 + r_{GBP})^2} = (2.00 \ CAD/GBP)\frac{(1.04)^2}{(1.07)^2} = 1.8894 \ CAD/GBP$$

$$F_2 = S \times \frac{(1 + r_{CAD})^3}{(1 + r_{GBP})^3} = (2.00 \ CAD/GBP)\frac{(1.04)^3}{(1.07)^3} = 1.8364 \ CAD/GBP$$

$$F_4 = S \times \frac{(1 + r_{CAD})^4}{(1 + r_{GBP})^4} = (2.00 \ CAD/GBP)\frac{(1.04)^4}{(1.07)^4} = 1.7850 \ CAD/GBP$$

FREE CASH FLOW CONVERSION.   Using these forward exchange rates, we can now calculate the expected free cash flows in CAD by multiplying the expected cash flows in GBP by the forward exchange rate, as shown in the spreadsheet in Table 31.2.

EXPECTED CAD FREE CASH FLOWS FROM ITYESI'S U.K. PROJECT

TABLE 31.2

SPREADSHEET

	0	1	2	3	4
CAD Free Cash Flow (million CAD)					
1 GBP Free Cash Flow (million GBP)	(17.500)	11.250	11.250	11.250	11.250
2 Forward Exchange Rate (CAD/GBP)	2.0000	1.9439	1.8894	1.8364	1.7850
3 CAD Value of GBP Free Cash Flow	(35.000)	21.869	21.256	20.660	20.081

THE VALUE OF ITYESI'S FOREIGN PROJECT WITH WACC.   With the cash flows of the U.K. project now expressed in CAD, we can value the foreign project as if it were a domestic CAD project. We proceed, as we did in Chapter 18, under the assumption that the market risk of the U.K. project is similar to that of the company as a whole; as a consequence, we can use Ityesi's costs of equity and debt in Canada to calculate the WACC.[4]

Ityesi has built up 20 million CAD in cash for investment needs and has debt of 320 million CAD, so its net debt is $D = 320 - 20 = 300$ million CAD. This amount is equal to the market value of its equity, implying a (net) debt-equity ratio of 1. Ityesi intends to maintain a similar (net) debt-equity ratio for the foreseeable future. The WACC thus assigns equal weights to equity and debt (Table 31.3).

ITYESI'S CURRENT MARKET VALUE BALANCE SHEET (MILLION CAD) AND COST OF CAPITAL WITHOUT THE U.K. PROJECT

TABLE 31.3

Assets		Liabilities		Cost of Capital	
Cash	20	Debt	320	Debt	6%
Existing Assets	600	Equity	300	Equity	10%
	620		620		

With Ityesi's cost of equity at 10% and its cost of debt at 6%, we calculate Ityesi's WACC as follows:

$$r_{wacc} = \frac{E}{E + D}r_E + \frac{D}{E + D}r_D(1 - \tau_C)$$
$$= (0.5)(10.0\%) + (0.5)(6.0\%)(1 - 40\%) = 6.8\%$$

We can now determine the value of the foreign project, including the tax shield from debt, by calculating the present value of the future free cash flows using the WACC:

$$\frac{21.869}{1.068} + \frac{21.256}{1.068^2} + \frac{20.660}{1.068^3} + \frac{20.081}{1.068^4} = 71.506 \text{ million CAD}$$

Because the upfront cost of launching the product line in dollars is only 35 million CAD, the net present value is $71.506 - 35 = 36.506$ million CAD. Thus Ityesi should undertake the U.K. project.

USING THE LAW OF ONE PRICE AS A ROBUSTNESS CHECK

To arrive at the NPV of Ityesi's project required making a number of assumptions—for example, that international markets are integrated, and that the exchange rate and the cash flows of the project are uncorrelated. The managers of Ityesi will naturally worry about whether these assumptions are justified. Luckily, there is a way to check the analysis.

Recall that there are two ways to compute the NPV of the foreign project. Ityesi could just have easily computed the foreign NPV by discounting the foreign cash flows at the

---

4. The risk of the foreign project is unlikely to be *exactly* the same as the risk of domestic projects (or the firm as a whole), because the foreign project contains residual exchange rate risk that the domestic projects often do not contain. In Ityesi's case, managers have determined that the additional risk premium for this risk is small, so for practical purposes they have chosen to ignore it and just use the domestic cost of capital.

foreign cost of capital and converting this result to a domestic NPV using the spot rate. Except for the last step, this method requires doing the same calculation we have performed throughout this book, that is, calculate the NPV of a (domestic) project. Determining the NPV requires knowing the cost of capital, in this case, the cost of capital for an investment in the United Kingdom. Recall that to estimate this cost of capital we use return data for publicly traded single-product companies—in this case, U.K. firms. For this method to provide the same answer as the alternative method, the estimate for the foreign cost of capital, r^*_{GBP}, must satisfy the Law of One Price, which from Eq. 31.4 implies:

$$(1 + r^*_{GBP}) = \frac{S}{F}(1 + r^*_{CAD}) \tag{31.5}$$

If it does not, then Ityesi's managers should be concerned that their simplifying assumptions in their analysis are not valid: Market frictions exist so that the market integration assumption is not a good approximation of reality, or perhaps there is a significant correlation between spot exchange rates and cash flows.

We can rewrite Eq. 31.5 as follows. Using the covered interest rate parity relation derived in Chapter 30 (Eq. 30.3), we have

$$\frac{S}{F} = \frac{1 + r_{GBP}}{1 + r_{CAD}} \tag{31.6}$$

where r_{GBP} and r_{CAD} are the foreign and domestic risk free interest rates, respectively. Combining Eqs. 31.5 and 31.6 and rearranging terms gives the foreign cost of capital in terms of the domestic cost of capital and interest rates:

The Foreign-Denominated Cost of Capital

$$r^*_{GBP} = \frac{1 + r_{GBP}}{1 + r_{CAD}}(1 + r^*_{CAD}) - 1 \tag{31.7}$$

If the simplifying assumptions Ityesi made in calculating the NPV of its U.K. project are valid, then the cost of capital estimate calculated using Eq. 31.7 will be close to the cost of capital estimate calculated directly using comparable single-product companies in the United Kingdom.

EXAMPLE **31.2**   INTERNATIONALIZING THE COST OF CAPITAL

Problem
Use the Law of One Price to infer the GBP WACC from Ityesi's CAD WACC. Verify that the NPV of Ityesi's project is the same when its GBP free cash flows are discounted at this WACC and converted at the spot rate.

Solution
Using Eq. 31.7 to compute the GBP WACC gives

$$r^*_{GBP} = \frac{1 + r_{GBP}}{1 + r_{CAD}}(1 + r^*_{CAD}) - 1 = \left(\frac{1.07}{1.04}\right)(1.068) - 1 = 0.0988$$

The GBP WACC is 9.88%.

We can now use Ityesi's GBP WACC to calculate the present value of the GBP free cash flows in Table 31.1:

$$\frac{11.250}{1.0988} + \frac{11.250}{1.0988^2} + \frac{11.250}{1.0988^3} + \frac{11.250}{1.0988^4} = 35.754 \text{ million GBP}$$

The NPV in GBP of the investment opportunity is $35.754 - 17.5 = 18.254$ million GBP. Converting this amount to CAD at the spot rate gives 18.25 million GBP × 2.00 CAD/GBP = 36.508 million CAD, which is exactly the NPV we calculated before except for a slight difference due to rounding.

CONCEPT CHECK

1. Explain the two methods we use to calculate the NPV of a foreign project.

2. When do these two methods give the same NPV of the foreign project?

31.3 VALUATION AND INTERNATIONAL TAXATION

In this chapter, we assume that Ityesi pays a corporate tax rate of 40% no matter where its earnings are generated. In practice, determining the corporate tax rate on foreign income is complicated because corporate income taxes must be paid to two national governments: the host government (the United Kingdom in this example) and the home government (Canada). If the foreign project is a separately incorporated subsidiary of the parent, the amount of taxes a firm pays generally depends on the amount of profits **repatriated** (brought back to the home country).

SINGLE FOREIGN PROJECT WITH IMMEDIATE REPATRIATION OF EARNINGS

We begin by assuming that the firm has a single foreign project and that all foreign profits are repatriated immediately. The general international arrangement prevailing with respect to taxation of corporate profits is that the host country gets the first opportunity to tax income produced within its borders. The home government then gets an opportunity to tax the income from a foreign project to the domestic firm. In particular, the home government must establish a tax policy specifying its treatment of foreign income and foreign taxes paid on that income. In addition, it needs to establish the timing of taxation.

Canadian tax policy requires Canadian corporations to pay taxes on their foreign income at the same rate as profits earned in Canada. However, a full tax credit is given for foreign taxes paid *up to* the amount of the Canadian tax liability. In other words, if the foreign tax rate is less than the Canadian tax rate, the company pays total taxes equal to the Canadian tax rate on its foreign earnings. In this case, all of the company's earnings are taxed at the same rate no matter where they are earned—the working assumption we used for Ityesi.

If the foreign tax rate exceeds the Canadian tax rate, companies must pay this higher rate on foreign earnings. Because the Canadian tax credit exceeds the amount of Canadian taxes owed, no tax is owed in Canada. Note that Canadian tax policy does not allow companies to apply the part of the tax credit that is not used to offset domestic taxes owed, so this extra tax credit is wasted. In this scenario, companies pay a higher tax rate on foreign income and a lower (Canadian) tax rate on income generated in Canada.

MULTIPLE FOREIGN PROJECTS AND DEFERRAL OF EARNINGS REPATRIATION

Thus far, we have assumed that the firm has only one foreign project and that it repatriates earnings immediately. Neither assumption is realistic. Firms can lower their taxes by pooling multiple foreign projects and deferring the repatriation of earnings. Let's begin by considering the benefits of pooling the income on all foreign projects.

POOLING MULTIPLE FOREIGN PROJECTS.   Under Canadian tax law, Canadian-based multinational corporations may use any excess tax credits generated in high-tax foreign countries to offset their net Canadian tax liabilities on earnings in low-tax foreign countries. Thus, if the Canadian tax rate exceeds the combined tax rate on all foreign income, it is valid to assume that the firm pays the same tax rate on all income no matter where it is earned. Otherwise, the firm must pay a higher tax rate on its foreign income.

DEFERRING REPATRIATION OF EARNINGS.   Now consider an opportunity to defer repatriation of foreign profits. This consideration is important because a Canadian tax liability is not incurred until the profits are brought back home if the foreign operation is set up as a separately incorporated subsidiary (rather than as a foreign branch). If a company chooses not to repatriate 12.5 million GBP in pre-tax earnings, for example, it effectively reinvests those earnings abroad and defers its Canadian tax liability. When the foreign tax rates exceed the Canadian tax rates, there are no benefits to deferral because in such a case there is no additional Canadian tax liability.

When the foreign tax rate is less than the Canadian tax rate, deferral can provide significant benefits. Deferring repatriation of earnings lowers the overall tax burden in much the same way as deferring capital gains lowers the tax burden imposed by the capital gains tax. Other benefits from deferral arise because the firm effectively gains a real option to repatriate income at times when repatriation might be cheaper. For example, we have already noted that by pooling foreign income, the firm effectively pays the combined tax rate on all foreign income. Because the income generated across countries changes, this combined tax rate will vary from year to year. In years in which it exceeds the Canadian tax rate, the repatriation of additional income does not incur an additional Canadian tax liability, so the earnings can be repatriated tax free.

CONCEPT CHECK
1. What tax rate should we use to value a foreign project?
2. How can a Canadian firm lower its taxes on foreign projects?

31.4   INTERNATIONALLY SEGMENTED CAPITAL MARKETS

To this point, we have worked under the assumption that international capital markets are integrated. Often, however, this assumption is not appropriate. In some countries, especially in the developing world, all investors do not have equal access to financial securities. In this section, we consider why countries' capital markets might not be integrated—a case called **segmented capital markets**.

Many of the interesting questions in international corporate finance address the issues that result when capital markets are internationally segmented. In this section, we briefly consider the main reasons for segmentation of the capital markets and the implications for international corporate finance.

DIFFERENTIAL ACCESS TO MARKETS

In some cases, a country's risk-free securities are internationally integrated but markets for a specific firm's securities are not. Firms may face differential access to markets if there is any kind of asymmetry with respect to information about them. For example, Ityesi may be well known in Canada and enjoy easy access to CAD equity and debt markets there because it regularly provides information to an established community of analysts tracking the firm. It may not be equally well known in the United Kingdom and, therefore, may have difficulty tapping into the GBP capital markets because it has no track record there. For this reason, investors in the United Kingdom may require a higher rate of return to persuade them to hold GBP stocks and bonds issued by the Canadian firm.

With differential access to national markets, Ityesi would face a higher GBP WACC than the GBP WACC implied by Eq. 31.7. Ityesi would then view the foreign project as less valuable if it raises capital in the United Kingdom rather than in Canada. In fact, to maximize shareholder value, the firm should raise capital at home; the method of valuing the foreign project as if it were a domestic project would then provide the correct NPV. Differential access to national capital markets is common enough that it provides the best explanation for the existence of **currency swaps**, which are like the interest rate swap contracts we discussed in Chapter 30, but with the holder receiving coupons in one currency and paying coupons denominated in a different currency. Currency swaps generally also have final face value payments, also in different currencies. Using a currency swap, a firm can borrow in the market where it has the best access to capital, and then "swap" the coupon and principal payments to whichever currency it would prefer to make payments in. Thus, swaps allow firms to mitigate their exchange rate risk exposure between assets and liabilities, while still making investments and raising funds in the most attractive locales.

MACRO-LEVEL DISTORTIONS

Markets for risk-free instruments may also be segmented. Important macroeconomic reasons for segmented capital markets include capital controls and foreign exchange controls that create barriers to international capital flows and thus segment national markets. Many countries regulate or limit capital inflows or outflows, and many do not allow their currencies to be freely converted into dollars, thereby creating capital market segmentation. Similarly, some countries restrict who can hold financial securities.

Political, legal, social, and cultural characteristics that differ across countries may require compensation in the form of a country risk premium. For example, the rate of interest paid on government bonds or other securities in a country with a tradition of weak enforcement of property rights is likely not really a risk-free rate. Instead, interest rates in the country will reflect a risk premium for the possibility of default, so relations such as covered interest rate parity will likely not hold exactly.

EXAMPLE 31.3   **RISKY GOVERNMENT BONDS**

Problem

For July 27, 2009, the spot exchange rate between Russian rubles and U.S. dollars was 30.9845 RUB/USD and the one-year forward exchange rate was 33.7382 RUB/USD. At the time, the yield on short-term Russian government bonds was about 11%, while the comparable one-year yield on U.S. Treasury securities was 0.5%. Using the covered interest parity relationship, calculate the implied one-year forward rate. Compare this rate with the actual forward rate, and explain why the two rates differ.

Solution

Using the covered interest parity formula, the implied forward rate is

$$F = S \times \frac{(1 + r_{RUB})}{(1 + r_{USD})} = 26.9975 \times \frac{1.06}{1.05} = 27.2546 \ RUB/USD$$

The implied forward rate is higher than the current spot rate because Russian government bonds have higher yields than U.S. government bonds. The difference between the implied forward rate and the actual forward rate likely reflects the default risk in Russian government bonds (the Russian government defaulted on its debt as recently as 1998). A holder of 100,000 RUB seeking a true risk-free investment could convert the RUB to USD, invest in U.S. Treasuries, and convert the proceeds back to RUB at a rate locked in with a forward contract. By doing so, the investor would earn

$$\frac{100,000 \ RUB}{26.9975 \ RUB/USD \ \text{today}} \times \frac{1.05 \ USD \ \text{in 1 yr}}{1 \ USD \ \text{today}} \times 26.9775 \ RUB/USD \ \text{in 1-yr}$$

$$= 104,922 \ RUB \ \text{in 1 yr}$$

for an effective RUB risk-free rate of 9.432%. The higher rate of 11% on Russian bonds reflects a credit spread of $11\% - 9.432\% = 1.568\%$ to compensate bondholders for default risk.

IMPLICATIONS

A segmented financial market has an important implication for international corporate finance: One country or currency has a higher rate of return than another country or currency, when the two rates are compared in the same currency. If the return difference results from a market friction such as capital controls, corporations can exploit this friction by setting up projects in the high-return country/currency and raising capital in the low-return country/currency. Of course, the extent to which corporations can capitalize on this strategy is naturally limited: If such a strategy were easy to implement, the return difference would quickly disappear as corporations competed to use the strategy. Nevertheless, certain corporations might realize a competitive advantage by implementing such a strategy. For example, as an incentive to invest, a foreign government might strike a deal with a particular corporation that relaxes capital controls for that corporation alone.

EXAMPLE 31.4

VALUING A FOREIGN ACQUISITION IN A SEGMENTED MARKET

Problem

Camacho Enterprises is a U.S. company that is considering expanding by acquiring Xtapa Inc., a firm in Mexico. The acquisition is expected to increase Camacho's free cash flows by 21 million MXN (Mexican pesos) the first year; this amount is then expected to grow at a rate of 8% per year. The price of the investment is 525 million MXN, which is 52.5 million USD at the current exchange rate of 10 MXN/USD. Based on an analysis in the Mexican market, Camacho has determined that the appropriate after-tax MXN WACC is 12%. If Camacho has also determined that its after-tax USD WACC for this expansion is 7.5%, what is the value of the Mexican acquisition? Assume that the Mexican and U.S. markets for risk-free securities are integrated and that the yield curve in both countries is flat. U.S. risk-free interest rates are 6%, and Mexican risk-free interest rates are 9%.

Solution

Let's begin by calculating the NPV of the expansion in MXN and converting the result into USD at the spot rate. Putting the free cash flows on a timeline:

The net present value of these cash flows at the MXN WACC is

$$NPV = \frac{21}{0.12 - 0.08} - 525 = 0$$

so the purchase is a zero-NPV transaction. Presumably, Camacho is competing with other Mexican companies for the purchase.

We can also compute the NPV in USD by converting the expected cash flows into USD using forward rates. The N-year forward rate (Eq. 30.3 in Chapter 30) expressed in MXN/USD is

$$F_N = S \times \frac{(1 + r_{MXN})^N}{(1 + r_{USD})^N} = 10 \times \left(\frac{1.09}{1.06}\right)^N = 10 \times 1.0283^N = 10.283 \times 1.0283^{N-1}$$

Thus the USD expected cash flows are the MXN cash flows (from the earlier timeline) converted at the appropriate forward rate (we divide by the forward rate because it is in MXN/USD):

$$C_{MXN}^N / F_N = \frac{21(1.08)^{N-1}}{10.283 \times 1.0283^{N-1}} = 2.0422 \times 1.0503^{N-1}$$

The USD expected cash flows are therefore

so the USD cash flows grow at about 5% per year. The NPV of these cash flows is

$$NPV = \frac{2.0422}{0.075 - 0.0503} - 52.5 = 30.18 \text{ million USD}$$

Which NPV more accurately represents the benefits of the expansion? The answer depends on the source of the difference. To compute the USD expected cash flows by converting the MXN expected cash flows at the forward rate, we must accept the assumption that spot rates and the project cash flows are uncorrelated. The difference might simply reflect that this assumption failed to hold. Another possibility is that the difference reflects estimation error in the respective WACC estimates.

If Camacho is relatively confident in its assumptions about spot rates and its WACC estimates, a third possibility is that Mexican and U.S. capital markets are not integrated. In this case, Camacho, because of its access to U.S. capital markets, might have a competitive advantage. Perhaps other companies with which it is competing for the purchase of Xtapa are all Mexican firms that do not have access to capital markets outside of Mexico. Hence Camacho can raise capital at a cheaper rate. Of course, this argument also requires that other U.S. companies not be competing for the purchase of Xtapa. Camacho, however, might have special knowledge of Xtapa's markets that other U.S.-based companies lack. This knowledge would give Camacho a competitive advantage in the product market over other U.S. companies and puts it on an equal footing in the product market with other Mexican companies. Because it has a competitive advantage in capital markets over other Mexican companies, the NPV of the purchase is positive for Camacho, but zero for the other bidders for Xtapa.

As Example 31.4 demonstrates, the existence of segmented capital markets makes many decisions in international corporate finance more complicated but potentially more lucrative for a firm that is well positioned to exploit the market segmentation.

CONCEPT CHECK
1. What is the main implication for international corporate finance of a segmented financial market?
2. What are the reasons for segmentation of the capital markets?

31.5 CAPITAL BUDGETING WITH EXCHANGE RISK

The final issue that arises when a firm is considering a foreign project is that the cash flows of the project may be affected by exchange rate risk. The risk is that the cash flows generated by the project will depend upon the future level of the exchange rate. A large part of international corporate finance addresses this foreign exchange risk. This section offers an overview with respect to valuation of foreign currency cash flows.

The working assumptions made thus far in this chapter are that the project's free cash flows are uncorrelated with the spot exchange rates. Such an assumption often makes sense if the firm operates as a local firm in the foreign market—it purchases its inputs and sells its outputs in that market, and price changes of the inputs and outputs are uncorrelated with exchange rates. However, many firms use imported inputs in their production processes or export some of their output to foreign countries. These scenarios alter the nature of a project's foreign exchange risk and, in turn, change the valuation of the foreign currency cash flows.

As an example, let's reconsider what happens if the Ityesi project in the United Kingdom imports some materials from Canada. In this case, the project's GBP free cash flows will be correlated with exchange rates. Assuming the cost of the material in Canada remains stable, if the value of a CAD appreciates against the GBP, the GBP cost of these materials will increase, thereby reducing the GBP free cash flows. The reverse is also true: If the CAD depreciates, then the GBP free cash flows will increase. Hence, our working assumption that changes in the free cash flows are uncorrelated with changes in the exchange rate is violated, and it is no longer appropriate to calculate the expected CAD free cash flows by converting the expected GBP free cash flows at the forward rate.

Whenever a project has cash flows that depend on the values of multiple currencies, the most convenient approach is to separate the cash flows according to the currency they depend on. For example, a fraction of Ityesi's manufacturing costs may be for inputs whose cost fluctuates with the value of the CAD. Specifically, suppose 5.625 million GBP of the costs are denominated in GBP, and an additional 20 million CAD (or 10 million GBP at the current exchange rate of 2.00 CAD/GBP) is for inputs whose price fluctuates with the value of the CAD. In this case, we would calculate Ityesi's GBP-denominated free cash flows excluding these CAD-based costs, as shown in Table 31.4.

If the revenues and costs in the spreadsheet in Table 31.4 are not affected by changes in the spot exchange rates, it makes sense to assume that changes in the free cash flows are uncorrelated with changes in the spot exchange rates. Hence we can convert the GBP-denominated free cash flows to equivalent CAD amounts using the forward exchange rate, as we did in Section 31.2. Table 31.5 spreadsheet performs this calculation, with the CAD value of the GBP-denominated free cash flow shown in line 3.

Next we add the CAD-based cash flows to determine the project's aggregate free cash flow in CAD terms. This calculation is done in lines 4 through 6 of Table 31.5. Note that we deduct Ityesi's CAD-denominated costs, and then add the tax shield associated with

ITYESI'S GBP FREE CASH FLOWS

TABLE 31.4

SPREADSHEET

	Year	0	1	2	3	4
Incremental Earnings Forecast (million GBP)						
1 Sales		—	37.500	37.500	37.500	37.500
2 Cost of Goods Sold		—	(5.625)	(5.625)	(5.625)	(5.625)
3 Gross Profit		—	31.875	31.875	31.875	31.875
4 Operating Expenses		(4.167)	(5.625)	(5.625)	(5.625)	(5.625)
5 Depreciation		—	(3.750)	(3.750)	(3.750)	(3.750)
6 EBIT		(4.167)	22.500	22.500	22.500	22.500
7 Income Tax at 40%		1.667	(9.000)	(9.000)	(9.000)	(9.000)
8 Unlevered Net Income		(2.500)	13.500	13.500	13.500	13.500
Free Cash Flow						
9 Plus: Depreciation		—	3.750	3.750	3.750	3.750
10 Less: Capital Expenditures		(15.000)	—	—	—	—
11 Less: Increases in NWC		—	—	—	—	—
12 GBP Free Cash Flow		(17.500)	17.250	17.250	17.250	17.250

these costs. Even if the taxes will be paid in GBP in the U.K., they will fluctuate with the CAD cost of the inputs and so can be viewed as a CAD-denominated cash flow.

Given the CAD-denominated free cash flow in line 6 of Table 31.5, we can now compute the NPV of the investment using Ityesi's CAD WACC:[5]

$$\frac{21.533}{1.068} + \frac{20.593}{1.068^2} + \frac{19.679}{1.068^3} + \frac{18.791}{1.068^4} - 35.000 = 33.812 \text{ million CAD}$$

The Ityesi example was simplified because we could easily isolate the cash flows that would vary perfectly with the CAD/GBP exchange rate from those that would be uncorrelated with the exchange rate. In practice, determining these sensitivities may be difficult. If historical data is available, the tools of regression can be used to identify the exchange rate risk of project cash flows, in much the same way that we used regression to identify the market risk of security returns in Part 4 of the text.

In this chapter, we have endeavoured to provide an introduction to international capital budgeting. This topic is sufficiently complicated that entire textbooks have been devoted to it. Hence, it is difficult to do this issue justice in a single-chapter treatment. Although we have provided a basic framework for approaching the problem, a reader who is seriously considering undertaking a foreign venture should consult one of the books listed for this chapter in the Textbook Resources section on MyFinanceLab.

EXPECTED CAD FREE CASH FLOWS FROM ITYESI'S U.K. PROJECT

TABLE 31.5

SPREADSHEET

	Year	0	1	2	3	4
CAD Free Cash Flow (million CAD)						
1 GBP Free Cash Flow (million GBP)		(17.500)	17.250	17.250	17.250	17.250
2 Forward Exchange Rate (CAD/GBP)		2.0000	1.9439	1.8894	1.8364	1.7850
3 CAD Value of GBP Free Cash Flow (1 × 2)		(35.000)	33.533	32.593	31.679	30.791
4 CAD Costs		—	(20.000)	(20.000)	(20.000)	(20.000)
5 Income Tax at 40%		—	8.000	8.000	8.000	8.000
6 Free Cash Flow		(35.000)	21.533	20.593	19.679	18.791

---

5. We again use the domestic WACC to discount the cash flows because we continue to assume that any additional risk premium for the exchange rate risk is small. If this assumption does not hold, then the CAD costs and the CAD value of the expected GBP free cash flows would have to be discounted at different rates to reflect the additional exchange rate risk in the GBP free cash flows.

INTERVIEW WITH BILL BARRETT

William (Bill) Barrett is co-chair of Barrett Corporation and CEO of Barrett Explorer. Barrett Corporation is a family business headquartered in Woodstock, New Brunswick, that distributes recreation and outdoor goods, consumer electronics, wireless broadband services, and other products.

QUESTION: What are the benefits to being international? What are the challenges?

ANSWER: When a business seeks growth, sooner or later it must look at the international market. In our global economy most businesses with any kind of brand inevitably need to look outside Canada because there is a limit to the opportunities within Canada. The challenge is that we know Canada better than the rest of the world. We force ourselves to become comfortable in new environments so we can manage the risks there.

In today's world you are usually involved in international business because so much production and manufacturing occurs in China. We have had long-standing relationships with Chinese companies and have been importing from China and Japan for 30 years. We have also invested to become partners in other businesses: one in India, another in Africa, in Europe, and in the United Kingdom. We have a "comfortableness" in dealing internationally.

QUESTION: What issues are important when a company goes international compared to when it is purely domestic?

ANSWER: In an international environment the most important thing is to have really good resources inside the countries in which you operate. You either find people from a country to represent you in that country, or you build a relationship with a firm inside that country that represents you. Another alternative is a joint venture. You need to respect how business is done in that country. Related to this is the fact that laws differ from country to country. You need to be working with law firms that have a global reach. Our law firms in Toronto and in London, England, both have affiliations with law firms in just about every country in the world.

QUESTION: How have currency exchange rates affected your company?

ANSWER: Currency fluctuations have huge implications. If the marketplace was used to buying something at $1 Canadian but now, due to an exchange rate change, it is $1.20 Canadian, that is a really tough situation to manage. Sometimes we hedge. We buy options on currency. We buy forwards on currency. We try to anticipate and protect ourselves by buying into the future. We never buy 100% into the future but we hedge 50 to 70% of our exposure.

QUESTION: Are there any important international tax considerations you face?

ANSWER: International tax rules affect where and how we do business. We are an Atlantic Canadian company. We form holding companies in various parts of the world depending upon the tax implication that we need to resolve. In a specific instance in India, we determined that by manufacturing in China and exporting to India, we would face a huge import duty. The solution was to manufacture in India; by doing so, we saved about 27% in tax.

QUESTION: How do you handle corruption?

ANSWER: So far we have been fortunate and have not had to deal with corruption to any significant degree. More important for us is the issue of the competence or incompetence of a potential business partner. We manage that by doing our due diligence so that we find out before it becomes an issue for us.

QUESTION: Do you get involved in joint ventures, licensing agreements, etc., or do you access other countries directly?

ANSWER: We do business in a variety of ways, including joint venture relationships, distribution relationships, and agency relationships. There are many countries that have such complex regulatory issues that a joint venture is the only practical way to go. In other situations, like the European Union, there is a common set of regulatory, tax, and deployment issues in terms of how people are hired, what your obligations are to them, and what their obligations are to you. In all of these situations you try to find the very best win for the individual, for yourself, for the company, and for the opportunity.

CONCEPT CHECK

1. What conditions cause the cash flows of a foreign project to be affected by exchange rate risk?

2. How do we make adjustments when a project has inputs and outputs in different currencies?

SUMMARY

1. The condition necessary to ensure internationally integrated capital markets is that the value of a foreign investment does not depend on the currency (home or foreign) used in the analysis.

2. Two methods are used to value foreign currency cash flows when markets are internationally integrated and uncertainty in spot exchange rates is uncorrelated with the foreign currency cash flows:

   a. Calculate the foreign currency value of a foreign project as the NPV of the expected foreign currency future cash flows discounted at the foreign cost of capital, and then convert the foreign currency NPV into the home currency using the current spot exchange rate.

   b. Compute the expected value of the foreign currency cash flows in the home currency by multiplying the expected value in the foreign currency by the forward exchange rates, and then compute the NPV of these home currency cash flows using the domestic cost of capital.

3. When markets are internationally integrated and uncertainty in spot exchange rates is uncorrelated with the foreign currency cash flows, the foreign currency (FOC) WACC and home currency (HOC) WACC are related as follows:

$$r_{FOC}^* = \frac{1 + r_{FOC}}{1 + r_{HOC}}(1 + r_{HOC}^*) - 1 \qquad (31.7)$$

4. A Canadian corporation pays the higher of the foreign or domestic tax rate on its foreign project, so project valuation should use the higher of these two rates as well. The Canadian corporation may be able to reduce its tax liability by undertaking foreign projects in other countries whose earnings can be pooled with those of the new project or by deferring the repatriation of earnings.

5. Capital markets might be internationally segmented. The implication is that one country or currency has a higher cost of capital than another country or currency, when the two are compared in the same currency.

6. When a project in a country has inputs and outputs in different currencies, the out-of-country denominated cash flows are likely to be correlated with changes in spot rates. To correctly value such projects, the foreign and domestic cash flows should be valued separately.

KEY TERMS

currency swaps *p. 1048*
internationally integrated capital
   market *p. 1041*

repatriated *p. 1046*
segmented capital markets *p. 1047*

PROBLEMS

Internationally Integrated Capital Markets

1. You are a Canadian investor who is trying to calculate the present value of a 5 million EUR (euro) cash inflow that will occur one year in the future. The spot exchange rate is 1.600 CAD/EUR and the forward rate is 1.5551 CAD/EUR. You estimate that the appropriate CAD discount rate for this cash flow is 4% and the appropriate EUR discount rate is 7%.

    a. What is the present value of the 5 million EUR cash inflow computed by first discounting the EUR and then converting it into CAD?

    b. What is the present value of the 5 million EUR cash inflow computed by first converting the cash flow into CAD and then discounting?

    c. What can you conclude about whether these markets are internationally integrated, based on your answers to parts a and b?

2. Mamma Mia Enterprises, a Canadian manufacturer of children's toys, has made a sale in Poland and is expecting a 4 million PLN cash inflow in one year. (The currency of Poland is the Polish new zloty. Poland is a member of the European Union, but has not yet adopted the euro.) The current spot rate is 2.040 PLN/CAD and the one-year forward rate is 2.055 PLN/CAD.

    a. What is the present value of Mamma Mia's 4 million PLN inflow computed by first discounting the cash flow at the appropriate PLN discount rate of 10% and then converting the result into CAD?

    b. What is the present value of Mamma Mia's 4 million PLN inflow computed by first converting the cash flow into CAD and then discounting at the appropriate CAD discount rate of 6%?

    c. What can you conclude about whether these markets are internationally integrated, based on your answers to parts a and b?

Valuation of Foreign Currency Cash Flows

 3. Etemadi Amalgamated, a U.S. manufacturing firm, is considering a new project in the Euro Zone. You are in Etemadi's corporate finance department and are responsible for deciding whether to undertake the project. The expected free cash flows, in EUR, are shown here:

Year	Free Cash Flow (million EUR)
0	−15
1	9
2	10
3	11
4	12

You know that the spot exchange rate is $S = 1.5$ USD/EUR. In addition, the risk-free interest rate on USD is 4% and the risk-free interest rate on EUR is 6%.

Assume that these markets are internationally integrated and the uncertainty in the free cash flows is not correlated with uncertainty in the exchange rate. You determine that the USD WACC for these cash flows is 8.5%. What is the USD present value of the project? Should Etemadi Amalgamated undertake the project?

EXCEL

4. Etemadi Amalgamated, the U.S. manufacturing company in Problem 3, is still considering a new project in the Euro Zone. All information presented in Problem 3 is still accurate, except the spot rate is now $S = 1.11$ USD/EUR, about 26% lower. What is the new present value of the project in USD? Should Etemadi Amalgamated undertake the project?

5. You work for a Canadian firm, and your boss has asked you to estimate the cost of capital for countries using the EUR. You know that $S = 1.6100$ CAD/EUR and $F_1 = 1.5807$. Suppose the CAD WACC for your company is known to be 8%. If these markets are internationally integrated, estimate the EUR cost of capital for a project with free cash flows that are uncorrelated with spot exchange rates. Assume the firm pays the same tax rate no matter where the cash flows are earned.

6. Montreal Light, a Canadian light fixtures manufacturer, is considering an investment in Japan. The CAD cost of equity for Montreal Light is 11%. You are in the corporate treasury department, and you need to know the comparable cost of equity in JPY for a project with free cash flows that are uncorrelated with spot exchange rates. The risk-free interest rates on CAD and JPY are $r_{CAD} = 5\%$ and $r_{JPY} = 1\%$, respectively. Montreal Light is willing to assume that capital markets are internationally integrated. What is the JPY cost of equity?

7. The dollar cost of debt for Javelin Consulting, a Canadian research firm, is 7.5%. The firm faces a tax rate of 30% on all income, no matter where it is earned. Managers in the firm need to know its JPY cost of debt because they are considering launching a new bond issue in Tokyo to raise money for a new investment there. The risk-free interest rates on CAD and JPY are $r_{CAD} = 5\%$ and $r_{JPY} = 1\%$, respectively. Javelin Consulting is willing to assume that capital markets are internationally integrated and that its free cash flows are uncorrelated with the CAD/JPY spot rate. What is Javelin Consulting's after-tax cost of debt in JPY? (*Hint:* Start by finding the after-tax cost of debt in CAD and then find the JPY equivalent.)

EXCEL

8. McCain Foods, a Canadian food processing and distribution company, is considering an investment in the Euro Zone. You are in McCain's corporate finance department and are responsible for deciding whether to undertake the project. The expected free cash flows, in EUR, are uncorrelated to the spot exchange rate and are shown here:

Year	Free Cash Flow (million EUR)
0	−25
1	12
2	14
3	15
4	15

The new project has similar CAD risk to McCain's other projects. The company knows that its overall CAD WACC is 9.5%, so it feels comfortable using this WACC for the project. The risk-free interest rate on CAD is 4.5% and the risk-free interest rate on EUR is 7%.

a. McCain is willing to assume that capital markets in Canada and the Euro Zone are internationally integrated. What is the company's EUR WACC?

b. What is the present value of the project in EUR?

9. Tailor Johnson, a U.S. maker of fine menswear, has a subsidiary in Ethiopia. This year, the subsidiary reported and repatriated earnings before interest and taxes (EBIT) of 100 million ETB (Ethiopian birrs). The current exchange rate is 8 ETB/USD or 0.125 USD/ETB. The Ethiopian tax rate on this activity is 25%. U.S. tax law requires Tailor Johnson to pay taxes on the Ethiopian earnings at the same rate as profits earned in the United States, which is currently 45%. However, the United States gives a full tax credit for foreign taxes paid up to the amount of the U.S. tax liability. What is Tailor Johnson's U.S. tax liability on its Ethiopian subsidiary?

*10. Tailor Johnson, the menswear company with a subsidiary in Ethiopia as described in Problem 9, is considering the tax benefits resulting from deferring repatriation of the earnings from the subsidiary. Under U.S. tax law, the U.S. tax liability is not incurred until the profits are brought back home. Tailor Johnson reasonably expects to defer repatriation for ten years, at which point the ETB earnings will be converted into USD at the prevailing spot rate, S_{10}, and the tax credit for Ethiopian taxes paid will still be converted at the exchange rate $S_1 = 0.125$ USD/ETB. Tailor Johnson's after-tax cost of debt is 5%.

   a. Suppose the exchange rate in ten years is identical to this year's exchange rate, so $S_{10} = 0.125$ USD/ETB. What is the present value of deferring the U.S. tax liability on Tailor Johnson's Ethiopian earnings for ten years?

   b. How will the exchange rate in ten years affect the actual amount of the U.S. tax liability? Write an equation for the U.S. tax liability as a function of the exchange rate S_{10}.

11. Qu'Appelle Enterprises, a Canadian import-export trading firm, is considering its international tax situation. Canadian tax law requires Canadian corporations to pay taxes on their foreign earnings at the same rate as profits earned in Canada; this rate is currently 35%. However, a full tax credit is given for the foreign taxes paid up to the amount of the Canadian tax liability. Qu'Appelle has major operations in Poland, where the tax rate is 20%, and in Sweden, where the tax rate is 60%. The profits, which are fully and immediately repatriated, and foreign taxes paid for the current year are shown here:

	Poland	Sweden
Earnings before interest and taxes (EBIT)	$80 million	$100 million
Host country taxes paid	$16 million	$60 million
Earnings before interest after taxes	$64 million	$40 million

   a. What is the Canadian tax liability on the earnings from the Polish subsidiary assuming the Swedish subsidiary did not exist?

   b. What is the Canadian tax liability on the earnings from the Swedish subsidiary assuming the Polish subsidiary did not exist?

   c. Under Canadian tax law, Qu'Appelle is able to pool the earnings from its operations in Poland and Sweden when computing its Canadian tax liability on foreign earnings. Total EBIT is thus $180 million and the total host country taxes paid is $76 million. What is the total Canadian tax liability on foreign earnings? Show how this relates to the answers in parts a and b.

Internationally Segmented Capital Markets

*12. Suppose the interest on Russian government bonds is 7.5% and the current exchange rate is 28 RUB per CAD. If the forward exchange rate is 28.5 RUB per CAD, and the current Canadian risk-free interest rate is 4.5%, what is the implied credit spread for Russian government bonds?

Capital Budgeting with Exchange Risk

 *13. Assume that in the original Ityesi example in Table 31.1 all sales actually occur in Canada and are projected to be 75 million CAD per year for four years. Keeping other costs the same and in GBP, calculate the NPV of the investment opportunity.

DATA CASE

You are a senior financial analyst with IBM in their capital budgeting division. IBM is considering expanding in Australia due to its positive business atmosphere and cultural similarities to the United States.

The new facility would require an initial investment in fixed assets of 5 billion AUD (Australian dollars) and an additional capital investment of 3% would be required each year in years 1–4. All capital investments would be depreciated straight line over the 5 years that the facility would operate. First-year revenues from the facility are expected to be 6 billion AUD and to grow at 10% per year. Cost of goods sold would be 40% of revenue; the other operating expenses would amount to 12% of revenue. Net working capital requirements would be 11% of sales and would be required the year prior to the actual revenues. All net working capital would be recovered at the end of the fifth year. Assume that the tax rates are the same in the two countries, that the two markets are internationally integrated, and that the cash flow uncertainty of the project is uncorrelated with changes in the exchange rate. Your team manager wants you to determine the NPV of the project in USD using a cost of capital of 12%.

1. Go to the NASDAQ Web site (www.nasdaq.com).
   a. Enter the stock symbol for IBM (IBM) in one of the boxes and click "Summary Quotes."
   b. Click "Financials" from the menu on the left. When the income statement appears, place the cursor inside the statement and right-click. Select "Export to Microsoft Excel" from the menu.

2. Obtain exchange rates and comparable interest rates for Australia at Bloomberg's Web site (www.bloomberg.com).
   a. Place the cursor on "Market Data" and click on "Currencies" from the drop-down menu. Export the currency table to Excel and paste it into the same spreadsheet as the IBM income statement.
   b. Go back to the Web page and click on "Rates & Bonds" from the menu on the left. Next click on "Australia" to get the interest rates for Australia. Right-click and export the table to Excel; paste it into the spreadsheet.
   c. Go back to the Web page and click on "U.S." Download the Treasury data and paste it into the spreadsheet.

3. You may have noticed that the one-year and four-year rates are not available at Bloomberg's Web site for the U.S. Treasury. Go to the U.S. Treasury Web site (www.treas.gov).
   a. To find the one-year rate, type "historic yield data" into the search box at the top of the page and select the second link that appears. Be sure it is *not* the link for the "real" rates.

Export the yields into Excel on the same spreadsheet as the other data. Add the one-year yield to the other Treasury rates.

    b. To find an estimate of the four-year yield, calculate the average of the three- and five-year yields from the Treasury yield curve.

4. In your Excel spreadsheet, create a new worksheet with a timeline for the project's expected cash flows.

    a. Compute the tax rate as the four-year average of IBM's annual income tax divided by annual earnings before tax.

    b. Determine the expected free cash flows of the project.

5. Note that the free cash flows you calculated in Question 4 are in AUD. Use Eq. 30.3 to determine the forward exchange rates for each of the five years of the project. Then use the forward rates to convert the cash flows to USD.

6. Compute the NPV of the project in USD using the 12% required return given by your team manager.

Glossary

$1.00 out lease A type of lease, also known as a finance lease, in which ownership of the asset transfers to the lessee at the end of the lease for a nominal cost of $1.00.

10-K The annual form that U.S. companies use to file their financial statements with the U.S. Securities and Exchange Commission (SEC).

10-Q The quarterly reporting form that U.S. companies use to file their financial statements with the U.S. Securities and Exchange Commission (SEC).

abandonment option An option for an investor to cease making investments in a project. Abandonment options can add value to a project because a firm can drop a project if it turns out to be unsuccessful.

absolute return *See* cash multiple.

accounts payable The amounts owed to creditors for products or services purchased with credit.

accounts payable days An expression of a firm's accounts payable in terms of the number of days' worth of cost of goods sold that the accounts payable represents.

accounts receivable Amounts owed to a firm by customers who have purchased goods or services on credit.

accounts receivable days An expression of a firm's accounts receivable in terms of the number of days' worth of sales that the accounts receivable represents.

acquirer (or bidder) A firm that, in a takeover, buys another firm.

acquisition premium Paid by an acquirer in a takeover, it is the percentage difference between the acquisition price and the premerger price of a target firm.

actuarially fair When the NPV from selling insurance is zero because the price of insurance equals the present value of the expected payment.

adjusted present value (APV) A valuation method to determine the levered value of an investment by first calculating its unlevered value (its value without any leverage) and then adding the value of the interest tax shield and deducting any costs that arise from other market imperfections.

adverse selection The idea that when the buyers and sellers have different information, the average quality of assets in the market will differ from the average quality overall.

after-tax interest rate Reflects the amount of interest an investor can keep after taxes have been deducted.

agency costs Costs that arise when there are conflicts of interest between a firm's stakeholders.

agency problem When decision makers, despite being hired as the agents of other stakeholders, put their own self-interest ahead of the interests of the stakeholders.

agency securities Securities issued by agencies of the U.S. government or by U.S. government-sponsored enterprises.

aggressive financing policy Financing part or all of a firm's permanent working capital with short-term debt.

aging schedule Categorizes a firm's accounts by the number of days they have been on the firm's books. It can be prepared using either the number of accounts or the dollar amount of the accounts receivable outstanding.

alpha The difference between a stock's expected return and its required return according to the security market line.

American options The most common kind of option, they allow their holders to exercise the option on any date up to, and including, the expiration date.

amortization A charge that captures the change in value of acquired assets. Like depreciation, amortization is not an actual cash expense.

amortizing loan A loan on which the borrower makes monthly payments that include interest on the loan plus some part of the loan balance.

angel investors Individual investors who buy equity in small private firms.

annual percentage rate (APR) Indicates the amount of interest earned in one year without the effect of compounding.

annual report The yearly summary of business sent by U.S. public companies to their shareholders that accompanies or includes the financial statement.

annuity A stream of equal periodic cash flows over a specified time period. These cash flows can be inflows of returns earned on investments or outflows of funds invested to earn future returns.

annuity spreadsheet An Excel spreadsheet that can compute any one of the five variables of *NPER, RATE, PV, PMT*, and *FV*. Given any four input variables the spreadsheet computes the fifth.

APR *See* annual precentage rate.

APT *See* Arbitrage Pricing Theory.

APV *See* adjusted present value.

arbitrage The practice of buying and selling equivalent goods or portfolios to take advantage of a price difference.

arbitrage opportunity Any situation in which it is possible to make a profit without taking any risk or making any investment.

Arbitrage Pricing Theory (APT) A model that uses more than one portfolio to capture systematic risk. The portfolios themselves can be thought of as either the risk factor itself or a portfolio of stocks correlated with an unobservable risk factor. Also referred to as a multifactor model.

articles of incorporation Documents that set out the terms and conditions of the corporation's ownership and existence.

ask (offer) price The price at which a market maker or specialist is willing to sell a security.

asset-backed bonds A type of secured corporate debt. Specific assets are pledged as collateral that bondholders have a direct claim to in the event of bankruptcy. Asset-backed bonds can be secured by any kind of asset.

asset-backed securities (ABS) Mortgage-backed securities, such as those guaranteed by the CMHC, are one type of asset-backed securities. Each security is backed by an underlying portfolio or pool of mortgages.

asset beta *See* unlevered beta.

asset class Categories defined by the Canada Revenue Agency to indicate types of depreciable properties that will be given the same treatment for capital cost allowance (CCA) calculations.

asset cost of capital The expected return required by the firm's investors to hold the firm's underlying assets; the weighted average of the firm's equity and debt costs of capital.

asset pool The sum of all assets in one asset class.

asset substitution problem When a firm faces financial distress, shareholders can gain from decisions that increase the risk of the firm sufficiently, even if they have negative NPV.

asset turnover   The ratio of sales to assets, a measure of how efficiently the firm is utilizing its assets to generate sales.

assets   The cash, inventory, property, plant and equipment, and other investments a company has made.

asymmetric information   A situation in which parties have different information. It can arise when, for example, managers have superior information to investors regarding the firm's future cash flows.

at-the-money   Describes options whose exercise prices are equal to the current stock price.

auction IPO   A method for selling new issues directly to the public. Rather than setting a price itself and then allocating shares to buyers, the underwriter in an auction IPO takes bids from investors and then sets the price to clear the market.

auditor   A neutral third party that corporations are required to hire to check the annual financial statements to ensure they are prepared according to GAAP, and to verify that the information is reliable.

availability float   How long it takes a bank to give a firm credit for customer payments the firm has deposited in the bank.

average annual return   The arithmetic average of an investment's realized returns for each year.

backdating   The practice of choosing the grant date of a stock option retroactively, so that the date of the grant would coincide with a date when the stock price was lower than its price at the time the grant was actually awarded. By backdating the option in this way, the executive receives a stock option that is already in-the-money.

balance sheet   A list of a firm's assets and liabilities that provides a snapshot of the firm's financial position at a given point in time.

balloon payment   A large payment that must be made on the maturity date of a bond.

bank rate   The interest rate at which the Bank of Canada lends to financial institutions.

Bankruptcy and Insolvency Act (BIA)   The Canadian act used by financially distressed companies and individuals to enter into bankruptcy for the purpose of reorganization or liquidation.

basis risk   The risk that the value of a security used to hedge and exposure will not track that exposure perfectly.

bearer bond   Similar to currency in that whoever physically holds this bond's certificate owns the bond. To receive a coupon payment, the holder of a bearer bond must provide explicit proof of ownership by literally clipping a coupon off the bond certificate and remitting it to the paying agent.

benchmark bonds   Bonds issued by the Government of Canada that state precise maturity dates and coupon rates. Other bond-issuers base their rates on these Government of Canada bonds.

best-efforts basis   For smaller initial public offerings (IPOs), a situation in which the underwriter does not guarantee that the stock will be sold, but instead tries to sell the stock for the best possible price. Often such deals have an all-or-none clause: either all of the shares are sold on the IPO, or the deal is called off.

beta (β)   The expected percentage change in the excess return of a security for a 1% change in the excess return of the market (or other benchmark) portfolio.

bid price   The price at which a market maker or specialist is willing to buy a security.

bid-ask spread   The amount by which the ask price exceeds the bid price.

bidder   *See* acquirer.

Binomial Option Pricing Model   A technique for pricing options based on the assumption that each period, the stock's return can take on only two values.

binomial tree   A timeline with two branches at every date representing the possible events that could happen at those times.

bird in the hand hypothesis   The thesis that firms choosing to pay higher current dividends will enjoy higher stock prices because shareholders prefer current dividends to future ones (with the same present value).

Black-Scholes Option Pricing Model   A technique for pricing European-style options when the stock can be traded continuously. It can be derived from the Binomial Option Pricing Model by allowing the length of each period shrink to zero.

blanket lien   *See* floating lien.

board of directors   A group elected by shareholders that has the ultimate decision-making authority in the corporation.

bond   A security sold by governments and corporations to raise money from investors today in exchange for the promised future payment.

bond indenture   States the terms of a bond as well as the amounts and dates of all payments to be made.

book building   A process used by underwriters for coming up with an offer price based on customers' expressions of interest.

book-to-market ratio   The ratio of the book value of equity to the market value of equity.

book value   The acquisition cost of an asset less its accumulated depreciation.

book value of equity   The difference between the book value of a firm's assets and its liabilities; also called stockholders' equity, it represents the net worth of a firm from an accounting perspective.

break-even   The level for which an investment has an NPV of zero.

break-even analysis   A calculation of the value of each parameter for which the NPV of the project is zero.

Bulldogs   A term for foreign bonds in the United Kingdom.

business income trust   A flow through entity that holds all the debt and equity securities of a corporation in trust for the trust's owners.

business interruption insurance   A type of insurance that protects a firm against the loss of earnings if the business is interrupted due to fire, accident, or some other insured peril.

business liability insurance   A type of insurance that covers the costs that result if some aspect of a business causes harm to a third party or someone else's property.

butterfly spread   An option portfolio that is long two calls with differing strike prices, and short two calls with a strike price equal to the average strike price of the first two calls.

buying stocks on margin (leverage)   Borrowing money to invest in stocks.

CCAA   *See* Companies' Creditors Arrangement Act.

callable annuity rate   The rate on a risk-free annuity that can be repaid (or called) at any time.

callable bonds   Bonds that contain a call provision that allows the issuer to repurchase the bonds at a predetermined price.

call date   The right (but not the obligation) of a bond issuer to retire outstanding bonds on (or after) a specific date.

call option   A financial option that gives its owner the right to buy an asset.

call price   A price specified at the issuance of a bond at which the issuer can redeem the bond.

Canada (make-whole) call provision   A bond call provision that sets the call price as the present value of the remaining coupons calculated using a rate that adjusts according to prevailing interest rates in the economy.

cannibalization   When sales of a firm's new product displace sales of one of its existing products.

CapEx   The original purchase price of an asset.

Capital Asset Pricing Model (CAPM)   An equilibrium model of the relationship between risk and return that characterizes a security's expected return based on its beta with the market portfolio.

capital budget   Lists all of the projects that a company plans to undertake during the next period.

capital budgeting   The process of analyzing investment opportunities and deciding which ones to accept.

capital cost allowance (CCA)   The Canada Revenue Agency method of depreciation used for tax purposes.

capital expenditures   Purchases of new property, plant, and equipment.

capital gain   The amount by which the sale price of an asset exceeds its initial purchase price.

capital gain rate   An expression of capital gain as a percentage of the initial price of the asset.

capital gains tax   A tax collected on the profit (the amount the sale price exceeds the original purchase price) from assets in the year in which the assets are sold.

capital (finance) lease   Long-term lease contract that obligates a firm to make regular lease payments in exchange for the use of an asset. Viewed as an acquisition for accounting purposes, the lessee lists the asset on its balance sheet and incurs depreciation expenses. The lessee also lists the present value of the future lease payments as a liability, and deducts the interest portion of the lease payment as an interest expense.

capital market line (CML)   When plotting expected returns versus volatility, the line from the risk-free investment through the efficient portfolio of risky stocks (the port-folio that has the highest possible Sharpe Ratio). In the context of the CAPM, it is the line from the risk-free investment through the market portfolio. It shows the highest possible expected return that can be obtained for any given volatility.

capital rationing   When funds are limited, there is said to be a capital rationing constraint.

capital structure   The relative proportions of debt, equity, and other securities that a firm has outstanding.

CAPM   *See* Capital Asset Pricing Model.

captured   Describes a board of directors whose monitoring duties have been compromised by connections or perceived loyalties to management.

carried interest   Fee representing general partners' share of any positive return generated by the fund.

carryback or carryforward   *See* tax loss carryforwards and carrybacks.

cascade effect   A situation in which traders ignore their own information hoping to profit from the information of others.

cash-and-carry strategy   A strategy used to lock in the future cost of an asset by buying the asset for cash today, and storing (or "carrying") it until a future date.

cash conversion cycle (CCC)   A measure of the cash cycle calculated as the sum of a firm's inventory days and accounts receivable days, less its accounts payable days.

cash cycle   The length of time between when a firm pays cash to purchase its initial inventory and when it receives cash from the sale of the output produced from that inventory.

cash management bills   Pure discount bonds that are issued with very short maturities: as short as one day and less than three months.

cash multiple (multiple of money, absolute return)   The ratio of the total cash received to the total cash invested.

cash offer   A type of seasoned equity offering (SEO) in which a firm offers the new shares to investors at large.

CCA rate   The proportion of undepreciated capital cost (UCC) that can be claimed as capital cost allowance (CCA) in a given tax year.

CCA tax shield   The tax savings that results from the ability to deduct CCA from taxable income.

Chapter 11   A common form of bankruptcy for large corporations in the U.S. in which all pending collection attempts are automatically suspended, and the firm's existing management is given the opportunity to propose a reorganization plan. While developing the plan, management continues to operate the business as usual. The creditors must vote to accept the plan, and it must be approved by the bankruptcy court. If an acceptable plan is not put forth, the court may ultimately force a Chapter 7 liquidation of the firm.

Chapter 7   A provision of the U.S. bankruptcy code in which a trustee is appointed to oversee the liquidation of a firm's assets through an auction. The proceeds from the liquidation are used to pay the firm's creditors, and the firm ceases to exist.

chief executive officer or CEO   The person charged with running the corporation by instituting the rules and policies set by the board of directors.

chief financial officer (CFO)   The most senior financial manager, who usually reports directly to the CEO.

clean price   A bond's cash price less an adjustment for accrued interest, the amount of the next coupon payment that has already accrued.

clientele effect   When the dividend policy of a firm reflects the tax preference of its investor clientele.

CML   *See* capital market line.

collateralized debt obligation (CDO)   The security that results when banks re-securitize other asset-backed securities.

collection float   The amount of time it takes for a firm to be able to use funds after a customer has paid for its goods.

commercial paper   Short-term, unsecured debt issued by large corporations that is usually a cheaper source of funds than a short-term bank loan. Most commercial paper has a face value of at least $100,000. Like long-term debt, commercial paper is rated by credit rating agencies.

committed line of credit   A legally binding agreement that obligates a bank to provide funds to a firm (up to a stated credit limit) as long as the firm satisfies any restrictions in the agreement.

common risk   Perfectly correlated risk.

Companies' Creditors Arrangement Act (CCAA)   The Canadian act used by financially distressed companies that owe $5 million or more to creditors to preempt formal bankruptcy under the BIA and seek protection from creditors so as to allow for a plan of arrangement (or reorganization) to be put forward.

compensating balance   An amount a firm's bank may require the firm to maintain in an account at the bank as compensation for services the bank may perform.

competitive market   A market in which goods can be bought and sold at the same price.

compounding   Computing the return on an investment over a long horizon by multiplying the return factors associated with each intervening period.

compound interest   The combined effect of earning interest on the original principal plus interest on accrued interest.

conglomerate merger   The type of merger in which the target and the acquirer operate in unrelated industries.

conservation of value principle   With perfect capital markets, financial transactions neither add nor destroy value, but instead represent a repackaging of risk (and therefore return).

conservative financing policy   When a firm finances its short-term needs with long-term debt.

consol   A bond that promises its owner a fixed cash flow every year, forever.

constant dividend growth model   A model for valuing a stock by viewing its dividends as a constant growth perpetuity.

constant interest coverage ratio When a firm keeps its interest payments equal to a target fraction of its free cash flows.

continuing pool An asset pool in which there exists positive undepreciated capital cost (UCC) and for which the company still owns assets.

continuous compounding The compounding of interest every instant (an infinite number of times per year).

conversion price The face value of a convertible bond divided by the number of shares received if the bond is converted.

conversion ratio The number of shares received upon conversion of a convertible bond, usually stated per $1000 face value.

convertible bonds Corporate bonds with a provision that gives the bondholder an option to convert each bond owned into a fixed number of shares of common stock.

convertible preferred stock A preferred stock that gives the owner an option to convert it into common stock on some future date.

corporate bonds Bonds issued by a corporation.

corporate governance The system of controls, regulations, and incentives designed to minimize agency costs between managers and investors and prevent corporate fraud.

corporate investor, corporate partner, strategic partner, strategic investor A corporation that invests in private companies.

corporation A legally defined, artificial being, separate from its owners.

correlation The covariance of the returns divided by the stan-dard deviation of each return; a measure of the common risk shared by stocks that does not depend on their volatility.

cost of capital The expected return available on securities with equivalent risk and term to a particular investment.

coupon bonds Bonds that pay regular coupon interest payments up to maturity, when the face value is also paid.

coupon-paying yield curve A plot of the yield of coupon bonds of different maturities.

coupon rate The percent of a bond's face value paid out as coupons over a one-year period. The coupon rate, expressed as an APR, is set by the issuer and stated on the bond certificate.

coupons The promised interest payments of a bond.

covariance The expected product of the deviation of each return from its mean.

covenants Restrictive clauses in a bond contract that limit the issuers from undercutting their ability to repay bonds.

covered interest parity equation States that the difference between the forward and spot exchange rates is related to the interest rate differential between the currencies.

credibility principle The principle that claims in one's self-interest are credible only if they are supported by actions that would be too costly to take if the claims were untrue.

credit default swap (CDS) When a buyer pays a premium to the seller (often in the form of periodic payments) and receives a payment from the seller to make up for the loss if the underlying bond defaults.

credit risk The risk of default by the issuer of any bond that is not default free; it is an indication that the bond's cash flows are not known with certainty.

cum dividend When a stock trades before the ex-dividend date, entitling anyone who buys the stock to the dividend.

cumulative abnormal return Measure of a stock's cumulative return relative to that predicted based on its beta, at the time of the event.

cumulative normal distribution The probability that an outcome from a standard normal distribution will be below a certain value.

currency forward contract A contract that sets a currency exchange rate, and an amount to exchange, in advance.

currency swaps A contract in which parties agree to exchange coupon payments and a final face value payment that are in different currencies.

currency timeline Indicates time horizontally by dates (as in a standard timeline) and currencies vertically (as in dollars and euros).

current assets Cash or assets that could be converted into cash within one year. This category includes marketable securities, accounts receivable, inventories, and pre-paid expenses such as rent and insurance.

current liabilities Liabilities that will be satisfied within one year. They include accounts payable, notes payable, short-term debt, current maturities of long-term debt, salary or taxes owed, and deferred or unearned revenue.

current ratio The ratio of current assets to current liabilities.

cut-off period If the payback period is less than a prespecified length of time, called the cut-off period, then you accept the project. Otherwise, you turn it down.

data snooping bias The idea that given enough characteristics, it will always be possible to find some characteristic that by pure chance happens to be correlated with the estimation error of a regression.

dealer paper Commercial paper that dealers sell to investors in exchange for a spread (or fee) for their services. The spread decreases the proceeds that the issuing firm receives, thereby increasing the effective cost of the paper.

debentures A type of unsecured corporate debt. Debentures typically have longer maturities (more than ten years) than notes, another type of unsecured corporate debt.

debt covenants Conditions of making a loan in which creditors place restrictions on actions that a firm can take.

debt holders Individuals or institutions who have lent money to a firm.

debt overhang When shareholders choose not to invest in a positive-NPV project because some of the gains from investment will accrue to debt holders.

debt-equity ratio The ratio of a firm's total amount of short- and long-term debt (including current maturities) to the value of its equity, which may be calculated based on market or book values.

debt-to-value ratio The fraction of a firm's enterprise value that corresponds to debt.

debtor-in-possession financing (DIP) New debt issued by a bankrupt firm; this debt is senior to all existing creditors, providing renewed access to financing to allow a firm that has filed for bankruptcy to keep operating.

decision node A node on a decision tree at which a decision is made, and so corresponds to a real option.

decision tree A graphical representation of future decisions and uncertainty resolution.

declaration date The date on which a public company's board of directors authorizes the payment of a dividend.

deductible A provision of an insurance policy in which an initial amount of loss is not covered by the policy and must be paid by the insured.

deep in-the-money Describes options that are in-the-money and for which the strike price and the stock price are very far apart.

deep out-of-the-money Describes options that are out-of-the-money and for which the strike price and the stock price are very far apart.

default When a firm fails to make the required interest or principal payments on its debt, or violates a debt covenant.

default spread   *See* credit spread.

depreciation   A yearly deduction a firm makes from the value of its fixed assets (other than land) over time according to a depreciation schedule that depends on an asset's life span.

derivative security   A security whose cash flows depend solely on the prices of other marketed assets.

diluted EPS   A firm's disclosure of its potential for dilution from options it has awarded which shows the earnings per share the company would have if the stock options were exercised.

dilution   An increase in the total number of shares that will divide a fixed amount of earnings; often occurs when stock options are exercised or convertible bonds are converted.

direct lease   A type of lease in which the lessor is not the manu-facturer, but is often an independent company that specializes in purchasing assets and leasing them to customers.

direct paper   Commercial paper that a firms sells directly to investors.

disbursement float   The amount of time it takes before a firm's payments to its suppliers actually result in a cash outflow for the firm.

discount   The amount by which a cash flow exceeds its present value.

discount factor   The value today of a dollar received in the future.

discount loan   A type of bridge loan in which the borrower is required to pay the interest at the beginning of the loan period. The lender deducts interest from the loan proceeds when the loan is made.

discount rate   The rate used to discount a stream of cash flows; the cost of capital of a stream of cash flows.

discounted free cash flow model   A method for estimating a firm's enterprise value by discounting its future free cash flow.

discounting   Finding the equivalent value today of a future cash flow by multiplying by a discount factor, or equivalently, dividing by 1 plus the discount rate.

distribution date   *See* payable date.

disposition effect   The tendency to hold on to stocks that have lost value and sell stocks that have risen in value since the time of purchase.

diversifiable risk   *See* firm-specific risk.

diversification   The averaging of independent risks in a large portfolio.

dividend payments   Payments made at the discretion of the corporation to its equity holders.

dividend payout rate   The fraction of a firm's earnings that the firm pays as dividends each year.

dividend puzzle   When firms continue to issue dividends despite their tax disadvantage.

dividend signalling hypothesis   The idea that dividend changes reflect managers' views about a firm's future earnings prospects.

dividend smoothing   The practice of maintaining relatively constant dividends.

dividend yield   The expected annual dividend of a stock divided by its current price. The dividend yield is the percentage return an investor expects to earn from the dividend paid by the stock.

dividend-capture theory   The theory that absent transaction costs, investors can trade shares at the time of the dividend so that non-taxed investors receive the dividend.

domestic bonds   Bonds issued by a local entity and traded in a local market, but purchased by foreigners. They are denominated in the local currency.

double-barreled   Describes municipal bonds for which the issuing government has strengthened its promise to pay by committing itself to using general revenue to pay off the bonds.

dual class shares   When one class of a firm's shares has superior voting rights over the other class.

DuPont Identity   Expression of the ROE in terms of the firms' profitability, asset efficiency, and leverage.

duration   The sensitivity of a bond's price to changes in interest rates. The value-weighted average maturity of a bond's cash flows.

duration mismatch   When the durations of a firm's assets and liabilities are significantly different.

duration-neutral portfolio   A portfolio with a zero duration.

Dutch auction   A share repurchase method in which the firm lists different prices at which it is prepared to buy shares, and shareholders in turn indicate how many shares they are willing to sell at each price. The firm then pays the lowest price at which it can buy back its desired number of shares.

dynamic trading strategy   A replication strategy based on the idea that an option payoff can be replicated by dynamically trading in a portfolio of the underlying stock and a risk-free bond.

EAR   *See* effective annual rate.

earnings per share (EPS)   A firm's net income divided by the total number of shares outstanding.

EBIT   A firm's earnings before interest and taxes are deducted.

EBIT break-even   The level of sales for which a project's EBIT is zero.

EBITDA   A computation of a firm's earnings before interest, taxes, depreciation, and amortization are deducted.

economic distress   A significant decline in the value of a firm's assets, whether or not the firm experiences financial distress due to leverage.

economies of scale   The savings a large company can enjoy from producing goods in high volume, that are not available to a small company.

economies of scope   Savings large companies can realize that come from combining the marketing and distribution of different types of related products.

effective annual rate (EAR)   The total amount of interest that will be earned at the end of one year.

effective dividend tax rate   The effective dividend tax rate measures the additional tax paid by the investor per dollar of after-tax capital gain income that is instead received as a dividend.

efficient frontier   The set of portfolios that can be formed from a given set of investments with the property that each portfolio has the highest possible expected return that can be attained without increasing its volatility.

efficient markets hypothesis   The idea that competition among investors works to eliminate all positive-NPV trading opportunities. It implies that securities will be fairly priced, based on their future cash flows, given all information that is available to investors.

efficient portfolio   A portfolio that contains only systematic risk. An efficient portfolio cannot be diversified further; there is no way to reduce the volatility of the portfolio without lowering its expected return. The efficient portfolio is the tangent portfolio, the portfolio with the highest Sharpe ratio in the economy.

empirical distribution   A plot showing the frequency of outcomes based on historical data.

energy trust   A flow through entity that holds resource properties directly or holds all the debt and equity securities of a resource corporation within the trust.

enterprise value   The total market value of a firm's equity and debt, less the value of its cash and marketable securities. It measures the value of the firm's underlying business.

EPS   *See* earnings per share.

equally weighted portfolio　A portfolio in which the same dollar amount is invested in each stock.

equal-ownership portfolio　A portfolio containing an equal fraction of the total number of shares outstanding of each security in the portfolio. Equivalent to a value-weighted portfolio.

equity　The collection of all the outstanding shares of a corporation.

equity holder (also shareholder or stockholder)　An owner of a share of stock in a corporation.

equity multiplier　Measure of leverage that indicates the value of assets held per dollar of shareholder equity.

equivalent annual benefit　The annual annuity payment over the life of an investment that has the same NPV as the investment.

equivalent annual benefit method　A method of choosing between projects with different lives by selecting the project with the higher equivalent annual benefit. It ignores the value of any real options because it assumes that both projects will be replaced on their original terms.

error term　Represents the deviation from the best-fitting line in a regression. It is zero on average and uncorrelated with any regressors.

ESO　*See* executive stock option.

Eurobonds　International bonds that are not denominated in the local currency of the country in which they are issued.

European options　Options that allow their holders to exercise the option only on the expiration date; holders cannot exercise before the expiration date.

evergreen credit　A revolving line of credit with no fixed maturity.

excess return　The difference between the average return for an investment and the average return for a risk-free investment.

exchange ratio　In a takeover, the number of bidder shares received in exchange for each target share.

exchange-traded fund　A security that trades directly on an exchange, like a stock, but represents ownership in a portfolio of stocks.

ex-dividend date　A date, two days prior to a dividend's record date, on or after which anyone buying the stock will not be eligible for the dividend.

execution risk　The risk that a misstep in the firm's execution may cause a project to fail to generate the forecasted cashflows.

executive stock option (ESO)　A common practice for compensating executives by granting them call options on their company's stock.

exercise price　*See* strike price.

exercising (an option)　When a holder of an option enforces the agreement and buys or sells a share of stock at the agreed-upon price.

exit strategy　An important consideration for investors in private companies, it details how they will eventually realize the return from their investment.

expected (mean) return　A computation for the return of a security based on the average payoff expected.

expiration date　The last date on which an option holder has the right to exercise the option.

face value　The notional amount of a bond used to compute its interest payments. The face value of the bond is generally due at the bond's maturity. Also called par value or principal amount.

factor betas　The sensitivity of the stock's excess return to the excess return of a factor portfolio, as computed in a multifactor regression.

factoring of accounts receivable　An arrangement in which a firm sells receivables to the lender (i.e., the factor), and the lender agrees to pay the firm the amount due from its customers at the end of the firm's payment period.

factor portfolios　Portfolios that can be combined to form an efficient portfolio.

factors　Firms that purchase the receivables of other companies and are the most common sources for secured short-term loans.

fair market value cap lease　A type of lease in which the lessee can purchase the asset at the minimum of its fair market value and a fixed price or "cap."

fair market value (FMV) lease　A type of lease that gives the lessee the option to purchase the asset at its fair market value at the termination of the lease.

Fama-French-Carhart (FFC) factor specification　A multi-factor model of risk and return in which the factor portfolios are the market, small-minus-big, high-minus- low, and PR1YR portfolios identified by Fama, French, and Carhart.

familiarity bias　The tendency of investors to favour investments in companies with which they are familiar.

FCFE　*See* free cash flow to equity.

FFC factor specification　*See* Fama-French-Carhart factor specification.

field warehouse　A warehouse arrangement that is operated by a third party, but is set up on the borrower's premises in a separate area. Inventory held in the field warehouse can be used as secure collateral for borrowing.

final prospectus　Part of the final registration statement prepared by a company prior to an IPO that contains all the details of the offering, including the number of shares offered and the offer price.

financial distress　When a firm has difficulty meeting its debt obligations.

financial option　A contract that gives its owner the right (but not the obligation) to purchase or sell an asset at a fixed price at some future date.

financial security　An investment opportunity that trades in a financial market.

financial statements　Firm-issued (usually quarterly and annually) accounting reports with past performance information.

firm commitment　An agreement between an underwriter and an issuing firm in which the underwriter guarantees that it will sell all of the stock at the offer price.

firm-specific, idiosyncratic, unsystematic, unique, or diversifiable risk　Fluctuations of a stock's return that are due to firm-specific news and are independent risks unrelated across stocks.

floating lien　A financial arrangement in which all of a firm's inventory is used to secure a loan.

floating rate　An interest rate or exchange rate that changes depending on supply and demand in the market.

floor planning　*See* trust receipts loan.

flow through entities　Business entities in which virtually all income produced by the business flows to the investors.

flow to equity (FTE)　A valuation method that calculates the free cash flow available to equity holders taking into account all payments to and from debt holders. The cash flows to equity holders are then discounted using the equity cost of capital.

FMV lease　*See* fair market value lease.

foreign bonds　Bonds issued by a foreign company in a local market and are intended for local investors. They are also denominated in the local currency.

forward exchange rate　The exchange rate set in a currency forward contract, it applies to an exchange that will occur in the future.

forward earnings　A firm's anticipated earnings over the coming 12 months.

forward P/E　A firm's price-earnings (P/E) ratio calculated using forward earnings.

free cash flow   The incremental effect of a project on a firm's available cash.

free cash flow hypothesis   The view that wasteful spending is more likely to occur when firms have high levels of cash flow in excess of what is needed after making all positive-NPV investments and payments to debt holders.

free cash flow to equity (FCFE)   The free cash flow that remains after adjusting for interest payments, debt issuance, and debt repayment.

freezeout merger   A situation in which the laws on tender offers allow an acquiring company to freeze existing shareholders out of the gains from merging by forcing non-tendering shareholders to sell their shares for the tender offer price.

friendly takeover   When a target's board of directors supports a merger, negotiates with potential acquirers, and agrees on a price that is ultimately put to a shareholder vote.

FTE   *See* flow to equity.

funding risk   The risk of incurring financial distress costs should a firm not be able to refinance its debt in a timely manner or at a reasonable rate.

future income tax   An account that shows taxes that have been recognized on the firm's financial statements but are not yet charged according to tax law.

future value   The value of a cash flow that is moved forward in time.

futures contract   A forward contract that is traded on an exchange.

GAAP   *See* Generally Accepted Accounting Principles.

general lien   *See* floating lien.

Generally Accepted Accounting Principles (GAAP)   A common set of rules and a standard format for public companies to use when they prepare their financial reports.

general obligation bonds   Bonds backed by the full faith and credit of a local government.

golden parachute   An extremely lucrative severance package that is guaranteed to a firm's senior managers in the event that the firm is taken over and the managers are let go.

goodwill   The difference between the price paid for a company and the book value assigned to its assets.

Government of Canada bonds   Long-term debt issued by the Government of Canada to provide financing for the government.

grey directors   Members of a board of directors who are not as directly connected to the firm as insiders are, but who have existing or potential business relationships with the firm.

greenmail   When a firm avoids a threat of takeover and removal of its management by a major shareholder by buying out the shareholder, often at a large premium over the current market price.

greenshoe provision (over-allotment allocation)   *See* over-allotment allocation.

gross margin   The third line of an income statement that represents the difference between a firm's sales revenues and its costs.

growing annuity   A stream of cash flows paid at regular intervals and growing at a constant rate, up to some final date.

growing perpetuity   A stream of cash flows that occurs at regular intervals and grows at a constant rate forever.

growth option   A real option to invest in the future. Because these options have value, they contribute to the value of any firm that has future possible investment opportunities.

half-year rule   As assets may be purchased at any time throughout a year, it can be assumed that on average an asset is owned for half a year during the first tax year of its ownership. Thus, the CRA allows only half of CapEx to generate CCA in the first tax year (the year in which a purchase takes place).

hedge   To reduce risk by holding contracts or securities whose payoffs are negatively correlated with some risk exposure.

herd behaviour   The tendency of investors to make similar trading errors by actively imitating other investors' actions.

high-minus-low (HML) portfolio   An annually updated portfolio that is long stocks with high book-to-market ratios and short stocks with low book-to-market ratios.

high-yield bonds   Bonds below investment grade which trade with a high yield to maturity to compensate investors for their high risk of default.

HML portfolio   *See* high-minus-low portfolio.

homemade leverage   When investors use leverage in their own portfolios to adjust the leverage choice made by a firm.

homogeneous expectations   A theoretical situation in which all investors have the same estimates concerning future investment returns.

horizontal merger   A merger in which the target and acquirer are in the same industry.

hostile takeover   A situation in which an individual or organization, sometimes referred to as a corporate raider, purchases a large fraction of a target corporation's stock and in doing so gets enough votes to replace the target's board of directors and its CEO.

hubris hypothesis   The idea that overconfident CEOs pursue mergers that have a low chance of creating value because they truly believe that their ability to manage is great enough to succeed.

hurdle rate   A higher discount rate created by the hurdle rate rule. If a project can jump the hurdle with a positive NPV at this higher discount rate, then it should be undertaken.

hurdle rate rule   Raises the discount rate by using a higher discount rate than the cost of capital to compute the NPV, but then applies the regular NPV rule: Invest whenever the NPV calculated using this higher discount rate is positive.

idiosyncratic risk   *See* firm-specific risk.

immunized portfolio   *See* duration-neutral portfolio.

immunizing   Adjusting a portfolio to make it duration neutral.

implied volatility   The volatility of an asset's return that is consistent with the quoted price of an option on the asset.

income statement   A list of a firm's revenues and expenses over a period of time.

income trust   *See* flow through entity.

incremental earnings   The amount by which a firm's earnings are expected to change as a result of an investment decision.

incremental IRR investment rule   Applies the IRR rule to the difference between the cash flows of two mutually exclusive alternatives (the *increment* to the cash flows of one investment over the other).

indenture   Included in a prospectus, it is a formal contract between a bond issuer and a trust company. The trust company represents the bondholders and makes sure that the terms of the indenture are enforced. In the case of default, the trust company represents the bondholders' interests.

independent (outside) directors   *See* outside directors.

independent risk   Risks that bear no relation to each other. If risks are independent, then knowing the outcome of one provides no information about the other. Independent risks are always uncorrelated, but the reverse need not be true.

index funds   Mutual funds that invest in stocks in proportion to their representation in a published index, such as the S&P 500 or S&P/TSX Composite Index.

inefficient portfolio   Describes a portfolio for which it is possible to find another portfolio that has higher expected return and lower volatility.

information node   A type of node on a decision tree indicating uncertainty that is out of the control of the decision maker.

initial public offering (IPO)   The process of selling stock to the public for the first time.

inside directors   Members of a board of directors who are employees, former employees, or family members of employees.

insider trading   Occurs when a person makes a trade based on privileged information.

insurance premium   The fee a firm pays to an insurance company for the purchase of an insurance policy.

interest coverage ratio   An assessment by lenders of a firm's leverage. Common ratios consider operating income, EBIT, or EBITDA as a multiple of the firm's interest expenses.

interest rate factor   One plus the interest rate, it is the rate of exchange between dollars today and dollars in the future.

interest rate swap   A contract in which two parties agree to exchange the coupons from two different types of loans.

interest tax shield   The reduction in taxes paid due to the tax deductibility of interest payments.

interim financial statement   Firm-issued accounting reports with past performance information that a firm issues periodically (usually quarterly and annually). Canadian public companies are required to file these reports with their provincial securities commissions.

internal rate of return (IRR)   The interest rate that sets the net present value of the cash flows equal to zero.

internal rate of return (IRR) investment rule   A decision rule that accepts any investment opportunity where IRR exceeds the opportunity cost of capital. This rule is only optimal in special circumstances, and often leads to errors if misapplied.

internationally integrated capital markets   When any investor can exchange currencies in any amount at the spot or forward rates and is free to purchase or sell any security in any amount in any country at its current market prices.

in-the-money   Describes an option whose value if immediately exercised would be positive.

intrinsic value   The amount by which an option is in-the-money, or zero if the option is out-of-the-money.

inventories   A firm's raw materials as well as its work-in-progress and finished goods.

investment-grade bonds   Bonds in the top four categories of creditworthiness with a low risk of default.

invoice price   *See* dirty price.

IPO   *See* initial public offering.

IRR   *See* internal rate of return.

IRR investment rule   *See* internal rate of return investment rule.

JIT inventory management   *See* "just-in-time" inventory management.

junk bonds   Bonds in one of the bottom five categories of creditworthiness (below investment grade) that have a high risk of default.

"just-in-time" (JIT) inventory management   When a firm acquires inventory precisely when needed so that its inventory balance is always zero, or very close to it.

key personnel insurance   A type of insurance that compensates a firm for the loss or unavoidable absence of crucial employees in the firm.

Law of One Price   In competitive markets, securities or portfolios with the same cash flows must have the same price.

LBO   *See* leveraged buyout.

lead underwriter   The primary banking firm responsible for managing a security issuance.

lease-equivalent loan   A loan that is required on the purchase of an asset that leaves the purchaser with the same net future obligations as a lease would entail.

lemons principle   When a seller has private information about the value of a good, buyers will discount the price they are willing to pay due to adverse selection.

lessee   The party in a lease liable for periodic payments in exchange for the right to use the asset.

lessor   The party in a lease who is entitled to the lease payments in exchange for lending the asset.

leverage   The amout of debt held in a portfolio or issued by a firm. *See also* buying stocks on margin.

leverage ratio   A measure of leverage obtained by looking at debt as proportion of value, or interest payments as a proportion of cash flows.

leveraged buyout (LBO)   When a group of private investors purchases all the equity of a public corporation and finances the purchase primarily with debt.

leveraged lease   A lease in which the lessor borrows from a bank or other lender to obtain the initial capital to purchase an asset, using the lease payments to pay interest and principal on the loan.

leveraged recapitalization   When a firm uses borrowed funds to pay a large special dividend or repurchase a significant amount of its outstanding shares.

levered equity   Equity in a firm with outstanding debt.

liabilities   A firm's obligations to its creditors.

LIBOR   *See* London Inter-Bank Offered Rate.

limited liability   When an investor's liability is limited to her initial investment.

limited liability partnership (LLP)   A partnership in which a partner's personal assets are protected from the negligent actions of other partners.

limited partnership   A partnership with two kinds of owners, general partners and limited partners.

line of credit   A bank loan arrangement in which a bank agrees to lend a firm any amount up to a stated maximum. This flexible agreement allows the firm to draw upon the line of credit whenever it chooses.

linear regression   The statistical technique that identifies the best-fitting line through a set of points.

liquid   Describes an investment that can easily be turned into cash because it can be sold immediately at a competitive market price.

liquidating dividend   A return of capital to shareholders from a business operation that is being terminated.

liquidation   Closing down a business and selling off all its assets; often the result of the business declaring bankruptcy.

liquidation value   The value of a firm after its assets are sold and liabilities paid.

liquidity risk   The risk of being forced to liquidate an investment (at a loss) because the cash is required to satisfy another obligation (most often a margin requirement).

LLP   *See* limited liability partnership.

loan origination fee   A bank charge that a borrower must pay to initiate a loan.

lockup   A restriction that prevents existing shareholders from selling their shares for some period (usually 180 days) after an IPO.

London Inter-Bank Offered Rate (LIBOR)   The rate of interest at which banks borrow funds from each other in the London interbank market. It is quoted for maturities of one day to one year for 10 major currencies.

long position   A positive investment in a security.

long-term debt   Any loan or debt obligation with a maturity of more than a year.

mail float   How long it takes a firm to receive a customer's payment check after the customer has mailed it.

management buyout   A leveraged buyout in which the buyer is the firm's own management.

management discussion and analysis (MD&A)   A preface to the financial statements in which a company's management discusses the recent year (or quarter), providing a background on the company and any significant events that may have occurred.

management entrenchment   A situation arising as the result of the separation of ownership and control in which managers may make decisions that benefit themselves at investors' expense.

management entrenchment theory   A theory that suggests managers choose a capital structure to avoid the discipline of debt and maintain their own job security.

maple bonds   A term for foreign bonds in Canada.

margin   Collateral that investors are required to post when buying or selling securities that could generate losses beyond the initial investment.

marginal corporate tax rate   The tax rate a firm will pay on an incremental dollar of pre-tax income.

market capitalization   The total market value of equity; equals the market price per share times the number of shares.

market index   The market value of a broad-based portfolio of securities.

market makers   Individuals on the trading floor of a stock exchange who match buyers with sellers.

market portfolio   A value-weighted portfolio of all shares of all stocks and securities in the market.

market proxy   A portfolio whose return is believed to closely track the true market portfolio.

market risk   *See* systematic risk.

market-to-book ratio (price-to-book [PB] ratio)   The ratio of a firm's market (equity) capitalization to the book value of its stockholders' equity.

market value balance sheet   similar to an accounting balance sheet, with two key distinctions: First, all assets and liabilities of the firm are included, even intangible assets such as reputation, brand name, or human capital that are missing from a standard accounting balance sheet; second, all values are current market values rather than historical costs.

market timing   View that the firm's A firm's overall capital structure depends in part on the market conditions that existed when it sought funding in the past.

marketable securities   Short-term, low-risk investments that can be easily sold and converted to cash (such as money market investments, like government debt, that mature within a year).

marking to market   Computing gains and losses each day based on the change in the market price of a futures contract.

martingale prices   *See* risk-neutral probabilities.

matching principle   States that a firm's short-term needs should be financed with short-term debt and long-term needs should be financed with long-term sources of funds.

maturity date   The final repayment date of a bond.

MD&A   *See* management discussion and analysis.

merger waves   Peaks of heavy activity followed by quiet troughs of few transactions in the takeover market.

merger-arbitrage spread   In a takeover, the difference between a target stock's price and the implied offer price.

method of comparables   An estimate of the value of a firm based on the value of other, comparable firms or other investments that are expected to generate very similar cash flows in the future.

momentum strategy   Buying stocks that have had past high returns, and (short) selling stocks that have had past low returns.

money manager   A person who charges investors a fee based on the amount of capital they have under management.

monitor   A person who oversees the company's activities while a plan of arrangement is being developed.

Monte Carlo simulation   A common technique for pricing derivative assets in which the expected payoff of the derivative security is estimated by calculating its average payoff after simulating many random paths for the underlying stock price. In the randomization, the risk neutral probabilities are used, and so the average payoff can be discounted at the risk-free rate to estimate the derivative security's value.

moral hazard   When purchasing insurance reduces a firm's incentive to avoid risk.

mortgage   A loan in which the borrower offers property as security for the lender.

mortgage bonds   A type of secured corporate debt. Real property is pledged as collateral that bondholders have a direct claim to in the event of bankruptcy.

mortgage-backed security (MBS)   An asset-backed security backed by home mortgages.

multifactor model   A model that uses more than one risk factor to capture risk. Also referred to as Arbitrage Pricing Theory (APT).

multiple of money   *See* cash multiple.

multiple regression   A regression with more than one independent variable.

municipal bonds   Bonds issued by local governments. In Canada, their interest is taxable by the Canada Revenue Agency. In the U.S., interest from "munis" (bonds issued by state or local governments) are not taxed by the Internal Revenue Service.

munis   The term used in the United States for interest from bonds issued by the state or municipal governments.

mutually dependent investments   Situation in which the value of one project depends upon the outcome of the others.

mutually exclusive projects   Projects that compete with one another; by accepting one, the others cannot be accepted.

natural hedge   When a firm can pass on cost increases to its customers or revenue decreases to its suppliers.

negative net additions   The situation when a continuing asset pool has asset purchases less than asset sales in the same tax year. (The UCC of the pool will decline but still remain positive.)

net debt   Total debt outstanding minus any cash balances.

net income or earnings   The last or "bottom line" of a firm's income statement that is a measure of the firm's income over a given period of time.

net investment   The firm's capital expenditures in excess of depreciation.

net present value (NPV)   The difference between the present value of a project or investment's benefits and the present value of its costs.

net profit margin   The ratio of net income to revenues, it shows the fraction of each dollar in revenues that is available to equity holders after the firm pays interest and taxes.

net working capital The difference between a firm's current assets and current liabilities that represents the capital available in the short term to run the business.

95% confidence interval A confidence interval gives a range of values which is likely to include an unknown parameter. If independent samples are taken repeatedly from the same population, then the true parameter will lie outside the 95% confidence interval 5% of the time. For a normal distribution, the interval corresponds to approximately 2 standard deviations on both sides of the mean.

no-arbitrage price In a normal market, when the price of a security equals the present value of the cash flows paid by the security.

nominal interest rates Interest rates quoted by banks and other financial institutions that indicate the rate at which money will grow if invested for a certain period of time.

non-tax lease A type of lease in which the lessee receives the depreciation deductions for tax purposes, and can also deduct the interest portion of the lease payments as an interest expense. The interest portion of the lease payment is interest income for the lessor.

normal market A competitive market in which there are no arbitrage opportunities.

notes A type of unsecured corporate debt. Notes typically are coupon bonds with maturities shorter than 10 years.

notional principal Used to calculate the coupon payments in an interest rate swap.

NPV *See* net present value.

NPV Decision Rule When choosing among investment alternatives, take the alternative with the highest NPV. Choosing this alternative is equivalent to receiving its NPV in cash today.

off-balance sheet transactions Transactions or arrangements that can have a material impact on a firm's future performance yet do not appear on the balance sheet.

offer price (offer) *See* ask price.

OID (original issue) discount *See* original issue discount.

open interest The total number of contracts of a particular option that has been written.

open market repurchase When a firm repurchases shares by buying its shares in the open market.

operating cycle The average length of time between when a firm originally receives its inventory and when it receives the cash back from selling its product.

operating income A firm's gross profit less its operating expenses.

operating lease A type of lease, viewed as a rental for accounting purposes, in which the lessee reports the entire lease payment as an operating expense. The lessee does not deduct a depreciation expense for the asset and does not report the asset, or the lease payment liability, on its balance sheet.

operating leverage Relative proportion of fixed versus variable costs.

operating margin The ratio of operating income to revenues, it reveals how much a company has earned from each dollar of sales before interest and taxes are deducted.

opportunity cost The value a resource could have provided in its best alternative use.

option delta The change in the price of an option given a $1 change in the price of the stock. The number of shares in the replicating portfolio for the option.

option premium The market price of the option.

option writer The seller of an option contract.

original issue discount (OID) Describes a coupon bond that is issued at a discount

out-of-the-money Describes an option that if exercised immediately, results in a loss of money.

outside (independent) directors Any member of a board of directors other than an inside or grey director.

over-allotment allocation (greenshoe provision) On an IPO, an option that allows the underwriter to issue more stock, usually amounting to 15% of the original offer size, at the IPO offer price.

overconfidence hypothesis The tendency of individual investors to trade too much based on the mistaken belief that they can pick winners and losers better than investment professionals.

overhead expenses Those expenses associated with activities that are not directly attributable to a single business activity but instead affect many different areas of a corporation.

overnight rate The overnight loan rate charged by banks with excess reserves at the Bank of Canada (called federal funds) to banks that need additional funds to meet reserve requirements. The federal funds rate is influenced by the Bank of Canada's monetary policy, and itself influences other interest rates in the market.

par A price at which coupon bonds trade that is equal to their face value.

partnership A sole proprietorship with more than one owner.

passive portfolio A portfolio that is not rebalanced in response to price changes.

payable date (distribution date) A date, generally within a month after the record date, on which a firm mails dividend checks to its registered stockholders.

payback investment rule The simplest investment rule. Only projects that pay back their initial investment within the payback period are undertaken.

payback period A specified amount of time used in the payback investment rule. Only investments that pay back their initial investment within this amount of time are undertaken.

payments pattern Information on the percentage of monthly sales that the firm collects in each month after the sale.

payout policy The way a firm chooses between the alternative ways to pay cash out to equity holders.

P/E *See* price-earnings ratio.

pecking order hypothesis The idea that managers will prefer to fund investments by first using retained earnings, then debt and equity only as a last resort.

perfect capital markets A set of conditions in which investors and firms can trade the same set of securities at competitive market prices with no frictions such as taxes, transaction costs, issuance costs, asymmetric information, or agency costs.

permanent working capital The amount that a firm must keep invested in its short-term assets to support its continuing operations.

perpetuity A stream of equal cash flows that occurs at regular intervals and lasts forever.

perquisites Benefits provided free of charge to managers of corporations.

plan of arrangement The proposed reorganization under the CCAA that allows a business to continue operations.

pledging of accounts receivable An agreement in which a lender accepts accounts receivable as collateral for a loan. The lender typically lends a percentage of the value of the accepted invoices.

poison pill A defense against a hostile takeover. It is a rights offering that gives the target shareholders the right to buy shares in either the target or an acquirer at a deeply discounted price.

policy limits   Those provisions of an insurance policy that limit the amount of loss that the policy covers regardless of the extent of the damage.

pool   An underlying portfolio of assets that back a pass-through security.

portfolio   A collection of securities.

portfolio insurance   A protective put written on a portfolio rather than a single stock. When the put does not itself trade, it is synthetically created by constructing a replicating portfolio.

portfolio weights   The fraction of the total investment in a portfolio held in each individual investment in the portfolio.

positive net additions   The situation when a continuing asset pool has asset purchases greater than asset sales in the same tax year. (The UCC of the pool will increase and remain positive.)

post-money valuation   At the issue of new equity, the value of the whole firm (old plus new shares) at the price the new equity is sold at.

precautionary balance   The amount of cash a firm holds to counter the uncertainty surrounding its future cash needs.

preferred stock   Preferred stock issued by mature companies such as banks usually has a preferential dividend and seniority in any liquidation and sometimes special voting rights. Preferred stock issued by young companies has seniority in any liquidation but typically does not pay cash dividends and contains a right to convert to common stock.

preliminary prospectus (red herring)   Part of the registration statement prepared by a company prior to an IPO that is circulated to investors before the stock is offered.

premium   A price at which coupon bonds trade that is greater than their face value. Also, the price a firm pays to purchase insurance, allowing the firm to exchange a random future loss for a certain upfront expense.

pre-money valuation   At the issuance of new equity, the value of a firm's prior shares outstanding at the price in the funding round.

prepackaged bankruptcy   A method for avoiding many of the legal and other direct costs of bankruptcy in which a firm first develops a reorganization plan with the agreement of its main creditors, and then files Chapter 11 to implement the plan.

present value (PV)   The value of a cost or benefit computed in terms of cash today.

pretax WACC   The weighted average cost of captial computed using the pretax cost of debt; it can be used to estimate the unlevered cost of captial for a firm that maintains a target leverage ratio.

price-earnings ratio (P/E)   The ratio of the market value of equity to the firm's earnings, or its share price to its earnings per share.

price-to-book (PB) ratio   *See* market-to-book ratio.

price-weighted portfolio   A portfolio that holds an equal number of shares of each stock, independent of their size.

primary market   Market used when a corporation itself issues new shares of stock and sells them to investors.

primary offering   New shares available in a public offering that raise new capital.

primary shares   New shares issued by a company in an equity offering.

prime rate   The rate banks charge their most creditworthy customers.

principal-agent problem   A problem that arises when employees in control (the agents) act in their own interest rather than in the interest of the owners (the principals).

PR1YR   *See* prior one-year momentum portfolio.

prior one-year momentum (PR1YR) portfolio   A self-financing portfolio that goes long on the top 30% of stocks with the highest prior year returns, and short on the 30% with the lowest prior year returns, each year.

private company   A company whose shares do not trade on a public market.

private debt   Debt that is not publicly traded.

private equity firm   A firm organized very similarly to venture capital firms that invests in the equity of existing privately held firms rather than startup companies.

private placement   A bond issue that is sold to a small group of investors rather than to the general public. Because a private placement does not need to be registered, it is less costly to issue.

probability distribution   A graph that provides the probability of every possible discrete state.

processing float   How long it takes a firm to process a customer's payment cheque and deposit it in the bank.

profitability index   Measures the NPV per unit of resource consumed.

profitability index rule   Recommends investment whenever the profitability index exceeds some predetermined number.

pro forma   Describes a statement that is not based on actual data but rather depicts a firm's financials under a given set of hypothetical assumptions.

project externalities   Indirect effects of a project that may increase or decrease the profits of other business activities of a firm.

promissory note   A written statement that indicates the amount of a loan, the date payment is due, and the interest rate.

property insurance   A type of insurance companies purchase to compensate them for losses to their assets due to fire, storm damage, vandalism, earthquakes, and other natural and environmental risks.

protective put   A long position in a put option held on a stock you already own.

provincial bonds   Securities issued by provincial governments and their Crown corporations (e.g., Hydro Quebec). Their interest is taxable income by the Canada Revenue Agency.

proxy fight   In a hostile takeover, when the acquirer attempts to convince the target's shareholders to unseat the target's board by using their proxy votes to support the acquirers' candidates for election to the target's board.

public companies   Those corporations whose stock is traded on a stock market or exchange, providing shareholders the ability to quickly and easily convert their investments in to cash.

public warehouse   A business that exists for the sole purpose of storing and tracking the inflow and outflow of inventory. If a lender extends a loan to a borrowing firm, based on the value of the inventory, this arrangement provides the lender with the tightest control over the inventory.

pure discount bonds   Zero-coupon bonds.

put option   A financial option that gives its owner the right to sell an asset for a fixed price up to (or on) a fixed date.

put-call parity   The relationship that gives the price of call option in terms of the price of put option plus the price of the underlying stock minus the present value of the strike price and the present value of any dividend payments.

PV   *See* present value.

pyramid structure   A way for an investor to control a corporation without owning 50% of the equity whereby the investor first creates a company in which he has a controlling interest. This company then owns a controlling interest in another company. The investor controls both companies, but may own as little as 25% of the second company.

quick ratio   The ratio of current assets other than inventory to current liabilities.

raider   The acquirer in a hostile takeover.

rational expectations   The idea that investors may have different information regarding expected returns, correlations, and volatilities, but that they correctly interpret that information and the information contained in market prices and adjust their estimates of expected returns in a rational way.

real estate investment trust (REIT)   A flow through entity that holds real estate properties directly or holds all the debt and equity securities of a corporation that owns real estate properties.

real interest rate   The rate of growth of purchasing power after adjusting for inflation.

real option   The right to make a particular business decision, such as a capital investment. A key distinction between real options and financial options is that real options, and the underlying assets on which they are based, are often not traded in competitive markets.

real return bonds   Bonds that have their payments adjusted for the effects of inflation.

realized return   The return that actually occurs over a particular time period.

record date   When a firm pays a dividend, only shareholders of record on this date receive the dividend.

red herring   *See* preliminary prospectus.

registered bonds   The issuer of this type of bond maintains a list of all holders of its bonds. Coupon and principal payments are made only to people on this list.

registration statement   A legal document that provides financial and other information about a company to investors, prior to a security issuance.

REIT   *See* real estate investment trust.

relative wealth concerns   When investors are concerned about the performance of their portfolio relative to that of their peers, rather than its absolute performance.

repatriated   Refers to the profits from a foreign project that a firm brings back to its home country.

replicating portfolio   A portfolio consisting of a stock and a risk-free bond that has the same value and payoffs in one period as an option written on the same stock.

required return   The expected return of an investment that is necessary to compensate for the risk of undertaking the investment.

residual value   An asset's market value at the end of a lease.

retained earnings   The difference between a firm's net income and the amount it spends on dividends.

retention rate   The fraction of a firm's current earnings that the firm retains.

return   The difference between the selling price and purchasing price of an asset plus any cash distributions expressed as a percentage of the buying price.

return of capital   When a firm, instead of paying dividends out of current earnings (or accumulated retained earnings), pays dividends from other sources, such as paid-in capital or through the liquidation of assets.

return on assets (ROA)   The ratio of net income to the total book value of the firm's assets.

return on equity (ROE)   The ratio of a firm's net income to the book value of its equity.

revenue bonds   Municipal bonds for which the local government can pledge as repayment revenues generated by specific projects.

reverse split   When the price of a company's stock falls too low and the company reduces the number of outstanding shares.

Revlon duties   State that if a change of control is going to occur, then directors must seek the highest value (they cannot favour one controlling entity over another based on anything other than value to shareholders.)

revolving line of credit   A credit commitment for a specific time period, typically two to three years, which a company can use as needed.

rights offer   A type of seasoned equity offering (SEO) in which a firm offers the new shares only to existing shareholders.

risk-arbitrageurs   Traders who, once a takeover offer is announced, speculate on the outcome of the deal.

risk-free interest rate   The interest rate at which money can be borrowed or lent without risk over a given period.

risk-neutral probabilities   The probability of future states that are consistent with current prices of securities assuming all investors are risk neutral. Also known as state-contingent prices, state prices, or martingale prices.

ROA   *See* return on assets.

road show   During an IPO, when a company's senior management and its underwriters travel around the country (and sometimes around the world) promoting the company and explaining their rationale for an offer price to the underwriters' largest customers, mainly institutional investors such as mutual funds and pension funds.

ROE   *See* return on equity.

sale and lease back   Describes a type of lease in which a firm already owns an asset it would prefer to lease. The firm receives cash from the sale of the asset and then makes lease payments to retain the use of the asset.

sales-type lease   A type of lease in which the lessor is the manufacturer (or a primary dealer) of the asset.

Samurai bonds   A term for foreign bonds in Japan.

Sarbanes-Oxley Act (SOX)   A 2002 Congressional act intended to improve the accuracy of information given to both boards and to shareholders.

scenario analysis   An important capital budgeting tool that determines how the NPV varies as a number of the underlying assumptions are changed simultaneously.

seasoned equity offering (SEO)   When a public company offers new shares for sale.

secondary market   Market shares continue to trade on after the initial transaction between the corporation and investors.

secondary offering   An equity offering of secondary shares.

secondary shares   Shares sold by existing shareholders in an equity offering.

secured debt (loan)   A type of corporate loan or debt security in which specific assets are pledged as a firm's collateral.

security   *See* financial security.

security interest   A classification of a lease in bankruptcy proceedings that assumes a firm has effective ownership of an asset and the asset is protected against seizure.

security market line (SML)   The pricing implication of the CAPM, it specifies a linear relation between the risk premium of a security and its beta with the market portfolio.

SEDAR   System for Electronic Document Analysis and Retrieval.

segmented capital markets   Capital markets that are not internationally integrated.

self-financing portfolio   A portfolio that costs nothing to construct.

seniority A bondholder's priority in claiming assets not already securing other debt.

sensation seeking The increase in trading activity due to an individual's desire for novel or intense risk-taking experiences.

sensitivity analysis An important capital budgeting tool that determines how the NPV varies as a single underlying assumption is changed.

SEO *See* seasoned equity offering.

Separate Trading of Registered Interest and Principal bonds *See* STRIP bonds.

Separation of Individual's Consumption Preferences from the Optimal Investment Decision Consumers' preferences for consumption spending through time are separate from their optimal investment decisions.

Separation of the Investment and Financing Decisions In a perfect market, the NPV of an investment decision can be evaluated separately from any financial transactions a firm is considering.

serial bonds A single issue of municipal bonds that are scheduled to mature serially over a period of years.

share repurchase A situation in which a firm uses cash to buy back its own stock.

shareholder (also stockholder or equity holder) An owner of a share of stock in a corporation.

shareholder wealth maximization A corporate objective that seeks to maximize the financial benefit to all persons holding stock in the corporation by maximizing the current value of a company's stock.

shareholders' equity, stockholders' equity An accounting measure of a firm's net worth that represents the difference between the firm's assets and its liabilities.

shirking Neglecting the responsibilities of managing a corporation.

short sale Selling a security you do not own.

signalling theory of debt The use of leverage as a way to signal information to investors.

simple interest Interest earned without the effect of compounding.

single-factor model A model using an efficient portfolio, capturing all systematic risk alone.

sinking fund A method for repaying a bond in which a company makes regular payments into a fund administered by a trustee over the life of the bond. These payments are then used to repurchase bonds.

size effect The observation that small stocks (or stocks with a high book-to-market ratio) have higher returns.

small-minus-big (SMB) portfolio A portfolio resulting from a trading strategy that each year buys a small market value portfolio and finances that position by selling short a large market value portfolio.

SMB portfolio *See* small-minus-big portfolio.

SML *See* security market line.

sole proprietorship A business owned and run by one person.

sovereign debt Debt issued by national governments.

sovereign wealth fund A pool of money controlled by a government. Such pools are usually raised from royalties, resource revenue, or taxes that have been collected.

SPE *See* special-purpose entity.

special dividend A one-time dividend payment a firm makes that is usually much larger than a regular dividend.

specialists Individuals on the trading floor of the NYSE who match buyers with sellers; also called market makers.

special-purpose entity (SPE) A separate business partnership created by a lessee for the sole purpose of obtaining a lease.

speculate When investors use securities to place a bet on the direction in which they believe the market is likely to move.

speculative bonds Bonds in one of the bottom five categories of creditworthiness that have a high risk of default.

spin-off When a firm sells a subsidiary by selling shares in the subsidiary alone.

spot exchange rate The current foreign exchange rate.

spot interest rates Default-free, zero-coupon yields.

staggered (classified) board In many public companies, a board of directors whose three-year terms are staggered so that only one-third of the directors are up for election each year.

stakeholder Any person with an interest in what a corporation does, including employees, customers, suppliers, the community, the government, and investors.

stakeholder model The explicit consideration most countries (other than the United States) give to other stakeholders besides equity holders, in particular, rank-and-file employees.

stakeholder satisfaction A corporate objective that seeks to meet the interests of all stakeholders of a corporation.

standard deviation A common method used to measure the risk of a probability distribution, it is the square root of the variance, the expected squared deviation from the mean.

standard error The standard deviation of the estimated value of the mean of the actual distribution around its true value; that is, it is the standard deviation of the average return.

state prices See risk-neutral probabilities.

state-contingent prices See risk-neutral probabilities.

statement of cash flows An accounting statement that shows how a firm has used the cash it earned during a set period.

statement of comprehensive income Statement showing the total income and expenses for a period by combining net income (or profit) from the income statement with information not reported on the income statement, such as gains and losses that affect equity through reserve or other accounts.

statement of financial performance Statement showing the firm's revenues and expenses over a period of time. See income statement.

statement of financial position List of the firm's assets and liabilities that provides a snapshot of the firm's financial position at a given point in time. *See* balance sheet.

statement of shareholders' equity An accounting statement that breaks down the shareholders' equity computed on the balance sheet into the amount that came from issuing new shares versus retained earnings.

stay Legal protection from creditors for a firm while it is developing a plan of arrangement.

stock The ownership or equity of a corporation divided into shares.

stock dividend *See* stock split.

stock exchanges *See* stock markets.

stock markets (also stock exchanges) Organized markets on which the shares of many corporations are traded.

stock options A form of compensation a firm gives to its employees that gives them the right to buy a certain number of shares of stock by a specific date at a specific price.

stock split (stock dividend) When a company issues a dividend in shares of stock rather than cash to its shareholders.

stock swap Merger deal when the target shareholders receive stock as payment for target shares.

stockholder (also shareholder or equity holder) An owner of a share of stock or equity in a corporation.

stock-out When a firm runs out of inventory, leading to lost sales.

straddle A portfolio that is long a call and a put on the same stock with the same exercise date and the strike price.

strangle A portfolio that is long a call and a put with the same exercise date but the strike price of the call exceeds the strike price of the put.

strategic investor *See* corporate investor.

strategic partner *See* corporate investor.

stream of cash flows A series of cash flows lasting several periods.

stretching the accounts payable When a firm ignores a payment due period and pays later.

strike (exercise) price The price at which an option holder buys or sells a share of stock when the option is exercised.

STRIP bonds (Separate Trading of Registered Interest and Principal) Zero-coupon government securities with maturities longer than one year that trade in the bond market.

subordinated debenture Debt that, in the event of a default, has a lower priority claim to the firm's assets than other outstanding debt.

subprime mortgages Mortgages for which borrowers do not meet typical credit standards, and thus have a high default probability. The CMHC will not insure these.

sunk cost Any unrecoverable cost for which a firm is already liable.

syndicate A group of underwriters who jointly underwrite and distribute a security issuance.

syndicated bank loan A single loan that is funded by a group of banks rather than just a single bank.

synthetic lease A lease that commonly uses a special-purpose entity (SPE) and is designed to obtain specific accounting and tax treatment.

systematic, undiversifiable, or market risk Fluctuations of a stock's return that are due to market-wide news representing common risk.

takeover Refers to two mechanisms, either a merger or an acquistion, by which ownership and control of a firm can change.

tangent portfolio A portfolio with the highest Sharpe ratio; the point of tangency to the efficient frontier of a line drawn from the risk-free asset; the market portfolio if the CAPM holds.

target A firm that is acquired by another in a merger or acquisition.

target leverage ratio When a firm adjusts its debt proportionally to a project's value or its cash flows (where the proportion need not remain constant). A constant market debt-equity ratio is a special case.

targeted repurchase When a firm purchases shares directly from a specific shareholder.

tax loss carryforwards and carrybacks Two features of the tax code that allow corporations to take losses during a current year and offset them against gains in nearby years. In Canada, companies can "carry back" losses for three years and "carry forward" losses for 20 years.

tax year The fiscal year relevant for tax and CCA calculations for the Canada Revenue Agency.

temporary working capital The difference between the actual level of short-term working capital needs and its permanent working capital requirements.

tender offer A public announcement of an offer to all existing security holders to buy back a specified amount of outstanding securities at a prespecified price over a prespecified period of time.

term The time remaining until the final repayment date of a bond.

term loan A bank loan that lasts for a specific term.

term sheet Summary of the structure of a merger transaction that includes details such as who will run the new company, the size and composition of the new board, the location of the headquarters, and the name of the new company.

term structure The relationship between the investment term and the interest rate.

terminal value (*See also* continuation value) The value of a project's remaining free cash flows beyond the forecast horizon. This amount represents the market value (as of the last forecast period) of the free cash flow from the project at all future dates.

terminating pool A group of assets in the same asset class in which the last asset is sold, or in which the post-sale UCC drops below zero.

thinly traded Term used to describe the low level of trading volume in stocks that attract little investor interest.

time value The difference between an option's price and its intrinsic value.

time value of money The difference in value between money today and money in the future; also, the observation that two cash flows at two different points in time have different values.

timeline A linear representation of the timing of (potential) cash flows.

toehold An initial ownership stake in a firm that a corporate raider can use to initiate a takeover attempt.

tombstone A newspaper advertisement in which an underwriter advertises a security issuance.

total payout model A firm's total payouts to equity holders (i.e., all the cash distributed as dividends and stock repurchases) are discounted and then divided by the current number of shares outstanding to determine the share price.

total return The sum of a stock's dividend yield and its capital gain rate.

trade credit The difference between receivables and payables that is the net amount of a firm's capital consumed as a result of those credit transactions; the credit that a firm extends to its customers.

tradeoff theory The firm picks its capital structure by trading off the benefits of the tax shield from debt against the costs of financial distress and agency costs.

trailing earnings A firm's earnings over the prior 12 months.

trailing P/E The computation of a firm's P/E using its trailing earnings.

tranches Different classes of securities that comprise a single bond issuance. All classes of securities are paid from the same cash flow source.

transaction cost The cost of executing a trade or transaction, normally including broker commissions or other fees.

transactions balance The amount of cash a firm needs to be able to pay its bills.

Treasury Bills Short-term (with a maturity of up to one year), zero-coupon debt, issued by the Government of Canada to provide financing for the government.

true lease A classification of a lease in bankruptcy proceedings in which the lessor retains ownership rights over an asset.

true tax lease A type of lease in which the lessor receives the depreciation deductions associated with the ownership of the asset. The lessee can deduct the full amount of the lease payments as an operating expense, and these lease payments are treated as revenue for the lessor.

trust receipts loan A type of loan in which distinguishable inventory items are held in a trust as security for the loan. As these items are sold, the firm remits the proceeds from their sale to the lender in repayment of the loan.

tunnelling A conflict of interest that arises when a shareholder who has a controlling interest in multiple firms moves profits (and hence dividends) away from companies in which he has relatively less cash flow rights toward firms in which he has relatively more cash flow rights.

UCC   *See* undepreciated capital cost.

uncommitted line of credit   A line of credit that does not legally bind a bank to provide the funds a borrower requests.

unconventional cash flows   Flows in which there is an upfront cash inflow followed by cash outflows.

undepreciated capital cost (UCC)   The balance, at a point in time, calculated by deducting an asset's current and prior CCA amounts from the original cost of the asset (the CapEx).

under-investment problem   A situation in which equity holders choose not to invest in a positive NPV project because the firm is in financial distress and the value of undertaking the investment opportunity will accrue to bondholders rather than themselves.

underwriter   An investment banking firm that manages a security issuance and designs its structure.

underwriting spread   Company-paid fee to underwriters based on the issue price.

undiversifiable risk   *See* systematic risk.

unique risk   *See* firm-specific risk.

unit holder   An owner of an income trust.

unlevered beta   Measures the risk of a firm were it unlevered; beta of the firm's assets; measures the market risk of the firm's business activities, ignoring any additional risk due to leverage.

unlevered cost of capital   The cost of capital of a firm, were it unlevered; for a firm that maintains a target leverage ratio, it can be estimated as the weighted average cost of capital computed without taking into account taxes (pre-tax WACC).

unlevered equity   Equity in a firm with no debt.

unlevered net income   Net income plus after-tax interest expense.

unlevered P/E ratio   The enterprise value of a firm divided by its unlevered net income in a particular year.

unsecured debt   A type of corporate debt that, in the event of a bankruptcy, gives bondholders a claim to only the assets of the firm that are not already pledged as collateral on other debt.

unsystematic risk   *See* firm-specific risk.

valuation multiple   A ratio of a firm's value to some measure of the firm's scale or cash flow.

valuation principle   The value of an asset to the firm or its investors is determined by its competitive market price: The benefits and costs of a decision should be evaluated using these market prices, and when the value of the benefits exceeds the value of the costs, the decision will increase the market value of the firm.

value additivity   A relationship determined by the Law of One Price, in which the price of an asset that consists of other assets must equal the sum of the prices of the other assets.

value stocks   Firms with low market-to-book ratios.

value-weighted portfolio   A portfolio in which each security is held in proportion to its market capitalization. Also called an equal-ownership portfolio, because it consists of the same fraction of the outstanding shares of each security.

variance   A method to measure the risk of a probability distribution, it is the expected squared deviation from the mean.

venture capital firm   A limited partnership that specializes in raising money to invest in the private equity of young firms.

venture capitalist   One of the general partners who work for and run a venture capital firm.

vertical integration   Refers to the merger of two companies in the same industry that make products required at different stages of the production cycle. Also, the merger of a firm and its supplier or a firm and its customer.

vertical merger   The type of merger when the target's industry buys or sells to the acquirer's industry.

volatility   The standard deviation of a return.

WACC   *See* weighted average cost of capital.

warehouse arrangement   When the inventory that serves as collateral for a loan is stored in a warehouse.

warrant   A call option written by the company itself on new stock. When a holder of a warrant exercises it and thereby purchases stock, the company delivers this stock by issuing new stock.

weighted average cost of capital (WACC)   The average of a firm's equity and after-tax cost of capital, weighted by the fraction of the firm's enterprise value that corresponds to equity and debt, respectively. Discounting free cash flows using the WACC computes their value including the interest tax shield.

white knight   A target company's defense against a hostile takeover attempt, in which it looks for another, friendlier company to acquire it.

white squire   A variant of the white knight defense, in which a large, passive investor or firm agrees to purchase a substantial block of shares in a target with special voting rights.

winner's curse   Refers to a situation in competitive bidding when the high bidder, by virtue of being the high bidder, has very likely overestimated the value of the item being bid on.

with recourse   A loan or lease in which the lender can claim all the borrower's assets in the event of a default and not just explicitly pledged collateral.

without recourse   A loan or lease in which the lender's claim on the borrower's assets in the event of a default is limited to only explicitly pledged collateral.

workout   A method for avoiding a declaration of bankruptcy in which a firm in financial distress negotiates directly with its creditors to reorganize.

Yankee bonds   A term for foreign bonds in the United States.

yield curve   A plot of bond yields as a function of the bonds' maturity date.

yield to call (YTC)   The yield of a callable bond calculated under the assumption that the bond will be called on the earliest call date.

yield to maturity (YTM)   The IRR of an investment in a bond that is held to its maturity date.

YTC   *See* yield to call.

YTM   *See* yield to maturity.

zero-coupon bond   A bond that makes only one payment at maturity.

zero-coupon yield curve   A plot of the yield of risk-free zero-coupon bonds (STRIP bonds) as a function of the bond's maturity date.

Index

KEY EQUATIONS